The First American Frontier

The First American Frontier

Advisory Editor: Dale Van Every

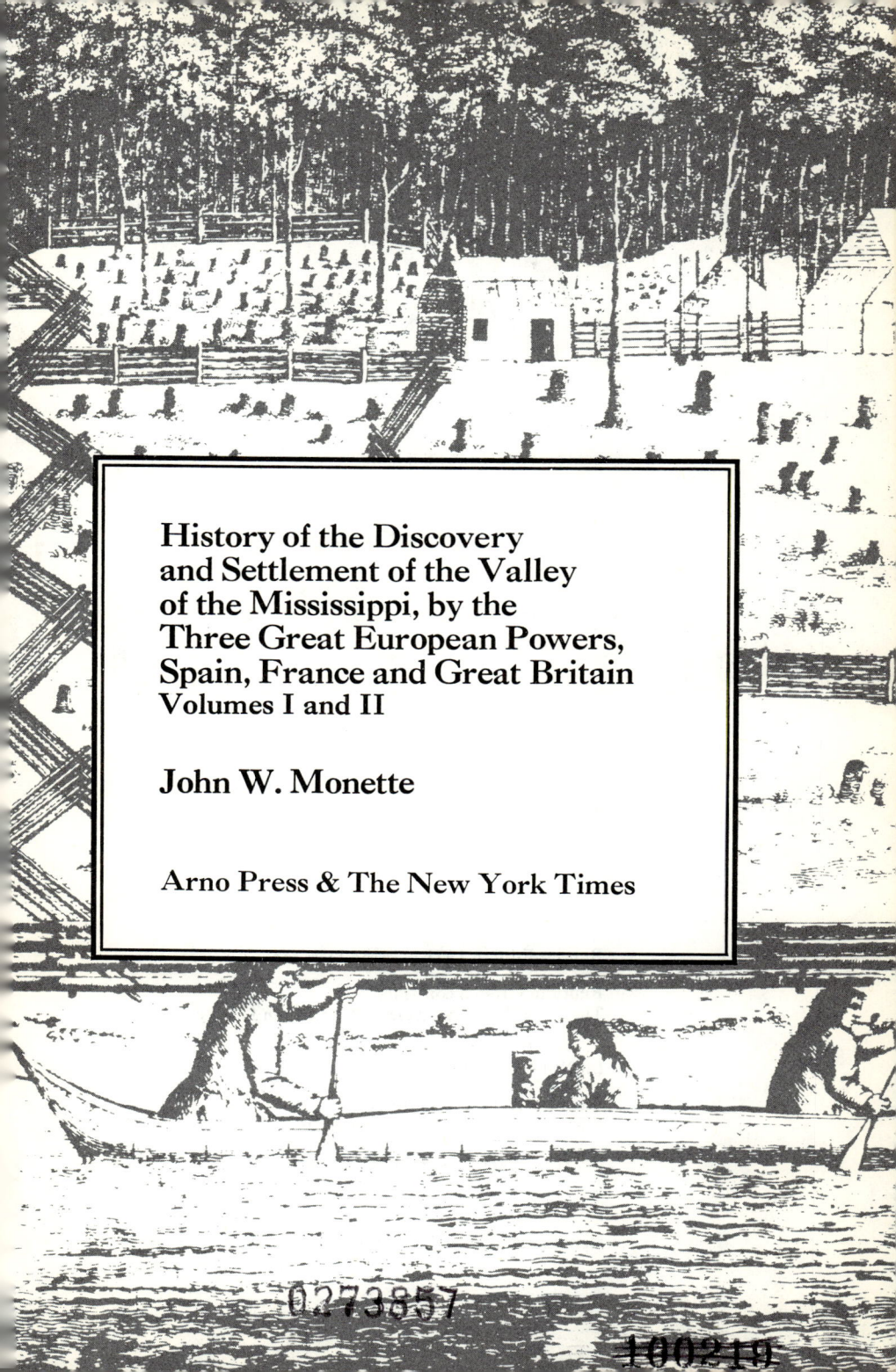

History of the Discovery
and Settlement of the Valley
of the Mississippi, by the
Three Great European Powers,
Spain, France and Great Britain
Volumes I and II

John W. Monette

Arno Press & The New York Times

Reprint Edition 1971 by Arno Press Inc.

Reprinted from a copy in
The State Historical Society of Wisconsin Library

LC # 78-146408
ISBN 0-405-02868-7

The First American Frontier
ISBN for complete set: 0-405-02820-2

See last pages of this volume for titles.

Manufactured in the United States of America

HISTORY

OF THE

DISCOVERY AND SETTLEMENT

OF

THE VALLEY OF THE MISSISSIPPI,

BY

THE THREE GREAT EUROPEAN POWERS,

SPAIN, FRANCE, AND GREAT BRITAIN,

AND

THE SUBSEQUENT OCCUPATION, SETTLEMENT, AND EXTENSION OF CIVIL GOVERNMENT BY

THE UNITED STATES,

UNTIL THE YEAR 1846.

BY

JOHN W. MONETTE, M.D.

"Westward the star of empire takes its way."

IN TWO VOLUMES.

VOL. I.

HARPER & BROTHERS, PUBLISHERS,
82 CLIFF STREET, NEW YORK.
1846.

Entered, according to Act of Congress, in the year 1846,
By HARPER & BROTHERS,
In the Clerk's Office of the Southern District of New York.

PREFACE.

The records of the first European colonies in the Valley of the Mississippi are distributed sparsely through the archives of foreign governments, and are to be found published only in fragments and hasty sketches, interspersed through miscellaneous works and periodicals, so that a connected and concise account of their rise and progress is not accessible to those who desire to trace their history. In like manner, the early records of the Anglo-American settlements west of the Alleghany Mountains, and their extension over the Valley of the Mississippi, are concealed chiefly among the archives of the several states and territories, or among the voluminous documents of the Federal government, thus placing any connected account of these infant colonies equally beyond the reach of common research. Other fragments, pertaining to the early history of the western settlements, are enveloped in private memoirs, narratives of individual observers loosely compiled, and meriting but slender claims to the confidence of the discerning reader.

Hence that portion of the reading public who are desirous of tracing the true history of past events in the rise and progress of the new states in the Valley of the Mississippi, free from the glosses and episodes of visionary writers, are excluded from any concise and connected history of the whole West, which discloses correctly the progressive changes, and notes the order in the chain of events, in their advance from isolated, feeble frontier colonies, to populous, wealthy, and enlightened states.

To supply this *desideratum*, and to present a concise and comprehensive detail, a complete but condensed narrative of American colonization west of the Alleghanies is the object of the present work. In this undertaking, the author has endeavored to connect the history of the French and Spanish colonies, which have had their important agency in the destiny of the American Republic, with those of the Anglo-Americans in their advance upon the tributaries of the Ohio River.

The blending of these three great branches of European emigration in North America has resulted in the formation of a great and powerful Republic, the wonder, if not the admiration, of the civilized world, teeming with an enterprising and ever-active population, proud of their origin from the three great nations that have successively held dominion in the Western World.

The advance of the Anglo-American population into the Valley of the Mississippi, its union with Gallic and Spanish colonies, the concurrent extension of Republican government over the subjects of absolute monarchies, and its benign influence upon the moral character and enlightened enterprise of mankind, afford a subject worthy the profound attention of the philosopher and the statesman. They present a new phenomenon in the science of human government, as to the development of human capabilities, when untrammeled by arbitrary power, and left free to the exercise of its own energies, under the fostering care of a free and liberal system of government. They exhibit the speedy and progressive conversion of a savage wilderness into a populous and highly-civilized country, inhabited by a people who have made all nature tributary to their aggrandizement as a nation, and in the promotion of domestic independence and social wealth, by the extension of navigation and commerce, and by the perfection of arts and sciences throughout the magnificent regions of central North America.

Such a result, heretofore, has been the work of many ages; and hence the early records of the rise and progress of most nations known to history have been lost in the uncertain mazes of tradition, until arms and commerce, arts and sciences, after the lapse of centuries, had given them renown and history. It has been left to the West to furnish the history of a new Republic, to present to the world the novel spectacle of a great nation formed by people coming from various portions of the globe, differing in manners, language, politics, and religion, and settling down quietly together, forming governments, constitutions, and laws, without bloodshed, violence, conquest, or invasion, and coalescing into one uniform, harmonious, and prosperous people. Never was there an experiment of greater moral grandeur, a more sublime spectacle of the harmonious development of the moral and political energies of a people left free to the unrestrained operation of enlightened public opinion, the great regulator of their forms of government, laws, and religion.

The history of the early pioneers of the West is full of thrilling interest and incident connected with their struggles for the occupancy of this great and fertile region, which they have left as a rich inheritance to their posterity. The only requital they ask at our hands is the gratitude with which their names and their virtues are cherished by their posterity, and the fidelity with which they are transmitted, as models of enterprise and perseverance, to future ages.

The last participants in the great drama of western civilization will soon have passed from the stage of action; and the only voice heard in their praise, the only tribute of gratitude and admiration for their merits, will be the impartial records of history, which should embalm their deeds of valor, their patient endurance, and their active virtues in the grateful remembrance of posterity.

The general tenor of this history is to trace the gradual and steady advance of the European colonies and settlements by their various routes into the central part of North America, and the progressive extension of the Anglo-American population and Republican government throughout the great Valley of the Mississippi and the southwest; to illustrate the progressive changes, and the rapid advance of population and civil government, from the rude and half-civilized pioneer up to flourishing cities and powerful states, extending over regions which a few years previously had been savage solitudes.

The plan of the work is simple, and grows out of the order in which the different colonies advanced in the occupation of the regions now comprised in the United States.

The *Spaniards* were the first exploring pioneers in the Valley of the Mississippi, and their early explorations and settlements furnish the subject of the *First Book,* or " Early Spanish Explorations."

The *French* were the first peaceful explorers and permanent colonists who occupied and settled the banks of the Mississippi River, subsequent to the hostile explorations of the Spaniards. The French colonies and explorations therefore furnish the subject of the *Second Book,* or " France in the Valley of the Mississippi."

Great Britain, the jealous rival of France, next extended her colonies into the western country, encroaching upon the discoveries and possessions of France, until finally, by force of arms, she expelled the French power from Canada and the Mississippi, and appropriated to her own use the whole eastern half of the valley, including the Floridas.

The progress of her colonies west of the Alleghanies, her fierce contests with the French and their savage allies, and her subsequent occupancy of the country, furnish the subjects of the *Third Book*, or "Great Britain in the Valley."

At the dismemberment of Louisiana in 1763, while Great Britain had secured the eastern portion of the province, except the Island of New Orleans, Spain had acquired all the western portion, including that island. Thus was Louisiana divided between Spain and Great Britain. Spain held dominion over the western portion of Louisiana and the Island of New Orleans, together with the Floridas, subsequent to 1781, until the close of the year 1803, when the Spanish dominion ceased in Louisiana. The acquisition, the occupancy, and the exercise of Spanish authority over this extensive province, until the final termination of the Spanish dominion on the Mississippi, furnish the subjects of the *Fourth Book*, or "Spain in the Valley."

Meantime, the "United States" on the Atlantic coast having declared their independence, which was recognized by Great Britain at the close of the Revolutionary war, succeeded to the territory claimed by Great Britain east of the Mississippi, as far south as the proper limits of Florida. The United States claimed dominion, and continued to extend civil jurisdiction in the formation of new states west of the Alleghany Mountains, gradually displacing the native savages from the country east of the Mississippi, and finally, by treaty negotiations, annexed all the Spanish provinces east and west of the Mississippi, as far as the Rio del Norté of Mexico.

The extension of settlements, the establishment of civil government, the increase of population, the wars and treaties with the native tribes, the acquisition of territory and the extension of dominion, the progress of agriculture, manufactures, trade, and commerce, aided by the potent influence of steam power, constitute the subjects comprised in the *Fifth Book*, or, "The United States in the Valley of the Mississippi."

Such is the general outline of the work which is now presented to the American public. For its completion and perfection, so far as the nature and extent of the plan will admit, and its faithful adherence to truth and accuracy, the author has spared neither labor nor expense, and he throws himself upon the generous approbation of the American people for the first systematic arrangement of this portion of the history of the United States.

CONTENTS OF VOL. I.

BOOK I.
EARLY EXPLORATIONS OF THE SPANIARDS IN THE VALLEY OF THE MISSISSIPPI.

CHAPTER I.
FIRST SPANISH DISCOVERIES IN FLORIDA.—A.D. 1512 TO 1538.

Argument.—The former undefined Extent of Florida.—Spirit of Enterprise and Discovery awakened in Europe by Spanish Conquests in the West Indies, Mexico, and Peru.—The romantic and unfortunate Expedition of Ponce de Leon into East Florida.—The Expedition and Disasters of Vasquez de Ayllon; his Avarice, Cruelty, and Death.—The disastrous Expedition of Pamphilo de Narvaez.—Preparations for the great and chivalrous Expedition, under Hernando de Soto, for the Conquest of Florida.—The Nature and Extent of this Enterprise.—De Soto's commanding Person and Influence.—The Expedition sails from Spain for the West Indies.—Other Arrangements and Preparations completed.—The Expedition sails from Havana, and arrives at the Bay of Espiritu Santo late in May, 1539, A.D.—A Synopsis of the Marches, Disasters, and Fate of the Expedition . . . . . . Page 1

CHAPTER II.
INVASION OF FLORIDA BY HERNANDO DE SOTO.—A.D. 1539 TO 1540.

Argument.—The Spanish Expedition at the Bay of Espiritu Santo.—Disasters commence.—De Soto invades the Territory of Hirhihigua.—Invades the Territories of Acuera; of Ocali; of Vitachuco. — Invades Osachile; the Cacique's Castle upon a fortified Mound.—Invasion of Appalaché.—The Expedition winters in Appalaché.—Various Incidents while here.—The Expedition marches in the Spring toward Western Georgia.—Invasion of the Territories of Copafi.—Capture of the Cacique.—His Person and Character.—His miraculous Escape.—Invasion of the Territory of Cofachiqui.—De Soto's Disappointment at the Poverty of the Natives.—Captures a Queen Regent.—Detains her as a Hostage, and carries her Westward in his March.—She effects her Escape near the eastern Limits of the Cherokee Country.—The Expedition upon the Sources of the Chattahoochy River.—Arrives on the head Waters of the Coosa River 16

CHAPTER III.
THE SPANISH EXPEDITION EAST OF THE MISSISSIPPI.—A.D. 1540 TO 1541.

Argument.—De Soto marches down the Coosa River.—The King, or Cacique, of Cosa.—De Soto enters the Territory of Tuscaluza. — Noble Person and lofty Bearing of Tuscaluza.—He is inveigled into De Soto's Train.—The Army marches through the Dominions of Tuscaluza.—The captive King is impatient and indignant at his Detention.—Resolves to secure his Liberty or die. — Reaches Mauvile with the Army.—De Soto apprehends Danger from the Native Warriors.—The severe and disastrous Battle of Mauvile. — Indian Courage and Desperation.—Deplorable Condition of the Spanish Army after the Battle.—De Soto resolves to advance to the Northwest.—Crosses the Tombigby River in the Face of an Indian Army.—Passes the Head Waters of Pearl River.—Enters the Chickasâ Country.—Takes Possession of a large Indian Town for his Winter-quarters.—The great Battle and Conflagration of Chicasâ.—Great Losses of the Spaniards.—The Army marches Westward to Chicaçilla, where they spend the remainder of the Winter.—They march Northwest to Alibamo.—Severe Battle of Alibamo.—They approach the Mississippi, or Rio Grande. —Preparations for crossing the great River.—Indian Hostilities and Opposition to their crossing.—The Army at length reach the western Side of the Rio Grande.— The probable Crossing-place . . . . Page 33

CHAPTER IV.

THE SPANISH EXPEDITION WEST OF THE MISSISSIPPI.—A.D. 1541 TO 1543.

Argument.—De Soto arrives upon the Banks of White River.—Incidents and Religious Ceremonies.—De Soto joins an Indian King in a hostile Expedition.—Marches with him Northeast to the Mississippi, near Helena.—Arrives at the Town of Capahâ.— Present Remains of Capahâ.—He returns to White River, and thence resumes his March to the West.—Winters high up the Arkansas in a cold Latitude.—Difficulties and Disasters there.—Returns to the Mississippi in the Spring.—Disasters begin to multiply.—He determines to leave the Country by descending the River.—New Hostilities by the Natives.—Difficulties increase, and Perplexities prey upon the iron Soul of De Soto.—He sickens and dies.—Affecting Scene before his Death.—He is finally deposited in the Mississippi, near the Mouth of the Arkansas.—His Eulogium.— Louis de Moscoso succeeds to the Command.—He marches Westward in search of the Mexican Settlements.—His fruitless Search.—Returns to the Mississippi.—Spends the Winter and Spring in Preparations for a Departure down the River.—Commences building Brigantines for descending the River.—He is greatly annoyed by hostile Indians.—Perilous Descent of the River in Boats and Brigantines.—Dangerous Voyage in the Gulf of Mexico.—The Remnant of the Expedition reach the Spanish Settlements of Mexico.—Reflections 47

CHAPTER V.

EARLY EXTENT AND SETTLEMENTS, WITH THE SUBSEQUENT BOUNDARIES AND SOVEREIGNTY OF FLORIDA.—A.D. 1544 TO 1845.

Argument.—Extent of Florida in 1560.—Spanish Missions and Settlements.—Ribault's French Colony in 1562.—Its Location on the Combahee River.—Destruction of the Colony.—Laudonnier's French Colony in 1564.—"Fort Carolana" built on the St. Mary's.—Destitute Condition of this Colony.—Timely Relief by Ribault.—Melendez is Adelantado of Florida in 1565.—He exterminates the French Colony.—St. Augustine founded.—Degourges ravages the Spanish Colony and captures the Forts.—Jesuit Missionaries introduced by Melendez.—Missions established in 1584.—St. Augustine plundered by Sir Francis Drake.—First Attempts at English Settlement, in 1585 and 1608.—English Colony of Virginia.—Carolina granted to Lord Clarendon and others.— St. Augustine plundered in 1665 by Captain Davis, an English Pirate.—English Settlement at "Charlestown," in 1679.—French Colonists arrive in Carolina, 1785-6.— Restricted Limits of Florida.—Spanish Settlements invaded by the English from Carolina.—Partisan Warfare continued.—Pensacola settled in 1696.—Boundary between Florida and Louisiana.—English Boundaries of Florida in 1764.—English Settlements in Florida.—Turnbull's Colony of New Smyrna.—His inhuman Tyranny.— Wretched Condition, and subsequent Liberation of his white Slaves.—English Agriculture in Florida.—Florida retroceded to Spain in 1783.—Extent of Florida claimed by Spain.—Extent claimed by the United States.—Claim of United States under the Purchase of Louisiana.—Baton Rouge District annexed to the State of Louisiana.—Fort Charlotte and Mobile District surrendered in 1813.—Florida restricted to the Perdido on the West.—Revolt and Occupancy of East Florida by "Patriots" in 1812.—Spain fails to preserve the Neutrality of Florida during the War with Great Britain.—Woodbine's Operations among the Seminoles of Florida after the War.—He builds a Negro Fort on the Appalachicola.—Negroes, Arms, Munitions, and Military Stores furnished from the British Fleet.—The Patriots of South America again occupy Amelia Island in 1817.—The Seminole War commences.—General Jackson prosecutes it successfully.—Captures St. Mark's.—Arbuthnot and Ambrister condemned and executed.—Their righteous Sentence and deserved Fate.—Jackson marches to Pensacola and expels the perfidious Spaniards.— He retires to private Life.—His Traits of Character.—Florida ceded to the United States in 1819.—Terms of Cession.—General Jackson is first American Governor, civil and military, of the Province.—Collision with Governor Calleava.—The first Grade of Territorial Government organized in 1822.—Indians removed from Middle Florida in 1824.—The second Grade organized in 1825.— Advance of white Population until 1835.—Hostilities by the Mickasukie Indians.—Military Movements and Operations.—Horrible Massacre of Major Dade's Detachment.—Indian Murders at Fort King.—Commencement of the "Florida War."—Gradual Removal of the Seminoles West of the Mississippi.—Increase of white Population until 1844.—State Constitution formed.—The State of Florida admitted into the Union in 1845 . Page 65

BOOK II.

FRANCE IN THE VALLEY OF THE MISSISSIPPI.

CHAPTER I.

ADVANCE OF THE FRENCH UPON THE ST. LAWRENCE, AND DISCOVERY OF THE MISSISSIPPI.—A.D. 1608 TO 1673.

Argument.—First Attempt of French Colonization in Canada.—First successful Settlement by Champlain in 1608.—His Explorations on the St. Lawrence and Lakes.— Indian Alliances against the Iroquois.—Advance of Catholic Missionaries.—Hostilities of the Iroquois.—Fathers Brebeuf and Daniel visit Sault St. Mary in 1634.— Character of Catholic Missionaries in Canada.—Sufferings of Father Raymbault among the Iroquois in 1642.—Of Father Bressani in 1643.—The Missionaries sustain the Colonies.—Death of Father Jouges among the Iroquois in 1646.—Others suffer Martyrdom in the same Field.—Jesuits and Monks flock to Canada in 1650 for the Missionary Field.—Le Moyne among the Mohawks in 1656.—Chaumonot and Dablon among the Onondagas.—René Mesnard among the Cayugas.—Missionaries killed and expelled by the Iroquois.—Montreal a Bishop's See in 1656.—Mesnard repairs to St. Mary's and Green Bay.—Dies in the Forest alone.—Canada a Royal Province in 1665.—Military Protection of Settlements.—Father Allouez among the Chippewas at St. Mary's.—Learns the Existence of the Mississippi in 1667.—Dablon and Marquette repair to St. Mary's in 1668.—Military Outposts of New France in 1670. —Missions in the Far West.—Marquette conceives the Design of discovering the Mississippi.—Plans his Voyage of Discovery in 1672.—M. Talon patronizes the Enterprise.—Marquette and Joliet conduct the Exploration in 1673.—They proceed by Way of Green Bay and Fox River to the Wisconsin.—Discovery of the Mississippi, June 17th, 1673.—Explore the Great River 1100 Miles.—They return by the Illinois River to Chicago Creek.—Marquette returns to his Mission, and Joliet to Quebec.—Joy in Canada at the Discovery.—Native Tribes known to the early Explorers of Illinois and Louisiana: Algonquin Tribes; Shawanese; Miamis; Illinois; Potawatamies; Ottawâs; Menomonies, Chippewas; Sioux; Sauks and Foxes; Chickasâs; Natchez; Choctâs 1 0

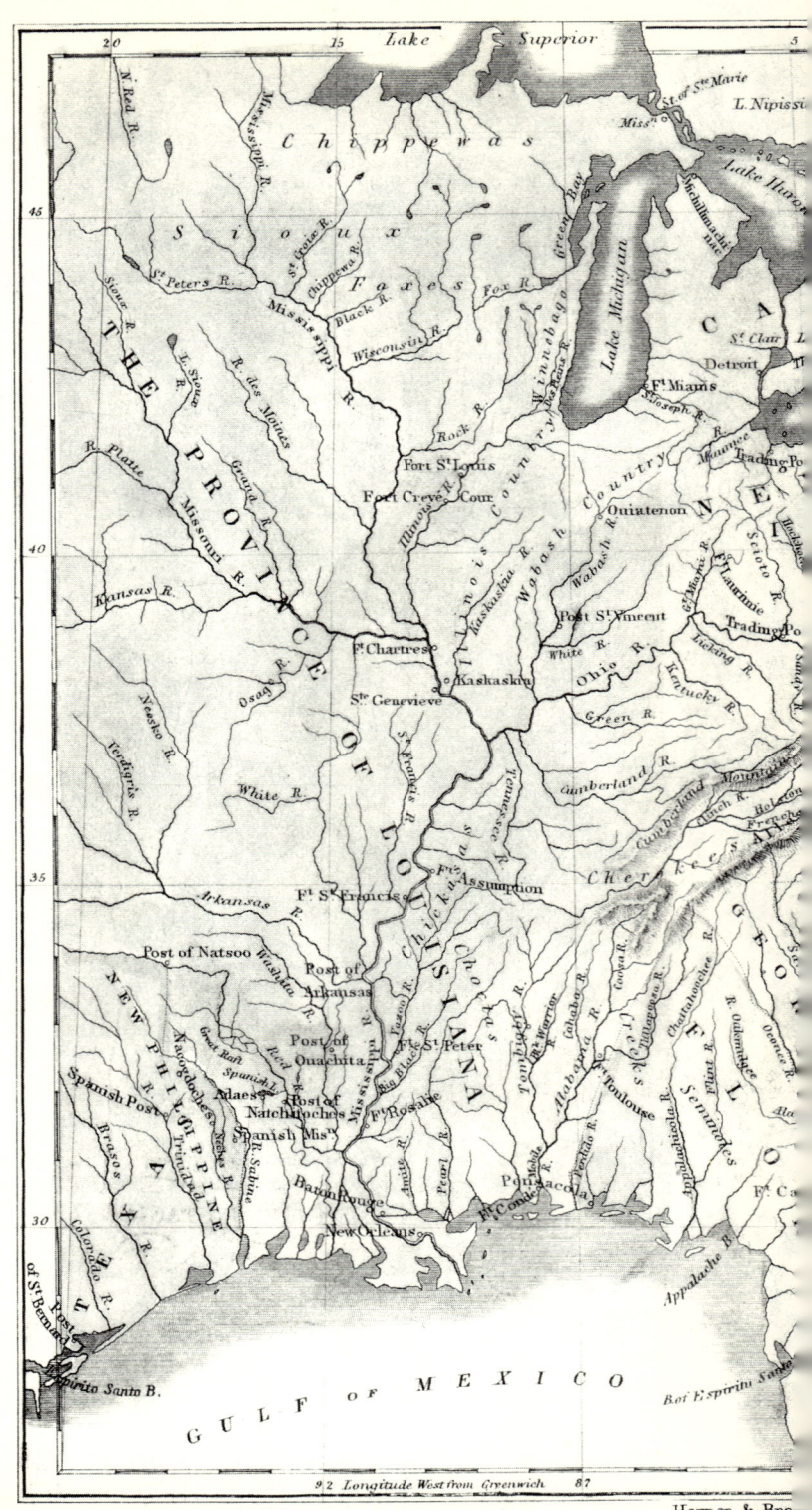

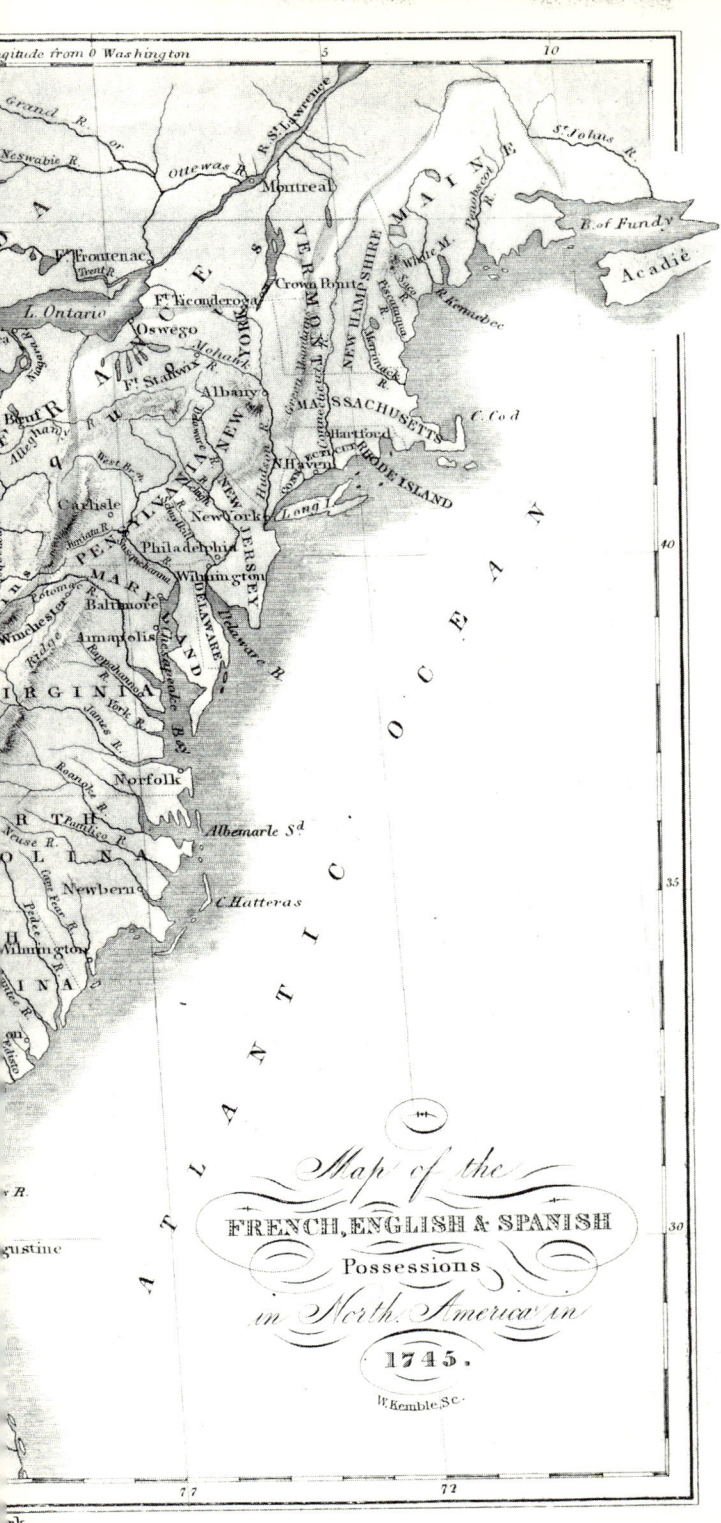

CHAPTER II.

EXPLORATION OF THE MISSISSIPPI RIVER BY LA SALLE: HIS COLONY ON THE COLORADO.—A.D. 1673 TO 1696.

Argument.—Character and Enterprise of La Salle.—His Ambition to complete the Exploration of the Mississippi.—His Plans approved by M. Talon, Intendant of New France.—La Salle sails for Europe.—Receives the King's Patronage.—Returns to Canada.—Repairs to Fort Frontenac and the Western Lakes in 1678.—Winters on the Niagara, and builds the Griffon in 1679.—Proceeds to Green Bay and freights the Griffon.—Visits the Miamis on St. Joseph's River.—Loss of the Griffon and Cargo.—Builds Fort Miami in 1680.—Builds Fort Crève Cœur.—Difficulties with Indians.—Mutiny among his Men.—Mutiny quelled and Indians reconciled.—Father Hennepin sent to explore the Mississippi. — La Salle returns to Fort Frontenac. — Rock Fort built on the Illinois.—Extent of Hennepin's Explorations in 1681.—Subsequently he explores the Mississippi as low as the Arkansas.—La Salle devotes his whole Energy to retrieve his Fortune. — Prepares for a final Exploration of the River to the Sea.—He enters the Mississippi, February 2, 1682.—He explores it to the Sea, and visits numerous Tribes of Indians.—Takes formal Possession of Lower Louisiana.—Returns to Canada.—Sails to Europe in October, 1782.—In Paris, organizes a Colony for the Mississippi.—Sails from Rochelle with his Colony, July 24, 1684.—Character and Numbers of the Colony. — Tedious and disastrous Voyage. — Sails West of the Mississippi, and is compelled to land in Western Texas.—Unavailing Searches for the Mississippi.—Builds "Fort St. Louis" on the Colorado, and takes formal Possession of Texas in 1685.—Deplorable Condition of the Colony.—La Salle finally determines to reach the Illinois and Canada by Land, in 1687.—Assassinated near the Trinity River.— The Remainder of the Colony are dispersed, and some reach the Illinois.—Spaniards search for the French Colony in vain, in 1689.—Illinois Country occupied by French after La Salle's Departure.—Wars in Canada with the Iroquois and English.—The Colonization of Lower Louisiana deferred until the Year 1698 . . . . Page 131

CHAPTER III.

ADVANCE OF THE FRENCH SETTLEMENTS FROM CANADA UPON THE UPPER MISSISSIPPI AND OHIO RIVERS, TO THE CLOSE OF THE FRENCH WAR.—A.D. 1696 TO 1764.

Argument.—Settlements near the Missions, and La Salle's Trading-posts on the Illinois.—At Peoria.—Kaskaskia.—Missionaries visit the Lower Mississippi.—Detroit settled in 1701, by La Motte Cadillac. — Peace with the Iroquois and Western Tribes.—English Jealousy.—Hostile Foxes humbled in 1713.—Settlements on the Upper Mississippi from 1712 to 1720.—Accession of Emigrants from Canada and Louisiana.—Renault and two hundred Miners arrive.—Trade between the Illinois and Mobile.—Agriculture in the Illinois and Wabash Countries.—Ohio River unexplored. — Fort Chartres built in 1721.—Villages in its Vicinity.—Jesuits' College at Kaskaskia.—Advance of the French South of the Niagara River.—On Ontario and Champlain.—Fort Niagara built in 1726.—Crown Point in 1727.—Ticonderoga in 1731.—Tuscarawas join the Five Nations.—Post St. Vincent's erected in 1735.—Presque Isle in 1740.—Agriculture of the Wabash in 1746.—English Jealousy.—Villages of the Illinois Country in 1751.—Population of Kaskaskia.—French advance to the Head Waters of the Alleghany River in 1753.—Forts Le Beuf, Venango, Sandusky.—Ohio Company of Virginia.—Gist visits the Ohio Region as Agent of the Company in 1753.—English Colonies remonstrate against the Advance of the French.—Major Washington Commissioner to Le Beuf.—His Mission unsuccessful.—Governor Dinwiddie rouses the People of Virginia to resist the French on the Ohio.—Captain Trent advances to the Ohio in 1754.—Lieutenant Ward's Detachment captured by the French.—Fort Duquesne erected by the French.—Colonel Washington marches a Detachment to the Monongahela.—Captures a Detachment under M. Jumonville, who is killed.—Colonel Washington surrenders "Fort Necessity" to the French, and retires to Fort Cumberland.—French Forbearance and Moderation.—Arrival of General Braddock at Alexandria.—Preparations for the Capture of Fort Duquesne.—General Braddock marches from Fort Cumberland for the Ohio.—Falls into an Ambuscade on the Monongahela, and utterly defeated.—French at Duquesne undisturbed for two Years.—General Forbes, in 1758, advances to the Ohio.—Occupies Fort Duquesne.—All Canada falls under the British Arms.—France relinquishes New France and Louisiana, by the Treaties of 1762 and 1763, to Spain and Great Britain . . . . Page 157

CHAPTER IV.

THE MANNERS AND CUSTOMS OF THE EARLY FRENCH SETTLERS IN THE ILLINOIS COUNTRY.—A.D. 1700 TO 1780.

Argument.—Extent of the "Illinois Country."—Conciliatory Policy of the French toward the Indian Tribes.—Their amicable Intercourse with the Natives.—Picture of primitive Happiness enjoyed by the Illinois French.—Their plain and homely Houses and rural Villages.—"Common Field," and Mode and Distribution of Labor.—Family Interests in the same.—"Commons," and its Uses.—Patriarchal Harmony and Contentment of these Communities.—Moral Influence of the System.—Equality and Happiness of the People. — The Paternal Homestead, and Patriarchal Families.—Costume: Male and Female.—Catholic Religion.—Equality.—Contentment.—Sabbath Amusements and Hilarity.—Trades and Professions.—Idiom.—Habits and Deportment.—Domestic Simplicity of Manners and Virtues.—The mild and indulgent Regime of Spain.—Facility of Incorporation with Indian Character.—English Authority introduced in 1765.—The Jurisdiction of the United States extended over them in 1804.—Their Objections to American Population and Laws . . . 181

CHAPTER V.

THE FIRST COLONIZATION OF LOUISIANA UNTIL THE CLOSE OF CROZAT'S MONOPOLY.—A.D. 1698 TO 1717.

Argument.—Retrospect of the Illinois Settlements.—D'Iberville undertakes to Colonize Lower Louisiana.—Sails with his Colony from Rochelle, September 24th, 1798.—Leaves the West Indies, and reaches Florida in January, 1699.—Casts anchor at Isle Dauphin.—Disembarks his Colony on Ship Island.—Sets out to explore the Mouth of the Mississippi.—Enters that River on the 2d of March.—Finds Letter of De Tonti to La Salle, dated 1685.—Returns by way of the Bayou Iberville to Bay of St. Louis.—Builds Fort Biloxi, May 2d.—Sails for France.—English Attempts to pre-occupy Louisiana.—The British King bribes Hennepin to lie.—British Colony arrives in the Mississippi.—Condition of the Colony at Biloxi.—Bienville superintends the Colony as Governor.—Explores the Channel of the Mississippi.—Iberville returns with another Colony.—Builds a Fort on the Bank of the River.—Ascends the River as far as the Natchez Tribe.—Selects a Site for Fort Rosalie.—The Natchez Indians.—Their Customs and Religious Ceremonies.—Interview with the "Great Sun."—Boundary between Louisiana and Florida compromised.—The Colony at Biloxi reduced by Sickness and Death.—Exploring Parties.—Unrivaled Water Communications.—Death of Sauvolle, Commandant.—Iberville retires to France.—His Death in 1706.—Extravagant Mining Credulity continues.—Explorations for Mines.—Feeble Condition of the Colony from 1704 to 1710.—Louisiana made Independent of Canada.—Bienville Governor-general.—Banks of the Mississippi neglected.—Crozat's Monopoly granted, 1712.—Extent of Louisiana defined in his Grant.—Population of the Colony in 1713.—Crozat's Enterprise, Zeal, and Plans of Trade.—He is excluded from Trade with Florida and Mexico.—Settlements extend.—Natchitoches on Red River settled.—Trading-posts established.—Disappointment and Failure of his Plans.—Expenditures of Crozat up to 1716.—Fort Rosalie built in 1716.—The new Governor, L'Epinai, arrives with Troops.—Crozat surrenders his Charter in 1717.—Condition of the Colony at his Surrender . . . . . Page 195

CHAPTER VI.
LOUISIANA UNDER THE "WESTERN COMPANY" UNTIL THE FAILURE OF LAW'S "MISSISSIPPI SCHEME."—A.D. 1717 TO 1722.

Argument.—Enthusiasm in France for colonizing the Mississippi.—The Western Company succeeds to the Monopoly of Louisiana.—Charter of the Company.—Its Privileges, Powers, and Term of Existence.—Extravagant Expectations of the Company. —Arrival of the Company's Officers, Troops, and some Colonists at Mobile.—Bienville appointed Governor.—He desires to extend Settlements upon the Mississippi.—Selects the Site of New Orleans.—Establishes a Military Post on it.—Company refuse to leave Mobile as Headquarters.—Mining Delusion excludes Agriculture.—Extensive Mining Arrangements in 1719.—Bienville's Agricultural Views embraced by the Company.—Dependent Condition of Louisiana.—Several large and small Colonies from France arrive.—The Spaniards establish Settlements and "Missions" east of the Rio del Norté.—La Harpe maintains his Post near Natchitoches.—Spanish Encroachments.—Correspondence of the Spanish Commandant, De la Corne, with La Harpe, in 1719.—Negro Slavery introduced into Louisiana by the Western Company.—Different early Importations from Guinea.—Value of Slaves.—Sources from which the African Slave-trade is supplied.—Changes in the Government of Louisiana in 1719.— Superior Council organized.—Headquarters removed to Biloxi.—Emigrants and Troops arrive in 1720.—War with Spain.—Operations at Mobile and Pensacola.— The latter captured and burned by the French.—Spanish Incursions from Santa Fé to the Missouri and Arkansas.—Fort Orleans built on the Missouri.—Plan of Defense for the Upper Mississippi.—Lesueur occupies a Post on the St. Peter's.—Fort Chartres commenced.—Becomes a strong Fortress.—Difficulties in Southwestern Louisiana.—Bienville resolves to occupy Texas.—His "Order" to Bernard La Harpe.—La Harpe's Occupation of the Bay of St. Bernard.—Indian Hostilities east of the Mississippi.—"Fort Condé" built on the Alabama.—Increase of Population by different Arrivals.—Colonies.—Convicts.—Females from the Houses of Correction in Paris.—Interdiction of Convicts to Louisiana.—Arrival of Emigrants and Slaves.—New Orleans becomes the Capital of the Province.—Embarrassment of the Western Company.— Sufferings of the Colonies and Scarcity of Food.—Revolt of Troops at Fort Condé.— New Orleans in 1723.—Picture of Law's celebrated Scheme.—Its Character.—False Basis.—Credit System.—Mining Delusion.—Schemes for procrastinating the Catastrophe.—Bursting of the "Bubble."—Calamitous Consequences of an inflated Currency
216

CHAPTER VII.
LOUISIANA UNDER THE "WESTERN COMPANY," FROM THE FAILURE OF LAW'S "MISSISSIPPI SCHEME" TO THE NATCHEZ MASSACRE.— A.D. 1723 TO 1729.

Argument.—State of the Colony of Louisiana.—Disastrous Effects of Law's Failure in 1722.—Origin of the "German Coast."—Louisiana divided into Nine Judicial Districts.—The Mining Delusion still haunts the Company.—First Outbreak of Hostilities among the Natchez Indians.—Bienville's stern and cruel Demands.—His Treachery and Revenge against the Natchez.—Their Feelings toward the French.— Threatening Attitude of Indian Tribes.—Crops and Plantations destroyed by Equinoctial Storm.—Colony threatened with Famine.—Swiss Troops Revolt.—Financial

Difficulties.—Population in 1723.—Royal Edicts for Relief of Debtors.—Prosperity in 1724-6.—Province supplied with Ecclesiastics and Nuns.—Chevalier Perrier appointed Governor of the Province.—Bienville retires.—Colonial Prosperity and Trade in 1726-7.—Indigo, Fig, and Orange introduced.—"Cassette Girls."—Land Titles recorded.—Prosperous Condition in 1728.—Population.—Trade.—Indications of Indian Hostilities disregarded by Company.—French Aggressions and Intolerance toward the Natchez Tribe.—Indian Impatience of Revenge.—French Indifference to Danger.—Chickasâ Conspiracy.—Chopart's Aggressions among the Natchez.—Conspiracy of the Natchez Chiefs for Revenge.—Chopart's Insensibility to Danger.—Colony on the St. Catharine destroyed by the Indians, November 28, 1792.—Massacre, and the Slain . . . . Page 245

CHAPTER VIII.

LOUISIANA UNDER "THE WESTERN COMPANY" AFTER THE NATCHEZ MASSACRE : EXTERMINATION OF THE NATCHEZ TRIBES.—A.D. 1729 TO 1733.

Argument.—Consternation in Louisiana after the Natchez Tragedy.—The Governor, M. Perrier, prepares to invade the Natchez Country.—Loubois leads on the French Troops and Allies.—Lesueur leads on the Choctâs.—Lesueur arrives on the St. Catharine with his Choctâ Allies.—They attack the Natchez Towns and return victoriously.—Loubois arrives with the Artillery.—After a short Siege, the Indians propose an Armistice.—Loubois permits the Natchez Warriors to escape him.—Erects a terraced Fort and retires to New Orleans.—The Natchez Tribes retire to Black River, and there Fortify themselves.—The Chickasâs espouse the Natchez Cause.—English Intrigue active among the Chickasâs.—Chouacas Tribe exterminated by the French and Negro Troops.—Negro Insurrection arrested.—Military Strength of the Province.—Small Re-enforcement arrives from France.—M. Perrier advances his Forces to Black River.—Invests the Natchez Strong-hold.—Negotiations for Capitulation.—The "Great Sun" and fifty-two Indians surrendered.—Perrier's Demand refused, and the Cannonade opens again.—The Besieged abandon the Fort during a dark and stormy Night.—Many are overtaken and captured.—The French Army return to New Orleans with their Prisoners.—The Prisoners are sold into West Indian Slavery.—The Remnant of the Natchez Tribe imbodies on Red River.—They attack the French Post at Natchitoches, and are repulsed with great Loss.—Termination of the Natchez War.—Personal Characteristics of this Tribe.—State of the Province at the Close of the War.—The Company resolve to surrender their Charter.—The King's Proclamation announces its Acceptance, April 10th, 1732.—Retrospect of the Province under the Company.—The Crown purchases the Company's Effects, and the Royal Government is established 263

CHAPTER IX.

LOUISIANA UNDER THE ROYAL GOVERNORS UNTIL THE CLOSE OF THE CHICKASÂ WAR.—A.D. 1733 TO 1741.

Argument.—Recapitulation of Chickasâ Hostilities, and English Intrigue from Carolina and Georgia.—Bienville reappointed Commandant-general of Louisiana.—He resolves to chastise the Chickasâs.—Demands a Surrender of the Natchez Refugees.—Prepares to invade the Chickasâ Country.—Indian Alliances formed with Choctâs.—Plan of Operations to invade from the North and South simultaneously.—Bienville, with the main Army and Allies, proceeds up the Tombigby.—Is delayed by Rains.—Marches to the Chickasâ Strong-hold.—Attacks the Fortress, and is repulsed with Loss.—Retires, and finally retreats down the Tombigby.—Defeat of D'Artaguette, with the Illinois Forces.—His Captivity and Death in the Chickasâ Country.—Bienville's Account of the Chickasâ Fort.—Chickasâs send Runners to apprise the English of their Victory over the French.—Bienville, overwhelmed with Chagrin, resolves on a second Invasion from the Mississippi.—The Plan of Invasion approved by the Minister of War.—The Grand Army proceeds up the Mississippi to Fort St. Francis.—Fort Assumption built on Fourth Chickasâ Bluff.—Delays from Sickness and Want of Provisions.—M. Celeron advances with a Detachment toward the Chickasâ Towns.—Concludes a Peace, by Bienville's Order, with a single Village.—Fort Assumption dismantled, and the Army descends to New Orleans.—Bienville retires under the Disgrace of a second Failure, and is superseded by the Marquis de Vaudreuil as Governor.—Retrospect of the Condition of the Province up to the Year 1741 . . . . Page 277

CHAPTER X.
CONDITION OF LOUISIANA FROM THE CLOSE OF THE CHICKASÂ WAR UNTIL THE TERMINATION OF THE FRENCH DOMINION.—A.D. 1741 TO 1764.

Argument.—Louisiana continues Prosperous and free from Indian Hostilities until the Close of the Acadian War.—Agriculture and Trade prosper under individual Enterprise.—Equinoctial Storm in 1745.—Rigorous Winter of 1748-9 killed the Orange-trees.—La Buissonière and Macarty Commandants at Fort Chartres.—Condition of Agricultural Settlements near New Orleans.—Staples, Rice, Indigo, Cotton, Tobacco.—Sugar-cane first introduced in 1751, and Sugar subsequently becomes a Staple Product.—The British resume their Intrigue with the Choctás and Chickasâs after the Close of the Acadian War.—Choctâs commence War.—Chickasâs resume Hostilities on the Mississippi.—Disturbances break out on the Ohio with the English Provinces.—Governor Vaudreuil invades the Chickasâ Country by way of the Tombigby.—Ravages their Towns and Fields.—Collisions between French and English on the Ohio.—Ohio Company's Grant leads to Hostilities.—Re-enforcement sent to Fort Chartres.—Lower Louisiana is prosperous.—Horrid Military Execution for Revolt at Cat Island.—British Inhumanity to the People of Acadia.—Origin of the "Acadian Coast" in 1755.—Louisiana suffers again from Paper Money in 1756.—The French abandon the Ohio Region.—Canada falls under the Arms of Britain in 1759, and many Canadians emigrate to Louisiana.—France relinquishes all Louisiana, by Treaties of 1762 and 1763, to Spain and Great Britain.—Great Britain takes possession of Florida and Eastern Louisiana in 1764-5.—Spain assumes Jurisdiction over Western Louisiana in 1765.—Extension of the Limits of West Florida by Great Britain.—Spain and Great Britain divide the Valley of the Mississippi, until the United States succeed, first to British, and then to Spanish Louisiana . . 294

BOOK III.
GREAT BRITAIN IN THE VALLEY OF THE MISSISSIPPI.
CHAPTER I.
EXPULSION OF THE FRENCH FROM THE OHIO REGION.—INDIAN HOSTILITIES UNTIL THE CLOSE OF PONTIAC'S WAR.—A.D. 1757 TO 1764.

Argument.—England persists in occupying the Upper Ohio Region.—The Frontier Anglo-American Settlements driven back in 1757.—Indian Hostilities West of the Blue Ridge.—Shawanese Incursions in 1757.—Sandy Creek Expedition under Colonel Lewis.—Peace established with the Cherokees.—Fort Loudon built on South Branch of Holston.—First White Settlements on the Holston in 1758.—Explorations of Dr.

CONTENTS.

Walker and others in 1758, and previously.—Forces for Reduction of Fort Duquesne. —Major Grant's Defeat at Fort Duquesne.—French and Indians attack Colonel Bouquet's Camp at Loyal Hanna.—General Forbes advances to Fort Duquesne.—Occupies the deserted Post.—" Fort Pitt" commenced.—Fort Burd erected on the Monongahela, 1759.—Cherokees resume Hostilities.—A Portion of the Cherokees averse to Hostilities.—Friendly Cherokee Deputation imprisoned at Fort George.—Cherokees attempt to rescue their Chiefs.—General Cherokee War provoked in 1760.— Capture and Massacre of Fort Loudon.—Colonel Grant invades the Cherokee Nation.—Peace with Cherokees restored in 1761.—British Arms victorious in New France and Canada.—English Settlements from Virginia and North Carolina advance upon the Waters of the Ohio in 1762–3.—Treaty of Paris confirms to England all Canada and Eastern Louisiana.—The Northwestern Indians refuse their Assent to the Treaty.—The "Six Nations."—Their territorial Limits.—The Western Tribes resolve to resist the Advance of the English Power.—The King's conciliatory Proclamation of 1763.—Locations and Grants made on the Waters of the Ohio; on Cheat River.—Indian League under Pontiac, the great Ottawâ Chief, or Emperor.— His Character and Plan of offensive Operations.—Catholic Missionaries and Jesuits not Instigators of the War.—Terrible Onset of Indian Hostilities.—Traders first Victims.—Capture of the Western Posts by Indians.—Capture of Presque Isle; of Fort Miamis; of Mackinaw.—Massacre of the Garrison and Inmates.—Siege of Fort Pitt.—Colonel Bouquet defeats Indian Ambuscade at Turtle Creek.—Protracted Siege of Detroit by Pontiac in Person.—The Defense by Major Gladwyn.—Incidents of Indian Warfare and savage Barbarity.—A Detachment of Troops with Supplies for Detroit cut off by Indians.—Captain Dalzel slain in a Sortie.—Exposed Condition of the western and southwestern Frontiers.—Indian Hostilities in Pennsylvania.— "Massacre of Wyoming."—Hostilities in Virginia, at Muddy Creek and Big Levels.—Attack on Fort Ligonier.— Fort Loudon.— Hostilities on Susquehanna; on Greenbrier and Jackson Rivers.—Terror of eastern Part of New York.—Marauding Bands of Indians on the southwestern Frontier.—Lawless white Men on the Frontiers.—Outrages and Massacres committed by the Paxton Boys.—Origin and Designs of this Banditti.—Military Movements of the English Forces toward the Frontier.—Advance of General Bradstreet to Niagara.—Treaty of Niagara.—Treaty of Detroit.—Pontiac opposes the Treaty.—Colonel Bouquet invades the Indian Country upon the Muskingum.—Forms a Treaty.—Treaty of the "German Flats" with the "Six Nations."—Peace proclaimed December 5th, 1764 . . . . Page 309

CHAPTER II.

ADVANCE OF THE ANGLO-AMERICAN POPULATION TO THE OHIO RIVER.—SETTLEMENTS AND EXPLORATIONS.—A.D. 1765 TO 1774.

Argument.—Settlements spring up near the military Routes and Posts.—Fort Pitt.— Fort Burd.—Isolated Condition of the Illinois Settlements.—Advance of white Settlements upon the Sources of the Susquehanna, Youghiogeny, and Monongahela; also upon New River and Greenbrier, Clinch and Holston.—Indian Territory on the Susquehanna, Alleghany, and Cheat Rivers.—Frontier Settlements of Virginia in 1766.—Emigration to the Monongahela in 1767.—Redstone Fort a garrisoned Post.— Increase of Emigration in 1768.—Settlements extend to the Sources of the two Kenhawas.—The colonial System of granting Lands east of the Ohio.—The Indians become impatient of the white Man's Advance.—Mode of conciliating Indians for their Lands.—Remonstrance of the Six Nations to the King's "Indian Agent."—The Subject of their Complaint laid before the provincial Legislature.—Treaties with northern and southern Indians ordered by royal Government.—"Treaty of Fort Stanwix." —The "Mississippi Company" of Virginia, 1769.—"Treaty of Hard Labor" with Cherokees.—Extensive Claims to Territory set up by the English under the "Treaty of Fort Stanwix" with the Six Nations.—Settlements advance to the Holston and Clinch Rivers.—Impatience of northern and southern Indians at the Advance of the

xviii   CONTENTS.

Whites.—Explorations of Dr. Walker west of Cumberland Mountains, in 1768; of Finley, in 1769; of Colonel Knox.—"Long-Hunters."—Western Emigration encouraged by royal colonial Governments.—Emigration to Holston, Clinch, and to West Florida, in 1770.—Fort Pitt a garrisoned Post.—Settlements at Redstone Fort, on Ohio, at Wheeling, and other Points, in 1770.—Enthusiasm of eastern Settlements for western Emigration.—Territory claimed by Virginia.—Emigrants from North Carolina advance upon the Sources of Holston River.—Impatience of the Cherokees. —"Treaty of Lochaber."—New boundary Line.—The four hundred acre Settlement Act of Virginia, passed in 1770.—"District of West Augusta" organized.—Cresap's Settlement at Redstone "Old Fort," in 1771.—Provisions fail.—The "Starving Year" of 1772.—Settlements on the Ohio above the Kenhawa.—Route from eastern Settlements to the Ohio.—Manner of traveling.—Emigration to the West increases greatly in 1773.—To Western Virginia.—To "Western District" of North Carolina. —To West Florida.—Numerous Surveyors sent out to Kentucky.—Thomas Bullitt, Hancock Taylor, M'Afee.—Surveys near Frankfort, Harrodsburg, and Danville.— Captain Bullitt at the Falls of Ohio.—Settlements on the Holston, East Tennessee.— Daniel Boone attempts to introduce white Families from North Carolina.—Driven back by Indians.—Emigration in 1774 to the Upper Ohio; on the Monongahela, Kenhawa, and Kentucky Regions.—Simon Kenton at May's Lick.—James Harrod at Harrodsburg.—West Augusta in 1774.—Outrages of lawless white Men provoke Indian Vengeance.—Wheeling Fort built.—Fort Fincastle.—Dr. Connolly Commandant of West Augusta . . . . Page 343

CHAPTER III.

LORD DUNMORE'S INDIAN WAR: EXTENSION OF THE WESTERN SETTLEMENTS FROM THE TREATY OF "CAMP CHARLOTTE" TO THE DECLARATION OF INDEPENDENCE.—A.D. 1774 TO 1776.

Argument.—The Indians reluctantly assent to Boundaries claimed by the Treaty of Fort Stanwix.—Outrages of lawless white Men provoke Indian Resentment.—Explorers and Land-jobbers.—Rumor of Indian Depredations circulated by them.—Alarm excited among Explorers.—Captain Cresap advises Violence, and heads a Party which murders some Indians above Wheeling and at Captina Creek.—Greathouse leads another Party against the Indians at Yellow Creek.—Other Murders preceding these. —Murder of "Bald Eagle" Chief.—Five Families at Bulltown.—Indian Revenge commences upon the Traders.—Consternation on the Frontier.—Settlements abandoned.—Union Station near Laurel Hill established.—Hostile Incursions of Indians. —Defensive Measures under Lord Dunmore.—The Wappatomica Campaign under General M'Donald.—Surveys and Explorations in Kentucky suspended in 1774.— Daniel Boone conducts Surveyors to old Settlements.—General Lewis marches down the Kenhawa.—Learns the Change of Dunmore's Plans.—The severe "Battle of the Point."—Loss of the Virginians and of Indians.—"Cornstalk," the King of the Shawanese.—Lord Dunmore's Advance to the Scioto.—"Camp Charlotte" fortified.—Operations against the Shawanese Towns.—Negotiations with the Indians.—General Lewis advances to the Scioto.—He indignantly obeys Dunmore's Order to halt.— Treaty of Camp Charlotte opened.—Speech of Cornstalk; of Logan.—Stipulations of this Treaty.—Peace proclaimed, January 7th, 1775.—Suspicions against Lord Dunmore.—Emigration revives in the West.—Explorations resumed in Kentucky.— Colonel Floyd on Bear-grass Creek.—Other Surveys and Settlements.—Settlements on the Holston and Clinch in 1775.—Preparations in Virginia and North Carolina for the Occupancy of Kentucky.—Patrick Henry and others.—Colonel Henderson and others.—Treaty of Watauga.—Colonel Henderson's Land Company.—Preparations for establishing the Colony of Transylvania.—Boone Pioneer of the Colony to Kentucky River.—Boonesborough erected.—Colonel Henderson leads out his Colony.—Boone leads another in the Fall.—"Plan of Boonesborough."—Logan's Fort built.—Company's Land-office.—Proprietary Government established in Transylvania, 1775.—Acts

CONTENTS. xix

of Legislature, second Session.—The Company memorialize the Federal Congress.—Opposition to the Proprietary Government.—Transylvania Republic merges into the State Government of Virginia.—Settlements begin to form on the north Side of Kentucky River.—Harrod's Station erected in 1776.—Colonel Harrod introduces the first Families from the Monongahela.—Declaration of American Independence.—Indian Hostilities begin in Kentucky.—Preparations for Defense.—Major George Rogers Clark superintends the Militia Organization. . . . . Page 368

CHAPTER IV.
BRITISH OCCUPANCY OF FLORIDA AND THE ILLINOIS COUNTRY.—CLOSE OF THE BRITISH DOMINION IN THE MISSISSIPPI VALLEY.—A.D. 1764 TO 1782.

Argument.—Extent of Florida and the Illinois Country under the British Dominion.—English Authority established in West Florida by Governor Johnston.—Major Loftus appointed Commandant of Illinois.—His Defeat above Tunica Bayou, and his Death.—Dissatisfaction of the French of West Florida.—Population in 1764.—Anglo-American Emigration to Florida encouraged.—Emigrants arrive from 1765 to 1770.—Great Increase of Emigrants in 1773 to 1776.—Settlements on east Side of the Mississippi.—British Military Posts in West Florida.—Monopoly of Trade by British Traders.—Emigration in 1775-6.—Agriculture encouraged.—British Tories in West Florida.—British Authority established in the *Illinois Country*, 1765.—St. Angé.—Captain Stirling.—French Population in 1765.—General Gage's Proclamation.—Major Frazer.—Colonel Reed.—Colonel Wilkins.—His Administration.—Grants of Land.—British Military Posts in the Northwest.—Detroit.—Kaskaskia.—Cahokia.—St. Vincent.—Prejudices of the Illinois French.—Detroit, Vincennes, and Kaskaskia the Sources of all the Indian Barbarities on the Western Frontier.—Reduction of these British Posts indispensable to the Security of the Virginia Frontier.—Plan of Colonel Clark's Expedition for their Reduction.—Colonel Clark leads his Expedition to Kaskaskia.—The Fort and Town taken by Surprise.—Stern Demeanor of the Commander toward the French.—Happy Results.—Cahokia surrenders to Captain Bowman.—Governor Rocheblave sent Prisoner to Virginia.—People of Vincennes declare for Virginia.—Indian Negotiations and Treaties on the Wabash.—Jurisdiction of Virginia extended over the Illinois Country.—"Illinois County."—Colonel Hamilton advances with a strong Force from Detroit.—Captain Helm capitulates.—Clark advances to recapture the Post.—Colonel Hamilton taken by Surprise.—Despairs of successful Defense, and capitulates.—Captain Helm captures a Detachment with Supplies from Detroit.—Colonel Hamilton sent Captive to Virginia.—Is placed in close Confinement in retaliation for his Inhumanity.—Colonel Clark contemplates the Capture of Detroit.—British Power expelled from the Illinois Country.—Difficulties begin in West Florida.—Captain Willing descends the Mississippi.—His Collision with the People at Natchez.—First Act of Hostility at Ellis Cliffs.—Spain espouses the American Cause.—Galvez invades West Florida.—Captures British Posts at Manchac, Baton Rouge, Natchez, and Mobile.—Is unsuccessful at Pensacola.—Pensacola captured in 1781.—All Florida submits to the Arms of Spain.—British Dominion ceases on the Mississippi

402

BOOK IV.
SPAIN IN THE VALLEY OF THE MISSISSIPPI.
CHAPTER I.

LOUISIANA UNDER THE DOMINION OF SPAIN FROM THE DISMEMBERMENT TO THE EXPULSION OF THE ENGLISH FROM FLORIDA.—A.D. 1763 TO 1783.

Argument.—Extent of Spanish Louisiana.—Repugnance of the French of West Florida to the English Dominion.—French Opposition to the Spanish Dominion in Louisiana.—Spain indulges their Prejudices by deferring her Jurisdiction.—Public Remonstrances and Petitions against the Transfer to Spain.—Jean Milhet sent a Delegate to Paris.—His Mission unsuccessful.—Arrival of Don Ulloa as Spanish Commissioner in New Orleans.—He delays the formal Transfer of the Province.—French Population in Louisiana in 1766.—Spanish Troops arrive for the different Posts.—Popular Excitement against Ulloa.—The Superior Council requires him to leave the Province or produce his Commission.—He retires on Board a Spanish Man-of-war.—Perilous Condition of the prominent Malecontents.—Second Convention.—Second Mission to Paris.—General O'Reilly arrives at the Balize with a strong Spanish Force.—He notifies Aubry of his Arrival and his Powers.—His Professions of Lenity.—Ceremony of Transfer, August 18th, 1769.—The Flag of Spain displaces that of France.—Population of Louisiana in 1769.—Settlements of Upper Louisiana.—Arrest of twelve prominent French Citizens.—Their Trials, Imprisonment, and Execution.—Spanish Jurisdiction formally introduced in the Province.—" Superior Council" superseded by the " Cabaldo."—Inferior Courts organized.—Rules of procedure in the Courts.—Spanish Emigrants arrive.—Summary of O'Reilly's Administration.—Subsequent Spanish Rule.—Commerce and Agriculture under Unzaga's mild Rule.—Population of Upper Louisiana in 1776.—Galvez Governor of Louisiana.—British Traders from Florida endeavor to monopolize the Trade of the Mississippi.—Spain favorable to the American Revolution.—Oliver Pollock and Captain Willing in New Orleans.—Spain espouses the War against Great Britain.—West Florida invaded by Governor Galvez.—Fort Charlotte captured in 1780.—Unsuccessful Attack on Pensacola.—Attack on St. Louis by British and Indians from Mackinaw.—Repulsed by Spaniards and Americans.—Bombardment and Capture of Pensacola, May 9th, 1781.—Surrender of West Florida.—Cession of East Florida to Spain.—Revolt in the Natchez District, and Capture of Fort Panmure in 1781.—Proceedings of the Spanish Authorities against the Insurgents.—Treaty of 1783 concluded.—Revival of Agricultural and commercial Enterprise . . . . Page 441

CHAPTER II.

LOUISIANA UNDER THE SPANISH DOMINION, FROM THE TREATY OF 1783 TO THE YEAR 1796.—A.D. 1783 TO 1796.

Argument.—Prosperous Condition of Louisiana after the War.—Population in 1785.—Galvez retires from Louisiana.—Don Miro succeeds to the provisional Government.—Judge of Residence.—Catholic Church in Louisiana.—Inquisition excluded.—Acadian Emigrants.—Indulgence to British Subjects in West Florida.—Irish Catholic Priests for the Natchez District.—Miro succeeds as Governor-general of Louisiana in 1786.—Arrival of the Commissioners of Georgia.—Georgia Act creating " Bourbon County."—Spanish Duties upon American river Trade.—Extension of American Settlements in the Ohio Region.—Claims of western People to free Navigation of the Mississippi.—Their Impatience under Spanish Imposts.—They contemplate the Invasion of Louisiana by military Force.—Nature and Extent of Spanish Imposts.—

CONTENTS. xxi

Relaxation of impost Duties.—Colonel Wilkinson's Agency in effecting Relaxation of revenue Laws.—Emigration of Americans to West Florida and Louisiana.—General Morgan's Colony.—" New Madrid" laid off.—Guardoqui urges rigid Execution of impost Regulations.—The Intendant rigorously enforces revenue Laws.—Louisiana threatened with military Invasion from Ohio Region.—Conflagration of New Orleans in 1788.—Supplies from the Ohio admitted by the river Trade.—Colonel Wilkinson engages in the tobacco Trade.—Emigration from Cumberland to Louisiana encouraged; also from the Ohio and the Illinois.—Population of Louisiana in 1788.—Emigration and Trade from the Ohio Region in 1789-90.—Policy recommended by Navarro to Spain.—Spain jealous of the Extension of the Federal Jurisdiction.—First Schools and Academies in New Orleans.—Baron Carondelet succeeds Miro as Governor of Louisiana.—Population of New Orleans in 1792.—Trade with Philadelphia. —Political Disturbances emanating from revolutionary France in 1793.—Genet's Intrigues and contemplated Invasion of Louisiana and Florida from the United States. —Defensive Movements of Baron Carondelet in Louisiana.—Measures of the Federal Government to suppress any hostile Movement.—Fort Barrancas commenced at the fourth Chickasâ Bluff.—Counter-plot of Carondelet for effecting a Separation of western People.—Don Rendon Intendant of Louisiana and Florida.—Louisiana and Florida an independent Bishopric.—Carondelet improves and fortifies the City of New Orleans; drains the back Swamps.—A navigable Canal.—" Canal Carondelet' completed.—The Indigo Crop fails, and Cotton, Sugar, and Tobacco succeed.—Louisiana relieved from Apprehension.—Genet's Agents arrested; himself recalled.— French Royalists propose to settle a Colony on the Washita.—Arrangements with Maison Rouge.—Alleged Grant and Colony of Maison Rouge.—Subsequent Litigation.—Adjudication and final Rejection of the Claim as fraudulent.—Grant to Baron de Bastrop.—Americans excluded from Louisiana and Florida.—Grant to Dubuque on Upper Mississippi.—Carondelet's Intrigues for the Separation of Kentucky from the Union.—Gayoso sent to negotiate with the Kentucky Conspirators.—Sebastian descends to Natchez and New Orleans.—Negro Insurrection discovered and suppressed in the Island of Point Coupée.—Negro Importation interdicted.—Don Morales is Intendant for 1796.—Baron Carondelet's last Effort to detach Kentucky in 1796.— Route to Upper Louisiana through the Bayou Barthelemy and St. Francis River
Page 465

CHAPTER III.

POLITICAL RELATIONS OF LOUISIANA WITH THE UNITED STATES, FROM THE TREATY OF 1783 TO THE TREATY OF MADRID.— A.D. 1783 TO 1795.

Argument.—Field of national Controversy opened by Treaty of 1783.—Construction of the Treaty by Spain.—Construction by United States.—Navigation of the Mississippi.—Claimed by the United States.—Spain claims the exclusive Right.—Denies Use of the River to the western People.—Restrictions and Duties exacted by Spanish Authorities.—Embarrassed Condition of the western People.—Jealous Apprehensions of Spain.—Condition of American Settlements.—Indian Tribes.—Policy pursued by Spain toward Kentucky.—Indignation of the western People.—Excitement by a Rumored abandonment of the Claim of the United States.—Change of Spanish Policy.— Governor Miro relaxes the Restrictions upon the western Trade.—His conciliatory Policy to western People in 1788-9.—Colonel Wilkinson's commercial Enterprise with New Orleans suspected.—Western People become reconciled to the Spanish Authorities.—Cumberland Settlements.—" Miro District."—Emigration from Kentucky and Cumberland encouraged.—Grants of Land in 1790.—Spanish Intrigue for separating the Western States.—Negotiations of the Federal Government.—Impatience of the western People.—Disaffection appears in Kentucky.—Negotiations by the Federal Government.—Spanish Emissaries embarrass Negotiations with Creek Indians, 1789-1790.—" Southwestern Territory" organized. — Baron Carondelet commences

CONTENTS.

his Intrigue with Kentucky, 1792.—Creeks instigated to Hostilities by Spanish emissaries.—Intrigues of M. Genet, the French Minister.—Threatened Invasion of East Florida from Georgia.—Spain procrastinates Negotiations while Carondelet operates upon the western People.—War with Spain apprehended by President Washington in 1794.—Baron Carondelet apprehends Danger from the western People.—Five political Parties in the West.—Powers, the Spanish emissary, sent to Kentucky.—Views of the Federal Government.—It restrains the western Excitement.—Carondelet renews his Mission to Kentucky in 1795.—Gayoso and Powers sent to negotiate with the Kentucky Conspirators.—The Mission Fails.—Prospects of Disunion blasted.—Sebastian visits New Orleans.—Overtures from the Spanish Court.—Thomas Pinckney Minister to Spain.—Treaty of Madrid signed, October 20th.—Stipulations in the Treaty relative to Boundary and the river Trade.—The Georgia Bubble.—"Yazoo Speculation."—Its Effects on Louisiana . . . . Page 493

CHAPTER IV.
POLITICAL RELATIONS BETWEEN THE UNITED STATES AND LOUISIANA, FROM THE TREATY OF MADRID TO THE SURRENDER OF THE NATCHEZ DISTRICT.—A.D. 1796 TO 1798.

Argument.—Treaty of Madrid merely a Measure of State Policy with Spain.—Her Intention to evade its Stipulations, if possible.—Intrigue with the western People.—The United States prepare in good Faith to carry out the Stipulations.—Colonel Ellicott, as Commissioner of the United States, arrives at Natchez.—His Military Escort left at Bayou Pierre.—Gayoso designates the 19th of March to begin the Line of Demarkation.—Ellicott encamps in Natchez.—Proceedings delayed by Baron Carondelet.—Ellicott orders down his Military Escort.—Gayoso suddenly ceases Preparations to evacuate the Fort Panmure.—Fortifies this Post.—Pretext for Change of Conduct.—Lieutenant M'Leary, with his Escort, arrives from Bayou Pierre.—Gayoso continues to strengthen his Defenses.—Indian Hostilities alleged as the Cause.—Next, a British Invasion from Canada apprehended.—Blount's Conspiracy, and its Explosion.—The People become excited.—Correspondence between the American Commissioner and Gayoso.—Advanced Guard under Lieutenant Pope arrives at Natchez.—Gayoso objects to the Presence of United States Troops at Natchez.—Other Reasons for Delay urged by Gayoso.—His Agents tamper with the Indians.—Popular Excitement increases.—The Governor-general issues his Proclamation, 24th of May.—Effects of this Proclamation.—Efforts of Gayoso to calm the popular Excitement.—Arrest and Imprisonment of Hannah.—This excites the People to Resistance.—Colonel Ellicott and Lieutenant Pope sustain the popular Commotion.—Gayoso's Proclamation of June 14th.—A public Meeting called.—Gayoso and his Family retire to the Fort.—Seeks an Interview with the American Commissioner.—" Committee of Public Safety" appointed.—This Committee recognized by Gayoso.—A " Permanent Committee" elected.—Opposition of Colonel Hutchens and others, who sustain Gayoso.—Ellicott retires to Washington.—Gayoso appointed Governor-general.—Retires to New Orleans.—Captain Guion arrives with United States Troops.—His Attempt to restore Harmony and Tranquillity.—The Policy of his Course.—The Posts of Nogales and Panmure evacuated in March, 1798.—The Line of Demarkation commenced in May, 1798, and completed next Year.—First organization of the Mississippi Territory.—Arrival of the Territorial Governor and Judges.—General Wilkinson arrives with United States Troops.—Retrospect of the Spanish Policy.—Pretexts for Delay, and the Intrigue with General Wilkinson again unsuccessful.—Return of Emissary Powers 516

CHAPTER V.

CLOSE OF THE SPANISH DOMINION IN LOUISIANA, AND THE FINAL TRANSFER OF THE PROVINCE TO THE UNITED STATES.—A.D. 1797 TO 1804.

Argument.—Prosperity of Louisiana unaffected by Hostilities in Europe.—Gayoso succeeds as Governor-general of Louisiana in 1797.—The King's Orders relative to Land Grants.—The Intendant alone empowered to make Grants.—French Privateers.—Daniel Clarke, Jr., recognized as Consul.—Harmony on the Spanish and American Borders.—Concordia.—Vidalia in 1799.—Death of Gayoso in 1799.—His Successors.—Colonel Ellicott's Eulogy of Gayoso.—Population of Upper Louisiana.—Its Trade and Commerce.—Harmony with the western People again disturbed by Morales.—Policy of Spain in restricting her Grants of Land.—Jealous of Military Adventurers.—Restrictions enforced by Morales.—His first Interdict of Deposit at New Orleans.—Western Indignation.—Capture of New Orleans contemplated.—American Troops in the Northwest.—Invasion of Louisiana abandoned by John Adams.—Filhiol and Fejeiro at Fort Miro, on the Washita.—Right of Deposit restored in 1801.—Again suspended in 1802.—Restored in 1803.—Approaching Change of Dominion in Louisiana.—The First Consul of the French Republic acquires the Province of Louisiana.—The French Occupation deferred one Year by European Wars.—Napoleon determines to sell the Province to the United States.—Negotiation for Sale commenced.—Mr. Jefferson's Instructions.—Treaty of Cession signed April 30th, 1803.—Amount of Purchase-money.—Terms of Payment.—Preparations for French Occupation.—The Form of Government prepared by French Prefect.—Arrival of Laussat, the Colonial Prefect.—His Proclamation.—Response of the People.—Proclamation of Governor Salcedo.—Rumor of Cession to United States.—Laussat appointed Commissioner of the French Republic.—Conditions of the Treaty of April 30th, 1803.—Preparations for Occupation by the United States.—Protest of the Spanish King.—Congress ratifies the Treaty.—Commissioners of the United States.—Preparations of French Commissioner.—Ceremony of Spanish Delivery.—Proclamation of the French Prefect.—Spanish Rule abolished and French Government instituted.—Volunteer Battalion for the Preservation of Order.—Preparations for Delivery to the United States.—Governor Claiborne and General Wilkinson arrive in New Orleans.—Ceremony of French Delivery to the United States, December 20th, 1803.—Remote Posts formally delivered subsequently to Agents of the French Prefect.—Major Stoddart takes Possession of Upper Louisiana, March 9th, 1804.—Condition and Boundaries of Louisiana.—Population of the Province.—Commerce.—Agricultural Products.—Trade and Manufactures of New Orleans . . . . Page 538

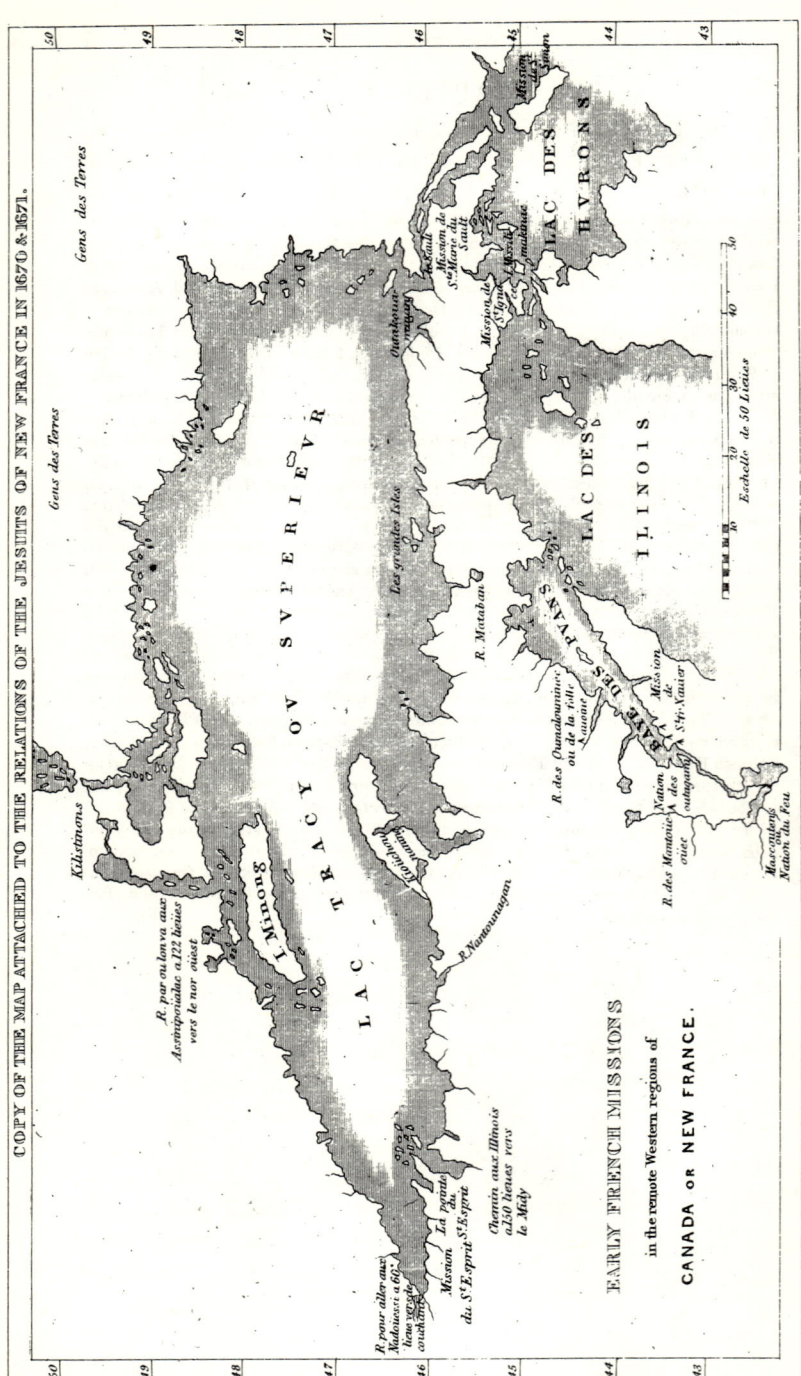

HISTORY

OF THE

DISCOVERY AND SETTLEMENT

OF THE

VALLEY OF THE MISSISSIPPI.

BOOK I.

EARLY EXPLORATIONS OF THE SPANIARDS IN THE VALLEY OF THE MISSISSIPPI.

CHAPTER I.

FIRST SPANISH DISCOVERIES IN FLORIDA.—A.D. 1512 TO 1538.

Argument.—The former undefined Extent of Florida.—Spirit of Enterprise and Discovery awakened in Europe by Spanish Conquests in the West Indies, Mexico, and Peru.—The romantic and unfortunate Expedition of Ponce de Leon into East Florida.—The Expedition and Disasters of Vasquez de Ayllon; his Avarice, Cruelty, and Death.—The disastrous Expedition of Pamphilo de Narvaez.—Preparations for the great and chivalrous Expedition, under Hernando de Soto, for the Conquest of Florida.—The Nature and Extent of this Enterprise.—De Soto's commanding Person and Influence.—The Expedition sails from Spain for the West Indies.—Other Arrangements and Preparations completed.—The Expedition sails from Havana, and arrives at the Bay of Espiritu Santo late in May, 1539, A.D.—A Synopsis of the Marches, Disasters, and Fate of the Expedition.

[A.D. 1512.] In the first explorations of North America, Florida, as originally claimed by Spain, comprised all that portion of the present territory of the United States which lies south of the state of New York. At a later period, until the French discovered Canada, and the pilgrims settled in New England, it comprised all that portion of the United States south of the present state of Virginia, or south of the parallel of latitude 36° 30′ north, and extending westward to the Spanish possessions of Mexico. These limits were successively restricted by other European powers, until Florida, early in the eighteenth century, comprised only a narrow strip of sea-coast on the northeast side of the Gulf of Mexico, chiefly south of

Vol. I.—A

latitude 31° north, and east of the Perdido River and Bay, and including the peninsula of East Florida.*

Within thirty years after the first discovery of America by Columbus, nearly all the great West India Islands, as well as the isthmus between North and South America, known as the Spanish Main, were explored and conquered by the Spaniards; yet, in that part of the Continent north of the Gulf of Mexico, few and imperfect discoveries had been made. During the early part of the sixteenth century, or between the years 1510 and 1540, numerous attempts had been made to explore, and some expeditions had been fitted out to conquer, the country lying east and north of the Mexican Gulf; but they had been disastrous and fruitless.

These expeditions generally set sail from Cuba, Hispaniola, or some of the larger islands, and, proceeding in a northward direction, touched upon the Bahama Isles, and upon the eastern coast of what is now East Florida, Georgia, and South Carolina. The islands were populous and wealthy, while the country north of the Mexican Gulf was an immense wilderness, inhabited only by a few scattering and hostile savages. Yet the belief obtained among the Spaniards that in the interior of this vast region there existed great and powerful empires, far more wealthy than those of Mexico and Peru. Those who had shared in the plunder of the latter countries, sighed for the still richer plunder which they believed to exist in Florida.† This belief was confirmed by the most incredible stories, told by navigators who, at different times, had touched upon those shores. Every disaster on that coast, and every failure of a new expedition, only served to inflame their avarice, and stimulate their spirit for adventure and wild enterprise. In Spain the enthusiasm of all classes for discovery and conquest was unbounded. In the beautiful language of Theodore Irving, "Never was the spirit of wild adventure more universally diffused than at the dawn of the sixteenth century. The won-

---

* See book i., chapter v., for the "Extent and Boundaries, &c., of Florida."

† See Irving's Conquest of Florida. This is an interesting work, in two vols., 12mo, written by Theodore Irving. It is handsomely devised and compiled from Spanish historians, and written in a most beautiful style. It treats chiefly of the explorations and adventures of Hernando de Soto, and his gallant band of cavaliers, who overrun Florida, as known at that time, between the years 1539 and 1542. It is compiled from the narrative of the Inca Garcilaso de la Vega, and others. Many portions of the narrative may appear like romance, but the adventures of De Soto were only romance acted out in real life. See vol. i., chap. i. and ii.

drous discoveries of Columbus and his hardy companions and followers, the descriptions of beautiful summer isles of the west, and the tales of unexplored regions of wealth, locked up in an unbounded wilderness, had an effect upon the imaginations of the young and adventurous, not unlike the preaching of the chivalric crusades for the recovery of the Holy Sepulcher. The gallant knight, the servile retainer, the soldier of fortune, the hooded friar, the pains-taking mechanic, the toilful husbandman, the loose profligate, and the hardy mariner, all were touched with the pervading passion; all left home, country, friends, wives, children, lovers, to seek some imaginary Eldorado, confidently expecting to return with countless treasure."

Fired with this enthusiasm, Spain and Portugal sent forth a continued succession of fleets and armies, led on by the proudest soldiers of the age. Every island in the Gulf of Mexico and in the Caribbean Sea, as well as Mexico, Peru, and Guatimala, were speedily explored, overrun, and plundered by their warlike and avaricious soldiers. The natives were consigned to every species of extortion, suffering, and cruel deaths, or to an ignominious slavery, worse to them than death itself. The immense riches accumulated by those who led on these conquests were such as to constrain belief in the most incredible tales of other lands. This state of mind prepared those of ardent and enthusiastic temperaments to receive as true the most extravagant tales of the unbounded wealth of the interior of Florida; while the dangers of the coast, and the terrible hostility of the natives, only served to confirm them in the belief of the immense wealth of that country, which was so strongly guarded by nature and so resolutely defended by man. The fortunate adventurer who had amassed unbounded wealth in Mexico and Peru, sighed for the transcendent riches of Florida. This delusion was not cured by twenty-five years of subsequent disaster and disappointment. The conquerors of Mexico and Peru vainly dreamed of new laurels to be gained in the wilds of Florida. Such was the state of feeling, and such the enthusiasm, which led to the disastrous attempts to explore and conquer a country which, until near the middle of the nineteenth century, was still in the possession of the indomitable savages.*

* The Indians were removed by the government of the United States, but not until

The following are some of the principal expeditions prepared and sent to these ill-fated shores in the first half of the sixteenth century.

1. *The Expedition of Ponce De Leon.*—The first adventurer who discovered the coast of Florida was Ponce de Leon, formerly a companion of Columbus, ex-governor of Porto Rico, and a gallant soldier of fortune. He sailed from Porto Rico on the 3d of March, 1512, upon a chimerical cruise, in search of the Fountain of Youth, whose waters, it was said, possessed the property of perpetuating youth beyond the power of time and disease. The Indian tradition placed this fountain in one of the Bahama Islands. After a long cruise in search of the island which contained the healing waters, he at length came upon the coast of a country of vast and unknown extent, which he supposed to be a large island. Land was seen on Palm Sunday (Pascha Florida), the 27th of March. From this circumstance, as well as the appearance of the forest, which was in full bloom, and brilliant with flowers, he called it *Florida*. The coast was dangerous and the weather tempestuous, and for many days he was compelled to avoid the shore. At length he effected a landing, which proved to be the east coast of Florida, a few miles north of the present site of St. Augustine. Having explored the dangerous and unknown shore and channels in the vicinity, and southward among the Bahama Islands, he returned to Porto Rico. Here he still burned with the desire of exploring and conquering his newly-discovered country. After a lapse of several years, and various delays, he received authority from the Emperor Charles V. to sail to Florida as the governor thereof, with the task of colonizing it, as the reward for his discovery, and other former services.

At length, in the year 1512, he set sail for Florida with two ships, to select a site for his new colony, and for the seat of his government. Where he landed is not known, but most probably somewhere in the vicinity of St. Augustine. Here he was soon attacked by the natives with the most implacable fury. Many of the Spaniards were killed; the remainder were driven to their vessels for safety. Among the latter was Ponce de

the year 1842, three hundred and three years after the invasion by De Soto. The Florida Indians were known in the nineteenth century as the "Seminoles" in East Florida, and the "Muskhogees" in Northern Florida, and in the southern and western parts of Georgia.

Leon, mortally wounded by an Indian arrow. He returned with the wreck of his expedition to Cuba, where he shortly afterward died. As the eloquent Bancroft remarks, "So ended the adventurer who had coveted immeasurable wealth, and had hoped for perpetual youth. The discoverer of Florida had desired immortality on earth, and gained only its shadow."*

[A.D. 1520.] 2. *Expedition of Vasquez de Ayllon.*—While the conquest of the islands and Mexico was progressing, the rich mines discovered required numerous able hands to bring forth the precious metals. For this purpose, it was proposed to capture as many of the hardy natives of the islands and of Florida as might be requisite to supply the demand of the mines with slaves. For this purpose, some wealthy miners fitted out a fleet of two vessels under Vasquez de Ayllon, in the year 1520, to cruise among the islands in quest of Indian slaves. This expedition reached the eastern coast of Florida, a little north of the first landing of Ponce de Leon, where the vessels were anchored in a river, in latitude 32° north, in a country called by the natives Chicorea. The river was called Jordan, and is probably the same now called the Savannah, or, as some think, the Combahee, in South Carolina. At this place Europeans were unknown to the natives, who admired the fair skins, the long beards, the splendid clothing, and the brilliant armor, no less than the huge vessels in which they came. But they fled in terror to their forests. The Spaniards soon dispelled their fears, and enticed them on board the vessels, where they traded beads and trinkets for marten skins, pearl, and some gold and silver. While on board, the unsuspecting Indians thronged the decks, gazing with admiration on every thing around them. As soon as a sufficient number had been enticed below the decks, the perfidious Spaniards closed the hatches, and made all sail for St. Domingo. Husbands were torn from their wives, parents from their children. Storms arose on the voyage; they were overtaken by disasters, and one vessel, with all on board, was lost: the other arrived safe. But the Indians on board remained sullen and gloomy; and, refusing all food, most of them died of famine and melancholy.

This enterprise only stimulated the cupidity of Vasquez de Ayllon to further outrages. He repaired to Spain, and sought from the emperor the government of Chicorea, with authority

* Hist. of United States, vol. i.

to subdue it by conquest. He obtained his request, and wasted his whole fortune in the preparation of his fleet and troops. [A.D. 1525.] He arrived in the mouth of the Jordan, with his fleet, in the year 1525, but soon his largest ship was stranded and lost. The natives, fired with revenge for former wrongs, meditated the entire destruction of their invaders. They dissembled their resentment, and, by acts of hospitality and friendship, gained the confidence of the Spaniards, who hoped former wrongs were forgotten. Vasquez was completely deceived, and believed the country already subdued to his sway. The natives invited the Spaniards to visit their village, nine miles distant, for festive entertainment. They accepted the invitation, and Vasquez permitted two hundred of his men to visit the village, while he remained with a small force to guard the ships. The natives entertained their guests with feasting and mirth for three days, until they were placed completely off their guard. That night the Indians arose upon them and massacred every soul. At daybreak they repaired to the harbor, and surprised Vasquez and his handful of guards. Only a few of them escaped to the ships, wounded and dismayed, and with all speed hastened back to St. Domingo. According to some accounts, Vasquez remained among the slain; according to others, he returned among the wounded to St. Domingo, where mortified pride, and the ruin of his fortune, hurried him, broken-hearted, to his grave. Thus signally were the natives of Chicorea avenged upon their cruel and perfidious enemies.*

[A.D. 1528.] 3. *Expedition of Pamphilo de Narvaez.*—Disasters from heaven, and hostility from men, were insufficient to deter the Spaniards from attempting the conquest of Florida. They still believed the interior was far more wealthy than Mexico. The next important expedition was conducted by Pamphilo de Narvaez, a man of no great prudence or reputation for virtue. He was authorized to subdue the country, over which he was appointed governor, with the title of adelantado, or commander-in-chief. His authority extended over all the country of Florida, from Cape Sable as far as the River of Palms, probably the Colorado in the west of Texas. He at length equipped his fleet of four ships, and a strong military force of four hundred foot and eighty horse: with this complement he set sail from Cuba in March, and on the 12th of

* Conquest of Florida, vol. i., p. 13–15.

April he anchored in an open bay in East Florida, called the Bay of Espiritu Santo, the modern Tampa Bay. Having lost some of his men by desertion among the islands, and some of his horses in a storm, he landed his forces for the conquest of the country, amounting to three hundred men and forty-five horses. He then formally took possession of the country in the name of his imperial master, and explored the region in the vicinity. Having found it barren, and but thinly inhabited, he determined to penetrate northwardly into the interior, in quest of some populous and wealthy empire like Mexico or Peru. The fleet was directed to seek some safe harbor and await his return, or to proceed to Havana and bring new supplies for the army. With these arrangements he plunged into the depths of an unknown and savage wilderness, blinded against the danger by the delusive hope of conquest and riches. At first he passed through an inhabited country, with fields of maize; afterward, for many days, they journeyed through desert solitudes, and often suffered the extremes of hunger, of exposure, and of despair. They crossed rapid rivers, on rafts and by swimming, exposed to frequent attacks from hordes of lurking savages. Their extreme cruelty to the Indians who fell into their hands secured to them the most implacable hostility. Some of their captives were compelled to act as guides; but they led the invaders through swamps and forests, through matted thickets and fallen trees, until their souls sickened at the idea of proceeding further. They were thus led on for many days by their treacherous and vindictive guides, who sought to bewilder them, and lead them beyond their own territory. Yet they were urged on by the hope of reaching the rich country, which, the guides declared, was still far ahead. This was the Appalachee country, which lay, probably, west of the head streams of the Suwanee River, in Georgia, between the Alapahaw and the Withlacoochy Rivers, and east of Flint River. This country was represented by the Indians as abounding in gold, and toward this the weary Spaniards bent their eager way. At length they arrived at the long-sought country, and in sight of the chief town; but, instead of a great city like Mexico, Narvaez was chagrined to find only a village of two hundred and forty huts and sheds. The natives fled at their approach, and with them, for a time, fled the delusion of gold. The Spaniards remained twenty-five days in the village, and were compelled to forage and plunder the country for subsistence; but they were harassed day and night, and numbers were cut off by the warlike natives, until despair began to brood over them. They now became more anxious for food than for gold; and the captives directed them southward, to the village of Auté, near the sea, where they represented the country as abounding in corn, vegetables, and fish, and the natives as peaceable and kind. This was distant nine days' march, and thither they turned their weary course. They were led through dismal swamps with deep lagoons, with the water often up to their breasts, the passage frequently obstructed by fallen timber, and beset with hordes of hostile and fierce savages. These were armed with bows of an enormous size, and hung continually upon their flanks and rear. At length, after incredible difficulties, they reached the village of Auté, which was deserted and burned by the natives at their approach. Some corn, however, remained, and this was more acceptable than gold. They were now within a day's march of the sea, probably in the vicinity of the present site of St. Mark's; their numbers were greatly reduced by disease, by privation, and by the savages. Only two thirds of their original number survived, and many of those were now ill, and disease was daily spreading among them. They had now traveled eight hundred miles of dismal wilderness from the point of their disembarkation, and knew not the part of the gulf upon which they had now arrived. Their hopes of conquest and wealth were at an end, and to retrace their steps in search of their ships would only be to hazard the lives of all the survivors. Having discovered an inlet one day's march from Auté, they determined to encamp there until they could construct a few rude barques, in which they might coast around in search of their ships. Desperation drove them to invention. A rude bellows and forge were constructed, and all the iron implements of every kind, even to their stirrups and spurs, were converted into nails, hatchets, and saws. Their shirts were made into sails, and cordage was made from palm bark and horse hair. They made pitch of pine rosin, and oakum of palm bark. Every man able to work joined in building the frail vessels; a horse was killed every three days for the laborers and the sick.

At length, after great exertion, they completed five vessels and embarked on the 22d of September, 1528, crowding their gunwales almost to the water's edge. They coasted along the unexplored shore for many days, suffering both with hunger and sickness. They were driven by storms on the water, and assailed by savages when they approached land, until they became wild and desperate. A storm sprung up in the night, and three vessels were dispersed and wrecked: only two remained. In one of these was Narvaez himself. After coasting the shore round for many days in the most forlorn condition, he landed, and sent all his men ashore in search of provisions, retaining with him only one sailor and a sick page. While they were on shore a severe gale sprang up from the north, and his vessel, without food or water, was driven out to sea, and never heard of afterward. Thus this ill-fated man reaped only suffering and privation, poverty and death, where he expected wealth, conquest, and glory; while the country of Florida, which he was to subdue and colonize, remained as inhospitable and unknown as before.

Out of the whole number who landed at the Bay of Espiritu Santo for this expedition, only five escaped, Alvar Nunez Cabexa de Vaca, and four of his companions. They were in the other barque that remained after the night storm, and were afterward cast upon the inhospitable shore; and, as Mr. Irving observes, " After the most singular and unparalleled hardships, they traversed the northern parts of Florida, crossed the Mississippi, the desert mountainous regions on the confines of Texas and the Rocky Mountains, passing from tribe to tribe of Indians, and often as slaves, until, at the end of several years, they succeeded in reaching the Spanish settlement of Compostella. From thence Alvar Nunez proceeded to Mexico, and ultimately arrived at Lisbon in 1537, nearly ten years after his embarkation with Pamphilo de Narvaez." The remainder of the crew, left on shore when Narvaez's barque was blown out to sea, were never heard of, and, in all probability, perished with hunger and by savage vengeance.*

Strange as it may appear, Alvar Nunez and his companions, after their forlorn wanderings and privations, and return to Europe, persisted in declaring Florida the richest country in the world; and their romantic narrations had the effect of still keeping alive the spirit of adventure for the conquest of

* Conquest of Florida, vol. i., p. 16–23.

a country so much richer than Mexico. Encouraged by these declarations, a new and more extensive expedition was set on foot, during the following year, under Hernando de Soto, one of the most distinguished and wealthy cavaliers of that age. De Soto had been a companion of Pizarro in the conquest of Peru, where he had amassed an immense fortune, and had won the most distinguished honors in the field of battle for his valor and his heroic achievements. Descended of noble blood, he maintained all the pomp and retinue of a Spanish nobleman of that day; his fame in the conquest of Peru had gained him a favorable standing with the Emperor Charles V., and he appeared at court with great pomp and splendor.

Fired with the enthusiasm which he had contributed to inspire, Alvar Nunez determined to join the contemplated expedition, and again to enter upon the conquest of Florida. A few months sufficed to light up all Spain with the enthusiasm of the enterprise.

The history of this expedition contains so much of romance and adventure, that it can hardly be believed by some as serious matter of fact. Yet this expedition for gold and conquest was unquestionably made; and it affords a sad proof of the proneness of human nature, under certain circumstances, to be carried away by the enthusiasm of the times, as if in expectation that the laws of nature, in the physical as well as the moral world, would be changed or subverted to subserve the imaginary wants of man.

Of all the enterprises undertaken in the spirit of wild adventure, none has surpassed, for hardihood and variety of incident, that of the renowned Hernando de Soto and his band of cavaliers. As Mr. Irving observes, "It was poetry put into action; it was the knight-errantry of the Old World carried into the depths of the American wilderness. The personal adventures, the feats of individual prowess, the picturesque descriptions of steel-clad cavaliers with lance and helm, and prancing steed, glittering through the wildernesses of Florida, Georgia, Alabama, and the prairies of the *Far West*, would seem to us mere fictions of romance, did they not come to us in the matter-of-fact narratives of those who were eye-witnesses, and who recorded minute memoranda of every day's incidents."[*]

The sixteenth century was an age of adventure, and all

---

[*] Conquest of Florida, vol. i., p. 24–36.

Europe was fired with the enthusiasm of American discovery and conquest. The populous islands of the West Indies, and the powerful and wealthy empires of Mexico and Peru, were early subdued and plundered of their immense riches by small but gallant bands of Spaniards. The whole of Europe resounded with the fame of Cortez and Pizarro, and those who had followed their standards had amassed riches and honors without number. The ambition of the young and chivalrous was inflamed to deeds of daring.

[A.D. 1538.] De Soto burned with ambition to signalize himself equally with Cortez and Pizarro, to whose fame his was only inferior. The only field for his enterprise was the rich and powerful countries supposed to exist in the interior of Florida, north of the Mexican Gulf. This country was still believed to abound in silver and gold, and to be extremely fertile in all the products of agriculture. Several expeditions had formerly failed to subdue its inhabitants and to possess its wealth: but chivalric adventurers were still ready to enter a crusade again into these regions for the sake of gaining wealth and honors, and to stake their lives and fortunes on the issue. A man suitable to lead and command such an expedition was all they required. De Soto was in every way qualified. In fame he almost equalled the conquerors of Mexico and Peru themselves; in courage and perseverance he was not less. He was in the prime of manhood, and only waited some fit opportunity to signalize himself, and hand down his fame to posterity equally brilliant with that of Cortez and Pizarro. About this time Alvar Nunez returned to Spain, with the tidings of the unfortunate fate of Pamphilo Narvaez and his followers. All the vague reports of the immense riches and fertility of Florida, which had been greedily received and accredited, were confirmed in glowing colors by Alvar Nunez. In his miraculous wanderings through the country for many years, he had explored the whole region, had become acquainted with the language, customs, and resources of the natives. He therefore would be the most valuable acquisition to the contemplated expedition.

The imagination and enthusiasm of De Soto took fire at the glowing representations of Alvar Nunez, and he determined to lead an expedition which should eclipse the fame of the great captains who had preceded him, and yield the immense riches which he so much coveted. The fate of all former expeditions to that inhospitable land only served to stimulate his ambition. He conceived that he possessed the energy and firmness to overcome all the obstacles and dangers which had caused the failure and destruction of former expeditions. He believed, too, that the barren coast, and the fierce hostility of the native tribes, were only so many obstacles placed by nature to protect and conceal the immense riches of the interior.

De Soto accordingly obtained permission and authority from the Emperor Charles to undertake the conquest of Florida at his own risk and expense. The emperor conferred upon him the title and office of governor and captain-general for life of Cuba and Florida. In the country of Florida which he should conquer he was appointed adelantado, an office comprising the whole civil and military authority, with a marquesite, and an estate in the country of thirty leagues in length and fifteen in breadth. A more splendid field of action, and a brighter prospect, presented to those who should engage in this expedition than any yet undertaken on the Continent. De Soto himself was transported with enthusiasm in the cause, and his enthusiasm and ardor were infused into all about him. So soon as it was announced that Hernando de Soto, one of the conquerors of Peru, was about to undertake the conquest of Florida, men of rank and wealth were foremost in offering the aid, not only of their personal services, but also of their money and fortunes. Soldiers of fortune, who had served with distinction in the wars against the Moors as well as in distant portions of the globe, were eager to join his standard in so splendid an undertaking. Young nobles, ambitious of distinction and wealth, cavaliers of experience, men of fortune, all volunteered in the intended conquest: some sold their whole estates to invest the proceeds in equipments for the expedition. None were more liberal in their contributions than De Soto himself, who exhausted his whole means in equipping the fleet, and in other requisites for the invasion. A troop of Portuguese cavaliers were among the volunteers for the enterprise; the whole of Spain was anxiously looking on the preparations for the expedition, and all was a brilliant display of arms and wealth. The number who presented themselves for the enterprise was far greater than could be received. From all the applicants De Soto selected the choicest spirits for his companions.

Many of the aspirants for fame and wealth, even those who had sacrificed their estates in preparing the expedition, were compelled to remain.

After nearly fourteen months spent in preparation for this enterprise, De Soto set sail from Spain on the 6th of April, 1538. His expedition consisted of nine hundred and fifty chosen Spaniards and Portuguese. A more gallant band had never been seen; scarcely one with gray hairs was among them. All were young and vigorous, and well fitted for the toils, hardships, and dangers of so adventurous an undertaking. In the enterprise, also, were enlisted twelve priests, eight clergymen of inferior rank, and four monks, most of them being relatives of the superior officers. This magnificent armament sailed from Spain in ten vessels, and in company with a fleet of twenty-six sail, bound for Mexico. They left the port amid the sounds of music, the blasts of trumpets, and the roar of artillery.*

After a prosperous voyage of near seven weeks, the expedition arrived at St. Jago de Cuba about the last of May. Their arrival spread general joy and rejoicing throughout the island, and for several days it was one scene of balls, masquerades, tilting-matches, bull-fights, contests of skill in horsemanship, and other chivalrous amusements. These being over, De Soto spent three months in a tour around the island, visiting the principal towns, and appointing officers of justice to rule in his absence. Most of the wealthy cavaliers were likewise furnishing themselves with the choicest horses and the most splendid trappings. The enthusiasm which prevailed in Spain spread likewise in Cuba, and many more of the wealthy and ambitious joined the expedition, and aided in furnishing every thing necessary for conquest and comfort. Late in August, the governor, De Soto, arrived at Havana, where he was joined by his family and all his troops. He continued here, engaged in the duties of his station as governor, for several months. In the mean time, he had sent a brigantine, manned with picked sailors and a trusty commander, to the coast of Florida, in search of a safe and commodious harbor, to which the expedition might sail direct on leaving Cuba. The object of this mission being accomplished, the brigantine returned, bringing four of the natives of Florida, who were detained to

* Irving's Conquest of Florida, vol. i., p. 35, 36.

learn the Spanish language, for the purpose of being employed as guides and interpreters. During this time the preparations for the expedition had been progressing with great diligence, and the number of additional volunteers had increased the whole force to one thousand men, including three hundred and fifty horsemen, besides the crews of the ships; the fleet consisted of eight large and three small vessels.

Every thing was provided that could possibly be necessary for conquest or for planting colonies. Artisans in wood and iron; iron in abundance, and a complete set of forging tools; men and apparatus for assaying gold and silver; a whip-saw and various tools for working in wood; live stock of different kinds, including three hundred head of swine for their colony, as well as food on their march, in case of emergency. Besides these, they provided every thing which the experience of former expeditions could suggest, or avarice and cruelty could dictate. Not only priests and learned men, but chemists and miners to procure and assay the precious metals. Chains and fetters for the captives, and even blood-hounds to assist in drawing them from their hiding-places, were among the articles provided for the conquest, while cards were supplied to amuse their leisure hours or to gratify their love of gaming. The fighting men were completely clad in steel armor glittering with gold; coats of mail, helmets, breast-plates, and shields for defense; and lances, broad-swords, and cimeters for offensive warfare. A few were armed with cross-bows, and eighteen with arquebuses; and one piece of ordnance was taken. Fire-arms were not then in general use; such as were used were imperfect, compared with those of modern times.

Thus provided and equipped, the expedition set sail from Havana on the 12th of May, 1539, as gayly as if it had been an excursion of a bridal party. Little did they dream of the dangers and hardships which they were about to encounter. In a fortnight the fleet arrived in the Bay of Espiritu Santo, which had been selected before. Here they cast anchor and prepared to disembark.*

The whole was a roving band of gallant freebooters in quest of plunder and of fortune; an army rendered cruel and ferocious by avarice, and ready to march to any point with slaughter where they might suppose an Indian village was stored with

* Conquest of Florida, vol. i., p. 54.

gold or other riches. Stimulated by the love of fame, and still more by the love of gold, they plunged into the savage wilds of East Florida, and thence northward into the southwest section of Georgia, through the country of the Seminoles, who were as warlike and ferocious then as at the present time. They marched and wandered for the first year in East Florida and in Georgia, east of Flint River, continually harassed and cut off by the natives. The Indians captured for guides led them through dismal forests and impassable swamps until they reached the Appalachee country, where they spent the first winter, about one hundred and thirty miles north of St. Mark's. The next year they traversed the State of Georgia northeastward, and north of the Altamaha River; thence they were led northwestward, in search of gold, to the barren regions of the Cherokees; thence down the valley of the Coosa River; and thence southwestward, down the Alabama Valley toward its junction with the Tombigby, where they met with the most terrible disaster from a desperate attack by an immense Indian host, in which many were killed, and nearly all their baggage was destroyed by fire. From this they marched northward, or, rather, northwestward, in the midst of winter, and spent the remainder of their second winter in the upper part of the State of Mississippi, near the Yalobusha, or Tallahatchy River. During the winter they were attacked by a large body of Indians in the Chickasâ country, and again burned out. In this attack many were killed, and nearly every thing in the way of clothing and armor was destroyed by fire. Many of their horses likewise were killed or burned to death. The hostile savages harassed them incessantly in all their marches and encampments, and every day diminished the numbers of this gallant band. They next bent their course north of west, until they struck the Mississippi River. They crossed it, and extended their march with the wreck of their army in a northwestern direction to the mountainous region north of the Arkansas, where they spent their third winter. Thence they returned to the Mississippi, where De Soto died from disease brought on by constant hardships, fatigue, and disappointed ambition. The remnant of the army again set out westward in hopes of reaching Mexico; and their fourth summer was spent in traversing the regions north of Red River. They finally returned to the Mississippi, near the mouth of the Arkansas River, where the remnant of three hundred and fifty men, worn down with privations, hardships, and savage warfare in body, and depressed in mind by anxiety, disappointments, and despair, finally constructed rude vessels, and, pursued by hostile Indians, floated down the Mississippi to the gulf; and thence coasting around toward Mexico, only two hundred and fifty men finally reached the Spanish settlements. During the whole of nearly four years, while they were in quest of gold east and west of the Mississippi, their sufferings were indescribable. They encountered one continued and successive scene of privations, toils, dangers, disasters, and despair. I have not enumerated sickness and death among their sufferings, for these were the only comforts to their spirits, which sickened at the very thoughts of life.

CHAPTER II.

INVASION OF FLORIDA BY HERNANDO DE SOTO.—A.D. 1539 TO 1540.

Argument.—The Spanish Expedition at the Bay of Espiritu Santo.—Disasters commence.—De Soto invades the Territory of Hirihigua.—Invades the Territories of Acuera; of Ocali; of Vitachuco.—Invades Osachile; the Cacique's Castle upon a fortified Mound.—Invasion of Appalaché.—The Expedition winters in Appalaché. —Various Incidents while here.—The Expedition marches in the Spring toward Western Georgia.—Invasion of the Territories of Copafi.—Capture of the Cacique. —His Person and Character.—His miraculous Escape.—Invasion of the Territory of Cofachiqui.—De Soto's Disappointment at the Poverty of the Natives.—Captures a Queen Regent.—Detains her as a Hostage, and carries her Westward in his March. —She effects her Escape near the eastern Limits of the Cherokee Country.—The Expedition upon the Sources of the Chattahoochy River.—Arrives on the head Waters of the Coosa River.

[A.D. 1539.] *De Soto in East Florida.*—The splendid expedition under De Soto arrived in the bay of Espiritu Santo on the 25th of May. As the fleet approached the coast, the Spaniards beheld the shore lighted up with alarm fires of the natives, who had perceived their approach; but as it entered the bay the Indians disappeared, and not one was seen for several days. These circumstances excited suspicion in the mind of De Soto, and caused him to be extremely cautious in his movements. After four days of delay and observation, he landed a body of three hundred men, most probably on the shore of that portion of the Bay of Espiritu Santo known as Hillsborough Bay. Here, with great pomp, he formally took possession of the country in the name of his imperial master, Charles V.; after which the detachment, in the joyful expectation of conquest and riches, encamped for the night in a state of careless security. Next morning, just before the dawn of day, the Indians, who had been secretly observing all their movements, assaulted the camp in vast numbers and with terrific yells. Unacquainted with such warfare, the whole detachment, panic-stricken, fled in great confusion toward the shipping. Many were wounded by arrows, and some were killed before they could reach the vessels. The Indians having dispersed, De Soto soon afterward disembarked the whole of his troops, and began his march into the interior by slow and cautious advances. The army had not proceeded more than six miles, when they came in sight of an Indian village governed by a chief named Hirihigua, who entertained for the Spaniards the most implacable hostility; the Indians fled at their approach; and the Spaniards, finding the town deserted, entered and plundered it of all that was left. Here De Soto remained with his army until he had somewhat explored the country, and completed his arrangements for advancing into the interior.

During the stay of the Spaniards at this post, Hirihigua and his warriors lost no opportunity of harassing them by day and by night. The savages burned with revenge against their invaders; yet they dreaded the terrible arms and horses of their enemies. De Soto, as a measure of policy, used every exertion and entreaty to appease the wrath of the vindictive chief, but all in vain. He endeavored by his interpreters, and by prisoners, discharged loaded with presents and favors, to gain his confidence and friendship. But to all their entreaties he answered scornfully, and upbraided his warriors for their intercession. His indignant reply in all cases was, "I want none of their speeches and promises; bring me their heads, and I will receive them joyfully." Ten years before, this chief had been treated with great cruelty and treachery by Pamphilo de Narvaez, after having shown great kindness to him and his army. Among other outrages, Narvaez had caused the mother of Hirihigua to be torn to pieces before his eyes by bloodhounds; after which he caused his own nose to be cut off or otherwise mutilated. The remembrance of these wrongs and

Vol. I.—B

cruelties was fresh in his mind. De Soto and his army were countrymen of Narvaez, and he held them answerable for the treachery of their predecessors.

Before advancing further into the country, De Soto determined to provide himself with guides and interpreters who were acquainted with the country. Having learned that a Spaniard by the name of Juan Ortiz, who had been left by the fleet of Narvaez nearly eleven years before, remained a prisoner and slave in a neighboring tribe, he determined to obtain possession of him; for he would understand both the Spanish and Indian languages; besides, he would be able to give much valuable information relative to the country, the number, and the customs of the Indians. After a hazardous enterprise by some of his bravest troopers, he obtained possession of this individual, and soon afterward took up his line of march toward the northeast, having left a garrison to hold the post of Hirihigua.

During their stay at the latter place, they had succeeded in capturing a number of Indians, who were chained and made to serve as guides, and porters of the baggage.

The army pursued an Indian trace, which traversed the low, marshy region south and east of the Hillsborough River, toward the northeast. Their guides led them through thick woods, with tangled vines and undergrowth, through swamps, marshes, and deep morasses, almost impassable for man or horse. Sometimes they passed over small quaking prairies, with a thick vegetable soil, and with water beneath. At first it would bear the horses, and then, yielding, leave them in a suffocating bog. When the woods were thick, and the path intricate, they were beset by hordes of savages lurking in ambush, who poured showers of arrows upon them, where neither cavalry nor foot could follow to attack. After several days of severe toil, and great perplexity in threading their way through almost impassable swamps and bogs, they at length came to a deep river, which was out of its banks from recent rains. On each side of the stream, for a mile and a half in width, was a low swamp, which was excessively boggy when not completely covered with water. Three days were spent in continued and fruitless attempts to find a firm crossing-place.* During the whole of this time, they were sorely harassed by continued

* Conquest of Florida, vol. i., chap. vii.-xiv.

assaults from hostile Indians, with terrific yells. They became impatient, and, in despair, suspecting their Indian guides of treachery, caused four of them to be torn to death by bloodhounds. The guides atoned with their lives for the errors of their enemies, and for the impassable nature of the country. Yet no obstacles could turn their course; other guides were selected, who finally led them across, where the bottom of the swamp was firm, but covered with water up to the knees, and often to the armpits. Still they pressed on, and at length reached the channel of the river, which was swarming with Indians in their canoes, darting through the inundated swamp and trees, and sending forth showers of arrows upon them. A rude Indian bridge, made by a tree felled in from each bank, and joined by a floating raft, enabled them to cross, while the horses were obliged to swim.

They were now, in all probability, on the Withlacoochy River, which has been made memorable in modern times by the disasters of the bravest troops of the United States.* They were probably in the region of the Wahoo Swamp, and, pursuing their route, they crossed from the south to the north side, and continued their march toward the north.

After almost incredible difficulties and perplexities, and after having lost several of their brave companions, the army arrived at the village of Acuera, a hostile and warlike cacique. This village was about thirty miles north of the Withlacoochy, or Amaxura River, situated in a beautiful and fertile bottom, environed by extensive fields of corn, and by gardens abounding in pumpkins, squashes, and other vines; besides beautiful copses of fruit-trees close at hand.

The Cacique Acuera and all his people fled to the forests, and would hold no intercourse with De Soto, who, by interpreters and captured Indians, with every token of peace and friendship, endeavored to gain a friendly interview. But the implacable chieftain returned only the most haughty and vaunting reproaches for the cruelty and treachery of his countrymen, Pamphilo de Narvaez and De Ayllon, in former times.

Near the village of Acuera, De Soto remained for twenty days, to recruit his men and horses after their perilous marches.

---

* It was on this ill-fated stream where the brave but unfortunate Major Dade, with his detachment of United States troops, was inhumanly butchered by the Seminoles and negroes on the 28th of December, 1835. — See Williams's Florida, p. 217, 218.

They found abundance of corn and other culinary vegetables in the adjoining fields, which were numerous and extensive. The camp was securely fortified, so as to prevent sudden surprise; yet the Indians ceased not, day or night, to harass them in every form of savage warfare. Small parties dared not leave the camp; for whoever loitered a hundred yards from it was picked off by the arrows of the Indians, concealed in the adjoining thickets. Those who were thus killed were beheaded, and their heads presented to their chief; and next morning the Spaniards would find the bodies quartered and hung upon trees, or stuck upon stakes in sight of their camp. Fourteen Spaniards thus lost their lives while encamped at Acuera; yet the Indians were so wary, that they were seldom taken or killed; the whole loss of the savages in twenty days did not exceed fifty warriors.

The Spaniards were now about seventy or eighty miles distant from Hillsborough Bay, in a due north direction, and about twelve miles southwest from Orange Lake. Having explored the country for many miles around, by detachments and foraging parties, De Soto determined to march for the country of Ocali, about forty miles further north. In the first thirty miles they passed over a thin, barren region, and some pine forests, probably northwest of the present site of Fort Micanopy, before they entered the fertile region of Ocali. For twenty miles further, they passed through a fruitful valley, thickly inhabited, and abounding in fields. At length they arrived at the chief town, called, after the country, Ocali. This was one of the most extensive towns in Florida, and contained six hundred houses. It was situated upon the south side of a river, in all probability the Suwanee, or the Santa Fé branch.

Here the Spaniards remained several days, finding plenty of corn, fruits, and other vegetables. The Indians were less hostile than most of those they had seen; but living in a fertile and open country, where the cavalry could act, the Spaniards had nothing to fear from their hostility, had they been otherwise. Having constructed a bridge across the river, and having captured about thirty Indians to serve as guides, De Soto set out northward with his army for the great country of Vitachuco, about forty miles distant, and called in the Portuguese narrative the Province of *Palache*.[*]

[*] Conquest of Florida, vol. i., chap. xv.–xviii.

The country of Vitachuco was a large territory, one hundred and fifty miles across, under the government of three brothers, but called after the eldest, who was cacique, or king. This country, no doubt, extended from the tribe last named to what is now the southern limit of Hamilton county, Florida. After three days' march through a more open country than that formerly traversed, they arrived at the frontier settlements of Vitachuco, and approached the first town, which was that of Ochile, one of the younger brothers. This town De Soto surprised at daybreak, and secured the chief and some of his principal warriors and attendants as prisoners. These were treated with every kindness and attention, for the purpose of securing, through them, a peaceable passage through the country of the other two brothers. This village was strongly fortified, and contained about fifty large houses.

After some days of delay they marched to the town of the second brother, and, through the messages and influence of the first, De Soto obtained a friendly reception. After this they marched toward the town of the cacique, or oldest brother, interpreters and messengers having been sent in advance. Vitachuco, however, was displeased with the kind reception given to the Spaniards by the younger brothers; he detained the messengers, and returned no answer. This haughty chieftain, during eight days, would receive no messenger nor compromise from the Spanish governor, but returned the most insulting and menacing messages. He warned him against the danger of violating his territory, and upbraided them with the treachery and cruelty of Narvaez. Finally, after great hostility and menaces, he appeared to have become reconciled to the Spaniards, and professed great friendship. He appeared anxious to atone for his former hostility by acts of kindness, in supplying their necessities, and accompanied them with professions of friendship, and unqualified submission to the wishes of De Soto. The latter, however, began to suspect a plot of treachery; and his suspicions, whether just or unfounded, terminated in the most dreadful slaughter of the natives.

Among the demonstrations of friendship and esteem toward De Soto, the cacique proposed, probably in the spirit of generous rivalry, to make a display before him of his power, and the number of warriors under his command, as well as the excellence of his tactics and evolutions, in a grand review. On a given day the whole of his warriors were assembled, to the number of several thousands, including nearly all his tribe. During the parade, De Soto desired that his warriors too should display ; the chief assented, and the Spaniards marched out with glittering arms and flying banners to the sound of martial music. They marched before the Indians, the infantry and cavalry duly arranged, when, upon a signal given by a blast of trumpets, they fell, sword in hand, upon the terrified and unsuspecting Indians. In three hours not less than five hundred of the warriors were numbered with the dead, and nine hundred were secured as prisoners and slaves. The remainder escaped to the woods, thickets, and a lake, which was near the town. Among the prisoners was Vitachuco himself, and many of his choicest warriors.

The town of Vitachuco was situated upon a lake, probably about twelve miles southeast of Suwanee River, where it forms the southern limit of Hamilton county. In this massacre the Indians defended themselves with great courage against the superior arms of the Spaniards and the terrible charges of their cavalry; but flight was their only safety.

A few days afterward, the captive Indians rose upon their treacherous invaders, preferring death to an ignominious slavery. This gave the Spaniards a pretext for putting to death, in cold blood, the whole of their prisoners. Some were tied to stakes and shot with arrows ; others were cut to pieces, or torn with dogs.

Whether De Soto was justifiable in this atrocious act, must ever remain unknown. He justified himself by a belief that the chief intended to play the same treachery upon him, and that he saved the lives of his men only by anticipating him in his cruel purpose. In favor of the Indian, it may be said, that his conduct in this case was only a specimen of the policy and conduct of the Spaniards in the conquest of Mexico and Peru, where De Soto learned his Indian morality. Pretexts were not wanting in other instances, when he wished to gratify his desire of pomp and power, or, it may be, to give his troops an easy revenge for all the toils, hardships, and conflicts they had encountered since their disembarkation. In favor of the Indians, it may be asked, if they came there prepared to exterminate their invaders, why were they unable to defend themselves against their attack ? The Indian princes were always anxious to impress Europeans with their strength and power; and if, in this case, the cacique designed treachery, his designs have been forever concealed by the known and terrible designs of his antagonist.

Five days after the massacre of Vitachuco, the Spaniards resumed their march northward, to a country called Osachile, after the name of its chief town, which was situated thirty miles north of Vitachuco. The fame of their treachery and cruelty, however, had preceded them, and had roused the savages to the most determined resistance. They had not marched more than twelve miles before they came to a large and deep river, which formed the boundary between the two countries. Here the Indians contested the passage; but the country being open, so that the cavalry could move, the savages were soon dispersed, and the army crossed at their leisure upon rafts constructed for the occasion. They marched partly through an open country, and at length arrived at the village of Osachile, containing about two hundred houses. The river crossed in this march was doubtless the Suwanee River. The Indians of this village having heard of the approach of the Spaniards, and knowing the terror of their arms, and the still greater terror of their warlike animals, had fled, and left the town, as usual, an easy capture. This village resembled most of those in Florida in the manner of its construction. The house of the chief was built upon a high artificial mound, or eminence, in a level country. The mound was large enough to contain on its level summit from five to ten houses for the chief and his family, with their attendants. Around the base of this eminence were the houses of the other chiefs and warriors of most distinction, and others successively in the order of their respective rank. The margin of the mound was fortified by pickets and other wooden barriers. The ascent was an avenue about fifteen feet wide, inclosed on each side by strong pickets made of trunks of trees, set deep into the ground. Within this passage were rude steps made of logs laid transversely, and partly buried in the ground. The other sides of the mound were steep, and inaccessible below the pickets on the margin.*

De Soto remained in this town only two days, as it was now getting late in the season, and he wished to reach the country

* Conquest of Florida, chap. xx.-xxi.

of Appalaché before winter. He learned at Osachile that a few days' march would bring him to that country, of which he had heard so much during his whole march. The natives always referred to it as the most fertile and populous of all countries, and as inhabited by the most warlike nation on the Continent. Besides, it was supposed to be near the gold region, where they were to reap the wealth for which they had undertaken their adventurous campaign. Only forty miles now intervened between the two countries; but nearly the whole of the intervening region was uninhabited. On the fourth day they arrived at the "*Great Morass.*" This was a wide swamp, covered with lofty trees, with a dense undergrowth of thorns, brambles, and vines, so interwoven as to form a perfect barrier to man or horse. In the center, or lowest part of this morass, was a large shallow lake, or sheet of water, more than a mile in width, and several miles in length. The trace led through this dismal region, scarcely wide enough for two to pass abreast, between two walls of matted vines and thorns nearly a hundred feet high. The advanced guard, in single file, penetrated but a small distance into this forest, when they were met by a band of hostile Indians. These defended the pass every step to the central lake, although only two or three of the front rank on each side could engage at one time. When they reached the lake, both parties having room to spread and form for action, the contest became general. The governor sent forward a re-enforcement, and attended it in person; for he was always in the hottest part of a battle. Still the Indians made a bold stand; and they also having received a strong re-enforcement, made the battle long and bloody. Both parties gradually spread out into the lake, and fought with great courage, nearly up to their waists in water. The lake abounded with a vast quantity of roots, cypress knees, bushes, briers, and fallen trees, over which they were liable to stumble at every step. It was the design of the Indians to check the progress of the Spaniards at this point, and prevent their further march into their country. The path led through the water to the opposite side of the lake, and here they might be embarrassed, and made to lose their way. But the courage of De Soto and his perseverance were equal to any obstacle that could be opposed, and he finally succeeded in driving off the Indians and passing the morass, which was altogether more than five miles across, being about two miles on each side of the lake. About forty yards in the middle of the lake was too deep to be forded without swimming. The Indians still met them in the narrow trace, or defile, on the other side of the lake, and resolutely defended every inch of the path until they emerged into more open and higher ground. Here likewise they made an obstinate resistance. Fearing the action of the cavalry, which would have more room for operating, they had obstructed the woods with fallen trees, and by vines and branches tied from one tree to another; and sheltering themselves among the trees, they plied the Spaniards with showers of arrows. The Indians, concealed among thickets, would spring forth as the enemy advanced, and rapidly discharge six or seven arrows each while a Spaniard could fire and re-load his arquebuse once. For six long miles were the Spaniards compelled here to toil and fight their way, without a possibility of taking vengeance until they should reach the open country. Two days were occupied in this perilous passage; but so soon as they did reach the open country they gave loose reins to their vengeance, pursued the Indians wherever they could be seen, cutting them down, or lancing them to death.

In this same morass Narvaez, in his expedition, was defeated by the Indians, and compelled to retreat toward the sea with the wreck of his army. Many of De Soto's brave men lost their lives here too, and many of them were severely wounded.

De Soto continued his march, and passed through many miles of inhabited country with numerous fields; at length he came to a deep river bordered by dense forests, which was the boundary between Osachile and Appalaché. This was, in all probability, the Oscilla River of the present day. This was the last difficult barrier against their advance; the Indians had assembled in large numbers to dispute the passage of the river. They strongly barricaded the road and banks of the river with palisades to prevent the passage of the cavalry, and here they fought with the fury of desperation; but at length were defeated by the intrepid Spaniards, who entered Palaché, or the Appalaché country, victoriously.

Having crossed the river, they pursued their march, with but little interruption, for nearly twelve miles, through alternate level lands and fertile fields, until they reached the chief town, Anhayca, which they found deserted. As usual, the Spaniards took possession, De Soto himself occupying the house of the cacique as his headquarters.*

Having found the province of Appalaché fruitful, and abounding with the most necessary articles for the sustenance and comfort of man and beast, De Soto determined to remain encamped at Anhayca until the severity of winter should be over. His army, accordingly, went into winter-quarters about the last of November.

The province of Palaché, or Appalaché, was extensive, and probably embraced a confederacy of tribes. According to the best authorities, it extended from the Appalachicola River around the north and northwest of Appalaché Bay; but as to its precise limits on the north and east, there is much uncertainty. In all their marches the Spaniards had no other mode of ascertaining the distances traveled over than by rough estimate; and often the difficulties of the route may have caused the distance to appear much greater than it was in reality. Besides, in passing over an unknown wilderness, inhabited by savages in open hostility, it is not likely that they could ascertain the boundaries and extent of any country or tribe, or even get the exact pronunciation of the names, where all were harsh, guttural sounds to them. That part of the province in which the town of Anhayca was situated is, by general assent, placed from about one hundred to one hundred and thirty miles north of the present site of St. Mark's. As to the immediate site of this town, nothing definite can be ascertained; but it was probably in the vicinity of some of the tributaries of the Suwanee River, or nearer the Flint. The Spaniards, pursuing their circuitous marches, considered it nine days' march from the sea, and near one hundred leagues north from the Bay of Espiritu Santo.

The province was populous, and had numerous villages and extensive fields. There was no gold in the country, and this was a sore disappointment to the Spaniards; but the former accounts continually given them of its fertility, and the extreme hostility and fierceness of the natives, were not exaggerated. Indeed, they were without doubt the most fierce and implacable of all the tribes they had yet seen. During their whole stay in this town, which was nearly four months, they were harassed with constant attacks, by day and by

---

* Conquest of Florida, vol. i., p. 159–162.

night, in the open woods, and in thick ambuscades. The Indians here, too, were in the habit of taking the scalps of those they killed, a custom not observed among the tribes in the latitude of Tampa Bay at that time. They ambuscaded foraging parties, harassed the encampment with nightly attacks and terrific yells, and also lay in wait continually to seize or shoot down with arrows any that ventured from the camp. The chief, whose name was Capafi, remained concealed in some strong-hold or fastness, from which he directed his plans against the Spaniards; but no intelligence of him could be obtained, nor would he receive any friendly overtures made to him.

While in winter-quarters at Anhayca, De Soto repeatedly sent out strong detachments through the surrounding country, to the distance of forty or fifty miles, to explore the country and inquire for the gold region. Some of these detachments were out as long as a week or ten days, and returned and reported the country on the north fertile, populous, and free from marshes. At length one of the most intrepid and persevering captains was dispatched southward with a strong detachment of horse and foot to reach the sea, which they had not seen since they left the Bay of Espiritu Santo. This detachment, after incredible difficulties and perplexities in deep swamps, marshes, &c., came to the village of Auté, and thence to the sea, at the place where Pamphilo de Narvaez made his last encampment, while building his rude brigantines to tempt the watery deep.

Here they were shown by the Indian guides the remains of his camp, of the forge, the troughs hewed out of trees for feeding their horses, the skeletons of the horses that died or were killed for food, and also the spot where ten of his men had been surprised and killed, besides many other melancholy mementoes.

[A.D. 1540.] De Soto being highly pleased at having found a harbor so convenient, sent the same intrepid Captain Juan de Anasco, with a detachment of thirty lancers, on the perilous route by land, back to the post of Hirihigua, to order on the garrison to headquarters, and the ships around to the Bay of Auté. All this was effected with much better success than might have been expected, considering the great distance, the impassable nature of the route, and the fierce hostility of the savages. The ships also arrived at the newly-discovered bay in safety.

Soon after the vessels arrived at this bay, De Soto dispatched an able officer with some of the smaller vessels to explore the coast westward for another convenient harbor, to which supplies and re-enforcements might be brought from Havana in the fall, when he would be further westward. This officer accomplished his mission by exploring the coast around for more than two hundred miles to the Bay of Achusi, which afforded a spacious, deep, and secure harbor. This bay is now known as Pensacola Bay. Here the fleet was directed to await his arrival in the fall, after having brought supplies from Havana.

While wintering at Anhayca, De Soto, being harassed by continual attacks from the fierce natives by day and by night, determined that the most effectual way to restrain their hostilities, and secure the lives of his men and horses, which were daily diminished, was to obtain possession of the person of their cacique, through whom he might control their hostile operations. It was the policy of the Spaniards—fully tested in Mexico—to obtain possession of the person of the king, or cacique, as a hostage, through whose authority they could restrain the Indians and effect other objects. De Soto was well aware of this fact, and in most cases, his first object in entering the territory of any tribe was to secure the chief, on account of the profound obedience and respect paid to him. Hence this was always a matter of first importance, whether accomplished by force, or by artifice and treachery. In most tribes through which they had yet passed, the terror of their cruelty had preceded them, and the chiefs and all their people fled from their villages to avoid Spanish treachery; for, although the sole object of the Spaniards was conquest and plunder, they were not averse to obtaining these upon as easy terms as possible; hence De Soto had made every effort and inquiry to discover where the chief, Capafi, concealed himself. At length he ascertained that the place of his retreat was in a dense and almost inaccessible forest, about twenty miles distant. De Soto, placing himself at the head of a strong detachment of horse and foot, set out to surprise and capture the cacique in his strong-hold. This was an enterprise of peculiar peril: the road lay through tangled thickets and treacherous morasses, which rendered it almost impassable to cavalry. At the end of three days, and after great difficulties, they reached this formidable retreat of the savage king. It consisted of a cleared space, in the midst of the almost impervious forest, which they had prepared for their camp. All around this space it was fortified in the strongest Indian manner. The only avenue to it was by one narrow path cut through the forest, and lined on both sides with dense thickets of vines, thorns, and undergrowth. About every hundred yards this path was strongly barricaded by trees, palisades, and vines, and at each barricade was posted a guard of the bravest warriors. Beyond these sat Capafi, strongly ensconced in the midst of his devoted warriors.*

De Soto commenced the attack; and, after acts of the most daring intrepidity by himself and his troop, they forced the narrow passage, and gained one barrier after another, amid the most galling showers of arrows from every quarter. Many of the Spaniards were severely wounded; but at length they gained the open space of the fort, where the cacique and his chief warriors were assembled. Here was the severest fight and the greatest havoc. The Indians seemed to offer themselves a willing sacrifice to the Spanish sabres for the protection of their chief; but at length, being overpowered by the superiority of the Spanish arms, they were mostly killed, and the remainder were taken prisoners. Among the latter was the cacique himself.

This chief, one of the most powerful of all the native princes, was an object of great curiosity to the Spaniards. He was so remarkably fat and unwieldy that he could not walk, but was carried by his attendants upon a litter wherever he desired to go. This was, however, probably more a matter of form than necessity; for, after several days of captivity, he effected his escape from the midst of his guards, as they alleged, by crawling off on his hands and knees while they were asleep. His devoted warriors, being concealed around the camp, soon carried him to a place of safety. The guards had undergone severe fatigue, and, overcome with sleep, had given way to slumber, believing it impossible for their unwieldy prisoner to escape; but when they awoke he was gone, and never seen again by them. To appease the anger of De Soto, and to excuse their own negligence, they invented and told some marvelous tales of his having been spirited away by magic.

De Soto in Georgia.—Early in March, 1540, De Soto broke up his winter-quarters, and set out for the northeast in search

* Conquest of Florida, vol. i., p. 182–185.

of the province of Cofachiqui, which was supposed, from Indian accounts, to be the rich country for which he was in search. He had been informed by the guides and other Indians that it lay a long distance off, toward the northeast, and that it abounded in gold, silver, and pearls. The expectation of these anticipated riches buoyed up the spirits of his troops, and led them cheerfully onward. They passed alternately through fertile fields and barren forests; through inhabited regions and deep wildernesses; through open, high woods, and deep, gloomy swamps; and often were in danger of starvation in remote and desolate forests. In their route, after the first few days, they found the tribes through which they passed friendly, hospitable, and confiding. The natives of these remote regions were unacquainted with the former cruelties and treachery of Pamphilo de Narvaez; hence they were less suspicious of the strange warriors. From Anhayca they passed northward, probably crossing the Flint River, and pursuing their march in the valley on the west side for nearly twenty days, until they reached the southern part of the Cherokee country, called Achalaque. Then they directed their route to the northeast, crossing, in the course of the next twenty days' march, two large rivers, in all probability the Ocmulgee and Oconee Rivers, not far from the vicinity of Macon and Milledgeville, in Georgia. As they passed up on the west side of the Flint River, De Soto had been informed by some Indian chief of a great and rich country to the west, called Cosa; but he determined to pursue his march to the northeast, in search of the province of Cofachiqui. In the remainder of this march he received every kindness and hospitality from the Indians that could be expected from unsophisticated human nature. The Spaniards, too, had learned, by their first year in Florida, that every encounter with the savages only increased the difficulties of their march, and reduced the number of their men and horses; hence they were careful to give as little offense to the natives as possible, and to commit fewer depredations upon their property.

At length, after an entire march and sojourn of more than two months, the Spanish army arrived in the province of Cofachiqui about the middle of May. This province was situated on the head waters of the Savannah River, and the chief town, probably, in the peninsula at the junction of the Broad and Savannah Rivers. They had, in their march, encountered many severe difficulties and hardships; and, having missed their way, they were lost three days in a desolate, uninhabited region, their guides bewildered, their provisions exhausted, and starvation staring them in the face. But they had now reached the termination of their perilous march. They found the country ruled by a beautiful Indian queen, or female cacique. She entertained the Spanish governor and his army with great ceremony, kindness, and even generosity. But the proud spirit of De Soto could not brook the mortification of finding the country inhabited by savages, and they destitute of gems and precious metals. He brooded over his disappointment, but concealed it from his troops; yet it was discernible in his morose conduct, and in his increased sternness to his men. Among the latter the disappointment was equally great, and showed itself in murmurs and acts of marauding upon the kind and hospitable Indians. They plundered their sacred depositories for the bones of their ancestors, and especially of the "illustrious dead." In the latter were deposited the most costly riches they possessed, which were numerous valuable pearls. These sacred relics were plundered for the jewels found, and for others which they hoped to find. These were the only riches to be found, and, although many and valuable, were to be obtained in large quantities only by plundering the vaults of the dead. The Indians abhorred the sacrilege, but were unable to punish the perpetrators. They began, however, to withhold the usual supplies of food and corn. The troops began to find new difficulties, and became more dissatisfied; they found, among the spoils of the cemetery of the chiefs, several old coats of mail and a dagger, which they learned had been obtained from the expedition of the cruel and unfortunate De Ayllon. They also learned that the sea-coast where he had landed was only ten or twelve days' journey distant, and that they were then upon the head streams of a river which was probably the Jordan, which entered the sea not far from Point St. Helena, the place selected by that unfortunate man for his colony. They therefore desired to form a colony here, and here to end their toils and their wars. But "De Soto was a man of few words and stern," and he determined to march toward the northwest, along the base of the mountain ranges, and thence proceed toward the Bay of Achusi, where he expected to meet his fleet with supplies.*

* Conquest of Florida, vol. i., p. 245-253.

Having refreshed his army and horses by a sojourn of a few weeks, he determined to set out for the northwest about the latter part of May. A difficulty having occurred between some of the soldiers and the Indians while he remained in this country, and the Indians having become distrustful and unfriendly, De Soto determined to adopt the policy found so successful in the conquest of Mexico and Peru, which was to obtain possession of the sovereign, and insure the friendship or forbearance of the subjects. He therefore obtained possession of the queen, and carried her upon his march through her dominions, as a hostage for the security of his men against any hostile designs of the Indians. All due respect and ceremony were extended to her, and she was surrounded by a numerous guard to prevent her escape or capture by her people. Through this means the Spaniards procured a safe march through the territory of Cofachiqui to the country of the Cherokees, called the province of Chalaque. Near the borders of this country the young queen effected her escape from the Spaniards, and returned to her own people. The Spaniards passed through the country of the Cherokees, and found them peaceable, domestic, and hospitable, and inhabiting rather a sterile region.

At first they feared and fled from the Spaniards; but, finding them friendly, they came forward and supplied them with every thing in their power for food. But they knew nothing of gold and silver. Passing westward over the head branches of the Chattahoochy River, after a march of about twenty-two days, the Spaniards arrived, about the 25th of June, at a village called Ichiaha, situated on the Etowee branch of the Coosa River, probably in that part of Georgia now designated as Floyd county. While here, the usual inquiries for gold and silver were made, and, having learned that yellow metal was found in a region forty or fifty miles to the north, De Soto remained here, and sent couriers in quest of the region supposed by Indian accounts to yield gold. At the end of ten days they returned without any intelligence of gold, and with no other booty than a buffalo rug. Having secured the friendship of this tribe, De Soto continued his march toward the southwest along the valley, and on the north side of the Coosa River nearly fifty miles, within the limits of the present state of Alabama.*

* Conquest of Florida, vol. ii., chap. iv.

CHAPTER III.

THE SPANISH EXPEDITION EAST OF THE MISSISSIPPI.—A.D. 1540 TO 1541.

Argument.—De Soto marches down the Coosa River.—The King, or Cacique, of Cosa. —De Soto enters the Territory of Tuscaluza.—Noble Person and lofty Bearing of Tuscaluza.—He is inveigled into De Soto's Train.—The Army marches through the Dominions of Tuscaluza.—The captive King is impatient and indignant at his Detention.—Resolves to secure his Liberty or die.—Reaches Mauvile with the Army. —De Soto apprehends Danger from the Native Warriors.—The severe and disastrous Battle of Mauvile.—Indian Courage and Desperation.—Deplorable Condition of the Spanish Army after the Battle.—De Soto resolves to advance to the Northwest.—Crosses the Tombigby River in the Face of an Indian Army.—Passes the Head Waters of Pearl River.—Enters the Chickasâ Country.—Takes Possession of a large Indian Town for his Winter-quarters.—The great Battle and Conflagration of Chicasâ.—Great Losses of the Spaniards.—The Army marches Westward to Chicaçilla, where they spend the remainder of the Winter.—They march Northwest to Alibamo.—Severe Battle of Alibamo.—They approach the Mississippi, or Rio Grande. —Preparations for crossing the great River.—Indian Hostilities and Opposition to their crossing.—The Army at length reach the western Side of the Rio Grande.— The probable Crossing-place.

[A.D. 1540.] *De Soto in Alabama.* — The Spanish army now crossed to the south side of the river, and pursued their march toward the province of Cosa. After easy marches for twenty-four days through the fertile regions and fields of this extensive province, they came, about the first of August, to the chief town, named Cosa, which, as well as the province, was called by the Spaniards after the Cacique Cosa. This town was delightfully situated upon a noble river, supposed to be the Coosa. It contained five hundred dwellings, some of which were spacious. The cacique, a noble-looking young Indian, borne upon a kind of litter by four attendants, and attended by one thousand warriors, came out to meet De Soto. The chief and his retinue, all adorned with lofty plumes, with mantles of marten-skins over their shoulders, and preceded by a band of music, presented a splendid and imposing appearance. The chief received De Soto with marks of great respect and with much ceremony; gave him a residence in a part of his own house, and quartered his soldiers in the town. Great kindness and friendship were shown by the Indians, and the whole army were abundantly supplied with every thing requisite for com-

Vol. I.—C.

fort and convenience. The fields in the vicinity were numerous and extensive, and the Spaniards spent several weeks in the neighborhood. Late in August, De Soto set out on his march southward. He was attended by a large number of the Cosa Indians, for the purpose of carrying the baggage, and accompanied by the cacique, who was taken, attended by a Spanish guard, under the guise of special honor, but, in fact, as a guarantee for the safety of the Spaniards against any treachery or hostile attack from the Indians. As usual, every attention was paid to the chief; a splendid mantle and a horse were allowed him; but still he was, in fact, a prisoner. The Indians, perceiving that their king was not at liberty to depart from his escort if he desired, had seriously meditated his release by the massacre of his detainers. Several acts indicative of hostile intentions had been committed by some of the Indians, who had been punished by De Soto, and put in chains. At the intercession of Cosa, they had been released, and a state of amicable feeling and confidence was restored. At the extreme of Cosa's dominions, De Soto dismissed the cacique with much profession of friendship and with presents.

Proceeding southward, he reached the confines of the territory of Tuscaluza, one of the most potent, proud, and warlike chieftains of the South. His sway, probably, extended over a large portion of South Alabama and Mississippi. "Tuscaluza had heard with solicitude of the approach of the Spaniards to his territories, and probably feared some hostility on their part, in combination with his rival, the Cacique of Cosa. He sent, therefore, his son, a youth eighteen years old, attended by a train of warriors, on an embassy to De Soto, proffering his friendship and services, and inviting him to his residence, which was only forty miles from the frontiers of Cosa." De Soto gladly accepted the offer. When he had advanced within five or six miles of the town where Tuscaluza was, he halted the army, and proceeded, in company with his staff, toward the town, where he found Tuscaluza prepared to receive him in great state. Posted upon the crest of a hill, which commanded a view of a rich and beautiful valley, he was seated on a kind of throne, or wooden stool, used by the caciques of the country. Around him stood one hundred of his principal men, dressed in rich mantles and plumes. Beside him was his standard-bearer, who bore, on the end of a lance, a dressed deer-skin, stretched out to the size of a buckler. It was of a yellow color, traversed by blue stripes. This was the great banner of this warrior chieftain, and the only military standard that the Spaniards met with throughout the whole expedition.*

This celebrated chieftain, who has given his name to a noble river, as well as the capital of Alabama, may claim a few words more. He was of extraordinary stature, being a foot taller than any of his attendants; he was about forty years of age; "his countenance was handsome, though severe, showing the loftiness and ferocity of his spirit, for which he was celebrated throughout all the country; he was broad across the shoulders, and small at the waist, and so admirably formed that the Spaniards declared him altogether the finest-looking Indian they had yet beheld."†

When De Soto approached, Tuscaluza rose and advanced twenty paces to receive him, although he took not the least notice of the officers and cavaliers who preceded him. The chieftain extended great kindness and friendship to De Soto and his troops. De Soto, as usual, suspected treachery from the cacique, and got possession of his person under the guise of honor and respect. He surrounded him with a guard; clothed him in a splendid scarlet robe, glittering with gold. After a few days, the Spaniards continued their march toward the Bay of Achusi. They desired Tuscaluza to accompany them through his dominions, for which purpose he was furnished with a horse to ride. Only one horse in the troop was found large enough for his use, and when seated upon this one his feet almost touched the ground. Proceeding southward, at the end of three days they arrived at the town of Tuscaluza, about forty miles from the point of his first interview. There the march assumed a northwestern direction, and crossed to the west side of the Alabama River. A few days afterward De Soto took up his line of march toward the southeast, until he arrived at the town of Mauvile, in company with the distinguished chief and his attendants.

The indignant savage, perceiving that he was detained a prisoner under the guise of friendship and pompous ceremony, burned with secret revenge; yet, like his European rival, dis-

---

* Conquest of Florida, vol. ii., ch. v. and vi.   † Ibid, vol. ii., p. 31.

sembling the greatest solicitude for the welfare of the Spaniards, Tuscaluza dispatched some of his attendants in advance to Mauvile, above the junction of the Alabama and Tombigby Rivers, under the pretext of ordering supplies and attendants for his Spanish friends; but instead of ordering supplies for the invaders, he summoned his warriors to rally to his rescue, for the expulsion or destruction of their enemies.

De Soto continued his march, and at length arrived in the vicinity of Mauvile, which was found to be a strongly-fortified town, on an extensive plain, and swarming with Indian warriors. From various incidents on the way, De Soto began seriously to suspect danger, and accordingly kept the cacique well guarded with twenty soldiers; yet the soldiers had seen so little danger from Indians for several months, that they could not be made to apprehend any then. The town of Mauvile, from which the modern name Mobile is derived, is situated on the north side of the Alabama River, in a fine plain, surrounded by a bend of the river, not a great distance above the junction of the Tombigby. This was the principal town in the dominions of Tuscaluza, and was strongly fortified. Here he and his chief warriors resided. The town contained eighty large houses, which were different from those of other towns. They were large sheds of reeds and straw, set upon posts, and covering a large surface of ground, inclosed by pickets; and some of them were large enough to accommodate from five hundred to a thousand persons. The whole was surrounded by a strong wall, made of a double row of large pickets, deeply set in the ground, bound together by ties, vines, and reeds, and cemented with mud and moss, and plastered over, so as to be impervious to arrows or darts, except at the port-holes left at proper distances. Every fifty yards around the wall was a kind of wooden tower, capable of containing six or seven warriors; there were only two gates or entrances, one on the east and one on the west extremity. Many of the pickets had taken root, and were growing with a profusion of branches and foliage. Such was the ancient town of Mauvile, or Mobile, where De Soto met his severest disaster, and where was fought the hardest Indian battle on record.

The Disastrous Battle of Mauvile.—During more than four weeks, while De Soto had been leisurely marching through the dominions of Tuscaluza, the latter was secretly maturing the plan which, as it appeared, he had previously conceived, for the entire destruction of the Spanish army. The van-guard, consisting of about half the cavalry and near two hundred infantry, under De Soto in person, reached the strong post of Mauvile at eight o'clock on the morning of the eighteenth of October, having left the main body of the army following slowly a few miles behind, under Luis de Moscoso. At the town, De Soto was met by a large body of warriors, painted, and splendidly dressed and equipped, preceded by a band of young females, with music, songs, and dancing. The governor and the cacique entered on horseback, side by side, and were received with great parade and respect. So soon as De Soto and his chief officers were provided with rooms, and the baggage was stowed away, Tuscaluza informed the governor that he wished to retire a short time to see his people, and make further arrangement for the remainder of the army. De Soto began to apprehend treachery, but was unable to detain the cacique. After an absence of an hour, De Soto sent a messenger to invite him to breakfast, as they had been in the habit of eating together. This finesse, used to obtain possession of the chief, was without success. Circumstances became more suspicious; some of De Soto's spies, who had been sent before him, came to him and informed him that there were a great many choice warriors concealed, perfectly armed, in large houses in remote parts of the town; and that the women were concealed in other large houses, remote from these. De Soto, certain that mischief was brewing, sent a messenger back to Luis de Moscoso, ordering him to advance rapidly with the main body of the army. At length, several messages having been sent to Tuscaluza without his notice, the messenger, who was not permitted to enter the house where he was, called out aloud from the door for the cacique. This was deemed disrespectful by his attendants, and was resented accordingly. Weapons were drawn by some of the Spaniards, and an Indian chief gave the war-whoop, which rang through the village. The warriors poured out from every house and from the plain around the town. In a short time the Spaniards and Indians were engaged in one general and deathly melée through the principal streets. The Spaniards fought with great courage and vigor against overpowering numbers. At length, finding themselves greatly annoyed by missiles of every kind from the house-tops, as well as from behind the houses, they fell back, disputing every inch of ground, until they reached the plain outside of the walls, where the cavalry, also, could act with more effect. So soon as they left the town the Indians plundered the baggage, and, releasing and unchaining the captives brought from Appalaché, furnished them with arms to assist in destroying their oppressors.

Swarms of warriors pressed upon the Spaniards in the plain with the utmost fury, discharging showers of arrows pointed with flint with great execution, notwithstanding their defensive armor. The battle raged with great fury backward and forward from the walls to the plain for several hours, when many of the Indians were disposed to shelter themselves from the furious charges of the cavalry by retreating within the walls. De Soto determined to break down the gates, and secure admission to his cavalry; this was soon done with axes, and the cavalry charged through, followed by a part of the infantry. The battle now raged fiercely within the walls, and the Spaniards set fire to the combustible houses covered with reeds and straw. These were soon wrapped in flames, and the town presented a scene of horrid carnage, smoke, and flame. The wind drove the flames and smoke furiously along the narrow streets, where hundreds were blinded or suffocated by the smoke, and burned to death. The fire spread to one large building in which were a thousand females, most of whom were consumed with it.

The battle still raged with great fury through the burning town and in the surrounding plain. The Indians disdained to yield or ask for quarter, although slaughtered in hundreds by the keen sabres of the Spaniards. Repeatedly repulsed, they as often renewed the attack, although certain to die in the charge.

This terrible strife and carnage had continued for near five hours. The gallant band of Spaniards were diminished in number, and those remaining were almost exhausted with fatigue, heat, and thirst. Scarcely able to attack, they collected together to stand and resist only the attacks of the numerous host of savages still swarming around them. At length they were relieved by the approach of De Moscoso with the main army, near the middle of the afternoon. The fresh troops attacked the Indians on all sides with great fury, and strewed the ground with piles of their dead bodies, while the fresh cavalry cut hideous lanes through their crowded masses. Toward the evening the females joined in the contest with the most determined fury, and threw themselves fearlessly upon the swords and spears of the Spaniards. The carnage ceased only with the setting sun; and every where the intrepid De Soto was in the hottest of the battle, always leading on the impetuous charges of the cavalry. This he continued to do even after he had been severely wounded by an arrow in the thigh.

"Such," says Theodore Irving, "was the deadly battle of Mauvile, one of the most sanguinary, considering the number of combatants, that had occurred among the discoverers of the New World. Forty-two Spaniards fell dead in the conflict; eighteen of them received their fatal wounds either in the eyes or in the mouth; for the Indians, finding their bodies cased in armor, aimed at their faces. Scarce one of the Spaniards but was more or less wounded, some of them in many places. Thirteen of the wounded died before their wounds could be dressed, and twenty-two afterward, so that in all eighty-two Spaniards were slain. To this loss must be added that of forty-two horses, killed by the Indians, and mourned as if they had been so many fellow-soldiers."*

The havoc among the Indians was almost incredible. Several thousands are said to have perished by fire and sword. The plain around the village was strewed with more than twenty-five hundred bodies. Within the walls the streets were blockaded up by the dead. A great number were consumed in the burning houses. In one large building a thousand persons perished, the flames having entered by the door, and prevented their escape, so that all were either burned or suffocated. The greater part of these were females.

The Indians fought with desperate courage. They had vowed to expel the invaders, or die in the attempt. Often, during the day, victory seemed certain in their favor; but it was as often snatched from them by the terrific charges of the cavalry. Still, their assaults were renewed with fresh ardor, until the whole field around, as well as the streets of the town, were covered with their dead bodies. The Spaniards fought like men who knew that they must conquer or die. Had it not

---

* Conquest of Florida, vol. ii., chap. vii.-ix. See, also, Williams's Florida, p. 166-70.

been for their superior arms and their defensive armor, as well as their excellent cavalry, not one Spaniard would have lived to witness the setting sun.

The number of wounds in all amounted to seventeen hundred that required a surgeon's care, being those about the joints and other parts attended with danger, besides many slighter ones left to the care of the common soldiers.

It is worthy of remark that the Indians used bows of great size and strength. So heavy were they, that often, when closely pressed, they would use their bows as clubs over the heads of the Spaniards, with such effect as to cause the blood to flow freely through their casques. The arrows were driven with great force, so as often to inflict severe wounds through their coats of mail, and in some instances to penetrate through the eyes and mouth, and out at the back of the head. Horses that were unprotected were covered with wounds, and many of them pierced through the body or to the heart.

It may appear strange that the Indians engaged around the strong-hold of Mauvile were so numerous; but these warriors were collected from all the confederated tribes of South Alabama and Mississippi, as well as Florida, and at a time when those tribes were far more populous than they have been within the past century. The occasion, too, was one of the most momentous which had occurred in their history, and which called the warriors from the most distant nations to make common cause against a common enemy.

"The situation of the Spaniards after the battle was truly deplorable. Most of them were severely wounded; all were exhausted by fatigue and hunger. The village was reduced to ashes around them, and all the baggage of the army, with its supplies of food and medicine, had been consumed in the houses." Not even a house or shed remained to shelter the wounded from the cold and dew of the night. Temporary sheds were erected against the remaining walls of the town, and covered with branches of trees and bushes, while straw was placed for their beds. Those who were least injured exerted themselves to attend and relieve those who were severely wounded. "Those who were able to bear arms patrolled as sentinels, and maintained a vigilant watch, expecting to be assailed" again in the night. "Thus they passed that wretched night, amid bitter lamentations and dying groans."

After eight days they were able to move into such of the Indian hamlets as were found in the vicinity, where they continued until the wounded men and horses were able to march. During this time, those that were able were obliged to forage in the vicinity to procure sustenance for the men and horses. In every direction they found dead and wounded Indians, who had escaped thus far after the carnage of the eighteenth of October. But they were not interrupted again by the savages while they remained in this region. The whole confederated tribes, having lost most of their choice warriors at Mauvile, dared not attempt to renew the contest.

Previous to the battle of Mauvile, De Soto was advancing toward the south to meet his ships with stores and provisions at the Bay of Achusi, now known as Pensacola Bay. But the disaster of Mauvile wrought deeply upon his pride and ambition; his troops were becoming discontented and mutinous. They were disappointed, because, instead of conquering rich kingdoms and regions abounding in gold mines, they had met with nothing in Florida but one privation and disaster after another, and found nothing but savage wilds, inhabited by the most fierçe and unconquerable tribes. They had now been near eighteen months in quest of gold, and yet they were solaced by the sight of no such metal. Their numbers had been greatly diminished by hardships, privation, and by savage foes, in all their marches; and for a month before they reached Mauvile a malignant disease had made its appearance among them, and many fell victims to its ravages. The elements, the country, and the natives all seemed combined against them, and they sighed to reach the ships, which were now known to have arrived at the Bay of Achusi, only seven days' march distant, by which they hoped to effect their escape from this inhospitable land. De Soto, learning all this, and knowing that his followers would desert him in hopes of obtaining a safe passage to Mexico or to the islands, and that he should be left blasted in reputation and fortune, determined to frustrate all such calculations by speedily plunging into the depths of the forest toward the north. He became morose, irritable, and discontented, and seemed anxious to finish his existence far from the reach of his friends in Havana, unless, by persevering, he might yet discover the object of his ambition. Accordingly, about one month after the great disaster of Mauvile, finding that his horses and men were now sufficiently recovered from their wounds to travel, he set out on his march toward the north near the last of November. He thus determined to silence all murmuring and complaint, and sternly gave orders to prepare to march northwardly, and punished all who dared to speak of the sea or the ships.

After five days' march they arrived at "a deep and wide river," which was in all probability the Tombigby, below the mouth of the Black Warrior. This they crossed after much delay and hard fighting with a large body of Indians, who disputed the passage for twelve days, until large boats were constructed to ferry the army across. This was probably in Marengo county, Alabama, not far from Chickasâ Creek. After this they marched on toward the northwest for five days more, when they came to another river, probably the Pearl, which was not so large as the first. Here they met with some opposition from the natives, and passed on in the province of Chicasâ, within the state of Mississippi.

De Soto in Mississippi.—The first river crossed by De Soto and his army after leaving Mauvile was "a deep and wide river," where they were vigorously opposed by a large body of Indians, who, stationed for six miles on the western bank, defeated every attempt to cross for twelve days, until the Spaniards had completed a very large scow, or ferry-boat, in which many of the infantry and cavalry could cross at each load. Some have erroneously supposed this was the Black Warrior itself; but De Soto directed his general course west of north from Mauvile, and, of course, he would not reach the Black Warrior, which was toward the northeast; besides, the latter river does not answer to the size and depth of the first river crossed in their march for Chicasâ.

The second river crossed in this march was probably the main Pearl River, somewhere in Leake county. Thence the course was more toward the north; and after eight or ten days' march in that direction, they came to the village of Chicasâ, situated in a beautiful plain, fertile and well watered, probably in the valley of the Yalobusha, and in that portion embraced in Yalobusha county. The expedition arrived at this village late in December, about one month after its departure from Mauvile. It was composed of about two hundred small houses or wigwams, which were abandoned by the Indians on the approach of the Spaniards. The winter had now set in, and the weather was extremely cold, attended with snow and ice. De Soto determined to remain in the village until spring. He accordingly built other houses, as the number then existing were insufficient to accommodate all his men, and inclosed the whole with strong pickets and other means of defense against any sudden attack from the Indians. The neighboring fields were extensive, and there was no scarcity of corn for the support of the army and horses. This was supposed by the Spaniards to have been the chief town of the Chicasà Indians, whose territory extended to the first river they crossed after leaving Mauvile.

[A.D. 1541.] For several weeks the Spaniards enjoyed comparative quiet from Indian hostility, as the savages appeared friendly, and did not venture to make any regular attacks or ambuscades. At length the continued aggressions from the troops in their foraging excursions, and the cruelties inflicted on those captured, impelled them to hostilities, for the purpose of expelling their insolent invaders. Several Indians, who had attempted to pillage about the camp, were shot to death; others had their hands cut off by De Soto's order, and were thus dismissed as warnings to their countrymen. The Spaniards, also, were now endeavoring to secure captives to serve as slaves, and to carry the baggage in their further march, instead of those they had lost at Mauvile. The forbearance of the savages was at length exhausted, and they determined to punish their oppressors at the peril of their lives. They began to make frequent false attacks at night, with terrific yells, to harass the Spaniards, as well as to place them off their guard when the intended main attack should be made. Finally, late in February, on a dark, cold, and windy night, the real attack was made, as usual, with terrific yells, the blowing of conchs and horns, and the war-whoop on every side of the encampment. Although the Spaniards were not taken by surprise, still it proved to them the severest disaster which had yet befallen them.*

Battle and Conflagration of Chicasà.—It was at a late hour of the night, only a few hours before day, when the Indians advanced in three divisions, and commenced the attack on all sides, having reached the inclosure unperceived. By means

* Conquest of Florida, vol. ii., p. 82–87.

of lighted matches attached to the arrows shot from their bows, and by ropes of hay set on fire and hurled on the combustible roofs made of reeds and straw, the whole village was soon on fire. The flames were spread with great rapidity by the wind, and in a short time the whole encampment was one scene of flame and confusion. The Spaniards were mostly roused from their slumbers by the war-whoops of the savages, and by the flames which were consuming the frail tenements over them. Many barely escaped with their lives, and without their clothes or armor. Bewildered by the spreading flames and the horrid yells and assaults of the savages, the first object was self-preservation, without system or order. As soon as they could prepare to act on the defensive, they made a most desperate resistance, every man doing his utmost to repel the hosts of savages which were pressing on all sides. At the first onset, many of the horses took fright and escaped into the plain, and others could not be released from the burning stables in which they were haltered. At length about one half of the cavalry was ready for action, and commenced the most desperate charges upon the thickest bodies of the Indians, until they were dispersed. But several hours elapsed before they were entirely repulsed, and the Spaniards suffered severely in every charge. On the morning their whole encampment was a scene of desolate confusion, and they themselves were in the most deplorable condition.

This night was more disastrous to the Spaniards than even the battle of Mauvile. For now, not only their baggage and clothing were destroyed, but their arms were burned or injured, and they had inflicted less injury upon the savages than at Mauvile, while they suffered almost as much themselves.

In this engagement and conflagration, the Spaniards lost forty men killed, besides some burned to death; fifty horses, also, were killed or burned to death. Those who survived this terrible night were mostly wounded and destitute of the necessary clothing for the season. The greater part of their herd of swine which they had taken with them were consumed in the flames of a large shed, covered with thatching, in which they had been inclosed. Their condition was truly deplorable. They were now nearly three hundred miles from their ships, with impassable rivers, swamps, and savage tribes intervening, destitute of clothing, half armed, and surrounded by hostile savages who desired their extermination. Their courage and fortitude in all these disasters and misfortunes are probably without a parallel in history. But it was chiefly to the bold, adventurous, and unconquerable spirit of Hernando de Soto that they were conducted through all these difficulties and sustained in all their privations.

After this disaster, the army soon removed to another village about three miles distant, called Chicaçilla, where they fortified themselves and remained until the last of March. Here they employed themselves in repairing and making saddles, re-tempering their swords which had been injured by the fire, in making lances, and shields of hides, and also in manufacturing a coarse fabric for clothing; for many were almost naked, and others had only skins and other garments taken from the Indians. During the whole time they remained in Chicaçilla, they were harassed with continual attacks by the Indians, and were obliged to keep out a strong guard all night to prevent another conflagration of their camp.

About the first of April, De Soto broke up his winter-quarters, and set out again toward the northwest. The first day's march westward brought them to the vicinity of a strongly fortified town called Alibamo, or, as the Portuguese narrator writes it, Alimamu. This is the town from which the River Alabama takes its name. It was situated on the east bank of a deep but narrow river, with high banks, in all probability the same now known as the Tallahatchy, and probably not far above the junction of the Yalobusha. This fortress was surrounded by a triple wall of pickets and earth, in a quadrangular form, about four hundred yards on each side, and intersected by other strong picket walls on the inside. The whole was a very strong post, and so constructed as to prevent the free operation of the cavalry should they once gain an entrance.

The next day this post was regularly attacked and carried by storm, with the slaughter of a large proportion of the garrison. The Indians, as usual, fought with great courage to the last; but when the Spaniards gained admission, they hewed down the savages with the most dreadful carnage, taking ample vengeance for their sufferings at Chicasâ. Vast numbers were likewise slain by the cavalry in the pursuit. The Spaniards lost fifteen men killed, besides many who were severely wounded.

The Spaniards remained in camp four days to recruit their strength and for the recovery of the wounded. Their next march was westward; and crossing the river at an easy ford, they left the province of Chicasâ. "For seven days they traversed an uninhabited country, abounding in swamps and forests, where they were often compelled to swim their horses in the route. At length, they came in sight of a village called Chisca, seated near a wide river. As this was the largest river they had yet seen, they called it the 'Rio Grande.' It was the same now called the Mississippi."

De Soto may be said to have been the first European who beheld the magnificent river which rolled its waters through the unbroken forest and splendid vegetation of a wide and deep alluvial soil. The lapse of three centuries has not changed the character of the stream. It was then described, as it now is, as more than a mile in width, flowing with a strong current, and by the weight of its waters forcing a channel of great depth. The water was described as being always muddy, and trees and timber were continually floating down the stream.*

Since their departure from the fortress of Alibamo, the Spaniards had traversed a vast and dense forest, "intersected by numerous streams;" doubtless the creeks and bayous of the Tallahatchy region. Wearied in the toilsome march, they remained several days in camp at the village of Chisca, near the Great River. "The river was low, and both banks were high." Incessantly harassed by the hostility of the natives, they resumed the line of march up the eastern bank, during four days; yet such was the tangled nature of the wooded country, that they advanced only twelve leagues in four days. Having found an open region, they encamped until boats should be built for crossing to the western side. Twenty days were required to build them in sufficient size and number to transport the army and horses. No sooner were the boats completed than De Soto began to cross his army to the western shore. Here new troubles were encountered. By this time a large body of savages had assembled on the opposite bank, while others swarmed upon the water in their war canoes to dispute the passage. The neighboring streams and bayous communicating with the river were covered with the savage fleet, and afforded to them secure retreats. The courage and en-

* Conquest of Florida, vol. ii., p. 98, 99.

terprise of De Soto did not desert him here. He at length succeeded, with the aid of a friendly chief, in obtaining for his whole army a safe passage.

"At this place," says the Portuguese historian, "the river was half a league from one shore to the other, so that a man standing still could not be seen from the opposite shore. It was of great depth, and of wonderful rapidity. It was very muddy, and was always filled with floating trees and timber, carried down by the force of the current."

Much doubt and uncertainty has obtained as to the precise point at which De Soto reached the Mississippi. It was evidently much below the latitude of Memphis, where he was toiling four days in advancing twelve leagues up the river, and seven days in his westward march, through swamps and deep forests, from the uplands east of the Tallahatchy. At no point above Helena are the highlands, on the east side of the river, more than ten or fifteen miles distant. The point where De Soto crossed the river was probably within thirty miles of Helena. The changes of the channel in the lapse of three hundred years may have been such as to defy identification now.

CHAPTER IV.

THE SPANISH EXPEDITION WEST OF THE MISSISSIPPI.—A.D. 1541 TO 1543.

Argument.—De Soto arrives upon the Banks of White River.—Incidents and Religious Ceremonies.—De Soto joins an Indian King in a hostile Expedition.—Marches with him Northeast to the Mississippi, near Helena.—Arrives at the Town of Capahá.—Present Remains of Capahá.—He returns to White River, and thence resumes his March to the West.—Winters high up the Arkansas in a cold Latitude.—Difficulties and Disasters there.—Returns to the Mississippi in the Spring.—Disasters begin to multiply.—He determines to leave the Country by descending the River.—New Hostilities by the Natives.—Difficulties increase, and Perplexities prey upon the iron Soul of De Soto.—He sickens and dies.—Affecting Scene before his Death.—He is finally deposited in the Mississippi, near the Mouth of the Arkansas.—His Eulogium.—Louis de Moscoso succeeds to the Command.—He marches Westward in search of the Mexican Settlements.—His fruitless Search.—Returns to the Mississippi.—Spends the Winter and Spring in Preparations for a Departure down the River.—Commences building Brigantines for descending the River.—He is greatly annoyed by hostile Indians.—Perilous Descent of the River in Boats and Brigantines.—Dangerous Voyage in the Gulf of Mexico.—The Remnant of the Expedition reach the Spanish Settlements of Mexico.—Reflections.

[A.D. 1541.] *De Soto in Arkansas.*—The whole expedition having safely crossed to the west side of the river, the boats were broken up for the nails and iron, and the army prepared to advance northwestward into the interior of what is now the State of Arkansas. After nearly five days' march through a level wilderness country, intersected in many places with streams, bayous, and lakes, many of which were not fordable, they descried a large Indian village containing about four hundred dwellings. It was situated on the banks of a river, bordered, as far as the eye could reach, with luxuriant fields of corn, and fruit-trees of different kinds.* This town was occupied by the tribe of Casqui, or Casquin; and the river upon which it was situated, in all probability, was White River, about one hundred and fifty miles above its junction with the Mississippi. They remained at this place six days, during which they were kindly supplied by the natives with all kinds of food. They then set out for the chief town, or residence, of the cacique, which was situated upon the same side of the river, about two days' march above the first town. In this distance, they passed through a beautiful rolling country, which was less alluvial than any they had passed since they left the highlands east of the Tallahatchy. They were received by the cacique and all his people with much ceremony and kindness. It was late in the month of May, and the weather was fine, but very warm. There had been no rain for many weeks, and the corn in the fields was beginning to suffer from drought. After several days, the cacique, with his attendants, came to De Soto with great solemnity, and desired him to pray to *his God* that he would send rain upon their parching fields, as they had entreated the Great Spirit in vain. De Soto promised to intercede in their favor for rain. He accordingly directed his carpenters to construct a very large cross; and, at the end of two days and much labor, a cross fifty feet high, and made from a pine-tree, was erected. The next morning the formal ceremony of intercession was to take place. The whole tribe was to be assembled to witness the ceremony from the opposite side of the river.

On the morning of the third day, the Spaniards formed a great and solemn procession, with the priests in front, chanting psalms and hymns. The most profound silence and solemnity pervaded the whole Indian hosts, as well as those who joined in the procession. The procession, consisting of more

* Conquest of Florida, vol. ii., p. 104–110.

than a thousand persons, including many Indians, advanced slowly in front of the cross, and there all silently knelt upon the ground, while two or three fervent prayers were offered up by the priests. After which the whole procession arose, two and two at a time, advanced to the foot of the cross, bowed the knee, and kissed the holy emblem. In returning, the same order was preserved, and the ceremonies closed with chanting a " *Te Deum Laudamus.*"

It so happened that on the following night the rain poured down abundantly; as the Spanish historian says, " To show those heathen that God doth hearken to those who call on him in truth." Next day the savages, to the number of thousands, moved by fervent gratitude to God for this favor, formed themselves into a procession before the cross in token of their gratitude, and the cacique expressed his grateful feelings to De Soto for his kind intercession. De Soto, in the true spirit of Christianity, directed him to " thank God, who had created the heavens and the earth, and who was the bestower of these and other far greater mercies."*

Having remained nine or ten days, enjoying the bountiful hospitality of this noble savage, De Soto set out toward the north and east, escorted by the cacique and several thousand of his warriors. After marching three days through open lands, " they came to a great swamp, rising on the borders, with a lake in the center too deep to be forded, and which formed a kind of gulf on the Mississippi, into which it emptied itself." Two days more brought them to some elevated ridges, beyond which they beheld the chief town of the Capahâ tribe. This town, which contained five hundred houses, was situated on an elevated piece of land, nearly surrounded by a deep bayou, which communicated with the Mississippi, or " Rio Grande," nine miles distant from the town. Here the Cacique Casqui and his warriors, who were in advance of the Spaniards, by committing the most inhuman cruelties involved the Spaniards in the most dangerous hostility with the tribe of Capahâ. After narrowly escaping utter destruction from this warlike tribe, it required the utmost of De Soto's tact and finesse to bring about a reconciliation with the chief and his warriors. Having finally succeeded, the army was hospitably received and entertained by the cacique for several days.

* Conquest of Florida, vol. ii., p. 111-115.

The town of Capahâ, in all probability, was situated a few miles south of the present town of Helena, in Arkansas, upon the west bank of the Mississippi.* The changes in the river channel since that time may have obliterated the ancient landmarks, and have thrown the river several miles further west at this particular point. The numerous old river lakes on the east side of the river are facts which corroborate the inference. The low grounds west of the Mississippi, which were traversed by De Soto in this portion of his marches, correspond well with the present region of the White River delta, and its tributary Big Creek.

In further confirmation of the inference that De Soto crossed the Mississippi near this point, the reader is referred to the present geography of the country in the vicinity of Helena, which will abundantly satisfy him of its correctness. Helena is on the west side of the river, ten miles by the river below the mouth of the St. Francis River, and twenty miles above the "Horse-shoe Bend," or eighty miles above the mouth of White River. It is situated on alluvial ground, which descends gently back to a low, boggy, cypress bayou, which meanders within a few rods of the town, and near the base of the uplands, which rise fifty or sixty feet above the alluvion. This bayou takes its origin from an old river-lake near the bluffs, a few miles above Helena, and winds on about fifteen miles below the town, where it unites with the river at "Horse-shoe Bend." Upon this bayou, which is called "Old-town Bayou," about eight miles below Helena, are found the remains of a large Indian town. These remains consist of mounds, embankments, and bricks of antique appearance and form. They are doubtless the remains of the old Indian town *Capahâ*.

The striking resemblance in the general features of the country about the Arkansas, White River, and the St. Francis, compared with that on Red River, the Washita, and the River au Bœuf, or the Tensas, as regards the general description of rivers, swamps, and high, rolling lands, has been the cause of much doubt and uncertainty among those who have attempted to trace the route of the Spanish army. Some have supposed that their first sojourning and marches west of the Mississippi was principally in the vicinity of New Madrid; some that it was near the Arkansas; and others that it must have

* Conquest of Florida, vol. ii., p. 115–124.

been as low down as Red River. This latter opinion is maintained by Judge Martin in his "History of Louisiana." In this he is most probably in error.

While in the territory of Capahâ, De Soto, having heard of a region to the north where salt abounded, and where, probably, gold might be found, sent two Spaniards with Indian guides to ascertain the prospects. After eleven days they returned, having been about one hundred leagues northwest, through a barren and hilly region abounding in buffaloes. They brought a supply of rock salt and some copper, but found no gold. Discouraged by this intelligence, De Soto determined to bear more toward the west. He finally returned to the village of Casqui, probably on White River, and thence, after a few days' rest, they advanced down the river, marching through a fertile and populous country for several days, or about one hundred miles, to the principal town of Quigate, where he arrived on the 4th of August. This town must have been on White River, about forty or fifty miles above its mouth.

Mr. Irving says, " From Quigate De Soto shaped his course to the northwest, in search of a province called Coligoa, lying at the foot of mountains, beyond which he thought there might be a gold region. After a march of several days through dreary forests and frequent marshes, they came to the village of Coligoa, on the margin of a small river." This must have been the Big Meto Creek, about fifty miles southeast of Little Rock.

At Coligoa, De Soto learned that the country to the north was thinly inhabited by Indians, but that vast herds of buffaloes ranged the country, and that toward the south there was a populous and fertile country called Cayas. Toward this country his march was next directed. After nine days' march, having passed a large river, he came to a village called Tanico, in the Cayas country. Here he found salt springs, and remained some days making salt, for want of which both men and horses had been suffering much. He was now probably on the head waters of Saline River, a branch of the Washita. From Tanico their march was next directed westward, and after several days' march through a wilderness country, they reached the chief town of the Tula tribe, situated between two streams, probably the Upper Ouachita and Little Missouri. Here the Spaniards were severely handled by the natives, who proved the fiercest tribe they had yet seen, for even the women fought as fiercely as the men. Some of their men having been killed, and many severely wounded, they were obliged to remain here twenty days, until the wounded were able to march. In the mean time, several exploring parties were sent in different directions; the country was populous, and the buffaloes were plenty.*

Having heard of the country of Autiamque, or Utiangue, toward the north, or northwest, the march was next thither. The distance was about two hundred and thirty or forty miles by the route marched over. "Five days of their journey was over a rough, mountainous country, closely wooded." At length they reached the chief town of Utiangue, after almost incessant skirmishes and ambuscades on the march. The town "contained numerous well-built houses, and was situated in a fine plain, watered by a wide, running river, the same that passed through the province of Cayas."

This "*wide, running river*" was doubtless the Arkansas, the same river crossed by them in their march southward three months before; and the portion of the river upon which this village was situated most likely was not more than fifty miles below Crawford court-house, in the State of Arkansas.

The town of Utiangue was found deserted by the Indians; but they had left it well supplied with corn, beans, dried fruit, and nuts. The country in the vicinity was fertile and well cultivated, and the forest abounded in game; yet the winter had already set in with great severity. The expedition was now on the north side of the Arkansas River, not far from the western boundary of the present State of Arkansas, in latitude about 36° north; they were exposed to the full force of the bleak winds which swept down from the great western desert. De Soto determined to take up his winter-quarters, and fortify the village against the inroads of the savages.

[A.D. 1542.] The winter continued to increase in severity, and the earth was covered with heavy falls of snow. "At one time the Spaniards were blocked up for more than a month, until at last fire-wood began to fail them," and all hands, with the horses, were compelled to turn out to open the way, and beat a path through the snow to a neighboring forest for a supply of fuel.

While in this country, they were exceedingly harassed by

* Conquest of Florida, vol. ii., p. 126–130.

the fierce natives, who would entertain no friendship, nor make any compromise with them. During the winter the chief interpreter, Juan Ortis, who had been obtained in Florida, died. This was a severe loss to the army, as he had been the only means by which any thing like an intelligible communication could be had with the native chiefs. Now this imperfect communication was destroyed; the Indian interpreters were comparatively ignorant of the Spanish language; hence, in their subsequent marches, they were led into many errors and misunderstandings with the Indians, not only as to countries, distances, routes, and rivers, but into many serious difficulties of another nature. De Soto began to despair of finding gold; he saw the difficulties that were gathering about him, and disasters had broken down his spirits. Bitterly did he repent having left the region near the sea-coast, of which none of the tribes he had seen for the last ten months could give any information. He was now in the midst of a vast wilderness, surrounded by hostile tribes; he had lost nearly half his men from war, or they had perished from hardships, disease, and accident of various kinds; the greater part of his horses had been killed, or had perished from the same causes; and the remainder were, many of them, lame and unfit for service, and had been without shoes for more than a year. " He was now too far from the sea to attempt reaching it by a direct march; but he determined to give over his wanderings in the interior, and make the best of his way back to the Rio Grande, or Mississippi. Here he would choose some suitable village on its banks for a fortified post, and establish himself, until he could build vessels to descend the river, and in these send some of his most trusty men to Cuba with tidings of his discoveries, and who should return with re-enforcements of men and horses, as well as of every thing necessary to establish a colony, and secure possession of the vast country they had discovered."*

As soon, therefore, as the winter was sufficiently over, he broke up his winter-quarters at Utiangue, and marched toward the Mississippi. After several days' march along the river on the south side, they halted ten days at an Indian town, until they built boats, and crossed the whole army over to the north or east side. This, probably, he did to reach the Mississippi near the point where he had left it. Their advance thence

* Conquest of Florida, vol ii., chap. xxv. and xxvi.

was "through a low region, and perplexed with swamps," so that the troops were often to the stirrups in mud and water, and sometimes were obliged to swim their horses. At length, after several days' march, they came to the village of Anilco, situated on "the same river that passed through the provinces of Cayas and Utiangue." There, learning that there was a populous and fertile country not far below the junction of these two great rivers, he determined to proceed toward it, in hopes the sea might be at no great distance. The chief town, Guachoya, he learned, was situated on the banks of the Mississippi, and this would be a suitable place for him to remain while building his vessels. He accordingly crossed the river at Anilco to the south side, and, after a march of four days over a hilly, uninhabited country, arrived at the village of Guachoya, on the Mississippi, about twenty miles below the mouth of the Arkansas. It was situated on two hills, one or two hundred yards from the river, and contained about three hundred houses, and was fortified around with strong palisades. De Soto took possession of the town, and finally succeeded in establishing terms of amity with the chief. Here he made diligent inquiry for the sea, but could gain no information. He at length sent an exploring party down the river to seek tidings of the sea; but after eight days' absence they returned, having advanced only forty-five miles, "on account of the great windings of the river, and the swamps and torrents with which it was bordered." Thus it seems that the river was full, and many sluices were putting out into the swamps and filling the bayous. It was now about the last of May, 1542.

Death of De Soto.—While at Guachoya, De Soto was indefatigable in urging preparations for fitting out his brigantines with dispatches to Cuba for supplies and re-enforcements. To sustain his army during this time, it was requisite he should find some country which had not been exhausted by them. For this purpose, one of his detachments crossed to the east side of the Mississippi, to a province which was said to be fertile and populous, and inhabited by a warlike tribe. They found it even so; the chief village contained five hundred houses; the cacique was exceedingly hostile, and threatened destruction to the Spaniards if they presumed to violate his territory. The Spaniards, knowing their own weakness and defenseless condition, used every effort to conciliate him and gain his friendship; but all in vain. In return for all his entreaties and proffers of friendship, De Soto was compelled to submit to taunts and gross insults, which, two years before, would have been resented by the most active warfare. Finding that the tribe, of which this cacique was chief, worshiped the sun, De Soto, anxious to avoid hostilities, and to receive their aid, sent a message to the cacique, and informed him that he and the Spaniards were children of the sun, and desired from him a visit as from a brother. But the haughty chief returned the scornful answer, " Tell him, *if he be the child of the sun, to dry up the river, and I will come over and do homage to him.*"—" But De Soto's spirits were failing him; he had brooded over his past error, in abandoning the sea-coast, until he was sick at heart; and, as he saw the perils of his situation increasing, new and powerful enemies springing up around him, while his scanty force was daily diminishing, he became anxious for the preservation of the residue of his followers, and desired to avoid all further warfare." A melancholy had seized upon his spirits, while the incessant fatigue of body and anxiety of mind, together with the influence of the climate, brought on a slow, wasting fever, which at length confined him to his bed. Still, De Soto was the vigilant commander, and from his sickbed gave all the necessary orders, and directed all the plans of movement. But his labors and anxieties were fast coming to a close; and being conscious of the near approach of death, he prepared himself to die like a soldier and a devout Catholic. Having made his will, and with great solemnity appointed and installed Luis de Moscoso as his successor, he called all his faithful officers to him, two and two, and bade them an affectionate farewell; begged forgiveness if at any time, in the discharge of his duty, he had been harsh toward them; and exhorted them to remain true to the king, courageous and affectionate to one another; he thanked them for the fidelity and constancy with which they adhered to his fortunes, and expressed deep regret that it was not in his power to reward them according to their merits.

He next called to him his soldiers, according to their rank, by twenties, and in like manner bade them adieu, with his blessing. He expired the next day, being about the fifth of June.

" Thus died Hernando De Soto, one of the bravest of the

many brave leaders who figured in the first discoveries, and distinguished themselves in the wild warfare of the Western World. How proud and promising had been the commencement of his career! How humble and hapless its close! Cut off in the very vigor and manhood of his days, at the age of forty-two years; perishing in a strange and savage land, amid the din and tumult of a camp, and with merely a few rough soldiers to attend him," while all were anxiously engaged in devising means of escape from their perilous condition in those inhospitable wilds.*

The death of De Soto overwhelmed his hardy veterans with sorrow; they had followed him nearly four years; and in all their sufferings he had suffered with them, and led them on through dangers which he equally shared. They mourned for him as for a father; and so much the more, because they could not give him a burial and such obsequies as were due his birth and rank: they also feared lest his remains should be insulted by the Indians after he was buried. The hostile Indians had been in the habit of searching for the bodies of Spaniards who had been buried; and when found, they would quarter them, and set them upon posts and trees as trophies. How much more eager would they be for the governor's body? To prevent this, they sought a retired spot near the village, where many pits and holes rendered the ground uneven; there they buried him secretly at the dead hour of the night. To conceal his grave from the Indians, they prepared the ground as if for a place of parade, and gave out word to the Indians that the governor was fast recovering from his illness. Finding, however, that the Indians suspected not only the death, but the burial-place of the governor, they determined to remove the body to a place of greater security: accordingly, the next night they disinterred it, and placed it in a strong and heavy coffin, made by excavating a cut of green oak, over the aperture of which they nailed a strong plank. The body, thus inclosed, was taken with great secrecy to the middle of the Mississippi, or "Rio Grande," and sunk in nineteen fathoms of water. Thus the first discoverer of the Mississippi made his grave in the bosom of its waters.†

No one was better qualified than De Soto to rule the hardy spirits under him. He was stern in command; agreeable in

* Conquest of Florida, vol. ii., chap. xxvii. † Idem, p. 170.

his common intercourse; lenient to mild offenses; gentle and courteous in his manners; patient and persevering under difficulties; and encouraging to those inclined to despond. Personally, he was valiant in the extreme, and with such a vigorous arm, that he is said to have hewn for himself a lane whenever he was pressed in battle. He became severe with the Indians; but a sense of necessity and danger caused him to be such. Under the influence and operation of those feelings, which were entertained by the Spaniards no less than by the "Pilgrims" of New England, more than a hundred years afterward, the poor savages were considered as scarcely entitled to the rights of humanity.*

The March of Moscoso West of the Mississippi.—Luis de Moscoso, having succeeded to the command of the remnant of De Soto's army, soon called a council of his officers to deliberate upon the best course to be pursued. Having received vague rumors from the Indians that, far to the west, there were other Spaniards roving from country to country, fighting and conquering the Indians, he concluded that they were his countrymen in Mexico, which might not be very remote. He accordingly abandoned the plan of De Soto, of descending the river to the sea, and determined to reach Mexico by land.

The expedition accordingly set out for the west about the middle of June. They passed near the salines of the Wachita River, where they tarried and supplied themselves with salt. Leaving this region, they pushed their march forward, and passed through the country of the Naguatax, now written Natchitoches, and which appears to have been high up Red River, in the southwest corner of the State of Arkansas. At length, after nearly three months, they came upon Red River, in the barrens north of the present country of Texas. In their marches, they were often misled and lost, and frequently were involved in bloody skirmishes.†

Continuing the march south of De Soto's route, they passed through a country abounding in buffaloes; beyond which they passed a sterile region, and came in sight of mountains, where the country was almost uninhabited. Here they halted, and sent light exploring parties, who penetrated in every direction nearly ninety miles further, and returned with information that

---

* See New England Wars with Indians; King Philip's War; Mather's Magnalia; General Church's Campaigns. † Conquest of Florida, vol. ii., p. 183–188.

the country grew worse as they advanced. In this region the natives lived in camps, scattered over the country, and depended upon hunting, fishing, and upon fruits, roots, and herbs, for their precarious subsistence. These were evidently the early ancestors of the Pawnees, Camanches, and other roving tribes of the West, who are the Tartars of North America.*

It was now late in October, and they had been nearly five months making their way across from the Mississippi, and had traversed regions which are unknown; and still they knew not where they were. Moscoso called a council of his officers to determine what was best to be done: much debate arose; many proud and high-minded cavaliers declared they would prefer perishing in the wilderness to returning to their friends in Europe and the West Indies, beggared and miserable, from an expedition undertaken with such high and vaunting anticipations. It was, however, determined at length to return, and retrace their steps to the Mississippi. Yet their return to the Mississippi presented only a dreary prospect to the wearied and forlorn adventurers, without the relief of novelty. The savage tribes, numerous and hostile, were chafed by former wrongs, and sought the opportunity for ample revenge. The country, exhausted and devastated in their advance, could afford them but little succor in their retreat. They returned by forced marches, in order to avoid preconcerted attacks by savages apprised of their approach. To avoid these attacks, and the danger of ambuscades, they were induced to march all day and a great portion of the night. Still they encountered almost daily attacks, in open skirmishes or in ambuscades. The Indians would waylay the road, and infest the rear; at night they would lurk about the camp, and shoot down, with their arrows, every soldier that chanced to leave the lines; and often, under the darkness of night, they would creep upon their hands and knees, and shoot down the sentinels on their posts.

Before they reached the vicinity of the Arkansas (for they struck across to that river) the winter had set in, and the cold was severe; heavy drenching rains were frequent; the cold winds benumbed them; yet, in their eagerness to reach the Mississippi, they pushed forward in all kinds of weather, traveling all day, and encamping at night, often drenched with rain

* Conquest of Florida, vol. ii., p. 198-200.

and covered with mud: still, they had afterward to sally forth in quest of food, at the imminent peril of their lives. At night, too, they often had no place to lie down, the ground being covered with mud and water from rains and the inundation of the streams, which were all full to overflowing. Sometimes, indeed, they were obliged to remain in low, wet places, where the infantry were nearly knee-deep in water, and the lancers remained upon their horses. With all this, they were nearly naked; all their European clothing had been burned or lost at the two great fires and battles of Mauvile and Chicasâ, except the tattered garments on their backs. Their clothing now consisted principally of skins belted around their bodies and over their shoulders; they were mostly bare-legged, and without shoes or sandals; sometimes they had made moccasins of skins after the manner of the Indians.

Besides all these sufferings and privations, they were often detained on the bank of a bayou, or river, for several days before they could pass. The streams being full, they had to make rafts and floats, upon which to cross, during the whole time harassed by swarms of Indians on both sides. Under these privations and sufferings, together with hearts and spirits broken with fatigue and disappointments, both men and horses began to sicken and die. Every day two, three, and at one time seven, Spaniards fell victims to the hardships of the journey. There were no means of carrying the sick and dying, for many of the horses were infirm, and those that were well were reserved to repel the constant attacks of the enemy. The sick and exhausted, therefore, dragged their steps forward as long as they could, and often died by the wayside; while the survivors, in their haste to press onward, scarce paused to give them burial, leaving them half covered with earth, and sometimes entirely unburied.

At length they reached the Mississippi, not far from the mouth of the Arkansas. At the sight of it the hearts of the poor wayworn Spaniards leaped within them for joy, for they considered it the highway by which they were to escape out of this land of disappointment, privation, and disaster. They determined to winter here, and make preparation to descend the Mississippi to the sea, in order to reach Mexico or some of the West India Islands.

Here they took possession of an Indian fortified town, more

by the good will of the Indians than by their own strength. The noble and chivalrous army of De Soto had been reduced, by war, disease, and famine, from one thousand to about tnree hundred and fifty men, in less than three years and a half of wandering over the unknown regions of the southwest. They had set out with high expectations in search of gold, of riches, and fame, and had found disasters, privations, and, most of them, a grave, in a savage land, as their only reward.

[A.D. 1543.] *Departure of the Spanish Expedition.*—As has been remarked before, Moscoso, in his retrograde march from the west, reached the Mississippi River not far above the mouth of the Arkansas. His men, worn out with privations and fatigue, rejoiced that they had reached the vicinity of the village of Aminoya, where they had expected to enjoy the comforts of peace and plenty. This hope had cheered up the last days of their march, although human nature had been almost exhausted with fatigue, famine, and privation. But many of them gained this place of refuge only to rest and die. The stimulus of anxiety, hope, and active life being remitted, they sunk into a state of lethargy and slow fever, of which nearly fifty died in a few days. Afterward, having become comfortably situated, the remainder began to recover their strength and spirits. They soon began to make preparations for finally leaving the country, where they had found nothing but disaster and death. Moscoso determined to build seven brigantines, during the winter and spring, and in them to descend the Mississippi to the sea, and thence seek the Spanish settlements in Cuba or Mexico. There remained among the remnant of the expedition one ship-carpenter and several other mechanics. These were employed in getting out timber for the vessels, and every soldier assisted in one capacity or another. Two large sheds were first erected to protect the workmen from rain, cold, and storms. Iron of every kind was gathered up to make nails; the fire-arms, which had become useless for want of powder, and even the iron stirrups of the troopers, were given up; the captives were released, and their chains and fetters were wrought into nails. Ropes were made from grass and bark furnished by the Indians. Other materials were prepared and wrought by others, and each man seemed emulous to excel in the aid he should contribute to the completion of the vessels. The Indians among whom they were sojourning were hospitable and kind, and furnished every thing which they could toward their support and comfort.*

But the hostile chief on the east side of the river, who conducted himself so haughtily toward De Soto in the previous spring, still maintained his hostile attitude. His fears were excited by the large vessels which his enemies were building so near his dominions, and which he readily supposed were intended to operate against his little fleet of pirogues. He accordingly used great exertion to form an extensive league with the neighboring tribes, with the design of exterminating their common enemy at one decisive blow. The Spaniards, apprised of the designs of the natives, doubled their industry and vigilance to avoid surprise and massacre. A sudden rise in the river, however, by inundating the low grounds, prevented the attack of the savages at the appointed time. After two months, the river having slowly subsided within its banks, the Indians again prepared to put their plans into execution. Moscoso having detected the treachery, as he supposed, inflicted great cruelties upon such of the hostile Indians as fell into his hands. On one occasion he caused the right hands of thirty to be cut off, and sent them back to their chief with this mutilation for their supposed treachery. The Indians continued their preparations for the extermination of their cruel invaders with unabated ardor.

Moscoso, finding his situation becoming daily more perilous, urged on the completion of his vessels, and made every preparation for a speedy departure. All the remaining hogs were killed and made into bacon, and twenty of the least valuable of the horses were slaughtered for the voyage. The vessels being nearly completed, a sudden rise of the river greatly facilitated the lanching. The vessels were merely large open barques, with bulwarks of plank and hides around the gunwales, to protect the men from the Indian arrows. The horses, of which only thirty remained, were likewise protected in boats, alongside the brigantines, with similar bulwarks. All things being ready, the Indian captives, to the number of thirty, were discharged; the remainder had perished in the toilsome marches from exposure, fatigue, and hunger.

Having taken an affectionate leave of the friendly chiefs and their people, Moscoso and his companions embarked, and com-

* Conquest of Florida, vol. ii., p. 217-218.

mitted themselves to the Mississippi on the second of July, 1543.

The numerous and gallant host of De Soto had dwindled down to less than three hundred and fifty men; their armor, once brilliant, was now battered and rusty; their rich, silken garments were now reduced to rags and tatters; and some were covered with skins like the native savages; with hopes once so buoyant, they were now forlorn, and despair was depicted in every countenance. This was the concluding piece of the great drama in which they had been engaged. Having wandered long in unknown lands, and among savage tribes, "they now were about to exchange the dangers of the wilderness for the dangers of the world of waters. They were now embarking upon a vast and unknown river, leading they knew not whither; they were to traverse, in frail barques, without chart or compass, great wastes of ocean to which they were strangers, bordered by savage coasts, in the vague hope of reaching some Christian shore, on which they would land as beggars."*

They at length were under weigh, but had not floated far, when they ascertained that the hostile chiefs had assembled all their forces some distance below to dispute the passage down the river. This was a new source of anxiety. They, however, proceeded, and were soon engaged in skirmishes with parties of the Indian canoes. Two days after they embarked, they came in sight of the combined Indian fleet, consisting of a great number of canoes, having from fourteen to twenty-four paddles each, and carrying from thirty to seventy men. The warriors were painted in the fantastic colors so common among Indians, and the pirogues carried them with great rapidity through the waters. For nearly two days they followed and hovered near the Spanish brigantines, with war songs and deafening yells. About noon, the second day, the Indian fleet made a disposition to attack, and formed themselves into three divisions, the van, center, and rear. One division at a time would glide rapidly past the brigantines, discharging, as they passed, a shower of arrows, by which many of the Spaniards were wounded, in spite of their breast-work of hides and boards. Each division, in like manner, made their successive charges, amid the terrific sound of their yells and war songs. They continued to hang upon the Spaniards, harassing them in this

* Conquest of Florida, vol. ii., p. 234-238.

manner, with continual attacks, during the evening and the greater part of the night. The attacks were renewed next day, and continued at intervals for several days and nights, until the Spaniards were worn out with fatigue and anxiety. During this time, although protected by the breast-work of boards and skins, and by shields made of skins and double mats, to resist the arrows, yet nearly every one was wounded. The horses, so well protected, were all killed but eight.

At length the Indians desisted from their attacks, and hovered along at the distance of a mile and a half or two miles in the rear. The Spaniards, supposing they had given up the contest, drew up to shore, and landed one hundred men at an Indian village to forage. No sooner had they entered the village with the eight horses, than the Indian fleet began to advance rapidly, and a host of savages from the woods rushed toward the village, so that they were barely able to escape to their vessels, leaving the horses on shore, where they were soon shot to death by Indian arrows. When the Spaniards saw them thus slaughtered before their eyes, they wept as for their own children.

On the sixteenth day of their voyage, while the Indian fleet was still hovering in sight, an unfortunate freak in five foolhardy young men caused the loss of forty-eight men, slain by the savages. These five men, without authority, and unknown to the governor, manned a pirogue and put off rapidly toward the enemy, in order to taunt and defy them. The fact being known to Moscoso, he immediately dispatched fifty men in three pirogues to bring them back, with a full determination to hang the leader as soon as he came on board. But the latter, supposing his daring had been approved, and that the detachment was sent to support his daring enterprise, pressed forward with all might to the Indian fleet. The Indians fell back, in order to draw them further from the brigantines; when, suddenly advancing in three divisions, they made a furious attack, and in a few minutes the whole detachment was surrounded and completely cut off by the savages; only seven escaped to the brigantines. Thus Fate seemed still to pursue the unfortunate adventurers with unnecessary disasters, resulting alone from their own rashness and folly.

At the end of twenty days from their embarkation on the river, they arrived in sight of the open sea; and, after coasting westward for fifty days, amid perils by sea and by land, they arrived at the town of Panuco, on the coast of Mexico. Here they were kindly received by the Spanish inhabitants, who were touched with pity at beholding this forlorn remnant of the gallant armament which had caused so much joy in its departure from Cuba.

They remained twenty-five days at Panuco; but the soldiers became gloomy and despondent at their situation; their proud hearts revolted at the idea of being objects of charity, and many affected a desire to return to Florida, which now, out of sight, presented itself to their imaginations as the most fertile country on earth, and possessed of many advantages not less valuable than gold itself. In the contemplation of these, for a time their sufferings and misfortunes were forgotten.

The viceroy sent for them to Mexico, where they were treated with great kindness and attention by the people; yet they became morose, despondent; and, as disappointed men do, they entertained much ill will, and mostly entered the armies of Mexico and Peru, hoping there to retrieve their fortunes.

Such was the end of the romantic and chivalrous expedition of Hernando de Soto within the early limits of Florida.

We have given more in detail the expedition and invasion of De Soto, because it was decidedly the most extensive, as well as the first exploration of the Valley of the Mississippi. Some have affected to consider the whole expedition too much characterized by romance and fiction to merit entire belief; but, independent of the internal evidence which abounds in the narrative, it is corroborated and sustained by the same weight of testimony which we have in the account of the conquest of Mexico and Peru by Cortez and Pizarro.

In all the devious marches and wanderings of the chivalrous band of De Soto, for nearly four years, through the vast regions east and west of the Mississippi, they exhibited the same unfeeling cruelty to the natives, and the same insatiable thirst for gold and plunder, which so strongly marked the conquerors of Mexico and Peru. When they found the savages poor or destitute, they plundered them of their little all, and then tortured them because they had no gold. The natives, at first friendly and hospitable, and comparatively unarmed, were compelled, by their exactions and cruelty, to make common cause against their proud invaders, although clothed in steel, and apparently armed with the thunderbolts of Jove.

CHAPTER V.

EARLY EXTENT AND SETTLEMENTS, WITH THE SUBSEQUENT BOUNDARIES AND SOVEREIGNTY OF FLORIDA.—A.D. 1544 TO 1845.

Argument.—Extent of Florida in 1560.—Spanish Missions and Settlements.—Ribault's French Colony in 1562.—Its Location on the Combahee River.—Destruction of the Colony.—Laudonnier's French Colony in 1564.—"Fort Carolina" built on the St. Mary's.—Destitute Condition of this Colony.—Timely Relief by Ribault.—Melendez is Adelantado of Florida in 1565.—He exterminates the French Colony.—St. Augustine founded.—Degourges ravages the Spanish Colony and captures the Forts.—Jesuit Missionaries introduced by Melendez.—Missions established in 1584.—St. Augustine plundered by Sir Francis Drake.—First Attempts at English Settlement, in 1585 and 1608.—English Colony of Virginia.—Carolina granted to Lord Clarendon and others.—St. Augustine plundered in 1665 by Captain Davis, an English Pirate.—English Settlement at "Charlestown," in 1679.—French Colonists arrive in Carolina, 1785–6.—Restricted Limits of Florida.—Spanish Settlements invaded by the English from Carolina.—Partisan Warfare continued.—Pensacola settled in 1696.—Boundary between Florida and Louisiana.—English Boundaries of Florida in 1764.—English Settlements in Florida.—Turnbull's Colony of New Smyrna.—His inhuman Tyranny.—Wretched Condition, and subsequent Liberation of his white Slaves.—English Agriculture in Florida.—Florida retroceded to Spain in 1783.—Extent of Florida claimed by Spain.—Extent claimed by the United States.—Claim of United States under the Purchase of Louisiana.—Baton Rouge District annexed to the State of Louisiana.—Fort Charlotte and Mobile District surrendered in 1813.—Florida restricted to the Perdido on the West.—Revolt and Occupancy of East Florida by "Patriots" in 1812.—Spain fails to preserve the Neutrality of Florida during the War with Great Britain.—Woodbine's Operations among the Seminoles of Florida after the War.—He builds a Negro Fort on the Appalachicola.—Negroes, Arms, Munitions, and Military Stores furnished from the British Fleet.—The Patriots of South America again occupy Amelia Island in 1817.—The Seminole War commences.—General Jackson prosecutes it successfully.—Captures St. Mark's.—Arbuthnot and Ambrister condemned and executed.—Their righteous Sentence and deserved Fate.—Jackson marches to Pensacola and expels the perfidious Spaniards.—He retires to private Life.—His Traits of Character.—Florida ceded to the United States in 1819.—Terms of Cession.—General Jackson is first American Governor, civil and military, of the Province.—Collision with Governor Calleava.—The first Grade of Territorial Government organized in 1822.—Indians removed from Middle Florida in 1824.—The second Grade organized in 1825.—Advance of white Population until 1835.—Hostilities by the Mickasukie Indians.—Military Movements and Operations.—Horrible Massacre of Major Dade's Detachment.—Indian Murders at Fort King.—Commencement of the "Florida War."—Gradual Removal of the Seminoles West of the Mississippi.—Increase of white Population until 1844.—State Constitution formed.—The State of Florida admitted into the Union in 1845.

[A.D. 1544.] FROM the close of the disastrous expedition of De Soto, Florida for many years, as claimed by Spain, embraced all the Atlantic coast as far north as the Gulf of St. Lawrence, where the French had made some unsuccessful attempts to plant colonies. No other European power pretended to claim the coast from Cape Sable on the south, to the

VOL. I.—E

Bay of Fundy on the north; nor did they attempt to establish colonies within these boundaries. For more than twenty years after the death of De Soto, Florida was abandoned by the crown of Spain as a vast wilderness province, too poor for conquest, and therefore unworthy of her arms. The fate of De Soto and his gallant army had convinced all that it was idle to dream of rich empires in the interior, where gold and silver were the plunder, and where fame and conquest were the rewards of the ambitious brave. The dread instilled by the fierce natives, and the insalubrity of the climate, had cooled the ardor of those who aspired to honor and wealth in Florida.

[A.D. 1560.] Nearly twenty years after De Soto traversed Eastern Florida, a few zealous Catholic missionaries attempted to plant the cross at several points along the Atlantic coast of the peninsula of Eastern Florida. They formed missionary settlements at St. Augustine and at other points on the St. John's River. The attempt, although hazardous, was not altogether in vain. Some lost their lives by disease; but others braved the inhospitable climate, and refused to abandon the holy undertaking, willing to sacrifice their lives in extending the kingdom of Christ.

[A.D. 1562.] Next, by necessity, a portion of the same vast region became the refuge of those who fled from the persecution and intolerance of the Catholic Church. Calvinism had spread widely in Europe, and had threatened the universal power of the pope. To check the spread of Calvin's heresy and the light of the Reformation, an unrelenting persecution was urged, with all the power and influence of the See of Rome. None distinguished themselves more by their unchristian and intemperate zeal in a rigorous persecution of the Calvinists than the bishops of France. Thousands of the best citizens and most enlightened men were compelled to abjure Calvinism or leave the country, in order to avoid persecution unto death.

Under these circumstances, Admiral Coligny, a patron of the French Calvinists, undertook to establish a colony of refugees upon the coast of Florida, north of any Spanish settlement. The colony embarked under the command of John Ribault, an experienced mariner. They set sail on the 18th day of February, 1562, in two of the king's ships, and first made land in the latitude of St. Augustine.* Advancing northwardly, they dis-

---

* See Williams's Florida, p. 169; also, Marshall's Life of Washington, *Introduction.*

covered the River St. Mary's, and, having spent a portion of the month of May on its banks, they called it the "River of May." It was not until nearly two centuries afterward that this river was recognized by Spain as the northern limit of Florida upon the Atlantic coast.

After a short stay, finding themselves within the limits of the Spanish missionary settlements, they determined to sail further north. Their next settlement was made a few miles above the St. Helena Sound, south of the Combahee River, and within the present limits of South Carolina. Here Ribault erected a fort, which he called Fort Carolana, in honor of Charles IX. of France. Having organized the colony and made suitable preparation for their safety and comfort, he set sail about the 15th of July for France, to report his success. He left M. Albert as his lieutenant, and twenty-six of his crew to keep possession of the fort. Political confusion and distraction in France withdrew his attention from the colony for near two years. During this time, the lieutenant, Albert, cultivated the friendship of the natives, who supplied the colony liberally with such articles as they possessed. Every exertion was used by him to restrain the avarice and licentiousness of the people. In his efforts to enforce justice to the Indians, he was met by a mutiny, in which he lost his life. Lachan, a turbulent demagogue, the author of the mutiny, assumed the command of the colony, which began rapidly to decline. Insubordination and want succeeded; the friendship and supplies of the natives were withheld, and the settlement was finally abandoned. They set sail for France, and after being becalmed at sea and reduced to the point of starvation, the survivors, picked up by an English vessel, were landed on the coast of England, destitute and helpless. Thus terminated the first French settlement in Florida.

[A.D. 1564.] Soon after this disastrous issue, Admiral Coligny projected another settlement, and obtained permission to send three ships to Florida, with a new colony of emigrants. This colony, which contained six hundred emigrants and soldiers, among whom were many of the nobility and the best blood of France, was placed under the command and superintendence of M. Laudonnier, who was also an experienced mariner. This colony was well supplied with provisions, arms, and agricultural implements. After a long and disastrous voyage in the month of June, the colony arrived at Fort Carolana: but the fort was abandoned. Fearing the resentment of the natives, Laudonnier declined to remain. He sailed south, and landed in the "River of May." Six leagues above the mouth, upon the south bank, he erected a fort, and called it also "Fort Carolana." No opportunity was lost, and no kind offices were spared, for securing the good will and friendship of the natives.*

[A.D. 1565.] An enthusiastic phrensy was the vice of the age, and the individuals in the new colony were by no means exempt from its influence. Many were blinded with the passion for sudden wealth, which still lured the credulous to Florida. Others were avaricious and dissolute, despising subordination in the sands and swamps of a savage wilderness. Instead of a patient and frugal industry, with judicious tillage of the earth, they rambled over the country in search of gold, silver, and precious stones. In this search, some had penetrated west as far as the Mississippi River.†

At length, having forfeited the confidence and hospitality of the natives, they were reduced to want and suffering. Dissensions sprang up, and, while one half were in danger of destruction by the natives and by famine, another portion, including the mariners, formed a mutiny, and the mutineers engaged in a piratical expedition against the neighboring settlements of Spain, while others were preparing to abandon the settlement and return to France.

In time to prevent the total destruction of the colony and the abandonment of Florida, Ribault arrived with a large supply of provisions, and such implements as were requisite for a new settlement. He assumed the command, endeavored to restore harmony and order, and to introduce economy and industrious habits among the colonists.

But the jealousy of Spain and the bigotry of Rome were aroused when it was known that a colony of *heretics* was established within the limits of Florida, a province of Spain, and a bishopric of Rome. The true faith had been almost excluded by nature and the natives; and should Calvinism be established there by a rival power? The Spanish court determined at once to exterminate the heresy with the colony. An expedi-

---

* Williams's Florida, p. 170. Also, Martin's Louisiana, vol. i., p. 21, 22.
† See Williams's Florida, p. 171.

tion was accordingly prepared in Spain, under Pedro Melendez de Avilés, for the conquest and colonization of Florida. In consideration of certain extensive grants and privileges, with the title of "Adelantado of Florida," he obligated himself to invade Florida with at least five hundred men, and to complete the conquest in three years; to explore the coast, harbors, and rivers; to establish a colony of five hundred souls, of whom one hundred should be married men; to introduce twelve ecclesiastics and four Jesuits, besides domestic animals and other supplies for a colony.

A direful destiny awaited the French Calvinists, and they had, through their predecessors, provoked the evil. Melendez was a man of cruel disposition, and accustomed to scenes of blood. The King of Spain was resolved to protect his Catholic subjects in his own dominions. The cause found no weak avenger in Melendez. He arrived on the coast on the twenty-eighth of August, 1565, and, having captured or dispersed the French cruisers off the coast, he landed near the present site of St. Augustine. Here, having ascertained the strength and position of the French colony on the south side of the St. Mary's River, a few miles from the coast, he deemed it his first duty to destroy the intruding heretics. After a rapid and secret march through the intervening woods and swamps, the colony was taken by surprise. The attack was made on the twenty-first of September, and, after a spirited resistance by the garrison, the fort was carried by storm, and the garrison put to the sword. During several days afterward the settlements were ravaged, and men, women, and children were put to death indiscriminately. The principal massacre occurred on St. Matthew's day, and the Spaniards commemorated it by naming the river St. Matheo.*

The whole number of French who fell in this carnage was about nine hundred. Many of the bodies were suspended from trees with this inscription, "*Not as Frenchmen, but as heretics!*"

After the destruction of the colony, Melendez returned to the present site of St. Augustine, where he built a town upon an inlet, to both of which he gave the name of St. Augustine. He

* The River St. Mary, the present northeastern boundary of East Florida, was doubtless the seat of the French settlements of this early period, and is the proper "River of May" of the French, and "St. Matheo" of the Spaniards. The settlements were chiefly on the south side, within ten miles of the river. Some have confounded the River of May with the St. John's. See Martin's Louisiana, vol. i., p. 19–23.

also built a fort for the protection of his colony. Another fort was erected, and a colony planted upon the ruins of the late French colony, on the River of May. St. Augustine is, therefore, the oldest town in the United States, having been built fifty years before any other town now remaining.

[A.D. 1569.] To retaliate this outrage of the Spaniards, a strong expedition was prepared by Dominic de Gourges, a Catholic, a man of wealth, who had seen much service in the wars with Spain, and had no love for Spaniards, having once been their prisoner, and by them consigned to the galleys. He was a suitable person to revenge the outrage upon his countrymen. He equipped, at his own expense, a military expedition, enlisted men for a twelve months' cruise, and set sail for Florida, alleging Africa to be the object of his enterprise. His real purpose was kept a profound secret until he reached the coast of Florida; then, in an animated and thrilling speech, he disclosed to his men the object of his voyage, and infused into them the deep revenge he entertained against the disgraceful conduct of the Spaniards three years before. Filled with his spirit, they desired to be led to the revenge of their slaughtered countrymen. Unsuspected by the Spaniards, he ascended the River St. Mary's for many miles into the interior, observing the settlements and forts as he advanced. Three forts protected the settlements; two had been mounted with the cannon taken from the French forts, and the entire garrison consisted of four hundred men.

At length, having secured the aid of a numerous body of Indians, he descended the river, attacked the forts by surprise, and carried them all by storm. The garrisons were put to the sword, besides many of the settlers who could not escape his fury.*

Having demolished the forts, burned the houses, and ravaged the settlements with fire and sword on both sides of the River St. Mary, and being sensible of his inability, with his small force, to retain the country permanently, he retired to the coast and set sail for France.

In imitation of his Spanish rival, he had suspended the bodies of some of his victims on trees, with this inscription, "Not as Spaniards, but as murderers." The act was disavowed by the government of France, which laid no claim to the conquest

---
* Williams's Florida, p. 174.   Martin's Louisiana, vol. i., p. 24, 25.

of De Gourges, nor to the country occupied by the French refugees.

[A.D. 1580.] Melendez heard of the destruction of his garrisons with extreme indignation; but the enemy had fled. He continued to govern the province for ten years, strengthened his position at St. Augustine, and used every effort to restore the colony to comfort and safety. He was also indefatigable in his exertions to conciliate the natives, and to reduce them to the Catholic faith. At his request, missionaries of every order were sent from Spain, but chiefly Franciscans. These men visited the remotest tribes, and, by their address, the mildness of their manners, and the simplicity of their lives, devoted to teaching the arts of civilization, obtained the entire ascendency over the savages. The Catholic religion, in 1584, was acknowledged by most of the tribes north of the Gulf of Mexico and east of the Mississippi.

[A.D. 1584.] This year many missions were established, and convents were founded in Middle Florida, and as far westward as the Mississippi. The ruins of many of those in Middle Florida now excite the investigation of the curious. Here was a great religious province chartered by the See of Rome under the Franciscan order, and known by the name of "St. Helena," whose representative government was fixed at St. Augustine.*

[A.D. 1585.] English arrogance and love of dominion viewed with jealousy the peaceful settlements of Spain which were springing up in Florida. Sir Francis Drake, on the 8th of May, 1585, with a large fleet, after ravaging and plundering the Spanish colonies in the West Indies, and at Carthagena, in the true spirit of a pirate, sailed for the feeble settlements upon the St. John's, in Florida. He attacked the forts at St. Augustine, which were abandoned to his superior force after a feeble resistance. The terrified people of the settlements fled to the woods for safety; and the English buccaneer, after ravaging the country, plundered Fort St. John of fourteen pieces of brass cannon, and the military chest, containing two thousand pounds sterling in money.†

Still the limits of Florida on the north were vague and undefined. Spain claimed all the coast northward indefinitely. St. Augustine is in latitude 29° 50′ north; but from the founding of this ancient town, the Spaniards made but little effort to

* Williams's Florida, p. 175. † Idem, p. 176.

extend their settlements north of the St. Mary's River, which is in latitude 30° 45' north. The first English settlement in Florida was attempted, unsuccessfully, in 1585, by Sir Humphrey Gilbert upon the Roanoke River, within the present limits of North Carolina. The second, equally unfortunate, was made by Sir Walter Raleigh, in 1608, upon James's River, within the present limits of Virginia. About the same time the first French settlements were attempted in Acadie, on the Bay of Fundy, at Port Royal, and upon the St. Lawrence below Montreal.

[A.D. 1651.] The English colony on James's River struggled against disasters and misfortunes for nearly twenty years; and in 1626, out of nine thousand emigrants sent from England, only eighteen hundred remained alive in the colony. Such was the first English colony, which began to encroach upon the undefined limits of Spanish Florida. In the next quarter of a century the population of the colony, supplied and sustained by religious and political persecution in the mother country, had augmented its numbers to more than twenty thousand souls, comprised within the royal province of Virginia, claiming the latitude of 36° as its southern boundary.

Spain, unable to oppose more than a feeble resistance to the encroachment of her powerful rival, acceded to the demands of England, and relinquished all claim to lands north of latitude 36° 30', the present southern boundary of Virginia.

Such was the first definite limit claimed by Spain as the northern boundary of Florida against the pretensions of rival powers. Yet the spirit for colonizing America having spread to England, she sought to establish other colonies upon the unappropriated coast of Florida, south of Virginia, as well as upon the coast north of the Chesapeake Bay. Disregarding any claim of Spain to the country north of her actual settlements, the English monarchs, after having established numerous colonies upon the coast north of Long Island Sound, resolved to occupy the unappropriated regions north of the Spanish settlements upon the River St. Matheo; nor was it long before the resolution was carried into effect.

[A.D. 1663.] The next English encroachment upon the limits of Florida was by Charles the Second, who granted to Lord Clarendon and others the absolute right and property in all lands from the thirty-sixth parallel of north latitude southward to the River St. Matheo, by which he intended the present St. Mary's River, in latitude 30° 45'. A short time afterward the king extended the limits of their grant on the south to the parallel of 29°, of course embracing the coast for nearly fifty miles south of St. Augustine. This grant, like many of the early English grants, with an utter ignorance of the interior, extended, according to the royal charter, westward to the "South Sea," or the Pacific Ocean.* Such was the ignorance of Europe as to the actual extent of North America as late as the middle of the seventeenth century.

This grant, so far as it conferred any right, embraced all the immense territory north of the Gulf of Mexico, and would have restricted Spain to the southern half of the peninsula of East Florida. The proprietors, however, for more than half a century, were unable to extend their settlements further south than the parallel of 32°, or to the north bank of the Savannah River; and Spain continued to claim the unappropriated country.

[A.D. 1665.] In the year 1665, Captain Davis, an English buccaneer, sailed from the West Indies, and attacked the Spanish settlement at St. Augustine. Meeting with no opposition, although the town was defended by an octagonal fort and two round towers, garrisoned by regular troops, he plundered the town, and retired with his booty.† No English settlement had then been made south of St. Helena Sound.

[A.D. 1679.] Fourteen years afterward, an English colony settled on Ashley River, and laid the foundation of a colonial capital, which was called "Charlestown," and the province was called Carolina, in honor of Charles II. of England, thus perpetuating the name of Fort *Carolana*, which had been named in honor of Charles IX. of France, one hundred years before.

[A.D. 1685.] The English colony of Carolina did not increase in population as was desired. In order to colonize the country more rapidly, the English crown permitted and encouraged the emigration of the French Calvinists, or "Huguenots," who were compelled to seek refuge out of France from the intolerance of Catholic persecution. The first emigration of these unfortunate people took place in the year 1685, when four hundred families arrived, consequent upon the revocation

---

* See Marshall's Life of Washington, vol. i., p. 180, 181, first edition.
† See Williams's Florida, p. 176.

of the "Edict of Nantz." Carolina subsequently received several other arrivals of these refugees from religious persecution, whose numbers served greatly to augment the population of the new English colony. The exiles from Catholic France were thus received under the protection of England, which had espoused the cause of the Reformers. Other colonies of French Calvinists arrived repeatedly in the next twenty years. Incorporated under English laws, with English subjects, they gave origin to some of the most intelligent, wealthy, and influential families which now adorn the State of South Carolina.

The Spaniards in vain remonstrated against encroachments upon their territory south of latitude 36° 30′. The British court refused to acknowledge their claim, and for years disregarded their remonstrances.

[A.D. 1690.] At length, to favor a peaceable adjustment of boundaries, Spain further relinquished all the territory north of latitude 33°, claiming only as far north as Cape Romain, or one degree north of the most southern settlements of the English.* Finally, exasperated at the persevering encroachments of their rival colony, and their intrigues with the native savages, the Spaniards resolved to imitate their example by exciting against the English settlements the hostility of the Indian tribes. Accordingly, until the close of the seventeenth century, mutual acts of partisan hostility and piratical war, aided by the Indian allies respectively, spread terror and desolation through the frontiers of the rival colonies. These expeditions were conducted by the English against the Spanish settlements on the St. Mary's and St. John's Rivers with great fury and destruction, and these beautiful regions again became a scene of blood and rapine.

[A.D. 1702.] At length, war having been declared between Spain and Great Britain, Governor Moore of Carolina, "thirsting for Spanish plunder," with an army of 1200 volunteers and Creek Indians, ravaged the whole settlements from the St. Mary to the St. John Rivers, and plundered St. Augustine itself.

[A.D. 1704.] Two years afterward, the same Governor Moore raised a force of one thousand Creek Indians and a few desperate white men, with whom he ravaged the Spanish settlements from Flint River to the Oklockony, and westward to the Appalachicola. A scene of general devastation mark-

* See Marshall's Life of Washington, vol. i., Introduction.

ed his route. The fort on the Oklockony, twenty miles from the sea, was captured with great slaughter. In the strife, the Governor of Appalachy, Don Juan Mexia, and the greater portion of the garrison, amounting to nearly four hundred men, were slain; the fort was burned to ashes; monasteries, convents, and missionary establishments alike sunk under the flames. Such of the inhabitants as escaped the tomahawk and scalping-knife were driven into a wretched captivity. Fourteen hundred Yamasses, who had been on friendly terms with the Spaniards, were driven into Georgia, and many of them were reduced to slavery.* Such have been the tender mercies of the English in all their conquests.

Meantime, Spain encountered another restriction upon the limits of Florida on the west. The French colonists from Canada on the extreme north had penetrated beyond the great lakes, and had explored the Mississippi to the Gulf of Mexico; a colony had been landed west of the Colorado, and the government of France had been actively engaged more than five years in establishing a permanent colony upon the Mississippi and upon the coast, more than fifty miles east of the great river.

Up to this time Spain had no rival in the west; and, fearing no opposition in that quarter, she had neglected to plant colonies west of the district of Appalachy. The whole coast, around the northern side of the Gulf of Mexico, from Tampico eastward to the Appalachicola River, nominally attached to the viceroyalty of Mexico, was in the sole occupancy of the Indian tribes, without a single Spanish settlement, except that of Pensacola, which had been established first in 1696, after the French had advanced upon the Mississippi.

The Spanish government, perceiving the advance of the French, had, in 1696, sent a colony of three hundred emigrants from Mexico to occupy the point; which subsequently, in 1699, was re-enforced, and placed in command of Don Andre de Riola, who proceeded to fortify the harbor and enlarge the settlement.

Meantime, after the arrangement of boundaries between the English and Spanish settlements on the Atlantic sea-board, a continual system of partisan and piratical warfare was maintained by the rival colonies, each instigating the numerous warlike savages in their vicinity to espouse their causes respectively. Hence, for nearly twenty years, these settlements, about

* Williams's Florida, p. 179.

three hundred miles asunder, were repeatedly ravaged by sword and fire.

At length the people of Carolina, dissatisfied with the proprietary government, and being again threatened with a formidable invasion from Havana, renounced all subjection to the proprietary government, and cast themselves upon the protection of the crown of Great Britain. Carolina was soon after annexed as the royal province of Carolina, extending from the Roanoke to the Savannah.

[A.D. 1732.] In the year 1732, for the convenience of the colonists, the province was divided into two governments, called North and South Carolina.* About this time, a new colony was projected in England for the settlement of the country south of the Savannah, as far as the Altamaha River. This region was to be called the province of "Georgia," in honor of George the Second. It was to be peopled chiefly by indigent but industrious families; and in the following year the town of Savannah was begun, soon after the arrival of the first emigrants, under the superintendence of General James Oglethorpe. The introduction of slaves was prohibited, in order to remove competition and to encourage free white labor.

[A.D. 1739.] The Spaniards persisted in their opposition to the English encroachments in Florida, and reciprocal partisan warfare again broke out between the rival colonies and their Indian allies.

Before the close of the year 1739, England and Spain were again involved in a general war, which extended to their American colonies in Florida. The following year an expedition under General Oglethorpe sailed from Georgia and South Carolina, for the invasion of the Spanish settlements near St. Augustine, in Florida. After partial success, the ultimate object of the expedition, the capture of St. Augustine, failed.

[A.D. 1742.] In 1742 a strong Spanish expedition, consisting of thirty-two sail, and conveying three thousand troops, invaded Georgia; and after producing great consternation and considerable ravages, they advanced up the Altamaha River, landed upon the island, and there erected fortifications, threatening the subjugation of the Carolinas and Virginia. But at the close of the war Georgia was still considered as extending southward to the River St. Mary.

* See Marshall's Life of Washington, vol. i., p. 308.

Meantime, on the west, as early as 1721, the Perdido River and Bay had been established as the eastern boundary of lower Louisiana; thus restricting the western limit of Florida to the same boundary which it now possesses as an independent state.

[A.D. 1763.] Such were the boundaries and sovereignty of Florida until the year 1763, when it fell under the dominion of the British crown, after the dismemberment of Louisiana. At the close of a protracted war, Great Britain, at the treaty of peace, became possessed of the whole of New France, and all that portion of the province of Louisiana lying upon the east side of the Mississippi, except the Island of New Orleans. At the same time, Spain, for valuable considerations, relinquished the province of Florida to the same power. Thus the dominion of Great Britain was extended over the whole territory east of the Mississippi, from its sources to the Gulf of Mexico, excepting only the Island of New Orleans.

[A.D. 1764.] The following year the British cabinet extended the limits of Florida on the west, by annexing to it all that part of Louisiana ceded by France on the east side of the Mississippi, and south of the Yazoo River. Thus Florida, under the English dominion, was again extended from the Atlantic Ocean to the Mississippi River. The province was also then first divided into two portions, called East and West Florida. West Florida, agreeably to the king's proclamation, was bounded on the north by a line drawn due east from the mouth of the Yazoo to the Chattahoochy River; the latter of which was made the boundary between East and West Florida. Each of these divisions was erected into a separate government, under different governors. Pensacola was the capital of West Florida, and St. Augustine of East Florida. This division, and these boundaries, remained unchanged for fifteen years, until West Florida was wrested from the British crown, in the years 1779 and 1781, by the victorious arms of Spain, under Don Galvez, from Louisiana.

English emigrants began to arrive in Florida; and several of the English nobility settled plantations on Hillsboro' River, on St. John's River, and on Amelia Island, in the peninsula of East Florida. Settlements were also made at Pensacola. Lord Rolle obtained a grant of land on St. John's River, to which he transported nearly three hundred miserable females, who were picked up in the purlieus of London. He hoped to reform them, and make them good members of society in his new colony of "Charlotia;" but death, in a few years, removed them from his charge.*

[A.D. 1767.] Doctor Turnbull, of notorious memory, and Sir William Duncan, tried a different experiment for peopling Florida. The former sailed for the Peloponnesus, and for the sum of four hundred pounds sterling, obtained permission of the Governor of Modon to convey to Florida a large number of Greek families. In 1767, he arrived with one small vessel, and took as many Greeks as he could obtain. On his way from Modon, he put in at the islands of Corsica and Minorca, and there procured several vessels, and augmented the number of his settlers to fifteen hundred. He agreed to carry them free of expense, to furnish them with good provisions and clothing, and, at the end of three years, to give to each head of a family fifty acres, and to each child twenty-five acres of land. If they should be dissatisfied at the end of six months, he agreed to send them back to their native country. These were the terms promised, but never complied with.

They had a long and tedious voyage of four months, and many of the old people died on the voyage. Twenty-nine died in one vessel. They arrived in Florida in the fall season, and a grant of sixty thousand acres of land for the settlement was made by the Governor of Florida. To shelter them through the winter, they built huts of palmetto, and proceeded to prepare the fields for the opening spring. The settlement was designated "New Smyrna," and its location was about four miles west of Musqueto Inlet, and seventy-four miles south of St. Augustine.

After a sufficient quantity of provisions had been raised, Turnbull directed his attention to the cultivation and manufacture of indigo, and reduced his ignorant and helpless foreigners to the most abject and disgraceful slavery. In five years they had nearly three thousand acres of good land in a fine state of cultivation; and the nett value of the indigo crop, for one year, amounted to three thousand one hundred and seventy-four dollars.

[A.D. 1770.] Turnbull's avarice seemed to increase with his prosperity; but he failed to comply with his agreements, or

* Williams's Florida, p. 188.

to fulfill his contracts. From the colonists he selected a few Italians, whom he made overseers and drivers; and they exercised over the remainder such cruelty and oppression as is known only under English masters. Men, women, and children, indiscriminately, were subjected to the lash, and to the most inhuman treatment and privations.*

Tasks were assigned them for the week as large as they could possibly perform. The food allowed the laborers was seven quarts of shelled corn per week for the whites; to the negroes on the plantations ten quarts per week were allowed. Saturday and Sunday were allowed to supply themselves with meat by fishing and hunting. The sick and invalids were allowed only three and a half quarts of corn per week.

Most of the Minorcans and Corsicans had brought a good supply of clothing with them; when these were worn out, they were furnished with one suit of Osnaburgs each year. One blanket and one pair of shoes, for the whole term, were given to the men; but none were allowed to the women, although many of them had been accustomed to live in comparatively easy circumstances in their own country.

[A.D. 1774.] For nine years were this people kept in ignominious bondage, ground down by a tyranny unequalled by the relentless Spaniards of St. Domingo. During the last three years they were supplied with no clothing at all, but were permitted to buy on credit at a public store belonging to the company, thus creating a debt which served as a pretext for their detention. On the most trifling occasions, they were beaten without mercy; and negroes were usually chosen as the instruments of diabolical cruelty, they being often compelled to beat and lacerate those who failed to perform their tasks, until many of them died. Sometimes, after having the skin scourged from their backs, they were left tied to trees all night, naked and exposed, for swarms of musquetoes to fatten on their blood and to aggravate their tortures. If induced by despair to run away, they were captured by the negroes of the neighboring plantations, who received a bounty for their apprehension and delivery. Some wandered off and sought an asylum in the woods, where they died of hunger and disease, or sought the protection of the Indians.

[A.D. 1776.] At the end of nine years, their number, including

* Williams's Florida, p. 188, 189.

the natural increase, was reduced to six hundred. These people, living under the protection of a nation which boasts its freedom, and that its very soil strips the shackles from the slave, were, by a mere accident, released from their cruel tyrant. Secluded, over-tasked, and isolated, they knew not their rights, nor the means of obtaining them. In the summer of 1776, some English gentlemen from St. Augustine, making an excursion down the coast, called at "New Smyrna" to see the improvements, especially a spacious stone mansion-house which had been commenced for the proprietor. Seeing the wretched and degraded condition of these people, one of the gentlemen observed, in the hearing of an intelligent boy, " that if these people knew their rights," they would not submit to such slavery. The boy repeated the remark to his mother, and she took counsel with her friends at night, to gain more intelligence on the subject.*

A plan was devised to send three individuals ostensibly to the coast to obtain a supply of turtle, but, in fact, to St. Augustine. They arrived in safety, and soon had an interview with Mr. Younge, the attorney-general of the province. They made known their business, and he promised them the protection guarantied to them by the laws. Governor Grant, who is supposed to have been personally connected with Turnbull in the slavery of these Greeks and Minorcans, had been superseded by Governor Tonyn, who sought to render himself popular by causing justice to be done to these long-injured people.

The messengers returned, after a few days, with the joyful intelligence that justice was in prospect; but the mission must be concealed, as well as the intelligence received. Although Turnbull was absent, they feared the overseers, and dreaded their cruelty. They met in secret, and chose M. Pallacier for their leader, and secretly arranged the plan of their departure. Upon a given day, formed into a phalanx, the armed and strong men guarding the women and children, they marched in a body toward St. Augustine. So secretly had the whole plan been concerted, that they were some miles on their way before the overseers discovered that the settlement was deserted.

Turnbull, their tyrannical master, having been informed of their departure, rode many miles after them, and overtook them before they reached St. Augustine; but his entreaties were unavailing to induce them to return. At St. Augustine they

* Williams's Florida, p. 188.

were supplied with provisions by the order of the governor; their case was tried before the judges, and their cause honestly advocated by the attorney-general. Turnbull could show no cause for their detention, and they were set at liberty;* but they had no redress for the wrongs which they had already endured upon British soil and under British jurisdiction.

To supply them with homes, they were offered lands for settlement near New Smyrna; but, fearing some treachery in Turnbull, they refused to return to that place. Grounds were, therefore, assigned them in the northern suburbs of St. Augustine, where they erected their houses, and cultivated gardens for the town supplies. The same grounds to this day are occupied by many of their descendants, who now constitute a respectable, and in some instances a wealthy and intelligent portion of the population of that city.†

[A.D. 1778.] During the occupancy of Florida by the English, under the fostering care of the government, agriculture made rapid progress. Sugar and rum became the staple products; sugar-cane was cultivated extensively both in East and in West Florida. The remains of the iron machinery and sugar furnaces may be seen to this day upon the old, deserted plantations. Indigo, protected by a bounty, was also a staple product of Florida.‡ Such was Florida under British dominion.

[A.D. 1783.] By the treaty of 1783, Great Britain acknowledged the independence of the United States with the Mississippi for their boundary on the west, and Florida on the south. But Florida had been retroceded to his Catholic majesty without defining its limits on the north; and Spain, having acquired West Florida by conquest before the cession, claimed the northern boundary as it existed under the British authorities in 1779, that is, bounded by a line to be drawn from the mouth of the Yazoo, due east to the Chattahoochy. His Catholic majesty could not concede to Great Britain the right to restrict the limits of a province already conquered, and the right of possession to which was recognized by the consideration stipulated in the treaty. He contended that the treaty, which fixed the southern limits of the United States at the 31st parallel of latitude, virtually ceded to them territory rightfully belonging to Spain, and was consequently to that extent null and void. It was upon this ground that his Catholic majesty continued to

---

* Williams's Florida, p. 189, 190.   † Idem, p. 190.   ‡ Idem, p. 191.

occupy and hold possession of the "Natchez district" for fifteen years after the treaty of 1783. But the United States persisted in their right to the limits specified in the treaty; and after ten years of fruitless negotiation, and a contemplated appeal to arms, when Spain was again at war with Great Britain, his Catholic majesty reluctantly consented to the treaty of Madrid, signed on the 20th day of October, 1795.

[A.D. 1795.] By this treaty the King of Spain, recognizing the claim of the United States to the 31st parallel of latitude as their southern boundary, entered into stipulations for the evacuation of the country and military posts situated north of that limit, so soon as the latitude should have been ascertained. For the purpose of ascertaining the proper boundary, commissioners on the part of each power were to meet within six months after the ratification of the treaty, to ascertain and mark out a proper line of demarkation. At length, after many vexatious delays, the Spanish authorities, in the spring of 1798, retired from the north side of this boundary, reluctantly yielding that which they found themselves unable to hold by force.*

The remainder of West Florida near the Mississippi, and south of the line of demarkation, continued under the Spanish dominion, and was organized into a government, known as "the District of Baton Rouge," under the administration of Don Carlos de Grandpré, lieutenant-governor, exercising the duties of civil and military commandant. These duties he continued to exercise for more than twelve years after the evacuation of the Natchez District, and until the expulsion of the Spanish authority from the banks of the Mississippi in December, 1810, and seven years after the province of Louisiana and the island of New Orleans had become the territory of the United States.†

[A.D. 1803.] Meantime the United States, having acquired from France the possession of the province of Louisiana, advanced a new claim to that portion of West Florida which extended westward from the Perdido River to the Mississippi, and north of the island of New Orleans. The boundaries of Louisiana, as received from France, were to be those which it possessed under the French crown in 1762, prior to the dismemberment, except such claim as might inure to Spain by the secret treaty of 1762, and to Great Britain by the treaty of

---

* See book iv., chap. iv., close of chapter.
† See book v., chap. xv., "Territory of Orleans."

1763. The Federal government never ceased to urge this claim with the Spanish crown as a valid reason for the restriction of the northern and western boundaries of West Florida.

[A.D. 1810.] In the mean time, the district of Baton Rouge had become settled by numerous emigrants from the western states and territories, in addition to a large number of Anglo-Americans, who had been grievously disappointed in finding themselves excluded from the jurisdiction of the United States, by the line of demarkation established under the treaty of Madrid. The whole population in the district, of Anglo-American descent, partial to the Federal government, and unwilling to submit to an absolute monarchy beyond the seas, was but little short of ten thousand persons. Surrounded as they were by Republican friends and Republican institutions, which they desired to enjoy, they could hardly be expected to remain loyal subjects of a foreign prince. At length the people revolted from their Spanish allegiance, and expelling their Spanish rulers, organized a provisional government, and claimed the protection of the United States. On the 7th of December, 1810, Governor Claiborne, of the territory of Orleans, by order of the President of the United States, took formal and peaceable possession of the country, with the troops of the Federal government. Soon afterward, all that portion of West Florida known as the Baton Rouge District, extending eastward to Pearl River, was, by act of Congress, annexed to the territory of Orleans, and finally became incorporated within the limits of the State of Louisiana.*

[A.D. 1813.] The residue of West Florida, eastward to the Perdido, remained under the Spanish jurisdiction, and in possession of the Spanish troops, until the spring of 1813. About this time war between the United States on one side, and Great Britain and her Indian allies on the other, was raging on the northern and southern frontiers of the United States. Apprehensive of the inability or the indisposition of the Spanish authorities to maintain a strict neutrality in the bays, inlets, and harbors west of Pensacola, Congress authorized the military occupation of the country, from the Pearl River to the Perdido, by the commander-in-chief of the seventh military district.†

By an order from the Secretary of War, and received by

---

* Martin's Louisiana, vol. ii., p. 299. See, also, book v., chap. xv. of this work, "Territory of Orleans."   † See Martin's Louisiana, vol. ii., p. 315.

General Wilkinson early in the year 1813, he was directed to take possession of all that portion of Florida west of the Perdido river and bay, and to extend the Federal jurisdiction over the same. He accordingly prepared to concentrate his forces for the capture of Fort Charlotte at Mobile. The naval forces in the vicinity of New Orleans were ordered to concentrate in the Bay of Mobile, while, at the head of a strong land force, he in person proceeded across the country from the Mississippi. On the 12th day of April the army encamped before the town of Mobile, and the commander-in-chief immediately dispatched a summons to the commandant of Fort Charlotte, couched in courteous language, but in a positive tone, demanding the evacuation of the fort.* The Spanish commandant, Don Cayetano Perez, seeing he was completely surrounded by sea and land, made no delay to enter into negotiations for an honorable capitulation. The article of capitulation was signed on the 14th, stipulating for the evacuation of the fort on the following day, together with the surrender of all the military stores, artillery,

---

* The following is a copy of the summons sent by General Wilkinson, viz.:
"Camp near Mobile, April 12th, 1813.

"SIR,—The troops of the United States under my command do not approach you as the enemy of Spain; but, by the order of the President, they come to relieve the garrison which you command from the occupancy of a post within the legitimate limits of those states. I therefore hope, sir, that you may peacefully retire from Fort Charlotte and from the bounds of the Mississippi territory (east of the Perdido River), with the garrison you command, and the public and private property which may appertain thereunto.

"I flatter myself that you will meet a proposition so reasonable and so just in the spirit with which it is offered, and that no time may be unnecessarily lost in carrying it into execution. My aide-de-camp, Major H. D. Piere, will present you this note, and, if convenient to you, will receive your answer. With due consideration and respect, I have the honor to be
"Your most obedient and humble servant,
"JAMES WILKINSON.
"To the officer commanding Fort Charlotte."

The following reply was returned, viz.:
"Fort Charlotte, Mobile, April 13th, 1813.

"MOST EXCELLENT SIR,—I have marked the contents of your letter of yesterday, and I have commissioned Lieutenant Don Francisco Morrison to confer with your excellency on the points in dispute.
"God preserve your excellency many years.
"CAYETANO PEREZ.
"His excellency Don James Wilkinson."

In the subsequent negotiation it was deemed expedient to leave the fort, and all the munitions and public property remaining in the hands of the United States, the value to be settled by commissioners of the two governments. See Wilkinson's Memoirs, vol. i., p. 508–512.

ammunition, arms, and munitions, to be accounted for by the United States at a fair valuation.

Among the supplies of the fort left with the American commander were thirty-seven heavy pieces of ordnance, seventeen swivels, brass and iron, besides a large amount of munitions of war, comprising solid balls of different sizes, bombs of divers kinds, small arms, and every variety of apparatus, offensive and defensive.

The Spanish garrison retired quietly on board their vessels and set sail for Pensacola; and the American troops, agreeably to stipulations, deferred entering the fort until the Spanish troops had departed.*

A few days afterward, General Wilkinson advanced eastward to the Perdido, and established a small post on its western bank, while another detachment was sent to fortify Mobile Point, afterward known as Fort Boyer. Thus terminated the dominion of Spain over the western portion of Florida.

Florida, thus restricted, remained a loyal Spanish province, without any other change of boundary, until it was finally ceded to the United States by the treaty of Washington in 1819. Yet it was not exempt from the revolutionary designs and operations of the revolted Spanish provinces of South America. The Patriots of South America, being engaged in a sanguinary war with the mother country, aided by adventurers from the United States and from Europe, omitted no opportunity for effecting the expulsion of the regal domination from the loyal provinces of Florida and Texas. To accomplish this purpose, several expeditions were successively fitted out in the ports of South America and the West Indies, to operate against the Spanish authorities in these two provinces.

The first expedition against East Florida entered the country through the St. Mary's, occupying the Port of Fernandina and the Island of Amelia. From this point operations were extended until the Patriot forces had extended their authority over the whole district comprised in the government of St. Augustine. But the government established by them was of short duration. It was on the 12th of April, 1812, that the Spanish governor, Don Jose Lopez, entered into terms of capitulation, by which he surrendered the Port of Fernandina, including the

* See Wilkinson's Memoirs, vol. i., 514-516.

whole island, and his entire command, to the "superior forces" of the Patriots. A provisional government was organized, and the authorities made formal application for admission into the Federal Union, as an integral portion of the United States.* But the government of the United States, true to its treaty obligations to Spain, declined to receive the province from the usurpers, and established a competent military force upon the St. Mary's, to enforce neutrality on the border, and to restrain any popular outbreak of the American people. At the same time, the American government proposed to the Spanish minister to take possession of the country in trust for the King of Spain, until his Catholic majesty should find himself in a condition to maintain the neutrality of the country, so as to secure the proper execution of the revenue laws of the United States against a band of smugglers by which the St. Mary's River was infested. General George Matthews and Colonel John M'Kee were authorized commissioners on the part of the United States.†

On the 12th of June, Sebastian Kinderlan, with a re-enforcement of royal troops, expelled the Patriots, and re-established the royal authority. The Federal troops, who had advanced to the south side of the St. Mary's, were ordered to retire within the limits of Georgia.‡

The foreign occupancy of Florida had become a source of great annoyance, not only to the Federal government, but to the western people in general. Surrounded, as it were, by the territory of the United States, with an extensive boundary, much of it designated only by a surveyor's line, separating two races so radically different, under civil and religious institutions so strongly repugnant to each other, it was certain the frontier people could never harmonize; and the Federal executive had for many years endeavored to prevent the collision of the advancing settlements by the peaceable acquisition of the whole of Florida; but Spain preferred to prolong her feeble authority over the province.

---

* The Patriot forces comprised an armament of nine gun-boats, with a full complement of marines and infantry, composed of adventurers from all countries, including a large proportion of Americans. The forces were under the command of Commodore Campbell and Colonel Ashley.

† A more extended account of the operations connected with the revolution upon the Island of Amelia may be found in Williams's Florida, p. 191–196. See, also, American State Papers, vol. ix., p. 41–46; and 156, 7, Boston edition of 1819.   ‡ Ibid.

At length the United States were involved in a war with Great Britain, who, disregarding the neutrality of the Spanish territory, introduced her emissaries through the Spanish ports, to arm the savages of Florida and the Mississippi territory against the defenseless frontier settlements.* In the progress of the war, the British fleets and armies destined for the invasion of the United States and the destruction of American ports were allowed to enter the ports, and to garrison the strong forts of West Florida, from which they operated upon the frontier settlements.

[A.D. 1815.] Nor did this violation of a neutral territory cease with the termination of the war. After the war had terminated, and the treaty of peace with Great Britain had been ratified, and after the savages had been vanquished, subdued, and had entered into amicable arrangements by a treaty of peace, the emissaries of Great Britain, armed with the powerful patronage of that government, continued with impunity to make Florida the theatre of renewed operations for involving the United States in the horrors of another Indian war.

It was in the spring of 1815, immediately after the promulgation of peace between the United States and Great Britain, that Captain Woodbine resumed his intrigues with the Indians of Florida, for the avowed purpose of instigating the Seminoles and Muskhogees to renew hostilities against the frontier settlements of Georgia and the Mississippi Territory. To the effects of his subsequent operations, under the directions of Colonel Nichols, an officer of his Britannic majesty's navy, and to his successors, Alexander Arbuthnot and Robert C. Ambrister, must be ascribed the existence of the "Seminole War," which resulted, finally, in the entire exclusion of all foreign dominion from Florida.

Adopting the opinion of Lord Castlereagh, that the ninth article of the treaty of Ghent virtually entitled the Creek Indians to a restoration of all the lands they had relinquished to the United States by the treaty of Fort Jackson in 1814, Captain Woodbine entered upon the arduous task of enforcing an admission of their claim.

Having conducted a colony of negro slaves to East Florida, he ascended the Appalachicola River, under the directions of Colonel Nichols, and commenced the construction of a strong

* See book v., chap. xiv., "Creek War."

fort, as the headquarters of his future operations. At this place he was abundantly supplied with artillery, munitions of war, arms, and ammunition from the British fleet, for the use of the savages in the contemplated enterprise.*

He immediately opened a correspondence with Colonel Benjamin Hawkins, Indian agent of the United States for the Creek nation. In a letter, dated April 28th, 1815, he announces himself as the advocate of the Indians, and notifies the United States agent that the Creek Indians had determined to demand the restoration of all the lands ceded to the United States by the treaty of Fort Jackson, agreeably to the provisions of the ninth article of the treaty of Ghent: " The Indians being independent allies of Great Britain."

In a subsequent communication, dated May 12th, he represents himself as " commanding his Britannic majesty's forces in the Floridas," and declares that " he has ordered the Indians to stand on the defensive, and having sent them a large supply of arms and ammunition, has told them to put to death without mercy any one molesting them." Again: " They have given their consent to wait your answer before *they take revenge;* but, sir, they are impatient for it, and are well armed, as the whole nation now is, and stored with ammunition and provis-

---

* The following document is selected from a large mass of documentary evidence transmitted to the War Department from the commanding general, showing the cause of the Seminole war, and referred by Congress to the committee on the forcible occupancy of Florida by General Jackson, viz.:

Deposition of Samuel Jervais.

Samuel Jervais, being duly sworn, states that he has been a sergeant of marines, in the British service, for thirteen years past; that "about a month ago he left Appalachicola, where he had been stationed for several months; that the English colonel, Nichols, had promised the hostile Indians at that place a supply of arms and ammunition, a large quantity of which *had been delivered to them* a few days before his departure, and *after* the news of peace between England and the United States had been confirmed and reached Appalachicola; that *among the articles delivered* were four twelve-pounder cannon, one howitzer, two cohorns, about three thousand stand of arms, and nearly three thousand barrels of powder and ball; that the British left with the Indians *between three and four hundred negroes,* taken from the United States, and chiefly from Louisiana; that the arms and ammunition were for the use of the Indians and negroes, and for the purpose, as he understood, of war with the United States; that the Indians were assured by the British commander that, according to the treaty of Ghent, all the lands ceded by the treaty with General Jackson were to be restored; otherwise the Indians must fight for them, and the British would in a short time assist them.

his
SAMUEL + JERVAIS."
mark.

Sworn to and subscribed before me, this 9th day of May, 1815,
L. JUDSON, J. P.

ions, having a *strong-hold* to retire upon in case superior force appears."

Soon afterward, in company with the "Prophet Francis," also called *Hillis-hadjo*, and a deputation of Creek chiefs, Colonel Nichols departed for England, for the purpose of forming a treaty of alliance, offensive and defensive, with the prince-regent. The formation of such treaty was prevented only by the remonstrance of the American minister, John Quincy Adams, then resident in London. The British premier, Lord Castlereagh, and the Earl of Bathurst, cautiously avoided any written correspondence on the subject; but Hillis-hadjo was received with attention, and, as a mark of distinction and favor, the prince-regent conferred upon him the rank of "brigadier-general in his majesty's service," together with a splendid suit of British uniform.*

[A.D. 1816.] Before the lapse of twelve months, Woodbine had completed his "strong-hold" on the bank of the Appalachicola, twenty-five miles above its mouth; it was now occupied by a garrison of more than one hundred negroes and a few Indians. Occasional hostilities had been committed against the American settlements, and military posts were established on the Chattahoochy for the protection of the Georgia frontier. Among these was "Camp Crawford," just above the Florida line. The supplies for this post were received by way of the river through the Spanish province, and by passing immediately under the guns of the negro fort which commanded the river.† The commandant of the fort was Garçon, a French

---

* All these facts, and many others, were fully established before the committee of Congress in 1819, in the investigation instituted upon the course pursued by General Jackson in taking military possession of Florida for the better protection of the frontiers. The subject of British intrigue in Florida, and the diabolical machinations of British agents in provoking the Seminoles to war, is discussed in a lucid and able manner in the excellent speech of the Hon. George Poindexter, in the House of Representatives of the United States on the 1st and 2d of February, 1819. This speech was an able vindication of General Jackson for his occupancy of the Spanish posts of St. Mark's and Pensacola.

This speech is contained in Williston's "Eloquence of the United States," vol. iii., p. 128–187. It was also published extensively in the newspapers of the day. See Mississippi State Gazette of May 8th and 12th, 1819.

† This fort was described as follows: viz., It was situated on a beautiful high bluff, with a large creek near the base, and protected by a swamp in the rear, which rendered the approach of artillery very difficult. The parapet was fifteen feet high and eighteen feet thick. It was defended by one thirty-two pounder, three twenty-four pounders, several of them inscribed "His Britannic majesty's frigate Cydnus," two nine pounders, two six pounders, and one elegant brass five and a half inch howitzer. It contained in its magazines a large amount of arms and ammunition. One magazine

negro, in connection with the Choctâ chief, "Red Sticks;" and within its walls were sheltered no less than two hundred negro women and children. Near the fort the fields were fine, and others extended up and down the river for nearly fifty miles.

From this general rendezvous, marauding expeditions had been sent out, not only against the defenseless settlements of the Georgia frontier, but also piratical excursions against trading vessels on the coast. Such was the prelude to the Seminole war.

On the 16th of August, Colonel Clinch, commanding at Camp Crawford, received intelligence that two transports laden with provisions, stores, and ordnance, convoyed by two gun-boats, were lying in the bay near the mouth of the river, awaiting an escort of United States troops from his command, as protection against the fort on the river. The instructions to Colonel Clinch required him, in case of opposition to the ascent of the vessels by the fort, to reduce it by military force.

Next day Colonel Clinch, with a detachment of two companies, under the command of Major Muhlenberg and Captain Z. Taylor, comprising one hundred and sixteen choice men, descended the river in order to conduct the supplies above the point of danger. On the 18th he was joined by Major M'Intosh with one hundred and fifty friendly Creeks, and on the following day by two other detachments of Indians, who had set out for the capture of negroes in the vicinity of the fort.

With this force he took up his position in the vicinity of the negro fort to await the ascent of Lieutenant Loomis with the transports and gun-boats. On the same evening an express from Lieutenant Loomis informed him that a watering party, near the mouth of the river, had been attacked by a detachment of negroes, who had killed one midshipman and two sailors, and captured a third. Colonel Clinch determined, without further delay, to invest the fort, and the Indians were directed to take their positions around the fort, and open upon it a scattering fire. The negro garrison commenced a terrible discharge of artillery, designed to frighten the Indians, and with no other injury to the besiegers. The demand of the Indians for the surrender of the fort was answered by Garçon with the

---

contained six hundred barrels of powder, and the other one hundred and sixty-three, besides about three thousand stand of arms, and other valuable property to a large amount.

utmost contempt, after which he hoisted the English jack. Such was the state of things until the arrival of the whole force of gun-boats and vessels from below.

It was on the 26th that the escort and convoy arrived within four miles of the fort, when preparations were made to take it by storm. For this purpose a battery was erected during the night, and early the next morning the two gun-boats, prepared for action, moved up in handsome style, and moored near the battery. In a few minutes they were saluted by a shot from a thirty-two pounder in the fort. This was the signal for the attack, and the fire was returned in gallant style. At the fifth discharge, *a hot shot* from gun-boat No. 154 penetrated the great magazine, and immediately the fort was blown up with the most awful explosion. The scene in the fort was horrible beyond description; nearly the whole of the inmates were involved in one indiscriminate destruction; not one sixth of the whole escaped. The cries of the wounded and dying, mingled with the shouts and yells of the Indians, rendered the confusion horrible in the extreme.

Three thousand stand of arms and six hundred barrels of powder were destroyed by the explosion. The whole amount of property destroyed and taken was not less than $200,000 in value. One magazine, containing one hundred and sixty-three barrels of powder, was saved by the victors. The negro commander, Garçon, and the Choctâ chief, "Red Sticks," were delivered to the Indians, who put them to a painful death.*
Woodbine had escaped the evening before.

On the following day, intelligence was received of the approach of a formidable body of hostile Seminoles. Finding Colonel Clinch well prepared to receive them, they prudently declined an attack. Preparations were immediately made by the State of Georgia and by the Federal government for the efficient protection of the exposed frontier.

Such was the commencement of the Seminole war in Florida.

General Gaines, of the United States army, commanding at Fort Scott, on the Georgia frontier, proceeded to chastise the hostile Seminoles. At the first Indian town attacked in December, on Clinch River, the evidences of British treachery were fully presented. In the cabin of Neamathla the chief was found a British uniform of scarlet cloth, with gold epau-

* Williams's Florida, p. 202, 203.

lets. According to the certificate found in the pocket, and signed by the secretary of Colonel Nichols, "Neamathla was a faithful British subject."*

The Seminoles, however, being deprived of their principal leaders, and especially the ferocious Woodbine, were frustrated in their operations; yet for more than twelve months they were prone to hostilities, and from time to time committed frequent murders and depredations upon the frontier settlements, which required the maintenance of an active surveillance on the part of the Federal troops to prevent any general concert of operation.

[A.D. 1817.] While these events were transpiring upon the Indian frontier, the Patriot forces again invaded East Florida, taking possession of Amelia Island, from which they contemplated the entire subjugation of the whole province. In the present case, the invasion was made by General Gregor M'Gregor and Admiral Aury, acting under the authority of the "United Provinces of New Grenada and Venezuela." Having learned that Spain contemplated ceding Florida to the United States, they deemed it an opportune occasion to wrest it from the Spanish crown. To this end they proceeded to augment their forces, by enlisting into their ranks every description of adventurers, embracing outlaws from the United States, slaves, smugglers, English emissaries, among whom was Captain Woodbine, and partisans picked up in the streets of Savannah, Charleston, and other ports of the United States. To induce the Federal government to be a silent spectator in the spoliation of the Spanish province, General M'Gregor attempted to forestall any movement on the part of the executive of the United States, by avowing it to be his object, after a temporary occupation, to provide for its annexation to the United States.

On the 30th of July, 1817, the Spanish governor entered into a capitulation for the surrender of the province to the Patriot forces; thus again excluding the authority of Spain.

But with his incongruous mass of reckless adventurers, no permanent government could be sustained. Dissensions arose; and General M'Gregor, having been supplanted by the artful intrigue of Hubbard, and having been induced to believe that his personal security was endangered by his enemies, retired

* Williams's Florida, p. 204.

from the command, and accompanied the notorious Woodbine to England. It was not long before Aury lost his influence, and retired also, leaving Hubbard in chief command.

The government, under the usurped authority, had but short duration. To prevent the lawless assemblage, which concentrated near the frontier of the United States, and interrupted the due operation of the revenue laws, the Federal government determined to take forcible possession of the country until Spain should be able to maintain her authority over it. Accordingly, on the first of January, 1818, in obedience to instructions, Major J. Bankhead and Commodore J. D. Henly, with a division of the land and naval forces of the United States, had expelled the Patriots and took possession of the country.*

In the mean time, the Seminoles had imbodied in large numbers upon the Clinch and Appalachicola Rivers, and upon the St. Mary's, near the frontiers of Georgia. In addition to the regular troops of the United States, the Georgia militia had been called into service, and were placed under the command of General Gaines. From the threatening attitude in this quarter, General Andrew Jackson was again called into the field as commander-in-chief of the troops operating in this quarter, with authority to call upon the executives of the adjacent states for such force as he might deem necessary for the subjugation of the Indian forces, estimated by General Gaines at twenty-seven hundred warriors.

[A.D. 1818.] Early in January following, he advanced into the Creek nation, at the head of a large body of Tennessee volunteers, on his route to the seat of war. On the 22d of January, he concluded a treaty of peace and alliance with the friendly Creeks, and early in February they agreed to march under their chief, Major M'Intosh, to fight the Seminoles in Georgia and Florida.

On the first of March, General Jackson, with the Tennessee volunteers and the friendly Creeks, arrived at Fort Scott, and took command of the army. A few days afterward, he took up his line of march, with the united forces, down the Appalachicola to Fort Gadsden. On the way the country was scoured by the friendly Indians, and by detachments of cavalry, which brought in a large number of prisoners from the Seminoles.

* See American State Papers, vol. xii., p. 390–416, Boston edition of 1819.

On the 26th of March, having received strong re-enforcements, he set out for the Mickasukie towns, in East Florida, his whole force amounting to five hundred regulars, one thousand militia, and one thousand eight hundred Indians. On the first of April, the Mickasukie towns were utterly destroyed; and the same fate soon afterward attended the Fowel towns, situated upon Mickasukie Lake and on the Oscilla River, both of which were inhabited by hostile Creeks. The Indians fled before the troops, and made but little resistance, leaving one thousand head of fine cattle and large quantities of corn.

At the Mickasukie towns, about fifty miles north of St. Mark's, were found nearly three hundred scalps, taken promiscuously from the heads of not only men and women, but of children and infants. Many of them were of quite recent date, and fifty of them were suspended over the council square, upon a painted war-pole.*

Receiving intelligence of the aid which had been given the Indians at St. Mark's, on the Appalachy River, General Jackson took up his line of march for that post. This post, situated six miles from Appalachy Bay, was defended by a strong Spanish fort, mounting twenty pieces of heavy ordnance. The agency of the officers of this post, and the people of the place, in abetting and supplying the Indians, was undoubted, and General Jackson demanded its immediate surrender. The commander capitulated, the garrison was permitted to retire to Pensacola, and the American troops took possession of the fort.

Among the prisoners captured near St. Mark's was the "Prophet Francis," or *Hillis-hadjo*, and another notorious Indian chief, both of whom were formally sentenced to death, and hung without delay.

In the vicinity of the Suwanee River, on the 18th of April, Robert C. Ambrister, a British agent under Alexander Arbuthnot, was captured, and kept in close confinement for further examination.

From St. Mark's the general took up his line of march for the Seminole towns on the Suwanee River, situated about one hundred and seven miles southeast of St. Mark's. In this vicinity were assembled a large body of Indians and negroes, amounting to about two thousand, acting under the orders of

---

* See Williams's Florida, p. 205; also, p. 214.

Arbuthnot, who was supplying them with arms, ammunition, and military stores. On the first appearance of the army at these towns, the Indians made a show of resistance; but they soon fled with precipitation eastward, and many took shelter under the walls of St. Augustine. The fugitives were pursued several miles until dark, when the troops encountered an encampment of three hundred and forty negroes, who fought with great desperation until eighty of them were killed, when the remainder fled. Three hundred Indian women and children were taken prisoners, and many others were killed by the Indians, to prevent their captivity.*

While here, the videttes succeeded in capturing the notorious Alexander Arbuthnot, who, ignorant of the proximity of the American forces, in a canoe, with two negroes and an Indian, had approached the American lines to reconnoiter, when he was captured by the videttes on duty. He was properly secured in camp, and next morning a detachment was sent to seize his schooner, laden with arms, ammunition, and valuable stores, then lying in Wakassee Bay, at the mouth of the Suwanee.

During the next ten days, Major M'Intosh, with his Indian warriors, scoured the country around, and was engaged in numerous skirmishes with the hostile Seminoles, of whom many were killed, besides a large number taken prisoners. Their resources were destroyed, and their towns and fields were ravaged with fire and sword.

On the first of May, a court-martial, with General Gaines presiding, found Arbuthnot and Ambrister guilty on three charges: 1. Exciting the negroes and Indians to commit murders upon the people of the United States; 2. Supplying them with arms and ammunition for offensive operations; 3. Acting as spies. General Jackson determined not to interpose his authority between the guilty and their doom, and they were sentenced to die; Ambrister by shooting, and Arbuthnot by hanging. The execution of the sentence was speedily enforced.†

* Williams's Florida, p. 206.

† After the destruction of the negro fort, Colonel Nichols, from the Island of New Providence, dispatched Alexander Arbuthnot, a British officer, to succeed Captain Woodbine in his diabolical operations. "He arrived in Florida in the guise of a British trader in the year 1817, and simultaneously the war-whoop resounded through the forests, and the blood of our citizens began to flow along the borders of Georgia and the Alabama Territory."—*Hon. George Poindexter's Speech on the Seminole War.*

In one of his letters, directed to the British minister, Mr. Bagot, resident at Wash-

Arbuthnot was justly considered the author of the Seminole war, under the direction of Woodbine, who escaped from justice in the United States to meet it in another country, and at a later date, from the hands of that race which had absorbed all his sympathies.*

Ambrister was a young man, apparently not over twenty-five years old, having a fine person, and holding the rank of lieutenant of marines in the British navy; but he died like a weak woman, repining at his merited fate. Although, in many parts of the United States and in England, sympathizers affected to censure the sentence of these two men, yet the Congress of the United States and the Parliament of Great Britain were constrained to sanction their execution as a merited doom, and permit their names to be consigned to infamy.

The war in this quarter having been thus brought to a close, General Jackson discharged the militia, whose term of service had nearly expired, and at the head of the regular troops, a few volunteers, and the friendly Indians under Major M'Intosh, marched for Pensacola, where his presence had become necessary. Parties of Indians in that vicinity had committed frequent murders, and had attacked boats conveying supplies for his army. The Governor of Pensacola had also refused to permit his vessels a free passage through the bay and up the Escambia River. Lieutenant Eddy, in charge of a boat loaded with provisions, had been attacked on the Escambia, in April, by Indians, who killed one and wounded two men. To chastise these outrages, Major Young, from Fort Montgomery, at the head of seventy-five mounted men, pursued the fugitives within one mile of Pensacola. Here, encountering them at the Bayou Texar, in a severe engagement, he slew thirty

---

ington City, he requested a supply of the following articles for the use of the Indians: viz.:

A quantity of powder, lead, muskets, and flints sufficient for arming one thousand Indians, as follows:

1000 muskets, and more smaller pieces, if possible.
10,000 flints, a portion for rifles, put up separate.
50 casks of gunpowder, a proportion for the rifle.
2000 knives, six to nine inches blade, of good quality.
1000 tomahawks, and one hundred pounds of vermilion.
2000 pounds lead, independent of ball, for muskets.—See *Congressional Documents connected with the Seminole War.*

* Woodbine, after his escape from the negro fort on the Appalachicola, fled to Mexico, where he remained until 1837, when he and his family were murdered at Campeachy by negroes. See Williams's Florida, p. 206.

of them, and took seventy-five prisoners. These Indians had been virtually protected by the Spanish authorities.

It was on the 24th of May that General Jackson reached the vicinity of Pensacola. Being assured of the conduct of the governor, who had refused to permit boats bearing the American flag, with provisions for his troops, to ascend the Escambia, while he countenanced the hostile attitude of the Indians, he determined to take effectual steps to remove these difficulties in future. To this effect, he determined to expel the perfidious Spaniards from Pensacola, as he had from St. Mark's.

Apprehensive of this measure, the governor sent a messenger to meet him as he approached Pensacola, warning him that the whole Spanish force would be brought to resist any such attempt. The general replied that he would return his answer in the morning, and continued his march. The governor well knew the man he had to deal with, and next morning, at nine o'clock, when General Jackson marched into the town, the governor had retired into the Fort Barancas, and left him undisputed possession of the place.

Three days afterward, the army marched to the Barancas, and took position about four hundred yards west of the fort. The night was spent in erecting a breast-work. In the morning the Spaniards opened upon it with two twenty-four pounders, and the Americans returned the fire actively from one howitzer, and made preparations to storm the fort. At three o'clock P.M. a flag from the fort conveyed the governor's proposition to capitulate. The capitulation was forthwith concluded and signed. The fort was surrendered, and the governor, with the garrison, was permitted peaceably to retire to Havana. The American troops occupied the post, and Colonel King was subsequently left in command at Pensacola.

On the 29th of May, the commander-in-chief issued his proclamation to the inhabitants of West Florida, including his general orders to the army. The following extract exhibits the tenor of that document,* viz.:

"Headquarters, Division of the South,
"Pensacola, May 29th, 1818.

"Major-general Andrew Jackson has found it necessary to take possession of Pensacola. He has not been prompted to this measure from a wish to extend the territorial limits of the

---

* See Mississippi State Gazette, June 20th, 1818.

United States, or from any unfriendly feeling on the part of the American Republic to the Spanish government. The Seminole Indians, inhabiting the territories of Spain, have, for more than two years past, visited our frontier settlers with all the horrors of savage massacre: helpless women have been butchered, and the cradle stained with the blood of innocence. These atrocities, it was expected, would have early attracted the attention of the Spanish government, and that, faithful to existing treaties, speedy measures would have been adopted for their suppression.

"The obligation to restrain them was acknowledged; but weakness was alleged, with a concession that, so far from being able to control, the Spanish authorities were often compelled, from policy or necessity, to issue munitions of war to these savages, thus enabling, if not exciting, them to raise the tomahawk against us. The immutable laws of self-defense, therefore, compelled the American government to take possession of those parts of the Floridas in which the Spanish authority could not be maintained. Pensacola was found in this situation, and will be held until Spain can furnish military strength sufficient to enforce existing treaties. Spanish subjects will be respected; Spanish laws will govern in all cases affecting property and person; a free toleration to all religions guarantied, and trade alike free to all nations."

Thus all West Florida was virtually occupied by the American troops; and detachments under Captains Girt and Bowles were sent to scour the country, from the Perdido on the west to the Uche and Holmes's Old Fields on the Chactahatchy. St. Augustine had likewise been occupied by General Gaines, acting under the orders of General Jackson.

Having thus concluded the Seminole war, General Jackson disposed of the regular troops, discharged the friendly Creeks, and marched the Tennessee volunteers home. Thus terminated the Seminole war, leaving all Florida in the occupancy of the United States.

Such was the celerity and decision of all General Jackson's movements. As a forcible writer on the Seminole war, in a Tennessee paper of that year, observes, "General Jackson is a more extraordinary person than has ever appeared in our history. Nature has seldom endowed man with a mind so powerful and comprehensive, or with a body better formed for activity, or capable of enduring greater privations, fatigue, and hardships. She has been equally kind to him in all the qualities of his heart. General Jackson has no ambition but for the good of his country: it occupies the whole of his views, to the exclusion of all selfish or ignoble considerations. Cradled in the war of the Revolution, nurtured amid the conflicts which subsequently took place between the Cherokees and the Tennesseeans, being always among a people who regard the application of force, *not* as the *ultima ratio regum*, but as the *first* resort of individuals who look upon courage as the greatest of human attributes, his character, on this stormy ocean, has acquired an extraordinary cast of vigor, with a conviction that we should never despair of effecting whatever is within the power of man to accomplish; and that courage, activity, and perseverance can overcome obstacles which, to ordinary minds, appear insuperable. In society, he is kind, frank, unaffected, and hospitable; endowed with much natural grace and politeness, without the mechanical gentility and artificial polish found in fashionable life."*

The course of General Jackson in the occupancy of Florida was severely attacked in Congress by a party of great zeal and activity, at the head of which was Henry Clay, then speaker of the House of Representatives; but the general was fully sustained by the president and his cabinet, and by an overwhelming majority in Congress. The people, from one end of the United States to the other, spoke out, and, through the State Legislatures and public meetings, vindicated the decisive and prompt measures adopted by the defender of the South.

[A.D. 1819.] While these things were transpiring on the southern frontier, the Federal government of the United States, well assured that the possession of the whole of the Floridas was indispensable to the peace and security of the Southern States, had been pressing an urgent negotiation for the purchase of the whole province from Spain. The possession had been restored to Spain, but the negotiation was continued with unremitting perseverance and with increasing firmness on the part of the American government, until the 22d of February, 1819, when a formal treaty of cession was signed on the part of the United States by John Quincy Adams, secretary of State, and on the part of the Spanish crown by Don Onis, res-

---

* See Mississippi State Gazette, September 9th, 1818.

ident Spanish minister near the American government. This treaty was rejected by the Spanish Cortes at their following session, but was subsequently ratified on the 24th of October, 1820. On the part of the American government, it was confirmed by the Senate on the 22d day of February, 1821.

The treaty stipulated, on the part of Spain, for and in consideration of *five millions of dollars*, paid by the United States to their citizens, as an indemnity due from Spain for spoliations on American commerce, to cede to the United States all the Floridas, with the islands adjacent, from the mouth of the St. Mary's River on the Atlantic coast to the Perdido Bay on the Gulf of Mexico. Under cover of this treaty, for the acquisition of Florida on the part of the United States, the great province of Louisiana was *dismembered*, and the important and extensive region of Texas was transferred to the Spanish crown. The western limit of Louisiana, on the Gulf of Mexico, was removed from the Rio Bravo del Norte, eastward five hundred miles, to the Sabine, without any consideration received on the part of the United States for a territory three times as extensive as the Floridas, and infinitely more valuable.

[A.D. 1821.] In this treaty, President Monroe, reluctantly yielding to the prejudices and interests of Northern politicians, consented to abandon for a time the extensive and fertile country west of the Sabine, in order to conciliate the approbation of the New England States* to the annexation of Florida, well

* From the earliest period of the Western settlements, after the adoption of the Federal Constitution in 1789, the jealousy of New England, and especially of Massachusetts, was awakened to the danger of losing her ascendency in the national government, and in the commercial importance of the country. With this view predominant, they have never failed, when opportunity offered, to embarrass the West in the national councils, and by all means to retard and restrict the extension of its settlements. The same narrow, interested policy induced them to throw every obstacle in the way, to prevent the acquisition of the free navigation of the Mississippi, previous to the treaty of Madrid and subsequently. The same interested policy prompted them to oppose, with great violence, the purchase of Louisiana, because, "lest," as was unblushingly said, "our New England lands become a desert, from the contagion of emigration;" and because "the politicians of the Northeastern States were *anxious to give such a shape to the Union as would secure the dominion over it to its Eastern section.*"—See Boston Centinel, Nov. 12, 1803.—See, also, Mr. Monroe's letter to Mr. Jefferson in 1820.

When Louisiana was finally acquired in 1803, these states, and Massachusetts especially, threatened to dissolve the Union and recede; in 1814 they desired to surrender to Great Britain the navigation of the Mississippi River, and virtually all beyond. The same policy predominated in the treaty of 1819, in which, to conciliate the New England States, upon the acquisition of Florida, three times as much Western territory was abandoned without equivalent or necessity. Now they acquiesced in being able to detach all beyond the Sabine. Again, in 1845, Massachusetts, through her Legislature, urged the most violent opposition to the annexation of Texas, threatening to se-

assured in his own mind that Texas must inevitably come into the Union whenever the advance of population should demand its use. To insure the respectful acquiescence of the American people, the memory of "the Father of his Country" was invoked at the signing and final ratification of the treaty. And, as if still further to shield himself from popular displeasure, the name of Jackson was to be identified with the acquisition of Florida, as its first governor and military commandant. But the stability of the Union increases with its extension; and a quarter of a century had scarcely elapsed when the American Union, having doubled its population, found its stability unshaken, and the whole of Texas and Florida embraced.

General Jackson, "acquiescing for the present" in the loss of Texas for the acquisition of Florida, repaired to his post; and on the 17th of June, 1821, he took possession of the same in the name of the United States, by the exchange of flags, and the usual formalities.

General Jackson immediately entered upon the duties of his office, as civil and military commandant and governor of Florida, invested by Congress with ample powers, legislative, judicial, and executive.*

From Pensacola, his headquarters, he issued several proclamations and ordinances regulating the administration of public justice. The territory was divided into two judicial districts, which continued to be known as East and West Florida, separated by the Suwanee River instead of the former boundary of the Appalachicola River. A court, with civil and criminal jurisdiction, was established in each.†

By the treaty the Spanish population were allowed a reasonable time to dispose of their estates and personal property previous to their departure, provided they did not wish to remain under the American government.

The American population began to advance rapidly into Florida, by sea from various portions of the Union, and by land from Georgia, Alabama, Mississippi, and from Tennessee. The State of Tennessee had long desired the expulsion of the Spaniards from Florida; hence the Tennessee volunteers had cheerfully entered the campaign under General Jackson, anxious to

cede from the Union, and declaring "that the re-annexation of Texas was a virtual dissolution of the Union."
* Williams's Florida, p. 207. † Idem, p. 208.

witness and aid in the humiliation of the perfidious Spaniards. They now were among the first to press in and occupy the country wrested from them. Before the close of the year 1822, the greater portion of the Spanish population had retired to Havana and Mexico.

Early in his administration of the government of Florida, Governor Jackson came into collision with the Spanish authorities still remaining in the country. Apprehending a renewal of the evasions and artifices practiced by the Spanish authorities relative to the surrender of the Natchez District in 1798, and relative to the factitious land-titles of Louisiana, Governor Jackson determined, by prompt measures, to suppress any such attempt. Having been informed that the ex-governor, Calleava, was about to transmit to Havana certain documents and archives pertaining to land-titles, in violation of the second article of the treaty of cession, he made a peremptory demand for their surrender, as the property of the United States. The ex-governor refusing to obey the demand, Governor Jackson issued an order for his arrest and confinement in the calaboose, and the documents were seized and taken from his house, where they had been boxed up for shipment. The ex-governor was then released.

Castilian pride was touched, and several Spanish officers, resenting the indignity to their late governor, sent to Governor Jackson a strong remonstrance against his procedure. The governor, considering it an unwarrantable interference with his authority, and highly offensive in language, issued an order for their immediate departure from the country, on pain of imprisonment. Twelve of them were accordingly compelled to sail for Havana, with but little time allowed for settling up their affairs and disposing of their property.*

[A.D. 1822.] General Jackson continued to administer the government, clothed with the general powers of the Spanish governors, until the following year, when the American population having increased to five thousand males, the first grade of territorial government, under the ordinance of 1787, was organized.

Under the new organization, William P. Duval was appointed governor, with a superior court in each district. A legislative council was organized, and held its first session in June,

---

* Williams's Florida, p. 208.

1822. At this session each district was divided into two counties, viz., West Florida into the counties of Escambia and Jackson, and East Florida into the counties of St. John's and Duval.

[A.D. 1824.] Two years afterward the present site of Tallahassee was selected and laid off as the permanent seat of the territorial government. The counties of Monroe and Gadsden were organized this year, and four other counties were laid off for subsequent organization, viz., the counties of Leon and Walton in West Florida, and Alachua and Nassau in East Florida.

[A.D. 1825.] The American population continued to increase in the principal settlements, and in the vicinity of Pensacola, St. Mark's, and St. Augustine, until the territory became entitled to the *second grade* of territorial government, under the ordinance of 1787. The territory was divided into thirteen election districts, and the people proceeded to elect their legislative assembly, which, having convened soon afterward, elected their first delegate to Congress.

Such had been the mass of emigrants and unacclimated persons into St. Augustine in 1821, that a mild epidemic yellow-fever was generated among the crowded population. The same thing occurred at Pensacola the following year. But it was not until the year 1825 that Pensacola received a dense population of unacclimated emigrants, when a most destructive epidemic yellow fever was generated, and swept off great numbers of the crowded population.

The native tribes of Indians still occupied the greater portion of the country, while the white settlements were concentrated in the vicinities of Pensacola, St. Mark's, Tallahassee, and St. Augustine. On the eighteenth of September, 1823, the Seminoles had, by the treaty of Moultrie Creek, ceded a large portion of lands in Middle Florida, and had agreed to retire south and east, upon the lands lying east of the Suwanee, and upon the Ocklawaha and Withlacoochy Rivers, preparatory to their final emigration from the territory. Thus the middle region of Florida gradually became open to the extension of the white settlements, and the Indians were mostly removed in the winter of 1824, excepting a few reservations to particular chiefs.*

* See Williams's Florida, p. 214.

[A.D. 1835.] The Mickasukie Indians had always been averse to leaving Middle Florida, and they had opposed the treaty of Moultrie Creek. After their removal in 1824, they still evinced great dissatisfaction, which induced the Federal government to extend the limits assigned them on the north, and to furnish them additional supplies, besides those already stipulated. Still they continued dissatisfied, and many of them, in 1835-6, became disposed to emigrate west of the Mississippi. Difficulties began to spring up between them and the white settlements, and the Indians, in revenge, began to commit depredations and murders upon the exposed frontiers. They began to kill or expel the agents of the army, the surveyors of the government, and the mail-carriers, and others who had frequented their country.

At length it was deemed prudent to station a strong military force within the Indian territory, to restrain the violence of the discontented. Fourteen companies of regular troops were ordered to hold themselves in readiness to march from different posts to Florida during the winter of 1835-6.

Most of these detachments, entering the country at different points, were greatly annoyed in their advance by bodies of Indians, who determined to dispute the passage of the streams and rivers. Hence several severe skirmishes occurred before they reached the points of their destination.

The most terrible of these ambuscades was that encountered by the ill-fated but brave detachment under Major Dade, which was totally cut off by the savages. Major Dade, on the 24th of December, 1835, marched from Tampa Bay with a detachment of three companies, comprising one hundred and thirty-nine men, for Fort King.* On the route they encountered much difficulty, from the heavy roads, in transporting their stores, and one piece of artillery. On the 28th they had reached an open pine country, six miles northeast of the Withlacoochy River. Suddenly, about mid-day, they were attacked on all sides with a continuous volley of small arms, accompanied by horrid yells, from an unseen enemy in the high grass; and so terrible was the first discharge, that Major Dade was killed, and nearly half his detachment disabled. The remainder, under Lieutenant Bassinger, sheltered themselves behind trees, while five or six discharges of canister from the

* Williams's Florida, p. 217, 218.

six pounder caused the Indians to disperse and retire. On their retreat, Captain Gardiner immediately commenced the erection of a triangular breast-work, by cutting down pine trees. In three quarters of an hour the savages returned in great numbers and with horrid yells. A cross-fire was immediately opened upon the unfinished breast-work with dreadful execution. Lieutenant Bassinger continued to fire his piece until all his artillerists were cut down by the enemy's fire, and until he fell wounded himself. Every man able to raise a gun continued to defend the spot after they were wounded.

At length the last man fell, when the savages rushed into the inclosure. Here, supposing all were dead, a large Indian made a speech to the warriors, who immediately proceeded to strip the arms and accoutrements from the soldiers, without any indignity to their bodies, and then retired. Thus in two hours this fine detachment of brave men had been annihilated.

Soon afterward, fifty negroes on horseback rode up to the breast-work, tied their horses, and began the horrid butchery. Did any man on the ground show signs of life, it was only to receive the negro's tomahawk into his brains, or to be stabbed to death with their knives, or otherwise to be cut and mutilated by the thick-lipped savages, amid demoniac yells and horrid blasphemies. Lieutenant Bassinger, still alive, sprung to his knees and begged his life of the negro savages; but they mocked his prayers, and mangled his body with their hatchets until death relieved him from their tortures.

After stripping the dead, the negroes dragged the field-piece to a neighboring pond, in which they concealed it; after which they shot the oxen, and burned the wagon and gun-carriage.

Two men, Clarke and Decouy, lay concealed among the dead bodies until night, when they crawled out and made their way toward Tampa Bay.* Next day Decouy was discovered and shot by an Indian; Clarke concealed himself in the bushes, and proceeded to Tampa next day, where he speedily recovered of his wounds. Another soldier, named Thomas, after lying half suffocated under the dead bodies all night, recovered, and finally succeeded in reaching the fort at Tampa Bay in safety.

Thus terminated this disastrous battle, in which only two

* Williams's Florida, p. 219.

men survived to tell the melancholy story of this detachment of as brave men as ever suffered under savage cruelty.

A free negro, named Lewis, formerly the property of General Clinch, had been the guide of Major Dade, and it was through his treachery that this fatal ambuscade succeeded. He fled to the Indians upon the first attack. The number of Indians engaged in this tragedy is unknown; but probably there were not less than three hundred, besides fifty negroes. They were commanded by Jumper and Micanopy. The officers slain in this massacre were Major Dade, Captain Frazier, Captain Gardiner, Lieutenant Bassinger, Lieutenant Mudge, Lieutenant Keys, Lieutenant Henderson, and Doctor Catlin.

On the same day that Major Dade was cut off, the Seminole chief, Powell, with twenty men, advanced to Fort King, and, within two hundred and fifty yards of the pickets, killed the suttler to the fort, Erastus Rodgers, and a party of friends, while at dinner. Among those slain with Rodgers were Suggs, Hitzler, General Wiley Thompson, the Indian agent, and Lieutenant Constantine Smith. Four others escaped. The body of General Thompson was pierced by fifteen balls, and that of Rodgers by sixteen, and their bodies were horribly mangled and mutilated afterward.

This was the commencement of the noted "Florida War," which cost the government much time and money before the savages were finally all taken and transported to their western homes, after many severe engagements, skirmishes, and individual rencounters. The government determined to press the war until the whole race should be removed or exterminated from Florida. The militia of Florida and Georgia were immediately called into service to protect the frontier settlements.

[A.D. 1836.] From this time the Federal government urged the war with vigor; the Indians were pursued and hunted from every point of the peninsula, and captured by families, by masses, and by surrender, and in every possible manner, during the next four years. Those who were captured or who surrendered were kept securely at the different posts, and sent by steam-boat loads under armed guards to their destination in the territory appropriated for the Indian tribes in the Far West, north of Red River.

[A.D. 1839.] The Florida war was prosecuted with varied

success, and chiefly south of the Suwanee River, until the year 1839, when it was terminated by the capture or surrender of the last remnant of the hostile tribes. During this period, the commanders of the United States forces had captured or received the voluntary surrender of warriors and families to the number of three thousand eight hundred and thirty souls, which were provided with all the necessaries and comforts of savage life, until they were finally removed by agents of the United States to the Indian territory west of the State of Arkansas.

[A.D. 1840.] From this time the occupancy of Florida by every portion of the Creek and Seminole Indians terminated, and the whole country was in the undisputed possession of the United States, and free to the advance of the white population, and the extension of settlements into the former Indian territory.

In 1839 the population had gradually increased under the territorial form of government, until the entire number, including slaves, amounted to nearly fifty thousand souls. The territorial jurisdiction had been extended over the whole territory, which had been divided into twenty organized counties, which were comprised in five judicial districts of the Federal court.*

The increase of population during the last ten years had been rapid, notwithstanding the dangers from Indian hostilities. The census of 1830 gave the entire population, exclusive of Indians, at 34,723 souls; and that of 1840 gave an aggregate of 54,477 souls, including 26,500 slaves and free negroes, the Indian tribes having been entirely removed.

Meantime the people of Florida had been desirous of establishing a state government, preparatory to admission into the Federal Union as an independent state. The territorial Legislature of 1838, representing the wishes of the people, had memorialized Congress for authority to form a state constitution. An act of Congress authorized the election of a convention for that purpose. On the 11th of January, 1839, the convention at Tallahassee adopted a constitution for the organization of a state government, which was duly submitted to the consideration of Congress. The general feature of this constitution was similar in its provisions to those of the slave-holding states, and, of course, legalized the bondage of the negro race within the limits of the proposed new state. In this re-

* See American Almanac for 1844, p. 291.

spect the constitution for Florida was more rigid than many other slave-holding states, prohibiting forever the emancipation of any negro slave in the state.

But the people of Florida were not permitted so soon to assume state sovereignty. There were features in the constitution designed to protect Southern rights and Southern interests, which necessarily encountered a strong opposition from Northern interests and feelings. The fact of the proposed new state being a Southern one, and a slave-holding one in its most rigid sense, created in the national Legislature a strong opposition to its admission into the Union as an independent state with less than thirty thousand free whites. Hence, Northern influences and prejudices were strongly arrayed against the measure; and they were sufficiently powerful to defeat the admission of the new state for nearly five years after it was constitutionally and legally entitled to assume the rank of an independent state.

[A.D. 1845.] During this time, the territorial government had continued in operation under the wise and judicious administration of Governor Richard C. Call, and his successor, Governor John Branch. In 1845, the population had greatly increased its numbers, so as to remove the opposition created by want of free white citizens; and a bill for the admission of "Iowa," a northern free state, coming before Congress, the friends of Florida rallied, and, by including Florida with Iowa in the same bill, succeeded in securing the passage of a joint resolution which made Florida an independent state. The act for the admission of both Iowa and Florida as independent states was approved March the 3d, 1845.* The Legislature of Florida accepted the act of Congress, with its conditions, and immediately Florida was an "independent state," upon an equal footing with the original states.

The limits and boundaries of Florida remain the same that were recognized while it was a province of Spain, and with which it was ceded to the United States in 1819.

Meantime Iowa remained without the pale of the Union, under the territorial form of government. The limits prescribed in her constitution having been restricted by Congress, the Legislature declined to accept the terms of admission, and submitted the decision to the vote of the people. The general

---

* See Acts of second session of the 28th Congress.

election held soon afterward confirmed the rejection of the terms by a large majority of the votes.

Florida became an independent state just twenty-four years after it became a territory of the United States. The same year witnessed the admission of Texas as an independent state of the American Union, and extending the Federal jurisdiction to the Rio del Norte; while Iowa, in the extreme north, was yet a territorial dependence. Strange that Texas, which was exchanged for Florida in 1819, should enter the Union simultaneously with it in 1845 as an independent state.*

The first general assembly of the State of Florida was convened at Tallahassee on the 23d of June, when James A. Berthelet, of Leon county, was unanimously elected president of the Senate, and Hugh Archer, of the same county, was also unanimously elected speaker of the House of Representatives; Thomas F. King was clerk of the Senate, and M. D. Papy, chief clerk of the Lower House. Both houses, soon after their organization, adopted resolutions in honor of the memory, and commemorating the death, of its first American governor, General Andrew Jackson.

The first executive of the state, Governor Mosely, was installed into office on the 25th of June, with all the solemnity of civic honors. His inaugural was strongly characterized by its pure Republican principles; while a banner presented and borne by the citizens as a temporary state flag, bearing the orange stripe of Florida, responded to the sentiment in the inscription, "Let us alone."†

The first session of the General Assembly continued until the 26th of July; no attempt at legislation was made further than what was necessary to put the machinery of state government in operation.‡

* See book v., chap. xvii., "Re-annexation of Texas."
† Weekly Union, No. 10, p. 148.   ‡ Idem, August 23d, 1845.

BOOK II.

FRANCE IN THE VALLEY OF THE MISSISSIPPI.

CHAPTER I.

ADVANCE OF THE FRENCH UPON THE ST. LAWRENCE, AND DISCOVERY OF THE MISSISSIPPI.—A.D. 1608 TO 1673.

Argument.—First Attempt of French Colonization in Canada.—First successful Settlement by Champlain in 1608.—His Explorations on the St. Lawrence and Lakes.—Indian Alliances against the Iroquois.—Advance of Catholic Missionaries.—Hostilities of the Iroquois.—Fathers Brebeuf and Daniel visit Sault St. Mary in 1634.—Character of Catholic Missionaries in Canada.—Sufferings of Raymbault among the Iroquois in 1642.—Of Father Bressani in 1643.—The Missionaries sustain the Colonies.—Death of Father Jouges among the Iroquois in 1646.—Others suffer Martyrdom in the same Field.—Jesuits and Monks flock to Canada in 1650 for the Missionary Field.—Le Moyne among the Mohawks in 1656.—Chaumonot and Dablon among the Onondagas.—René Mesnard among the Cayugas.—Missionaries killed and expelled by the Iroquois.—Montreal a Bishop's See in 1656.—Mesnard repairs to St. Mary's and Green Bay.—Dies in the Forest alone.—Canada a Royal Province in 1665.—Military Protection of Settlements.—Father Allouez among the Chippewas at St. Mary's.—Learns the Existence of the Mississippi in 1667.—Dablon and Marquette repair to St. Mary's in 1668.—Military Outposts of New France in 1670.—Missions in the Far West.—Marquette conceives the Design of discovering the Mississippi.—Plans his Voyage of Discovery in 1672.—M. Talon patronizes the Enterprise.—Marquette and Joliet conduct the Exploration in 1673.—They proceed by Way of Green Bay and Fox River to the Wisconsin.—Discovery of the Mississippi, June 17th, 1673.—Explore the Great River 1100 Miles.—They return by the Illinois River to Chicago Creek.—Marquette returns to his Mission, and Joliet to Quebec.—Joy in Canada at the Discovery.—Native Tribes known to the early Explorers of Illinois and Louisiana: Algonquin Tribes; Shawanese; Miamis; Illinois; Potawatamies; Ottawâs; Menomonies; Chippewas; Sioux; Sauks and Foxes; Chickasâs; Natchez; Choctâs.

As early as the year 1535, before De Soto arrived in Florida, the French had made several unsuccessful attempts to form settlements along the northeast coast of North America. The same year Jacques Cartier conducted an exploring expedition to the Gulf of St. Lawrence. He ascended the great river of the North as far as the Island of Orleans. He first called the spacious gulf into which the river discharged the "Gulf of St. Lawrence;" the name has since been extended to the whole river. The country along both shores he also first called "New France." Six years afterward, Cartier and La Roche de Robertval led out a colony from France, to form a settlement in the newly-discovered country. They failed in the attempt. The inclemency of the climate and the hostility of the natives defeated all their plans. For several years afterward, other colonies were led out to form settlements along the shores of the St. Lawrence, as well as upon the Atlantic coast, south and southwest of the Gulf of St. Lawrence, and known as "Acadie" and "Cape Breton;" yet such was the inclemency of the climate and the fierceness of the Indian tribes, that the colonists were compelled to abandon their settlements, or submit to perish of hunger, or die by the hand of the savages.

[A.D. 1608.] France had been too much involved in wars in Europe to expend her resources in making explorations and settlements in distant, unknown regions. More than sixty years had elapsed after Cartier's first voyage up the St. Lawrence, when the spirit of adventure revived in France. Again men were found willing to tempt the rigors of the climate and the dangers of those inhospitable regions. A colony was conducted by Samuel Champlain to the shores of the St. Lawrence. A bold and experienced mariner, he advanced up that river, in the summer of 1608, about three hundred and sixty miles, to the Island of Orleans.* The same summer, in July, he cleared the ground, and erected a few cabins to shelter his little colony from the rigors of a Canadian winter. This was the foundation of the city of Quebec, which was cotemporaneous with the first settlement in Virginia, upon James's River.

The same year, Champlain, in hopes of securing the friendship and confidence of the Huron and Algonquin tribes, was induced to aid them, with a few of his troops, in a war expedition against the Iroquois confederacy, then inhabiting the country south of the St. Lawrence, on both sides of the lake, which still perpetuates his name. The Hurons and Algonquins inhabited the northern shores of the St. Lawrence and of Lake Ontario. With the aid of the French soldiers, they obtained a victory over their enemies, near the Sorel River. By this means Champlain secured the friendship of the Algon-

---

* Martin's Louisiana, vol. i., p. 38, octavo edition of 1827.
This is a valuable repository of many historical events and transactions connected with the early history of the settlements in the provinces of New France and Louisiana. The author, Judge Francois Xavier Martin, has evinced much research in collecting the incidents of the early history of these provinces; but he has not been clear and concise in his arrangement, which is often defective and irregular. The work preserves the character of annals, although, from a want of strict care in the author, or negligence in the printer, events are often detailed under erroneous years; and the reader is apt to be confused, or misled by erroneous dates. Not writing in his native tongue, the author could not be expected to conform to the strict idiom of the English language. He has, however, left us a valuable store-house for the future historian.

quin tribes for his people, but entailed upon their descendants, for ninety years, the implacable hostility of the more warlike Iroquois.*

[A.D. 1615.] Difficulties and privations innumerable awaited the feeble colony, but fortitude and perseverance sustained them through the darkest hour. Each closing year brought them additional emigrants, and their numbers slowly increased. Restricted in their advances south of the St. Lawrence, the colony was confined to the rigorous climate of Quebec; yet Champlain, before the close of the year 1615, had explored Lake Huron by way of the Ottawâ River and lakes. Fourteen years after the settlement was made, the city of Quebec was a small hamlet containing but fifty inhabitants, men, women, and children. Six years later, Quebec contained only one hundred souls, upon the point of starvation, whose only wealth was a few furs and peltries purchased of the Indians.

[A.D. 1628.] For many years after their first settlement, Champlain continued to conduct the affairs of the little colony. When Iroquois hostilities did not prevent, he explored the regions and rivers for many miles on both sides of the St. Lawrence, and even to the southern extremity of Lake Champlain. Every year found his little colony slowly increasing in numbers, and their settlements gradually but slowly extending.

[A.D. 1632.] But it was impossible to advance settlements into the wilderness without the aid of that spirit of meekness, benevolence, and perseverance which characterized the early missionaries of the Catholic Church in this part of America.

The genius of Champlain, whose comprehensive mind planned enduring establishments for French commerce, and a career of discovery that should carry the lilies of the Bourbons to the extremity of North America, could devise no method of building up the dominion of France in Canada but an alliance with the Hurons, or of confirming that alliance by the establishment of missions. " Such a policy was congenial to the

* Champlain had been many years engaged as a mariner in exploring the northern coasts near the Gulf of St. Lawrence, comprising the provinces now known as Nova Scotia, New Brunswick, and Cape Breton, south of the Gulf of St. Lawrence, which were embraced in a grant made by Henry IV. of France to a company of merchants, and others of Rouen, of whom Pontgrave and Chauvin were principal. In 1608, Samuel Champlain conducted a colony up the St. Lawrence, and on the third of July laid the foundation of Quebec. Champlain for many years afterward superintended the colony, and in 1613 had advanced his settlements up the river and laid out Montreal. See Martin's Louisiana, vol. i., p. 34–39, and 45.

Catholic Church, and was favored by the conditions of the charter itself, which recognized the neophyte among the savages as an enfranchised citizen of France." " Thus it was neither commercial enterprise nor royal ambition which carried the power of France into the heart of our Continent: the motive was religion."*

[A.D. 1633.] In 1633, twenty-five years after the first settlement, Champlain was still governor of New France. The colony, notwithstanding its gradual increase, encountered dangers and privations under the most adverse circumstances. The inclemency of the climate enabled them to procure but scanty sustenance from the soil, and the constant state of hostilities among the great powers of Europe cut off all supplies from the mother country. Nor was this all: the early enmity of the Iroquois continued to increase. Seldom did a single year pass without some hostile incursion or depredation upon the settlements, from Quebec to Montreal.

Water-courses, lakes, and rivers are the high-ways of Nature; and especially to uncivilized man, or to civilized man beyond the reach of civilization, they are favorite routes. To those who have no axes, the thick jungle is impervious; emigration by water suits the genius of civilized life no less than the savage; canoes are older than wagons, and ships than chariots; a gulf, a strait, the sea intervening between islands, divide less than the matted forest. Civilized man, no less than the savage, emigrates by sea and by rivers; and in America he has advanced from Cape Breton to Fon du Lac, and from the coast of Florida he has ascended the Mississippi, two thousand miles above the mouth of the Missouri, while interior portions of New York and Ohio were still a wilderness. To man beyond the reach of civilization, no path is free but the sea, the lake, or the river.

[A.D. 1634.] As early as the year 1634, the French Jesuits, Brebeuf and Daniel, had penetrated the dangerous wilds as far as the Straits of St. Mary and the southern shore of Lake Superior. Their avenue to the West was by the Ottawâ and French Rivers of Lower Canada. At that time, and for forty years afterward, the continued hostilities of the Five Nations,

---

* See Bancroft's History of the United States, vol. iii., p. 121; also p. 327. This is a work of rare merit; and to the eloquent author we are indebted for much valuable historical matter pertaining to the early settlements of France in North America. In the following chapters we have made free extracts from his excellent pages.

and especially of the Mohawks, had excluded the French from the navigation of the St. Lawrence and Lake Ontario. All the country south of Lakes Ontario and Erie was unknown, except as the abode of their implacable enemies. On Lake Erie the French had not lanched even a canoe, for the war parties of the Iroquois occupied all the avenues near the lakes, and death was the forfeit of the adventurous missionary and trader south of Ontario.

"Within three years after the second occupation of Canada, the number of Jesuit priests in the province reached fifteen; and every tradition bears testimony to their worth. They had the faults of ascetic superstition, but the horrors of a Canadian life in the wilderness were resisted by an invincible, passive courage, and a deep, internal tranquillity. Away from the amenities of life, away from the opportunities of vain-glory, they became dead to the world, and possessed their souls in unalterable peace."*

[A.D. 1636.] The unwearied Jesuits of the Catholic Church were always in advance of civilization. "The history of their labors is connected with the origin of every celebrated town in the annals of French America; not a river was entered, not a cape was turned, but a Jesuit led the way."†

[A.D. 1640]. Although certain privation and suffering were their lot, and martyrdom might be the crown of their labors, they ventured into the remotest regions and among the most warlike tribes. In the autumn of 1640, Charles Raymbault and Claude Pijart advanced to the Huron missions, destined for service among the Algonquins of the north and west. Although the continual wars of the Mohawks, or the Five Nations, completely excluded them from the route of the southern lakes, the unwearied missionaries of the Catholic Church continued to penetrate a thousand miles by the northern route to the west, among the remote Algonquin tribes, and already missionary stations had been formed upon the northern shores of Lake Huron.‡

The route to the west passed over by Brebeuf and the early missionaries was more than three hundred leagues from Quebec, by the Ottawâ River, to the Straits of St. Mary. This avenue led "through a region horrible with forests. All day long they must wade or handle the oar. At five-and-thirty

* Bancroft, vol. iii., p. 122. † Idem, p. 122. ‡ Idem, p. 145.

water-falls the canoes were to be carried on the shoulders for leagues through thickest woods and over the roughest regions; fifty times they were to be dragged by hand through shallows and rapids over sharpest stones."*

Nor were the privations of heat, cold, hunger, thirst, and disease all they had to encounter. The hostilities of the Iroquois were more terrible than all these. The advantages of a western route, by way of Lakes Ontario and Erie, were early seen by the missionaries; but the fixed hostility and the power of the Five Nations left no hope of success for gaining a safe intercourse by the St. Lawrence.

[A.D. 1641.] The following autumn, Charles Raymbault, having visited Quebec, proceeded by the Ottawâ route, in company with Isaac Jouges, to the Straits of St. Mary, to establish a mission at that point. The former died soon afterward, the victim of a lingering consumption; the latter was captured the following year by the Mohawks upon the St. Lawrence as he returned from Quebec to St. Mary's. Carried prisoner to the banks of the Mohawk River, he suffered all the tortures which Indian vengeance could inflict upon their enemies. "In several villages he was compelled to run the gantlet, and tortured with hunger and thirst, and every torment which petulant youth could inflict. Surviving all these, he was retained a captive until humanely ransomed by the Dutch on Hudson's River."

[A.D. 1643.] A similar fate awaited Father Bressani. Taken prisoner while on his way to the Hurons; beaten, mangled, mutilated; driven barefoot over rough paths, through briers and thickets; scourged by a whole village; burned, tortured, and scarred, he was an eye-witness to the fate of one of his companions, who was boiled and eaten. Yet some mysterious awe protected his life, and he, too, was humanely rescued by the Dutch.†

Such were the horrors which the French encountered from the Iroquois in their first attempts to penetrate to the West; but the fearless Jesuit led the way, and finally, after the lapse of more than half a century, gained the friendship of the warlike Five Nations.

[A.D. 1646.] The whole strength of the colony lay in the missions. The government was weakened by the royal jealousy; the population hardly increased; there was no military

* Bancroft, vol. iii., p. 122. † Idem, p. 134.

force; and the trading company deriving no revenue, except from Indian trade and traffic in skins, could make no great expenditures for defense, or for promoting colonization. Thus the missionaries were left almost alone to contend with the myriads of braves who roamed over the basin of the St. Lawrence. Many had lost their lives in the wilderness, victims of savage cruelty, or of hunger, cold, and the dangers of the western wilds.*

[A.D. 1647.] Father Jouges, sacrificing his life to an effort to reconcile the Iroquois, volunteered as an envoy of peace to the Mohawks. He arrived in peace among them, but soon afterward was killed by them as an enchanter, who had blighted their fields. The death-blow he received with tranquillity; his head was hung upon the palisades of the village, and his body thrown into the Mohawk River.†

[A.D. 1649.] This was the signal of war, and the following year the missionary villages of the French along the St. Lawrence and Ottawâ were destroyed, and their inmates cruelly murdered, or tortured by fire unto death. The hostile incursions of the Iroquois for five years against the settlements upon the St. Lawrence, as well as upon the Ottawâ and Lake Huron, were terrible and destructive. Many were butchered in the general carnage, and others were reserved for the lingering tortures of the slow fire. Among these, the intrepid and meek Brebeuf and Lallemand suffered tortures indescribable.

[A.D. 1650.] Thus had the Jesuits penetrated into the country on the south side of Lake Ontario, where they had gained a precarious and dangerous field of operations, and where martyrdom might have been deemed the certain test of their zeal. But instead of being discouraged at the prospect of suffering and death, the enthusiasm of all France seemed to have awakened to the vast field now opened in New France for the triumphs of the cross, in the conversion of savage tribes, who roamed in the remote wilds beyond the Western lakes. Jesuits and monks of every order began to flock to Quebec and Montreal, ready to commence the work of Christian benevolence.

[A.D. 1655.] At length the Iroquois themselves seemed wearied of the strife, and manifested a willingness for peace and friendship with the French. The Jesuits lost no opportunity of introducing Christianity and its benign doctrines among

* Bancroft, vol. iii., p. 137.   † Idem, p. 138.

their warlike and vindictive tribes: the first opening which presented for the accomplishment of so desirable an object was seized with ardor by the devoted missionaries of the cross, ever ready to brave new dangers and new privations. With all her deformities, let us yet pay a merited tribute to the Church of Rome. Zealous, earnest, untiring in her efforts to evangelize the world, she carried the cross forward, she rallied around it; for there were pure spirits in the midst of her; men full of the power of God and holiness, who practically illustrated the doctrines they taught; and well might the Protestant world be counseled by the Catholic, in the vigor with which his missionary operations were conducted among the untutored savages.

[A.D. 1656.] La Moyne had settled himself upon the banks of the Mohawk, selecting this river for his abode, in the vain hope of infusing the gentle spirit of civilization into the savage nature of the Mohawk tribe. Chaumonot, an Italian priest, and Claude Dablon, a missionary from France, were hospitably welcomed to the principal village of the Onondagas. A general convocation of the tribe greeted them with joy and songs of welcome, as the bearers of a "heavenly message." A chapel at once sprung into existence, formed by hewed logs, and hung with bark and mats; and there, in the heart of New York, the solemn services of the Roman Church were chanted as securely as in any part of Christendom. The Onondagas dwelt upon the Oswego River, and its basin was deemed a part of the dominions of France.*

A colony of fifty Frenchmen soon embarked for Onondaga, and received a hearty welcome from the rejoicing Indians. The Cayugas also desired a missionary, and they received the fearless René Mesnard. In their village a chapel was erected, with mats for tapestry, and there the pictures of the Savior and the Virgin Mother were unfolded to the admiring children of the wilderness.

[A.D. 1657.] The Oneidas also listened to the missionary, and early in the year 1657 Chaumonot reached the more fertile and more densely populated land of the Senecas; and the influence of France and the missionaries was felt from the Mohawk to the Genesee River.†

But the savage nature of the tribes was unchanged. A war

* Bancroft, vol. iii., p. 144.   † Idem, p. 144.

of extermination at this very time was waged by the Iroquois against the Eries, a nation in the northern portion of the present State of Ohio. Prisoners were brought home to the villages and delivered to the flames; and what could the missionaries expect from nations who could burn even children, with the refinements of tortures? Yet they pressed in the steps of their countrymen, who had been boiled and roasted; they made their home among cannibals; hunger, and thirst, and nakedness were to be endured, and fever and sickness had already visited their little colony.*

[A.D. 1658.] It was not until the colony in New France was fifty years old, that it possessed sufficient strength to repel successfully the incursions of their southern enemies. In 1659, the settlements about Montreal were deemed sufficiently secure to be erected into a bishop's see. The same year, Francis de Leval, as bishop of Montreal, arrived with a large supply of ecclesiastics from France. These were exclusive of the Jesuits and recollêt monks, who, up to this time, were the only spiritual guides in the province. A seminary under the bishop's charge was established at Montreal, and another at Quebec.† The Church of Rome was established in the center of New France. The rites and ceremonies of the Catholic Church were extended to the remote West. The monk, by acts of self-denial, sought salvation for himself; the Jesuit plunged into the secular affairs of men, to maintain the interests of the Church.

The Franciscan, as a mendicant order, being excluded from the newly-discovered world, the office of converting the natives of New France was intrusted to the Jesuits; and their missionaries continued to defy every danger and to endure every toil. The pleasures of life and the opportunities of vain-glory were too remote to influence their lives or to affect their character.

Yet the missionaries could not control the angry passions of men. Border collisions again broke out: the Oneidas murdered three Frenchmen, and the French retaliated by seizing Iroquois. A conspiracy among the Onondagas compelled the French to abandon their chapel, their cabins, and their dwellings in the valley of the Oswego. The Mohawks compelled Le Moyne to return, and the French and the Five Nations were once more at war. Such was the issue of the most successful attempt at French colonization in western New York as late as

* Bancroft, vol. iii., p. 145.   † Martin's Louisiana, vol. i., p. 65, 66.

1660. The extension of British power over the Dutch of New Amsterdam was a guarantee that France could never regain the mastery. Many zealous missionaries terminated their courageous course and their lives in all the agonies of Indian torture, but with unwavering confidence in God.

[A.D. 1660.] The Iroquois, in the mean time, aided by European arms received from Albany, had exterminated the Eries, and had carried their conquests as far as the Miamis. The western tribes desired commerce; and, forced by the necessity of the case, sought an alliance with the French, that they might be enabled to resist the Iroquois. The French traders had penetrated as far west as Lake Superior and Green Bay; and a deputation of three hundred Algonquins, in sixty canoes, laden with peltry, returned with them to Quebec. Jesuit missionaries were commissioned to form alliances with the numerous tribes in the remote West. The Bishop of Quebec, Francis de Leval himself, kindled with zeal to engage in the mission to the remote tribes; but the lot fell upon René Mesnard. Every personal motive seemed to retain him at Quebec, but "powerful instincts" impelled him to the enterprise.

"Obedient to his vows, the aged man entered upon the path that was red with the blood of his predecessors, and made haste to scatter the seeds of truth through the wilderness, although the sower cast his seed in weeping."

After a residence of eight months among the tribes on the southern shore of Lake Superior, he yielded to the invitations of the Hurons in the Isle of St. Michael, and departed with one attendant for the Bay of Chegoimegon. On his route, while his attendant was engaged in transporting a canoe across the portage of the Kawena Lake, he was lost in the forest, and was never again seen. Long afterward, the cassock and breviary of René Mesnard were kept as amulets among the Sioux.

As late as 1660, such were the horrors and the vengeance of the Iroquois, aided by their English allies, that the settlements upon the St. Lawrence had well-nigh been abandoned. The missionary spirit alone prevented that result, and subsequently prevailed in acquiring for the French the friendship and alliance of the Five Nations.

[A.D. 1662.] Peace with the Five Nations was at length partially confirmed, and the missionaries had resumed their efforts to form a mission among the Iroquois, but the Mohawks would not be appeased, and Montreal was not safe. The "Hundred Associates," to whom New France had been committed, resolved to surrender the province to the king. Under the auspices of Colbert, it was conceded to the company of the West Indies. After various efforts at fit appointments, the year 1665 saw the colony of New France first protected by a royal regiment, with the aged but indefatigable Tracy as viceroy; with Courcelles, a veteran soldier, as governor, and with M. Talon, a man of business and integrity, as intendant and representative of the king in civil affairs.*

[A.D. 1665.] The war with the Iroquois was to be renewed with more vigor when the emergency might require it, and the savages soon found the power of the French on the St. Lawrence was to be feared and conciliated.

From the year 1664 the colony in New France began to gain a footing on the south side of the St. Lawrence. The Iroquois began to recede from the shores of that river, and from those of Lake Champlain. French settlements began to extend up the Chambly, or Sorel River, and trading posts were established on the east side of Lake Champlain, and south of the Upper St. Lawrence, and within the limits of the present state of New York.† By the year 1665, small French settlements, or trading posts, extended as far south as Lake George; several years previously, a fort had been erected upon the Chambly River to check the incursions of the Iroquois upon Quebec by that route. This had broken up their incursions from that quarter, but they soon found new routes to the settlements on the St. Lawrence. In these, also, they were met and checked by forts. They next sought the route by way of Lake Ontario, and down the St. Lawrence. Their approach to the settlements was always by water in their war-canoes, through the lakes and tributary streams of the St. Lawrence. To command the St. Lawrence against their incursions from Lake Ontario, Fort Cataracoui was subsequently built in 1670, near the present site of Kingston, in Upper Canada, and near the point where the river flows from the lake.

[A.D. 1669.] For two years past, Father Claude Allouez, who had embarked by the way of the Ottawâ, had been on the southern shores of Lake Superior, and had extended his inquiries and missionary labors among the Chippewas; had instituted

* Martin's Louisiana, vol. i., p. 72. † Idem, p. 73.

peace between them and the Sioux; and with the Potawatamies, Sacs, and Foxes, who flocked to him, he had formed the basis of a lasting alliance of commerce, and mutual defense against the Iroquois. He had also learned from the remote tribes of a great river further to the west, known by the natives as the *Mesasippi,* or "Great River," which, as yet, no Frenchman had seen.

Allouez now returned to Quebec to urge the establishment of permanent missions, which should be accompanied by little colonies of French emigrants, who were willing to venture into the remote West upon the shores of Lakes Huron and Michigan.

Peace now prevailed, and favored the progress of the French dominion; a recruit of missionaries had arrived from France, and among them was James Marquette. Claude Dablon and James Marquette repaired to the Chippewas, at the "Sault," to establish the mission of St. Marie. This formed the oldest settlement by Europeans within the present limits of Michigan.* A mission was also opened at Green Bay, still further west. In this remote region these devoted missionaries remained, "mingling happiness with suffering, and winning enduring glory by their fearless perseverance."†

[A.D. 1670.] Such had been the continued hostility of the Iroquois tribes until late in the seventeenth century, aided and excited by the English colonies of New England and New York, that the French missions and settlements had extended more than a thousand miles westward on the lakes, and even to the Mississippi, fifteen hundred miles west of Quebec, before they had extended one hundred miles south and east of the St. Lawrence. Surprising as it may appear to the reader, still it is nevertheless true, that the French colonies in the Illinois country, and upon the Wabash, were carrying on a profitable trade with the settlements on the Lower Mississippi, and about Mobile, before a permanent settlement had been effected on the southern shores of Lake Champlain. About the time that Fort Cataracoui was built near the outlet of Lake Ontario, traders and voyagers had begun to penetrate the Chambly River to Lake Champlain. Fifty years elapsed from that time before the French settlements extended as far south as Crown Point and Ticonderoga. Then they began to settle west of the Green Mountains, and on the eastern shore of Champlain.

* Bancroft, vol. iii., p. 152.   * Idem, p. 150–152.

To the east they could see the towering peaks of the Green Mountains, "Verd Monts," from which the State of Vermont takes its name.

The colony of New France had now increased to eight thousand souls, chiefly settled on the St. Lawrence, from Quebec to within one hundred miles of Lake Ontario. For many years Fort Cataracoui remained a remote frontier post; but traders and *voyageurs* began to visit the remote tribes of the West on the southern shores of the great lakes, as far as the western limit of the present State of Ohio. In those remote regions the native tribes were less hostile, and were well disposed to receive and trade with the French, who soon penetrated in their trading voyages as far as Lake Michigan and Green Bay. The Jesuits, or Catholic missionaries, were always in advance of the trading establishments. As early as 1660, one year after the arrival of the Bishop of Montreal, they had penetrated as far as the Straits of Mackinac, where they now pursued the even tenor of their way among the benighted children of the forest. Each missionary had collected around him a few converted Indians, who gladly received their affectionate instructions in the elements of Catholic faith. By their kind offices and paternal regard, no less than by their pious and unostentatious benevolence, they gained the confidence of the Indians, and prepared the way for their more worldly-minded countrymen. Although from these western tribes, as before observed, the missionaries had learned, in 1667, that still further to the west was an extensive and delightful region, beyond which was a great river, known to them as the *Mesasippi*, or "Great River," yet of this great river, and the regions near it, the missionaries could obtain but imperfect accounts; they could not learn to what point it flowed, nor into what sea it discharged; but they ascertained "that it flowed neither toward the north nor toward the east."* The Count de Frontenac this year entered upon his duties as Governor of New France, and successor of M. Courcelles.

As yet, no Frenchman had ever advanced beyond Fox River of Green Bay. All beyond was a region of romance, unknown or mystified by Indian tradition. The ardent entertained hopes that the great river might afford an easy and direct route to China, or, at least, into the South Pacific Ocean. This was

---

* Martin's Louisiana, vol. i., p. 76.

one of the bubbles of the age. Every nation of Western Europe had been enthusiastic with the hope of discovering a direct route by water to China, and all had searched for it in vain. It was believed by some that the pioneers of New France would have all the glory of the great discovery, and be the first to reap the advantages of the direct trade. To the disappointment of the commercial world, this route still remains as much unknown as it was two hundred years ago; and such it will remain until it is opened by way of the Oregon River or the Bay of California.

[A.D. 1672.] "The purpose of discovering the Mississippi sprung from Marquette himself. He had resolved on attempting it in the autumn of 1669, and had selected a young Illinois as his companion; and, by his instruction, he became familiar with the dialect of that tribe."* His proposed discovery of the great river of the West had been favorably received by the intendant of New France, who was willing to aid him in the enterprise.

[A.D. 1673.] At length, M. Talon, the first intendant, was on the point of retiring to France, after a long and useful service in the province. Ambitious to close his career with the brilliant discovery of the great storied river of the West, he determined to set on foot an expedition to this effect. For this purpose, he selected M. Joliet, a trader of Quebec, to conduct the enterprise. He was a man of intelligence and great experience in Indian affairs, and possessed an enterprising and energetic spirit. Father Marquette, a recollêt monk, and still a missionary among the Hurons, was likewise engaged to accompany the expedition. He was the very soul of the enterprise, to insure a favorable reception among the distant tribes. He had long been among the Indians, a thousand miles in advance of civilization; he knew well their manners, feelings, and language, and how to conciliate the suspicious Indian into confidence and love. He was one of the worthy Catholics who spent many years among the western tribes, and built up among them their little churches, in which they were regarded as fathers and friends. Father Marquette had endeared himself to the savages in a remarkable manner, not only by his apostolical piety, but by his tender affection for them, and his kind offices in all their distresses. Such was the veneration of the

* Bancroft, vol. iii., 153.

savages for this good man, that for years after his death, when overtaken in their frail bark canoes by the storms on Lake Michigan, it is said they "called upon the name of Marquette, and the winds ceased and the waves were still."* Among these unsophisticated children of Nature, he pursued the noiseless tenor of his way until the spring of 1673, when he was required to join M. Joliet in the hazardous enterprise of exploring the great river of the unknown West.

With five other Frenchmen, these two adventurous men resolved to enter upon the expedition and make their way to the great river. All preparations for the voyage having been completed, this little band of hardy spirits, on the 13th day of May, 1673, set out from Michilimackinac, the missionary station of Father Marquette. Having coasted along the western shore of Lake Michigan for many days, they entered the Bay of the Puants, now known as Green Bay. Here they entered Fox River of the lakes, and ascended, paddling their canoes up the rapid stream, and occasionally dragging them over the rapids. At length they arrived at a village of the Fox River Indians, the extreme limit of missionary labor in those western regions, where Allouez had already planted the cross.

Marquette and Joliet were introduced with due ceremony before the chiefs in council, where the father made known the object of their visit. "My companion," said the venerable Marquette, "is an envoy of France, to discover new countries; and I am an ambassador from God, to enlighten them with the Gospel."† The council received them with favor; and, having made a few presents, Marquette requested two guides for their journey on the morrow. The guides were granted to conduct them across the portage to the Wisconsin River, which was said to flow into the great river; yet the council deemed their voyage hazardous in the extreme. They reached the portage, and their light canoes were carried on their backs across the dividing ridge to the Wisconsin. They stood on the banks of the Wisconsin and in the valley of the Mississippi; France and Christianity stood side by side. No Frenchman had yet been beyond this point. The Indian guides refused to proceed further, and determined to return. They endeavored to dissuade the holy father from his perilous voyage among unknown and fierce nations of Indians, who would destroy him without

---

* Charlevoix's Letters. † Bancroft's United States, vol. iii., p. 156.

cause. Tradition told of monsters in the great river that would swallow both man and his canoe; also of a demon, or *manitou*, that buried in the boiling waters all who ventured upon them. Marquette thanked them for their good advice; but he could not follow it, "since the salvation of souls was at stake, for which he would be overjoyed to give his life."

The Indian guides left them. "The guides returned," says the gentle Marquette, "leaving us alone in this unknown land, in the hands of Providence."* They prepared to pursue their perilous voyage to the Mississippi, strangers among unknown tribes.

They began to float down the rapid Wisconsin, and seven days brought them to the great river, which they entered on the 17th of June, 1673.† They descended the river, observing the splendid country on both sides, and the beautiful and verdant isles which divide the channel. About one hundred miles below the mouth of the Wisconsin, an Indian path, or trail, was discovered on the western shore. Marquette and his fellow-envoy determined to trace the path, and form some acquaintance with the tribes of that region. At length, after a walk of several miles, they came in sight of an Indian town, or village. Commending themselves to God, they determined to make themselves known by a loud cry. Four elders of the village advance to meet them, and conduct them into the village. They are presented to the council, and "Marquette published to them the one true God, their Creator. He spoke also of the great captain of the French, the governor of Canada," who had humbled the "Five Nations" of the Iroquois, and compelled them to peace. This was good news to these remote savages, and procured them a hearty welcome and a plentiful feast. Six days were spent among these hospitable savages; nor could they depart without the "peace-pipe," the sacred calumet, suspended from the neck of Marquette, brilliant with beauteous feathers, which was to be his safeguard among strange tribes. They float down the stream, and pass the "most beautiful confluence of rivers in the world," where the transparent Mississippi mingles reluctantly with the turbid Missouri, the Pekitanoni of the Indians. They pass, also, the

* Bancroft, vol. iii., p. 157.
† Martin says, they reached the Mississippi on the 7th of July; but he is so often in error in relation to dates, that his authority must yield when it conflicts with other sources of information. See Martin, vol. i., p. 77.

confluence of the Ohio, which was afterward known for many years as the Wabash, and which likewise mingles its bright waters reluctantly with the turbid flood.

They continued their descent with the rapid current until the sun became oppressive and insects intolerable, and where the canes become so thick that the buffalo can not break through them. They approached a village of the Michigamies, in latitude 33°. Armed with bows and arrows, with axes and clubs, and bent on war, the natives, with terrific whoops and yells, advanced in their war-canoes to assault the helpless party. Marquette advanced, holding the sacred calumet aloft, and thus brought safety to his companions. The meek father says, "God touched the hearts" of the old, and they restrained the young. After several days spent in refreshing themselves with the generous hospitality of this village, the party proceeded to the village of Akansea, beyond the limits of the Algonquin dialects. Here they conversed by an interpreter; and having made inquiries of the Indians relative to the course of the river, and the distance to the sea, they determined to return to Canada. It was now about the middle of July. They had been on the Mississippi about four weeks, and had descended about eleven hundred miles from the mouth of the Wisconsin.

But difficulties had increased as they descended; and they were among tribes whose language they did not understand. Their provisions, too, were well-nigh exhausted, and the course of the river was sufficiently ascertained. The object of their mission was in a great measure accomplished, and they determined to venture no further among unknown tribes, where disasters and death might overtake them.

They began to ascend the river; and after several weeks of hard toil against a strong current, and exposed to numerous privations, they reached the mouth of the Illinois River in safety.

Here they ascertained from the Indians that this river afforded a much more direct and easy route to the great lakes than that through the Wisconsin. They therefore began to ascend the gentle stream. After two weeks more they crossed over from the head streams of the Des-pleins branch of the Illinois into the Chicago Creek, through which they entered Lake Michigan. Here Joliet and Marquette parted; the one across to the Miami Indians of Lake Erie, on his way to Quebec, to make known the success of the expedition; the other to his missionary post among the Hurons.* In September the father joined his little flock, and soon afterward M. Joliet arrived at Quebec.

This was the first time that any white man had floated upon the Mississippi for one hundred and thirty years, since the disastrous voyage of Luis de Moscoso, with the remains of De Soto's chivalrous expedition, in 1543.

The discoveries of M. Joliet and Father Marquette filled all New France with rejoicing. A *Te Deum* was chanted in the Cathedral. M. Joliet was suitably rewarded by a grant of the Island of Anticosti, in the St. Lawrence; Father Marquette desired no other reward than an approving conscience that he had been doing good. It was for a time believed that the long-desired route to China had been discovered. The jealousy and fears entertained toward the English colonies, which now covered the whole Atlantic coast north of Florida, caused these early discoveries to be concealed, as far as practicable, from general publicity in Europe. England then, as now, was prone to seize and appropriate the discoveries of others to herself.

Such was the first discovery of the Mississippi by the French from Canada; a discovery which gave to France a conventional claim to occupy and settle all the regions lying upon the great river itself, as well as upon its great tributaries.

[A.D. 1680.] The native occupants of the Illinois country and the western portion of New France, as seen by the first Jesuit missionaries upon Lake Michigan, were similar in all respects to the tribes previously known to them on the St. Lawrence; for the first aspect of the original inhabitants of the United States was uniform. "Between the Indians of Florida and Canada the difference was scarcely perceptible. Their manners and institutions, as well as their organization, had a common physiognomy; and, before their languages began to be known, there was no safe method of grouping the nations into families. But when the vast variety of dialects came to be compared, there were found east of the Mississippi not more than eight radically distinct languages, of which five still constitute the speech of powerful communities, and three are known only as memorials of tribes that have almost disappeared from the earth."†

* Martin's Louisiana, vol. i., p. 78.
† Bancroft's History of the United States, vol. iii., p. 237.

The Algonquin tongue, which existed not only on the St. Lawrence, but also on the Des Moines, was most widely diffused. It was heard from Cape Fear to the land of the Esquimaux; from the Cumberland River of Kentucky to the southern bank of the Missinnippi, a thousand miles northwest from the sources of the Mississippi.

The *Shawanese* connected the southeastern Algonquins with those of the west. "The basin of the Cumberland River is marked by the earliest French geographers as the home of this restless nation of wanderers. A part of them afterward had their 'cabins' and their 'springs' in the neighborhood of Winchester. Their principal band removed their hunting-fields in Kentucky to the head waters of one of the great rivers of South Carolina; and, at a later day, an encampment of four hundred and fifty of them, who had been straggling in the woods for four years, was found not far north of the head waters of Mobile River, on their way to the country of the Muskhogees." "So desolate was the wilderness, that a vagabond tribe could wander undisturbed from Cumberland River to Alabama, from the head waters of the Santee to the Susquehanna."*

The *Miamis* were more stable, and their own traditions preserve the memory of their ancient limits. "My father," said the Miami orator, Little Turtle, at Greenville, in 1795, "kindled the first fire at Detroit; from thence he extended his lines to the head waters of the Scioto; from thence to its mouth; from thence down the Ohio to the mouth of the Wabash; and from thence to Chicago, on Lake Michigan. These are the boundaries within which the prints of my ancestors' houses are seen."

The forests beyond Detroit were at first found unoccupied, or, it may be, roamed over by bands too feeble to attract a trader or to win a missionary. The "Ottawâs, Algonquin fugitives from the basin of the magnificent river whose name commemorates them, fled to the Bay of Saginaw, and took possession of the whole north as a derelict country; yet the Miamis occupied its southern moiety, and their principal mission was founded by Allouez on the banks of the St. Joseph's, within the present state of Michigan."

"The *Illinois* were kindred to the Miamis, and their country

* Bancroft's History of the United States, vol. iii., p. 241.

lay between the Wabash, the Ohio, and the Mississippi. Marquette found a village of them on the Des Moines; but its occupants soon withdrew to the east side of the Mississippi. Kaskaskia, Cahokia, and Peoria still preserve the names of the principal bands, of which the original strength has been greatly exaggerated. The vague tales of a considerable population vanished before the accurate observation of the missionaries, who found in the wide wilderness of Illinois scarcely three or four villages. On the discovery of America, the number of the scattered tenants of the territory, which now forms the states of Ohio and Michigan, of Indiana, Illinois, and Kentucky, could hardly have exceeded eighteen thousand."*

In the early part of the eighteenth century, the *Potawatamies* had crowded the Miamis from their dwellings at Chicago; the intruders came from the islands near the entrance of Green Bay, and were a branch of the great nation of Chippewas. That nation held the country from the mouth of Green Bay to the head waters of Lake Superior, and were early visited by the French at Sault St. Marie and Chegoimegon. "They adopted into their tribes many of the Ottawâs from Upper Canada, and were themselves often included under that name by the early French writers."

"Ottawâ is but the Algonquin word for 'trader,' and Mascoutins are but 'dwellers in the prairie.' The latter hardly implies a band of Indians distinct from the Chippewas; but history recognizes as a separate Algonquin tribe, near Green Bay, the Menomonies, who were found there in 1669, and retained their ancient territory long after the period of French and English supremacy, and who prove their high antiquity as a nation by the singular character of their dialect."†

"Southwest of the Menomonies, the restless Sauks and Foxes, ever dreaded by the French, held the passes from Green Bay and Fox River to the Mississippi, and with insatiate avidity roamed in pursuit of contest over the whole country, between the Wisconsin and the upper branches of the Illinois. The Shawanese are said to have an affinity with this nation; that the Kickapoos, who established themselves by conquest in the north of Illinois, are but a branch of it, is demonstrated by their speech."

Northwest of the Sauks and Foxes, and west of the Chippe-

* Bancroft's U. States, vol. iii., p. 241.   † Idem, p. 242.

was, bands of the Sioux, or Dahcotas, had encamped in the prairies east of the Mississippi, vagrants between the head waters of Lake Superior and the Falls of St. Anthony. They were a branch of the great family which, dwelling for the most part west of the Mississippi and Red River of the north, extended from the Saskatchawan to lands south of the Arkansas. Hennepin was among them in his expedition to the north in 1680; Joseph Marest and another Jesuit visited them in 1687, and again in 1689. There seemed to be a hereditary warfare between them and the Chippewas. "Like other Western and Southern tribes, their population appears of late to have increased."

South and southwest of the Shawanese were the Chickasâs, a warlike and powerful tribe of savages, extending from the banks of the Mississippi eastward to the Muscle Shoals of Tennessee River. These tribes were visited by Marquette, and again by La Salle, in his exploration of the Lower Mississippi. At first they were friends of the French, but having been won to the English interests by traders and emissaries from Carolina, they became the most constant and most successful enemies of the French colonies in Louisiana.

South of the Chickasâs was the Natchez tribe, occupying the country on the east side of the Mississippi, between the Yazoo and the Pearl River, and the most civilized of any tribe seen by Iberville in Louisiana. West and south of the Natchez was the powerful tribe of the Choctâs, the constant friends of the early French colonies on the Mississippi and Mobile Rivers.

Such is the brief outline of the native tribes first known to the early French colonies in Louisiana, and whose friendship they continued to preserve in a remarkable manner, until the close of their dominion on the Mississippi, excepting only the Natchez and Chickasâ nations.

CHAPTER II.

EXPLORATION OF THE MISSISSIPPI RIVER BY LA SALLE: HIS COLONY ON THE COLORADO.—A.D. 1673 TO 1696.

Argument.—Character and Enterprise of La Salle.—His Ambition to complete the Exploration of the Mississippi.—His Plans approved by M. Talon, Intendant of New France.—La Salle sails for Europe.—Receives the King's Patronage.—Returns to Canada.—Repairs to Fort Frontenac and the Western Lakes in 1678.—Winters on the Niagara, and builds the Griffon in 1679.—Proceeds to Green Bay and freights the Griffon.—Visits the Miamis on St. Joseph's River.—Loss of the Griffon and Cargo.—Builds Fort Miami in 1680.—Builds Fort Crève Cœur.—Difficulties with Indians.—Mutiny among his Men.—Mutiny quelled and Indians reconciled.—Father Hennepin sent to explore the Mississippi. — La Salle returns to Fort Frontenac. — Rock Fort built on the Illinois.—Extent of Hennepin's Explorations in 1681.—Subsequently he explores the Mississippi as low as the Arkansas.—La Salle devotes his whole Energy to retrieve his Fortune. — Prepares for a final Exploration of the River to the Sea.—He enters the Mississippi, February 2, 1682.—He explores it to the Sea, and visits numerous Tribes of Indians.—Takes formal Possession of Lower Louisiana.—Returns to Canada.—Sails to Europe in October, 1782.—In Paris, organizes a Colony for the Mississippi.—Sails from Rochelle with his Colony, July 24, 1684.—Character and Numbers of the Colony. — Tedious and disastrous Voyage. — Sails West of the Mississippi, and is compelled to land in Western Texas.—Unavailing Searches for the Mississippi.—Builds "Fort St. Louis" on the Colorado, and takes formal Possession of Texas in 1685.—Deplorable Condition of the Colony.—La Salle finally determines to reach the Illinois and Canada by Land, in 1687.—Assassinated near the Trinity River.—The Remainder of the Colony are dispersed, and some reach the Illinois.—Spaniards search for the French Colony in vain, in 1689.—Illinois Country occupied by French after La Salle's Departure.—Wars in Canada with the Iroquois and English.—The Colonization of Lower Louisiana deferred until the Year 1698.

[A.D. 1673.] THE first ebullition of joy in New France, after the discovery of the great river of the West by Father Marquette and M. Joliet, soon subsided. The colonial government manifested but little interest in prosecuting the discovery for five years. At length a private individual undertook to complete the exploration to the sea. This individual was Monsieur la Salle, a native of Rouen in Normandy. He had been a man of letters and of fortune, but had renounced his patrimony and joined the order of Jesuits. "After profiting by the discipline of their schools, and obtaining their praise for purity and diligence, he had taken his discharge of the fraternity, and with no companions but poverty and a boundless spirit of enterprise," he came to New France in quest of fame and fortune.*

* Bancroft's History of the United States, vol. iii., p. 162.

At first he established himself as a fur trader at La Chiné, near Montreal. But he was ready and willing to engage in any enterprise that would gratify his ambition and reward his toil. He resolved to prosecute the discovery and exploration of the Mississippi as an enterprise worthy of his ambition. He entertained the belief advanced by Father Marquette, that some of the western tributaries of the great river would afford a direct route to the South Sea, and thence to China. This subject still was agitated in Europe, and all were interested in knowing the fact. To avoid a long and dangerous voyage around the Cape of Good Hope, or of Cape Horn, was surely an object of deep concern to the commercial world. La Salle was a man of extraordinary courage and perseverance, and hence was well adapted for the exploration of remote and unknown regions. M. Joutel declares "his constancy and courage, his extraordinary knowledge in the arts and sciences, rendered him fit for any thing; and besides this, he possessed an indefatigable body, which made him surmount all difficulties."

[A.D. 1678.] Such was the man who was eager to enter upon the new enterprise of exploring the "great river" to its mouth, which he believed must be in the Gulf of Mexico. He communicated his views to the Count de Frontenac, then governor of New France. He urged upon him the propriety of sending colonies westward, and of protecting them by adequate fortifications against the hostilities of the Indians. He portrayed, with all the ardor of his temperament, the advantages that would result from such a policy; that it would not only benefit and strengthen New France, but also aggrandize France herself. The count readily entered into all his views, and approved all his plans for the accomplishment of his designs. But the execution of them required heavy disbursements, which the provincial authorities could not order. He resolved, therefore, to send La Salle to France, that he might there explain his views and advocate his plans before the court. La Salle arrived in France, and lost no time in presenting himself before the minister. He was fortunate, and received a favorable audience. Letters of nobility were granted by the king, with authority to prosecute his projected discoveries. He was appointed proprietor and commandant of Fort Cataracoui, afterward called Frontenac, near the eastern extremity of Lake

Frontenac, or Ontario, and upon the present site of Kingston. Yet no money was appropriated; for this he was to depend upon his own resources and industry.*

Having engaged the aid of the Chevalier de Tonti, and about thirty colonists, including several mechanics, he set sail from France for the St. Lawrence. After a prosperous voyage, he arrived at Quebec on the 25th of September, 1678. Thence he proceeded to Fort Frontenac. The fort was neglected and dismantled. The first labor was to rebuild the works and place the whole in a proper military condition.† Here he remained some weeks, making preparations for his tour to the Far West. In all his preparations and plans, he evinced such business-like dispatch, and such prompt enterprise and undaunted firmness, that the colonial government became more and more convinced that he possessed the proper spirit and genius for the arduous undertaking. "He sent forward men to prepare the minds of the remote tribes for his coming, by well-chosen words and gifts."

A barque of ten tons having been built, La Salle and his party left Fort Frontenac on the 18th of November, 1678, upon his Western tour. For the means of defraying the expenses of the expedition, his principal dependence was upon his success in trading with the Indians. He had supplied himself with a large amount of goods and articles adapted to the Indian trade, which he expected to barter for rich furs and skins. After a tedious and dangerous voyage in that tempestuous season, they reached the western extremity of Lake Frontenac. The winter had now set in with great severity, and he was compelled to go into winter-quarters with his small party near the Falls of Niagara. The delay here was turned to advantage. During the winter, he was constantly employed in making further provision for the expedition. Exploring parties, under the Chevalier de Tonti, were sent to reconnoiter the country, to conciliate the Indians, to open a friendly intercourse with them, and to make further inquiries of the route to the Mississippi. La Salle himself returned to Fort Frontenac for an additional supply of provisions, goods, and ammunition. He also brought with him, the following spring, three recollêt monks, to administer to the spiritual wants of his people, and to aid in the enterprise. One of these was "Father Louis Hennepin, a Francis-

* See Martin's Louisiana, vol. i., p. 83.   † Idem, p. 85, 86.

can friar, a man full of ambition for discoveries and fame; daring, hardy, energetic, vain, and self-exaggerating almost to madness." He was more inclined to promote his own fame for great deeds than to advance the cause of truth. He had been a missionary among the Indians about Fort Frontenac; he had made frequent visits among the Iroquois, south of Lake Ontario, and on the sources of the Alleghany, and had learned much of Indian character and customs.

[A.D. 1679.] The barque brought from Fort Frontenac could not be taken over the Falls of Niagara: of course another must be built above them. The "Griffon," of sixty tons, was begun upon Lake Erie, near the mouth of the Tonnewanto Creek, but it required six months for its completion. During this time La Salle was not idle. He sent exploring parties into the different tribes of Indians south and west of the lakes, to make arrangements for collecting furs and opening a profitable trade. Father Hennepin performed his part by preaching and conciliating the natives, and by gaining information of the country. At length, on the seventh of August, 1679, the Griffon was finished, and the expedition set sail for the Straits of Mackinac. Sailing over Lake Erie and between the verdant isles of the majestic Detroit, they arrived on the 28th, in health and fine spirits.* Here they remained two weeks, while La Salle was making his arrangements and collecting furs. They sailed from the straits about the middle of September, and on the eighth of October they landed in the Bay of the Puants, or Green Bay. Here La Salle, having completed the stock for a cargo, sent the Griffon back to Lake Erie, richly freighted with furs and peltries, with instructions to meet him on its return at the mouth of the river of the Miamis, the present St. Joseph's of Michigan.

In the mean time, he proceeded by land through the tribes south of Green Bay, and thence around to the Miami Indians, on the southeast of the lake. Here he entered into engagements for opening a trade with the Miamis of the River St. Joseph.

He obtained permission of them to erect a stockade fort and a trading-post on that river, near its entrance into Lake Michigan. This was known afterward as the Fort of the Miamis; for the use of which, he expected a supply of goods from Lake Erie upon the return of the Griffon in December following.

* Bancroft's U. States, vol. iii., p. 164.

Here he waited impatiently for the return of the Griffon. At length December came; yet nothing was heard of the vessel. La Salle coasted out in search of her, and set up beacons near the shore to direct her course. Still the vessel did not arrive, and supplies of all kinds were beginning to fail. He left a garrison of ten men in the Fort Miami, with instructions for the commander of the Griffon upon her arrival.* With the remainder of his force, consisting of thirty-four men, including the Cnevalier de Tonti, he set out for the Illinois River. While himself and some others passed over by land, the remainder of the party, with the boats and canoes, paddled up the St. Joseph's River for four days, and then by a portage crossed over to the head branch of the Kankakee River, which they descended to the Illinois. Thence the whole party descended that placid river until they came to a large Indian village, which they supposed to be one hundred and fifty miles from the Mississippi. The Indians were kind and hospitable; they supplied the party abundantly with corn and meats. This village was near the expansion of the Illinois River, known as Lake Peoria, where Fort St. Louis was afterward built.

It was now about Christmas; and the party proceeded about sixty miles further down the river, where they were well received by the Indians. Believing this a good point for a trading-post, La Salle obtained permission to build a fort. He accordingly remained to complete the work. It was now late in January, 1680, when he first received intelligence from the Griffon. She had been wrecked on the voyage home, and all his rich cargo was lost. This circumstance, together with the appearance of discontent among his men, foreboding mutiny, so dispelled his hopes and depressed his spirits, that he called the fort "Crève Cœur," or Broken Heart.†

[A.D. 1680.] Up to this time, his undertaking, although arduous, appeared to be prosperous. He had extended his explorations westward fifteen hundred miles beyond the settlements. The country had been examined, forts were erected, and the friendship of the savages had been secured. But now a dark cloud overspread his prospects. His men appeared worn out and disgusted with an expedition which had already engaged them more than a year; the issue still appeared to them hazardous, or at least uncertain. They were not willing

* Martin's Louisiana, vol. i., p. 88, 89. † Idem.

to spend their lives in a deep wilderness, among savages, without guides, and often without food. This dissatisfaction at length broke out into open murmurs against the projector of the expedition, the author of all their troubles, who had led them into a fatiguing, perilous, and, to them, an apparently useless ramble, remote from civilization and all the endearments of social life.

Nothing escaped the quick penetration of La Salle.* He had soon perceived that discontent and mischief were fomented among his men; that a storm was impending, and must be calmed. He went into the midst of them; he assured them of good treatment, and ultimate success; he placed before them the hope of glory and wealth; he pointed them to the successful example of the Spaniards in Mexico and Peru; but they were not so easily appeased. The mutineers represented to their comrades how idle it was to continue slaves to the caprice and dupes to the idle visions and imaginary hopes of leader who seemed to consider the dangers already passed only as pledges which demanded still greater sacrifices from them.

They asked whether they could expect any other reward for their protracted slavery than misery and indigence. What could be expected, at the end of a ramble almost to the confines of the earth, and to inaccessible seas, but to be obliged to return poorer and more miserable than when they first set out? They said the only means of avoiding the impending calamity was to return while they had sufficient strength, to part from a man who sought their ruin and his own, and to abandon him to his laborious and useless discoveries. They adverted to the difficulty of return when their leader, by his intelligence, influence, and intrigues, should have secured the means of apprehending and punishing them as deserters, and that it would be impossible to proceed without provisions or resources of any kind. It was suggested to cut the tree up by the roots, and to end their misery by the death of its author, and that thus they might avail themselves of the fruits of their

---

* It may be well here to remark, that Martin, in the whole of La Salle's explorations, discoveries, and trade among the Western tribes, is negligent of dates; places transactions, generally, one year earlier than they really transpired. Thus, he makes La Salle's first voyage down the Mississippi to take place in the year 1681, whereas Bancroft establishes the time to be in the spring of 1682. See Martin, vol. i., p. 86, and on to p. 102.

own labor and fatigues. Those who were in favor of such steps were not in sufficient number to effect their object. They, however, determined to endeavor to induce the Indians to rise against La Salle, hoping that they might reap the advantage to be derived from his murder without appearing to have participated in the crime.*

The leaders of the mutineers, approaching the natives with apparent concern and confidence, said that, grateful for their hospitality heretofore extended, they were alarmed at the danger which threatened them; that La Salle had entered into strong engagements with the Iroquois, their greatest enemies; that he had advanced into their country now to ascertain their strength, to build a fort, and to keep them in subjection; that, in his meditated return to Fort Frontenac, he had no other object than to convey to the Iroquois the information he had gained, and to invite them to make a rapid irruption into the country, while his force was among them to co-operate with the Iroquois.†

The Indians, of course, attached much truth to the allegations of these men. La Salle instantly discovered a change of conduct in the Indians, but he knew not the cause. He at length succeeded in obtaining a declaration of the cause of their cold reserve. After communicating his reasons for suspecting perfidy in some of his men, he showed how impossible it was that he could be connected with the Iroquois; that he considered that nation as perfidious, lawless, cruel, revengeful, and thirsting for human blood; and, as such, that neither credit nor safety would dictate such an alliance with those brutal savages; and, moreover, that he had frankly announced his views to the Illinois on his first arrival among them; that the smallness of his force precluded the belief of an intention to subdue any tribe. The open and ingenuous calmness with which he spoke gained him credence, and the impression previously made by the mutineers appeared to be entirely effaced from the minds of the Indians.‡

This success, however, was of short duration. An emissary had been sent from a neighboring tribe, the Mascotins, secretly, to the Illinois, to stir them up against La Salle and his party.

By great art, he had nearly convinced them that La Salle

* Martin's Louisiana, vol. i., p. 90–91. † Idem, p. 92–93.
‡ Idem, p. 93–94.

was in alliance with the Iroquois, and almost succeeded in his efforts to induce the Illinois to cut off the whole party. The suggestions of this emissary, corresponding with the rumors circulated by the disaffected of his own party, had well-nigh effected his destruction. The suspicions which La Salle, by his candor and address, had allayed, were suddenly revived, and the chiefs spent the night in deliberation. In the morning, all the delusory hopes he had entertained on the apparent return of confidence were dispelled on his perceiving the cold reserve of the chiefs and the unconcealed distrust and indignation of others. He vainly endeavored to discover the immediate cause of the change, and began to think of the propriety of intrenching his party in the fort. Alarmed and surprised, and unable to remain in suspense, he boldly advanced into the midst of the Indians, who were gathered into small groups, and speaking their language sufficiently well to be understood, he demanded the cause of the coolness and distrust now seen on their brows. He said they had parted on the preceding evening in peace and friendship, and now he found them armed, and some of them ready to fall upon him; that he was naked and unarmed in the midst of them, a willing and ready sacrifice to their vengeance, if he could be convicted of any designs against them.

Moved by his open and undaunted demeanor, the Indians pointed to the deputy of the Mascotins, who had been sent to apprise them of his schemes and his connection with their enemies. Rushing boldly toward him, La Salle, in an imperious tone, demanded what evidence or reason existed for this alleged connection. The Mascotin coldly replied that, in circumstances where the safety of a nation was concerned, full evidence was not always required to convict suspicious characters; that the smallest circumstances often justified precautions; and as the address of the turbulent and seditious consisted in dissembling their schemes, the duty of the chiefs consisted in adopting measures to prevent their success; that, in the present case, his past negotiation or trade with the Iroquois, his intended return to Fort Frontenac, and the fort he had just built, were sufficient presumptions to induce the Illinois to apprehend danger, and to take the steps necessary to avoid being taken in the snare he seemed to have prepared. By a display of great address and firmness, La Salle finally gave sufficient assurance that he entertained no hostile designs against them, and that he had no such connection with the Iroquois as ought to prejudice the Illinois against him.

A good understanding with the Indians was at length restored, and his own men became so far reconciled that they promised to remain at the fort on duty, while an exploring party should advance toward the sources of the Mississippi. Still they were inclined to defeat the object of this expedition, and subsequently sought occasion to take off the leaders of it by poison placed in their food; but the attempt was detected before any fatal effects were produced, and thus they failed to accomplish their object.

Having arranged the expedition for the Upper Mississippi, La Salle, in the month of March, with a sack of parched corn, a musket, a shot-pouch and powder-horn, for defense and to procure food, a blanket, and deer-skins for moccasins, with three companions, set out on foot for Fort Frontenac, trudging through melting snows and marshes, through thickets and forests, upon the ridge which divides the waters of the Ohio from those of the lakes.*

The exploring party for the Mississippi consisted of Father Louis Hennepin, M. Dugay, and six other Frenchmen, as oarsmen and woodsmen. Leaving Fort Crève Cœur on the 28th of February, they descended the Illinois in the midst of winter. For ten days they were detained at the mouth by floating ice in the Mississippi, after which they proceeded to ascend the river. They continued their voyage in their canoes more than eight hundred miles, when their progress was arrested by great falls in the river, which were named by the Franciscan the "Falls of St. Anthony," in honor of his patron saint, St. Anthony of Padua. On a tree near the cataract, he engraved the cross and the arms of France. For several weeks the party rambled through the regions above the falls, exploring the country and its rivers, but never reaching the real sources of the great river, as Hennepin falsely affirmed. The whole party, during their sojourn in these parts, was held by the Sioux in a short captivity, from which they at length escaped. Descending the Mississippi to the mouth of the Wisconsin, Hennepin and his companions returned by way of the Wisconsin and Fox Rivers to the French mission at Green Bay.†

* Bancroft's U. States, vol. iii., p. 166. † Idem, p. 167.

Toward the close of summer, Father Hennepin, desirous of accomplishing the whole of La Salle's wishes, with a party of five men set out on a voyage of exploration down the river, vainly expecting to trace and to examine the country to the sea. Entering the Mississippi again by way of the Wisconsin, the party descended, occasionally paddling their canoes, and again floating with the current, until they reached the mouth of the Arkansas River, the point formerly reached by Marquette and Joliet. Here it was ascertained from the Indians that the distance to the sea was still very great—much greater than had been anticipated. Father Hennepin deemed it best to return to the Illinois, and thence to Fort Crève Cœur. Late in the autumn he reached the posts upon the Upper Illinois.

This was the extent of Father Hennepin's discoveries on the Mississippi; yet, after the death of La Salle, he endeavored to claim the principal credit of the explorations to the sea.* The account of his voyage to the mouth of the Mississippi, published in London in 1699, was a manifest fiction, and the result of British intrigue with the Franciscan. The whole distance from the mouth of the Arkansas to the Falls of St. Anthony is but little short of fifteen hundred miles. Over this distance Hennepin had passed twice, an entire distance of nearly three thousand miles, upon a vast, unknown river, and among unknown savage tribes. This was truly an enterprise worthy of La Salle himself; and, after all fair allowance for Father Hennepin's propensity to exaggerate, he is still entitled to our admiration and respect for his enterprise and perseverance.

During the exploring voyage of Hennepin and M. Dugay,

---

* Hennepin, after this expedition, retired to Canada, and soon afterward he set sail for France. He there published a splendid account of the newly-discovered country of "Louisiana," which he so called in honor of Louis XIV. This work he dedicated to the French minister, Colbert. It contained an account of his discoveries under La Salle, in which he makes no claim to have descended the river lower than the Arkansas. Several years subsequently, not meeting with that patronage which he expected in France, he visited England, and was soon taken into the pay of King William, who declared "that he would leap over twenty stumbling-blocks" to accomplish his designs in America. The King of England desired to set up a claim to the discovery of the Mississippi, and to the whole of Louisiana, through Father Hennepin's discoveries. He therefore induced him to write a *new* account of his explorations, and so modify its details as to favor the pretensions of the English king. This account was published in London in 1699. It is in this that he first claims to have explored the river to its mouth. The whole narrative, in this respect, bears evidence of its own falseness, and with the French procured for him the title of "the great liar." See Martin's Louisiana, vol. i. Also, Bancroft's History of the United States, vol. iii., p. 167. Stoddart's Sketches of Louisiana, p. 16.

La Salle was busily engaged in visiting and repairing his forts, and in bringing forward supplies of goods and ammunition to his trading-posts. His visits extended likewise to the tribes west and south of Lake Michigan, and south of Erie. He knew it was all-important to keep up a good understanding with these numerous tribes, lest all might be lost by the hostility which had already been partially excited against him.

In the mean time, soon after the departure of Hennepin's party in February, La Salle had placed the Chevalier de Tonti in command at Fort Crève Cœur, with instructions to fortify "Rock Fort," on the Illinois, during his contemplated absence at Fort Frontenac. The point to be thus fortified was a partially isolated "cliff, rising two hundred feet above the river, which flows near its base, in the center of a lovely country of verdant prairies, bordered by distant slopes, richly tufted with oak and black walnut, and the noblest trees of the American forest." This rocky eminence may now be seen, near the northern bank, rising above the beautiful plain, through which the Illinois flows, and within four miles below the mouth of Fox River. This spot, near five miles below the town of Ottawâ, a few years since was selected by some enterprising Yankees as the site of a town, which they designated with the appropriate name of "Gibraltar;" but it remains yet, as it was in the days of La Salle, only an impregnable site for a fortress. La Salle, compelled by necessity, determined to defer the further exploration of the great river until he could retrieve his former losses, restore confidence and authority among his men, and induce a state of friendship among the Indians. To this important end he resolved to devote his energies and his undivided attention. His debts were pressing, and as yet he had realized nothing, after great outlays and great expenses, besides the loss of two years spent in privation and toil.

After a long and toilsome journey, visiting the Iroquois nations in his route, he arrived at Fort Frontenac in June, after having established amicable relations with the western portion of this confederacy. The remainder of the summer was spent in conducting his trading operations, and in extending his influence among the remote tribes of the West. In the fall, he flattered himself that his trading-posts were established, that a friendly intercourse had been opened, and that peace prevailed among the tribes, giving a more encouraging aspect to his general affairs.

But he was again doomed to disappointment. About the first of September, hostilities had broken out between some of the Iroquois tribes and those on the Illinois. The position of the French between the opposing bands was dangerous in the extreme, and De Tonti deemed it prudent to withdraw from the seat of war to a place of greater security. He accordingly retired with his little force to Fort Miami, on the St. Joseph's River of Lake Michigan, where he arrived about the middle of September. Here he continued until peace was established, and La Salle's contemplated exploration was necessarily deferred.

[A.D. 1681.] In the spring of 1681, La Salle set out from Fort Frontenac for the West. He at length reached the country of the Miamis; and, having made due arrangements, he set out from that post with De Tonti for Fort Crève Cœur, on the Upper Illinois. The following summer was spent in traversing the country, visiting and supplying his trading-posts, in efforts to reconcile the hostile tribes, and in opening a free trade and intercourse with the Illinois and Miami tribes. These preparations having been made, he began to make his arrangements for completing the exploration of the great river to its mouth. To the river, concurring with Father Hennepin, he had given the name of "St. Louis," and to the country through which it flowed that of "Louisiana," both in honor of the King of France. The enterprise was one which had engaged his thoughts and had influenced his plans for the last two years, and he now determined to complete the undertaking. Before he could set out, he was obliged once more to return to Fort Frontenac to complete his arrangements. His stay was of short duration, and on the 20th of November he left Fort Frontenac on his return to the Illinois country. Having to visit his posts, and make other arrangements for his long absence, he did not arrive at Fort Crève Cœur until the beginning of January following. Here a few days were spent in preparing for his departure, and a further delay of a few days was caused by the inclemency of the winter; yet on the 2d day of February, 1682, La Salle and his little band of voyagers and explorers, a band of hardy adventurers, were floating on the broad bosom of the Mississippi.

[A.D. 1682.] As M. Dugay and Father Hennepin had already explored the upper portion of the river, La Salle determined to lose no time in prosecuting the exploration down to the sea. Having descended to the mouth of the Missouri, he remained some days, endeavoring to obtain such information as the Indians could give of that great Western tributary, which received the name of "St. Philip." The party next delayed a few days at the mouth of the Ohio, where La Salle made some arrangements for trade and intercourse with the Indians. Thence they proceeded down to the first Chickasâ bluffs. Here La Salle entered into amicable arrangements for opening a trade with the Chickasâ Indians, where he established a trading-post, and obtained permission to build a stockade fort. This he designed as a point of rendezvous for traders from the Illinois country, passing to the lower posts on the river. This post was called "Fort Prud'homme," in honor of the man who, with a small garrison, was left in command. The next stop made by the party was at the mouth of the Arkansas River, which was the extreme limit of former discoveries. Here he tarried several days, and then proceeded to a village of the Tensas Indians, where he displayed the emblem of Christianity to the admiring natives. This village was upon the banks of a lake, some distance back from the river, and was probably the same now known as "Lake Providence," from which the Tensas River has its source. Here he was received with much kindness and hospitality by the Indians; and, consequently, remained several days in friendly intercourse with them. Thence he continued his voyage down, and visited each of the tribes on the banks as he passed. On the 27th of March he arrived at the mouth of Red River. Here, likewise, he made a short stay, and then proceeded down the Mississippi to its confluence with the Gulf of Mexico. He reached this destination on the 7th of April, after a tedious voyage among unknown tribes for more than twelve hundred miles below the Illinois. By occasional accessions of French and Indians, the party now amounted to nearly sixty persons; some were engaged in providing for their comfort and sustenance; and others, with La Salle, were engaged for several days in exploring the inlets and sea-marshes along the coast, and in making other necessary observations. La Salle then ascended the river with his party until firm land was found, where he determined to tarry some days until his men could refresh themselves after their toilsome voyage. A few days served to revive the hardy pioneers, when they prepared to celebrate the glory of France in the possession of the newly-discovered province. La Salle took formal possession of the country, planted the arms of France, erected the cross, and calling the country "Louisiana," in honor of the King of France, he closed the ceremony with a display of the solemn and imposing rites of the Catholic Church. Thus France and Christianity entered the valley of the Mississippi hand in hand.*

* See Martin's Louisiana, vol. i., p. 100, 101.
The following inscription and *procès verbal* are copied by Mr. Sparks from a MS. in the Department of Marine, at Paris, viz.:
"A column was erected, and the arms of France were affixed with this inscription:

'LOUIS LE GRAND,
ROI DE FRANCE ET NAVARRE, REGNE;
LE NEUVIEME AVRIL, 1682.'"

The following ceremonies were then performed, viz.:
"The whole party, under arms, chanted the *Te Deum*, the *Exaudiat*, the *Domine Salvum fac Regem*; and then, after a salute of fire-arms, and cries of *Vive le roi*, the column was erected by M. de la Salle, who, standing near it, said with a loud voice in French, 'In the name of the most high, mighty, invincible, and victorious prince, Louis the Great, by the grace of God king of France and Navarre, fourteenth of that name, this ninth day of April, one thousand six hundred and eighty-two, I, in virtue of the commission of his majesty, which I hold in my hand, and which may be seen by all whom it may concern, have taken, and do now take, in the name of his majesty, and of his successors to the crown, possession of this country of Louisiana, the seas, harbors, ports, bays, adjacent straits, and all the nations, peoples, provinces, cities, towns, villages, mines, minerals, fisheries, streams, and rivers comprised in the extent of said Louisiana, from the mouth of the great River St. Louis, on the eastern side, otherwise called Ohio, Alighin, Siporé, or Chuckagoná, and this with the consent of the Chouanons, Chickachas, and other people dwelling therein, with whom we have made alliance; as also along the River Colbert, or Mississippi, and rivers which discharge themselves therein, from its source beyond the country of the Kious or Nadouessious, and this with their consent, and with the consent of the Motantees, Illinois, Mesigameas, Coroas, and Natchez, which are the most considerable nations dwelling therein, with whom we also have made alliance, either by ourselves, or by others in our behalf, as far as its mouth at the Sea or Gulf of Mexico, about the twenty-seventh degree of the elevation of the North Pole, and also to the mouth of the River of Palms; upon the assurance which we have received from all these nations, that we are the first Europeans who have descended or ascended the said River Colbert, hereby protesting against all those who may in future undertake to invade any or all these countries, people, or lands above described, to the prejudice of the right of his majesty, acquired by the consent of the nations herein named. Of which, and of all that can be ceded, I hereby take to witness those who hear me, and demand the act of the notary as required by law.'

"To which the whole assembly responded with shouts of *Vive le roi*, and with salutes of fire-arms. Moreover, the Sieur de la Salle caused to be buried at the foot of the tree to which the cross was attached, a leaden plate with the arms of France, and the following Latin inscription:

'LUDOVICUS MAGNUS REGNAT,
NONO APRILIS, CIƆ IƆC LXXXII.

ROBERTUS CAVALIER, CVM DOMINO DE TONTI, LEGATO, R. P. ZENOBIO MEMBRE, RE-
COLLECTO, ET VIGINTI GALLIS, PRIMIS HOC FLVMEN, INDE AB ILLINEORVM PAGO ENAV-
IGAVIT, EJVSQVE OSTIVM FECIT PERVIVM, NONO APRILIS, ANNO CIƆ IƆC LXXXII.'"

La Salle descended the Mississippi, and his sagacious eye, as he floated on its flood, when he formed a cabin on the first Chickasâ bluff, as he raised the cross on the bank of the Arkansas, and as he planted the arms of France near the Gulf of Mexico, beheld the future affluence of emigrants; he heard in the distance the footsteps of the advancing multitude that were coming to take possession of the valley.*

At length, La Salle and his party began to ascend the river on their return to the Illinois country. Advancing slowly against the strong current of the Mississippi, they made land in the Natchez country, where they tarried several days; but, having discovered a treacherous design among the Natchez Indians for cutting off the whole party, La Salle determined to proceed without further delay. Their next tarry was in the country of their old friends, the Tensas Indians, nearly two hundred miles above the Natchez villages. Here they were again hospitably received, and bountifully supplied with such provisions and comforts as the Indians could give. On the 12th of May they resumed their voyage, and proceeded to Fort Prud'homme, among the Chickasâs. Here La Salle was taken sick; and, being unable to travel, he remained nearly two months with his party, after having dispatched the Chevalier de Tonti with twenty men, including Indians, to announce his success to the posts upon the Illinois, and to take command of the forts and settlements until his return.

The whole ceremony was witnessed by attendants, and certified in a *procès verbal*, which concludes in the following words, viz.:

"After which the Sieur de la Salle said, that his majesty, as eldest son of the Church, would annex no country to his crown without making it his chief care to establish the Christian religion therein, and that its symbol must now be planted; which was accordingly done at once by erecting a cross, before which the *Vexilla* and the *Domine Salvum fac Regem* were sung. Whereupon the ceremony was concluded with cries of *Vive le roi.*

"Of all and every of the above, the said Sieur de la Salle having required of us an instrument, we have delivered to him the same, signed by us, and by the undersigned witnesses, this ninth day of April, one thousand six hundred and eighty-two.

"La Metaire, *Notary.*
"De la Salle.
P. Zenobe, *Recollét Missionary.*
Henry de Tonti.
Francois de Boisrondet.
Jean Bourdon.
Sieur d'Autray.
Jacques Cauchois.
Piere You.
Gilles Meucret.
Jean Michel, *Surgeon.*
Jean Mas.
Jean Dulignon.
Nicholas de la Salle."

See *Sparks's Life of La Salle,* p. 199, 200.

* Bancroft's U. States, vol. iii., 168, and Martin's Louisiana, vol. i.; p. 104.

At length La Salle, having recovered his health, set out upon his upward voyage, and reached the Illinois country near the last of September. Father Zenobé was sent to France with dispatches for the king, and to represent the vast importance which would accrue to France by peopling the immense country of Louisiana with Frenchmen; to report the extraordinary beauty of the virgin plains and valleys, the lakes and rivers of the great West, as they came from the hands of the Creator, deemed by all not unlike the "garden of paradise."

[A.D. 1683.] Several months were spent by La Salle in organizing his trading-posts, in providing for their future operations, in selecting his agents, and visiting the principal tribes. This at length having been accomplished, he gave the chief control of the Illinois country to the Chevalier de Tonti, as commandant of "Fort St. Louis," and superintendent of the whole trade of Illinois and Louisiana, during his absence on a visit to Fort Frontenac, for the purpose of supplying his establishments for the fall and winter trade.

Father Zenobé was still in Paris; and the enemies of La Salle, jealous of his enterprise and his growing fame, had sought to prejudice the minister against the importance of his discoveries. He had been represented as "an ambitious, plotting, restless character, full of schemes of self-aggrandizement." Similar representations were made by Le Ferre de la Barré, governor of Canada, in his official dispatches. Zenobé did not fail to expose the grounds of opposition to La Salle.* But the Sieur resolved in person to appear before the minister in Paris, and to develop fully his discoveries and his plans of colonization to the king.

Accordingly, late in the autumn of 1683, he set sail from Quebec for France, with vast schemes to be laid before the ministry for the colonization of Louisiana. But his enemies were not idle in their efforts to frustrate his plans. Yet Father Zenobé and the Count de Frontenac were in Paris, with all their influence in his favor; and the minister, Seignelay, son of Colbert, was inclined to enter heartily into all his plans.

La Salle arrived in Paris near the close of the year, and hastened to present his claims to the minister's attention. After great delays and obstacles, he at length met with a favora-

---

* See Southern Quarterly Review of Charleston, S. C., No. xiii., January 7th, 1845, p. 90–98.

ble reception at court. The ministers became convinced of the importance of his discoveries, and of the energy of his character in extending their American possessions. Much attention was therefore shown him at court, and at length his plan of settling a colony at the mouth of St. Louis, or Mississippi River, was approved.

[A.D. 1684.] More than six months were spent in France in preparations for conducting a suitable colony for the occupancy of Louisiana; and under the countenance of the crown, adventurers readily joined the contemplated enterprise. The government had resolved to supply the colonists with implements and provisions, and to afford them safe transports free of expense, together with a detachment of troops for their protection.*

By the 24th of July, 1684, La Salle, having collected together his colony of adventurers, set sail from the port of Rochelle in company with a large fleet of merchantmen. For the conveyance of the colony to the banks of the Mississippi, the government had furnished four vessels, under the command of M. Beaujeu, a man of an imperious and stubborn disposition.

The whole colony which embarked for the Gulf of Mexico, under the superintendence of La Salle, for the occupancy of Louisiana, consisted of two hundred and eighty persons, of all ranks and ages. Among them were one hundred soldiers, under the command of M. Joutel; thirty volunteers, including the young Cavalier, and the rash and passionate Moranget, nephews of La Salle; six ecclesiastics, including a brother of La Salle; twenty families, including young women, liberally supplied with provisions, implements of husbandry, and money; and also a number of mechanics of various arts, who had embarked their fortunes in the enterprise.

Such was the physical strength of the colony which was to plant the standard of France and Christianity in the newly-discovered province of Louisiana; but the moral worth of the colony was strangely complicated. The mechanics were poor workmen, ill versed in their art; the soldiers, though under Joutel, a man of courage and truth, and afterward the historian of the enterprise, were themselves spiritless vagabonds, without discipline and without experience; the volunteers were restless, with indefinite expectations; and, most of all, Beaujeu,

* Bancroft's Hist. of the U. States, vol. iii., p. 168.

the naval commander, was deficient in judgment, envious, self-willed, and foolishly proud.*

Early in the voyage, a variance sprung up between the naval commander and La Salle. This was only the beginning of continual differences between these two men; and in every instance on record the judgment of La Salle was right.

After a long voyage, with tedious calms, the little fleet arrived in the West India Seas. Before they reached Hispaniola, they were scattered by a storm, and Spanish privateers captured one of their vessels. The fleet remained several weeks in the vicinity of Hispaniola and Cuba, for the purpose of procuring further supplies for the colony, and for gaining information relative to the direction of the mouth of the St. Louis River. Its longitude was unknown to the mariners, and its direction from Hispaniola was uncertain. While at Hispaniola, La Salle was delayed and cruelly frustrated by the perverseness of Beaujeu, and many of the colonists sickened and died from exposure to the climate. But disappointment, grief, and intemperance were strong predisposing causes, and La Salle already saw the shadow of his coming misfortunes. The fleet sailed at length from St. Domingo, on the 25th of November, for the Mississippi. On the 10th of January, the fleet must have been near the mouth of the Mississippi; but La Salle thought not, and they sailed westward. Presently, perceiving his error, La Salle desired to return; but Beaujeu refused, and thus they sailed westward, and still to the west, till they reached the Bay of Matagorda, which proved to be seven degrees, or more than four hundred miles, west of the Mississippi.

[A.D. 1685.] At length they came in sight of land, at the distance of six leagues. The coast was unknown, and none could ascertain the longitude; the latitude was 29° 10′ north, but whether east or west of the Mississippi, none could tell. La Salle persisted that the river was far to the east of them. Soon after, they were overtaken by a storm, and one vessel, with a large supply of provisions, implements of husbandry, and ammunition, was wrecked and lost. All were anxious and distressed; but M. Beaujeu, the commander of the fleet, had differed with La Salle on the voyage; both were imperious and unyielding, and the breach had widened daily. The naval commander had conducted the colony to the shores of the Mexican

---

* Bancroft, vol. iii., p. 169. See, also, Martin, vol. i., p. 104.

Gulf, and refusing to be longer delayed after his duty had been performed, he resolved to return to France, and to leave La Salle to locate his colony, and to discover his great river. Impatient and resentful, he caused the little colony to be landed at the first convenient harbor, and set sail for Europe, leaving the wretched colony, of about two hundred and thirty souls, destitute and helpless, in an unknown and savage wilderness, huddled together in a rude fort made of the fragments of their wrecked vessel.

The bay near which they were left proved to be a portion of the present Bay of Matagorda, on the west side of the Colorado, and near eight hundred miles, by the indentations of the coast, west of the Mississippi.

For weeks La Salle continued to search for the hidden river, by coasting along the shore east and west, and by expeditions by land for the same object. In the mean time, his colony remained encamped near the Matagorda Bay. About the middle of March, the Indians began to exhibit a hostile attitude, and to threaten the destruction of the colony. At length, late in April, he moved fifteen miles further up the river, where a rude fort was erected for the protection of the people against Indian massacre, and here they opened a field and a garden for corn, beans, and vegetables. This settlement and fort were called "St. Louis," and comprised the first French settlement in Texas.

Here La Salle planted the arms of France, erected the cross, and formally took possession of the country in the name of his king. This settlement of the country, thus formally occupied, made Texas a portion of Louisiana,* and gave to France a claim which had never been relinquished when Louisiana fell into the possession of the United States, nearly one hundred and twenty years afterward.

Having secured his little colony from savage massacre, he began to extend his explorations in search of the Mississippi. Parties were dispatched toward the east and toward the west, in hopes of gaining some intelligence of the river. La Salle at length set out himself to seek the Mississippi, in canoes, with an ample crew; but after an absence of four months, and having explored the coast for one hundred and fifty leagues, he returned to his colony with the remnant of his detachment, un-

* Darby's Louisiana, p. 16.

successful, himself in rags, and having lost thirteen men in the expedition.* Yet his presence was sufficient to inspire hope in the desponding colony, and he continued indefatigable in his exertions to discover the river, which he still believed to be east of them.

[A.D. 1686.] The colony had been on the Colorado more than a year, and La Salle determined to seek the Spanish settlements of Northern Mexico. For this purpose, "in April, 1686, he plunged into the wilderness with twenty companions, lured by the brilliant fiction of the rich mines of St. Barbe, the El Dorado of Northern Mexico. Here, among the Cenis Indians, he obtained five horses, and supplies of maize and beans. He found no mines, but a country unsurpassed for beauty of climate and exuberant fertility."

"On his return, he heard of the wreck of the little barque which had remained with the colony, and he heard it unmoved. Heaven and man seemed his enemies, and with the giant energy of an indomitable will, having lost his hopes of fortune, his hopes of fame, with his colony diminished to about forty souls, among whom discontent had given birth to plans of crime, with no European nearer than the River Panuco, no French nearer than the Illinois, he resolved to travel on foot to his countrymen at the North, and to return from Canada to renew his colony in Texas.†

The colony began to suffer; the depredations and hostility of the Indians had prevented the advantages which they had hoped from their little crop, and they suffered for food. The summer was past, and the winter was not remote, and La Salle determined to make an effort to reach the Illinois country. From the Indians he had learned that the Spanish settlements of Western Mexico were within four or five hundred miles on the west. This convinced him that he was certainly west of the Mississippi, yet he dared not make their situation known to the Mexican authorities, for France and Spain were now at war: his only alternative was to seek the Illinois country.

Having made preparation to search for this remote region, he set out with a party of twenty men, some time in the month of October. He proceeded in a general northeast direction about four hundred miles, through unknown lands, and tribes speaking a strange language. Having proceeded thus far, he was

* Martin's Louisiana, vol. i., p. 106–110.   † Bancroft's U. States, vol. iii., p. 172.

taken sick, his provisions and ammunition began to fail, and he was compelled to retrace his steps to his fort on the Colorado. During the winter following, he was indefatigable in supplying his colony with every requisite afforded by the country, and in placing it in the best condition to make a good and plentiful crop the ensuing spring. But time passed off slowly, under gloomy apprehensions.

[A.D. 1687.] La Salle at length became impatient, vexed, harassed, and discouraged. Small incidents vexed him much; his men became impatient and censorious upon him as the author of all their misfortunes; and he, in turn, became harsh and severe to his men. They had been compelled with him, in his unavailing searches, to encounter the marshes, the bayous, swollen creeks, and the inhospitable deserts of western Texas. They had been in this unknown region for more than two years; many of their number had died, having suffered much from the climate, and other privations incident to their condition; others had been killed by the Indians, until the colony was reduced to less than forty persons.*

The remainder had become desperate in the hopelessness of their condition, when La Salle at last, in January, determined, as a last effort, again to seek relief from the Illinois settlements, toward the northeast, or from France herself. With this determination, he set out early in March upon the perilous journey, accompanied by sixteen men, provided with wild horses obtained from the Cenis Indians for their baggage, clothed in skins, and in shoes made of green buffalo hides. Thus equipped, the party set out, through wide prairies and woods, following the buffalo paths for roads, confiding in the courage of their leader, and hoping to win favor with the savages. The remnant of the colony, including twenty men, were to remain at Fort St. Louis, and await their return.

They had proceeded probably three hundred miles, and were upon some of the western branches of the Trinity, when they encamped to recruit their exhausted frames and to procure game for their sustenance in the progress of their journey. Dissatisfaction and jealousy among his companions finally ripened into mutiny. Two men upon a hunting excursion murdered Moranget, the nephew of La Salle; and three days af-

* Some account of La Salle's colony may be seen in Stoddart's Sketches of Louisiana, p. 20-23.

ter, when La Salle, led by the hovering of the vultures, was in search of his missing nephew's murdered body, concealed in the grass, he fell without uttering a word, shot dead by Dehault, one of his men, who was skulking in the high grass. The 'ong-suppressed feelings of revenge and mutiny in one of the conspirators, Leotat the surgeon, gave vent in the expression, as La Salle fell, "You are down now, grand bashaw! you are down now!" and they proceeded to despoil his body, which was left naked upon the prairie to be devoured by wild beasts.

Thus perished the Chevalier la Salle, one of the most enterprising, indefatigable, and persevering of all the early explorers of the Continent of America. He was a man whom no misfortune could daunt and no terror could alarm, a martyr to the cause of truth and to the welfare of his country. Yet, to the sorrow of France, and the everlasting ignominy of the unfeeling and treacherous Beaujeu, he was compelled to die a murdered exile, after suffering in mental anxiety and in physical toil more than a thousand deaths.

The murderers themselves soon after met their fate from the hands of their companions. Joutel, with the surviving nephew of La Salle, and others, in all but seven, obtained a guide for the Arkansas, and, proceeding in a northeastern direction, they came upon a French post, erected by De Tonti,[*] where a hut was tenanted by two Frenchmen, near the present post of Arkansas, sixty miles from the Mississippi. The weary pilgrims some time afterward reached the Illinois, there content to spend the remainder of their lives. But after a delay of four months, they set out for Quebec, to report the disasters of the colony. On the ninth of October, 1687, about seven months after the death of La Salle, they arrived at Quebec.

The remnant of the colony left at the Bay of St. Bernard either died of famine and disease, or were taken captive or destroyed by the Indians. They were never heard of afterward.[*]

---

[*] This party, according to other authorities, consisted of Joutel, Cavalier, brother of La Salle, Father Athanasius, and seven others. They made their way northward, and reached the country of the Nassonites or Nassonians, high up Red River. Further on they found the Cenis or Cenesians, who furnished them with horses and guides to the Arkansas. Among the Cenis they were joined by four Frenchmen who had deserted the year before, and had escaped to the Indians. See a full account given in Stoddart's Sketches of Louisiana, p. 22, 23.

† Stoddart, following the authority of a manuscript of La Harpe, says the remnant of this colony was seized by Spanish cruisers in 1689, and by them carried to Mexico. This is probably the truth.—Sketches of Louisiana, p. 24.

The Chevalier De Tonti, having heard of La Salle's arrival in the West Indies, on his voyage for the mouth of the Mississippi, had descended by way of the Illinois with a detachment of men and supplies, to meet the colony. But when he reached the mouth of the river, he found no trace of La Salle or his colony. After an anxious, long, and vain search for his friend, he returned to the Illinois, and thence to Fort Frontenac.

[A.D. 1689.] In 1689, the Mexican authorities, having heard of the French colony on the Bay of St. Bernard, sent a detachment of troops, under Don Alonzo de Leon, to search for them; but when they arrived at the site of " Fort St. Louis," no white man was found. Having heard that the French had retired to the country of the Assinais Indians, near Red River, Don Alonzo proceeded toward the Assinais towns, where he was courteously received by the natives, but the French were not to be found; and, after a delay of some days, enjoying the hospitality of the Indians, he set out on his return, having designated this part of the country " Texas," or *friends*. Thirty years afterward, the Spaniards sent missionaries to this portion of the country, where they at subsequent periods established military posts, or *presidios*, around which grew up the first Spanish settlements in Texas.*

Thus ended the first attempt of the French to settle the regions of the Lower Mississippi. The same fortune attended all the first European settlements in North America, until they began to be sufficiently numerous and powerful to withstand the natives and the climate. From the death of La Salle the whole region on both sides of the Mississippi, from its source to its mouth, and for an indefinite extent east and west, was known as Louisiana, and the river itself as the St. Louis River: both in honor of Louis XIV., king of France.

The further prosecution of discoveries on the Lower Mississippi was interrupted, until the year 1698, by the harassing and bloody war kept up against the province of Canada from 1689 to 1696, by the Iroquois Indians and the British colonies[†] of New England and New York.

But the occupation of the Illinois never was discontinued from the time La Salle returned from Frontenac, in 1681. Joutel found a garrison at Fort St. Louis, on the Illinois, in 1687, and in 1689 La Houtan bears testimony that it still con-

* Martin's Louisiana, vol. i., p. 126, 127.   † Idem, p. 122–138.

tinued. In 1796 a public document proves its existence; and it was the wish of Louis XIV. to preserve it in a good condition; and when Tonti, in 1700, again descended the Mississippi, he was attended by twenty Canadians, residents on the Illinois.*

From the time of La Salle's departure from France, in 1684, with his colony, for the Mississippi, the jealousy of England had been awakened against the extension of the French dominion in North America; to arrest which, the usual intrigue of the English cabinet was put in operation.

About that time, the English began to excite the Iroquois tribes of Indians to hostilities against the French settlements on the St. Lawrence. In 1687, the cabinet of St. James was using every exertion, by court intrigue and diplomatic negotiation, to lull the French court and the province of Canada into a fatal security. It affected an anxious desire to conclude a treaty of neutral friendship and peace between their respective colonies, while the Governor of New York was secretly and treacherously intriguing with the Iroquois tribes, and endeavoring to excite their jealousy and hostility against the French on the St. Lawrence. He endeavored to induce them to make sudden and unexpected attacks and incursions against their defenseless settlements, and promised, in that case, not to desert his red allies in any event.

New France was a feeble colony in the midst of hostile savages. The actual French settlements, as yet, had not extended upon the lakes. "West of Montreal, the principal French posts, and those but inconsiderable ones, were at Frontenac, at Mackinaw, and on the Illinois. At Niagara there was a wavering purpose of maintaining a post, but no permanent occupation. So weak were the garrisons, that the English traders, with an escort of Indians, had ventured even to Mackinaw, and, by means of the Senecas, obtained a large share of the commerce of the lakes. In self-defence, French diplomacy had attempted to pervade the West, and concert an alliance with all the tribes from Lake Ontario to the Mississippi. The traders were summoned even from the plains of the Sioux; and Tonti and the Illinois were, by way of the Ohio and the Alleghany, to precipitate themselves on the Senecas, while the French should come from Montreal, and the Ottawâs and other Algonquins,

---

* Bancroft's Hist. of the U. States, vol. iii., p. 195.

under Ducantaye, the vigilant commander at Mackinaw, should descend from Michigan. But the power of the Illinois was broken; the Hurons and Ottawâs were almost ready to become the allies of the Senecas. The savages still held the keys of the great West; intercourse existed but by means of the forest rangers, who penetrated the barren heaths around Hudson's Bay, the morasses of the northwest, and the homes of the Sioux and Miamis—the recesses of every forest where there was an Indian with skins to sell. 'God alone could have saved Canada this year,' wrote Denonville in 1688. But for the missions at the West, Illinois would have been abandoned, the fort at Mackinaw lost, and a general rising of the natives would have completed the ruin of New France."* Such was the danger of the French settlements of Canada from the hostilities of the Indian tribes.

The following year the English began to make open demonstration of hostilities in Hudson's Bay and Acadie, while the Indians of the Five Nations began to be very troublesome in their attacks on the French settlements and the trade of the St. Lawrence. The whole population of all Canada was only 11,249 souls,[†] exposed to Indian hostility and English intrigue.

On the 7th of June, the following year, the Count de Frontenac was appointed governor-general of New France. Difficulties were increasing between the two courts, and warlike preparations were progressing in the province of New France. During this time the Iroquois, or Five Nations, instigated by their English neighbors of New York, had been preparing a secret expedition against the upper settlements of the St. Lawrence. On the 25th of August, 1689, they made a sudden, unexpected, and terrible irruption, with fifteen hundred warriors, into the Island of Montreal. The whole island was ravaged with fire and sword; all the settlements were destroyed; the town and fort of Montreal were taken; all the victims who fell into the hands of the Indians were butchered with unheard-of cruelties.

After spreading blood, horror, and consternation in every direction until October, they retired, with threats that not one Frenchman should be found living in Canada at the opening of the next spring. In the mean time, England had formally declared war against France. From this time, the war against

* Bancroft's U. States, vol. iii., p. 178.   † Martin's Louisiana, vol. i., p. 126–128.

New France was waged with vigor and perseverance, both by England and the Iroquois tribes, until the year 1696, when the treaty of Ryswick put a close to hostilities. While the English fleets and troops had ravaged all the province on the sea-board, and up the St. Lawrence as far as Quebec and Montreal, the Iroquois allies had repeatedly ravaged the upper settlements, yet at the close of this war the population of Canada had increased to 13,000 souls.*

[A.D. 1696.] After many vacillations relative to their course of policy with the French, the Western tribes became settled in their determination. The prudence of the memorable La Motte Cadillac, who had been appointed governor at Mackinaw, confirmed the friendship of the neighboring tribes, and a party of Ottawâs, Potawatamies, and Chippewâs surprised and routed a band of Iroquois, returning with piles of beaver and scalps as trophies.

Soon afterward, Frontenac, then seventy-four years old, conducted an invasion against the Onondagas and Oneidas. He ravaged their country, destroyed the corn, burned their villages, and caused the enemies of the French to seek safety in flight. In August he encamped near the Salt Springs, upon the site of Salina. Frontenac refused to push his victorious arms against the Cayugas; he declined to risk more, as if uncertain of the result. "It was time for him to repose," and the army returned to Montreal. He had humbled, but not subdued, the Five Nations, and left them to suffer from a famine. They were left to recover their lands and their spirit, having pushed hostilities so far that no negotiation for peace was likely to succeed.†

[A.D. 1697.] So soon as this war was fairly terminated, France proceeded to occupy and settle the Valley of the Mississippi, pushing her colonies into it from the North and South at the same time. In the North they entered from Canada and the lakes, by way of the Illinois and Wabash Rivers; at the South they advanced from Mobile Bay and River, and through the passes of the Mississippi at the Balize.

* Martin's Louisiana, vol. i., p. 137.   † Bancroft's U. States, vol. iii., p. 191.

CHAPTER III.

ADVANCE OF THE FRENCH SETTLEMENTS FROM CANADA UPON THE UPPER MISSISSIPPI AND OHIO RIVERS, TO THE CLOSE OF THE FRENCH WAR.—A.D. 1696 TO 1764.

Argument.—Settlements near the Missions, and La Salle's Trading-posts on the Illinois.—At Peoria.—Kaskaskia.—Missionaries visit the Lower Mississippi.—Detroit settled in 1701, by La Motte Cadillac.—Peace with the Iroquois and Western Tribes.—English Jealousy.—Hostile Foxes humbled in 1713.—Settlements on the Upper Mississippi from 1712 to 1720.—Accession of Emigrants from Canada and Louisiana.—Renault and two hundred Miners arrive.—Trade between the Illinois and Mobile.—Agriculture in the Illinois and Wabash Countries.—Ohio River unexplored.—Fort Chartres built in 1721.—Villages in its Vicinity.—Jesuits' College at Kaskaskia.—Advance of the French South of the Niagara River.—On Ontario and Champlain.—Fort Niagara built in 1726.—Crown Point in 1727.—Ticonderoga in 1731.—Tuscarawas join the Five Nations.—Post St. Vincent's erected in 1735.—Presque Isle in 1740.—Agriculture of the Wabash in 1746.—English Jealousy.—Villages of the Illinois Country in 1751.—Population of Kaskaskia.—French advance to the Head Waters of the Alleghany River in 1753.—Forts Le Beuf, Venango, Sandusky.—Ohio Company of Virginia.—Gist visits the Ohio Region as Agent of the Company in 1753.—English Colonies remonstrate against the Advance of the French.—Major Washington Commissioner to Le Beuf.—His Mission unsuccessful.—Governor Dinwiddie rouses the People of Virginia to resist the French on the Ohio.—Captain Trent advances to the Ohio in 1754.—Lieutenant Ward's Detachment captured by the French.—Fort Duquesne erected by the French.—Colonel Washington marches a Detachment to the Monongahela.—Captures a Detachment under M. Jumonville, who is killed.—Colonel Washington surrenders "Fort Necessity" to the French, and retires to Fort Cumberland.—French Forbearance and Moderation.—Arrival of General Braddock at Alexandria.—Preparations for the Capture of Fort Duquesne.—General Braddock marches from Fort Cumberland for the Ohio.—Falls into an Ambuscade on the Monongahela, and utterly defeated.—French at Duquesne undisturbed for two Years.—General Forbes, in 1758, advances to the Ohio.—Occupies Fort Duquesne.—All Canada falls under the British Arms.—France relinquishes New France and Louisiana, by the Treaties of 1762 and 1763, to Spain and Great Britain.

[A.D. 1696–1700.] THE trading-posts established by La Salle, and the missions south and southwest of Lake Michigan, were points of attraction around which emigrants and adventurers from Canada were annually collected, until each became a small French settlement. The frequent visits of La Salle among the Miami Indians, and those on the Illinois, had prepared the way for further intercourse and trade by his successors. The glowing descriptions of the country given by him and his predecessors had been such, that the imaginations of adventurers were filled with the ideas of a terrestrial paradise in the delightful regions of the Illinois and the Mississippi. The climate, too, was said to be comparatively mild, and the forests to abound in the choicest products of fruits, which yielded a spontaneous supply. Such descriptions served as strong temptations to the inhabitant of the cold and comparatively sterile shores of the St. Lawrence and the lakes. Adventurers continued to advance from the older settlements of Quebec and Montreal to the more fertile and temperate region in the Far West. Their route was through the lakes first traversed by Marquette in 1673, and by La Salle in 1679, and through the Straits of Mackinaw to the mouth of the St. Joseph's River of Michigan, and to Chicago Creek of Illinois. From these points they passed over the dividing ridge to the head branches of the Illinois, the Des Pleins on the west, and the Kankakee on the east. There were still living many who had traversed these routes with La Salle in the various journeys which he made in this region; others had volunteered to accompany the Chevalier de Tonti in his fruitless search for the unfortunate La Salle and his colony, which had been lost in Texas. Some of these still lingered in the Illinois country in the capacity of settlers, traders, or *voyageurs*. The route had become familiar, and civilized communities had been formed at several points upon the Illinois and Mississippi. Before the close of the seventeenth century, "Old Kaskaskia" had been founded in the "terrestrial paradise," and many desired to leave Canada to enter its delightful abodes. Missionary stations had grown into regular parishes. They had been formed on the Illinois as high as Peoria Lake, and Fathers Gravier and Marest had long had the care of their little flock; and up to the year 1705, they had a colony of converted Indians near Lake Peoria, who shared their apostolic care. Nor were other points west and south of the Illinois country neglected. Kaskaskia had already become a populous and happy village, and other settlements and towns were rapidly rising into note. Missionaries, at this early day, had penetrated west of the Mississippi, and south as far as the mouth of Red River. Fathers Montigny and Davion had visited the Yazoo and Tansas Indians, and had established a missionary station near the promontory of Fort Adams, which for many years afterward was known as "La Roche à Davion." St. Comé had likewise established a mission among the Natchez Indians.[*]

[*] Martin's Louisiana, vol. i., p. 148–152.

Such had been the inveterate hostility of the Five Nations until this time, that the whole region south of the lakes, from Fort Frontenac to Green Bay, was a savage wilderness, traversed only by a few hardy traders and missionaries. Not a French village or settlement existed south of the great lakes, from the St. Lawrence to the Illinois country on the west. Yet many of the Western tribes were kind and hospitable to the French emigrants, and mutual confidence prevailed. Amity was confirmed by treaties formally made with the principal tribes. In the summer of the year 1700, the Ottawâs and Hurons from Mackinaw assembled at Montreal; and the four upper nations of the Iroquois " sent deputies to Montreal to weep for the French who had fallen in the war."* After a rapid negotiation, peace was ratified between the Iroquois on one side, and France and her Western allies on the other. " A written treaty was made, to which each nation placed for itself a symbol: the Senecas and Onondagas drew a spider; the Cayugas, a calumet; the Oneidas, a forked stick; and the Mohawks, a bear." It was declared, also, " that war should cease between the French allies and the Sioux; that peace should reach beyond the Mississippi."†

Thus did France open the way for the peaceful extension of her settlements into the western parts of Upper Canada. " In the summer of 1701, in the month of June, De la Motte Cadillac, with a Jesuit missionary and one hundred men, took possession of the site of Detroit, and formed a settlement" on the beautiful river of the lakes. " The country on the Detroit River and Lake St. Clair was deemed the loveliest in Canada." France now claimed all the country south of the lakes, and upon all the streams occupied by the tribes in alliance with her, and comprising all the territory drained by the lakes and the St. Lawrence; and this extensive region was called Canada, or New France.

The jealousy and bigotry of England never slept. No effort was omitted which might stir up hostilities between the " Five Nations" and the French of Canada. New York claimed all the territory south of Lake Ontario; and the provincial government looked with jealous suspicion upon all friendly intercourse between the Indians and the French traders or missionaries. In the autumn of the year 1700, after the treaty of

* Bancroft's Hist. of U. States, vol. iii., p. 193.　　　† Idem, p. 194.

Montreal with four of the Iroquois nations, in the belief that "the influence of the Jesuits gave to France its only power over the Five Nations, the Legislature of New York made a law for hanging every popish priest that should come voluntarily into the province."* This might be said to be the first act of legislative intolerance in New York.

[A.D. 1705.] The elder Marquis de Vaudreuil was now governor of Canada, and had lost no opportunity for securing the friendship of the Five Nations of New York. The four Western nations south of Lake Ontario still adhered to the French interests. The Mohawks and some Eastern towns alone were under British influence.

[A.D. 1712.] Mutual friendship and confidence continued between the French and all the Western tribes; and emigrants from the St. Lawrence continued to advance, by way of the lakes, to Detroit, and to the Illinois country. Towns had grown up near the missionary stations and trading-posts: "Old Kaskaskia" had become the capital of the Illinois country. As early as the year 1712, land-titles were issued for a "common field" at Kaskaskia; and deeds and titles came in use to designate the acquisitions of private enterprise. The traders had already opened a commerce in skins and furs with the remote port of Isle Dauphin, in Mobile Bay. Intercourse was opened between Quebec of the North and the infant colony of Louisiana in the South; the latter being a dependence of Canada, or New France.

[A.D. 1713.] England, in 1711, had declared war against France, and vainly endeavored to restrict her pretensions south of the St. Lawrence and the Eastern lakes. Along the Atlantic coast war had been waged, with alternate success, between the colonies of New England and of New France; and each were aided by their savage allies respectively. But in the West, France had triumphed over Indian hostility, until English and Mohawk emissaries had penetrated to the Far West, to excite the restless Algonquins to war against them. With none of these was peace more uncertain than with the Ottogamies, or Foxes, "a nation passionate and untamable, springing into new life from every defeat, and although reduced in the number of their warriors, yet present every where, by their ferocious enterprise and savage daring." It was not until the year 1713

* Bancroft's U. States, vol. iii., p. 194.

that they were finally subdued. Resolving to burn Detroit, they had pitched their lodgings near the fort, which M. Dubuisson, with but twenty Frenchmen, defended. Aware of their intention, he summoned his Indian allies from the chase; and about the middle of May, Ottawâs and Hurons, Potawatamies and one branch of the Sacks, Illinois, Menomonies, and even Osages and Missouris, each nation with its own ensign, came to his relief. So wide was the influence of the missionaries in the West. "Father," said they, "behold thy children compass thee around. We will, if need be, gladly die for our father; only take care of our wives and our children, and spread a little grass over our bodies, to protect them against the flies."

"The warriors of the Fox nation, far from destroying Detroit, were themselves besieged, and at last compelled to surrender at discretion. Those who bore arms were ruthlessly murdered; the rest were distributed among the confederates as slaves, to be saved or massacred at the will of their masters."*

[A.D. 1719.] Population was extending from Mobile upon the Mississippi; and soon after, M. Crozat received the monopoly of trade in Louisiana; his trading-posts were established in the Illinois country, and trade began to assume the regular channels of commerce. Under the Western Company, soon afterward, Philippe Francis Renault, "director-general of the mines of Louisiana," with two hundred miners and artificers, arrived in the Illinois country. This arrival gave a great accession to the French population, and introduced many useful mechanics into the settlements. Illinois was deemed by the company to be a region of mines immensely valuable, which were to enrich the capitalists of Europe.

Fortunately, the hopes of the company concerning the valuable products of the mines were doomed to disappointment, and the public mind was directed more intensely to agriculture. Mines there were, of iron, lead, copper, and perhaps of silver and gold; but they were reserved for a race of men who were to live a century after the dissolution of the company, when monopolies should cease. The richest mines of the country, at this early period, were found in the prolific and inexhaustible soil, which was free to the industry of all classes. Thus an overruling Providence shaped the destiny of the country, which was to become the granary for nations.

* Bancroft's U. States, vol. iii., p. 224.

[A.D. 1720.] By the year 1720, a lucrative trade had sprung up between the Illinois country and the province of Lower Louisiana. Not only the furs and peltries of the Northern tribes, but the grain, flour, and other agricultural products of the Upper Mississippi, were transported down the river to Mobile, and thence to the West Indies and to Europe; and in return, the luxuries and refinements of European capitals were carried to the banks of the Illinois and Kaskaskia Rivers.*

Agriculture had been early introduced around the missionary stations upon the Illinois and at " Old Kaskaskia," and many of the grains of Europe had been naturalized to the climate. Wheat had been found to succeed well as a staple product. The maize, or Indian corn, was in its native soil. The culinary vegetables of the Old World, as well as of the New, yielded a most abundant product. The forest produced the native vine in great profusion, besides many luxuries unknown to Europe. The soil was productive beyond all belief, and a moderate toil supplied every comfort, and richly rewarded the care of the husbandman. Compared with New France, the climate was mild in summer, and the rigors of a Canadian winter unknown. In such a region, should we wonder if, in their peaceful and contented villages, with all the charities of Christianity to soften the ills of life, they should have deemed this region a " terrestrial paradise ?"

Nor had the early French confined their discoveries and settlements to the Illinois country. As early as the year 1705, traders and hunters had penetrated the fertile regions of the Wabash; and from this region, at this early date, fifteen thousand hides and skins had been collected, and sent to Mobile for the European market. In the year 1716, the French population on the Wabash had become sufficiently numerous to constitute an important settlement, which kept up a lucrative trade with Mobile by means of traders and voyageurs.† Nor was the route from Lake Erie unknown. For many years this route had been familiar to the *voyageurs* and *courriers du bois*, who ascended the Miami of the Lake by the St. Mary's branch, and, after a portage of three leagues, passed the summit level, and floated down a shallow branch of the Wabash. In the year 1718 this route had been used for two years;‡ for it was established in the year 1716.

* Martin, vol. i., p. 164–188. † Idem.
‡ Bancroft's U. States, vol. iii., p. 346.

At this early period the Ohio River was comparatively unknown, and all that portion below the mouth of the Wabash was known as the continuation of the Wabash River. The Ohio, above that point, was known, only by report, as the "River of the Iroquois," which was often called the *Hoio* by the Indians. In the French maps of that day, the Ohio River did not occupy half the space allotted to the Illinois. Father Hennepin, in his early missionary labors, and a few other daring missionaries, had visited some of the northern tributaries of the Ohio before the exploration of the Mississippi, under the direction of La Salle; but such had been the implacable hostility of the Iroquois confederacy to the French colonists, that the greater portion of the Ohio River was imperfectly known for nearly forty years after the first exploration of the Mississippi.

Settlements continued to be formed upon the Mississippi below the mouth of the Illinois, and France resolved to circumvent the English provinces on the Atlantic coast by a cordon of military posts, from the lakes of Canada on the north to the Gulf of Mexico on the south, as first suggested by La Salle himself, on his visit to Paris in the year 1684. His plans were now about to be adopted, for the purpose of occupying the great Valley of the Mississippi before any Englishman had crossed the mountains from their Atlantic colonies. This same year the commandant on the Illinois, M. Boisbriant, removed his headquarters to the bank of the Mississippi, twenty-five miles below the village of Kaskaskia.*

The first important step in the accomplishment of this great object was taken in the year 1720. Near the close of this year, arrangements were made for the construction of a strong fortress in the Illinois country, to serve as the headquarters of Upper Louisiana. The site had been selected, and Fort Chartres was begun, on the east side of the Mississippi, about sixty-five miles below the mouth of the Missouri. It was designed by the ministers to be one of the strongest fortresses on the continent, and its walls were built of strong and solid masonry. At the end of eighteen months, and after great labor and expense, Fort Chartres was completed. Its massy ruins, one hundred years afterward, were overgrown with vines and forest-trees, almost impenetrable to the traveler.

* See Martin's Louisiana, vol. i., p. 224.

[A.D. 1725.] Soon after the construction of Fort Chartres, the villages of Cahokia, Prairie du Rocher, and some others, sprung into note in its vicinity. All the settlements from the Illinois to the Kaskaskia continued to extend and multiply. In the year 1721, the Jesuits had established a monastery and a college in the village of Kaskaskia. Four years afterward, the village of Kaskaskia became a chartered town; and a grant of Louis XV. guarantied the "commons" as the pasture-grounds for the stock of the town. Emigrants, under the favor and protection of the crown, continued to settle the fertile region of the "American Bottom," and Fort Chartres became, not only the headquarters of the commandant in Upper Louisiana, but the center of life and fashion in the West. It was for many years the most celebrated fortress in all the Valley of the Mississippi.

Although the French had made but little advance upon the upper tributaries of the Ohio, yet they had obtained a footing in the Iroquois country, south of Lake Ontario, and east of Niagara River, early in the eighteenth century. Missionaries and traders had penetrated into the interior as far as the sources of the Alleghany River. Joncaire, a French trader and agent, had been many years in the country south of the west end of Ontario; and in the year 1721 he had been adopted as a Seneca, and built his house on the site of Lewistown, where La Salle had erected his rude palisade forty years before. He had acquired the confidence of the Senecas, and exerted great influence over them.* In 1726 Fort Niagara was built, near the mouth of Niagara River, and the French flag waved over its walls, the key to Lake Erie.

Although the English had not crossed the mountains, they had early disputed with France her claim to the territory west of Lake Champlain and south of the St. Lawrence. In the treaty of Ryswick, in 1697, England had failed to obtain from France a relinquishment of her dominion over the territory lying south of the St. Lawrence River and Lake Ontario. Ten years afterward, the French and English provinces were engaged in a sanguinary war, which was terminated by the treaty of Utrecht in 1713. This treaty had left the southern limit of Canada unchanged, and the Iroquois confederacy more firm in their adherence to the French interests. French trad-

* Bancroft's U. States, vol. iii., p. 341.

ers and Jesuit missionaries had free intercourse among many of the Western bands and tribes, as well as among those upon the head waters of the Alleghany River; and while the English agent, Burnet, had built a trading-post at Oswego, near the eastern end of Lake Ontario, in 1722,* the French were extending trading-posts and missions along the shores of Lake Champlain, and as far south as Lake George, in the eastern part of the province of New York, as well as upon many of the southern tributaries of Lakes Erie and Ontario. As early as the year 1724, settlements had been extended as far as Crown Point, on the west side of Champlain; and this point was strongly fortified in 1727.† Four years after, in 1731, Ticonderoga, on the west side of the lake, was a strong French fortress; and the Mohawks looked upon the French as their allies and protectors.

The feeling of the Five Nations toward the English had been more or less alienated, since the treaty of Utrecht, by the addition of another nation to the confederacy. This was the hostile part of the Tuscaroras, from the western part of North Carolina. The Tuscaroras were once a formidable tribe; but having been embroiled in hostilities with the English of Carolina, and having their power weakened and their tribe divided by British intrigue, the hostile party left their country, to join their kindred in the western part of New York. They arrived there late in the summer of 1713; and having been welcomed by the confederates, they settled in the vicinity of Oneida Lake, and were adopted into the confederacy as the *sixth nation*. Harassed as they had been by the English of Carolina, they were not likely to form any alliance with them in New York.‡ From this time the confederacy was known as the "Six Nations."

[A.D. 1735.] The settlements upon the Illinois and Wabash Rivers continued to increase, and were successively protected by military posts. In the year 1735 the post of Vincennes was erected, and in later times was called Post St. Vincent.§ For many years it was an important military station. It was situated on the bank of the Wabash, one hundred and fifty miles above its mouth, and was designed to command the lower settlements. The upper settlements at this time were sparsely

* Bancroft's U. States, vol. iii., p. 342. † Idem, p. 193, 194.
‡ Idem, p. 322. § Idem, p. 346.

distributed upon the river and its tributaries, nearly three hundred miles above Vincennes.

[A.D. 1740.] The year 1740 found the French settlements extending south from Lake Erie, upon its southern tributaries, and upon the sources of the Ohio. Forts and military posts began to appear along the northern bank of the Ohio, and generally near the junction of its principal tributaries. Presque Isle, upon the present site of Erie, in Pennsylvania, became a military post almost coeval with that of St. Vincent on the Wabash. From Presque Isle a chain of posts extended down the Alleghany to the junction of the Monongahela, and thence to the mouth of the Wabash.

[A.D. 1746.] In the year 1746, agriculture on the Wabash was still flourishing, and the same year six hundred barrels of flour were manufactured and shipped to the city of New Orleans, besides large quantities of hides, peltry, tallow, and bees' wax.* The Upper Wabash, almost to its source, had become the seat of a large settlement of quiet, industrious people, who were mainly devoted to agriculture, but enjoying also the bounty of nature, found profusely in the forests, as well as in the beautiful lakes and rivers. The climate here, like that on the Illinois, was more congenial than was to be found in the regions of Canada.

The settlements in the Illinois country continued to increase. Those on the Illinois alone, in the year 1730, embraced one hundred and forty French families, besides about six hundred converted Indians,† many traders, voyageurs, and *courriers du bois*. The Jesuit college at Kaskaskia continued to flourish, until the irruption of hostilities with Great Britain.

[A.D. 1749.] It was not until the year 1749 that the French authorities regularly explored the Ohio River, to ascertain its distance and relative position to the Atlantic colonies of Great Britain. They now explored the country east of the Ohio, and upon its tributaries eastward to their sources in the Alleghany Mountains. Alliances of friendship and trade were formed with the various tribes and towns west of the mountains,‡ and within the western portions of the provinces of New York, Pennsylvania, and Virginia, as claimed under their royal charters.

---

* Martin's Louisiana, vol. i., p. 316.   † North American Review
‡ See Stoddart's Sketches of Louisiana, p. 66.

[A.D. 1750.] The ever-watchful eye of England had been directed to the rapid extension of the French settlements south and west of the lakes. The court of St. James became impatient again to measure arms with France in America, to cross the Alleghany Mountains, and to contend for the fertile and boundless valleys of the West. The settlements of the English provinces were as yet restricted to a narrow and comparatively unproductive strip of territory east of those mountains, and England pretended to claim westward to the Pacific Ocean. She sought every occasion to enlist the savages in her interest, and to incite them to hostilities against the French. She took steps to rouse her colonies into a provincial war in the West, in hope of curtailing the growing power of France in the Valley of the Mississippi. To stimulate personal interest and individual enterprise, a large grant had already been made to the "Ohio Company," to be located on the waters of the Ohio River, to the extent of six hundred thousand acres of choice lands.

The French did not recede from their possessions, but advanced upon the "River of the Iroquois," which to their delighted eyes became the "Belle Rivière" of the West. The Iroquois confederacy had now become reconciled to the French, and many were willing to join them in resisting the claims and encroachments of the English provinces west of the mountains.

[A.D. 1751.] Up to this time, the "Illinois country," east of the Upper Mississippi, contained six distinct settlements, with their respective villages. These were, 1. Cahokia, near the mouth of Cahokia Creek, and nearly five miles below the present site of St. Louis; 2. St. Philip, forty-five miles below the last, and four miles above Fort Chartres, on the east side of the Mississippi; 3. Fort Chartres, on the east bank of the Mississippi, twelve miles above Kaskaskia; 4. Kaskaskia, situated upon the Kaskaskia River, five miles above its mouth, upon a peninsula, and within two miles of the Mississippi River; 5. Prairie du Rocher, near Fort Chartres; 6. St. Geneviève, on the west side of the Mississippi, and about one mile from its bank, upon Gabarre Creek. These are among the oldest towns in what was long known as the Illinois country. Kaskaskia in its best days, under the French regime, was quite a large town, containing two or three thousand inhabitants. But after it passed from the crown of France, its population for many years did not exceed fifteen hundred souls. Under the

British dominion the population decreased to four hundred and sixty souls, in 1773.

[A.D. 1753.] The French court was well aware of the importance of the great Western valley. It was now known that if there were no rich mines of gold and silver north of the Ohio and east of the Mississippi, there was a more inexhaustible mine in the fertility of the soil and the mildness of the climate. A spirit of agricultural industry had been infused into the Western settlements; in a few years more, Upper Louisiana, which embraced the Ohio region, might become the store-house for France and Western Europe. These advantages were not to be lost without an effort. Nor was the court of Versailles unapprised of the determination of England to secure to herself these valuable resources. Jealous of every movement of the French toward the "Belle Rivière," the British government protested against the occupation of the territories south of the lakes, which they claimed as a part of their Atlantic provinces. The French had explored a portion of the country more than half a century before, and their colonies on the Illinois and Mississippi were more than fifty years old, while the English had not a single settlement west of the mountains. France was resolved to establish her claim by actual possession and military occupation. The Marquis of Duquesne, governor of Canada, determined to secure the beautiful region on the head waters of the Alleghany River, and south of Lake Erie. Presque Isle was strongly fortified; a fort was erected at Lake *Le Beuf*, fifteen miles from Presque Isle; another, superintended by Legardeur St. Pierre, a knight of St. Louis, was built at the mouth of French Creek, known as Fort Venango.* Others were in a state of progression on the Sandusky River, and at suitable points on the Ohio. The Governor of New France determined not only to hold military possession of the country, but likewise to restrict the English settlements to the eastern side of the mountains.

The ministers of the British crown had watched with jealous apprehension the advances of the French from Canada to the Ohio River. Border wars and disturbances began to spring up between the subjects of the respective powers. England, desirous of enlisting individual interest and enterprise in settling the Ohio country, had made a liberal offer of lands west

---

* Martin's Louisiana, vol. i., p. 322.

of the mountains. The "Ohio Company," formed of wealthy gentlemen chiefly from Virginia, prepared to locate their grant of six hundred thousand acres in select tracts on the waters of the Monongahela, and in the vicinity of the Ohio itself, including a portion of the region already occupied by the French.* At this time no English settlement existed west of the Alleghany Mountains, although traders and emissaries from Virginia had occasionally traversed the country.†

The French now held actual possession of all the northern and western portions of New York, along the southern shores of the St. Lawrence, of Lakes Ontario and Erie, besides all the eastern and western shores of Lake Champlain, and northward to the St. Lawrence. The former allies of the English were still in the French interest, from the Niagara to the Wabash. The English colonies were restricted to the Green Mountains in the north and to the Alleghany ranges in the south, as their western boundaries. Crown Point and Ticonderoga, on Lake Champlain, were then strong French posts. In Virginia but few settlements had extended west of the Blue Ridge. The site of the old town of Winchester was then a dense forest, although Virginia claimed jurisdiction westward to the Mississippi. The remote frontier post of "Fort Cumberland," in Maryland, had not been erected, and the route by Will's Creek was scarcely known. All beyond and to the west was a savage wilderness, except the French settlements on the north side of the Ohio.

Although the British provinces claimed westward to the Mississippi, the whole region west of the Blue Ridge was unknown to them except by rumor, and the statements of a few traders or emissaries, who, at remote intervals, had visited the West. Occasionally adventurers from Pennsylvania and New York had penetrated to the Miami Indians for the purpose of trade, or from a native propensity for solitary rambles.

The "Ohio Company," which had been formed as early as 1748, now dispatched Christopher Gist, a frontier settler, as an agent, to explore the country, and to report the result of his explorations and discoveries. As a pretext for this arduous and dangerous enterprise, he was sent in the capacity of a trader, whose ostensible object was to carry on a friendly traf-

* Sparks's Writings of Washington, vol. i.; also vol. ii., Appendix, "Ohio Company."
† Martin's Louisiana, vol. i., p. 160.

fick with the Indians, but in fact to gain over their good-will to the English, by presents of guns, ammunition, and trinkets, whereby a neutrality, if not an alliance, might be secured in case of any collision between the English and French colonies. But the principal object of Mr. Gist's visit was to spy out the movements and plans of the French, and the state of feeling among the tribes. For this purpose, he penetrated by land to the Ohio River, and thence down that stream as far as the mouth of the Great Miami.* Thence he explored the country near the Miami as far north as the towns of the Twightwees, or Miami Indians, whose hunting-grounds were then upon Loramie's Creek, about fifty miles north of Dayton, in the State of Ohio.

After a short sojourn among these western Indians, Gist returned to Virginia, having accomplished but little, and having acquired but little satisfactory information relative to the principal object of his mission, and yet not without serious alarm for his personal safety.† He represented the French to be in great force on the southern shore of Lake Erie, at several points from Sandusky River to Presque Isle; also upon French Creek, a tributary of the Alleghany River. Notwithstanding this intelligence, the company established a small trading-post the following year upon Loramie's Creek. This, however, was soon afterward broken up by the French.

For several years the provinces of Virginia, Pennsylvania, and New York had been much agitated by the advance of the French south of Lake Erie, and from an apprehension of hostilities by the Indian tribes within the territory claimed by those provinces respectively. In this state of things, the British minister, apprehensive of a rupture in this quarter, had instructed the royal governor of Virginia to build two forts near the Ohio River, for the double purpose of keeping the French in check, and of securing the friendship of the Indians by driving off lawless intruders. At the same time, thirty pieces of light artillery and eighty barrels of powder were shipped from England for the use of these forts when constructed.‡ But in this England was too late: the Governor of Canada had already anticipated this movement by several French forts, which commanded the country north and west of the Ohio.

---

* See "Cincinnati in 1841," p. 14, 15.   † Sparks's Writings of Washington, vol. i.
‡ Sparks's Life of Washington, vol. i., p. 21.

When this was made known to the Governor of Virginia, he resolved to take a decided stand. He determined first to send a special commissioner to remonstrate with the French commandant south of the lakes against the encroachments made by the French posts and settlements upon the territory claimed by his Britannic majesty. Accordingly, Major George Washington was duly commissioned, and sent to the headquarters of the French commandant. After a long and toilsome journey through an uninhabited wilderness, he reached Fort Venango, on the present site of the town of Franklin, in the State of Pennsylvania. But the commandant was at Lake le Beuf, whither Major Washington proceeded without delay. He had been instructed to demand of the French commandant the objects and designs of his government, and to assert the claims of Virginia in the name and by the authority of the British crown. He was also privately instructed to examine carefully and report such points in his route as were suitable for military posts, and especially "the Forks," or the point at the junction of the Alleghany and Monongahela Rivers.

He reached the headquarters at Le Beuf in the middle of December, and laid his instructions before M. de St. Pierre. But little satisfaction was obtained. France claimed the country by the right of discovery and settlement, as well as by military possession. These are the strongest of all titles to a savage country. England claimed it by virtue of her first royal charters, and especially that of Virginia, which extended its limits "westward to the South Sea," or Pacific Ocean, at a time when the distance was unknown, and was supposed to be not very remote. France could not recognize such a claim in opposition to her own.

On the same principle, England might claim, not only all the lands east of the Mississippi, but those also beyond it. France admitted the claims of England to extend westward to the sources of all the Atlantic rivers, and even to the most western ranges of the Alleghany Mountains. She denied that Great Britain could justly claim beyond that limit, especially as the country had been discovered, explored, and settled by colonies from New France long before England knew of such a country as the Ohio Valley.

The commissioner, Major Washington, was treated with the utmost courtesy, but his demands were disregarded. In reply to the demands of the Governor of Virginia, the Chevalier M. de St. Pierre, commandant south of the lakes, replied in the most courteous terms, " That the summons could not be complied with, as it did not belong to him to discuss treaties; that the message should have been sent to the Marquis Duquesne, governor of New France, under whose instructions he acted, and whose orders he should be careful to obey."* Washington returned, and, after a tedious and difficult journey, mostly on foot, in the dead of winter, reached Williamsburg, the seat of the provincial government, on the 16th of January, 1754.

[A.D. 1754.] The result of the mission was of course unsatisfactory. Governor Dinwiddie used every means to rouse the patriotic enthusiasm and the indignation of the people against the invaders of his majesty's dominions. He caused Major Washington's journal to be published, to show the insidious designs of the French, and no means were left untried to excite the people to rise and expel the invaders. Troops were raised by calls for volunteers, as well as by enlistments, and a liberal bounty in lands was guarantied to the soldiers. Major Washington was commissioned a lieutenant colonel in the provincial army; military stores and munitions were collected and pushed forward toward the frontiers: a military post was built at Will's Creek, and known as Fort Cumberland.†

The governors of New York, Pennsylvania, Maryland, and North Carolina were invoked to make common cause against the enemies of the British crown. " The Ohio Company," in which the governor was doubtless deeply interested, lent its utmost aid and influence. It aided to push forward a company of troops, under Captain Trent, to take possession of the country near the Monongahela, and southward to the Ohio.

The governor's instructions were of a warlike character: no less than " to drive away, kill, and destroy, or seize as prisoners all persons not subjects of the King of Great Britain who should attempt to take possession of lands on the Ohio, or any of its tributaries."‡

Captain Trent detached Lieutenant Ward, with forty men, to occupy and fortify " the Forks," or point of land immediately above the junction of the Alleghany and Monongahela Rivers. This point had been recommended by Major Washington as a suitable position for a military post, and it had

* Sparks's Writings of Washington, vol. i., p. 30.   † Idem, p. 36, 37.   ‡ Ibidem.

been determined to occupy it with a fort and trading-post. Lieutenant Ward had no sooner accomplished the object for which he was detached, than he was compelled to abandon the enterprise and surrender the post to the French. The latter had been apprised of the movements from the provinces against them, as well as of the small force which had been advanced to the Ohio and Monongahela. They resolved to defeat such designs, and to prevent the occupation of the country by English troops. War was not their desire, if they could maintain their rights without it.

It was about the middle of April that the bold Contrecœur descended the Alleghany River with a strong force of French and Indians. The alarm of the detachment under Lieutenant Ward magnified the hostile force to one thousand French and Indian warriors, with a fleet of three hundred canoes, thirty barges, and eighteen pieces of cannon. Resistance was vain. Lieutenant Ward was compelled to surrender the post without a semblance of defense. The French desired to avoid hostilities; and Lieutenant Ward and his detachment were permitted quietly to evacuate the position, and, with their arms and military stores, peaceably to return to the frontier post of Fort Cumberland. The French commander began to erect a regular and strong fortification at "the Forks," which he called "Fort Duquesne," in honor of the Governor of Canada and New France. In a few months it became one of the strongest fortified places west of the mountains, and but little inferior to Fort Chartres itself.

The result of Lieutenant Ward's expedition caused great excitement in Virginia and the neighboring provinces. Troops were expeditiously raised and pushed forward to Fort Cumberland. Virginia determined to enforce her claims by an appeal to arms; and she was well assured that England would rejoice to make it a national war. England had long sought occasion to humble the growing power of her rival in North America. The occasion and pretext had now arrived. France was determined not to yield, unless by the fate of arms, to the domineering claims of Great Britain. She accordingly began the construction of forts in most of the prominent points south of the lakes and north of the Ohio. In each new post was stationed a small garrison; others were re-enforced; and preparations were made daily for the approaching contest. The

Indian tribes, were conciliated; and some were united into an alliance offensive and defensive.

The provinces were in a state of high excitement, and troops were organizing more or less from New York to North Carolina. A strong detachment of Virginia troops, under Colonel Washington, was advanced into the country near the Monongahela. At the Great Meadows, about thirty miles southeast from Fort Duquesne, Colonel Washington received intelligence that a detachment of French troops from Fort Duquesne, under M. Jumonville, were reconnoitering the country, for the purpose of capturing such English as might have entered the disputed territory. This detachment consisted of fifty men, including some Indians. Colonel Washington sought to surprise this small force, and finally succeeded on the 28th of May. M. Jumonville and ten of his men were killed, and twenty-two were taken prisoners; and but few escaped. This was doubtless a rash movement on the part of Colonel Washington, and scarcely to be justified; for the French, taken by surprise, were not inclined to resist.*

The French account of this affair, which is uncontroverted, and admitted by Mr. Sparks, declares that the detachment of M. Jumonville were surprised by a very superior force, while totally unconscious that an enemy was near; that the first intimation of the presence of any hostile force was a volley from their fire-arms, while engaged in their camp duties; that the fire was repeated, notwithstanding their submission and their imploring attitude, until they were compelled to fire in self-protection, by which the Virginians had one man killed and two wounded.†

The disaster of M. Jumonville's detachment, and the hostile attitude of the provincial troops, were soon known at the head-quarters of the French commandant, and a retaliation and reprisal were concerted. No delay was necessary or proper; but as the provincials were represented in great force, he deemed it proper to draw re-enforcements from other points nearer the lake and Presque Isle. Colonel Washington, apprehending an attack from a stronger force, immediately fell

---

* Martin errs greatly in reference to this transaction. He says *Jumonville alone* was killed, and all the party surrendered; but the account by Sparks, in his "Writings of Washington," gives the true state of facts, taken from the French archives, which we have followed. See Sparks, vol. i., p. 36–40; also, Martin, vol. i., p. 324.

† Sparks's Life of Washington, vol. i., p. 46, 47.

back to the Great Meadows, a few miles west of Uniontown, and near the western side of the Laurel Ridge. Here he erected a fortified camp, and called it "Fort Necessity." By this time he received a re-enforcement, which augmented his force to something over four hundred men.*

Preparations were made for resisting an attack, which was daily apprehended, and the camp was protected by a breastwork and surrounded by a ditch.

On the 3d of July, early in the morning, the French and Indians made their appearance before the fort and upon the adjacent hills; but the attack was not commenced until about ten o'clock in the forenoon. The investing force consisted of about nine hundred men, including French and Indians, under the command of a brother of M. Jumonville, M. Villiers, who had left Fort Chartres with the express purpose of revenging the death of his brother.† The attack was urged with great impetuosity and perseverance, and as vigorously resisted. During the attack, which continued until sunset, the French and Indians fought with great ardor from their positions, concealed behind trees, or lying in the tall grass which covered the meadow. The Virginians fought partly from behind their breast-work and partly from the ditch which surrounded the fort. At sunset a flag was sent to the fort demanding its surrender. Considering the danger of his situation, Colonel Washington agreed to enter upon terms of capitulation, in order to preserve the remainder of his detachment, which had bravely defended themselves for nine hours, under a most destructive fire.

The loss of the Americans in this severe engagement was fifty-eight killed and wounded, besides the loss of two independent companies, increasing their entire loss to seventy killed and wounded.‡

Articles of capitulation were drawn up and signed, with the following stipulations, viz.: the fort was to be surrendered upon honorable terms; the troops were permitted to march out with their arms and baggage, and to retire unmolested to the nearest post on the eastern side of the mountains, upon the express condition that no further settlements or forts should be attempted by the English west of the mountains for one year. The French faithfully observed the conditions, and Colonel

---

* Sparks's Life of Washington, vol. i., p. 52. † Martin's Louisiana, vol. i., p. 324.
‡ Marshall's Life of Washington, vol. ii., p. 11.

Washington marched his detachment to Fort Cumberland, on Will's Creek, near the present town of Cumberland, in Maryland. Thus the whole Western country was again left in the possession of the French and their Indian allies.

In all the first collisions between the French and English, in the contest which ensued, the former were uniformly mild and conciliating in their resistance to British aggression; yet they were firm in maintaining their rightful claim to the country. The encroachments of the English were resisted, at first, with courtesy and good feeling. The Governor of Canada had remonstrated with the governors of New York and Pennsylvania against their claims to the territory south of Lake Erie. He protested against their right to occupy the country, and warned them against encroachments, and declared that, were his protestations and warnings disregarded, he should be obliged by his duty to seize all intruders and send them prisoners to Canada.*

As an evidence of the kind and peaceable feeling entertained by the French in the beginning of their struggle for the great Ohio region, we need only cite the facts in relation to the capture and release of Lieutenant Trent, with his whole detachment, who were permitted to retire, with all their arms, equipage, and military stores, to the nearest English settlements; or the capture and release of Colonel Washington and his army, after the slaughter of M. Jumonville and his party. These facts prove unquestionably that they were reluctant to shed blood in the contest.

[A.D. 1755.] During the winter, General Braddock had arrived in the Potomac, with a large regular army from England, for the effectual invasion and conquest of the Ohio country. This army encamped near Alexandria until the severity of winter should cease, and a body of provincial troops could be organized for marching orders. In the mean time, the army was provided with every thing requisite for their comfort, and for the complete subjugation of the territory on the upper portion of the Ohio River. Such an army had never been seen in the provinces. As soon as the spring had sufficiently opened, regardless of the stipulations in the surrender of "Fort Necessity," General Braddock set out from Alexandria, with two regiments of British regulars and one brigade

* Martin's Louisiana, vol. i., p. 319.

of Virginia light troops, for the reduction of the French fortress Duquesne.

His march was directed to Fort Cumberland, where he arrived with the army about the middle of May. Here he was joined by two independent companies from New York, and the whole force, exclusive of provincials, now consisted of two royal regiments of five hundred men each, one of which was commanded by Sir Peter Halket, and the other by Colonel Dunbar. Both regiments were furnished with a fine train of artillery, and abundant military stores and munitions. The provincial troops consisted of about one thousand effective men, furnished by the provinces of Virginia, New York, and Pennsylvania.

Having been detained at Will's Creek about three weeks for supplies and horses for transportation, General Braddock set out with the whole army upon his march through the wilderness. The army was divided into two divisions: the first, under the commander in person, consisted of twelve hundred men, as the advanced division; the second, commanded by Colonel Dunbar, was ordered to follow by slow marches.

After nearly four weeks of slow and regular marches through the wilderness, the advanced division, in fine health and spirits, arrived, on the 8th of July, at the junction of the Youghiogeny and Monongahela Rivers. The officers and troops eagerly pressed forward, in the belief that in a few hours more they should victoriously enter the walls of Fort Duquesne.

On the morning of the 9th of July the army had reached the last crossing of the Monongahela, within ten miles of the French fort. Here they tarried until noon, and having again set out after their repast, they had just crossed the river, and were slowly advancing in marching order along a defile near the river, thoughtless of danger, when the advancing column was suddenly arrested by a furious fire of musketry and small arms on all sides from an unseen foe, consisting of about eight hundred Frenchmen and Indians.

The whole column was instantly thrown into the utmost confusion and consternation. A total rout and defeat ensued, with the loss of all the artillery, camp equipage, stores, and papers. About three hundred and fifty men were killed on the ground, and about four hundred were badly wounded, many of them mortally. Besides these, twenty-six officers were killed, and thirty-seven were wounded. Among the latter was General

Braddock himself, mortally wounded, who died a few days afterward at Camp Dunbar, near fifty miles in the rear.

The loss sustained by the forces under General Braddock was not altogether the work of the enemy. The panic and consternation of the British troops at the onset were indescribable. The provincials, who were accustomed to Indian warfare, immediately sheltered themselves, after the Indian fashion, behind trees and other objects, from which they kept up a constant fire upon such of the enemy as were visible. The regulars, on the contrary, formed themselves into close columns, which were continually thinned by the incessant fire of the invisible foe. At length, utterly confounded by the slaughter and the panic, which extended to the officers, they collected into squads, and fired furiously and indiscriminately at every point where the crack of a rifle or the smoke of a gun indicated a combatant. The men in the front ranks were often shot down by their terror-stricken companions in the rear. In the same way, every party of provincials who engaged the enemy from their coverts drew upon themselves the fire of the regulars, as well as the enemy in front. Those who were most active in resisting the enemy were almost certain to perish by the hands of their friends. In this way, Captain Waggoner, of the Virginia troops, who had taken an advanced position near the Indians, with eighty men, was driven from his position by the united fire of the Indians and British regulars, after the loss of fifty of his men.

General Braddock himself, in all probability, was killed by one of the indignant provincials. The general had cut down a provincial, for disobeying orders in sheltering himself from the enemy's fire. The brother, who witnessed the act, determined to avenge his death, and awaited the first opportunity, when he lodged his ball in the body of his overbearing commander.* The name of the provincial who is supposed to have fired at Braddock was Thomas Fawcett. Colonel Washington himself declared that many of the brave provincials were killed by the "cowardly British regulars."

The whole force under the command of General Braddock on the Monongahela, including the provincial militia and volunteers from Virginia, Pennsylvania, and New York, was about twenty-five hundred men, of whom two thousand were effective

---

* See Gordon's History of Pennsylvania, p. 303, 304. Also, Appendix, p. 613.

troops. Of these, one thousand belonged to the royal regiments, and the remainder were furnished by the colonies.

The advanced division, which sustained the attack and slaughter in this memorable defeat, was composed of at least twelve hundred effective men. About noon, on the 9th day of July, this division crossed the Monongahela in fine spirits, confident of an easy victory, and the capture of Fort Duquesne within a few hours. What a melancholy doom lay behind the bright hopes and the brilliant pageant of that day.*

M. de Contrecœur, commandant of Fort Duquesne, had received early and continual intelligence of Braddock's arrival in Virginia, and of his regular advance. West of Will's Creek, the French and Indian scouts were constantly abroad, and observed and reported every movement to the commandant, who devised his measures accordingly. Feeling himself wholly unable, with his limited resources, to offer any effectual resistance to such a formidable foe, he despaired of making a regular defense. At this time, M. de Beaujeu, a captain in the French service, proposed to head a detachment of French and Indians, to meet the advancing force and to harass their march. He did not expect to draw them into a general engagement, but only to embarrass and retard their advance. Yet such was the apprehension of the savages, that this attempt was deemed hopeless and hazardous, and with difficulty the Indians were persuaded to engage in the enterprise. At length, seeing him firm in his determination, they consented to accompany him, and to aid in forming an ambuscade, but little dreaming of victory. The ambuscade had scarcely been distributed, when the advancing column was seen crossing the river, within a few hundred yards of the defile where the men were distributed.†

The disasters of the Monongahela put an end to the military operations of Great Britain west of the mountains for more than two years. In the mean time, her efforts were redoubled to reduce the French posts near the great lakes and on the St. Lawrence. The fate of war began to crown the English arms with success, and by the close of the year 1758, France had lost all her strong-holds on the lakes and south of them.

While France was victorious upon the Ohio, her arms were advancing with varied success from the St. Lawrence south-

---

* See Sparks's Writings of Washington, vol. ii., p. 468–470. Also, vol. i., p. 66.
† See Butler's Kentucky, 2d ed., p. 30.

ward upon Lake Champlain. In the spring of 1755, Sir William Johnson had erected "Fort William Henry" upon the southern extremity of Lake George, named in honor of George III. This was the extreme frontier of the English settlements in this quarter, and the French lost no opportunity to transfer the war to the east, and upon the shores of Lakes Champlain and George. Fort William Henry was protected by a garrison commanded by Colonel Williams, and was within the territory claimed by France. The Baron Dieskau, the commander of Eastern Canada, determined to reduce the fort and exclude the English.

On the 6th of September, at the head of eighteen hundred Indians and Canadian French, he advanced to the attack, but was most signally defeated, with the loss of many of his brave men, yielding himself a martyr to the cause.*

[A.D. 1758.] The new British minister, William Pitt, had taken the most energetic means to retrieve the honor of the British arms. A numerous and well-disciplined army had been dispatched to Virginia, where it was re-enforced by large bodies of provincial troops under the most experienced officers. This army, well supplied with every thing requisite, and numbering about seven thousand men, began to advance from Carlisle, in Pennsylvania, toward the Monongahela. The French commandant at Fort Duquesne, being duly apprised of the advance of the enemy, and finding himself without assistance or re-enforcement from Canada, deemed it folly to attempt resistance with his feeble force. He accordingly retained possession of the fort, but was prepared to abandon it without resistance whenever the British army should begin to make its appearance. The main body of the latter was within one day's march of the confluence, when the commandant, with his troops, artillery, munitions, and stores, embarked in boats provided for the occasion; and having dismantled the works, he set fire to the buildings at night, and departed down the Ohio in a blaze of light, to join the French troops on the Mississippi.

As he descended the Ohio, he stationed a detachment of troops under M. Massac, at a commanding eminence on the north bank of the river, nearly fifty miles above its mouth, to erect a stockade, which was called Fort Massac.†

---

* See Western Pioneer, vol. ii., p. 12, 13.
† Martin's Louisiana, vol. i., p. 333.

[A.D. 1760.] The war was continued upon the St. Lawrence and near the great lakes for more than two years afterward; when France, having lost all her Canadian territories, was compelled to terminate hostilities by a treaty which deprived her of all her continental possessions in North America.

[A.D. 1763.] By the treaty of Paris, she relinquished in favor of Great Britain all claim to Canada and New France, embracing all the territory east of the Mississippi from its source to the Bayou Iberville. By a secret treaty made previously with the King of Spain, the French king had ceded to the Spanish crown all the remainder of his American possessions on the Mississippi, embracing all Western Louisiana and the Island of Orleans.

Thus ended the dominion of France in North America, and with it terminated all the plans for extended empire on the Mississippi. Hard as seemed their lot, the French population in Louisiana and New France were compelled to submit to the hated power of England; and many Canadians, to avoid this alternative, resolved to abandon their homes and relatives in Canada, and seek the mild paternal rule of France in Western Louisiana.

CHAPTER IV.

THE MANNERS AND CUSTOMS OF THE EARLY FRENCH SETTLERS IN THE ILLINOIS COUNTRY.—A.D. 1700 TO 1780.

Argument.—Extent of the "Illinois Country."—Conciliatory Policy of the French toward the Indian Tribes.—Their amicable Intercourse with the Natives.—Picture of primitive Happiness enjoyed by the Illinois French.—Their plain and homely Houses and rural Villages.—"Common Field," and Mode and Distribution of Labor.—Family Interests in the same.—"Commons," and its Uses.—Patriarchal Harmony and Contentment of these Communities.—Moral Influence of the System.—Equality and Happiness of the People.—The Paternal Homestead, and Patriarchal Families.—Costume: Male and Female.—Catholic Religion.—Equality.—Contentment.—Sabbath Amusements and Hilarity.—Trades and Professions.—Idiom.—Habits and Deportment.—Domestic Simplicity of Manners and Virtues.—The mild and indulgent Regime of Spain.—Facility of Incorporation with Indian Character.—English Authority introduced in 1765.—The Jurisdiction of the United States extended over them in 1804.—Their Objections to American Population and Laws.

[A.D. 1700–1740.] For many years the term "Illinois country" embraced all the region east of the Upper Mississippi as far as Lake Michigan, and from the Wisconsin on the north to the Ohio on the south. The extent of the Illinois country under the French varied but little from the extent of the present State of Illinois. At a later date, its limits on the east were restricted by the "Wabash country," which was erected into a separate government, under the commandant of " Post of St. Vincent," on the Wabash River.

In all the settlements of the French on the Illinois and Wabash Rivers, as well as in Louisiana, they adopted a policy at once singular and benevolent; a policy well adapted to insure unity and harmony among themselves, and to secure the good will and friendship of the numerous tribes in the Northwest by which they were surrounded. They seemed, indeed, constituted to harmonize in all their habits and feelings with the Indians among whom they took up their abode. They had left behind them, among the colonists near the Atlantic border, avarice, that ruling passion of European emigrants in the New World, which has too often sought its gratification in plundering the natives of their little patrimony and the comforts of savage life.

Hence, while other colonies were continually embroiled with the natives in exterminating wars, the Illinois French, who sought peace and friendship, lived in harmony and mutual confidence with the surrounding tribes.

In all their migrations and explorations to the remotest rivers and hunting-grounds, they associated with the Indians " like a band of brothers," as equally the children of the same great Father of all. Free from that selfish feeling which prompts men to associate in separate communities, with distinct and discordant interests, each endeavoring to monopolize all the advantages of time and circumstances, they lived among themselves as one common brotherhood, and yet shared with the Indians their sufferings and their hospitality. Providence smiled upon the happy union of the white man of Europe with the red man of the American wilderness.

The early French on the Illinois were remarkable for their talent of ingratiating themselves with the warlike tribes around them, and for their easy amalgamation in manners, and customs, and blood. Unlike most other European emigrants, who commonly preferred to settle in sparse settlements, remote from each other, the French manifested in a high degree, at the same time, habits both social and vagrant. They settled in compact villages, although isolated, in the midst of a wilderness a thousand miles remote from the dense settlements of Canada. On the margin of a prairie, or on the bank of some gentle stream, their villages sprung up in long, narrow streets, with each family homestead so contiguous that the merry and sociable villagers could carry on their voluble conversation, each from his own door or balcony. The young men and voyageurs, proud of their influence among the remote tribes of Indians, delighted in the long and merry voyages, and sought adventures in the distant travels of the fur-trade. After months of absence upon the sources of the longest rivers and tributaries among their savage friends, they returned to their village with stores of furs and peltries, prepared to narrate their hardy adventures and the thrilling incidents of their perilous voyage. Their return was greeted with smiling faces, and signalized by balls and dances, at which the whole village assembled, to see the great travelers, and hear the fertile rehearsal of wonderful adventures and strange sights in remote countries.*

Such were the scenes at "Old Kaskaskia," at Cahokia, Prairie du Rocher, and a few other points on the Upper Mississippi, from the year 1720 to the year 1765; and, in later times, at the villages of Fort Chartres, St. Geneviève, St. Louis, and St. Charles; and at St. Vincent on the Wabash, as well as many other points on the Lower Mississippi; at the Post of Natchitoches on Red River, and the Post of Washita on the Washita River; as well as upon the La Fourche, Fausse Rivière, and the coast above New Orleans.

Their settlements were usually in the form of small, compact patriarchal villages, like one great family assembled around their old men and patriarchs. Their houses were simple, plain, and uniform. Each homestead was surrounded by its own separate inclosure of a rude picket fence, adjoining or contiguous to others on the right and left. The houses were generally one story high, surrounded by sheds, or galleries; the walls were constructed of a rude frame-work, having upright corner-posts and studs, connected horizontally by means of numerous cross-ties, not unlike the rounds in a ladder. These served to hold the "cat and clay" with which the interstices were filled, and with which the walls were made, and rudely plastered with the hand. "Cat and clay" is formed by mud, or clay, made into soft mortar, which is then intimately

* See Flint's Geography, vol. i., p. 161-2.

blended with cut straw or Spanish moss, cut fine, instead of hair. The chimney was made of similar materials, and was formed by four long corner-posts, converging toward the top to about one half, or less than the space below.

These abodes of happiness were generally situated on the margin of a beautiful prairie, and beside some clear stream of running water, or on the bank of a river or bayou, near some rich, alluvial bottom, which supplied the grounds for the "common field" and "commons."

The "common field" consisted of a large contiguous inclosure, reserved for the common use of the village, inclosed by one common fence for the benefit of all. In this field, which sometimes consisted of several hundred acres, each villager and head of a family had assigned to him a certain portion of ground, for the use of himself and family, as a field and garden. The extent of the field was proportionate to the number of persons or families in the village. The subdivisions were in due proportion to the number of members in each family. Each individual, or family, labored and reaped the product of his own allotment for his own use.

If the inclosure became ruinous, or was neglected contiguous to the plat of any family, or individual, so as to endanger the general interest, that individual, or family, forfeited their claim to the use of the common field; and their interest was assigned to another person, who would be less negligent.

Each individual, or head of a family, so long as he conformed to the regulations and requisitions of the village, retained his interest in the common field in fee simple, transferable by sale, gift, or otherwise; liable, however, to the general regulations which might be adopted by the village.

The season for ploughing, planting, reaping, and other agricultural operations in the "common field," was regulated by special enactments, or by a public ordinance, and to take place simultaneously in each village: even the form and manner of door-yards, gardens, and stable-yards, and other arrangements for mutual benefit, and the convenience of all, were regulated by special enactment of the little village senate. These were often in such shape and connection as to form a partial protection, like a picketed camp, against any hostile irruption of Indians, provided such event might ever occur.

Near the village, and around the common field, was an extensive open scope of lands reserved for "commons," or a common pasture-ground. This consisted of several hundreds, and often of thousands, of acres uninclosed, and free for the use of all as a common pasture, as well as for the supply of fuel and timber. Yet no one could take possession of any portion of it, or appropriate it to his own individual use, without the general consent of the villagers. To the indigent, however, who came to settle among them, and to newly-married pairs, appropriations were often made from portions of the "commons" contiguous to the common field, and situated so that it might subsequently be taken into it by extending the inclosure, provided the individuals proved themselves acceptable members of their community.

In making grants of land for the use of a village or community, the commandant always took special care to cause a reservation to be specially designated for a "common field" and a "commons." These were deemed indispensable requisites for every large French village. The same custom was observed by the Spanish authorities after the dominion of Spain was extended over Louisiana.

Nothing was better calculated to improve the simple and benevolent feelings of unsophisticated human nature, to maintain the blessings of peace and harmony, and the prevalence of brotherly love, than the forms of life and the domestic usages which prevailed in these early French villages. Under this benign influence, peace and competence smiled upon them; joy and mirth beamed from every countenance; contentment sat on every brow. The natural affluence which pervaded the whole village was common to all. The prolific soil, solicited by gentle labor as a mere matter of recreation, yielded abundance of all the necessaries of life, except those which were derived from the still more prolific waters and the chase. With all these advantages, and all these easy enjoyments, in a climate of great benignity, remote from the strife and conflicting interests of a dense population, what should prevent them from esteeming the Illinois a "terrestrial paradise," as La Salle had termed it in 1682?

How enviable the condition of these children of nature, with but little more care and anxiety of mind than is experienced by the fowls of the air, compared with the toil and anxiety of refined civilization; in which the mind is continually harassed by the goadings of avarice, and by the incessant efforts to accumulate wealth and honors on the one hand, or, on the other, is straitened under the influence of penury and want, by a constant harassing anxiety in procuring the bare necessaries of life, with the constant apprehension of still greater want, as is often seen in the crowded cities of Europe!

In the early French settlements the commons abounded with herds of domestic animals—with cattle, horses, sheep, swine, and others tamed from the forest, which wandered at large— and was used as a general store-house, from which all were freely supplied; while corroding care was banished from hearts as light as those of the beasts that roamed the fields.

In the happy enjoyment of such a life, time glides rapidly on; and to age death came a hasty, but not unwelcome messenger, for they hoped for a still better world beyond the grave.

Care was a stranger in the villages, and was rarely entertained many days as a guest. Amusements, festivals, and holydays were frequent, and served to dispel dull care, when an unwelcome visitor. In the light fantastic dance, the young and the gay were active participants, while the serene and smiling countenance of the aged patriarch, and his companion in years, and even of the "reverend father," lent a sanction and a blessing upon the innocent amusement and useful recreation. The amusements past, all could cheerfully unite in offering up to God the simple gratitude of the heart for his unbounded mercies.

Fathers, and mothers, and grand-sires enjoyed no higher pleasure than to witness the innocent mirth of their children, and their aged eyes beamed with tranquil delight while they beheld the happiness of the young. Religion was the link which united the joys of life to those of eternity; and with hearts doubly devout, the young and the old, the "reverend father" and the unlettered child, could all retire from a scene of innocent mirth, and humbly render the homage of their hearts to the Supreme Ruler of the universe.

Nor were these festive enjoyments confined to any sex or condition. In the dance all participated, from the youngest to the oldest, the bond and the free; even the black slave was equally interested in the general enjoyment, and was happy because he saw his master happy; and the master, in turn, was pleased to witness the enjoyment of the slave. The mutual dependence of each upon the other, in their respective spheres, contributed to produce a state of mutual harmony and attachment. It has been almost a proverb, that the world did not exhibit an example of a more contented and happy race than the negro slaves of the early French in the Illinois country.* The numerous festivals of the Catholic Church tended strongly to foster the mutual interchange of friendly feelings among those who were thus removed beyond the reach and influence of wealth and power.

In religion all were Catholics, and revered the pope as the great head of the Church, who held the keys of heaven and of purgatory, and dispensed his favors or his frowns through the priests, who were their friends and counselors, and whom they esteemed as "reverend fathers." They knew no difference of sects, nor

"Doctrines framed to suit the varying hour."

Ardently attached to their spiritual guides, religion became one of the great rules of social life. They observed strictly all the outward rites and ceremonies of the Romish Church, and their lives corresponded with their professions. Ignorant of creeds, except the "Apostles' Creed," they were not skillful disputants; but holydays and festivals were never forgotten or neglected. Gratitude to God, the religion of the heart, and love to mankind, is found more often in the rude stages of civilized life than in the blandishments of wealth, and among the accumulated temptations of refinement and intelligence.

As has been observed by Major Stoddart, who was lieutenant-governor of Upper Louisiana in 1804, "Perhaps the levities displayed, and the amusements pursued by the French people on Sundays, may be considered by some to border upon licentiousness. They attend mass in the morning with great devotion; but after the exercises of church are over, they usually collect in parties and pass away their time in social and merry intercourse. They play at billiards and other games, and to balls and assemblies the Sundays are particularly devoted. To those educated in regular and pious Protestant habits such parties and amusements appear unseasonable, strange, and odious, if not prophetic of some signal curse on the work-

---

* See "The Far West." This is a very interesting little work, in two volumes, 12mo, by an anonymous author. It was published in 1837 or 1838. It contains some fine sketches of the Western country, of Western manners and customs, and many graphic descriptions of the natural beauties of the West, chiefly on the region of the Upper Mississippi.

ers of iniquity. It must, however, be confessed that the French people, on those days, avoid all intemperate and immoral excesses, and conduct themselves with apparent decorum. They are of opinion that there is true and undefiled religion in their amusements, much more, indeed, than they can see in certain night conferences and obscure meetings in various parts among the tombs.

"When questioned relative to their gayety on Sundays, they will answer, that men were made for happiness, and that the more they are able to enjoy themselves, the more acceptable they are to their Creator. They are of opinion that a sullen countenance, attention to gloomy subjects, a set form of speech, and a stiff behavior, are more indicative of hypocrisy than of religion; and they say they have often remarked that those who practice these singularities on Sunday will most assuredly cheat and defraud their neighbors during the remainder of the week.

"Such are the religious sentiments of a people void of superstition; of a people prone to hospitality, urbanity of manners, and innocent recreation, and who present their daily orisons at the throne of Grace with as much confidence of success as the most devout Puritan in Christendom."*

The *costume* of the early French was plain, simple, and unique, differing but little from that of the Creole and Acadian French of Louisiana at the present time, as seen upon the Lafourche, the Teche, and in the Acadian settlements of Oppelousas and Attakapas.

The winter dress of the men was generally a coarse blanket *capote*, drawn over their shirt and long vest. The capote served the double purpose of cloak and hat; for the hood, attached to the collar behind, hung upon the back and shoulders as a cape, and, when desired, it served to cover the whole head from intense cold. Most commonly, in summer, and especially among the boatmen, *voyageurs*, and *courriers du bois*, the head was enveloped in a blue handkerchief, turban-like, as a protection from solar heat and noxious insects. The same material, of lighter quality, and fancy colors, wreathed with bright-colored ribbons, and sometimes flowers, formed the fancy headdress of the females on festive occasions: at other times they also used the handkerchief in the more patriarchal style.

* See Stoddart's Sketches of Louisiana, p. 316, 317.

The dress of the matrons was simple and plain; the old-fashioned short jacket and petticoat, varied to suit the diversities of taste, was the most common over-dress of the women. The feet in winter were protected by Indian moccasins, or the more unwieldy clog-shoe; but in summer, and in dry weather, the foot was left uncovered and free, except on festive occasions and holydays, when it was adorned with the light moccasin, gorgeously ornamented with brilliants of porcupine quills, shells, beads, or lace, ingeniously wrought over the front instead of buckles, and on the side flaps.

The *idiom* of these villagers, especially in those of the Illinois country and Upper Louisiana, was in many points different from that of the European French, both in the pronunciation and in the signification of words. In general terms, the Illinois idiom seemed destitute of that nervous and animated brilliancy of expression peculiar to the Parisian French. In the Creole French of Louisiana, at this time, there is perceptible a slow, drawling, or nasal sound of many words, which gives to conversation a languid air, not often seen in Europe. Yet the Creole French tongue is more pure than might have been expected, after a protracted separation of nearly a century from the parent country, and much of the time under a foreign dominion, with the introduction of a foreign language among them.*

Under the French dominion, the government was mild and paternal; a mixture of civil and military rule, without the technicalities of the one or the severity of the other. The commandant was invested with despotic authority; yet he rarely exercised his power otherwise than in a kind and paternal manner, and for the general welfare of his people. In return, he received not only their obedience and respect, but also their love.

The peculiar manners and customs of these French settlements at first, and for an age afterward, isolated, and a thousand miles from any other civilized community, became characteristic and hereditary with their descendants, even to the present time. From their first settlement on the Illinois and at Kaskaskia, one hundred and fifty years ago, they have uniformly enjoyed the confidence and friendship of the Indian tribes. From long intercourse, and by assimilating themselves

* See "The Far West."

in a great measure to the habits and customs of the native tribes, and by their peaceable and conciliatory characters, they had become almost identified as brothers. While the Anglo-Saxon race was establishing colonies along the Atlantic coast, from the close of the seventeenth century to the middle of the eighteenth, ever restless and discontented, were struggling with the savage occupants for the sterile and sandy shores of Virginia and New England, and the rocky barriers of the interior, the French, far removed from civilization, in the very heart of the continent, and surrounded by every thing in nature which could fascinate the eye or delight the fancy, in peace and friendship with the tribes, lived contented, happy, and prosperous, in the full enjoyment of the "terrestrial paradise of America."[*]

In the appearance of the "patriarchal homestead," among the country settlements, there was something peculiarly interesting, which reminds us strongly of a primitive simplicity but rarely seen in the present day. The patriarchal homestead of detached settlements stands in the middle of a spacious inclosure, used as a common yard for several generations. This inclosure may contain one or two acres, and sometimes less; it is the residence of the oldest member of the family, who possibly has occupied it for more than half a century. Each child or grand-child, who, having arrived at the years of maturity, and become the head of a family, may be found settled in a small thatched or mud cottage at one side of the paternal inclosure, rears up a flourishing young family, which, with their increase, are branches of the original family, having a community of interest and feeling. At length, the aged patriarch becomes surrounded by a dozen growing families of his own lineage, until the third and fourth generations will be found living in perfect harmony, each family occupying its own cottage around the patriarchal roof. Scenes of this kind are yet seen upon the French coast above and below New Orleans, upon the Lafourche, the Teche, and other French settlements of Louisiana, in the region of Oppelousas and Attakapas.

As their lands were generally held in common, and vacant lands were free to all, the relation of landlord and tenant was unknown; vested rights of chartered companies were equally unknown, and no inflated and unfeeling aristocracy lorded it over the humble poor, reduced to a dependent and servile peas-

[*] See "The Far West," vol. ii., p. 155.

antry. The wealth of all consisted in their good name, and in their unrestrained freedom to enjoy the bounties of nature. Some possessed more personal property than others; but wealth gave no exclusive privileges. Superiority depended alone upon superior merit.

The common people, in their ordinary deportment, were often characterized by a calm, thoughtful gravity, and the saturnine severity of the Spaniard, rather than the levity characteristic of the French; yet, in their amusements and fêtes, they exhibited all the gayety of the natives of France. Their saturnine gravity was probably a habit, adopted from the Indian tribes with whom they daily held intercourse, and in whose sense of propriety levity of deportment on ordinary occasions is esteemed not only unbecoming, but unmanly. The calm, quiet tenor of their lives, remote from the active bustle of civilized life and business, imparted to their character, to their feelings, to their general manners, and even to their very language, a languid softness which contrasted strongly with the anxious and restless activity of the Anglo-Saxon race, which is fast succeeding to the occupancy of their happy abodes. With them hospitality was hardly esteemed a virtue, because it was a *duty* which all cheerfully performed. Taverns were unknown, and every house supplied the deficiency. The statute-book, the judiciary, and courts of law, with their prisons and instruments of punishment, were unknown; as were also the crimes for which they are erected among the civilized nations of Europe. Learning and science were terms beyond their comprehension, and their technicalities were unheard. Schools were few, and *learned men* were rare; the priest was their oracle in matters of learning, as well as in the forms and observances of religion. The village school was the great source and fountain of book-knowledge, and there the rising generation might acquire all the elements of a complete education for a French villager.

On politics and the affairs of the nation they never suffered their minds to feel a moment's anxiety, believing implicitly that France ruled the world, and all must be right. Worldly honors and distinctions were bubbles unworthy a moment's consideration or a moment's anxiety. Without commerce, they knew not, nor desired to know, the luxuries and the refinements of civilized communities. Thus day after day passed by in contentment and peaceful indolence. The distinction of wealth or rank was almost unknown; all were upon a natural equality, all dressed alike, and all met as equals at their fêtes and in their ball-rooms.

The virtues of their primitive simplicity were many. Punctuality and honesty in their dealings, politeness and hospitality to strangers, were habitual; friendship and cordiality toward neighbors was general; and all seemed as members of one great family, connected by the strong ties of consanguinity. Wives were kind and affectionate; in all respects, they were equal to their husbands, and held an influence superior to the females in most civilized countries. They had entire control in all domestic concerns, and were the chief and supreme umpires in all doubtful cases. Did a case of casuistry arise, who so well able to divine the truth, or so well qualified to enforce the decision, as the better half?

Among the villagers, we have said, there were few distinctions; the more enterprising became, of course, more wealthy, by trade and traffic with the Indians, in the purchase and sale of furs, peltries, and other commodities supplied by the native tribes.

The "*traders*" kept a heterogeneous stock of goods in their largest room, where their assortment was fully displayed to the gaze of the purchasers. The young men of enterprise, wishing to see the world, sought occupation and gratification as *voyageurs* or boatmen, as agents for the traders, or as hunters, to visit the remote tribes upon the furthest sources of the Mississippi and the Missouri, in company with the trading expeditions which annually set out from the Illinois country.

Mechanic trades, as a means of livelihood, were almost unknown; the great business of all was agriculture, and the care of their herds and flocks, their cattle, their horses, their sheep, and their swine, and each man was his own mechanic.[*]

Thus lived the French in New France and Louisiana, until after the Canadian provinces had been wrested from the French crown by the arms of England, and the English power was extended over the Illinois in 1765. But a change came over their peaceful abodes. Should Frenchmen submit to the hated dominion of England, their most inveterate national enemy? Many preferred to leave their homes and their fields, and to

[*] See "The Far West," vol. i., p. 163.

seek new abodes under the dominion of France, which still prevailed west of the Mississippi. The French settlements of the Illinois then began to decline; and, to prevent their entire abandonment, the English governor, instructed by his government, gave assurances that their religion should be protected, and their rights and property remain inviolate under the dominion of Great Britain. Many consented to remain; but many retired to Western Louisiana. Then it was that the French settlements began to extend upon the west side of the Mississippi, within the present limits of the State of Missouri.

But their peace was soon interrupted here. Rumor soon proclaimed that all Western and Southern Louisiana had been ceded to Spain. The rumor was too true; for already they were subjects of the Spanish king. Although the Spanish authority was not formally extended over them for five years, yet these five years were years of trouble, suspense, and disappointment.

The government of Spain, like that of France, was mild and paternal; nor did the Spanish authorities care to interfere with the established usages and customs of the French population, but extended every indulgence which could be desired from a kind and lenient government. A few years served to dispel all dissatisfaction at the change of rulers, and the French villagers and voyageurs, for thirty years more, continued to enjoy their "terrestrial paradise," under their ancient forms of government and the Catholic religion, on the west side of the Mississippi.

Nor was their peace again disturbed until the Anglo-Americans from the United States began to approach the Mississippi in the regions of the Illinois and Old Kaskaskia. This approach, however, was only the precursor of a new era, with themselves, in Upper Louisiana, and of a total change in their happy and retired mode of life. A few years brought the unwelcome news that all Louisiana had been ceded to the United States, and that soon a new system of jurisdiction was to be extended over them.

Previous to the cession of Louisiana to the United States in 1803, the French had become assimilated in feelings with their Spanish rulers, who wisely combined the laws of Spain and France. "The laws of Spain were introduced only so far as related, generally, to municipal arrangement and real estate;

while the common law of France governed all contracts of a social nature, modified by, and interwoven with, the customs of the people. Each district had its commandant, and each village its syndic; besides judges in civil affairs for the province and officers of the *militia*, a small body of which was stationed in every district, though too inconsiderable to afford much protection to the inhabitants. These rulers were appointed by the governor at New Orleans, to whom there was the right of an appeal. The lieutenant-governor, who resided at St. Louis, was commander of the troops. Thus the government was a mixture of civil and military; and though arbitrary to the last degree, yet we are told the rod of domination was so light as scarcely to be felt.

"However this may be, it is certain they did not well relish, at first, the change in the administration of justice when they came under the jurisdiction of the United States. The delays and the uncertainty attendant on trial by jury, and the multifarious technicalities of our jurisprudence, they could not well comprehend, either as to its import or utility; and it is not strange that they should have preferred the more prompt and less expensive decisions of the Spanish tribunals."*

* Stoddart's Louisiana.

CHAPTER V.

THE FIRST COLONIZATION OF LOUISIANA UNTIL THE CLOSE OF CROZAT'S MONOPOLY.—A.D. 1698 TO 1717.

Argument.—Retrospect of the Illinois Settlements.—D'Iberville undertakes to Colonize Lower Louisiana.—Sails with his Colony from Rochelle, September 24th, 1798.—Leaves the West Indies, and reaches Florida in January, 1699.—Casts anchor at Isle Dauphin.—Disembarks his Colony on Ship Island.—Sets out to explore the Mouth of the Mississippi.—Enters that River on the 2d of March.—Finds Letter of De Tonti to La Salle, dated 1685.—Returns by way of the Bayou Iberville to Bay of St. Louis.—Builds Fort Biloxi, May 2d.—Sails for France.—English Attempts to pre-occupy Louisiana.—The British King bribes Hennepin to lie.—British Colony arrives in the Mississippi.—Condition of the Colony at Biloxi.—Bienville superintends the Colony as Governor.—Explores the Channel of the Mississippi.—Iberville returns with another Colony.—Builds a Fort on the Bank of the River.—Ascends the River as far as the Natchez Tribe.—Selects a Site for Fort Rosalie.—The Natchez Indians.—Their Customs and Religious Ceremonies.—Interview with the "Great Sun."—Boundary between Louisiana and Florida compromised.—The Colony at Biloxi reduced by Sickness and Death.—Exploring Parties.—Unrivaled Water Communications.—Death of Sauvolle, Commandant.—Iberville retires to France.—His Death in 1706.—Extravagant Mining Credulity continues.—Explorations for Mines.—Feeble Condition of the Colony from 1704 to 1710.—Louisiana made Independent of Canada.—Bienville Governor-general.—Banks of the Mississippi neglected.—Crozat's Monopoly granted, 1712.—Extent of Louisiana defined in his Grant.—Population of the Colony in 1713.—Crozat's Enterprise, Zeal, and Plans of Trade.—He is excluded from Trade with Florida and Mexico.—Settlements extend.—Natchitoches on Red River settled.—Trading-posts established.—Disappointment and Failure of his Plans.—Expenditures of Crozat up to 1716.—Fort Rosalie built in 1716.—The new Governor, L'Epinai, arrives with Troops.—Crozat surrenders his Charter in 1717.—Condition of the Colony at his Surrender.

WE have already seen that, from the exploration of the Mississippi by La Salle, in 1682, emigrants, *voyageurs*, and traders from Canada continued to visit and occupy portions of the Illinois region, as well as a few points on the Upper Mississippi. Many of those who had first accompanied La Salle in his perilous advance south and west of Lake Michigan became permanent settlers, attached to the mild climate and the prolific soil. Thus small French settlements began to be made in the vicinity of La Salle's trading-posts more than a thousand miles in advance of the settlements of Canada, where the unambitious white man dwelt in peace with the red man of the wilderness. Other restless spirits and hardy adventurers from Canada longed to see the region which had been described by La Salle and others as the most delightful country on earth. The veteran Chevalier de Tonti had remained in command on the Illinois while La Salle was in France organizing his colony for Lower Louisiana; and in 1685, having heard of his arrival with his colony in the West Indies, he had descended the river with a party of Canadians and Indians to greet him and his colony at the mouth of the Mississippi. Finding no vestige of his colony, and unable to obtain any certain intelligence of his fate, he returned to the Illinois, where he remained at the head of affairs until the year 1700, when he descended the river again with twenty Canadians to greet the new colony of Iberville.* Occasionally, before this time, the traders and voyageurs, as well as the Jesuit missionaries, had descended the river from the Illinois country to the Chickasâ and Natchez Indians; but after the arrival of Iberville's colony, these adventurous voyages were more frequent.

[A.D. 1698.] The court of France had been engaged in wars and political intrigues, and nothing toward colonizing Louisiana had been effected since the disastrous expedition of La Salle. Twelve years had elapsed, but his discoveries and his unfortunate fate had not been forgotten. At length, in 1698, an expedition for colonizing the region of the Lower Mississippi was set on foot by the French king. It was placed under the command of M. d'Iberville, who had been an experienced and distinguished naval commander in the French wars of Canada, and a successful agent in establishing colonies in Canada, Acadie, and Cape Breton. D'Iberville was a man well qualified for the undertaking; his judgment was mature, his manner stern, and his decision and action prompt in the execution of his plans.

He was willing, after encountering the snows and icebergs of Hudson's Bay and St. Lawrence, to transfer the theatre of his operations to the burning sands of Florida. Desirous of distinction also in the South, and willing to serve his country in any sphere, he accepted the trust of colonizing the Lower Mississippi. The Spaniards had already formed a settlement and taken formal possession of the coast of West Florida, and Pensacola had become a fortified town, with a colony of three hundred Spaniards from Vera Cruz.

In the summer of 1798, D'Iberville entered upon the command of the enterprise of colonizing Louisiana. With his little

* Bancroft, vol. iii., p. 195.

fleet of two frigates, rating thirty guns each, and two smaller vessels, bearing a company of marines and two hundred colonists, including a few women and children, he prepared to set sail from France for the mouth of the Mississippi. The colonists were mostly soldiers who had served in the armies of France, and had received an honorable discharge. They were well supplied with provisions and implements requisite for opening settlements in the wilderness.

It was on the 24th day of September, 1798, that this colony sailed from Rochelle.* A long and tedious voyage of seventy-two days gave them a safe anchorage in the harbor of Cape François, in the Island of St. Domingo. To D'Iberville the governor gave a hearty welcome, and bore a willing testimony to his good judgment.†

[A.D. 1699.] A large additional ship of war, rating fifty guns, commanded by Chateaumorant, was detailed to escort the fleet to the shores of Louisiana; and on the first of January, 1699, the colony, thus protected, set sail from St. Domingo in search of the mouth of the Mississippi. After twenty-four days, the fleet cast anchor off the Island of St. Rose, a few miles east of the bay, known to De Soto one hundred and sixty years before as the Bay of Achusi, and subsequently designated by the Spaniards as the Bay of St. Mary de Galve.‡ A few miles up the bay was the Spanish settlement of Pensacola, protected by a strong fort and ample garrison. The fleet cruised off the mouth of Pensacola Bay for several days; but the Spanish governor, obedient to his orders, and to the maxims of the commercial system, would permit no foreign vessel to enter the harbor. Sailing further to the west, the fleet anchored off the island first called Massacre, and known to the French subsequently as Dauphin Island, lying west of the present Bay of Mobile. A few days afterward the fleet sailed westward, and the water near the coast being too shallow for the large vessel from the St. Domingo station, that vessel returned, and the frigates anchored near the Chandaleur Groups, while Iberville explored the channel between Ship Island and Cat Island, and, with his colony, landed upon Ship Island, off the mouth of the Pascagoula River. Here he erected huts for his people; and afterward discovered, by coasting in boats

---

* Martin's Louisiana, vol. i., p. 141. † Bancroft, vol. iii., p. 200.
‡ Bancroft, vol. iii., p. 353.

along the shore, the Pascagoula River, and the tribe of Biloxi Indians.

Having explored the coast, and ascertained from the natives the probable course and distance of the outlet of the great river St. Louis, or, as it was latterly known to the French, the "Hidden River," Iberville, on the 27th day of February, set out from Ship Island in boats, to explore the mouth, which had, as yet, never been entered from the sea. In two large barges, one commanded by himself and one by his brother Bienville, each carrying twenty-four men, Iberville moved south and westward along the coast. Three days brought them to the Balize, and they entered, on the second day of March, a wide river flowing into the sea. Father Athanase, a Franciscan, who had been a companion of La Salle in his exploring voyage in 1682, declared this to be the true River St. Louis. The water was turbid, and moved in a vast volume to the sea, its surface bearing down large quantities of floating timber. It could be no other than the Perdido, or "Hidden River." Iberville doubted the father's opinion. He expected to have seen a more expansive mouth, and could not believe this to be the mighty river of the West. The barges, however, were directed to proceed up the stream, and soon afterward he concurred in the opinion of the worthy father. As they advanced, all doubt was dispelled when he beheld in the hands of the Indians, near Bayou Goula, articles which had been distributed by La Salle in 1682; here, also, safely preserved by the wondering natives, he found a letter, written in 1685 by De Tonti to La Salle. Not far from this, as they ascended, he saw in the possession of the natives a portion of a coat of mail, which, in all probability, had remained in the country since the disastrous expedition of De Soto, one hundred and sixty years before. The letter of De Tonti was dated April 20th, 1685, and expressed the extreme disappointment of the chevalier in failing to meet La Salle with his colony, which he knew had already sailed from France. In this letter the chevalier further stated that he had departed from Canada for the St. Louis River, by way of the lakes and Illinois; that he had descended the river to the sea, with a party of twenty-five Canadian French and thirty Indians, in order to join the colony which La Salle had led from France for the settlement of Louisiana; that, having continued near the mouth, as had been previously agreed, and not having been able to obtain any intelligence of him or his colony, he had returned to the Illinois.*

After several days spent in exploring.the country, and holding intercourse with the Indian tribes near the mouth of Red River, Iberville, with his party, descended the river to the outlet of Bayou Iberville, or Manchac. Here being informed of an inland route through to the Bay of St. Louis, he first explored the pass through Bayou Manchac and Lakes Maurepas and Pontchartrain, and returned to the settlement on Ship Island, which names were then given by Iberville himself.

Soon afterward, Iberville selected a site, and began to erect a fort upon the northeast shore of the Bay of Biloxi, about fifteen miles north of Ship Island. Here, upon a sandy shore, and under a burning sun, upon a pine barren, he settled his colony, about eighty miles northeast from the present city of New Orleans. This occupation, protected by a fort, under the command of Sauvolle, with four bastions, and defended by twelve cannon, was the sign of French jurisdiction, which was to extend from the Bay of Pensacola on the east to the Rio del Norte on the west.†

Having thus located his colony, and protected them from the danger of Indian treachery and hostility, he made other provision for their comfort and security, and then set sail for France, leaving his two brothers, Sauvolle and Bienville, as his lieutenants; the first to command the fort, and the other as general superintendent of the colony under him.

The movements in France for the colonization of Louisiana had not been unobserved by England. The jealous eye of that grasping power had been observing closely the preparations for colonizing Louisiana and the shores of the Mississippi. "Father Louis Hennepin had been taken into British pay under William III., and had published his new work, in which, to bar the French claim of discovery, he had, with impudent false-

* Martin, vol. i., p. 143, 144.

† According to Martin, Bancroft, and others, the present Bay of Biloxi is the point where Iberville made his first location on the main land, and erected his fort, defended by twelve pieces of cannon; but Stoddart says this fort, afterward known as "old Biloxi," was upon the *Perdido Bay*, twelve miles west of Pensacola. As the French subsequently claimed to the Perdido River and Bay, which was finally agreed upon as the boundary between Louisiana and Florida, in consequence of a prior occupation, we incline to the opinion that Stoddart, who was personally acquainted with the coast, is correct. See Sketches of Louisiana, p. 24, 26, 42, and 136, 137; see, also, Martin, vol. i., p. 145, and Bancroft, vol. iii., p. 201.

hood, claimed to have himself first descended the Mississippi to the sea." Then it was he interpolated his former narrative with a journal of his pretended voyage down the river. This had been published in London, at the very time the fort at Biloxi was in progress; and at once an exploring expedition and colony, under the auspices of Coxe, a proprietor of New Jersey, was dispatched also to explore the mouths of the Mississippi, under the escort of a British vessel of war,‡ commanded by Captain Barr.

The condition of the French colony on Ship Island and on the Bay of Biloxi was far from pleasant. The barren sands of the coast promised but little in point of agriculture, and the burning suns of the tropics made many sigh for the cool breezes of Hudson's Bay. A truce with the Spaniards of Pensacola might be obtained, but the Indians were also to be conciliated. The latter had already been visited on the Mississippi by Fathers Montigny and Davion, and were considered allies of the French.

Bienville, during the absence of Iberville, lost no opportunity of extending his explorations, and was indefatigable in his exertions to secure the prosperity and perpetuity of the colony. Every opportunity of conciliating the native tribes, as he explored the bays and rivers upon the coast, was duly improved, by attaching them to the French interest, and impressing them with the magnificence of France.

In September, while exploring the channel of the Mississippi, with his boats and lead-lines, a few miles below the present site of New Orleans, Bienville perceived a British corvette of twelve guns slowly moving up the stream. Nothing daunted at his defenseless condition, he sent a flag on board the English ship to Captain Barr, informing him that he was within the dominions of his most Christian majesty; that if he persisted in ascending the river, he should be compelled by his duty to use the force at his command to resist their advance: he signified that there were strong defenses a few miles above, and that he had ample means to enforce obedience to his demands. The Britons grumbled and turned about, but declared that Captain Wood had discovered the river and country nearly fifty years before,† and that they would return with force sufficient to main-

* Bancroft's United States, vol. iii., p. 202. Also, Martin, vol. i., p. 149.
† N. A. Review, Jan. 7, No. 1839.

tain their claim. The English had seen with a jealous eye the advances of the French from Canada to the Upper Mississippi, and now they were making active advances upon the Lower Mississippi. The British crown was anxious to prevent these latter advances into what was claimed as a part of the British provinces. England was willing to supplant the French in the occupancy of the country, and to reap the advantages of their discoveries. But the attempt on the part of Captain Barr to explore the Mississippi was abandoned, and he was seen no more by the French. The point at which he made his return, in commemoration of that circumstance, has since been known as the "English Turn."*

Having failed to dislodge the French from the Mississippi, the English authorities in Carolina subsequently lost no opportunity for annoying the settlements on the Mobile, through the Indian tribes. Yet England still held a nominal claim westward to the Mississippi, while Spain could only protest against the separation of what she was pleased to call the government of Mexico; for France was destined to hold the Valley of the Mississippi, as it were in trust, for a people yet unborn, as an asylum for oppressed humanity.

During the past summer, sickness and bilious fever had made sad ravages among the unacclimated Europeans and Canadians. Many had died from diseases incident to the climate; and the troops had also suffered severely, and their numbers had been greatly reduced. Above all, the commandant of Fort Biloxi, M. Sauvolle, had died during the summer, leaving the youthful Bienville sole commandant and superintendent of the province.

But early in December following, D'Iberville returned with an additional colony and a detachment of troops, in company with several vessels of war.† Up to this time, the principal settlements had been at Ship Island and on the Bay of Biloxi; others had been begun at the Bay of St. Louis and on the Bay of Mobile. These were made as a matter of convenience, to

---

* Martin's Louisiana, vol. i., p. 149.

† Among the colonists and officers of the province were St. Denys and Maton, with sixty Canadians. In this arrival came also Lesueur, a geologist who had been sent out to examine some greenish earth which had been seen high up the Mississippi by Dugay and Hennepin in 1680. Iberville brought the king's commission to Bienville as governor of the province, and Boisbriant as commander of the fort. Martin, vol. i., p. 150, 151.

hold and occupy the country; for his principal object was to colonize the banks of the Mississippi itself. When he learned that the English meditated a settlement on that river, and had sent an exploring expedition to examine its channels and shores, he resolved no longer to defer the occupation of the river by a military post. Accordingly, on the 17th of January, 1700, he set out from the Bay of St. Louis for the exploration of the Mississippi, in search of a suitable site for a fort. He soon selected a point, supposed to be above ordinary high water, about fifty-four miles above the mouth, and about thirty-eight miles below the present city of New Orleans. Upon this ridge, not far from Poverty Point, he located a small colony and erected a small fort.*

[A.D. 1700.] About the middle of February, the veteran Chevalier de Tonti arrived on the Lower Mississippi, with a party of Canadian French from the Illinois. He found Iberville at his newly-erected fort, arranging the settlements for the colonization of the Lower Mississippi. The experience of De Tonti, his knowledge of the Indian language and customs, and his acquaintance with several tribes on the river, rendered him a valuable acquisition to the new colony. With his aid, Iberville determined to ascend the river and explore the country upon its banks, and form friendly alliances with the native tribes of the interior. Accordingly, he hastened to detail a suitable party, in company with De Tonti and Bienville, to ascend the river in barges and canoes. The voyage was continued as far as the Natchez tribe, nearly four hundred miles from the mouth. On the voyage, D'Iberville landed at various points, and formed friendly alliances with such tribes as were seen; thereby securing for his colony the friendship and hospitality of the natives, and receiving in person an earnest of future friendly intercourse. He had commenced the exploration of Red River as he passed up, but determined to defer it to a future time.

D'Iberville was well pleased with the Natchez tribe and with their country. This tribe was found to be powerful and highly improved: they had made considerable advances toward civilization; yet, by recent wars, they had been reduced to about twelve hundred warriors. The Natchez country was deemed the most desirable in the province; suitable for the principal colony, and for the headquarters of the future

* Martin's Louisiana, vol. i., p. 151.

provincial government; and here he selected an elevated bluff as the site for the future capital of the province. It was the bluff where the city of Natchez now stands. The site was distinguished by the name of "Rosalie," in honor of the Countess of Pontchartrain, who had received that name at the baptismal fount.* He designed to establish a fort at this point, as the sign of French jurisdiction; but Fort Rosalie was not erected by his successors until sixteen years afterward. The Count of Pontchartrain had been the friend and patron of Iberville's plan of colonizing the Mississippi, which received all the aid which his influence as minister of marine affairs could give.

In many particulars, the Natchez tribes differed, in the time of Iberville, from the neighboring tribes and nations, both in their appearance and in their mode of civilization. They exerted an extensive influence over the neighboring tribes, several of which were in alliance with them. Of all these allies, the Tensas were strongest in their resemblance, in their persons, their manners, and their religion.

Their religion, in some respects, resembled that of the fire-worshipers of Persia. Fire was the emblem of their divinity; the sun was their god: their chiefs were called "suns," and their king was called the "Great Sun." In their principal temple a perpetual fire was kept burning by the ministering priest, who likewise offered sacrifices of the first fruits of the chase. In extreme cases, they offered sacrifices of infant children, to appease the wrath of the deity. While Iberville was there, one of the temples was struck by lightning and set on fire. The keeper of the fane solicited the squaws to throw their little ones into the fire to appease the angry divinity, and four infants were thus sacrificed before the French could prevail on them to desist from the horrid rites.†

After Iberville reached the Natchez tribe, the Great Sun, or king of the confederacy, having heard of the approach of the French commandant, determined to pay him a visit in person. As he advanced to the quarters of Iberville, he was borne upon the shoulders of some of his men, and attended by a great retinue of his people. He bade Iberville a hearty welcome, and showed him the most marked attention and kindness during his stay. A treaty of friendship was concluded, with permission

* Martin's Louisiana, vol. i., p. 152. † Idem.

to build a fort and to establish a trading-post among them; which was, however, deferred many years.

"The grand chief of the tribe was revered as of the family of the sun, and he could trace his descent with certainty from the nobles; for the inheritance of power was traced exclusively through the female line. Hard by the temple, on an artificial mound of earth, stood the hut of the 'Great Sun;' around it were grouped the cabins of the tribe. There, for untold years, the savage had freely whispered his tale of love; had wooed his bride, by purchase, from her father; had placed his trust in his manitous; had turned at daybreak toward the East, to hail and worship the beams of morning; had listened to the revelations of dreams; had invoked the aid of the medicine-men to dance the medicine-dance; had won titles of honor by prowess in war, and had tortured and burned his prisoners. There were the fields where, in spring, the whole tribe had gone forth to cultivate the maize and vines; there the scenes of the glad festival at the gathering of the harvest; there the natural amphitheatres, where councils were convened and embassies were received, and the calumet of reconciliation passed in solemn ceremony from lip to lip; there the dead had been arrayed in their proudest apparel," supplied with food for their long journey; and there the requiem was chanted by women, in mournful strains, over their bones; and there, too, when a great sun died, persons of the same age were strangled, as his escort into the realms of shades.*

D'Iberville returned to the fort erecting above the mouth of the Mississippi, while Bienville, accompanied by St. Denys, a few Canadians, and a number of Indians, ascended Red River as far as the Yatassee tribe of Indians, who then dwelt chiefly upon the south side of Red River, upon the Bayou Pierre, about thirty miles above the site of the present town of Natchitoches. After a short time spent on the north side of Red River, in the vicinity of the salines, Bienville returned, leaving St. Denys to prosecute the exploration of the country on Red River far into the West.

Soon afterward, late in April, Lesueur set out with twenty men and Indian guides for the country of the Sioux, high up the Mississippi, in quest of mineral wealth.†

---

* Bancroft's History of the United States, vol. iii., p. 359, 360.
† Martin, vol. i., p. 153. Stoddart's Sketches, p. 27.

[A.D. 1701.] The Spanish governor at Pensacola, unable to expel the French by force, continued to remonstrate against their settlements within the limits of Florida. The English had departed from the Mississippi, and more was now to be apprehended from the Spaniards than from the English.

[A.D. 1702.] Although Iberville considered the colonization of the banks of the Mississippi his chief object, yet the headquarters of the commandant remained at Biloxi. In the spring of 1702, war had been declared by England against France and Spain, and by order of the King of France the headquarters of the commandant were removed to the western bank of the Mobile River. This was the first European settlement within the present State of Alabama. The Spanish settlement at Pensacola was not remote; but as England was now the common enemy, the French and Spanish commandants arranged their boundary between Mobile and Pensacola Bays to be the Perdido River, and both concurred in resisting the common enemy.

Dauphin Island Harbor, near the entrance of Mobile Bay, was used as a convenient station for the fleet during the summer; and although in a sterile pine region, it served as an excellent shelter for the ships, and for many years afterward it was an important port.

English emissaries from Carolina and Virginia penetrated westward to the head waters of the Tombigby and Alabama Rivers, and excited the Indian tribes to hostilities against the Spanish and French settlements near the coast. Others from Virginia penetrated westward to the Wabash, and excited the northwestern Indians against the settlements and traders of the Illinois country.* Instigated by them, the Coroas had killed the Jesuit Foucault, a missionary among the Natchez.

The whole colony of Southern Louisiana as yet did not number thirty families besides soldiers.† Bilious fevers had cut off many of the first emigrants, and famine and Indian hostility now threatened the remainder. But Iberville had been indefatigable in his exertions to protect and provide for the colony. He had, by his detachments, partially explored the remotest regions; the channels and passes of the Mississippi had been explored; the outlets and bayous of the Atchafalaya, Plaquemines, La Fourche, and Manchac, as well as the lake routes,

* Martin's Louisiana, vol. i., p. 159-164. † Bancroft, vol. iii., p. 205.

had been discovered; aided by the Canadian French, the great tributaries of the Mississippi had been explored for more than a thousand miles; the Indian tribes had been conciliated, and were the friends of the French; and missionary stations had been established among them by Jesuits from Canada. The general extent and natural resources of the province were known. St. Denys, in the year 1700, had explored Red River, with a party of French and Indians, for nearly a thousand miles. Other parties had explored the lower portions of the Washita and Yazoo. The Arkansas River had likewise been explored far above the present town of Little Rock. Lesueur had likewise explored the Upper Mississippi as far as the St. Peter's River, in search of precious metals of silver and gold.* But all their dreams of precious stones and metals led them only into the remote wilds of the West, to sicken and die, or to return filled with disappointment.

In all the explorations and excursions throughout this vast province, the splendid water-courses, the great high-ways of nature, afforded, by means of boats and canoes, facilities of travel unsurpassed in the world. The light canoe, propelled by the vigorous arm of the voyageur, traversed the most rapid streams with speed but little inferior to the power of steam. Did a rapid or perpendicular fall obstruct the channel, the same sturdy hands dragged the light canoe over the rapid, or carried it around the falls and over the portage.

[A.D. 1704.] The colony had suffered much from sickness. We have said Sauvolle had fallen an early victim to bilious fever, leaving the youthful Bienville in command of the province. D'Iberville, attacked with yellow fever in the West Indies, had escaped with his life; but his health was gone. Unable to sustain the influence of a tropical climate, he had retired to France; after more than a year, he attempted to do service in the West Indies, but here he was attacked with a

---

* Nothing was done the first two years except to explore the country and form friendly alliances with the numerous tribes of Indians. Stoddart, on the authority of a MS. narrative of La Harpe, during his long service, says that Lesueur ascended the St. Peter's River to the mouth of the Blue Earth River, where in 1702 he erected a fort, called "L'Huillier," in latitude 44° 13′ north, which was abandoned the next year on account of the hostility of the Sioux. Other posts on the Upper Mississippi, above the Wisconsin, were abandoned at the same time.

A settlement and mission were established on the Washita, probably at Sicily Island, in 1703, and another on the Yazoo.—See Sketches of Louisiana. p. 27.

In 1705, the mineral explorers ascended the Missouri as far as the Kanzas River, and finding the Indians friendly, they erected a fort on an island above the mouth of the Osage River.—Idem, p. 28.

severe disease, which terminated his life at Havana, early in July, 1706. In him the colony, as well as the French navy, lost a hero worthy their regret.* Thus perished the bold and persevering founder of the province of Louisiana, a martyr to the glory of France, as La Salle had been a few years before.

[A.D. 1710.] Louisiana was as yet only a vast wilderness, nominally under the jurisdiction of France. During the first ten years of the colony, the population had been repeatedly augmented by additional emigrants from France, and some from Canada. Yet they merely lived; prosper they could not, since agriculture was neglected, and the improvident emigrants were scattered over a vast country, vainly searching for gold and silver and precious stones, or seeking wealth in the paltry traffick of furs and skins purchased of the Indians. Those who remained stationary were settled upon the barren shores of Mobile, of Biloxi, and of St. Louis Bay, with an uncertain dependence upon hunting and fishing, or the precarious bounty of the savages. Many of them, with childish confidence, seemed to have expected annual supplies from France, or that the natives would continue to supply their wants. Led away by the most unreasonable hopes as to the spontaneous products of the country, they deemed labor or provident attention on their part wholly superfluous. They even entertained the belief that the wool of the buffalo, which abounded in the prairies, would yield a valuable commodity for export. Instead of building comfortable houses for permanent residence, they roamed to the most remote regions in quest of mines of precious metals. Every new specimen of earth, to their distempered imaginations, was some valuable mineral; every brilliant ore or carburet was pure gold. Nor was the government of France free from the delusion. The ministry had directed that a number of buffaloes should be caught and tamed, to propagate their species in France, for the sake of their wool. Large quantities of earths were shipped to France from the Upper Mississippi, to be assayed by experienced smelters, in hopes of proving it a valuable oxyd of some precious metal. The most extravagant tales of designing men were received with the greediness of entire belief;† rewards were paid to those who gave intelligence of valuable mines, and extravagant discoveries multiplied in proportion to the rewards offered.

* Bancroft, vol. iii., p. 205. † Martin's Louisiana, vol. i., p. 155.

Hence it is not strange that the colony suffered from want little short of starvation. Several times the colony was driven to extreme suffering for want of the necessary staff of life; and in the year 1701, disease had succeeded to famine, for most of the colonists had sickened, and death had reduced the entire number to one hundred and fifty souls. Three years afterward, or in the year 1704, the same suffering was experienced for food. The horrors of famine and pestilence combined were averted only by the timely relief afforded by the Spanish governor of Pensacola.* For many years the colony was much harassed by Indian hostilities, incited by the British emissaries and traders from Carolina; instead of increasing the number of settlers in compact settlements, the colonial government was anxious to spread them thinly over a vast territory; hence they were easily cut off by the savages. The first maritime trade with the colony was in January, 1709, ten years after the landing of Iberville's colony. This was by a vessel laden with provisions, brandy, and tobacco from Havana, for the purpose of trade;† but the colonists had nothing to barter but hides and peltries, obtained from the natives.

The whole history of the small colonies in Louisiana, for ten years, had been only a tissue of the friendly or hostile relations between detached parties or settlements, and the different Indian tribes; of difficulties encountered by the settlers in their continual efforts to extend the power and influence of France over the savages by treaty or by trade. But now they began to perceive their error. They became convinced that the wealth of Louisiana was in the soil, susceptible of producing every thing requisite for any community. When agriculture began to flourish, provisions became plenty. The colony soon assumed the appearance of a regularly-organized community. Indian girls were employed as servants in private families; twenty negro slaves were now in the colony, and other evidences of luxury appeared. Yet the male population, refusing to labor, amused themselves in every species of idleness. The colony now presented a population of only three hundred and eighty souls, distributed into five settlements, remote from each other. These were on Ship Island, Cat Island, at Biloxi, Mobile, and on the Mississippi. The meager soil of the islands and of the coast, the marshes of the Mississippi,

---

* Martin's Louisiana, vol. i., p. 161, 162.   † Idem, p. 169.

where D'Iberville had erected a small fort, at the mercy of every flood of the river, and the noxious insects and reptiles, no less than the sighing of the pines near Mobile, warned the new emigrants to seek homes further inland. The French court began likewise to see that a change in the government and general policy of the province of Louisiana was requisite. The colony, so far, had failed to meet the expectations of the crown or the people of France, and a change was indispensable.

Heretofore the settlements of Louisiana had been a dependence on New France or Canada, although separated by a wilderness of two thousand miles in extent. Now it was to be made an independent government, responsible only to the crown, and comprising also the Illinois country under its jurisdiction.

[A.D. 1711.] The government of Louisiana was accordingly placed in the hands of a governor-general. The headquarters, or seat of the colonial government, was established at Mobile, and a new fort was erected upon the site of the present city of Mobile.* Dirou d'Artaguette, as commissary ordonnateur, arrived early in the year 1711, and entered upon his duties. De Muys, the governor-general, had died on the voyage.

It was determined that the colonists should depend upon their own exertions and industry for the principal necessaries of life; that agriculture should be fostered, and that the land, which heretofore had been neglected, should be taxed to supply those necessaries; that France would supply only such articles as could not be produced in the province. But the settlements were as yet confined to a few sandy islands, and to the sterile coast from Mobile Bay westward to the Bay of St. Louis, and they could not hope to succeed in tilling a barren soil; although the lakes and bays supplied them in abundance with all kinds of fish and water-fowl, they required bread, the product of a generous earth.

Bienville had been appointed governor-general of the province; he had before seen the necessity of agricultural settlements, and his eye had rested upon the deep alluvions of the Mississippi, which were covered with heavy forests and an impenetrable undergrowth of cane, vines, and briers. To remove these, not only time, but vast labor, was required. Yet Bienville had seen that no agricultural colony could prosper near

* Bancroft, vol. iii., p. 343.

Mobile, and he sought to form settlements on the Mississippi alluvions.

Although exploring parties had been sent to the remotest portions of the province; although every Indian tribe had been visited, yet not one permanent settlement had been made on the banks of the Mississippi; not one vestige of civilized life had been made upon the most fertile regions of the vast province; not one field or village greeted the traveler's eye, if we except the small fort of Iberville, toward the mouth, which had now been abandoned. The government of France, embarrassed and burdened with debt, was unable to maintain the helpless colony.

[A.D. 1712.] In France, it was still believed that Louisiana presented a rich field for enterprise and speculation. The court, therefore, determined to place the resources of the province under the influence of individual enterprise. For this purpose, a grant of exclusive privileges, in all the commerce of the province, for a term of fifteen years, was made to Anthony Crozat, a rich and influential merchant of France. His charter was dated September 26th, 1712. At this time the limits of Louisiana, as claimed by France, were very extensive. As specified in the charter of Crozat, it was "bounded by New Mexico on the west, by the English lands of Carolina on the east, including all the establishments, ports, havens, rivers, and principally the port and haven of the Isle of Dauphin, heretofore called Massacre; the River St. Louis, heretofore called Mississippi, from the edge of the sea as far as the Illinois, together with the River St. Philip, heretofore called Missouri, the River St. Jerome, heretofore called Wabash, with all the lands, lakes, and rivers mediately or immediately flowing into any part of the River St. Louis or Mississippi."*

Thus Louisiana, as claimed by France, at that early period embraced all the immense regions of the United States, from the Alleghany Mountains on the east, to the Rocky Mountains on the west, and northward to the great lakes of Canada. As Bancroft observes, " Louisiana was held to embrace the whole Valley of the Mississippi. Not a fountain bubbled on the west of the Alleghanies but was claimed as being within the French empire. Half a mile from the head of the southern branch of the Savannah River is 'Herbert's Spring,' which flows into

* Martin's Louisiana, vol. i., p. 178, 179. See, also, Stoddard, p. 133–135.

the Mississippi; strangers who drank of it would say that they had tasted French waters."*

On the west, France claimed to the Bay of St. Bernard, fifty miles west of the Rio Colorado, where La Salle, in 1685, located his unfortunate colony, the remains of which, if any remained, are supposed to have been destroyed or carried off by the Spaniards in 1689.† A large portion of the states of Mississippi and Alabama, not drained by the Mississippi River, were also a part of Louisiana, and so remained for more than sixty years, or until the dismemberment in 1763.

Up to this time, in thirteen years, there had been not less than twenty-five hundred settlers of all kinds introduced into Louisiana, who had been distributed in distant explorations and scattered settlements on the coast west of Mobile. Many had died; some had remained in the Illinois country. Yet the colony had been a source of great expense to the crown. Already 689,000 livres, or about $170,000,‡ had been expended, when the value of money was not reduced by paper.

[A.D. 1713.] The French population in all this region was still only a few hundred indolent and ignorant colonists, besides a few troops in the forts. At the time Crozat's charter was granted, the whole number of settlers in Lower Louisiana consisted chiefly of twenty-eight families, whose occupation, besides fishing and hunting, was the cultivation of small tracts of sterile lands for gardens, in the pine regions around the bays of Biloxi, St. Louis, and Mobile. The soldiers, distributed in the several garrisoned forts, consisted of one hundred and seventy-five men, comprising two companies of infantry with fifty men in each, and seventy-five Canadian volunteers. There were also at this time twenty negro slaves, a few Jesuits and Franciscans, and king's officers. The whole number of Europeans in Lower Louisiana was three hundred and eighty souls, and about three hundred head of cattle. There were also a few settlements on the Kaskaskia and Wabash Rivers, as well as upon the Illinois. Such was the feeble condition of the colony in Louisiana, the whole commerce of which was secured to M. Crozat as a monopoly, together with the privilege of working all the mines.

Yet Crozat entered upon the enterprise with zeal and ac-

* Bancroft, vol. iii., p. 343. † Martin's Louisiana, vol. i., p. 203.
‡ Stoddart's Sketches, p. 29.

tivity. He expected to derive great profit from the fur-trade and traffick with the Indians. But the prospect of discovering rich mines of gold and silver held out to his enraptured vision sources of boundless wealth, and tempted enterprise and expense. In the line of commercial trade, the demands of the Spanish settlements of New Mexico, Florida, and the West Indies promised the most certain revenue of the precious metals. The commerce of these countries he vainly hoped to monopolize by favor, intrigue, or otherwise.

Among the many exclusive privileges granted by his charter, besides the trade and commerce of the province, and of all the Indian tribes, and the exclusive privilege of working all the mines of precious metals, was that of importing from the coast of Africa, for sale, one ship-load of negroes every year.

" La Motte Cadillac, now royal governor of Louisiana, became his partner; and the merchant proprietary of Detroit sought fortune by discovering mines and encroaching on the colonial monopolies of Spain." "But the latter attempt met with no success whatever."* A vessel was sent to Vera Cruz with a rich cargo for sale, but it was not allowed to dispose of its merchandise, and every Spanish harbor in the Gulf of Mexico was closed against the vessels of Crozat. The occupation of Louisiana itself was deemed an encroachment upon Spanish territory.

Failing in this quarter, M. Crozat caused settlements or trading-posts to be made in the most remote parts of the province, while explorations were extended into the most distant known tribes. Under St. Denys, a settlement and trading-post was established on Red River, on the site of the present town of Natchitoches, in the present State of Louisiana. St. Denys also explored Red River much further, and advanced on a tour of observation as far as the Rio Bravo del Norte, the present western limit of Texas.† About the same time, a

---

* Bancroft, vol. iii., p. 347.

† St. Denys, in 1714, was dispatched with thirty men to Natchitoches, for the purpose of forming a settlement. He was also instructed to explore the country westward, and to observe the movements of the Spaniards on the Rio Bravo, and to see whether they had advanced over that river into Louisiana. He found that they had formed a settlement on the west side of the Rio Bravo, where they had erected a fort, which was called the *presidio* of St. John the Baptist. No settlement had then been made by them east of that river; but they claimed jurisdiction over the country eastward to Red River, under the name of the province of "Texas," signifying "friends," because the Indians were friendly.

small settlement and trading-post was established on the Yazoo, and on Sicily Island, and high up the Washita, on the site of the present town of Monroe, afterward known as the "post of Washita." M. Charleville, one of M. Crozat's traders, penetrated the Shawanese tribes, then known as the "Chouanoes," upon the Cumberland River. His store was situated upon a mound near the present site of Nashville, on the west side of the Cumberland River, near French-lick Creek, and about seventy yards from each stream.*

[A.D. 1714.] Soon afterward, with the aid of a band of Choctâs, a fort was built on the Coosa River, two leagues above the mouth of the Tallapoosa, upon an isthmus, where both streams approach within a few hundred yards of each other. This post was nearly four hundred miles above the mouth of the Alabama River; a garrison was placed in it, and the post was subsequently called "Fort Toulouse." The site was the same occupied by "Fort Jackson" just one hundred years afterward.

[A.D. 1715.] In all his calculations and expectations, M. Crozat was doomed to be sadly disappointed. After nearly three years spent in fruitless negotiations with the Spanish viceroy of Mexico relative to commercial intercourse with the Spanish ports on the Gulf of Mexico, and after much delay, vexation, and expense, his vessels were prohibited from trading in any of the Spanish ports. He then attempted to institute commercial relations by land for supplying the interior provinces of New Mexico; but his goods were seized and his agents imprisoned, after a persevering effort of nearly five years.†

The same year, more effectually to hold the country, the French established a small post and mission upon the upper tributaries of the Sabine: the post was known as the post "Le Dout," and was in existence until the treaty of 1763, when Louisiana was ceded to Spain. Another small post had also been erected about thirty miles west of the present town of Nacogdoches, which also was kept up for many years.

During the first thirty years after the settlement of Louisiana, the French commandants kept a watchful eye upon the Spaniards, and sent frequent detachments to the western parts of Texas.—See Stoddart's Sketches, p. 30, 31, and 41.

* See Haywood's History of Tennessee.

† In 1715, La Motte sent St. Denys as envoy to Mexico, to negotiate a treaty of colonial commerce with the viceroy. In this he was successful; and friendly relations were established between the French of Louisiana and the Spanish settlements of the Rio Bravo during the years 1716 and 1717. In 1718, St. Denys was again in Mexico as agent of La Motte and Crozat, with valuable merchandise to exchange for such articles and commodities as were useful in Louisiana. But the viceroy had died, and his successor, regardless of treaty obligations, seized St. Denys as a smuggler and spy,

The trade with the Indians also failed to meet his expectations. The English emissaries from Carolina were active in their efforts to excite the tribes east of the Mississippi to hostilities against the French. Where this was impracticable, they endeavored to annoy the French trade by supplying the same articles at reduced prices. The mines of Louisiana were principally of lead, copper, and iron, all of which were found in great abundance; but they were not profitable. Much money had been spent in searching for gold and silver, without any recompense. Failing to realize any profit from all his contemplated resources, he was unable to meet his engagements with his workmen, agents, and troops, and dissatisfaction ensued. He had expended 425,000 livres in his operations, and had realized from all the sources of trade only 300,000, leaving him the loser of 125,000 livres, or about $30,000.* His partner, La Motte, the governor, had died recently.

[A.D. 1716.] As yet no permanent settlement had been made at Natchez. A few traders and hunters had frequented that beautiful region, and some stragglers had taken up their abode among the Natchez Indians. A difficulty had occurred, and some Frenchmen had been plundered, and one or two had been murdered. A feeling of hostility manifesting itself among some of the tribe, it was deemed expedient and prudent to erect a fort and to place a small garrison in the Natchez country. Bienville, who was now again governor of the province, repaired to the Natchez tribe in June, and, after settling the difficulty with much sternness and severity, he began the erection of the fort, which had been previously ordered by the king's government. A garrison of eighteen men, under the command of M. Pailloux, was left to defend the post and protect the traders.†

This fort was erected on the site selected by his brother Iberville sixteen years before, and the name by him selected was now confirmed, and the post was called "Fort Rosalie." This fort was situated remote from the bluff which overlooks the river. Its site was probably near the eastern limit of the

---

confined him in a dungeon, and confiscated his goods as contraband. St. Denys, for more than two years, had been married to a Spanish lady of noble descent; and at length the viceroy, to satisfy popular feeling, liberated him to the city bounds. In September, 1718, he escaped on horseback, and at length, after more than six months, reached Louisiana in April, 1719.—See Stoddart's Sketches, p. 33, 34; also, Martin's Louisiana, vol. i., p. 191.   * Idem, p. 35.   † Martin's Louisiana, vol. i., p. 190.

present city of Natchez. This gave Natchez precedence, as a settlement, over every other upon the Mississippi south of the Illinois country.

[A.D. 1717.] Early in the following year, L'Epinai arrived at Mobile as governor of the province, with M. Hubert, ordonnateur-commissaire. The same arrival brought also fifty emigrants for the establishment of new settlements, and three companies of infantry to re-enforce the garrisons at the different posts.

Through the intrigue of England, the Spanish ports were now all closed against Crozat's vessels, and the interior being cut off from his trade, his plans had all failed. He had been indefatigable in urging his commercial operations; but loss or misfortune lay in his path, and none of his plans prospered. At length, despairing of the ultimate success of his enterprise in a savage country, and having already expended large sums of money without any profit, Crozat determined to abandon the whole scheme. He accordingly petitioned the king to revoke his charter, or to permit him to surrender it to the crown. The king complied with his request, and accepted the surrender of his charter in August, 1717. The government of the colony reverted solely into the hands of the king's officers, and Crozat retired to France.

During the period of Crozat's charter, the colony continued to languish; the settlements increased slowly, and were confined chiefly to the River and Bay of Mobile, and other parts of the coast westward from Biloxi. Two small settlements had been commenced on Red River, near Natchitoches and at Alexandria. Although Crozat had introduced many settlers, so that the entire European population had nearly doubled their numbers, yet the whole number of colonists was still only seven hundred souls, of all ages, sexes, and colors. Several small forts had been erected. Among them was the one on the Coosa River, called Fort Toulouse, and the other at Natchez, known as Fort Rosalie. These were merely blockhouses, inclosed with palisades to protect the inmates from surprise by the Indians, and to shelter the traders, with their goods and families.

As Mr. Bancroft observes, "For the advancement of the colony, Crozat accomplished nothing. The only prosperity which it possessed grew out of the enterprise of humble individuals, who had succeeded in establishing a little barter between themselves and the natives, and a petty trade with neighboring European settlements. These small sources of prosperity were cut off by the profitless but fatal monopoly of the Parisian merchant. The Indians were too powerful to be resisted by his factors. The English gradually appropriated the trade with the natives, and every Frenchman in Louisiana, except his agents, fomented opposition to his privileges. Crozat resigned his charter."*

CHAPTER VI.

LOUISIANA UNDER THE "WESTERN COMPANY" UNTIL THE FAILURE OF LAW'S "MISSISSIPPI SCHEME."—A.D. 1717 TO 1722.

Argument.—Enthusiasm in France for colonizing the Mississippi.—The Western Company succeeds to the Monopoly of Louisiana.—Charter of the Company.—Its Privileges, Powers, and Term of Existence.—Extravagant Expectations of the Company.—Arrival of the Company's Officers, Troops, and some Colonists at Mobile.—Bienville appointed Governor.—He desires to extend Settlements upon the Mississippi.—Selects the Site of New Orleans.—Establishes a Military Post on it.—Company refuse to leave Mobile as Headquarters.—Mining Delusion excludes Agriculture.—Extensive Mining Arrangements in 1719.—Bienville's Agricultural Views embraced by the Company.—Dependent Condition of Louisiana.—Several large and small Colonies from France arrive.—The Spaniards establish Settlements and "Missions" east of the Rio del Norte.—La Harpe maintains his Post near Natchitoches.—Spanish Encroachments.—Correspondence of the Spanish Commandant, De la Corne, with La Harpe, in 1719.—Negro Slavery introduced into Louisiana by the Western Company.—Different early Importations from Guinea.—Value of Slaves.—Sources from which the African Slave-trade is supplied.—Changes in the Government of Louisiana in 1719.—Superior Council organized.— Headquarters removed to Biloxi.— Emigrants and Troops arrive in 1720.—War with Spain.—Operations at Mobile and Pensacola.—The latter captured and burned by the French.—Spanish Incursions from Santa Fé to the Missouri and Arkansas.—Fort Orleans built on the Missouri.—Plan of Defense for the Upper Mississippi.—Lesueur occupies a Post on the St. Peter's.—Fort Chartres commenced.—Becomes a strong Fortress.—Difficulties in Southwestern Louisiana.—Bienville resolves to occupy Texas.—His "Order" to Bernard La Harpe.—La Harpe's Occupation of the Bay of St. Bernard.—Indian Hostilities east of the Mississippi.—" Fort Condé" built on the Alabama.—Increase of Population by different Arrivals.—Colonies.—Convicts.—Females from the Houses of Correction in Paris.—Interdiction of Convicts to Louisiana.—Arrival of Emigrants and Slaves.—New Orleans becomes the Capital of the Province.—Embarrassment of the Western Company.—Sufferings of the Colonies and Scarcity of Food.—Revolt of Troops at Fort Condé.—New Orleans in 1723.—Picture of Law's celebrated Scheme.—Its Character.—False Basis.—Credit System.—Mining Delusion.—Schemes for procrastinating the Catastrophe.—Bursting of the "Bubble."—Calamitous Consequences of an inflated Currency.

[A.D. 1717.] "The Valley of the Mississippi inflamed the imagination of France; anticipating the future, the French na-

------
* Hist. of United States, vol. iii., p. 348.

tion beheld the certain opulence of coming ages as within their immediate grasp; and John Law, who possessed the entire confidence of the regent, obtained the whole control of the commerce of Louisiana and Canada."* Trade, commerce, and inexhaustible wealth were to spring up in the solitudes of America.

No sooner had Crozat surrendered his charter, than others were anxious and ready to enter the same field of adventurous enterprise. A company was organized and received the royal charter, under the name of the "Western Company," connected with Law's Bank of France, and sharing its privileges. This charter conferred upon the Western Company much more extensive powers and privileges than those granted to M. Crozat. The plan of this company was not unlike that of the British "East India Company," and possessed powers and privileges nearly equal. But the plunder of a savage wilderness could not yield such immense revenues as an ancient, wealthy, and effeminate empire. Hence the French West India Company ultimately failed in its operations.

The Western Company had a legal existence, by the charter, of twenty-five years. It was vested with the exclusive privilege of the entire commerce of Louisiana and New France, and with authority to enforce its rights. It was authorized to monopolize the trade of all the colonies in the provinces, and of all the Indian tribes within the limits of that extensive region, even to the remotest source of every stream tributary in any wise to the Mississippi and Mobile Rivers; to make treaties with the Indian tribes; to declare and prosecute war against them in defense of the colony; to grant lands, to erect forts, to levy troops, to raise recruits, and to open and work all mines of precious metals or stones which might be discovered in the province. It was permitted and authorized to nominate and present men for the office of governor, and for commanders of the troops, and to commission the latter, subject to the king's approval; to remove inferior judges and civil officers; to build and equip ships of war, and to cast cannon. The king also granted for the use of the company all the forts, magazines, guns, ammunition, and vessels pertaining to the province.†

Among the obligations imposed upon the company was the stipulation to introduce into the province of Louisiana, within

* Bancroft's U. States, vol. iii., p. 349.   † Martin's Louisiana, vol. i., p. 200–202.

the period of their chartered privileges, six thousand white persons and three thousand negro slaves, and to protect the settlements against Indian hostilities.

It was vainly hoped, on the part of France, that the Western Company would exert a powerful influence in colonizing the vast regions of the Mississippi Valley, while the company looked forward to certain inexhaustible sources of wealth: but what are exclusive privileges in a savage wilderness? Where there are few and destitute settlements, of what value are the spoils?

[A.D. 1718.] In the following spring, early, three of the company's ships arrived in the port of Mobile, having on board M. Boisbriant, the king's lieutenant for Louisiana, bearing the king's commission to M. Bienville as governor of the province, M. Hubert, "director-general" of the company's affairs, besides three companies of infantry, and sixty-nine colonists. Such was the first step of the company to subdue the great Valley of the Mississippi.*

Bienville again entered upon his duties as governor and lieutenant-general of the province. He still deemed it expedient to remove the headquarters of the colonial government from the sterile regions near Mobile Bay, and to establish it upon the banks of the St. Louis or Mississippi River. Upon the sterile lands around Mobile Bay, and the Bays of St. Louis and Biloxi, no agricultural colony could prosper, and without agriculture the province could not be sustained. Upon the fertile alluvions, and the rich hills bordering on the Mississippi and its tributaries, an agricultural community might succeed, and supply the whole colony with all the products necessary to sustain life, and yield a competence to the emigrating colonies. He accordingly resolved to encourage the extension of settlements upon the banks of the Mississippi itself.

In view of this object, he selected a site for a town, and placed fifty men to clear off the grounds, as the location of the future capital of the province, and to erect barracks for the troops. The ground selected was that which is now covered by the lower portion, or French part, of the present city of New Orleans; a name given by Bienville in honor of the dissolute but generous regent of France, and a name which it retains to this day. But M. Hubert, the director-general of

* Martin's Louisiana, vol. i., p. 202.

the company, refused to remove the offices and the warehouse of the company from Mobile. Of course, Bienville's new settlement remained but little more than a small military post, remote from the settlements. Next spring the river overflowed its banks, the new settlement was completely inundated, and the site seemed to present an uncertain location for a city. The troops were stationed again at Mobile; yet, subsequently, a small military post was renewed at New Orleans, although for three years Bienville's headquarters remained at Mobile. M. Hubert could not agree that the commercial depôt of the company should be removed from a sea-port which afforded a direct intercourse with the West Indies, whence they could derive the earliest intelligence from France. M. Hubert considered the site of New Orleans an inland point, remote from maritime advantages, and subject to frequent inundations, which must render it unhealthy. Agriculture was not the object of the company, so much as trade and the rich mines supposed to exist in the interior.

The delusion which dreamed of rich mines of silver and gold in Louisiana still haunted the minds of the company and its agents. The most influential men in the province were eager to encourage the search for the precious metals. Notwithstanding the failure of Crozat, the company were willing to believe that the failure resulted more from unskillful assayers than from absence of gold. To remedy this defect, a numerous company of miners and assayers, not less than two hundred in number, was to be sent to Upper Louisiana, under the direction of Francis Renault, "director-general of the mines of Louisiana." Every agent and every trader was required carefully to observe and report the presence of any rich ores which might be discovered in their distant rambles. The inexhaustible soil was neglected as a too tardy source of wealth.*

Yet Bienville, confident that the prosperity of the colony depended upon its agricultural resources, and knowing that nothing was to be expected by the company from free trade with the Mexican provinces or Florida, persisted in his efforts to transfer the colonists to the banks of the Mississippi. The disastrous experiment of M. Crozat was sufficient evidence of this fact; and what was to be gained by the exclusive commerce and trade of a colony which consisted of only a few

* Martin's Louisiana, vol. i., p. 210–216.

hundred indigent, lazy people, scattered thinly over a savage wilderness? Such was the reasoning of Bienville.

The attainment of riches from the mines of precious metals in Upper Louisiana was equally preposterous. Mines there were, of purest lead, of iron, of copper, and other metals; but not of gold or silver. At length the directory concurred with Bienville, that, after the fur trade with the Indians, the next most desirable source of revenue to the company would spring from a densely settled country of civilized people. It became, therefore, an object of primary importance to encourage the emigration of industrious and useful citizens from France, who should establish regular agricultural settlements upon the fertile lands which spread through the alluvions of the Mississippi, its large tributaries and bayous. To accomplish this object, large grants of land were made to influential and enterprising men, for the purpose of establishing new colonies upon the Mississippi. The largest grants were located upon the banks of the river, within three hundred miles above New Orleans; others were located upon Red River, upon the Washita, upon the Yazoo, and upon the Arkansas. The grant on the Arkansas was made to the noted John Law himself, the Scotch financier, who was now at the head of the Bank of France, and controlled the financial operations of the company as well as of France. Law stipulated to colonize the Arkansas with fifteen hundred German emigrants from Provençe, in France, and to keep up a sufficient military force for their protection against Indian hostility. Other grants were upon similar conditions; the number of emigrants to be furnished were proportioned to the extent of the grant.* A change in the condition of the colony was about to be introduced by the new policy which had been adopted; and preparations were active in France, by the different grantees, in collecting their emigrants who were willing to visit the great Valley of the Mississippi.

Although, up to this time, agriculture had been entirely neg-

* Among the grants made for colonies was one to John Law, of twelve miles square, upon the Arkansas; one on the Yazoo to Leblanc and others; one to M. Hubert and others, merchants of St. Malves; one to Bernard de la Harpe, above Natchitoches; one to De Meuse, at Point Coupée; one to St. Reiné, at the Tunicas; one to Dirou D'Artaguette, at Baton Rouge; one to Paris Duvernay, at Bayou Manchac, on the west side of the river; one to Du Muys, at Tchoupitoulas; one to the Marquis d'Anconis; one to the Marquis d'Artagnac, at Cannes Brulée; one to De la Housaie and La Houpe, on the opposite side; one to Madame de Mezières; one to Madame de Chaumonot, at Pascagoula.—See Martin's Louisiana, vol. i., p. 207.

lected in Lower Louisiana, yet upon the Illinois and Wabash agricultural products had become staples of a valuable trade. In the South, although blessed with a soil unsurpassed in fertility, and a climate inferior to none in the world for agricultural productions, the colonists had been dependent on France, or upon the caprice of chance and circumstances, for all their supplies. Instead of locating themselves upon the fertile hills above Bayou Manchac, or upon the deep alluvions of the river, they had all disembarked upon the crystalline sands of Dauphin Island, where they were often reduced to a state of want and suffering by any accidental interruption in the arrival of supplies expected from France.

Whatever the mines of Upper Louisiana might ultimately yield, it had become evident that the true wealth of Louisiana had been entirely neglected. This neglect had several times reduced the infant colony to the verge of destruction. Twenty years had now elapsed since the first settlement of Louisiana by Iberville, and yet the people were dependent upon France for all their supplies, except such as were derived from the chase or the prolific waters, unless supplied from the precarious bounty of the savages. Thrice had the colony been on the verge of famine; and fortune, not their own enterprise, rescued them from starvation.

Meantime the Spaniards were advancing from Mexico to the east side of the Rio del Norte, and were establishing their claims to the province of Texas by actual occupation. During the last two years, they had established several "missions," or fortified settlements, in Western Texas; and others were contemplated as far east as the Adaës, near Natchitoches, and upon the Delta of Red River. Advancing from the "Mission of St. John Baptist," on the Del Norte, they had erected the mission of San Antonio de Bexar, on the northeast side of the San Antonio River. Advancing still further, they erected the "Mission of La Bahia," on the San Antonio River, not thirty miles north of the Bay of St. Bernard, which they designated *Espiritu Santo*, and near the present town of Goliad. These towns are the oldest Spanish settlements in Texas, and were occupied as early as the year 1716. During the Spanish dominion over Louisiana, they became places of great importance. Goliad, as its name implies, was "the place of strength." One hundred years after its first settlement, "it contained sev eral thousand inhabitants," and, situated upon a high, rocky bluff, upon the bank of the San Antonio River, " its fortifications, which were built almost entirely of stone" by the Spaniards, were deemed impregnable.

Soon after the establishment of these posts, the Spaniards advanced to Nacogdoches, upon the waters of the Angelina, a tributary of the Neches. Having established a "mission" at this point also, they advanced eastward to the Adaës, in the vicinity of the present town of Natchitoches. Here they established the "Mission of San Miguel de Linarez," upon the banks of the Adaës, and the settlement is still commemorated in the adjacent lake, now known as "Spanish Lake."*

Such were the advances of the Spaniards toward the Mississippi as early as the years 1716 and 1718.

Among the most noted "missions" of Western Texas, in subsequent years, were those of the Alamo, in Bexar; San José and Conception, situated a few miles below the city of San Antonio; and Espiritu Santo, near Goliad.

The French kept a jealous eye toward the approaches of the Spaniards from Mexico; but such was the feeble condition of the colonies in Louisiana, that the country west of the Mississippi had not been occupied until the year 1718, when emigrants began to arrive for that portion of the province.

[A.D. 1719.] During the past year, Bernard de la Harpe had received a grant for a colony on Red River, near the present site of Natchitoches. Late in the autumn he arrived with a colony of sixty settlers, and near the close of December reached the point of his location. He had orders to occupy the country with a military post, and to explore it westward. Having selected his situation, in January he began to make a permanent settlement, and to construct a military post on the present site of Natchitoches. From this point,

* Martin's Louisiana, vol. i., p. 204-209. In 1718, the principal eastern settlement of Mexico was the Presidio of St. John the Baptist, six miles west of the Rio del Norte. The same year settlements and missions were extended into the western portion of Louisiana, or what was known to the Spaniards as the province of "Texas." A mission was established among the Adaës Indians, within twenty miles of the Natchitoches tribe. This was the mission of San Miguel de Linarez. The following year, 1719, two friars, accompanied by a few soldiers, joined the mission among the Adaës, to catechise them, among whom several Frenchmen had settled. At the same time, the Spaniards had established several missions among the Assinais Indians, residing about thirty miles east of Nacogdoches, or nearly one hundred and forty miles west of Red River, and in the region designated by them New Philippine.—See Stoddart, p. 142. Also Moore's Texas, ed. 1840, p. 74.

subsequently, during the summer, he explored the country westward, far into the province of Texas, and lost no opportunity of conciliating the Western tribes, and of opening with them a friendly intercourse by means of trading-posts established among them.

Early in the spring, other colonies began to arrive for some of the principal grants. Among these, the first large colony was that of M. Dubuisson, who arrived in April at Mobile, with sixty families, to settle a grant made to Paris Duvernay, on the right bank, or west side, of the Mississippi, opposite the Bayou Manchac, or Iberville. In June one of the company's vessels arrived, with upward of eight hundred emigrants, for different grants and settlements. These proceeded from the harbor of Dauphin Island, by way of the Bay of St. Louis, through Lakes Pontchartrain and Maurepas, to the Mississippi, as the others had done, to seek their respective locations. Among them were seventy emigrants for the settlement of a grant made to M. de la Housaie, on the Mississippi, opposite to the Cannes Brulée Bayou; also, seventy settlers for a grant made to M. de la Houpe, adjoining the last. Among them were also twelve small colonies, of fifteen persons each, for the settlement of twelve other small grants; also thirty young men, to serve as clerks at the different offices and dépôts of the company. This vessel also contained a number of convicts from Paris, whose sentence had been commuted to transportation.

In the autumn, sixty emigrants arrived at Mobile, for the settlement of M. de la Harpe on Red River. About the same time, M. Brizart arrived, with a colony for a settlement upon the Yazoo River, where Fort St. Peter was afterward built. Besides those who came as colonists for particular grants, there were, from time to time, many arrivals of individuals and families from France, who were at liberty to choose their own locations and settle at pleasure. Accessions of this kind continued gradually to increase the numbers of the several colonies.

Among the valuable emigrants of this year, we must not omit a colony of miners, two hundred in number, under the direction of Philip Francis Renault, son of Philip Renault, a noted iron-founder at Consobre, near Maubeuge, in France. Renault, as "director-general of the mines" under the Western

Company, with his colony, proceeded to the Illinois country, where he entered upon the duties of his office. As the mining interest never prospered, many of these, subsequently, were incorporated with the villagers and agriculturists of the Illinois country. Others engaged in mining operations on the east and west banks, far above the Wisconsin River.

The jealousy of Spain kept a watchful eye upon the advance of the French settlements west of the Mississippi. On the east, the line between Louisiana and Florida had been mutually arranged, and the Perdido was the dividing stream; but on the west no such arrangement had been made. While France claimed westward as far as the Bay of St. Bernard, west of the Colorado River, Spain claimed the territory eastward, from Mexico nearly to the Mississippi itself. The Spanish authorities had advanced their settlements, as before observed, from Texas as far east as the village of Adaës, on the Bayou Adaës, near "Spanish Lake," and within nine miles of Natchitoches, where La Harpe had erected a military post, and was now establishing a regular French colony.

Such was the state of claims and boundaries between the French province of Louisiana and the Spanish province of Texas in January, 1719, when La Harpe arrived at Natchitoches. Having ascertained that the Spanish commandant of Texas, Don Martin de la Corne, had established several missions in Western Louisiana, forming a chain of settlements from Nacogdoches to the Adaës, and was also preparing to form a settlement on Red River, at the Caddo village, La Harpe determined to act with promptness and decision. He proceeded, early in February, to explore and occupy the river and country above the Spanish settlements. On the 21st of April, with a detachment of troops, he had proceeded as far as the Yatassee village, one hundred and fifty leagues by the river above Natchitoches. Here he established a trading-post for the company, and on the 27th he laid the foundation of a fort at the Natsoo village.[*] This post was about two hundred miles above the head of the Great Raft, and near the parallel of 33° 30' north latitude, and probably not far from the mouth of North Little River, in the southern angle of the present county of Hempstead, in the State of Arkansas.

The Spanish commandant of Texas remonstrated against

[*] Darby's Louisiana, p. 22. See, also, Stoddart's Sketches, p. 142–145.

this intrusion upon the territory of his province; and in June La Harpe received from Don de la Corne the following laconic communication, requiring him to abandon the country, which was claimed as a part of the Spanish province of Texas, viz.:

"Monsieur,—I am very sensible of the politeness that M. de Bienville and yourself have had the goodness to show me. The order I have received from the king, my master, is, to maintain a good understanding with the French of Louisiana. My own inclinations lead me equally to afford them all the services that depend upon me; but I am compelled to say, that your arrival at the Nassonite village surprises me very much. Your governor could not have been ignorant that the post you occupy belongs to my government, and that all the lands west of the Nassonites depend upon New Mexico. I recommend you to give advice of this to M. Bienville, or you will force me to oblige you to abandon lands that the French have no right to occupy. I have the honor to be, sir,

"De la Corne.

"Trinity River, May 20, 1719."

To which the gallant La Harpe returned the following answer, viz.:

"Monsieur,—The order of his Catholic majesty, to maintain a good understanding with the French of Louisiana, and the kind intentions you have yourself expressed toward them, accord but little with your proceedings. Permit me to inform you that M. de Bienville is perfectly informed of the limits of his government, and is very certain that the post of Nassonite depends not upon the dominions of his Catholic majesty. He knows, also, that the province of Lastekas, of which you say you are governor, is a part of Louisiana. M. de la Salle took possession in 1685, in the name of his most Christian majesty; and since the above epoch, possession has been renewed from time to time.

"Respecting the post of Nassonite, I can not comprehend by what right you pretend that it forms a part of New Mexico. I beg leave to represent to you, that Don Antoine du Miroir, who discovered New Mexico in 1683, never penetrated east of that province or the Rio Bravo. It was the French who first made alliances with the savage tribes in this region; and it is natural to conclude that a river which flows into the Mississippi, and the lands it waters, belong to the king, my master.

Vol. I.—P

"If you will do me the pleasure to come into this quarter, I will convince you that I hold a post which I know how to defend. I have the honor to be, sir,

"DE LA HARPE.*

"Nassonite, July 8, 1719."

The French continued to hold the country in question, notwithstanding all the remonstrances of the Spaniards, and never ceased to claim the jurisdiction westward to the Rio del Norte, up to the cession of Louisiana to Spain in 1762. For several years, the Spanish post and settlement on the Trinity was maintained; but the settlement of the Adaës, near the French post of Natchitoches, was abandoned. Each commandant at their respective posts, on Red River and on the Trinity, resolved to permit the other quietly to occupy his post, and to secure each the friendship and alliance of the neighboring tribes, while war was ravaging the seaboard of Florida and Louisiana.

Experiments had shown that the fertile soil of the Mississippi, as well as the climate, were well adapted to the cultivation of tobacco, rice, and indigo. But laborers were few, and the climate sickly to European emigrants. The European constitution was ill adapted to endure the labors of the field during the long summers and under the burning suns of Louisiana, and to withstand the chilling dews and fogs of night. In the attempt many had sickened and died, and the survivors deemed life and health more precious than the redundant wealth of the fields.†

Negroes from Africa had been successfully employed in the fields and in the low grounds of Virginia and Carolina, as well as in the Islands of Cuba and Hispaniola, under a tropical sun.‡ Experience had proved that, by nature, they were well adapted to withstand such a climate as that of Louisiana. Under these considerations, the company resolved to introduce African negroes to cultivate the fields, and to open plantations among the dense undergrowth and heavy forests of the Mississippi. Two ships were accordingly dispatched to the coast of Africa for a

---

* See Darby's Louisiana, p. 23, 24. The correspondence between the French and Spanish commandants is placed by Martin among the occurrences of 1720. See Martin's Louisiana, vol. i., p. 219–223. This, however, is an error. The inquiring reader may consult the "American State Papers," Boston edition of 1819, vol. xii., p. 106, 107, for the elaborate discussion of the Louisiana boundaries, by Don Onis and John Q. Adams.   † Darby's Louisiana, p. 22.   ‡ Martin's Louisiana, vol. i., p. 210.

cargo of slaves. These vessels made a prosperous voyage, and late in autumn they returned with five hundred African negroes, in company with three vessels of war. They disembarked at Pensacola, which had been captured from the Spaniards by the French troops of Louisiana soon after the irruption of hostilities.

With a portion of the slaves which were sent to New Orleans the directors of the company opened a large plantation on the west bank of the river, nearly opposite the post at New Orleans. This was done as an example to others, and to test the advantages which were to be derived from this species of labor. This was the first extensive slave plantation in Louisiana, owned, too, by a company with chartered privileges. The remainder of the cargo was sold to emigrants and opulent settlers in different parts of the province, but chiefly for the agricultural settlements on the Lower Mississippi.

Such was the first importation of African slaves into Louisiana as a cargo from Guinea; and for several years the importation of negroes was one of the most profitable monopolies of the company. During Crozat's monopoly but few slaves had been introduced, and those by private persons as domestic property. Although Crozat's charter conferred the privilege of introducing " one ship-load of negroes annually," it does not appear that he availed himself of the privilege.

[A.D. 1720–1722.] The second cargo of slaves introduced into Louisiana consisted of five hundred African negroes, which arrived in the company's ships at Mobile during the summer of 1720. The third cargo, consisting also of five hundred Africans, arrived at Mobile on the first of April, 1721.* The fourth cargo of slaves consisted of two hundred and ninety African negroes on board a Guineaman, which arrived at Mobile in the spring of 1722. The fifth cargo of slaves arrived in another Guineaman in August following, and consisted of three hundred African negroes.

During the existence of the company, for several years afterward, their agents continued to supply the demand for slaves in the agricultural interest of Louisiana from the same source, the number varying from one to three hundred annually. The common price for a good negro man was about one hundred and fifty dollars, or about six hundred livres. For a healthy

* Martin's Louisiana, vol. i., p. 234.

woman, the ordinary price was about one hundred and twenty-five dollars, or five hundred livres;* the livre being equal to twenty-five cents Federal money. Such was the origin of African slavery in Louisiana.

While France and Spain, during the next half century, were endeavoring to supply their American colonies with negro slaves as laborers on their plantations, England, true to her system of monopolies, was contending for the monopoly of the slave-trade in the supply, not only of her own provinces, but also those of France and Spain. To this policy of England, encouraged by British legislation, and fostered by royal favor, posterity owes the fact that one sixth of the population of the United States, a moiety of those who now dwell in the states and territories nearest the Gulf of Mexico, are descendants of Africans.

The colored men imported into the American colonies were sought all along the African coast, for thirty degrees together, from Cape Blanco to Loango St. Paul's, from the great Desert of Sahara to the kingdom of Angola, or, perhaps, even to the borders of the land of the Caffres. They were chiefly gathered from gangs that were marched from the far interior, so that the freight of a single ship might be composed of persons of different languages, and of nations altogether strange to each other. Nor was there uniformity of complexion: of those brought to our country, some were from tribes of which the skin was a tawny-yellow; others varied, not only in the hues of the skin, but in the diversities of features which abound in Africa among the varieties of the negro race.†

"The purchases in Africa were made in part of convicts punished with slavery, or mulcted in a fine, which was discharged by the proceeds of their sale; of debtors sold, though but rarely, into foreign bondage; of children sold by their parents; of kidnapped villagers; of captives taken in war. Hence the sea-coast and the confines of hostile nations were laid waste. But the chief source of supply was from swarms of those born in a state of slavery; for the despotisms, the superstitions, and the usages of Africa had multiplied bondage."

"In the upper countries, on the Senegal and Gambia, three fourths of the inhabitants were not free; and the slave's master was absolute lord of the slave's children:" Hence the

---

* Martin's Louisiana, vol. i., p. 217.   † Bancroft, vol. iii., p. 402.

European slave-trader only converted their bondage into a servitude among Christians instead of pagans and Mohammedans. "In the healthy and fertile uplands of Western Africa, under a tropical sun, the reproductive power of the prolific race, combined with the imperfect development of its moral faculties, gave to human life in the eye of man himself an inferior value. Humanity did not respect itself in any of its forms in the individual, in the family, or in the nation."*

Among the changes ordered by the directory of the company was the removal of the headquarters of the commandant-general to Biloxi Bay, now known as New Biloxi. Accordingly, in December following, a detachment of troops was sent to build a principal dépôt, erect barracks, and dwellings for the officers and commandant-general.

Another change introduced into the government of Louisiana this year was the institution of a "Superior Council," agreeably to an edict of the king issued in September. The Council at headquarters had heretofore been the sole tribunal in the colony for the adjudication of civil and criminal cases. Now the increase of population and the extension of settlements required judicial tribunals in various portions of the province. The directors of the company, or its agents, with two of the most notable inhabitants of the vicinity, were constituted inferior courts in remote parts of the province for all civil cases. The same, with four of the principal inhabitants, might act in criminal cases, subject to an appeal to the Superior Council.†

The Superior Council was composed of the commandant-general, the king's two lieutenants, a senior counselor, three other counselors, the attorney-general, and a clerk, associated with such of the company's directors as might be in the province. The quorum was fixed at three members in civil, and five in criminal cases. All cases, original as well as appellate, as the last resort, were acted upon, and judgments given without costs to the parties litigant.‡ Such was one of the advantages enjoyed under the royal government of France and Spain.

[A.D. 1720.] Early in February, 1720, five hundred and eighty-two emigrants arrived at Mobile for the settlements in different portions of Louisiana. Among these were many females taken from the hospital-general of Paris. They served

---

* Bancroft, vol. iii., p. 403.   † Martin, vol. i., p. 215, 216.   ‡ Idem, p. 215.

to augment the population of the colony, and might ultimately contribute largely to the permanent strength of the province; yet they were not likely to add much to the elevation of character and the moral worth of the settlements.*

During the summer the colony received a large increase of population by the arrivals of settlers for the different grants. Among them were a colony of sixty settlers for the grant of St. Catharine among the Natchez Indians. They were followed soon afterward by two hundred and fifty others, for the same grant, in charge of Bouteux. Every arrival now brought colonies for the respective grants. Within a few months preceding the winter, the arrivals for the different grants amounted to five hundred and fifty settlers, besides workmen, soldiers, and officers.†

New interests were daily awakened in France by the enthusiastic proprietors, and new prospects of wealth were held out to induce emigration. Hence the colony continued to augment its population rapidly. White European emigrants, allured by the hope of wealth, and fascinated by the glowing descriptions of the magnificence of the country, continued to come, and every month witnessed their arrival.

In the mean time, since March, 1719, war had raged between France and Spain, and the province of Louisiana became involved in hostilities with the Spaniards of Florida and Mexico. The settlements of Louisiana had presented a continual scene of military display and hostile preparation. So soon as war had broken out, Bienville determined to reduce Pensacola by force of arms before re-enforcements should arrive from Mexico. Accordingly, in April, he had assembled his forces, with a party of Canadians, and about four hundred Indians; with these, and a few armed vessels, he made a sudden descent on Pensacola. The fort was assailed from the harbor by the armed vessels, and by the French infantry and Indians from land; and after a severe attack, and a brave resistance of five hours, the commandant surrendered to the French forces. Bienville held possession near forty days, when the arrival of a powerful Spanish armament off the bay compelled him to abandon the place and retire to Mobile. Here he was blockaded for thirteen days, in the port of Isle Dauphin, by a superior Spanish squadron, which vainly attempted to subdue

* Martin, vol. i., p. 224. † Idem, p. 226.

the French posts on Dauphin Island by a furious bombardment.*

The war continued to harass the frontier settlements of Louisiana contiguous to the Spanish provinces. In September, M. de Serigny had received orders to reduce the fort and town of Pensacola. The whole disposable force of Louisiana was now required to invest the fort on the land side, while the fleet advanced by sea. Bienville, with his land forces, and a considerable body of Indians, again advanced from Mobile to Pensacola. After a close investment by land and sea, the fort and town were carried by assault. The citizens were spared, but the town was given up to the pillage of the Indians. Besides the artillery and munitions of war, the French took eighteen hundred prisoners. Soon afterward, several Spanish vessels, laden with stores and provisions, entered the port, ignorant of its occupation by the French, and they were likewise captured. But the French occupancy was of short duration, for the apprehended arrival of a large fleet from Vera Cruz induced the French commander to burn the town, blow up the forts, and to retire to the port of Mobile.

Nor was the war with the Spaniards confined to the sea-coast and the deltas of the Mississippi and Red River. The traders and hunters from Santa Fé had discovered the route across the great American desert, and detachments of cavalry had penetrated across the upper branches of the Arkansas to the Missouri, and to the Upper Mississippi, and had witnessed the advance of the French in that quarter. The Missouri tribes inhabiting this region were in alliance with the French, and espoused their interests. To check their advance in this quarter, the Spanish authorities had planned the extermination of the Missouris and the French settlements, to be replaced by a Spanish colony from Mexico. Their plan was to excite the Osages to war with the Missouris, and then take part with them in the contest. For this purpose, an expedition was fitted out from Santa Fé for the Missouri. It was a moving caravan of the desert—armed men, horses, mules, families, women, priests, with herds of cattle and swine to serve for food on the route, and to serve for increase in the new col-

* Stoddart's Sketches, p. 37, 38. After vainly attempting to reduce the French posts and fort of Isle Dauphin, the approach of a large French fleet, under M. de Serigny, caused the Spaniards to abandon the blockade and retire to Pensacola.—Stoddart, p. 39.

ony. In their march they lost the proper route, the guides became bewildered, and led them to the Missouri tribes instead of the Osages. Unconscious of their mistake, as both tribes spoke the same language, they believed themselves among the Osages instead of their enemies, and without reserve disclosed their designs against the Missouris, and supplied them with arms and ammunition to aid in their extermination. The wily savages perceived the fatal mistake, but encouraged the error. They requested two days to assemble their warriors for the contemplated expedition, in which they were rejoiced to engage. The appointed time had nearly elapsed, and the following morning was the time to march. More than one hundred muskets were distributed among the warriors; but to the Spaniards the next morning never rose. Before the dawn of light the Missouris fell upon their treacherous enemies, and dispatched them with an indiscriminate slaughter. The priest alone was spared; his dress had spoke him a man of peace, and he was reserved to bear the sad tidings to Mexico. Thus the Spanish treachery came home upon their own heads.[*]

This disaster apprised the commandant-general of Louisiana of the designs of the Spaniards to advance into Upper Louisiana. To arrest any further attempt, a French post was designed for the Missouri. In due time, M. Burgmont, with a detachment of troops, was dispatched from Mobile to the Missouri River. He took possession of an island in that river, above the mouth of the Osage, upon which he built a fort, which he called "Fort Orleans."

War continued to rage between the rival powers, and the maritime portions of Louisiana and Florida were the theatre of colonial hostilities. The Indian tribes had been leagued in with the interests of the respective colonies, and carried on their marauding excursions against the enemies of their respective friends.

The late expedition from Santa Fé to the Missouri, although overwhelmed with disaster, evinced the possibility of other expeditions by the same route for the destruction of the French settlements in the Illinois country or Upper Louisiana. Fort Orleans, high up the Missouri, was already in progress as an outpost; but to protect these important settlements from a disastrous invasion, it was deemed expedient to erect a strong

---

[*] Stoddart, p. 39. See, also, Wetmore's Gazetteer of Missouri, ed. 1837, p. 200.

military post upon the Mississippi itself. The Lower Mississippi, also, had been threatened from the same quarter. The necessity of securing the western bank of that river against the hostile incursions of the Spaniards, was evident to the Western Company as well as to Bienville, the royal commandant. Hence, after the demolition of Pensacola, the attention of the company was directed to an extensive plan of defense against the inroads of the Spaniards from Mexico. A chain of forts was begun, to keep open a communication from the mouth to the sources of the Mississippi.

M. Paugér, a royal engineer, proceeded to make a complete survey of the mouth of the Mississippi, and all the passes, bars, and channels below the present site of New Orleans city. By this survey, it was ascertained that the site selected by Bienville might be made a commercial port; that the practicability of bringing shipping up the river was beyond a doubt.* The point selected by him three years before was now about to become the great commercial port of the province. The advantages of a port on the river were manifest to all, and the "directory," unable to withstand the force of Bienville's influence and the evidence of their own senses, yielded a reluctant assent to the removal of the company's principal dépôt and their offices to New Orleans.

About the same time, Lesueur, with a detachment of ninety men, advanced up the Mississippi, and up the St. Peter's River to the Blue Earth River among the Sioux, by his estimate, a distance of seven hundred and sixty leagues from the sea; and there, at the mouth of the Blue Earth, he erected a fort and a trading-post for the company; and, with all the usual formalities, he took possession of the country in the name of his most Christian majesty.†

At the same time, the commandant of the Illinois country, M. Boisbriant. under instructions from the king, commenced the erection of a strong fortress on the east bank of the Mississippi, about twenty-five miles below Kaskaskia. This fort, which was not completed until eighteen months afterward, was called "Fort Chartres," and was designed as the headquarters of the commandant of Upper Louisiana. It was a regular fortress, built of solid masonry, and was deemed one of the strongest French posts in North America for many years afterward.

* Martin's Louisiana, vol. i., p. 233. † Idem.

It was completely impregnable to any power which could then have been brought against it.*

[A.D. 1721.] Having secured Upper Louisiana from Spanish invasion, the colonial authorities, with the hearty concurrence of the directory, proceeded to secure the occupation of the country west of the Mississippi, as far as the Colorado, and eastward to the sources of the Mobile River. The company had never lost sight of Western Louisiana, although the Spaniards had claimed it as a part of New Mexico, and had established temporary posts and missions as far east as the Trinity and the Sabine Rivers. The directory considered it a part of Louisiana, over which they claimed a monopoly of the Indian trade, and from which they desired the exclusion of the Spanish missions. During the past year, Bernard de la Harpe, one of the most enterprising commandants of Louisiana, had led an exploring detachment from the Mississippi to the Rio Bravo del Norte; he had traversed the country from the Washita and Arkansas westward to the sources of Red River. After a tour of six months, and a laborious ramble of more than fifteen hundred miles, visiting the different tribes of Indians in his route, he returned to New Orleans in the month of January, 1721, to report the result of his explorations to the colonial government.

From the first operations of the company, the directory had evinced great anxiety for the occupation of the western frontier, with settlements and colonies west of the Sabine; but Bienville, adhering to his policy of concentrating the settlements near the Mississippi, had declined sending colonies to a remote wilderness, where they would be exposed alike to the

* For the gratification of the curious, we give a more particular account of this principal French fortress on the Mississippi. It was begun in 1720, and completed eighteen months afterward. It was erected in the vicinity of Prairie du Rocher, and was originally one mile and a half from the river bank. Its form was quadrilateral, with four bastions built of stone, and well cemented with lime. Each side was three hundred and forty feet in length; the walls were three feet thick and fifteen feet high. Within the walls were spacious stone barracks, a spacious magazine, two deep wells, and such buildings as are common in such posts. The port-holes, or loops, were formed by four solid blocks of freestone properly shaped. The cornices and casements about the gates were of the same material. It was greatly repaired and enlarged in 1750.

In 1770, the river broke through its banks and formed a channel near one of the bastions, and in two years afterward, two bastions being undermined, the English abandoned it in 1772. It was then suffered to fall to decay, and in 1809 it was a splendid ruin, grown over in its area with forest-trees, vines, and weeds. Some of the trees then were from seven to twelve inches in diameter. See Stoddart's Sketches, p. 234.

A good description of this fort, as it appeared in 1765 and in 1829, may be seen in Hall's Sketches of the West, vol. i., p. 154–157.

hostility of the Indians and the treachery of the Spaniards. At length, yielding to their urgent desires, he resolved to take formal possession of the country on the Colorado, and near the Bay of St. Bernard.

Accordingly, on the 10th of August, 1721, he issued the following order to M. de la Harpe, viz. :*

"Order.

"We, Jean Baptiste de Bienville, chevalier of the military order of St. Louis, and commandant-general for the king in the province of Louisiana:

"It is hereby decreed that M. de la Harpe, commandant of the Bay of St. Bernard, shall embark in the packet, the 'Subtile,' commanded by Beranger, with a detachment of twenty soldiers, under M. de Belile, and shall proceed forthwith to the Bay of St. Bernard, belonging to this province, and take possession in the name of the king; and the Western Company shall plant the arms of the king in the ground, and build a fort upon whatsoever spot appears most advantageous for the defense of the place.

"If the Spaniards or any other nation have taken possession, M. de la Harpe will signify to them that they have no right to the country, it being known that possession was taken in 1685 by M. de la Salle, in the name of the King of France, &c.   "Bienville.

"August 10th, 1721."

La Harpe proceeded upon the hazardous enterprise, and established the post agreeably to his orders; but the Indians were in alliance with the Spaniards, and strongly opposed the settlement. Unwilling to expose his colony to savage massacre, he determined to abandon so perilous a place. In October following he returned to New Orleans, and reported to the commandant-general that he had coasted three hundred leagues west of the Mississippi, and that on the 27th of August he had entered a fine bay, with eleven feet water at half tide; that his weak force and the hostility of the savages prevented him from making a permanent establishment; that the bay known to the French as the Bay of St. Bernard was the same known to the Spaniards as the bay of Espiritu Santo, and is in latitude 29° 12' north, and in longitude 282° east from Ferro. He also gave

* See Darby's Louisiana, p. 25.

the extent of Louisiana upon the Gulf of Mexico, from this bay eastward, at about one hundred and sixty leagues.*

The colonial government continued to claim the territory westward to the Colorado and beyond, and several attempts were subsequently made to establish settlements west of the Sabine. Settlements were also attempted, with subsequent failure, high up Red River, and upon the Upper Arkansas.

The Spaniards, in the mean time, pushed their settlements and missions eastward to the Colorado ; and parties of Spanish cavalry from Santa Fé had infested the region west of the Sabine, until the French were compelled to retire toward the Mississippi.

In the mean time, forts and trading-posts were extended eastward upon the waters of the Tombigby and Alabama Rivers. The fort at Mobile was removed to the west shore of the Mobile Bay, and, being strongly fortified, was called " Fort Condé." The fort on Biloxi Bay was enlarged, and called " Fort St. Louis." Another fort was advanced into the Indian country, to the head of navigation on the Alabama River, two leagues above the mouth of the Tallapoosa ; this was called " Fort Toulouse."†

In each of these were placed suitable garrisons to defend them against Indian hostility, and to protect the agents of the company from the depredations of the savages, instigated by British traders from Carolina. Trading-posts were established with the friendly Choctâs upon the Tombigby, and upon the Pearl and Pascagoula Rivers.

In the mean time, during the war, which had now terminated, between the French and Spanish kings, the colonies of Louisiana had suffered much, and the company had become greatly embarrassed by the interruption of trade and the hostilities of the Indians ; yet they had exerted themselves with energy to sustain the colonies in the province. The population had been gradually augmented by emigrants introduced by the company's ships, besides convicts and indigent females from the houses of correction in Paris, introduced by the king's vessels. But the former of these classes were not desirable emigrants for a new colony, and, upon the petition of the directory, the king had interdicted the transportation of convicts to Louisi-

---

* Darby's Louisiana, first ed., p. 28. Also, Stoddart, p. 39, 40.
† See Martin's Louisiana. Also, Bancroft, vol. iii., p. 348, 349.

ana after the 9th day of May, 1720.* The latter were not so objectionable; for, although they would add but little to the good morals of the colonists, they were a valuable acquisition to a new and growing colony. Several hundred of these indigent females, taken from the hospital-general and the houses of correction, were subsequently introduced into Louisiana, and contributed largely to the future population.

Emigrants for the different colonies had arrived during the past year. Early in January, one of the company's ships had arrived at Mobile with three hundred settlers for Madame Chaumonot's grant on the Pascagoula River. In February, another vessel had arrived with one hundred emigrants and passengers for different colonies and grants on the Mississippi; also with them came eighty girls from the Salpêtrière, a house of correction in Paris. Early in March, one of the company's vessels had arrived at Mobile, with two hundred emigrants for John Law's grant on the Arkansas. They proceeded from Mobile, by way of the lakes and Iberville Bayou, to the Mississippi, and thence to the Arkansas. A portion of them settled about sixty miles above the mouth of that river, at a point long afterward known as the "Post of Arkansas." Others advanced further up the river, and settled upon the margins of the great prairies which lie southeast of Little Rock.

[A.D. 1722.] The numerous arrivals of colonists and emigrants during the last two years had increased the population so rapidly in the new and uncultivated country, which had not yet developed its agricultural resources, that the supply of grain and breadstuffs was insufficient for their supply. A scarcity, bordering on famine, was the consequence. Supplies from France were irregular and insufficient; and the troops and many of the colonists were compelled to disperse among the friendly tribes of Indians, in order to procure food and sustenance. Others were compelled to sustain themselves and their families by the precarious supplies derived from fishing and hunting. Distress and gloom overspread the settlements; many sickened and died for want of wholesome food, added to the influence of a new and unhealthy climate. Yet emigrants from France continued to arrive. Near the first of June, one vessel arrived at Mobile with two hundred and fifty emigrants for the different settlements.

* Martin's Louisiana, vol. i., p. 224.

Bienville urged his agricultural settlements as the only protection against such dearth in future. Negroes continued to arrive for the agricultural establishments, which were opening on the river alluvions, the governor having already abandoned Mobile and St. Louis Bay.

Instead of the sterile sands of Mobile and Biloxi, he had caused the colonies to be located upon the fertile alluvions of the Mississippi; and he now prepared to remove the headquarters of the provincial government to New Orleans. With the consent of the directory, the company's principal establishment was also to be removed to New Orleans early in November following; and buildings for the governor and for the company's officers, and warehouses, were to be erected.

[A.D. 1723.] The following year opened with New Orleans the provincial and commercial capital of Louisiana. The superior judgment of Bienville, relative to the great commercial advantages of New Orleans over Mobile and Biloxi, has been approved by the verdict of posterity. The site which, according to the interested judgment of M. Hubert,* "never would be any thing more than a dépôt for goods" under a privileged company, has in less than a century become the great commercial emporium of a powerful union of states which have sprung up in the Valley of the Mississippi, and also the political capital of one of the richest states in that union.

Yet the company had become greatly embarrassed in their financial affairs. The war with Spain, for two years, had cut off all maritime commerce; the inland trade with the Spanish provinces of Mexico and Florida had been entirely prohibited; many of the Indian tribes, influenced by emissaries from Mexico, Florida, and from the English settlements of Carolina, had shown a hostile attitude, and had committed depredations upon the trade of the interior; the troops in garrison, suffering under privations and want, had become disgusted with their situation, and were disaffected; the garrison at Fort Toulouse had revolted during the last year, and out of twenty-six soldiers, twenty departed for the English settlements of Carolina; but overtaken by Villemont, the commandant, with a body of Choctâs, some of the unhappy wretches were put to death

---

* M. Hubert had been director-general of the company's affairs, and personally was interested in a large planting establishment upon the grant formerly made to him on the St. Catharine Creek, in the Natchez country, where he had desired to establish the headquarters of the colonial government, and a principal dépôt of the company.

on the spot; part were reserved for a more ignominious death, and, conducted to Mobile, were retained to grace a military execution. Even the wilderness could not moderate the barbarism of military discipline.

About the same time, the hostile bands of the Chickasâs had destroyed Fort St. Peter, on the Yazoo, and had massacred the garrison and colony with indiscriminate butchery.* The Creeks, on the head waters of the Alabama, and the Chickasâs of the Tombigby, had likewise evinced hostile intentions, under the instigation of English traders. War had also broken out among the tribes on the Missouri and Upper Mississippi Rivers, and threatened the interruption of trade in that quarter.

Under all these embarrassments, the company struggled on, in hopes of more propitious times. The expenses already had far exceeded the proceeds of every branch of trade. Before the beginning of the year 1722, the expenditures had amounted to 1,163,256 livres, or nearly $366,000, without any equivalent return.† Now the heaviest loss had come upon them, from the failure of Law's financial schemes, which had spread confusion into every department of the company's affairs; for they were intimately blended with his "Bubble," known as the "Mississippi Scheme."

In the mean time, settlements were concentrating around New Orleans; cabins, houses, a church, and other public buildings had been rapidly progressing for the residence of the governor, the company's agents, and their commercial operations. In January, when visited by Charlevoix, it contained, besides the church, the company's warehouse, and a few other wooden buildings, near one hundred cabins, and about two hundred inhabitants, besides troops and government officers.‡ The population increased continually, and soon after the first of August, this year, the public buildings for the governor and the company having been completed, Bienville removed his headquarters to the city, and in November following, Delorme, the director-general of the company, removed the stores and offices under his control from the Bay of Biloxi to the same point.§

The embarrassed condition of the company caused them to resort to various means and devices to enable them to continue their operations, and to increase their available resources.

---

* See Martin, vol. i., p. 252. Also, Stoddart, p. 47.   † See Stoddart, p. 36.
‡ Martin, vol. i., p. 246.   § Martin, vol. i., p. 252.

The price of negro slaves, of which they held the monopoly, was increased from six hundred livres for men to six hundred and seventy livres, or from about one hundred and fifty to nearly one hundred and seventy dollars, payable in three annual instalments, of rice and tobacco. Rice was receivable at twelve livres per barrel, and tobacco at twenty-six livres per hundred pounds. The value of the Mexican dollar was made equivalent to four livres in all transactions with the company's agents in Louisiana; the livre was thus made equivalent to twenty-five cents of the Federal money of the United States.*

But the failure of " Law's Mississippi Scheme" did not, in Louisiana, fall upon the Western Company alone. Its disastrous consequences were experienced in every part of the province, from the slave and the humblest peasant up to the governor himself, and the wealthy proprietors in the oldest settlements. That it may serve as a beacon-light to future legislators, to warn them from the disastrous consequences which result from legislative enactments, designed to expand the circulating medium, but which, in reality, only drive the real currency of a country from circulation by substituting a fictitious representative, we subjoin the following graphic sketch from the inimitable work of the eloquent Bancroft.

" The Mississippi Scheme" was a system of credit, devised and proposed by John Law, a native of Scotland, for the purpose of extricating the French government from the embarrassment under which it struggled by reason of the enormous state debt. " The debt which Louis XIV. bequeathed to his successor, after arbitrary reductions, exceeded two thousand millions of livres; and, to meet the annual interest of eighty millions, the surplus revenues of the state did not yield more than nine millions; hence the national securities were of uncertain value, and the national burdens exceeded the national resources. In this period of depression, John Law proposed to the regent a credit system, which should liberate the state from its enormous burden, not by loans, on which interest must be paid—not by taxes, that would be burdensome to the people, but by a system which should bring all the money of France on deposit. It was the faith of Law that the currency of a country is but the representative of its moving wealth; that this representative need not, in itself, possess an intrinsic value,

* Martin, vol. i., p. 246, 256.

but may be made, not of stamped metals only, but of shells or paper; that where gold and silver are the only circulating medium, the wealth of a nation may at once be indefinitely increased by an arbitrary infusion of paper; that credit consists in the excess of circulation over immediate resources; and that the advantage of credit is in the direct ratio of that excess. Applying these maxims to all France, he gradually planned the whimsically gigantic project of collecting all the gold and silver of the kingdom into one bank. At first, from his private bank, having a nominal capital of six million livres (of which a part was payable in government notes), bills were emitted with moderation; and while the despotic government had been arbitrarily changing the value of its coin, his notes, being payable in coin, at an unvarying standard of weight and fineness, bore a small premium. When Crozat resigned the commerce of Louisiana, it was transferred to the 'Western Company,' or Company of the Mississippi, instituted under the auspices of Law. The stock of the corporation was fixed at two hundred thousand shares, of five hundred livres each, to be paid in any certificates of public debt. Thus nearly one hundred millions of the most depreciated of the public stocks were suddenly absorbed. The government thus changed the character of its obligations from an indebtedness to individuals to an indebtedness to a favored company of its own creation. Through the bank of Law, the interest on the debt was discharged punctually, and, in consequence, the evidences of debts, which were received in payment for stock, rose rapidly from a depreciation of two thirds to par value. Although the union of the bank, with the hazards of a commercial company, was an omen of the fate of 'the system,' public credit seemed restored as if by miracle."*

The mines, and commerce, and boundless extent of Louisiana were now invoked to sustain the public credit and the bank. "The human mind is full of trust; men in masses always have faith in the approach of better times; humanity abounds in hope. The Valley of the Mississippi inflamed the imagination of France; anticipating the future, the French nation beheld the certain opulence of coming ages as within their immediate grasp; and John Law, who possessed the entire confidence of

* Bancroft, vol. iii., p. 349–351.

the regent, obtained the whole control of the commerce of Louisiana and Canada."*

"The ill success of La Salle, of Iberville, of Crozat, the fruitlessness of the long search for the mines of St. Barbe, were notorious; yet tales were revived of the wealth of Louisiana; its ingôts of gold had been seen in Paris. The vision of a fertile empire, with its plantations, manors, cities, and busy wharves, a monopoly of commerce throughout all French North America, the certain products of the richest silver mines, and mountains of gold, were blended in the French mind into one boundless promise of untold treasures. The regent, who saw opening before him unlimited resources, the nobility, the churchmen, who competed for favors from the privileged institution, the stock-jobbers, including dukes and peers, marshals and bishops, women of rank, statesmen and courtiers, eager to profit by the sudden and indefinite rise of stocks, conspired to reverence Law as the greatest man of the age."†

"In January of 1719, the bank of Law became, by a negotiation with the regent, the Bank of France, and a government which had almost absolute power of legislation, conspired to give the widest extension to what was called credit. The contest between paper and specie began to rage, the one buoyed up by despotic power, the other appealing to common sense. Within four years a succession of decrees changed the relative value of the livre not less than fifty times, that, from disgust at fluctuation, paper at a fixed rate might be preferred. All taxes were to be collected in paper; at least, paper was made the legal tender in all payments. To win the little gold and silver that was hoarded by the humbler classes, small bills as low even as ten livres were put in circulation."‡

To absorb the enormous issues, a new scheme was put in operation. Two kinds of paper bills, payable on demand, and certificates of stock, were put abroad together. To absorb its issues, new shares of the Mississippi, or Western Company, were constantly created and offered for sale, under its new name of "Company of the Indies." "The extravagance of hope was nourished by the successive surrender to that corporation of additional monopolies. The trade in Africans, the trade on the Indian seas, the sale of tobacco, the profits of the royal mint, the profits of farming, the whole revenue of France, till

* Bancroft, vol. iii., p. 349. † Ibidem, p. 350, 351. ‡ Ibidem, p. 355.

a promise of a dividend of forty per cent. from a company which had the custody of all the revenues, and the benefit of all the commerce of France, obtained belief, and the shares which might be issued after a payment of a first instalment of five hundred livres rose in price a thousand per cent. Avarice became a phrensy, its fury seized every member of the royal family, men of letters, prelates, women. Early in the morning, the exchange opened with beat of drum and sound of bell, and closed at night on avidity that could not slumber. To doubt the wealth of Louisiana provoked anger. New Orleans was famous at Paris as a beautiful city almost before the canebrakes began to be cut down. The hypocrisy of manners, which, in the old age of Louis XIV., made religion become a fashion, revolted to libertinism, and licentious pleasure was become the parent of an equally licentious cupidity." The system perpetuated its own absurdities, and plunged its votaries still further into ruin. "In the course of sixteen months more than two thousand millions of bills were emitted. The extravagances of stock-jobbing were increased by the latent distrust alike of the shares and of the bills; men purchased stock because they feared the end of the paper system, and because, with the bills, they could purchase nothing else."* The fraud grew too apparent, and the Parliament protested that the people were robbed and defrauded of nearly their whole income. "To stifle doubt, Law, who had made himself a Catholic, was appointed comptroller-general; and the new minister of finance perfected the triumph of paper by a decree that no person or corporation should have on hand more than five hundred livres in specie; the rest must be exchanged for paper, and all payments, except for sums under one hundred livres, must be paid in paper. Terror and the dread of informers brought, within three weeks, forty-four millions into the bank. In March, a decree of council fixed the value of the stock at nine thousand livres for five hundred, and forbade certain corporations to invest money in any thing else; all circulation of gold and silver, except for change, was prohibited; all payments must be made in paper, except for sums under ten livres. He who should have attempted to convert a bill into specie would have exposed his specie to forfeiture, and himself to fines. Confidence disappeared, and in May, bankruptcy was avowed by a decree which reduced the value of bank notes by a moiety."

* Bancroft, vol. iii., p. 356.

"When men are greatly in the wrong, and especially when they have embarked their fortunes in their error, they wilfully resist light. So it had been with the French people; they remained faithful to their delusion, till France was impoverished, public and private credit subverted, the income of capitalists annihilated, and labor left without employment; while, in the midst of the universal wretchedness of the middling class, a few wary speculators gloried in the unjust acquisition and enjoyment of immense wealth."[*]

"Such was the issue of Law's celebrated system, which left the world a lesson which the world was slow to learn, that the enlargement of the circulation quickens industry *so long only* as the enlargement continues, for prices then rise, and every kind of labor is remunerated; that, when this increase springs from artificial causes, it must meet with a check, and be followed by a reaction; that, when the reaction begins, the high remunerating prices decline, labor fails to find an equivalent, and each evil opposite to the previous advantages ensues; that, therefore, every artificial expansion of the currency, every expansion resting on credit alone, is a source of confusion and ultimate loss to the community, and brings benefits to none but those who are skillful in foreseeing and profiting by the fluctuations."

Such was the state of things in Louisiana for several years after the downfall of Law, and his system of finance in France and French America. Who then would have believed that in less than one hundred and fifteen years from that time, the Valley of the Mississippi would have been the theatre of delusions almost as great, under a new system of credit held out by a hundred banking institutions and chartered monopolies, as rotten and as baseless as Law's Bank of France? Such was the currency of the Valley of the Mississippi, among five millions of people, for four years after the year 1834.

[*] Bancroft, vol. iii., p. 357.

CHAPTER VII.

LOUISIANA UNDER THE "WESTERN COMPANY," FROM THE FAILURE OF LAW'S "MISSISSIPPI SCHEME" TO THE NATCHEZ MASSACRE.—A.D. 1723 TO 1729.

Argument.—State of the Colony of Louisiana.—Disastrous Effects of Law's Failure in 1722.—Origin of the "German Coast."—Louisiana divided into Nine Judicial Districts.—The Mining Delusion still haunts the Company.—First Outbreak of Hostilities among the Natchez Indians.—Bienville's stern and cruel Demands.—His Treachery and Revenge against the Natchez.—Their Feelings toward the French.—Threatening Attitude of Indian Tribes.—Crops and Plantations destroyed by Equinoctial Storm.—Colony threatened with Famine.—Swiss Troops Revolt.—Financial Difficulties.—Population in 1723.—Royal Edicts for Relief of Debtors.—Prosperity in 1724–6.—Province supplied with Ecclesiastics and Nuns.—Chevalier Perrier appointed Governor of the Province.—Bienville retires.—Colonial Prosperity and Trade in 1726–7.—Indigo, Fig, and Orange introduced.—"Cassette Girls."—Land Titles recorded.—Prosperous Condition in 1728.—Population.—Trade.—Indications of Indian Hostilities disregarded by Company.—French Aggressions and Intolerance toward the Natchez Tribe.—Indian Impatience of Revenge.—French Indifference to Danger.—Chickasâ Conspiracy.—Chopart's Aggressions among the Natchez.—Conspiracy of the Natchez Chiefs for Revenge.—Chopart's Insensibility to Danger.—Colony on the St. Catharine destroyed by the Indians, November 28, 1792.—Massacre, and the Slain.

[A.D. 1723.] The failure of Law's financial schemes fell heavily upon Louisiana. The rapid expansion of the circulating medium throughout the province during the first three years of his operations, and the consequent sudden prostration of all business upon his failure, involved the interests of the company, and embarrassed their operations for advancing the population and prosperity of the province. Although emigrants from France and Canada continued to arrive at New Orleans and upon the Illinois, yet the remote settlements in Lower Louisiana, such as those upon the Arkansas, the Yazoo, and the Washita, were in a great measure deserted by the starving and discontented colonists.

The number of settlers remaining at Law's grant on the Arkansas in 1722 had been reported by La Harpe at forty souls. The settlement at Fort St. Peter was still more feeble, with only thirty acres of land in cultivation; that on the Washita was but little better.

So soon as Law's failure affected the regular supplies to his colony on the Arkansas, they were on the verge of starvation, and were neglected by his agents. Disappointed in their expectations, and finding themselves deserted in the midst of savages, who viewed them with a jealous eye, they resolved to abandon their settlement, and, if possible, return to Europe. They were chiefly Germans from Provençe, and, situated remote from the other French settlements, they departed for New Orleans, determined to seek passage in the first vessel bound for France. The directors of the company, and the commandant-general, unwilling to permit the pernicious influence of their example in leaving the province, induced them to remain and settle near New Orleans. For this purpose, a grant of sufficient land was made for their use, and was located about twenty miles above New Orleans, on both sides of the river. This land was allotted to them as a permanent home, and was divided among them in such tracts as they individually required. This was the beginning of the "German Coast" of Louisiana, which, for several years afterward, supplied the city of New Orleans and the troops with rich horticultural products.*

Heretofore Louisiana had been a subordinate dependence, under the jurisdiction of the Governor-general of Canada. It was now determined to erect it into an independent government; and accordingly, early in the year 1723, the province of Louisiana was divided into nine districts, for civil and military purposes. Each was under the jurisdiction of a commandant and a judge, who administered the military and civil concerns of their respective districts.† Sometimes the same person filled both offices.

Notwithstanding the company had embarked largely in agriculture, and had established large plantations on the river, still it refused to abandon the idea of discovering boundless wealth in the mines of Missouri. They still believed that gold and silver mines were to be found in the Illinois country, al-

* Martin's Louisiana, vol. i., p. 246.
† The nine military districts were as follows, viz.:

1. District of the Alibamons.	6. District of the Yazoo.
2. " of Mobile.	7. " " Illinois and Wabash.
3. " " Biloxi.	
4. " " New Orleans.	8. " " Arkansas.
5. " " Natchez.	9. " " Natchitoches.

M. Boisbriant, who arrived in March, 1723, was the king's lieutenant; Bienville was governor and commandant-general; M. Loubois, a knight of St. Louis, was commandant at Fort St. Louis, on the Biloxi; M. Latour, lieutenant-general of the province; De lorme, director-general of the company.—Martin, vol. i., p. 246-7.

though M. Renault, "director-general of the mines," had failed to discover them with his company of two hundred miners. Desire begets credulity; and the directory, ever ready to receive and encourage extravagant accounts of mines, offered rewards proportionate to the importance of the discovery. With such incentives, they could not fail to be amused with the most marvelous exhilarating discoveries. Men are prone to deception without reward; and how much more for recompense! In this way the attention of the company continued to be diverted to the search of mines in distant regions, as far as the sources of the St. Peter's, the Arkansas, the tributaries of the Missouri, and even to the Rocky Mountains,* while they neglected the increasing hostile indications among the Chickasâs, the Natchez, and other tribes immediately contiguous to their principal settlements. Under the mining delusion these indications were deemed unworthy of serious attention. Anxious to establish trading-posts with remote and unknown tribes, they neglected to protect their settlements from hostile tribes at their very doors, while their own uncontrolled agents were fanning the flame of discord among their allies on the Lower Mississippi.

This year witnessed the first outbreak among the Natchez Indians, and many of the settlers on the St. Catharine were murdered by the hostile warriors. The difficulty began in a quarrel between a warrior and a sergeant in Fort Rosalie. One Indian was killed, and another was wounded, by an unprovoked fire from the guard. To revenge this outrage, the Indians committed frequent depredations upon the settlements, and at different times had killed a number of the settlers on the St. Catharine. One act of violence brings on another, and at length a party of eighty warriors made a bold attack upon the settlements, but were finally repulsed with the loss of seven of their number. They had, however, killed or taken away a number of horses, hogs, and cattle from the plantations, and had captured and murdered two planters, whose heads were afterward found severed, and their bodies dishonored.†

---

* Martin, vol. i., p. 252.

† A few days after the difficulty, M. Guenot, superintendent of the St. Catharine grant, while riding in the road, was shot and wounded by an Indian from his concealment. Next day, the Indians attempted to seize a cart-load of provisions, which was guarded by a few soldiers. The Indians concealed themselves in the high grass, and by the first fire killed one negro and wounded another.—Martin, vol. i., p. 244.

At length a chief, called the "Stung Serpent," interposed his influence and authority, and with difficulty he finally succeeded in putting a stop to further revenge. Soon afterward, with other principal "suns," he came to Fort Rosalie to arrange affairs, and to prevent further hostilities. A reconciliation took place, which was ratified by sundry presents made by the French to the chiefs. The whole matter was subsequently laid before Bienville, the commandant-general. He approved the treaty, and ratified the stipulations entered into by his inferior officers, and all former animosities between the Indians and the French appeared to have been consigned to oblivion. But Bienville secretly determined to inflict a severe chastisement upon the tribe.* Having placed the Indians off their guard, and removed all apprehension of danger from their minds by friendly assurances, he made his arrangements to take them by surprise. Accordingly, a few months afterward, suddenly and unexpectedly, Bienville arrived at Fort Rosalie with seven hundred troops. An attack was immediately made upon their villages, and the defenseless and unsuspecting natives were slain without mercy, and their towns consumed by fire. During four days, detachments of troops were ravaging the country, laying waste their fields, burning their houses, and killing such as fell into their hands. At length Bienville agreed to desist from further hostilities, provided the "suns" would deliver to him a certain obnoxious chief, who held the title of a sun.† No alternative but submission was left them; they must surrender another victim to the French vengeance, and that victim a Sun, or they must sacrifice their people and their families to the armed soldiery of the French. At length they consented to hold a council, and several of the chiefs waited upon him, and proposed to surrender common warriors as vicarious sacrifices, instead of the "sun." Bienville sternly refused: the chiefs and suns of the council were forcibly detained, and some of them confined in irons, until the obnoxious chief or his head should be produced. In hopes of preserving the life of the sun, a warrior volunteered to die in his place, and his head

---

* In recording the difficulties between the Natchez Indians and the French of St Catharine, Martin has strangely confused dates and transactions. Part of the occurrences by him are placed under the year 1716, and part under the year 1723 (see vol i., p. 189, 190, and 254). This confusion of dates in Martin's Louisiana is by no means uncommon. See Stoddart's Sketches, p. 47, 48, for a proper detail of Natchez difficulties. * Stoddart's Sketches, p. 48.

was carried to Bienville; but he refused to receive the supposititious head. Another warrior volunteered to die, and his head was presented to the inexorable Frenchman. This, in like manner, was refused. Nothing but the veritable head of the obnoxious sun would be received. By the laws and usages of the Indians, a full atonement had been made, and a full ransom had been paid for the life of the sun; but Bienville was inexorable for the blood of the sun. At length the sun resolved to surrender himself, and thus procure the release of his companions, who were still held as hostages for his delivery. Having succeeded in his stern demands, he released the captive suns and returned triumphant to New Orleans, having reaped all his laurels from peaceable and unresisting Indians.

From this time, the Natchez Indians despaired of ever being able to live in peace with the French. They saw that all their former friendships, their favors, and their forbearance were repaid by every species of personal injury, ingratitude, and usurpation; they saw plainly that either themselves or the French must be totally destroyed, and it was the dictate of nature to consult their own safety. They had found that the intolerance and the usurpation of the French increased with their numbers and power; hence they became, in their intercourse, shy, reserved, and distrustful; yet, resolved upon ultimate revenge, they were cautious in devising the means of future vengeance and safety. Such was the state of things among the Natchez Indians until the summer of 1729, when a new aggression on the part of the French compelled them to resist, and to resolve upon the defense of their homes, and the graves of their fathers.*

The Chickasâs had again exhibited hostile indications, and omitted no occasion to harass the settlement on the Yazoo. The post on the Yazoo was a stockade, feebly defended by less than twenty men. Fort Rosalie was but little better than a pile of rotten timbers, garrisoned by sixteen soldiers. Yet the company seemed to enjoy confident security, although Bienville had not failed to warn their agents of the danger. The Spaniards, also, were advancing their settlements rapidly into Western Louisiana.†

Yet the impending vengeance of the Indian tribes was still withheld. Their unwelcome neighbors disregarded their displeasure, and added provocation to injury. Thus commenced

* Stoddart's Sketches, p. 49. † Martin, vol. i., p. 256.

the first breach of peace and confidence between the Natchez tribes and the French of Louisiana.

In addition to all the other misfortunes of the times, which operated severely upon the people of Louisiana, was that of a terrible equinoctial storm on the 11th of September. The crops had just approached maturity, and the whole southern portion of the province was greatly injured. Such was the violence of the storm at New Orleans, that the church, the hospital, and thirty houses were leveled with the ground; three vessels lying in the river were thrown ashore and nearly destroyed. Much damage was sustained at Mobile, Biloxi, and Natchez. Several vessels at Biloxi were entirely lost. The crops of rice were destroyed; many houses of the planters were blown down, and their plantations otherwise injured. The scarcity of provisions, in consequence, was greatly increased, and famine seemed to stare them in the face. Supplies from France were cut off by the financial embarrassments of the mother-country consequent upon the failure of Law's schemes; and many began to despair at the continuation of the untoward circumstances which brooded over the colony. Many, discouraged at these things, longed to see once more the vine-clad hills of France. Even the troops began to evince a spirit of insubordination and revolt. This was a new source of alarm. Fort Toulouse, among the Alibamons, had been deserted by the garrison, who attempted to escape to their friends in Carolina. More recently, a serious revolt had occurred close to headquarters; nor were those in command so fortunate as to capture and punish the offenders. A company of Swiss troops had been placed on board a schooner in the Bay of Biloxi, in order to sail to the new headquarters at New Orleans. But they dreaded the dangers and privations of the Mississippi swamps no less than the sterile sands and lagoons of Biloxi, and their hearts were set upon seeing the desirable settlements of South Carolina. No sooner had the schooner left the bay, than the officers and soldiers, rising in open revolt, compelled the master and crew to sail for Charleston where they all finally arrived in safety, with all their baggage, arms, and munitions.*

To multiply the resources of the province and extend its agriculture, this year, at the request of a number of planters, the

* Martin, vol. i., p. 255.

company procured a supply of indigo seeds. It had been ascertained that the soil and climate of Louisiana were well adapted to the cultivation of indigo; and many were anxious to embark in the enterprise. The following year may be said to be the period when indigo was introduced as a staple product of Louisiana.

[A.D. 1724.] In the last six years the company had introduced four thousand and forty-four settlers into the province, besides one hundred and fifty galley-slaves, and several hundred females from the different houses of correction of Paris, and fourteen hundred and forty-one African slaves. The agricultural resources of the country were just beginning to develop the real wealth of Louisiana; but it was now only that the people began to feel the full effects of the financial experiments of the Scotch financier.

It was now perceived that his paper money, or his representative of money, which had been so extensively introduced into the whole business of Louisiana, had, in fact, not only reduced the nominal value of silver and gold, but that it had driven both from circulation and from the province. The nominal value of every species of property had increased with the supply of the paper representative. The facilities of obtaining this imperfect representative of money had removed all the restraints which a prudent economy and long experience had established for the regulation of business and the proper accumulation of property.

A raging thirst for the rapid accumulation of wealth had followed; this had begotten a spirit of extravagance and speculation, upon which had been ingrafted the most ruinous credit system. This system had been approaching a crisis for more than twelve months. Now the crisis was past: the only circulating medium had suddenly become depreciated, and ceased to represent half the silver formerly represented by it. Very soon creditors refused to receive it at any rate of discount, and it became utterly useless. Specie was scarce, and now became proportionably increased in its relative value. The people were left deeply involved in heavy debts, contracted when the relative value of silver had been reduced and a vast amount of the fictitious representative was in circulation: now they were to pay only in specie: this was equivalent to an onerous augmentation of their debts beyond the possibility of payment.

Legislative interference was loudly demanded; and the only relief possible depended upon a reduction of the amounts owed, or in facilitating the payment of them. The latter mode was adopted by the king.*

The accounts throughout the province had heretofore been kept and estimated in livres as the unit denominated in their money transactions. By several edicts of the king, progressive in their operation, Mexican dollars were made the principal circulating medium. This being effected, the next step was to increase the *relative* value of Mexican dollars in Louisiana. From long custom and usage, each Mexican dollar was equal to four livres. Mexican dollars became the sole circulating medium; and, for the benefit of debtors, the king issued his edict, declaring that the legal value of every Mexican dollar in Louisiana should be equal to seven and a half livres, and should be a legal tender in that ratio. This was justice to the debtor, but the creditor complained that injustice was done to him. The debtor was favored at the expense of the creditor. Still, in its general effects and operation in the province, it might be called sheer justice between man and man. At length, by other edicts of the king, the relative value of a Mexican dollar was gradually reduced to its former value of four livres, and all within the space of ten months.

Such are the consequences of all attempts to inflate the currency by arbitrary and factitious representations of money.

The upper portion of Louisiana was harassed with Indian hostilities, on the part of hostile tribes on the western side of the Missouri River, probably instigated by the Spanish emissaries from Mexico. During the state of hostile feeling among these tribes, the "Fort Orleans," on the Missouri River, was utterly destroyed, and the garrison and the little colony contiguous were totally exterminated by some unknown bands; thus sharing the same fate experienced by the Spanish colony, in the same region, about three years before.†

[A.D. 1725.] Bienville continued to administer the government with great firmness, and often with great wisdom. The settlements gradually revived, and the province continued gradually to augment its population, while the embarrassments of the last two years had nearly passed over. Before the close of the year 1725, the province had in a great measure recovered from the effects of financial embarrassments.

* Martin, vol. i., p. 256–7. † Stoddart's Louisiana, p. 45, 46.

[A.D. 1726.] During the following year, agriculture began to flourish, and a healthy state of trade began to pervade every department of the province. Emigrants, both from Canada and France, continued to arrive.

Early in this year, the company made arrangements with the Jesuits to supply the different posts and settlements with priests, missionaries, and ecclesiastics. Father Petit, superior of the Jesuits, was to reside in New Orleans. The Jesuits engaged to keep at least fourteen priests of their order in the colony, besides missionaries at the different posts, and especially at St. Peter's, on the Yazoo, for the purpose of forming friendly alliances with the Indians, and to propagate the Catholic faith among them. They were to be paid and provided for by the company's agents. Arrangements were also made for the introduction of a number of Ursuline nuns, to take charge of the education of females and the care of a hospital, assisted by several other sisters of charity; but they did not arrive in the city until the summer of the following year.*

In the autumn, the government of Louisiana passed out of the hands of Bienville, who was superseded by M. Perrier as commandant-general of the province. Bienville, with great propriety, has been called the father of Louisiana. He arrived in 1799 at Dauphin Island, as a midshipman, at the age of eighteen years. Three years afterward, he succeeded Sauvolle, an elder brother, as governor of the province and commandant of Fort St. Louis; and, with but two intermissions, he had been invested with the office of governor and commandant-general of the province ever since.

The province continued to improve in prosperity for nearly two years after M. Perrier entered upon the duties of governor. Emigrants from France and Canada continued to swell the general population, and to augment the resources of the province. The agricultural products of the older settlements, in the Illinois country and on the Wabash, yielded a bountiful supply to the new colonies and settlements on the Lower Mississippi. In these regions, wheat, flour, maize, beef, pork, bacon, leather, tallow, hides, bees' wax, bears' oil, and many other useful articles, were produced in abundance. In Lower Louisiana, tobacco and rice had been produced in considerable quantities; and indigo, which had been introduced within

* Martin's Louisiana, vol. i., p. 261-264.

three years, had already become a valuable staple product. The fig-tree had been introduced from Provençe, and the orange-tree from Hispaniola,* and both were now common about New Orleans.

In the month of December, the company's ships brought over a number of poor young girls, but of good moral character, as emigrants to the colony. Each of them was supplied with a small box, or "cassette," containing a few articles of clothing, from which they were known as the girls "*de la cassette*," and were placed under the care of the nuns until they could be provided for in marriage.†

Already lands had become valuable in the settlements, and litigation began to test the validity of titles; and, to prevent the frequent recurrence of disputed claims, the directory issued an order requiring those holding grants to come forward and have them duly authenticated, under penalty of fine and forfeiture. Larger grants, not properly improved, were reduced; or, on failure to comply with the terms, were formally revoked.

[A.D. 1728.] The colony was now in its highest prosperity. Although it had languished until placed under the control of the Western Company, yet under their management it had reached a degree of population, and advance in agriculture and commerce, highly creditable to the company and honorable to France.

The company now had controlled the province for eleven years; they had raised it from a few hundred idle, indolent, and improvident settlers around the Bay of Mobile, and along the coast west of that place, near the Bays of Biloxi and St. Louis, to a flourishing colony of several thousand souls, many of whom were industrious, enterprising, and productive citizens. In the year 1717, when the company took charge, agriculture had been neglected and was almost unknown, except a few small gardens for private use. The rich alluvions of the Mississippi had presented no attractions for the indolent settlers; all had collected on the barren shores from the Bay of Mobile westward, or had wandered over the vast regions in search of traffick with the Indians. Now agriculture had begun to flourish on the fertile alluvions of the river, capitalists had become interested in the staple products of the soil, and considerable portions of rice,

* Martin's Louisiana, vol. i., p. 263.   † Idem, p. 265.

tobacco, and indigo had already been exported. Eighteen hundred negro slaves had been imported from Africa, and twenty-five hundred redemptioners, or laborers from France, had been introduced, liable to serve three years for those who paid the expenses of their emigration. The military force in the province had been augmented from less than three hundred to eight hundred and fifty troops.* Settlements were formed on the Mississippi, and the city of New Orleans had become a large commercial port. Many pleasant cottages lined the banks of the river for more than twenty miles above the city; settlements had grown up on Red River, and on the Washita, at Natchez, and on the Yazoo. In the Illinois and Wabash countries there had been a large accession to the agricultural population, and an active trade had sprung up from the Illinois and Wabash countries to the ports of New Orleans and Mobile. Each settlement had now been provided with a regular government for the administration of justice; religious instruction had been provided for each settlement; clergymen and chapels were common in the old settlements, and missions were established in the new. But a severe check to colonial prosperity was soon to be experienced.

For several years a spirit of jealous dissatisfaction had appeared among several of the Indian tribes east of the Mississippi. The Chickasâs had never been sincerely friendly to the French, and were continually urged to hostilities by English emissaries from Carolina. The Natchez, and other tribes south of them, although in alliance with the French, had several times wavered in their friendship, and were only restrained by fear. This state of feeling among the tribes had been observed for years by the commandant-general, who had often urged upon the directory of the company the necessity of preparing more effectually to protect the settlements. M. Perrier, since his appointment, had also urged upon them the necessity of carrying out the suggestions of Bienville. The directory, however, had disregarded all his admonitions and plans of defense. They deemed his apprehensions as groundless, and possibly somewhat influenced by a desire to increase the number of troops under his command, in order to magnify his own importance and to acquire a more active command.† Thus they inferred that he would willingly embroil the province in

* Martin, vol. i., p. 266. † Idem, p. 270.

an Indian war, that he might display his military skill and prowess in conducting it to a successful termination. Still M. Perrier continued to warn them of the necessity of preparing to meet the impending danger. But his warnings were unheeded. The directory could see nothing in the occasional murders and depredations of the Indians, more than had been common from the earliest periods of the colony.

Notwithstanding all the signs of restless impatience on the part of the Indian tribes, the French officers and agents took no prudent steps to soothe their hostile feelings, or to quiet their jealous apprehensions. The Indian plainly saw the rapid strides of ambition, which sought to possess their entire country, and which must ultimately, if not arrested, prove the destruction of their nation, or their expulsion from the land of their fathers. On the other hand, the French appeared to view the Indians as beings without rights, whom they might strip of their lands and homes at pleasure. Every aggression on the part of the French only served to rouse up the slumbering vengeance of the savage, and to impress upon him more firmly the necessity of revenge, and the maintenance of his rights and his liberty. The impatience with which the Indian beheld his insolent oppressor, and the destroyer of his peace, was but little calculated to cause him to conciliate the unwelcome guests. Such were the feelings mutually existing between the French and the Natchez Indians.

The French, influenced by mercenary motives, had no forbearance for what they considered insolence in the Indian. Hence they became arrogant, domineering, and unjust in their demands, and dealt with them in no measured harshness. Trivial offenses and depredations were punished with extreme rigor upon the savage; but his demands for justice against the white man were disregarded, and revenge was left to rankle in his breast. Above all, the commandant at Fort Rosalie, M. Chopart, had long been obnoxious to the Natchez chiefs, and he, in turn, took pleasure in making them feel his power when opportunity offered for harassing them.

This state of reciprocal ill-will became known to the English agents and emissaries from Carolina, who hoped to see their European rivals embroiled with the numerous tribes east of the Mississippi. Nothing, of course, was done by them to prevent a result so much desired by the British cabinet.

Instead of giving due attention to these things, the company had been preparing expeditions to explore the Missouri River in search of silver and gold mines, or sending exploring detachments into the remote western portions of Louisiana. The forts near the sea-board, which were mostly beyond the danger of Indian hostilities, employed nearly all the efficient force of the province, while those in the midst of the disaffected Indians were in a decayed state, and but feebly defended.

In this state of affairs the Chickasâs, who had always entertained a jealous hostility to the French, conceived the propriety of an attempt to exterminate the defenseless colony. For this purpose, the chiefs devised a plan of extermination, and with much secrecy and address engaged several of the other tribes in the conspiracy. The Natchez chiefs engaged with ardor in the plan; so did many of the Choctâs and Yazoo tribes, as well as those upon the Tensas west of the Mississippi. The conspirators attempted to engage the Northern tribes in a similar and simultaneous conspiracy against the French settlements in the Illinois and Wabash countries. Attempts were made also by the Chickasâs to excite the small tribes in the vicinity of Red River and north of the Bayou Iberville. Such were the general feelings of the Indians preceding the fatal massacre of the French settlements.

The Chickasâ conspiracy, however, was never carried into effect. From some unknown cause, it was frustrated before the period for execution arrived; or, as some suppose, the period had not arrived when the Natchez chiefs, from some unforeseen cause, were induced to anticipate the day. It is certain that the Chickasâs were displeased at their exclusion from a participation in the massacre. They also suspected the Choctâs of treachery.* Various tales have been invented to account for the manner in which the Natchez massacre superseded the Chickasâ conspiracy. The general impression is, that the number of days to elapse, after the new noon, previous to the general massacre, was designated by a bundle of reeds, one of which was to be withdrawn every day by a chief; and that each tribe or village had this record; and that, by accident or design, the bundle at the Natchez towns had been robbed of several reeds, thereby accelerating the day. Possibly the Natchez chiefs, in their premature attack, may

* Martin's Louisiana, vol. i., p. 270, 271.

have been instigated by some new and unexpected aggression; or, possibly, they may have been influenced by the arrival of a large supply of ammunition, military stores, and goods, which had been received at the company's warehouse near Fort Rosalie.* Certain it was that the Chickasâs took a deep interest in the success of the enterprise.

Chopart became more and more obnoxious to the Natchez chiefs. His arbitrary and despotic conduct toward them cherished in the savage a growing impatience for revenge, while a disdainful resentment caused him to exercise his brief authority with increasing severity against the Indians.†

It was but recently that Chopart had made new aggressions upon the Indians' rights. Early in the summer, he had required the Indians to abandon one of their villages, that he might occupy the site with a plantation. This was the village of the " White Apple" chief, which spread over nearly three miles in extent.‡ Chopart summoned the "sun," and required him to cause their huts to be removed to some other place, and their fields to be laid waste. The indignant chief replied, " that their fathers, for many years, had occupied that ground, and that it was good for their children still to remain on the same." The commandant resorted to threats of violence to enforce his commands, and the chief retired and called a council to determine the proper course of policy. At length, after a promise of one basket of corn and one hen for every cabin, after the corn should have matured and the fowls were grown, for indulgence until that time, Chopart condescended to grant a respite to his commands.

* Martin's Louisiana, vol. i., p. 272, 273.

† Such had been the overbearing conduct of M. Chopart, that the chiefs had formerly complained to the commandant-general, M. Perrier, who had summoned M. Chopart to New Orleans to answer for his conduct. He had succeeded in explaining matters to the governor in such manner as to justify himself with the commandant-general, who subsequently reinstated him in his command at Fort Rosalie. On his return, he indulged in many vexatious exactions upon the Indians, to gratify his spite; and as a part of this course, demanded the removal of their village.—See Stoddart, p. 49.

‡ It was no uncommon thing, in the early explorations of the Spaniards and French, in Louisiana and Florida, to see Indian villages scattered for miles along a fertile plain, each cabin or house surrounded by extensive fields of corn, pumpkins, beans, &c. De Soto, in Florida, passed through some towns, which, with their fields, spread out for five or six miles. Since the encroachments of the white man, these scattered villages are more rare.

The site of the White Apple village was situated about twelve miles south of the present city of Natchez, near the mouth of Second Creek, and three miles east of the Mississippi. The site was occupied by the plantation of Colonel Anthony Hutchens, an early emigrant to Florida. All vestiges of Indian industry have disappeared, except some mounds in the vicinity.

Time passed slowly, and all appeared quiet and peaceable; but the nation was highly incensed at the unjust demand. As the time approached for the destruction of their village, the chiefs sat in council, to devise the most proper course for resenting the injury and defending their rights. It was determined not to limit their revenge to the obnoxious individual, but to effect the total overthrow of the whole colony. The settlement was to be destroyed; the men were to be put to death, and the women and children were to be reduced to slavery. The plan was to be confided alone to the warriors and chiefs. Runners were sent to every village, both of the Natchez and their confederates, with the signal of preparation. Bundles of reeds were prepared, each having an equal number. One of these bundles was to be sent to every village, with instructions to keep it until the new moon. Then, for every day afterward, at the rising of the sun, one reed was to be withdrawn, until only one remained. The attack was to be made on the day that the last reed was withdrawn. The plan, thus arranged, awaited only the fatal day.*

Suspicion of some fatal conspiracy was afloat in the settlements; many feared the rankling vengeance of the savage, and various indications seemed to apprise them of some approaching catastrophe; but they were unheeded by the commandant of Fort Rosalie, whose avarice and self-will blinded his perception of visible danger.

Chopart had been warned of the approaching danger; but he affected to despise it, and is said to have threatened violence to his monitor. The settlements, accordingly, remained in doubtful security, and unprotected, until the fatal day disclosed the bloody tragedy. The Indians, under their respective chiefs, were prepared to make the preconcerted attack on the different portions of the settlements. At the St. Catharine's settlement, the signal was to be given by the "Great Sun" from Fort Rosalie. The signal to the surrounding settlements was to be the smoke and flames of the fort and the adjacent buildings, accompanied by the shouts and yells of the victorious warriors.

The corn and poultry had been paid for the respite to the devoted village, and to all appearance the Indians and French were inclined to mutual friendship and forbearance;† but they

---

* See Stoddart's Louisiana, p. 50, 51.

† Stoddart states that the massacre was arranged to take place at the time of pay-

remembered the deceptive truce of Bienville six years before, and now they were resolved to improve upon his example.

Indian tradition asserts that the preconcerted massacre was kept a profound secret, confined only to the chiefs and warriors, and that none others were permitted to have any knowledge of the plan; that the women especially were excluded from a knowledge of the conspiracy; that at length the wife of a chief, or sun, from various appearances, suspected that some momentous enterprise was in contemplation, and, after various artifices and devices, she succeeded in gleaning from her son the contemplated plan of massacre. She immediately took steps to communicate to the white men the imminent danger which awaited them. The information was communicated to the commandant of Fort Rosalie, M. Chopart, who derided the fears of his informant, and threatened with punishment those who should give currency to the rumor.*

Under this fatal security, the whole colony was left entirely unguarded and unprepared for danger; some were in their houses, some in the fields, and others dispersed through the settlements. The fort itself was not in a state of defense, and the garrison was negligent and unsuspicious of the danger so near at hand. The women and children, as usual, were engaged in the ordinary avocations of domestic employments, thoughtless and unconcerned as to the calamity which was about to overtake them.

Such was the state of things in the province until near the close of November, 1729. At length the fatal day arrived. It was the 28th day of the month. Early in the morning the Great Sun repaired, with a few chosen warriors, to Fort Rosalie, and all were well armed with knives and other concealed weapons.

The company had recently sent up a large supply of powder and lead, and provisions for the use of the post. The Indians had recourse to stratagem to procure a supply of ammunition, pretending they were preparing for a great hunting excursion. Before they set out, they wished to purchase a

ing the tribute to the commandant; but it is not probable that the payment of the tribute would have been deferred until the last of November, when the corn would have been ripe for gathering, in this latitude, by the middle of September, at furthest. The probability is, that the tribute had been paid in due time, to quiet suspicion.—See Stoddart, p. 51.

* See Martin's Louisiana, vol. i., p. 271; and Stoddart's Sketches, p. 51, 52.

supply of ammunition, and they had brought corn and poultry to barter for powder and lead. Having placed the garrison off their guard, a number of Indians were permitted to enter the fort, and others were distributed about the company's warehouse. Upon a certain signal from the Great Sun, the Indians immediately drew their concealed weapons, and commenced the carnage by one simultaneous and furious massacre of the garrison, and all who were in and near the warehouse.*

Other parties, distributed through the contiguous settlements, carried on the bloody work in every house as soon as the smoke was seen to rise from the houses near the fort.

The massacre commenced at nine o'clock in the morning, and before noon the whole of the male population of the French colony on St. Catharine (consisting of about seven hundred souls) were sleeping the sleep of death. The slaves were spared for the service of the victors, and the females and children were reserved as prisoners of war. Chopart fell among the first victims; and, as the chiefs disdained to stain their hands with his despised blood, he was dispatched by the hand of a common Indian. Two mechanics, a tailor and a carpenter, were spared, because they might be useful to the Indians.

While the massacre was progressing, the Great Sun seated himself in the spacious warehouse of the company, and, with apparent unconcern and complacency, sat and smoked his pipe while his warriors were depositing the heads of the French garrison in a pyramid at his feet. The head of Chopart was placed in the center, surmounting those of his officers and soldiers. So soon as the warriors informed the Great Sun that the last Frenchman had ceased to live, he commanded the pillage to commence. The negro slaves were employed in bringing out the plunder for distribution. The powder and military stores were reserved for public use in future emergencies.

While the ardent spirits remained, the day and the night alike presented one continued scene of savage triumph and drunken revelry. With horrid yells they spent their orgies in dancing over the mangled bodies of their enemies, which lay strewed in every quarter where they had fallen in the general carnage. Here, unburied, they remained a prey for dogs and

* See Martin's Louisiana, vol. i., p. 272, 273; and Stoddart's Sketches.

hungry vultures. Every vestige of the houses and dwellings in all the settlements was reduced to ashes.*

Two soldiers only, who happened to be absent in the woods at the time of the massacre, escaped to bear the melancholy tidings to New Orleans. As they approached the fort and heard the deafening yells of the savages, and saw the columns of smoke and flame ascending from the buildings, they well judged the fate of their countrymen. They concealed themselves until they could procure a boat or canoe to descend the river to New Orleans, where they arrived a few days afterward, and told the sad story of the colony on the St. Catharine.

The same fate was shared by the colony on the Yazoo, near Fort St. Peter, and by those on the Washita, at Sicily Island, and near the present town of Monroe. Dismay and terror were spread over every settlement in the province. New Orleans was filled with mourning and sadness for the fate of friends and countrymen.

The whole number of victims slain in this massacre amounted to more than two hundred men, besides a few women and some negroes, who attempted to defend their masters. Ninety-two women and one hundred and fifty-five children were taken prisoners. Among the victims were Father Poisson, the Jesuit missionary; Laloire, the principal agent of the company; M. Kollys and son, who had purchased M. Hubert's interest, and had just arrived to take possession.†

* Martin's Louisiana, vol. i., p. 272, 273.   † Idem, p. 272.

CHAPTER VIII.

LOUISIANA UNDER "THE WESTERN COMPANY" AFTER THE NATCHEZ MASSACRE: EXTERMINATION OF THE NATCHEZ TRIBES.—A.D. 1729 TO 1733.

Argument.—Consternation in Louisiana after the Natchez Tragedy.—The Governor, M. Perrier, prepares to invade the Natchez Country.—Loubois leads on the French Troops and Allies.—Lesueur leads on the Choctâs.—Lesueur arrives on the St. Catharine with his Choctâ Allies.—They attack the Natchez Towns and return victoriously.—Loubois arrives with the Artillery.—After a short Siege, the Indians propose an Armistice.—Loubois permits the Natchez Warriors to escape him.—Erects a terraced Fort and retires to New Orleans.—The Natchez Tribes retire to Black River, and there Fortify themselves.—The Chickasâs espouse the Natchez Cause.—English Intrigue active among the Chickasâs.—Chouacas Tribe exterminated by the French and Negro Troops.—Negro Insurrection arrested.—Military Strength of the Province.—Small Re-enforcement arrives from France.—M. Perrier advances his Forces to Black River.—Invests the Natchez Strong-hold.—Negotiations for Capitulation.—The "Great Sun" and fifty-two Indians surrendered.—Perrier's Demand refused, and the Cannonade opens again.—The Besieged abandon the Fort during a dark and stormy Night.—Many are overtaken and captured.—The French Army return to New Orleans with their Prisoners.—The Prisoners are sold into West Indian Slavery.—The Remnant of the Natchez Tribe imbodies on Red River.—They attack the French Post at Natchitoches, and are repulsed with great Loss.—Termination of the Natchez War.—Personal Characteristics of this Tribe.—State of the Province at the Close of the War.—The Company resolve to surrender their Charter.—The King's Proclamation announces its Acceptance, April 10th, 1732.—Retrospect of the Province under the Company.—The Crown purchases the Company's Effects, and the Royal Government is established.

[A.D. 1729.] So soon as the Natchez disaster was known at New Orleans, the whole city and settlements presented a scene of general commotion and consternation. M. Perrier, the commandant-general, made the most active preparations for avenging the loss of the French settlements by waging a war of extermination against the tribes concerned in the conspiracy. A vessel was immediately dispatched to France for troops and military supplies. Two vessels were ordered up the river as far as Bayou Tunica, to observe the movements of the savages and to afford protection to such individuals as may have escaped the tomahawk and scalping-knife in any of the settlements. Couriers were dispatched to Mobile, to Red River, and to Fort Chartres, in the Illinois country, to summon the several commanders to prepare for co-operation with their respective commands. Emissaries and agents were sent to the Choctâs, and to all the tribes in alliance with the

French from the head waters of the Alabama to the Cumberland, and even to the Illinois tribes. Every house in the city, and every plantation, was furnished with arms and ammunition for defense out of the company's store-house; the city was fortified, and placed in a state of complete military defense against any possible attack of savages.*

The brave and enterprising Lesueur, ever ready to engage in remote excursions, had gone to rouse and organize the Choctâs on the Tombigby for an immediate campaign, while M. Perrier prepared to march with the troops drawn from the posts and settlements near Mobile and Red River. Three hundred regular troops were taken from the posts, and three hundred militia from the lower settlements joined his standard for the invasion of the Natchez country. But just as M. Perrier was about to take up the line of march for the hostile towns, his attention was suddenly arrested by an alarming danger close at hand. The late disaster, and the contemplated departure of the troops and most of the able-bodied men from the settlements, had prompted some of the slaves on the large plantations to improve the occasion by an attempt to overpower the whites and assert their liberty. To suppress the threatened insurrection, and to punish the instigators of the plot, M. Perrier was compelled to defer his departure for a few days.

In the mean time, the Chevalier M. Loubois, with the main body of troops, set out for the Natchez country, in order to effect a junction with Lesueur and his Choctâ allies from the east. As he proceeded northward, he received re-enforcements at Baton Rouge and Point Coupée, besides a few Tunica Indians in the vicinity of Red River.

[A.D. 1730.] As Loubois advanced toward the Natchez towns, he was met by two Natchez chiefs with proposals for peace; though, doubtless, their real object was to spy out his forces, and to devise some plan of treachery. Their terms were extraordinary and arrogant, and the assurance with which they were urged induced M. Loubois to advance cautiously, lest he might be overpowered by their superior numbers.

As the condition of peace, with the surrender of their prisoners and a general amnesty, they demanded no less than two hundred barrels of powder, two thousand flints, four thousand bullets, two hundred knives, and an equal number of axes, hoes,

* Martin's Louisiana, vol. i., p. 276.

shirts, coats, and pieces of ginghams; besides twenty laced coats, twenty laced hats with plumes, twenty barrels of brandy, and as many of wine.*

Loubois could view the extraordinary proposition in no other light than a bold attempt at defiance against the French forces, and he continued his march with caution, awaiting reenforcements from below.

In the mean time, the ever-successful Lesueur had won the Choctâs to his aid, and, advancing from the Tombigby with six hundred warriors, had augmented his force near Pearl River to twelve hundred auxiliaries. With this formidable body of allies he arrived upon the St. Catharine on the morning of the 28th of January. Here he encamped, vainly to await the arrival of the forces under M. Loubois, who had not yet entered the Natchez country.

The Indian runners soon brought intelligence that the Natchez chiefs were utterly ignorant of the arrival of the Choctâ warriors from the east, and were spending the night in carousals and dancing. This intelligence coming to the ears of the warriors, they became impatient, and, disregarding all restraint, next morning about daybreak, in spite of Lesueur's urgent entreaties, they fell upon the Natchez villages with great fury. After a conflict of three hours they returned to camp, bringing, as the trophies of their prowess, sixty Indian scalps, and eighteen Indian prisoners, besides fifty-one women and children, and two men rescued from captivity. The men were the two mechanics who had been spared in the general massacre of November.

The Choctâs also recovered from captivity one hundred and six negro slaves. Their loss in this affair, having found their enemies unprepared for defense, was only two warriors killed and eight wounded.† After skirmishing a few days, most of the warriors dispersed, and returned to their towns.

The Natchez warriors, now apprised of the hostile movements against them, lost no further time in idle carousal, but proceeded with great diligence to secure their women and children by a strongly-fortified camp. All their military art was put in requisition, and all the available labor, to secure themselves against the attacks of the Choctâ warriors and the strong military force advancing from New Orleans.

* Martin's Louisiana, vol. i., p. 277.   † Idem, p. 278.

The interval for defensive operations was short; for in ten days, Loubois, with a force of fourteen hundred men, including French and Indians, appeared before the Indian strong-hold. Yet, by this time, the Natchez warriors had intrenched themselves strongly, and were determined upon a brave resistance. The besieging force was nearly eleven hundred Frenchmen, besides three hundred Indians, and such of the Choctâs under Lesueur as still remained to take part in the contest.

The fort was regularly invested; trenches were opened, and the artillery was planted upon the batteries. But on the seventh day of the investment, and after many skirmishes by the Indian allies, in which the Natchez warriors fought with great desperation, the besieged sent a flag with propositions for a conditional surrender of prisoners.

The proposition stipulated that the Natchez chiefs would surrender the remaining French prisoners, to the number of more than two hundred souls, provided the artillery were removed from before the fort and the siege abandoned. At the same time, they declared that a refusal to meet their proposition should be followed by the immediate destruction of all their prisoners by fire.

In order to preserve the lives of the helpless victims still in their power, Loubois consented to accede to their terms. A suspension of hostilities for ten days was agreed upon, for the purpose of conducting the negotiations.

Yet Loubois designed to wreak his vengeance upon the hostile Indians so soon as the prisoners should have been secured. As yet, but little damage had been effected by the artillery, although eleven field-pieces were at his command. The engineers were inexperienced, and his supply of ammunition had become nearly exhausted. Meanwhile, he was exerting every means to hasten forward a supply of ammunition and military stores from New Orleans.

The Indians, suspecting treachery on the part of the French, resolved to improve the occasion during the suspension of hostilities, and provide for their own escape.

At length, on the 25th of February, negotiations had been concluded. The artillery had been removed, the batteries demolished, and the prisoners were to be surrendered on the following day in front of the fort.

During the night of the 25th, the Natchez chiefs and warriors, with their women and children, together with their plunder and personal effects, silently retired from their intrenchments, leaving a small guard with the prisoners until daybreak, and before morning they had crossed the river and were beyond pursuit. M. Perrier found the prisoners in the fort agreeably to the treaty, but the enemy had fled. The French were astonished at the dextrous manœuver, but it was useless to pursue the fugitives.

A few days afterward, M. Loubois advanced to the bluff on the bank of the river and commenced a terraced fort, which was supplied with cannon and munitions, and a garrison of one hundred and twenty men.* This was the beginning of the terraced Fort Rosalie, the remains of which are still visible on the brink of the bluff, just below the city of Natchez. After a military occupancy of nearly seventy years by the troops of France, Great Britain, Spain, and the United States successively, this fort was finally abandoned about the year 1800.

Having left Fort Rosalie in command of his lieutenant, M. Loubois dismissed his Indian allies, and returned with the Southern troops to New Orleans, where he delivered the rescued prisoners into the arms of their sympathizing friends.

The further prosecution of the Natchez war was deferred until re-enforcements and supplies should have arrived from France. Although hostilities for the present were suspended, the Indians were well assured in their own minds that a terrible vengeance was still meditated against them. To escape the fury of their enemies, they determined to abandon their homes and their country, with the bones and ashes of their ancestors, and seek safety and protection among their red brethren west of the Mississippi. This vengeance was the more to be dreaded, since the French had succeeded in securing the alliance of several powerful tribes of the South, as well as those upon the Illinois and Wabash rivers.

Under these circumstances, the whole tribe resolved to disperse from the eastern side of the Mississippi. The largest portion, led by the Great Sun and the principal chiefs, sought an asylum and a place of defense upon the Lower Washita, on "the point" between Little River and the Washita, just below the mouth of Little River, where the Washita assumes the name of Black River. On the peninsula rises a lofty terraced mound

* Stoddart's Sketches of Louisiana, p. 58. Also, Martin, vol. i., p. 279.

of earth, surrounded at irregular distances, from three to six hundred yards, with many smaller mounds and embankments, which are the remains of the Natchez earthworks in their first retreat. The whole area embraced in these remains is probably not short of four hundred acres, comprising, besides the large mound, twelve smaller ones. This point, when securely fortified by the Indians, must have been one of the strongest Indian fortresses ever known to white men; and here the Natchez "suns," with the flower of their nation, determined to make a stand to meet the coming storm.* Yet other portions of the tribe sought an asylum among the Chickasâs, who were willing to espouse their cause.†

[A.D. 1731.] It was not long before the warlike Chickasâs, urged by their Natchez allies and refugees, began their preparations to meet the vengeance of the French in defense of their friends; and the English of Carolina did not long withhold their counsel from the wavering Chickasâs.

The jealousy of England toward the French colonies in Louisiana had never slept. Although domestic troubles between the people and the proprietaries of Carolina had given the French a temporary exemption from English intrigue among the Chickasâs and some of the more southern tribes, yet the English traders and emissaries in the Chickasâ nation were ever ready to seize any occasion to annoy the French. Affairs in Carolina had now been settled, except collisions on the South with the Spaniards of Florida and their Indian allies. Treaties of peace and amity had been concluded with the tribes of the interior, as far as the Muskhogees, or Creeks. During the past year, the proprietaries had sold out their interest to the crown, and a royal governor had been duly installed over Carolina.

* This point, at the junction of the Washita and Little River, is a remarkable point, such as was generally termed by the French "Trois Rivières," or *three rivers*; because, unlike the ordinary confluence of two streams, it presents the appearance of *three rivers* coming together. The union of the Washita and Little River forms Black River, which immediately receives the Tensas from the east. Thus *three rivers* unite to form the *fourth*. These are all deep and wide rivers.

The principal central mound, or terrace, is about one hundred yards long and fifty wide at the base. It rises as a pyramid to the height of thirty feet, then recedes, with a terrace on every side, and rises more than thirty feet higher in a conical form. Major Stoddart, who examined it in 1804, estimated the elevation of the principal summit at eighty feet. The author viewed it in 1844, when, having been cleared of the trees and undergrowth, it was in cultivation. The traces of circumvallation are very evident, and the smaller mounds stand around at unequal distances, varying from two hundred to six hundred yards from the central turret.

† See Martin's Louisiana, vol. i., p. 280–283. Also, Stoddart's Sketches, p. 58.

No sooner had the royal government been fully established, than it attempted, by treaties of peace and alliance, to convert the tribes on the Western frontiers of Carolina into subjects and allies of Great Britain.

"Early in the year 1730, Sir Alexander Cummings, a special envoy, guided by Indian traders to the Keowee River, summoned a general convention of the chiefs of the Cherokee nation to meet at Nequassee, in the Valley of the Tennessee. They came together in the month of April, and were told that King George was their sovereign."* English traders had already established themselves among the Chickasâs, who also became the steadfast allies of the English. This relation to England necessarily implied a settled hostility to the French.

Preparations for prosecuting the Natchez war engaged a large share of M. Perrier's attention, and he lost no opportunity of urging the matter before the company. Yet the whole effective force in the province, at this time, consisted of only six hundred and fifty French troops and two hundred Swiss mercenaries, distributed in ten different forts and military posts. The militia of the province, exclusive of the Illinois country, amounted to eight hundred men.† These comprised the whole available force with which M. Perrier was to carry on his contemplated war of extermination. The Indian allies would augment the whole to nearly two thousand men and warriors.

In the mean time, a new danger had sprung up at home, in the midst of the settlements near New Orleans. This difficulty proceeded from their own jealousy and imprudence. Highly susceptible to imaginary indications of savage hostility since the Natchez tragedy, the French had suspected the fidelity of the Chouacâs, a small tribe of Indians inhabiting the country between the English Turn and Lake Barataria, below New Orleans. Believing them in secret alliance with the Chickasâs, they deemed it necessary to exterminate them, in order to avoid their enmity. For this purpose, a body of negro slaves were armed and drilled to march against this devoted tribe. The negroes were accordingly led against the defenseless villages and settlements of the unsuspecting natives, who, taken by surprise, were involved in one general and indiscriminate massacre of men, women, and children.

* Bancroft's United States, vol. iii., p. 332.
† Martin's Louisiana, vol. i., p. 281, 282.

This bloody work completed, the negroes, well pleased with their new calling, were loth to resign the musket for the hoe. At length it was ascertained that they had been planning an actual insurrection and massacre of the white settlements near New Orleans. But a timely discovery of the plot, and the prompt execution of the ringleaders and prominent abettors, sufficed to prevent the contemplated tragedy.*

In the mean time, M. Perrier had ordered a requisition of troops and militia for the campaign against the Natchez stronghold on Black River. He had issued his proclamation calling out every able-bodied man, and conjuring them to arm and equip themselves in readiness to join his standard in the contemplated campaign.

Expecting re-enforcements from France, the people of New Orleans were highly rejoiced, on the 10th of August, upon hearing the arrival of one of the company's ships off the Balize, with troops and supplies for the colonies, under the command of M. Perrier de Salvert, brother of the commandant-general. But the re-enforcement was small, and the aid inefficient. The whole number of troops was only three companies of marines, comprising one hundred and eighty men. These, with the regular troops maintained in the province, amounted to less than one thousand men; a small force with which to garrison at least five or six forts, and protect numerous remote and exposed settlements.

The commandant-general was highly mortified at this small re-enforcement; yet he determined to prosecute a vigorous campaign for the chastisement of the Natchez warriors on Black River. He sought aid in person from the friendly tribes near Fort Condé, and among the Choctâs. He then returned to New Orleans, and completed his levy of the militia; but the whole number of the enrollment from the Wabash to Mobile did not exceed eight hundred men. These would yield a small effective force in actual service in prosecuting a war in the heart of an enemy's country, and in the midst of powerful tribes. By the middle of November, the whole number of troops mustered into service amounted to six hundred and fifty, including regulars and volunteers, leaving only a small garrison in each of the important forts.

The Natchez refugees and the hostile Chickasâs, during the past year, had lost no opportunity of harassing the settlements

* Martin's Louisiana, vol. i., p. 282.

within their reach. Every Frenchman who fell into their hands upon the river, or near any remote settlement, suffered the most barbarous and cruel tortures. Such had been the dangers and horrors of the river route, that, for a time, the river trade and intercourse had been almost abandoned, and the Illinois settlements were virtually cut off from Lower Louisiana. Many persons captured by the Natchez warriors upon the river had been burned at the stake with the cruel tortures of slow fire.

On the 15th of November, the army, six hundred and fifty in number, left New Orleans for the strong-hold of the Natchez tribe on Black River. On the way, they were joined by three hundred and fifty Indian warriors, increasing the entire force to one thousand men.

[A.D. 1732.] Early in January the army reached the mouth of Black River, and proceeded slowly up its broad and gentle stream. On the 20th of January they came in sight of the enemy's principal fort. The troops were disembarked, and the fort was invested. On the following day the field-pieces and artillerists were landed, and the siege was regularly opened. For three days the besieged made a spirited resistance; but on the 25th a flag of truce was suspended from the fort, just as the artillery was prepared to open upon it; yet M. Perrier rejected all propositions unless the "suns" and war-chiefs were delivered into his hands, and threatened utter destruction to all in case of refusal. At length, after a protracted negotiation, the Indians surrendered the Great Sun and one war-chief; but M. Perrier refused to extend quarters to the tribes unless others were also surrendered. Not being in a situation to dictate terms, they at length consented to surrender sixty-five men and about two hundred women and children, upon condition that their lives should be spared. But these sternly refused to leave their intrenchments unless the artillery was withdrawn from before the fort; they likewise demanded that the Indian allies, who were guarding the avenues of escape, should also be withdrawn. These demands were refused by the French commander, and the artillery opened a furious cannonade against the works; but it was soon silenced by heavy rain, which continued until night, when clouds and wind thickened to a tempest. Soon after dark, it was ascertained that the enemy were abandoning their strong-hold under the shelter of the tempestuous night. They were now making their escape up Little River, and through the dense forests and swamps toward Catahoola Lake. The Indian allies were sent in rapid pursuit, and they at length captured about one hundred of the fugitives. Further pursuit was abandoned by M. Perrier, and he proceeded next day to demolish the outworks of the deserted fort. Soon afterward the Indian allies were dismissed, and the French commander prepared to return with his army and his prisoners to New Orleans. He arrived in the city on the 5th of February, accompanied by four hundred and twenty-seven captives of the Natchez tribe, among whom were the Great Sun and several principal war-chiefs.*

The Great Sun and his companions were soon afterward shipped to St. Domingo and sold as slaves. Such was the termination of this expedition, and such was the fate of the Great Sun and nearly half of his nation. Although in two campaigns they had lost many of their tribe by captivity and death, yet nearly one half of the entire nation remained; but being dispersed in detached parties, they were compelled to seek safety from the vengeance of the French. Some retired west of the Washita, some to Red River, and some joined the Chickasâs east of the Mississippi. Nearly three hundred individuals, including seventy warriors, had retired to the region west of Catahoola Lake, and others passed up the Washita. One chief, with forty warriors, had gone to join the Chickasâs, taking with them their women and children. The Yazoos and Coroas, tribes of the Natchez confederacy, were still able to bring a few warriors into the field.†

Although reduced and dispersed, the Natchez warriors had not been conquered. A few months served to recover them from their late reverses, and they still breathed vengeance against their destroyers; hence the Natchez war was not yet terminated, and the invincible courage of the warriors could be subdued only by extermination.

Toward the close of summer, the warriors, who had retired from the strong-hold upon Black River and Catahoola Lake, with other wandering bands of the dispersed tribes, collected into one body near the remote settlements of Natchitoches, on Red River. Here they determined to make another bold stand against their French enemies. Their united force comprised

* Martin's Louisiana, vol. i., p. 287. † Idem.

about two hundred warriors, burning with revenge for their disasters at Natchez and on Black River, for the loss of their Great Suns and chiefs, as well as their wives and children, who had now been sold into hopeless slavery in St. Domingo. Their first operations were directed against the French posts and settlements at Natchitoches.

The post of Natchitoches was commanded by St. Denys, a bold and intrepid officer, of great experience in Indian affairs. The hostile warriors designed the utter destruction of this remote post and settlement; but St. Denys, apprised of their designs and movements, had made ample preparation for the defense of his post. He had re-enforced his garrison by the enlistment of a few Spaniards, and others willing to serve under his command; the fort was repaired, and placed in a state of complete defense; at the same time, having secured the aid of a body of friendly Indians from the neighboring tribes, he now deemed himself able to withstand any assault which might be made by the hostile warriors.

Nor was he long in suspense as to their movements. The Natchez warriors at length approached the post, and made a furious assault upon the works; but, after a hard-fought battle of several hours, they were repulsed with great loss by the vigorous resistance of the garrison. Failing in the attack upon the fortified post, they retired to wreak their vengeance upon the Natchitoches Indians, a weak tribe in the vicinity, who were in alliance with the French. The Natchitoches village, being deserted, was entered by the hostile warriors, who proceeded forthwith to fortify it as a strong-hold for future defense.

These movements were closely observed by the vigilant St. Denys, and he lost no time in his preparations to dislodge them from their new position. Having re-enforced his detachment by volunteers, and a few more friendly Indians from the regions south of Natchitoches, he advanced to the attack of the Natchez intrenchments. By a vigorous assault, the outworks were carried by storm, and the whole fortress was soon in possession of the assailants. The Natchez warriors made a vigorous resistance, during which ninety-two of their braves, including all of their head chiefs, were slain. The remainder, overpowered by the numbers and impetuosity of the French and their allies, escaped by flight.

Thus St. Denys, with his limited resources, by his indomitable energy and courage in this brilliant achievement, had accomplished more in bringing the Natchez war to a close than the commandant-general, with the whole resources of the province. This was, in fact, the closing scene in the war, and the blow which completed the final dispersion and annihilation of the Natchez Indians as a distinct tribe.

[A.D. 1733.] The scattered remnants of the tribe sought an asylum among the Chickasâs and other tribes who were hostile to the French. Since that time, the individuality of the Natchez tribe has been swallowed up in the nations with whom they were incorporated. Yet no tribe has left so proud a memorial of their courage, their independent spirit, and their contempt of death in defense of their rights and liberties. The city of Natchez is their monument, standing upon the field of their glory. Such is the brief history of the Natchez Indians, who are now considered extinct. In refinement and intelligence, they were equal, if not superior, to any other tribe north of Mexico. In courage and stratagem, they were inferior to none. Their form was noble and commanding; their stature was seldom under six feet, and their persons were straight and athletic. Their countenance indicated more intelligence than is commonly found in savages. The head was compressed from the os frontis to the occiput, so that the forehead appeared high and retreating, while the occiput was compressed almost in a line with the neck and shoulders. This peculiarity, as well as their straight, erect form, is ascribed to the pressure of bandages during infancy. Some of the remaining individuals of the Natchez tribe were in the town of Natchez as late as the year 1782, or more than half a century after the Natchez massacre.*

To the great joy of the whole province, a partial and temporary peace with the Indian tribes now succeeded. For three years, the whole population had been in a state of continual alarm and apprehension. Every thing had presented the appearance of hostile array and military parade. The troops in the province having been insufficient for the protection of the

* The venerable Christopher Miller, of Natchez, remembers to have seen a number of Natchez warriors in the village of Natchez as late as the year 1782, during the Spanish dominion. He had also seen several of them previous to that time, at the post of Arkansas, on the Arkansas River, under Spanish occupancy. He testifies to their commanding form and noble stature, no less than to their remarkably lofty and retreating forehead.

settlements and remote posts, and at the same time to keep down the rebellious spirit of the slaves, the population was drained of its most efficient members to fill the ranks of distant expeditions, leaving the settlements at the mercy of the small tribes in their immediate vicinity. This state of things was now, fortunately, terminated for a time, and the respite was essentially necessary for the safety of the province.

But the company had been involved in enormous expenses in conducting the military defense of the settlements, and in prosecuting the Natchez war. Their losses, by Indian depredations at Natchez and other points, in the first outbreak of hostilities, had also been great. The disturbance of harmony with other remote tribes, consequent upon the Natchez war, was such as precluded any profitable trade with them, and diminished the success of trade at the remote posts. This state of things, following upon the disasters consequent upon Law's failure, alarmed the directory, who, believing that they were not secure from similar disasters in future, determined to surrender their charter into the hands of the crown, and abandon the further prosecution of their scheme. Obedient to the wishes of the "Company of the Indies," who could invest their capital more profitably in traffick and conquest upon the coasts of Guinea and Hindostan, they had petitioned the king to permit them to surrender their charter and retire from the American wilderness. The petition was readily granted, and the king had issued his proclamation, declaring the whole province of Louisiana free to all his subjects, with equal privileges and rights as to trade and commerce. This proclamation was issued on the 10th day of April, 1732, and had taken effect from its date. From this time the Western Company, which was, in fact, only a branch of the "Company of the Indies," was absorbed in the parent monopoly.

During fifteen years the Western Company had held the control and monopoly of the mines and commerce of the province. They exercised all the rights of proprietors, subject only to the approbation of the king; yet the advantage derived was not proportionate to their outlay and their expectations. For the last three years, it had been a source of continual expense and harassing vexation. During this period, the population of the province had increased but little; yet from the time when the company first assumed the control, in 1717, the province had greatly changed. At that period, scarcely seven hundred souls, of all ages, sexes, and colors, formed the civilized population of this vast province; now the number of the colonists exceeded five thousand souls, among whom were many men of worth and enterprise. The whole number of slaves had increased from twenty souls to more than two thousand. The settlements were rapidly extending upon the fertile alluvions of the Mississippi, of Red River, of the Washita, and the Arkansas, besides the fine agricultural settlements upon the Illinois and Wabash Rivers.*

M. Salmon, as commissioner in behalf of the king, received formal possession of Louisiana from the company. The crown also purchased, through the commissioner, all the effects of the company in the province at a fair valuation, amounting to about sixty thousand dollars. The property thus transferred to the crown consisted of their warehouses, goods, stock in trade, plantations, with two hundred and sixty negroes, and all the appendages of their planting establishments.†

Under the new organization of the government, M. Perrier retained the appointment of commandant-general, and M. Salmon commissaire-ordonnateur. Loubois and D'Artaguette, both of whom had distinguished themselves in the Natchez war, were the king's lieutenants, the first for Louisiana, and the second for the Illinois country.

At this time, the settlements of Lower Louisiana had extended, at various points on the Mississippi, above New Orleans. At the German Coast, the river bank on both sides was lined by a large number of handsome cottages. Large settlements and plantations had been opened at Manchac, Baton Rouge, and Point Coupée, besides many others more remote from the city. At Natchez, settlements had extended upon the St. Catharine and upon Second Creek, from its sources to the Homochitto River.

The culture of rice was extensive; tobacco and indigo had succeeded well, and formed articles of export. A flourishing trade from the Illinois and Wabash countries increased the

* Martin's Louisiana, vol. i., p. 288, 289.

† In the valuation of the company's property, negroes were valued at an average of seven hundred livres, or one hundred and seventy-five dollars each. Horses were valued at fifty-seven livres, or fourteen dollars twenty-five cents each. Rice, of which there were eight thousand barrels, was rated at three livres, or seventy-five cents per hundred pounds. The value of a horse was estimated equal to nineteen hundred pounds of rice.—See Martin's Louisiana, vol. i., p. 292.

commercial importance of Louisiana. Civil government was organized, and religious instruction had been amply supplied in the different settlements. This, of course, was the Catholic faith, taught under the superintendence of the vicar-general at New Orleans, as a portion of the diocese of the Bishop of Quebec.*

The Illinois and Wabash countries, comprising all the settlements on the Upper Mississippi, from "Fort Chartres" and Kaskaskia eastward to the Wabash, and south of Lake Michigan, contained many flourishing settlements devoted to agriculture and the Indian trade.

CHAPTER IX.

LOUISIANA UNDER THE ROYAL GOVERNORS UNTIL THE CLOSE OF THE CHICKASÂ WAR.—A.D. 1733 TO 1741.

Argument.—Recapitulation of Chickasâ Hostilities, and English Intrigue from Carolina and Georgia.—Bienville reappointed Commandant-general of Louisiana.—He resolves to chastise the Chickasâs.—Demands a Surrender of the Natchez Refugees.—Prepares to invade the Chickasâ Country.—Indian Alliances formed with Choctâs.—Plan of Operations to invade from the North and South simultaneously.—Bienville, with the main Army and Allies, proceeds up the Tombigby.—Is delayed by Rains.—Marches to the Chickasâ Strong-hold.—Attacks the Fortress, and is repulsed with Loss.—Retires, and finally retreats down the Tombigby.—Defeat of D'Artaguette, with the Illinois Forces.—His Captivity and Death in the Chickasâ Country.—Bienville's Account of the Chickasâ Fort.—Chickasâs send Runners to apprise the English of their Victory over the French.—Bienville, overwhelmed with Chagrin, resolves on a second Invasion from the Mississippi.—The Plan of Invasion approved by the Minister of War.—The Grand Army proceeds up the Mississippi to Fort St. Francis.—Fort Assumption built on Fourth Chickasâ Bluff.—Delays from Sickness and Want of Provisions.—M. Celeron advances with a Detachment toward the Chickasâ Towns.—Concludes a Peace, by Bienville's Order, with a single Village.—Fort Assumption dismantled, and the Army descends to New Orleans.—Bienville retires under the Disgrace of a second Failure, and is superseded by the Marquis de Vaudreuil as Governor.—Retrospect of the Condition of the Province up to the Year 1741.

[A.D. 1733.] FROM the first settlement of Louisiana, the Chickasâ Indians, occupying all the northern half of the present State of Mississippi, and all the western half of Tennessee, had often manifested feelings inimical to the French. This feeling was known, however, to proceed from British intrigue, carried on by traders and emissaries from Carolina, which then comprised the present states of North and South

---

* Martin's Louisiana, vol. i., p. 289.

Carolina. Aware of the bias thus produced in the minds of the Chickasâs toward the French settlements, agents and emissaries, during Crozat's monopoly, as well as under the Western Company, had endeavored to reconcile them, and to secure their neutrality, if not their friendship, by mild and amicable means. Efforts were made to establish a reciprocal intercourse with them, by means of trading-posts and formal negotiations. But the result of all such overtures was, at most, a temporary friendship, or a disguised hostility. Within the first twenty years after Iberville planted his colony on the Bay of Mobile, the Chickasâs had several times been instrumental in instigating smaller tribes and bands into hostilities against the French, while they assumed an attitude of disguised friendship. On the Mississippi, as well as upon the Tombigby, their depredations upon the traders, and occasionally their murders at remote, unprotected points, had been subjects of remonstrance and of special negotiation. Influenced by British emissaries and traders from Carolina, they had almost entirely excluded French traders, and the agents both of M. Crozat and the Western Company. In this manner did the English authorities of Carolina attempt to arrest the extension of the French settlements east of the Lower Mississippi.

The Chickasâ nation constituted a rendezvous for British emissaries, whence they might operate through the contiguous tribes; and when opportunity might offer, they could penetrate the territory of tribes in friendship and alliance with the French. In this manner, remote settlements were often placed in extreme danger by any sudden hostility excited in the contiguous tribes. As early as the year 1715, a British emissary named Young had penetrated from the Chickasâ country through all the small tribes then inhabiting the southwestern portion of the present State of Mississippi, and thence through the tribes from New Orleans to Pascagoula Bay. This man having been captured by the agent of M. Crozat, was sent a prisoner to Mobile.* The object of his mission was to form a general conspiracy or league among the tribes, for the total expulsion of the French from Louisiana. The same object was attempted by others; but, fortunately, their efforts were unsuccessful.

Such attempts on the part of the English served as a full

* Martin's Louisiana, vol. i., p. 185.

justification on the part of the French to seek means of retaliation. For this purpose, in self-defense, they had encouraged the confederacy of the Yamases and the other tribes of Western Georgia, in their hostilities against the English settlements of Carolina the same year.

Eight years afterward, the Chickasâs near the Mississippi had resumed their hostilities upon the traders and voyageurs who conducted the commerce between Mobile and the Illinois country. After many such murders and robberies had been committed by them, Bienville succeeded in restoring peace and a temporary security to the river trade, without any general rupture with this nation. In a short time, however, restless desperadoes in the West resumed their attempts to harass and interrupt the river trade. This state of things had continued, with occasional intermissions, until about the close of the year 1729. About this time the Chickasâs began their efforts to form a conspiracy among all the tribes south of them, for the destruction of the French settlements throughout Lower Louisiana. In this conspiracy, the Natchez tribe had been originally only a consenting party, the Chickasâs being the principals, until circumstances urged the former to become principals in the memorable massacre of November, 1729. During the war, which resulted in the annihilation of the Natchez tribe, although the Chickasâs took no active part in the contest, they had received and given protection to the refugees of that tribe, as well as to many fugitive negroes who had escaped to them after the Natchez massacre. They also had given a refuge to the hostile warriors who escaped the arms of M. Perrier on Black River, and of St. Denys at Natchitoches, in the autumn of 1732. Such was the prelude to the Chickasâ war.

The province of Carolina, in 1732, had been divided into North and South Carolina, for the greater convenience of the royal government. The proprietaries having formally sold out their claims to the crown, from that time North and South Carolina were distinct royal provinces, under a newly-organized government of the king.* Nor was this the only movement made by the English crown to secure a footing north of the Gulf of Mexico and westward to the Mississippi. By a royal charter of George II., a new province had been planned, to embrace all the unoccupied country upon the Atlantic coast

---

* Marshall's Life of Washington; Introduction, vol. i., p. 308.

between the Savannah and Altamaha Rivers, and to extend from their sources westward to the Mississippi, thus interfering directly with the claims of both Spain and France.* In honor of the British king, it had been called the Province of Georgia. A colony prepared in England, under General James Oglethorpe, for its settlement, had arrived in the summer of 1733, and was located on the Savannah River, where the town of Savannah was laid off. Thus commenced the British province of Georgia, which received annual accessions to its population by successive colonies from the mother country.

[A.D. 1734.] No sooner had this colony been located than Oglethorpe set himself to forming friendly alliances with the neighboring tribes. In a short time his agents had secured the alliance of the different branches of the Muskhogees, the Yamases, and Cherokees. The following year, Red Shoes, a Choctâ chief, made a visit to Oglethorpe, in order to open an advantageous trade for his tribe. "We came a great way," said he, "and we are a great nation. The French are building forts about us against our liking. We have long traded with them, but they are poor in goods: we desire that a trade may be opened between us and you." And when a commerce with them began, the English coveted the harbors on the Gulf of Mexico, which rightfully belonged to Spain and France. Such was the beginning of British encroachments upon the limits of Louisiana.†

The Natchez refugees, still thirsting for vengeance, urged the Chickasâs to open hostilities. Encouraged by the English traders and emissaries, the Chickasâs again commenced depredations and murders upon the French commerce on the Mississippi. Before another year elapsed, they threw off all disguise, and openly espoused the Natchez cause. They also dispatched some of the most sagacious and artful of the negroes who had escaped from the Natchez settlements, as emissaries well calculated to sow the seeds of insurrection among the slaves on the plantations near New Orleans. They were to insinuate themselves among the slaves, and to encourage them to a bold and vigorous effort to obtain their freedom by the destruction of their masters; to represent to them their own liberty, and the ease with which the whole slave population could be speedily emancipated, when they might find a secure

* Bancroft's History of the United States, vol. iii., p. 419–421.   † Idem, p. 423.

refuge, if necessary, with their friends among the Chickasàs. Several of these emissaries had penetrated to the plantations near New Orleans, and especially to that formerly belonging to the Western Company, on which there were two hundred and fifty slaves.* Such are the intrigues, and such the means ever used by the British government to accomplish their designs against those they doom to destruction.

The contagion of their seduction spread among the negroes with surprising rapidity. They held meetings for night parties and dancing, unsuspected by their owners, wherever the desired intercourse between the leaders could be effected. A plan was actually laid, and a time appointed when they were to collect from all parts around the city of New Orleans, which was to be burned and the people massacred by one party, while another party were to seize the king's arsenal and magazines, from which they were to supply themselves with arms and ammunition. From this point they were to carry conflagration and slaughter along the river coast, until they should be joined by parties of Chickasâs, who were to hold themselves in readiness at some convenient point on the river above. The plot was discovered in time to prevent its contemplated execution. The ringleaders were taken, and executed in the most exemplary manner, as a warning and terror to others.

In the mean time, the intercourse by the river between New Orleans and the Illinois country was so hazardous, by reason of Indian murders and robberies, that the river commerce was virtually suspended, and the colonies were kept in a state of continual alarm.

[A.D. 1735.] Such had been the state of things early in the year 1734, when Bienville was again commissioned by the king as governor and commandant-general of Louisiana. Early in the autumn he arrived at New Orleans, and entered upon the duties of his office. Bienville, in his old age, still felt a thirst for military fame; he also coveted the honor of humbling the tribes which had espoused the Natchez cause, and who had afforded them an asylum from the vengeance of the French.

During his absence from the province the horrible massacre of the French colony on the St. Catharine had taken place, besides numerous other Indian outrages. During his former administration all the tribes had been kept in due subjection, or

* Martin's Louisiana, vol. i., p. 295, 296.

were held under proper restraint. But so soon as he left for Europe, Indian outrages commenced; murders and depredations were frequent; the whole province was kept in a state of continual alarm and apprehension of Indian aggression; the navigation of the Mississippi was virtually cut off, and communications with the upper province interrupted. None of these things had been permitted during his presence in the province. He had now returned, and he doubted not that his name alone would be a check upon the Indians, and a terror to the Natchez refugees. Thus he may have reasoned with himself. Accordingly, soon after his arrival in New Orleans, he dispatched an officer to the principal village of the Chickasâs, demanding from them the surrender of the Natchez refugees who had been received among them. In reply to his demand, he was informed that the Natchez Indians had been incorporated with the Chickasâ tribe, and could not be given up.

Upon the reception of this intelligence, Bienville determined to inflict signal chastisement upon the Chickasâs themselves, by invading and laying waste their country with a powerful army. The whole force of the province was now to be arrayed against them. The government of France itself had given directions for the invasion, and the royal eye was turned anxiously upon the coming contest.*

In the mean time, the Natchez refugees and a few hostile Chickasâs continued to harass the river trade by their repeated robberies and murders upon the traders and voyageurs. At length the Mississippi was not a safe route between the remote portions of the province; few only of those who ventured to ascend the river were so fortunate as to escape the bandits by whom it was infested.

Bienville determined to lose no time in bringing his forces into the field, and in executing summary vengeance upon the Chickasâ nation. He had made a levy of troops from all the settlements upon the Upper and Lower Mississippi, and from Mobile. An officer had been sent duly authorized to solicit the aid and alliance of the Choctâs, and to secure their co-operation in the contemplated expedition. The Choctâ chiefs, conducted by the emissary, met Bienville in council at "Fort Condé," and contracted to lead a large body of their warriors to "Fort Tombigby," which was to be erected in their own

* Bancroft's United States, vol. iii., p. 365.

country, about two hundred and fifty miles above Mobile, upon the west bank of the Tombigby River.

An officer was also dispatched with a detachment of troops to erect the stockade and the necessary buildings for a military dépôt, which would serve as a general rendezvous for the eastern division of the army. An order was likewise sent to M. d'Artaguette, commandant at Fort Chartres, and son of the Chevalier d'Artaguette, to march his whole disposable force for the Chickasâ nation, including all the troops and Indians which could be collected from the Illinois and Wabash countries. With these he was to form a junction with the grand army about the 10th of May, between the sources of the Yazoo and the Tombigby Rivers.*

The plan of operations was as follows: Bienville, with the whole force of Louisiana and the Choctâs from the Tombigby, were to ascend that river to the junction of its principal head streams, the east and west forks, supplied with military stores and artillery. Here he was to advance across the country in a northwest direction toward the strong-hold of the Chickasâs, which was upon the head waters of the Tallahatchy. D'Artaguette, with the Illinois forces, was to descend the Mississippi to the last Chickasâ bluff, there disembark, and traverse the country in a southeast direction to the sources of the Tallahatchy. The two divisions of the army were to be near the dividing ridges about the 10th of May, when further operations would be concerted.

[A.D. 1736.] In the mean time, Bienville was absorbed in the object of collecting a strong force at Fort Condé, preparatory to the invasion of the Chickasâ country. Early in the spring of 1736, the troops moved from New Orleans for Mobile in thirty barges and thirty large pirogues. On the 10th of March they arrived at Fort Condé, where they remained preparing for the expedition until the 4th of April, when they commenced the voyage up the Tombigby. Ten days brought the army to Fort Tombigby. Here they were joined by six hundred Choctâ warriors, and ten days afterward six hundred more arrived, increasing the whole number of these auxiliaries to twelve hundred.† Rains and inclement weather multiplied the difficulties and delays of the invading host. An army unemployed becomes restless and discontented, and military discipline in a state of idleness will rarely quiet the discontented mind.

* Bancroft, vol. iii., p. 365. † Martin's Louisiana, vol. i., p. 302, 303.

Already some of the advanced guard, sent to construct Fort Tombigby for the rendezvous, had attempted to escape and enjoy the liberty of the wilderness; but they were taken, and in the wilds of Alabama, condemned by a court-martial, they were shot, a warning to the discontented.

Such had been the unavoidable delays, that Bienville did not leave Fort Tombigby until the 4th of May, only six days previous to the junction which D'Artaguette was instructed to make with him upon the sources of the Tallahatchy. The boats and barges moved slowly up the tortuous stream, while the light infantry and the Indian auxiliaries advanced by land across the country. From Fort Tombigby to the junction of the East and West Forks, where the artillery and munitions of war were to be deposited, was but little short of two hundred and fifty miles, following the meanders of the stream. To reach this destination required near twenty days of toil before the little fleet could make the point for disembarking the troops and munitions of war. At length, upon the banks of the Tombigby, not far from the site of the present town of Cotton-gin Port, and nearly five hundred miles, by the river, from Mobile, Bienville disembarked his supplies, and erected a stockade fort for the protection of the sick, the baggage, the military stores, and the artillery. The nearest Chickasâ town was twenty-seven miles distant, in a northwestern direction,[*] and probably within a few miles of the present town of Pontotoc. The town was known to be well fortified, and was situated, probably, upon the bank of Pontotoc Creek, in the northern part of Mississippi, and in the central portion of Pontotoc county, which perpetuate the name of the Indian strong-hold.

The stockade having been completed, and a sufficient guard having been detailed for its defense, Bienville commenced his march with the army in two columns, flanked by the Choctâ warriors, in search of the enemy. Then it was that "the solitudes of the quiet forests and blooming prairies, between the sources of the Tombigby and Tallahatchy, were disturbed by the march of the army toward the strong-hold of their ancient enemy."[†] On the evening of the 25th of May, the army encamped within one league of the Indian citadel. Next morning, before day, the Choctâs advanced to surprise the enemy's

---

[*] Bancroft, vol. iii., p. 366. Martin says the Chickasâ fort lay northeast from the point of debarkation. See vol. i., p. 303.   [†] Bancroft, vol. iii., p. 366.

post; but the Chickasâs were on the alert, and their intrenchments were strong. The Choctâ warriors, after vainly assailing its impregnable defenses, retired from the assault. About noon the French army advanced in battle array, and posted themselves in full view of the fort, ready for the fearful assault. The British flag was seen waving over its ramparts, and it was known that British traders and emissaries were in the fort, conducting the defense.*

About one o'clock the French column, prepared with hand-grenades for the conflagration of the buildings, advanced to the charge with the cheering shout of "*Vive le roi.*" Twice during the day was the assault renewed with fire and sword, and twice were their columns repulsed by the terrible fire from the fort. Four hours had the battle raged around the intrenchments, without success or hope of victory. Many had fallen among the slain, many were severely wounded, and the number of killed and wounded were multiplying rapidly. Bienville, despairing of success without the aid of artillery, and seeing his brave troops constantly falling in the unequal contest, ordered a retreat to be sounded, and drew off his forces. The retreat was led off in excellent order, but the slain were left upon their gory battle-field. Such was the result of this day's contest. The French in the assaults had thirty-two men killed, and sixty-one were wounded. Among the slain were four officers of rank.

The army retired to their camp, one league distant, and spent the evening and night in throwing up an intrenchment around it for their more perfect security.

Next morning the Choctâs advanced to skirmish with parties of Chickasâs; as they approached the fort, they beheld the bodies of the French who had fallen in the assaults of the previous day, quartered and impaled upon the stockades of the fort.

Three days were spent in the fortified camp, but no further serious attempt was made to dislodge the enemy from their strong-hold. Surrounded by the hostile warriors in the midst of the enemy's country, Bienville received no tidings of the northern division from the Illinois, or of the arrival of D'Artaguette among the Chickasâs. Chagrin at his unexpected repulse completely overwhelmed the veteran chief, and, despairing of his ability to reduce the formidable position occupied by his warlike enemies, he determined to abandon the enterprise and re-

* Martin's Louisiana, vol. i., p. 301, 302.

turn to New Orleans. On the 29th of May he broke up his encampment and took up the retrograde line of march, and on the following day halted at the head of Tombigby, where his stores and artillery had been deposited. Here he made but little delay previous to his final departure from the Chickasâ country. On the 31st he dismissed the Choctâs with kind words and presents, when, after throwing his cannon into the Tombigby, with his army he floated down the river ingloriously to Fort Condé.* Near the last of June, he entered the Bayou St. John on his return to New Orleans, covered with defeat and shame.

In the mean time, where was the young and chivalrous D'Artaguette? He and his brave companions were sleeping the quiet sleep of death in the land from which Bienville had ingloriously fled.

D'Artaguette, the pride and flower of Canada, had convened the tribes of the Illinois at Fort Chartres; he had unfolded to them the plans and designs of the great French captain against the Chickasâs, and invoked their friendly aid. At his summons, the friendly chiefs, the tawny envoys of the North, with "Chicago" at their head, had descended the Mississippi to New Orleans, and there had presented the pipe of peace and friendship to the governor. " This," said Chicago to M. Perrier, as he concluded an alliance offensive and defensive, " this is the pipe of peace or war. You have but to speak, and our braves will strike the nations that are your foes."† They had made haste to return, and had punctually convened their braves under Artaguette. Chicago was the Illinois chief from the shore of Lake Michigan, whose monument was reared, a century afterward, upon the site of his village, and whose name is perpetuated in the most flourishing city of Illinois.

In due time, D'Artaguette and his lieutenant, the gallant Vincennes, from the Wabash, with their respective forces and Indian allies, had descended the Mississippi to the last Chickasâ bluff, and, agreeably to his orders, had penetrated the Chickasâ country. The fearless heroes had cautiously, and unobserved, penetrated from the bluffs eastward into the heart of the Chickasâ country, and, on the evening before the appointed 10th of May, had encamped among the sources of the Yalobusha, probably not six miles east of the present town of Pontotoc, near

---

* Bancroft's United States, vol. iii., p. 366. † Ibidem, p. 365.

the appointed place of rendezvous, and not more than thirty miles from the point of Bienville's debarkation. Here, ready for co-operation with the commander-in-chief, D'Artaguette and his brave troops were prepared to maintain the arms and the honor of France.

With his lieutenant Vincennes, the youthful Voisin, and his spiritual guide and friend, the Jesuit Senat, D'Artaguette sought in vain for intelligence of his commander. But he maintained his post, and from the 9th until the 20th of May he encamped in sight of the enemy, until his Indian auxiliaries, becoming impatient for war and plunder, refused all further restraint. D'Artaguette then consented to lead them to the attack. His plans were wisely devised and vigorously executed; but, unsupported by the main army, what could he effect against a powerful enemy?

The attack was made with great fury against a fortified village; the Chickasâs were driven from their town and the fort which defended it; at the second town, the intrepid youth was equally successful. A third fort was attacked, and, in the moment of victory, he received a severe wound, and soon after another, by which he fell disabled. He distinguished himself, as he had done before in the Natchez war, by acts of great valor and deeds of noble daring. "The red men of Illinois, dismayed at the check, fled precipitately. Voisin, a lad but sixteen years old, conducted the retreat, having the enemy at his heels for five-and-twenty leagues, and marching forty-five leagues without food, while his men carried with them such of the wounded as could bear the fatigue." But the unhappy D'Artaguette was left weltering in his blood, and around him lay others of his bravest troops.* The Jesuit Senat might have fled; but he remained to receive the last sigh of the wounded, regardless of danger, and mindful only of duty. "Vincennes, too, the Canadian, refused to fly, and shared the captivity of his gallant leader."†

* Bancroft's History of the United States, vol. iii., p. 366, 367. See, also, Martin's Louisiana, vol. i., p. 303, 304.

† The troops from Illinois in this campaign, as they advanced to the attack, had their bodies protected in front, from the arrows of the Chickasâs, by wool-sacks, or quilted cushions made of wool, suspended before their bodies. This novel, and yet very useful kind of armor, was discovered by the British traders in the fort, who directed the Chickasâs to shoot at their heads and legs.—Stoddart, p. 63.

Prescott, in his "Conquest of Mexico" by Hernando Cortez, describes a similar protection made of cotton, and used by the Spaniards against the arrows and missiles of the Mexican Indians.

D'Artaguette and his valiant companions who fell into the hands of the Chickasâs were treated with great kindness and attention; their wounds were dressed by the Indians, who watched over them with fraternal tenderness, and they were received into the cabins of the victors in hopes of a great ransom from Bienville, who was known to be advancing by way of the Tombigby with a powerful army. But the same day brought the intelligence of the advance and the discomfiture of the commander-in-chief. His retreat and final departure soon followed, and the Chickasâs, elated with their success, and despairing of the expected ransom, resolved to sacrifice the victims to savage triumph and revenge. The prisoners were taken to a neighboring field, and, while one was left to relate their fate to their countrymen, the young and intrepid D'Artaguette, and the heroic Vincennes, whose name is borne by the oldest town in Indiana, and will be perpetuated as long as the Wabash shall flow by the dwellings of civilized men, and the faithful Senat, true to his mission, were, with their companions, each tied to a stake. Here they were tortured before slow and intermitting fires, until death mercifully released them from their protracted torments.* Such were the sufferings of the leaders of the northern division, at the very time that Bienville had commenced his inglorious voyage down the Tombigby: and such is the early history of the white man in Mississippi.

Thus the magnificent parade of Bienville, and his pompous threats against the Chickasâs, terminated in a complete failure of the expedition, and brought a cloud of disgrace upon his military fame. The Chickasâs proved themselves then the true descendants of the powerful and warlike nation which had encountered the steel-clad chivalry of De Soto, two hundred years before. The French allege that the fort, attacked by the forces under Bienville, was constructed of large and tall palisades planted in the ground, and perforated with numerous loop-holes for firing upon an approaching enemy; and that a strong platform of boards, covered with earth, extended around the inside, so as to protect the defenders from the hand-grenades used by the French in the assault. The British traders and emissaries had taught them the art of fortifying their villages, and of making regular defenses against field artillery.

It was not until early in July, and soon after his arrival at

* Martin's Louisiana, vol. i., p. 304.

New Orleans, that Bienville learned by rumor the sad fate of D'Artaguette and his companions in arms, who had been sacrificed to his strict obedience to military orders, and to the inexcusable want of energy in the commander-in-chief.

The English settlements in Georgia were apprised of this disastrous expedition of the French within a few weeks after Bienville reached New Orleans; for the Chickasâs, elated with their victory over the French, sent runners the same summer to narrate to Oglethorpe, on the Savannah, how they had met and defeated the French in two divisions, and what lingering torments they had inflicted upon the captives. "Ever attached to the English, they now sent their deputation of thirty warriors, with their civil sachem and war-chief, to make an alliance with Oglethorpe, whose fame had reached the Mississippi. They brought for him an Indian chaplet, made from the spoils of their enemies, glittering with feathers of many hues, and enriched with the horns of buffaloes."*

[A.D. 1737.] Bienville, mortified with the result of his late unsuccessful campaign against the Chickasâs in the East, determined to retrieve his honor and the glory of France by a more powerful invasion from the West. With but little grounds for the assurance, he hoped that the route of D'Artaguette was more accessible, and that victory might attend his arms where fortune had smiled upon the intrepid commandant of Fort Chartres. A plan of an expedition against the Chickasâs with a grand army, by way of the Chickasâ Bluffs, was devised and laid before the minister for his sanction.

[A.D. 1738.] The approbation of the minister was transmitted to Bienville near the close of the following year, and he began to put in operation his plans for humbling the pride and power of his late fierce antagonists. Great preparations were set on foot throughout the whole province, and far exceeding any thing of the kind which had been seen in Louisiana from its first settlement. The signal of preparation was given, and the commandants throughout the province had their orders from the commandant-general himself. The spring of 1739 was the time for the contemplated grand invasion.

[A.D. 1739.] The route of the contemplated invasion was from the lower Chickasâ Bluff, on the east bank of the Mississippi, eastward to the principal towns, about two hundred miles

* Bancroft's United States, vol. iii., p. 433.

distant, on the sources of the Tallahatchy and Tombigby Rivers. A fort was ordered as the point of general rendezvous for the grand army, near the mouth of the St. Francis River, on the west side of the Mississippi. Here the allied army was to have its general dépôt for baggage, the sick, and military stores. Troops, together with large bodies of friendly Indians, were to be drawn from all the posts, settlements, and regions contiguous to the Lower Mississippi and Mobile. These were to be joined at the mouth of the St. Francis by all the troops and Indian allies to be mustered from the Illinois and Wabash countries, under their respective commanders.

All things being in readiness about the last of May, the main army began to leave New Orleans for the rendezvous at the mouth of the St. Francis. They embarked in a fleet of boats and barges, and slowly moved up the strong current of the Mississippi until the last of June, when they reached Fort St. Francis. This division of the army consisted of Louisiana militia and regular troops, besides a few companies of marines, and more than sixteen hundred Indian allies. The division from the Illinois and Wabash, commanded by La Buissonière, commandant of Fort Chartres, comprised about two hundred men, including regulars, militia, and some cadets from Canada, besides about three hundred Indian allies under the command of M. Celeron and M. St. Laurent, his lieutenants. The entire force now at Bienville's command was about twelve hundred whites, and nearly twenty-five hundred Indians and negroes, giving a grand total of three thousand seven hundred fighting men.

With but little delay, the army was crossed over to the east bank of the Mississippi, where "Fort Assumption" was built, near the mouth of the Margot, or Wolf River, as a convenient dépôt for the sick, the baggage, and military stores. This fort, however, was delayed in its completion until the middle of August.* By this time, sickness and the autumnal fevers began to make fearful ravages in the ranks, both among the Europeans and the Canadians. Those who escaped disease, as well as those who had recovered from its attack, were debilitated and unfit for active service. The cool, bracing air of early winter and the purifying frosts were anxiously expected, as the best restoratives against the debilitating effects of a long

* Martin's Louisiana, vol. i., p. 307.

summer upon their northern constitutions. Early winter came, and found the ranks more than decimated; and while the atmosphere became wholesome and elastic, and the troops began to assume their wonted vigor, a new enemy threatened them with annihilation. This was famine; for the supplies of provisions had begun to fail, and all were reduced to short allowance. The invasion of the Chickasâ country must now be delayed until supplies were received from New Orleans and from Fort Chartres. Thus was the expedition against the Chickasâ towns deferred until the middle of March following, when a large portion of the white troops were so much debilitated by exposure to the inclemency of winter, and by the want of wholesome food, that not more than two hundred effective men could be mustered who were able to take up the line of march with the Indian and negro warriors toward the Chickasâ towns. With these, M. Celeron had orders to march against the Chickasâs, and was specially instructed to lose no opportunity of treating for peace. As he advanced, the Chickasâs, at first sight, supposed the whole French army was close behind them, and, as a measure of safety, sued for peace. M. Celeron, taking advantage of their alarm, entered into a treaty of peace and friendship.*

[A.D. 1740.] The Indians promised to remain the true friends of the French, and declared they would renounce the English, who had incited them to hostilities. M. Celeron, in the name of Bienville, promised peace to the Chickasâ nation; and a deputation of chiefs and warriors accompanied his return march, to consummate the bonds of peace by a regular treaty, to be concluded at Fort Assumption. Here Bienville entered into negotiations, which were ratified, after the Indian custom, with presents and festivity.

Fort Assumption was dismantled; the army retired to Fort St. Francis, on the western bank of the Mississippi. Here Bienville, having discharged his Northern troops and the Indian allies, prepared again to float ingloriously down the Mississippi with the main army. Thus ended the second invasion of the Chickasâ country, begun by Bienville to retrieve his military fame, but which sunk it lower than it had been before.

After a long and expensive preparation in two campaigns; after the loss of many lives, many slain in battle, and far more

* Martin's Louisiana, vol. i., p. 308, 309.

ingloriously swept off by disease and famine, the war was discontinued, and a treaty of peace had been concluded with the chiefs and warriors of a single town, and without a single laurel upon the commander's brow.

This campaign closed the military career of Bienville in Louisiana. He had been bold, ardent, and an able commander in his youth; but, cooled in his ardor by the snows of thirty-six winters in the service, he was ill qualified for the arduous duties of conducting an army through a wilderness of swamps and dense forests, remote from the facilities of civilized life. To contend with the wily savage in his own native forests requires the energies of the iron-hearted warrior in the prime of manhood and in the vigor of health.

To crown the misfortune of two disastrous campaigns, Bienville, the following spring, was succeeded in the government of Louisiana by the Marquis de Vaudreuil, who was appointed governor and commandant-general. Thus the public career of Bienville, who for nearly forty years, a few short intervals excepted, had controlled the affairs of Louisiana, terminated under a cloud of censure, and the disapprobation of his sovereign. Such are the vicissitudes of fortune, which assail the high as well as the humble.

The population and wealth of Louisiana for the last five years had continued to increase gradually, notwithstanding the hostile attitude of the Chickasâs and the reverses of two unsuccessful campaigns. The settlements had gradually extended and multiplied upon Red River, and upon the Washita, as well as upon the Upper and Lower Mississippi. Agricultural productions, adapted to the climate, both in the upper and lower portions of the province, were important items in the commerce with the parent country. About this time cotton was introduced as an agricultural product of Louisiana, but for many years it was cultivated only in small quantities.*

[A.D. 1741.] The emigration from France continued to swell the population of New France and Louisiana. Every arrival from France was the harbinger of a new settlement, or the extension of the old. Many Canadians, retiring from the rigors of the long winters on the St. Lawrence, sought the comparatively mild climate of the Wabash and the Illinois countries. While the Chickasâs, instigated by British intrigue, had

* Stoddart's Sketches of Louisiana, p. 65.

kept up a state of continual hostilities from the Yazoo to the Ohio, the tribes north of the Ohio, and to the very sources of the Alleghany River, were mostly in friendly alliance with the French, and received their traders and missionaries into almost every village. French settlements from Canada began to extend south of the Western lakes upon the streams which flow into Lake Erie and Lake Michigan, and trading-posts were slowly passing the dividing plains upon the tributaries of the Ohio, within the limits of the present States of Ohio and Indiana. The Illinois country, embracing much of the present State of Illinois, likewise derived emigrants from Canada, as well as through Lower Louisiana. The traders and voyageurs, in their continual intercourse and traffick, penetrated the remotest tributaries of the Mississippi, and maintained a friendly attitude with the remotest tribes.

Many of the tropical fruits and luxuries had been introduced into the settlements. The fig-tree and the orange-tree had already begun to adorn the residences of the colonists, as well as to supply them with delicious fruit; the yam and the varieties of the West India sweet potato were already a certain crop for the sustenance of their numerous families.

CHAPTER X.

CONDITION OF LOUISIANA FROM THE CLOSE OF THE CHICKASÂ WAR UNTIL THE TERMINATION OF THE FRENCH DOMINION.—A.D. 1741 TO 1764.

Argument.—Louisiana continues Prosperous and free from Indian Hostilities until the Close of the Acadian War.—Agriculture and Trade prosper under individual Enterprise.—Equinoctial Storm in 1745.—Rigorous Winter of 1748-9 killed the Orange-trees.—La Buissonière and Macarty Commandants at Fort Chartres.—Condition of Agricultural Settlements near New Orleans.—Staples, Rice, Indigo, Cotton, Tobacco.—Sugar-cane first introduced in 1751, and Sugar subsequently becomes a Staple Product.—The British resume their Intrigue with the Choctâs and Chickasâs after the Close of the Acadian War.—Choctâs commence War.—Chickasâs resume Hostilities on the Mississippi.—Disturbances break out on the Ohio with the English Provinces.—Governor Vaudreuil invades the Chickasâ Country by way of the Tombigby.—Ravages their Towns and Fields.—Collisions between French and English on the Ohio.—Ohio Company's Grant leads to Hostilities.—Re-enforcement sent to Fort Chartres.—Lower Louisiana is prosperous.—Horrid Military Execution for Revolt at Cat Island.—British Inhumanity to the People of Acadia.—Origin of the "Acadian Coast" in 1755.—Louisiana suffers again from Paper Money in 1756.—The French abandon the Ohio Region.—Canada falls under the Arms of Britain in 1759, and many Canadians emigrate to Louisiana.—France relinquishes all Louisiana, by Treaties of 1762 and 1763, to Spain and Great Britain.—Great Britain takes possession of Florida and Eastern Louisiana in 1764-5.—Spain assumes Jurisdiction over Western Louisiana in 1765.—Extension of the Limits of West Florida by Great Britain.—Spain and Great Britain divide the Valley of the Mississippi, until the United States succeed, first to British, and then to Spanish Louisiana.

[A.D. 1741.] For ten years after the close of the Chickasâ war, the settlements of Louisiana were comparatively free from Indian hostilities. The English provinces along the Atlantic coast, during the greatest portion of this time, were involved with the mother country in prosecuting the Northern or Acadian war, against the French provinces south of the St. Lawrence and north of New England. The remote province of Louisiana and the Illinois country, inaccessible alike to British fleets and armies, remained free from Indian hostilities.

During this period, the French of Louisiana and of the Illinois country had succeeded in establishing amicable relations with all the tribes west of the Alleghany Mountains, from the sources of the Alleghany and the Tennessee Rivers to the Missouri, and from the sources of the Mississippi to New Orleans and Texas. The whole Valley of the Mississippi had yielded to the dominion of France, and the native tribes had become her allies.

As early as the year 1742, the defense of the country being in the hands of the king's officers and troops, the Indian tribes generally observed a respectful neutrality, or a friendly and commercial attitude. Free from danger and apprehension of Indian violence, agriculture continued to flourish, and commerce, freed from the shackles of monopolies, began rapidly to extend its influence, and to multiply its objects under the stimulus of individual enterprise. Capitalists embarked with alacrity into agriculture and commerce. The trade between the northern and southern portions of Louisiana had greatly augmented, as well as that from New Orleans to France and foreign countries. Regular cargoes of flour, bacon, pork, hides, leather, tallow, bear's oil, and lumber were annually transported down the Mississippi in keel-boats and barges to New Orleans and Mobile, whence they were shipped to France and the West Indies. In their return voyages, these boats and barges, from New Orleans and Mobile, supplied the Illinois and Wabash countries with rice, indigo, tobacco, sugar, cotton, and European fabrics. The two extremes of Louisiana produced and supplied each other alternately with the necessaries and comforts of life required by each respectively. The mutual exchange of commodities kept up a constant and active communication from one end of the province to the other. Boats, barges, and pirogues were daily plying from one point to another, freighted with the rude products of a new and growing country. The great high-ways of commerce were the deep and solitary channels of the Mississippi and its hundreds of tributaries.

[A.D. 1745.] Such was the growing condition of Louisiana, until hostilities again broke out between the English and French provinces, ten years after the Acadian war.

In the mean time, the settlements had been liable to occasional disasters and unforeseen dangers, which affect alike the colony in its infancy and the more powerful state. In the fall of the year 1745, a destructive storm swept over the settlements of Lower Louisiana, and laid waste the plantations, destroying a large proportion of the crops. The rice crop especially, one of the most important in Lower Louisiana, was nearly destroyed. Rice, for several years, had been an important substitute for bread, and the destruction of this crop reduced many poor emigrants to absolute want. Yet the necessities of the lower country were supplied by timely relief from the Illinois country and from the Wabash. Their boats annually descended early in December, and returned in February. The supply of breadstuff from Upper Louisiana this year, by some accounts, is given at four thousand sacks,* containing, probably, one hundred pounds each.

[A.D. 1747–8.] Louisiana continued to prosper, and the settlements continued to extend upon the Wabash and upon the tributaries of the Illinois and the Upper Mississippi, and even as far as the upper tributaries of the Ohio. The prosperity of the province continued without interruption until the renewal of hostilities by the English provinces.

[A.D. 1749.] The winter of 1748–9 was remarkable for its uncommon rigor, both in Upper and Lower Louisiana. Such was the severity of the cold, that the thriving groves of orange-trees on the river coast, above and below New Orleans, were entirely killed.

[A.D. 1750.] For several years past, the government of the settlements on the Upper Mississippi and Illinois had been conducted by La Buissonière, commandant at Fort Chartres, where he had succeeded the unfortunate Chevalier D'Artaguette.

[A.D. 1751.] In the following autumn, 1751, he was succeeded in the command of Fort Chartres by the Chevalier Macarty, who left New Orleans on the 20th of August, with a small detachment of troops for re-enforcing the posts on the Mississippi and Ohio Rivers.† He continued to retain the command in this quarter until the close of the French dominion on the Ohio.

[A.D. 1752.] The settlements on the Lower Mississippi continued to augment in population, by the frequent arrivals of emigrant colonies from France and the West India Islands. The spirit of enterprise and agricultural industry began to develop the resources of the country, and to increase the wealth and happiness of the people. Plantations lined the banks of the river for twenty miles below, and for a much greater distance above the city. In this distance the whole coast was in a fine state of cultivation, and nearly the whole was securely protected by levees against the floods of the river. The principal staples of this section were rice, indigo, corn, and tobac-

* Martin's Louisiana, vol. i., p. 316. † Idem, p. 321–324.

co. Rice and indigo were the chief crops up to the year 1750, about which time cotton had been introduced, and became soon after an important item in the agricultural products of Lower Louisiana and the Illinois country; yet, from the extreme difficulty of separating the cotton from the seed, it did not constitute, in any portion of the country, the entire product of any plantation, but was cultivated in small quantities, by almost every family, as a useful article for domestic consumption.

Tobacco was cultivated in considerable quantities in the uplands near Baton Rouge and in the settlements of the Natchez country. To encourage the extensive cultivation of tobacco, the royal government offered a moderate bounty on the article, and the farmer-general of the king was authorized to receive into the king's warehouses all the tobacco raised in the province, at the rate of thirty livres per hundred pounds, equal to about seven dollars the hundred weight.*

About this time a cotton-gin, invented by M. Dubreuil, which facilitated the operation of separating the cotton fiber from the seed, created an epoch in the cultivation of cotton in Louisiana, and it began to enter more largely into the product of the plantations.

Sugar-cane had not yet been introduced as a staple product of Louisiana. The first attempt to cultivate the sugar-cane in the province was made by the Jesuits in the year 1751. This year they had introduced a quantity of cane from St. Domingo, together with several negroes who were acquainted with the process of manufacturing sugar from the juice. They opened a small plantation on the banks of the Mississippi, just above the old city of New Orleans, and within the limits of the second municipality.† The following year attempts were made by others to cultivate the plant and to manufacture it into sugar. Satisfied with the success of the first attempts, many others soon afterward commenced its culture, and within a few years most of the plantations above and below the city, for many miles, had introduced the culture of cane on a small scale, by way of experiment. Several years elapsed, when the Jesuits and some others, having succeeded even above their expectations, M. Dubreuil, a man of capital and enterprise, was induced, in 1758, to open a sugar plantation on a large scale. He erected the first sugar-mill in Louisiana

---

* Martin's Louisiana, vol. i., p. 320.   † Idem.

upon his plantation, which occupied the lands now covered by the lower part of the city of New Orleans, and known as the " Suburb of St. Marigny," below the third municipality. The enterprise of M. Dubreuil having rewarded him with an abundant crop and a ready sale, others were anxious to embark in the same enterprise with large capital.

Thus, before the close of the year 1760, sugar-cane had been fairly introduced as one of the staple products of Louisiana; yet the art of making sugar was in its infancy. The sugar which was made was consumed wholly in the province, and was of very inferior quality, for want of a knowledge of the granulating process. Before the year 1765, M. Dubreuil, M. Destrechan, and others, had succeeded in making sugar which answered all the purposes of home consumption. Still, the planters had not learned the art of giving it a fine, dry, granulated appearance, such as was produced in the West Indies. The whole product of the province had been, heretofore, barely sufficient for domestic consumption; but in the year 1765 one ship-load of sugar was exported to France; yet so imperfect had been the granulating process, that one half of it escaped from the casks as leakage before the vessel reached her destination.* This was the first export of sugar from Louisiana, and the commencement of her trade in her most valuable staple, which has since continued to increase up to the present time, until the annual crop of sugar made in Louisiana varied, between the years 1840 and 1845, from 110,000 to 115,000 hogsheads, besides as many barrels of molasses.†

In the mean time, the British emissaries from the Atlantic provinces resumed their efforts to rouse the Chickasâs to a renewal of hostilities against the French of Louisiana, as well as against the trade carried on between the colonies on the Upper Mississippi and the city of New Orleans. The Northern or Acadian war had been terminated, and peace had been restored between the two powers, England and France, by the treaty of Aix la Chapelle, on the 18th day of October, 1748. Tranquillity had been likewise restored to all the British provinces along the Atlantic coast, and they now again had leisure to indulge in their former practices of intrigue with the Southern Indians, and especially with the Choctâs and Chickasâs.

* Martin's Louisiana, vol. i., p. 320:
† See New Orleans Annual Commercial Price-current for 1840–1843, &c.

Traders and agents from Carolina and Georgia introduced vast quantities of British goods and commodities of Indian trade, and abundantly supplied almost every Choctâ and Chickasâ village as far west as the Yazoo and Mississippi Rivers, and wholly within the territory claimed by France.* British trading-posts were established in some of the towns, and protected by regular fortifications, which the English had instructed them to build.†

The traders and emissaries lost no opportunity to poison the minds of these tribes against the French of Louisiana. As early as 1750, they had succeeded in rousing the Choctâs into actual hostilities with their old allies the French. This war, however, was brought to a close, and the Choctâs being conciliated, again entered into a treaty of peace with their old friends before the beginning of the year 1751.‡ Yet the English emissaries continued their intrigues with the Chickasâs, losing no opportunity of exciting them to hostilities and depredations upon the French settlements and trade from the Tombigby River to the Mississippi. Simultaneously with these movements in the South, the province of Virginia, under the influence of the "Ohio Company," and Governor Robert Dinwiddie, a member of the company, led the way in making similar encroachments and intrigues, supported by military force, upon the eastern tributaries of the Upper Ohio River. In this latter region, agents, emissaries, and traders were distributed for the purpose of gaining the Indians over to the English interest, and to induce them to exclude the French traders from the Ohio region. Thus the object of the British authorities was to excite finally the whole of the Northern and Southern tribes simultaneously against the French settlements, from Mobile and New Orleans to Canada.

* The English never had acquired any right to the territory west of the mountains from the Monongahela on the north to the Alabama and Tombigby on the south. The French had discovered and explored the whole regions claimed by them; and treaties with the different tribes inhabiting the same gave them a right of jurisdiction or sovereignty over the country superior to any claim which England could set up. The French had explored most of the immense territory comprised in Louisiana, as defined in Crozat's charter, as early as the year 1720, twelve years before the first English settlement in Georgia, and when the settlements on the remote frontiers of Virginia did not extend as far west as the Blue Ridge. In opposition to this right of possession, England had no other claim than the former royal grants, made to individuals and companies, for vast regions of unexplored and unknown lands already in possession of the French.   † Martin's Louisiana, vol. i., p. 321, 322.

‡ Governor Vaudreuil's Report to Ministry, January 12th, 1751, among the French Colonial Records in the Library of the State of Louisiana.—Documents Nos. 230 and 248.

To protect the settlements of the South against the incursions of the Chickasâs, which were now becoming very annoying to the province of Louisiana, the governor, the Marquis de Vaudreuil, determined to march a strong force into the heart of the Chickasâ country. The force collected and organized for this expedition amounted to seven hundred regulars and militia, besides a large body of Choctâs and other Indian allies from the waters of the Tombigby and Alabama Rivers. The route of invasion was the same which had been pursued by Bienville in the year 1736. The fort formerly built by him on the Tombigby was repaired and enlarged for the general rendezvous. From this point he marched into the Chickasâ country, resolved to chastise them severely for their depredations.

Yet, like all other expeditions against the Chickasâs, it was destined to prove a failure. The Chickasâs, instructed by their English friends, had learned the best mode of fortifying their towns. They were flanked by regular block-houses, surrounded by a deep and wide ditch, within which was a tall and strong palisade inclosure. In the towns thus protected, the Indians chose to remain behind their defenses, and not to venture into the open plain against the overwhelming force of the French. The marquis, unprovided with artillery to effect a breach in the works, and having in several assaults failed to injure the enemy, or to draw them from their coverts, determined that it was useless to spend time in an ineffectual siege. He concluded, therefore, to destroy their resources by laying waste the country, ravaging their fields, burning their corn and their deserted villages. This object being accomplished as far as practicable, he caused a strong detachment to be stationed as a garrison in the fort on the Tombigby, as a barrier against future incursions from that quarter. Matters being thus arranged, he set out on his return to New Orleans, by no means pleased with the laurels he had won from the Chickasâs.

Among the benevolent efforts of the king's government to promote the increase of population in Louisiana, for many years under the royal governors, was the humane policy of sending every year at the royal expense a large number of worthy but poor girls to the province, in charge of suitable agents or guardians, with instructions to bestow them in marriage, together with a small dowry, to such of the soldiers as by their good behavior were entitled to an honorable discharge from the service. The dowry allotted to each soldier who married one of these females was a small tract of land, one cow and calf, one cock and five hens, a gun and ammunition, an ax and a hoe, together with a supply of garden seeds. Thus the newly-married pair were enabled to begin the world as independent heads of families.* Thus commenced many useful and worthy families of the French population of Louisiana previous to the year 1751, which witnessed the last arrival of these young females.

About this time the difficulties between the French posts and settlements on the head streams of the Alleghany and the upper portion of the Ohio, and the provincial authorities of Virginia, in favor of the "Ohio Company," and some other interested individuals, began to assume a more threatening attitude. The French continued to advance from Presque Isle, of Lake Erie, upon the tributaries of the Alleghany, and their advance was protected by military posts properly fortified. The grant originally made by the British crown to the Ohio Company in the year 1748, for six hundred thousand acres of land, had been transferred chiefly to the Washington family and to Governor Dinwiddie.† These persons, not more than ten in number, endeavored, by all the influences within their control, to rouse the hostile feelings of the English colonists in Virginia, Pennsylvania, and New York against the encroachments of the French, with such effect that a collision and active hostilities between the troops of the two powers were ultimately produced.

[A.D. 1753.] Near the close of the year 1753, the Marquis de Vaudreuil was advanced to the governor-generalship of New France, or Canada, when M. Kerlerec, a captain in the royal navy, succeeded him as Governor of Louisiana. M. Auberville was commissaire-ordonnateur.

[A.D. 1754.] At length the collisions between the advanced traders and military detachments of France and Virginia upon the head waters of the Ohio had brought on a state of actual hostilities between the troops of England and France. The first hostile act was on the part of the Virginians, under the command of Lieutenant-colonel Washington. It consisted in

* Martin's Louisiana, vol. i., p. 321.
† See Sparks's Writings of Washington, vol. i. and ii. A full account of the grant to the Ohio Company, and of some other royal grants west of the mountains, may be seen in vol. ii., p. 478–485.

the attack and capture of a small detachment of French troops under the command of M. Jumonville, after having slain one third of their number, including their commander.*

France began now to re-enforce her troops on the Ohio, preparatory to a military defense of the country. In the autumn of the same year, M. Favrot, with four companies, of fifty men each, with a large supply of provisions and ammunition, was dispatched from New Orleans to the headquarters of Fort Chartres, for the use of the posts on the Ohio.

During the past year strict military discipline and subordination were rigidly enforced, and sometimes with extreme rigor. In the summer, the soldiers of a military post on Cat Island, exasperated at the cruelty and avarice of their commander, M. Roux, rebelled against his authority and put him to death. Afterward, failing in their object of reaching the English settlements of Carolina, they were captured by a band of Choctâs sent in pursuit, and brought back for punishment, except one, who killed himself rather than submit. The most horrid military execution was inflicted upon the ringleaders; two were broken upon the wheel, and one, who was a Swiss from the regiment of Karrer, after the immemorial usage of his country, was placed alive in a wooden coffin, and by two sergeants sawed in two with the whip-saw.

The colonial authorities were active in their efforts to place the province in the most defensible condition, and the governor, M. Kerlerec, and the ordonnateur, M. Auberville, made active preparations to work the lead and copper mines of Illinois. These mines were known to be inexhaustible, and the minister was desired to send additional miners from Paris.

Emigrants still continued to arrive from France, and among the arrivals of the year 1754 were a large number of families from Lorrain for a settlement in the parish of Des Allemands.†

From this time began the contest between France and England for the possession of the Valley of the Mississippi, a contest which was waged with varied success for eight years, until finally the tide of war set in favor of Great Britain, and France was compelled at length to surrender first one, and then another of her military positions in New France; until at last,

---

* For a more full account of this transaction, see chap. iii. of this book.—See, also, Martin, vol. i., p. 324–326.

† Colonial Records in State Library of Louisiana, Doc. No. 240.

driven by stern necessity, the king sought peace at the expense of a treaty which confirmed to Great Britain the whole of Canada, or New France, and all the eastern half of Louisiana.

[A.D. 1755.] Although the province of Louisiana was involved in the prosecution of this war, yet her remote situation and her inaccessible position secured her settlements and towns from the horrors of invasion, with its attendant rapine and bloodshed. The Mississippi and Ohio Rivers were the great high-ways of intercourse between New Orleans and the seat of war upon the lakes and the St. Lawrence, and these were in the exclusive possession of the French and their Indian allies until 1759.

Early in this war, the cruel jealousy and the wicked policy of the English court prompted them to perpetrate one of those national atrocities which have so long tarnished the honor of British conquests. In the war which was terminated by the treaty of Aix la Chapelle, France had ceded to Great Britain the whole province of Acadié, comprising the present provinces of New Brunswick and Nova Scotia. Now, when that power had resolved to possess herself of the whole of Canada, lest the poor Acadians, on their bleak, sterile, and rocky shores, should sympathize with their brethren on the St. Lawrence, and make common cause with Canada, England resolved to exterminate them as a people. Although she shrunk from the atrocity of a wholesale murder in cold blood, yet she deemed it consistent with her policy, before they had offered any resistance, or had evinced a disposition to reject her authority, to tear them away from their homes and possessions, and throw them helpless and destitute upon that mercy which protects the fowls of the air.

To accomplish this purpose, a number of vessels were dispatched to Acadié, where they were filled with the poor, kidnapped inhabitants, who were torn by armed ruffians, in the character of British soldiers, from their houses and possessions, and ruthlessly transported to distant regions. Here, less merciful to them than to the kidnapped Africans, who are provided with masters and a home, the English threw them, forlorn and destitute, upon the wide world for a support, caring but little whether they lived or died. Hundreds, nay, thousands, of these wretched people, thus barbarously torn from their homes and from their country, were landed in detached parties on different points of the barren and sandy coast of Delaware, New Jersey, Maryland, and Virginia. Destitute and helpless, like so many dumb beasts, they were turned loose to shift for themselves, or to perish of hunger and cold.*

Lest a lingering desire of home might prompt them to seek again their country and former abodes, they had been stripped of all the money and available means by which they might have returned, their fields and inclosures had been laid waste, their houses and possessions were burned before their eyes—thus at once sweeping away the last inducement for return. Upon the barren shores of the British provinces were these wretched people turned loose to wander they knew not where; strangers in manners and language, they had no other hope, or protection from famine and death, than the generous sympathy of the Anglo-Americans. From these they received generous aid, and their necessities were liberally supplied by the public authorities, as well as by individuals. Yet they were among those who spoke the language of their oppressors, although endued with better hearts.

A wilderness of more than a thousand miles in extent separated them from their countrymen on the Illinois, yet they determined to seek some land where the spotless banner of France still waved for their protection. Loathing all connection with those who bore even the name of their oppressors, they determined to turn their faces toward the West, and took up their weary pilgrimage through the trackless wilderness across the Alleghany Mountains to the Ohio River. After a tedious and painful march of several weeks, they arrived upon the banks of the "Belle Rivière," upon whose gentle current, provided with boats and barges, they floated down to the Mississippi, whose majestic flood soon conveyed them to their countrymen of New Orleans.

The arrival of the Acadians in New Orleans was equalled only by the scene presented by the women and children who had been rescued from the Natchez Indians twenty-five years before. All houses, and hearts too, were open to relieve their distress and to minister to their wants. Charity herself walked the streets personified in acts of kindness. The governor and ordonnateur-commissaire ordered a portion of land to be allotted to each family for their permanent homes. Thus a settle-

* Martin, vol. i., p. 326–329.

ment was formed on both sides of the river, a short distance above the German coast, formerly assigned to the colonists of Law from the Arkansas; each family was supplied with implements of husbandry, seeds, and rations from the king's stores, until they could procure means for their own support. The settlement thus formed was known and designated as the "Acadian Coast," where many of their descendants are found at this day, who have lost but little of their paternal hatred for the English name.*

[A.D. 1756.] The province of Louisiana, although remote from the seat of war, labored under many pecuniary embarrassments, growing out of the war waged in Canada. The whole country was literally inundated with government drafts and notes which it was unable to redeem. The embarrassments were such as necessarily result from a bankrupt treasury and a ruinous paper currency, ever fluctuating and of uncertain value. This embarrassment continued to increase until the close of the war by the treaty of 1763.

[A.D. 1758.] In the autumn of the year 1758, the French being compelled to abandon the post of Fort Duquesne on the Ohio, the garrison and military stores arrived at New Orleans about the 1st of December, when new barracks were erected for them in the city.

[A.D. 1759.] Early in the spring of 1759, Fort Massac was built by the French, on the right bank of the Ohio, about forty miles above its mouth, and continued to be occupied by the French as a garrison post until after the termination of the war.

In the mean time, the tide of war in the northeast had set against France, and the arms of Great Britain had been triumphant in Canada. One strong-hold after another had been lost to France, and it became evident that all Canada would fall under the dominion of Great Britain. Under these prospects, a large number of Canadian French determined to escape such a calamity as they deemed the British yoke, by abandoning their country and joining their countrymen in Louisiana. Many of them, accordingly, departed from Canada by way of the lakes, and thence through the Wabash and Illinois Rivers to the Mississippi. Those who reached Lower Louisiana sought settlements mostly west of the Mississippi, on the bayous and

* Martin's Louisiana, vol. i., p. 329.

prairies of Attackapas, Oppelousas, and Avoyelles.* This emigration added a large population to Lower Louisiana, and also augmented the settlements on the Upper Mississippi. Louisiana continued under the administration of Kerlerec until the close of the war, and his government was prompt and energetic.

[A.D. 1760.] Although Spain had made common cause with France against Great Britain, the latter had completed the conquest of Canada, during the year 1760, by the reduction of Montreal. The fortresses of Quebec, Ticonderoga, Crown Point, and Niagara, had fallen under the British arms during the summer and autumn of the previous year.†

[A.D. 1762.] At length hostilities ceased between the three great powers; and peace was ratified by the treaty of Paris, dated the 16th of February, 1763. By this treaty, France ceded and confirmed to Great Britain all her northern provinces, commonly known as New France, or Canada; embracing all the countries contiguous to the great lakes and the St. Lawrence River to its mouth, together with all the territory, forts, and settlements south of the St. Lawrence, including Acadié and Cape Breton on the Atlantic coast, south of the Gulf of St. Lawrence. France also ceded to Great Britain all that portion of Louisiana lying on the east side of the Mississippi River, from its source to the Bayou Iberville, or Manchac. The irrevocable boundary between the English and French provinces was to be an imaginary line along the middle of the Mississippi River, from its source to the Bayou Manchac; thence along said bayou and the Amité River to Lake Maurepas; thence through the middle of Lakes Maurepas, Pontchartrain, and Borgne to the sea. France also ceded the port and river of Mobile. In the mean time, Spain had ceded to Great Britain the whole of Florida, then embracing all the coast east of the Perdido River and Bay, to the St. Mary's River on the Atlantic coast. Thus, by this treaty, England acquired virtual possession of all North America east of the Mississippi River; and by the stipulations of the treaty, the navigation of the river, from its source to its mouth, was to remain forever free to the subjects of both powers.

[A.D. 1763.] In the mean time, the King of France, by a secret treaty, ratified on the 3d of November, 1762, had agreed

---

* Martin's Louisiana, vol. i., p. 336.
† For the reduction of Fort Duquesne on the Ohio, see chap. iii. of book ii.

to cede and deliver to the King of Spain the residue of Louisiana, embracing all the territory on the west side of the Mississippi to its remotest tributaries, and including the Island of New Orleans on the east side, south of the Bayou Manchac.

This completed the dismemberment of Louisiana, which was thus divided between Great Britain and Spain. The jurisdiction of each of these powers was subsequently extended over their respective portions.

By a decree of the king in council, dated October 7th, 1763, Florida was divided into two governments, known as East Florida and West Florida. West Florida, by this decree, was to extend from the Mississippi, north of the Bayou Iberville, eastward to the Chattahoochy River; bounded on the north by the thirty-first parallel of latitude, and on the south by the Gulf of Mexico. East Florida was bounded by the Chattahoochy on the west, and extended to the Atlantic on the east; comprising the whole peninsula as far north as the St. Mary's River, or the southern boundary of Georgia.

In February following, Captain George Johnston, of the British army, took formal possession of West Florida in the name of the British king. Pensacola was made the capital of West Florida, and St. Augustine of East Florida.

Soon after Governor Johnston entered upon his duties, the Court of St. James was informed that there were important settlements on the east side of the Mississippi, which were north of the thirty-first parallel of latitude, the northern boundary of West Florida. To embrace these settlements, a second decree of the king in council was issued on the 10th of June, 1764, extending the northern limit of West Florida as far as the mouth of the Yazoo River. The northern limit was henceforth to be an imaginary line drawn due east from the mouth of the Yazoo to the Chattahoochy River.*

That portion of Louisiana north of the Yazoo remained a portion of the Illinois government. The jurisdiction of Great Britain was not formally extended over the settlements on the Upper Mississippi and Illinois until the year 1765, when Captain Sterling, from Detroit, assumed the duties of commandant of Fort Chartres, and governor of the Illinois settlements.†

In the mean time, Spain had formally assumed possession of Western Louisiana, including the Island of New Orleans. The

---

* Martin's Louisiana, vol. i., p. 342, 343. † See book iii., chap. iv., of this work.

disappointed inhabitants yielded a reluctant obedience to the Spanish authority, and the civil jurisdiction of Spain was not enforced in Upper Louisiana until the year 1769.*

Thus terminated the dominion and power of France in North America. From the first permanent settlements on the St. Lawrence, she had held Canada, or New France, nearly one hundred and fifty years; she had discovered, occupied, and held dominion over the Valley of the Mississippi more than eighty years, until it had become a flourishing and important province.

The entire continental possessions of France in North America originally comprised New France, or Canada, with the provinces of Cape Breton and Acadié, south of the Gulf of St. Lawrence on the north, embracing the whole Valley of the St. Lawrence and the Great Lakes; in the west and south, the vast province of Louisiana, comprising the whole Valley of the Mississippi.

[A.D. 1764.] From this time the Valley of the Mississippi was virtually divided between the two great European powers of Great Britain and Spain. The dominion of the former was destined to be of short duration, and to be superseded by a new power heretofore unknown, a power which was ultimately to swallow up the dominion of Spain also. This new power was to be the United States of America, the land of freedom and the rights of man, the bulwark of human liberty and the asylum for the oppressed. This great confederated Republic now holds dominion over the whole Valley of the Mississippi, from the sea to its remotest tributaries.

* See book iv., chap. i., of this work.

BOOK III.
GREAT BRITAIN IN THE VALLEY OF THE MISSISSIPPI.

CHAPTER I.

EXPULSION OF THE FRENCH FROM THE OHIO REGION.—INDIAN HOSTILITIES UNTIL THE CLOSE OF PONTIAC'S WAR.—A.D. 1757 TO 1764.

Argument.—England persists in occupying the Upper Ohio Region.—The Frontier Anglo-American Settlements driven back in 1757.—Indian Hostilities West of the Blue Ridge.—Shawanese Incursions in 1757.—Sandy Creek Expedition under Colonel Lewis.—Peace established with the Cherokees.—Fort Loudon built on South Branch of Holston.—First White Settlements on the Holston in 1758.—Explorations of Dr. Walker and others in 1758, and previously.—Forces for Reduction of Fort Duquesne. —Major Grant's Defeat at Fort Duquesne.—French and Indians attack Colonel Bouquet's Camp at Loyal Hanna.—General Forbes advances to Fort Duquesne.—Occupies the deserted Post.—" Fort Pitt" commenced.—Fort Burd erected on the Monongahela, 1759.—Cherokees resume Hostilities.—A Portion of the Cherokees averse to Hostilities.—Friendly Cherokee Deputation imprisoned at Fort George.—Cherokees attempt to rescue their Chiefs.—General Cherokee War provoked in 1760.— Capture and Massacre of Fort Loudon.—Colonel Grant invades the Cherokee Nation.—Peace with Cherokees restored in 1761.—British Arms victorious in New France and Canada.—English Settlements from Virginia and North Carolina advance upon the Waters of the Ohio in 1762-3.—Treaty of Paris confirms to England all Canada and Eastern Louisiana.— The Northwestern Indians refuse their Assent to the Treaty.—The " Six Nations."—Their territorial Limits.—The Western Tribes resolve to resist the Advance of the English Power.—The King's conciliatory Proclamation of 1763.—Locations and Grants made on the Waters of the Ohio; on Cheat River.—Indian League under Pontiac, the great Ottawá Chief, or Emperor.— His Character and Plan of offensive Operations.—Catholic Missionaries and Jesuits not Instigators of the War.—Terrible Onset of Indian Hostilities.—Traders first Victims.—Capture of the Western Posts by Indians.—Capture of Presque Isle; of Fort Miamis ; of Mackinaw.—Massacre of the Garrison and Inmates.—Siege of Fort Pitt.—Colonel Bouquet defeats Indian Ambuscade at Turtle Creek.—Protracted Siege of Detroit by Pontiac in Person.—The Defense by Major Gladwyn.—Incidents of Indian Warfare and savage Barbarity.—A Detachment of Troops with Supplies for Detroit cut off by Indians.—Captain Dalzel slain in a Sortie.—Exposed Condition of the western and southwestern Frontiers.—Indian Hostilities in Pennsylvania.— "Massacre of Wyoming."—Hostilities in Virginia, at Muddy Creek and Big Levels.—Attack on Fort Ligonier.— Fort Loudon.— Hostilities on Susquehanna; on Greenbrier and Jackson Rivers.—Terror of eastern Part of New York.—Marauding Bands of Indians on the southwestern Frontier.—Lawless white Men on the Frontiers.—Outrages and Massacres committed by the Paxton Boys.—Origin and Designs of this Banditti.—Military Movements of the English Forces toward the Frontier.—Advance of General Bradstreet to Niagara.—Treaty of Niagara.—Treaty of Detroit.—Pontiac opposes the Treaty.—Colonel Bouquet invades the Indian Country upon the Muskingum.—Forms a Treaty.—Treaty of the " German Flats" with the " Six Nations."—Peace proclaimed December 5th, 1764.

[A.D. 1757.] IN another portion of this work,* we have shown that Great Britain had omitted no opportunity for ex-

* See book ii., chapter iii., "Advance cf the French upon the Upper Ohio," &c.

pelling her powerful rival from the beautiful and fertile regions drained by the Ohio. We have shown that she had never ceased to urge her claim to the regions west of the mountains which were virtually in the possession of France; that royal grants had been made to individuals and companies for extensive bodies of land upon the eastern tributaries of the Ohio, for the encouragement of emigration to that quarter;* that English subjects had sent agents to explore the country, and to establish trading-posts among the Indian tribes; that the French had refused to acknowledge the claim of Great Britain to any lands west of the mountains, and had driven back the agent and traders of the Ohio Company; that subsequently they had captured two detachments of troops, sent out under the authority of the province of Virginia; and, finally, that they had, in the summer of 1755, routed and totally defeated a large combined army of provincials and royal troops, under the command of General Braddock.

These successive reverses in this quarter, besides others of a similar character in other parts of Canada and New France, had put a check to the military operations of Great Britain west of the mountains for three years. During this period, the frontier settlements of Pennsylvania and Virginia east of the mountains were kept in a state of continual apprehension from Indian incursions, robberies, and murders. The government of Great Britain was absorbed in the contest with France on the ocean, and upon the St. Lawrence and other eastern portions of New France. The provinces were left to contend against the savages, without aid or control, until Fortune had begun to smile again upon the British arms. Remote from each other and from the older settlements, the frontier population of Pennsylvania and Virginia was compelled to fall back and relinquish the country to the French and their savage allies

* The grant made to the Ohio Company in 1748 was only one out of several grants made about that time. Several grants further south were of older date. Among these were those made to lands lying upon the sources of the Kentucky or Louisa River, the Cumberland, Clinch, and Holston Rivers, and within the present limits of Eastern Kentucky and East Tennessee. It was for the purpose of exploring the lands comprised in these grants that several parties of woodsmen and hunters from North Carolina, under Colonels Wood, Patton, and Buchanan, and those under Captain Charles Campbell and Dr. Walker, were made between the years 1745 and 1750. All these persons were largely interested in grants; and as early as 1755, they had led out about fifty families for settlements west of the mountains; but after the commencement of the French War, in 1755, they were compelled to retire until after Pontiac's War. In 1765 they returned to the West.—See Guthrie's Geography, vol. ii., p. 472.

The most western English settlements at that time had not reached the sources of the Susquehanna, the Potomac, the Shenandoah, James, and Roanoke Rivers; yet they were exposed during the whole of the French war to the continual incursions of the "Six Nations" and their confederates northwest of the Ohio River. Among the latter, the Shawanese were the most powerful and the most inveterate enemies of the Virginians. From the banks of the Scioto and Miami Rivers, they would penetrate the vast mountain wilderness of western Virginia, advancing up the eastern tributaries of the Ohio to the dividing summits, not less than five hundred miles from their towns; from these elevations they would descend upon the settlements situated on the tributaries of the Atlantic rivers, spreading consternation, rapine, and death through the unprotected immigrants. The settlements on the sources of the Yadkin, the French Broad and New River, also, had been driven back by the Cherokees, who joined the northern Indians as allies of France.

At this time, the whole valley between the Blue Ridge and the Alleghany ranges was a desolate frontier region, where the inhabitants were cooped up in forts for protection, or, to avoid starvation, had fled toward the eastern settlements. The present town of Winchester occupies the site of a stockade fort, erected in the year 1756, to "protect the inhabitants from the barbarities daily committed by the French Indians."* Staunton and Fincastle were then frontier posts, harassed by constant inroads of the savage war-parties. Nor was it until the next year that Winchester was made a military post, when "Fort Loudon" was erected as a regular stockade post.†

In making incursions upon the western settlements of Virginia, along her wide frontier, the Indians generally pursued two routes, one up the Valley of the Great Kenhawa, and the other up the Valley of the Big Sandy. Those war-parties who pursued the former route passed up the Kenhawa to the mouth of Greenbrier River; thence, following that river to its sources, they passed the dividing summits and descended upon the sources of the Potomac and Shenandoah, harassing the valley settlements from Winchester on the north to Staunton on the south. Others of the same party, following the main valley of the Ken-

---
* See Butler's History of Kentucky, Introduction, p. 39.
† Marshall's Washington, vol. ii., first edition, p. 23–26.

hawa, where it assumes the name of New River, to its sources, descended upon the settlements dispersed upon the numerous tributaries of James River and the Roanoke.

Those who took the Big Sandy Creek route ascended that stream to the mountains, and easily passed from the dividing highlands down upon the settlements sparsely scattered upon the head waters of the Staunton and Dan Rivers, and upon the sources of the Roanoke.

By the latter route, in the fall of 1757, a party of Shawanese from the Scioto towns had penetrated to the sources of the Roanoke, and had exterminated a whole settlement. To avenge this destructive inroad, and to prevent a repetition of it, the Governor of Virginia, Robert Dinwiddie, under Colonel Andrew Lewis, of Botetourt county, organized an expedition against the Scioto towns for the purpose of chastising the Shawanese, and of establishing, on his return, a fort at the mouth of the Great Sandy, as a barrier against future inroads.

Colonel Lewis without delay organized his expedition, and proceeded from Salem, the point of rendezvous, across New River to the Great Sandy late in the fall, with supplies inadequate for so distant a march through an uninhabited country. Before the troops reached the vicinity of the Ohio River, their salt provisions were exhausted, and they were driven to the necessity of supplying their wants by the labor of the chase, and by such game as their hunters could supply. Fortunately, deer, bear, and buffaloes were found sufficient for their immediate wants. When they had reached within ten miles of the Ohio River, they were overtaken by an express from Lieutenant-governor Fauquier, commanding Colonel Lewis to abandon the further prosecution of the campaign, to return to the settlements, and there disband his troops.

With great reluctance, this band of brave backwoodsmen consented to return, but not until they had reached the Ohio, in hopes of meeting the enemy. Many were in favor of proceeding, notwithstanding the orders of the lieutenant-governor. These orders, however, had been dictated by a proper regard for the safety of this little army, and the propriety of them was fully proven by the sequel. Notwithstanding the early retrograde movement toward the settlements, they were, by the severity of winter, on their return march, reduced to the verge of starvation in the midst of the wilderness. The supplies for the expedition had been completely exhausted, and life was barely sustained by the small quantities of wild game and beech nuts found in the woods. But these were taken from them by the deep snow which soon covered the mountains: the flesh of the pack-horses was then their only dependence for sustenance; and when, at length, this supply failed, every piece of skin, hide, or leather was sought and devoured with great voracity. Before they reached the settlements, they had become so emaciated by fatigue and starvation that they could hardly command strength to pursue their march. What would have been their fate had they advanced two hundred miles further into the wilderness, requiring three or four weeks more of toil and privation, if perchance they should have escaped the fury of the savages? However, they all finally, under their able and energetic conductor, Colonel Lewis, arrived in safety at their homes. This fruitless and hazardous expedition for many years afterward was designated as the "Sandy Creek voyage."*

Such was the second expedition to the West, in which Colonel Lewis had served an arduous and hazardous campaign; the first being the disastrous expedition under General Braddock two years before.

In the mean time, the Cherokees of the South had been conciliated and won over from the French interest. Before the close of the summer of 1757 they had entered into treaty stipulations for peace and friendship, and had consented for the establishment of a fort in the heart of their country. The same autumn "Fort Loudon," named in honor of the Earl of Loudon, who was then commander-in-chief of his majesty's forces in America, was built and left in charge of a suitable garrison. Its situation was upon the north bank of the Little Tennessee, or Watauga River, about one mile above the mouth of Tellico River, and within the present limits of Monroe county, in East Tennessee. The garrison, in the spring of 1758, was augmented to two hundred men, and was intended for the protection of the exposed frontier, as well as to prevent and neutralize French intrigue in this quarter. The same year adventurers and camp-followers advanced into this remote region, and established a small settlement in the immediate vicinity of the fort, which in a few months, by the arrival of traders and hunters, grew into a thriving village. This fort and settlement

* Butler's History of Kentucky, Introduction, p. 40.

were about one hundred and ten miles west of the frontier post of Fort "Prince George," on the Keowee River, a branch of the Savannah.*

[A.D. 1758.] The same autumn, Colonel Burd, with a detachment of troops, advanced into the Cherokee country about one hundred miles north of Fort Loudon, and erected the first English fort upon the Holston River. This fort was located upon a beautiful eminence, nearly opposite the upper end of Long Island, within the present limits of Sullivan county, in East Tennessee. A garrison was maintained in this post the whole of next year, during which time a thriving village settlement sprung up around the fort, comprising a number of mechanics and artisans, for the convenience of the Indians.†

During the summer of 1758, Dr. T. Walker, of Virginia, a man of intelligence and enterprise, made a second tour of exploration‡ into Powell's Valley, and across the head waters of Clinch River, and, passing the Cumberland Mountains, traversed the eastern portion of the present State of Kentucky, crossing in his route the head streams of the Kentucky River, which he called Louisa River; yet he did not see the fairest portion of Kentucky, on the lower valley of that fine river. This exploration resulted in no attempt to form settlements, and further explorations were precluded by the state of Indian hostilities in the West.

Such was the condition of the southern frontier until the close of the year 1759. The extreme western frontier settlements of Virginia and North Carolina were nearly one hundred miles east of the remote posts of Loudon and Long Island; yet the English vainly supposed they had virtual control over the country watered by the great southern branches of the Ohio.

The same year, 1758, the Shawanese warriors resumed their

* See Drake's Book of the Indians, book iv., p. 28.

† See Flint's Geography and Hist. of the Mississippi Valley, vol. ii., p. 19. First ed., 1828.

‡ As early as 1748, Dr. Walker, in company with Colonels Wood, Patton, and Buchanan, and Captain Charles Campbell, and a number of hunters and woodsmen, made an exploring tour upon the Western waters. Passing Powell's Valley, he gave the name of "Cumberland" to the lofty range of mountains on the west. Tracing this range in a southwestern direction, he came to a remarkable depression in the chain; through this he passed, calling it "Cumberland Gap." On the western side of the range he found a beautiful mountain stream, which he named "Cumberland River:" all in honor of the Duke of Cumberland, then prime minister of England.—See Winterbotham's America, vol. iii., p. 25, 26. Also, Marshall's History of Kentucky, vol. i., p. 6. Hall's Sketches of the West, vol. i., p. 239, 240.

incursions against the frontier population east of the mountains. These war-parties, accompanied by a few Canadian French, penetrated the settlements west of the Blue Ridge, and death and desolation marked their path. Dividing into smaller parties as they approached the settlements, they dispersed, and quietly and cautiously penetrated the remotest habitations, unobserved and unsuspected, until the blow was struck, when they as slyly departed. In this manner no less than sixty persons were killed during the summer of 1758, in the county of Augusta alone.

Meantime the British forces were concentrating in Pennsylvania for the reduction of the French posts on the Ohio. The British arms had been attended by one disaster after another, almost from the beginning of the war, and upon the Ohio another disaster awaited them; although, on the Atlantic sea-board, fortune had begun to smile propitiously.

Great preparations had been made by the mother country, as well as by the provinces, to fit out a strong expedition to the French posts on the Ohio. In July, General Forbes, at the head of an army of about seven thousand men, set out from Carlisle for Raystown, on the west side of the mountains.† About the middle of September, the advanced guard of twenty-five hundred men, commanded by Colonel Bouquet, was encamped at Loyal Hanna, fifty miles west of Raystown. From this point Colonel Bouquet dispatched Major Grant with eight hundred men, consisting of one regiment of Scottish Highlanders, and three hundred provincials under Colonel Andrew Lewis, of Botetourt county, Virginia, for the purpose of reconnoitering the country in the vicinity of Fort Duquesne.

On the 13th of September Major Grant had crossed the Monongahela, and advanced down the river within two miles of the French fort, where he encamped for the night. Determined to surprise the French garrison, next morning very early he advanced toward the fortress, leaving the provincials in camp, lest they might share in the glory of the achievement. Upon an eminence which overlooks the confluence, within six hundred yards of Fort Duquesne, with an incautious bravado, he first announced his presence to the enemy by the sound of the reveille drums. The French, pleased with his critical sit-

* Marshall's Life of Washington, vol. ii., p. 24-26, and 40.
† See Sparks's Writings of Washington, vol. ii., p. 289.

uation, made no display of troops; but silently marching from the fort to the water's edge, and dividing into two columns, they marched up the channel of both rivers, under the concealment of the river banks, and the heavy forest and dense undergrowth with which they were covered, until they gained the rear of Major Grant's position. Then suddenly converging and ascending the heights in the rear of the enemy, the united columns, with a numerous body of Indians on the flanks, suddenly gave the war-shout, and rushed to the attack. A scene of carnage ensued. The terrified Caledonians were thrown into irretrievable confusion, and were cut down without mercy by infuriate savages as they attempted to force their way through the French line. In less than one hour no less than two hundred and seventy Caledonians fell victims to the united fury of the rifle, the tomahawk, and scalping-knife. Many of those who escaped were wounded, and Major Grant and many others were taken captive.*

The regiment was rescued from utter destruction by the prompt advance of Colonel Lewis and his provincials, who, at the first report of the fire-arms, apprehensive of a severe engagement, without orders hastened to their relief, and arrested the victorious pursuit of the Indians. Such was the cause and issue of "Grant's Defeat" in 1758.

After this sanguinary affair, the remnant of the Highland regiment, perfectly satisfied with their first lesson in Indian warfare, were glad to place themselves under the protection of the provincials, and make a precipitate retreat to the main army at Loyal Hanna, leaving the French once more victorious on the Ohio.

The scene of this disastrous battle was long known as "Grant's Hill," in the rear of the city of Pittsburgh; and the hill itself, which was removed in 1844 to enlarge the city, is still commemorated by "Grant-street."

Nor was it long before the French, with their allies, advanced to meet the royal forces. Emboldened by the success at Grant's Hill, they hung upon the rear and flanks of the retreating detachment until it reached the camp at Loyal Hanna. On the 11th of October, they made a furious attack upon Colonel

* See American Pioneer, vol. i., p. 303. This valuable periodical was published monthly, first at Chillicothe, and then at Cincinnati, Ohio; but was discontinued after 1843. The design was to collect and record historical incidents and personal reminiscences of the early pioneers of the Ohio region.

Bouquet's encampment, where he was in command of twelve hundred men. After a severe engagement of four hours' duration, the enemy was repulsed, but not until the English had lost sixty-seven men killed and wounded.

On the 24th of October, General Forbes began to move the main army westward to Loyal Hanna.* On the 13th of November, he detached Colonel Armstrong with one thousand men, to advance by regular marches to Fort Duquesne; and on the 17th, with the main army, he proceeded toward the French fortress, leaving strong detachments to garrison Raystown and Loyal Hanna. On the 24th of November, the advanced detachment marched into Fort Duquesne without resistance; for it had been dismantled and burned by the French, who abandoned it only when defense was impracticable against the overwhelming force which was advancing against it, and within one day's march.†

The French commandant, who had been well informed of every movement of the British army since its departure from Carlisle, conscious of his inability successfully to defend the post against such overwhelming numbers, had dismantled the fort and set the buildings on fire previous to its evacuation. Having thus rendered it useless to the enemy, he embarked his command of about five hundred men, together with the ordnance and military stores, in boats and barges upon the Ohio, and descended that river to its mouth, whence he soon afterward descended to New Orleans.‡

As the French commander descended the Ohio, he made a halt about forty miles from the mouth, and, on a beautiful eminence on the north bank of the river, commenced a fort, and left a detachment of one hundred men as a garrison. The post was called "Fort Massac," in honor of the commander, M. Massac, who superintended its construction. This was the last fort erected by the French on the Ohio, and it was occupied by a garrison of French troops until the evacuation of the country under the stipulations of the treaty of Paris. Such

---

* The whole army under General Forbes, designed to operate upon the French posts near the Ohio, was composed of the following royal troops and provincials, viz.:

  1. Royal Americans,   350 men. | 3. Virginians,   2600 men.
  2. Scotch Highlanders, 1200 " | 4. Pennsylvanians, 2700 "

besides wagoners, sutlers, and camp followers to the number of 1000 souls.—See Gordon's History of Pennsylvania, p. 366–369.

† Gordon's Pennsylvania, p. 366, 367.   ‡ Martin's Louisiana, vol. i., p. 333.

was the origin of Fort Massac, divested of the romance which fable has thrown around its name.

Fort Duquesne was repaired by the orders of General Forbes; after which the name was changed to "Fort Pitt," in honor of the great William Pitt, the prime minister of Great Britain, by whose wise and energetic administration the fortunes of the war in America had been so signally changed.

A garrison of four hundred and fifty provincial troops, under the command of General Mercer, was left in the post as the key to the whole Ohio region. Thus commenced the first establishment of British power upon the waters of the Ohio River, consequent upon the expulsion of the French.

After the fall of Fort Duquesne, the minor posts situated on the northwest side of the Ohio were successively abandoned by the French commandants, leaving them an easy conquest to the superior forces of the English commanders. The French troops, retiring before the advance of the English forces, descended the Ohio River from all the posts south of the lakes, and concentrated on the Lower Ohio. The Indian allies were compelled to suspend hostilities, and reluctantly to enter into terms of peace with their English enemies. Many of the unprotected settlements upon the tributaries of the Alleghany, the Sandusky, and the Scioto abandoned their homes, and retired upon the settlements of the Wabash and Illinois countries, and some descended the Mississippi to Lower Louisiana.

Actual hostilities upon the Upper Ohio were virtually terminated by the evacuation of Fort Duquesne; and the whole region on both sides of the river being in the actual occupancy of the English troops, emigrants began again to explore the remote regions west of the Alleghany Mountains, and upon the upper tributaries of the Ohio.

[A.D. 1759.] Early in the spring of 1759, several new English posts were established upon the east side of the Ohio, as a protection to the advancing population, and for observing the movements of the hostile tribes upon the waters of the Monongahela. One of the most important of these was that which subsequently was known as "Redstone Old Fort." The site of this fort was the earthworks of an aboriginal fortification, situated upon the margin of an eminence which overlooks the Monongahela from the north side of Dunlop's Creek. Having been selected as an eligible site for a military post, Colonel

Burd, with two hundred men, was ordered to open a road from Braddock's "old trace," on the best route to the Monongahela at this point. The same summer witnessed the completion of the fort, which, after its founder, was named "Fort Burd." Captain Paull, with a small garrison, continued to hold command until after the ratification of the treaty of peace, in 1763. At a later period, it was discontinued as a military post, and received the name of "Redstone Old Fort," from the red sandstone found in a bluff below.* Around this point was subsequently concentrated one of the first English settlements on the Monongahela.

Although driven from the upper tributaries of the Ohio, the French did not abandon the country further south. They made another effort to eject the English from the Cherokee country. Emissaries were dispatched to rouse the Cherokees from their new alliance, and to induce them again to resume the tomahawk as an ally of France. If the Cherokees, as a nation undivided, could be marshalled against the English, France might yet retain Louisiana from the grasp of England; and it was known that a portion of the nation was ready to strike the enemies of France.†

The Cherokees, obedient to the call of the French envoys, again put on their armor. In a few weeks the frontiers of North and South Carolina were reeking under the incursions of the war-parties from the Cherokee nation; and the provinces were actively employed in defending the unprotected settlements. It was resolved to invade the Cherokee country with a powerful army, and to chastise the nation by ravaging their country and destroying their towns. This being known in the Cherokee nation, of which a large portion was not hostile, but desirous of averting the contemplated invasion, a plan was devised to prevent such a calamity. For this purpose,

* American Pioneer, vol. ii., p. 59–62, where a full history of this fort and the first Redstone settlement may be seen.

† Most of the Cherokees had been pacific and espoused the English cause; some of them had joined the English in their campaigns to the Ohio; but, having been treated improperly, as they supposed, and very imperfectly supplied, they retired to their towns. During the French war, the Legislature of North Carolina had authorized a premium for the scalps of hostile Indians. As it was impossible to distinguish the scalp of a friendly Indian from one that was hostile, and as the former were much more easily procured, the lawless Western people, the Germans especially, frequently shot friendly Cherokees for their scalps. In one season nearly forty Cherokees had been thus cruelly murdered. They became greatly disaffected toward the English, as the French well knew.—See Drake's Book of Indians, book iv., p. 28. Grahame, vol. iv., p. 67.

they sent thirty chiefs upon an embassy of peace. Their route lay by way of Fort Prince George, on the Savannah, where Governor Lyttleton was encamped with eleven hundred men. At this post the Indian envoys were forcibly detained, and compelled to sign a treaty; and for the fulfillment of its stipulations, to which they unwillingly assented, twenty-two of their number were held as hostages for the surrender of those Indians who had committed recent murders upon the frontiers. This unjust and impolitic act roused the indignation and vengeance of the whole Cherokee nation, and led to general hostilities.*

[A.D. 1760.] The first movement on the part of the Indians, after the hostages had been in close imprisonment for nearly two months, was an attempt, by stratagem, to liberate their chiefs from confinement in the fort. In the attempt, the commandant of the fort and one or two soldiers were wounded. In retaliation, the prisoners were soon afterward taken out and deliberately shot.

The whole Cherokee nation immediately flew to arms, and for a time they waged a most unrelenting and bloody war against the frontier settlements of Virginia and North Carolina.

The first general movement of the hostile Indians in this quarter was the capture of "Fort Loudon," with its garrison of two hundred men. The latter, after a protracted siege, had been reduced to the horrors of famine, after having consumed their horses and dogs for food. It was not until then that the commandant agreed to capitulate, upon condition that the garrison should be permitted to march with their arms, unmolested, to the nearest white settlements. The Indians stipulated that this privilege should be granted upon the surrender of the fort; but they violated their obligations.

Agreeably to treaty stipulations, the fort was surrendered on the 7th day of August, and the troops had proceeded one day's march up the Tellico, where they encamped for the night, fifteen miles from Fort Loudon, and on the route to Fort George. Here, on the banks of the Tellico River, at daybreak next morning, they were surrounded and attacked by nearly five hundred Indian warriors, with the most hideous yells, as they rushed, tomahawk in hand, upon the feeble and emaciated troops. Resistance was vain: the captain and thirty of his men fell at the first fire, and the greatest portion of the re-

* Drake's Book of the Indians, book iv., p. 28, 29.

mainder were massacred upon the spot. Captain Stewart, with a few others, were spared, and carried into a captivity worse than death.*

Hostilities, with all the horrors of Indian warfare, were urged with ruthless barbarity by the vindictive Cherokees against the frontier population of Virginia, as well as of North and South Carolina, for nearly two years. The warlike Cherokees at this time held possession of all the regions upon the sources of the Tennessee River and its tributaries, as far south and west as the Muscle Shoals; and France, under them as her allies, had claimed all the southwestern portion of Virginia and North Carolina as a part of Louisiana.

During the period of hostilities in this portion of the western frontier, the white population, which had been extending upon the sources of the Holston and Clinch, and upon the sources of the French Broad, were driven back upon the older settlements east of the mountains.

During the summer of 1761, a strong force, under Colonel Grant, invaded the Cherokee country, and the savages, flying before him, left the country an easy conquest. Marching through the nation, he laid waste their fields, burned their towns, and, destroying their resources, compelled them to sue for peace. Near the close of the year peace was restored upon the southwestern frontier of the provinces, and emigrants were again ready to advance into their deserted settlements.

[A.D. 1761.] During the two years which had elapsed since the expulsion of the French from the Ohio region, and the possession of the key to the Western country by the English troops at Fort Pitt, the most rapid and brilliant successes had attended the British arms in Canada, and in the region south of the St. Lawrence and upon the lakes. The whole region east and west of Lake Champlain, and westward to Lake Erie, was already subjected to the dominion of Great Britain. The strong fortresses of Ticonderoga and Crown Point had been captured in August, 1759, and in September following Fort Niagara, at the western extremity of Lake Ontario, and Quebec, the Gibraltar of North America, had yielded to her victorious arms. With them fell the French power south of the lakes. Next year Montreal fell, and with it the whole of Canada.†

---

* Gordon's History of Pennsylvania, p. 388. Also, Drake's Book of Indians, book iv., p. 51. † Martin's Louisiana, vol. i., p. 236.

[A.D. 1762.] The people of Northern Virginia began to advance from the sources of the Potomac over the mountains, upon the head waters of the Monongahela; from the sources of James River they were crossing the dividing ridges, and descending upon the Greenbrier, New River, and other tributaries of the Kenhawa. Others, from the Roanoke and from North Carolina, were advancing westward upon the sources of the Staunton, Dan, Yadkin, Catawba, and Broad Rivers, along the eastern base of the Blue Mountains, with wishful eyes upon the beautiful country of the Cherokees.

Pennsylvania was sending her emigrants westward upon the tributaries of the Susquehanna, while other hardy pioneers from Virginia, Maryland, and Pennsylvania were advancing by the military roads to form settlements on the Monongahela, near Fort Pitt, and upon its eastern tributaries. But the region of Western Virginia, drained by the tributaries of the Holston and Clinch, were still savage wilds, in the occupancy of the native tribes, excluding even the most resolute pioneer. The embryo settlements, formerly made on the Tellico and on the Holston, near Long Island, had been destroyed or abandoned.

[A.D. 1763.] At length, in the following year, France was obliged to acknowledge the loss of her empire in America. The treaty of Paris, on the 16th of February, 1763, ceded to Great Britain all Canada, and all the French claim to the whole region east of the Mississippi River, as far south as the southern limit of Georgia.

But the treaty of Paris made no stipulation for the tribes who had been in alliance with France, and who claimed to be independent nations, and the real occupants of the territory ceded by France. They had been no party to the treaty of peace, and they refused to be bound by any transfer which the French king should make of their country to their enemies, the English.

We have already seen that the dominion of Great Britain, by the treaty of Paris, was recognized over all the territory east of the Mississippi, from its source to the Bayou Iberville,* including all the French settlements in the Illinois country, and upon the tributaries of the Ohio. During the contest which preceded the treaty of Paris, most of the Indian tribes occupying the vast region from Lake Champlain on the east,

* See book ii., chap. iii.

to the Mississippi on the west, had either been engaged as allies and auxiliaries to the French arms, or had observed a suspicious neutrality. Among the most powerful of these auxiliaries was the confederacy known to the French as the Iroquois, and to the English as the "Six Nations," then inhabiting the northern and western portions of New York and part of Pennsylvania. Some bands of the Six Nations dwelt on the sources of the Ohio south of Lake Erie, and others as far west as the Cuyahoga River, on Lake Erie. Other tribes further west, upon the tributaries both of the Ohio and of the Upper Mississippi, were in alliance with, or under the control of the Six Nations.* These also entertained the same hostile feeling toward the English settlements. But the Cherokees of the South had buried the hatchet, and again had entered into a treaty of peace and friendship with the English.

During the war between the French and English provinces, the French had duly impressed the Indians with the inordinate desire of the English to possess their western lands. This grasping propensity of England to occupy these fine lands, in the eye of the Indian, was the chief cause of the war in which General Braddock had fallen. The French, of course, had no such objects to accomplish. Under this belief, the Indians had entered heartily into the war, in expectation of restricting the English settlements to the east side of the mountains. In their alliance, the French had pledged themselves to defend and protect the Indians in their rights, and in the occupancy of their territory and hunting-grounds eastward to the western ranges of the Alleghany Mountains.

The Indians were well apprised that, in the treaty of Paris, ceding the whole country to England, including all their lands south of the lakes and westward to the Mississippi River, without their assent, the King of France, vanquished and driven from all his strong-holds, had been compelled to accede to such

---

* The Six Nations originally occupied and held dominion over a very extensive territory. After the close of the French war, but especially after the treaty of the "German Flats" in 1764, they entered into alliance with the English. "The limits of their lands or country included all the nations and tribes which were subject to them by conquest or otherwise: they extended from the south part of Lake Champlain, in latitude 44° north, to the borders of Carolina, in latitude 36°, comprehending all Pennsylvania and the adjacent countries. The Six Nations themselves are seated between the forty-second and forty-third parallels of north latitude, north and east of Pennsylvania, within the bounds of New York government, and on the rivers which run into Lake Ontario."—See Proud's History of Pennsylvania, vol. ii., p. 293, 294.

terms as were dictated by the conquerors. Hence it was that France, unable to obtain for her Indian allies any favorable stipulations, had been compelled to leave them to contend alone with the colossal power of their enemies. Although exasperated at the ungenerous desertion of the French, and left to contend single-handed with the English provinces, the Indians were not dismayed, but were rather roused to desperation in their determination to resist the advance of the white settlements west of the mountains. They had no reasonable hope that the inordinate pretensions heretofore set up by the British provinces to the Ohio country would be withdrawn or in any wise abated, since their right had been acknowledged by France.

England claimed for her colonies only the right of dominion or jurisdiction; but the Indians could perceive no distinction between the right of jurisdiction and the right of possession. They inferred, correctly judging from the past, that the English intended to dispossess them of the whole country so soon as they could find it convenient to occupy it with their colonial settlements. This belief was strongly confirmed by the fact that British troops were distributed in all the old French posts as far west as Detroit and Green Bay. They also beheld the erection of other strong forts in the very heart of their country. One fort had been built at Bedford, more than two hundred miles west of Philadelphia; another was erected at Ligonier; another, called Fort Pitt, on the site of the old French Fort Duquesne. The forts at Niagara, Presque Isle, Detroit, St. Joseph's, and Mackinaw were repaired, and garrisoned with British troops.

Other forts were being erected upon the waters of the Susquehanna River, and upon lands claimed by the Indians. Thus the red men saw themselves circumvented by a strong line of forts on the north and east, while those of Bedford, Ligonier, and Pitt threatened the speedy extension of the white settlements into the heart of their country.*

Under these circumstances, the native proprietors and occupants of the country from time immemorial were compelled to choose between the only three alternatives: first, the prospect of being driven to the inhospitable regions north and west of the lakes; secondly, to negotiate with the English for permission to remain upon their own lands; or, thirdly, to take up

* Doddridge's Notes on Virginia, p. 215.

arms in defense of them.* Their native courage and love of independence, sustained by the justness of their cause, prompted them to adopt the last alternative. All former experience taught them that finally they should be overcome, if not exterminated, by their intolerant enemy; yet they determined to assert their rights, although they might be crushed in the attempt to maintain them against their powerful oppressors. They preferred death to ignoble dependence or a cowardly peace.

To remove, so far as appearances might avail, any apparent grounds for apprehension, on the part of the Indians, that the British government designed to extend its jurisdiction over the Indian territory, the proclamation of King George III. was issued in the year 1763, prohibiting all the provincial governors from granting lands, or issuing land-warrants to be located upon any territory lying west of the mountains, or west of the sources of those streams which flow into the Atlantic. The same proclamation prohibited, also, all settlements by the subjects of Great Britain in the provinces west of the sources of the Atlantic streams.†

This proclamation, however, as was admitted by Colonel George Washington and Chancellor Livingston, was intended merely to quiet the jealous apprehensions of the Indians against the advance of the white settlements on the western side of the mountains. It was not in any wise designed really to check the ultimate occupation of the country. Virginia, agreeably to Colonel Washington's opinion, "viewing the proclamation in no other light than as a temporary expedient to quiet the minds

* Doddridge's Notes on Virginia, p. 215, 216.

† The following extract contains the prohibition alluded to in this proclamation of the king, dated October 7th, 1763, viz.:

"And whereas great frauds and abuses have been committed in purchasing lands of the Indians, to the great prejudice of our interests and to the great dissatisfaction of the said Indians; in order, therefore, to prevent such irregularities for the future, and to the end that the Indians may be convinced of our justice and determined resolution to remove all reasonable cause of discontent, we do, with the advice of our privy council, strictly enjoin and require that no private person do presume to make any purchase from the said Indians of any lands reserved to the said Indians within those parts of our colonies where we have thought proper to allow settlements. But that, if at any time any of the Indians should be inclined to dispose of the said lands, the same shall be purchased only for us in our name, at some public meeting or assembly of the said Indians, to be held for that purpose by the governor or commander-in-chief of our colony respectively, within the limits of any proprietors, conformably to such directions and instructions as we or they shall think proper to give for that purpose."—See Brown's History of Illinois, p. 210.

of the Indians," soon afterward " patented considerable tracts of land on the Ohio, far beyond the Appalachian Mountains."*

In the mean time, agents and surveyors had been busily engaged, whenever Indian forbearance permitted, in searching out the finest lands east and southeast of the Ohio, and making surveys or locations of them in such tracts as might be desired to complete the *quantum* originally granted to the Ohio Company, and also to complete the complement of other private grants and military bounties for service in the late French war.

The master spirit of Pontiac was busily engaged, during this time, in preparing his plan of hostile operations against the English provinces, the execution of which has rendered the year 1763, as well as the name of Pontiac, memorable in the annals of Indian hostilities in the West.

Pontiac, or Pondiac, was an Ottawâ chief, partly of French descent (having declared that he would live and die a Frenchman), and an unwavering enemy to the British power. He was a savage of the noblest mold, equal, at least, to King Philip of former times, or Tecumseh of later date. In point of native talent, courage, magnanimity, and integrity, he will compare, without prejudice, with the most renowned of civilized potentates and conquerors. During the series of Indian wars against the English colonies and armies, from the Acadian war in 1747 up to the general league of the Western tribes in 1763, he appears to have exercised the influence and power of an emperor, and by this name he was sometimes known.† He had fought with the French, at the head of his Indian allies, against the English in the year 1747. He had likewise been a conspicuous commander of the Indian forces in the defense of Fort Duquesne, and took an active part in the memorable defeat of the British and provincial army under General Braddock in 1755.

After the fall of Canada and the humiliation of the French, he burned with an inveterate hatred to the English people. When, after the treaty of 1763, the British troops began to take possession of the northwestern posts, he began to exert himself in uniting and rousing the Indian tribes in one common cause against them, whereby he hoped to put a check

* See Sparks's Writings of Washington, vol. ii., p. 347–349.
† Major Rogers's Account.—See Thatcher's Indian Biography, vol. ii., p. 84.

to the advance of their settlements into the Indian country. The general plan to effect this object comprised the capture and massacre of all the western garrisons, and the extermination of the western settlements from the lakes on the north to the southern limits of Carolina. In this general league of the savages Pontiac had engaged all the tribes inhabiting the whole region west of this extensive frontier and back to the Mississippi. The league formed by him in this great undertaking was more extensive than any which had ever been known upon the Continent. In all his plans to effect the great object of the league, he seemed to exercise the power of an absolute dictator. Well acquainted with the geography of the whole region, he planned each attack, and assigned to each band and leader their respective stations and duties.

The general hostile rising of the savages was to be nearly simultaneous against all the posts and settlements. Nor were active hostilities long delayed. By the first of May the Indians were in full motion throughout the extensive frontier. All the military posts and forts, before the middle of May, were either captured or closely invested by an Indian siege. Besides a great number of trading-posts which had fallen, with their owners and occupants, in the first assaults, nine British forts were captured, and the garrisons chiefly massacred with Indian triumph, while others, more strongly fortified or more effectually defended, environed by hosts of hostile savages, and cut off from all communication with the settlements east of the mountains, suffered with famine and the continual apprehension of Indian massacre.

The English historians, biased by their insuperable prejudice and hatred against Catholicism, and their jealousy of papal supremacy, have ascribed the war of Pontiac to the influence of French missionaries and Jesuits among the Indian tribes. Yet nothing is more erroneous than such an inference. Those missionaries of the Catholic Church were doubtless the advocates of peace and mercy, but their influence was insufficient to extinguish revenge from the savage breast, roused by wanton and atrocious murders perpetrated by the whites,* who were protected and encouraged in their encroachments by British troops.

* Several wanton murders had been committed by the whites upon the peaceable Indians near the Susquehanna after the peace of 1763. These, although perpetrated by lawless frontier white men, served to rouse up the Indian's revenge, and his suspicions of treachery and hostility on the part of the whites.

Hostilities once commenced, the whole Indian confederacy bent every energy to its effectual prosecution. As Dr. Doddridge observes, "Never did military commanders of any nation display more skill, or their troops more steady and determined courage, than did those red men of the wilderness in the prosecution of their gigantic plan for the recovery of their country from the possession of the English." It was a war of extermination on a large scale, where a few destitute savage tribes, in defense of their country and their homes, were arrayed against the colossal power and resources of the mistress of the civilized world; a contest where human nature, in its simplest state, was the antagonist of wealth, civilization, and arts, and where the wild man was obliged to call to his aid all the power of stratagem, treachery, revenge, and cruelty against the innocent, the helpless, and the unoffending. Such is the stern mode of savage warfare, which knows no mercy to the feeble, the aged, or the infant; where the youthful mother and her tender infant are alike doomed to the fate of the tomahawk and scalping-knife.

The spirit which animated Pontiac, the Indian emperor in this struggle, may be conceived by the following extract of a speech made by him before a grand council of the Western tribes. After an eloquent and powerful appeal to the warriors against the advance of the British power, he declared that he had been requested by their father, the French king, to aid him in driving out the English, and he repeated to them the will of the Great Spirit, communicated in a dream to a Delaware chief. The Great Spirit had said to him, "Why do you suffer these dogs in red coats to enter your country and take the lands I have given *to you?* Drive them from it! drive them! and when you are in trouble, I will help you."*

Among the forts or military posts captured by the Indians during the early part of May, were those of Ouiatenon, Green Bay, Mackinaw, St. Joseph's, Miami, Sandusky, Presque Isle, Le Beuf, and Venango. Some had been taken by open attack, others by stratagem and treachery; and in nearly all of them the garrisons had shared the fate of Indian victory, their bodies mangled in triumph, and their blood quaffed in rage.

Besides those posts which fell before the victorious savages, no less than six were beleaguered for many weeks or months,

* Thatcher's Lives of the Indians, vol. ii., p. 86, Family Library edition.

until they were finally relieved by re-enforcements from the older settlements and from England. The principal of these were Detroit, Ligonier, Bedford, Cumberland, and Loudon, most of which were reduced to great extremities before relief reached them. Niagara was deemed impregnable to the savages, and was not attacked.

In addition to the destruction of life and property at the forts and in their immediate vicinity, the frontier settlements west of the Blue Ridge, from the Susquehanna to the sources of the Roanoke, were broken up with indiscriminate massacre, where the people could not effect their timely escape. Those who escaped were crowded into fortified stations, or retired with their families to the more secure parts of the old settlements east of the mountains. "The English traders among the Indians were the first victims in this contest. Out of one hundred and twenty of them, only two or three escaped the general destruction. The posts of Presque Isle, St. Joseph, and Mackinaw were taken, with a general slaughter of the garrisons."

Such was the general result; the detail of some of the scenes in the western regions may give some idea of the nature of an Indian war. "The work of extirpation was commenced on or about the same time from north to south, and from east to west. Nine British forts were captured. Some of the garrisons were completely surprised and massacred on the spot; a few individuals, in other cases, escaped. The officer who commanded at Presque Isle defended himself two days. During this time the savages are said to have set fire to his blockhouse about fifty times, but the flames were as often extinguished by the soldiers. It was then undermined and a train laid for an explosion, when a capitulation was proposed and agreed upon, after which a part of the garrison was carried captive to the northwest."*

In the treachery put in operation against the posts, the prominent object was, first, to obtain possession of the commanders, or officers, previous to any actual hostile attack. This was attempted, and sometimes successfully, by parties of Indians gaining admission under pretense of business or friendship; at other times they were enticed from the fort without any apprehension of danger. At Miami, on the Maumee River, the commandant was induced, by the entreaties and cries of a squaw, to

* Thatcher's Indian Biography, vol. ii., p. 87.

accompany her two hundred yards from the fort, to relieve a man who, she said, was wounded and dying. He went for the purpose of relieving the dying man, and found his own death from a party of Indians in ambuscade. The fort was afterward captured, and the garrison massacred.*

At Mackinaw a more subtle policy was adopted. This was a very important post, standing on the south side of the Strait of Michilimackinac, between Lakes Huron and Michigan. It was a place of deposit, and the point of departure between the upper and lower countries, and here the traders always assembled on their voyages to and from Montreal. The post was situated on a fine plain near the water-level, and consisted of a stockade inclosing nearly two acres, and about thirty small houses, occupied by as many families. The bastions were mounted with two small brass pieces of ordnance, and the garrison consisted of about ninety-five men. Near the time for the contemplated attack, numerous Indians, apparently quite friendly, began to collect about the fort. At length, under pretense of celebrating the king's birthday, they made arrangements for a great game of *baggatiwà*, or Indian ball, resembling the common game of racket, in which each party strives to carry the ball to the opposite boundary of the field. It was pretended that a great wager was at stake for the victorious party. Nearly two hundred Indians were engaged on each side. The play was about to commence near the fort, and many from it were induced to come out as spectators. In the midst of the play, when all were apparently intent upon the game, and engaged in the most violent exercises of rivalry, the ball was, as if by accident, thrown within the stockade. Each party, eager to excel, were allowed to pass directly into the fort in pursuit of the ball. Immediately after they had entered the fort, the war-whoop was given, and each Indian, drawing his concealed weapons, began the indiscriminate massacre of every Englishman in the fort. The French were not molested. Henry, an eye-witness, states that, after having been engaged writing for nearly half an hour, he was suddenly aroused by a loud war-cry, and great noise and general confusion. Going to his window, he saw a crowd of Indians within the fort, furiously cutting down and scalping every Englishman they found; and he could plainly witness the last struggles of some of his particu-

* Thatcher's Indian Biography, vol. ii., p. 88.

lar acquaintances. Some of them he saw fall, and more than one struggling between the knees of the savages, who were holding them in this manner, and tearing off their scalps while they were yet alive. All show of resistance was soon over, and the cry was heard through the fort, "All is finished!" While this scene of blood was passing, several of the Canadian villagers were seen looking out upon the scene quite composed, and neither interfering nor being molested.

After the massacre was over, and all the English had been hunted up, the scene of savage revelry commenced. Here the observer, who had been fortunately concealed in a Frenchman's house, beheld the most ferocious and foul triumphs ot the savages. The dead were scalped and mangled; the dying were writhing and shrieking under the unsatiated knife and reeking tomahawk. Some, from the bodies of their victims ripped open, were drinking the blood scooped up in the hollow of their hands, and quaffed amid the shouts and rage of victory.*

Fort Pitt was likewise invested, and closely besieged for nearly three months. All communication with the eastern settlements being intercepted by the lurking bands of Indians, and all succor by re-enforcement being impracticable, the garrison for many weeks was an isolated community, nearly three hundred miles from the settlements, and surrounded by fierce bands of hostile savages. Reduced to the greatest extremities, starvation or Indian massacre seemed their only doom. To them starvation was less terrible than to become the objects of Indian vengeance, and this heroic band determined to resist so long as a man might remain, and die, if need be, by famine. During this time every road was intercepted to prevent intercourse between Fort Ligonier and the beleaguered post. All messengers who attempted to penetrate from Fort Pitt were either killed by the Indians, or were compelled to return to the fort by the lurking Indians on the way. During this time the fort was continually beset by a host of savages, who made daily attacks upon the stockade, while their sharp-shooters, lying concealed under the banks of the Monongahela and Alleghany Rivers, poured a destructive volley of bullets whenever any of the garrison dared to expose any part of their persons over the piquets or outside the inclosure.† Lighted ar-

* Thatcher's Ind. Biog., vol. ii., p. 88–92.   † Gordon's Hist. of Pennsylvania, p. 399.

rows were daily shot upon the stockade and houses for burning them down.

At length, General Amherst, commander-in-chief of his majesty's forces in North America, detached a strong re-enforcement with three hundred and forty horses, loaded with supplies and ammunition, under Colonel Bouquet, for the relief of the garrison. This whole detachment, of more than six hundred men, had well-nigh been cut off by the savages within a few miles of the fort. As usual, the savages, by their runners and spies, became well apprised of every movement made by any portion of the English armies. They accordingly selected a dangerous defile on Turtle Creek, and only about fifteen miles from Fort Pitt, as a suitable place to cut off the advancing re-enforcement. Through this defile the detachment must necessarily pass, and here, on the 4th of August, the Indian ambuscade was laid. Nothing but the extraordinary courage and presence of mind in the commander, seconded by his brave troops, saved the corps from utter destruction. After having sustained a desperate contest for several hours, until the mantle of night spread its protection over them, they stood upon their guard until the morning light. After several hours' hard fighting again in the morning, Colonel Bouquet resolved to practice the Indian stratagem upon the savages. Carefully posting four companies in ambuscade, he feigned a rapid retreat with the troops who were actively engaged. The Indians, as if sure of victory, pressed forward after the retreating enemy, without order, and thoughtless of danger, until suddenly the terrible fire in their rear convinced them that they were between two fires. Instantly thrown into the greatest consternation and confusion, they fled precipitately from the field of action. The loss of the English was severe; one hundred men were killed and wounded. That of the Indians was equally severe, and some of their most distinguished chiefs were slain. The detachment arrived at Fort Pitt four days afterward,* and the Indians dispersed.

In the mean time, Detroit was beleaguered by a formidable body of western savages, under the immediate command of Pontiac himself. The Indians appeared before this post on the 8th of May, and the siege, with innumerable attacks, was continued without intermission until the last of August; and, with

---

* Doddridge's Notes, p. 218, 219. Gordon's Pennsylvania, p. 401, 402.

occasional relaxations only, from that time until next spring, altogether about twelve months. After the last of August, many of the allies and warriors of Pontiac, wearied with the toil and privations of the siege, retired to their towns and families.

Detroit was one of the most important of the western posts, although, like most of them, its garrison had been reduced during the apparent pacification of the Indian tribes, immediately preceding the outbreak of hostilities. At the time of the siege it was a rich object for savage plunder, far exceeding any other western post, being at that time the general dépôt of goods and merchandise for the whole Indian trade, to the value of nearly half a million of pounds sterling. Many of the western traders had arrived, and were moving forward to monopolize the Indian fur trade. The fort was a stockaded village on the bank of the Detroit River, with bastions mounting six small pieces of ordnance, and defended by a garrison of one hundred and thirty men, besides about forty persons who were connected with the fur trade.

On the 8th of May, Pontiac presented himself before the fort with three hundred Ottawâ and Chippewa warriors, and demanded of the commandant, Major Gladwyn, a council. The commandant refused to admit the whole force of Pontiac, but consented to admit him and forty of his associates, who should hold a council with him in the fort. The main body of the Indians retired to their camp, about one mile distant, when Pontiac and his forty associates were admitted. In the mean time, Major Gladwyn, having received intimation of treachery and hostile intentions from an Indian squaw, had put the fort and garrison in a state of complete defense. Pontiac and his warriors, all secretly armed, entered the fort; but, seeing the troops under arms, and every man at his post, he inquired, "Why all this parade of arms?" and finally declined to give the signal for the massacre to his warriors. Their secret arms were soon after discovered by Major Gladwyn, when he dismissed Pontiac and his band from the fort, with reproaches for his treachery. As they retired from the gate, they gave the Indian yell, and discharged their short fire-arms upon the fort with little or no injury. The Indians under the command of Pontiac immediately proceeded to the houses in the vicinity of the fort, and commenced an indiscriminate massacre of such persons as were found outside of the stockade. The night was spent in savage revelry over the helpless victims of their revenge, while others lurked about the fort, under the darkness of the night, and secreted themselves behind houses, fences, and trees for an opportunity to shoot down any who should venture to expose themselves from the fort after daylight.

The next day Pontiac renewed his efforts and stratagems to induce the officers of the fort to meet him in council beyond the reach of the small arms of the garrison. One officer, who voluntarily went out to meet the chiefs with three attendants, was detained and subsequently put to death.

On the 10th of May the Indians made a resolute attack upon the fort, and kept up a brisk fire the whole day from behind houses, fences, barns, and trees, within gunshot of the palisades, while the main body of the savage army was kept at a respectful distance by the ordnance of the fort. The force of the savages was rapidly increasing every day, and already amounted to about seven hundred warriors. Major Gladwyn began to apprehend serious danger to the garrison and inmates of the stockade, and contemplated secretly leaving the post, and descending the river with his command; but being informed by an experienced Frenchman that the Indians never contemplate an open assault in daylight and in the face of cannon, he determined to remain and defend the fort to the last extremity. From this time every person in the fort capable of duty was closely employed to prevent any secret attack, and to avoid any stratagem laid for them either by night or by day.

At length Pontiac demanded the surrender of the fort by capitulation, requiring the British to lay down their arms, and march out as the French had done. This being refused, he renewed his attacks with increased vigor and frequency. So unremitted were his attacks for several weeks, that neither officers nor men were allowed to take off their clothes to sleep, all being continually engaged about the ramparts. During this time the whole number of effective men, exclusive of sick and wounded, and including two vessels in the river, was only one hundred and twelve.

Every plan of annoyance was put in operation. Floating fire-rafts were repeatedly prepared and sent against the vessels in the river for the purpose of destroying them, and with great difficulty they were preserved from the flames. Parties were continually hovering near the fort under some concealment, for the purpose of taking off, by their marksmen, any who might incautiously expose themselves in the fort, while other detached parties scoured the country around in every direction, to intercept every kind of aid or succor intended for the garrison.

In the month of June, a detachment of fifty men, with a supply of provisions from Niagara, on their voyage to Detroit had been entirely cut off, and the supplies captured by the Indians. Soon afterward, another detachment of one hundred men, with a supply of provisions and ammunition from Fort Niagara, had reached the Detroit River, within half a day's sail of the fort, when, having landed and encamped for the night, they were attacked by a strong party of Indians and entirely defeated, with the loss of their commander and seventy men, besides the supplies, which fell into the hands of the Indians, along with a few prisoners.*

Scenes of unparalleled barbarity continued to be perpetrated in the vicinity of the fort upon every Englishman whom they could intercept. It was a matter of almost daily occurrence for the garrison to behold the dead and mangled bodies of their countrymen floating past the fort; every family and individual in the vicinity had been murdered in the most horrid manner, and every habitation destroyed by fire.

On the 26th of July, a re-enforcement, under Captain Dalzel, from Niagara, amounting to two hundred and fifty regular troops, succeeded in reaching the fort in safety. On the same evening a sally was made by three hundred men against the Indian breast-work within less than a mile from the fort. This detachment was fiercely encountered by the savages and furiously repulsed, with the loss of seventy men killed and forty wounded. Captain Dalzel was among the slain.†

The whole number of troops lost during the siege of Detroit was but little short of three hundred, besides individuals unconnected with the army; the exact number, however, has never been correctly ascertained.

While these things were transpiring at the military posts, the whole frontier settlements, from north to south, were desolated with fire and blood. In Pennsylvania, "the whole country west of Shippensburg became the prey of the fierce barbarians. They set fire to houses, barns, corn, hay, and every thing

---

* See Doddridge, p. 217, 218. Also, Thatcher's Indian Biography, vol. ii., p. 92-107
† Idem.

which was combustible. The wretched inhabitants, whom they surprised at night, at their meals, or in the labors of the field, were massacred with the utmost cruelty and barbarity; and those who fled were scarcely more happy. Overwhelmed by sorrow, without shelter, or the means of transportation, their tardy flight was impeded by fainting women and weeping children. The inhabitants of Shippensburg and Carlisle, now become the barrier towns, opened their hearts and their houses to their afflicted brethren. In the towns, every stable and hovel was crowded with miserable refugees, who, having lost their houses, their cattle, and their harvest, were reduced from independence and happiness to beggary and despair. The streets were filled with people; the men distracted by grief for their losses, and the desire of revenge, more poignant from the disconsolate females and bereaved children who wailed around them. For some miles on both sides of the Susquehanna, many families, with their cattle, sought shelter in the woods, being unable to find it in the towns." The city of Philadelphia, as well as the adjoining counties, contributed largely to their relief.*

This state of things in Pennsylvania is only a specimen of what existed for more than eight hundred miles along the western frontier, as far south as Maryland and Virginia.

Among the hostilities in Pennsylvania during the early part of this war, we must enumerate the horrible massacre of the whole population of the Valley of Wyoming, on the east branch of the Susquehanna. At the same time, all the great branches of the Susquehanna were in the sole occupancy of the hostile Indians.

The plan of the Indian hostilities had embraced not only the destruction of all the western population, but likewise all the grain and growing crops, so as effectually to prevent a return of the inhabitants, who had generally fled from their homes to seek safety among the older settlements.

Among the first massacres in Western Virginia during this war were those of "Muddy Creek" and "Big Levels," upon the upper tributaries of the Greenbrier River. The people of these remote settlements, distant alike from the Atlantic border and from the country occupied by the Indians, had received no intelligence of a renewal of hostilities until they were overwhelmed in destruction. Presuming that the treaty

* Gordon's History of Pennsylvania, p. 399.

of 1763 had pacified the whole Indian confederacy, the settlers in these remote regions entertained no apprehension of danger. In this state of security, they felt no alarm when they beheld their settlement visited by nearly sixty Indians under the guise of friendship. The Indians were received with that cordial hospitality so common to the frontier people.

At Muddy Creek, suddenly, and without any previous hostile indication, after a refreshing meal, they commenced killing all the men in the settlement, and made prisoners of the women and children.

Having secured the prisoners under a suitable guard, the party proceeded to the "Big Levels," about fifteen miles distant, and before any intimation of the fate of Muddy Creek had preceded them. At this settlement they were treated with great hospitality and friendship. Archibald Glendennen gave them a sumptuous feast upon a fat elk which he had recently killed. At the conclusion of their feast, they began, without ceremony or provocation, to murder all the men, and to secure the women and children as prisoners, as they had done at Muddy Creek.*

In the massacre at Big Levels, the signal was given by a chief, as follows: An old woman, who had a sore leg, showed it to the Indian, and requested his advice how it might be cured. After examining the sore, without ceremony he drew his hatchet, and laid her lifeless at his feet by a single blow upon the head. This was the signal for the general assault, and the massacre was instantly commenced.

When these disasters became known in Botetourt county several days afterward, a party of volunteer armed men assembled, who went to the desolate settlements and buried the dead bodies, which, till that time, lay scattered where they had fallen, except that of Glendennen, which had been imperfectly buried by his wife.†

As late as the 22d of June, the Indians were still committing

---

* Doddridge's Notes, p. 222.

† Mrs. Glendennen was among the prisoners. She boldly charged the Indians with cowardice, and upbraided them with treachery in assuming the mask of friendship to commit murder. One of the Indians, exasperated with her boldness and the truth of her charge, brandished his tomahawk over her head, and then slapped her husband's scalp in her face. Next day, after marching ten miles with the captives, she escaped from the Indians in passing a thicket, leaving her infant with the enemy. Her absence soon after was discovered by the cry of the child for its mother, when one of the savages, taking the child in his hands, and saying he would soon bring *the cow to her calf*,

Vol. I.—Y

depredations and murders in the vicinity of Fort Cumberland, on the Potomac; and nine persons had been killed within the last ten days. At this time the whole population of this region, to the number of nearly five hundred families, on the frontiers, poor and destitute, leaving all behind, had fled to the eastern settlements.* Indeed, the whole western frontier, for nearly a thousand miles, from north to south, presented a scene of unprecedented terror and flight.

On the 23d of June, Fort Ligonier, on the west side of the Laurel Hill, and sixty miles east of Fort Pitt, was invested by a large body of Indians, who kept up a vigorous attack for twenty-four hours. On the 27th of July, Fort Loudon, on the site of the present town of Winchester, in Virginia, and not more than one hundred feet square, contained more than two hundred women and children, who had sought its shelter from the scalping-knife.

At this time, Shippensburg and Carlisle, in Pennsylvania, not thirty miles west of Harrisburg, were frontier towns; and all the remote settlements west of them had been broken up, and the inhabitants had fled eastward for safety. The few who remained were secured in stations, or strong palisade inclosures, from the midnight attacks of savage bands prowling for scalps and plunder.

At the same time, "Greenbrier River and Jackson River were depopulated," and nearly three hundred persons had been killed or taken prisoners by the Indians. Not one family was found on their plantations on this frontier, for three hundred miles in length and one hundred in width. By the consternation which had spread in this region, nearly twenty thousand persons were thrown out of house and home, to seek shelter and safety east of the mountains.†

Late in July, such was the state of public apprehension and alarm at the secret incursions of scalping parties of Indians, that the smallest circumstance often caused great alarm. In the eastern part of New York, about the last of July, a party of men having returned from a deer hunt over the western hills, in the vicinity of Goshen, suddenly fired four guns in quick

---

dashed out its brains against a tree. The mother having made her escape, returned to the settlement and imperfectly buried her husband, when she found herself the only survivor remaining of both settlements, alone in the midst of a dreary wilderness, and surrounded by the mangled bodies of her friends and neighbors.—Doddridge, p. 223.

* Thatcher's Indian Biography, vol. i., p. 112.   † Idem, p. 113.

succession at a flock of partridges. The reports having been heard in the vicinity, were supposed to indicate the approach of Indians, and alarm-guns were fired over the whole neighborhood, and the people commenced an immediate and general flight, until the whole settlements were in utter confusion and consternation. Those in their houses gathered up what they could carry, and with their children sought safety in flight; those who were with their teams in the fields cut the horses loose in haste, and made their escape with them; those who had no boats to cross the river plunged in with their wives or children on their backs. In this manner the consternation spread from one to another, until nearly five hundred families had left their homes and property, as they supposed, to the mercy of the Indians. Some continued their flight to the borders of New England before they were undeceived.

Early in October, about twenty persons had been killed by Indians in the vicinity of Allenstown and Bethlehem, on Lehigh River, in Pennsylvania; and such was the general consternation, that "most of the people in the vicinity had fled from their habitations."*

It is not our design to recount all the deeds of blood and cruelty perpetrated upon the frontier people by the hostile Indians. The feelings of humanity are shocked, and recoil at the recitation of them. The sketch already given may serve to convey a faint idea of the calamities endured by the wretched inhabitants subject to the horrors of Indian warfare.

During the following winter, detached scalping parties of Indians continued to traverse the border regions, and to prowl about the forts on the western parts of Pennsylvania, Virginia, and North Carolina, committing such depredations and murders as served to keep the whole exposed population in a state of continual dread and fearful apprehension for their personal safety.

Although the savages at all times, in their hostile incursions upon the settlements, commit the most inhuman barbarities upon the helpless and unprotected, there are among the frontier people occasionally men equally depraved, and who in deeds of blood are scarcely superior to the most ferocious savages. In some instances, indeed, the whites, exasperated to phrensy by the repeated murders atrociously perpetrated upon

* See Thatcher's Indian Biography, vol. ii., p. 113, 114.

their friends and relatives by the savages, have been impelled, by feelings of revenge, to deeds of blood at which humanity weeps. Such was the phrensied revenge of the "Paxton Boys." These desperadoes, prompted by a fanatical delusion, that the massacre of Wyoming was a judgment from God for "sparing the Canaanites in the land," organized themselves into a bandit corps, and, disregarding law or any civil authority of the state, proceeded to commit the most revolting barbarities upon the peaceable and innocent Conestago Indians, as a retaliation for the acts perpetrated by the hostile tribes. Dr. Doddridge says, "They rivaled the most ferocious of the Indians themselves in deeds of cruelty which have dishonored the history of our country; shedding innocent blood without the slightest provocation, in deeds of the most atrocious barbarity."*

The Conestago Indians were the remains of the Conestago tribe, the early friends of William Penn, whose descendants, for more than a century, had lived in peace and friendship with the whites. This remnant of a tribe, about forty in number, were the first victims of this infuriate and demoniacal band. They were murdered in cold blood, in the midst of a civil government too weak to protect the weakest.

The same vengeance would have been wreaked equally upon the peaceable and inoffensive Christian Indians of the villages of Wequetank and Nain, had not the state authorities at length succeeded in protecting them.†

[A.D. 1764.] Such had been the disasters to the British

* Doddridge's Notes on Virginia, p. 220.

† Although this subject is properly beyond the limits of our prescribed history, yet, as it is connected with the Indian hostilities of 1763, we will take this further notice of this bandit corps. This band, laboring under a delusion which had been encouraged by certain fanatics, that it was their duty to exterminate the Indians, as Joshua did the Canaanites of old, organized into a military band, and set all law at defiance. On the 14th day of December, 1763, fifty-seven of these men, in military array, entered the Conestago village about daybreak, and immediately, with the most cruel barbarity, murdered every soul that was found in the village, amounting in all to fourteen, including women and children. The remainder of them happened to be absent about the white settlements, and were taken in charge by the civil authorities, who placed them in the jail of Lancaster for protection. But this precaution was unavailing; the Paxton Boys broke open the jail, and murdered the whole, to the additional number of nearly twenty. In vain did the poor, defenseless creatures, upon their knees, protest their innocence and implore mercy. Nor did the death of these victims satisfy these fiends in human shape; they mangled the dead bodies with scalping-knives and tomahawks in the most savage and brutal manner. Even the children were scalped, and their feet and hands chopped off with tomahawks. The authorities of Pennsylvania removed the Indians of Wequetank and Nain, under a strong guard, to Phil-

arms, and such the consternation and slaughter in the provinces during the past year, that the English government, as well as the provinces, had determined to prosecute the war with vigor, and to give security to the frontier settlements during the next campaign by carrying the war, with fire and desolation, into the enemy's country.

Early in the spring, active preparations were in operation throughout the provinces for the chastisement of the hostile Indians, and for the protection of the frontiers from the merciless fury of savage warfare. Troops were fast concentrating upon the remote posts near the lakes, and upon the Ohio region.

Early in June, General Bradstreet, with three thousand troops, reached Fort Niagara on his route to re-enforce the garrisons in the western posts. While at Niagara, the Indians from the northwest made overtures for peace, and the general demanded of them a grand council, to confirm their professions by a treaty of peace. At length nearly two thousand Indians were assembled near Fort Niagara, and among them were representatives and chiefs from twenty-two nations, and embracing those from eleven of the remote northwestern tribes. A treaty was soon after concluded between his majesty's superintendent of Indian affairs, Sir William Johnson, on the part of Great Britain, and the chiefs, sachems, and warriors of the respective tribes. The treaty stipulates for peace and friendship, and a cession of certain lands to Great Britain lying south of Lakes Ontario and Erie.* But Pontiac was not there, nor would he sanction the treaty.

General Bradstreet sailed from Detroit, and, after a narrow escape from shipwreck with his whole army on Lake Erie, off the present city of Cleveland, he arrived safely at Detroit. Af-

---

adelphia, where they remained under guard, either in the barracks or state-prison, for more than one year, or from November, 1763, to December, 1764. During this time, the Paxton Boys assembled in force several times for the purpose of assaulting the barracks and wresting the helpless Indians from the guard, to gratify their thirst for blood. The preparation and show of firmness by the military in their defense prevented an assault. In this instance, as in all other outrages against the rights and persons of the Indians, the civil authorities of the States have interfered in their behalf against the ferocity of the white man.

The Paxton Boys at length began to commit outrages upon their fellow-citizens; and such was the terror inspired by their acts and threats, that no man felt safe to act or speak against them.—See Doddridge's Notes.

For a more full account of this bandit clan and their fanaticism, see Proud's History of Pennsylvania, vol. ii., p. 325–330. Also, Gordon's Pennsylvania, p. 405.

* Gordon's History of Pennsylvania, p. 438.

ter making several incursions against hostile towns, and chastising several bands of hostile warriors, opposed to the late treaty, overtures of peace were received from them. Negotiations for a truce were opened, which soon after resulted in a peace with all the northwestern tribes, except the Shawanese and Delawares of the Scioto. Pontiac would take no part in the treaty, and remained adverse to peace. Soon afterward he retired to the Illinois River, where he still meditated vengeance against the English for nearly twelve months afterward. He continued to reside on the Illinois until the summer of 1767, when he was assassinated in the council-house by a Peoria chief.*

In the mean time, Colonel Bouquet invaded the Indian country south of Lake Erie, and upon the branches of the Muskingum River. Marching from Fort Pitt on the 3d of October, he advanced through the Indian territory, spreading terror and death among the savages, destroying their fields and burning their towns, until the 25th of October, when he encamped at the Forks, or junction of the Tuscarawa and Walhonding Rivers.† Here he received overtures of peace, which were accepted, and he dictated his terms to the hostile tribes of the Delawares, Senecas, and Shawanese.‡

The surrender of prisoners, which had been one of the first requisitions, took place soon afterward; the Indians surrendered two hundred and six prisoners, men, women, and children, and delivered over hostages for the surrender of others. Peace being thus ratified with these tribes, Colonel Bouquet returned with his victorious army and his rescued captives to Fort Pitt, to the great joy of all the provinces.

General Stanwix, who had succeeded to the command of the northwestern army, had taken measures for convening a grand council of the western tribes, and specially of the Six Nations and their confederates, to be held in the month of November, at the "German Flats," on the Mohawk River. The council accordingly convened, and the chiefs, warriors, and sachems of the Six Nations therein ratified and confirmed the previous treaty of Niagara, and entered into a general article of friendship and alliance with the British crown, as they had formerly done with the King of France.

By this treaty, designated as the "Treaty of the German

---

* Thatcher's Indian Biography, vol. ii., p. 107. † Gordon's Pennsylvania, p. 436.
‡ American Pioneer, vol. i., p. 240.

Flats," the Six Nations ceded extensive tracts of land to the English provinces of New York and Pennsylvania. On the 5th day of December following, the treaty was proclaimed throughout the provinces, and peace was established with the Six Nations and their confederates.

CHAPTER II.

ADVANCE OF THE ANGLO-AMERICAN POPULATION TO THE OHIO RIVER.—SETTLEMENTS AND EXPLORATIONS.—A.D. 1765 TO 1774.

Argument.—Settlements spring up near the military Routes and Posts.—Fort Pitt.—Fort Burd.—Isolated Condition of the Illinois Settlements.—Advance of white Settlements upon the Sources of the Susquehanna, Youghiogeny, and Monongahela; also upon New River and Greenbrier, Clinch and Holston.—Indian Territory on the Susquehanna, Alleghany, and Cheat Rivers.—Frontier Settlements of Virginia in 1766.—Emigration to the Monongahela in 1767.—Redstone Fort a garrisoned Post.—Increase of Emigration in 1768.—Settlements extend to the Sources of the two Kenhawas.—The colonial System of granting Lands east of the Ohio.—The Indians become impatient of the white Man's Advance.—Mode of conciliating Indians for their Lands.—Remonstrance of the Six Nations to the King's "Indian Agent."—The Subject of their Complaint laid before the provincial Legislature.—Treaties with northern and southern Indians ordered by royal Government.—"Treaty of Fort Stanwix."—The "Mississippi Company" of Virginia, 1769.—"Treaty of Hard Labor" with Cherokees.—Extensive Claims to Territory set up by the English under the "Treaty of Fort Stanwix" with the Six Nations.—Settlements advance to the Holston and Clinch Rivers.—Impatience of northern and southern Indians at the Advance of the Whites.—Explorations of Dr. Walker west of Cumberland Mountains, in 1768; of Finley, in 1769; of Colonel Knox.—"Long-Hunters."—Western Emigration encouraged by royal colonial Governments.—Emigration to Holston, Clinch, and to West Florida, in 1770.—Fort Pitt a garrisoned Post.—Settlements at Redstone Fort, on Ohio, at Wheeling, and other Points, in 1770.—Enthusiasm of eastern Settlements for western Emigration.—Territory claimed by Virginia.—Emigrants from North Carolina advance upon the Sources of Holston River.—Impatience of the Cherokees.—"Treaty of Lochaber."—New boundary Line.—The four hundred acre Settlement Act of Virginia, passed in 1770.—"District of West Augusta" organized.—Cresap's Settlement at Redstone "Old Fort," in 1771.—Provisions fail.—The "Starving Year" of 1772.—Settlements on the Ohio above the Kenhawa.—Route from eastern Settlements to the Ohio.—Manner of traveling.—Emigration to the West increases greatly in 1773.—To Western Virginia.—To "Western District" of North Carolina.—To West Florida.—Numerous Surveyors sent out to Kentucky.—Thomas Bullitt, Hancock Taylor, M'Afee.—Surveys near Frankfort, Harrodsburg, and Danville.—Captain Bullitt at the Falls of Ohio.—Settlements on the Holston, East Tennessee.—Daniel Boone attempts to introduce white Families from North Carolina.—Driven back by Indians.—Emigration in 1774 to the Upper Ohio; on the Monongahela, Kenhawa, and Kentucky Regions.—Simon Kenton at May's Lick.—James Harrod at Harrodsburg.—West Augusta in 1774.—Outrages of lawless white Men provoke Indian Vengeance.—Wheeling Fort built.—Fort Fincastle.—Dr. Connolly Commandant of West Augusta.

[A.D. 1765.] No sooner had peace with the northwestern Indians been established, than the restless population of the provinces began to move forward to the western side of the mountains. Settlements soon began to spring up around the military posts and upon the roads leading to these remote points. The garrisons were in the receipt of their monthly pay, which they drew only to expend; and those who could most contribute to the wants and comforts of the troops were sure to receive their money. A few months of peace and security served to produce the germs of trading and manufacturing towns near the military posts; and agricultural pursuits became indispensable to their subsistence and comfort. The garrisons, no less than the frontier villagers, required the aid of the various mechanical trades adapted to new settlements, as well as the more indispensable articles of grain and culinary vegetables, with the flesh of domestic animals, and milk. Hence the husbandman derived employment and profit by a residence near the remote posts. The route to each, from the old settlements, was traveled by troops and caravans with supplies, conducted by government agents, and followed by hundreds of adventurers who were anxious to explore the beautiful and fertile regions of the Ohio and its great tributaries. This gave occasion for taverns, or public houses, on the road; and to support these in a manner adequate to the demands of the increasing intercourse, farms were opened, mills were erected, and mechanics were employed. Hence settlements were gradually formed along the main routes which led from the eastern settlements westward through the wilderness. At first they were at distances for a day's journey; but these distances were soon divided, and "half-way houses" sprung up at the distance of half a day's travel; these distances were again reduced by intermediate houses, which enabled the emigrant and traveler to consult his ease and convenience in making his journey. The increasing spirit for western emigration from the Atlantic provinces soon brought crowds of families and adventurers from the sandy shores of Delaware and Maryland, to seek ease and competence upon the fertile valleys and bottoms west of the mountains. The intelligent and virtuous, reared in ease and competence, allured by the glowing descriptions of the fertile West, sought to better their condition in a new region; the profligate and vicious, impatient of the wholesome restraints of law and good government, also sought the remote population where those restraints are unknown.

[A.D. 1766.] Thus, in a few years after the close of Pontiac's war, small settlements had extended upon all the great routes to the west; those from the north converging to Fort Pitt, and those from the south leading to the head waters of the Holston and Clinch Rivers. Already a town had been laid out on the east bank of the Monongahela, within two hundred yards of Fort Pitt, upon the site of a village which had been destroyed two years before by the hostile savages.* A route had been opened to the Monongahela, in the vicinity of "Redstone Old Fort," near the mouth of Dunlap's Creek, seventy miles above Fort Pitt. This point was soon to become an important place of embarkation for emigrants from the Atlantic seaboard, in their advance to the Ohio River and the western country generally.†

These were the extreme frontier settlements of the British provinces in this quarter. Beyond them, and more than a thousand miles in advance of any organized colonial government, were the isolated settlements on the Wabash and Illinois Rivers, comprising a few poor and ignorant French colonies. They had fallen under the dominion of the English crown, but they were not regarded as a part of the English settlements. They formed only small detached military colonies, speaking a foreign language, and having little or no intercourse with the restless emigrants which were now crowding toward the Ohio. Hence they were visited only occasionally by officers or agents of the government, or by Indian traders and adventurers, to gratify a thirst for pecuniary gain, or an innate desire for distant rambles.‡

* See Imlay's America, Lond. ed., 1797, p. 448. This is quite a large and valuable work upon the early history, settlements, and statistics of the western country, up to the year 1786, by Major Imlay, formerly an officer in the British service. He made the tour of the western country about the year 1786, and collected and arranged such sketches of the western country and statistics as were accessible at that period.

† See American Pioneer, vol. ii., p. 59–62.

‡ Except the commandants sent to these posts, probably the first regular British agent sent to these remote settlements was Colonel George Croghan, by way of Fort Pitt and the Ohio River, in the summer of 1765. Accompanied by a party of English soldiers, and deputies from the Shawanese, Delawares, and Senecas, and a party of friendly Indians, he set out in boats from Fort Pitt on the 15th of May, upon a mission to the western tribes, for the purpose of opening a friendly intercourse and trade with them, and to take observations of the country and the tribes inhabiting the western regions. The party coasted slowly down the Ohio, and on the 23d of May they encamped at the mouth of the Scioto, where they remained several days, awaiting the arrival of several French traders whose attendance at this point was expected. On the 30th they descended to the mouth of Licking River, and on the 31st they visited the Bigbone Lick, on the south side of the Ohio; here they witnessed the wide beaten roads

Settlements were now advancing rapidly from eastern portions of Pennsylvania, Maryland, and Virginia, and emigrants were pressing forward upon the upper tributaries of the Monongahela, upon the Youghiogeny or "Yough," and upon the great branches of Cheat River. On the south, the frontier counties of Virginia and North Carolina were pouring forth their hardy pioneers, who were still advancing, and already settling the fertile regions upon the head waters of New River, west of the mountains, as well as upon the sources of the Greenbrier. Others, full of enterprise and love of western adventure, were exploring the country drained by the great branches of Clinch River, and were forming remote, isolated settlements in Powell's Valley, still further north and west, and also upon the waters of the North Fork of Holston, in the regions near the present towns of Abington and Wytheville.

At this time the principal sources of the Susquehanna in New York and in Pennsylvania, as well as the whole region drained by the Alleghany River and its tributaries, were deep Indian solitudes, wholly in possession of the native tribes, and rarely frequented by the most advanced pioneer. A large portion

leading from the lick to the upper portion of Licking River, made by the herds of buffalo which then frequented the country. On the first of June they were at the "falls of the Ohio;" on the 6th of June they arrived at the mouth of the Wabash. Here they found a breast-work, supposed to have been erected by the Indians. Six miles further, they encamped at a place called the "Old Shawanese Village," upon or near the present site of Shawneetown, which perpetuates its name. At this place they remained six days, for the purpose of opening a friendly intercourse and trade with the Wabash tribes; and while here, Colonel Croghan sent messengers with dispatches for Lord Frazer, who had gone from Fort Pitt as commandant at Fort Chartres, and also to M. St. Angé, the former French commandant at that place.

On the 6th of June, at daybreak, they were attacked by a party of eighty warriors, chiefly Kickapoos and Musquatamies, by whom several of the party were killed, and nearly all of the remainder wounded. Besides, they were plundered of all their clothing, provisions, goods, and money. From this point they set out for Vincennes by land; and, passing through wooded hills and uplands, and wide-spreading prairies, they arrived at the post of St. Vincent on the 9th of June. Here they found eighty or ninety French families settled upon the east bank of the river, where they tarried several days. From St. Vincent they proceeded by land up the Wabash for 210 miles to Ouiatenon. the upper French settlement, which was also protected by a small fort. The settlement at this place comprised about fourteen families. They arrived at this post on the 23d of June, and remained some days, forming amicable relations and instituting commercial arrangements. From this point they set out for the region of the Maumee, and passing over the dividing ridges between the head-streams of the Wabash and the Maumee, they descended the latter stream to the lake. After some delay on the shores of Lake Erie, they set out by water to Detroit, where they arrived on the 17th of August. Detroit then was a large stockaded village, containing about eighty houses of all kinds.—For a copy of Croghan's Journal, see Butler's Kentucky, second edition, Appendix, 459-471.

of the regions lying upon the Cheat and Monongahela Rivers was still in possession of the Indians, and had never been relinquished by treaty, although the impatient Anglo-Americans were already crowding them from its beautiful valleys and romantic hills.

In Virginia, the counties of Rockbridge, Augusta, Greenbrier, and Frederic, lying west of the Blue Ridge, were frontier regions, occupied by a sparse population, exposed to the dangers of savage massacre upon any sudden outbreak of Indian vengeance; the towns of Staunton, Lexington, and Winchester were remote frontier trading-posts, inhabited by a few pioneers, who formed a connecting link between the Indians and the eastern people of Virginia. Not ten years before, Winchester had been an extreme frontier stockade post, erected for the protection of a few wretched families who were crowded into it, and were in daily apprehension of Indian massacre.* Staunton had been first laid off as a town in the year 1761, and was still a frontier village; Cumberland, in Maryland, also was a frontier military post, more than sixty miles in advance of the old settlements near Hagerstown, and fifty miles in the rear of the settlements which were then advancing upon the sources of the Youghiogeny and Cheat Rivers.

[A.D. 1767.] The following year witnessed a gradual advance of settlements down the valleys of the Youghiogeny and Cheat Rivers, and upon the Monongahela itself. This region soon became a focus of emigration from Maryland, Pennsylvania, and Northern Virginia; and the fine undulating bottoms and rolling intervals, with their limpid streams, leaping along over rocky bottoms, figured in the narratives of those who returned to visit their eastern friends, until all were filled with the bright visions of future wealth which seemed to open to their excited fancy. The intelligent, the enterprising, and the young were foremost in the throng which eagerly looked beyond the mountains for wealth and happiness, and the old and sedate could not remain behind their children and friends.

To protect the growing settlements, and check their impatient advances, as much as to observe the disposition and movements of the jealous savages, a small military post had been erected at Redstone Old Fort, and was still occupied by a suitable garrison.† The Indians looked with a jealous eye upon the ad-

* Sparks's Writings of Washington, vol. ii., p. 151, 161; vol. xxiv., 241–250.
† See Butler's History of Kentucky, second edition, p. 48, Introduction.

vance of the countless immigrants, no less than the formation of new settlements and stockades in the heart of their territory, which they had never relinquished formally to the white man.

Still the tide of emigration continued to move to the West, and settlements began to multiply upon the lower tributaries of the Monongahela, while others were busily engaged in exploring other regions for the location of future settlements, to be taken up subsequently by military warrants, by special grants, and by right of settlement or first occupancy.

[A.D. 1768.] With the approbation of the British crown, the provincial government had issued script and military warrants without number since the close of Pontiac's war, besides many extensive claims anterior to that period. All these were to be located upon the waters of the Ohio, within the region claimed to be within the chartered limits of Virginia and Pennsylvania, and hundreds of surveyors and agents were constantly employed in exploring, selecting, and locating for the respective claimants. Some grants had been made before the French war, and hundreds of military warrants had been issued before the French troops retired from Fort Duquesne. In none of the provinces had the infatuation for western lands been carried to a greater extent than in the province of Virginia. In a report made to the executive council of Virginia in 1757, by John Blair, secretary of the council, he states, the quantity of lands then entered to companies and individuals, as indicated by the records, amounted to *three millions of acres*, a large portion of which had been granted as early as the year 1754.* Subsequent to the treaty of German Flats, in 1764, the number of grants and land-warrants issued by the colonial authorities multiplied astonishingly.

It is impossible to form a correct estimate of the land mania which seemed to pervade the middle colonies, from the commencement of the first explorations on the Ohio until the beginning of Lord Dunmore's war in 1774. The province of Virginia invariably took the lead in all movements for the occupancy of the western lands. As early as 1744, two commissioners from Virginia, Colonel Thomas Lee and Colonel William Beverly, with others from Pennsylvania and Maryland, convened a portion of the Six Nations at Lancaster, Pennsylvania, for the purpose of treating with them for the sale and

---

* See North American Review, No. 104, for July, 1839, p. 100.

relinquishment of large bodies of land extending west of the settlements in the three provinces, from the Susquehanna to the Potomac. After a liberal use of whisky-punch, "bumbo," and wine, of which the Indians partook freely, the treaty was duly read and signed by the parties respectively. The amount paid the Indians for signing this treaty was two hundred and twenty pounds on the part of Maryland, and two hundred pounds on the part of Virginia, both in Pennsylvania currency, besides sundry presents, and abundance of whisky-punch and "bumbo."

When it was afterward ascertained that the Indians charged fraud in the treaty, and denied the relinquishment of the *extensive regions* claimed by the provinces in virtue of its stipulations, an effort was made to reconcile and appease the indignation of the savages by means of a subsequent treaty. For this purpose, three commissioners from Virginia, Colonels Fry, Lomax, and Patton, with others from the other two provinces, repaired to "Logstown," on the north bank of the Ohio, seventeen miles below the mouth of the Monongahela. The few Indians who attended this treaty, and others subsequently held at Winchester and other places, indignantly refused to ratify the treaty of Lancaster, although urged thereto by earnest entreaties, supported by the promise of money, and many valuable presents and trinkets for Indian use.

In all these treaties, whether ratified or rejected, the Virginians appear to have been determined to coerce a relinquishment of the Indian lands, either by fair means or foul, and no effort of negotiation or intrigue was omitted to accomplish this purpose.

Notwithstanding the Indian title had not been extinguished to the lands which were already occupied by settlements, which were gradually extending over them, the tide of emigration still flowed into the West, and parties of woodsmen, explorers, and surveyors were distributed over the whole country east of the upper portion of the Ohio. Regardless of the Indians' rights, and deaf to their remonstrances, the settlements and explorations continued to advance. Occasionally, lawless men committed outrages upon the persons and property of the Indians, and thereby provoked the tribes generally to unite and assert their rights, as the common cause of the whole confederacy. Beyond the restraints of law, the evil propensities of disorderly men were virtually encouraged to indulge in additional encroachments upon the unprotected Indians. Outrages upon their persons and property in these remote regions consequently became more frequent.

The Indians, finding themselves without recourse or appeal to any tribunal, at length became impatient and exasperated at the repeated aggressions of lawless white men. They had expressed their dissatisfaction in no measured terms, and evinced a strong inclination to resist the encroachment of the whites by a resort to arms, as the *certain mode of enforcing* respect to their demands and to their rights. Heretofore they had repeatedly remonstrated to the agents of the British crown specially charged with the Indian affairs, and to the commandants of the western posts; but their representations had been disregarded, and their injuries unredressed, until self-preservation and revenge began to rouse them from their temporary slumber.

By the opening of the spring of 1768, the Indians along the whole line of the western frontier, from the sources of the Susquehanna to those of the Tennessee, became exasperated, and united in their determination to check further encroachments, and to enforce an observance of their rights. Still they refrained from open hostilities, while the restless population of the Atlantic border continued to press forward into the Ohio country, regardless alike of the rights of the Indians and the proclamation of the king,* issued five years previously.

At length, on the 6th of May, a deputation of the "Six Nations" presented to the "deputy superintendent of Indian affairs" at Fort Pitt a formal remonstrance against the continued encroachments of the whites upon lands which of right, and without doubt, belonged to the Indians. That officer with promptness forwarded the remonstrance to the colonial government, and the whole subject was laid before the royal government without delay. On the 31st of May, the president of the king's council of Virginia brought the subject before the representatives of the province for their immediate action, as one which endangered the peace and security of the colony.

In his communication to the colonial Legislature, he informed them "That a set of men, regardless of the laws of natural jus-

---

* This refers to the proclamation of 1763, prohibiting settlements beyond the sources of the Atlantic streams, and which was still in force.

tice, unmindful of the duties they owe to society, and in contempt of the royal proclamations, have dared to settle themselves upon the lands near Redstone Creek and Cheat River, *which are the property of the Indians;* and notwithstanding the repeated warnings of the danger of such lawless proceedings, and the strict and spirited injunctions to desist and quit their unjust possessions, they still remain unmoved, and seem to defy the orders, and even the powers of the government."*

The authority of the colonial government was exerted to quiet the jealous apprehensions of the Indians, and to restrain further acts of aggression on the part of the frontier people, until the royal government should act in the matter.

At length, the subject having been duly considered by the royal government, orders were issued near the close of summer to Sir William Johnson, " superintendent of Northern Indian affairs," instructing him to call together the chiefs, warriors, and sachems of the tribes more especially interested, for the purpose of purchasing from them the lands already occupied by the king's subjects.

Agreeably to these instructions, Sir William Johnson convened the delegates of the Six Nations and their confederates at Fort Stanwix,† where a treaty of peace and relinquishment of lands was concluded in the month of November following. By this treaty, as the English allege, for and in consideration of certain goods of divers kinds, and other valuable presents to them paid, the Indians did relinquish to the king large bodies of land in the provinces of Pennsylvania and Virginia, extending from the Alleghany Mountains westward to the Ohio River, and thence westward, on the south side of the same, to the mouth of the Cherokee or Tennessee River. This construction of the treaty was firmly resisted by the Indians, as being a fraud upon them.

At the same time, John Stewart, Esq., " superintendent of Southern Indian affairs," had received instructions to assemble the Southern Indians in like manner, for the purpose of establishing a boundary line between them and the whites. He accordingly concluded a treaty with the Cherokees at " Hard Labor," in South Carolina, on the 14th day of October. By this

* See Butler's Kentucky, Appendix, p. 475.

† Fort Stanwix occupied the site of the present town of Utica, formerly Fort Schuyler, in Oneida county, New York, high up the Mohawk River. See American Pioneer, vol. ii., p. 391.

treaty, the Cherokees agreed that the southwestern boundary of Virginia should be a line "extending from the point where the northern line of North Carolina intersects the Cherokee hunting-grounds, about thirty-six miles east of Long Island, in the Holston River, and thence extending in a direct course, north by east, to Chiswell's Mine, on the east bank of the Kenhawa River, and thence down that stream to its junction with the Ohio River."

[A.D. 1769.] This line, however, did not include all the settlements then existing within the present limits of the State of Virginia. Those formed northwest of the Holston, and upon the branches of Clinch and Powell's Rivers, were still within the limits of the Indian territory. This fact being ascertained, a subsequent treaty became necessary for the adjustment of a new boundary, and the remuneration of the savages for an additional extent of country.

A large portion of the lands south of the Ohio, claimed by the English in virtue of the treaty of Fort Stanwix, were, in fact, lands to which the Six Nations had *no exclusive claim*, they being the "common hunting-grounds" of the Cherokees and Chickasâs also. Yet the Ohio River was urged as the proper boundary between the white settlements and the Indians on the west, and the latter were finally compelled to acquiesce in the English construction of the limits.*

Yet, at the time of the treaty at Fort Stanwix, the Indians never intended to relinquish all the lands between the mountains and the Ohio River. They were compelled first to admit the English construction, and afterward to plead it against further encroachments. The Cherokees had been peaceable and friendly since the close of the French war; but the western people of North Carolina and Virginia were again beginning to encroach upon them.† Settlements were advancing upon the sources of the Holston and Clinch Rivers, and upon the waters of Powell's River, east of the Cumberland Mountains, and beyond the established boundary. Although the Cherokees refrained from open war, yet they looked with a jealous eye upon the advances which the white population were now beginning to make upon the waters flowing westward.

The treaty of Fort Stanwix had quieted apprehension on

* Butler's Kentucky, Introduction, p. 50-52.   † Idem, p. 49.

account of Indian hostility in the north, at the same time it had given a *new impulse* to the spirit of emigration and exploration westward. The Indian title was claimed to have been extinguished to all lands east and south of the Ohio to an indefinite extent. Fame had represented the country west of the Cumberland Mountains as one of boundless fertility and inconceivable beauty; yet it was three hundred miles in advance of the most remote frontier settlements, and was claimed as the common hunting-grounds of the Northern and Southern Indians. That portion of Kentucky between the Kentucky and Cumberland Rivers could not be claimed under any treaty; it was the undisputed territory of the native tribes, and was claimed exclusively by the Cherokees and Chickasâs as their common hunting-ground. As both these tribes were powerful and warlike, they had excluded the white man's advance from this region; yet there were men of fearless spirit and hardy enterprise in the western settlements of North Carolina and Virginia, who were willing to "tempt the dangerous wilds," and to explore the enchanted plains of Kentucky. Still the "garden of Kentucky" was unknown to the white man, or known only by rumor; one Englishman only had seen the matchless country.

But the treaty of Fort Stanwix having revived the spirit of western emigration in a tenfold degree, explorers fearlessly penetrated this most remote district. The whole system of land speculation received a new impulse; new companies were formed on the most magnificent scale, and persons of all ranks and conditions embarked in the enterprise of a land crusade to the West. Companies were formed, and sent their united petitions to the king, praying for enormous grants, scarcely inferior to the early colonial charters. Among these was the first Anglo-American "Mississippi Company," formed and conducted chiefly by Francis Lightfoot Lee, Richard Henry Lee, George Washington, and Arthur Lee, all wealthy Virginians, besides nearly fifty other petitioners, who were to be joint stockholders in the contemplated grant. The grant required in this petition was no less than two and a half millions of acres, to be located upon the waters of the Ohio.* Arthur Lee, as special agent for the company, in December repaired

---

* Butler's Kentucky.—See Appendix, p. 175–177, for a copy of this petition and names.

with all haste to London, to lay the memorial and petition before the ministers; but finally, after great efforts and protracted delays, the company failed in their object. Yet Colonel George Washington, with his faithful and indefatigable agent and principal surveyor, Major William Crawford, were eagerly engaged, with hundreds of other claimants, in locating former grants and military warrants, until Indian hostilities again checked their operations.

About this time the first adventurers from North Carolina and Southern Virginia began to explore the valleys and plains northwest of the Cumberland Mountains, within the southern limits of the present State of Kentucky. During the summer of 1768, the fearless John Finley, an Indian trader from North Carolina, had pursued the route of Dr. Walker by way of Cumberland Gap, and had penetrated as far north and west as the Kentucky River. Here, on an eminence near the mouth of a tributary called Red River, he had erected a hut and opened a friendly intercourse with the Indians. He had also explored some of the beautiful plains of Kentucky, which he described in glowing colors to Daniel Boone, a hunter and woodsman settled upon the Yadkin River. In the fall of 1769, he returned to his former post, with Daniel Boone and John Stewart, accompanied by a party of hunters, who followed him as their guide, upon a hunting excursion. They pursued their route by way of the Holston River and Cumberland Gap, crossed Cumberland River near the mountains, and penetrated as far as Finley's trading-post, within the present limits of Clarke county, in the State of Kentucky. Here, from a lofty eminence on the north side of the Kentucky River, Daniel Boone first beheld "the beautiful level of Kentucky." The plains and forests abounded with wild beasts of every kind; deer and elks were common; the buffalo was seen in herds; and the plains were covered with the "richest verdure."

[A.D. 1770.] Stewart left his bones in Kentucky, the first victim of Indian resentment to the white man's advance into "the dark and bloody ground." Finley and Boone returned to the banks of the Yadkin. Their friends and neighbors were 'enraptured with the glowing descriptions given of the delightful country which they had discovered, and their imaginations were inflamed with the wonderful products which were yielded in such bountiful profusion. The sterile hills and rocky mountains of North Carolina began to lose their interest when compared with the fertile plains of Kentucky.

Nor did the southern portion of Kentucky escape exploration. The same summer had witnessed an excursion, conducted by Colonel James Knox, of North Carolina, to the remote regions west of the Cumberland Mountains. With a party of nine hunters and woodsmen, he passed the Cumberland Gap, and penetrated westward to the sources of Green River and upon the lower portion of the Cumberland, nearly one hundred miles south of the eminence from which Boone first beheld the plains of Kentucky. This party under Colonel Knox was absent several months, and was known among the western people of North Carolina as "*Long Hunters.*"*

While these explorations were being made in Kentucky, nearly three hundred miles west of the most advanced settlements of Virginia and North Carolina, and while the population was rapidly augmenting upon the sources of the Monongahela and Greenbrier from Northern Virginia and Maryland, the hardy pioneers of North Carolina were moving forward and forming settlements upon the Nolichucky, the French Broad, the Watauga, and other branches of the Holston, and upon the sources of New River. Others, filled with the spirit of emigration, deigned not to limit their movements to a few hundred miles. The Mississippi itself did not limit their journey. The English possessed the Floridas and the Illinois country. West Florida was bounded on the west, for more than two hundred miles, by the Mississippi River, and the branches of the Holston opened a direct water communication for nearly two thousand miles of circuitous but easy navigation. The crown of Great Britain desired to see the colonial population flow into Florida, and had held out inducements for settlers to emigrate from Carolina. Those emigrating from the western parts of North Carolina and Virginia could advance by land to the Holston, and there commence their voyage in flat-boats or barges, at Long Island, in the Cherokee nation, one hundred and fifty miles, by water, above the mouth of the French Broad.† The point of destination in West Florida was the upland region in the vicinity of the Walnut Hills, of Natchez, Bayou Sara, and Baton Rouge.

The British government, since the treaties of 1768, had

* Butler's Kentucky, p. 18, 19. † Imlay's America, p. 499

thrown off all disguise as to the occupancy of the western country, and the most alluring inducements were held out to western emigration. Western posts were maintained with military garrisons for the protection of the remote settlements against the effects of Indian jealousy and revenge. Although no evidence existed of any hostile designs on the part of the savages, Fort Pitt was occupied by two companies of "Royal Irish Infantry," under command of Captain Edmonson. This post at this time was a regular stockade fort, on two sides facing the Alleghany and Monongahela, defended by blockhouses and bastions. On the land side was a regular brick wall mounted with cannon, and surrounded by a wide and deep ditch.*

Before the close of the year 1770, settlements had advanced upon the Youghiogeny and Monongahela below the Red Stone Old Fort, and westward to the Ohio. They approached the Monongahela chiefly by Braddock's "Old Road," and to Red Stone Old Fort by the route opened by Colonel Burd ten years before. Brook county, in the western neck of Virginia, and Washington county, in Western Pennsylvania, had already received their first Anglo-American population. Others, still more daring, had descended the Ohio as far as Wheeling, and had commenced settlements in the limits of the present county of Ohio, more than ninety miles below Fort Pitt by the river channel. Among those who reached these remote regions for frontier residences were the three brothers, Jonathan, Ebenezer, and Silas Zane, besides many other woodsmen and pioneers. The same year Ebenezer Zane selected the present site of Wheeling as his location; another settlement was formed at the same time on Wheeling Creek, near the "Forks," a few miles above its mouth.†

Explorations for future settlements and locations of land were spreading upon the *western tributaries* of the Monongahela, upon the upper branches of the Great Kenhawa, the Greenbrier, and New Rivers, and also upon the Little Kenhawa, and upon Gauly River. The prospect of wealth and future independence in the fertile regions west of the mountains was sought in exchange for the comforts and conveniences of the older settlements, laboriously drawn from a meager soil.

---

* Sparks's Writings of Washington, vol. ii., p. 518.
† Butler's Kentucky, Introduction, p. 48, 49.

The West was a virgin soil, which would more than repay the temporary inconveniences of a new settlement, and afford a prospect of future competence to a rising family.

The same tide of emigration continued from the southern portions of Virginia and from North Carolina, flowing beyond the sources of the Yadkin and Catawba, and upon the upper branches of the north fork of Holston, and upon the tributaries of Clinch River, beyond the limits assigned to the white inhabitants by the treaty of Hard Labor in 1768. The settlements on Powell's River, and other western branches of Clinch River, were within the Indian territory, and the Cherokees began to remonstrate against the encroachment. To avoid Indian resentment, and to remove all occasion for hostilities on the part of the Cherokees, the superintendent of "Southern Indian Affairs" was instructed to convene a council of the chiefs, warriors, and head men of the nation, for the purpose of establishing *a new boundary* further west. Accordingly, the treaty of Lochaber was concluded and signed on the 18th of October, 1770, by which the Cherokees consent to a new boundary, to include the white population on Clinch River.

The *new line* commenced on the south branch of Holston River, six miles east of Long Island; thence it extended in a northwardly course to the mouth of the Great Kenhawa.[*] This was to be the western limit for the settlements of Virginia and North Carolina; and as yet the whole southwestern portion of Virginia was a wild and savage wilderness, with only a few scattered inhabitants upon the head waters of Holston and Clinch Rivers. The site of the present town of Abington was a frontier settlement.

The provincial Legislature of Virginia at its next session passed an act, which received the sanction of the royal governor, for the encouragement of western emigration. This act allowed every actual settler having a log-cabin erected, and any portion of ground in cultivation, the right to four hundred acres of land, so located as to include his improvement. A subsequent act extended the privilege much further, allowing the owner and occupant of each four hundred acre tract the preference right of purchasing one thousand acres adjoining him, at such cost as scarcely exceeded the expense of selecting it, and

---

[*] See Butler's Kentucky, p. 51. Also, Hall's Sketches, vol. ii., p. 256; and Treaty of Lochaber, p. 260.

having it designated by a regular survey. These acts greatly encouraged emigration to the West, where every man, with industry and perseverance, could not fail to secure himself a comfortable home, and a valuable estate for his children. Other provinces enacted similar laws for the purpose of occupying their western lands. Crowds of emigrants immediately advanced to secure the proffered bounty; and settlements and explorations rapidly spread upon all the eastern tributaries of the Ohio, from the Alleghany to the Cumberland River.

[A.D. 1771.] In the "District of West Augusta," the population of Virginia had already advanced from the extreme sources of the Monongahela westward to the Ohio River, and from Fort Pitt down to Big Grave Creek, and in many points still further. The remote, isolated settlements were provided with a strong block-house, or a secure stockade inclosing a compact village, or "station," for the general defense of the little colony. Although no hostile demonstrations had been made by the Indians, it was deemed requisite to observe every prudential measure to secure the helpless families against surprise and massacre.*

Among the emigrants upon the Monongahela, under the provision of the late pre-emption law for four hundred acres, was Captain Michael Cresap, who had been a soldier in the French war under Braddock, and in the subsequent campaign.* He was a man of undoubted courage, and had been an active defender of the frontier settlements during Pontiac's war. In the year 1771, he settled upon the site of Redstone Old Fort as his pre-emption claim, and erected the first shingled-roof house ever built in the town of Brownsville.

During the year 1771, such was the throng of emigrants to the new settlements in Western Virginia, upon the Youghiogeny, Monongahela, and Upper Ohio, as low as Big Grave Creek, that an alarming scarcity of every kind of breadstuff ensued. To such an extent had this dearth attained, that for more than six months, at least half of the entire population were compelled to sustain life by the use of meats, roots, vegetables, and milk, to the entire exclusion of all bread and grains. This period became memorable, in the history of the early population of this part of the country, as the "starving year." Nor did the settlements recover from the exhaustion,

* See American Pioneer, vol. ii., p. 62.

under the constant influx of immigrants, until the close of the year 1773, when abundant crops restored a supply of grain.

[A.D. 1772.] As yet the habitations were but sparsely distributed upon the Ohio below Big Grave Creek, and the whole region between the upper branches of the Monongahela and the Little Kenhawa was wholly in the occupancy of the Indians, except surveyors and exploring parties, who were continually traversing the country. The settlements were becoming more dense upon the branches of Cheat, the East branch of the Monongahela, and in Tygart's Valley, and also upon the upper tributaries of Greenbrier, Gauly, and Elk Rivers. The west branch of the Monongahela was wholly in the Indian country.

The tide of emigration to the Upper Ohio and the Youghiogeny advanced across the mountains through Pennsylvania, by way of Forts Bedford, Ligonier, and Loyal Hanna, while those from Virginia and Maryland advanced by way of Fort Cumberland and Redstone Old Fort. At that early period the greater portions of these routes lay through an uninhabited wilderness for more than two hundred miles. A wagon road was unknown west of the eastern settlements, and all beyond was a solitary horse-path, or "trace," winding through defiles and over mountains almost inaccessible.

Hence the early immigrants in the West were compelled to travel on horseback, in single file, carrying their small patrimony and personal effects upon the backs of pack-horses, driven likewise in single file. Most of those who traversed these "dangerous wilds" at this early period were fortunately encumbered with but a scanty share of this world's goods requiring transportation, unless it were "the poor man's boon," a thriving family. In most cases, one or two pack-horses were amply sufficient to bear all the personal effects across the mountains, and these were commonly but little more than a frying-pan or an iron pot, a wheel, a hoe, an ax, an auger, and a saw, besides a few blankets and bedding. The indispensable portion of each man's personal equipment was his rifle; his shot-pouch and powder-horn were a part of his wearing apparel.

If the pioneer emigrant were so happy as to possess a wife and a few children, an extra horse carried the one with her dowry, and another pack-horse, bestrode by two large hampers, bore the children to their western homes.

[A.D. 1773.] The next spring opened with a still stronger tide of emigration for the waters of the Ohio, both on the northern and on the southern limits of Virginia. The habitations upon the numerous branches and tributaries of the Ohio continued to multiply and extend. Those upon the sources of the Greenbrier and Gauly were gradually extending down those rivers, and upon the upper tributaries of the Little Kenhawa and Elk Rivers. Further west, upon the latter streams, companies of surveyors and explorers were busily engaged in selecting and locating lands for future settlements.*

Nor did the emigrants and explorers stop on the waters of the Upper Ohio. Hundreds were looking far beyond the present limits of Virginia. The British province of West Florida offered advantages not less than those of the Ohio region, and might be free from Indian hostilities and dangers. The mild and sunny climate of the Lower Mississippi had its charms for others, and there were not a few who had left their homes near the Atlantic coast, and were on their journey for the south. Before the summer of 1773 had passed, four hundred families from the Atlantic seaboard advanced through the wilderness to the Monongahela and Ohio Rivers, and descended in boats for the Natchez country.† During this year, also, in England a pamphlet had been published, in which the author highly extolled "the advantages of a settlement on the Ohio in North America."

During the early part of the summer, Lord Dunmore had sent out several parties of surveyors upon the Great Kenhawa, while others were sent as far west as the "Falls of Ohio," to locate military land-warrants and grants in the delightful regions upon the Kentucky River. Locations were made the same summer on the south side of the Kentucky River, near Frankfort, and as far south as the present town of Danville.‡

Among the enterprising pioneer surveyors sent to Kentucky this summer, were Hancock Taylor and Captain Thomas Bullitt, who, with a party of surveyors from southwestern Virginia, crossed the mountains to the Ohio River, by way of the Great Kenhawa. They reached the vicinity of the Ohio in the month of May, after which they spent several weeks in making surveys and explorations on the Kenhawa, until the 1st of July. About

---

* Butler's Kentucky, chap. ii., p. 20.   † Holmes's Annals, vol. ii., p. 185, 186.
‡ Butler's Kentucky, p. 23.

this time they were joined by the three brothers, James, George, and Robert M'Afee, who had left Botetourt county early in June, and had traveled westward across the country to New River, and thence along that river to the Kenhawa. Early in July this whole company of surveyors and woodsmen descended the Ohio in boats to "the falls." Here they soon afterward separated to their respective surveying districts.

The three M'Afees, with their party, proceeded in their boats and canoes up the Ohio to the mouth of Kentucky River, which they ascended as far as the site of the present city of Frankfort. Here they landed and encamped, and on the 16th day of July made their first survey of a tract of six hundred acres, including the ground upon which the city of Frankfort stands. This was the first survey made by white men on the Kentucky River. Other surveys were subsequently made by this company in the same vicinity, and further south, in the vicinity of Harrodsburg and Danville, and upon the sources of Salt River.*

In the mean time, Captain Bullitt had made his camp near the mouth of Bear-grass Creek; and, having made several locations and surveys in that vicinity, he resolved to provide for his future safety by conciliating the Indians, and thus preventing their jealous suspicions and revenge at the near approach of the white man's camp. He accordingly proceeded alone and on foot to the nearest Shawanese town on the Scioto, for the purpose of forming a friendly acquaintance with the Indians. He succeeded in his hazardous undertaking, and produced in the minds of the chiefs a favorable impression as to his feelings and object, before suspicion in the savage had ripened into jealousy.

After his return to camp, he proceeded in the month of August to lay off the plan for a town near the site of the present city of Louisville. This was the first town laid off in Kentucky by the early pioneers.

The tide of emigration was equally strong to the western portions of North Carolina, and within the limits now comprised in the eastern portion of East Tennessee. Settlements had extended down the north branch of Holston, upon the Nolichucky, French Broad, and Clinch Rivers, and, before the close of the year 1773, had spread along the western base of the Alleghany range, in a southwestern direction, for nearly one hundred and

* Butler's History of Kentucky, p. 20-22.

twenty miles, and nearly as far west as Long Island in the south fork of Holston.* South of Holston River settlements were rapidly extending upon the tributaries of the French Broad.

This year witnessed the first attempt to introduce white females and families into Kentucky, and the first decided indication from the Indians that *they would resist* the occupancy of the country. The fame of Kentucky had spread through the western settlements of North Carolina, and the restless population upon the waters of the Yadkin, New River, and Holston having heard the glowing accounts given by Boone and Finley, and confirmed by other hunters and pioneers, began to loathe their barren hills and contracted valleys, and to sigh for the beautiful and fertile plains of Kentucky; but as yet no family had ever attempted to advance west of the Cumberland range of mountains, although residences had already been made in Powell's Valley and on Powell's River, on the eastern side. That range was considered the boundary between the whites and the Cherokee hunting-grounds, as established by the treaty of Lochaber in 1770. The savage was jealous of further encroachments, and would not quietly permit intrusion under any pretext.

Late in the month of September, Daniel Boone, having collected a little colony of five families besides his own, willing to venture beyond the Cumberland Mountains, left the peaceful banks of the Yadkin to try the dangerous wilds of Kentucky. With these, equipped in pioneer style, the women and children mounted, with their baggage and luggage in the center of the procession, he proceeded on the hazardous journey for the southern portion of Kentucky, claimed by the warlike Cherokees.

After a tedious and hazardous travel of near two hundred miles over the most elevated and mountainous region of North Carolina and Southern Virginia, they reached Powell's Valley, on the east side of Cumberland range. Here they made a short stay before leaving the last vestige of civilized life, and little suspecting the dangers which lay before them in their journey. But the Indians, ever jealous of the white man's approach, had observed all their movements, and were cautiously preparing to cut them off at the proper time, should they continue to advance beyond the limits assigned for the white settlers.†

* See Winterbotham's America, vol. ii., p. 25, 26.
† At this time a few families had settled on Clinch River, about fifteen miles south-

Boone proceeded with his little colony, and as he advanced toward Cumberland Gap, about the 5th day of October, he was joined in Powell's Valley by forty armed hunters, who were anxious to explore the newly-discovered country west of the Cumberland range of mountains. The whole now formed a caravan of nearly eighty persons in number, and had advanced with fine spirits and joyful hearts until the 10th of October, when suddenly, while passing a narrow defile, they were startled by the terrific yell of Indians in ambuscade, by whom they were furiously assailed. The men flew to the protection of the helpless women and children, while others rushed to encounter the enemy in their coverts. A scene of confusion and consternation for a moment ensued; but the Indians, surprised at the fierce and resolute resistance of the men, soon fled in every direction.

The first fire of the Indians had killed six men and wounded the seventh. Among the first was the oldest son of Daniel Boone, a youth nearly twenty years old. This was a sad presage of the dangers before them, and the whole party fell back forty miles, to the nearest settlement on the Clinch River. Here the emigrant families remained until the termination of Lord Dunmore's war, near the close of the following year.*

[A.D. 1774.] But the country bordering upon the Ohio was considered free for emigrants from the older settlements. The Indian title had been extinguished by the treaty of Fort Stanwix, and by the laws of Virginia each emigrant was entitled to a fine landed estate, for the sole consideration of designating his selection by a small improvement upon it. Nor was it long before hundreds of hardy and fearless emigrants, from the western counties of Virginia and from the new settlements on the Monongahela and Kenhawa, determined to secure portions of the fertile regions of Kentucky. Parties of surveyors and pioneers began to descend the Ohio, for the purpose of making improvements and locations for future residences and farms.

The following spring presented upon the waters of the Monongahela and the sources of the two Kenhawas a continual scene of emigration, of parties of surveyors and explorers, dis-

west of Powell's Valley, which was the frontier settlement on this route, or within the limits of the Cherokee nation.

* See Marshall's Kentucky, vol. i., p. 20, 21. Butler's Kentucky, p. 28. Also, Flint's Life of Boone, p. 80.

tributed over all the region southwest of the principal forks of the Monongahela, and westward to the Ohio and the Great Kenhawa Rivers. Other parties were advancing further south, and westward to Kentucky; and a large number of surveyors and woodsmen had been sent to that region by Lord Dunmore, for the purpose of locating and selecting lands under royal grants and military warrants.

Among the first explorers and pioneers of Kentucky during the year 1774, we may enumerate Simon Kenton and his party, who explored the country from Limestone Creek, at the present site of Maysville, traversing the buffalo trace as far as the Lower Blue Licks. This trace he found opened by the herds of buffaloes, like a wide, beaten road, from May's Lick to the Licking River. Buffaloes were still common, and elk were frequently seen browsing upon the hills near the licks.*

Kenton returned to May's Lick, and selected a tract of land, upon which he made a "tomahawk improvement," including a camp and an acre of planted corn, near the present site of the town of Washington. But Indian hostilities, especially from the Shawanese, were already begun in Kentucky. Returning one evening to his camp from the day's excursion, he found that his companion, who had been left to guard the camp, had been killed and scalped, and his body, half consumed by fire, was still smoking upon the pyre.† His first care was to secure himself from ambuscade; after which, he was compelled to seek safety by retiring from Kentucky, and abandoning his improvement until the danger from the Indians should be less imminent.

As yet, no permanent settlement had been made in Kentucky, nor did the Indians intend to permit them to be made in their favorite hunting-grounds. No white man's house, *for residence*, had yet been erected, although hundreds had explored the country upon the Kentucky River, and marked their "tomahawk improvements." During the summer, however, James Harrod, from the Monongahela, selected a place, afterward known as "*Harrod's Station*," six miles from the present town of Harrodsburg, and soon afterward he erected the first house for a residence ever built by a white man in Kentucky. With his party, he had descended the Ohio in boats and canoes to the mouth of Kentucky River, which he ascended as far as

* M'Donald's Life of Kenton, ed. of 1843.   † Butler's Kentucky, p. 23.

"Harrod's Landing," where he disembarked for his settlement.*

Heretofore the principal object of all the explorers upon the waters of the Kentucky River had been to make pre-emption, or "tomahawk improvements," or to locate lands already granted by the provincial authorities. Tracts so selected were run off by the compass, or bounded by some branch or water-course, and marked by blazing a few trees with the tomahawk, planting a patch of corn, or erecting a temporary hut. Either of these was sufficient to indicate that the land had been already appropriated by an inchoate title. The house erected by James Harrod was a regular log-house, designed for the future residence of his family, when circumstances would justify their removal.

The jurisdiction of Virginia had already been extended over the whole region upon the Youghiogeny and Monongahela, as far as the settlements extended, and westward to the Ohio River, north of Big Grave Creek, under the name of the "District of West Augusta."† The country south of Grave Creek was uninhabited by white men, and remained in the full possession of the native Indians.‡ West Augusta, as a district of Virginia, for several years comprised all the western inhabitants from the Little Kenhawa northward to Fort Pitt.

The settlements west of the Monongahela, and upon the Ohio above the present site of Wheeling, had been steadily increasing their population. Numerous parties of surveyors and explorers were advancing upon the waters of the Little and the Great Kenhawa, and westward to the Ohio. The whole country was overrun by parties of pioneers and explorers, to the great annoyance of the Indians, who claimed the possession of the lands; but the whites disregarded both their claims and their remonstrances.

But a sad reverse was about to overtake the western settlements, and a signal check put to their advance. The hardy pioneers, in their new homes in the wilderness, amid all the hardships and privations of a frontier life, were about to en-

---

* Butler's Kentucky, p. 26. † American Pioneer, vol. ii., p. 303–306.
‡ Dr. Briscoe, a wealthy planter from Virginia, had formed a settlement at the mouth of the Little Kenhawa, composed of several families and a number of negro slaves, which was commenced in 1773; at the same time, a settlement was first made at Big Grave Creek. Both were abandoned in 1774.—See M'Donald's Life of Kenton, p. 205.

counter all the horrors of *an Indian war*—a war of *extermination*, which knows no mercy, even to the infant and its defenseless mother.

Since the treaty of Fort Stanwix, six years had elapsed, and the Indians had gradually retired from the eastern sources and tributaries of the Monongahela, and were slowly removing to the west side of the Ohio. They were still inclined to maintain a friendly intercourse with the whites, although jealous of the encroachments, and grieved to see the rapid advance and the unfeeling deportment of the settlers toward their waning tribes; they seldom gave occasion for outrage or bloodshed. Although they had often been the subjects of injustice and aggression from the petty tyranny of unprincipled men, they had not been charged with any overt act of hostility.

In a frontier country, and among a population of such opposite races of men, one small act of injustice brings on another, until both become arrayed in deadly hostility. So in relation to the war which was about to break forth. Small things were only the precursors of the most atrocious acts. A petty theft from a lawless white man involves two nations in a war of extermination. Injustice and aggravated aggression are sure to be on the side of power; and the Indians had submitted patiently until resistance became a virtue, and vengeance was taken into their own hands. In this manner, the aggressions of the reckless emigrants of Western Virginia brought on that series of Indian hostilities comprised under the name of "Lord Dunmore's war."

This spring witnessed the erection of a fort at Wheeling for the protection of the frontier people. It was brought about in the following manner: A party of near one hundred emigrants from Eastern Virginia had arrived upon the Ohio on their way to Kentucky. About the latter part of April they were encamped near the mouth of the Little Kenhawa. Apprehensive of an outbreak of Indian treachery, they were induced to defer their location in Kentucky until the hostile attitude of the Shawanese should be changed. Captain Michael Cresap, of Redstone Old Fort, being in their vicinity making a settlement, advised the party to retire nearer the older settlements, for greater security from Indian barbarities. They accordingly retired to the bank of the Ohio River, just above the mouth of Wheeling Creek, where they commenced the construction of a stockade fort for their mutual protection. The situation of this stockade was a few hundred yards above Wheeling Creek, and near the site of the present city of Wheeling. The plan of the fort was prepared by Major George Rogers Clark, who was one of the party.* The work was immediately commenced under the superintendence of Ebenezer Zane and John Caldwell, two experienced frontier men, who had already made improvements and a settlement on Wheeling Creek. The fort, when completed, was called "Fort Fincastle," and was designed as a place of security for the settlers in that vicinity; and during the war which followed, they had ample need of its protection.

In the mean time, the attitude of the Indians foreboded hostilities, requiring the settlements to be placed in a condition to avoid surprise. To this effect, Doctor Connolly, the royal "captain commandant of West Augusta," then at Pittsburgh, authorized Captain Michael Cresap, an experienced and brave Indian fighter, to use his influence with this party of emigrants, and induce them to "cover the country with scouts until the inhabitants could fortify themselves." Accordingly, reconnoitering or scouting parties were sent out in all directions, and the settlers proceeded to fortify the stations. Captain Cresap took command of Fort Fincastle.†

* Among the party of fearless pioneers were also Joseph Bowman, Hugh M'Gary, and many others who afterward figured in the settlement of Kentucky.
† American Pioneer, vol. ii., p. 303.

CHAPTER III.

LORD DUNMORE'S INDIAN WAR: EXTENSION OF THE WESTERN SETTLEMENTS FROM THE TREATY OF "CAMP CHARLOTTE" TO THE DECLARATION OF INDEPENDENCE.—A.D. 1774 TO 1776.

Argument.—The Indians reluctantly assent to Boundaries claimed by the Treaty of Fort Stanwix.—Outrages of lawless white Men provoke Indian Resentment.—Explorers and Land-jobbers.—Rumor of Indian Depredations circulated by them.—Alarm excited among Explorers.—Captain Cresap advises Violence, and heads a Party which murders some Indians above Wheeling and at Captina Creek.—Greathouse leads another Party against the Indians at Yellow Creek.—Other Murders preceding these.—Murder of "Bald Eagle" Chief.—Five Families at Bulltown.—Indian Revenge commences upon the Traders.—Consternation on the Frontier.—Settlements abandoned.—Union Station near Laurel Hill established.—Hostile Incursions of Indians.—Defensive Measures under Lord Dunmore.—The Wappatomica Campaign under General M'Donald.—Surveys and Explorations in Kentucky suspended in 1774.—Daniel Boone conducts Surveyors to old Settlements.—General Lewis marches down the Kenhawa.—Learns the Change of Dunmore's Plans.—The severe "Battle of the Point."—Loss of the Virginians and of Indians.—"Cornstalk," the King of the Shawanese.—Lord Dunmore's Advance to the Scioto.—"Camp Charlotte" fortified.—Operations against the Shawanese Towns.—Negotiations with the Indians.—General Lewis advances to the Scioto.—He indignantly obeys Dunmore's Order to halt.—Treaty of Camp Charlotte opened.—Speech of Cornstalk; of Logan.—Stipulations of this Treaty.—Peace proclaimed, January 7th, 1775.—Suspicions against Lord Dunmore.—Emigration revives in the West.—Explorations resumed in Kentucky.—Colonel Floyd on Bear-grass Creek.—Other Surveys and Settlements.—Settlements on the Holston and Clinch in 1775.—Preparations in Virginia and North Carolina for the Occupancy of Kentucky.—Patrick Henry and others.—Colonel Henderson and others.—Treaty of Watauga.—Colonel Henderson's Land Company.—Preparations for establishing the Colony of Transylvania.—Boone Pioneer of the Colony to Kentucky River.—Boonesborough erected.—Colonel Henderson leads out his Colony.—Boone leads another in the Fall.—"Plan of Boonesborough."—Logan's Fort built.—Company's Land-office.—Proprietary Government established in Transylvania, 1775.—Acts of Legislature, second Session.—The Company memorialize the Federal Congress.—Opposition to the Proprietary Government.—Transylvania Republic merges into the State Government of Virginia.—Settlements begin to form on the north Side of Kentucky River.—Harrod's Station erected in 1776.—Colonel Harrod introduces the first Families from the Monongahela.—Declaration of American Independence.—Indian Hostilities begin in Kentucky.—Preparations for Defense.—Major George Rogers Clark superintends the Militia Organization.

[A.D. 1774.] As we have shown, the Indian tribes west of the Ohio seemed disposed, for a time, quietly to submit to their fate, and permit the white inhabitants to occupy all the territory east of the Ohio River. But at length the whites, by one act of aggression after another, roused up the sleeping vengeance of the savage to active war. The immediate provocation to hostilities was an unprovoked and wanton murder of two parties of peaceable Indians by a reckless band of white men, living on the east side of the Ohio, in the settlements above and below Wheeling.

It is a fact which has been verified by all experience, from the first occupancy of the British colonies in North America up to the present time, that when the tide of emigration sets strong toward the wilderness occupied by the native tribes, a large proportion of the most lawless and worthless part of the population is carried in advance of the older settlements, like driftwood upon a swollen river. Hence it is almost impossible for the civil authorities to restrain acts of lawless violence in such persons on the extreme confines of civilization. Men who are impatient of the wholesome restraints of law and social order naturally seek those parts of a civilized community where the arm of the civil authority is weakened by distance, or where they find themselves beyond the reach of civil government. Hence the extreme frontier settlements are always more or less composed of a population which, from their natural and depraved propensities, are prone to keep up a spirit of hostility with the neighboring savages, to the great detriment of the better classes of emigrants.

In the settlements which were crowding upon the east side of the Ohio, there were many individuals such as we have described, and who kept in advance of the more orderly and virtuous portion of the community.

The particulars of the outrages which roused the Indians to hostile revenge in the summer of 1774, and at the record of which humanity weeps, are as follows: In the month of April, a rumor obtained circulation that some Indians had stolen several horses from a party of land-jobbers near the Ohio and Kenhawa Rivers. This report, doubtless, may have had some foundation in truth, but it was propagated by designing and evil men. Some, affecting to believe the rumor true, deduced from the facts a hostile intention on the part of the Indians against the white settlements. The object in view appears to have been a breach of the friendly state of feeling between the white inhabitants and the Indian tribes residing on the west side of the Ohio. Although the Indians had always looked with a jealous eye upon the advance of the white population, yet there is no reasonable ground to suspect, on this occasion, any hostile designs on their part against the settlements previous to the outrages which were the immediate cause of the war.

Vol. I.—A a

Near the last of April the land-jobbers, the bane of all new countries, collected in considerable numbers at Wheeling, alleging the apprehension of a hostile attack from the Indians. The true cause, no doubt, was cowardice and conscious guilt, if not a desire to embroil the savages in a war of extermination. A few days afterward, it was known that two Indians, with their families, were descending the river a few miles above Wheeling. Upon learning this fact, Captain Cresap, who had command of Fort Fincastle, proposed to kill the Indians without further inquiry. Colonel Zane, the proprietor of Wheeling, vehemently opposed any such proposition. He represented in glowing colors the extreme folly and atrocity of such conduct; he declared that the wanton murder of those Indians would stir up a bloody revenge against the settlements, and bring a fierce Indian war, with all its horrors, upon the innocent frontier inhabitants, which would cause the name of Cresap to be held in execration by hundreds of widows and orphans; but his voice and counsel were disregarded, and Captain Cresap, with his party, proceeded to execute their blood-thirsty designs. The party of Indians were met a few miles above the town, and deliberately shot in their canoes. These reckless men then returned to Wheeling in the bloody canoes of their murdered victims; and when questioned, they significantly replied that the Indians "had fallen overboard into the river."

This first murder only served to stimulate them to further deeds of blood. The same evening rumor informed them of an Indian camp near the mouth of Captina Creek, a few miles below Wheeling. The same party, with some others, set out and descended the river to the Indian camp. Here they deliberately shot several Indians in cold blood, and by whose attempt to defend themselves one of Cresap's men was severely wounded.*

A few days after this second murder had been perpetrated, another still more atrocious was committed upon a party of Indians near the mouth of Yellow Creek, and about forty miles above Wheeling. Daniel Greathouse, affecting to apprehend danger for "Baker's Bottom," on the east side of the river, not far from an Indian camp near Yellow Creek, collected a party of thirty-two men, and proceeded up to Baker's Bottom. Here the party concealed themselves near the bank of the river, while their commander, Greathouse, crossed the river alone,

* Doddridge's Notes, p. 226–229. See American Pioneer, vol. i., p. 8.

under the mask of friendship, to spy out the Indian force, and to ascertain their numbers and position. While approaching the camp, an Indian woman advised him to return and to depart speedily, for the warriors, highly exasperated at the late murders, were drinking, and might do him some injury. He returned to his party, and reported the Indians too strong for an open attack. Baker had been in the habit of selling whisky to the Indians, and was therefore a fit tool for Greathouse in his contemplated treachery and murder. A plan was agreed on that Baker should freely supply with whisky all who could be decoyed over the river. At length many were decoyed over, all of whom were made beastly drunk. In this condition, Greathouse and a few others of his party fell upon them, and murdered them in cold blood. The squaw who had given Greathouse the friendly advice near the Indian camp was one of the victims of this bloody tragedy. Others from the camp, attracted by the reports of the guns, came to seek their friends, but they were deliberately shot while crossing the river.

Doddridge observes, "It is but justice to state, that out of the party of thirty-two, only five or six were actually engaged in this atrocious murder." We should feel no desire to screen the memories of the guilty twenty-five, who would permit a few desperate fellows among them to perpetrate deliberate and outrageous murder, which they might profess to abhor. But their names are not permitted to be inscribed upon the page of history. Their posterity, of course, are exempt from the odium which attached to the men who could permit a diabolical outrage of this kind without interference. Virtue, so feeble in the cause of justice and humanity, is a curse rather than a blessing to its possessors.

The murders perpetrated at Captina and Yellow Creeks included the whole family of the generous and unfortunate Logan, who became noted in the war which followed. He had long been the friend of the whites, and the advocate of peace among his red brethren. He now became vindictive, and proved himself a bold and active warrior against the Virginia frontier.*

* Soon after the murders at Captina and Yellow Creeks by the parties under Cresap and Greathouse, the authorities of Pennsylvania took the precaution to dispatch messengers to the Indians to inform them that those outrages were not committed by Pennsylvanians, and that the government of Pennsylvania disavowed and condemned them, and therefore were not the proper objects of their revenge. This timely notice given to the Indians is probably the reason why the war was not carried on against the frontier settlements of Pennsylvania, but was directed chiefly against those of Virginia,

Nor were the murders at Captina and Yellow Creeks the first or only outrages of the whites upon the Indians. Other murders equally atrocious had been perpetrated by the lawless whites with impunity. Such was the force of public sentiment; such the prejudices and animosity of the frontier population against the Indians, that no redress could be obtained from the civil authorities for injuries inflicted upon them by white men. Previous to the Captina tragedy, a white man had been committed to prison in Winchester charged with the willful murder of a peaceable Indian; but an armed mob surrounded the jail, and forcibly released the prisoner from the custody of the law. Again, an old and distinguished chief, called "Bald Eagle," who had long been friendly toward the whites, had lived with them, and had hunted with them, being alone in the woods near the Monongahela, was attacked by three white men and killed. Afterward, they placed the lifeless body of their victim in a sitting posture in his canoe, and sent it adrift down the stream.

At "Bulltown," on the Little Kenhawa, there were five Indian families, who had lived and hunted with the whites near Buchanan's River and upon Hacker's Creek. These families were all killed by lawless individuals, under a pretext of revenging the deaths of a white family which had been murdered by a party of hostile Indians on Gauly River. The white inhabitants of Bulltown remonstrated strongly against the designs which these men entertained against these innocent Indians, whom they had long known, and whom they believed above suspicion. But all was in vain; their skins were Indian, and they were all deliberately shot, and their bodies thrown into the river by these desperadoes.*

Immediately after the murders at Captina and Yellow Creeks, the smothered fire of revenge broke out into open hostilities. The Shawanese, on the Scioto, were principals in the war; and the warriors of other northern and western tribes entered into alliance with them. They first murdered all the traders and white men found within the Indian country. A young man, taken by the Indians near the falls of Muskingum, was killed, and his body, cut into fragments, was scattered to the

where all manner of savage barbarities were inflicted.—See Gordon's History of Pennsylvania, p. 475.

* See Butler's History of Kentucky, Introduction, p. 53, 54.

four winds. Savage fury and revenge knew no bounds, and the innocent families upon the frontiers were doomed to destruction.*

Consternation spread through all the frontier settlements, from the sources of the Monongahela to the Kenhawa; the settlers fled from their homes toward the mountains; others retired into forts and stations. Fort Pitt and Redstone Fort were among their asylums.

The settlements within striking distance of the Ohio were entirely deserted. The greater portion of the women and children were removed from fifty to one hundred miles back from the frontier border, and safely lodged in "stations" and fortified camps near the mountains, while the men were compelled to expose themselves to innumerable hardships and privations to procure food for their families and to protect them from the marauding bands of hostile Indians. A large fortified station, near the present site of Uniontown, in Pennsylvania, at the western base of the Laurel Hill, was hardly deemed secure from Indian attack. As remote from the eastern settlements as from savage danger, they were destitute of supplies and the necessaries of life, except what the wilderness itself afforded. This resource was scanty indeed, amid the howling blasts of an inclement winter; and famine seemed to covet what had been wrested from the vengeance of the Indian.

A few days had been sufficient to prove that the alarm was not without cause. The Indians immediately had commenced the warfare by detached parties, scouring the whole country, murdering the remaining inhabitants, and laying waste every settlement within one day's march of the Ohio River.† The

---

* Butler's Kentucky, Introduction, p. 56.

† The Indian "declaration of war" was made by Logan himself, on the 21st of July, 1774, in company with a party of eight warriors. Having advanced into the settlements on the Upper Monongahela, and having killed one man and taken two prisoners on the 12th of July, he returned on the 21st, and left at the house of William Robinson, whose family had been murdered, "the war club," to which was attached a note, written by a white prisoner who had been adopted into Logan's family, in the following words, viz.:

"CAPTAIN CRESAP—

"Why did you kill my people on Yellow Creek? The white people killed my kin at Conestago a great while ago, and I thought nothing of that. But you have killed my kin again on Yellow Creek, and took my cousin prisoner. Then I thought I must kill too; and I have been three times to war since: but the Indians are not angry; it is only myself. CAPTAIN JOHN LOGAN.

"July 21, 1774."

—See American Pioneer, vol. i., p. 18.

colonial Legislature of Virginia was in session, when it was electrified by an express from the "District of West Augusta," near the Ohio River, apprising them that an "Indian war" had already been commenced; that the tomahawk and scalping-knife were already doing their bloody work upon the frontier people.

Provision was to be immediately made for the emergency. Lord Dunmore, governor of the province of Virginia, lost no time in delay, but immediately put in operation a system of defense for arresting Indian hostilities upon the settlements. A powerful and vigorous campaign was planned for the invasion of the Indian country west of the Ohio. Orders were immediately sent to General Andrew Lewis,* of Botetourt county, to raise with all possible dispatch four regiments of militia and volunteers from the southwestern counties, to rendezvous at Camp Union, in the Greenbrier country. This was to be the "Southern Division" of the invading army, and General Andrew Lewis, a veteran in the French war, was commander. He was ordered to march down the Great Kenhawa to the bank of the Ohio, and there to join the "Northern Division," under the earl in person. In the mean time, Lord Dunmore was actively engaged in raising troops in the northern counties west of the Blue Ridge, to advance from Fort Cumberland, by way of Redstone Old Fort, to the Ohio at Pittsburgh, whence he was to descend in boats to the Kenhawa. This was the original plan of the campaign.

While these plans were maturing under the provincial authorities in the eastern portion of Virginia, by command of the royal governor, General Angus M'Donald had been organizing the western people on the Youghiogeny and Monongahela for their own defense. Agreeably to the orders of Lord Dunmore, General M'Donald had collected a body of four hundred volunteers, who made their rendezvous at Wheeling Creek, in

* General Lewis was one of the most experienced and efficient provincial commanders that Virginia had yet produced. Such was the high opinion which General Washington entertained of his military abilities, that he recommended him as a suitable person to fill the office of commander-in-chief of the Revolutionary armies, which was tendered to himself. He had been a captain in the detachment under Washington at Little Meadows in 1754. He was also a companion of Washington in the fatal campaign under General Braddock, in 1755; he commanded the detachment of Virginia which, in 1758, rescued Major Grant's regiment of Highlanders from complete annihilation, when the latter was so signally defeated on the heights above Fort Duquesne. See Hall's Sketches of the West, vol. i., p. 204.

June. From this point it was resolved to invade the Indian country upon the head waters of the Muskingum River, and to destroy the Wappatomica towns situated on the river, about sixteen miles below the junction of the Tuscarawa and Walhonding, within the present State of Ohio. The little army thus collected descended the Ohio to the mouth of Captina Creek, and thence proceeded by the most direct route westwardly to the Indian towns. The march was irregular, and discipline was but feebly enforced. A few days brought them near the object of the expedition. Within six miles of the Indian town, while the army were carelessly advancing, they were assailed by about fifty Indian warriors in ambuscade, and thrown into some confusion. A skirmish ensued, and the Indians fled, with the loss of one warrior killed, besides several wounded. The whites, having lost two men killed and eight wounded, pressed forward to the towns, and found them deserted. But the Indians had only retired across the river and laid an ambuscade for their invaders. By a fortunate accident, this was discovered by the whites, who thus escaped a disastrous defeat. Light skirmishes with detached parties comprised the subsequent offensive operations of this expedition. The Indians from these towns at length having sued for peace, the commander of the expedition granted their request, upon the surrender of five chiefs as hostages. Of these, two escaped soon afterward.

The commander, finding he would be short of provisions, burned the Indian towns, destroyed the fields of growing corn, and returned with the utmost dispatch to Wheeling.*

Such was the result of this half-organized expedition, and such had been its effects upon the Indians on the Muskingum, that hostile parties infested the march of the retreating army, causing every kind of annoyance, and inflicting the most cruel barbarities upon such persons as fell into their hands. The pursuit by marauding parties of the Indians continued almost to the very banks of the Ohio. Thus ended the first military movement of this iniquitous war, serving to exasperate rather than to subdue the Indians.

During the summer, the operations of the western emigrants in exploring the country, making improvements and locations of land on the east and south side of the Ohio, were completely

* Doddridge's Notes, p. 241, 242, 243. Butler's Kentucky, Introduction, p. 57.

checked by the outbreak of Indian hostilities. Those who had advanced into the wilderness near the Ohio, and into the region on the Kentucky River, had retired into the more secure situations, or had taken an active part in the military operations in progress. Among the latter were many of the first settlers of Kentucky, who were engaged as scouts and rangers upon the exposed settlements on the Monongahela and Upper Ohio, or had connected themselves with the army preparing on the Greenbrier under General Lewis. Among the brave frontier men engaged in the defense of the settlements were Major George Rogers Clark, Robert Patterson, and Simon Kenton, who afterward became distinguished soldiers of Kentucky. Besides these, were many others equally meritorious, who were then just entering upon their career of usefulness and military service in Kentucky.

Daniel Boone, the fearless woodsman and pioneer of Kentucky, had been engaged in June to advance, accompanied by Michael Stoner, his sole companion, from the banks of the Clinch River, through a trackless wilderness, a distance of four hundred miles, to "the falls" of Ohio, to conduct a party of surveyors and explorers into the older settlements of Virginia. This service he had performed at the request of Lord Dunmore, making the whole trip of eight hundred miles in sixty-two days, without any accident or loss. After performing this duty, and after conducting the surveyors and others safely to the settlements, he joined the southern division of the army under General Lewis, and marched to the mouth of the Kenhawa.*

In the mean time, General Lewis, having collected at Camp Union three regiments† of volunteers and militia from the counties of Augusta, Botetourt, and Fincastle, set out on the 11th day of September upon his march for the designated point of rendezvous. Colonel Williamson, with another regiment, was to follow a few days afterward.

The route of General Lewis lay through a trackless wilderness down the Valley of the Kenhawa. The route being impassable for wagons, the whole camp equipage, military stores, provisions, and even the sick, were conveyed upon the backs of pack-horses. For twenty-five days the march slowly advanced through a rugged country, where a pathway had never

---

* See Butler's Kentucky, p. 28. Also, Flint's Life of Boone, p. 82.
† American Pioneer, vol. i., p. 382.

been opened. At the head of a pioneer party, Captain Arbuckle, the only white man who had ever traversed these wild and romantic regions, advanced as their guide through this dreary wilderness. The route led over rugged mountains, through deep defiles and mountain gorges, until they reached the Valley of the Lower Kenhawa. At length the tedious march of one hundred and sixty miles was completed, and the army encamped on the banks of the Ohio on the 6th of October.* The point selected for the camp was the peninsula above the mouth of the Great Kenhawa, upon the site of the present town of Point Pleasant.

The march had been a laborious one, and the privations of the gallant army had been extreme. During the whole route, such had been the scarcity of provisions, that select hunters had been kept out on daily service, in order to add the flesh of the elk, the bear, and the deer to their scanty allowance. At the mouth of the Kenhawa they had expected to receive a plentiful supply from Fort Pitt, with the "northern division" under Lord Dunmore. But here they were doomed to disappointment and new dangers in a region infested with hostile savages. Lord Dunmore had not arrived with his division, nor had supplies been forwarded by him.

In obedience to his orders, General Lewis remained in camp; but, having no intelligence from his lordship, he dispatched messengers up the Ohio in search of his encampment, or of such information as could be obtained. Select parties of hunters were kept constantly on duty to supply food for the troops, who were already suffering from short allowance.

At length, on the 9th of October, three messengers from the commander-in-chief arrived in camp. From them General Lewis ascertained that his lordship had duly arrived at Wheeling, where he had concluded to change his plan of operations. He had now determined to descend the Ohio in boats and barges to the mouth of Hocking River, and there erect a stockade fort for the protection of the sick, the military stores, and boats, under a suitable guard. To this point General Lewis was ordered to march, while his lordship, with the northern division, would ascend the Hocking River to "the falls," and

---

* American Pioneer, p. 381. Doddridge says it was the 10th of October instead of the 6th. For an account of General Lewis's expedition from "Camp Union," see Hall's Sketches, vol. i., p. 199.

thence, marching across the dividing ridges to the Scioto Valley, would advance to the Shawanese towns on that river. General Lewis was ordered to join the main army with his division, near the lower Shawanese towns on the Scioto.

The force commanded by General Lewis was about twelve hundred men of every kind, including two companies of Colonel Christian's regiment, which had joined the main body at "the Point." Colonel Christian, with about three hundred men, had encamped about half a day's march in the rear.

Next morning, about daylight, two privates, who had been out hunting before day, fell in with a large body of hostile Indians, who were about two miles above the camp, and marching directly for it. One of these men was killed by the fire from the Indians, the other escaped to the camp.* The alarm was instantly given, and the troops were put in motion. This timely notice saved the army from a disastrous defeat. A few moments afterward, two other scouts or hunters came flying to camp, and confirmed the statement of the first, declaring that they had "seen a body of Indians covering five acres of ground, as closely as they could stand." The truth of this statement could not long remain in doubt, for the Indians were pressing forward to the attack.

The only salvation for the whole army depended upon the firmness of the commander and the courage of his troops. General Lewis was equal to the occasion, and his troops were a full match for the Indians themselves. Two detachments, under Colonels Flemming and Charles Lewis, were immediately ordered forward to meet the enemy and break the force of his assault upon the camp. These detachments had not proceeded more than four hundred yards, when they encountered the enemy advancing upon them in two parallel lines near the bank of the Ohio. The engagement was immediately opened by a tremendous fire from the savages, and the detachments, being closely pressed, began to fall back. At this critical moment, Colonel Fields brought his regiment into action in gallant style, and checked the advance of the Indian line.

General Lewis had been prompt in his arrangements for de-

---

* These two men belonged to Captain Russel's company, and to Colonel Christian's regiment. The other two belonged to Captain Evan Shelby's company, also of Colonel Christian's regiment, the only two companies of his regiment engaged in the battle. The latter two privates were James Robertson and Valentine Sevier, subsequently distinguished in the settlement of Tennessee.

fense, and the whole army was soon formed, ready for action. The first and second lines were promptly supported by the main line, and the action soon became general and furious.

In the first onset, the sun had just risen above the horizon, when the terrific yells of the savages and their destructive fire indicated the deadly nature of the contest before them. Colonels Flemming and Lewis valiantly encouraged their men to maintain the contest, while the incessant fire of the Indians was spreading death through their ranks at every moment. The main line advanced, and the Indians in turn began to recoil and to fall back. But Colonels Flemming and Lewis had been mortally wounded in the first assault, although they refused to leave the field until the main line came to their relief.

The Indians, extending their line entirely across the peninsula, from the Ohio to the Kenhawa, took position behind a rude breast-work of trees, old logs, and bushes, previously formed, and continued the deadly strife with unwavering courage.

In this condition, the gallant Virginians, cut off from retreat on every side, and pressed by a powerful enemy in front, maintained their position until evening. The battle had raged with unprecedented fury and obstinacy, each line alternately receding or advancing as the fate of war seemed to balance between the two armies, until evening was far advanced, and the sun was just above the western horizon. Ten hours had the rifle been doing its murderous work in the hands of the unerring savage, and the no less skillful marksmen of Western Virginia. The whole plain was strewed with the dead and wounded enemies, strangely commingled where they had fallen, as each line advanced and had been alternately driven back. The forest-trees which covered the field of carnage presented on every side numerous signs of the leaden messengers of death, which had passed like a hailstorm between the contending armies. Thus had the battle raged with equal success, until the sun began to decline behind the western hills, when General Lewis ordered three companies* to advance up the Kenhawa River, under the shelter of the bank and undergrowth, until they had gained the rear of the In-

* These were the companies of Captains Isaac Shelby, George Mathews, and John Stewart. At the beginning of the battle, Isaac Shelby was lieutenant in his father's company; but his father having taken command on the death of his colonel, early in the engagement, Isaac advanced to the command of his company.—American Pioneer, vol. i., p. 381-383.

dian line. From that point they were to pour an incessant fire upon the enemy's rear, while their fire would be a signal for renewed efforts by their fellow-soldiers in the main line. This order having been executed with great promptness and ardor, the savages, panic-stricken at the terrible fire in their rear, and believing that they were now attacked by the whole of Colonel Christian's re-enforcement, fled with great precipitation across the Ohio, and retreated to their towns sixty miles up the Scioto.

The battle of the Kenhawa, or of "the Point," as it is sometimes designated, has by general consent been admitted to have been one of the most sanguinary and well-contested battles which have marked the annals of Indian warfare in the West. On the part of the Virginians, twelve commissioned officers were killed or wounded, seventy-five non-commissioned officers and privates were killed, and one hundred and forty-one were wounded.*

The greater portion of Colonel Christian's regiment did not reach the field of battle until near midnight, when their presence gave security to the repose of the wearied and almost exhausted troops who had borne the heat and burden of battle, and who could then retire to rest, leaving their wounded and dying companions in the charge of their friends.

It has never been ascertained what was the force of the Indians engaged in this battle, or what was their entire loss. The field of battle next day presented twenty-one Indian bodies left upon the ground, besides twelve others severely wounded, who had concealed themselves among the brush and logs. Many had been thrown into the river during the engagement, and it is highly probable that the entire Indian loss was but little inferior to that of the whites.

This Indian force was composed of the flower of the tribes inhabiting the present State of Ohio, commanded by the most distinguished chiefs among the western tribes. Among them

* Colonel Charles Lewis, one of the bravest and most meritorious officers, who commanded one of the advanced detachments, was mortally wounded early in the engagement, but he continued to cheer on his men to victory until he was removed from the field. Colonel Flemming fell severely wounded early in the engagement, but continued to encourage his men until he also was carried off the field. Colonel Fields, a valuable officer, was killed on the field of battle. Captains Buford, Murray, Ward, Wilson, and M'Lannahan were also killed; also Lieutenants Allen, Goldsby, Dillon, and several other subaltern officers.—See Doddridge, p. 231. Also, Thatcher's Lives of the Indians, vol. ii., p. 169, 170.

was "Cornstalk," the great Shawanese war-chief, who was commander-in-chief, aided by his son Ellinipsico, Red Hawk, a Delaware, Chiyawee, a Wyandot, and Logan, a Cayuga chief.* Cornstalk had opposed the war, and had advocated a truce on the eve of battle. Being overruled by his associates in command, he sternly declared, "Since you *will fight, you shall fight,*" and he conducted the engagement with great skill and courage. During the rage of battle, his voice was frequently heard above the din of war and amid the carnage, cheering on his warriors with the stern command, in his native tongue, "*Be strong! be strong!*" When an Indian faltered in his duty, Cornstalk instantly cut him down, as a warning to others.

A few days were required for the troops to recruit their exhausted frames, and restore the sick and wounded, before the division could be placed in a marching condition.

In the mean time, Lord Dunmore, with nearly twelve hundred men, had descended the Ohio from Fort Pitt, in one hundred canoes and several large boats, to the mouth of the Hocking River, where he had erected "Fort Gore," a stockade for the protection of his military stores and the invalids, which were left in charge of a detachment of provincial troops. From this point he ascended the Hocking to the falls, near the present town of Athens. From that place he directed his march across the country westward to the Scioto, where he encamped within a few miles of the Shawanese towns. Here, upon the eastern side of the Scioto, in the margin of the Piqua plains, near Sippoo Creek, he established his camp, which was regularly environed by a deep ditch encircling twelve acres of ground. Within was a regular stockade inclosure, in the center of which was the citadel, or headquarters, comprising about one acre, and occupied by the commander-in-chief and his superior officers. The position, thus fortified, was called "Camp Charlotte," in honor of the British queen.†

---

* Butler's Kentucky, p. 61.

† Atwater's History of Ohio, p. 115. There has been some difference of opinion as to the locality of Camp Charlotte; but recent examinations and inquiries by the "Logan Historical Society" of Chillicothe have resulted in the conviction that the site is comprised in a tract of land formerly belonging to Mr. Winship, upon Sippoo Creek, five miles east of Westfall, in Ross county, Ohio.

Mr. Caleb Atwater says, the camp was within three miles of a principal Shawanese town; other towns were within one day's march. The site of the present town of Frankfort, formerly "Old Town," or old Chillicothe, on the north fork of Paint Creek, was an important Shawanese town during the first emigration to the northwest side of

From this place, as headquarters, the Earl sent out his detachments against different towns on the waters of the Scioto, several of which were destroyed and burned. Among the incursions made by these detachments was one under Major William Crawford, with three hundred men, for the destruction of a Mingo town,* which was attacked with great energy, and utterly destroyed.

Such had been the sanguinary character of the battle of the Kenhawa, with only one division of the provincial army, which was concentrating upon the waters of the Scioto, that the Indians declined to continue the contest with the united forces. Hence, after the bloody "battle of the Point," the chiefs lost no time in making overtures of peace to the commander-in-chief, before the arrival of the vindictive troops under General Lewis. At length, after repeated overtures, and after the destruction of several of their towns, Lord Dunmore consented to order an armistice, preparatory to a general treaty of peace. In the mean time, every precaution was taken to avoid surprise and the danger of Indian treachery. But the southern division little thought of peace until they had again faced the enemy in the field.

Yet, having given the Indians an assurance of peace, his lordship dispatched a messenger to General Lewis, who was advancing with his division, with instructions to halt and encamp until further orders, and to observe the armistice which had been proclaimed. Smarting under their recent loss, and burning with revenge for an opportunity to inflict severe chastisement upon their enemies, the troops of General Lewis's division received the order with surprise and indignation. Gen-

---

the Ohio, between the years 1786 and 1790. This town was probably the principal Shawanese town, which was nearest Camp Charlotte. Mr. Felix Renick, one of the early settlers and pioneers in Ohio, concurs with the text. He locates Lord Dunmore's camp on Sippoo Creek, on the east side of the Scioto, about five miles south of Circleville and five miles east of Westfall. Mr. Renick informs us that he was upon the site of Lord Dunmore's camp, as well as that of General Lewis, in the year 1801, before the country was settled by white men. He says he has received the oral testimony of several persons who were in the campaign under Lord Dunmore, and they confirm this location. The same pioneer locates General Lewis's camp upon Congo Creek, a branch of Sippoo, two and a half miles distant from Camp Charlotte.—See American Pioneer, vol. i., p. 329–332; also, vol. ii., p. 37–42. The earth-works of a similar camp may be seen one mile above Chillicothe, on the Scioto.

* Butler's History of Kentucky, Introduction, p. 63. The term "Mingo" and "Mingoes" was the common phrase in the West to designate any or all of the tribes constituting the confederacy of the "Six Nations." A "Mingo chief" was a chief of some one of the Six Nations, not a confederate.

eral Lewis refused to obey, and prepared to continue his march. A second order was sent by a second messenger, who was directed to reiterate the same peremptorily. The order was again disregarded by the indignant general, who continued his march toward Camp Charlotte. Finally, Lord Dunmore in person, as commander-in-chief, hastened to meet the advancing troops, and personally, in presence of his staff, gave General Lewis a peremptory order to halt and encamp. The order was then reluctantly obeyed.

At length matters were arranged, and the council was held in the center of the camp, or in the "citadel" of headquarters, into which only eighteen unarmed chiefs and warriors were admitted at any one time.* The council having been convened, the deliberations were opened by Cornstalk in a short and energetic speech, delivered with great dignity, and in a tone so loud as to be heard over the whole camp, as if designed for the whole army. "He recited the former power of the Indians, the number of their tribes, compared with their present wretched condition, and their diminished numbers; he referred to the treaty of Fort Stanwix, and the cessions of territory then made by them to the whites; to the lawless encroachments of the whites upon their lands, contrary to all treaty stipulations; to the patient forbearance of the Indians for years under wrongs exercised toward them by the frontier people. He said the Indians knew their weakness in a contest with the whites, and they *desired only justice;* that the war was *not sought by the Indians,* but was *forced upon them;* for it was commenced by the whites without previous notice; that, under the circumstances, they would have merited the contempt of the whites for cowardice if they had failed to retaliate the unprovoked and treacherous murders at Captina and Yellow Creeks; that the war was the work of the whites, for the Indians desired peace."

The terms of peace were soon arranged, and their prisoners were surrendered into the hands of the provincial army. But

---

* Atwater's History of Ohio, p. 114. This is one of the early histories of Ohio, by Caleb Atwater. It contains some sketches of the early history of this state, loosely written and irregularly arranged. It embraces portions of the natural as well as the political history of Ohio; but it has been compiled with so little attention to accuracy, that it can not be depended upon unless it is corroborated by other authentic history. Although such is its general character, it is useful as a work of reference relative to matters which admit of but little discrepancy.

Logan, the Cayuga chief, still indignant at the murder of his family, refused to attend the council, or to be seen as a suppliant among the other chiefs.

Yet to General Gibson,* who was sent as an envoy to the Shawanese towns, after a private interview, and "after shedding abundance of tears," he delivered the following speech, which was committed to paper for Lord Dunmore, viz.: "I appeal to any white man to say if ever he entered Logan's cabin hungry, and he gave him nothing to eat; if ever he came cold and naked, and he clothed him not. During the course of the last long and bloody war, Logan remained idle in his cabin, an advocate for peace. Such was my love for the whites, that my countrymen pointed at me as they passed, and said, 'Logan is the *friend of white men.*' I had even thought to have lived with you, but for the injuries of one man. Captain Cresap the last spring, in cold blood, and unprovoked, murdered all the relations of Logan, *sparing not even my women and children.* There runs not a drop of my blood in the veins of any living creature. This called on me for revenge. I have sought it; I have killed many; I have fully glutted my vengeance. For my country, I rejoice at the beams of peace; but do not harbor a thought that mine is the joy of fear. Logan never felt fear. He will not turn on his heel to save his life. Who is there to mourn for Logan? Not one!"†

This speech, which is so well known as a specimen of native eloquence, is the condensed version given by Mr. Jefferson in

---

* General Gibson subsequently took an active part in the Indian war on the western frontier, from the Declaration of Independence to the close of the war in 1784. In an affidavit, made at Pittsburgh on the 4th of April, 1800, he states that the Indians sent a white man, by the name of Elliott (probably the same who was subsequently British Indian agent on the Maumee), to meet Lord Dunmore with a flag of truce when within fifteen miles of the Shawanese towns. Subsequently, General Gibson, being sent as an envoy to the Indian towns, saw the great Cornstalk and Logan in a conference. At length Logan took him aside to a copse of woods at a short distance, and there, "after shedding abundance of tears," while sitting upon a log, he delivered the speech, which is so well known, to be handed to Lord Dunmore.—See American Pioneer, vol. i., p. 18, 19.

† See Doddridge's Notes. In the speech of Logan we have substituted the word "captain" for colonel, as there were two persons of the same name, the father and the son. Colonel Cresap, the father, was not in any wise implicated in the Captina or Yellow Creek murders. Captain Michael Cresap, commandant of Fort Fincastle, first instigated the tragedy at Captina; but he was not with the party at Baker's Bottom, by whom Logan's family was killed. Greathouse and Baker were alone chargeable for this murder.—See American Pioneer, vol. i., p. 14–18; also, p. 64, &c. The "last long and bloody war" alluded to was Pontiac's war in 1763–4, after the close of the French war.

his "Notes on Virginia," published first in 1784. Other versions give a more extended copy, with some additional sentiments, which were doubtless contained in the speech delivered by Logan to General Gibson.

The principal stipulations on the part of the Indians in the treaty of Camp Charlotte were, besides those of peace and amity generally, that they should surrender into the hands of the whites, within a specified time, all the prisoners held by them in captivity; that they should abstain from all hostilities against the frontier settlements east and southeast of the Ohio River; that they should recognize the Ohio River as the proper boundary between the white population and the Indian hunting-grounds; and that the Indians should not hunt on the east and southeast side of the Ohio.

After the negotiations of the treaty had been concluded, and the prisoners had been duly surrendered, presents were distributed among the Indians who were assembled at the treaty, and they were dismissed with the smiles of the royal governor. Soon afterward the troops were put in motion for the post of Fort Pitt, previous to their return to their respective homes. They were soon afterward disbanded, and Lord Dunmore returned to Williamsburg, the seat of the provincial government.

[A.D. 1775.] On the 23d of January following, he issued his proclamation announcing the ratification of the treaty of peace with the Western Indians. He gave public notice that the Indians had agreed to withdraw their hunting-parties from the lands east of the Ohio River, and that they would offer no molestation to any white person peaceably ascending or descending the Ohio. All emigrants were forewarned against trespassing upon the Indian lands *on the west side of the river*.

Thus was the Ohio River, for the first time, *acknowledged by the Indians* as the boundary between the white man's territory and the Indian hunting-grounds.

The transactions of the late campaign appear to have laid the foundation for all the bitter feelings and outbreak of popular indignation which subsequently caused Lord Dunmore to abandon the country, and seek protection on board his majesty's fleet.

Whether any just grounds existed for the suspicion or not, it was believed by many, and probably by General Lewis and his Virginia troops, that, while the governor was at Wheeling, about the first of October, he received from the royal government dispatches instructing him to terminate the war speedily with the hostile tribes, and to make such terms with them as *might secure their alliance in favor of England* against the colonies, in case the growing difficulties with them should terminate in a state of open war. General Washington and Chief-justice Marshall, it is affirmed, never ceased to believe that such were his orders, and that his conduct was dictated by a desire to secure the alliance of the savages against the colonies, whenever hostilities between them and the mother country should take place.*

Notwithstanding the difficulties between the mother country and the colonies were daily increasing, yet the spirit of western emigration, which had received a temporary check from the late Indian war, revived, and continued to lead hundreds of families from each of the Middle and Southern States into the regions drained by the tributaries of the Ohio. Although emigrants were crowding into the country now comprised in western portions of Pennsylvania and Virginia, yet this region did not limit the explorations for new settlements. Several hundred miles lower down the Ohio, in the vicinity of the falls, many surveyors and explorers had penetrated the fertile plains on the Kentucky River previous to the late Indian war. During Indian hostilities they had been compelled to abandon these remote regions, and to retire into the settled portions of Western Virginia and Pennsylvania. Now, since peace was restored, the former explorers and surveyors returned, and with them new adventurers, to seek homes and settlements to which they might subsequently remove their families. A small cabin, and an acre of ground in cultivation, gave each a preference right, which he might leave and resume at pleasure. This was the extent of improvement required by the provisions of the act of the Virginia Legislature, and gave to each settler a settlement right to four hundred acres of land, including his improvement. By this species of inchoate title, as well as by large grants from the royal governors, and by military land-warrants of different dates, was a large portion of Central Kentucky covered before the close of the year 1775. Most of the settlement rights, grants, and warrants located during this year were laid upon

* See Atwater's History of Ohio, p. 118.

the elevated rolling plains which extend from east to west between the main branches of Licking and Salt Rivers, but especially within fifty miles of the Kentucky River, for nearly two hundred miles above its mouth. Yet there had been no families introduced into Kentucky; all were pioneers and explorers, preparing the way for the advance of subsequent emigration and settlements. Among the locations were many large grants from the royal governor, Lord Dunmore.

Among the prominent pioneers and explorers of Kentucky, during the year 1775, was Colonel John Floyd, a surveyor from Eastern Virginia. He had made a visit of exploration to Kentucky during the previous year, when the irruption of Indian hostilities had driven in the remote settlers. He now returned to the West, to pursue his vocation as a surveyor, in locating claims and land-warrants, and to select for himself a permanent home for future residence. For himself he made a location within six miles of "the falls" of the Ohio, and established his "camp" on Bear-grass Creek, at a place subsequently known as "Floyd's Station."

Among the hundreds of settlers who were now pressing forward into Kentucky, none, more than Colonel Floyd, were endowed with that courage and perseverance so indispensable to a frontier life; and he soon proved himself a useful and valuable member of the new and growing settlements in this quarter. Such was the state of emigration and settlement in this portion of Western Virginia.

In the southern portion of Virginia and in the adjacent province of North Carolina the tide of western emigration was equally strong. People from the older settlements were pressing forward in great numbers upon the numerous branches of the Clinch, on the *southeast side of* the Cumberland Mountains. The pioneers in this region were anxious to *advance beyond* the Cumberland Mountains into the unexplored regions which had been discovered upon the waters of the Cumberland River and upon the tributaries of the Kentucky River. This region as yet had been but little explored by emigrants and pioneers. It was nearly fifty miles south of the principal locations made on the Kentucky River, and within the limits of the Cherokee hunting-grounds. It had never been relinquished to the whites, and the Indians were jealous of any advances made by them west of the Cumberland Mountains. Those who ventured upon the forbidden territory found death the forfeiture of their temerity. To gain a footing in this region, the permission of the Cherokees must be obtained. The attempt of Daniel Boone to introduce a colony without their consent had been signally rebuked two years before.

In view of this prerequisite, associations of influential men and capitalists were formed in Virginia and North Carolina, for the purpose of obtaining the Indian title to these lands by treaty and purchase. Early in the spring of 1774, Patrick Henry, with the Hon. William Byrd, John Page, Esq., and Colonel William Christian, had contemplated the purchase of the lands south of the Kentucky River from the Cherokees. But Indian hostilities on the Ohio, and political difficulties with the royal government, added to the uncertainty of the royal confirmation to any title obtained by individuals treating with the Indian tribes, prevented the consummation of their designs.*

A project of the same character was undertaken soon afterward by Colonel Richard Henderson and other influential men of Hillsborough, in North Carolina. Their plans were also deferred until the close of Lord Dunmore's Indian war.

Yet Daniel Boone had not been discouraged by the failure of his attempt to introduce a colony upon the south side of the Kentucky River in the fall of 1773. He still resolved to take possession of the beautiful regions west of Cumberland Gap, but not without the consent of the Cherokees.† In his first attempt he had lost his son and several of his neighbors by his rash advance into the Indian territory, and he was unwilling to incur the same danger again. Measures were taken, accordingly, to conciliate the favor and consent of the Cherokees‡ previous to a second advance.

Soon after the close of the late Indian war upon the Ohio, Daniel Boone had urged upon Colonel Richard Henderson, of North Carolina, and others, who were anxious to settle a colony south of the Kentucky River, the propriety of obtaining the consent of the Cherokees by formal purchase: hence Colonel

---

* Hall's Sketches of the West, vol. i., p. 249.

† The country on the north, as well as on the south side of the Cumberland River, had been the residence and the hunting-grounds of the Chouanoes, or Shawanese; and the Cumberland River had been known to the French as the River of the Chouanoes, or Shawanese, for many years after the Shawanese were expelled by the Cherokees, which was between the years 1715 and 1718. It had now been in the possession of the Cherokees for fifty-five years.

‡ Butler's History of Kentucky, Introduction, p. 66. Also, the Life of Daniel Boone, by Timothy Flint, p. 82, 83.

Henderson, and several other men of capital and enterprise, formed themselves into a company* for the purchase and settlement of the country west of Cumberland Gap. Soon afterward, Colonel Henderson and Colonel Nathaniel Hart, in company with the hunter and woodsman, Daniel Boone, proceeded to the Cherokee towns, and proposed a general council to be held in the spring, for the purpose of purchasing the Indian title to the lands lying between the Cumberland and Kentucky Rivers. Arrangements were accordingly made for convening a general council in the following spring of 1775.

Subsequently, on the 17th of March, a treaty was concluded and signed by Richard Henderson, Nathaniel Hart, and J. Luttrell, agents for the company, on the one part, and by certain chiefs and warriors of the Cherokee nation on the other part, at the "Sycamore Shoals" of the Watauga River, within the present limits of Carter county, in East Tennessee. Twelve hundred Indians are said to have been assembled on the treaty ground.

By this treaty the Indians agreed to cede and relinquish to Richard Henderson and his associates all the lands lying between the Kentucky and Cumberland Rivers, from their sources to their mouths respectively. In consideration of this cession, it is alleged that ten thousand pounds sterling in goods had been duly paid before the signing of the treaty.†

But the treaty having been made and entered into by private individuals, without any authority from the States of Virginia or North Carolina, was in itself null and void, so far as it claimed to vest the title of lands in those individuals; for at that early date the colonial government claimed the sole power to treat with the Indian tribes, and to purchase their lands, as one of the prerogatives of sovereignty.

Yet the company, regardless of consequences, proceeded to take possession of their unlawful purchase. The new colony was to be known and designated as "Transylvania in America." No efforts or means were spared to induce emigrants to make permanent settlements. The spirit of emigration from North Carolina and Virginia was active, and pioneers were anxious to lead the way in locating a colony.

* This land company consisted of the following persons, viz.: Richard Henderson, Thomas Hart, John Williams, James Hogg, Nathaniel Hart, David Hart, Leonard H. Bullock, John Luttrell, and William Johnston.
† Butler's Kentucky, p. 67, 68. See, also, Hall's Sketches, vol. i., p. 250, 251.

Daniel Boone, with a party of about twenty hunters and woodsmen, was sent in advance, to open and blaze a road from Holston River, through the southern wilderness, to the Kentucky River, north of the present town of Richmond, in Madison county, Kentucky. They had proceeded on the route with their labor until within fifteen miles of the termination, when they were attacked by a party of Indians, who killed two of their number and wounded two others. On the 23d of March they were again attacked by another party of Indians, who killed two more of their number and wounded three others. A few days afterward, Boone and the remainder of his party, in all sixteen men, arrived on the bank of the Kentucky River, and prepared immediately to erect a "station," or *fortified village*. This work was commenced on the first day of April, and progressed steadily until the first of June, when it was urged to completion, under the immediate superintendence of Colonel Henderson.

In the mean time, Colonel Henderson, by the way of Powell's Valley, had arrived with forty armed men and forty packhorses, besides many adventurers who sought the protection of such a numerous caravan to the west. This colony, having left Powell's Valley in April, had arrived upon the banks of the Kentucky River early in May.

Shortly afterward, Boone, leaving the fort in charge of Colonel Henderson and his companions, set out upon his return to the Holston settlements for his family, and such emigrants as were inclined to accompany him to the new settlement. In the autumn he conducted his family, with a few others, through the wilderness to the banks of the Kentucky River. They took up their residence in the "station," which had now been called "Boonesborough," a name which the place retains to this day. Daniel Boone's wife and two daughters may be considered the first white women who made their residence in Kentucky.

Soon afterward, Colonel Calloway and his family, with a few other emigrants, arrived at Boonesborough, and the population increased from day to day by the arrival of other pioneer settlers and adventurers, who made their residence at or near this station.[*] Such was the beginning of the first settlement in Kentucky, on the site of the present town of Boonesborough.

[*] See Life of Boone, p. 83. This is a small duodecimo volume of 250 pages, com-

The following sketch of the fortified station of Boonesborough will give the reader an idea of the general character of "stations" for the protection of the surrounding settlements during Indian hostilities. It is taken from Judge Hall's "Sketches of the West."

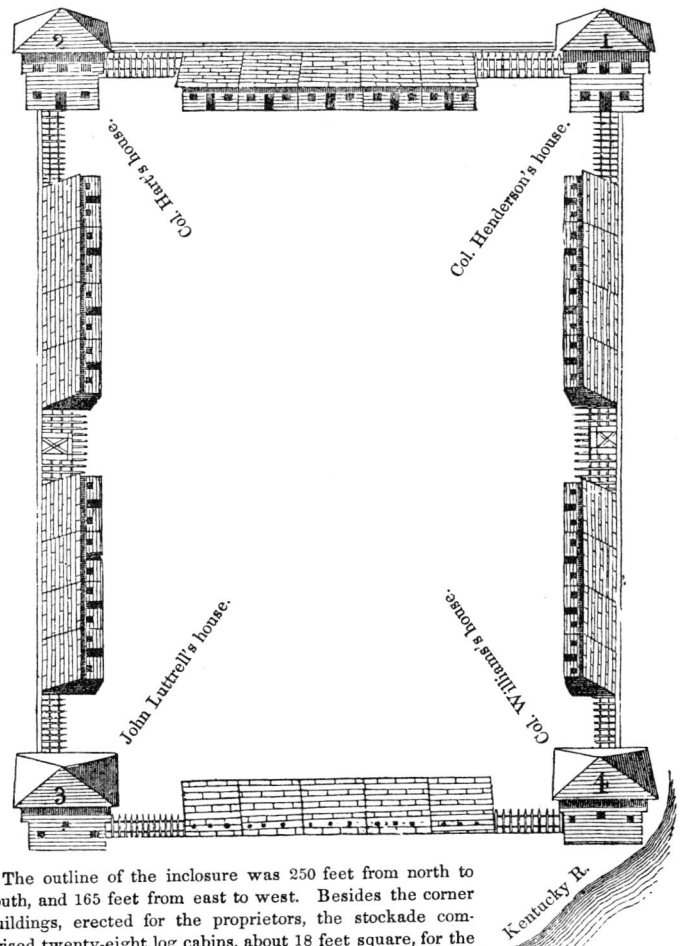

The outline of the inclosure was 250 feet from north to south, and 165 feet from east to west. Besides the corner buildings, erected for the proprietors, the stockade comprised twenty-eight log cabins, about 18 feet square, for the use of families pertaining to the colony. The outside wall of each was built up close, and was made bullet-proof, without doors or windows, and raised 12 feet in height, from which the roof, with a single slope, declined to the inner wall, 8 feet high: the doors and window-openings were wholly within the stockade: the fronts of the cabins all faced the central area, or common yard. Two secure gateways, on opposite sides, guarded the entrance.

The lawless character of the "Treaty of the Watauga," and the purchase of Transylvania, did not escape the watchful eye of Governor Dunmore. No sooner had he been apprised of the facts, than he issued his proclamation against the purchase of "Richard Henderson, and other disorderly persons," in which he declared the purchase null and void, vesting in them no right of title whatever, the title and sovereignty of the same remaining exclusively in the government of Virginia, as a portion of her territory. This gave rise to much difficulty between the proprietors and those who held their land-titles.

Yet emigrants from North Carolina had continued to visit the new settlements of Transylvania, and made almost daily accessions to the resident population. The Shawanese, although expelled from the occupancy of the country north of Cumberland, still retained a claim to the lands as a hunting-ground, common to them and the Cherokees, and they had, at the treaty of Camp Charlotte, reluctantly yielded their consent to the white man's advance. Hence straggling parties of Shawanese, as well as a few Cherokees who infested these regions, took every opportunity to harass the advance of the settlers. The route by which the emigrants from North Carolina advanced was exposed to depredations and murders, which these tribes could occasionally commit with impunity. And as the Indians continued to evince a hostile disposition toward the settlement, it was deemed advisable to take all precautions for its protection against any combined attack which might be contemplated by the savages. Hence, about the first of May, another fortified station, or "Fort," had been commenced near the present site of Stanford, in Lincoln county, under the control and command of Colonel Benjamin Logan. This fort for many years constituted an important defense for the population in this part of the country, and it was afterward known as "Logan's Fort," a name given in honor of its founder.[*] This was the second settlement and station in Kentucky.

In the mean time, regardless of the governor's proclamation, the company claimed the right of title to the soil, and lands were sold or leased by the proprietors on terms that might be termed liberal to emigrants, reserving to themselves one half

piled by Timothy Flint, and published in Cincinnati. It is an excellent picture of frontier life and the perils of savage warfare, and, with the exception of some exaggerations and fancy sketches of border incident, is authentic history.

[*] Butler's Hist. of Kentucky, p. 30.

of all the gold and silver, the lead, copper, and sulphur mines which might subsequently be discovered.* With this reservation, and the additional payment of a small nominal rent, deeds were drawn up and executed with great formality, and full of the old English law-verbiage. The company also opened accounts with the purchasers and settlers, and furnished them, on reasonable terms and at fair prices, with ammunition and such other articles as were requisite for the general defense. Toward the liquidation of these accounts, each settler was allowed a credit of fifty cents per day for all military service, for serving as rangers or scouts, for opening roads, and for public hunting. Powder was charged at two dollars and sixty cents per pound, and lead at sixteen and two third cents per pound; prices certainly not unreasonable in that remote region.†

A land-office was established for the regular entry of all sales made under the authority of the company; surveyors, clerks, and chain carriers, all duly sworn, were appointed by the "agent of the company." The manner of surveys was also established, to be governed, as a general rule, "by the four cardinal points, except where rivers or mountains so intervene as to render it too inconvenient."‡ An officer was appointed whose duty corresponded to that of secretary of state in the colonial government. The "agent" of the company was Colonel John Williams, of North Carolina.

As early as the 23d of May, a proprietary government had been organized at Boonesborough by the election of a house of delegates, consisting of eighteen persons, chosen from the four settlements on the south side of Kentucky River, including

* The settlements on the north and northeast side of Kentucky River, at this early period, were known as the "Crown lands," in contradistinction to the Transylvania purchase. Many transient adventurers having visited the West, in company with the colonies and armed caravans, spent their time, as interest or inclination directed, among the settlers on the company's lands, or among those on the crown lands.

† Butler's Kentucky, p. 30–32.

‡ See Hall's Sketches of the West, vol. ii., Appendix. This is a valuable collection of historical sketches of the Western settlements, incidents, and character of Western life, by Judge James Hall, of Indiana. Although it is presented to the public (edition of 1835) as "sketches," it is useful for the many valuable incidents of Western history, which the author has collected and arranged under appropriate heads. Some portions of it are written in a style interesting to the general reader, rather than an exact detail of connected historical facts. Although in some portions the author has not been very accurate as to unimportant facts in history, he has greatly contributed to aid the future historian. Those who desire to see a more full account of the transactions of the company proprietors of Transylvania during the existence of their government, will find valuable records of the same in the Appendix of 54 pages, in vol. ii. of Hall's Sketches.

Boonesborough and Harrodsburg.* After a session of nearly one week, they adjourned, having enacted a number of laws for the good government of the colony, independent of the jurisdiction of Virginia. Among the objects for which this convention was assembled was that of adopting *a written compact*, defining the powers and prerogatives of the proprietors, and the rights and privileges of the colonists. The proprietors made a formal exhibit of their title-deed to the soil from the Cherokee Indians, and desired it to be spread upon their journal as a public record.†

The proprietors then entered into a written compact for securing the rights of the colonists, beginning with the following preamble, viz.:

"Whereas it is highly necessary for the peace of the proprietors, and the security of the people of this colony, that the powers of the one, and the liberties of the other, be ascertained; We, Richard Henderson, Nathaniel Hart, and John Luttrell, in behalf of ourselves, as well as of the other proprietors of Transylvania, on the one part, and the representatives of the people of the colony on the other part, do most solemnly enter into the following agreement and compact, to wit," &c. The following are some of the conditions and provisions of this contract, or *constitution*, which was signed by the three proprietors above recited on the part of the company, and by Thomas Slaughter, chairman, on the part of the convention, viz.:

"1. The election of delegates in the colony shall be annual.

"2. Perfect religious freedom and general toleration.

"3. The judges of the superior courts to be appointed by the proprietors, but to be *paid by the people*, and *to them an-*

---

* See Hall's Sketches, vol. i., p. 264, 265, 266. It might be interesting to the general reader to know the names of the prominent men of this first little republic in Kentucky, who composed the convention to define their rights and powers. They were as follows:

For Boonesborough: Squire Boone, Daniel Boone, William Cocke, Samuel Henderson, William Moore, and Richard Calloway.

For Harrodsburg: Thomas Slaughter, John Lythe, Valentine Harmon, and James Douglass.

For the Town of St. Asaph: John Todd, Alexander Spotswood Dandridge, John Floyd, and Samuel Wood.

For Boiling Spring Settlement: James Harrod, Nathan Hammond, Isaac Davis, and Azariah Davis.

Colonel Thomas Slaughter was unanimously chosen *chairman*, and Matthew Jewett *clerk*.

† For a condensed historical sketch of the legislative proceedings of the Transylvania Republic, see Hall's Sketches, vol. i., p. 264-276. Also, Butler's Kentucky, Introduction, p. 68.

swerable for mal-conduct: the *judges of the inferior courts* to *be recommended by the people*, and to be *commissioned by the proprietors.*

"4. The legislative authority, when the colony shall be more mature, to consist of *three* branches, to wit: 1st. A house of delegates, *elected by the people;* 2d. A council of freehold residents, not exceeding twelve in number; 3d. The proprietors.

"5. The convention shall have the sole power to raise and appropriate all public moneys, and of electing their own treasurer."

Thus commenced the first civilized government in Kentucky, and such were some of the fundamental principles of a Republican form of civil government, which planted in the remote West those germs of civil and religious liberty which had already taken deep root in the Atlantic provinces.

The second session of the convention convened on the first Thursday in September following, at Boonesborough. At this session the convention, after formally acknowledging the authority of the proprietors, Richard Henderson and company, proceeded to establish courts of justice and rules of proceeding in the same; they also enacted a militia law, an attachment law, a law for preserving the game, and for the appointment of civil and military officers.

In the mean time, at a meeting of the proprietors, held at Oxford, in the county of Granville, North Carolina, on the 25th day of September, 1775, certain resolutions were adopted for the good government of the colony. Among them was one appointing Colonel John Williams, a member of the company, general agent in behalf of the proprietors, and defining his duties and powers, and the manner of supplying his place with a successor. James Hogg, another member of the company, was appointed a delegate of the company to the continental Congress, with a memorial to that body setting forth their claims to the territory of Transylvania, and professing an ardent attachment to the cause for which they were contending, and claiming their protection as a portion of the great country represented by them.

Soon afterward, in the winter of 1775–6, a memorial, or petition, signed by nearly ninety men deeply interested in the affairs of Transylvania, was sent to the convention of Virginia, remonstrating against the authority of the Company, and praying to be protected against the legal enforcement of their obligations, given for lands to which no valid titles could be given.

The emigrants to the Transylvania colony had continued to increase its numbers from the time that the town of Boonesborough was completed. Before the first of November the entire occupants of all the settlements was estimated at three hundred persons, the majority of whom were efficient men for the defense of the inhabitants. The whole quantity of land in cultivation was two hundred and thirty acres, chiefly planted in corn. The amount of lands entered in the land-office by individuals amounted to five hundred and sixty thousand acres.* But many of the adventurers were already impatient to return to the quiet haunts of domestic life in the settlements east of the Cumberland Mountains.

Up to this period the southwestern angle of Virginia was a frontier region, with a few sparse habitations distributed on the northern branches of Holston River and upon the branches of Clinch River, comprising most of the present counties of Wythe, Smyth, Washington, Russell, Lee, and Scott. The contiguous portion of North Carolina, comprising the present counties of Washington, Sullivan, Carter, and Johnson, was also a frontier region, comprised in the " Western District" of North Carolina, extending indefinitely westward, even to the Mississippi. Powell's Valley was nearly three hundred miles from the older settlements east of the mountains, and about one hundred and forty miles distant from the extreme western settlements of Transylvania.

But the attempt to establish a proprietary government received no sanction from the province of Virginia, nor from the provincial Congress, nor subsequently from the Legislature of the State of Virginia, although the company's agents were indefatigable in their efforts to obtain the sanction of the two latter legislative bodies.† The majority of the people of Transylvania never had cordially approved and supported the proprietary government, and to a portion of them it was decidedly unacceptable from the first organization. The rapid spread of the Revolutionary opinions through the colonies

---

* See Butler's Kentucky, Introduction, p. 68, 69.
† See Butler's Kentucky, Introduction, p. 68, 69. Also, Hall's Sketches, vol. i., p. 276, 277.

greatly augmented the number of disaffected in Transylvania, until the proprietary government was virtually rejected. Colonel Henderson and his associates finding it impracticable to sustain themselves in the executive station which they had assumed, at length abandoned their pretensions, and sought pecuniary indemnity from Virginia, in consideration of having extinguished Indian title. This they finally obtained, after many years of delay.*

[A.D. 1776.] The jurisdiction of Virginia was formally extended over the whole colony of Transylvania during the following year, to the great satisfaction of the people. Such was the fate of the first attempt to establish a privileged class and a landed aristocracy in Kentucky.

In the mean time, pioneer settlers were crowding into the beautiful plains on the northeast and west side of the Kentucky River, between thirty and fifty miles north of Boonesborough. They were still exploring the country, and making locations and surveys, lodging in temporary camps, and without families or domestic encumbrances, and exposed to the incursions and depredations of the northwestern Indians.

The few females who had as yet ventured into these remote settlements, and the small number of permanent residences which had been erected, were on the south side of the Kentucky River, in the vicinity of Boonesborough, Logan's Fort, and "Harrod's Station." Near the latter place, a fort or fortified station was in progress of erection, preparatory to the introduction of the families next year. This fort was not completed until March following, when it formed the third regular

* Hall's Sketches, vol. i., p. 277–280. The company had been very active in their efforts to obtain an acknowledgment of their claims by the continental Congress, as well as by the Legislature of the State of Virginia. On the 25th of September, 1775, James Hogg, Esq., had been appointed a delegate to the Congress, with a memorial from the company; but his efforts were unsuccessful.

Although the proprietors had been liberal in their first sales of land to settlers, and had made generous donations to meritorious individuals, yet they soon afterward became more exorbitant in their demands for lands, surveying, and terms of tenure. The people became dissatisfied, and their fears were aroused at the uncertainty of the title under which the proprietors themselves held the lands. They at length refused to submit to obligations entered into with the agent of the company, in consideration of lands which belonged, in fact, to the state. Hence the people of the colony threw themselves upon the protection of the government of Virginia, by a memorial sent to the "Convention of the Colony of Virginia," with the signatures of eighty-six men of the colony. Among these were the names of James Harrod, William Harrod, Levi Harrod, William Wood, Thomas Wilson, John Hardin, John Helm, and others who have left large families to perpetuate their names.—See Hall's Sketches, vol. ii., p. 236–240; also, 249–254.

station in Kentucky, Boonesborough and Logan's Fort being the first and second.

During the winter, several murders and assaults had been committed by parties of Indians who had been lurking about the settlements; these, however, were only marauding parties of Shawanese, without the sanction of their chiefs. Yet there were indications of dissatisfaction among the northwestern tribes at the rapid advance of the whites into their choice hunting-grounds, where, from time immemorial, the bear, the deer, the elk, and the buffalo had their winter resort, in the luxuriant cane which covered its extensive plains and bottoms, and served both for food and a shelter from the blasts of winter. Should this fine region, the paradise of the Indian hunter, be given up to the whites without a struggle? The Indian thought not; and the British agents at Detroit, in the Illinois country and in the Cherokee nation, were soon ready to aid them to harass, and, if possible, to break up these advanced settlements. The Indians began to find that the English agents and commandants of the northwestern posts were disposed to encourage them in their hostility against the frontier people. Of course, the stations, the roads, the frequented paths, and traces near the settlements, began to be infested with lurking bands of Indians, who never failed to attack individuals when it could be done with impunity. Hence the inhabitants were compelled to adopt measures of precaution to prevent frequent disasters from the wily savage.

As spring began to open, the tide of emigration began to move toward Kentucky. Many families from the Monongahela were now willing to venture into the country, under the protection of the three strongly-fortified stations which were now ready for their reception. Thus women and children began to swell the numbers of those who had already gone as pioneers to Kentucky. A few slaves, also, were introduced, with some personal property and domestic utensils. Among the first families introduced by way of the Ohio River, from the settlements on the Monongahela, was that of Colonel James Harrod. Ever active, and full of daring enterprise, having completed his station and a house for a private residence, he proceeded to the Monongahela for his family and a colony of settlers. Early in the summer, he returned by way of the Ohio to the Kentucky River, in a boat freighted with a number of families besides his own, all destined for Harrod's Station. Among the families thus introduced were those of Denton, M'Gary, and Hogan, all valuable citizens for a frontier community. Other families followed in the course of the summer, increasing the number of females at Harrod's Station to something like thirty. This was the first introduction of females into this portion of the Kentucky settlements.

In the mean time, difficulties between the colonies and the British crown had ripened into bloodshed and open rebellion against the regal power. The colonies, through their delegates in general Congress convened, had declared themselves free and *independent states;* to maintain which declaration, a furious war was already raging along the Atlantic coast. Soon after the commencement of hostilities by the British forces on the Atlantic seaboard, the northwestern Indians, instigated by British agents and emissaries from Detroit, Vincennes, and Kaskaskia, had commenced a state of desultory warfare against the exposed settlements of Kentucky and Western Virginia. These settlements, including those of Pennsylvania, were now scattered sparsely over a frontier region not less than seven hundred miles in extent, from the Alleghany River to the falls of the Ohio. This extensive frontier was again to be exposed to the constant and terrible incursions of the Mingoes, and the warlike Shawanese residing upon the waters of the Scioto, Miami, and Wabash Rivers. Such was the condition of the northwestern frontier after the opening of the Revolutionary war. The exposed inhabitants were necessarily active in their preparations to protect themselves from the impending storm of savage vengeance which was lowering in the western horizon, induced through the instrumentality of British intrigue among the northwestern tribes.

The first indication of determined hostility on the part of the northwestern Indians in Kentucky occurred on the 7th of July. Again, on the 14th of July, a party of Indians, almost in sight of the station, captured the daughter of Daniel Boone, and two daughters of Colonel Calloway, who had strolled a few hundred yards from the stockade, upon the banks of the Kentucky River. Daniel Boone, with a party of eight men, pursued the savages, and, after two days of pursuit, succeeded in re-capturing the girls and in killing two of the Indians.

After this occurrence the stations were placed in a more

secure state of defense, the women and children collected into the stockades, and measures taken for guarding against surprise from Indian incursions. The detached settlements were abandoned, and their occupants retired to stronger stations. Many who were able retired east of the mountains, or to situations less exposed on the Monongahela, where they imparted to others a portion of their enthusiasm for the glorious country of Kentucky.*

Among the prominent visitors of Kentucky this summer was Major George Rogers Clark, from Virginia, who had been appointed to superintend the defense of the Kentucky settlements. In this employment he spent the summer at Harrod's Station and Boonesborough alternately, organizing military companies for their common protection.

Major Clark was one of Nature's noblemen; with a mind of extraordinary compass, he possessed also a robust frame and an iron constitution. He had already seen much service in the Indian wars. He had served in the old French war under General Braddock; in Pontiac's war he was no idle spectator; and in Lord Dunmore's war he was an active field-officer from first to last. Such was the man whose military genius was to be the bulwark of the western frontier.

On the Carolina frontier a similar state of things existed. Early in the year 1776, the people of the "Western District," with indignation and noble firmness, rejected the proffered protection of the royal government, and chose to adhere to the cause of the colonies in sustaining the measures of the Continental Congress in support of their independence. This, in the eye of the royal authorities, placed them on the same footing with the people of the northwestern frontier, and beyond the pale of civilized warfare. Through the influence of Sir John Stewart, British superintendent of southern Indian affairs, a formidable invasion of these settlements by the Cherokees was devised *for the depopulation of the country.* But the Indians were ultimately defeated in the subsequent operations of Virginia and Carolina for the defense of the frontiers.†

* See Butler's Kentucky, p. 32, 33. Also, Flint's Life of Boone, p. 98.
† See Winterbotham's America, vol. ii., p. 26.

Vol. I.—C c

CHAPTER IV.

BRITISH OCCUPANCY OF FLORIDA AND THE ILLINOIS COUNTRY.— CLOSE OF THE BRITISH DOMINION IN THE MISSISSIPPI VALLEY.— A.D. 1764 TO 1782.

Argument.—Extent of Florida and the Illinois Country under the British Dominion.— English Authority established in West Florida by Governor Johnston.—Major Loftus appointed Commandant of Illinois.—His Defeat above Tunica Bayou, and his Death.— Dissatisfaction of the French of West Florida.—Population in 1764.—Anglo-American Emigration to Florida encouraged.—Emigrants arrive from 1765 to 1770.—Great Increase of Emigrants in 1773 to 1776.—Settlements on east Side of the Mississippi. —British Military Posts in West Florida.—Monopoly of Trade by British Traders.— Emigration in 1775-6.—Agriculture encouraged.—British Tories in West Florida.— British Authority established in the *Illinois Country*, 1765.—St. Angé.—Captain Stirling.—French Population in 1765.—General Gage's Proclamation.—Major Frazer. —Colonel Reed.—Colonel Wilkins.—His Administration.—Grants of Land.—British Military Posts in the Northwest.—Detroit.—Kaskaskia.—Cahokia.—St. Vincent.— Prejudices of the Illinois French.—Detroit, Vincennes, and Kaskaskia the Sources of all the Indian Barbarities on the Western Frontier.—Reduction of these British Posts indispensable to the Security of the Virginia Frontier.—Plan of Colonel Clark's Expedition for their Reduction.—Colonel Clark leads his Expedition to Kaskaskia.— The Fort and Town taken by Surprise.—Stern Demeanor of the Commander toward the French.—Happy Results.—Cahokia surrenders to Captain Bowman.—Governor Rocheblave sent Prisoner to Virginia.—People of Vincennes declare for Virginia.— Indian Negotiations and Treaties on the Wabash.—Jurisdiction of Virginia extended over the Illinois Country.—"Illinois County."—Colonel Hamilton advances with a strong Force from Detroit.—Captain Helm capitulates.—Clark advances to recapture the Post.—Colonel Hamilton taken by Surprise.—Despairs of successful Defense, and capitulates.—Captain Helm captures a Detachment with Supplies from Detroit. —Colonel Hamilton sent Captive to Virginia.—Is placed in close Confinement in retaliation for his Inhumanity.—Colonel Clark contemplates the Capture of Detroit.— British Power expelled from the Illinois Country.—Difficulties begin in West Florida. —Captain Willing descends the Mississippi.—His Collision with the People at Natchez.—First Act of Hostility at Ellis Cliffs.—Spain espouses the American Cause. —Galvez invades West Florida.—Captures British Posts at Manchac, Baton Rouge, Natchez, and Mobile.—Is unsuccessful at Pensacola.—Pensacola captured in 1781.—All Florida submits to the Arms of Spain.—British Dominion ceases on the Mississippi.

[A.D. 1764.] As has been observed heretofore,* the province of West Florida, under the British dominion, comprised a large extent of territory on the east side of the Mississippi River, between the mouth of the Yazoo and the Bayou Manchac, and extending eastward to the Chattahoochy River. East of Lake Maurepas, it comprised all the coast and ports on the Gulf of Mexico to Appalachicola Bay. The whole formed one government under the commandant, or governor,

---

* See book ii., chap. x.; also, book i., chap. v.

whose headquarters were at Pensacola, the capital of the province.

Early in February, 1764, Captain George Johnston arrived at Pensacola, in company with a regiment of troops, to take formal possession of the province, of which he had been appointed civil and military governor. The French posts of Fort Condé, Toulouse, Baton Rouge, and Rosalie, at Natchez, were soon afterward garrisoned with British troops. Another fort was built during the year upon the north bank of the Bayou Manchac, or Iberville, near its junction with the Mississippi, and was subsequently known as "Fort Bute," in honor of the Earl of Bute, who had been chosen prime minister by George the Third.

Governor Johnston, after his arrival, had issued his proclamation announcing his powers and the limits of his jurisdiction, after which measures were taken to reorganize the civil government under English commandants and magistrates; superior courts were organized under English judges.*

The "Illinois country," comprising the region between the Upper Mississippi and the Wabash River, differed in extent but little from the present limits of the State of Illinois. The settlements in that region were isolated, in the midst of a boundless wilderness, inhabited by the few native tribes who roamed over its extensive plains and forests. Kaskaskia was the principal town and settlement, and Fort Chartres had long been the headquarters of the French commandant.

West Florida.—On the 27th of February, Major Loftus, who had been stationed at the outlet of Bayou Manchac, was dispatched from that point with four hundred men for the posts in the Illinois country, of which he had been appointed commandant. With his detachment, he set out from Manchac to ascend the river in ten sixteen-oared barges or keels; and after three weeks of toil against the strong current of the river, he had just reached the point of highlands which touch the river for three miles on the east, about ten miles above the mouth of Red River. Here, in the contracted channel of the river, the deep, strong current sweeps for five miles around a bend at the base of the bluff. The heights on the east, which rise abruptly from the water's edge, as well as the low alluvial bank on the west side, were

* Martin's Louisiana, vol. i., p. 342, 343. Also, see Gentleman's Magazine, London, 1764.

clothed in heavy forests, with impenetrable thickets of cane undergrowth. At this point, concealed on both sides of the river, were assembled a large number of the Tunica Indians in ambuscade, awaiting the approach of the English army in their toilsome and slow advance against the majestic flood. These Indians, former confederates of France, had imbibed the Frenchman's hatred of British dominion, which had not been placated by the imperious English. As the last galley entered the ambuscade, the astonished English troops were suddenly assailed along the whole line with a destructive discharge of fire-arms and arrows, accompanied with most terrific yells from the unseen savages. The whole fleet, thrown into confusion, after an ineffectual attempt at resistance against the unseen foe, fell back with the current beyond the reach of the enemy.

A large number of the men were killed and wounded. Among the slain was the commandant, Major Loftus himself, after witnessing the fall of numbers of his brave troops. The expedition to the Illinois country failed, and the remnant of the detachment dropped down with the current to the point of embarkation, from which they were subsequently ordered to Mobile. Such was the defeat of Major Loftus; and the attempt to occupy the Illinois country was abandoned until after the general pacification of the northwestern Indians subsequent to Pontiac's war and the treaty of the German Flats.

The point on the Mississippi where this disaster occurred was known subsequently, during the British dominion, as "Loftus's Heights;" at a later date the hills were occupied by Fort Adams, which name is still retained by the village at the base of the bluff. So soon as it was known that the English jurisdiction was extended over the settlements on the east side of the Mississippi as far as the Walnut Hills, great dissatisfaction was expressed by the French population, which was at that time quite numerous in that section of country. Many determined to retire across the river, where the jurisdiction of France was still exercised over the people. Yet, after having been assured that they should be protected in their religion, rights, and property, many consented to remain and test the fair promises of their new rulers. Others resolved to be reconciled by no assurances, and obstinately refused to submit themselves to the hated dominion of England. Those who preferred to submit to the doubtful rule of France in Louisiana retired west of the river, and south of the Bayou Manchac.

[A.D. 1765.] After the extension of the British dominion over West Florida, and until the outbreak of hostilities against the United Colonies on the Atlantic border, the English authorities gave every encouragement, and held out strong inducements to emigration from the Atlantic provinces, and especially from the Carolinas and Georgia. It had been ascertained that no country could excel that portion of Florida which extended upon the Mississippi River, and the people of North Carolina and Georgia began to seek a route through the interior, and down the Mississippi, to the new province of West Florida. They were not averse to exchange the sterile pine lands near the Atlantic coast for the rich alluvions and the fertile hills of the Natchez country. Many began to explore the route across to the upper branches of the Holston and Tennessee Rivers, through the Indian country to the Mississippi. The Tennessee and Ohio Rivers were found to afford fine navigation, and an easy route to Florida. Those who came received liberal grants of land in the region of rich uplands extending from the Yazoo to Baton Rouge. From these early emigrants are descended some of the oldest American families now inhabiting this portion of the present states of Mississippi and Louisiana.

Emigrants soon began to arrive from the provinces near the Atlantic seaboard, and from Great Britain and Ireland, as well as from the British colonies in the West Indies. Among the first colonies which arrived in this portion of West Florida was one from the banks of the Roanoke, in North Carolina, which formed settlements upon the first highlands north of the Iberville Bayou, and thence northward to the vicinity of Baton Rouge. This was probably the first Anglo-American colony which settled upon the banks of the Mississippi.*

[A.D. 1768.] During the next three years numerous emigrants arrived from Georgia and the Carolinas, as well as from New Jersey, and settled in the regions drained by the Bayou Sara, the Homochitto, and the Bayou Pierre, comprising the upland region from Baton Rouge to Grand Gulf Hills, and generally within fifteen or twenty miles from the immediate bank of the Mississippi. A few years afterward, a colony of Scotch

* Martin's Louisiana, vol. i., p. 343.

Highlanders from North Carolina arrived, and formed a settlement upon the upper branches of the Homochitto, about thirty miles eastward from Natchez. At a subsequent date others arrived from Scotland and increased the settlement, which afterward assumed the name of Scotia, or New Scotland. The people of this settlement still preserve much of their Highland character, and not a few of the older branches of families yet speak their native Gaelic tongue.

[A.D. 1770.] About the year 1770, emigrants began to arrive from the British provinces of North America by way of the Ohio and Mississippi Rivers; yet it was not until the year 1773 that the greatest number of emigrants advanced by this route. A large portion advanced from New Jersey, Delaware, and Virginia westward to the Monongahela and the Upper Ohio, while another portion, from North and South Carolina, advanced westward to the Holston and Cumberland Rivers, and thence to the Ohio. The disturbances growing out of the Revolutionary war prevented further emigration after the year 1777.

The British authority on the Lower Mississippi was sustained by several military posts with ample garrisons. Of these the principal were Fort Charlotte, at Mobile, formerly called Fort Condé; Fort Bute, on the north side of the Iberville, erected in 1765; the post of Baton Rouge, and Fort Panmure, at Natchez, formerly called Fort Rosalie.

With these supporters of her power, England began to encourage her citizens to monopolize the trade of the Lower Mississippi, and to introduce large quantities of slaves from Africa. From Fort Bute the English traders supplied the settlements of Louisiana with English articles of trade, and with slaves, which had been prohibited by the Spanish government. The latter were introduced from the coast of Guinea, by way of Lakes Pontchartrain and Maurepas, and thence up the Amite and Iberville.*

To check this illicit trade with the Spanish subjects within the Spanish dominion, and to embarrass the operations of the English traders from Fort Bute, the Spanish governor, Don Ulloa, ordered a small fort to be constructed on the south bank of the Iberville, or Manchac, opposite, and distant about four hundred yards from Fort Bute.

* Martin's Louisiana, vol. i., p. 354.

The entire French population in this portion of the former province of Louisiana, at the period of its dismemberment, was in all probability not less than two thousand persons, including about twelve hundred slaves.

[A.D. 1775.] West Florida continued under the government of the commandant at Pensacola, a mere military province, unlike those on the Atlantic seaboard, which were provided with a regular system of colonial government, under laws enacted by a colonial Legislature elected by the people, subject only to the approval of the king.

The cultivation of cotton, which had been introduced by the French, was encouraged by the whole commercial policy of the parent country. Slaves were freely introduced as an article of trade, for the extension of the staple products of cotton, indigo, and sugar.*

From the year 1773 to 1775, not less than four hundred families arrived in West Florida by way of the Ohio and Mississippi Rivers.† Many of these were from the New England States, and from Virginia and Maryland, who followed in the tide of emigration which had begun to set toward the Monongahela and the Upper Ohio. Among the emigrants from New England was a colony introduced by General Thaddeus Lyman, of Connecticut. He had been a brave and energetic commander during the Canadian wars, and had obtained a large grant from the king to be located in West Florida. After many difficulties and embarrassments, and after selecting a location on the Yazoo and other points, he finally chose another upon the waters of Bayou Pierre.‡ The grant called for twenty thousand acres, and covered the land from the Grand Gulf Hills eastward upon the Bayou Pierre, including the junction of the north and south forks, within one mile of the present town of Port Gibson. Upon this location he proceeded to settle his little colony; but, embarrassed with pecuniary difficulties, he was soon afterward compelled to abandon the further prosecu-

* Stoddart's Louisiana, p. 74.
† See Holmes's Annals of the United States, vol. ii., p. 183, 184.
‡ Martin erroneously makes the location of this grant to General Lyman at the Walnut Hills. Although he explored the country near this point, and as far as the Yazoo River, yet the records of the United States Land-office at Washington, Mississippi, the seat of the territorial government from 1800 to 1817, show that the location was made upon the Bayou Pierre, in the present county of Claiborne, Mississippi. In this case, the king's *mandamus* was made in favor of Thaddeus Lyman, and was dated February 2d, 1775, for twenty thousand acres.—See Martin's Louisiana, vol. ii., p. 35.

tion of the enterprise, and with a few friends, who, like himself, had become old and discouraged, retired to a private settlement made in the vicinity of Fort Panmure.

Other British grants were made in the Natchez district of West Florida about this time; but, owing to the growing difficulties between the provinces and the mother country, or to some other cause, they were never fully confirmed, or were re-granted by the Spanish authorities, who soon afterward succeeded to the government of Florida.*

[A.D. 1776.] At the commencement of the war of the Revolution, Florida adhered to the British crown, and gave no aid or countenance to the Atlantic provinces in their struggle for independence. The English population of West Florida being loyal subjects of the British monarchy, became odious in the eyes of the confederated colonists, and obnoxious to their indignant resentment, such as they meted out to "British Tories." Yet they took no active part in the contest against the colonies. The political animosities of the new states waxed strong against such of their citizens as continued to adhere to the royal cause, and they receiving but little favor, and often gross indignities from their Republican neighbors, in many instances retired westward, and made their way down the Mississippi, seeking security and peace among their loyal countrymen in West Florida, under the protection of the British flag. Hence, about this time, the settlements on the east side of the Mississippi, from the Walnut Hills to Baton Rouge, received a considerable accession to its Anglo-American population. Here they continued to enjoy peace and security until after the arms of Virginia began to be triumphant in the West.

The Illinois Country.—The activity and zeal of the British

* Among the British grants in the "Natchez District," now on file in the land-office in Washington, Mississippi, are the following:

1st. "Ogden's Mandamus," made in favor of Amos Ogden, for twenty-five thousand acres, located on the north side of the Homochitto River, dated October 27th, 1772.

2d. "Lyman's Mandamus," made to Thaddeus Lyman, and dated February 2d, 1775, for twenty thousand acres, located on the Bayou Pierre.

3d. "Grant" to Doctor John Lorimer for two thousand acres, dated May 6th, 1776.

4th. "Grant" to William Grant for one thousand acres, dated May 6th, 1776, near the Walnut Hills.

5th. "Grant" to William Garnier, dated May 28th, 1779, for five thousand acres, located on the Homochitto.

6th. "Grant" to Augustin Provost, dated December 31st, 1776, for five thousand acres, located on Cole's Creek.

Besides these, there are many smaller grants, varying from five hundred to one thousand acres.

officers at the different posts northwest of the Ohio, instigating and leading their savage allies against the feeble settlements east of the Ohio in their murderous incursions, was the chief cause which prematurely involved the Illinois population in the war of the Revolution, and hastened the downfall of the royal authority in this portion of the American possessions, and also accelerated the loss of Florida. As we have elsewhere observed,* the British dominion was not formally extended over the Illinois and Wabash countries until the spring of 1765. After the defeat which Major Loftus had experienced in March of the preceding year, the attempt to send troops and a commandant to that region had been deferred, and the French commandant, St. Angé, at Fort Chartres, continued to exercise authority under the laws and usages of France as formerly, although it was known that the country was a British province.

[A.D. 1765.] Early in the spring of 1765, Captain Stirling, of the British army, arrived by way of Detroit, and took command of Fort Chartres, as commandant of the Illinois country, under the orders of General Gage, commander-in-chief of his majesty's forces in America. He was authorized to receive the allegiance of his majesty's new Catholic subjects, and to institute an organized government, by introducing the English laws and usages among the people. He was also instructed to guaranty to the French population, who desired to remain under the dominion of Great Britain, the free enjoyment of their liberty and property, the free exercise of their religious opinions, and the observance of all the rites and ceremonies of the Catholic Church. At the same time, he was instructed to grant permission freely to all who desired to retire to the French settlements on the west side of the Mississippi, together with the unrestrained removal of their personal property. On entering upon his official duties, he made known to the inhabitants the proclamation of General Gage, the provisions of which he was authorized to enforce. In this affectionate proclamation the commander-in-chief did not fail to close with the humane admonition to the inhabitants that, "by a wise and prudent demeanor, by avoiding all cause of complaint," and by "acting in concert with his majesty's officers," they might "save themselves from the *scourge of a bloody war*."†

* See book ii., chap. x., near the close of the chapter.

† The following is a copy of General Gage's proclamation to the inhabitants of the Illinois country, viz. :

St. Angé delivered to him in due form the fortress of Fort Chartres, and the whole territory eastward to the Ohio River, after which he and his garrison of one and twenty men retired across the river to the village of St. Louis. Many of the French, preferring to leave their houses and fields and to follow their beloved commandant, promptly declined to become subjects of Great Britain. Those who retired west of the Mississippi settled chiefly about the vicinity of St. Louis and St. Geneviève, the latter being then a village of nearly twelve years' standing.* The former had been selected two years before, as a dépôt for the Fur Company of Louisiana.

The French population of the whole Illinois country, from the Mississippi eastward to the Wabash, at this time were proba-

---

"PROCLAMATION.

"Whereas, by the peace concluded at Paris, the 10th of February, 1763, the country of the Illinois has been ceded to his Britannic majesty, and the taking possession of the said country of the Illinois, by the troops of his majesty, though delayed, has been determined upon; we have found it good to make known to the inhabitants:

"That his majesty grants to the inhabitants of the Illinois the liberty of the Catholic religion, as it has already been granted to his subjects in Canada. He has consequently given the most precise and effective orders, to the end that his new Roman Catholic subjects of the Illinois may exercise the worship of their religion, according to the rites of the Romish Church, in the same manner as in Canada.

"That his majesty, moreover, agrees that the French inhabitants or others, who have been subjects of the most Christian king (the King of France), may retire in full safety and freedom, wherever they please, even to New Orleans, or any other part of Louisiana; although it should happen that the Spaniards take possession of it in the name of his Catholic majesty (the King of Spain), and they may sell their estates, provided it be to subjects of his majesty, and transport their effects, as well as their persons, without restraint upon their emigration, under any pretense whatever, except in consequence of debts, or of criminal processes.

"That those who choose to retain their lands and become subjects of his majesty, shall enjoy the same rights and privileges, the same security for their persons and effects, and the liberty of trade, as the old subjects of the king.

"That they are commanded by these presents to take the oath of fidelity and obedience to his majesty, in presence of Sieur Stirling, captain of the Highland regiment, the bearer hereof, and furnished with our full powers for this purpose.

"That we recommend forcibly to the inhabitants to conduct themselves like good and faithful subjects, avoiding, by a wise and prudent demeanor, all cause of complaint against them.

"That they act in concert with his majesty's officers, so that his troops may take peaceable possession of all the forts, and order be kept in the country. By this means alone they will spare his majesty the necessity of recurring to force of arms, and will find themselves saved from the scourge of a bloody war, and of all the evils which the march of an enemy into their country would draw after it.

"We direct that these presents be read, published, and posted up in the usual places.

"Done and given at headquarters, New York, signed with our hand, sealed with our seal and arms, and countersigned by our secretary, this 30th of December, 1764.

"THOMAS GAGE.

"By his excellency, G. Maturin."

* Martin's Louisiana, vol. i., p. 321.

bly not less than five thousand persons, including about five hundred negro slaves. The number was subsequently diminished by emigration to Louisiana, which was not replaced by English emigrants. Ten years afterward, the population of Kaskaskia was estimated at but little over one hundred families, that of Cahokia fifty families, and of Prairie Dupont and Prairie du Rocher each fourteen families.

Three months after the arrival of Captain Stirling, he died, and left the office of commandant vacant on the east side of the Mississippi. In this state of things, the excellent commandant, St. Angé, returned to Fort Chartres, and resumed the duties of his former office until a successor to Captain Stirling should arrive from the commander-in-chief. Not long afterward, Major Frazer, from Fort Pitt, arrived as commandant, and exercised an arbitrary authority until next spring, when he was relieved by Colonel Reed, who also exercised his authority for eighteen months* in an oppressive and despotic manner.

[A.D. 1767.] The region of the Illinois and Upper Mississippi received but few emigrants from the British provinces, and the population in that quarter remained, during the British dominion, as isolated French settlements in the heart of an immense savage wilderness, having only occasional intercourse with Detroit, Fort Pitt, and New Orleans, by means of agents and traders.

[A.D. 1768.] On the 5th of September, 1768, Colonel Reed, to the great joy of the French, was superseded by Lieutenant-colonel Wilkins. He proceeded to organize regular courts of justice for the administration of the laws, in all matters of debt and property. The first court, announced by his proclamation of November 21st, consisted of seven judges, who held their first term at Fort Chartres on the 6th of December following.† The people claimed, as British subjects, the right of trial by jury; but the governor refused his sanction. Subsequently, like his predecessors, he was disposed to inflict upon the people a series of military oppressions, rather than cause an impartial administration of justice. The French gradually became alienated from the English authorities, and many retired to their friends in Louisiana, west of the Mississippi.

* See Peck's Gazetteer of Illinois, p. 86. Peck, Brown, and others call this commandant erroneously Major Farmer.

† See Brown's History of Illinois, p. 214. Also, American State Papers, vol. ii., land laws, p. 113 and 180.

[A.D. 1769.] Early in the following year he began to transcend his authority in making extensive grants of land to a number of British officers and favorites; and " for the better settlement of the colony, and the better to promote his majesty's service," he modestly consented to become " interested in one sixth part thereof." Thus he would have appropriated one third of all the lands in Illinois; and some of these fraudulent grants were subsequently confirmed by the American authorities.*

Previous to the year 1778, Detroit was the headquarters of the western posts; they were all subordinate to the commandant at Detroit. From this point a trace led westward by way of the Maumee, and across to the Upper Wabash, and thence to Post St. Vincent; and thence a similar trace, or Indian path, led westward to Kaskaskia, and other points upon the Upper Mississippi. There was likewise between all these posts an admirable communication by water, which, although more circuitous, served for the transportation of military stores and munitions of war.

Detroit at this time was a village containing about one hundred houses, ranged upon narrow streets crossing each other at right angles, and containing about eight hundred inhabitants, chiefly French. The whole village was surrounded by a stockade nearly one mile in circuit, and defended by block-houses and bastions at the angles. The entire settlements within ten miles of the town comprised about two thousand inhabitants, residing near the banks of the Detroit River and its small tributaries.† The greater portion of these were Canadian French.

The headquarters of the Illinois country, previous to the year 1772, was Fort Chartres: subsequently, "Fort Gage," a wooden stockaded fort opposite the town of Kaskaskia, and on the east bank of the Kaskaskia River, was the headquarters of the commandant of Illinois.

At Cahokia, on the bank of the Mississippi, three miles below St. Louis, was a small post, dependent upon Fort Gage. Kaskaskia itself was three miles from the bank of the Mississippi, on the west side of the Kaskaskia River, about five miles above its mouth, and nearly sixty-five miles below St. Louis. It was the oldest settlement in the Illinois country, known as

---

* See Peck's Gazetteer of Illinois, p. 86. Martin's Louisiana, vol. i., p. 345 and 355.
† Imlay's America, London edition of 1797, p. 505, 506.

"Old Kaskaskia," often designated by the French sobriquet *Au Kâ*, or, inversed, Kâ-hō.

On the Wabash, about one hundred and fifty miles above its mouth, was the post of "Fort Sackville." This post, on the west side of the Wabash, nearly opposite the old town of Vincennes, was a regular stockade, with bastions and a few pieces of cannon, in charge of an officer with a small garrison. It was the old French St. Vincent, designated by the French often as "*Au Poste.*" It was on the direct line of communication between Detroit and Kaskaskia.

The whole region northwest of the Ohio was commanded by these posts. Around them the Indians congregated annually to receive their presents and winter supplies from the British agents, and to barter their skins and furs with the traders.

The only white inhabitants in all this region were composed of a few ignorant, half-civilized French, who had remained in the country after the British authority was extended over it, and a few Tory emigrants from the revolutionary states, who had fled from the displeasure and the vengeance of their indignant countrymen.

The poor patriarchal French, unsophisticated by the vices and intrigues of refined civilization, knew nothing of the people in the revolted provinces, except what they had learned through their brethren of Canada, or through their new English masters. The former had been engaged with New England in almost continual border wars for nearly a century; and there was nothing in these wars, instigated and controlled by British cupidity, in anywise calculated to instill into the Canadians any exalted ideas of the "*Bostonais*," who were now proclaimed by their own king as outlawed rebels.

With the British authorities in this region, it had been the uniform policy, from the beginning of the Revolutionary war, to prevent any intercourse between the French population and the revolted provinces which had renounced the British dominion. It was well known to the commandants that the revolted provinces themselves could not entertain toward England a more implacable hatred than was hereditary in the French. Beyond the reach of aid or protection from the English forces, the authorities in these regions employed every moral means to reconcile the French to their new allegiance, and to conciliate their national prejudices. At the same time, they did not fail carefully to instill into their minds the utmost horror of the fierce and ruthless character of the provincial rebels, who were more to be dreaded than even the hostile Indians themselves; and of all these rebel "Bostonais," none were more terrible than the Virginia "long-knives."*

[A.D. 1778.] *The Loss of the Illinois Country.*—From the first act of hostilities by the royal troops against the revolted colonies, the northwestern savages had been associated as allies of Great Britain, and had been employed by the British commanders to lay waste the western frontiers of Virginia and Pennsylvania, on the east side of the Ohio. After a bloody partisan warfare of nearly two years upon the western settlements, the Governor of Virginia adopted the plan of Major George Rogers Clark for suppressing the terrible incursions of the northwestern Indians.†

Moreover, Virginia, in virtue of her royal charter, claimed all the territory westward between the parallels of 36° 30' and 40° north latitude, as far as the Mississippi; and the British posts on the Wabash, the Illinois, and the Upper Mississippi were considered properly within the chartered limits of Virginia. These posts, as subordinate to Detroit, were found to be the actual source of all the Indian incursions which had been sent against the exposed frontier of Virginia west of the mountains, from Fort Pitt southward to the Kentucky River. From these points the British officers and emissaries operated upon the Indian tribes, which were dispersed over the whole northwestern

* Butler's History of Kentucky, chap. iii.

† During the years 1775 and 1776, Lord Dunmore, the royal governor of Virginia, driven by public odium from his capital, had been compelled by his fears to seek an asylum on board one of his majesty's ships-of-war, from which he planned the destruction of the frontier settlements near the Ohio River and its tributaries. For this purpose, through a special agent and emissary, Dr. John Connolly, former commandant at Fort Pitt and of the district of "West Augusta," an enterprising and audacious man, his lordship concerted measures with the commandants of Detroit and Fort Gage for the purpose of arming the northwestern savages against the defenseless frontier inhabitants. Connolly with impunity passed the western settlements, in possession of secret orders from Lord Dunmore to the commandants and agents of the West for carrying out his plan of operations in this quarter. In this nefarious employment, Connolly, during the years 1775 and 1776, aided by the "Loyalists," had passed to and from Detroit several times, keeping his correspondence with Lord Dunmore and other "Tories" a profound secret, until he was finally detected and arrested on the borders of Maryland, on his route to Detroit; and his papers were published by order of Congress. His capture and the disclosures made by his correspondence led to the expedition of Colonel Clark against the post of Kaskaskia, and the final interruption of the British operations northwest of the Ohio.—See Botta's History of the American War of Independence, vol. i., p. 250.

territory, from the Ohio and the great lakes westward to the Upper Mississippi: from these points were planned and supplied the numerous hostile incursions which had spread desolation and blood along the wide frontier east of the Ohio; and these were the points at which the savages were supplied with arms, ammunition, and clothing, to enable them to carry on their murderous warfare into the remote settlements. To these points, too, they carried their captives, torn from their families, and the scalps of their murdered victims, as trophies of their prowess and evidence of their industry.

As the numerous settlements scattered over an extensive frontier region could not be protected against the midnight prowlings of small detached parties penetrating every portion of the country unseen, the only effectual means of security was to dry up the fountain, or, in Western phrase, to *cut up the tree by the roots.* At length the governor, Patrick Henry, with the Executive Council, prompted and guided by the genius and enterprise of Colonel George R. Clark, set on foot a secret expedition for the reduction of the British posts on the Upper Mississippi and upon the Wabash Rivers. What the commonwealth lacked in men and means was fully supplied by the courage and daring intrepidity of her frontier defenders. The expedition for the reduction of these posts, these fountains of Indian massacre, was intrusted to Colonel Clark, yet with strict injunctions to *treat with humanity* such of the enemy as the chances of war might place in his power.*

* The following is a copy of the instructions issued to Colonel Clark for his government in the projected expedition, viz.:

"*Virginia in Council, Williamsburg, January 2d,* 1778.
"Lieutenant-colonel George Rogers Clark,—

"You are to proceed with all convenient speed to raise seven companies of soldiers, to consist of fifty men each, officered in the usual manner, and armed most properly for the enterprise, and with this force attack the British fort at Kaskaskia.

"It is conjectured that there are many pieces of cannon and military stores to considerable amount at that place, the taking and preservation of which would be a valuable acquisition to the state. If you are so fortunate, therefore, as to succeed in your expedition, you will take every possible measure to secure the artillery and stores, and whatever may advantage the state.

"For the transportation of the troops, provisions, &c., down the Ohio, you are to apply to the commanding officer at Fort Pitt for boats; and during the whole transaction you are to take especial care to keep the true destination of your force secret; its success depends upon this. Orders are therefore given to secure the two men from Kaskaskia. Similar conduct will be proper in similar cases.

"*It is earnestly desired that you show humanity to such British subjects and other persons as fall in your hands. If the white inhabitants of that post and the neighborhood will give undoubted evidence of their attachment to this state (for it is certain they*

The entire expedition was to consist at most of three hundred and fifty men, or seven companies of fifty men each, or such portion of them as could be enlisted for the enterprise. Yet that number could not be spared from the exposed frontier settlements, and he was compelled at last to execute the hazardous enterprise with less than half the number authorized by the governor.

With no other means than twelve hundred dollars in depreciated paper, and an order for transports and supplies of powder and ammunition, and a promised bounty of three hundred acres of land to each private, Colonel Clark, in January, set out from Williamsburg for Fort Pitt. Encountering great difficulties in recruiting his companies from settlements already too feeble for their own protection, he succeeded, by extraordinary exertions, in assembling at the Falls of the Ohio less than six incomplete companies about the middle of June. Selecting from his whole force four companies of picked men, under well-known captains, he prepared to descend the river upon the hazardous enterprise. The companies were commanded by Captains Montgomery, Bowman, Helm, and Harrod; and each man, after the Indian custom, was armed with a rifle, tomahawk, and scalping-knife. About the 24th of June he commenced his voyage down the river, after communicating to his officers the object and design of the expedition. The whole was conveyed in a number of keel-boats, and the destination was Kaskaskia.

live within its limits) *by taking the test prescribed by law*, and by every other way and means in their power, *let them be treated as fellow-citizens, and their persons and property duly secured*. Assistance and protection against all enemies whatever shall be afforded them, and the Commonwealth of Virginia is pledged to accomplish it. But if these people will not accede to these reasonable demands, they must feel the miseries of war, under the *direction of that humanity that has hitherto distinguished Americans, and which it is expected you will ever consider the rule of your conduct, and from which you are in no instance to depart.*

"The corps you are to command are to receive the pay and allowance of militia, and to act under the laws and regulations of this state now in force as militia. The inhabitants at this post will be informed by you, that, in case they accede to the offers of becoming citizens of this commonwealth, a proper garrison will be maintained among them, and every attention bestowed to render their commerce beneficial, the fairest prospects being opened to the dominions of France and Spain.

"It is in contemplation to establish a post near the mouth of the Ohio. Cannon will be wanted to fortify it. Part of those at Kaskaskia will be easily brought thither, or otherwise secured, as circumstances may make necessary.

"You are to apply to General Hand for powder and lead necessary for this expedition. If he can not supply it, the person who has that which Captain Lynn brought from Orleans can. Lead was sent to Hampshire by my orders, and that may be delivered to you. Wishing you success, I am, sir,

"Your humble servant, P. HENRY."

Arrangements for additional supplies had been made by the Federal authorities, through Captain William Lynn and Captain James Willing, to be obtained from the Spaniards in New Orleans, for the supply of all the posts in the region of the Ohio, as well as for the expedition to the Upper Mississippi.

About the last of June the expedition arrived at the "Old Cherokee Fort," below the mouth of the Tennessee, and about forty miles above the mouth of the Ohio. At this point important information was received relative to the actual condition of the British posts on the Upper Mississippi. Here, having obtained experienced guides through the wilderness, Colonel Clark determined to march through by land and take Kaskaskia by surprise. Having sunk his boats for concealment, he set out with his force, and plunged through the pathless wilderness, across extensive low grounds and marshes, a distance of nearly one hundred and twenty miles, each man bearing upon his back his scanty rations, baggage, and camp equipage, and encouraged by the dauntless energy of their commander, who shared equally with his soldiers every hardship, and led the way.

After a laborious and difficult march of several days through a trackless wilderness of swamps, flats, open woods, and prairies, in which even the guides were bewildered, they arrived, unperceived, in the vicinity of Kaskaskia, on the evening of July 4th, 1778. To avoid discovery, the troops remained concealed in the woods on the east side of Kaskaskia River, within two miles of the town, until night had obscured their movements from observation. Having procured boats for crossing the river, about midnight Colonel Clark prepared to advance against the enemy. Addressing his men in a short and sententious speech, he concluded by reminding them "that the town and fort were to be taken at all hazards." A portion of the troops, under command of the fearless Captain Helm, crossed the river to the town, and, having taken it by surprise, the principal street was secured while the inhabitants were asleep in their beds. Every avenue was guarded before they were apprised of their captivity.

On the opposite side of the river, Fort Gage was secured in like manner by the remainder of the force, under Colonel Clark himself. The garrison and the sleeping commandant, Lieutenant-governor Rocheblave, were awakened from their peaceful slumbers only to find themselves prisoners of war. Apprehending no danger at this remote point, not even a sentinel was on duty, nor a gate secured. Colonel Clark, leading his column, was conducted silently by a guide he had captured, through a postern gate into the open fort, and while with his sturdy warriors he surrounded the sleeping garrison and controlled the defenses of the post, the fearless Simon Kenton, at the head of a file of men, advanced softly to the apartment of the commander. While quietly reposing by his wife, he was aroused by a gentle touch only to behold his own captivity, and to order the unconditional surrender of the fort and its defenders.*

The town of Kaskaskia, containing about two hundred and fifty houses, was completely surrounded, and every avenue securely guarded to prevent escape or intercourse; runners were sent to warn the people in the French tongue that every enemy found in the streets would be instantly shot down; at the same time, they were convinced, by the terrible shout and yelling of the troops around the town, that they were all prisoners of war. A strict patrol was kept on duty during the night throughout the town, and a sergeant's guard, passing through the streets and entering every house, succeeded in completely disarming the inhabitants in the course of two hours. The troops in the suburbs of the place were directed to keep up, during the remainder of the night, a continual tumult and whooping, after the Indian fashion, while the inhabitants were required to observe the most profound silence. All intercourse from house to house was strictly prohibited, and the terror inspired was general and appalling. At the same time, Colonel Clark had full possession of the fort and its artillery, which commanded the whole town from the opposite side of the river.

Such was the work of the first night, during which, in the true spirit of generous chivalry, this handful of brave backwoodsmen accomplished one of the most important conquests in the West, without the shedding of one drop of blood, or committing the slightest outrage upon the conquered people.† The

---

* Approaching the fort, a solitary light issued from a house outside the stockade, and a corporal's guard was dispatched to secure the party in the house. Among them was a Pennsylvanian, who entertained but little affection for the English name, and who cheerfully served as a guide to Kenton's detachment, entering the stockade through a small postern gate.—See Hall's Sketches of the West, vol. ii., p. 118, 119. Also, Butler's Kentucky, p. 53–55.

† There has been much discrepancy among authors relative to the actual force of Colonel Clark's expedition, which proceeded from the "Falls of Ohio" with him for the

wife of M. Rocheblave, under the courtesy of the warrior to female prerogative, artfully concealed his public papers, which Colonel Clark did not succeed in obtaining.

On the day following, Colonel Clark proceeded to organize the affairs of the conquered post. Having obtained ample intelligence of the state of the defenses in the vicinity, and having properly secured his prisoners and all suspicious persons, he ordered the troops to be withdrawn from the town behind an eminence in view. All communication between suspicious persons and the troops was strictly prohibited, and several militia officers in the British service were unceremoniously placed in irons. An air of stern severity and prompt decision was assumed by the colonel, which struck terror into the citizens; every movement was made with the most rigid military discipline, enforced by the severest penalties; the most unqualified submission was required from every individual in the town, which was placed under strict martial law; his words were few and stern; and a general gloom appeared to gather over every countenance. They were now prisoners of war to that inexorable enemy, whom they had been taught to view as the most terrible of the " Bostonais," and all their fears and apprehensions were about to be realized.

At length the village priest, Father Gibault, at the head of six principal men of the town, was deputed to wait upon the American commander to supplicate his mercy and to deprecate his vengeance. They were introduced to him at his quarters, where he and his officers were seated. At the first sight of the sturdy warriors, Father Gibault and his associates for some minutes were almost speechless; all their fears and prejudices were more than realized in the rough and severe features of the men, no less than in their tattered and soiled apparel. The

reduction of Kaskaskia. Some give the number at three hundred men, and others less. The fact is as follows: that with all his efforts and extraordinary exertions, he succeeded in recruiting only four companies at his rendezvous on Corn Island, after having succeeded in raising an additional number of twenty men from the vicinity of "the falls," and from Harrod's Station. It was here he became acquainted with the brave Captain Montgomery, "an Irishman, and full of fight," who engaged in the enterprise with great ardor; also, Simon Kenton, a pioneer of Kentucky, and a number of resolute pioneers. After a number of desertions and the rejection of the faint-hearted, there remained only one hundred and fifty-three fighting men, according to General Kenton's statement, who served through the campaign. These were organized into four incomplete companies, under the four captains named in the text.—See M'Donald's Sketches of Simon Kenton and others, p. 219. This is probably the most authentic account of this extraordinary expedition.—See Hall's Sketches of the West, vol. ii., p. 118.

reverend father at length spoke, and stated that they had one small request to make of the American commander, which they desired as a special favor.

As the people expected to be torn from each other, and probably separated forever, they begged, through him, to be permitted first to assemble in the church to take a farewell of each other. Their request was granted; but they were warned not to attempt to leave the town. The colonel's replies were laconic and austere. The deputation were disposed to continue the interview; but, with a wave of the hand, they were informed that he had no leisure for further intercourse, and they retired. The whole village attended at church, and at length retired to their houses. The deputation again waited upon Colonel Clark, and tendered "their thanks for the indulgence they had received." They further continued, "they were sensible that theirs was the fate of war, and they could well submit to lose their property;" but they prayed not to be separated from their wives and children, and that something might be allowed for their support. They declared that heretofore in their conduct they had only obeyed their commandants, as their duty required; that they were ignorant of the nature of the contest between the United States and Great Britain; and that many of them felt more favorably inclined toward the people of the United States than they dared avow.

At this time, when their anxiety and fears were most excited, they were thus sternly addressed by the commander: "Do you mistake us for savages? From your language, surely you do. Do you think Americans will strip women and children, and take the bread out of their mouths? My countrymen disdain to make war upon helpless innocence. To prevent the horrors of Indian butchery upon our own wives and children, we have taken arms and penetrated to this remote strong-hold of Indian and British barbarity, and not for despicable plunder. The King of France has now united his powerful arms with those of America, and the contest will soon be ended. The people of Kaskaskia may side with either party; their property and families shall be safe; their religion shall not be molested by Americans. To verify my words, go tell your fellow-citizens they are at liberty to do as they please, without apprehension of danger from me. I know they are convinced since my arrival that they have been misinformed by British officers as to the character of Americans. Your friends shall be released from confinement."

The deputation attempted to apologize for the imputation implied against the American character, but it was unnecessary; they were desired to communicate his declaration to the people. In a few moments the gloom and dejection of the whole town was changed into the extravagance of joy. The bells rang their loudest peals, and the church was crowded with grateful hearts offering up to God their devout thanks for their unexpected deliverance from all the horrors they had anticipated.

The people, thus relieved from a state of fearful anxiety and bitter suspense, made the most unreserved expressions of their admiration for the generous conduct of the American commander and his brave associates in arms; at the same time they professed their firm attachment to the cause and government of the United States, and of the commonwealth of Virginia especially.

On the evening of the same day, Colonel Clark dispatched a detachment of troops under Captain Bowman to surprise and capture the post and village of Cahokia, on the banks of the Mississippi. The capture of this post was effected with the same secrecy and celerity which characterized the movements upon Kaskaskia. In this measure Captain Bowman was aided by many of the citizens of the latter place, who volunteered to serve as guides, and to lend their friendly influence with their countrymen at Cahokia to insure the successful issue of the enterprise.* The people gladly espoused the American cause.

Every post and settlement on the Upper Mississippi having been secured, Colonel Clark proceeded to reorganize the civil government by placing in office chiefly those who were citizens of the country. The people rejoiced at the change, and acknowledged themselves a colony dependent on Virginia, well pleased with the protection of the United States, which were now at war with the hereditary enemy of France.†

In the mean time, Colonel Clark had dispatched Captain Montgomery with his imperious and insolent prisoner, Governor Rocheblave, under a strong guard, to Richmond, to be dealt with as a prisoner of war. Simon Kenton, with dispatches to Kentucky, was directed to take the post of St. Vincent in his route,

---

* Butler's Kentucky, p. 57, 58.   † See M'Donald's Sketches, p. 220.

and by a confidential messenger transmit to Kaskaskia a minute account of the condition of that post and the feelings of the people. In this hazardous duty, Kenton acquitted himself with his usual intrepidity. Having reconnoitered the post and town for three nights, lying concealed by day, he transmitted the result of his discoveries to his commander, and proceeded on his route to "the Falls."

On the 18th of July, the inhabitants of Vincennes, at the recommendation of Father Gibault, parish priest of Kaskaskia, threw off their allegiance to the King of Great Britain, and voluntarily declared themselves citizens of the United States and of the State of Virginia. The commandant of the Wabash, Captain Abbot, being absent at Detroit, and the post at Vincennes being protected by only a small garrison, Colonel Clark early in August, having appointed Captain Helm commandant of Fort Sackville, and "agent for Indian affairs in the department of the Wabash," dispatched him with a small garrison, to take possession of the post of St. Vincent, and to await the arrival of re-enforcements from Virginia. The new commandant was received with acclamation by the people, and entered upon his official duties. Instructed by Colonel Clark, he soon succeeded, by his address and influence, in convening an Indian council, attended by the great Wabash chief Tobacco, or "Grand Door," with whom, after some delay, he effected a treaty, which conciliated the Wabash tribes as far north as Ouiatenon and the Wea towns.

September came, and but few recruits from Virginia arrived. A new difficulty now presented to the commander; the troops had been enlisted for only three months, and the term of service with the greatest portion of them was about to expire. To remedy this difficulty, he exercised the full extent of his discretionary powers, and in the emergency determined to re-enlist upon new terms such of his men as were willing to continue in the service. Seventy of his men, including Simon Kenton, determined to return to Kentucky; the remainder re-entered the service, associated with one company of the resident inhabitants under their own officers. With these he organized two garrisons, one under Captain Williams at Kaskaskia, and one under Captain Bowman at Cahokia.

Colonel William Linn, who had entered the campaign as a volunteer, returned to Kentucky in charge of the discharged recruits, with orders to erect a stockade at the "Falls of the Ohio." The sovereignty of Virginia was fully extended over the Illinois and Wabash countries, as known to the British authorities.

Before the close of September, Colonel Clark had commenced his negotiations with the Indian tribes occupying the regions drained by the Illinois and Upper Mississippi Rivers. Believing it impolitic, and a mistaken estimate of the Indian character, to invite them to treaties of peace and friendship, he lost no opportunity of impressing them with the power of the Americans and the high sense of honor which regulated all their military operations, no less than the unalterable determination to punish their enemies. Long acquainted with the Indian character, he maintained his dignified and stern reserve until they should ask for peace and treaties; and he fought them fiercely until they did sue for peace. When he treated with them, he avoided many presents, because they evinced to the Indian that those who gave them were moved by fear of their vengeance. In all his negotiations with the Indians, he impressed them by his manner, his fearless and stern reserve, as well as by his prompt decision, with a fear and terror of his authority which had been entirely unknown before.*

* To give the reader some idea of Colonel Clark's manner of intercourse with the Indians, the following sketch of an interview and speech may be taken. At the first of his treaties, the different parties of white and red men were assembled, when the Indians, being petitioners, opened the council by a chief, who advanced to the table at which Colonel Clark was sitting, "with the belt of peace in his hand; another followed with the sacred pipe; and a third with a fire to light it. The pipe, when lighted, was presented to the heavens, then to the earth, and completing the circle, was presented to all the spirits, invoking them to witness what was about to take place. The pipe was then proffered to Colonel Clark, and afterward to every one present." These formalities past, the orator addressed himself to the Indians as follows: "Warriors, you ought to be thankful that the Great Spirit has taken pity on you, has cleared the sky, and opened your ears and hearts so that you may hear the truth. We have been deceived by bad birds flying through the land (British emissaries), but we will take up the bloody hatchet no more against the long-knife, and we hope that, as the Great Spirit has brought us together for good, as he is good, so we may be received as friends, and peace may take the place of the bloody belt." The speaker then threw down the bloody belt of wampum and flags which they had received from the British, and stamped on them in token of their rejection. To this Colonel Clark guardedly and coldly replied, that "he had paid attention to what had been said, and would next day give them an answer, when he hoped the hearts of all people would be ready to receive the truth; but he recommended them to keep prepared for the result of this council, upon which their very existence depended."

"He desired them not to permit any of his people to shake hands with them, as peace was not yet made, for it was time enough to give the hand when the heart could be given too."

An Indian chief replied, "Such were the feelings of men who had but one heart, and

In October following, the jurisdiction of Virginia was formally extended over all the settlements on the Wabash and the Upper Mississippi, by the organization of the "County of Illinois," and the appointment of Colonel John Todd as civil commandant, and lieutenant-colonel of the county.*

The services of Colonel Clark and his brave companions were highly approved by the Legislature of Virginia, as expressed in a resolution of thanks to them "for their extraordinary resolution and perseverance in so hazardous an enterprise, and for the important services thereby rendered to their country."†

The Indian tribes in the vicinity of all the northwestern British posts had been panic-stricken at the daring courage of the Virginia troops. The name of Clark struck terror into their chiefs, because of his sleepless vigilance and his rapid movements. Indian hostilities on the southeast side of the Ohio, for a time, had almost ceased, and many of the Indians most intimate with the French population proposed to take up arms against the English; but Colonel Clark desired no such allies in a civilized war, and their offer was rejected.

Before the middle of December, all appearance of Indian hostility had vanished; the people of Vincennes remained firmly attached to the cause of the United States, and in their allegiance to the commonwealth of Virginia. Captain Helm was left with only two soldiers and a few volunteer militia to protect the fort at Vincennes. The whole regular force at Kaskaskia and Cahokia was reduced to less than one hundred men.

It was not long before this state of things was made known

who did not speak with a forked tongue." The council rose until next day, when Colonel Clark delivered a speech, of which the following is a specimen:

"Men and warriors! pay attention to my words. You informed me yesterday that the Great Spirit had brought us together, and you hoped, as he was good, it would be for good. I, too, hope the same, and expect each party to stand to what is agreed upon, whether it be peace or war, and hereafter prove ourselves worthy of the attention of the Great Spirit. I am a man and a warrior, not a counselor; I carry war in my right hand, and in my left peace. I am sent by the great council of the long-knife and their friends to take possession of all the towns owned by the English in this country, and to watch the motions of the red people. I come to bloody the paths of those who attempt to stop the course of the river, and to clear the roads between us and those who desire peace, so that women and children may walk in them without striking their feet against any thing. I am ordered to call upon the Great Fire for warriors enough to darken the land, that the red people may hear nothing but the sound of birds that live on blood. I know there is a mist before your eyes; I will dispel the clouds, that you may see clearly the cause of the war between the Great Fire and the English."—See Butler's Kentucky, p. 67, 68.

* Butler's Kentucky, p. 64, 65. † Idem, p. 61

to Governor Hamilton, commandant at Detroit. Alarmed at the rapid successes of the Virginia troops, and mortified at the disasters of the British arms, he determined to make an energetic invasion of the Illinois country, and retrieve the honor of his majesty's arms by the recapture of all the posts on the Wabash and Illinois, and by leading Colonel Clark and his followers captive to Detroit.

Having assembled six hundred Indian warriors, in addition to his force of eighty regular soldiers and some Canadian militia, he set out upon the expedition to Vincennes. Ascending the Maumee to the sources of the St. Mary's River, and crossing over to the Wabash, he made a rapid descent, and approached the post at Vincennes about the middle of December. Captain Helm and his associates, though few in number, were upon duty, and witnessed the savage host which swarmed around the approaching column of red-coated Britons.*
The British commander, having determined to carry the fort by assault, and to exterminate the feeble garrison, advanced to the attack.

But Captain Helm was not to be alarmed from the presence of mind belonging to a backwoods warrior. With an air of confidence, and as if supported by hundreds of defenders in the fort, he sprang upon a bastion containing a well-charged six-pounder ranged to the advancing enemy, and with a voice of thunder, as he brandished his match in the air, he commanded the column to "*halt*," or he would blow them to atoms. Surprised at such daring, and fearing a desperate resistance by the garrison, which possibly might far exceed his expectation, the British commander ordered a halt until a parley was opened. To the demand for the surrender of the fort, Captain Helm replied, that, with the full "honors of war," he would surrender the post, but otherwise he would resist while a man lived to shoulder his rifle. The Briton agreed to allow him all the "honors of war;" and when the fort was thrown open, Captain Helm and five men, with due formality, marched out and laid down their arms before the astonished commander.

The people of Vincennes, of course, were obliged again to acknowledge the authority of England and renounce that of the United States and Virginia. Captain Helm and one other American were retained as prisoners of war, the other three

* Butler's Kentucky, p. 78, 79, note.

being volunteer citizens of Vincennes. Here ended the efficient operations of Colonel Hamilton toward the discomfiture of Colonel Clark.

The winter had now set in with much rain and snow, creating obstacles to a military invasion almost insurmountable. Colonel Hamilton, therefore, determined to postpone the re-capture of Kaskaskia and its dependences until the opening of spring, when he expected a re-enforcement of two hundred warriors from Michillimackinac, and five hundred Cherokees and Chickasâs from the South.* In the mean time, he determined to give employment to his northern allies, who now, to the number of four hundred, were eager to commence their operations against the frontier population west of the mountains. For this purpose, they were sent out in detached parties and small bands, intending to spread over the border settlements of Western Virginia and Pennsylvania, to harass the exposed inhabitants, and to plunder and collect scalps until spring, when the governor would be ready to lead them, with the other Indian allies, against the American posts from Kaskaskia to Fort Pitt, scouring the whole frontier as they passed.

Such were the arrangements of Colonel Hamilton for prosecuting the enterprise of capturing Colonel Clark and his handful of backwoodsmen at Kaskaskia, and subsequently of prostrating the American settlements on the Ohio, by "sweeping Kentucky and Virginia" on his route to Fort Pitt.

[A.D. 1779.] Late in January following, Colonel Clark received intelligence that Colonel Hamilton was at Vincennes, with only eighty soldiers under his command, and was unsupported by his savage allies, yet contemplating the reduction of the post at Kaskaskia in the spring. To avoid the disagreeable alternative of being captured and led a prisoner to Detroit, he determined to make an energetic movement with such forces as he could raise, and anticipate his rival's designs by capturing Fort Sackville and sending Colonel Hamilton a prisoner to the capital of Virginia.

For this purpose, with great expedition, he prepared to make

* Arrangements had been made for a general council with the Cherokees and Chickasâs at the mouth of the Tennessee, and the Indians were to bring with them down the Tennessee large supplies of corn for the grand expedition which was to rendezvous at this point. This grand council, of course, was broken up by the unexpected movements of Colonel Clark, and thus the operations of the Northern and Southern Indians were at once thwarted.

a sudden and unexpected march to Vincennes with his whole disposable force. This force, increased by two companies raised in Kaskaskia and Cahokia, and such recruits as he could muster within ten days, amounted to only one hundred and seventy men. Preparations for the expedition were made without delay; two companies were immediately raised and organized to re-enforce his command; one from Kaskaskia, commanded by Captain Charleville, and one from Cahokia, commanded by Captain M'Carty. His force was thus increased to one hundred and seventy men. A large keel-boat was fitted up as a galley, and mounted with two four-pounder cannon and four swivels, and furnished with a suitable supply of provisions, ammunition, and military stores. This vessel was placed under the command of Captain John Rodgers, with a company of forty-six men, with orders to penetrate up the Wabash within a few miles of the mouth of White River, and there to take up his position and wait for further orders, permitting none to pass up or down the river.

On the 7th of February, Colonel Clark, with the remainder of his force, amounting to one hundred and thirty men, set out upon a perilous march of one hundred and fifty miles through the wilderness northeast to Vincennes. The route was an Indian trace, which lay through deep forests and prairies; the weather was uncommonly wet; the water-courses were out of their banks; and the larger streams had inundated their bottoms from bluff to bluff, often three or four miles in width; but the hardy backwoodsmen, under their intrepid and persevering leader, pressed forward in spite of every obstacle. On foot, with their rifles on their shoulders, and their knapsacks filled with parched corn and jerked beef, for six days they advanced along the trace, through forests, marshes, ponds, swollen streams, and inundated lowlands, for nearly one hundred miles, when they arrived at the crossings of the Little Wabash, where the bottoms, to the width of three miles, were inundated to the depth of "three feet, never under two, and frequently over four." Through these lowlands the whole battalion were compelled to march, often feeling for the trace with their feet, and carrying their arms and ammunition over their heads to protect them from the water.

Five days more brought them to the Wabash, just below the mouth of the Embarrass River, and nine miles below the post of Vincennes. Here great difficulty was encountered in crossing the river. No boats were within reach, and the galley had not arrived. Nearly two days were spent in unavailing efforts to cross the river; the men became discouraged, and starvation seemed to await them in their present situation. At length, on the evening of the 20th, a boat was captured, and preparations for crossing the low grounds and the river commenced. After great difficulty in crossing the river, they traversed low grounds by wading often up to their armpits, and reached the opposite highlands nearly exhausted by fatigue, fasting, and cold.* Here they remained to recruit their exhausted bodies, and to prepare for their appearance before Fort Sackville. Such had been their hardships by day and at night, by hunger and exposure in the water, that the comparative mildness of the season alone prevented this gallant little band from perishing almost in sight of the object of their toils.†

On the evening of the 23d, Colonel Clark dispatched a message to the people of Vincennes, informing them that he should take possession of the town that night, and that no violence would be used against those who abstained from aiding the enemy, and urging all the friends of the King of England to repair to the fort, and to fight like men.

At twilight the troops were paraded with flags and martial music around the summit of a contiguous eminence, in order to display their lines, and to augment their numbers in the eyes of the people, while a detachment of fourteen men were sent to begin the attack upon the fort with the rifle. When the attack was first made, the British commander was not aware that any enemy was at hand, until the sharp crack of the rifle announced their presence, and warned him to his post.

When the attack commenced, Colonel Hamilton and his prisoner, Captain Helm, were amusing themselves over a social game of cards and apple-toddy. At the crack of the rifle, Captain Helm, as if inspired by the sound, sprung to his feet, and, with the usual expletive, exclaimed, "It is Clark, and we shall all be his prisoners!" The town of Vincennes, on the east side of the Wabash, immediately surrendered, and many of the inhabitants gladly assisted in the investment of the fort.

A constant fire by moonlight from the marksmen, securely

* Butler's Kentucky, p. 81-83.
† See Jefferson's Correspondence, Randolph's ed., vol. i., p. 451, 452.

posted out of reach of the guns of the fort, took down every man who dared to expose his person above the walls. About midnight, when the moon had declined behind the western hills, and darkness had spread its mantle over the besiegers, Colonel Clark ordered a deep ditch opened within rifle shot of the fort, to shield his men from the fire of the enemy during the following day. Before the next dawn of day, the riflemen were securely sheltered in the ditch, from which they poured a continued volley of well-directed balls into the port-holes, and without the loss of a man silenced two pieces of cannon in fifteen minutes.* Every gunner who presented himself to direct the cannon was immediately killed by the unseen riflemen firing through the port-holes, until, terror-stricken at the unerring aim, they abandoned the batteries.

Eighteen hours had the garrison been exposed to this destructive fire, when Colonel Clark sent a menacing summons to the commander, demanding the surrender of the fort.† After a protracted conference relative to the terms of capitulation, Colonel Hamilton signed the article late in the evening of the 24th of February, and on the following day, Colonel Clark, at the head of two companies, entered the fort victoriously, while Captains Bowman and M'Carty, with their companies, received the prisoners.

In the first assault, one of Colonel Clark's men was wounded by a shot from the port-holes, who was the only man injured on the part of the assailants. During the siege on the second day, a war-party of Western Indians, ignorant of the presence of Colonel Clark, arrived from an excursion against the Kentucky settlements, bringing with them two white prisoners, and encamped in the vicinity of the fort. Colonel Clark soon resolved to give them battle, and detached a party, who encountered the savages, and in a short time completely routed them,

---

* See Colonel Clark's Report, Jefferson's Correspondence, vol. i., p. 551.

† The following is a copy of the summons sent by Colonel Clark to his British antagonist, viz.:

"SIR,—In order to save yourself from the impending storm which now threatens you, I order you immediately to surrender yourself, with all your garrison, stores, &c., for, if I am obliged to storm, you may depend on such treatment as is justly due to a murderer. Beware of destroying stores of any kind, or any papers or letters that are in your possession, or injuring any house in town, for, by Heaven! if you do, there shall be no mercy shown you.

"G. R. CLARK."

—See North American Review, No. 105, October, 1839, p. 301.

with the loss of nine warriors, besides the recapture of the two white prisoners. The remainder of the Indians, surprised at the courage and impetuosity of the American troops, fled with precipitation.

The humbled pride of the haughty commander of Detroit, upon his unexpected reverses, was but half concealed when, in signing the articles of capitulation, with affected complacency he declared, that in the surrender he was greatly influenced by the " *known generosity of his enemy.*"*

The articles stipulated for the surrender of Fort Sackville, with its military stores and ordnance, together with its entire dependences, including the whole force under his command, as prisoners of war.

After a few days, intelligence was received that an escort of forty men, convoying a large amount of merchandise, including goods for the Indians and supplies for the army, was advancing by way of the Wabash from Detroit. With the utmost dispatch Colonel Clark took measures to intercept and capture the rich cargo and the escort, before the commander should receive intelligence of the fall of the post at Vincennes. With the secrecy and dispatch so characteristic of all Colonel Clark's military operations, Captain Helm, the late British prisoner, at the head of sixty men, was on his way to intercept the unsuspecting detachment. The ever-successful captain, after a few days' absence, returned in charge of the entire escort, prisoners of war, and the cargo, amounting to ten thousand pounds in value, all of which had been captured without the loss of a man in the enterprise.

The private soldiers surrendered by Colonel Hamilton were dismissed on parole, many of them being Canadian French. But Colonel Hamilton himself, Major Hay, and a few other officers of lower grade, as company for Governor Rocheblave, were sent in charge of Captain Williams, under guard, to the capital of Virginia, prisoners of war, there to meet the just indignation of an outraged people from the hands of the civil authorities.

Having organized a provisional government at Vincennes and its dependences, Colonel Clark returned to Kaskaskia.

While at Vincennes, Colonel Clark had planned a campaign for the capture of Detroit, which was finally abandoned on ac-

* See Jefferson's Correspondence, vol. i., p. 164, &c.

count of the remote situation of the post and the difficulty of procuring supplies at that distant point, and for want of sufficient re-enforcements from the settlements on the Ohio. At that time, having entered into treaty stipulations with most of the northwestern tribes, he had for the expedition the proffered service of several thousand warriors who were anxious to turn their arms against the British power in Canada, and to fight under the standard of the great American chief. But Colonel Clark was unwilling to conduct a savage invasion against the frontiers of Canada, and the enterprise was finally abandoned. An expedition for the reduction of Detroit, the great store-house of Indian warfare, had also been contemplated by General M'Intosh the same year from Fort Pitt. The object, however, was virtually accomplished by the captivity of the commandant and his army at Vincennes.

The executive council of Virginia, pleased with the opportunity of avenging the numerous wrongs, cruelties, and murders inflicted upon the frontier people, by retaliating condign punishment upon the authors and prime instigators of all those barbarities, consigned Governor Hamilton and his associates to close imprisonment in irons.

This sentence of the Executive Council was passed upon them for the following reasons,* viz.:

"1st. In retaliation for cruel treatment of our captive citizens by the enemy generally.

"2d. For the barbarous species of warfare which he himself and his savage allies carried on in our western frontier.

"3d. For particular acts of barbarity of which he himself was personally guilty toward some of our citizens when in his power."†

---

* See Jefferson's Correspondence, vol. i., p. 162, 168, 185, and 453.

† During the whole course of the Revolutionary war, the British officers and agents permitted and instigated the Indians to indulge in every species of cruelty and barbarity against the American people within their reach. The following extract from the journals of the Executive Council of Virginia will throw some light upon the conduct of these agents of a Christian power. Among these, captured by Colonel Clark at Vincennes, were Governor Hamilton, of Detroit, Major Hay, Philip Dejean, justice of the peace for Detroit, and William Lamothe, captain of volunteers. The proceedings of the Executive Council on the 18th of June, 1779, "relative to the case of Henry Hamilton, Esq., who has acted for some years past as lieutenant-governor of the settlements at and about Detroit, and commandant of the British garrison there," &c.

"The council find that Governor Hamilton has executed his task of exciting the Indians to perpetrate their accustomed cruelties on the citizens of the United States, *without distinction of age, sex, or condition,* with an eagerness and avidity which evince that the general nature of his charge harmonized with his peculiar disposition," &c.

Although numerous attempts to harass the frontier settlements of Pennsylvania and Virginia by savage incursions were made at Detroit subsequently, no attempt was ever made to recover the posts on the Wabash and Upper Mississippi. The

---

The journal continues to declare that "the uniform tenor of his cruelty is established by numerous documents and ample testimony. At the time of his capture, it appears he had sent considerable bodies of Indians against the border population of these states, and had actually appointed a great council to meet him at (the mouth of) Tennessee, to concert the operations of this present campaign. They find that his treatment of our citizens and soldiers, taken and carried within the limits of his command, *has been cruel and inhuman;* that in the case of John Dodge, a citizen of these states, which has been particularly stated to this board, *he loaded him with irons, threw him into a dungeon, without bedding, without straw, without fire,* in the dead of winter and in the severe climate of Detroit; that in that state he wasted with incessant expectations of death; that when the rigors of his situation had brought him so low that death seemed likely to withdraw him from their power, he was taken out and somewhat attended to, until a little mended, and before he had recovered ability to walk, was again returned to his *dungeon, in which a hole only seven inches square was cut for the admission of air,* and the same load of irons put upon him; that appearing a second time in imminent danger of being lost to them, he was again taken from his dungeon, in which he had lain from January until June, with the intermission of a few weeks only, before mentioned. That Governor Hamilton gave standing rewards for *scalps*, but *offered none for prisoners;* which induced the Indians, after making their captives carry their baggage into the neighborhood of the fort, *there to put them to death and carry their scalps to the governor,* who welcomed their return and success by a discharge of cannon; that when a prisoner, who had been destined to death by the Indians, was dextrously withdrawn by a fellow-prisoner, from pure humanity, after the fire was kindled, and himself tied to the stake, a large reward was offered for the discovery of the victim; and when his place of concealment was known, Dejean, being sent with a party of soldiers, surrounded the house and took the unhappy victim and his deliverer, and threw them into jail, where the former soon expired, under perpetual assurances from Dejean that he was to be again restored to the Indians for execution; and the latter, when discharged, was bitterly reprimanded by Governor Hamilton. It appears that Dejean was upon all occasions the willing and cordial instrument of Governor Hamilton, acting both as judge and keeper of the jail; instigating and urging him, by malicious insinuations and untruths, to increase rather than relax his severities; and heightening the cruelty of his orders by his manner of executing them; offering at one time a reward to one man to be hangman for another, threatening his life on refusal, and taking from his prisoners the little property their opportunities enabled them to acquire.

"It appears that Lamothe was captain of the volunteer scalping-parties of Indians and whites who went from time to time, under general orders *to spare neither men, women, nor children.*" These are only a few circumstances from many others.

"They have seen that the conduct of the British officers, both civil and military, has, in the whole course of this war, been savage and unprecedented among civilized nations; that our officers taken by them have been confined in crowded jails, loathsome dungeons and prison-ships, loaded with irons, supplied often with no food, generally with too little for the sustenance of nature, and that little sometimes unsound and unwholesome, whereby numbers have perished," &c. Therefore, "this board has resolved to advise the governor that the said Henry Hamilton, Philip Dejean, and William Lamothe, prisoners of war, be put in irons, confined in the dungeon of the public jail, debarred the use of pen, ink, and paper, and excluded from all converse, except with their keepers; and the governor orders accordingly; they being some of those very individuals who, having distinguished themselves personally in this line of cruel conduct, are fit subjects to begin with in the work of retaliation."—See Jefferson's Correspondence, vol. i., p. 456–458.

civil and military jurisdiction of Virginia was extended over the whole country, until after the close of the Revolutionary war, as the "County of Illinois." This county had been organized early in the spring of 1779.

By the treaty of peace, Great Britain renounced all claim to the whole territory east of the Mississippi.

Thus terminated forever the dominion of Great Britain in the Illinois and Wabash countries, with the loss of three military posts, which commanded the whole northwestern territory of the United States.

To the Americans the conquest was doubly important, because the victories on the Upper Mississippi were won without bloodshed or military devastation; and while the conquest secured the hearts of the people as well as the country, it was only a sure presage of similar reverses to the British arms upon the Lower Mississippi.

The Loss of West Florida.—From the commencement of the Revolutionary war until the spring of 1778, the people of West Florida had remained free from any participation in the war which had been raging along the Atlantic seaboard and upon the western frontier, or Ohio region. During the summer of 1777, the Federal government, having secured the friendship and favorable consideration of the Spanish authorities of Louisiana, had made arrangements, through Oliver Pollock, the American agent in New Orleans, for supplies of ammunition, military stores, and munitions of war for the western posts. Supplies of this kind, including several small field-pieces of artillery, transported up the Mississippi and Ohio Rivers in keel-boats and barges, under the command of American officers, had been received at Fort Pitt in the autumn of the same year. The Spanish possessions on the west side of the river, and the constant intercourse between New Orleans and Upper Louisiana, by means of the river commerce, greatly facilitated the American officers in the arduous enterprise of transporting military stores upon a river which was partly claimed by the English, and which was occupied by numerous English settlements, with several military posts, for more than two hundred miles below the mouth of the Yazoo. The Spaniards had an undoubted right to the river navigation; but not so with the Americans. The latter encountered great hazard, and often imminent danger, in navigating the river, or in attempting to

Vol. I.—E e

evade the vigilance of the English commandants, being sometimes compelled to procure their supplies through Spanish bargemen beyond the surveillance of the British posts on the Lower Mississippi.

Nevertheless, through the enterprise and discretion of Captain William Lynn, Colonel Rodgers, Captain James Willing, and Captain Benham, the American posts on the Ohio and Upper Mississippi were repeatedly supplied during the years 1777, 1778, and 1779 with military stores and supplies from New Orleans.

It was in one of these expeditions, in the winter and spring of 1778, that Captain Willing descended the Mississippi with a detachment of fifty men, in two keel-boats, for supplies from New Orleans for the western posts. The King of Spain was on terms of peace with the United States, and maintained a neutral attitude as to Great Britain. Captain Willing, although in the service of the United States, which were engaged in a deadly war with Great Britain, was willing to consider the English settlements on the east side of the river, below the Yazoo, as neutrals in the war, taking no active agency either for or against the United States; yet as he was necessarily, in self-defense, compelled to observe the greatest circumspection and precaution, to avoid the vigilance of the English agent in New Orleans, who was closely observing any violation of neutrality in the Spanish authorities, and who had remonstrated with the Governor of Louisiana relative to former supplies obtained by agents of the United States, Captain Willing deemed it prudent that he should have some assurance, as he descended to New Orleans, that the people of the Natchez district would observe a strict neutrality on their part. In order to place this question beyond doubt, he landed at Natchez, where he had formerly resided for several years before the war, and having obtained an interview with some of the citizens, he took the sense of the town in a public meeting, and with the general approbation entered into a written convention of neutrality.

The convention having been concluded and signed, Captain Willing prepared to descend on his perilous enterprise; but it was not long before he was informed that several individuals, repugnant to the convention, would not be governed by its provisions. Having satisfied himself that the opposition of these men would be highly prejudicial to his operations, he determined to place them in military custody, and thereby secure their neutrality by preventing interference with his operations. To accomplish this object, he dispatched, at night, a corporal's guard, under the direction of a faithful guide, to the dwellings of the most obnoxious of the Loyalists, who were conveyed, together with some of their slaves and other personal property, to his headquarters on board his vessel, where they were detained under guard until a satisfactory assurance was given that they would not violate the convention of neutrality. This assurance having been given, they were set at liberty, and their property restored. To this there was only one exception. One individual, a pensioner of the king, from his known energy of character, his strong attachment to the royal cause, and his zealous efforts to promote the interests of his majesty's government, Captain Willing retained in custody, and conveyed him to the city of New Orleans. After a few days, the captain was induced to give him the liberty of the city upon his parole until his return to Natchez. Disregarding his parole, which he may have deemed only a release from an unlawful restraint, he returned to the vicinity of Natchez, resolved to seek revenge by taking redress in his own hands.

These transactions led to the first overt act of hostility on the part of West Florida against the troops of the United States, and placed the people of the district in the attitude of parties in the war. It was but a short time before Spain became involved with England in the war; and Florida then stood to Spain in the relation of an enemy's country, and became a legitimate object for conquest.

It was not many weeks afterward, when the first act of open hostility by the people of the Natchez district against the American troops occurred at Ellis's Cliffs, a short distance below the mouth of the St. Catharine Creek. This was a wanton attack, made by about twenty-five men in ambuscade, upon the troops and crew of one of Captain Willing's boats on their return from New Orleans.* The boat, advancing against the

* Whether Captain Willing was taken prisoner by the English while on the Lower Mississippi or not, I have not been able to ascertain, but am inclined to believe he must have been captured before he left West Florida, in 1778. One thing is certain: in the spring of 1779 he was a prisoner of war, and was kept in rigorous confinement, and a portion of the time in irons, in the British army. He was exchanged near the close of the year 1779, at the same time that Colonel Hamilton, of Detroit, M. Rocheblave, of Kaskaskia, and others were exchanged. His rigorous treatment by the ene-

strong current, was decoyed to the shore where the ambuscade was laid, when a sudden volley from the concealed party killed five men and wounded several others.* The boat immediately made land, and the crew surrendered. This boat was commanded by Lieutenant Reuben Harrison, who had been instructed to take his position for a short time at Natchez, in order to secure a strict observance of neutrality. Hostilities were suppressed by the judicious interference of others.

It would hardly be deemed strange, under these circumstances, if Captain Willing subsequently, on his return to Natchez, did land and pay his respects to his former adversary, by levying a heavy contribution upon his vindictive enemy for the use and benefit of the American service.

The wanton attack upon Captain Willing's boat and men was an outrage upon the officers of the United States, which accelerated the determination of the Spanish authorities of Louisiana to make active preparations for the entire subjugation of that portion of Louisiana which had been annexed to West Florida. The influence of Captain Willing was exerted with great industry, and was seconded by many influential Americans then resident in the country, to induce the Spanish governor, upon the first intelligence of a rupture between the English and Spanish courts, to make a vigorous campaign at the onset, and reduce the British posts before they could re-

my was retaliated on Colonel Hamilton and others.—See Jefferson's Correspondence, vol. i., letter xii., p. 169.

* The party in concealment had been awaiting the expected arrival of this boat, which was known to be a few miles below. An ambuscade was formed, and two persons were unconcealed, to entice the boat near the shore. The boat was seen for several miles below, as she slowly toiled up the strong current. In an affidavit made by James Truly before William Ferguson, Esq., on the 6th of November, 1797, in Fairchild's precinct, he declares, "he has resided in the Natchez district since 1773, and is well acquainted in that vicinity; and that the party was commanded by Colonel Hutchens. That the party was concealed in the bushes and cane, while Captains Hooper and Bingaman remained upon the shore to hail the boat; that when the signal for enticing the boat over was made, some one urged that they should fire upon them as soon as they came in reach, without speaking; but that the people objected, and said it would be time to fire when they found there was a necessity; when they appointed Captains Hooper and Bingaman to remain unconcealed by the water-side (the rest being concealed), to know their intentions; but when Lieutenant Harrison came near enough to speak, and discovered that he had been basely decoyed over, he spoke aloud, and said he desired all those who were *friends of the United States* to separate from those who were not; in answer to which, Captain Hooper ordered all those on board who were *friendly to the Natchez* (English) to fall below the gunwale or jump ashore. In the confusion which ensued, a volley was fired from all sides, and five Americans were killed; the rest jumped ashore and called for quarter."—See Ellicott's Journal, p. 131, 132.

ceive aid, and while the Republicans in the province were highly exasperated at the treacherous breach of neutrality in the Natchez district. Many persons in West Florida were emigrants from North Carolina, Virginia, and the Middle States, and others were from the New England States, who took a lively interest in the struggle of their friends near the Atlantic seaboard. Such were anxious to see the British power excluded from the Mississippi in the south, as it had been already on the north, by the individual State of Virginia alone. Hence the military operations of Governor Galvez, for the reduction of the British posts of West Florida in 1779, were accompanied by a large number of patriotic Americans from the districts of Natchez and Baton Rouge, as well as from the Illinois country, who contributed the whole weight of their influence and personal services in the enterprise.*

While England had been waging war vigorously against the colonies, France and Spain were not indifferent spectators of the contest. Circumstances connected with the operations of the British arms against the colonies gave rise to a hostile collision between the French and English governments; and Spain, by an attempt of friendly intercession between England and France, gave offense to the English cabinet, and soon afterward became involved in the war as an ally of France. Having declared war against Great Britain, his Catholic majesty resolved upon the re-annexation of Florida to the province of Louisiana. Don Bernard de Galvez, colonel in the armies of Spain and governor of Louisiana, a man of genius and daring ambition for military distinction, having received the earliest intimation of the declaration of war, concerted measures for the immediate subjugation of all that portion of West Florida contiguous to the Mississippi.†

Such was the energy and dispatch of the Spanish governor, that on the first of September he was before Fort Bute with an army of fourteen hundred men. The commandant refused to capitulate, and made a brave resistance for five days, when the fort was carried by storm and utterly demolished.

From this point, the Spanish governor, re-enforced by several hundred militia, including a large number of patriotic Americans, marched northward to Baton Rouge, the strongest British

---

* Martin's Louisiana, vol. ii., p. 48.
† See Stoddart's Louisiana, p. 75, 76. Also, book iv., chap. i., of this work.

post on the Mississippi. This post was garrisoned with four hundred regular troops, besides one hundred militia; and the arsenal was abundantly supplied with arms, ordnance, and all kinds of military stores. Many of the troops, however, were disabled by sickness and consequent debility, reducing the real strength of the garrison far below its numerical force. The fort was immediately invested; and on the 21st of September the Spanish batteries opened upon the works, and after a brisk cannonade and bombardment of two hours and a half, the commandant, Colonel Dickinson, proposed to capitulate, and terms were speedily arranged.

In this capitulation, Colonel Dickinson surrendered to the King of Spain, not only the post of Baton Rouge, but also all that portion of West Florida near the Mississippi River, including Fort Panmure at Natchez, one small fort and garrison on the Amite, and another at Thompson's Creek. Thus Spain became possessed of West Florida eastward to Pearl River, and Great Britain lost the last remnant of teritory in the Mississippi Valley. From this time, all that portion of West Florida south of latitude 31° north, and west of Pearl River, was known as the Florida district of Louisiana, under the Spanish dominion for more than thirty years, when the people revolted and expelled the Spanish authorities preparatory to its annexation to the United States; that portion north of latitude 31° was peaceably surrendered to the United States in 1798.

The King of Spain, well pleased with the success of Don Galvez, as a mark of approbation for his energetic conquest, conferred upon him the rank and title of brigadier-general, and confided to his judgment and valor the enterprise of reducing the remaining English posts in Florida near the Gulf of Mexico.

[A.D. 1780.] Preparations were urged during the winter, and early in March following General Galvez arrived with a strong force before "Fort Charlotte," at Mobile. The commandant refused to surrender, and a regular investment commenced. After a severe cannonade, the commander, on the 14th of March, was compelled to surrender to the Spanish arms. In the capitulation was comprised all the territory dependent upon this post, or from Pearl River to the Perdido.

The same year the Spaniards of Upper Louisiana, assisted by Colonel Clark from Kaskaskia, repulsed an attack made upon St. Louis by a large body of Indians from Mackinaw, under the command of the commandant of that post.*

The only remaining post in West Florida was that of Pensacola, the headquarters of the governor. This was a regular fortress, defended by a strong garrison, and was not to be reduced without heavy artillery and ample military stores, which the Spanish commandant could not at once command. Consequently, he returned to New Orleans to provide for the reduction of this important post, whereby the whole of West Florida would be again restored to the crown of Spain.

During the remainder of this year the intrepid Galvez was unremitting in his efforts to reduce Pensacola. Twice had he advanced his forces by land and sea to the investment of the devoted post, and twice had his utmost efforts failed to effect a breach in the walls, or to compel the commander to capitulate, although reduced to the greatest extremities. At length he determined to withdraw his forces to Mobile and New Orleans, and at Havana seek re-enforcements and a heavy train of artillery from the powerful armament which was expected in that port under the command of Admiral Solano.

[A.D. 1781.] But it was not until the last of February following that he had sufficiently completed his preparations, and set out for the harbor of Pensacola. Having encountered a severe gale on the way, with considerable injury to his fleet, he did not reach the Bay of Pensacola until the 9th of March, when he proceeded to invest the British fortress by land and sea. Yet such was the terrible cannonade kept up by the garrison upon the Spanish fleet, that it was not until the 19th of March that the vessels of war could take their position to bombard the fort.

Having at length completed several land batteries in the rear of the fort, by which the enemy's fire was diverted from the fleet, the vessels immediately took their position and opened the bombardment. The garrison bravely defended the fortress to the last extremity, although the fire from the united batteries of the fleet and land was so destructive that the men were repeatedly driven from their guns. Yet for more than thirty days the garrison continued to resist every renewed assault of the Spaniards, until the 8th of May, when a shot from one of the Spanish batteries lodged in the magazine, producing a most

* See book iv., chap iii., of this work, for a full account of this expedition.

awful explosion, and completely demolishing their works. They were now completely exposed to the enemy's fire, and deprived of their ammunition; and further resistance being impracticable, the commandant, Colonel Campbell, proposed to capitulate. A suspension of hostilities accordingly took place, and on the 9th, articles of capitulation were signed and exchanged. In this capitulation Colonel Campbell, after a heroic defense, surrendered the Fort and Port of Pensacola, including the garrison of eight hundred men, and all the stores and ordnance, together with the whole province of West Florida.*

East Florida subsequently yielded to the victorious arms of his Catholic majesty, and the whole of Florida, including the eastern and western districts, were fully confirmed to the crown of Spain by the treaty of peace in 1783.

Thus terminated the British dominion upon the Lower Mississippi, two years after its termination upon the Ohio and in the Illinois country, and after an occupancy of less than twenty years from the expulsion of the French from the same region.

For the acquisition of this great and fertile region, Great Britain had contended with France for more than sixty years, at an immense cost of blood and treasure, expended in no less than five long and expensive wars, and great human suffering by sea and land. The occupancy was but short, and after a vexatious possession of less than one third the period she had been engaged in the contest for its acquisition, she was doomed by the inexorable decree of fate to be exiled from it, together with all her extensive provinces contiguous. Such are the great political revolutions by which an all-wise Providence sees proper to rule the great moral universe of mankind in fulfilling the destinies of nations.

* Martin's Louisiana. Also, Stoddart, p. 78.
Stoddart says the capitulation included "about one thousand men." The whole number in the garrison and vicinity of Pensacola was about that number; but during the siege about one hundred of the English had been killed, and double that number had been severely wounded. The Spanish loss, of course, was much less.—Stoddart, p. 79.

BOOK IV.

SPAIN IN THE VALLEY OF THE MISSISSIPPI.

CHAPTER I.

LOUISIANA UNDER THE DOMINION OF SPAIN FROM THE DISMEMBERMENT TO THE EXPULSION OF THE ENGLISH FROM FLORIDA.—A.D. 1763 TO 1783.

Argument.—Extent of Spanish Louisiana.—Repugnance of the French of West Florida to the English Dominion.—French Opposition to the Spanish Dominion in Louisiana.—Spain indulges their Prejudices by deferring her Jurisdiction.—Public Remonstrances and Petitions against the Transfer to Spain.—Jean Milhet sent a Delegate to Paris.—His Mission unsuccessful.—Arrival of Don Ulloa as Spanish Commissioner in New Orleans.—He delays the formal Transfer of the Province.—French Population in Louisiana in 1766.—Spanish Troops arrive for the different Posts.—Popular Excitement against Ulloa.—The Superior Council requires him to leave the Province or produce his Commission.—He retires on Board a Spanish Man-of-war.—Perilous Condition of the prominent Malecontents.—Second Convention.—Second Mission to Paris.—General O'Reilly arrives at the Balize with a strong Spanish Force.—He notifies Aubry of his Arrival and his Powers.—His Professions of Lenity.—Ceremony of Transfer, August 18th, 1769.—The Flag of Spain displaces that of France.—Population of Louisiana in 1769.—Settlements of Upper Louisiana.—Arrest of twelve prominent French Citizens.—Their Trials, Imprisonment, and Execution.—Spanish Jurisdiction formally introduced in the Province.—"Superior Council" superseded by the "Cabaldo."—Inferior Courts organized.—Rules of procedure in the Courts.—Spanish Emigrants arrive.—Summary of O'Reilly's Administration.—Subsequent Spanish Rule.—Commerce and Agriculture under Unzaga's mild Rule.—Population of Upper Louisiana in 1776.—Galvez Governor of Louisiana.—British Traders from Florida endeavor to monopolize the Trade of the Mississippi.—Spain favorable to the American Revolution.—Oliver Pollock and Captain Willing in New Orleans.—Spain espouses the War against Great Britain.—West Florida invaded by Governor Galvez.—Fort Charlotte captured in 1780.—Unsuccessful Attack on Pensacola.—Attack on St. Louis by British and Indians from Mackinaw.—Repulsed by Spaniards and Americans.—Bombardment and Capture of Pensacola, May 9th, 1781.—Surrender of West Florida.—Cession of East Florida to Spain.—Revolt in the Natchez District, and Capture of Fort Panmure in 1781.—Proceedings of the Spanish Authorities against the Insurgents.—Treaty of 1783 concluded.—Revival of Agricultural and commercial Enterprise.

[A.D. 1763.] THE boundaries of Spanish Louisiana, after the dismemberment, comprised, as we have already stated,* all that vast unknown region west of the Mississippi River, from its sources to the Gulf of Mexico, and extending westward to the extreme sources of all its great western tributaries among the Rocky Mountains. It included, also, the Island of New Orleans, on the east side of the Mississippi, and south of the Bayou Iberville. On the Gulf of Mexico it comprised the whole

* See book ii., chap. x., of this work.

coast, from Lake Borgne on the east, to the Bay of St. Bernard and the Colorado River on the west, with an unsettled claim to the territory westward to the Rio Bravo del Norte. Of course, it included the Mississippi River, with the western bank above the Iberville, and both banks from the Iberville to the Balize.

The troops of Great Britain had already taken possession of Florida, and that portion of Louisiana lying east of the Mississippi, and north of the Iberville or Manchac Bayou. Many of the French in that region, dissatisfied with the idea of coming under the dominion of England, had retired to the western side of the river, believing they would still be within the dominion of France. But soon it became rumored that Western Louisiana also had been ceded to a foreign power. Many became highly excited and greatly alarmed when it was intimated that this portion of Louisiana had been ceded to the crown of Spain. These rumors were confirmed by dispatches from the French court early in October, 1763, announcing the cession of Western Louisiana to his Catholic majesty. M. de Abadie, the governor and director-general *ad interim*, was furnished with instructions by which he was to be governed in surrendering the province into the hands of the authorized agents of Spain, when they should be duly empowered and commissioned to receive it from him.

In the mean time, such was the state of excitement and dissatisfaction among the French population of Louisiana, that for nearly two years subsequently no active measures were taken by the Spanish crown to take formal possession of the province. It was hoped by the court of Madrid that a few months would suffice to cool down the excitement, and to allay the dissatisfaction which had manifested itself so generally in the province ; hence it had been deemed expedient to permit the former French authorities to administer the civil government under the laws and usages of France, as if it were still a French dependence. But the people seemed unwilling to abandon their prejudices, or in any wise to become reconciled to the change of dominion.*

Under these circumstances, the court of Madrid declined to press the formal delivery of the province and the extension of the Spanish jurisdiction. Yet the population evinced no dis-

---

* Martin's Louisiana, vol. i., p. 348, 349.

position to submit peaceably to the Spanish dominion: but a determination to resist was plainly indicated among all classes. All the prominent citizens seemed still to retain their first impressions and prejudices against a foreign yoke, and all joined in deprecating subjection to the Spanish king. They still hoped to avert the fulfillment of the treaty by appeals and petitions to the throne of France, and they left untried no effort by which they hoped to influence the royal decision.

Early in the year 1765, a general meeting of the principal inhabitants and planters of the province convened in the city of New Orleans, for the purpose of discussing freely the subject of their distracted condition, and for sending to the throne of France their united appeals and prayers for the royal interposition in their behalf. The meeting was attended by a numerous assemblage, and the whole subject was freely discussed before the people, when it was resolved unanimously to send M. Jean Milhet, a wealthy merchant, as a delegate to France, to lay their memorial at the feet of the king.

In their petition they entreated the king to make such arrangements with his Catholic majesty as might obviate the necessity of a separation of his faithful subjects from the paternal rule of France. M. Milhet arrived in Paris, and, to give effect to his embassy, he appeared before the prime minister in company with the aged Bienville, "the father of Louisiana," now in his eighty-seventh year, whose entreaties were joined with those of the whole province; but the complaints and remonstrances of the Spanish court had preceded them, and had prepared the minister and the king to disregard their petitions.

[A.D. 1766.] The minister was averse to the prayer of the petitioners, and artfully prevented M. Milhet from an interview with the king. After many unavailing efforts on his part, M. Milhet, discouraged at the apathy of the court, returned to Louisiana, and reported the result of his unsuccessful mission. Still the people would not despair until the result of a second mission should be known. But the second mission of M. Milhet the following year was equally unsuccessful, and all hope of evading the Spanish yoke began to vanish.

Two years had now elapsed since D'Abadie, the director-general of the province, had received instructions for the delivery of the country to the proper authorities of his Catholic majesty. The delusive hope of remaining under the dominion of France did not forsake them until late in the month of July, when a formal notice was received to the director-general in New Orleans, by a messenger from Havana, that Don Antonio de Ulloa, commissioner of his Catholic majesty, would repair to New Orleans in the autumn for the purpose of receiving formal possession of the province.

Accordingly, he arrived in New Orleans, accompanied by two companies of Spanish infantry, where he was received by the people with constrained and silent respect. Perceiving the remaining dissatisfaction, and the violence of the popular prejudice against the Spanish authority, Don Ulloa deemed it prudent to refrain from the exercise of his authority, and declined to present his commission for receiving possession of the province until he should be sustained by such re-enforcements from Havana as would justify the departure of the French troops. Until the arrival of such troops from Havana, he determined to spend a few weeks in visiting the different military posts of Louisiana, and especially the old Spanish settlement of the Adaës, and the post at Natchitoches.

The population of Spanish Louisiana at this time was estimated at something more than ten thousand souls, of whom five thousand five hundred and fifty-six were whites; the remainder were negro slaves. Among the whites were nearly one thousand nine hundred men capable of bearing arms, and one thousand four hundred and forty-four marriageable women, besides one thousand three hundred and seventy-five boys, and one thousand two hundred and forty girls.*

[A.D. 1767.] At length the troops expected from Havana arrived; but still Don Ulloa declined to produce his commission, and deferring the formal reception of the province, distributed the troops among the different military posts, to relieve the French troops on duty. The Spanish government doubtless desired to effect the transfer of sovereignty with as little violence to the prejudices of the people as was practicable, and quietly to occupy the military posts while the civil jurisdiction was undisturbed, until the people should gradually become reconciled to the new order of government. Yet the delays and the temporizing movements of Don Ulloa served only to irritate the unsettled and suspicious apprehensions of the people. Many anxiously expected the return of M. Milhet,

* Martin's Louisiana, vol. i., p. 354.

who was still in France; and a lingering hope still remained that his efforts might yet be successful in averting the transfer. At length he returned, a second time unsuccessful, when all hope suddenly vanished. Many became desperate; and others, exasperated at their disappointment, began to manifest their opposition to Don Ulloa, who still declined a public official recognition of his authority as commissioner. Yet he was upon intimate terms with the French director-general, Mons. Aubry, who had succeeded D'Abadie; and the people became jealous of the influence which he might exert against them. Public meetings were held in the different settlements and in the city. Each meeting elected delegates to a general meeting, or convention, to be held in New Orleans. This convention resolved to petition the Superior Council to direct Don Ulloa and the principal Spanish officers to leave the province. The petition was signed by five hundred and fifty of the most wealthy and respectable citizens and planters. Ulloa was denounced, and threatened as a disturber of the peace, and all viewed his presence in the province with jealousy and suspicion. Many believed the formal reception of the province was designedly delayed for state purposes, and none knew how deeply they might be interested personally in the result.

[A.D. 1768.] During the summer of 1768, rumor gave notice of the arrival of a powerful Spanish fleet at Havana, and that its ultimate destination was the province of Louisiana. Strong apprehensions were aroused in the public mind. Many expected the people would be driven to open resistance, with all its consequent horrors. The English authorities of West Florida were consulted for aid, in case matters were urged to extremities; but no encouragement was given. At length, on the 29th of October, the popular anxiety and excitement became so extreme, that the Superior Council, overruling the opposition and protest of Aubry, the president, deemed it expedient to require Don Ulloa to produce his commission and credentials from the Spanish court, for verification and record in the minutes of their proceedings, or to depart from the province within one month. This decree of the council was sustained by the inhabitants of the city of New Orleans and of the German coast, and six hundred armed men stood ready to enforce obedience to the order. Under these alarming appearances, and the increasing discontent of the people, Don Ulloa determined, without further delay, to retire from Louisiana into the Island of Cuba. He retired on board one of the king's vessels then moored opposite the city, where he remained until night of the following day, when the cables were cut by the populace and the vessel was set adrift. Other Spanish vessels soon left the port.*

Things had now remained in this state of anxious suspense for nearly three years. The people determined, since the Spanish vessels and commissioner were gone, to make one more effort with the King of France to avert the dreaded transfer. A mere difference of opinion, and a discontented mind, had now become an offense against the authority of Spain; and the consequences to them, personally, might well be apprehended as any thing but desirable, especially to such as had been most active in expressing their dissatisfaction. A general meeting, or convention, of all the delegates from the parishes was again convened at New Orleans. From this convention two members were selected, and commissioned to repair with all haste and lay the petition and entreaties from the province of Louisiana once more before the king. The two delegates selected were M. St. Lette, of Natchitoches, and M. La Sassier, a member of the Superior Council.†

[A.D. 1769.] In March following, the Spanish intendant for Louisiana arrived at Havana; but learning from Don Ulloa the popular excitement and the general discontent, he declined proceeding to New Orleans, and finally returned to Spain. The delegates had proceeded to Paris; but the voyage across the Atlantic had been long and tedious, and they arrived too late. A large Spanish force was in readiness to sail for the Mississippi, to silence all opposition against the dominion of Spain. Apprehending much resistance in the province, the King of Spain had prepared a formidable army, to proceed to Louisiana under one of his most energetic generals. Don Alexander O'Reilly, lieutenant-general in the armies of Spain, had been appointed governor and captain-general of the province of Louisiana by the king's commission, dated at Aranjuez, April 16, 1769. With a strong military force at his disposal, he was now on the Atlantic, sailing for the mouth of the Mississippi.

At New Orleans, things remained tranquil until the 23d of

---

* Martin's Louisiana, vol. i., p. 358, 359. † Idem, p. 359.

July, when intelligence was received that a strong Spanish armament, with four thousand five hundred troops on board, had arrived at the Balize, on their way to New Orleans. On the day following, Governor Aubry received by express a dispatch from Don Alexander O'Reilly, commander of the Spanish forces, notifying him that he was duly authorized to receive formal possession of the province of Louisiana in the name of the King of Spain. He expressed himself desirous of maintaining a good understanding between the authorities of Spain and the people of Louisiana, but with a firm determination to put down all opposition, and to extend the jurisdiction of his sovereign over the province.*

On the 27th of July, a meeting of the citizens was convened, from whom were selected three persons, M. Grandmaison, town-major, Lafrenière, attorney-general, and M. Mazent, a wealthy planter, as delegates to Don O'Reilly, informing him of their determination to abandon the province, and praying only the favor of permission to remove, with their effects, within two years. The Spanish captain-general received the delegates with courtesy, and returned a conciliatory reply. He promised that all former occurrences should be forgotten; that to all who proved themselves good citizens, and yielded a proper obedience to the Spanish authority, all former acts should be buried in oblivion, and all offenses should be forgiven to those who returned to their duty.

In the mean time, the people of the German and Acadian coasts were still in arms, and refused to submit to the Spanish government. A considerable body of them, conducted by M. Villière, had marched down to the city, where they arrived on the first of August.

About two weeks afterward, the Spanish armament cast anchor before the city of New Orleans; and in two days more the troops finally disembarked, and were marched into the public square in front of the government buildings. Here, on the 18th of August, in presence of a large concourse of people, and before the troops of both powers, the public ceremony of delivering the province to the Spanish governor was performed, when the flag of France slowly descended from the top of the flag-staff, greeting that of Spain as it mounted aloft before the assembled multitude, and was cheered by the troops

* See Martin's Louisiana, vol. i, p. 361.

of both nations. The Spanish authority was forthwith proclaimed dominant over the whole province.*

Thus was Louisiana, on the 18th of August, 1769, and about seventy years after its first colonization under Iberville, forever lost to France. During the period of its colonial dependence on France, it had slowly augmented its population from a few destitute fishermen and hunters to a flourishing colony of twelve thousand souls, distributed in several important settlements, besides the city and vicinity of New Orleans.

At this period there had been for many years quite a lucrative trade between the Illinois country and Lower Louisiana in the mutual exchange of their respective commodities. For more than ten years past, Louisiana had carried on quite a respectable foreign trade through the ports of New Orleans and Mobile. During the last year, the exports of the province were valued at two hundred and fifty thousand dollars, embracing the following articles and amounts respectively, viz.: Indigo, valued at one hundred thousand dollars; deer-skins, to the value of eighty thousand dollars; lumber, to the value of fifty thousand dollars; and other miscellaneous articles, to the value of twenty thousand dollars.* Cotton and sugar had not become articles of export.

Don O'Reilly entered upon the discharge of the duties pertaining to his station with every outward mark of respect from all classes of the population. Tranquillity soon prevailed over the whole province; but great anxiety was entertained by many as to the subsequent policy and designs of the new governor.

The first act of his administration was to order a complete census of the city of New Orleans. This was accomplished with great accuracy, and presented an aggregate of 3190 souls. Of these, 1803 persons were free whites; 31 were free blacks; 68 were of mixed blood; 1225 were slaves, and 60 were domesticated Indians. The city contained 468 houses of all descriptions.

The population of the province, exclusive of New Orleans, amounted to ten thousand two hundred and forty-eight souls, exclusive of about fifteen hundred souls who were comprised in the district of West Florida, under the dominion of Great Britain.

* Martin, vol. i., p. 362.   Stoddart's Louisiana, p. 72.   † Martin, vol. i., p. 363.

Thus the aggregate population of Spanish Louisiana at the period of the transfer, including the settlements on the Upper Mississippi, was about thirteen thousand five hundred and forty souls.*

Up to this time but few habitations had been made on the west bank of the Mississippi above the mouth of the Ohio. The oldest of these was St. Geneviève, first settled by a few French families in the year 1751. There were several other small settlements of more recent date, but none of much importance except St. Louis, which received its principal population after the cession of the Illinois country to Great Britain, as did most of the other small towns in this quarter. The site of St. Louis was first selected for a town by M. la Clede, in the year 1764, when it was made the general dépôt for the fur-trade.

Although Governor O'Reilly had promised pardon to all who submitted quietly to his authority, and oblivion for all past offenses, he had resolved to except and to punish the principal instigators of the late discontent, and the former opposition to the Spanish authority. This determination was artfully concealed until about the last of August, when, by an act of treachery and dissimulation, he first made known his designs by the arrest of four of the most prominent citizens of the province. These were M. Focault, former commissary-general and ordonnateur, M. de Noyant and M. Boisblanc, two members of the former Superior Council, M. la Frenière, former attorney-general, and M. Brand, the king's printer.

These men, confiding in his professions of esteem and friendship, accepted an invitation to attend his levée; and, while enjoying the hospitality of his house, were, with true Spanish treachery, invited by O'Reilly himself into an adjoining apartment, where they soon found themselves surrounded by a body

---

* The population, as given by Martin, is as follows:

Parishes and Settlements, exclusive of New Orleans.

1. Below the city on the river	570	Brought forward,	7678
2. Bayou St. John and Gentilly	307	9. Attakapas	409
3. Tchoupitoulas	4192	10. Avoyelles	314
4. St. Charles	639	11. Natchitoches	811
5. St. Jean Baptiste	544	12. Rapides	47
6. La Fourche	267	13. Washita	110
7. Iberville	376	14. Arkansas	88
8. Point Coupée	783	15. St. Louis, or Upper Louisiana	891
Carried forward,	7678		10348

—See Martin's Louisiana, vol. ii., p. 3.

of grenadiers with fixed bayonets, the commander of which, informing them that they were the king's prisoners, conveyed them under a military guard to places of confinement, there to await their trial.

O'Reilly had determined to make an example of eight other prominent individuals concerned in the opposition to Don Ulloa's authority. Within a few days afterward, this number was completed by the arrest of the following persons, agreeably to his order, viz.: M. Marquis, officer of the troop; M. Doucet, a lawyer; Messrs. Villierè, Mazent, and Petit, planters; and Messrs. John Milhet, Joseph Milhet, Caresse, and Poupet, merchants.

Soon after the arrest of M. Villière, while in confinement on board a man-of-war, he was visited by his wife, who was not permitted to enter his apartment. Indignant at the outrage, and frantic with despair, he attempted to force his way to her, when a struggle with the guards ensued, and he was killed. Still she was not permitted to witness his last moments, and, to aggravate her frantic grief, his bloody shirt was afterward thrown out to her, as evidence of his death, with an order for her immediate departure from the ship. Such was a specimen of the lenity which others might expect from the mercy of O'Reilly.

The remaining eleven prisoners were soon put upon a formal trial, charged with having aided and abetted an insurrection against the king's authority, as provided by the laws of Castile and Spain, which were unknown in Louisiana. The trials which followed were hasty, arbitrary, and tyrannical in the extreme, evincing the vindictive resolution of the captain-general to make an example of those who had been active in the late revolt.

They all pleaded against the jurisdiction, and declined to be tried by the laws of Spain, which had not been extended over the province at the time of the alleged insurrection. They claimed to have been subjects of the King of France; that the French flag was then waving over the province; and that their acts had been in accordance with their allegiance and duty to the King of France: that they owed no allegiance to the King of Spain until the Spanish authority had been proclaimed, and the Spanish flag and laws had duly superseded those of France; that the acts charged could not constitute an offense against the Spanish laws while those of France retained their empire over the province; that Ulloa had never made known his authority, but had studiously concealed it, if, indeed, he were clothed with any; that O'Reilly could not claim or expect obedience from the people until he had made known to them his character and powers; and that no act was charged against them after this manifestation of his authority.

The plea was sustained relative to several who had been officers of the former government, but was overruled in relation to De Noyant, La Frenière, Marquis, Joseph Milhet, and Caresse, who were formally convicted, and by O'Reilly sentenced to be hanged, with confiscation of property.

This severity, impolitic as it was cruel and uncalled for, was justified by O'Reilly as necessary to protect the province against other and more daring combinations, which might convulse the peace of the country unless such offenders were brought to punishment. Such was the plea of necessity with which he vindicated his acts of cruel revenge, if not his atrocious treachery.

Consternation and fear fell upon all the French residents, and none could deem themselves safe against arbitrary power; and from the sullen silence observed by O'Reilly, they knew not how far he might be disposed to wreak his vengeance upon those who might be obnoxious to his displeasure.*

The victims enjoyed but a short respite between conviction and the execution of their sentence. O'Reilly remained inexorable to the most earnest entreaties from persons of every rank in the community, that he would suspend the sentence of death until the royal clemency could be implored. The only concession he would grant was the commutation of death by hanging to death by fire-arms, or military execution.

On the 28th of September all the troops were under arms, and were paraded through the streets until noon, when they were stationed in martial order along the levée and in the public square. Alarm and apprehension spread through the city, and many of the inhabitants fled into the country. The troops were kept under arms until three o'clock in the afternoon, when the victims were marched to a small square in front of the barracks, where they were bound to stakes and blindfolded. In a few moments more a loud discharge of musketry announced to the remaining inhabitants that their friends were

* Martin's Louisiana, vol. ii., p. 5–7.

no more.* Thus terminated the sacrifice of the first victims of O'Reilly's tyranny.

The proceedings against the other prisoners were suspended for a few weeks, after which the following persons were sentenced to imprisonment in the Moro Castle at Havana for different terms, viz.: Messieurs Boisblanc, John Milhet, Petit, and Poupet. It was not long before they were shipped to Havana, to take their cells in the Moro Castle, where they remained until the following year, when they were discharged by order of the king.†

O'Reilly proceeded to abolish the French courts and the municipal regulations, and to substitute those of Spain. On the 21st of November he issued his proclamation for the abolition of the Superior Council, which he alleged had been deeply implicated in the former treasonable movements against the Spanish authority, as appeared from the testimony elicited during the late trials.

In place of the Superior Council, he established the Cabaldo, constituted of six perpetual regidors, two ordinary alcaldes, one attorney-general syndic, and one clerk. The offices of perpetual regidors and clerk were to be acquired by purchase, and, on certain conditions, were transferable. The ordinary alcaldes and attorney-general syndic were to be chosen on the first day of every year by the Cabaldo, and might be re-eligible by the unanimous vote of the Cabaldo. Thus the high court was made virtually perpetual and self-constituted. The inferior civil offices were filled chiefly with French citizens of Louisiana.

The ordinary alcaldes were vested with judicial powers individually within the city, in common civil and criminal cases. The attorney-general syndic was not a prosecuting officer of the crown, as his title might seem to indicate, but his duty was to propose to the Cabaldo such measures as the interests of the people required, and to defend their rights from invasion.

The Cabaldo was a high court and a legislative council, at which the governor presided. In its judicial capacity it exercised only appellate jurisdiction, in appeals carried up from the alcalde courts. The Cabaldo sat every Friday, and it was subject to be convened at any time by a call from the governor.‡

The Cabaldo being duly organized, the governor surrendered the chair, or the presidency in that body, to Don Louis de Un-

---

* Martin's Louisiana, vol. ii., p. 5–7. † Idem, p. 8. ‡ Idem, p. 9, 10

zaga, colonel in the regiment of Havana, who had been designated as the future governor of the province after O'Reilly's departure.*

The next step taken by O'Reilly in organizing the new government was to cause a set of instructions to be prepared for the regulation of proceedings in civil and criminal cases, to be conducted in the courts agreeably to the laws and usages of Castile and the Indies. Other minor regulations were prepared for the government of the probate courts and the succession of estates. A commandant, with the rank of captain, was appointed for each parish, with authority to exercise a mixed civil and military jurisdiction; being an officer of the peace, he had authority to enforce all general police regulations, and to decide all controversies in which the amount did not exceed twenty dollars. The Spanish language was made the tongue in which the judicial records throughout the province were to be kept and the proceedings conducted.†

The Spanish authority and laws were now duly enforced, without further arrests or executions, and confidence began slowly to be established in the minds of the French population. Spanish emigrants soon began to arrive in great numbers from Spain, the Indies, and the American provinces, by which the population of the city and province was augmented so rapidly as to produce a general and alarming scarcity of provisions. Flour in the city rose in value to twenty dollars per barrel,‡ and other provisions in proportion.

[A.D. 1770.] During the short period of O'Reilly's power, although exercised with great rigor and severity, he introduced many useful regulations, and enacted many salutary laws, which he caused to be published for the use of the province. Numerous grants of land were made and located on the western bank of the Mississippi, and in the prairies west of the Atchafalaya and Teche.

---

* Martin's Louisiana, vol. ii., p. 12, 13.   † Idem, p. 14, 15.

‡ At this time, during the extreme scarcity of breadstuffs, Oliver Pollock, from Baltimore, arrived with a cargo of flour, which he offered to General O'Reilly upon his own terms, for the use of the troops and city. But O'Reilly declining to receive it on those terms, Pollock sold it to him at fifteen dollars per barrel. O'Reilly was so pleased at the purchase, that he granted to Pollock the free trade of Louisiana as long as he lived, and promised to report his generosity to the king. The advantages of this trade were enjoyed by Pollock for several years afterward, and placed him in a situation, subsequently, to act for the United States as "agent" for supplying the western posts on the Ohio and Upper Mississippi.—See book iii., chap. iv., of this work. Also, Martin's Louisiana, vol. ii., p. 12.

The "black code," *code noir,* formerly given by Louis XV., was re-enacted for the protection and government of the slaves. Foreigners were prohibited from passing through the domain without a passport from the governor, and the people were prevented from trading with individuals descending the river from the United States. Many of the local regulations and ordinances were particularly oppressive to the French, but they had permission to retire from the province quietly whenever they saw proper. Many, of course, availed themselves of this privilege, and abandoned a country where their situation was rendered more precarious, from a remaining suspicion of their disaffection to the Spanish authority, entertained by a governor who had clearly shown himself despotic, arbitrary, and treacherous. They preferred the alternative of departing to the Island of St. Domingo, the nearest French colony, where they could enjoy personal safety among their own countrymen, and free from suspicion.

But when the tyrant found that he was effectually driving from the province many valuable citizens, merchants, mechanics, and planters, he determined to put a check to this kind of emigration by refusing to issue passports. Hence many were compelled to remain and abide the concealed vengeance of a vindictive governor. By such means he suppressed the manifestation of a desire to emigrate, but did not eradicate it from the discontented mind.*

The province was, however, soon relieved from further anxiety, and the fear of O'Reilly's vengeance. At the end of one year he was superseded in the command of the province by Don Antonio Maria Bucarelly as "Captain-general of Louisiana." O'Reilly returned to Spain under the severe displeasure of his sovereign, Charles III., who forbade his appearance at court.

The subsequent government of Spain in Louisiana was generally mild and paternal, partly military and partly civil. The governor exercised both civil and military authority. The captain-general was commander of all the military posts and of the troops of the province. The intendant superintended the administration of the revenue laws, and not unfrequently

---

* An excellent synopsis of the civil and military polity of Spain in Louisiana may be seen in Stoddart's Sketches of Louisiana, from p. 270 to 290, to which the reader is referred for a more full account of the minutiæ of the Spanish provincial government.

this duty was exercised by the governor himself. The governor exercised judicial powers in such civil cases as might be brought before him. The affairs of the Church were committed to the charge of the vicar-general. In each parish there was a military officer, or commandant, whose duty was to attend to the police of the parish, and to preserve the peace. He also exercised most of the duties which are usually assigned to magistrates and notaries public in the United States, and had jurisdiction in all civil cases where the matter in dispute did not exceed twenty dollars in value.

The Captain-general of Cuba, under the king, exercised a general supervision of the province as intermediate between the crown and the king's officers in Louisiana.

[A.D. 1771.] The commerce of Louisiana, under the restrictions imposed by O'Reilly, continued to languish for two years, but it soon afterward began to revive under the judicious policy of Unzaga, who soon rescinded most of those restrictions which were in force during the first months of his administration.* He also encouraged agricultural industry and enterprise, by such means as were within his power, and thereby gave an impulse to agricultural enterprise, which had been almost entirely suppressed under his predecessor. Notwithstanding the restrictions of the royal schedule in 1766, he wisely permitted the planters to supply themselves with slaves for the cultivation of their estates from the British traders in West Florida.

[A.D. 1773.] After three years the province began to assume a state of general prosperity, and, under the judicious moderation and wise administration of Unzaga, the French population had gradually become reconciled to the Spanish dominion and to the Spanish authorities. Emigrants from Spain and her provinces also continued to flock to Louisiana under the mild and pacific rule of Unzaga, who soon afterward received from the king the commission of brigadier-general, and "Intendant of Louisiana," as a special mark of the approbation and confidence of his royal master, in addition to his office of governor of the province.†

[A.D. 1775.] During Unzaga's administration, the population on the Lower Mississippi, as well as in Upper Louisiana, had steadily increased, and before the close of the year 1775

* Martin's Louisiana, vol. ii., p. 25, 26.   † Idem, p. 31, 34.

the town of St. Louis had augmented its population to eight hundred persons. The number of houses was one hundred and twenty, including many good stone buildings. The people of St. Louis possessed large numbers of domestic stock, and especially horses and horned cattle, which ranged at large upon the fertile prairies for miles in the vicinity. St. Geneviève, at the same time, contained a population of four hundred and sixty persons, and about one hundred houses of every description.*

[A.D. 1776.] The mild and benevolent rule of Unzaga continued in Louisiana until the close of the year 1776, when, having received from the king the appointment of Captain-general of Caraccas, he was succeeded as Governor of Louisiana by Don Bernard de Galvez, a colonel in the "Regiment of Louisiana," and connected with the ruling nobles of Spain and the provinces. He entered upon the exercise of his office on the first day of January, 1777, at a time when England was waging a bloody and cruel war against her American provinces. As a Spaniard, he had no predilection for the English monarchy, and his sympathies were enlisted for the colonies, which were struggling against the power and tyranny of the British crown.

The province of Louisiana at this time was prosperous, and carried on quite an active trade with the French and Spanish colonies in the West Indies, to promote which, during the past year, the King of Spain had granted permission for French vessels from the West Indies to trade direct with the city of New Orleans, and, under certain restrictions, with the planters on the coast above the city. The cultivation of tobacco, as a valuable staple product, was encouraged by the royal government, which instructed the liberal purchase of crops to be received into the royal warehouses.†

[A.D. 1777.] The same year witnessed the first regular commercial intercourse between the ports of the United States and the city of New Orleans. The pioneer in this commerce was Oliver Pollock, a citizen of Baltimore, who had been residing in the city of New Orleans since the close of O'Reilly's administration.‡ During the year 1777 he received the appointment of United States agent in New Orleans for the purchase and supply of military stores, ammunition, and munitions of

---
* Imlay's America, p. 501, 502, ed. of 1797.
† Martin's Louisiana, vol. ii., p. 40.   ‡ Idem, p. 12 and 40.

war for the use of the American posts upon the Ohio frontier, as well as subsequently for those in the Illinois country. Being an active and energetic man of business, and an enterprising merchant of New Orleans, he soon received the favorable attention of Governor Galvez, which greatly facilitated his commercial operations in behalf of the Federal government, and enabled him to render important services to the cause of the American Revolution.

[A.D. 1779.] A few months elapsed, when France and Spain were involved in the war with Great Britain in favor of the American colonies. England, having taken offense at the action of the French court in relation to the revolted provinces, by a recognition of their independence, declared war against France herself. Subsequently, the King of Spain, in order to bring about a general pacification, proposed, through his minister in London, to the English cabinet, a general amnesty of peace, to be settled for a term of years, by a conference of ministers from the belligerent powers, to be convened at Madrid, and that those of the United States should be admitted upon an equality with others. But England could not brook the indignity, and, in very unequivocal language, and in no very courteous manner, rejected the Spanish minister's proposition. The latter, offended at the reception of his Catholic majesty's good offices to put a close to the war, without ceremony departed from London and returned to Madrid. With imprudent haste the English cabinet issued letters of marque and reprisal against the Spanish commerce, and the King of Spain was soon compelled to take an active part in the existing war. On the 8th of May, 1779, his Catholic majesty formally declared war against Great Britain, and took measures to commence active operations against the common enemy.*

A portion of the loyal British provinces immediately contiguous to Louisiana had already commenced hostilities against the American authorities, which placed them in the attitude of enemies to Spain and the United States, and as such rendered the province of West Florida a legitimate object of conquest.

From the first occupancy of Louisiana by the Spanish authorities, much annoyance had been experienced from the advance of the British settlements and posts on the Lower Mis-

* Martin's Louisiana, vol. ii., p. 47.

sissippi. The subjects of Great Britain, entering the river by way of the Amité and Iberville, introduced into the Spanish settlements near the Mississippi, as well as into those which were more remote, contraband goods and articles of merchandise, which entirely evaded the revenue laws of Spain, and thus created for themselves an entire monopoly of the trade with the province, through their trading-posts established upon the east bank of the river, as high as the mouth of the Yazoo. Such had been the annoyance of the Spanish authorities, that any event which might remove a troublesome neighbor and restore the eastern bank of the river to the Spanish dominion could not be otherwise than hailed with satisfaction.

The court of Spain had viewed with concealed satisfaction the revolt of the English provinces along the Atlantic coast, and secretly desired to see them successful in their resistance to British tyranny and power. Hence the Spanish authorities of Louisiana had offered no impediment to the agents of the United States in their efforts to procure military supplies in New Orleans for the western posts on the Ohio.

The governor and captain-general of Louisiana was early notified of the war, and was instructed to proceed vigorously against the British posts in West Florida. After some opposition and consequent delay from the Cabaldo, Galvez succeeded in organizing about fourteen hundred men ready to take the field. With these he marched against the English Fort Bute, on the north side of the Manchac, and carried it by assault on the 7th of September.* From this point, having received a re-enforcement of six hundred militia, he marched to Baton Rouge, the principal British post on the river. The post at this place was well supplied with arms, military stores, and provisions, and was garrisoned by four hundred regular troops and one hundred militia. After a cannonade of two hours and a half, the commandant, Colonel Dickinson, on the 21st of September, surrendered not only this post, but also Fort Panmure, at Natchez; also, a fort on the Amité, and one small post on Thompson's Creek, together with all this portion of West Florida.† Thus all that part of West Florida, now comprising the parishes of Baton Rouge and Feliciana, came under the dominion of Spain as a part of Louisiana, which had been severed in 1763.

* Martin, vol. ii., p. 48, 49. † Idem, p. 49.

[A.D. 1780.] For his soldier-like conduct at the Manchac and at Baton Rouge, and for the successes which attended his movements, the King of Spain conferred upon Don Galvez the commission of brigadier-general of the royal forces of Louisiana, with orders to prosecute the further reduction of the British power in West Florida. Having made preparation during the winter, and having received re-enforcements from Havana, he was ready in January to sail for the reduction of Fort Charlotte, at Mobile. On the voyage to Mobile Bay, he narrowly escaped utter destruction of his fleet by a violent gale in the Gulf of Mexico; and after tedious delays, he succeeded in making a landing of his troops, artillery, and military stores on the east bank of the river, near the British fort. Six strong batteries were erected, from which the fort could be bombarded with great effect. The batteries opened upon the fort, and a practicable breach having been made, the commandant capitulated on the 14th of March, without further resistance. The reduction of this post being effected, Galvez returned to New Orleans to concert measures for the reduction of Pensacola, the capital of West Florida, which was defended by the strongest fortress in the province. The remainder of the year was spent, during a protracted siege, in fruitless attempts to reduce the place.

At length Galvez, finding all his efforts ineffectual for the reduction of the post, suspended further operations until he should receive re-enforcements, together with a train of heavy battering cannon and a naval force, to aid in the final reduction of this important point.

In the mean time, while the Spanish arms had been triumphant on the Lower Mississippi and in West Florida, the settlements of Upper Louisiana, and the town of St. Louis, had been exposed to an invasion, concerted and put in motion at the British post of Mackinaw, on the northwestern lakes of Canada.

The British commandant at Michillimackinac, hearing of the disasters of the British arms in Florida, conceived the idea of leading an expedition upon his own responsibility against the Spanish settlements of St. Louis. Early in the spring he had assembled one hundred and forty regular British troops and Canadian Frenchmen, and fourteen hundred Indian warriors for the campaign. From the southern extremity of Lake Michigan this host of savages, under British leaders, marched across to the Mississippi, and encamped within a few miles of St. Louis. The town had been fortified for temporary defense, and the hostile host made a regular Indian investment of the place. Skirmishes and desultory attacks continued for several days, during which many were killed, and others were taken captive by the Indians. Much of the stock of cattle and horses belonging to the place was killed or carried off.

The people at length, believing a general attack was contemplated, and having lost confidence in their commandant's courage, or in his preparations for defense, sent a special request to Colonel Clark, then commanding at Kaskaskia, to come to their aid with such force as he could assemble. Colonel Clark immediately made preparation to march to their relief. Having assembled nearly five hundred men under his command, he marched to the bank of the Mississippi, a short distance below the town of St. Louis. Here he remained encamped for further observations. On the 6th of May the grand Indian attack was made, when Colonel Clark, crossing the river, marched up to the town to take part in the engagement. The sight of the Americans, or the " Long-knives," as they were called, under the command of the well-known Colonel Clark, caused the savages to abandon the attack and seek safety in flight. They refused to participate in any further hostilities, and reproached the British commandant with duplicity in having assured them that he would march them to fight the Spaniards only, whereas now they were brought against the Spaniards and the Americans. They soon afterward abandoned the British standard, and returned to their towns, near Lakes Superior and Michigan.

During the siege, which continued about a week, nearly sixty persons were killed in the town and vicinity, and about thirty persons had been captured by the Indians. The timely arrival of Colonel Clark rescued these and twenty other prisoners, which they had taken in their advance. Such was the invasion of Upper Louisiana in 1780 from Mackinaw.*

* The attack on St. Louis was in May, 1780, but Judge Hall erroneously makes it in 1778, at which time Colonel Clark had not been on the Upper Mississippi.

The people of St. Louis, having heard that this expedition from Michillimackinac was in preparation in the fall of 1779, had fortified the town with a rude stockade six feet high, made by two rows of upright palisades a few feet apart, filled in with earth. The outline of the stockade described a semicircle around the place, resting its

[A.D. 1781.] During the winter General Galvez had been indefatigable in his preparations for the effectual reduction of Pensacola. He had repaired to Havana for the requisite reenforcements and munitions of war, together with a strong naval force. At length, on the 28th of February, 1781, he set sail from the West Indies for the coast of Florida, to co-operate with the forces from Louisiana. The armament from Havana comprised one man-of-war, two frigates, and a number of transports, and off the coast of Louisiana he was joined by the land and naval forces from New Orleans. On the 9th of March the whole armament appeared before the port of Pensacola, when the fort opened a heavy fire upon such vessels as ventured within the range of its guns.

A regular investment commenced, and the works progressed with great activity until the first of April, when several batteries were ready to open upon the fort. The cannonade commenced with great vivacity, and with decided effect; but the garrison made a determined resistance, and all the efforts of the Spanish forces were insufficient to compel a surrender, until the 9th of May, when the lodgment of a bomb-shell exploded the magazine, and rendered all further resistance in vain. The commander then proposed to capitulate. Terms of capitulation were arranged and signed on the same day.*

By the articles of capitulation, the English commander surrendered to his Catholic majesty the fortress and port of Pensacola, together with the garrison of eight hundred men, as prisoners of war, and the whole of the dependence of West Florida. The whole of East and West Florida was confirmed to Spain by the subsequent treaty of 1783. Thus terminated the last vestige of British power upon the Lower Mississippi, after an occupancy of nearly nineteen years.†

During the protracted investment of Pensacola, a partial revolt of the English colonists in the Natchez District had well-

---

two extremities upon the river, above and below the town, flanked by one small fort at each extremity. Three gates gave opening to the country in the rear, each defended by a piece of ordnance kept continually well charged. When the attack was first made, the people, having supposed it abandoned, were not fully prepared to meet it; hence the number of persons killed and captured. The invading host was led on by English and Canadians, and consisted chiefly of Ojibeways, Menomonies, Winnebagoes, Sioux, and Sauks.—See Martin, vol. ii., p. 53; Life of Black Hawk, Extract in "Western Pilot," p. 138–142; Stoddart's Sketches, p. 79, 80; and Hall's Sketches, vol. i., p. 111, 112.

* See book iii., chap. iv., of this work.   † See Martin's Louisiana, vol. ii., p. 61.

nigh brought upon them the vengeance of their conquerors, the Spaniards of Louisiana.

These men having learned by rumor that a powerful British armament was off the coast of Florida for the recovery of his majesty's posts and possessions on the Lower Mississippi, and believing the cause of England already triumphant in Florida, determined to evince their zeal for his Britannic majesty's service by overpowering the Spanish garrison in Fort Panmure, and restoring the British flag over that portion of the province. Accordingly, having organized themselves under military officers, and having secured the co-operation of a large number of Choctâ warriors, they repaired, on the 22d of April, to an eminence above the town of Natchez, and in full view of Fort Panmure, where they raised the British flag, and commenced their operations for the capture of the Spanish post.

During the night they approached the fort, and planted their cannon so as to bear upon the works; but a heavy fire from the artillery of the fort next morning soon compelled them to retire. During the following day and night, a moderate cannonade was continued between the garrison and their besiegers.

On the 29th of April, the commandant sent a flag from the fort to the insurgents, representing to them the danger to which they exposed themselves by an open rebellion against their lawful sovereign, at the same time tendering to them the royal clemency, provided they would deliver up their leaders and disperse. They promised an answer next day.

Next day the garrison was induced to believe that the fort had been undermined from the deep ravine contiguous, with a powerful mine, the train of which was to be ignited on the following day; whereupon the commandant; seeing his supply of provisions and ammunition was nearly exhausted, and his men worn down with fatigue and watching, proposed to capitulate, upon condition that he should be permitted peaceably to retire from the fort, and march his troops without molestation to Baton Rouge. These terms were accepted by the insurgents, and the fort was surrendered to them.

A few days brought intelligence that the fleet which had arrived was a Spanish re-enforcement for Galvez, and that Pensacola had fallen into his hands by the fate of war.

This brought consternation to the insurgents, who deemed it

expedient to provide for their own safety before they were within reach of Spanish vengeance. Among the insurgents were General Lyman and many of his colony, as well as others from Ogden's colony, on the Homochitto, who immediately sought safety by flight from the country. Mindful of the fate of O'Reilly's victims ten years before, they determined to elude the vengeance of the Spanish governor by seeking the protection of the nearest British post in Georgia, upon the Savannah River. Without loss of time, they took up their pilgrimage, men, women, and children, with such of their effects as were available, through the Indian wilderness to the western parts of Georgia, through the Creek nation, of whose friendship they had no assurance. After a long and distressing journey of one hundred and thirty days, they reached the settlements on the Savannah, exhausted with fatigue, exposure, and privations.*

Others took refuge in the Indian nation, some of whom subsequently fell into the hands of the Spanish authorities, and were treated as rebels against the king's government.

On the 29th of July, Don Carlos de Grandpre, "lieutenant-colonel in the regiment of Louisiana," entered upon his duties as "civil and military commandant of the post and district of Natchez," when measures were immediately instituted for the punishment of such of the late insurgents as were within reach of the Spanish authorities. Arrests, seizures, and confiscations commenced.† During the months of September and October, the goods, chattels, effects, and dues of every kind, pertaining to more than twenty "fugitive rebels," had been seized for confiscation. Some of these were men of wealth, especially George Rappleje and Jacob Blomart. Before the middle of November,

* Martin's Louisiana, vol. ii., p. 63-65.

† The MS. Spanish records at Natchez exhibit a list of the "fugitive rebels," and the proceedings against such as were arrested. Those who had fled the country were Philip Alston, John Ogg, Christian Bingaman, Caleb Hansbrough, Thaddeus Lyman, John Watkins, William Case, John Turner, Thomas James, Philip Mulkey, Ebenezer Gosset, Thompson Lyman, Nathaniel Johnson.

The following were "leaders of the rebellion," who were prisoners in New Orleans on the 16th of November, awaiting their trials, viz.:
1. John Alston, who was arrested in the Indian nation.
2. Jacob Blomart, "chief of the rebels."
3. John Smith, "lieutenant of rebels."
4. Jacob Winfrey, "captain of rebels."
5. William Eason.
6. Parker Caradine.
7. George Rappleje.
—See MS. Spanish records at Natchez, in Probate Court, book A.

seven of the leaders were prisoners in close confinement in New Orleans, " charged with the crime of attempting to promote a general rebellion" against his Catholic majesty's government in the " District of Natchez." Seven were convicted and sentenced to death, but were subsequently reprieved by the governor-general. Thus terminated the first revolt of the Anglo-Americans in Florida. The second, nearly thirty years afterward, was more fortunate.

[A.D. 1782.] Meantime, the plenipotentiaries of the belligerent powers were engaged at Paris in negotiations for a general peace in Europe and America. On the 20th of November, 1782, the provisional treaty of peace between the United States and Great Britain was executed. This treaty established the southern limit of the United States to be the 31st parallel of north latitude, from the Mississippi eastward to the St. Mary's River of East Florida.*

[A.D. 1783.] On the 20th day of January, 1783, the preliminary articles of peace between Great Britain on the one side, and France and Spain on the other, were signed by their respective plenipotentiaries at Paris, and hostilities in Louisiana and Florida ceased. In September following, the definitive articles of peace were signed by the same parties and the United States respectively, for the final ratification of their respective governments.

By this treaty Great Britain confirmed to Spain the whole of the Floridas south of the 31st degree of latitude, reserving the right that all British subjects then resident in Florida should be allowed the period of eighteen months from the ratification of the treaty to sell their property and close their business, provided they desired to retire from the province.†

Meantime, the provinces of Louisiana and the Floridas, under the Spanish dominion, returned to a state of peace and repose, when military parade and martial display gave place to domestic cares, and the excitement of trade, agriculture, and individual enterprise. Emigration from the Spanish provinces of Mexico and the West Indies continued to augment the population as well as the commerce of the country, and enterprising emigrants from the United States began to arrive also.

---

* See Walker's Reports of Supreme Court of Mississippi, p. 63, note.
† Martin, vol. ii., p. 72.

CHAPTER II.

LOUISIANA UNDER THE SPANISH DOMINION, FROM THE TREATY OF 1783 TO THE YEAR 1796.—A.D. 1783 TO 1796.

Argument.—Prosperous Condition of Louisiana after the War.—Population in 1785.—Galvez retires from Louisiana.—Don Miro succeeds to the provisional Government.—Judge of Residence.—Catholic Church in Louisiana.—Inquisition excluded.—Acadian Emigrants.—Indulgence to British Subjects in West Florida.—Irish Catholic Priests for the Natchez District.—Miro succeeds as Governor-general of Louisiana in 1786.—Arrival of the Commissioners of Georgia.—Georgia Act creating "Bourbon County."—Spanish Duties upon American river Trade.—Extension of American Settlements in the Ohio Region.—Claims of western People to free Navigation of the Mississippi.—Their Impatience under Spanish Imposts.—They contemplate the Invasion of Louisiana by military Force.—Nature and Extent of Spanish Imposts.—Relaxation of impost Duties.—Colonel Wilkinson's Agency in effecting Relaxation of revenue Laws.—Emigration of Americans to West Florida and Louisiana.—General Morgan's Colony.—"New Madrid" laid off.—Guardoqui urges rigid Execution of impost Regulations.—The Intendant rigorously enforces revenue Laws.—Louisiana threatened with military Invasion from Ohio Region.—Conflagration of New Orleans in 1788.—Supplies from the Ohio admitted by the river Trade.—Colonel Wilkinson engages in the tobacco Trade.—Emigration from Cumberland to Louisiana encouraged; also from the Ohio and the Illinois.—Population of Louisiana in 1788.—Emigration and Trade from the Ohio Region in 1789–90.—Policy recommended by Navarro to Spain.—Spain jealous of the Extension of the Federal Jurisdiction.—First Schools and Academies in New Orleans.—Baron Carondelet succeeds Miro as Governor of Louisiana.—Population of New Orleans in 1792.—Trade with Philadelphia.—Political Disturbances emanating from revolutionary France in 1793.—Genet's Intrigues and contemplated Invasion of Louisiana and Florida from the United States.—Defensive Movements of Baron Carondelet in Louisiana.—Measures of the Federal Government to suppress any hostile Movement.—Fort Barrancas commenced at the fourth Chickasá Bluff.—Counter-plot of Carondelet for effecting a Separation of western People.—Don Rendon Intendant of Louisiana and Florida.—Louisiana and Florida an independent Bishopric.—Carondelet improves and fortifies the City of New Orleans; drains the back Swamps.—A navigable Canal.—"Canal Carondelet" completed.—The Indigo Crop fails, and Cotton, Sugar, and Tobacco succeed.—Louisiana relieved from Apprehension.—Genet's Agents arrested; himself recalled.—French Royalists propose to settle a Colony on the Washita.—Arrangements with Maison Rouge.—Alleged Grant and Colony of Maison Rouge.—Subsequent Litigation.—Adjudication and final Rejection of the Claim as fraudulent.—Grant to Baron de Bastrop.—Americans excluded from Louisiana and Florida.—Grant to Dubuque on Upper Mississippi.—Carondelet's Intrigues for the Separation of Kentucky from the Union.—Gayoso sent to negotiate with the Kentucky Conspirators.—Sebastian descends to Natchez and New Orleans.—Negro Insurrection discovered and suppressed in the Island of Point Coupée.—Negro Importation interdicted.—Don Morales is Intendant for 1796.—Baron Carondelet's last Effort to detach Kentucky in 1796.—Route to Upper Louisiana through the Bayou Barthelemy and St. Francis River.

[A.D. 1784.] LOUISIANA, relieved from the danger and privations of active warfare, began to prosper as a Spanish province. Emigration from Spain, the West Indies, and Mexico

VOL. I.—G G

continued to augment the population in all the settlements. Trade from the interior, and commerce with foreign ports and with the colonial dominions of Spain, began to develop the resources of the country, and to increase the strength and wealth of the settlements.

[A.D. 1785.] In the spring of 1785, according to a census by order of Governor Galvez, the population of the whole province of Louisiana, including the Natchez and Baton Rouge districts of West Florida, exclusive of Indians, was over thirty-three thousand souls. Of this amount, Lower Louisiana, exclusive of the Florida districts, contained 28,047 persons, including the population of New Orleans, which was 4980 souls. The West Florida districts contained 3477, and Upper Louisiana 1491 souls.* Thus the province, in fifteen years from the departure of O'Reilly, had more than doubled its population.

The greater portion of this increase of population was not altogether the result of emigration from Spain and the Spanish possessions near the Gulf of Mexico, but there had been many French emigrants from France and the French West India Islands, consequent upon certain privileges which had been extended to the French population for several years past. Among these were the privilege of serving in the "Royal Regiment of Louisiana," and of filling many of the inferior civil offices in the royal government.

In the course of the summer following, Governor Galvez retired from the province of Louisiana, to enter upon the duties of "Captain-general of Cuba," to which office he had been promoted by the king. The province of Louisiana and the two Floridas were to remain attached to his government, under his lieutenants, until a regular appointment should be made. On his departure from Louisiana, he was succeeded in the administration of the government by Don Estevan Miro, "colonel of the Regiment of Louisiana," who, having been appointed Judge of Residence† for Galvez, was intrusted with the duties

* Martin's Louisiana, vol. ii., p. 77.

† This office was peculiar to the Spanish colonial government and polity. In the Spanish colonies, "Judge of Residence" was a wise and salutary provision for investigating the official conduct of any crown officer *after* he had retired from office, either by removal, promotion, or death. The judge of residence, after having made full inquiry into his official acts, made a full and formal report of the same to the "Council of the Indies" for the king. This provision was intended to act as a wise and salutary check upon the officer, and to insure a zealous and upright discharge of his official duties. Knowing that his whole administration was to be scrutinized by an officer, who

of governor until a successor should be regularly appointed by the king.

The Catholic Church had already been established in Louisiana, and its influence was felt in every Spanish and French settlement; but it was not until the year 1785 that the successor of St. Peter attempted to introduce the terrors of the Holy Office to sustain the true faith against foreign heresies.

Heretofore the church establishment was supported by funds from the royal treasury, as a portion of the government establishment, and consisted of sixteen curates, four assistants, and six nuns, under the control of the vicar-general of Louisiana.* To give greater effect to their doctrines, and to check the progress of heresy, which was apprehended from the constant intercourse with the western people of the United States, it had been deemed expedient by the head of the Catholic Church to introduce the Inquisition into Louisiana. A clergyman of New Orleans was accordingly appointed "Commissary of the Holy Office" in that city. But Governor Miro, having been instructed by the king to prohibit the exercise of all inquisitorial functions in the province, notified the commissary of his instructions, and forbade him to exercise the duties of his office. But the "reverend father," deeming it his duty to obey his spiritual rather than his temporal master, entered upon the exercise of his commission. The governor, firm to his duty and obedient to his instructions, determined to remove him from the province, and soon afterward, without any other warning, the zealous ecclesiastic, while enjoying the slumbers of midnight, was suddenly aroused by an officer at the head of eighteen grenadiers, who conveyed him safely on board a vessel ready to sail for Spain, and by daylight next morning he was upon his voyage for Europe.† Thus was the first and *the only attempt* to establish the Inquisition in Louisiana effectually suppressed, although no other religion was tolerated.

During the same year, the province received an accession to its population by the arrival of a large number of Acadian French families, introduced by the King of France to enable

---

might be strict in the disclosure of his errors, his partiality, his avarice, or his injustice, it was to be expected that he would be prompted to an upright discharge of his duties; yet experience proves that, under the Spanish colonial government, this end was not always attained; for the rapid accumulation of large fortunes by the Spanish governors was not uncommon.—See Martin, vol. ii., p. 76.

* Martin, vol. ii., p. 80, 81. † Idem, p. 84.

them to join their friends, who, to escape the English dominion, had emigrated from their country to Louisiana in the year 1755. They were located upon grants of land made by the Spanish authorities, chiefly upon the Terre aux Beufs, upon the Bayou Lafourche, and in the districts of Oppelousas and Attackapas, where their descendants still reside. The whole number of persons in this importation was about three thousand five hundred souls, comprising the greater portion of the remainder of the original French population of that country.

During the same year, many of the English residents retired from West Florida, and especially from the districts of Natchez and Baton Rouge. Yet, as the period specified in the treaty of 1783 for their departure had elapsed, and many were still unprepared to remove, the acting governor, Miro, had granted an extension of the time, to enable them to complete their arrangements for their final departure from the province. The King of Spain not only approved the act of the governor, but signified his pleasure that such of the British subjects as desired to remain in the country should be entitled to all the rights and privileges of Spanish subjects by taking the oath of allegiance to the Spanish crown, and promising not to leave their respective districts without the permission of the governor.

[A.D. 1786.] To favor those who might desire to remain in the settlements of Natchez and Bayou Sara, where there were many Irish emigrants, the king directed that these districts should be supplied with Irish Catholic priests, in order to afford them the privileges of the Catholic Church. The priests arrived early in the following spring, and entered upon the duties of their office.

Early in the summer of 1786, Miro received his commission from the king as "Governor, civil and military, of Louisiana and West Florida," and on the 2d of June he issued his *bando de buen gobierno*,* setting forth his powers and the general principles of his administration of the government. Soon afterward he published several general regulations for the preservation of good order and religious decorum in the province,

---

* A *bando de buen gobierno* is a proclamation which the governor of a Spanish province generally issues when first entering upon the duties of his new office. The object is to make known the principles which are to regulate his future intercourse with the people of his province, and to notify them of any new ordinances or police regulations necessary to be enforced. It is literally an inaugural address.—See Martin, vol. ii., p. 86.

together with sundry police regulations for the government of the city of New Orleans. Among these were ordinances prohibiting concubinage, and incontinence as a livelihood, and providing for the enforcement of all laws for the suppression of gambling, duelling, and the wearing of dirks, pistols, and concealed weapons.

Under his wise administration the province continued to enjoy a high degree of prosperity; population and commerce increased, the river trade with Upper Louisiana, and the settlements upon the Ohio and its tributaries, had become active, and the Spanish dominion upon the Mississippi appeared to be increasing continually in importance and power.

In the mean time, the serious attention of the Spanish authorities was attracted to the growing power of the United States, whose western settlements were coming in collision with those of Louisiana and Florida.

The State of Georgia claimed the whole southern portion of the United States, from the Atlantic to the Mississippi River, bounded on the south by the thirty-first parallel of latitude. Hence all the territory near the Mississippi on the east side, from Loftus's Heights northward for several hundred miles, was properly the territory of Georgia. But this whole region was in the possession of Spain, with a population of nearly ten thousand souls.

This subject had not been overlooked by the state government, and commissioners on the part of Georgia had arrived at New Orleans, during the autumn of 1785, with a demand for the surrender of the territory, and the establishment of the line stipulated in the treaty of 1783. The subject, however, had been referred to the Federal government for settlement and amicable negotiation.

The commissioners notified the Spanish governor " that on the 7th of February, 1785, the Legislature of Georgia had passed an act, which provided for the erection of a county, by the name of 'Bourbon county,' near the Mississippi, comprising all the lands below the mouth of the Yazoo, to which the Indian title had been extinguished; and that said act provided, that whenever a land-office should be established in said county, the persons occupying any of said lands, being citizens of the United States, or of any friendly power, should have a preference claim allowed and reserved to them: provided *they* *actually lived on and cultivated said lands.*" The subject, however, having been referred to the Federal government for negotiation, the act of February 7th, 1785, was repealed on the first day of February, 1788.*

An active trade from the population on the Ohio had forced itself down the Mississippi to every part of Louisiana and West Florida, and the people of these western settlements claimed the natural right to the use of the river through the province of Louisiana; although, in the eyes of Spain, they were unquestionably citizens of a foreign power. It had early become a matter of great interest to the Spanish authorities to derive a large revenue from this trade by the imposition of transit and port duties, besides harbor duties, and such other expenses as were unavoidable in trade. A revenue officer, with a suitable guard and a military post, was established at New Madrid and other points, at which all boats were required to make land and comply with the revenue laws, which were enforced with rigor, even to seizure and confiscation of the cargo.

The western people were multiplying rapidly, and their surplus products adapted to the Louisiana trade continued to increase astonishingly, and forced their way down the Mississippi. The river duties, which by them were deemed oppressive and unjust, were collected and extorted by the officials of Louisiana, supported by military force. The western people believed these duties exorbitant, and the many restrictions which were imposed oppressive and unjust toward those who possessed a natural right to navigate the river free of all such impositions. Under these impressions, it is not strange that many of the sturdy Republicans should resist these exactions, and disregard the attempts of the Spanish authorities to enforce them. In this manner, it frequently happened that persons were seized, fined, and imprisoned, with other vexatious delays and expenses; and sometimes their cargoes were confiscated as contraband, or forfeited, and the owners or supercargoes were discharged, penniless, to find their way home.†

[A.D. 1787.] Repeated occurrences of this kind in the lapse of two years, from 1785 to 1787, had greatly incensed the western people, and disseminated a general feeling of revenge

---

* See American State Papers, folio edition, vol. i., Public Lands, p. 120. The Georgia act was entitled, "An act for laying out a district of land situate on the River Mississippi, and within the bounds of this state, into a county, to be called '*Bourbon.*'"— See Toulmin's Digest, p. 464. † Martin, vol. ii., p. 90, 91.

throughout the whole Ohio region, from the sources of the Monongahela to those of the Tennessee and Cumberland Rivers. To such an extent had this vindictive feeling been carried in Kentucky and upon the Cumberland River, that a military invasion of Louisiana was devised for redressing the wrongs of the western people, and seizing the port of New Orleans ; provided the Federal government failed to obtain from Spain, by negotiation, such commercial privileges in Louisiana as were indispensable to the prosperity of the western people.

Such had been the excitement in Kentucky and Tennessee, as early as the spring of 1787, that the Spanish governor became seriously apprehensive of an invasion from Kentucky, in defiance of the Federal authority. At the same time, the western people, indignant at the neglect of the Federal government in not securing for them the free use of the Mississippi, were strongly tempted to separate from the Atlantic States, and to secure for themselves an independent form of government, which would enable them to obtain from Spain, under one form or another, those commercial advantages which they were determined to possess.

It was under these circumstances that Colonel James Wilkinson, an enterprising merchant of Kentucky, and a man of fine talents and address, made arrangements with the Spanish authorities to descend to New Orleans with several boats loaded with tobacco, flour, and other articles of western production. Having reached New Orleans in safety, he obtained an interview with the governor, and at length succeeded in securing for himself and a few friends permission to trade with the city, and to introduce free of duties many articles of western production adapted to the Louisiana market.*

* The exactions of the Spanish government were in the shape of heavy transit and port duties on all produce and articles of trade descending the Mississippi from any of the western settlements upon the Ohio and its numerous tributaries. Every article thus introduced into Louisiana, of which Western Tennessee was claimed as a portion, and all kinds of trade descending the river, were compelled to pay an excise duty to the government, varying at different times, according to the arbitrary will of the intendant, or the orders of the king, from *six to twenty-five per cent. ad valorem.* For the collection of this duty, a military force, with revenue officers, was stationed at New Madrid, and other points below, by whom every boat was compelled to land and submit to have their cargoes overhauled, and sometimes, when deception was suspected, to have them unloaded, in order that the Spanish officers might be satisfied of the cargo, upon which to assess the duties. When duties were thus paid, and papers furnished, the boat was required to land at each post below, and exhibit the evidence of having paid duties; refusal to do so exposed them to be fired into from the batteries, or to be pursued, and subjected to heavy fines, imprisonment, and confiscations. The latter penalty was a

In making concessions in favor of the western people, Governor Miro desired to avail himself of the talents and popularity of Colonel Wilkinson in Kentucky and Tennessee for conciliating the hostile feelings and the inimical prejudices which had been excited against the Spanish authorities. Through him, in addition to the relaxation of the restrictions upon the river trade, and an abatement on the transit duties, the governor proposed to encourage emigration from Kentucky and the Cumberland settlements, to the parishes of West Florida contiguous to the Mississippi.*

The Spanish minister, Don Diego Guardoqui, apprised of the governor's views, and conceiving that he might derive a pecuniary advantage from such a state of things, readily assented to the policy, and became deeply interested in promoting the proposed plans for securing harmony of feeling between the western people and the Spanish authorities of Louisiana. The intendant of Louisiana, agreeably to the views of the governor, had consented to relax the revenue laws, and indirectly to sanction occasional violations of a rigorous and oppressive law.

This state of things continued for nearly two years, when Guardoqui, perceiving that his expectations, in a pecuniary point of view, were not realized, determined to require the rigid execution of the revenue laws upon the river trade.

"While Colonel Wilkinson was in New Orleans, in June, 1787, Governor Miro requested him to give his sentiments freely, in writing, respecting the political interests of Spain and the Americans of the United States inhabiting the regions upon the western waters. This he did at length in a document of fifteen or twenty pages, which the governor transmitted to Madrid to be laid before the King of Spain.

favorite measure with the Spanish officers; for, in that case, they generally managed to appropriate the spoils to their private use.

* See Butler's History of Kentucky, passim. In several portions of this work we have been compelled, in making references to authority, to depend chiefly on Butler's History of Kentucky, which embraces most of the early history of Western Virginia and Kentucky, which is imbodied in the first volume of Humphrey Marshall's History of the state. The material facts and incidents are certainly imbodied in Butler's History of Kentucky, which comprises much western history besides that properly belonging to that state. It is only to be regretted that Mr. Butler did not devote more time and attention to a systematic order of arrangement, to a perspicuous, dignified, and comprehensive phraseology so becoming the history of a member of this young and glorious Republic. Had his work been prepared with that patient care and mature reflection which would have enabled him to present the useful matter therein contained in that clear, concise, and lucid manner which characterizes our ablest historians, he would have merited and received the gratitude of the Great West.

"In this document he urges the natural right of the western people to follow the current of rivers flowing through their country to the sea. He states the extent of the country, the richness of the soil, abounding in choice productions proper for foreign markets, to which they have no means of conveying them should the Mississippi be shut against them. He sets forth the advantages which Spain might derive from allowing them the free use of the river. He proceeded to show the rapid increase of population in the western country, and the eagerness with which every individual looked forward to the navigation of that river; he described the general abhorrence with which they received the intelligence that Congress was about to sacrifice their dearest interest by ceding to Spain, for twenty years, the navigation of the Mississippi; and represents it as a fact that they are on the point of separating themselves entirely from the Union on that account; he addressed himself to the governor's fears by an ominous display of their strength; and argues the impolicy of Spain in being so blind to her own interest as to refuse them an amicable participation in the navigation of the river, thereby forcing them into violent measures. He assures the Spanish governor that, in case of such alternative, 'Great Britain stands ready, with expanded arms, to receive them,' and to assist their efforts to accomplish that object, and quotes a conversation with a member of the British Parliament to that effect. He states the facility with which the province of Louisiana might be invaded by the united forces of the English and Americans, the former advancing from Canada by way of the Illinois River, and the latter by way of the Ohio River; also, the practicability of proceeding from Louisiana to Mexico, in a march of twenty days; that in case of such invasion, Great Britain will aim at the possession of Louisiana and New Orleans, and leave the navigation of the river free to the Americans. He urged forcibly the danger of the Spanish interests in North America, with Great Britain in possession of the Mississippi, as she was already in possession of the St. Lawrence and the great lakes. He concluded with an apology for the freedom with which he had expressed his views by the governor's particular request; that such as they are, they are from a man 'whose head may err, but whose heart can not deceive.'"[*]

[*] Butler's History of Kentucky, 2d ed., p. 519, 520, Appendix.

These views accorded so nearly with those which had been already suggested by the condition of things on the Mississippi and in the West, that they were unhesitatingly adopted as the correct principles for the government of his Catholic majesty's officers charged with the administration of affairs in Louisiana.

The object of Colonel Wilkinson, in this statement of the relative feelings and interests of the two countries, was evidently to impress upon the Spanish government forcibly the importance of granting to the American people of the West those commercial privileges which Spain could not long withhold with safety to her dominion on the Mississippi. In doing this, he deemed it expedient to operate upon not only their fears, but their interests and their love of self-preservation. Hence he held out to the Spanish governor the possibility of an alliance between the western country and Louisiana.

Nor was the latter mistaken in his views as to the proper manner in which these concessions were to be effected. The statement of Colonel Wilkinson, and the influence of his address and talents, were the first efficient means which led to the change of policy in the government of Louisiana. Through Colonel Wilkinson's negotiation and his diplomatic address, the governor was convinced of the policy of conciliating the western people, and of attaching them as far as practicable to the Spanish government. For this purpose, he granted permission for Americans from Kentucky and the Cumberland River to emigrate to West Florida and establish themselves under the protection of Spain, with liberal grants of land, and other privileges granted only to the most favored nations. At the same time, the intendant of Louisiana, with the approbation of the governor and of the minister, Don Guardoqui, near the Federal government, relaxed the exactions required by the revenue laws, and extended special indulgences to favored persons from Kentucky and the Cumberland. While these things were exerting a salutary influence in conciliating these growing and populous settlements, the Spanish minister conceived the plan for effecting a political union between the western people and the province of Louisiana. The first step toward the accomplishment of this desirable object was the plan of forming American settlements in Upper Louisiana, as well as in the Florida district of Lower Louisiana.*

* Martin's Louisiana, vol. ii., p. 90, 91.

[A.D. 1788.] A large American settlement was to be formed on the west side of the Mississippi, between the mouth of the Ohio and the St. Francis River. General Morgan, an American citizen, received a large grant of land about seventy miles below the mouth of the Ohio, upon which he was to introduce and settle an American colony. Soon afterward, General Morgan arrived with his colony, and located it about seventy miles below the mouth of the Ohio, upon the ancient alluvions which extend westward to the White Water Creek, within the present county of New Madrid, in Missouri. Here, upon the beautiful rolling plains, he laid off the plan of a magnificent city, which, in honor of the Spanish capital, he called " New Madrid." The extent and plan of the new city was but little, if any, inferior to the old capital which it was to commemorate. Spacious streets, extensive public squares, avenues, and promenades were tastefully laid off to magnify and adorn the future city. In less than twelve months from its first location, it had assumed, according to Major Stoddart, the appearance of a regularly built town, with numerous temporary houses distributed over a high and beautiful undulatory plain. Its latitude was determined to be 36° 30' north. In the center of the site, and about one mile from the Mississippi, was a beautiful lake, to be inclosed by the future streets of the city.

This policy was continued for nearly two years, in hopes of gaining over the western people to an adherence to the Spanish interests. Nor was it wholly unsuccessful. In the mean time, many individuals in Kentucky, as well as on the Cumberland, had become favorably impressed toward a union with Louisiana under the Spanish crown, and a very large portion of them had been highly dissatisfied with the policy of the Federal government, because it had failed to secure for them the free navigation of the river, either by formal negotiation or by force of arms.

But this state of mitigated feeling toward the Spanish authorities was of but short duration. Don Diego Guardoqui, the minister, had failed to derive that pecuniary advantage which he had expected from his connivance at repeated infractions of the revenue laws. As if the facts had just come to his knowledge, he now affected great indignation at the remissness of the intendant, who had permitted these delinquencies; and, in an official communication, severely reprimanded his dereliction of duty, and threatened to represent his conduct and his delinquencies to the court at Madrid. The intendant, alarmed for the safety of his office, resumed the rigorous enforcement of the revenue laws. Seizures, confiscations, delays, and imprisonments, affecting owners, supercargoes, and crews of flatboats descending the river, became frequent and embarrassing ; and Louisiana was again menaced with invasion from the Ohio. Hundreds of fiery spirits in Kentucky and on the Cumberland were anxious to embark in the enterprise.

In the mean time, the city of New Orleans had been nearly destroyed by fire. On the 21st of March, about three o'clock in the afternoon, the chapel of a Spaniard in Chartres-street took fire, and, by a strong wind, it soon spread over the city, until nine hundred houses were consumed, besides an immense amount of property of every description. This was the severest calamity which had ever befallen the city, and threw the whole province into want and embarrassment.* Provisions of all kinds became scarce, and great distress prevailed in the city. To prevent actual suffering and famine, the government was obliged to take measures for supplying the necessities of the people. A contract was opened for the supply of a large quantity of flour from the Ohio region, upon which large advances of money were made, and, as an additional inducement to traders and boatmen, the privilege of introducing other articles was granted to those who brought cargoes of flour.

The embarrassment and privations occasioned by this unforeseen calamity in the city admonished the governor of the necessity of relaxing all the commercial restrictions upon the river trade, and of releasing those individuals who had been imprisoned for former violations of the revenue laws, and to restore the property previously seized and confiscated.

About this time an arrangement was entered into with Colonel Wilkinson for the introduction of one or more boat-loads of tobacco annually into the city. Permission was also extended to emigrants from the settlements upon the Wabash, Kentucky, or Cumberland Rivers, to settle in Louisiana, upon condition of their paying a duty of twenty-five *per cent.* upon all property introduced for sale. Slaves, stock, provisions for two years, farming utensils and implements, were to be free from any duty whatever. Lands for the settlement of farms and

* Martin, vol. ii., p. 97.

for residences were freely tendered to those who were willing to become Spanish subjects. Many American citizens, encouraged by these conditions, and allured by the mild climate and the productive soil of West Florida, removed, with their families and effects, to that country, and became incorporated as Spanish subjects.

During the year 1788 the jurisdiction of the United States was extended over the Northwestern Territory, which comprised the whole country from the Ohio northwestwardly to the Great Lakes and the Mississippi. By the ordinance of 1787, for the organization of this territory, involuntary servitude or slavery was forever abolished within its limits. Many of the French settlers in the Illinois country were in the possession of negro slaves, introduced under the French jurisdiction, which tolerated slavery, as did that of Virginia afterward. Unwilling now to be stripped of a valuable species of property by subsequent legislation, they determined to remove into the Spanish dominion west of the Mississippi, where negro slavery was free from restrictions.

The population of Louisiana for several years had been gradually increasing in number, from Spain and France and their dependences, no less than from the United States, and the census taken during the year 1788 presented an aggregate population of 42,611 souls in Louisiana and the West Florida districts. This aggregate indicated an increase of nearly ten thousand persons since the census of 1785, the greater portion of whom were Spanish immigrants and French Acadians, introduced two years before; the remainder were chiefly Americans, who had settled in the West Florida districts.

The whole population by this census is divided into the following classes and numbers, viz.: free whites, 19,445; free persons of color, 1701; slaves, 21,465.*

* See Martin, vol. ii., p. 99, 100. This population was distributed over the province in the following order, viz.:

I. *Lower Louisiana.*

1. City of New Orleans	5338
2. Below the city to the Balize	2378
3. Terre aux Beufs	661
4. Bayous St. John and Gentilly	772
5. Barrataria	40
6. Tchoupitoulas Parish	7589
7. Parish of St. Charles	2381
8. St. John Baptist	1368
9. St. James	1551
10. La Fourche	1164
11. La Fourche Interior	1500
12. Iberville	944
13. Point Coupée Parish	2004
14. Oppelousas	1985
15. Attakapas	2541
16. New Iberia	190
17. Washita	232
18. Rapides	147

From the year 1788 we may date the settled policy of Spain, through her colonial and diplomatic authorities, to endeavor, by intrigue and diplomacy, to acquire the western portion of the United States. The king, having approved the judicious policy of Governor Miro relative to the indulgences extended to the western people, relieved him from the interference of the intendant by the resignation of Navarro, and the union of his duties and authority in the governor himself. Navarro, in the mean time, had endeavored to rouse the court of Madrid to the danger to be apprehended from the increasing power of the United States.* He had portrayed in strong colors the ambition of the Federal government on the subject of western territory, and the thirst for conquest, which, he asserted, would be gratified only by the extension of their dominion to the shores of the Pacific Ocean. He also recommended, as the only true policy for Spain to pursue, the necessity of dismembering the Federal union by procuring the separation of the western country from the Atlantic States. This accomplished, the danger of the Spanish provinces from the encroachments of the Federal power would immediately cease, and Spain would be at liberty to enter into negotiations mutually advantageous to Louisiana and the western people, who were impatient of the delays and failures of the Federal government to promote their interests.

To effect this object, he recommended the judicious distribution of pensions to prominent individuals of Kentucky, and an extension of commercial privileges to the western people generally. The judicious control of these means, in his opinion, would make it no difficult matter for Spain to arrest forever the designs of the United States for extending their territory in the West, while it would greatly augment the power of Spain in Louisiana, and immensely increase its resources. The suggestions of the minister were well received at court, and

19. Avoyelles	209	III. *West Florida.*	
20. Natchitoches	1021	1. Manchac and Galveston	552
21. Arkansas Settlements	119	2. Baton Rouge	682
II. *In Upper Louisiana.*		3. Feliciana	730
		4. Natchez	2679
1. St. Geneviève	896	5. Mobile	1468
2. St. Louis	1197	6. Pensacola	265

* In this respect Navarro seemed to have had a prophetic vision into futurity, and to have foreseen the events which were to transpire more than half a century afterward, when Texas and Oregon were finally embraced in the limits of the Federal jurisdiction, permanently in 1846.

formed the basis of the subsequent policy of Spain and Louisiana toward the Federal government and the western people respectively, until the "Treaty of Madrid," seven years afterward.*

[A.D. 1789.] Thus commenced that series of intrigues and vexatious court delays on the part of Spain, which characterized the political relations of that power toward the United States until the final evacuation of the Natchez District ten years afterward; a state of uncertain peace, which for years continued to disturb the harmony of the two countries, and to destroy mutual confidence.† Nor were persons of talent and influence wanting in Kentucky who were willing to promote the designs of Spain in producing a separation of the West, for the purpose of effecting a political and commercial alliance with Louisiana under the protection of Spain.

Under the adopted policy of Spain relative to emigration from the United States, and the river trade, the population continued to advance west of the mountains, and emigration to Louisiana and West Florida began to add hundreds annually to the population of the province.

At the same time, a new impulse was given to the trade of the western people with the Spanish provinces generally, through the port of New Orleans. The surplus products of the settlements on the Monongahela, the Ohio, the Kentucky, and Cumberland Rivers consisted of flour, pork, beef, whisky, apples, cider, lumber, horses, cattle, and many other agricultural and manufactured products, which met with a ready sale in New Orleans, as well as other points upon the river.‡ An active trade in breadstuffs had likewise been opened with the city of Philadelphia by sea, and a state of general good feeling existed between the western people and the Spanish authorities in Louisiana.

Enterprise was awakened in the West, and capital freely invested in rearing those products most in demand in Louisiana and the Spanish provinces throughout the Continent, as well as in the West India Islands, and men of enterprise and capital embarked their means in the navigation of the river and in the extension of western commerce.

[A.D. 1790.] For two years this state of amicable trade

* Martin's Louisiana, vol. ii., p. 100, &c. See, also, Butler's Kentucky.
† See Butler's Kentucky. ‡ Martin's Louisiana, vol. ii., p. 103.

continued, and from all these settlements emigrants and adventurers continued to descend, upon every spring flood, in company with the regular trading-boats from the Ohio. Many of them, well pleased with the climate and the agricultural facilities of the country, remained and entered into the cultivation of tobacco, cotton, and indigo, then the most valuable staples of Louisiana. Others, who had contemplated a permanent residence in the Florida districts, averse to the tenets and rites of the Catholic Church, to which all were required to adhere, yielding to their prejudices, returned to the United States, to enjoy freedom of opinion in their religious sentiments and the church rituals.

But Spain had become jealous of the advance of the Federal power, and the Spanish authorities became highly disquieted by the extension of the Federal jurisdiction over the "Southwestern Territory," and the relinquishment of sovereignty over the same by the State of North Carolina. About the same time, the commissioners of the Federal government had succeeded in concluding a treaty of peace and boundary with the chiefs of the Creek nation, and which had been fully ratified by them in the city of New York. To counteract the effects of this treaty, the Spanish authorities immediately instituted a negotiation with the Creeks, by which they were induced to prohibit the opening of the boundary line stipulated in the treaty. Thus, for more than a year subsequently, did the Creeks refuse to ratify the boundary line* stipulated in the treaty, and many of them had been induced by the Spanish emissaries to assume a hostile attitude toward the United States.

[A.D. 1791.] Hence, during the years 1790 and 1791, the intercourse between the western people of the United States and those of Louisiana was greatly embarrassed by the continuation of Indian hostilities upon the northwestern frontier, and also upon the southwestern borders of the Cumberland settlements. Such had been the hostile operations of the northern Indians, that a succession of military expeditions had been arrayed against them, and had penetrated to the center of their country. The southern Indians had now taken up arms against the southern frontier, for the avowed purpose of arresting the further advance of the Federal power.

Heretofore but little attention had been given to education

* Martin's Louisiana, vol. ii., p. 106.

in Louisiana; schools were few, and confined exclusively to the wealthy, or were under the control of the clergy, where the expenses of education effectually excluded the great mass of the people. The only school in New Orleans was one under the control of the priests, taught by a few Spanish nuns who arrived soon after O'Reilly's departure. During the autumn of 1791, however, a number of French refugees from the massacre of St. Domingo arrived in New Orleans, and, being destitute of property, were compelled to seek a livelihood in the capacity of teachers. Many of them having been well educated, became valuable citizens of Louisiana, and contributed greatly to the subsequent introduction of schools in the province. The same catastrophe in St. Domingo furnished New Orleans with the first regular dramatic corps.

[A.D. 1792.] The same year closed the mild and judicious administration of Governor Miro in Louisiana. Being promoted to the Mexican provinces, he retired from Louisiana, esteemed and regretted no less by the people of the province than by those of Kentucky and the Cumberland settlements. He was succeeded in the government of Louisiana by Don Francisco Louis Hector, Baron de Carondelet, who exercised the offices of governor and intendant. On the 22d of January, 1792, he issued his *bando de buen gobierno*. In it was set forth the general policy of his future administration, besides several new regulations for the city police. He also instituted regulations for lighting the streets, and for organizing fire companies for the protection of the city from the calamity of destructive fires.

In July following, he issued his proclamation, by order of the king, establishing sundry wholesome and humane regulations for the treatment of slaves, tending greatly to meliorate their general condition.*

The city of New Orleans continued to augment in population and to extend its commerce. By the census of 1792, it was found to contain nearly six thousand inhabitants, with a proportionate increase in commercial importance.

The new governor, imitating the example of his predecessor, continued to extend commercial facilities to the western people, and to encourage the existing trade between the city of Philadelphia and New Orleans. Although contrary to instructions from the minister of finance, yet such was the general ad-

* Martin, vol. ii., p. 112.

vantage of this policy to the city of New Orleans, and to the whole province indirectly, that the king subsequently justified him in the partial infraction of the revenue laws relative to the western people. In accordance with the same amicable commercial policy with the people of the United States, before the close of the year 1792 the governor had permitted several merchants from Philadelphia to establish commercial houses in New Orleans for conducting the American commerce of the city.*

[A.D. 1793.] About this time the political disturbances in France began to affect, not only the United States, but Louisiana also. France and Spain were at war; and French emissaries sought, through the prejudice which had been roused against the Spaniards relative to the navigation of the Mississippi, to instigate an invasion of Louisiana and Florida by the people of the United States, and, if practicable, even a separation of the Western States, and an alliance with Louisiana under the dominion and protection of France. Connected with this scheme, a revolt of the French population of Louisiana against the Spanish authority was contemplated.

Such was the menacing attitude of affairs in Louisiana, that Governor Carondelet deemed it expedient to adopt all prudent measures for placing the province in a proper state of defense against foreign as well domestic enemies. The old fortifications near the city were superseded by two new forts commenced upon the bank of the river, one above and the other immediately below the city. Three redoubts defended the back part of the city, the central one being the principal. At the middle of each flank was also a battery; and the whole was surrounded by a deep ditch, within which was a strong palisade barrier.† Other forts, at different points on the river, above and below, were likewise placed in a proper state of defense.

The militia were also organized and trained, ready for service at the shortest notice. The governor reported the number of militia fit for service in the province as between five and six thousand men, and that the provincial authorities could at any time within three weeks concentrate three thousand men in any part of the province.‡

---

* Martin, vol. ii., p. 115. † Idem, p. 117.
‡ The militia were organized as follows:
1. In New Orleans there were five companies of volunteers, one company of artillery, and two companies of riflemen, each containing one hundred men.

Meantime the revolutionary spirit of France had begun to extend its influence into Louisiana. The political zealots of Jacobinical France were eager to commence a crusade for the recovery of their estranged countrymen of Louisiana under the dominion of France, and to release them from the thraldom of the Spanish dominion. At the head of these political fanatics was M. Genet, the French minister near the government of the United States. This fiery and indiscreet functionary of Republican France endeavored to rouse the people of the United States into an unlawful invasion of Louisiana and Florida. For this purpose, under the authority of the French Republic, he issued commissions to a number of men as officers in the French armies, with authority to raise troops in the United States for the contemplated invasion and revolution of Louisiana. The principal field of M. Genet's operations was the western country, especially in Kentucky and Tennessee. Seizing upon the excited prejudices of the western people, his agents were active in descanting upon the incalculable advantages which would accrue to the whole country by a separation from the Federal Union and an alliance with Louisiana under the protection of France. Many of the western people of the United States were seduced by his emissaries to espouse the schemes of the French agitator, and troops were actually imbodied upon the southern frontier of Georgia. An emissary had been dispatched to the Creek nation, and had enlisted a large body of Creek warriors in the enterprise.*

[A.D. 1794.] Although the Federal government of the United States had used the utmost vigilance and decision in arresting the contemplated treasonable expedition, the Governor of Louisiana neglected no measure for putting his province in a proper state of defense to meet the threatened danger. The fortifications around the city of New Orleans were progressing

---

2. Between the city and the Balize were four companies of one hundred men each.
3. The "legion of the Mississippi," comprising the militia on both sides of the river, from the vicinity of the city up to Point Coupée, constituted ten companies of fusiliers, four companies of dragoons, and two companies of grenadiers, each of one hundred men.
    4. At Avoyelles, one company of infantry.
    5. At Washita, one company of cavalry.
    6. At the Illinois, two companies of cavalry and two companies of infantry.
    7. At the German and Acadian coasts, one regiment of one thousand men.
    8. At Mobile, one company of infantry and one company of cavalry.—See Martin, vol. ii., p. 117, 118.

* See Martin's Louisiana, vol. ii., p. 123. Also, American State Papers, vol. x., Boston edition of 1817. See, also, chap. iii. of this book.

daily toward completion; the forts at Natchez, Walnut Hills, and New Madrid were re-enforced, and a treaty was concluded with the Chickasâs, by which the alliance of that nation was secured, and permission obtained for the establishment of a military post near the mouth of the Margot or Wolf River, upon the fourth Chickasâ Bluff, which was soon afterward occupied by a stockade fort.*

The militia throughout the province were kept in a state of complete organization, and the people were exhorted to a faithful adherence to their duty and allegiance to his Catholic majesty, to resist every attempt to excite rebellion, or in any wise to favor the military invasion designed by the adherents of France. To carry out measures for insuring the peace and due observance of the law, he issued his proclamation about the first of June, strictly requiring the enforcement of certain police regulations throughout the province.†

Yet the French population of Louisiana, influenced by reports of the successes and victories of the French arms on the Continent of Europe, the extension of Republican principles throughout France, and the successful experiment of free government in the United States, were for a time elated with the prospect of a speedy emancipation from absolute monarchy. But, restrained by the strong arm of a military despotism, with its watchful agents, no overt act of rebellion was disclosed in Louisiana, and soon afterward the agents of Genet were arrested by the Federal authorities, and by their demand Genet himself was recalled by his government.‡

To counteract the effects of Genet's intrigues in the West, and to conciliate the feelings and prejudices of the western people

* The treaty with the Chickasâs was conducted by Manuel Gayoso de Lemos, commandant and lieutenant-governor of the Natchez District. The Chickasâs ceded to him the fourth bluff, with the view of erecting thereon a fort, which was to be kept in good repair for the purpose of protecting Louisiana from any invasion which might proceed from the United States. Although a stockade was commenced soon afterward, it was not completed until May, 1795, when it was called "Fort San Ferdinando de Barancas." It was situated upon the peninsula formed by the junction of the Margot and the Mississippi. In June, 1795, the Baron de Carondelet wrote to Maison Rouge, "that the strong fort at the post of 'Echore Margot,' defended by eight pieces of eight-pounder cannon, was completed on the 31st of May, 1795, when the Spanish flag was hoisted, and saluted by repeated discharges of cannon from the shore as well as from the galleys in the river."—See report of case, United States, plaintiffs in error, v. Coxe and King, Supreme United States District Court, Louisiana, 1843, p. 93.

† Martin's Louisiana, vol. ii., p. 126, 127.

‡ See Martin's Louisiana. Butler's Kentucky. Also, book iv., chapter iii., of this work.

toward the Spanish authorities of Louisiana, the governor again relaxed the restrictions upon the river trade, and extended important privileges to men of enterprise, preparatory to another attempt to win over the western people to the dominion of Spain.

For this purpose, he employed Thomas Powers, an intelligent Englishman, who had become a subject of his Catholic majesty, and who was dispatched as a secret emissary to Kentucky, for the purpose of conspiring with some of the leading men of that state relative to the best measures for securing the friendship and favor of the people toward an alliance with Louisiana under the Spanish monarchy. His ostensible business, however, appeared to be the collection of materials for a natural history of the western country. Under this pretext, he penetrated as far as the interior of Kentucky, where he held many private conferences with some of the most prominent men in the state, who were favorably inclined to his plans. In this visit, his real and principal object, so far as practicable, was to remove the predilections in favor of a French alliance, to hold out stronger inducements for an alliance with Spain, and to ascertain the general state of feeling in relation to each of these projects, together with any general information relative to the strength of the Federal government in the West.*

In the alliance with Louisiana, he was authorized to promise every thing desired by the people; and also to give assurance of the readiness of the colonial government to *furnish arms, ammunition, and money* to sustain them in the attempt to throw off the authority of the Federal government.

Meantime, the people of Louisiana, relieved from apprehension relative to the French conspiracy, had become reconciled to the mild and judicious administration of his Catholic majesty's government, by which his French subjects were admitted to all the privileges pertaining to his Spanish colonists.

The internal administration of government, the ecclesiastical as well as the civil authority, became firmly and quietly established, and the officers of the same exerted themselves to promote the prosperity and general welfare of the province. The intendant for the year 1794 was Don Francisco de Rendon. The pope, having erected Louisiana and Florida into an independent bishopric, the worthy Don Louis Penalvert was in-

* Martin, vol. ii., p. 123, 124. Also, book iv., chap. iii., of this work.

stalled bishop of the diocese, with two additional canons to the corps of the provincial clergy.

The bishop having established his Cathedral in the city of New Orleans, Don Almonaster, a perpetual regidor and alferez-real, at his own individual cost, completed the Cathedral church edifice, which had been commenced two years previously.* The same venerable relic of former years still remains in front of the public square in the French municipality.

[A.D. 1795.] At the same time, the Baron de Carondelet was laudably exerting himself to enlarge, beautify, and fortify the city. Early in May, 1794, he had given public notice of his intention to open a canal in the rear of the city, for the double purpose of draining the marshes and ponds in that vicinity, and opening a navigable communication with the sea. This canal, communicating with a branch of the Bayou St. John, would effectually accomplish the latter object, to the great commercial advantage of the city, while it would also remove one great source of annoyance and disease proceeding from the generation of innumerable swarms of musquetoes and marsh miasma from the stagnant pools.

To accomplish this important undertaking for the advantage of the city, he proposed to accept the voluntary contribution of such slave labor as the planters and others in the vicinity might be willing to give. The month of June had been announced as the time for beginning the work, at which time sixty negro slaves were sent by the patriotic inhabitants, and the canal was commenced. The work progressed rapidly; but the depth of the canal was only six feet.† The convicts and a few slaves continued to labor upon the work during the remainder of the year, until it was opened to the intersection of the Bayou St. John, through which a navigable route lay to Lake Pontchartrain. The following year the plan of making the canal navigable up to the city was concurred in, and the governor made a second call upon the patriotism and public spirit of the people for additional labor. To this call a generous response was given, and one hundred and fifty negroes were sent to expedite the work. The excavation was now made to the width of fifteen feet, with a depth sufficient to admit small vessels up to the vicinity of the ramparts on the rear of the city. In November the governor made one more call

* Martin, vol. ii., p. 122–126.   † Idem, p. 124, 125.

for aid from the planters within fifteen miles of the city, assuring them that with eight days' work from the same number of hands he would be able to render the canal navigable for small vessels up to the " basin," which had been excavated near the ramparts of the city. The labor was cheerfully contributed, and the canal was in successful operation during the following winter. Early in the spring a number of schooners came up and moored in the " basin." Thus, in the autumn of 1795, was there a navigable canal route opened from the city, by way of the lakes, to the sea; and the spring of 1796 witnessed ships at anchor in the rear of the city. In honor of the projector and patron, the Cabaldo, by a decree, designated it as " Canal Carondelet,"* a name which it retains to this day.

[A.D. 1796.] The completion of the canal by the governor was considered a presage of the future grandeur and commerce of New Orleans, which was to become the great emporium of Louisiana; but it could hardly have entered his imagination that it was to become the great commercial emporium of the whole Valley of the Mississippi, under a free and independent Republic. A change was also about to be introduced in the great agricultural staples of the province.

During the last two years, 1793 and 1794, such had been the ravages of the insects in destroying the indigo plant, that planters were compelled to turn their attention to some other staple product. Up to this time, indigo had been one of the most valuable staples; but now it gave place gradually to the cultivation of sugar, tobacco, and cotton, which were deemed a more certain crop. Indigo, as a crop, had formerly been liable to a partial failure from the vicissitudes of the seasons; but for the last two years the insect had nearly destroyed the entire crop. In the year 1794, whole fields of indigo were stripped of their foliage by these destructive vermin, leaving only the naked stalks and stems.†

[A.D. 1795.] During the summer of 1795 a number of French royalists arrived in New Orleans, and professed to desire an asylum for many of their friends, who had arrived in the United States and advanced westward to join their countrymen near Gallipolis, on the Ohio. Among these exiled royalists were two noblemen, designated as the Marquis de Maison Rouge and the Baron de Bastrop. The marquis proposed to

---

* Martin, vol. ii., p. 128–131. † Idem, p. 125.

settle a colony of French upon the banks of the Washita; for which he undertook to introduce thirty French families from the Ohio for the cultivation of wheat and the manufacture of flour. But the nobleman was poor and destitute, and, withal, wanting in energy and character; consequently, he was unable to advance the means of introducing and locating his colony. The Baron de Carondelet, deeming it a favorable opportunity for settling the banks of the Washita with an industrious agricultural population, tendered his aid, upon the most liberal and advantageous terms for the marquis. For this purpose, the governor proposed to enter into an agreement jointly with the intendant and royal treasurer, to pay to the order of the marquis for every French Royalist family introduced and settled upon the Washita, and consisting of at least two persons capable of agricultural or mechanical labor, the sum of two hundred dollars. Besides this amount advanced to the marquis, the governor agreed to give every such family, for their use and benefit, four hundred acres of land, and to refund the actual expense of emigration from New Madrid. The conditions of the agreement were subsequently approved by the king. But the marquis never completed the location of his colony; having taken up his residence near the post of Miro, he spent a few years in poverty and obscurity, until 1799, when he died in indigent circumstances, having entirely failed to establish his agricultural colony.

During the last three years of his life his only means of subsistence appears to have been the pension drawn from the Spanish treasury, in the shape of compensation under his contract, for three or four families, including two Anglo-American, which he alleged to have introduced and settled near him.

Such is the foundation upon which was reared, after his death, a noted *land-claim* on the Washita for thirty square leagues of land, embracing both banks of the Washita for nearly thirty miles below the post of Miro. This claim, comprising an aggregate of more than 200,000 acres, was known and designated as the "Maison Rouge grant," covering some of the most splendid alluvions in Louisiana.*

The claim made its first appearance about the year 1806, soon after the constrained departure of the surveyor-general Don Trudeau, and many other Spanish *ex-officials*, from Louisi-

* See Martin's Louisiana, vol. ii., p. 129 and 137.

ana, in 1805.* The claim passed into the hands of Daniel Clarke and Daniel Coxe; and, subsequently, many other persons claiming through them have been largely interested in its confirmation by the United States.†

Consequently, for the next forty years it became a fruitful source of embarrassment to the settlement of the country, as well as to the legislation of the Federal and State governments. By the Congress of the United States, the question of title was referred to the decision of the judicial tribunals. The United States District Court of Louisiana, having adjudicated the case fully, decided certain points at issue in favor of the claimants; but the Supreme Court of the United States, in its final decision, adjudged and decreed *the claim* to be utterly null and void.‡

* See vol. ii., book v., chap. xv., "Territory of Orleans."

† According to Martin, this "grant," as originally claimed by the heirs-at-law, or assignees of Maison Rouge, comprised only thirty thousand acres; subsequently, the claim set up comprised more than two hundred and thirty thousand acres, and extended below the town of Monroe (the Spanish post of Miro, subsequently the post of Washita) more than fifty miles by the meanders of the river.

From the testimony introduced in the District Court in 1844-5, it appears that the inception of the claim dates back to the year 1802 or 1803, about three years after the death of the alleged *grantee*, and at a period when many of the Spanish officials, apprised of the approaching termination of the Spanish dominion in Louisiana, were actively employed for the benefit of their friends and favorites, as well as for their own pecuniary advantage, in fabricating land-titles for alleged previous grants during the legal existence of the Spanish authority. It is clearly shown that, during the *quasi interregnum*, the Spanish officials prepared hundreds of spurious Spanish titles, which were thrown into the market to the highest bidder *for what they would bring*, and large sums of money from time to time had been raised upon them, from that time to the final adjudication in the spring of 1845; each new claimant or adventurer in the speculation nominally augmenting the value of the general claim, because he increased the influence which could be brought to operate in the final decision of the question of confirmation, whether by Congress or otherwise. The final decision demonstrates that the Supreme Court of the United States is entirely beyond the reach of combined wealth.

‡ To test the principles involved in the main question, the parties claimant mutually agreed to present the case in the name of Richard King, a purchaser, holding under Daniel Coxe, of Philadelphia. The case came up for adjudication in New Orleans in 1844; finally disposed in 1845.

The testimony most important was as follows: On the 17th of March, 1795, Governor Carondelet and the intendant, Don Francisco de Rendon, contracted with the Marquis de Maison Rouge, a poor nobleman of France, for the introduction of twenty or thirty French families for a stipulated amount of money, and a certain quantity of land to each settler; the terms were approved by the king on the 14th of July following; the marquis, neglecting to avail himself of the liberal terms, settles near Miro in June, 1798, and dies late in 1799. In the year 1801 Louisiana is ceded conditionally to the French Republic, but is not formally delivered until near the close of the year 1803. For several months previous to the delivery to the French commissioner, it was known in Louisiana and the United States that it had been ceded to the United States, and required only the formality of passing through the French commissioner, being already the property of the United States. The Spanish officers hold office for the emolument pertaining to it, and for the opportunities which their official authority gives them for

A similar grant is alleged to have been made to the Baron de Bastrop the year after the grant of Maison Rouge, and under similar conditions, which, in like manner, were never complied with on his part.* One was also made the same year to Julien Dubuque, upon the Upper Mississippi, for nine square leagues above the mouth of the Little Macoketta River. This was in the heart of a rich mining region, and comprised what the proprietor termed the " Mines of Spain."

The De Bastrop claim, like that of Maison Rouge, has never been recognized by the government of the United States.

Among the events of this year, none tended so much to disturb the tranquillity and domestic prosperity of the province as the difficulty of controlling the slaves. These people, inured

accumulating wealth, directly or indirectly, through their official transactions, &c. Again, in the first adjudication of Spanish land-claims under the Federal government, the validity of the claims were decided by a majority of a board of three commissioners, before whom oral and documentary testimony was adduced to establish the claim. Claims not contested, of course, were not closely investigated; the oath of one or more persons established a claim not contested. The Maison Rouge claim was not adjudicated by the commissioners, who conceived it beyond their jurisdiction. This claim was owned by Louis Bouligny and others, the alleged heirs at law or assignees of Don Vincente Fernandez Fejeiro, former commandant of the post of Washita from the year 1800 to 1804. Louis Bouligny was at the post of Washita during the years 1802 and 1803, and was, in fact, a joint partner with Fejeiro in the Maison Rouge claim, which turns out to be for thirty square leagues of land. During these same years the commandant, Fejeiro, had made several visits to the city of New Orleans.

The title papers presented by the claimants purported to be,

1. A "plat survey, and corners," without any proper courses, distances, &c., made and certified by Don Carlos Laveau Trudeau, surveyor-general of Louisiana, bearing date June 14th, 1797.

2. A Spanish patent, or *titulo in formo*, dated June 20th, 1797, and calling for *thirty superficial leagues of land*.

On the part of the United States, it was shown that the Maison Rouge claim, if authentic, could not exceed four thousand acres previous to the death of the grantee.

John Filhiol, formerly commandant at Fort Miro from the year 1783 to 1800, " and an honest man," had no knowledge of any grant or survey for thirty square leagues to any person or persons; nor does he believe that *Maison Rouge ever claimed* such amount.

It is charged that this large amount was procured in fraud by said Bouligny and Fejeiro; that the plats of survey and the documentary evidence are false and fraudulent, and procured after the death of Maison Rouge.

It was proven that the Spanish governor-general himself had no authority to make such a grant; also, that the said "Don Vincente Fejeiro, in the spring of 1804, of his *own absolute will*, made a number of sales and transfers of land to different inhabitants, which were not asked from, or ever granted by the Spanish government;" that a " few days before the arrival of the American officer appointed to take possession of Fort Miro, this same Don Vincente Fejeiro called together a number of the oldest and most respectable inhabitants of his district, and persuaded them to make these abominable sales and transfers to each other; however, with one exception, not a single man has attempted to use them, but appeared to scorn and detest the vile, intriguing spirit of him who seduced them."—See Printed Case, No. 99, United States, Plaintiffs in Error, *versus* D. Coxe and R. King, Supreme Court of the United States.

* See Martin, vol. ii., p. 132.

to toil and hardships, and conscious of their physical strength, were prone to rebel against the feeble authority by which they were surrounded, and upon any emergency they were apt to take advantage of their physical power, in districts where the slave population was five times as numerous as the whites.

A few years only had elapsed since the horrible tragedy of St. Domingo had transpired, in which a whole race had asserted their freedom, and had expelled or exterminated their enslavers. They had assumed a national independence by their fearless daring; should the slave of Louisiana continue to submit patiently to his thraldom? The theme was one which required only the reckless intrepidity of a desperate leader to rouse the minds of the slaves of Louisiana to the hopeless effort of throwing off their bondage. Such was the motive which was urged by a few daring slaves who had heard of the catastrophe of St. Domingo. A conspiracy was put on foot, in like manner, to exterminate the white population in Louisiana. The plot originated upon the plantation of Julien Poydras, situated upon the island of Point Coupée, while the proprietor was absent on a visit to the United States.

The insurgents designed to murder all the whites of the parish indiscriminately; but a disagreement among the leaders as to the day for commencing the massacre gave occasion for the discovery of the plot before it had entirely matured; the execution of the whole conspiracy was therefore defeated, and promptly suppressed. The militia were immediately under arms, and were soon re-enforced by the regular troops. The slaves had imbodied and made a furious resistance. Twenty-five of them were killed before they were subdued. Upon the surviving ringleaders the full rigor of the law was enforced. In the subsequent trials fifty were found guilty, and were condemned to death. Of these, nine were hung in different parts of the parish of Point Coupee; nine others were taken down the river, and one of them was hung and left suspended at each parish church, as a warning to others. Many of the conspirators, who were less guilty, were severely whipped and discharged.* Thus terminated the first fruits of the St. Domingo tragedy within the present limits of the United States.

Such had been the general excitement and apprehension of the people at the imminent danger from which they had escaped,

* The insurrection of the slaves in the French portion of St. Domingo took place on

that all resolved to take measures for preventing a recurrence of similar danger. The Cabaldo soon afterward petitioned the king for his prohibition against the further introduction of negroes from any portion of the world.*

During the year 1795, the authorities of Louisiana experienced much anxiety in regard to the continued advance of the western settlements of the United States. This advance was not only upon the region of the Ohio; it caused a direct conflict of jurisdiction upon the immediate bank of the Lower Mississippi. This was the period of the famous "Yazoo speculation," under the impulse of which the State of Georgia chartered the "Mississippi Company," and had erected the whole settled portion of the Natchez District into the "County of Bourbon." Although the act was subsequently repealed, it had thrown a large number of Anglo-American adventurers within the Spanish dominion. It was about this time that his Catholic majesty issued his schedule prohibiting the emigration of American citizens to Louisiana.

About the same time, apprehending hostilities on the part of the United States, and an interruption of the intercourse with Upper Louisiana by way of the Mississippi River, the Baron de Carondelet was diligent in preparing to meet the emergency. Additional posts were established upon the Upper Mississippi, and at several points below the mouth of the Ohio. Also, while he was establishing military posts at the mouth of the Ohio, New Madrid, the Echore Margot, Walnut Hills, and Natchez, he was providing for another route to Upper Louisiana, entirely west of the Mississippi River. This route was by way of the Washita River and Bayou Barthelemy to the Arkansas River, and thence by way of White River, the St. Francis, and its great eastern tributary, White Water Creek. By this route he had discovered that a practicable water communication, with short portages, could be opened from New Orleans to the settlements of Upper Louisiana.†

During the following year, the intendant of the province was

---

the night of the 23d of August, 1791. Hundreds of families were butchered by the infuriated negroes, and many escaped only with their lives on board the ships in the harbors, or fled to the Spanish part of the island for protection. Many ultimately came to Louisiana under Spanish dominion, and some fled to the United States.—See Marshall's Life of Washington, vol. v., p. 368, 1st ed., and Martin, vol. ii., p. 109. Also, Marbois's Louisiana, p. 186–200. * Martin's Louisiana, vol. ii., p. 135.

† This route had been explored by experienced hunters and voyageurs, showing the Barthelemy navigable to within a few miles of Pine Bluffs, on the Arkansas.

Don Juan Beneventura Morales, who had succeeded Don Rendon. Morales had entered upon the duties of his office with a firm determination to enforce the revenue laws rigorously against the river trade from the United States, and to prohibit entirely emigration from the Western States to Louisiana, as directed by the king's schedule.

CHAPTER III.

POLITICAL RELATIONS OF LOUISIANA WITH THE UNITED STATES, FROM THE TREATY OF 1783 TO THE TREATY OF MADRID.— A.D. 1783 TO 1795.

Argument.—Field of national Controversy opened by Treaty of 1783.—Construction of the Treaty by Spain.—Construction by United States.—Navigation of the Mississippi.—Claimed by the United States.—Spain claims the exclusive Right.—Denies Use of the River to the western People.—Restrictions and Duties exacted by Spanish Authorities.—Embarrassed Condition of the western People.—Jealous Apprehensions of Spain.—Condition of American Settlements.—Indian Tribes.—Policy pursued by Spain toward Kentucky.—Indignation of the western People.—Excitement by a Rumored abandonment of the Claim of the United States.—Change of Spanish Policy.—Governor Miro relaxes the Restrictions upon the western Trade.—His conciliatory Policy to western People in 1788-9.—Colonel Wilkinson's commercial Enterprise with New Orleans suspected.—Western People become reconciled to the Spanish Authorities.—Cumberland Settlements.—" Miro District."—Emigration from Kentucky and Cumberland encouraged.—Grants of Land in 1790.—Spanish Intrigue for separating the Western States.—Negotiations of the Federal Government.—Impatience of the western People.—Disaffection appears in Kentucky.—Negotiations by the Federal Government.—Spanish Emissaries embarrass Negotiations with Creek Indians, 1789-1790.—" Southwestern Territory" organized. — Baron Carondelet commences his Intrigue with Kentucky, 1792.—Creeks instigated to Hostilities by Spanish emissaries.—Intrigues of M. Genet, the French Minister.—Threatened Invasion of East Florida from Georgia.—Spain procrastinates Negotiations while Carondelet operates upon the western People.—War with Spain apprehended by President Washington in 1794.—Baron Carondelet apprehends Danger from the western People.—Five political Parties in the West.—Powers, the Spanish emissary, sent to Kentucky.—Views of the Federal Government.—It restrains the western Excitement.—Carondelet renews his Mission to Kentucky in 1795.—Gayoso and Powers sent to negotiate with the Kentucky Conspirators.—The Mission Fails.—Prospects of Disunion blasted.—Sebastian visits New Orleans.—Overtures from the Spanish Court.—Thomas Pinckney Minister to Spain.—Treaty of Madrid signed, October 20th.—Stipulations in the Treaty relative to Boundary and the river Trade.—The Georgia Bubble – "Yazoo Speculation."—Its Effects on Louisiana.

[AD. 1783.] THE stipulations in the treaty of 1783, between the powers of Great Britain and of the United States, France, and Spain, opened a wide field of controversy between the Federal government and the court of Madrid, and the issue was made upon two principal points, deeply affecting the interests of the western portion of the United States. These were, *first*, the right of the western people to the free navigation and trade of the Mississippi; and, *second*, the establishment of the southern boundary of the United States under the provisions of the treaty. This controversy, which arose soon after the general peace, was continued with strong animosity on both sides, and with but little intermission, for nearly twelve years, until finally arranged by the treaty of Madrid in 1795.*

By the treaty signed September 3d, 1783, Great Britain relinquished to the United States all the territory on the east side of the Mississippi, from its sources to the 31st parallel of north latitude, which was to be the boundary of Florida on the north.

With this relinquishment, of course, was ceded all the previous rights of Great Britain to the free navigation of the river to its mouth, as derived from previous treaties with France and Spain. The United States, therefore, claimed the free navigation of the river to the mouth.

At the same time, Great Britain had ceded to Spain all the Floridas, comprising all the territory east of the Mississippi, and south of the southern limit of the United States. Hence Spain possessed all the territory on the west side of the river, and Florida on the east; and the river, for the last three hundred miles, flowed wholly within the dominions of Spain. His Catholic majesty therefore claimed the exclusive right to the use of the river below the southern limit of the United States.

Independent of this principle, Spain refused to recognize the southern boundary of the United States as extending further south than the old British boundary of Florida, which was an imaginary line extending from the mouth of the Yazoo due east to the Chattahoochy, or in latitude thirty-two degrees twenty-eight minutes north. As the treaty of 1783, in the cession of Florida to Spain, designated no boundaries, but presumed that of the United States, Spain demanded Florida with its British boundaries, alleging that England, by the treaty, confirmed to her the dominion of Florida, which was then in her possession as a conquered province.

* The first negotiation on the subject was opened by John Jay, on the part of the United States, on the 26th day of July, 1785, with the Spanish minister, Don Guardoqui. The negotiation was protracted in a very unsatisfactory manner until 1789.—See American State Papers, vol. x., p. 107, Boston edition.

In 1791, negotiations were renewed at Madrid by William Short and William Carmichael, charges to Madrid and Paris, duly authorized as commissioners, December 22d, 1791.

[A.D. 1784.] Yet Spain had been a party to the triple treaty, and had acquiesced in the article which had stipulated for the 31st parallel as the southern limit of the United States; and they now demanded the specified boundary. Nor could it be doubted that both Great Britain and the United States, in the treaty, contemplated the 31st parallel as the northern limit of Florida.

In reference to the free navigation of the Mississippi, the United States asserted a natural right, independent of any claim derived through Great Britain. The American people occupied and exercised dominion over the whole eastern portion of the Mississippi Valley, comprising all the country drained by its great eastern tributaries, and the east bank as low as the northern limit of Florida. This gave to them the natural right to follow the current of their rivers to the sea, as established by the admitted laws of nations.

The use of the river was necessary and absolutely indispensable to the western settlements, which were now fast rising into political importance. Situated as they were, no power on earth could prevent the final appropriation of the river below them to their use, when their numbers should enable them to maintain their rights by force.

Such were the questions at issue between Spain and the United States; and concession on the part of the former, or war on the part of the latter, was the only alternative by which the question was to be finally decided.

Spain was jealous of the growing power and the increasing population of the United States. The western country was rapidly filling up with a hardy and restless population, which was already encroaching upon the limits of the Spanish provinces. Their political principles, too, were at war with the laws, usages, and policy of Spain. To concede the free navigation of the river to them under such circumstances would be little less than political suicide; for it would be throwing open the flood-gates for a political inundation of Louisiana and her monarchical institutions. Such were the views of the two powers.

[A.D. 1785.] The tide of immigration was already setting strongly to the West. Kentucky alone contained about twelve thousand inhabitants; and within the present limits of Tennessee there were still more populous settlements upon the Holston and Clinch Rivers, and which were advancing upon the Cumberland. If it were not possible for Spain to check the advance of this tide, it certainly was impolitic to invite it into her dominions. Her only true policy was, to use every means in her power to embarrass the western people while connected with the Federal government, and at the same time to hold out strong inducements to them in favor of a separation from the Atlantic States and an alliance with Louisiana under the Spanish crown, whereby they would secure for themselves all the privileges and advantages which they so much desired.

Circumstances were favorable to such a policy. The settlements of Kentucky and Tennessee were isolated, cut off from the populous parts of the Atlantic States by a vast wilderness and lofty mountain ranges, which virtually removed them nearly six hundred miles from their respective state capitals. They were imperfectly protected from Indian hostility by the Federal government; they were without the advantages of trade and commerce, while their country was every where intersected by navigable streams, and abounded in all the valuable products for foreign markets. The ties on one side were weak, and on the other the inducements were strong. Under these circumstances, Spain did not for a moment hesitate in her course of policy, believing she would be able, ultimately, to goad the western people into a separation from the Federal Union.

Previous to the close of the war of Independence, the settlements in the western country were few and weak, surrounded by powerful tribes of hostile Indians, many of whom, on the south, were in alliance with the Spanish provinces. All the region south of Tennessee was a savage wilderness, and Spain claimed the territory as a part of Louisiana and Florida. But since the close of the war, settlements had been advancing into the West in a manner without a parallel. The whole country appeared in motion for the Mississippi. The United States had been entering into treaties of peace and amity with Indian tribes over whom Spain claimed to exercise protection and sovereignty.

The Spanish king had never entertained any sincere friendship for the American people. In the war of the Revolution, his Catholic majesty, yielding to the solicitations of the King of France, and prompted by his own jealous hostility to the

English power, had consented to make common cause with France and the revolted colonies against Great Britain; yet it was not for any good will he entertained for the people of the colonies, except so far as he might add to his own dominions, by humbling his powerful rival and repossessing the Floridas. Although he had been successful, and had subjugated Florida, he appeared to regret the aid which had been incidentally rendered to the United States, which now seemed to presage a more formidable obstacle to the peace and integrity of the Spanish provinces than the power of England herself. Hence the extreme reluctance with which his Catholic majesty ratified the treaty of 1783, which confirmed the independence and defined the boundaries of the new power.*

For the whole West there was but one great outlet to the ocean, and that was through the province of Louisiana and by way of the port of New Orleans. This circumstance alone must, of necessity, at length lead to difficulties between the Spanish authorities and the people of the United States. Indications of this were already too plain to be mistaken. The western people had already begun to *demand as a right* the free navigation of the Mississippi, the great river of Louisiana.

[A.D. 1786.] Three years after the ratification of the treaty of 1783, Spain occupied both banks of the Mississippi below the Ohio, and no less than four Spanish posts confirmed the military occupation of the eastern bank, and the governor and intendant of Louisiana were required to enforce the laws of Spain, in the collection of heavy duties on all imports by way of the river from the Ohio region. These duties were arbitrary, and often extremely heavy and unjust; but an excise officer, supported by a military force, was stationed at every commandant's headquarters on the river to enforce the collection of the revenue. Every boat descending the river was compelled to make land, and submit to the revenue exactions, with only such relaxations and modifications as the commandant saw fit to admit. All violations of these arbitrary regulations and restrictions thus imposed were met with seizure and imprisonment, and often by confiscation of the whole cargo to the use and benefit of the officers of the crown, who valued their offices in proportion to the profit derived from them.*

* See Sparks's Writings of Washington, vol. i., p. 466.
† The Spanish authorities in Louisiana seldom failed to use their offices and author-

This system of exaction upon the trade of the western people became exceedingly oppressive under the arbitrary power of the excise men; many acts of oppression and unjust exaction would of course take place from time to time, and the western boatmen had not been well schooled in submission to arbitrary rule. Many, disdaining to submit to the arrogant demands of the Spanish officials, were from time to time exposed to their official resentment, which occasionally ended, not with a mere temporary delay and embarrassment, but sometimes brought upon the offender the penalty of confiscation of property, and a vexatious imprisonment. Repeated occurrences of this kind soon spread great indignation among the trading portion of the western people, and made them impatient for that revenge which might be inflicted by a military invasion of Louisiana and the capture of New Orleans, which would give them the control of the whole commerce of the river.

As early as 1785, the Federal government, through John Jay, their commissioner, opened a negotiation with the Spanish minister, Don Guardoqui, relative to these embarrassments to the prosperity of the western people; but the Spanish minister, in behalf of his government, persisted in his refusal to concede any of the points in controversy, and, after a fruitless negotiation of twelve months, Mr. Jay had almost consented to waive the right of the western people to the free navigation of the Mississippi *for twenty years*, provided *Spain would concede their claims* at the expiration of that period.

[A.D. 1787.] It was about the close of the year 1786 that the rumor obtained currency in the West that the Federal government, regardless of the interests of the western people, was

---

ity for their private gain and emolument, with but few scruples for the impartial rights of the crown in competition with their own pecuniary interests. The estimate of Spanish integrity in the discharge of their official duties varied but little, in the time of Governor Miro, from the account given of it by Daniel Clarke, the American consul, twenty-five years afterward, in 1803. He says, "the auditors of war, and the assessors of government and intendancy, have always *been corrupt*, and to them only must be attributed the mal-administration of justice; for the governor and other judges, who are unacquainted with the law, seldom dare to act contrary to the opinions they give. Hence, when the auditor or assessor was bribed, suitors had to complain of delays and infamous decisions. But all the officers will plunder when the opportunity offers; they are all venal. A bargain can be made with the governor, the intendant, a judge, or a collector, and all others down to a constable. If ever an officer be displeased at the offer of money, *it is not because it is offered*, but because circumstances *compel him to refuse*. Instead of spurning the man who offers a bribe, he looks on him with additional favor, which encourages him to make a second offer when a better opportunity may present for its acceptance.—See Martin, vol. ii., p. 210.

about to conclude a treaty with the Spanish minister, in which the United States *were to abandon their claim* to the free navigation of the Mississippi *for twenty years*, to conciliate the good will of Spain. The very possibility of abandoning their rightful claims produced the highest degree of excitement in all the western settlements, which not only endangered the safety of Louisiana, but caused great anxiety to the Federal government itself for several years subsequently.

The indignation of the western people had been fully aroused, and they had determined *no longer to submit to* the vacillating negotiation of the Federal government, which could for a moment hesitate to urge the immediate recognition of their rights. The feelings of indignation were expended in a determination to plan a military invasion of Louisiana, which should compel Spain to concede their demands without delay.

This state of things had continued nearly a year, when Governor Miro entered upon the duties of his office. Perceiving the tendency of the policy heretofore pursued by the government of Louisiana toward the American people, he resolved to adopt a different course during his administration. With the consent and approbation of the Spanish minister, Don Guardoqui, resident at the seat of the Federal government, he resolved to relax the import and transit duties on the river trade from the western settlements. He accordingly granted the privilege of free trade to certain persons, and relaxed many of the oppressive restrictions heretofore imposed upon Americans visiting the province of Louisiana. Among these were the privileges granted to Colonel James Wilkinson, between the years 1787 and 1790, of a free trade in tobacco, flour, and other western productions, besides the privilege of introducing several hundreds of American families into Louisiana and the West Florida districts.*

[A.D. 1788.] Scarcely one year had elapsed after the extension of these indulgences to the western people, when Miro began to experience great opposition to his policy from the Spanish minister, who had failed to realize the pecuniary advantages which he had anticipated from this state of things.†
The same opposition was also experienced from the intendant,

---

* See Butler's History of Kentucky, p. 154–170.

† Don Guardoqui retired from his mission at the close of the old Confederation, in 1789.

Don Navarro, who had been influenced by the minister to require a rigid execution of the revenue laws and regulations. The opposition from the latter quarter, however, ceased with the close of the year 1788, when Navarro retired to Spain, leaving Governor Miro, by the king's command, invested with authority to discharge the duties of intendant in addition to his other prerogatives. This new arrangement tended greatly to calm the anxious excitement among the western people, who esteemed Governor Miro as their friend and benefactor.

[A.D. 1789.] Colonel Wilkinson, with an eye to his individual interests, had correctly represented the western people, and had entered into arrangements with Governor Miro for the *exclusive* supply of tobacco from Kentucky for the Mexican market; and he continued, for several years after 1787, to send his annual cargoes of tobacco and other western produce to the New Orleans market. In 1789 he received from New Orleans a large amount of specie, estimated at *ten thousand Spanish dollars*, shipped to him at Danville, in Kentucky, for the ostensible purpose of purchasing tobacco for his engagements with Governor Miro. But suspicions were awakened in Kentucky, and many believed that Wilkinson was in the secret service of Spain, for the purpose of winning over the western people to the Spanish dominion, and that he received an annual pension from the Spanish king, concealed under commercial remittances made to him on account of his tobacco monopoly. Unfortunately, subsequent developments were not calculated to remove this impression.

[A.D. 1791.] Until the year 1791, the same mild and conciliatory policy was maintained by Governor Miro toward the western people, not only of Kentucky, but also those on the Holston and Cumberland Rivers, in the Southwestern Territory, and also to those of Western Virginia and Pennsylvania, on the Monongahela. Many of the most fiery spirits became reconciled to the Spanish authorities, and entertained for Miro himself an affectionate regard. The prevalence of these feelings among the people on the Cumberland River was fully evinced in designating one of their judicial districts by the name of "Miro District."*

Many of the people of Kentucky and Tennessee, although

---

* See Martin's Louisiana, vol. ii., p. 110.

satisfied with the Spanish authorities, and pleased with the commercial privileges extended by Governor Miro, were unwilling to submit to the species of vassalage implied by the manner in which the river commerce was enjoyed. They claimed all these advantages, not as special favors, *but as common and indefeasible rights.*

To allay anxiety on that point, indulgences were extended to emigrants desirous of settling in Louisiana, and various inducements were held out to those who were willing to submit to the Spanish dominion. Grants of land were promised to such as desired to make their permanent residence in Louisiana, while intimations were secretly disseminated among the unsuspecting people that the Spanish government would grant to them as a community *every commercial advantage and privilege* which could be desired, provided they were disconnected from the Federal government east of the mountains. The Spanish minister resident in the United States had been bold enough to declare unequivocally to his confidential correspondents, that unless the western people, and especially those of Kentucky, would *declare themselves independent* of the Federal government, and *establish for themselves* an independent form of government, Spain never would allow them the free navigation of the Mississippi: "But upon those terms *he was authorized*, and would engage to open the navigation of the river, for the exportation of their products and manufactures, on terms of mutual advantage."* The same intimations were zealously disseminated among the people of all the western settlements by persons supposed to have been secretly in the employment and pay of the Governor of Louisiana.

Such were the conflicting interests and feelings of the western people, and the secret designs of the Spanish government; such were the intrigues and plans of the Spanish governor to effect a separation of the western people from the Federal Union, by alienating them from their allegiance, and winning over their feelings, no less than their interests, to the dominion of Spain. Many were seduced from the Federal government, but a greater number remained firm in their adherence to the Union.

In the mean time, the subject had been one of deep interest

* Butler's Kentucky, p. 177, &c.

to the Federal government. Congress, under the old confederation, had early brought the subject before the Spanish cabinet. In the year 1787, that body had directed the Secretary of Foreign Affairs to open a negotiation with the Spanish minister resident in the United States, and to press upon his *serious attention* the danger of an interruption of the good understanding existing between the two countries. He was also instructed and "required expressly to stipulate for both the territory of the United States, agreeably to the boundary of 1783, and the *free navigation of the Mississippi*, from its source to its mouth."

In the negotiation which ensued, Guardoqui, the Spanish minister, replied, that the Spanish king "*never would permit any foreign power* to use that river, both banks of which belonged to him."*

[A.D. 1792.] After fruitless attempts at negotiation for several years, all further efforts were suspended; as Guardoqui, having refused to consent to any treaty whatever on the subject which would require Spain to acknowledge in the United States any *right* to the free navigation of the Mississippi River, had retired to Spain.

The great mass of the western people, in the mean time, became impatient of the restraints and exactions which had been again imposed upon their commerce, and were highly exasperated against the authorities of Louisiana. The population upon all the great tributaries of the Ohio, next the mountains, had greatly multiplied; and the augmented agricultural products demanded an outlet adequate to the supply. On the east, commerce and export were entirely cut off by lofty ranges of mountains. On the west, the great branches of the Ohio gave them a direct and easy transportation from their doors to the Mississippi, and by that river to every part of the habitable globe. In fact, the Mississippi was the natural outlet for the whole West, and yet it was held and controlled by a power which claimed *exclusive* navigation upon it, because it held possession of the mouth.

Many, in their impatience at the privations imposed upon the river commerce, censured the tardiness of the Federal government and its want of energy, because Spain was not required

* Jay's Life, vol. i., p. 235, 236.

imperatively to concede the right of free navigation to the people of the United States. Some, prompted more by interest than honorable independence, began to devise means of conciliating the favor of Spain, at the expense of patriotism at home. They became disaffected toward the policy of the Federal government, because its negotiation had failed to secure to them their rights; and, despairing of more efficient measures by the government, began to look to the Spanish authorities themselves for relief. This relief had been secretly promised to them by men who were in the interest of Spain.

In the forcible language of General Wilkinson, such had been the precarious condition of the western settlements, that they seemed to labor under *every disadvantage*, political as well as natural; " open to savage depredations, exposed to the jealousies of the Spanish government, unprotected by the old confederation, and denied the navigation of the Mississippi, the only practical channel by which the productions of their labor could find a market," could it be a matter of surprise if they did reluctantly consent to abandon country and friends for relief?

But the Federal government had not been neglectful of their interests, and was now prepared for more vigorous negotiations. In the month of September, 1788, a resolution of Congress had declared " that the free navigation of the Mississippi is a clear and essential right of the United States, and that the same ought to be considered and supported as such." To this declaration a response was gladly echoed from the whole West, and from all the Southern States. The negotiation to this effect had been pressed under the old confederation without effect, until the Spanish minister retired to Spain upon the change of the Federal government. The president, under the new confederation, had kept up a constant negotiation through the American ministers, Mr. Carmichael and Mr. Short, resident at Madrid. These ministers had been charged specially to negotiate for the *cession of West Florida* near the Mississippi, *and the Island of New Orleans*, including the city of New Orleans, and the whole eastern bank of the river to the sea, which were to be obtained *at any cost*, provided the free use of the river through Louisiana *could not be obtained otherwise.**

---

* For an account of this instruction, see Marshall's Life of Washington, vol. v., p. 278 first edition.

But the King of Spain little thought of giving up the empire of the Mississippi. In 1783, he had, with great reluctance, given his assent to the treaty establishing the western and southern boundary of the United States, but with no intention of surrendering to them the territory which had been claimed as a part of his dominions east of the Mississippi. The Spanish minister, in his negotiation on the subject, had pretended to deny any right accruing to the United States, east of the Lower Mississippi, in virtue of the treaty of 1783, because, up to the declaration of independence, Great Britain had prohibited the settlement of lands west of the sources of the Atlantic streams. To sustain this position, he referred to the king's proclamation of 1763, prohibiting all settlements west of the mountains, and which had been cited by the last royal governor of Virginia, to bar the claims of the Transylvania Company in 1776.* Acting under this assumption, and presuming the Indian tribes to be independent nations, possessing the rightful sovereignty of the country occupied by them, Spain lost no opportunity, by means of agents and emissaries, to prevent the sale and transfer of territory from the Indians to the United States. Thus, while Spain, by negotiation, procrastinated any definite understanding with the United States relative to the claims under the treaty of 1783, she determined to check the advance of the settlements, and prevent the origin of any other title to the country through the Indian right.†

[A.D. 1793.] The Cumberland settlements were now included within the limits of the "Southwestern Territory," under the jurisdiction of the Federal government, protected by military posts and an organized militia. This advance of the Federal jurisdiction, extending to the Mississippi River, placed the people of Tennessee, who were on the head waters of the Holston and Clinch Rivers, and upon the Cumberland River, beyond the influence of Spanish intrigue and allurements; but Kentucky was still a district attached to the State of Virginia, and holding no separate political relation to the United States; and her citizens were impatient of a change in the form of their government which would release them from the condition of a mere colony of Virginia. This state of things stimulated

---

* See book iii., chap iii., of this work, near the close of the chapter, *i. e.*, the Transylvania purchase by Henderson and Co.

† See book v., chapter viii., of this work, viz., "Indian Relations," &c.

the Governor of Louisiana to renew the intrigues of Guardoqui for detaching Kentucky from the Federal Union, by holding out strong inducements for an alliance with Louisiana under the protection of Spain.

The Baron de Carondelet, having succeeded Miro as Governor of Louisiana, entered upon the duties of his office early in January, 1792. The condition of the western country, and the unsettled state of political feeling among the people, not only of Kentucky, but also of Western Pennsylvania, encouraged him to hope for ultimate success in accomplishing an object which was greatly desired by Spain. Hence he entered, with great ardor and perseverance, upon a regular and systematic plan of operations for this purpose. Nor did he cease his operations or despair of success until after the final ratification of the treaty of Madrid, nearly three years afterward. The intrigues of the baron and his emissaries were directed to Kentucky perseveringly, until nearly three years after that state had been admitted as an independent member of the Federal Union.*

In the mean time, he had succeeded in sowing the seeds of disaffection widely through the western settlements. Many were induced to favor the views and plans of the Spanish governor, and desired a separation from the Atlantic States.

Nor were the intrigues and operations of the Baron confined to the white settlements alone. Still further to arrest the advance of the white population in the " Southwestern Territory," in a region over which the Federal jurisdiction had been formally extended, emissaries had been sent to the Creek Indians in the western parts of Georgia to alienate them from their alliance with the United States. A treaty of peace and friendship had been concluded by the United States, in the year 1790, with M'Gillivray and other principal Creek chiefs, stipulating for a cession of territory and the establishment of a line of demarkation, to be surveyed and marked the following year; but before the time for running the line of demarkation had arrived, M'Gillivray, prompted by Spanish intrigue, had been induced to disavow the treaty, and to forbid the establishment of a line of demarkation. In the mean time, he had been taken into the Spanish service, with the rank and pay of a brigadier-general. Through his influence a war party had

* See book v., chap. vi., "Political Condition of Kentucky," &c.

been formed in the Creek nation, and hostilities had been commenced against the frontier settlements on the Holston and Cumberland Rivers. A hostile incursion of Creeks and Cherokees had actually penetrated the Holston settlement, and invested the stockade at Knoxville.*

This state of Indian hostility was known to have proceeded from Spanish intrigue in Florida and Louisiana, and the people of the "Southwestern Territory" became more than ever clamorous for the invasion of Louisiana by the Federal government. The Creeks were not reduced to peace until after the victory of General Wayne over the northwestern Indians, in the autumn of 1794, when, apprehending a similar visit, they made overtures, and entered into a treaty of peace and friendship with the Federal government.

[A.D. 1794.] The collision of interests between the people of the western country and the authorities of Spain in Louisiana soon became more apparent, and Spain began seriously to apprehend an invasion of Louisiana from the United States. To stir up this state of feeling more effectually against Spain, emissaries from France were now in the United States, all anxious to wrest Louisiana from the Spanish crown, and to place it again under the dominion of Republican France.† Their efforts to this effect, through the people of the United States, although instigated and directed by the French minister, M. Genet, were promptly arrested by the authorities of the United States.‡

Under the influence of the French minister, M. Genet, and his emissaries in the United States, a strong French party had been formed, not only in the Western States, but also in the South. The frontiers of Georgia were lighted up with a flame of enthusiasm for the invasion of East Florida, while the western people were preparing to invade Louisiana and West Florida from the Ohio region. At the head of the "French Legion," in Georgia, for the invasion of Florida, was General George Clark, of Georgia, a man of strong passions, of violent antipathies against the English, and of warm partialities for the

---

* See book v., chap. vii., "Indian Hostilities and early Settlements in Southwestern Territory."   † See book iv., chap. ii., of this work.

‡ The reader will find an interesting account of the character, temperament, and reception of the French minister, M. Genet, in the United States, in 1793, in Marshall's Life of Washington, vol. v., p. 409–412, first edition. Also, his official acts and insolence, idem, p. 413–450. Also, his intrigues with the southern and western people, idem, p. 452, &c.

French.* It was understood that M. Genet was to be appointed major-general, and to serve as commander-in-chief. The Creek Indians were to be enlisted in the cause by agents sent into the nation. Such was the state of affairs on the Georgia frontier, that the Spanish governor of East Florida, alarmed at the threatening aspect, had made his complaint to the Governor of Georgia, who, on the 5th of March, 1794, had issued his proclamation against the unlawful enterprise.†

* American State Papers, Boston edition, vol. iii., p. 230.

† The active state of hostile preparations against East Florida may be inferred from the dispatches of the officers of the United States army to the War Department. Major Henry Gaither, commandant of the Federal troops on the St. Mary's, dispatched a letter, dated April 13th, 1794, to the department, with information that the French had many friends in Georgia, and that their preparations for the invasion of Florida were active; that the French sloop-of-war Las Casas, of eighteen guns, recently arrived from Charleston, with two hundred men on board, mostly French, and one company of infantry, and that she was then lying within musket-shot of the fort, at anchor. They report thirteen sail, equally large and well supplied, that are soon to arrive from the United States. They have a recruiting post at Temple, eighteen miles above Fort St. Mary, where they have eighty men, and shortly expect three hundred more from the upper part of Georgia. Major Gaither, having withheld his approbation to their proceedings, was apprehensive of danger, and began to make additional defenses.—See American State Papers, Boston edition, vol. ii., p. 52.

A dispatch from Fort Fidius, dated April 18th, 1794, asserts that "officers have been appointed, and are now acting under the authority of the French Republic. Parties of recruits have already reached the rendezvous appointed for them; several men of this corps have crossed the Oconee, and are encamped opposite Greensborough. A small party was for some days opposite the Rock Landing; they have since marched to Carr's Bluff, to join those assembled at that place. The general rendezvous, we are told, is on the St. Mary's River. An agent is appointed to furnish the supplies, and he has, for that purpose, received ten thousand dollars. A person, who was formerly the contractor's clerk at this post, is employed by him to purchase four thousand rations of provisions. He has gone down the country to execute this business." A Colonel Carr and Major Williamson showed Captain Martin "a letter of instructions which they had received from General Clark, directing them to repair to Fort Philips, the Rock Landing, and Carr's Bluff, for the purpose of paying to the French legion an allowance for mileage from their homes to the place of rendezvous." The late Lieutenant Bird, who is now a captain in said legion, commands the men who are encamped on the Oconee, opposite to Greensborough. Major Williamson says that General Clark would cross the Oconee in ten days from that time, to take the command, and that Colonel Carr would be one of the adventurers. "Major Williamson has been employed as paymaster."—Idem, p. 52.

"Colonel Carr stated that large detachments had marched from the back settlements of South Carolina and from the State of Kentucky, and that the men were to be engaged for three months, and were to receive bounties of land in the provinces of East and West Florida, and in Louisiana, which they were to conquer from the Spaniards."—Idem, p. 53.

On the 6th of May, 1794, General Clark was on the Georgia side of St. Mary's with two hundred men, and their numbers were daily increasing, preparatory to crossing into Florida, and taking the oath of allegiance on Amelia Island, where the French had landed a few men, and were making preparations. Colonel Hammond, from Savannah, formerly of the Continental army, is one of the principal officers. The people of Savannah are strongly opposed to the enterprise. Intercourse with Kentucky and

The Spanish government was no less fearful of the invasion of Louisiana than of the introduction of political principles which might influence the western provinces of Mexico; but the firm and decided tone now assumed by the executive of the Federal government was such that Spain perceived plainly the negotiation must be brought to a *speedy close*, or *war would be inevitable*. It became evident that any policy for the separation of the western country from the Federal Union must be put into speedy operation, or it *must inevitably fail*. In the mean time, Spanish posts, with Spanish garrisons, occupied the country on the east side of the Mississippi, as far north as the present site of Memphis. The western and southern people, with all the checks of the Federal authorities, had been barely restrained from open violence against Louisiana. The President of the United States himself, under the impression that war with the Spanish provinces would be *forced upon him*, had begun to make preparations for the conflict, and had required from the proper departments such statistical information as would enable him to prepare for any emergency.*

The excitement among the western people was extreme, and large military forces were concentrated upon the Ohio River for the purpose of prosecuting the Indian war on the northwestern frontier. This had greatly increased the anxiety of the Governor of Louisiana, who now feared an invasion on every spring flood which descended from the Ohio River, since the Federal troops had been victorious over the northwestern savages.

The views and political feelings of the people of Kentucky and Tennessee, relative to the most salutary policy, were various and discordant, each proposing relief to their embarrassments by a different mode of action. During the period of this excitement, the people of Kentucky, and the West generally, were ranged under one or other of the following "five parties:"

1st. For separation from the Union and the formation of an independent Republic, which should form a treaty of alliance and commerce with Spain.

Tennessee by way of the "Wilderness Road" to Georgia and Carolina was extensive, &c.

* General Washington, believing a war probable, and being determined not to be taken unprepared, had provided the necessary information relative to the military force, and means of defense and offense, possessed by the Spanish provinces, and the preparation necessary on the part of the United States for subduing Florida and Louisiana.—See Marshall's Life of Washington, vol. v., p. 465; also, p. 475, first edition.

2d. For annexing the country to the province of Louisiana, and submitting to the introduction of the Spanish laws and forms of civil jurisprudence.

3d. For actual war with Spain, the capture of New Orleans, and the whole district of West Florida.

4th. For active and forcible measures by Congress, to compel Spain, by force of arms or by hostile array, to yield the privileges and rights which had been so long refused by negotiation.

5th. To solicit France to procure a retrocession of Louisiana, and to extend her protection over Kentucky and the Cumberland settlements.*

This unsettled and divided state of public feeling among the western people presented to the mind of Governor Carondelet a favorable opportunity for a successful mission to Kentucky, for the purpose of sounding the feelings of the people upon the subject of an alliance with Louisiana, under the protection of Spain. Accordingly, he made his first attempt at intrigue with the people of Kentucky through an artful emissary. This emissary was an intelligent and intriguing Englishman, who had become a Spanish subject, and who was devoted to the interests of Spain. This man, under the authority of the Governor of Louisiana, proceeded on the doubtful and hazardous enterprise of sowing the seeds of sedition among the western people, at a time when Western Pennsylvania was greatly agitated by the "excise on distilled spirits," commonly known as the "whisky insurrection."† The spirit of resistance to the Federal government, in the enforcement of the iniquitous law, had developed itself in open insurrection, which was quelled only by the presence of an army of twelve thousand troops from the Eastern States. No time could have been more propitious for the enterprise of separating Kentucky and the western country generally. Besides the insurrection in Western Pennsylvania, and the divided feelings of the people of Kentucky and Cumberland, the whole northwestern tribes of Indians had been engaged in open war, instigated and aided by British agents and traders from Canada; the Federal government was embarrassed by tedious and vexatious negotiations with Great Britain, with Spain, and even with France. The

---

* Martin's Louisiana, vol. ii., p. 101.
† See book v., chap. v., "Political Condition of Western Pennsylvania."

stipulations of the treaty of 1783 were violated by England on the northwestern boundary, and by Spain on the southwestern limit; Great Britain still held the northwestern posts, and Spain the southern territory; both powers seemed to unite in the purpose of restricting the western limits, and each power had her emissary in the West, one from Baron Carondelet and one from Lord Dorchester, on a mission of political intrigue with the western people.*

Yet, so far as the Federal government was concerned, Spain was on terms of peace and amity. The great national questions of boundary and the free navigation of the Mississippi were still unsettled, and afforded subjects of protracted negotiation. Spain, having an eye to the separation of the western country, and desirous of waiting the result of the prevailing difficulties in the West, had deemed it most politic to defer any definite negotiation upon the subject, which might ultimately endanger the peace and safety of Louisiana. In the mean time, the restrictions and exactions upon the commerce and trade of the river had been again enforced with rigor; and " Spain had persisted in withholding all the rights and privileges of that navigation from the citizens of the United States. There were various grounds of policy for the refusal; but probably the most operative was a secret hope that the western people, weary of these obstacles to their commerce, and dissatisfied with the national government for not removing them, might sooner or later dissever themselves from the Union, and form a separate republic, which would fall under the control of Spain."†

[A.D. 1795.] Under these influences, it is not strange that the court of Madrid should have resorted to its usual policy of procrastination and court delays. Another consideration bearing on the general question was the state of the Indian tribes in the West. Those on the northwest had been for several years in open war against the frontier settlements, and those on the southwestern frontier were far from friendly to the American settlements. The hostilities of those on the northwest, instigated by British emissaries, and those on the southwest, under the influence of Spanish agents, might ultimately compel a separation.

---

* See Marshall's Life of Washington, vol. v., p. 460–462, first edition.
† Sparks's Writings of Washington, vol. i., p. 467.

The Federal government was fully apprised of the conflicting interests in the West, upon which foreign emissaries might operate to accomplish a dismemberment of the Union. Although there might be apparently strong reasons for complaint, and for a partial alienation of feeling in the western people toward the Federal government, still the President confided in the virtue and patriotism of the people, their inveterate repugnance to regal authority, and their attachment to their friends east of the mountains, doubly cemented by the presence and influence of hundreds of revolutionary officers and soldiers, who had taken up their residence in the West. Determined to maintain the rights of the western people with the whole power of the Federal government, President Washington had assumed a firm and decided tone, and persisted in urging upon the Spanish crown the necessity of a speedy adjustment of all the points under negotiation.

Still the Baron de Carondelet did not despair of final success in severing the Western from the Eastern States. Early in the year 1795, relieved from the apprehension of danger from a French and Kentucky invasion of Louisiana, he determined, while the court of Madrid was procrastinating the negotiation with the Federal government, to press his secret negotiations with the disaffected of Kentucky and the West generally. Believing the Federal authority already tottering in Western Pennsylvania, and almost disregarded in Kentucky, he deemed the present juncture highly auspicious to his designs.

Accordingly, having been apprised by Powers of the state of popular feeling in Kentucky, he despatched Don Manuel Gayoso, a brigadier-general in the armies of Spain, and Lieutenant-governor of Natchez and its dependences, to the mouth of the Ohio as a special agent, authorized to negotiate with the leading conspirators of Kentucky relative to the weighty matters in contemplation.

In this mission was associated Thomas Powers, the former emissary to Kentucky, who had been successful in his former mission, and had made arrangements with the four most prominent conspirators, Sebastian, Innis, Murray, and Nicholas, to meet the Baron's commissioner at some point near the mouth of the Ohio. By appointment, they were to meet Powers at the Red Banks on the Ohio, the site of the present town of Hendersonville in Kentucky.

To conceal the real object of the lieutenant-governor's visit to Upper Louisiana, he conducted a detachment of troops for re-enforcing the different posts, for completing the stockade fort at the fourth Chickasâ Bluff, and commencing one just below the mouth of the Ohio. While engaged in these duties, Powers was dispatched in a fine Spanish row-barge to meet his engagement at the Red Banks. But the mission failed in its object. The increasing danger, from public indignation against those who had been suspected of conspiring for an alliance with Spain, consequent upon a separation from the Federal Union, had now become imminent and alarming; the Federal army under General Wayne was now victorious over the savages; the people were relieved from Indian hostilities on every frontier; the authority of the Federal government in Western Pennsylvania had been restored, and the people of Kentucky relied upon their victorious troops to vindicate their rights on the Mississippi, under the authority of the United States; and Kentucky had now been an independent state for nearly two years. An alliance with Louisiana under the Spanish crown had now become preposterous in the extreme, and the conspirators of Kentucky prudently declined appearing at the Red Banks.

Judge Sebastian was the only Kentuckian who attended on the part of the conspirators to meet the Spanish emissary; but he, as if deluded to his own ruin, consented to descend the river to hold an interview with the Spanish commissioner, Gayoso, at the mouth of the Ohio. But as an unexpected change in the face of affairs had taken place, Gayoso declined to negotiate definitely with Sebastian, and induced him to continue his voyage to New Orleans, and there confer with the baron in person. After a sojourn of several weeks at Natchez, and some time in New Orleans, Sebastian took passage by sea for Philadelphia, on his return to Kentucky.*

In the mean time, Spain had become embarrassed in the European wars, and, fearing hostilities on the part of the United States against Louisiana, had intimated, through the Spanish minister at Philadelphia, that negotiations might now be expedited on the great points in controversy, provided a regular envoy of high grade were sent to the court of Madrid. President Washington lost no time in delay; in November, 1794, he

* Martin's Louisiana, vol. ii., p. 126.

had nominated Mr. Thomas Pinckney as minister plenipotentiary and envoy extraordinary to the court of Madrid. His nomination had been confirmed by the Senate, and the following summer he repaired to Spain. Negotiations were soon opened with the Spanish court, and in due time a treaty was prepared, which was signed on the 20th day of October, 1795, covering the whole ground of controversy which had engaged the attention of both countries for nearly ten years.†

The principal stipulations of the treaty on this subject were as follows, viz.:

1. The *second* article stipulates that the future boundary between the United States and the Floridas shall be the thirty-first parallel of north latitude, from the Mississippi eastward to the Chattahoochy River; thence along a line running due east, from the mouth of Flint River to the head of the St. Mary's River, and thence down the middle of that river to the Atlantic Ocean; and that, within six months after the ratification of the treaty, the troops and garrisons of each power shall be withdrawn to its own side of this boundary, and the people shall be at liberty to retire with all their effects, if they desire so to do.

2. The *third* article stipulates that each party, respectively, shall appoint one commissioner and one surveyor, with a suitable military guard of equal numbers, well provided with instruments and assistants, who shall meet at Natchez within six months after the mutual ratification of the treaty, and proceed thence to *run and mark* the said southern boundary of the United States.

3. The *fourth* article stipulates that the middle of the Mississippi River shall be the western boundary of the United States, from its source to the intersection of the said " line of demarkation." The King of Spain also stipulates that the whole width of said river, from its source to the sea, shall be free to the people of the United States.

4. The *fifth* article stipulates that each party shall require and enforce peace and neutrality among the Indian tribes inhabiting their territories respectively.

5. The King of Spain stipulates and agrees to permit the people of the United States, *for the term of three years*, to use the port of New Orleans as a place of deposit for their produce and merchandise, and to export the same free from all duty or

* Marshall's Life of Washington, vol. v., p. 641, first edition.

Vol. I.—K k

charge, except a reasonable consideration to be paid for storage and other incidental expenses; that the term of three years may, by subsequent negotiation, be extended; or, instead, some other point in the island of New Orleans shall be designated as a place of deposit for the American trade. Other commercial advantages were likewise held out as within the reach of negotiation.*

This treaty was duly ratified by the Senate in March following, and the Federal executive proceeded to make the necessary arrangements for the fulfillment of all the stipulations on the part of the United States.

In the mean time, the whole state of Georgia had been in a state of excitement to expel the Spaniards from the western and southern limits of that state, as defined by the treaty of 1783. According to the royal charter and the treaty of 1783, Georgia laid claim to all the territory on her western frontier, extending to the Mississippi River on the west, and southward to the thirty-first degree of north latitude. This claim embraced all the Natchez District upon the Mississippi, from the sources of the Yazoo and Tombigby Rivers to their mouths. This whole region, however, was held and claimed by Spain as a part of West Florida. The fine lands, watered by these large rivers and their tributaries, had been represented as the paradise of the South. Popular excitement to enjoy and possess the delightful regions which properly belonged to the State of Georgia had been fanned into a flame of enthusiasm, which resulted in the wildest schemes of avarice and speculation. The contagion spread through the whole state, and even to North Carolina and Virginia; it pervaded the halls of legislation, and polluted the integrity of the legislative body. Authority by the Georgia Legislature was given to visionary men, to enthusiasts, and to speculators, to inundate the country with scores of adventurers and emigrants. The state had sent commissioners to the Spanish governor with a formal demand for the surrender and evacuation of the territory east of the Mississippi and north of the proper limit of Florida. The de-

---

* See American State Papers, folio ed., Foreign Affairs, vol. i., p. 547–549. See, also, Martin's Louisiana, vol. ii., p. 129, 130. Martin, however, errs in his term for which Spain stipulated the use of the port of New Orleans as a place of deposit. The treaty itself, in the American State Papers, specifies "*three years*" as the term of deposit, which may be extended. Martin gives the term stipulated erroneously at "ten years."

mand had been disregarded by the Spanish authorities, and the Legislature had proceeded to provide for its occupation, by organizing that portion near the Mississippi into the "county of Bourbon," under the jurisdiction of the State of Georgia. "The Yazoo speculation" was set on foot, in which more than seven millions of acres of the finest lands in the world were thrown into a second "Mississippi scheme," to be obtained for a mere trifle, and to serve as fountains of future riches. The "Mississippi Company" was chartered with the control of more than three millions of acres, at the rate of two and a half cents per acre, to be paid into the state treasury. The stock comprised forty shares of seventy-five thousand acres each, controlled by a company of seven men as stockholders.* Besides this company under the authority of the state, seventy-five sub-shares, in the shape of land-script, were issued to about seventy other individuals; each sub-share called for twenty-eight thousand acres, giving an aggregate of more than three millions of acres.

The act of the Georgia Legislature establishing this great scheme of speculation was passed on the 7th day of January, 1795. The next session of the Legislature not only repealed the act, but declared the whole null and void, as having been obtained by fraud and corruption. The act repealing and rescinding all parts of the charter passed on the 13th day of February, 1796, and directed all grants made by the Mississippi Company, all certificates of stock issued by the authority of said act, and all records of the same, to be cancelled and destroyed, and all moneys paid into the state treasury to be refunded.†

The former act of the Georgia Legislature infringed upon the prerogatives of the Federal government in assuming the power to settle a question of national boundary, and to involve the Union in war with a friendly power. Now the treaty of Madrid, on the part of the Federal executive, had amicably ar-

* As it may be interesting to some readers to become more fully acquainted with the whole history of the "Yazoo speculation," as it is called, we refer them to a full account of all the documentary evidence furnished to the Federal government on the subject, and published by order of Congress, among the "American State Papers," folio edition, vol. i., "Public Lands," p. 129–146.

The Mississippi Company, chartered January 7th, 1795, was composed of James Gunn, Matthew M'Allister, George Walker, Zachariah Coxe, Jacob Waldburger, William Longstreet, and Wade Hampton.

Among the sub-shareholders were nineteen prominent members of the Legislature, who had voted for the scheme, or, as it has been sometimes called, the "Yazoo Bubble." —See American State Papers, vol. i., Public Lands, p. 128, 129.

† See American State Papers, vol. i., Public Lands, p. 122.

ranged the question of boundary, by which a peaceable surrender had been secured.

Yet this procedure on the part of the Georgia Legislature had greatly tended to embarrass the prospects of the Spanish authorities in their contemplated retention of the country. Hundreds of fiery spirits and enterprising men had sought the Mississippi by way of the Yazoo and Tombigby, and, under the influence of the Yazoo speculation, had reached the settlements known as the Natchez District.

CHAPTER IV.

POLITICAL RELATIONS BETWEEN THE UNITED STATES AND LOUISIANA, FROM THE TREATY OF MADRID TO THE SURRENDER OF THE NATCHEZ DISTRICT.—A.D. 1796 TO 1798.

Argument.—Treaty of Madrid merely a Measure of State Policy with Spain.—Her Intention to evade its Stipulations, if possible.—Intrigue with the western People.—The United States prepare in good Faith to carry out the Stipulations.—Colonel Ellicott, as Commissioner of the United States, arrives at Natchez.—His Military Escort left at Bayou Pierre.—Gayoso designates the 19th of March to begin the Line of Demarkation.—Ellicott encamps in Natchez.—Proceedings delayed by Baron Carondelet.—Ellicott orders down his Military Escort.—Gayoso suddenly ceases Preparations to evacuate the Fort Panmure.—Fortifies this Post.—Pretext for Change of Conduct.—Lieutenant M'Leary, with his Escort, arrives from Bayou Pierre.—Gayoso continues to strengthen his Defenses.—Indian Hostilities alleged as the Cause.—Next, a British Invasion from Canada apprehended.—Blount's Conspiracy, and its Explosion.—The People become excited.—Correspondence between the American Commissioner and Gayoso.—Advanced Guard under Lieutenant Pope arrives at Natchez.—Gayoso objects to the Presence of United States Troops at Natchez.—Other Reasons for Delay urged by Gayoso.—His Agents tamper with the Indians.—Popular Excitement increases.—The Governor-general issues his Proclamation, 24th of May.—Effects of this Proclamation.—Efforts of Gayoso to calm the popular Excitement.—Arrest and Imprisonment of Hannah.—This excites the People to Resistance.—Colonel Ellicott and Lieutenant Pope sustain the popular Commotion.—Gayoso's Proclamation of June 14th.—A public Meeting called.—Gayoso and his Family retire to the Fort.—Seeks an Interview with the American Commissioner.—" Committee of Public Safety" appointed.—This Committee recognized by Gayoso.—A " Permanent Committee" elected.—Opposition of Colonel Hutchens and others, who sustain Gayoso.—Ellicott retires to Washington.—Gayoso appointed Governor-general.—Retires to New Orleans.—Captain Guion arrives with United States Troops.—His Attempt to restore Harmony and Tranquillity.—The Policy of his Course.—The Posts of Nogales and Panmure evacuated in March, 1798.—The Line of Demarkation commenced in May, 1798, and completed next Year.—First organization of the Mississippi Territory.—Arrival of the Territorial Governor and Judges.—General Wilkinson arrives with United States Troops.—Retrospect of the Spanish Policy.—Pretexts for Delay, and the Intrigue with General Wilkinson again unsuccessful.—Return of Emissary Powers.

[A.D. 1796.] As has been already observed, the difficulties which had sprung up between the United States and Spain, relative to the navigation of the Mississippi and the southern boundary of Georgia, appeared to have been settled by the treaty of Madrid. But, although Spain suspended her restrictions upon the river trade after this treaty had been duly ratified, it was quite apparent that the king never intended to surrender the territory east of the Mississippi and north of latitude 31°, provided any contingency would enable him to hold possession.* The King of Spain had been compelled, by the pressure of political embarrassments, both in Europe and in the United States, to yield a reluctant assent to the treaty, as the only means by which he could preserve the province of Louisiana from invasion, and conciliate the hostile feelings of the western people of the United States. The provincial authorities in Louisiana seemed to view the late treaty on the part of Spain as a mere measure of policy and court finesse, to propitiate the neutrality of the Federal government and satisfy the American people until her European embarrassments should have been surmounted.

Spain, incited by France, had been upon the verge of a war with Great Britain; and already the British authorities in Canada had planned an invasion of Upper Louisiana, by way of the lakes and the Illinois River, whenever hostilities should be formally proclaimed. To prevent this invasion was one object to be gained by acceding to the treaty of Madrid, which would place the neutral territory of a friendly power in the way of military invasion. In the mean time, the Baron de Carondelet, regardless of the treaty stipulations which had been made on the part of his government, again dispatched his emissary, Powers, to Kentucky and the Northwestern Territory, with a large amount of money, to foment disaffection in the West, and to encourage those who still desired a separation from the Union.

As has been observed in the preceding chapter, the treaty stipulated that each government should appoint one commissioner and one principal surveyor, who should meet at Natchez within six months after the ratification of the treaty, or about the first of October, 1796.†

The commissioners and surveyors, duly appointed, were to

---

* Martin's Louisiana, vol. ii., p. 138, 139.

† For a full account of this treaty and the accompanying documents, see "The American State Papers," "*Foreign Relations*," folio edition. vol. i., p. 533–551.

proceed from Natchez to ascertain the point on the east bank of the Mississippi which is intersected by the thirty-first parallel of north latitude. From that point on the said parallel they should cause to be run, opened, and marked "a proper line of demarkation," eastward to the Chattahoochy River. After this line should have been thus established, the troops of Spain were to be withdrawn from the forts and territory north of this line, and the country formally surrendered to the commissioner of the United States.

In the mean time, the President of the United States had appointed Colonel Andrew Ellicott, as commissioner on the part of the Federal government, to meet the Spanish commissioner at the place and time designated in the treaty, to be accompanied by a small detachment of troops from the western army. Don Manuel Gayoso de Lemos, commandant of Fort Panmure, and governor of the Natchez dependences, was appointed commissioner on the part of Spain, under the orders of the Baron de Carondelet, governor-general of Louisiana and the Floridas.*

About the middle of September, Colonel Ellicott departed from Philadelphia for the West, on his way to meet the Spanish commissioner at Natchez. At Pittsburgh he obtained his corps of thirty woodsmen, armed with rifles, and descended the Ohio in a barge conveying his instruments, baggage, and stores, to be followed soon afterward by a military escort of thirty men, to be furnished by Colonel Butler, commanding at Pittsburgh. Delayed on the Ohio by extreme low water, and other unavoidable circumstances, he did not reach the Mississippi until the 22d of December, where he was again detained by ice, which had now closed both rivers. On the 31st of January, 1797, having received his military escort and supplies, he descended the Mississippi, and on the 24th of February arrived at Natchez, having touched at each of the Spanish posts on the way, and having left his military escort at the Bayou Pierre, at the special request of Governor Gayoso.

[A.D. 1797.] In the mean time, the governor-general, as well as Lieutenant-governor Gayoso, had been duly notified of the approach of the American commissioner. The several commandants on the river had been instructed to use every effort short of compulsion, under one pretext or another, to retard his advance.

* Stoddart's Sketches of Louisiana, p. 89. Ellicott's Journal, p. 26-38.

After a polite and formal reception from Governor Gayoso, Colonel Ellicott announced the object of his mission, and desired the co-operation of the Spanish commissioner in ascertaining the point on the Mississippi at which the line of demarkation should commence. At an interview next day, upon the urgent solicitation of Colonel Ellicott, Gayoso reluctantly appointed the 19th day of March as the time for commencing the line of demarkation, at which time both commissioners should repair to Clarksville, on the Mississippi, near Bayou Tunica. This point had been ascertained, by astronomical observation, to be near the intersection of the thirty-first parallel of north latitude.

Three days after Colonel Ellicott's arrival he had pitched his tent, and located his camp upon an eminence within the limits of the present city of Natchez, and about five hundred yards north of Fort Panmure, which was strongly fortified, and occupied by a garrison of Spanish troops. At this point, not far from the present intersection of Wall and Jefferson streets, he hoisted the flag of the United States, and having commenced his astronomical observations, he found the latitude of his markee to be 31° 33' 46" north, or about thirty-nine miles north of the intersection of the thirty-first parallel of latitude, and the proper point for commencing the line of demarkation.*

In the mean time, the governor-general had been apprised of the arrival of the commissioner of the United States, duly authorized to co-operate in establishing the line of demarkation. But it was soon apparent that he declined any immediate action in the matter, alleging important business in New Orleans, which would prevent his presence at the time designated by Gayoso. At the same time, he held out various inducements to draw the American commissioner to New Orleans. Colonel Ellicott, however, declined to leave the point designated in the treaty, and remained at Natchez. The military escort under Lieutenant M'Leary was ordered from the Bayou Pierre, and reached Natchez on the 15th of March. The commandant encamped upon the eminence contiguous to Colonel Ellicott's flag, and soon afterward he appeared at the head of his men before Panmure, and formally demanded the surrender of the post to the troops of the United States.

Gayoso, until this time, had been apparently making preparations for evacuating the post; the artillery and stores were

* See Ellicott's Journal, p. 41–50.

removed from the fort, and other preparations indicated the speedy withdrawal of the troops. But suddenly the artillery and stores were returned to the fort *by night*, the cannon were remounted, and the fort was again placed in a state of defense.* This movement, and others subsequently made, were doubtless the result of secret orders from Governor Carondelet at New Orleans.

Gayoso soon afterward proceeded to strengthen the defenses at Natchez and Walnut Hills, and to re-enforce the garrisons from New Orleans; but Colonel Ellicott formally protested against his proceedings, as a violation of good faith toward the United States, and calculated to embarrass and procrastinate the object of his mission. In reply, Gayoso alleged that his defensive measures were prompted by apprehensions of Indian hostilities. At a subsequent period, he alleged a threatened invasion of Louisiana from Canada as the cause of his defensive preparations. Under the latter pretext, for several months Gayoso continued to fortify the different posts on the Mississippi above Natchez, and to re-enforce their garrisons. Thus the meeting of the commissioners for establishing the line of demarkation was indefinitely postponed.

The American commissioner became highly exasperated at the various pretexts for procrastination advanced by the Spanish governor, and the artifices employed to induce him to retire from the point designated in the treaty.† An angry correspondence had already commenced between the commissioners, and Lieutenant M'Leary had begun to fortify his camp. Great excitement began to prevail among the people of the district, under the apprehension that the Spaniards did not intend to surrender the country to the United States. Colonel Ellicott and Lieutenant M'Leary maintained their position, anxiously awaiting the arrival of an advanced guard of United States troops, which were known to be on their way from Fort Massac.

In the mean time, General Wayne had advanced the army of occupation to Fort Massac, there to await further orders. From this point, near the last of March, Lieutenant Piercy Smith Pope, with a detachment of forty men, was ordered to descend the Mississippi and to keep within supporting distance of Colonel Ellicott. This detachment arrived at the Walnut Hills early in April, when Lieutenant Pope reported himself to

* Ellicott's Journal, p. 54–58. † Idem, 50–58.

Colonel Ellicott, and encamped near the Spanish fort, in compliance with a request from Gayoso, through the commandant of that post.

On the 17th of April Colonel Ellicott was first apprised of the arrival of Lieutenant Pope at the Walnut Hills, and he immediately dispatched a messenger requesting him to advance to his relief without delay. On the 24th of April Lieutenant Pope, with his detachment, arrived at Natchez, and was escorted from the upper landing to the camp of the American commissioner by Lieutenant M‘Leary's company.*

But the Spanish governor strongly remonstrated against the presence of the United States troops, intrenched within sight of the Spanish fort, and immediately under the eye of the Spanish authorities. He therefore desired that Colonel Ellicott, with the detachments of troops and his woodsmen, would remove to Clarksville, near the point for their future operations; but the American commissioner declined leaving the point designated in the treaty. Gayoso at length desired him to accept comfortable buildings for himself and the troops at " Villa Gayoso," a Spanish church and village near the bluff, about fifteen miles above Natchez; but the American commissioner preferred the more appropriate shelter of the tent, in the open air; and Lieutenant Pope proceeded to complete the intrenchments of their camp. Soon afterward, he deemed it expedient to augment his force by voluntary enlistment, and by the apprehension of some deserters from the northern army, who had found an asylum among the Spaniards. This, again, was a new cause of remonstrance from the Spanish governor.

But the American commissioner, from various sources of information, and from the general tenor of the lieutenant-governor's correspondence, believed that the governor-general did not intend to evacuate the posts and surrender the country, in compliance with the terms of the treaty. The correspondence between the commissioners continued, and while the Spaniard was fruitful in pretexts and expedients for delay and equivocation, the American was no less ready to expose the fallacy of every pretext, and to urge the futility of his reasons for further delays.

It was the last of May when the proclamation of the Baron Carondelet announced that the delivery of the country, and the

* See Ellicott's Journal, p. 79, 80.

evacuation of the posts on the Mississippi, were delayed on account of a threatened invasion by British troops from Canada by way of the Illinois River. This apprehension on the part of the Spanish governor was not without foundation. Although Colonel Ellicott was inclined to disbelieve the rumor, and ascribe it to the fears and credulity of the Spaniards, yet the actual state of facts, unknown to the American commissioner, were sufficient to excite apprehension in the mind of the governor.

On the 6th of October preceding, Spain, having entered into an alliance with the French Republic, had declared war against Great Britain, and that power had entered into treaty with the United States the preceding year, by which the latter conceded the free navigation of the Mississippi. Might not the United States make common cause with the English of Canada to expel the Spaniards from the Mississippi? To the Spanish governor the enterprise did not appear impossible.*

* At this time there was a strong military force in Canada, and there were persons in the United States who would gladly have joined even a British invasion of Louisiana; and although the British cabinet disavowed any such intentions, the provincial authorities of Canada no doubt seriously contemplated such an event, as did men of influence in the United States. At the very time that Gayoso was deferring the fulfillment of the treaty, his allusion to a British invasion was not without foundation. As was subsequently ascertained, Senator William Blount, from Tennessee, who had enjoyed the confidence of the Federal government as " Governor of the Southwestern Territory and Indian agent," and was intimately acquainted with the southern country, people, and Indian tribes, where he had great influence, conceived the design of a conspiracy to aid the British forces of Canada by way of Lake Michigan, Chicago, and the Illinois River, to invade Louisiana and capture New Orleans. The troops of Great Britain in Canada had actually embarked from Quebec for the lakes. Blount's plan of operations contemplated a strong re-enforcement from the Ohio, the Tennessee, and Cumberland Rivers, with supplies of military stores and provisions, to meet the invading forces at the mouth of the Ohio. Blount, having disclosed his plans to Mr. Liston, the British minister, was referred by him directly to the British cabinet. The cautious mystery of the American senator led to his detection, and, having been found guilty of entertaining the treasonable plot, he was unanimously expelled from the United States Senate.—See Marbois's Louisiana, p. 163-165. See, also, Blount's letter to a confederate named Carey, American State Papers, vol. iii., p. 335, Boston edition. Martin's Louisiana, vol. ii., p. 139.

Subjects of Great Britain residing in Florida and in the Natchez District, and whose names were on the British pension list, were doubtless privy to this contemplated enterprise. Colonel Hutchens had proposed to Lieutenant Pope, early in 1797, to engage in the enterprise of capturing Governor Gayoso, and conveying him secretly to the Chickasâ nation, and to capture Fort Panmure with volunteers who were ready to engage in the undertaking. Mr. Rapelje, a British subject, supposed to be connected in Blount's conspiracy, and in the English interest, came to Colonel Hutchens and spent several days with him about this time, after which he proceeded to Mobile and Pensacola. At the latter place, he remained in confidential intercourse with the British house of Panton, Leslie, & Co., Indian traders, until the explosion of Blount's schemes.—See Ellicott's Journal, p. 64, 65, and 73.

At one time Gayoso alleged that, as the treaty of Madrid did not specify the " condition" in which the posts were to be delivered, it became necessary to wait until instructions on that point should be received from the king. If the king directed them to be delivered with all the ordnance and stores, or if he required them to be dismantled before delivery, he only waited to execute his pleasure ; and in the mean time, it would be necessary to dispatch an envoy to General Wayne, commander-in-chief, with a request that he would not urge the delivery until instructions should arrive from the king.

At another time he alleged that, as the treaty contained no guarantee of property to those who desired to retire beyond the American jurisdiction, it would be necessary to settle that point by a new treaty. At another time it was seriously urged that a scrupulous observance of the treaty of Madrid could not be demanded, because the United States had not acted in good faith toward Spain in conceding to Great Britain, by the treaty of London, November 19th, 1794, the free navigation of the Mississippi, although nearly a year previously.*

In the early period of the correspondence, before the arrival of Lieutenant Pope, the Spanish governor had endeavored to alarm the American commissioner by apprehensions of Indian hostility, alleged to have been excited by the presence of American troops. To give a plausibility to the rumor, and to excite apprehension of danger to be encountered from that quarter, swarms of drunken Indians were made to parade the town with every demonstration of displeasure at the presence of the American troops. Several times the savages paraded before the American intrenchments with drawn knives, and with the most threatening demonstrations. To quiet them into neutrality until the arrival of the re-enforcement under Lieutenant Pope, Colonel Ellicott was obliged to conciliate their hostility by distributing rations among them, together with such presents as their cupidity might fancy.

Only a few weeks elapsed before it was ascertained beyond doubt that emissaries had been sent to the neighboring tribes to rouse their vengeance against the extension of the Federal jurisdiction and the introduction of troops.†

The object of the Spanish governor was delay, in the vain

* Ellicott's Journal, p. 94–96. Also, American State Papers, Foreign Affairs, folio edition. † See Ellicott.

hope that some fortunate event might yet avert the necessity of surrendering the country. It was with regret the Spanish authorities beheld this presage of the entire loss of Louisiana in the surrender of this important portion of its territory. Believing that all hope in the West had not yet fled, the governor-general had caused these vexatious delays, until his emissary should return from Detroit and report the state of feeling upon the Ohio and its tributaries. Moreover, new hope had sprung up since the arrival of the American commissioner ; for General Wayne had died, and General Wilkinson had succeeded as commander-in-chief in the Northwest. Some event might yet transpire to defeat the obligations of the treaty, and secure to Spain the integrity of Louisiana.

At length the people became highly excited at the delays and perfidy of the Spaniards for deferring the fulfillment of the treaty stipulations. The district north of the line of demarkation contained at this time about four thousand inhabitants, the greater portion of whom were emigrants from the United States, or the remains of former British colonies from the Atlantic provinces. Many had emigrated from Kentucky and Tennessee, for the express purpose of becoming citizens under the American government. Most of them became impatient for the departure of the Spanish authorities, and the establishment of the free government of the United States. Settlements extended from the Bayou Pierre south to the line of demarkation, and eastward to the sources of the Bayou Pierre, Cole's Creek, St. Catharine, Homochitto, and Buffalo. Many of them had taken an active part in evincing their opposition to the continuance of the Spanish authorities, and had thus rendered themselves highly obnoxious to their resentment. Some had evinced a willingness to attempt their expulsion by force, and to capture Fort Panmure itself.

The governor-general's proclamation of the 24th of May was intended to quiet public excitement and to allay fears of future vengeance from the Spanish authorities, by assuring the people that the terms of the treaty would be faithfully performed so soon as the danger of the threatened British invasion should have passed. But the proclamation failed to produce the desired effect; instead of calming the excitement, Colonel Ellicott observes, after the proclamation, " the public mind might be compared to inflammable gas, which required only a spark to produce an explosion."

Colonel Ellicott, and those attached to his commission, continued to use every prudent means for tranquilizing the people, and for inducing them quietly and peaceably to await the regular action of the Spanish authorities.

Yet the people perceived no movement for the speedy evacuation of the military posts, or the surrender of the country. Many despaired of seeing the American authority established in the district; and others, having, by their zeal and activity in favor of the Federal jurisdiction, rendered themselves obnoxious to the resentment of the Spanish authorities, contemplated a removal back to the Western States. To calm these apprehensions, Gayoso gave notice that he had received from the Baron de Carondelet, governor of Louisiana, instructions for the removal of the artillery and military stores from the forts which were north of the line of demarkation.

Although the popular excitement and dissatisfaction were extreme, and the inclination to resist was strong, yet there was no open resistance until the 9th day of June. On this day Mr. Hannah, a preacher of the Baptist denomination, and an American citizen, was seized by the Spanish authorities, and, under some pretext, was confined in a small guard-house within the Spanish fort, with his feet in the stocks. This was like fire to an explosive train. The people considered this act an infringement of the liberty of the people of the United States. If not so, it certainly evinced a determination to enforce vigorously the authority of Spain in the country. Under this impression they flew to arms, and the commandant and his principal officers, with their families, were compelled to take refuge in the Spanish fort. The people organized themselves into military companies, and chose officers to command them. An instantaneous change had taken place, and "in the short space of less than ten hours the authority of the governor was confined to the small compass of the fort."*

The excitement spread into the surrounding country: public meetings were held, and violent measures contemplated. At this time Governor Gayoso, through his fort major, Stephen Minor, requested a private interview with the American com-

* Gayoso, in most of the correspondence and transactions relative to the delivery of the forts and the surrender of the Natchez District, is called "governor" by way of eminence; yet up to August, 1797, he was lieutenant-governor of the Natchez dependences. After August, 1797, he succeeded the Baron de Carondelet as governor of Louisiana and the Floridas.

missioner. The latter determined to have no communication with the Spanish governor except such as was strictly official. Lieutenant Pope further informed him that he should " repel by force any attempt made to imprison those who claim the privileges of citizens of the United States." He also notified the people of his intentions, and assured them of his " protection and support against any arbitrary military force which might be brought to operate against them, or in any wise to infringe their rights as American citizens."

At this time it was supposed Gayoso might order re-enforcements from other posts on the river to aid in maintaining his authority. Lieutenant Pope had resolved to permit no such re-enforcement, and he called on the people to sustain him in repelling any attempt to re-enforce the garrison in Fort Panmure.*

On the 14th of June, Governor Gayoso issued his proclamation, exhorting the people to a quiet and peaceable submission to the authority of his Catholic majesty until the difficulties between the two governments could be properly arranged. At the same time, he promised the utmost lenity, and a pardon to all who repented of their misdeeds, and, as an evidence of repentance, abstained from all acts calculated to disturb the public peace.

The people, already highly irritated by delays and disap-

* Letter of Lieutenant Pope, transmitted by Colonel Hutchens to the Department of State.—American State Papers, Boston edition, vol. iii., p. 350.

"*Natchez Camp, June* 12*th*, 1797.
"FELLOW-CITIZENS OF THE DISTRICT OF NATCHEZ,—

" Having received information that a number of you will be collected at my friend Bealk's, in conformity to an indirect invitation sent to you for that purpose, I have now positively to make the declaration to you that I have made this evening to Governor Gayoso, that I will, at all hazards, protect the citizens of the United States from every act of hostility; I mean such as reside north of the thirty-first degree of north latitude, or within thirty-nine miles due south of Natchez. I now, therefore, call on you in the most solemn manner *to come forward, assert your rights,* and you may rely on my sincere co-operation to accomplish that desirable object.

" I shall expect your assistance to repel any troops or hostile parties that may make an attempt to land for the purpose of re-enforcing this garrison, or for other purposes detrimental to the inhabitants of this country. PIERCY S. POPE,
"Commanding United States Troops, Natchez."

" From the present alarming situation of this country, I fully approve of Lieutenant Pope's letter of this date to his fellow-citizens assembled at Mr. Bealk's.
"ANDREW ELLICOTT,
"June 12th, 1797."   "Commissioner of United States."

"A true copy. Examined per THOMAS M. GREEN."
—See American State Papers, "Foreign Affairs." Also, Ellicott's Journal p. 96, 97.

pointed hopes, took great exceptions to the word "repentance," as highly offensive to free citizens of the United States. Things now assumed a serious aspect, and the opposition to Spanish authority had taken a regular form of rebellion. A number of respectable militia companies were organized, and ready to take the field at the first notice, and open hostilities seemed inevitable. Both parties were in a continual state of preparation to repel force by force. Gayoso made great exertions to re-enforce his garrison, but without success, while the militia were drilling throughout the settlements. Confined to the walls of his fortress, and too weak for offensive operations, he interceded with the American commissioner to use his influence in calming the popular excitement.* But Colonel Ellicott felt little sympathy for the unpleasant position which he had brought upon himself.

In the mean time a public meeting had been announced, to be held at Benjamin Bealk's, on the Nashville road, eight miles from Natchez. This meeting was assembled on the 20th of June, and was attended by many of the inhabitants. The subject of the existing difficulties was discussed, and the meeting dispersed after appointing a "committee of public safety," consisting of seven prominent men, to represent the people thereafter in any negotiation with the Spanish authorities. No measures adopted by the Spanish governor should have the force of law until the concurrence of this committee should render it obligatory.†

Up to this time, the Spanish commandant, as well as the American, kept each an active patrol continually on duty; and during the greater portion of the time, since the first of May, a heavy piece of ordnance in the Spanish fort had been brought to bear upon the American commissioner's tent, which was in full view.

On the 18th of June, while all was excitement and apprehension, the governor, confined within the narrow limits of the fort, desired an interview with the American commissioner at the house of Captain Minor. To meet this appointment, Gayoso, in great trepidation, "having left the fort by a circuitous

---

* Martin's Louisiana, vol. ii., p. 146, 147. Also, see Ellicott's Journal, p. 85–116.

† The Committee of Public Safety was composed of the following persons, viz.: Anthony Hutchens, Bernard Lintot, Isaac Gailliard, Cato West, William Ratliff, Gabriel Benoist, and Joseph Bernard, to which Colonel Ellicott and Lieutenant Pope were unanimously added.—Ellicott's Journal, p. 114.

route, made his way through thickets and cane-brakes to the rear or north side of Minor's plantation, and thence through a corn-field to the back of the house, and entered the parlor undiscovered." Such were the visible marks of anxiety in his person, that Colonel Ellicott says his feelings never were more affected than when he beheld the governor. "The humiliating state to which he was reduced by a people whose affections he had courted, and whose gratitude he expected, had made a strong and visible impression upon his mind and countenance. Having been educated with high ideas of command and prerogative, served only to render his present situation more poignant and distressing.*"

The "Committee of Public Safety," agreeably to their instructions, presented themselves before Gayoso in their official capacity, for his recognition and approbation. He did not hesitate to recognize them as representatives of the people, and cheerfully acceded to their demand that none of the people should be injured or prosecuted for the part they had taken in the late movements against the Spanish authority; also, that they should be exempt from serving in the Spanish militia, unless in case of riots or Indian hostilities. The proceedings of the public meeting, the recognition of the "committee" by the governor, and his acquiescence in their demands, had all tended greatly to quiet public apprehension and to allay the popular excitement.

Yet there were persons in the committee whose fidelity to the United States was suspected by Colonel Ellicott; and one of them was particularly objectionable to him and Lieutenant Pope. In order to insure harmony, he prevailed upon the governor to dissolve the committee, and to authorize the election of another, by proclamation, which should be permanent. A new committee, consisting of nine members, was accordingly elected about the first of July, "permanent" in its character, and created by virtue of the Spanish authority. The organization of this committee was highly gratifying to Colonel Ellicott, who declared that "this committee was the finishing-stroke to the Spanish authority and jurisdiction."†

---

* Ellicott, p. 109–113.

† The permanent committee was composed of Joseph Bernard, Judge Peter B. Bruin, Daniel Clarke, Gabriel Benoist, Philander Smith, Isaac Gailliard, Roger Dixon, William Ratliff, and Frederic Kimball, all firm Republicans, and strongly attached to the United States, except F. Kimball, who was deemed doubtful. Joseph Bernard presided

One of the most active opposers of the measures and policy of the American commissioner was Colonel Anthony Hutchens, who sustained the general policy of Gayoso and highly censured the course of Lieutenant Pope.

Colonel Hutchens had been a loyal subject of the crown of Great Britain during the British dominion in West Florida, had enjoyed the post of confidential correspondent to the British minister, and was enrolled on the pension list as a reduced half-pay British officer, up to the period of the establishment of the Federal jurisdiction, when he acquiesced and became a valuable citizen.

The efforts of Colonel Hutchens, during the early periods of the popular excitements in 1797, no doubt had a salutary influence in checking the outbreak of popular indignation in acts of open violence. Without some such modifying influence, the people, irritated by delays and apprehension of personal danger from Spanish perfidy, would scarcely have been restrained.*

During the autumn, for the health and comfort of his men, Colonel Ellicott removed his corps and escort to the banks of the St. Catharine, about seven miles northeast of Natchez, where he erected huts for his men near a beautiful spring which gushes out from a dell in the northern limits of the present town of Washington, and which, for many years afterward, was known as "Ellicott's Spring." He remained at this encampment until the 27th of September, and during his stay he made the survey and plat of the present town of Washington for the proprietor, John Foster.†

On the 26th day of July, Gayoso received his commission as Governor-general of Louisiana and Florida, and successor of the Baron Carondelet, who was promoted to the government of the Mexican provinces. Four days afterward he departed for New Orleans, having appointed Captain Stephen Minor temporary commandant of the fort.

with great ability and general satisfaction, until the 20th of September, when he died, and was succeeded by Gabriel Benoist, who discharged the duties of president with singular ability, assiduity, and integrity. For the character of those who opposed the Federal jurisdiction, see Ellicott's Journal, p. 116, 117, 152. Also, Stoddart, p. 94–96.

* Colonel Hutchens was very active in opposing the movements of Colonel Ellicott and Lieutenant Pope. These public officers, irritated by delays, and well apprised of the secret motives which prompted the official conduct of the Spanish governor, were sometimes induced to transcend the bounds of a prudent, dignified intercourse ; and as such they received the censure of some American authorities, who were not fully acquainted with all the causes of excitement and delay on the part of the Spanish authorities. † See Ellicott's Journal, Appendix, p. 17, 18.

Soon afterward, Colonel Grandpre was appointed to the office of lieutenant-governor at Natchez; but his presence being unacceptable to the majority of the people, and at the request of the permanent committee, the governor permitting Captain Minor to continue in the exercise of his duties as civil and military commandant, Colonel Grandpre did not make his appearance at Natchez. The powers of the permanent committee were duly recognized by Captain Minor; and harmony being again restored in the district, Lieutenant Pope, with his command, retired a few miles into the country.*

Most of those who had been opposed to the extension of the Federal jurisdiction, finding their wishes and opposition unavailing, quietly submitted to the established change.

In the mean time, the commander-in-chief, General Wilkinson, having been apprised of the delay in regard to the evacuation of the forts, determined to re-enforce the advanced guard at Natchez. For this purpose, early in the winter, he dispatched Captain Isaac Guion, a veteran of the Revolutionary war, with a re-enforcement from Fort Massac, with orders to descend the Mississippi to Natchez, and there to assume the command in that quarter. Before the close of December, Captain Guion, with his detachment, arrived at Natchez, and assumed the command. His first efforts were directed toward the suppression of any public manifestation of disrespect to the Spanish authorities, and to allay any remains of popular ill-will which might exist toward the Spanish troops. He proceeded, also, to disconcert what he considered the improper measures of the permanent committee, which he rudely threatened to disperse by military force.

Captain Guion, no doubt incredulous of the Spanish perfidy, and ignorant of their many pretexts for delay, deemed it proper to exalt the Spanish authorities to a decent respect in the eyes of the people. Yet, having resumed their former consequence, and having no further pretext for delay, they still deferred the final evacuation of the forts and the survey for the line of demarkation,† until Captain Guion himself became impatient.

---

* Colonel Grandpre, a Spanish officer, was appointed to the government of the Natchez District in November, 1797, as successor of Gayoso; but the permanent committee unanimously adopted a resolution declaring that his presence would not be acceptable, and notified the governor-general accordingly, and Colonel Grandpre never made his appearance at Natchez. He was afterward appointed to the government of Baton Rouge by the Spanish authorities.—See Ellicott, p. 161.

† Captain Guion was a great admirer of General Wilkinson, and no friend of Gen-

[A.D. 1798.] Finally, on the 10th of January, 1798, nearly eleven months after his arrival, Colonel Ellicott received notice from the governor-general at New Orleans that official instructions from his Catholic majesty had been received directing the surrender of the territory north of the line of demarkation, and the evacuation of the forts north of the thirty-first parallel of latitude, agreeably to the treaty stipulations. The post at the mouth of Wolf River, near the present site of Memphis, had been dismantled and evacuated during the preceding autumn, and the only forts now to be evacuated were those of Nogales and Natchez.

This order, it will be perceived, had not been issued until the last ray of hope had vanished, and Thomas Powers had made his final report against the practicability of a separation of the Western States, and all prospect of success had been abandoned.

Yet delays were not terminated. Since instructions had been received, January, February, and the greater portion of March had elapsed, and the Spanish garrisons still occupied the forts. At length, on the 23d of March, when Captain Guion had almost determined to take the forts by assault, the Fort Nogales was evacuated, and the garrison descended the river to Natchez. Here it retired into Fort Panmure, and remained for six days longer, previous to its final evacuation. During this time, the commander studiously concealed the time of his intended departure, while Captain Guion looked with impatience to the near approach of the first day of April, which he declared should not witness the Spanish garrison in the fort.

At length, on the 29th of March, about midnight, the Spanish drums began to sound the note of preparation; and at four o'clock next morning, having previously sent the artillery, stores, and baggage on board their boats and galleys, the troops marched out of the fort to the river bank. Before the morning light they had embarked, and were several miles below Natchez, on their voyage to New Orleans. The fort

eral Wayne. The dispatch borne by him to Governor Gayoso from General Wilkinson contained the following sentence, which Gayoso quoted to Colonel Ellicott, in his efforts to associate Captain Guion in the commission for running the boundary line, viz.: "This officer's experience and good sense, and the powers with which he is elevated by the President of the United States, conspire to promise a happy result to his command, in which I flatter myself I shall not be disappointed."—See Ellicott's Journal, p. 165-175. Also, Wilkinson's Memoirs, vol. i., p. 434.

was stripped of its terrors, and the gate was thrown open. Thus, instead of retiring amid the salutes of the American troops in open day, they retired by night, as if cautiously retreating from a powerful enemy.*

Soon after the evacuation of the fort at Natchez, Governor Gayoso issued his orders from New Orleans, directing the commissioners on the part of Spain, Stephen Minor and Sir William Dunbar, to repair to the Bayou Tunica and join the American commissioner in opening the line of demarkation. Colonel Ellicott, with his woodsmen and escort, in the mean time, repaired to Tunica Bayou, six miles below Fort Adams, and having located his camp, commenced his astronomical observations on the 6th of May. He proceeded to run and mark the line; and on the 21st of May he was joined by Captain Minor, with a party of woodsmen; and on the 26th, by Mr. Dunbar, astronomical commissioner for his Catholic majesty. On the 21st of June, Governor Gayoso, with his secretary and several Spanish officers, joined the commission at their camp, twelve miles east of the river.† The principal surveyor on the part of his Catholic majesty was Thomas Powers, late emissary to the Ohio; on the part of the United States was Major Thomas Freeman, subsequently United States surveyor-general south of Tennessee. Gayoso approved the manner in which the work had progressed, and directed its continuation. It progressed regularly until the last of August, when Sir William Dunbar resigned his commission and returned home.‡ On account of Indian disturbances, the line across East Florida was not completed until the following year. After the resignation of his colleague, Captain Minor continued to discharge the duties of principal commissioner on the part of his Catholic majesty.§

In the mean time, by an act of Congress approved April 7th, 1798, the territory surrendered had been erected into a

* The Spaniards studiously concealed the time of their intended departure. On the 29th of March, late in the evening, Colonel Ellicott, through a confidential channel, learned that the evacuation was to take place that night, or next morning before day. In consequence of which information he rose very early next morning, and at four o'clock A.M. walked toward the fort, which he approached just as the rear-guard was passing the gates. The gate being left open, he entered the fort, and from the parapet he had the pleasure of witnessing the boats and galleys leave the shore and get under way. Before daylight the whole fleet was out of sight.—Ellicott's Journal, p. 176. Also, Martin's Louisiana, vol. ii., p. 156. † Ellicott, Appendix, p. 49.

‡ Martin's Louisiana, vol. ii., p. 158. Also, Ellicott, Appendix, p. 56, 57.
§ Ellicott, p. 180.

territorial government, to be known and designated as the "Mississippi Territory." Its boundaries were the Mississippi on the west, the thirty-first parallel of latitude on the south, and on the north a line drawn due east from the mouth of the Yazoo to the Chattahoochy River.

By an act of Congress approved May 10th, the Mississippi Territory was organized into a territorial government of the "first grade." The first territorial governor, Winthrop Sargent, former secretary of the Northwestern Territory, and the territorial judges, arrived at Natchez on the 6th day of August, 1798, and on the 26th day of the same month General Wilkinson arrived with the Federal army, and established his headquarters at Natchez. Soon afterward he established the post of " Fort Adams," six miles above the line of demarkation.*

Governor Sargent made his residence near Natchez, and proceeded to establish the Federal government in the country, as he had heretofore done under Governor St. Clair in the Northwestern Territory.†

Thus terminated the train of vexatious difficulties and embarrassments from the Spanish authorities, originating from the treaty of 1783, and thus began the "Mississippi Territory," which was not admitted into the Federal Union until December, 1817,‡ after a tedious probation of nearly twenty years under the territorial grades.

It may be well to take a brief retrospect of the court intrigues and official manœuvers on the part of Spain in executing the stipulations of this treaty. Never were Spanish duplicity and perfidy more flagrant than in the transactions of the years 1796 and 1797, in relation to the surrender of the Natchez District and the evacuation of the military posts, preparatory to the establishment of the line of demarkation. All the delays in the accomplishment of these objects were preconcerted and studiously conducted, in the vain hope that future events would so transpire that Spain would still retain possession of this portion of Louisiana. The Spanish court still believed "that the western people might yet be induced to separate from their Atlantic brethren," and hence the surrender was delayed to the last moment.

The treaty of Madrid had been signed and ratified as a last

---

* Ellicott, p. 186. Martin, vol. ii., p. 156, 157. See, also, Wilkinson's Memoirs, vol. i., p. 434.   † See book v., chap. ix., of this work.   ‡ Idem, chap. xii.

resort, the only means of avoiding an open rupture with the United States, and the consequent invasion of Louisiana. The Spanish king never intended to fulfill the stipulations of the treaty, if compliance were avoidable. At the very time that his minister was negotiating the treaty, his pensioned emissaries were busily employed in sowing the seeds of revolt in the western country, and were endeavoring, by secret intrigue, to produce a separation of the States of Kentucky and Tennessee from the Federal Union.* On this errand Thomas Powers had been sent repeatedly to Kentucky and the Ohio region, with authority to contract, on the part of the Spanish king, for the liberal distribution of money to any amount not exceeding one hundred thousand dollars, to be appropriated *as he might see proper.* He was also authorized to promise an equal amount to procure arms and military stores, besides twenty pieces of artillery, with powder and ball, to enable them to resist the Federal power, provided they would form a "government wholly unconnected with the Atlantic States."†

All this the king would cheerfully have done to aid the western people to absolve themselves from their dependence upon the Atlantic States, and to unite themselves with the provinces of Spain. The only consideration required by the King of Spain was the extension of the northern limit of West Florida as far as the mouth of the Yazoo, to its old British boundary,‡ leaving the whole territory north of that latitude wholly to the people of the contemplated republic. As a further inducement, the king had authorized the promise that all the restrictions heretofore imposed upon the river trade should be removed, and other important advantages and privileges would be granted, which would give them a decided advantage over the Atlantic States. Thus, they were reminded that, as an independent government, in alliance with Spain, " they would find themselves in a situation infinitely more advantageous for their commercial relations than they could be, were the treaty of Madrid carried into effect."§

Such were a few of the specimens of Spanish faith and Spanish diplomacy with the United States during this tedious and vexed negotiation, which began soon after the close of the Rev-

---

* Martin's Louisiana, vol. ii., p. 150–152.   † Idem, p. 144, 145.
‡ Martin's Louisiana, vol. ii., p. 144. Also, Butler's Kentucky, p. 245–247.
§ Butler's History of Kentucky, p. 247, first edition.

olutionary war, and continued, with but little interruption, until the spring of 1798.

The western people, even those who had favored the overtures held out by the Spanish emissaries, had become satisfied with the treaty of Madrid, by which they had acquired all they had claimed or desired, the free navigation of the Mississippi; they preferred to enjoy these advantages under their own free government, rather than, by receiving them in a separate condition, become the vassals of Spain. Satisfied with the Federal Union, they desired no other alliance.*

It was not until the 4th of September, 1797, that Powers finally failed in his negotiation with Benjamin Sebastian and others of Kentucky. During the summer of 1797, he had penetrated through Kentucky on the line of the northwestern posts as far as Detroit, the headquarters of General Wilkinson, then commander-in-chief of the northwestern army. His ostensible business, on this occasion, was to bear to General Wilkinson a remonstrance against pressing the delivery of the forts on the Mississippi until it should be clearly ascertained " whether they were to be dismantled before delivery ;" but his real object was to press General Wilkinson into the Spanish conspiracy, with the whole weight of his power and authority as commander-in-chief of the army, in sustaining the separation.†

In his journey to Detroit, Powers passed by way of Fort Greenville, and reached the vicinity of Detroit on the 16th day of August; but, being informed that General Wilkinson was absent at Michillimackinac, he did not enter the fort. A few days afterward Wilkinson returned, and having heard of Powers's arrival, caused him to be arrested and brought to the fort, and thus secured the Baron de Carondelet's dispatches; after which he hurried him off, under an escort commanded by Captain Shaumburg, by way of the Wabash, to Fort Massac, in order to avoid interception by the Federal authorities.‡

In the mean time, the Federal government had been apprised of the embassy of Powers, and instructions had been issued to the governor of the Northwestern Territory to cause him to be arrested and sent a prisoner to Philadelphia.§

---

* See Burnet's Letters, p. 67–69, Cincinnati edition of 1839.
† Martin, vol. ii., p. 143.   ‡ Martin, vol. ii., p. 151.
§ On the 5th of June, at Natchez, during the time of the greatest excitement, it was ascertained that the Englishman Powers, a subject of his Catholic majesty, had been

The temerity of this last intrigue, put in operation by the Governor of Louisiana, astonishes every reflecting mind. But General Wilkinson was a talented and ambitious man; he had received many favors from the Spanish governors nearly ten years before; he had received exclusive privileges in the commerce with Louisiana; a long and confidential intercourse had existed between him and Governor Miro; he was known to have indulged a predilection for the Spanish authority, and was ambitious of power and distinction; he was now at the head of the western armies, and, with the power and influence of his station, he might effectually bring about a separation of the West, the formation of a new republic, of which he himself might be the supreme ruler, and conduct the alliance with Spain. Such may have been the reasoning of Baron de Carondelet at this late period.

But General Wilkinson had already proceeded too far in his treasonable intrigues and correspondence with the Spanish governor, and the suspicions of his own government rested upon him. The brilliant prospects, and the bright hopes of becoming the head of a new confederation, had vanished from his imagination, and he was now anxious to retain his command, and with it his standing as a patriotic citizen of the United States. Hence, in the summer of 1797, he had given to Mr. Powers a cold reception; he had informed him that the time for a separation had passed by; that now the project of the Baron would be chimerical in the extreme; that the western people, by the late treaty, had obtained all they had desired, and that now they entertained no desire for an alliance with either Spain or France; that the political ferment which existed four years previously had entirely subsided; and that,

---

secretly dispatched to Kentucky by the governor-general. Colonel Ellicott and others were active in their efforts to circumvent his movements, by dispatching letters to prominent persons in Kentucky and the Northwestern Territory, and giving them notice of his character and designs. Colonel Ellicott also wrote to the executive department of the Federal government, conveying the suspicions which were entertained against Powers, and the object of his mission. Before he left Kentucky his danger became imminent, and with difficulty he escaped arrest by a sudden departure in the night. A plan was laid to honor him with a coat of "tar and feathers" by the patriotic people of Kentucky. Early in September he set out from Detroit, and reached New Orleans in October following. After his arrival at New Orleans he reported his own views and those of Judge Sebastian as decidedly favorable to the success of the enterprise of separating the Western States, and also the opinion of General Wilkinson, that it was impracticable. Compare Ellicott, p. 98, &c. Also, Burnet's Letters, ed. of 1839, p. 68. Martin's Louisiana, vol. ii., p. 151, 152.

so far from desiring an alliance with Louisiana under the Spanish crown, the people of Kentucky, prior to the treaty of Madrid, had proposed to invade Louisiana with an army of ten thousand men, to be put in motion upon the first open rupture between the two governments; and that now they were highly exasperated at the spoliations committed upon the American commerce by French privateers, who brought their prizes into the port of New Orleans for condemnation and confiscation. He gave it as his opinion that the governor-general would therefore consult his own interest, and the interest of his Catholic majesty, by an immediate compliance with the terms of the treaty.*

General Wilkinson also complained that his connection and his correspondence with the Spanish governor had been divulged; that all his plans had been defeated, and the labor of ten years had been lost; that he had now burned all his correspondence and destroyed his ciphers, and that duty and honor forbid a continuance of the intercourse. Yet he still indulged the hope of being able to manifest his confidence in the Baron; for it was probable that he would receive from the Federal government the appointment of governor over the Natchez District when surrendered agreeably to treaty, when he should not want an opportunity of promoting his political projects.†

* Martin's Louisiana, vol. ii., p. 151.   † Idem, p. 152.

CHAPTER V.

CLOSE OF THE SPANISH DOMINION IN LOUISIANA, AND THE FINAL TRANSFER OF THE PROVINCE TO THE UNITED STATES.—A.D. 1797 TO 1804.

Argument.—Prosperity of Louisiana unaffected by Hostilities in Europe.—Gayoso succeeds as Governor-general of Louisiana in 1797.—The King's Orders relative to Land Grants.—The Intendant alone empowered to make Grants.—French Privateers.—Daniel Clarke, Jr., recognized as Consul.—Harmony on the Spanish and American Borders.—Concordia.—Vidalia in 1799.—Death of Gayoso in 1799.—His Successors.—Colonel Ellicott's Eulogy of Gayoso.—Population of Upper Louisiana.—Its Trade and Commerce.—Harmony with the western People again disturbed by Morales.—Policy of Spain in restricting her Grants of Land.—Jealous of Military Adventurers.—Restrictions enforced by Morales.—His first Interdict of Deposit at New Orleans.—Western Indignation.—Capture of New Orleans contemplated.—American Troops in the Northwest.—Invasion of Louisiana abandoned by John Adams.—Filhiol and Fejeiro at Fort Miro, on the Washita.—Right of Deposit restored in 1801.—Again suspended in 1802.—Restored in 1803.—Approaching Change of Dominion in Louisiana.—The First Consul of the French Republic acquires the Province of Louisiana.—The French Occupation deferred one Year by European Wars.—Napoleon determines to sell the Province to the United States.—Negotiation for Sale commenced.—Mr. Jefferson's Instructions.—Treaty of Cession signed April 30th, 1803.—Amount of Purchase-money.—Terms of Payment.—Preparations for French Occupation.—The Form of Government prepared by French Prefect.—Arrival of Laussat, the Colonial Prefect.—His Proclamation.—Response of the People.—Proclamation of Governor Salcedo.—Rumor of Cession to United States.—Laussat appointed Commissioner of the French Republic.—Conditions of the Treaty of April 30th, 1803.—Preparations for Occupation by the United States.—Protest of the Spanish King.—Congress ratifies the Treaty.—Commissioners of the United States.—Preparations of French Commissioner.—Ceremony of Spanish Delivery.—Proclamation of the French Prefect.—Spanish Rule abolished and French Government instituted.—Volunteer Battalion for the Preservation of Order.—Preparations for Delivery to the United States.—Governor Claiborne and General Wilkinson arrive in New Orleans.—Ceremony of French Delivery to the United States, December 20th, 1803.—Remote Posts formally delivered subsequently to Agents of the French Prefect.—Major Stoddart takes Possession of Upper Louisiana, March 9th, 1804.—Condition and Boundaries of Louisiana.—Population of the Province.—Commerce.—Agricultural Products.—Trade and Manufactures of New Orleans.

[A.D. 1797.] ALTHOUGH Spain had become deeply involved in the continental wars of Europe, the contest was confined chiefly to interior and maritime parts of that continent and the adjacent coasts of Africa, Syria, and the Grecian Isles of the Mediterranean Sea.[*] Louisiana continued to enjoy peace and prosperity, interrupted only by the jealous fears excited at the rapid extension of the American settlements upon the great eastern tributaries of the Mississippi.

[*] Martin, vol. ii., p. 139.

Nor was this jealous apprehension in any wise diminished by the compulsory relinquishment of the Natchez District, which was now open to the unrestrained tide of emigration from the whole West.

The new governor-general, Gayoso de Lemos, entered upon the duties of his office on the first of August, and devoted himself assiduously to the promotion of good government and tranquillity within the limits of his jurisdiction. Among the first objects requiring his attention was the restoration of harmony and good feeling between the American and Spanish authorities preparatory to the establishment of the *line of demarkation*.

[A.D. 1798.] It was not until January following that he issued his *bando de buen gobierno*. It contained no new regulations of importance except his determination to enforce a strict observance of the commands of the king respecting the future appropriation of lands to the use of Spanish subjects exclusively, and the prohibition of foreign immigration to the province.

Next day he issued his instructions to the different commandants, comprised in seventeen articles, defining all the provisions and regulations to be observed in future grants.* Heretofore, the authority for granting lands to settlers and emigrants had, by the king's order, dated August, 1770, been vested in the civil and military commandants, with the concurrent approbation of the governor-general. But this authority was now to be revoked, and confided exclusively to the intendant. Thus an entire change in the general policy of the land system was introduced.

About this time, the first regular commercial agent or American consul was recognized in the city of New Orleans.

" The French privateers had now become very troublesome to the trade of the United States in the West Indies and about the Gulf of Mexico. A number of our captured vessels were taken into the port of New Orleans, condemned and confiscated, with their cargoes, at a trifling price, our seamen treated in a most shameful manner, and our trade otherwise brought into great jeopardy."†

" This subject became a matter of serious consideration, and the United States having neither consul nor vice-consul at that

---
* See Martin, vol. ii., p. 153–155, where these regulations are given in full.
† Ellicott's Journal, p. 173.

port," Colonel Ellicott, the American commissioner, interested himself with the authorities of Louisiana in procuring from them the privilege of recognizing Daniel Clarke, Jr., a respectable merchant of that place, as consul for the United States, until the president should make a regular appointment. Whereupon, by the order of Governor Gayoso, Daniel Clarke was received as "Consul for the United States," and regarded as such by the merchants and officers of his Catholic majesty.*

"The firm and manly conduct of Mr. Clarke in a short time put a new face upon our commerce in that quarter, and obtained from the Spanish authorities some privileges not before enjoyed." In effecting this desirable object, Colonel Ellicott and Mr. Clarke had opened a voluminous correspondence with Governor Gayoso upon the various subjects which invited discussion, in all of which the governor evinced a sincere desire to promote the commerce of the city.

The agency of Mr. Clarke was so acceptable that the thanks of the President of the United States was tendered him through Colonel Ellicott, and he was requested to continue his good offices in favor of the American citizens until a regular consul and vice-consul should be duly appointed. Mr. Clarke accordingly continued to exercise the duties of the office until the regular appointment of Evan Jones consul, and Mr. Huling vice-consul the spring following. Upon the accession of Mr. Jefferson to the presidency, he appointed Daniel Clarke consul, highly approving his former services in that capacity.†

The line of demarkation having been established near the Mississippi, such of the inhabitants of the Natchez District as were so inclined quietly retired within the jurisdiction of the Spanish authorities. To insure a proper observance of a friendly neutrality, General Wilkinson, early in the autumn, established a military post on the east bank of the river, at Loftus's Heights, a few miles above the line of demarkation, subsequently known as Fort Adams. Other posts, with a small garrison in each, were distributed upon the line eastward. The headquarters of the American commander were at Natchez; and a new Spanish post was erected on the west bank of the river, opposite Fort Panmure. A convention was entered into between the American commander, General Wilkinson, and the Governor-general of Louisiana, for the mutual surrender of

---

* See Ellicott's Journal, p. 174. † Idem. Also, Martin, vol. ii., p. 158.

deserters. Also, a similar convention was concluded between the Governor of the Mississippi Territory, at Natchez, and Don Jose Vidal, on the west side of the river, for the mutual surrender of fugitive slaves. A spirit of mutual good feeling and amicable intercourse seemed to prevail between the civil and military authorities of both governments, which was suitably commemorated by the Spanish commandant opposite Fort Panmure in designating his post as "Fort Concord." The name has since been perpetuated in the rich parish of Concordia, while its excellent commandant is commemorated in the village of Vidalia, which occupies the site of the post.

During this state of things, the intercourse of American citizens in Louisiana was free and amicable, and the increase of western emigration and trade greatly augmented the commercial importance of the city of New Orleans.

Such was the state of things in Louisiana until the close of the year 1798, after which an important change ensued. Consequent upon the orders from the king revoking the authority of commandants to grant lands, the royal schedule was received, bearing date 21st of October, 1798, requiring the most rigid observance of all restrictions heretofore decreed. This was only a prelude to other movements more materially affecting the interests of the western people, and the ultimate object of which was to prevent the emigration of American citizens to the Spanish dominions.

[A.D. 1799.] The Spanish authorities were extremely jealous of the approach of the American population, and many new restrictions were imposed upon those who desired to establish themselves within the Spanish jurisdiction. All former privileges permitted to citizens of the United States were discontinued, and many of the restrictions relative to grants of land were deemed peculiarly oppressive, and framed to operate specially upon the western people.

Under the new system of distributing the royal domain, the regulations provided that no grant of land should be made to a trader, or any one who was not engaged in some regular employment, or in some agricultural or mechanical business. All persons without this qualification were excluded from all residence in Louisiana, which embraced also the settlements on the west side of the Mississippi, from the mouth of the Arkansas to that of the Missouri. No minister of the Gospel, nor preacher of any Protestant denomination whatever, was permitted to settle within the bounds of the province. The Catholic religion was supported by law, and, being a part of the regal government, was tolerated to the exclusion of all others.

Every immigrant for settlement was required, immediately after his arrival, to take the oath of allegiance to the Spanish crown, and to locate himself near some old Spanish settlement, under the eye of a Spanish commandant. No foreigner should receive a grant of land unless he possessed money, slaves, or valuable property, until he had been in the country four years, engaged in some useful and honest employment.

The prejudices of the Spanish authorities ran high against Americans of a certain class. Military adventurers who had served in the war of the Revolution, or in the western campaigns against the Indians, were highly obnoxious to the Spanish authorities. Hundreds of these, both soldiers and officers, had spread over the new settlements on the waters of the Ohio, and too often made their appearance in New Orleans and other portions of Louisiana. Those were particularly obnoxious as immigrants whose profession or avocation gave them influence over their fellow-men; hence lawyers and ministers of the Gospel were excluded. Those who were closely employed in laborious trades, or who had large families to support, or who had large possessions, were not likely to be engaged in any plans for subverting the king's authority; but military officers, disbanded soldiers, politicians, and men of that cast, could not be too carefully excluded from the province. Such were the sagacious inferences which prompted the Spanish policy after the final surrender of the Natchez District.

In carrying out the requisitions of the royal schedule relative to appropriations of land, persons who had received grants previously to the new regulations were prohibited from selling or in any wise transferring their claims until they had resided thereon three years; and no sale should be valid without the consent and approbation of the intendant. In no case should the quantity of land to any one family exceed eight hundred arpens; and petitions for grants must be written in the Spanish language. No title was to be considered complete, after the order of survey and occupancy, until, by a formal application, the claimant should receive *a regular title*, or final confirmation of the claim, known to the Spaniards as *titulo in formo.* These and other regulations for enforcing the views of the king had not been published until they were made known by the proclamation of the intendant, Don Morales, issued on the 17th day of July, 1799. They were comprised in thirty-eight articles.*

But the most ominous act of the intendant for the peace and security of Louisiana was an ill-advised and arbitrary *interdict* of the right of deposit at New Orleans, contrary to the stipulations of the treaty of Madrid. The effect on the western people of the United States was embarrassing in the extreme; and being a direct violation of their rights, as secured by treaty, it excited the highest degree of indignation throughout the whole western country, the consequences of which might have been the military invasion of Louisiana by the Federal troops, had not fate already decreed another mode by which Louisiana should submit to the Federal power.

The treaty of Madrid secured to the people of the United States the right of deposit in New Orleans for their commodities for *three years* from the ratification; and the King of Spain therein obligated himself, at the expiration of three years, to extend the time, or to designate some *other suitable point* within the Island of New Orleans, as a place of deposit.†

Such were the excitement and indignation of the western people, and specially of Kentucky and Tennessee, that it was with difficulty the Federal authorities could restrain them from an unlawful expedition against Louisiana for the capture of New Orleans. President Adams, swayed by the popular will in the West, had fully determined to take such measures as would coerce the Spanish authorities to open a dépôt for the American trade.

With an eye to this object, President Adams caused three regiments of the regular army to be concentrated upon the Lower Ohio, with orders to be held in readiness for any emergency. Congress soon afterward, for the ostensible purpose of avenging the French spoliations upon the American commerce, authorized the army to be increased by the enlistment of twelve regiments, to serve "during the continuance of difficulties with the French Republic." The troops concentrated

---

* See Martin's Louisiana, vol. ii., p. 159–170, where these regulations may be seen in detail.   † Idem, p. 158.

near the mouth of the Ohio were required to keep their boats in repair, ready for any service required of them.* At the same time, the commander-in-chief, General Wilkinson, was summoned to the seat of the Federal government, in order to hold an interview with the cabinet, with the design of arranging the plan of operations for a campaign against Louisiana. General Washington had been appointed provisional commander-in-chief of the new establishment, and General Knox, the former secretary of war, was appointed a major-general, and Generals Hamilton and Pinckney were appointed lieutenant-generals under General Washington.† Every thing was urged with great energy during much excitement in the West, and the whole object was first to redress the wrongs upon American rights and commerce on the Mississippi, which were more pressing than those from France on the ocean.

The success of the contemplated enterprise required the utmost secrecy, lest, by rousing the suspicions of Spain, Louisiana should be placed in a state of complete defense.‡

Such was the state of things on the Ohio during the year 1799, and such was the danger which secretly menaced Louisiana and the city of New Orleans. Political changes, and the strong indications of popular preference for Mr. Jefferson, induced Mr. Adams to abandon the enterprise, and leave the whole to the direction of his successor. At his recommendation, Congress directed the abandonment of the expedition, and the recruits were disbanded.

In the mean time, Louisiana was scarcely conscious of the danger which menaced her. The amiable Gayoso had died on the 18th of July, and was succeeded by Don Maria Vidal as civil governor, the Marquis de Casa Calvo as commandant-general, and Don Ramon de Lopez y' Angullo, a knight of the order of Charles III., as intendant of the provinces.§

The death of Governor Gayoso was deemed a great loss to the interests of the western people of the United States. Many of them who were engaged in the trade of the Mississippi had received from him particular attention, frequently partaking of that hospitality for which he was so remarkable. "As the governor of an arbitrary monarch, he was certainly entitled to great merit. It appeared, in an eminent degree, to be his pride to ren-

---

* Stoddart's Sketches of Louisiana, p. 100, 101.
† Martin's Louisiana, vol. ii., p. 173.   ‡ Idem, p. 174.   § Idem, p. 172.

der the situation of those over whom he was appointed to preside as easy and comfortable as possible ; and in a particular manner he directed his attention to the improvement of the country by opening roads, which he considered the arteries of commerce. He was educated in Great Britain, and retained to a considerable degree, until his death, the manners and customs of that nation, especially in his style of living. In his conversation he was easy and affable, and his politeness was of that superior cast which showed it to be the effect of early habit, rather than an accomplishment merely intended to render him agreeable. His passions were naturally so strong, and his temper so remarkably quick, that they sometimes hurried him into difficulties from which he was not easily extricated. It was frequently remarked of him, as a singularity, that he was neither concerned in traffick, nor in the habit of taking douceurs, which was too frequently the case with other officers of his Catholic majesty in Louisiana. He was fond of show and parade, in which he indulged to the great injury of his fortune, and not a little to his reputation as a good paymaster. He was a tender husband, an affectionate parent, and a good master." Such is the character given him by Colonel Ellicott, who ascribes all his difficulties with him to his instructions from his superiors, and who declares him to have been an accomplished gentleman.*

Meantime difficulties with the United States fortunately were averted by the timely disavowal of the intendant's interdict by his Catholic majesty, and the right of deposit was promptly restored by his successor, Don Ramon de Lopez, until otherwise ordered by the king.†

The population of Louisiana continued to increase ; that portion known as Upper Louisiana had augmented its population in a ratio far exceeding the remainder of the province. The settlements upon the Upper Mississippi, including the post at New Madrid, were now attached to the government of Upper Louisiana. The census of this portion of the province, taken by order of the lieutenant-governor and commandant-general of Upper Louisiana, Don Carlos Dehault Delassus, at the close of the year 1799, presents the entire population at more than six thousand souls, including eight hundred and eighty slaves and

* Ellicott's Journal, p. 215, 216.
† Martin's Louisiana, vol. ii., p. 176. Also, Marbois's Louisiana, p. 219.

one hundred and ninety-seven free persons of color.* During this year, there were in Upper Louisiana thirty-four marriages, one hundred and ninety one births, and fifty-two deaths.

The commerce of Upper Louisiana had also increased in a similar ratio, and a brisk trade had been established between St. Louis and New Orleans, as well as with the American settlements on the Ohio, Cumberland, and Tennessee Rivers. The annual crops yielded about eighty-eight thousand minots of wheat, eighty-four thousand minots of Indian corn, and twenty-eight thousand six hundred and twenty-seven pounds of tobacco. About seventeen hundred quintals of lead were produced from the mines, and about one thousand barrels of salt were made from the salines. The fur-trade yielded an annual value of about seventy thousand dollars.† The greater portion of the lead exported was for the Ohio settlements, including those on the Cumberland and Tennessee Rivers.

[A.D. 1800.] The right of deposit having been restored by the new intendant, trade and free intercourse had again taken place, and general harmony prevailed between the western people and the Spanish settlements on the Upper Mississippi, as well as in the rich and productive regions of the Delta. The bitter animosities and the spirit of revenge which had filled the western people, in consequence of former duties and restrictions, as well as the late interdict, had now subsided into a laudable desire for the peaceable acquisition of property, through the channels of lawful trade and enterprise. This state of mutual prosperity and friendly intercourse between the people of the United States and those of Louisiana continued, with but little interruption, for nearly two years, until the second interdict in the autumn of 1802.

* This population was distributed through the settlements as follows:

1. St. Louis . . . . . . 925 souls.	8. St. Geneviève . . . . 949 souls.
2. Carondelet . . . . . 184 "	9. New Bourbon . . . . 560 "
3. St. Charles . . . . . 875 "	10. Cape Girardeau . . . . 521 "
4. St. Fernando . . . . . 276 "	11. New Madrid . . . . . 782 "
5. Marias des Liards . . . 376 "	12. Little Prairie . . . . 49 "
6. Maramee . . . . . . 115 "	
7. St. Andrew . . . . . 393 "	Total, 6,028

—See Martin, vol. ii., p. 172.

† Martin, vol. ii., p. 173. The principal items in the fur-trade were as follows, with their relative value, viz.:

1754 bundles deer-skins, at $40	$70,160
8 " bear-skins, at 32	256
18 " buffalo robes, at 30	540

Total, $70,956

During this year, among the changes of officers in Louisiana, may be noted that of commandant at the post of Miro, on the Washita. John Filhiol, who had held the command since 1783, resigned his office, and was succeeded by Don Vincente Fernandez Fejeiro, a man of intriguing and avaricious disposition. During the time he held this post, subsequently, and until the close of the Spanish dominion, he lost no opportunity of enriching himself and his friends by a fraudulent abuse of his official station, in fabricating grants of land and the final titles to the same.* From such causes large bodies of land for more than forty years have been withheld from sale and settlement, to the great detriment of the state, if not a fraud upon the Federal government.

[A.D. 1801.] About the middle of June, 1801, the government of Louisiana was committed to other hands by the appointment of the king. The Marquis de Casa Calvo returned to Havana, and was succeeded by Don Juan Manuel de Salcedo, a brigadier-general in the armies of Spain, as Governor of Louisiana. Ramon de Lopez, the intendant, also returned to Havana, leaving the duties of his office to be discharged by Morales, the contador.†

[A.D. 1802.] It did not require the spirit of prophecy to predict the speedy termination of Spanish power on the Mississippi. The rapid extension of the American settlements, the increasing trade from the Western States, and the restless character of the people were such, that the king could not fail to perceive that, unless the flood of immigration could be arrested, Louisiana would ultimately be inundated and lost. To prevent such a result, he required of the provincial authorities a rigid enforcement of former regulations relative to land-grants, from which he required every American citizen to be utterly excluded. To enforce this principle, he signified his displeasure that the Baron de Bastrop had relinquished a moiety of his interest in the grant east of the Washita, by associating himself in the claim with Morehouse, an American citizen, which was a virtual violation of one of the conditions in the grant, which vitiated the grant from its inception.

On the 18th of July, 1802, another schedule of the king com-

* See Report of Case No. 99, District Court of Louisiana, carried to United States Supreme Court, "United States, plaintiffs in error, vs. Richard King and Daniel Coxe." passim.

† Martin, vol. ii., p. 178.

prised a positive prohibition against any grant of land, under any circumstances, to any citizen of the United States.*

In the mean time, rumors had reached Louisiana that the province had been ceded to France, and that the dominion of Spain was soon to give place to that of France.

Morales was again intendant, and suspecting the approaching termination of the Spanish authority on the Mississippi, resolved once more to evince his inveterate repugnance to the American people by again issuing *his interdict* suspending the right of deposit at New Orleans. His proclamation to this effect was dated October 16th, 1802,† and published in the city.

This act of arbitrary power again roused the indignation of the western people, and again suspended the commerce with New Orleans. The embarrassments and losses of those engaged in the river trade were extensive, and spread consternation through the Western States. The restrained indignation of the people vented itself in appeals, petitions, and even curses, upon the Federal government, for the protracted embarrassments of the West. It was a subject in which the whole United States now began to take a deep interest, and Congress was prepared to sustain the wishes of the people and vindicate their rights.

The subject was early brought before that body, and on the 7th of January, 1803, the House of Representatives, with great unanimity, passed the following resolution, viz.:

"*Resolved*, that this House receive with great sensibility the information of a disposition in certain officers of the Spanish government at New Orleans to obstruct the navigation of the Mississippi River, as secured to the United States by the most solemn stipulations."

The resolution proceeds to declare the firm determination of Congress to sustain the executive of the United States in such measures as he shall adopt for asserting the rights, and vindicating the injuries of the American citizens; at the same time declaring their unalterable determination to maintain the boundaries, and the rights of navigation and commerce through the River Mississippi, as established by existing treaties.

It was not long before the suspension of the western trade began to embarrass the city of New Orleans itself, as well as

---

* Martin, vol. ii., p. 180.
† See American State Papers, vol. iv., p. 483, Boston edition.

its dependences in remote parts of the province. The sudden diminution of the supplies of flour, and other western productions necessary for the daily sustenance of the population, had produced great scarcity and exorbitant prices, almost approaching famine. To counteract the effect of his own indiscretion, Morales was induced, on the 5th of February, to issue his proclamation granting to the western people the privilege of importing flour and provisions into Louisiana, subject to a duty of only *six per cent. ad valorem*, and exportable only in Spanish bottoms. But the Americans were not solicitous to embrace such advantages.

This interdict of Morales, near the close of the year 1802, was among the last acts of arbitrary power exercised by the Spanish authorities against the American people and the western commerce. This interdict, also, was disapproved by the king, and by his command the right of deposit was restored March 3d, 1803.*

[A.D. 1803.] But the power and dominion of Spain were about to cease upon the Mississippi. The French nation had never approved the transfer to Spain in 1762. The loss of Louisiana had been viewed as the greatest calamity to the French nation, the result of an ignominious war, and a dishonorable peace under a weak and corrupt government. Since the downfall of the Bourbon dynasty, the sympathies of Republican France had never lost sight of their estranged countrymen, subject, as they conceived, to foreign bondage on the Mississippi. The exertions of the French minister and his agents, in the years 1793 and 1794, for their disenthrallment, had been defeated only by the vigilance of the Baron de Carondelet, and the active co-operation of the authorities of the United States. Now the colossal power of France, under the guiding genius of Napoleon, had made the crowned heads of Europe tremble, and his edicts were supreme law to Southern Europe. Spain became involved in the wars in Europe, and her monarch had been compelled to yield to the dictation of Napoleon, who had resolved to restore to the French empire the ancient province of Louisiana, and thus to extend the dominion of France again upon the Mississippi.

By the third article of the treaty of Ildefonso, concluded on the first of October, 1800, between the King of Spain and the

---

* Martin, vol. ii., p. 181. Also, Marbois's Louisiana, p. 219, 220, and 245.

First Consul of the French Republic, and which was subsequently confirmed and ratified by treaty at Madrid on the 21st of March, 1801, the King of Spain had ceded, and had obligated himself to deliver to the first consul, within six months after the full and entire execution of certain stipulations therein specified in relation to the Duke of Parma, the colony and province of Louisiana, with the same extent which it had in the former possession of France, and which it then had in the possession of Spain after the fulfillment of all existing treaties by them.* Napoleon had complied with his obligations, and waited only a favorable opportunity to take possession of the great province on the Mississippi. Elated by the acquisition of a country so extensive and valuable, and which was to reinstate France in the best portion of her American possessions, he had made great preparations formally to extend over it the dominion of France in a manner commensurate with the power of the Republic. A large fleet had been assembled in the ports of Holland, and a land force of twenty-five thousand men had been advanced to the north of France, ready to sail for the Mississippi. But various embarrassments delayed the contemplated departure of the fleet and troops. The English, suspecting the destination of the armament, or fearing an invasion of their own coast, had concentrated a powerful fleet in the British Channel, for the purpose of observing the movements, and to prevent the sailing of the French armament, or to capture it whenever it should enter upon its voyage. Thus nearly twelve months had passed in delays and embarrassments, while Louisiana continued in the possession of Spain.

At length Napoleon, hard pressed by continual wars in Europe, intercepted by the English fleets in the British Channel, cut off from regular intercourse with remote provinces and dependences, determined to abandon the enterprise of transporting a large land and naval force to the Mississippi. Believing that England, with her immense navy, would infest the coast of Louisiana and blockade her ports, so soon as it was recognized as a province of France, and that all attempts to occupy and

---

* Napoleon had stipulated to settle upon the Duke of Parma, the son-in-law of his Catholic majesty, the sovereignty of the Kingdom of Tuscany, with the title of "King of Etruria," in consideration of the retrocession of Louisiana to France. The Kingdom of Tuscany, with its rich revenues, was estimated at one hundred millions of francs, which was the consideration for the retrocession of Louisiana.—See Martin, vol. ii., p. 175. Marbois's Louisiana, p. 170, 171.

defend it against invasion would only be the withdrawal of his troops and resources from his capital, without adding strength to the Republic, he determined to abandon Louisiana, and concentrate his resources for the defense of France in his contest with the powers of Europe on the Continent.

Louisiana was a vast province, sparsely inhabited, and utterly unable to defend herself against the formidable power of the British navy, by which it might be devastated, if known to be a province of France. Humanity, no less than policy, dictated the propriety of an effort to shield it from the horrors of an English invasion.

Under these circumstances, Napoleon determined to sacrifice his ambition and his glory in the acquisition of Louisiana to the necessity of the times, and to throw the whole province into the hands of the United States before its alienation from the Spanish crown should have been known to the enemies of France. The United States were the friends of the French people, the inveterate enemies of British power, and the rivals of British manufactures and commerce; the possession of Louisiana by the United States would therefore tend to raise up a barrier to the extension of British power in America. The United States, in possession of Louisiana, which they were well able to defend, would indirectly weaken the power of Great Britain, by raising up a powerful rival on the ocean, and an enemy to the extension of British power in the Gulf of Mexico. The amount of available resources which might be derived from the United States in consideration of the transfer of Louisiana, would enable him to prosecute his European wars with vigor and effect. Such was the reasoning of Napoleon.

Accordingly, near the close of the year 1802, he instructed M. Talleyrand and M. Marbois, minister of finance, to propose to Mr. Robert R. Livingston, resident minister of the United States in Paris, a strictly confidential negotiation for this purpose. Mr. Jefferson, then President of the United States, highly pleased with so favorable an opportunity of terminating forever all the difficulties growing out of the Spanish occupancy of Louisiana, determined to spare no means for securing the prize. The negotiation was urged with prudent promptitude, and in March following James Monroe was associated with Mr. Livingston to press the negotiation to a speedy consummation.

At an interview with the American minister, Napoleon frankly "confessed his inability to retain Louisiana; he declared that, were it possible by any means to retain it, he certainly never would consent to alienate a province so extensive and valuable; but he knew it could not be retained without immense treasure and blood expended in its defense. He declared that he was compelled to provide for the safety of Louisiana before it should come into his hands, and that he was desirous of giving the United States a magnificent bargain, an empire for a mere trifle."*

The American minister seized upon the opportunity of securing for the United States so valuable an acquisition. Dispatches were transmitted to the American government, and the negotiation was formally commenced in anticipation of instructions upon the important subject.

The first consul demanded one hundred millions of francs, but his minister might consider fifty millions of francs as the extreme minimum price demanded for the province of Louisiana. The minister demanded eighty millions of francs as his price, and the American ministers evinced but little disposition to reduce the amount. The negotiation for several months, under Mr. Jefferson's instructions, had been conducted with great secrecy, until the treaty was fully consummated, and all the terms and stipulations had been fully arranged. The purchase was finally effected for sixty millions of francs, to be paid by the United States in stocks, bearing six per cent. interest, and redeemable in three annual instalments, after the expiration of fifteen years, besides the assumption, on the part of the United States, of the payment of certain indemnities claimed by their citizens for French spoliations, to an amount not exceeding twenty millions of francs.† The dollar of the United States

---

* Marbois's History of Louisiana. This is an excellent disquisition or historical essay upon the early history of Louisiana as a province of France, its political changes, and the negotiations preceding its sale and transfer to the United States. It contains, however, but little historical narrative touching its internal history, its trade, boundaries, or natural resources, either under the French or Spanish regime. It is the work of M. Barbé Marbois, American edition, 1830, Philadelphia.

† The terms of sale, as finally agreed on, were, that the United States should pay sixty millions of francs in stocks bearing six per cent. interest, irredeemable for fifteen years, afterward to be discharged in three equal annual instalments, the interest to be paid in Europe. The principal, if France thought proper to sell the stock, to be disposed of as should conduce most to the credit of the American funds.

The United States also assumed to pay to their citizens a sum not exceeding twenty millions of francs, in discharge of claims due to them from France under the conven-

was receivable and negotiable at a value equal to five livres and eight sous.

The treaty was at length concluded, and signed by the ministers of each power on the 30th day of April, 1803. By this treaty the first consul, in consideration of the foregoing sums to be paid by the United States, and certain commercial privileges to French and Spanish commerce, ceded to them forever, in full sovereignty, the province of Louisiana, with all its rights and appurtenances in full, and in the same manner as they had been acquired by the Republic from his Catholic majesty.* The first consul obligated himself to give possession by formal delivery of the province within six·months from the date of the treaty. Such had been the negotiations in Europe to settle the political destiny of Louisiana.

In the mean time, the Spanish authorities of Louisiana, ignorant of the transfer of the province to the United States, had been making every preparation for the reception of the French commissioner, and for the delivery of the province to him in the name of the French Republic. General Victor had been appointed commissioner on the part of the French Republic for receiving possession of Louisiana, and was daily expected, with the French troops under his command; but on the 24th of March a vessel arrived from Havre de Grace, having on board the baggage of M. Laussat, the colonial prefect, who was to precede the captain-general and commissioner, with a special mission for providing supplies for the troops, and making arrangements for the organization of the new government under the authority of the Republic. The same vessel brought intelligence of the form of government which had been provided for the province under its new master. The principal executive officers were to be a captain-general, a colonial prefect, and a commissary of justice.

The captain-general was to be invested with all the powers heretofore exercised by governors-general under the Spanish dominion. In his absence, the duties of his office were to devolve upon the colonial prefect, or upon the highest military officer.†

The colonial prefect was invested with authority to control

tion of the year 1800, and also to exempt the productions, manufactures, and vessels of France and Spain, in the direct trade from those countries respectively, to all the ports of the ceded territory, for a term of twelve years.—Martin, vol. ii., p. 192.

* See Martin, vol. ii., 190–192. † Idem, p. 182, 183.

and administer the finances, and to supervise the acts of all the officers of the administration; powers similar, and more extensive than those heretofore exercised by the Spanish intendant, including those exercised, also, by the former French commissaries-general and ordonnateurs.

The commissary of justice was to be clothed with authority to superintend all the courts of justice, and the ministerial duties of all officers of the law; to preside and vote in any court; to regulate the conduct of all clerks and officers of the courts; to superintend the preparation of a civil and criminal code; to make monthly reports upon all these matters to the captain-general, or to the minister.*

Such was the outline of the government designed for Louisiana under the authority of the first consul; a form of government which had not gone fully into operation when it was superseded by the jurisdiction of the United States.

About the same time a French national vessel had arrived at the Balize, with M. Laussat, the colonial prefect, on board. Upon intelligence of this arrival, Governor Salcedo dispatched the government barge under Morales, with a captain and lieutenant of infantry, to congratulate and welcome the representative of the French Republic, and to escort him to the city. He arrived on the 26th of March, and was conducted to the government-house, where he met a cordial reception from Salcedo and Morales, surrounded by the staff of the regular army and of the militia, and by the heads of the clergy. At this interview, M. Laussat announced the determination of the French Republic to use every effort to promote the prosperity of the province; to preserve order; to maintain the laws; to respect the treaties with the Indian tribes; and to protect public worship without any change of religion. He also informed those present that the land and naval forces under General Victor had sailed from Holland, as he supposed, about the last of January, and would, in all probability, reach New Orleans before the middle of April.† Great joy was evinced by the French population at the prospect of a speedy reunion with France.

A few days afterward, the colonial prefect issued a proclamation in the name of the French Republic. In this, after alluding to the weak and corrupt government which, nearly forty years before, after an ignominious war, had yielded to a

---

* See Martin, vol. ii., p. 185.   † Idem, p. 185, 186.

dishonorable peace, with the separation of Louisiana from France, he informed the people that France was again triumphant, and that, amid the prodigious victories and triumphs of the late Revolution, France and all Frenchmen had cast an affectionate eye to estranged Louisiana, and that the fond mother was again about to embrace her long-lost offspring, and wipe out the disgrace of the former separation; that he who now controlled the destinies of France was no less remarkable for the love and confidence inspired by his wisdom, and the happiness of his people, than for the terror infused into his enemies by the rapidity and irresistible glory of his victories; and that the whole energies of his great mind would be devoted to the happiness and prosperity of the people of Louisiana, and to the development of the unbounded natural resources peculiar to the province. He concluded by a flattering encomium upon the fidelity, courage, and patriotism of the people of Louisiana, to whom he recommended the worthy and highly honorable magistrates with whom he was associated in the government.*

A few days afterward, M. Laussat received an address, signed by a number of the most respectable citizens of the city and province, expressing in very flattering terms, in behalf of the people, the joy inspired by his arrival, as the harbinger of their deliverance and reunion with France.†

On the 10th of April, the Marquis de Casa Calvo, having been associated with Salcedo as commissioner on the part of Spain for the delivery of Louisiana, returned from a visit to Havana, and entered upon the duties of his office.

On the 18th of May Salcedo issued his proclamation announcing the intention of his Catholic majesty to surrender the province to the French Republic; but that his paternal regard would accompany the people, as he had made ample arrangements with the latter for their protection and future prosperity.

In this proclamation the governor recited the limits of Louisiana, as embraced in the contemplated surrender, to include all Louisiana west of the Mississippi and the Island of New Orleans on the east side, it being the same ceded to Spain by France at the peace of 1763. The settlements on the east side of the Mississippi, between the Bayou Manchac and the thirty-first parallel of latitude, would still pertain to the government of West Florida.‡ This was the Spanish construction of the

* Martin, vol. ii., p. 187, 188. † Idem. ‡ Idem, p. 189.

limits of Louisiana; but the United States subsequently claimed other territory east of the Mississippi.

Every thing now seemed ready for the formal delivery of the province, awaiting only the arrival of General Victor with the troops. The tri-colored cockade was already in the hands of hundreds, ready to be attached to every hat as soon as the French flag should supersede that of Spain, and each Frenchman considered himself a member of the French Republic.

The first of June arrived, and no tidings were received of the approach of General Victor. At length a vessel from Bordeaux brought intelligence that the province had been sold by the first consul, Bonaparte, to the United States.*

In the mean time, Bonaparte, having declined sending General Victor and his troops to Louisiana, had made other provision for the delivery of the province. On the sixth day of June, he had appointed M. Laussat as commissioner on the part of France for receiving the formal delivery of Louisiana. To him, also, were sent instructions for the transfer of the same into the hands of the American commissioners, agreeably to the treaty of April 30th, 1803.†

The government of the United States, in the mean time, had taken measures to secure the prompt delivery of the province, and the extension of the Federal jurisdiction over the country. Large bodies of troops had been concentrating in the southern

* Martin, vol. ii., p. 190.

† 1. The treaty of Paris included in the cession of Louisiana all the islands adjacent to Louisiana; all public lots, squares, vacant lands; all public buildings, barracks, forts, and fortifications; all archives, public papers, and documents relating to the domain and sovereignty of the province.

2. It is also provided that the inhabitants of the ceded territory shall be incorporated into the Federal Union, and as soon as possible they shall be admitted to the enjoyment of all the rights and immunities of citizens of the United States, under the provisions of the Federal Constitution.

3. France is to appoint a commissioner, and send him to Louisiana for the purpose of receiving possession of the province from Spain, and to deliver it over, in the name of the French Republic, to the commissioners, or agents of the United States.

4. Immediately after the formal transfer and delivery to the United States, the commissioner of France is to deliver up all military posts in New Orleans and throughout the province, and withdraw the troops of France.

5. Commercial privileges were to be extended by the United States to French and Spanish ships entering the ports of Louisiana for twelve years, during which they were to pay no higher duties than citizens of the United States coming directly from the same countries.

6. By two separate articles of convention, of the same date with the treaty, the conditions for the payments severally to be made to the French Republic and to the American citizens are fully set forth.—See Martin's Louisiana, vol. ii., p. 191, 192. Also, Marbois's Louisiana, p. 403–412.

portion of the Mississippi Territory, north of the West Florida line, in the vicinity of Natchez and Fort Adams.

Only a few months had elapsed when the unwelcome intelligence of the cession to the United States reached the King of Spain. Indignant at the contemplated transfer, he instructed his minister at Washington City, the Marquis de Casa Yurujo, to remonstrate with the government, and to file with the Department of State his formal protest against the transfer; representing the conditions on which it had been transferred to the first consul, which would now impair the claim of the United States; for the first consul had stipulated with his Catholic majesty that Louisiana never should be alienated from France.

The Federal government disregarded the remonstrance and protest of the Spanish court; yet the first consul, as well as the President of the United States, upon this ground entertained serious apprehensions lest the King of Spain should carry out his opposition by instructing the governor and captain-general of Louisiana to refuse the formal transfer and delivery of the province.*

Anticipating such opposition from the King of Spain, and for the purpose of meeting any contingency on this ground, Mr. Jefferson, President of the United States, convened Congress about the middle of October, and laid the whole matter of the treaty relative to the purchase of Louisiana before the Senate. The treaty was ratified on the 21st of October, and after due deliberation, Congress resolved to sustain the president in his views of urging the transfer and delivery, agreeably to the stipulations of treaty with the French Republic. By an act passed October 30th, the president was authorized to take possession of the ceded territory, and to maintain over the same the authority of the United States, under such persons as he might au-

* The American minister had been instructed to ascertain from the Spanish court whether any such order was likely to be given: the possibility of a refusal on the part of the Spanish authorities to surrender to the United States had been suggested to the first consul; but he declared that no refusal on their part need be apprehended; that he would permit no such thing, and that he guarantied the delivery. No indication of the kind was evinced at any subsequent period of the transactions; and early in January following, several weeks after the final transfer and delivery to the United States, the Spanish minister at Washington gave assurance to the Department of State that his sovereign had given no order whatever for opposing the delivery of Louisiana, and the rumor to that effect of the preceding year was entirely groundless. The minister added, that he was commanded to make it known that his majesty had since thought it proper to renounce his protest, although made justly and upon proper grounds; thus affording "a new proof of his benevolence and friendship for the United States."—See Martin, vol. ii., p. 239.

thorize to exercise a provisional civil and military jurisdiction in the province. To this end he was empowered to employ such portion of the navy and army of the United States, and of the militia of the neighboring states and territories, as he might deem requisite.*

The president proceeded to complete his arrangements for the delivery, final transfer, and occupation of the province by the United States. On the part of the United States, the commissioners appointed by him were Governor William C. C. Claiborne, of the Mississippi Territory, and General James Wilkinson, commander-in-chief of the army. Governor Claiborne was also authorized to exercise provisionally all the civil authority pertaining to the former Spanish governor and intendant, for the preservation of order and the protection of persons and property.†

The colonial prefect, and commissioner on the part of the French Republic, M. Laussat, had remained in Louisiana from the period of his arrival in March, engaged in the duties of his commission, preparing the minds of the people for the approaching change of government, first as a province of France, and finally as a dependence of the American Republic.

At length, further delay being unnecessary, the ceremonies and formality of delivery from the crown of Spain to the French Republic were, by appointment, to take place in the city of New Orleans on the 30th day of November. On the morning of that day the Spanish flag was displayed from a lofty flag-staff in the center of the public square. At noon the Spanish regiment of Louisiana and a company of Mexican dragoons were drawn up before the City Hall, on the right, and the militia of the city on the left. The commissioners of Spain, Governor Salcedo and the Marquis de Casa Calvo, proceeded to the front of the City Hall, where they were soon afterward joined by the French commissioner, M. Laussat. The latter produced an order from his Catholic majesty directing the delivery of the province of Louisiana to the authorized agent of the first consul. Salcedo, in exchange, immediately presented him with the keys of the city. The Marquis de Casa Calvo then proclaimed that those of his majesty's subjects who preferred to

---

* Martin, vol. ii., p. 193. See, also, Marbois, p. 322–324.

† Martin, vol. ii., p. 193. See, also, American State Papers, folio edition, vol. on Foreign Affairs, p. 61, 62. Also, Stoddart's Sketches, p. 103.

remain under the authority of the French Republic were henceforth absolved from their allegiance to the crown of Spain. The three commissioners then advanced to the main balcony in front of the City Hall, when the Spanish flag gradually descended during the salute of a discharge of artillery. The flag of France soon afterward ascended to the head of the flag-staff, saluted by another discharge of artillery. Thus terminated the Spanish dominion in Louisiana, after a lapse of more than thirty-four years.*

The dominion of France had again resumed its sway, and M. Laussat immediately issued his proclamation to the people. It informed them that the mission on which he came to Louisiana had given rise to many fond hopes and honorable expectations in his mind relative to their reunion with the mother country; but the face of things had changed, and he now was commissioned shortly to perform a duty which, although less pleasing to him, was far more advantageous to them; that although the flag of the French Republic was displayed, and the sound of her cannon had announced the return of the French dominion, it was comparatively for a moment, for he was shortly to deliver the province into the hands of the commissioners of the United States.†

In reference to this change, he remarked, that circumstances of great moment had given a new direction to the benevolent views and intentions of France toward Louisiana; that the province had been ceded to the United States, as the surest pledge of increasing friendship between the two Republics, and of the future aggrandizement of Louisiana. He drew their attention to that provision in the treaty of cession which secured to them the rank of an independent member of the Federal Union, and congratulated them upon the happy result of becoming an important part of a nation which had already become powerful, and distinguished for their industry, patriotism, and intelligence. He alluded to that feature in the new arrangement which would place the government in their own hands, secure from the cupidity and malversation in office of those sent to govern them from a remote parent-country, surrounded by facilities of concealment operating as a temptation, which too often corrupts the most virtuous rulers. They were about to pass under a government which made all its rulers

* Martin, vol. ii., p. 195. † Idem, p. 195, 196.

dependent upon the will of the people, expressed through their suffrages at the ballot-box. He adverted to the many advantages of a free and independent form of government, affording to them the immense facilities of the trade which their location near the outlet of the Mississippi would throw into their hands ; the trade of the great river of the United States, bearing upon its surface the wealth of rich and populous states, and conferring upon them commercial advantages and privileges which they could not possibly enjoy under the colonial government of France.*

The same day M. Laussat, as colonial prefect, issued a number of proclamations and orders in relation to the government of the province, abolishing the old regnancy, and substituting the jurisdiction of France and the forms of the French jurisprudence. The Cabaldo was abolished, and a municipality was organized in its stead. The municipality consisted of a mayor and two adjuncts, with ten members. The office of mayor was conferred upon M. Boré, and that of adjuncts upon M. Destrehan and M. Sauve. The members appointed were, Messieurs Livaudais, Petit Cavelier, Villière, Jones, Fortier, Donaldson, Faurie, Allard, Tuveaud, and Watkins. M. Derbigny was appointed secretary, and M. Labatut was treasurer.†

The Black Code, except such portions as were incompatible with the Constitution and laws of the United States, was declared to be still in force.

Soon afterward, the Spanish troops were withdrawn, and the military posts were evacuated. In the city and suburbs of New Orleans there were four military posts, or forts, relinquished by the Spanish troops, which might be exposed to the depredations, and equally so to the unlawful occupancy of disaffected persons and nocturnal disturbers of the peace. The troops of the United States designed for the occupation of these forts not having arrived within the limits of the ceded province, many were apprehensive of outrage and violence from the numbers of lawless and disaffected populace. These were composed of the lowest class of Spaniards, Mexicans, and free persons of color which infested the city, and other disorderly persons, and desperadoes of all nations, who, released from the restraint of a standing army, might be prompted, by the hope of pillage, to fire the city, or to commit other violence.

* Martin, vol. ii., p. 196.   † Idem, p. 197.

To guard against any such attempt, and to preserve order in the city, a number of enterprising young Americans associated themselves into a volunteer battalion, to be placed under the command of Daniél Clarke, junior, the American consul. Their first muster was at Davis's rope-walk, on Canal-street, where they were joined by a number of patriotic young Creole Frenchmen, who continued to serve until the battalion was finally discharged. Having organized, they placed themselves under their commander, and proceeded to the headquarters of the colonial prefect, and made a formal tender of their services for the purpose of preserving order in the city, and for the occupancy of the forts until the arrival of the American commissioners and troops. The battalion continued to increase, by the voluntary enrollment of Americans and French Creoles, until the entire number exceeded three hundred men. The Americans were chiefly captains and mates of vessels, supercargoes, merchants, clerks, and seamen belonging to vessels in port. The French, by their zeal, vigilance, and patriotism during their term of service, proved themselves worthy of American citizenship.[*]

Their services were gladly accepted, and detachments from their number were detailed upon regular tours of duty in patrolling the city by day and by night, and in maintaining guard in the forts, until the 17th of December, when the American troops had arrived in the vicinity of the city.[†]

In the mean time, Governor Claiborne had been preparing to advance down to New Orleans to consummate the delivery of

---

[*] This volunteer battalion was formed at the instance of the following gentlemen, then resident in New Orleans, viz.: George Martin, since parish judge of St. Landry, Colonel Reuben Kemper, George King, George Newman, Benjamin Morgan, Daniel Clarke, American consul, Dr. William Flood, since a distinguished physician of New Orleans, Maunsel White, and Woodson Wren, present postmaster in Natchez. But few of the original members of the battalion are living at this time, which is now forty-one years since the delivery of Louisiana to the United States commissioners. There were two of the survivors still living in Adams county, Mississippi, in February, 1845. These are Woodson Wren and George Newman. Martin states this battalion to have been composed of only one hundred and twenty Americans; but Dr. Wren and George Newman, Esq., both members of the battalion, sustain the authority of the text.

[†] The city was defended by four strong forts, situated at each corner, and nearly half a mile apart. Forts St. Charles and St. Louis were regular fortresses, above and below the city, near the bank of the river. Each was built of brick, surrounded by a ditch and glacis; the ditch was deep and filled with water, over which were drawbridges. Those in the rear of the city were regular stockades, securely fortified. These forts were thrown open and evacuated by the Spanish garrisons upon the surrender of the province to the French prefect.

Louisiana to the Federal government. Five hundred Tennessee militia, under Colonel Dougherty, had advanced as far as Natchez, where they were awaiting further orders. The volunteer troop of the Mississippi Territory had received orders to hold themselves in readiness to march on the 10th of December, in company with the volunteers from Tennessee.

At Fort Adams, Governor Claiborne met with his colleague, General Wilkinson, who had just returned from a tour in the Choctâ nation. The troops at this post were put in motion, and pursued their march with the volunteers toward New Orleans. On the 17th of December, they encamped within two miles of the city. On the following day the commissioners, Claiborne and Wilkinson, presented themselves to the French prefect in a formal introductory visit, which was returned at the American camp next day by the colonial prefect, attended by the municipality and a number of militia officers. The following Monday, December 20th, was fixed as the day for the formal delivery of the province to the United States.*

On Monday morning, at sunrise, the tri-colored flag was elevated to the summit of the flag-staff in the public square. At eleven o'clock A.M. the militia paraded near it, and precisely at noon the commissioners of the United States, at the head of the American troops, entered the city. The regular troops formed on the opposite side of the square, facing the militia. At this time the colonial prefect, attended by his secretary and a number of French citizens, advanced from his quarters to the City Hall, saluted as he approached by a discharge of artillery. At the City Hall a large concourse of the most respectable citizens awaited his approach. Here, in the presence of the assembled multitude, the prefect delivered to the American commissioners the keys of the city, emblematic of the formal delivery of the province.†

He then declared that such of the inhabitants as desired to pass under the government of the United States were absolved from their allegiance to the French Republic.

Governor Claiborne then arose and offered to the people of Louisiana his congratulations on the auspicious event which had placed them beyond the reach of chance. He assured them that the people of the United States received them as brothers, and would hasten to extend to them the benefits of the free in-

* Martin, vol. ii., p. 198. † Idem, p. 199.

stitutions which had formed the basis of our unexampled prosperity, and that, in the mean time, they should be protected in their liberty, their property, and their religion; their agriculture should be encouraged, and their commerce favored.

The tri-colored flag of France slowly descended, meeting the rising flag of the United States at half-mast. After the pause of a few minutes, the flag of France descended to the ground, and the star-spangled banner rose to the summit of the flag-staff, saluted by the roar of artillery and the joyful response of the American people, accompanied by a full band of martial music to the air of "Hail Columbia."* The windows, balconies, and corridors of the vicinity were crowded with "ladies, brilliant beyond comparison," each with the American flag in miniature proudly waving over their heads.

The same day Governor Claiborne issued his proclamation announcing the supremacy of the Federal jurisdiction over the province, and the termination of all foreign dominion. He exhorted the people to be firm in their allegiance to the government of the United States, and obedient to the laws which were to be extended over them; he assured them that their liberty, their rights, and their property should be protected against all violence from any quarter, and that in due time they should be entitled to all the rights and privileges of an independent state government.

[A.D. 1804.] The formal delivery of the remote posts and their dependencies took place during the following spring. On the 12th of January the post of Concord was delivered, with great ceremony and form, by the Spanish commandant, Stephen Minor, into the hands of Major Ferdinand L. Claiborne, special agent of the French colonial prefect, and agent of Governor Claiborne, in behalf of the United States. Having been duly authorized for this purpose, Major Claiborne, accompanied by a detachment of Tennessee volunteers under Captain Russel, and the volunteer company of Captain Nicholls from Natchez, and a procession of the citizens of Natchez, headed by the mayor of the city, presented himself before the fort, which was formally delivered by the exchange of flags, with the usual interchange of ceremonies by the respective commandants.†

A few days afterward, the post of Washita was delivered in

---

* Martin's Louisiana, vol. ii., p. 199. Also, Natchez Herald, January 3d, 1804.
† See Natchez Herald, January 14th, 1804.

like manner by the Spanish commandant, Don Vincente Francisco Fejeiro, to Captain Bomar, agent of the United States. On the 9th of March the post of St. Louis, with the province of Upper Louisiana, was formally delivered by the Spanish lieutenant-governor to Major Amos Stoddart, commissioned as representative of the French Republic, in which capacity, on the following day, he formally delivered the post and district to the agent of the United States. Major Stoddart having been appointed also civil and military commandant of Upper Louisiana, with the authority and prerogatives of the former Spanish lieutenant-governor, immediately entered upon the duties of his office.* In his proclamation he adverted to the auspicious events which had made them a portion of the American Republic, and had elevated them from the rank of colonial subjects to free and independent citizens, the rights and privileges of which would be soon extended to them. He expressed his confidence in their patriotism and submission to the laws; the prejudices and resentments of former times had been buried in oblivion, and they were now united to the great Republican family by a bond of mutual interest, for the advancement of the common happiness, and a generous rivalry for commercial prosperity and national independence.

Thus the authority of the United States was peaceably extended over the whole province of Louisiana, comprising one of the most fertile and magnificent regions on earth, whose limits had never been definitively established. It was the interest of Spain to restrict its limits as much as practicable, and it was the interest of the United States to construe its boundaries with the utmost latitude.

The West Florida district lying south of the line of demarkation, and west of the Perdido River and Bay, was retained by Spain as a portion of Florida. The western portion of this district, lying between the Mississippi and Pearl Rivers, was erected into the "Government of Baton Rouge," which was administered by the lieutenant-governor, Don Carlos de Grandpré, comprising the posts of Manchac, Thompson's Creek, and Bayou Sara, until the 7th of December, 1810, when the people renounced the dominion of Spain, and claimed the protection of the United States.†

---

* Stoddart's Sketches of Louisiana, p. 106, 107.
† See book v., chapter xv., "Territory of Orleans," &c.

Hence the difficulties relative to boundaries between Spain and the United States were again opened. Spain still held dominion over the Mexican provinces west of Louisiana, and over the Floridas on the east. The western limits of Florida, previous to the peace of 1763, were the *Perdido* River and Bay; the territory west of the Perdido, and north of the Bayou Iberville and lakes, previous to 1763, had been a portion of Louisiana under the dominion of France, and was never attached to Spanish Florida. By the dismemberment of 1763, Great Britain became possessed of this portion of Louisiana; and by the king's order in council in the following year, it was annexed to the government of West Florida, and as such it was subsequently ceded to Spain by the treaty of 1783. This was the origin of the Spanish claim to the territory west of Mobile.

The United States purchased Louisiana with the boundaries acknowledged while in possession of France originally, before the dismemberment, and with such boundaries as properly pertained to it, after the due observance of all subsequent treaties. Hence the United States claimed Louisiana as extending to the Perdido on the east, and north to the southern limit of the United States, as established by the treaty of 1783. On the west side of the Mississippi they claimed to the Rio del Norte, the western boundary claimed by France previous to the treaty of 1762 with Spain. Thus the United States claimed Louisiana as comprising the whole country on the Gulf of Mexico, from the Bay of Mobile inclusive to the western limit of Texas.*

The population of the province of Louisiana, near the close of the year 1803, according to a report made to the Secretary of State by the American consul at New Orleans, gives a grand total of about forty-nine thousand and five hundred souls, including the West Florida district and the ports of Mobile and Pensacola. Of this amount, the city of New Orleans contained about eight thousand souls; Mobile and its dependencies eight hundred and ten souls; Pensacola four hundred and four souls; Baton Rouge and Galveston one thousand seven hundred and sixty souls; Upper Louisiana six thousand and twenty-eight souls, the same as it contained in 1799.† These estimates, of course, exclude the numerous tribes and remnants of native Indians remaining in different portions of the province.

The commerce and trade of New Orleans had become extens-

---

* Martin, vol. ii., p. 201, 202.   Stoddart, p. 112–114.   † Martin, vol. ii., p. 205.

ive, not only with foreign countries and European colonies, but especially with the Atlantic ports of the United States, and the Western States upon the waters of the Ohio. During the year 1802, two hundred and fifty vessels of all kinds entered the Mississippi all of which were merchantmen, except eighteen public armed vessels. Of the former, one hundred and seventy were American, and ninety-seven were Spanish.* The river trade from the Western States and Upper Louisiana was conveyed in not less than five hundred flat-boats and barges annually.

The annual products of agriculture in Louisiana had already become extensive and valuable, consisting chiefly of sugar and cotton. Both these products had increased greatly within the last few years. The cotton crop of 1802 yielded twenty thousand bales, each weighing about three hundred pounds; the sugar crop of the same year yielded five thousand hogsheads of sugar, weighing each about one thousand pounds, and five thousand casks of molasses, each containing about fifty gallons. The indigo crop had diminished gradually to about three thousand pounds.†

Manufactures, connected with the agricultural products of the province, had begun to assume a permanent footing near the city of New Orleans. About one dozen distilleries for the manufacture of taffia from molasses were in operation, producing about two hundred thousand gallons of this liquor annually. One sugar-refinery in the city likewise produced annually nearly two hundred thousand pounds of loaf-sugar. But few manufactories of importance existed in other branches of business.

The trade of New Orleans comprised not only the products of Louisiana, but also of the Western States and territories. The exports of 1802, including the western products, amounted to forty thousand tons. It consisted chiefly of flour, pork, salt beef, tobacco, cotton, sugar, molasses, peltries, naval stores, and lumber. The principal articles were as follows: fifty thousand barrels of flour, three thousand barrels of salt beef and pork, two thousand hogsheads of tobacco, thirty-four thousand bales of cotton, four thousand hogsheads of sugar, and eight hundred casks of molasses.‡

The whole province of Louisiana was now a dependency of the United States, under the government of the Federal au-

---

* Martin, vol. ii., p. 234.   † Idem, p. 234.   ‡ Idem, p. 236.

thorities, until provision should be made for organizing the population into a regular system of Republican government, agreeably to the Constitution and laws of the United States. The first legislation of Congress on this subject was an act for the organization of a territorial government within the "Territory of Orleans."*

* See vol. ii., book v., chap. xv., for the continuation of the history of Louisiana under the United States, the organization of the " *Territory of Orleans,*" and the admission of the " *State of Louisiana*" into the Union.

END OF VOL. I.

HISTORY

OF THE

DISCOVERY AND SETTLEMENT

OF

THE VALLEY OF THE MISSISSIPPI,

BY

THE THREE GREAT EUROPEAN POWERS,

SPAIN, FRANCE, AND GREAT BRITAIN,

AND

THE SUBSEQUENT OCCUPATION, SETTLEMENT, AND EXTENSION OF
CIVIL GOVERNMENT BY

THE UNITED STATES,

UNTIL THE YEAR 1846.

BY

JOHN W. MONETTE, M.D.

"Westward the star of empire takes its way."

IN TWO VOLUMES.
VOL. II.

HARPER & BROTHERS, PUBLISHERS,
82 CLIFF STREET, NEW YORK.
1846.

Entered, according to Act of Congress, in the year 1846,
By HARPER & BROTHERS,
In the Clerk's Office of the Southern District of New York.

CONTENTS OF VOL. II.

BOOK V.
THE UNITED STATES IN THE VALLEY OF THE MISSISSIPPI.

CHAPTER I.
MANNERS AND CUSTOMS OF THE FRONTIER POPULATION EAST AND SOUTH OF THE OHIO RIVER.—A.D. 1770 TO 1810.

Argument.—Condition of the frontier Settlements of western Pennsylvania and Virginia. — Characteristic Traits of the Pioneers generally. — *Manners and Customs:* 1. *Costume* of the Hunters: the Hunting-shirt; Pantaloons; Breech-cloth and Leggins; Moccasin. — 2. *Habitation:* the Log Cabin; its Location; internal Appearance.—3. *Employments:* the respective Duties of Man and Wife.—4. *Diet:* Meats; wild Game; Bread; Pone; Journey-cake; Hog and Hommony; Substitutes for Tea and Coffee.—5. *Settlement Rights:* Nature and Extent; tomahawk Improvements. —6. *Fort, or Station:* Form and Construction; its Location and Use; Stations in Kentucky.—7. *Hunters:* Science of Hunting; a hunting Camp; Game; Hides; Peltries.—8. *Caravans:* annual Trips to Baltimore and Frederic; Equipment of Caravan; solitary Route across the Mountains; Order of March; Fare.—9. *The moral Sense:* state of Morals; natural Honesty and Sense of Honor the supreme Law; force of Public Opinion; "Lynch Law;" "Regulators."—10. *Social Virtues:* Hospitality; Sociality; Conviviality; a marriage Party; Sports and Amusements.—11. *Boatmen:* general Character; Costume; Habits; peculiar Traits of Character.—12. *National Character:* Diversity of People and Languages blended; Peculiarities of Feelings and Habits neutralized; Influence of free Government upon the Enterprise and moral Character.—13. *Religious Traits:* Religion disconnected with civil Power; Ministers dependent for Support upon their own Merit; religious "Awakenings," or "Revivals," in the West; "Camp-meeting" Scene; Origin of Camp Meetings in Kentucky and Tennessee; Camp Meeting at Cane Ridge; at Desha's Creek; at Cabin Creek; astonishing Influence of sylvan Preaching, and the attendant Circumstances; extraordinary Conversions; Disturbance of mental and nervous Systems

Page 1

CHAPTER II.
INDIAN WARFARE, AND ITS EFFECTS UPON THE FRONTIER PEOPLE. —EMINENT PIONEERS OF KENTUCKY.—A.D. 1775 TO 1794.

Argument.—Man in his natural Condition the Creature of Circumstances, in Habits, Feeling, and Character.—The hostile Attitude and Jealousy of the Six Nations.— Their Neutrality secured by "Treaty of German Flats," in 1776.—Indians paid to violate treaty Stipulations by the British Commissioners at Oswego in 1777, and take up Arms against the frontier People.—The frontier People become daring and vindictive.—Influence of Indian Warfare upon Manners and Usages of the Whites.— Compelled to adopt the Indian Revenge.—Volunteer Defense of the West.—Personal Characteristics of frontier Soldiers. — Athletic Form and Strength.—Patience of Toil and Privation.—Recuperative Powers of the System.—State of Feeling on the Frontiers.—Exterminating Policy of Indians.—Cruelty of British Tories.—Spirit of Revenge in the People.—Their domestic Enjoyments.—Indian scalping Parties on

the Frontier.—Their cautious and destructive Movements.—Renegade white Men associated with Indians.
Indian Implements of War.—The Rifle.—The Scalping-knife.—Tomahawk.—Battle-ax.—War-club.—Declaration of War.—*Torture.*—Running the Gantlet.—Torture at the Stake by Fire.
Eminent Pioneers of Kentucky.—1. Daniel Boone.—His Nativity and early Habits.—Personal Traits of Character.—His first Acquaintance with Kentucky in 1769 and 1771.—At Watauga in 1775.—Opens a Road from Holston to Kentucky River.—Captain at Boonesborough until 1778.—Captured by Indians at Blue Licks.—His Captivity and Escape.—An active Defender of Kentucky until 1783.—Abandons Kentucky in 1800.—Settles in Missouri.—His Remains and those of his Wife removed to Kentucky in 1845.—2. Simon Kenton.—His Character as a fearless Pioneer.—Nativity and Early Habits.—Youthful Indiscretion and subsequent Hardships.—A Hunter in Kentucky.—A Hunter in Western Virginia.—Attached to Dunmore's Army.—Becomes "a Hunter of Kentucky."—His personal Appearance at the Age of twenty-one Years.—His benevolent Disposition.—Attached to Kentucky Stations.—Accompanies Colonel Clark to Kaskaskia.—Returns to Harrod's Station.—Visits the Paint Creek Towns.—Captured by Indians.—Wild Horse Torture.—Divers Tortures and Punishments suffered during his Captivity.—Sold in Detroit.—Escapes to Kentucky.—Serves under Colonel Clark in 1780 and 1782.—An active partisan Warrior until 1792.—Encounters *Tecumseh*.—Serves in Wayne's Army.—Abandons Kentucky in 1802.—Removes to Ohio.—Serves under Colonel Shelby in 1813.—Died in 1836.—3. Robert Patterson.—Nativity, early Life, and Habits.—Serves in Dunmore's Army.—A prominent Pioneer of Kentucky in 1776.—Erects a Station on the Site of Lexington in 1779.—Active Defender of Kentucky during the Indian War.—4. Major George Rogers Clark.—His early frontier Services.—His Character and Military Genius.—Superintends the Defense of Kentucky from 1776 to 1782.—Reduction of British Posts in 1778, 1779 . . . . Page 30

CHAPTER III.

EXTENSION OF VIRGINIA SETTLEMENTS AND JURISDICTION TO THE MISSISSIPPI.—INDIAN HOSTILITIES UPON THE OHIO.—A.D. 1776 TO 1780.

Argument.—Retrospect of the frontier Settlements of Western Virginia, Pennsylvania, North Carolina, and Kentucky in 1776.—Check to these Settlements by hostile Cherokees.—Cherokee War.—Three-fold Invasion of Cherokee Country.—" Treaty of Dewett's Corner."—" Treaty of Long Island," on Holston.—Cherokees retire from ceded Territory.—Hostilities of Northwestern Tribes.—Kentucky Stations supplied with Powder by Major Clark.—Posts on the Ohio.—Attack on M'Clellan's Station, December, 1776.—Hostilities in West Augusta.—County of Kentucky erected.—Militia Organization in 1777.—District of West Augusta divided into three Counties.—Ohio County organized.—Settlements in West Augusta.—The Indians attack Harrod's Station; also, Logan's Fort and Boonesborough.—Militia organization in Ohio County.—Memorable Siege of Boonesborough from July 4th to September.—Captain Logan's Re-enforcement from North Carolina.—Colonel John Bowman's Re-enforcement.—County of Kentucky organized.—Militia Organization.—Extent of Kentucky County.—Colonel Henderson indemnified for Loss of Transylvania.—Indian Hostilities near the Ohio.—Cornstalk, Ellinipsico, and Red Hawk killed at Point Pleasant.—Condition of Wheeling Fort.—" Fort Henry."—Situation and Importance of this Fort.—Attacked by four hundred Indians under Simon Girty.—Loss of the Garrison near the Fort.—Incidents of Indian Warfare.—Major M'Cullock.—Captain Mason.—Major Clark plans the Reduction of Kaskaskia.—The Expedition proceeds from "the Falls."—Surprise and Capture of Kaskaskia and "Fort Gage."—Suspension of Civil Government in West Augusta.—Martial Law suspended.—Courts organized.—Attorneys and Attorney-general.— Daniel Boone and twenty-seven Men captured at

CONTENTS. vii

Blue Licks.—His Captivity among the Indians.—His Escape and Return to Boonesborough.—Makes an Incursion to Paint Creek.—Boonesborough invested by large Indian Force, August, 1778.—Defense and Incidents of the Siege.—" Fort M'Intosh" erected.—" Fort Laurens" erected.—Protracted Siege of Fort Laurens.—Court of Land Commissioners established in Kentucky, 1779.—First Settlement at Lexington, Bryant's Station, Forks of Licking, and on Sources of Salt River.—Massacre of Colonel Rodgers and ninety Men on the Ohio.—Colonel Bowman's unsuccessful Expedition to the Miami Towns.—Emigration to Kentucky.—Arrival of Immigrants in 1779. —Scarcity of Provisions.—Depreciation of Paper Currency.—Distress of Emigrants until 1780.—Defenses on the Ohio.—" Fort Nelson."—Colonel Slaughter.—Landed Interest in Kentucky.—The Indians capture Ruddle's and Martin's Stations, and retire.—Destruction of the Moravian Towns on the Coshocton.—Massacre of Captives and friendly Moravians.—Colonel Clark invades the Shawanese Country in 1780.— Militia Organization in 1780.—Colonel Clark erects "Fort Jefferson" on the Mississippi.—Southern Boundary of Virginia extended to the Mississippi . Page 80

CHAPTER IV.

INDIAN WARS ON THE OHIO. — EXTENSION OF THE AMERICAN SETTLEMENTS EAST AND SOUTH OF THE OHIO.—A.D. 1781 TO 1784.

Argument.—Severe Winter of 1780–81.—Scarcity in Kentucky.—Kentucky divided into three Counties.—Indian Hostilities on Bear-grass Creek.—Attack on Boone's and M'Afee's Stations.—Indians contemplate utter Destruction of Kentucky Settlements.—Chickasâs attack Fort Jefferson in 1780.—Counties of Kentucky organized. —General Clark's gun-boat Defense on the Ohio River.—Abundant Crops of 1781. —Indian Hostilities renewed in the Spring of 1782.—Estill's Defeat.—Last Survivor of his Party.—Indian Hostilities continued.—Laherty's Defeat.—Indian Invasion, under Simon Girty, on Bryant's Station.—Disastrous Battle of Blue Licks.—Colonel Logan buries the Dead. *Upper Ohio.*—Settlements of West Augusta harassed.— Wheeling Campaign against the Moravian Towns.—Horrible Massacre of peaceable Indians.—Former Position of the Moravian Towns.—Previous Admonitions neglected. —Disastrous Campaign against Moravians on Sandusky.—Colonel Crawford and Dr. Knight captured.—Execution and horrid Torture of Colonel Crawford.—British Agency the Source of Indian Hostilities.—Attack on Wheeling Fort, and on Rice's Fort. *Lower Ohio.*—General Clark invades the Indian Country in 1782.—Effects of this Invasion.—Domestic Prosperity of Kentucky.—Settlements extend North of Licking.—Flood of Emigration sets into Kentucky.—The "District of Kentucky" organized.—Peace with Great Britain announced.—Extent of the Kentucky Settlements in 1783.—Population and Moral Condition of the Settlements.—Settlements extend North of Licking River in 1784–85.—Settlements in Western Virginia . 119

CHAPTER V.

INDIAN HOSTILITIES ON THE OHIO.—PREDATORY INCURSIONS INTO KENTUCKY, AND PARTISAN WARFARE.—A.D. 1785 TO 1793.

Argument.—The Shawanese resume predatory Incursions.—Indian Horse-stealing.— Object and Extent of these Depredations.—The Continuance of them provokes Invasion of the Indian Country in 1786.—Plan of Campaign under General Clark and Colonel Logan.—Colonel Logan destroys Scioto and Mad River Towns.—General Clark advances to the Wabash.—His further Operations frustrated for Want of Supplies.—A Mutiny ensues.—He returns inglorious to Kentucky.—His Sun sets.—Virginia comes to his Relief.—The Shawanese commence active Hostilities.—Exposed Condition of Settlements in Mason County in 1787.—Colonel Todd invades the Paint Creek Towns.—Simon Kenton as a Partisan Warrior.—Emigration in 1788.—Indians harass the Ohio Frontier of Kentucky and Western Virginia.—Depredations and

CONTENTS.

Murders on the Ohio from 1788 to 1790.—Population of Kentucky in 1791.—Partisan Warfare from 1790 to 1791.—General Harmar's Efforts to suppress Indian Hostilities.—The Campaigns of 1790 and 1791 divert Hostilities from the Kentucky Frontier.—Indian Hostility and partisan Warfare in Kentucky renewed in 1792-93.—Kenton makes an Incursion upon the Little Miami, and encounters Tecumseh.—Severe night Skirmish with Tecumseh in 1792.—Kenton continues his partisan Warfare in 1793.—Makes an Incursion to Paint Creek.—Intercepts and kills a marauding Party of Indians at Holt's Creek on the Ohio, and recovers a large Number of Horses
Page 147

CHAPTER VI.

POLITICAL CONDITION OF THE "DISTRICT OF KENTUCKY," FROM 1783 UNTIL ITS ADMISSION INTO THE FEDERAL UNION AS AN INDEPENDENT STATE.—A.D. 1783 TO 1794.

Argument.—Retrospect of the political Condition of the District.—Causes for political Discontent.—The People desire an independent State Government.—*First* Convention in 1784.—*Second* Convention in May, 1785.—*Third* Convention recommended.—Great Emigration to Kentucky in 1786.—Improved Condition of the Kentucky Settlements in 1786.—Measures adopted by the third Convention.—Action of the Virginia Legislature in favor of Separation.—Requisite Action by Kentucky unavoidably delayed.—*Fourth* Convention appointed for August, 1787.—First Newspaper in Kentucky.—Agricultural and commercial Prosperity in 1787.—Navigation of the Mississippi commenced.—*Fifth* Convention held in September, 1787.—*Sixth* Convention in July, 1788.—Diversity of political Sentiment.—Political Parties.—Action of the sixth Convention.—Prominent Men.—Corresponding Action of the Virginia Legislature.—Final Action of this Convention, and Application for Assent of Congress.—Assent of Congress granted February 4th, 1791.—Boundaries of the new State.—First State Governor and Legislature convened June 4th, 1792, for the organization of State Government.—Causes of the protracted delay of Separation.—A new Experiment in Political Philosophy.—Notice of political Parties.—Foreign Influence.—Spanish Intrigue.—Increasing Trade with New Orleans.—The fluctuating Policy of Spain with regard to the Navigation of the Mississippi.—Genet's Intrigue for the Invasion of Louisiana in 1793-94.—Measures taken by the Federal Government to suppress the contemplated Invasion.—Reluctance of Governor Shelby to interfere in the Plans of Genet.—Increasing Population of Kentucky in 1794.—New Counties organized.—Kentucky levies for the Campaign in the Northwestern Territory.—Advantages derived by Kentucky from Treaties of London and Madrid.—Last Efforts of Spain to detach Kentucky from the Union.—Progressive Wealth and Population of Kentucky.—Governors of Kentucky 168

CHAPTER VII.

THE EARLY SETTLEMENT AND POLITICAL CONDITION OF WESTERN PENNSYLVANIA.—A.D. 1783 TO 1796.

Argument.—Jurisdiction of Pennsylvania extended to the Ohio.—"Westmoreland County" organized.—"Washington County" organized.—Emigration to the Monongahela and Youghiogeny.—Town of Pittsburgh laid out.—Brownsville laid out; becomes an important Point.—First Newspaper in the West.—Pittsburgh becomes a Market Town in 1788.—Trade and Manufactures spring up.—It derives great Importance as a military Dépôt in 1790.—Prosperous Condition of Settlements on the Monongahela.—Pittsburgh becomes an important manufacturing and trading Town.—Agricultural Prosperity of Monongahela Settlements.—Effects of Spanish Restrictions on the Mississippi.—"Excise Law" odious.—Disaffection toward Federal Government.—French Influence in the West.—Resistance to Excise on Whisky.—Difficulties encountered by excise Officers.—General Neville appointed Superintendent of excise Customs.—His moral Worth and Popularity insufficient to sustain him.—His House burned by a Mob.—Other Outrages perpetrated by the Mob.—Character of the Insurgents.—A Meeting of the Militia.—A Convention proposed.—Measures adopted by the President of the United States.—Proposed Amnesty.—Convention at Parkinson's Ferry.—Alarm of the insurgent Leaders.—Effects of General Wayne's Victory on the Maumee.—Commissioners appointed by the President.—Troops levied to suppress the Insurrection.—Fourteen thousand Troops advance to Pittsburgh.—The Insurrection is suppressed.—Insurgents dispersed.—Inquisitorial Court established.—Three hundred Insurgents arrested.—The Troops discharged.—Pittsburgh incorporated in 1794.—Quietude of Frontiers, and Advance of Population.—Uninhabited Region west of Alleghany River.—Emigration encouraged.—"Population Company."—Their Grant. — State Grants to actual Settlers. — Conflict of State Grants with the Company's Privileges.—First Paper Mill on the Monongahela.—Manufactures increase . . . . Page 192

CHAPTER VIII.

INDIAN RELATIONS AND TREATIES WITH THE UNITED STATES, FROM THE TREATY OF PARIS TO THE "TREATY OF GREENVILLE."—A.D. 1783 TO 1795.

Argument.—Retrospect relative to the Northwestern Boundary.—Reluctantly assented to in the Treaty of 1783 by Great Britain.—Disregard of Treaty Stipulations relative to the Northwestern Posts by British Cabinet.—British and Indian Alliance during the Revolutionary War.—Western Feeling toward the Indians.—Jealousy of the Indians at the rapid Advance of the White Settlements.—Measures of Congress to conciliate Indian Jealousy.—Preliminary Steps for Treaties with all the Tribes.—Treaties by individual States prior to 1784.—Treaty of Fort Stanwix, and the Treaty Line.—Treaty of Fort M'Intosh, and Boundary Line.—Treaty of the Miami with the Shawanese, and their Cession of Lands.—Treaties of Hopewell with Southern Indians.—Cherokee Treaty.—Choctâ Treaty.—Chickasâ Treaty.—Extent of Country and Number of Warriors of each Nation respectively.—Dissatisfaction of the Six Nations relative to the Treaty of Fort Stanwix.—Their Grievances.—Preparations for a new Treaty.—Treaty of Fort Harmar in 1789.—The Shawanese refuse to attend.—Shawanese encouraged to Hostilities by British Traders at Detroit.—Connivance of the British Government at these Intrigues.—Hostilities commenced upon the Ohio Frontier.—Pacific Overtures of Governor St. Clair.—Unsettled Condition of the Southern Indians.—The Cherokees.—Encroachments of the Cumberland Settlements.—Treaty of Holston, July 2d, 1791.—Creek Disturbances.—Measures to conciliate the Creeks.—The Treaty of New York with M'Gillivray and other Creek Chiefs.—Efforts of Spanish Agents to embarrass the Negotiations.—M'Gillivray's Opposition.—The Creeks instigated to War.—Cherokees commence Hostilities.—Spanish Intrigue with Creeks and Cherokees.—Creek Preparation for Hostilities against Cumberland Settlements.—Bowles, a Creek Chief.—Indian Tribes generally make Overtures for Peace and Friendship after Wayne's Victory.—Treaty with Six Nations in 1794.—Treaty of Greenville in 1795, comprising all Northwestern Tribes.—Termination of Indian Wars 212

CHAPTER IX.

EXTENSION OF THE FIRST WHITE SETTLEMENTS ACROSS THE OHIO, UNTIL THE CLOSE OF THE INDIAN WARS.—A.D. 1787 TO 1794.

Argument.—Claims of Virginia and other States to "Northwestern Territory" relinquished, with certain Reservations.—"Connecticut Reserve."—Virginia military District.—"Northwestern Territory" laid off by Ordinance of 1787.—Territorial Government provided.—Partial Occupation by United States.—First Settlement on the Muskingum.—Putnam's Colony, from Connecticut, arrives at Fort Harmar April 17th,

1788.—Character of the Colonists.—Second Colony arrives July 2d.—Celebration of 4th of July in the Wilderness.—First Clergyman, Daniel Story.—Governor St. Clair and territorial Officers arrive.—Territorial Government organized.—"Washington County" laid off.—Arrival of Emigrants.—*Campus Martius*.—Settlements formed at Belpre and Newberry.—Emigration to Kentucky.—Miami Settlements.—Symmes's Purchase on the Miami.—Settlement at Columbia.—Settlement at Cincinnati.—Fort Washington commenced.—Its Form and Dimensions.—" County of Hamilton" organized.—Squire M'Millan.—Colerain Settlement.—Headquarters established at Fort Washington.—" Knox County" organized.—"St. Clair County" organized.—Population of Settlements on Muskingum and Miami in 1790.—Indian Hostilities commence. —Defensive Measures adopted.—Indians exasperated at the unsuccessful Expedition of General Harmar.—Destruction of Settlement of Big Bottom, January 2d, 1791. —Attack on Wolf Creek Settlement.—Attack on Colerain Station.—Nathaniel Massie settles Manchester, on the Ohio.—French Settlement at Gallipolis, March, 1791. —Fraud of the "Scioto Company."—General St. Clair also unsuccessful.—Indian Audacity and Hostilities increase.—President Washington adopts more energetic Measures with the Indians.—Indian Outrages multiply in 1792.—Cincinnati in 1793. —Its Importance as a military Dépôt.—First Presbyterian Pastor.—Indian Hostilities in 1793.—Martial Law paramount.—First Newspaper in Northwestern Territory.—General Wayne takes Command of the Army.—Confidence restored to the western People.—Troops concentrate in the Miami Country.—Advanced Posts established.—Indians defeated and reduced to great Distress.—Settlements again advance . . . . Page 236

CHAPTER X.

EARLY SETTLEMENT AND INDIAN HOSTILITIES IN THE "SOUTH-WESTERN TERRITORY," UNTIL ITS ADMISSION INTO THE FEDERAL UNION AS THE STATE OF TENNESSEE.—A.D. 1776 TO 1796.

Argument.—Retrospect of the First Settlements of East Tennessee.—First Settlements on Cumberland River.—Cherokee Hostilities in 1780.—North Carolina encourages Emigration to the Cumberland in 1783.—Military Land District erected.— Chickasâ Cession in 1784.—Increased Emigration to Holston and Cumberland in 1785.—Political Difficulties in Washington District.—Attempted Organization of the "Republic of Frankland."—Colonel John Sevier attainted for Treason, and restored to his Rights.—Authority of North Carolina sustained.—Spanish Influence in the Cumberland Settlements.—Population of Washington and Miro Districts in 1789.— North Carolina cedes her Western Territory to the Federal Government.—" Southwestern Territory" organized in 1790.—Indian Hostilities commence.—Efforts of the Federal Government to maintain Peace.—Rapid Increase of Emigration Westward in 1791.—Indian Hostilities in 1791 to 1793.—Spanish Intrigue with the Indians.— Colonel Sevier and General Robertson conduct Defenses.—Population of Southwestern Territory in 1794.—Population of the Territory in 1795.—Second Grade of Territorial Government assumed.—State Constitution adopted in 1796.—" State of Tennessee" admitted into the Union.—Features of Constitution.—Progressive Increase of Population and Extension of Settlements to the Mississippi until 1840.— Displacement of the Indian Tribes.—West Tennessee and Memphis.—Population and Enterprise.—Colonies sent out from Tennessee 265

CHAPTER XI.

INDIAN WARS AND MILITARY OPERATIONS BY THE UNITED STATES NORTH OF THE OHIO RIVER.—A.D. 1787 TO 1795.

Argument.—Unsettled State of the Indian Tribes from 1784 to 1790.—Extent of Indian Depredation and Murders up to 1790.—General Harmar prepares to invade the Indian Country.—Advances to the Maumee.—Is defeated in two Engagements.—Retreats to Fort Washington.—Indian Hostilities renewed.—General Scott marches an Expedition against the Wabash Towns.—Colonel Wilkinson leads another against the Towns on Eel River and Tippecanoe.—General St. Clair prepares to invade the Maumee Country.—Marches toward the St. Mary's.—Meets with a disastrous Defeat.—Terrible Onset of the Savages.—Their Number and Allies.—The Remnant of the Army arrives at Fort Washington.—Colonel Wilkinson commands at Fort Washington.—He proceeds from Fort Jefferson to the Scene of the Defeat.—Overtures of Peace tendered to the Indians in 1792.—The Federal Government authorize a strong Force for the Humiliation of the Savages.—General Wayne Commander-in-chief.—Indians continue their hostile Demonstrations.—Excited by British Emissaries.—General Wayne concentrates his Forces at Fort Greenville.—The advanced Posts harassed by Indians.—Plan of Encampment at Greenville.—Lord Dorchester.—President Washington's Views of Indian Tactics.—Fort Recovery built.—Is attacked by Indians in 1793.—General Scott arrives with the mounted Riflemen.—General Wayne takes up the Line of March for the Maumee.—" Fort Defiance" commenced.—" Fort Deposit" at the Head of the Rapids.—Force concentrated at this Point.—Battle of the Miami, August 20th, 1794.—Utter Defeat of the Savages.—The Army returns to Fort Defiance, which is strongly fortified.—Army advances to Miami Villages.—Fort Wayne erected.—Army retires to Winter-quarters at Greenville.—Indians sue for Peace . . . . Page 284

CHAPTER XII.

ADVANCE OF THE WHITE POPULATION INTO THE NORTHWESTERN TERRITORY.—ADMISSION OF THE "STATE OF OHIO" INTO THE FEDERAL UNION.—A.D. 1795 TO 1804.

Argument.—Security of the frontier Population after the Treaty of Greenville.—Amicable Intercourse with the Indians.—Emigrants advance upon the Muskingum, Scioto, and Miami Rivers.—Population of Northwestern Territory in 1796.—Of Cincinnati in 1797.—Population advances into the Virginia Military District.—Nathaniel Massie, Pioneer of Scioto Valley.—Chillicothe first Settled.—Tribute to Memory of Massie.—First Mail-route opened from Wheeling to Limestone.—Population advances to the "Western Reserve."—" County of Wayne" organized.—Old French Settlements near Detroit.—Traits of Character in French Population.—Retrospect of Northwestern Territory in 1796.—Extension of Settlements up the Scioto and Muskingum Valleys.—" Adams County" organized.—" Ross County" organized.—Condition of Chillicothe in 1798.—Extreme Settlements north of Chillicothe.—Herman Blannerhasset emigrates to Ohio in 1798.—His Traits of Character.—Blannerhasset's Island.—Steubenville laid off and settled.—Territorial Population in 1798.—*Second Grade* of Government assumed.—First Territorial Legislature.—Public Surveys.—Counties of Trumbull and Fairfield organized.—Belmont County organized.—Indiana Territory organized into a separate Government.—Congress authorizes a Convention to form a State Constitution.—Convention assembles and adopts a Constitution.—" State of Ohio" admitted into the Union.—State Government organized March 1st, 1803.—Character and Merits of Governor St. Clair.—New Counties organized.—Governors of Ohio.—Subsequent Increase of Population and Extension of Civil Government.—Population in 1840.—Character of Emigration to Ohio . . 311

CHAPTER XIII.

"THE MISSISSIPPI TERRITORY" FROM ITS FIRST ORGANIZATION TO THE COMMENCEMENT OF THE CREEK WAR. — A.D. 1798 TO 1813.

Argument.—Original Extent of the Mississippi Territory.—First Governor and Territorial Judges.—Authority and Jurisdiction of the same —Arrival of the United States

Troops under General Wilkinson.—*First* Grade of Territorial Government organized in 1799.—Extent of the White Settlements and Indian Territory.—Adams and Pickering Counties organized. — Population in 1799. — Washington County organized on the Mobile River.—*Second* Grade of Territorial Government in 1800.—The Federal Army in the Mississippi Territory.—Indian Treaties in 1801.—Treaty of Fort Adams.—Treaty of Chickasâ Bluffs.—Governor Claiborne enters upon his Duties.—The Counties of Claiborne, Jefferson, and Wilkinson organized in 1802.—First System of Jurisprudence.—First Newspapers in Mississippi.—"Articles of Agreement and Cession" by Georgia.—Extent of Georgia Claim.—Adjudication of Private Claims by Commissioners.—Land Offices.—Surveyor-general's Office organized.—Enlargement of Territorial Limits.—Indian Nations included.—Legislative Care for the Encouragement of Education.—First College and first Academy chartered.—The Robber Mason killed.—Emigration in 1803, in anticipation of the Occupation of Louisiana.—Governor Claiborne Commissioner.—Commissioners and Troops advance toward New Orleans.—Protestant Religion introduced in Mississippi Territory.—Washington County erected into a Judicial District.—Harry Toulmin, Judge. —First Delegate to Congress.—Robert Williams, Governor.—First City Charter of Natchez.—Spanish Exactions on the Mobile.—First Natchez Hospital.—Border Collisions.—Abduction of the Kempers.—Indian Treaties in 1805 : with the Chickasâs ; with the Cherokees ; Creeks ; Choctâs. — First "Choctâ Purchase."— Extent of White Settlements in 1806.—Spanish Encroachments on the Sabine.—Militia Movements in Mississippi.—Burr's Conspiracy in the West.—Burr prepares to descend the Mississippi.—President's Proclamation.—General Wilkinson protects New Orleans.—Defensive Measures of Governor Mead in the Mississippi Territory.—Burr appears before the Superior Court.—Patriotic Citizens of Wilkinson County.—Abortive Attempt to arraign Burr.—He escapes from Custody.—Is arrested near Fort Stoddart.—Sent to Richmond, Virginia.—Emigration to Mississippi induced by Burr's Plans.—Agriculture in the Territory in 1807.—Cotton the Staple Product.—Cotton Receipts negotiable by Law.—First Digest of Territorial Laws.—First Road across to Tombigby.—Lands on the Upper Tombigby.—Condition of the Tombigby Settlements.—Patriotism of the Inhabitants.—Governor Williams.—First White Settlements in "Madison County."—First Bank in the Territory in 1809.—Population in 1810.—Revolution in District of Baton Rouge.—First Brigade of Militia in 1812.—Tennessee Volunteers under General Jackson.—General Wilkinson occupies Fort Charlotte.—Mobile District annexed to the Mississippi Territory . . Page 339

CHAPTER XIV.

THE "MISSISSIPPI TERRITORY," FROM THE BEGINNING OF THE CREEK WAR UNTIL THE ADMISSION OF THE STATES OF "MISSISSIPPI" AND "ALABAMA" INTO THE FEDERAL UNION.—A.D. 1813 TO 1819.

Argument.—British Policy of instigating savage Warfare.—Population and Settlements in 1813.—Origin of Creek Hostilities.—Prosperous Condition of the Creeks in 1812.—British Instigation from Canada.—Tecumseh stirs up a war Party in the Creek Nation.—Tombigby Settlements menaced by hostile Creeks.—Deluded Security of Colonel Hawkins and General Flournoy.—General Claiborne advances to the Tombigby.—Judge Toulmin's Opinion of the true State of the Indian Affairs.—Disposition of Troops under General Claiborne.—Condition of Affairs on the Alabama in August.—General Claiborne's Letter.—Major Beasly admonished of Danger.—Attack and Massacre of Mims's Fort.—Number of Whites slain.—Loss of Indians.—Consternation produced by the Disaster.—Wretched Condition of the Inhabitants.—Marauding Bands of Indians ravage the Country.—Employment of the Choctâs urged as indispensably necessary.—General Claiborne secures the Co-operation of the Choctâs under Mushulatubbe and Pushmataha.—Spanish Treachery detected.—British Supplies for Indians sent to Pensacola.—The Army advances to Fort Claiborne.—Advances to the Holy Ground, and defeats Creeks under Weatherford.—The Georgia Troops under General

CONTENTS. xiii

Floyd invade eastern Part of the Creek Nation.—Tennessee Troops invade the northern Part.—General Jackson advances to Fort Strother, on the Coosa.—Battle of Tallushatches.—Battle of Talladega.—Creeks supplied for the War by British Agents.—Battle of Emuckfaw.—Battle of Enotochopco.—Battle of the Horse-shoe, or Tohopeka.—The Power of the Creeks humbled.—Invasion of the Hickory Grounds.—"Fort Jackson" built.—Submission of the hostile Chiefs.—Surrender of Weatherford.—Treaty of Fort Jackson.—Its Conditions and Requirements.—Colonel Nichols in Florida.—General Jackson Commander-in-chief in 7th military District.—British Emissaries among the Florida Indians.—Jackson advances to Mobile.—Defense of Fort Bowyer against British Fleet.—Expels the British Forces from Pensacola.—Tribute of Esteem to General Jackson.—Advance of white Population into the Indian Country.—Settlements north and south of Tennessee River; upon Sources of Tombigby.—Monroe County organized.—Population of Madison County in 1815.—The Creeks instigated by British Emissaries to reject the Treaty of Fort Jackson.—Population of the Territory in 1816.—Application for Authority to form a state Government.—Indian Treaties in 1816.—Territory divided.—" State of Mississippi" admitted into the Union.—Choctâ Cession by Treaty of Doak's Stand.—Ceded Territory organized into Counties.—Permanent state Capital selected.—"City of Jackson."—County of Monroe annexed.—Final Extension of the state Jurisdiction within the entire Limits.—Summary of Indian Treaties within the Mississippi Territory.—Governors of Mississippi.—*Alabama Territory* organized.—State of Alabama admitted into the Union.—Subsequent increase of Population . . . . . Page 391

CHAPTER XV.

THE "TERRITORY OF ORLEANS" FROM ITS FIRST ORGANIZATION UNTIL AFTER ITS ADMISSION INTO THE UNION AS THE "STATE OF LOUISIANA."—A.D. 1804 TO 1815.

Argument.—William C. C. Claiborne Governor-general of the Province of Louisiana.—General James Wilkinson Commander-in-chief of the Army.—Emigrants from the United States.—Governor Claiborne's judicious Administration.—Territorial Government provided for the "Territory of Orleans."—Plan of Government obnoxious to the People.—Volunteer Companies patronized by the Governor.—Expressions of popular Discontent by the French Population.—Territorial Government instituted.—First Territorial Legislature.—First Bank created.—Territorial Legislature modified.—Discontent in Baton Rouge District.—Abduction of the Kempers.—Their Release.—Spanish Exactions on the Mobile River, and Aggressions West of the Mississippi in 1805.—Spanish Officers in New Orleans.—They contemplate the Mississippi south of Red River as their eastern Boundary.—Re-enforcements in Texas and Florida.—Policy of the Federal Government.—Advance of the Spanish Troops to Red River.—Movements of United States Troops.—Spanish Troops on the Bayou Pierre and Arroyo Hondo.—Remonstrances of Governor Claiborne.—General Wilkinson advances the Army to Natchitoches.—His Negotiation with General Herrera.—Spaniards retire West of the Sabine.—Wilkinson proceeds to New Orleans to intercept Burr's Operations.—His energetic Measures against the Conspirators.—Zealous co-operation of Governor Claiborne.—His Proclamation. — Arrest of Dr. Bollman and others.—Great popular Excitement.—Conflict of the civil and military Authorities.—Affected Zeal of Judges Workman and Hall for the Supremacy of the civil Power.—Efforts made by Persons clothed with civil Authority to embarrass General Wilkinson, and to protect the Conspirators.—Burr utterly circumvented in the Mississippi Territory.—Lieutenant Pike's exploring Party returns from Santa Fé.—Object of his Exploration.—Wilkinson's Position relative to Burr's Enterprise *not criminal.*—The Organization of the Territorial Government completed.—Great Mortality of the Troops under General Wilkinson.—Revolt in District of Baton Rouge in 1810.—Spanish Authority expelled.—A Provisional Government established by the People.— The Baton Rouge District annexed to the Territory of Orleans.—Revolt among Slaves above New Orleans in 1811.—State Government authorized.—Constitution adopted.—Some of its Features.—"State of Louisiana" admitted into the Union.—Baton Rouge District annexed.—State Government organized.—General Wilkinson acquitted by a Court of Inquiry.—Advance of American Population into Louisiana.—General Wilkinson's Activity in providing for maritime Defense of Louisiana against British Invasion.—Louisiana threatened by a powerful Armament.—General Jackson Commander-in-chief.—He arrives at New Orleans.—His extraordinary Efforts for the effectual Defense of the City.—Suppresses a spirit of Despondency by efficient Measures.—The Enemy advances by Way of the Lakes.—Encounters American Gun-boats.—Martial Law proclaimed.—The Enemy advances through Bayou Bienvenu.—American Army concentrated at New Orleans.—Active Hostilities commence.—Efforts of the Enemy previous to January 8th.—Patriotic Devotion of American Citizens in New Orleans.—Grand Attack upon the American Lines on the 8th.—Repulse of the Enemy's bombarding Squadron at Fort St. Philip.—The British Army retires from the Scene of its Disasters.—The Watchword "Booty and Beauty."—Arbitrary Exercise of civil Authority by Judge Hall.—The unjust Fine disclaimed by the American People after thirty Years.—Population of Louisiana in 1815.—Extent of Settlements.—Agricultural Resources.—Governors until 1816

Page 448

CHAPTER XVI.

PROGRESSIVE EXTENSION OF THE FEDERAL JURISDICTION OVER THE "NORTHWESTERN TERRITORY" TO THE MISSISSIPPI.—A.D. 1800 TO 1845.

Argument.—The Origins of three States in Northwestern Territory.—Indiana.—Illinois.—Michigan.—"Indiana Territory" organized.—Indian Treaties.—"Illinois Territory" organized.—Michigan Territory organized.—Condition of these Territories in 1811.—Shawanese threaten Hostilities.—United States Troops advance with Governor Harrison toward the Prophet's Town.—Harrison contemplates a Treaty.—Unfortunate Battle of Tippecanoe.—Beginning of the Indian War in the West.—Emigration to Indiana and Illinois in 1816.—"State of Indiana" admitted into the Union.—"State of Illinois" admitted into the Union.—Progressive Increase of Population in these States.—Treaties for Extinguishment of Indian Title.—Michigan Territory until 1832.—Emigration to Michigan and Wisconsin.—Commercial and Agricultural Advantages of Michigan discovered.—Increase of Population.—Extension of Settlements.—"State of Michigan" admitted.—"Wisconsin Territory" organized.—Population and Resources of Wisconsin.—"Territory of Iowa" organized in 1838.—Rapid Extension of Population into Wisconsin and Iowa.—Aggregate Population of the States and Territories comprised in original Limits of Northwestern Territory.—Commerce on the Lakes.—Advance of Population and Education in the State of Michigan.—Emigration to Wisconsin and Iowa Territories in 1840-43.—Wisconsin applies for Admission into the Union 519

CHAPTER XVII.

EXTENSION OF THE FEDERAL UNION WEST OF THE MISSISSIPPI, AND THE RE-ANNEXATION OF TEXAS.—A.D. 1803 TO 1846.

Argument.—Retrospect of the Province of Louisiana.—"Territory of Orleans" and District of Louisiana.—Increase of Population in the Territory of Orleans and District of Louisiana.—Remote Missouri Regions explored by Lewis and Clark.—Lieutenant Pike explores the Upper Mississippi and the Arkansas Rivers.—Population advances into the District.—Settlements extend upon the Arkansas and Missouri.—Missouri Territory organized in 1812.—New Impulse to Emigration in 1815.—Indian Treaties.—Population of Missouri Territory in 1817.—"Territory of Arkansas" or-

CONTENTS.

ganized in 1819.—French Settlement incorporated with the American Population.—St. Louis as a commercial Point.—The People of Missouri Territory apply for a State Government in 1819.—Strong Opposition in Congress.—Stormy Debates on the "Missouri Question" in 1819-1829.—Convention and State Government authorized in 1820.—Constitution adopted, and State Government organized.—"State of Missouri" admitted into the Union under Restriction in 1821.—Population, Agriculture, and Commerce of Missouri until 1836.—Emigration to Arkansas Territory in 1835-36.—"State of Arkansas" admitted into the Union.—Features of the Constitution.—Governors of Arkansas.—State of Missouri, and City of St. Louis from 1838 to 1845.—Emigration west of the Mississippi; to Louisiana; to "Iowa District."—"Territory of Iowa" organized.—"Iowa City."—Increased Emigration to Territory of Iowa, from 1839 to 1844.—State Constitution authorized.—Features of Constitution.—Iowa rejects Terms of Admission.—Florida and Texas admitted.—Iowa forms another Constitution in 1846.—Emigration through Nebraska Territory to Oregon, from 1842 to 1845.

Re-annexation of Texas.—Former Condition of Texas as a Spanish Province.—Adheres to the Mexican Confederation of 1824.—Departments and Settlements in 1832.—Mexican Grants for European and American Colonies.—Population in 1834.—Texas and Coahuila form one Mexican State.—Texas secedes from the dictatorial Authority of Santa Anna, and is invaded by General Cos.—Texas declares herself Independent in 1836.—Is invaded by Santa Anna.—Santa Anna recognizes her Independence.—It is recognized by United States and the European Powers.—Emigration to Texas greatly increases.—The People of Texas desire Annexation to the United States.—Second Application in 1837.—Mexico, prompted by Santa Anna, repudiates his Acts in Texas.—Third Application of Texas met by an Overture from the United States in 1844.—President Tyler's Treaty of Annexation.—Mr. Shannon, Minister to Mexico.—His fruitless Mission.—Mr. Thompson sent as Envoy.—Returns unsuccessful.—Captain Elliott becomes an active Diplomatist against Annexation.—Hostile Attitude of Mexico.—Captain Elliott's Zeal in Diplomacy.—Intrigue of the British and French Ministers.—Annexation consummated.—The Protection of United States invoked against Mexican Invasion.—Army of Occupation at Corpus Christi.—Advances to the Rio del Norte . . . . Page 542

HISTORY

OF THE

DISCOVERY AND SETTLEMENT

OF THE

VALLEY OF THE MISSISSIPPI.

BOOK V.

THE UNITED STATES IN THE VALLEY OF THE MISSISSIPPI.

CHAPTER I.

MANNERS AND CUSTOMS OF THE FRONTIER POPULATION EAST AND SOUTH OF THE OHIO RIVER.—A.D. 1770 TO 1810.

Argument.—Condition of the frontier Settlements of western Pennsylvania and Virginia. — Characteristic Traits of the Pioneers generally. — *Manners and Customs:* 1. *Costume* of the Hunters: the Hunting-shirt; Pantaloons; Breech-cloth and Leggins; Moccasin. — 2. *Habitation:* the Log Cabin; its Location; internal Appearance.—3. *Employments:* the respective Duties of Man and Wife.—4. *Diet:* Meats; wild Game; Bread; Pone, Journey-cake; Hog and Hommony; Substitutes for Tea and Coffee.—5. *Settlement Rights:* Nature and Extent; tomahawk Improvements. —6. *Fort, or Station:* Form and Construction; its Location and Use; Stations in Kentucky.—7. *Hunters:* Science of Hunting; a hunting Camp; Game; Hides; Peltries.—8. *Caravans:* annual Trips to Baltimore and Frederic; Equipment of Caravan; solitary Route across the Mountains; Order of March; Fare.—9. *The moral Sense:* state of Morals; natural Honesty and Sense of Honor the supreme Law; force of Public Opinion; "Lynch Law;" "Regulators."—10. *Social Virtues:* Hospitality; Sociality; Conviviality; a marriage Party; Sports and Amusements.—11. *Boatmen:* general Character; Costume; Habits; peculiar Traits of Character.—12. *National Character:* Diversity of People and Languages blended; Peculiarities of Feelings and Habits neutralized; Influence of free Government upon the Enterprise and moral Character.—13. *Religious Traits:* Religion disconnected with civil Power; Ministers dependent for Support upon their own Merit; religious "Awakenings," or "Revivals," in the West; "Camp-meeting" Scene; Origin of Camp Meetings in Kentucky and Tennessee; Camp Meeting at Cane Ridge; at Desha's Creek; at Cabin Creek; astonishing Influence of sylvan Preaching, and the attendant Circumstances; extraordinary Conversions; Disturbance of mental and nervous Systems.

WHATEVER pertains to manners and customs of the early pioneer settlers on the tributary waters of the Ohio, applies, with nearly equal correctness, to the early white population of all the western half of Pennsylvania and Virginia, no less

VOL. II.—A

than to Kentucky and Tennessee, from the year 1770 to 1794, and to the white settlements northwest of the Ohio, until the termination of the Indian war by the victorious arms of General Anthony Wayne. All the settlements on the northwest, as well as those on the southeast side of the Ohio, during the hostilities of the western tribes, were placed in nearly the same circumstances in every thing pertaining to frontier life.

[A.D. 1770–1794.] One general trait has always characterized most of the frontier settlers contiguous to hostile tribes of Indians, and that is a daring, fearless, and enterprising spirit; a hardy, robust, and patient constitution, unaccustomed to the refinements, luxuries, or comforts of the older Atlantic colonies. The circumstances by which they were surrounded were such as tended to form constitutions capable of enduring almost any privation or bodily exposure without danger of serious disadvantage, mentally or physically.

Such qualifications were indispensable to those whose situation compelled them to brave the inclemency of the seasons, far remote from civilized life, and to contend with the fierce beasts of prey, and with the wily savage in his native haunts and forests. The pioneer who advances into the American wilderness against the consent of the fierce and vindictive savage, must possess no ordinary share of courage, and an iron constitution to sustain him.

To form a proper estimate of the character of the western pioneer, we must view him in all the relations of life, under the circumstances in which he is placed; examine him in his manners, customs, mode of life; in his pursuits, pastimes, and his domestic relations. Living in constant intercourse with the savage tribes, his costume, manner of life, habits, and customs were necessarily half savage and half civilized, and often the whole character of the savage was assumed.

1. The costume of the pioneer was simple, plain, and well adapted for use, comfort, and durability, and not unlike that of the native savages. The ordinary apparel of the hunter consisted of a peltry cap, pantaloons, buckskin moccasins, and a hunting-shirt, girded with a leather belt. Over this was worn the cross-belt of the shot-pouch and powder-horn, crossing from the left shoulder to the right side. On actual hunting duty, and during inclement weather, a pair of "leggins" were closely wrapped upon the legs and lower portion of the thighs,

of dressed deer-skin made smooth and firm. The pantaloons, worn tight and close to the legs, were made of domestic linsey, or tow-linen, but more commonly of soft and pliant dressed buckskin, which was both elastic and durable.

Sometimes, instead of pantaloons, the hunter adopted the "long leggins" of the Indian, which extended to the upper part of the thighs, while the breech and loins were covered with the more convenient breech-cloth of the savage, secured by a girdle around the waist. This covering was formed by a piece of cloth or linen, nearly a yard long, and eight or ten inches wide, passed between the thighs, with the two extremities carried under the belt, in front and rear, and the loose ends hanging over the girdle behind and before served as ornamental flaps. These flaps were often ornamented with coarse embroidery. The leggins were attached by straps, or suspenders, to the same girdle. With this dress, the upper part of the thighs and hips, for the sake of free action, were partially exposed, unless covered by the skirt of the hunting-shirt.

After the settlements had advanced to some degree of civilized refinement, this costume, formed of dressed buckskin, had been adopted by the young beaux as a fancy dress to display their fine forms and persons. To do this more effectually, it has been no uncommon occurrence for them to make their appearance in church during public worship, and gravely take their seat in the congregation, or stand gazing with stoical indifference, in imitation of Indian curiosity, but not contributing in the least to the sedate devotion of the young ladies present.*

The *hunting-shirt* was a characteristic article of costume among the western emigrants. Although many declined assuming the leggins and breech-cloth of the Indian, and still adhered to the pantaloons and breeches of their ancestors, all adopted the hunting-shirt as an overcoat, peculiarly adapted to their frontier mode of life, from its comparative simplicity of form, and its convenience in their rambles and hunting excursions through brush and the forests. Hence, as Dr. Doddridge observes, "the hunting-shirt was universally worn. It was a kind of loose frock, reaching half way down the thighs, with large sleeves, open before, and so wide as to lap over a foot

* See Doddridge's Notes on Western Virginia, p. 115. This is a valuable little work in one volume 12mo, treating of the early settlements near the Ohio River, the manners and customs of the people, and the Indian wars in that region, by Rev. Joseph Doddridge, ed. 1825, Wellsburg, Virginia.

or more when belted. The cape was large, and sometimes handsomely fringed with a raveled piece of cloth, different in color from the hunting-shirt itself." The bosom of this dress, above the belt which encircled the waist, served as a wallet to carry a chunk of bread and "jerked beef," cakes, tow for the gun, and other necessaries for a hunter and warrior. The belt, which was always tied behind, served to hold the dress close and in order. On the right side was suspended a tomahawk, and on the left a scalping-knife, each in a leathern case.

The hunting-shirt was generally made of linsey, sometimes of coarse linen, and occasionally a very fine one for summer was made of calico, or of dressed deer-skins for winter; the latter were very warm in cold and dry weather, but were not well adapted for rain. Sometimes the deer-skin hunting-shirt was ornamented with numerous tassels and bands of fringed deer-skin around the skirts, the cape, and even around the sleeves near the shoulders and wrists.

Under the hunting-shirt was often worn an ordinary vest, made of the same material, while a common cotton or linen shirt was worn next the skin. Such was the apparel adapted to freedom of action, and to the life of a hunter.

The "moccasins" are Indian coverings for the feet instead of shoes. These were made of thick, dressed buckskin, in a single piece, gathered by a single seam on top of the foot from the toe to the instep, and by another from the bottom of the heel to the top without gathers, as high as the ankle joint, or higher. Flaps were left on each side, which, in cold weather, could be closely adjusted around the ankle and lower part of the leg; but in dry weather these flaps were permitted to hang down over the upper side of the foot. These flaps in the Indian moccasin were often highly ornamented by a species of figures, embroidered with variegated porcupine quills and shells, similar to our modern bead-work; in fact, many of them were handsomely covered with the brilliant colors of bead embroidery.

In cold weather the moccasin was well stuffed around the feet with loose deer-hair, wool, or leaves, to protect the feet from the inclement weather. The seams in this covering for the feet were sewed and gathered by means of an awl and thongs of buckskin, or the sinews of the deer, which were known by the general term of "*whangs.*" Every hunter's shot-pouch was supplied with a rude moccasin-awl and a roll of buckskin, and whangs for mending and patching his moccasins at night. It was the use of buckskin moccasins in wet weather, and cold spring thaws, doubtless, that laid the foundation for the inveterate cases of rheumatism so common among the early settlers of the Ohio region.*

2. *Habitations.*—The log cabin was the primitive abode of the agricultural population which first advanced west of the mountains upon the waters of the Ohio. These habitations of the western settlements were rude and simple, and well adapted to the circumstances by which they were surrounded. Almost the only tools possessed by the first settlers were axes, hatchets, knives, and a few augers. They had neither saw-mills nor carpenters, nails nor glass, bricks nor masons. Each house erected was of similar construction, and consisted of one or more log pens, in the shape of a square or parallelogram, with the logs notched at each end, and riding transversely on each other, forming the body of the house. The logs were cut to one length, and were selected of nearly the same size; they were put up, either round, and with the bark on, or were neatly hewed on two sides, just as the taste and means of the builder might prompt. After the pen was raised to the height of eight or ten feet from the foundation, the gable ends were carried up with ridge poles extending lengthwise for the support of the clap-board roof. The clap-board shingles were laid in regular courses, over each of which a weight pole was laid, and retained in its place by short blocks of wood at right angles intervening.

The roof being completed, a door was cut out and faced, and also a window, if it were deemed necessary or desirable.

The spaces between the logs of the house were closed by "chinking," or small blocks of wood riding upon each other, and afterward daubed and plastered with tempered clay or mud. An opening was also cut out for the chimney, and a wooden square stack, of small pieces of wood, rudely dove-tailed to one end of the house, was built up, tapering to the top. It was so connected with the house as to form a large fireplace and chimney literally outside of the house. This chimney was chinked, daubed, and plastered similar to the house, except that the plastering was chiefly inside, and quite thick, to protect the wood-

* See Doddridge's Notes, p. 114.

en structure from the action of the fire within. The jambs and back of the fireplace were also further secured by three upright, large, flat stones laid in mud.

The earth was often the only floor, but more commonly the floor was made of "puncheons," or slabs split from logs, hewed smooth on the upper side, and resting bedded upon poles raised above ground. The "loft," or attic story, sometimes had a puncheon floor, and a rude ladder in one corner served as a stairway. The door was made of thick clap-boards split from oak logs, and pinned to cross-pieces, and were hung upon wooden hinges, and fastened by a wooden latch. The open door or the broad chimney admitted light by day, and a rousing fire and a bear-grease lamp, or a buffalo-tallow candle, were their resource at night.

As soon as the mechanic and merchant appeared, sashes with two or four lights of glass might be seen set into gaps cut through the side logs. Cotemporaneously, old barrels began to constitute the tops of chimneys, and joists and plank, sawed by hand, took the place of puncheons.*

At first log cabins were built in villages or clusters, and surrounded with stockades formed by logs set upright in the ground, and made bullet-proof for mutual protection against Indian surprise and massacre.

The location of the house was generally in some vale or dell, near a running stream of water, or near some permanent spring. Thus they consulted their own convenience in obtaining a constant supply of water, and also, considering that every thing coming to the house from abroad is more easily carried "down hill" than up, the house was seldom placed upon an eminence. In all the first locations the bottoms were selected, and the contiguous ridges formed the boundaries of the tract. This continued until the system of square surveys was introduced, when the boundaries of tracts were straight lines, and not the natural features of the country.

The inside appearance of a frontier habitation was also unique, and adapted to the circumstances of the times. Bureaus, side-boards, and armors were unknown, and so were their uses. The whole furniture of a room consisted of one home-made bedstead, and one trundle bedstead under it for children, both well furnished with bear skins and buffalo robes

* See Kendall's Life of Jackson, p. 74, 75.

instead of blankets; a few split-bottom chairs, and a few three-legged stools, a small movable bench or table, supported by two pairs of cross-legs, for the family meals; a shelf and water-bucket near the door. The naked wood and clay walls, instead of the ornamental paper and tapestry of the cities, were embellished with the whole wealth of the family wardrobe. The frocks, dresses, and bed-gowns of the women, the hunting-shirts, pantaloons, and arms of the men, all were suspended around the walls from wooden hooks and pegs, and served as a good index to the industry and neatness of the mistress of the house. The cooking utensils and table furniture consisted of a few iron pots, "pewter plates and dishes," spoons, knives and forks, which had been transported from the east with their salt and iron; besides these, a few wooden bowls, or "trenchers," "noggins and gourds," completed the list of cooking and eating utensils.*

The domestic employments of the women were chiefly in the household affairs. They milked the cows, and prepared food and clothing for the family; washed the clothing, and regulated the *minutiæ* of domestic affairs.

3. The *employment* of families was arranged by common custom. The husband was chiefly engaged in procuring food and materials for clothing; in erecting cabins and inclosures; in clearing and cultivating the land; and in building forts and stations for mutual protection against Indian hostilities. Much of his time in the cold season was spent in roaming the forests in quest of deer, bear, or other game, with which the unfrequented forests abounded. The dressed skin of the bear, the buffalo, and the deer, with its coat of long and shaggy hair, often served the double purpose of bed and blanket, and much more effectually protected the delicate from the rigors of winter.

As the settlements advanced in age and improvement, during the cessation of Indian hostilities, the exceptions to these general remarks became more frequent.

4. The *diet* was plain and homely. Wild game constituted the chief portion of animal food. The flesh of the bear was highly prized, and could easily be made a good substitute for beef and bacon; the deer yielded the most delicious venison, far preferable to veal; occasionally the flesh of an elk or buffalo supplied the place of fresh beef. The flesh of the partridge,

* Doddridge, p. 108, 109.

the wild pigeon, the pheasant, the wild turkey, and the like, yielded a more delicious fare than any domestic fowl. The squirrel, the rabbit, the opossum, and many other smaller quadrupeds, supplied the delicacies of veal, lamb, mutton, and pork.

Corn-meal, pounded in a wooden mortar, or ground in a hand-mill of steel, supplied the place of flour, and all the preparations of wheat. The dough, properly prepared, was spread upon a piece of shaved clap-board from three to four inches wide, and from fifteen to twenty inches long, and baked upon the hearth. When both sides were perfectly done, it was called "journey-cake," or *Johnny-cake.* A journey-cake board was an indispensable implement of frontier cooking. Johnny-cake and pone were the only varieties of bread used among the early frontier settlements for breakfast and dinner. At supper, milk and mush were the standard dish. When milk was not plenty, the lack was supplied by the substantial dish of hommony, or pounded corn thoroughly boiled. Sometimes maple molasses or bear's oil, and the gravy from fried meat, served as a substitute for milk in the regular supper dish.*

After domestic stock began to multiply, one of the standing dishes in western Pennsylvania and Kentucky was "hog and hommony." Vegetables at length began to be cultivated in abundance, and every garden yielded a supply of common culinary vegetables, such as pease, beans, lettuce, radishes, cabbage, and many other choice articles; while the "truck-patch" close by furnished a supply of roasting ears, squashes, pumpkins, and potatoes. The standard "dinner dish" at log-rollings, house-raisings, and harvest days was a large "pot-pie," inclosing minced meats, birds, or fruits.

Tea and coffee were unknown, and many of the native frontier inhabitants attained to the age of manhood without having ever seen or tasted these luxuries; yet the root and bark of the sassafras furnished a valuable substitute for the exotic from China, while parched rye and beans formed a substitute for coffee. In many of the remotest settlements, such articles as tea-cups and saucers were unknown. At length the manufactures and agricultural products of the older settlements, and cattle and hogs, were introduced, and the frontier manners yielded to the civilized.

* Doddridge, p. 109.

5. *Settlement Rights.*—In forming settlements and making locations of land, each settler had a valid claim under the provisions of the Virginia laws. One of these allowed to each emigrant as a settlement right four hundred acres of land, besides a preference right to one thousand acres more contiguous. The boundary lines between any contiguous settlement rights were generally adjusted amicably by the parties interested, before actual survey was made. In these adjustments, they were guided chiefly by the ridges or water courses, or some other natural boundary. In this manner, much of the country of western Pennsylvania and Virginia was parceled out among settlers, and subsequently nearly all the country between the Muskingum and the Ohio on the east.* These settlement rights were often selected and marked with the initials of the claimant's name on several beech-trees near "his clearing," where he had cut down a few trees, and probably erected a small hut, often many months before he took up his actual residence on the land. Yet these "tomahawk rights," as they were called, were recognized by other emigrants, and none would trespass upon them. Some were contented with one settlement right, and made no efforts to enlarge their landed estates; while others, as in all new countries, having a desire for accumulating wealth in landed estates, became speculators in lands, and purchased up great numbers of inchoate titles, in hopes of future gain in their augmented value.

During the continuance of Indian hostilities, every neighborhood was provided with a "stockade fort" for the common protection, to which all retired upon any alarm of Indian incursion. As all the frontier settlements west of the Blue Ridge, from the commencement of the French war in 1754, with only short intermissions, were continually exposed to Indian hostilities, in one form or another, "*the Fort*," or "Station," became a characteristic feature in the western settlements. In Western Pennsylvania and in Western Virginia, north of the Big Sandy, these stockades were commonly denominated "forts," while in Kentucky and Tennessee, in later times, they were known by the name of "stations."

6. *The Fort* or *Station.*—A station, in most cases, was constructed for the protection of a large number of families, as a safe retreat in time of danger. It consisted of an inclosure of

---

* See Doddridge, p. 102-105.

cabins, stockades, and block-houses, embracing about two acres or more, in the shape of a parallelogram or square; the inclosure being formed generally by cabins on two sides and by stockades on two sides. A large station sometimes presented three sides inclosed with cabins, the windows and doors all on the inner side. The outside wall of the cabin was generally ten or twelve feet high, without external openings, and perfectly bullet-proof, with the roof sloping downward to the inside. The cabins otherwise were finished in the usual manner, for the residence of families. The gate or entrance was a strong puncheon door between the parallel walls of adjoining cabins, and protected by a platform and sentry-box above. The remainder of the inclosure was completed by strong palisades set in the ground, with their sharpened points standing ten feet above ground. The whole inclosure, cabins and stockades, was provided with port-holes for defensive firing. In time of danger the gate was closed, and securely barricaded each day at sunset. During the day, if no immediate danger threatened, the inmates dispersed to their several homes or employments, until nightfall again approached.

Some larger stations in Kentucky were securely fortified against the most formidable attacks of the largest Indian army. Such were defended at the opposite angles by block-houses, or bastions, built of hewed logs, two stories high, and extending a few feet beyond the line or outer range of the stockade, each bastion commanding two sides of the stockade. These block-houses were bullet-proof, and provided with double sets of port-holes for defense, and so arranged that the riflemen could at all times clear the walls in case of assault, and prevent any secret lodgment near them.

Some small settlements were protected by a single block-house, surrounded by a strong palisade inclosure, so as to form a secure retreat for the families in case of Indian alarm. Every station or fort, however, was invariably located near some permanent spring or water course.

In Kentucky the stations were generally large, and protected a greater number of families, who in time of danger lived in the cabins of the station as in a fortified village, having their little farms and improvements in the immediate vicinity, upon which they remained engaged in the labors of husbandry during the day, returning to the fort for safety at night. Sometimes the stations in Kentucky contained three parallel rows of cabins, the two outer rows being connected by the line of palisades. As the Indians were without artillery, and had very little desire to take any fortified place by storm, these stockades proved amply sufficient to withstand all the attacks which they could make with their rifles and small arms. Many of these stations during the Indian hostilities were invested by large bodies of warriors, sometimes for several weeks together, yet it was a rare occurrence for one of them to be captured.

In the absence of Indian alarms and "signs," the people left the station and dispersed upon their respective farms and improvements, and resided in their own individual residences. But so soon as any alarm was given, or any "Indian sign" was found, they again retired into the station for security.

7. *The Hunter.*—" Hunting" constituted an important feature in the life of a western emigrant. By this means he supplied his family with a large proportion of their subsistence. Often their chief food was derived from the woods; while the skins and furs taken from the game supplied them with the only convertible medium of currency and exchange for the purchase of rifles, salt, and iron from the settlements east of the mountains. The "fall" and early part of the winter were the seasons for hunting the deer, and the whole winter and part of the spring for bears and animals which yield furs. The fur was said to be good in every month in whose name the letter *r* is found; besides, the annoyance and danger from Indian hostilities was less apprehended during the winter than in any other season. Every man, who was a farmer and husbandman in summer and autumn, became a hunter in winter. " As soon as the leaves were pretty well down, and the weather became rainy, accompanied with light snows, these men, after acting the part of husbandmen, so far as the state of the war permitted, began to feel that they were hunters. They became uneasy at home. Every thing about them became disagreeable. The house was too warm, the feather bed was too soft, and even the good wife, for the time, was not thought a good companion. The mind of the hunter was wholly occupied with the camp and the chase."

A hunting party being formed, " a day was soon appointed for the march of the little cavalcade to the camp. Two or three horses, furnished with pack-saddles, were loaded with

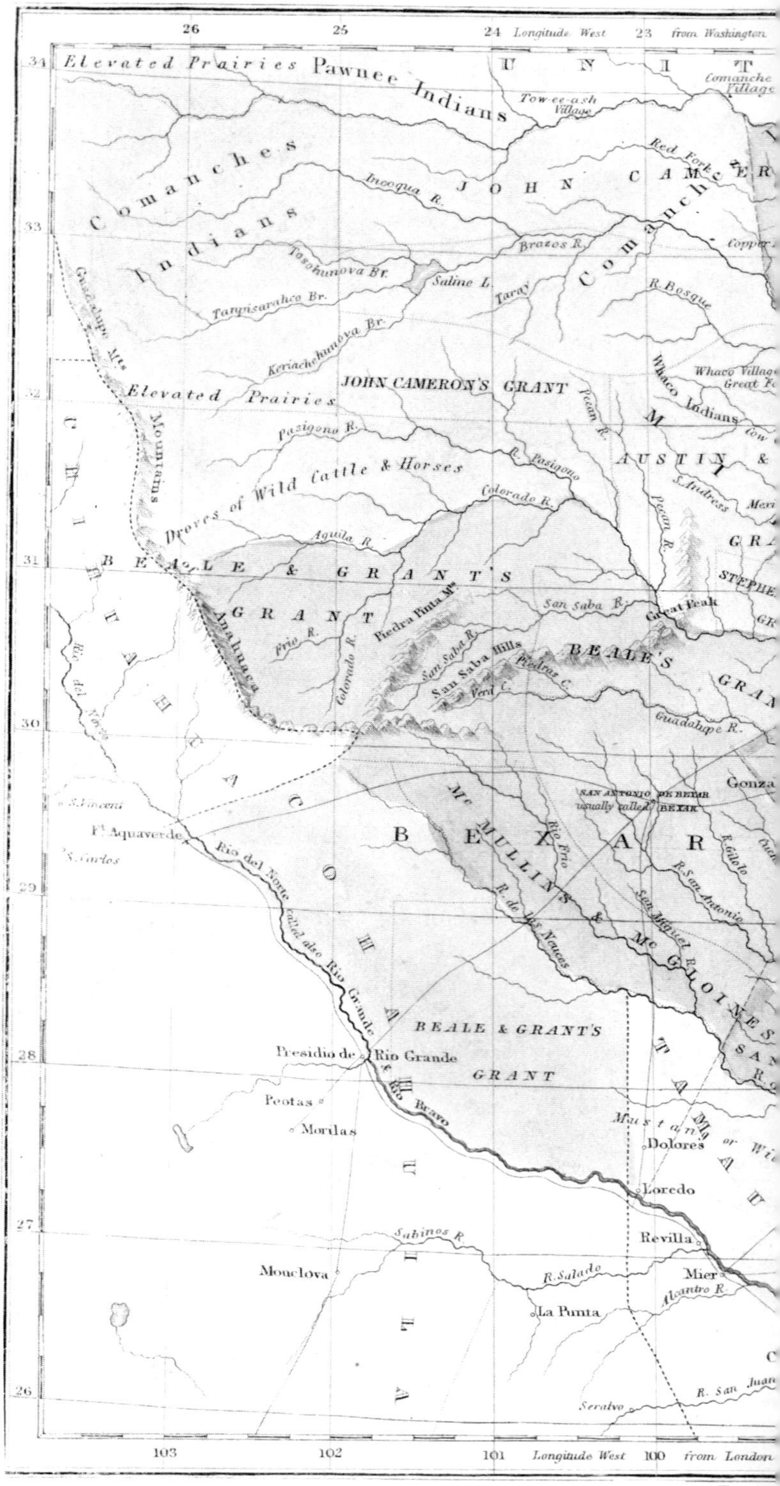

26
25
24 Longitude West
23
from Washington
34
33
32
31
30
29
28
27
26
Elevated Prairies
Pawnee Indians
Tow-ee-ash Village
Comanche Village
Comanches Indians
Red Fork
Inocqua R.
JOHN CAMERON'S GRANT
Comanches
Brazos R.
Tosohunova Br.
Saline L.
Taray
R. Bosque
Tanpisarahco Br.
Guadalupe Mts
Keriachehunova Br.
Whaco Village
Elevated Prairies
Mountains
Whaco Indians
Pecan R.
Pasigono R.
R. Pasigono
AUSTIN &
Droves of Wild Cattle & Horses
S. Andress
Colorado R.
Pecan R.
Aguila R.
BEALE & GRANT'S GRANT
San Saba R.
Great Peak
Frio R.
Colorado R.
Piedra Pinta Mts
San Saba R.
San Saba Hills
BEALE'S
Piedras C.
Verd C.
Rio del Norte
Guadalupe R.
SAN ANTONIO DE BEXAR usually called BEXAR
S. Vincent
Ft. Aquaverde
S. Carlos
Rio del Norte
BEXAR
Mc MULLINS & Mc GLOINES
Rio Frio
R. Gilolo
R. San Antonio
R. de los Neuces
San Miguel R.
Rio del Norte called also Rio Grande
BEALE & GRANT'S GRANT
Presidio de Rio Grande
Rio Bravo
Peotas
Morilas
Dolores
Loredo
Sabinos R.
Revilla
Mouclova
R. Salado
Mier
Alcantro R.
La Punta
R. San Juan
Seralvo
103
102
101 Longitude West
100
from London

Harper

TEXAS.
In 1836.

flour, Indian meal, blankets, and every thing else requisite for the use of the hunter."*

The *hunting camp* is at length erected in a suitable situation; in some valley or dell protected by hills from the northern blasts, as well as from discovery by Indians. The hunting camp is a half-faced cabin, made of logs or stakes driven into the ground, inclosed on three sides with slabs, bark, or skins, and covered on top with the same, the roof sloping from the open front backward. In front is the log fire; inside are the slabs, moss, and skins for the bed. Sometimes a hunting camp serves for several years, especially when made with care.

"Hunting was not a mere ramble in pursuit of game," without skill and calculation. The hunter must be skilled in the nature and habits of the animals he expects to take, in the weather, and their predilections; in what situation the game is to be found, whether on hill-sides, bottoms, or on high hills. In stormy weather the deer always seek the most sheltered places, and on the leeward side of hills; in rainy weather, with but little wind, they generally keep in the open woods, and on the highest ground.

It is requisite, also, to know the direction of the lightest winds, the cardinal points, and many other hunting sciences, which none but hunters know, to enable them to traverse the pathless forest in search of game. "The whole business of hunting consists in a succession of intrigues. From morning to night the hunter must be on the alert to gain the windward of his game," in order to avoid discovery. If a deer were killed, it was skinned and hung up out of the reach of wolves, and the chase was resumed and pursued until evening, when he returned toward the camp and prepared to cook the supper The supper being ended, the adventures of the day furnish a theme for the tales of the evening. The spike buck, the two and three pronged buck, the doe, and the barren doe figure through the tales and anecdotes of the day. After hunting some time in the same range, the hunter becomes acquainted with all the "gangs" or herds of deer in that range, and can easily recognize each when he sees them. The manœuvers of these are themes of discourse. Often some old buck, by his superior sagacity and watchfulness, has saved his little gang from the hunter's skill by giving timely notice of his approach.

* Doddridge's Notes, p. 124.

The cunning of the hunter and that of the old buck are often staked against each other; and not unfrequently, at the close of the hunting season, the old fellow is left the free, uninjured tenant of the forest; but if his rival succeeds in bringing him down, it is a victory followed by no small share of boasting on the part of the conqueror.*

Is the weather unsuited to the chase? the skins and carcasses of the game can be brought in, and a proper disposition made of them. Some hunters refrain from the chase on the Sabbath from motives of piety; others, from a superstitious belief that it brings "bad luck" to hunt on the Sabbath. Nor do those who revere the day, and abstain from their usual labors, lose their reward; for they are sure of a prosperous hunting season.

The spoils of the hunting season, the skins and furs taken during the winter, constitute the stock in trade for the purchase of sundry articles which are necessary in a new and wilderness country. Of these the most indispensable were salt, iron utensils, and implements. To purchase these, every family carefully preserved the furs and skins collected during the whole year, for the purpose of sending them over the mountains to be bartered for such necessaries as were not to be had in the wilderness. For this purpose, it was customary, in the western settlements of Pennsylvania and Virginia, from the Kenhawa to the Alleghany River, every fall, for each little neighborhood of a few families to dispatch "a caravan" to the settlements east of the mountains. Unlike their prototypes which traverse the deserts of Africa, they were generally few in number, and their merchandise of but little comparative value.

8. The *caravan*, when organized, consisted of a master, two or three young men, and one or two boys; a few horses, with pack-saddles on their backs, stuffed bells on their necks, and a pair of hickory-withe hopples attached to each pack-saddle. On each pack-saddle was secured a bag of shelled corn for provender on the way, to be deposited at convenient distances for the return route. A large wallet, well filled with bread, jerked bear's meat, or boiled ham and cheese, contained the provision for the drivers. Thus equipped, the cavalcade set out from the wilderness east of the Ohio for Baltimore, Freder-

* Doddridge's Notes, p. 126, 127.

ic, Hagerstown, or Oldtown in early times, and subsequently to Fort Cumberland and Winchester.

As these places successively, in the order of their names, became the marts of the western trade, the whole amount of hides and peltries, ginseng, snakeroot, and bear's grease were exchanged or bartered for salt, nails, and other articles of iron, and occasionally for a few pewter plates and dishes for the table. The bartering for the settlement being finished, the caravan was ready for its retrograde march. Each horse without a rider carried two bushels of salt, weighing eighty-four pounds to the bushel, besides a few light articles superadded.

The caravan route from the Ohio River to Frederic crossed the stupendous ranges of the Alleghany Mountains as they rise, mountain behind mountain, in the distant prospect. The path, scarcely two feet wide, and traveled by horses in single file, wound over hill and dale, through mountain defile, over craggy steeps, beneath impending rocks, and around points of dizzy heights, where one false step might hurl horse and rider into the abyss below. To prevent such accidents, the bulky baggage was removed in passing the dangerous defiles, to secure the horse from being thrown from his scanty foothold. This route, selected by experienced woodsmen, differed but little from that selected for turnpikes and rail-roads by professed engineers at a much later day.* Such was the danger in passing the mountain ranges from the old settlements of Pennsylvania, Maryland, and Virginia, to the settlements then forming on the branches of the Monongahela, the "Yough," and the Upper Ohio.

The order of the march, going and returning, was the same. The horses with their packs were marched along in single file, the foremost led by the leader of the caravan, while each successive horse was tethered to the pack-saddle of the horse before him. A driver followed behind to keep an eye upon the proper adjustment of the packs, and to urge on any horse that was disposed to lag. In this way two men could manage a caravan of ten or fifteen horses, each carrying about two hundred pounds burden. When night came, a temporary camp and a camp fire protected the weary travelers; while the horses, released of their burdens, with hopples on their feet, and their bell-clappers loosed, were turned loose to graze near the camp.

* See M'Donald's Life of Kenton, p. 72.

Salt, in the frontier settlements near the Ohio, was an expensive article for a backwoodsman; for a bushel of alum salt was equivalent to a good cow and calf. The salines of Kenhawa were then unknown, and the cattle multiplied without money.

In those early days, in the dawn of civilization in the West, the manners and customs, as well as the sense of propriety, were regulated by the state of things in the wilderness. A backwoodsman, in his first trip to Baltimore, could not conceive a more awkward predicament than the loss of his horse-bell and his hopples when about to enter the city.* Children who had been raised on the frontiers, when they reached the settlements east of the mountains, were surprised to find that all houses were not made of logs and chinked with mud; that all dishes and table-ware were not of pewter and wood. To them the luxuries of tea and coffee were nauseous or unknown; and they "wondered how people could show a fondness for such slops," which neither had gust for the palate nor "stuck to the ribs." The cups and saucers from which it was drank were themselves but emblems of a depraved taste and unmanly luxury, or, at most, were adapted to the effeminate or the sick.†

9. The *state of morals* was as might be expected; men were untrammeled by law or gospel; each man did that which was right in his own eyes. The line which separates Western Pennsylvania from Virginia was not defined, and for many years the civil jurisdiction of both states was withheld. Hence natural justice, and the sense of right and wrong, were unsophisticated by lawyers and courts, magistrates, sheriffs, or constables. "Their own consciences were a law unto themselves;" and if they erred, "it was human to err." Public opinion was the aggregate of individual judgment, and ruled with the force of the purest democracy. In those times, each man who could shoulder his rifle was a citizen-soldier, and as such was valued as a defender of his country, and ranked among her heroes. Conscious of his own importance, each man considered his neighbor his equal, and each was anxious to merit the general esteem. Industry in hunting or work, bravery and fortitude in war, honesty, candor, and hospitality in private life, entitled a man to his full share of public honor and confidence, which

---

* See Doddridge's Notes, p. 122.   † Idem, p. 110–112.

was never withheld. The incorrigible offender received the sentence which the majesty of moral virtue pronounces against vice and turpitude, and he was " hated from society." Courage was a virtue, and military duty was performed with alacrity. He that refused to appear in arms, fully equipped, at a moment's notice, found public censure resting upon him, and he was " hated from the place." Did a neighbor wish to erect a cabin, or to roll his logs, or to gather his harvest, each man was a willing hand, and in turn received aid from others. At such places an idler or an indifferent spectator dared not approach, or the contempt of the hardy pioneers settled upon him. Did any contract a debt, it was paid in labor or by the exchange of commodities; and the force of the moral sense, sustained by public sentiment, was a stronger guarantee than all the forms of law, which often serve as a protection against honest demands. Did a man want a bushel of salt, he received it in exchange for a cow and calf. So equal was the distribution of their scanty wealth, that no one envied that of his neighbor: if any were in want, they freely received from those who could give. Was any so base as to steal, with these advantages, " the law of Moses" was enforced, and forty stripes, save one, were freely given; but if the theft were small, in memory of the " old thirteen," as his reward, thirteen stripes disgraced his back. But such was the impression, and so firmly were the stripes applied, that they were not likely soon to fade away. In the absence of a judge and court, and the forms of law, " Judge Lynch" was sure to mete his just deserts to every disturber of the peace.

Lynch Law.—Although the pioneers in the West were a hardy, enterprising, honest race of men, yet the frontier settlements are often a retreat for loose and unprincipled individuals from the old settlements, who, if not familiar with crime, have very blunt perceptions of virtue. The genuine pioneer, the woodsman, is independent, brave, and upright; but, as the jackal follows in the footsteps of the lion, so the sturdy hunter is followed by the miscreant destitute of noble qualities; men who are the pests of the human race, averse to labor, impatient of the wholesome restraints of law, or the courtesies of civilized life. Some, indeed, are desperadoes, flying from justice, to escape the grasp of the law in older settlements; and in the frontier settlements he bids the civil law defiance. For such intruders the frontiers had a law of their own, a *lex loci*, known as *Lynch law*, which seldom failed to purge the community of his unwelcome presence. Its operation was often indispensable when a horse-thief, a counterfeiter, or other desperate vagabond infested a neighborhood, evading justice by cunning, or by a strong, audacious arm, or by the number of his confederates. The citizens formed themselves into a regulating party, commonly known as "*regulators*," a kind of holy brotherhood, whose duty required them to purge the neighborhood of such unruly members. Mounted, armed, and commanded by a leader, they proceeded to arrest the object of their mission. Night was the season for their official acts. Chief-justice "Birch" established his tribunal under a forest canopy; before him the culprit was arraigned, and with form and ceremony tried, and, as a matter of course, convicted. Sentence was pronounced, and without delay the penalty was inflicted, without stint or mercy. Tied securely to a tree, he was made to feel the rod, dealt by many sturdy hands, until justice was satisfied. If perchance he were an old offender, or had claims to the title of a "British Tory," his wounds were dressed, not with oil and wine, but with "tar and feathers." As the culprit retired from this ordeal, he was informed by Judge Lynch that the operation would be repeated in a few days unless he withdrew from the jurisdiction of the court. If there were confederates in crime, this warning served for all.

This tribunal was resorted to only in extreme cases; and, although liable to occasional abuse, it was a great protection to honest people against the most abandoned intruders, who defied the usual forms of law.*

10. *Social Virtues.*—Hospitality was a duty as well as a virtue; with the stranger or wayfaring man, they would readily divide their rough fare without pay or reward. In their settlements all lived together in harmony and rude simplicity. Warm and constant in their friendships, they lived and worked, feasted or suffered together in cordial harmony.

Was a man's honor or integrity impeached, the offender must prove his manhood on the spot. If he were unable to fight at fisticuff, or "rough and tumble," his friend must maintain the contest in his place. When the contest was decided, the combatants, reconciled, often shook hands, and there the

* See Hall's Sketches of the West, vol. ii., p. 88-92.

matter ended. Pitched battles between two rival heroes sometimes were seen, when fists, and feet, and teeth were used; but knives and fire-arms were deemed dishonorable and base.

In these rude settlements female virtue was safe without the protection of law. Each brother and kinsman was the prompt avenger of a sister's wrongs, and the penalty was not delayed by the slow process of law; but a want of chivalry in defense of female weakness was never known.

A *marriage* was the signal of a general jubilee among the friends of both parties. Days passed in anxious expectation of the appointed festival, when all hearts were to indulge in mirth and feasting.

At the appointed time, the rustic guests began to arrive from every quarter, males and females on horseback and on foot. No broad-cloth or beaver adorned their persons. Men were clad in their western dress, shoe-packs, or moccasins, leather breeches, leggins, and hunting-shirts. The women were dressed in their best, in linsey petticoats or gowns, coarse shoes, home-made stockings, handkerchiefs on their necks, and, if the weather was very cold, with leather gloves or woolen mittens on their hands. Few were able to adorn themselves with buckles, rings, or ruffles. Their horse caparisons were of the same rude stamp. The company, thus arrayed, began to arrive in single file about noon, when the rustic mirth began: with the swains, the bottle was an indispensable companion, and each made frequent draughts upon its inspiration.

The marriage ceremony over, all sat down to a wholesome dinner of backwoods fare. Beef, pork, fowls, baked or roasted, and sometimes venison or bear's meat, loaded the rustic board, together with vegetables of all kinds in great profusion; rude pies, pastry, and fruits served for dessert. The dinner past, a rustic dance engaged the joyous friends until the dawn of the following day, when they began to separate for their respective homes.

In sketching these traits of pioneer life, we have left much untold, which may be found in the excellent Notes of Dr. Doddridge. But such traits of pioneer life have long since vanished from Western Virginia, and are scarcely to be found, at this time, even in the remote West; yet, as they did exist, they constitute an important portion of early pioneer history, and as such demand a passing notice, without which the history of the pioneers would be incomplete.

The *sports* were characteristic of the frontier mode of life. Running, jumping, and wrestling were the pastimes of the boys as well as of the men. Throwing the tomahawk was common, and gave skill in the arts of war. When the stock of ammunition would permit, the men preferred the more warlike exercise of the rifle, with which the diameter of a cent upon a target was pierced at the distance of fifty steps at every shot by half the men present, and some could lodge two successive balls in the same place. The best marksman always took the prize, for which all were zealous competitors.

After the settlements had become more dense on the Monongahela and on the Ohio, a new class of men sprung up, whose life was unique in the West. This was the class of

11. *Boatmen.*—These were a hardy, fearless set of men, who always kept just in advance of civilization and luxury. They were athletic, persevering, and patient of privations. They traversed in their pirogues, barges, or keels, the longest rivers, penetrated the most remote wilderness upon their watery routes, and kept up a trade and intercourse between the most distant points. Accustomed to every species of exposure and privation, they despised ease and luxury. Clothed in the costume of the wilderness, and armed in western style, they were always ready to exchange the labors of the oar for offensive or defensive war. Exposed to the double force of the direct and reflected rays of the sun upon the water, their complexion was swarthy, and often but little fairer than the Indians. Often, from an exposure of their bodies without shirts, their complexion, from the head to the waist, was the same.

Steam had not exerted its magic influence on the western waters, and the rich cargoes which ascended the Mississippi in keel-boats and barges were propelled by human labor for nearly two thousand miles, slowly advancing against the strong current of these rivers. The boatmen, with their bodies naked to the waist, spent the long and tedious days traversing the "running board," and pushing with their whole force against their strong setting-poles firmly fixed against the shoulder. Thus, with their heads suspended nearly to the track on the running-board, they propelled their freighted barge up the long and tedious route of the river. After a hard day's toil, at night they took their "fillee," or ration of whisky, swallowed their homely supper of meat half burned and bread half baked, and retiring to sleep, they stretched themselves upon the deck, without covering, under the open canopy of heaven, or probably enveloped in a blanket, until the steersman's horn called them to their morning "fillee" and their toil.

Hard and fatiguing was the life of a boatman; yet it was rare that any of them ever changed his vocation. There was a charm in the excesses, in the frolicks, and in the fightings which they anticipated at the end of the voyage, which cheered them on. Of weariness none would complain; but rising from his hard bed by the first dawn of day, and reanimated by his morning draught, he was prepared to hear and obey the wonted order, "Stand to your poles and set off!" The boatmen were masters of the winding-horn and the fiddle, and as the boat moved off from her moorings, some, to cheer their labors, or to "scare off the devil and secure good luck," would wind the animating blast of the horn, which, mingling with the sweet music of the fiddle, and reverberating along the sounding shores, greeted the solitary dwellers on the banks with news from New Orleans.

Their athletic labors gave strength incredible to their muscles, which they were vain to exhibit, and fist-fighting was their pastime. He who could boast that he had never been whipped was bound to fight whoever disputed his manhood. Keel-boatmen and barge-men looked upon rafts-men and flat-boatmen as their natural enemies, and a meeting was the prelude to a "battle-royal." They were great sticklers for "fair play," and whoever was worsted in battle must abide the issue without assistance.

Their arrival in port was a general jubilee, where hundreds often met together for diversion and frolick. Their assemblages were often riotous and lawless to extremes, when the civil authorities were defied for days together. Had their numbers increased with the population of the West, they would have endangered the peace of the country; but the first steam-boat that ascended the Ohio sounded their death-knell, and they have been buried in the tide, never more to rise.

12. *National Character.*—Here we design to sketch in the western people the perceptible, but slight peculiarities which are the results of the peculiar circumstances and conditions of western pioneer life, and the influx of eastern and foreign immigration.

[A.D. 1795–1810.] The people of the Mississippi Valley are constituted from all nations, characters, languages, and conditions of men. Not a nation of Europe, not a class in all those nations, except royalty, which has not its full representation here; not a state in the Union which has not sent out its colonies to people more western regions; not a sect or denomination of Christians who have not their churches and their ministers here. The subjects of despotic monarchies, and the citizens of the freest republics in the world, all commingle here, and unite to form one people, unique in feeling, character, and genius. The Puritan of the North, the planter of the South, the German and the Iberian, the Briton and the Gaul, and even the sable sons of Africa and the northern Swede, all are here, each bringing with him his peculiar prejudices, local attachments, and predilections, and side by side they have set down together, and have gradually become assimilated in language, feelings, manners, and usages. Mutual prejudices have been effaced by contact and intimate connection, and the people, thus released from the narrow prejudices of birth and education, become more liberal, enlarged in feeling, more affectionate and agreeable, and, of course, more unprejudiced than a people who have long been unique in birth, education, and national character.

The rough, sturdy, and simple habits of the western people, living in a new and wilderness country, amid that abundance which God and Nature provide, and requiring only their own industry and exertion, give to them that fearless independence of thought and action which constitutes a characteristic trait in the American pioneers. Accustomed to the fascinating, but faithless intercourse of refined society and of great cities, men acquire habits of thought and feeling, and are subject to those restraints which give them a different mental development from the fearless, unrestrained freedom of feeling which characterizes the native of the great Valley of the Mississippi. Here candor, truth, sincerity, independence, and equality predominate over the more degenerate traits of character inculcated in old and densely-populated countries. Inhabiting a country of immense extent, with boundless prairies and forests, and traversed by the most magnificent rivers of the globe, their ideas travel, and distance is correspondingly enlarged. Free to roam at will through the whole extent, with facilities unheard of in the

Old World, with them the field of ordinary travel is one which, in Europe, would embrace many nations and languages. Accustomed to the independent control of property and their own actions, the western people become habitually more ardent, more energetic, and more enterprising than the serfs and minions of arbitrary power. The constant toils and active life, prompted by interest and a hope of personal gain, in a salubrious and fertile country, give energy of action and a patient endurance unknown to human nature chained in its efforts and limited in its aspirations.*

13. *The Religious Character.*—The experiment is being made in this vast region of future empires upon a broad scale, which will test the question whether religion, as a national trait, can be maintained without legislative aid, or a union with the civil power. Men are here left free to adopt such religious views and tenets as they choose, and the laws protect every man alike in his religious opinions. Ministers of the Gospel and priests, being presumed as devoted to humanity, charity, and general benevolence, are precluded by many of the state constitutions from any active participation in the legislative authority, and their compensation depends upon the voluntary aid of those among whom they labor in charity and love. In a wide country, with large districts as yet sparsely populated, there are comparatively few stationary ministers; yet there are thousands, embracing all denominations, who traverse the whole country, forming an itinerant corps, who visit in rotation, within their respective bounds, every settlement, town, and village. Unsustained by the rigid precepts of law in any privileges, perquisites, fixed revenue, prescribed reverence or authority, except such as is voluntarily acknowledged, the clergy find that success depends upon the due cultivation of popular talents. Zeal for the great cause, mixed, perhaps, with a spice of earthly ambition, the innate sense of emulation, and laudable pride, a desire of distinction among their cotemporaries and brethren, prompt them to seek popularity, and to study all the arts and means of winning the popular favor. Traveling from month to month through dark forests, with such ample time for deep thought as they amble slowly along the lonesome horse-path or unfrequented road, they naturally acquire a pensive and romantic turn of thought and expression, which is often favorable to el-

* Flint's Geography, p. 140–145.

oquence. Hence this preaching is of a highly popular cast, its first aim being to excite the feelings and mold them to their own: hence, too, excitements, or, in religious parlance, "awakenings," or "revivals," are common in all this region. Living remote from each other, and spending much of their time in domestic solitude in vast forests or wide-spreading prairies, the "appointment" for preaching is often looked upon as a gala day or a pleasing change, which brings together the auditors from remote points, and gratifies a feeling of curiosity, which prompts them to associate and interchange cordial congratulations.

Religious excitements sometimes pervade a town or settlement, or even an extensive section of country, simultaneously. People in every direction are fired with a desire to be present at the appointed time and place of meeting. They assemble as to an imposing spectacle; they pour in from their woods and remote seclusions to witness the assemblage, and to hear the new preacher, whose eloquence and fame have preceded him. The preaching has a scenic effect; it is a theme of earnest discussion, with apt illustrations, forcible arguments, and undaunted zeal. The people are naturally more sensitive and enthusiastic than in older countries. A man of rude, boisterous, but native eloquence rises among these children of the forest, and of simple nature, with his voice pitched to the highest tones, and his utterance thrilling with that awful theme to which each string of the human heart responds, and while the woods echo his vehement declamations, his audience is alternately dissolved in tears, awed to profound ecstasy of feeling, or, falling convulsed by spasms, attest the power of western pulpit eloquence.

In no instance are these effects more striking than at a regular "camp meeting." No one who has not seen and observed for himself can imagine how profoundly the preachers have understood what produces effect among the western people, and how well they have practiced upon it. Suppose the scene to be in one of those regions where religious excitements have been frequent and extensive, in one of the beautiful, fertile, and finely watered valleys of Tennessee, surrounded by grand and towering mountains. The notice has been circulated for several weeks or months, and all are eager to attend the long-expected occasion. The country, perhaps, for fifty miles around, is excited with the cheerful anticipation of the approaching festival of religious feeling and social friendship. On the appointed day, coaches, chaises, wagons, carts, people on horseback and on foot, in multitudes, with provision-wagons, tents, matresses, household implements, and cooking utensils, are seen hurrying from every direction toward the central point. It is in the midst of a grove of beautiful, lofty, umbrageous trees, natural to the western country, clothed in their deepest verdure, and near some sparkling stream or gushing fountain, which supplies the host with wholesome water for man and beast. The encampment spreads through the forest over hundreds of acres, and soon the sylvan village springs up as if by magic; the line of tents and booths is pitched in a semicircle, or in a four-sided parallelogram, inclosing an area of two acres or more, for the arrangement of seats and aisles around the rude pulpit and altar for the thronging multitude, all eager to hear the heavenly message.

Toward night the hour of solemn service approaches, when the vast sylvan bower of the deep umbrageous forest is illuminated by numerous lamps suspended around the line of tents which encircles the public area, besides the frequent altars distributed over the same, which send forth a glare of light from their fagot fires upon the worshiping throng and the majestic forest with an imposing effect, which elevates the soul to fit converse with its creator, God.

"The scenery of the most brilliant theatre in the world is only a painting for children compared to this. Meantime, the multitudes, with the highest excitement of social feeling, added to the general enthusiasm of expectation, pass from tent to tent, and interchange apostolic greetings and embraces, and talk of the approaching solemnities. A few minutes suffice to finish the evening repast, when the moon (for they take thought to appoint the meeting at the proper time of the moon) begins to show its disk above the dark summits of the mountains, and a few stars are seen glimmering in the west, and the service begins. The whole constitutes a temple worthy of the grandeur of God. An old man in a dress of the quaintest simplicity ascends a platform, wipes the dust from his spectacles, and, in a voice of suppressed emotion, gives out the hymn, of which the whole assembled multitude can recite the words, to be sung with an air in which every voice can join. We should esteem meanly the heart that would not thrill as the song is heard, 'like the sound of many waters,' echoing among the hills and mountains." The service proceeds. " The hoary orator talks of God, of eternity, of a judgment to come, and of all that is impressive beyond. He speaks of his 'experiences,' his toils and his travels, his persecutions and his welcomes, and how many he has seen in hope, in peace, and triumph gathered to their fathers; and when he speaks of the short space that remains to him, his only regret is that he can no more proclaim, in the silence of death, the unsearchable riches and mercies of his crucified Redeemer."*

"No wonder, as the speaker pauses to dash the gathering moisture from his own eye, that his audience is dissolved in tears, or uttering exclamations of penitence. Nor is it cause for admiration that many who poised themselves on an estimation of a higher intellect and a nobler insensibility than the crowd, catch the infectious feeling, and become women and children in their turn, while others, 'who came to mock, remain to pray.'"

And who constitute the audience, and who are the speakers?
"A host of preachers of different denominations are there, some in the earnest vigor and aspiring desires of youth, waiting an opportunity for display; others are there who have proclaimed the Gospel as pilgrims of the cross, from the remotest lakes of Canada on the north to the shores of the Mexican Gulf on the south, and who are ready to utter the words, the feelings, and experience which they have treasured up in a traveling ministry of fifty years, and whose accents, trembling with age, still more impressively than their words, announce that they will soon travel and preach no more on earth."†

But the ambitious and the wealthy, too, are there; for in this region opinion is all-powerful. They are there, either to extend their influence, or lest even their absence might prejudice their good name. Aspirants for office are there, to electioneer and to gain popularity. Vast numbers are there from simple curiosity, and merely to enjoy the spectacle. The young and beautiful are there, with mixed motives, which it were best not to scrutinize severely. Children are there, and their young eyes glisten with intense interest of eager curiosity. The middle-aged fathers and mothers are there, with the sober view of

* Flint's Geography, p. 145, 146.   † Idem.

people whose plans of life are fixed, and who wait calmly to hear. Men and women of hoary hairs are there, with such thoughts, it may be hoped, as their years invite. Such is the congregation, consisting of thousands.*

CAMP MEETINGS IN THE WEST.

It was about the year 1800 that camp meetings were introduced in the western country, and for several years afterward they became a remarkable feature in the religious exercises of several denominations of Christians, but with none more than the Presbyterians and Methodists. The operations of the Spirit at these meetings were often remarkable and extraordinary to an astonishing degree. Conversions were exceedingly numerous and effectual, producing in most cases a thorough change in the disposition, feelings, and conduct of the individuals, which continued through subsequent life. At some of these meetings, which were continued from five to ten days, no less than forty or fifty persons professed conversion by a powerful and extraordinary change. During the revivals, which often extended over wide sections of country, several hundreds, and even thousands, were operated upon in like manner.

The *first* important camp meeting on record was held at "Cane Ridge," in Tennessee, in the summer of 1799. The revivals and protracted meetings which had preceded it caused it to be attended by a vast concourse of people, encamped in the dense forest, where the religious exercises were continued day and night. This novel mode of worshiping God excited great attention, and people flocked to it from a distance of fifty and sixty miles ; many came from Lexington, Kentucky, a distance of one hundred and eighty miles. At night the grove was illuminated with lighted candles, lamps, and torches. The stillness of the night, the serenity of the heavens, the vast concourse of attentive worshipers wrapped in the deep solemnity which covered every countenance, the pointed and earnest manner in which the preachers, in different portions of the vast concourse, exhorted the people to repentance, prayer, and faith, denouncing the terrors of the law upon the impenitent, produced the most awfully-solemn sensations in the minds of all present. A general scene of penitential sorrow, mingled with the ecstasy of joy and gladness,

* Flint's Geography, p. 147.

spread over the encampment, such as had never been seen before. During this meeting one hundred persons professed a thorough conversion, and thousands were deeply impressed with the solemnities of the occasion.

At this meeting about three thousand persons fell under the power which overshadowed the encampment. Among them were several Presbyterian ministers, who had before possessed, by their own confessions, only a speculative knowledge of religion and its influences.

Such was the vast concourse at this meeting, that it was estimated at twenty thousand persons. As no one man's voice could reach half the audience, the people assembled into several large congregations, in different portions of the encampment, and were addressed by as many speakers at one and the same time. The whole grove became vocal with the praise of God and the cries of the penitent. At night the scene became peculiarly awful and solemn. The long ranges of tents, the glare of the illuminated forest from the midst of the encampment, the moving masses of anxious and admiring people passing to and fro, some preaching, some praying for mercy, others, in the ecstasy of joy, praising God for his pardoning love, produced a scene of indescribable awe and solemnity.*

The majority were wrought upon by a silent, inward awakening, to a solemn concern for salvation, which brought them from "a state of nature to a state of grace." In some, however, the inward concern and mental agony occasioned the most extraordinary effects upon the whole physical system.

The next important camp meeting was on Desha's Creek, near Cumberland River. This meeting was attended by many thousands of people from the distance of fifty and sixty miles. The same scenes were again witnessed in a still more remarkable manner. Hundreds were struck down insensible and powerless, as by lightning, under the solemn exercises; others fell "like corn before a storm of wind," in the most intense mental agony. From this state, after a longer or shorter time, they would rise, "with divine joy beaming in their countenances," praising God in strains of ecstasy and earnest exhortation, which was perfectly irresistible to the most obdurate sinner. Speaking the pure and heavenly feelings of the heart, and burning with rapture, their words were "sharper than a two-

* Bangs's History of Methodism, vol. ii., p. 109.

edged sword" in piercing the heart and extorting the cry, "What shall I do to be saved?" In many of these impassioned and burning exhortations, the young and modest females, as well as the sterner sex, were endued with a fluency and a power of eloquence which "confounded the wisdom of the learned" and subdued the most stubborn hearts.

Curiosity was excited far and near, and the newspapers of that day abounded with descriptions of the operations exhibited in this work, both defending and condemning the reality of the astonishing influences there operating. Yet all tended to excite public curiosity to the gratification of a desire to be eyewitnesses of the phenomena said to have been exhibited.*

Not only the openly profane, the carnal-minded, the irreligious, but the formal professor, beheld these strange exercises with mingled emotions of pity and abhorrence. The natural enmity of the carnal mind, the pride of philosophy, and the prejudices of education and religious bigotry created a formidable array of opposition, which was displayed in a variety of modes. Some would scoff, others would philosophize; some would dogmatize in terms of religious intolerance while they beheld those manifestations which, by the friends of the cause, were believed to be the true power and grace of God.

Yet all arguments on these points were answered by a fact which none could deny: that those, in many instances, who had been most violent in their opposition, and most vociferous in their denunciations against the "wild-fire" and hypocrisy of the converts, had subsequently yielded to its influence, and had become convinced of its power; in such it had melted their hearts within them, and caused them to fall down upon their faces and to worship God, "declaring that of a truth God is here." Blasphemers, scoffers, persecutors, and bigoted dogmatizers were struck dumb; and "the tongue of the dumb was made to sing," and the enemies of the work became living witnesses of its power and divine influence.

[A.D. 1801.] At Cabin Creek, Kentucky, in the summer of 1801, twenty thousand persons are said to have attended the camp meeting, and but few escaped its influence and its mysterious power. On the third night multitudes fell, and remained unconscious of external objects for hours together; and, to prevent their being trodden under foot by the crowd, they

---

* Bangs's History of Methodism, vol. ii., p. 110.

were carried and collected into one of the squares of the meeting-house in the charge of their friends, until they should pass through the strange phenomena of their conversion.* Those who have witnessed these scenes can recall the picture faintly in their minds, but it is impossible to impart the conception to those who have never been present to witness for themselves. It is impossible to revive the thrilling sensations produced by the solemn melody reverberating through the sounding forest and echoed from the surrounding hills, bearing aloft the swelling anthems of thousands, rolling like the sound of many waters, wave after wave, and in sweet, melodious harmony, rising up to heaven.

> "The groves were God's first temples: ere man learn'd
> To hew the shaft or lay the architrave,
> And spread the roof above them; ere he framed
> The lofty vault to gather and roll back
> The sound of anthems, in the shady grove,
> Amid the tow'ring oaks, he raised his voice,
> And offer'd to the Mightiest solemn praise
> And supplication."

The ministers who led the way in these exciting revivals were William and John M'Ghee, the Rev. Messrs. Gready, Hoge, and Rankin, of the Presbyterian Church, and William M'Kendree, William Burke, John Sale, and Benjamin Lakin, of the Methodist Church.†

---

* The feelings and mental exercises on these occasions are contagious, and often spread like an epidemic through the congregation. I have myself witnessed them with mingled sensations of admiration and surprise; but it is no feigned condition, for many are involuntarily smitten down.

The most common affection is an ecstasy, or mental revery, attended with a sudden deprivation of muscular power and consciousness of external relations and objects, similar to a protracted catalepsy. Yet the mind appears wholly abstracted and absorbed in delightful contemplations, which often light up the countenance with a heavenly radiance scarcely less than angelic. This condition continues for several hours, and often for one or two days, during which time all the animal and voluntary functions appear to be entirely suspended.

One of the most singular and alarming affections which sometimes occurs in times of great excitements and revivals, is a spasmodic affection attended with the most violent and alarming convulsions. These affections are common to both sexes, but most frequent in vigorous, athletic men. The contortions of body, and the violent, rapid, and irregular flexion and extension of the limbs, trunk, spine, and neck, are such as apparently to threaten instant and universal dislocation of the joints. The muscular contractions are supernatural and violent, requiring the strength of several men to control them and to prevent serious bodily injury. The flexions and vibratory motion in the neck and spine have been seen so strong and violent as to cause the disheveled hair of ladies to lash and crack like a whip, perfectly audible at the distance of twenty feet.

Whether these things can be accounted for on the principles of *Mesmerism*, we pretend not to decide; but there appears to be a similar disturbance in the equal and natural distribution of the nervous influence and power.

† See Bangs's History of Methodism, vol. ii., p. 110–112.

CHAPTER II.

INDIAN WARFARE, AND ITS EFFECTS UPON THE FRONTIER PEOPLE.
—EMINENT PIONEERS OF KENTUCKY.—A.D. 1775 TO 1794.

Argument.—Man in his natural Condition the Creature of Circumstances, in Habits, Feeling, and Character.—The hostile Attitude and Jealousy of the Six Nations.— Their Neutrality secured by " Treaty of German Flats," in 1776.—Indians paid to violate treaty Stipulations by the British Commissioners at Oswego in 1777, and take up Arms against the frontier People.—The frontier People become daring and vindictive.—Influence of Indian Warfare upon Manners and Usages of the Whites.— Compelled to adopt the Indian Revenge.—Volunteer Defense of the West.—Personal Characteristics of frontier Soldiers. — Athletic Form and Strength.— Patience of Toil and Privation.—Recuperative Powers of the System.—State of Feeling on the Frontiers.—Exterminating Policy of Indians.—Cruelty of British Tories.—Spirit of Revenge in the People.—Their domestic Enjoyments.—Indian scalping Parties on the Frontier.—Their cautious and destructive Movements.—Renegade white Men associated with Indians.
Indian Implements of War.—The Rifle.—The Scalping-knife.—Tomahawk—Battle-ax.—War-club.—Declaration of War.—*Torture.*—Running the Gantlet.—Torture at the Stake by Fire.
Eminent Pioneers of Kentucky.—1. Daniel Boone.—His Nativity and early Habits.— Personal Traits of Character.—His first Acquaintance with Kentucky in 1769 and 1771.—At Watauga in 1775.—Opens a Road from Holston to Kentucky River.— Captain at Boonesborough until 1778.—Captured by Indians at Blue Licks.—His Captivity and Escape.—An active Defender of Kentucky until 1783.—Abandons Kentucky in 1800.—Settles in Missouri.—His Remains and those of his Wife removed to Kentucky in 1845.—2. Simon Kenton.—His Character as a fearless Pioneer.—Nativity and Early Habits.—Youthful Indiscretion and subsequent Hardships. —A Hunter in Kentucky.—A Hunter in Western Virginia.—Attached to Dunmore's Army.—Becomes " a Hunter of Kentucky."—His personal Appearance at the Age of twenty-one Years.—His benevolent Disposition.—Attached to Kentucky Stations. —Accompanies Colonel Clark to Kaskaskia.—Returns to Harrod's Station.—Visits the Paint Creek Towns.—Captured by Indians.—Wild Horse Torture.—Divers Tortures and Punishments suffered during his Captivity.—Sold in Detroit.—Escapes to Kentucky.—Serves under Colonel Clark in 1780 and 1782.—An active partisan Warrior until 1792.—Encounters *Tecumseh.*—Serves in Wayne's Army.— Abandons Kentucky in 1802.—Removes to Ohio.—Serves under Colonel Shelby in 1813.—Died in 1836.—3. Robert Patterson.—Nativity, early Life, and Habits.—Serves in Dunmore's Army.—A prominent Pioneer of Kentucky in 1776.—Erects a Station on the Site of Lexington in 1779.—Active Defender of Kentucky during the Indian War.—4. Major George Rogers Clark.—His early frontier Services.—His Character and Military Genius.—Superintends the Defense of Kentucky from 1776 to 1782.—Reduction of British Posts in 1778, 1779.

[A.D. 1775.] MAN is the creature of the moral and physical circumstances with which he is surrounded. As these vary, or as any peculiar circumstances predominate, so will be the physical development, and the moral and social character. Labor, toil, and constant exposure to hardships and dangers, give strength and firmness to the muscles, and develop the full stature of the body. Men accustomed from youth to brave every danger from man and beast, exposed to the constant inroads and assaults of the savages, compelled to be on the alert at all times and places, in order to prevent surprise and death, and often driven by necessity and imminent danger to engage in fearful encounters with the wily Indian in defense of their families or friends, of necessity became bold, fearless, and implacable, eager only for vengeance or victory, whether gained by open war or stratagem.

Contending with civilized foes, man becomes imbued with all the feelings and principles of enlightened warfare, as practiced by civilized nations; but contending with the naked savage in his native forests and mountain defiles, he necessarily becomes assimilated in feelings, habits, and customs, and is compelled to meet all the savage wiles and artifices with similar caution and circumspection; he is likewise compelled to adopt their policy of extermination toward their enemies.

As a beautiful writer has observed, " The success of the early adventurers to the West is almost a miracle in colonization. Nation has heretofore precipitated itself upon nation, conquered the occupants of the soil, and seized upon their possessions; but in this case isolated emigrants, without the benefit of military or civil organization, relying upon their own bravery and skill, and with such assistance from men equally daring as accident might furnish, seized and held an extensive country, and laid the foundation of powerful states. The waste of life by incessant war was more than supplied by a constant stream of new-comers, until the aboriginal race, weakened and discouraged by contending with enemies whom no disaster or defeat appeared to diminish or dishearten, gave up in despair, and attempted by peace to save themselves from extermination."[*]

The Indians, at the close of Lord Dunmore's war, had been compelled to yield to the demands of the whites, and to acknowledge the Ohio River as the western boundary of the white settlements. The hostilities which had terminated with the treaty of Camp Charlotte had served only to renew the feelings of mutual enmity between the white man and the savage. These feelings of mutual enmity and jealousy were but imperfectly satisfied on either side by that treaty, for the royal governor had an eye to future events which were likely to transpire between the mother country and the colonies. Thus,

[*] Kendall's Life of Jackson, p. 80.

in 1776, there existed between the frontier people and the savages a feeling of mutual jealousy and mutual suspicion, which was only restrained for a time by the proclamation of the governor.

Many permanent settlements had been established on the banks of the Ohio, above Wheeling, and on many of the tributaries of the Kenhawa and Kentucky Rivers. The Indians looked upon all these advances with a jealous eye, but their remonstrances were disregarded; and when they found, year after year, that these settlements continued to increase, and that with every increase came additional claims for lands still further west, the jealousy of the savage ripened into settled revenge, and a fixed determination to arrest the white man's advance.

The wars which had raged from 1755 to 1764 had roused up the whole northwestern tribes to the importance of protecting their country from the white man's grasp. After a delusive calm of ten years, the advances under Lord Dunmore's administration had roused the Indians again to a general war, and their hostility to the whites was only quieted by another delusive peace, which had been entered into by the royal governor in view of ulterior arrangements, in case the colonial disturbances should result in open war.

[A.D. 1776.] Such was the state of Indian feeling at the opening of the Revolutionary war; the Indians were content to remain quiet and see the mother country destroy her own colonies, which had been so annoying to their peace and security. Yet the active part taken by the colonists in the war under Lord Dunmore was such as to leave no good will for them in the breast of the Indian, and they could scarcely desire the colonists to be triumphant. The colonists, however, in contending with the mother country, desired no contest with the Indian; yet, having rendered themselves obnoxious to the Indian resentment by their former efforts in favor of Great Britain for the occupancy of the West, it was deemed expedient by Congress to conciliate the Six Nations, and secure their neutrality by formal treaty.

To this end, provision had been made for a treaty early in the summer of 1776, and General Schuyler, duly authorized and provided, repaired to the "German Flats," where, early in June, the chiefs, warriors, and sachems of the Six Nations were assembled in council. After due negotiation, a treaty was formed and signed on the 14th of June, 1776, in which the Indians stipulated to observe a strict neutrality in the war which had been commenced by England. Such was the relation existing between the Six Nations and the United States in the early part of the Revolutionary war. But British rapacity, intolerance, and barbarism could not tolerate such a state of neutrality.

[A.D. 1777.] "About one year afterward, a messenger from the British commissioners arrived among the Indian tribes, requesting all the Indians to attend a grand council to be held soon at Oswego, on Lake Ontario. The council convened, and the British commissioners informed the chiefs that the object in calling a council of the Six Nations was to engage their assistance in subduing the rebels, the people of the States, who had risen up against the good king, their master, and were about to rob him of a great part of his possessions. The commissioners added, that they would amply reward the Indians for all their services.*

" The chiefs then informed the commissioners of the nature and extent of the treaty into which they had entered with the people of the States the year before; informing them, also, that they should not violate it now by taking up the hatchet against them. The commissioners continued their entreaties without success until they addressed their avarice and their appetites. They told the Indians that the people of the States were few in number, and easily subdued; and that, on account of their disobedience to the king, they justly merited all the punishment which *white men and Indians* could possibly inflict upon them. They added, that the king was rich and powerful, both in subjects and money; that his *rum was as plenty as the water in Lake Ontario;* that his men were as numerous as the sands on the lake shore; that if the Indians would assist in the war until the close, as the friends of the king, they should never want for money or goods." "Upon such persuasion, the chiefs at length concluded a treaty with the British commissioners, in which, for certain considerations stipulated, they agreed to take up arms against the rebels, and continue in his majesty's service until they were subdued."

* See Narrative of the White Woman, and quoted by Mr. Buckingham, the English traveler, as unquestionable historical truth.—Travels in America, vol. ii., p. 179–183.

As soon as the treaty was concluded, the commissioners made a present to each Indian, consisting of one suit of clothes, a brass kettle, a gun, a tomahawk, a scalping-knife, a quantity of powder and lead, and *one piece of gold*, promising likewise *a bounty on every scalp which should be brought in.* Such is the price of blood and rapine with Great Britain.

In a few weeks the warriors, "full of fire and war, and anxious to encounter their enemies," sallied forth against the unsuspecting settlements of New York and Pennsylvania, and their deeds were inscribed with the scalping-knife in characters of blood upon the fields of Wyoming and Cherry Valley, along the banks of the Mohawk, and in the Valley of the Susquehanna, in massacres unparalleled in the history of Indian warfare.* Thus began the Indian war of the Revolution, prompted, sustained, and encouraged by *British gold and British rum.*

At the same time, orders were issued to Sir John Stewart, his majesty's agent for southern Indian affairs, commanding him to stir up the Cherokees against the frontier settlements of Virginia and the two Carolinas, occupying the territory drained by the sources of the Holston, Broad, Tugeloo, and French Broad.

The flame of Indian war was lighted up simultaneously west of the mountains and against all the settlements upon the waters of the Ohio. These feeble settlements, remote from the dense population and from succor, without defense or support, were thrown, as an isolated portion of the States, entirely upon their own resources for the support of their families in the wilderness, and for the protection of their homes and lives from savage massacre and rapine. Unprovided with the means of regular warfare, they were compelled to associate for mutual protection and defense with the limited means at command. Surrounded by hostile savages in every quarter, whose secret approaches and whose vengeance none could foresee or know, they were compelled to depend upon their own courage and energy of character in order to maintain an existence against the exterminating warfare of these allies of the British king. The mode of Indian warfare itself suggested their only course. To protect themselves from midnight slaughter, they were compelled to secure themselves in forts and stations, where the women and children could enjoy comparative security, while the men, armed always in the Indian manner, went out to meet

* See Buckingham's Travels in the United States, vol. ii., p. 179–183.

the enemy in their secret approach and in their hiding-places, whether in the recesses of the mountains or in the dense forests. Thus detached parties of two or three, and sometimes seven, were kept on constant duty as "rangers," or "spies," in traversing the forests in every direction, to prevent surprise at the stations and forts. None but the strong, the active, and the courageous dared engage in these excursions; the remainder cocupied the stations and forts as permanent garrisons, and as guards to protect those who were engaged in the labors of the field, or in the avocations of domestic employments.

Every residence, however humble, became thus a fortified station; every man, woman, and child able to raise a gun, or ax, or club, in case of assault, became a combatant in defense of their castle, and every able-bodied man or youth was a soldier of necessity. During hostilities, every day was spent in anxious apprehension, and each night was a time of suspense and watching, uncertain who might survive the night. Life, in such a condition, was a forced state of existence against the dangers of the tomahawk and rifle, for no retreat was safe, no shelter secure, and no caution effectual against the insidious advances and midnight sallies of the ever-watchful savage. The private paths, the springs, the fields, and the hunting-grounds were all waylaid by parties of Indians, who remained quietly in their hiding-places for days to secure the devoted victim who might incautiously frequent those places. To cut off supplies, the gardens and the fields were laid waste at night, the stock were killed in the woods, and the game was destroyed around them by lurking savages. The bear and the panther, and the most ravenous beasts of prey, were less an object of dread than the Indian, thirsting for human blood, and bent on extermination.

Every recent massacre of helpless innocence and female weakness; every ruined family; every depredation and conflagrated dwelling; every daring incursion and new alarm, served but to increase the white man's terror of the horrid warfare, and to stimulate his vengeance to deeds of blood against the omnipresent foe. To remain at home and in their fortified stations was to starve and make themselves an easy prey to their enemies, or to invite an attack from united numbers, which would overwhelm all in one promiscuous carnage; hence the active, the strong, and the daring scoured the woods for miles in every direction, to discover any approaches that might be made, and, in case of large numbers discovered, to give the alarm, and prevent surprise to the respective stations.

Were offensive operations in force required, where no regular government existed, and where no military organization had been formed, each man volunteered his individual patriotism, and devised ways and means for the general defense; each man became a private soldier, supplied and equipped himself, and entered the expedition to aid in the enterprise. The bold and experienced were, by general consent, placed in command, and all submitted to a cheerful obedience. If the object was the destruction of a remote Indian town, probably two hundred miles distant, and known to be the dwelling-place of hostile bands which had repeatedly laid waste the settlements with conflagration and blood, all were eager to engage in the enterprise. Fathers, sons, brothers, and relatives, all were ready to march to the destruction of the devoted town. Were the numbers required less than the voluntary levy, the leader selected the chosen men and the skillful warriors, leaving the remainder to defend the stations. Thus a portion of the pioneers were compelled to seek danger at a remote distance in order to secure safety for those at home. Every man was a soldier by profession and by daily practice. The frontiers were strictly military cantons for nearly forty years; every man from boyhood was a soldier, and civil government was a mere interlude between the great acts.

Courage, stimulated by the constant demands for active enterprise, unfolded to each man a knowledge of his powers and capacity. Mutual dependence, sincere friendship, and strict confidence in times of danger, cemented them into a band of brothers. The circumstances by which they were surrounded served admirably to develop all those manly traits and noble qualities which, united, constitute "nature's noblemen," such as are rarely seen in dense communities. Early and constant exercise, and habitual exposure to the labors of frontier life, in constitutions naturally vigorous, gave a noble development to their forms and physical stature.

The superiority of the early pioneers and hunters of the West was too apparent to escape the notice of the most careless observer. In stature of body, in strength and activity, in swiftness in the chase, in patient endurance of cold, hunger and fatigue, in dexterity with the tomahawk and rifle, no set of men probably ever excelled them. Not only were their corporeal developments of the finest proportions, but their daring and active mode of life, and the dangers which they encountered and surmounted from youth to manhood, stamped upon the countenance an open, frank, and fearless air of expression, which was the true index to the soul. Such were Daniel Boone, Simon Kenton, George Rogers Clark, Joseph Bowman, Robert Patterson, Benjamin Logan, James Harrod, Ebenezer Zane, Jonathan Zane, Adam Poe, Captain Whitley, Leonard Helm, John Sevier, Isaac Shelby, and many others who distinguished themselves in the darkest hours of savage danger.

These men, as were hundreds of their associates, emigrants to the western country, were persons of robust forms, of great strength, full of courage and fearless adventure. Such only could survive and withstand the hardships necessarily encountered in the western wilds, beset by savages in every direction. Hence, in the emigration from the older states, the choice spirits, the bone and sinew of the country, and the iron hearts only were attracted to the western frontier during these times of danger and privation. A detachment of these men, marshaled in the West, appeared like giants compared to common men, or like the towering grenadiers among common troops, and when experienced in Indian warfare, were more than equal to the savages themselves.

Not only did they excel in vigor of body and in physical development, but the firmness of muscle was peculiar, and all the powers of life within were endued with uncommon vigor and energy. The recuperative powers of the constitution, the *vis medicatrix naturæ*, was active beyond all former example among a civilized people. The restorative power of the vital energy was such, that wounds of a serious character, lacerations, incisions, contusions, and even gun-shot wounds, healed speedily and with remarkable facility. Wounds which, in a dense population or in a highly-civilized community, would inevitably have been attended with gangrene and sloughing, among these frontier people produced only a temporary inconvenience, and healed by the first intention, with inflammation barely sufficient to produce a healthy granulation; many have recovered after having been tomahawked and scalped; and

Simon Kenton recovered and lived to old age after thrice enduring the ordeal of "running the gantlet" in its worst form.

Few persons living in the old settlements, remote from frontier dangers and privations during Indian hostilities, can properly appreciate the horrors of Indian warfare, such as was encountered by the frontier people of Western Virginia, Pennsylvania, Kentucky, and Tennessee; no painting of the historian can fully describe them, and his most glowing descriptions fall far short of the stern reality.

The life of the frontier settler was one of fearful danger; a continual contest with a foe who recognized no rules of civilized warfare, and knew no mercy to his enemy but that of extermination. In civilized warfare, those not found in arms may be safe from the death-blow of the soldier; no civilized warrior dishonors his sword with the blood of helpless infancy, old age, or female weakness. He aims his blows at those only who are arrayed against him in open war. But the Indian kills indiscriminately. His object is the total extermination of his enemies, and children are equally the victims of his vengeance; because if males, they may become warriors, and mothers if females. The unborn infant is his enemy also; and it is not sufficient that it should cease to exist with its murdered mother, but it must be torn from its mother's womb, to share with her the horrors of savage vengeance.

[A.D. 1778.] The Indian takes no prisoners; if he deviate from this rule, avarice, not mercy, prompts the deed. He spares the lives of such as fall into his hands because his Christian allies of Canada will pay him more for the living prisoner than for his dead scalp. But perhaps the victim is reserved only for torture, to grace the horrid festival and furnish the young warriors with an opportunity to feast their eyes upon the dying agonies of an enemy to the Indian race, and to gloat upon the pangs which the slow fire inflicts upon the white man. The prisoner may be reserved, though rarely, to strengthen the tribe and to fill the place of a fallen warrior. The cruelty of the savage otherwise knows no bounds; his revenge toward his enemies is insatiable.

The confines between the white man and the savage presents human nature in its most revolting aspect. The white man insensibly, and by necessity, adopts the ferocity and the cruelty of his savage competitor for the forests; and each is alternately excited with a spirit of the most vindictive revenge, a thirst for human blood which can be satiated only by the indiscriminate destruction of all ages, sexes, and conditions.

Man, in his primitive state, is by nature a savage, and in his wars knows no object except the extermination of his enemies in one form or another. When civilized man comes in collision with the savage, all the usages and maxims of civilization, calculated to ameliorate the horrors of war, are abandoned, and civilized man becomes in all these respects a savage in his mode of warfare, in his unrestrained passions, and in his cruel excesses. Too often, indeed, under the contagion of example, we find that civilized man degenerates into the most inhuman barbarian, not excelled by the most ruthless savage. Instances of this kind were of frequent occurrence during the war of the Revolution, exemplified in the persons of the "British Tories," who fought with the Indian allies against the defenseless frontier settlements.*

Nor can it be concealed that the American pioneer, smarting under the loss of friends and relatives murdered by the savages under every species of savage torture, burning with revenge for repeated incursions and murders upon the settlements, from which they had escaped with impunity, should sometimes wreak his vengeance, when occasion offered, with an unsparing

* Instances of this kind were not uncommon during the Indian wars of the Revolution, when British Tories and Indians fought side by side against the Americans.

As a specimen of the inhumanity of a "British Tory," compared to that of the savage himself, we cite the following as one out of many others. "It occurred in the attack of the British Rangers, under Colonel Butler, and is given in Salmon's Narrative, and corroborated by several other authorities."

"'A party of Indians in the British employ had entered a house, and killed and scalped a mother and a large family of children. This was at a spot on the west side of the Genesee River, where a small town called Leicester now stands. The Indians had just completed their work of death, when some Royalists belonging to their party came up and discovered an infant still alive in the cradle. An Indian warrior noted for his barbarity approached the cradle with his uplifted hatchet: the babe looked up in his face and smiled; the feelings of nature triumphed over the ferocity of the savage; the hatchet fell from his hand, and he was in the act of stooping down to take the infant in his arms, when a *Royalist*, cursing the Indian for his humanity, took up the child on the point of his bayonet, and as he held it up, struggling in the agonies of death, he exclaimed, 'This, too, is a rebel.'"—See Buckingham's Travels in America, vol. ii., p. 180; quoted from Narrative of "White Woman."

Another instance of extraordinary barbarity in a "British Tory," or renegade Pennsylvanian, was in the person of *Simon Girty*, who retired from Fort Pitt to the Muskingum, and thence to the Sandusky River, identifying himself with the Indians in their most atrocious cruelties, and conducting some of the most desolating incursions of the savages against the frontier people; and who distinguished himself among the western tribes for his enterprise and daring against the settlements, and for the zeal with which he inflicted his vengeance upon his countrymen in many bloody fields.

hand. Humanity is the same in all ages under the same circumstances. The atrocities perpetrated upon the Ohio from 1777 to 1782, and in Tennessee and the Northwestern Territory as late as 1790 and 1794, no less than the inhuman barbarities of the River Raisin in 1812, were sufficient to provoke human nature to a revenge which was truly insatiable. Hence, in their successes over their savage foes, the backwoods soldier has repaid them "an eye for an eye, and a tooth for a tooth."

[A.D. 1780.] Nor was the frontier settler himself proof against the example set by the savages and their British allies. More than once it has happened that the pioneer warrior, in defending his home, and in revenging the deaths of his murdered family or of his friends, has transcended the bounds of justifiable revenge, and, yielding to the impulses of outraged humanity, has inflicted the most signal and summary death upon unresisting Indians. History does not furnish an instance in which a civilized people, waging war with savages or barbarians, have not adopted the mode of warfare necessary to place them on an equality with their antagonists. It is impossible to adapt civilized warfare to the chastisement of savages.

How can the unprotected people of the frontiers meet a savage war of extermination and cruelty? Can it be met and resisted by the lenient maxims and usages of civilized warfare? In the face of the most horrid scenes of indiscriminate slaughter, the wholesale murder of settlements in cold blood, in the face of the most atrocious murders of friends and relatives, whose ghastly wounds, inflicted by the tomahawk and scalping-knife, were crying to Heaven for vengeance, shall the guilty authors be treated as civilized men? or shall they be treated as human beings? The pioneer who has witnessed these enormities will answer, that every principle of self-preservation requires the adoption of the Indian mode of revenge in its most destructive features. Civilized warfare is inefficient with the savage, and to adhere to it in a war with them is patiently to submit to self-immolation at the shrine of savage vengeance.

For forty years was the strife continued along the frontier settlements of New York, Pennsylvania, Virginia, and North Carolina, from the first hostilities under the royal governor, Robert Dinwiddie, in 1754, to the close of the Indian hostilities by General Wayne at Fort Greenville, in August, 1795. The tribes engaged in these hostilities were alternately the "Six

Nations," and their confederates the Shawanese, the Cherokees, the Creeks, and Chickasâs. During this time but few intervals of peace were known, and for the greater portion of the time the pioneer settler was constantly menaced with the tomahawk and scalping-knife, over a scope of country extending from the sources of the Alleghany River on the north to the sources of the Cumberland and Tennessee on the south.

To the inhabitants of cities and countries long settled and cultivated, it seems wonderful that any of their race should voluntarily seek the hardships which were necessarily encountered by the early emigrants to the West. That wonder is increased by the consideration that it was at the hazard of their lives, and in the midst of incessant war. With the rifle in one hand and the ax in the other, they traversed the wilderness and erected their scattered stations. Party after party was attacked and butchered on the road through the wilderness. Boat after boat was captured, and whole families were massacred upon the Ohio River and its tributaries. Scarcely a station escaped repeated sieges by the lurking savages. Some were taken and burned; and the inmates, men, women, and children, were tomahawked, or carried prisoners to the Indian towns. The men were waylaid and shot while cultivating their crops, the women and little children were captured or murdered in their cabins while their husbands and sons were in the forest or the field. Still the adventurous pioneer advanced, and thousands from the older settlements seemed to covet the danger, which certainly had its pleasures, though mingled with bitterness.

"But could there be happiness or comfort in such dwellings, and such a state of society? To those who are accustomed to modern refinements the truth appears like fable. The early occupants of log cabins in the 'bloody land' were among the most happy of mankind. Exercise and excitement gave them health; they were practically equal; common danger made them mutually dependent; brilliant hopes of future wealth and distinction led them on; and as there was ample room for all, and as each new-comer increased individual and general security, there was little room for that envy, jealousy, and hatred which constitute a large portion of human misery in older societies. Never were the story, the joke, the song, and the laugh better enjoyed than upon the hewed blocks or puncheon stools around the roaring log fire of the early western settler. The lyre of Apollo was not hailed with more delight in primitive Greece than the advent of the first fiddler among the dwellers of the wilderness; and the polished daughters of the East never enjoyed themselves half so well moving to the music of a full band, upon the elastic floor of their ornamented ball-room, as did the daughters of the emigrants keeping time to a self-taught fiddler on the bare earth or puncheon floor of the primitive log cabin. The smile of the polished beauty is the wave of the lake where the zephyr plays gently over it, and her movement is the gentle stream which drains it; but the laugh of the log cabin is the gush of nature's fountain, and its movement its leaping waters."*

Such were the merry hearts of the frontier people in the absence of Indian hostilities and dangers. The intervals of peace were short and uncertain, but they were seasons of refreshment, which all enjoyed as a season of rest.

Yet they lived in continual apprehension of danger and death. "The wars of the red man were terrible; not from their numbers, for on any one expedition they rarely exceeded forty men; it was the parties of six or seven which were most to be dreaded. Skill consisted in surprising the enemy. They follow his trail, to kill when he sleeps; or they lie in ambush near a village, and watch for an opportunity of suddenly surprising an individual, or, it may be, a woman and her children, and with three strokes to each the scalps of the victims are suddenly taken off, and the brave flies back with his companions to hang the trophies in his cabin, to go from village to village, exulting in procession, to hear orators recount his deeds to the elders and the chief people, and by the number of scalps gained with his own hand to gain the high war titles of honor. Nay, parties of but two or three were not uncommon. Clad in skins, with a supply of red paint, a bow and quiver full of arrows, they would roam through the wild forest as a barque would over the ocean; for days and weeks they would hang on the skirts of their enemy, waiting the moment for striking a blow. From the heart of the Six Nations two young warriors would thread the wilderness of the South, would go through the glades of Pennsylvania, the valleys of Western Virginia, and steal within the mountain fastnesses of

* See Kendall's Life of Jackson, p. 78-81.

the Cherokees. There they would hide themselves in the clefts of rocks, and change their place of concealment, till, provided with scalps enough to astonish their village, they would bound over the ledges and hurry home. It was the danger of such inroads in time of war that made every white family on the frontier insecure."*

The state of Indian hostilities is one of terror to the stoutest heart, because the feeble, the unprotected, and the sleeping families are their chief victims. During a state of active hostilities against an extended frontier settlement, the Indians seldom appear in great force, or desire to meet the white man in the field of battle. If an Indian army approach the settlements, it is only to divide into numerous bands or scalping parties, for distribution against each unprotected habitation, which may become an easy prey to their wiles. These parties separate, and skulk through dense forests, concealed behind trees, bushes, logs, stumps, or in cane-brakes and tall grass, until some victim, unconscious of his approach, hears but the crack of the rifle announcing his own instant death. By night, a fearless band will gain a covert, in full view of some unsuspecting settlement, from which they can observe every movement, until evening twilight approaches, when they advance and sacrifice every soul to their vengeance.

When they appear in great force before a fort or station, where many families are congregated for protection, after the first assault scarce an Indian is seen by the besieged. Without cannon or scaling-ladders, their hope of carrying the place is predicated upon stratagem, or upon starving the inmates into capitulation. They waylay every path, and stop the supplies of water and food, and cut off their victims in detail, without exposing themselves to danger. They kill the cattle, destroy the hogs, steal the horses, plunder every thing which can be of use to them; burn the deserted houses, the barns, the stacks of grain and hay, and cut off all intercourse with those who might render them aid. The chief glory of the savage warrior is to inflict the greatest injury upon his enemy with the least injury or exposure to himself; hence he deems it an act of superior merit to destroy the unwary, the sleeping, and the unresisting victim. Although he often engages in acts of fearless daring, it is not his policy to expose his person; hence,

* Bancroft, vol. iii., p. 281, 282.

cunning, stratagem, and secret assaults are the means by which he effects the destruction of the unprotected. It is a maxim with him never to attack unless he possesses every advantage; and if this can be obtained by cunning, treachery, or stratagem, it redounds so much the more to his fame as a warrior.

While the scalping parties are traversing the country of an enemy, every precaution is observed to leave no " sign" or trace of their route; not a bush or twig is broken, not a stick or log is moved, not a stone disturbed, not a portion of any thing used by an Indian is dropped; not even his lodging-place for the night, or his excrement, is suffered to be exposed, lest the white man, skilled equally with himself in tracing the secret courses of his advance, might follow his trail, and take him unawares, or when asleep. Lest he should leave " a sign," he dispenses with fire, with food, with the choicest game, which may pass him undisturbed; for no indication of his route must remain to point his course to an enemy. He utters no sound above a whisper, lest some skillful hunter may be at hand and catch the sound. He walks slowly and cautiously along, and sees the minutest animal or bird that crosses the path, as far as the eye can reach; he sees every leaf that falls, every warbler that carols in the woods, and every branch that is disturbed in the forest. While he sees and hears every thing, nothing, not even the watchful tenant of the forest, sees or hears him. If any moving object in the vista of the forest attracts his eye, he becomes as motionless as a statue, and is scarcely discerned from the inanimate objects around him. Such is the character of an Indian brave as he pursues his way in search of his enemies, and such is the character of the pioneer scout, or " spy," who traverses the forests to watch the approach of the lurking foe.

An Indian army can not long keep the field and remain imbodied; hence, when they imbody for any great enterprise, they proceed rapidly in the direct course, governed by the cardinal points as to the direction, and come suddenly upon their object. A furious assault is made: if upon a " station," swarming on every side, with horrid yells, they thicken around the walls, enter the unguarded gate, or scale the palisades, and, overpowering the feeble garrison within, reduce the whole to a promiscuous scene of carnage and flame. The inmates, probably unconscious of the approaching host, had been engaged in the ordinary avocations of domestic life, and, taken by surprise, each defends himself and his friends with such means and weapons as are at hand, without any order or preconcerted arrangement. If the station falls under the attack, the inmates and defenders are mostly put to death with indiscriminate slaughter, the houses and defenses are destroyed by fire, when the victors, laden with the spoil, and assisted by such ablebodied prisoners as might be useful to carry off the plunder, depart speedily to their towns.

If the inmates of the station have fortunately received timely intelligence of their approach, the gates are closed, every point is manned, and the men, women, and children are assigned to their proper posts and duties, while the active defenders give their savage assailants a warm and warlike reception. The Indians, perceiving the danger of persisting in the attack, retire from the reach of the fire-arms of the fort, and conceal themselves in the neighboring forest. Each man being his own commissary, and having no supplies of provision, the host is compelled to spread out in search of game and other kinds of food, while a few chosen warriors alternately remain to keep up a strict ambuscade around the fort, lest any should escape and bear intelligence to other stations for assistance and re-enforcements, or lest any should get out at night to procure sustenance for their families. Thus for many days, and sometimes for many weeks, the siege is maintained by bands of Indians alternately relieving each other, while the whole region around, for twenty miles or more, is infested with lurking bands of warriors, whose whole operations are little better than the adventures of thieves and robbers. A successful attack, or a rich supply of plunder, would itself disperse the most formidable army of Indians; for the warriors, as soon as loaded with plunder, can not be restrained from returning to their towns.*

The horrors of Indian massacre none can describe: the scene of triumph and savage revelry over the mangled bodies of their victims, in a successful enterprise against large numbers, beggars description, and presents them more as fiends incarnate than as human beings. Scenes of this character were witnessed in the war of Pontiac in 1763, when the frontier

* See Flint's Life of Daniel Boone, p. 98, 99. Also, Kendall's Life of Jackson, p. 80.

posts toward Canada, from Niagara to Chicago, were simultaneously assailed by the allied savages.*

The most revolting influences of Indian association upon the white man is witnessed in the *renegade* who has become an outcast from his own people, and, with hatred to his own race, and vindictive toward those he may have injured, retires to the Indian towns, stimulates them to deeds of blood and rapine against his country, and enters with fiendish zeal upon the horrid warfare of the savage. Such men there were along the frontiers in advance of civilization, from which their misdeeds or their lawless propensities had driven them; men who, associating with the savage, found ample pretexts under British authority to wreak their vengeance, side by side with the Indian, against their own countrymen who had become enemies to regal power. These were the frontier British Tories and agents among the Indians. Imbued with all the worst passions of civilized man, they became, in their savage state, the most cruel, the most implacable, and blood-thirsty of the hostile warriors. Adopting the dress, the arms, the manners, and the life of the savage, they also wore the ornaments and paint of the Indian, not excepting the slitting of the ears and nose for the savage pendants.

Among this class of men none were more notorious than Simon Girty, a renegade Pennsylvanian, who was a hunter and trader near Fort Pitt at the commencement of the Revolutionary war. A man of enterprise and daring disposition, he shunned the intercourse of civilized life; and when the Indian tribes took up the hatchet, he retired to the towns upon the Muskingum and Scioto, and, finally, to those between the sources of the Miami and Sandusky Rivers. Here he was actively engaged in planning, organizing, and leading on many of the most powerful Indian incursions against the settlements on the Ohio north and south of Wheeling, as well as against those upon the Kentucky River. Before the close of the war, his name had become notorious as a fierce and cruel warrior, and a chief among the hostile savages. Not only did he organize their warriors and lead them to battle, but he often attended, if he did not preside, at the horrid scenes of torture at the stake.

Savage Implements of War.—The savage warrior, preparatory to the excursion of a war-party, paints his face fantastically

* See book iii., chap. i., of this work.

with vermilion and blue stripes, ornaments his head with feathers from the eagle, the owl, and the hawk, fantastically interwoven with his scalp-lock, and then prepares for his enterprise. Thus decked, and armed with his rifle, or the bow and arrows, his tomahawk, and scalping-knife, he celebrates the war-dance, and proceeds to avenge his tribe upon their enemies.

1. The *rifle* is indispensable to every warrior who can procure fire-arms; this accompanies him in all his excursions of every kind and of every distance, and none is more skillful in its use than the Indian.

Where the rifle is not obtainable, the bow and arrow, in the hand of the warrior, is not less deadly in its effects as an offensive weapon in a close engagement, no less than in pursuit and in retreat; it is more efficient than the rifle itself, because its deadly shafts are hurled with greater frequency.

2. The *scalping-knife* is a part of his dress; it is worn in his belt at all times, and is a substitute for the dagger in all cases of close personal contest. It serves the uses of a knife in all cases: being large and sharp, it is a butcher-knife in killing his game, in skinning and dressing the bear, the deer, or the buffalo; but its most terrible use is to butcher helpless human beings, to cut their throats from ear to ear, to disembowel them, and otherwise to mangle their bodies. Its chief and indispensable use, however, and from which it derives its ominous name, is to strip the scalp from the heads of his victims as the trophies of his prowess.

3. The *tomahawk* is a small, narrow hatchet, not unlike those used by plasterers, having a cutting edge on one side and a hammer on the other. With the first he cleaves open the skull of his enemy as he stands or runs; with the other he knocks him in the head after he has fallen, as a butcher would a steer at the bull-ring, to extinguish life. Sometimes the tomahawk is hollow, and serves likewise for a pipe, in which he smokes his tobacco.

The tomahawk is also used as a missile, and is often thrown at the enemy before he comes into close quarters. Such is the practiced skill in throwing this weapon, that the warrior can plant its edge fast in a sapling not six inches in diameter at the distance of thirty yards. Such is his unerring aim, that he seldom fails to plant it in the head or body of the victim at whom it is thrown. This is a terrible weapon in the hands of the Indian in a promiscuous massacre of an overpowered army or captured station.

4. The *battle-ax* of the Indian is still more horrid in its use. It is formed of an angular club, about two and a half feet in length, the angle of one hundred and fifty degrees, being about ten inches from the large extremity. On the outer angle, or curve, is inserted securely a flat, sharp, triangular piece of iron about three inches long. This answers the double purpose of a tomahawk and scalping-knife. In pursuit or close attack it is equally destructive with the hatchet; and when the victim is down, one stroke across the neck, under the ear, divides the carotids, jugulars, and wind-pipe, and death is certain. Instruments of this kind were abundantly used by the savages on the Ohio frontier, and in the Kentucky and Cumberland settlements.*

5. *The Bow and Arrow.*—This weapon is still used in war by the Indians west of the Mississippi. It is a destructive weapon, and in the hands of the savage was often more annoying and effectual than the rifle itself, especially in a general assault in the open field, or in the rout and pursuit of a retreating army. With his bow and quiver the savage could discharge half a score of deadly arrows as he ran, while his companion with the rifle would stop to load. Every arrow which took effect was nearly as fatal as a rifle-ball, and in a mêlée and rout it could be thrown with more unerring effect.

The arrow, whether pointed with steel or stone, was rendered fatal by the envenomed point. The force with which it was sent made its wound deep and effectual. The Indian arrow will pierce a man through; and often a single arrow is fatal to the buffalo, piercing him to his heart; and the rapidity with which these shafts are sent makes them terrible to a routed foe.

Torture is a part of savage warfare. If an enemy have been noted as a warrior, or if a white man, taken in battle or captured by ambuscade, is a distinguished leader, and has been efficient in repelling the Indian incursions, they commemorate his capture by the horrid rites of torture. The same fate is doomed to the first prisoners taken in spring, upon the opening of the campaign.

1. *Torture by Fire at the Stake.*—The victim is taken to the appointed place for celebrating this savage festival, where the

* See American Pioneer, vol. ii., p. 109.

assembled chiefs, warriors, and the whole population of the villages have convened to witness the approaching tragedy. The victim is stripped to the waist, and his face painted black. In the center of a circle of fagots stands a green sapling, to serve as a stake for the burning. With his arms pinioned, he is led into the circle and haltered to the stake, when the women and children, provided with switches, sticks, and clubs, approach and commence their part of the torture, assailing him furiously with their sticks and other implements. If he falls or reels under the innumerable blows inflicted, or recoils from their force, it serves only to excite the greatest mirth and merriment to his juvenile and feminine tormentors. In this manner he is exposed to this species of torture until he is exhausted, or until the incarnate fiends around him are wearied in their amusement, and retire. During this initiatory ceremony, the mirth and gratification experienced by his tormentors at the sufferings inflicted are expressed in repeated peals of laughter and other signs of merriment, while the warriors look on with unconcern and indifference.

The signal of a more terrible ordeal is at length given. The victim is disengaged from the stake or sapling, and secured to it by a green grape-vine tether or wet rope ten or twelve feet in length. This gives him a circle of twenty or thirty feet in diameter around the stake, which can be traversed alternately back and forth under the infliction of subsequent tortures. His head is now enveloped in a soft clay cap, to protect his brain from the immediate action of the fire, which otherwise might prevent his protracted sufferings. His feet are covered with bear-skin moccasins, having the hair outside to protect them from the burning coals which may become scattered over the area of the circle. The fagots, placed in a circle around the stake, are at length set on fire, and the blazing element soon completes a circle a few feet outside of the circle described by his tether. The prisoner, constantly shunning the fire, retreats from one point to another, and is scourged around the stake forth and backward for the amusement of the youth and old women, exposing every part of his body successively to the action of the fire, until the surface is literally roasted. During this part of the process, the youths and squaws indulge in the free and boisterous mirth at the struggles, screams, and the agony of the victim, while the crowd of spectators look on
Vol. II.—D

with complacency and unconcern. At length, after this ceremony has continued half an hour or more, the victim, exhausted with suffering, becomes faint or insensible, reels to and fro, or falls upon the ground. To rouse his latent sensibilities, and to quicken his movements, the warriors, and even the squaws, step into the ring, and by the application of firebrands to his skin, or by piercing his body with blazing fagots of pine, endeavor to rouse him to renewed efforts.

If the victim be an Indian warrior, he is now goaded to perfect fury; he sweeps around the extent of his circle, kicking, biting, and stamping with inconceivable rage. As he sweeps around, the women and children fly from him with great merriment, and give place to fresh tormentors. At other times the warrior will bear all their torments without disclosing a single indication of pain, sullenly smoking his pipe, while he scornfully derides his tormentors by singing, or applying to them the most reproachful epithets, of which none is more degrading than the term of *old women* or *squaws*.

As the victim becomes faint and exhausted, the cap of clay is removed from his head, and burning coals and hot embers are poured over the head; at other times the scalp itself is removed with the scalping-knife, and hot embers poured over the bleeding skull.[*] At length some old warrior takes pity upon him, and with one blow of the tomahawk releases him from his agony.

2. The *Gantlet.*—This is likewise a severe ordeal, but not invariably fatal. This torture is likewise inflicted upon the prisoners who are deemed worthy such distinguished honor. The mode of conducting this torture is as follows: The inhabitants of one or more villages assemble near a council-house, and young and old, male and female, are formed in two parallel lines facing each other, and about ten feet apart, extending from three to six hundred yards in length, and terminating within fifty yards of the council-house, and comprising from one to five hundred individuals. The victim is taken to the remote extremity, and stripped of any clothing which might furnish protection from the blows and stripes aimed at his body, and thus he stands ready for sacrifice.

Each person in the lines has prepared himself, or herself, with some weapon or implement with which they intend to in-

---

[*] See Flint's Life of Boone, p. 140, 141.

flict a blow or wound as he passes in his race to the council-house. The women and boys have switches, rods, or sticks; the men have sticks, clubs, paddles, and sometimes knives, with which they seek to inflict some injury as he passes. All things having been duly arranged, the signal is given, the victim takes his position at the extremity of the two lines, his race is pointed out to him, and he is told to exert himself and do his best; that if he make his way alive to the council-house, it shall be to him an asylum not to be violated. He is scourged by those around him, and commanded to run for his life. As he progresses, every one endeavors to inflict a blow as he approaches; and many a severe buffet, and many a stripe, and many a heavy blow, and sometimes a deep wound by knives, does he receive before he reaches the goal of his desire. None but the vigorous and active can expect to reach the " council-house," and few who expect it ever succeed. The repeated blows, which fall thick and heavy upon him, seldom fail to arrest his career before he has run more than half his race.*

Simon Kenton, one of the most athletic of the Kentucky pioneer warriors, succeeded in reaching the council-house in three different towns, where he was compelled to submit to this species of torture while a prisoner among the Indians.

Declaration of War.—This ceremony, with the Mingoes, was at once singular and terribly expressive. When it had been determined in council to declare war against an enemy, a formal declaration of their intention was made in their peculiar style. A chief in command of a party of warriors proceeds to the vicinity of some small settlement, where they kill and scalp all that fall into their hands, burn the houses, and completely lay waste the enclosures, and secure the plunder preparatory to their return. The *war-club* is then placed in some conspicuous place, where it can not fail to be seen by those who come to pay the last tribute of sepulture to their friends. The pioneer, seeing the emblem, knows well the fearful import. The symbol near the silent dead and smoking ruins gives an indication which can not be misunderstood. It declares that a national war has begun, and that the havoc near is only a notice of future visitations still more terrible. This symbol was left by Logan, the Cayuga chief, in the beginning of Lord Dunmore's war in Western Virginia. The same symbol was also left, in

---

* See Flint's Life of Boone, p. 176. Also, M'Donald's Life of Simon Kenton.

the same manner, at the Big Bottom, on the Muskingum, in the winter of 1790 and 1791 ; a full warning of the dangers which threatened them.*

The *war-club* is not a weapon of war, as its name would seem to imply. It is purely symbolical, indicating that the ball has been thrown and the game has commenced. The symbol consists of the club, or bandy. It is about three feet and a half long, with each end terminating in a reversed curve, not unlike the human clavicle. In the concave extremity of one end is a large wooden ball, firmly attached to the club. This ball is about the size of a four-pound iron shot. The whole is a neat piece of workmanship, and prepared with care by the savage.

The best illustration of the manners and customs of the frontier people during savage hostilities, and their characteristic traits connected with border life, will be found in a condensed summary, a comprehensive sketch of their lives and actions. Hence, for the purpose of presenting the reader with the tissue of dangers, toils, privations, and sufferings encountered by those who opened the way for civilization in the West, we will sketch the biography of some of the prominent " hunters of Kentucky," as exhibited in the lives of Daniel Boone, Simon Kenton, Robert Patterson, and George Rogers Clark ; the three former, bold, experienced hunters and woodsmen in their earlier years, gradually rising to rank as soldiers and warriors ; the fourth, a bold, towering, and successful commander in the warfare of the wilderness.

[A.D. 1769.] *Daniel Boone,* reared upon the frontiers of North Carolina and Virginia, west of the mountains, a woodsman and hunter by nature and habit, was a man of strongly-marked character. A bold and skillful hunter from his youth, shunning the dense settlements, and preferring to rove in the solitary wilderness, he became associated in his views and feelings with all that was wild, romantic, and aboriginal. Endued by nature with remarkable equanimity of feeling, which assimilated him to his red brothers of the forest, and trained from youth, by his avocation as a hunter, to traverse deep solitudes remote from social life, his countenance assumed that demure cast, which, like that of the Indian, knows no change from inward emotions, and preserves a changeless uniformity in every

* See American Pioneer, vol. ii., p. 109.

vicissitude of fate or fortune. Yet in his domestic intercourse he was sociable and kind, his manners were plain and unassuming, and his benevolence embraced the whole circle of his acquaintance. With great bodily vigor, with indomitable courage, and with perseverance which never faltered in his object, he was peculiarly adapted to be the pioneer to civilization in the West, while his talents for social life fitted him for the relative and social duties which necessarily devolved upon him, surrounded by a frontier population.*

Grave, taciturn, and retiring, he courted not the presence of the crowd, or the excitements of popular assemblies, but the excitement of the battle-strife, and the daring adventures of the chase, subduing the denizens of the forest, whether man or beast, were his chief ambition, and the great business of his life.

In the summer of 1769, prompted by wealthy men of North Carolina, speculators in western lands, and allured by the glowing descriptions of Finley as to the abundance of game and the magnificence of the western wilderness, Boone plunged into the remote wilds of Kentucky, in company with John Finley, John Stuart, and three other companions, upon a protracted hunting expedition. Here, in the wilderness, two hundred miles west of the Cumberland Mountains, and three hundred miles from the frontier settlements of North Carolina, the party separated into two divisions, Boone and Stuart taking one course, and the remaining three taking another, for the purpose of compassing a more extensive hunting range and scope of exploration. Boone and Stuart advanced westward almost to the sources of Salt River, where they found the buffalo, elk, and deer in great abundance. Bearing north, they saw Kentucky River, and with astonishment beheld its smooth channel cut out to the depth of three hundred feet in the solid rock, through which its placid waters gently moved. Here, from a lofty eminence, they beheld the beautiful plain of Kentucky. Intending to return and rejoin their party, they set out from Kentucky River; but they had proceeded only a short distance, when a party of Indians, suddenly springing from a cane-brake, seized and bound them as prisoners, depriving them of their arms, ammunition, and clothing. Close prisoners with the Indians, they were marched several days on the Canada route, when, by their knowledge of Indian character, they succeeded in making

* See Flint's Life of Boone, passim.

their escape, and recovering their rifles while the savages were asleep, when they pressed forward in their return route, and at length established themselves in a hunting-camp, preparatory to the winter's toil. Here they were soon joined by Boone's brother and a small party from North Carolina, who, spending the winter in a regular hunting tour, exhibited a fair specimen of " Kentucky hunters," securing skins and peltries, and faring sumptuously on wild flesh without bread.

[A.D. 1770.] In the spring the proceeds of the winter's hunt were sent by the brother of Boone and his companions to the eastern market, and Daniel Boone and Stuart remained sole occupants of Kentucky. But they were upon forbidden ground. It was the " common hunting-grounds" of the Shawanese from the north, and of the Cherokees from the south, upon which no white man could safely establish himself. An intruder upon the rights of the savage, Boone required all his tact and experience as a hunter to avoid being discovered by the vindictive red man of the forest. The Indians were upon his trail and his haunts, and his place of rest was daily changed to insure his safety. More than once had his camp been plundered by the lurking savage in his absence, while the wily foe laid in wait near it for his return. Still Boone, superior to the red man in his own element, continued to elude pursuit. At length he was encountered by the Indians, and the first fire laid Stuart dead at his feet, when Boone, disappearing in the thick cane-brake, without arms, ammunition, or clothing, eluded his pursuers and secured his escape. Then followed the trying time of the wary hunter. Alone in the wilderness, without the means of procuring sustenance, or of defense against beasts of prey, without weapons or hunting implements, he roamed sole white tenant of the " dark and bloody ground," compelled to starve, or to subsist upon roots, shrubs, and fruits. Thus did Daniel Boone spend the summer of 1770, until fortunately relieved by his brother's return in the autumn.*

[A.D. 1772.] The next two years were spent in hunting excursions and expeditions on the extreme western frontier of North Carolina, and in frequent intercourse with the Cherokee Indians. Still haunted by the images of the glorious fertility and abundance of Kentucky, he determined to encounter the peril of conducting a colony into that remote and inhospitable

* See Hall's Sketches of the West, vol. i., p. 241–244; also, 279, 280.

region.* Having advanced one hundred and forty miles, near the western side of Cumberland Gap, he was assailed by Indians; and after a skirmish, in which his son and some others were killed, he was compelled to fall back to the settlements on Holston. But the occupation of Kentucky was not abandoned; he only waited a more propitious time. During the latter part of this year he was interested in the success of the projected colony of Transylvania, under the superintendence of Colonel Richard Henderson and company.

In the spring of 1775, after the close of the Indian war, he accompanied Richard Henderson and company to the Watauga, to assist in conducting the treaty for the relinquishment of the lands south of the Kentucky River. After the close of the treaty, he was the first man to advance beyond the Cumberland Gap, and, with twenty hunters and woodsmen, he proceeded to open and mark a trace more than two hundred miles through the wilderness to the banks of the Kentucky River. This was the first "blazed trace" in Kentucky. Notwithstanding the Cherokee cession, the route was infested by hostile Indians; and although several of his party were killed in repeated attacks of Indians, yet he continued to advance, and laid the foundation of Boonesborough. Returning to North Carolina, he led out in the fall the first regular colony.

He was an active and useful member of the little Republic of Transylvania until the following year, when it was merged in the "county of Kentucky." In 1777 he was appointed captain, and served in defense of the settlements on Kentucky River until the close of Indian hostilities. In the month of January, 1778, he and twenty-eight men under his command were captured by the savages, and six months he remained a prisoner among the Indians of Canada. Excelling the Indians themselves in every quality which exalts an Indian warrior, he became a favorite among them, and was adopted into their tribe as a brave. Gaining daily upon their confidence, he became their most expert and confidential hunter, and obtained his liberty to go at large with the warriors. Evincing cheerfulness, and a feigned attachment for the Indian mode of life, Boone was hardly suspected by the savages of entertaining a wish to return to Kentucky. But Kentucky and Boonesborough were the idols of his heart; and he secretly longed

* Flint's Life of Daniel Boone, p. 48–72.

for the opportunity of presenting himself to his family and friends.

In June, 1778, when the British and Indians had assembled a strong force for the invasion of Kentucky and the destruction of Boonesborough, he determined to give the alarm, and thus prevent a disastrous surprise. Seeking the first opportunity, he escaped from a regular hunting-tour, and with one meal in his wallet directed his eager steps toward Kentucky. From the head waters of the Great Miami, traversing the wilderness alone on foot, more than one hundred and fifty miles in six days, along the most unfrequented routes, he reached Boonesborough in advance of the Indian host, and gave the first intelligence of the approaching danger.

The escape of the prisoner not only gave the notice for preparation to his friends, but it likewise deferred the contemplated attack; for, knowing that the enemy, apprised of their approach, would be prepared, they thought success hopeless.

In August, 1782, he was commander of a company, and, obedient to the orders of his superiors, but against his own better judgment, advanced against the concealed savages in the disastrous battle of the Blue Licks. In the heat of the engagement, he came into a personal and mortal conflict with a powerful Shawanese warrior, and in the struggle laid him dead at his side.

[A.D. 1785.] After the close of the Indian wars, he remained a plain and retired farmer, enjoying the domestic comforts of rural life in the country which he had explored, settled, and so nobly defended. But it was not to be his abiding place. While lands were cheap and plenty, and exposed to constant dangers from hostile savages, his right to the possession and occupancy of a small portion was not disputed; but when settlements were extended, and a dense population had filled the country, and Indian dangers were past, lands became valuable, and titles were examined and compared. The hardy pioneer, the hunter, or the woodsman, unskilled in the technicalities of law, and the intricacies of land-titles and judicial procedure, was compelled to give way to the avarice of the speculator, the land-jobber, and the script-holder. The possession of paper titles, or script, from the Atlantic seaboard, when the whole West was in the possession of the hostile Indians, had more virtue in them, and gave a better title to the emigrant stranger, than the actual possession and conquest of the country; and those who had expelled the savages, and encountered all the horrors of a frontier life in holding possession of the country, were, in their old age, compelled to surrender the result of all their toils to some fortunate heir, born to be an unworthy script-holder and legal robber of the pioneer. In all litigation relative to land-titles in Kentucky, the law leaned to the non-resident script-holder; and Boone, who could conceive no title better than conquest and actual possession, was stripped of his lands by legal decisions, while his personal estate was exhausted in payment of costs for the unjust decisions.

No wonder that Boone, in his old age, driven from lands which he so well deserved to inherit, retired in disgust from civilized society, and sought an asylum in the remote wilds of the West, beyond the reach of the land-jobber and script-holder! In early life he had found independence and justice in the wilds of the West, and he resolved to enjoy it still in advance of civilization.

Hence, in the year 1800, taking his faithful rifle and his family, ejected from their homes, and bidding farewell to Kentucky, as he had to North Carolina thirty years before, he took up his pilgrimage to the far West, beyond the Mississippi, and sought a last resting-place on the banks of the Missouri, within the dominion of Spain. Here, in advance of civilization, and beyond the reach of a crowded population, he spent the residue of his days, where he was quietly gathered home to his fathers before he had again felt the approach of the advancing multitude.

But he was not forgotten in Kentucky; there was still virtue in that noble state duly to appreciate his merits, and a generous spirit of patriotism could not permit his bones to remain in the wilds of Missouri. The patriotic citizens of Frankfort, in the summer of 1845, transferred his mortal remains from their resting-place in Missouri, and deposited them under a monument erected to perpetuate the memories of the first pioneers of Kentucky.* Henceforth the mortal remains of Daniel

---

* The design of removing the bones of Daniel Boone and his wife, to be finally deposited in Kentucky, originated with the "Cemetery Society of Frankfort." The association appointed Thomas L. Crittenden, Esq., and Colonel William Boone, a committee for the removal of the remains of Colonel Daniel Boone and his wife from their resting-place on the lands of Harvey Griswold, in Warren county, Missouri, to Frankfort, Kentucky, for the purpose of enabling said society to render appropriate honors

Boone, and those of Rebecca Bryan, who had been the wife of his bosom for more than forty-five years, the companion and solace of his life, and his theme in death, shall remain inseparable until the general resurrection.

2. *Simon Kenton* was one of the most fearless and the most successful of the Indian fighters in Kentucky, not excepting Daniel Boone himself. No man among all the daring pioneers of the West encountered the savage foe in so many ways and on so many bloody fields. No one man in his own person encountered as many dangers, as many privations, and as many hair-breadth escapes in defense of the western settlements, from the very first dawn of civilization upon the Ohio. Others may have distinguished themselves by their usefulness in any one sphere of action, or in one or more important engagements with the savages; but with Kenton it was one uninterrupted train of operations, a continued scene of perils unknown to any other man. Rarely deigning to shelter himself in forts and stations, he preferred to encounter the enemy in the open forest, depending alone for success upon his superior strength, skill, and prowess. The child of adversity and the sport of fortune, his life can not fail to present an impressive picture of the dangers, privations, and horrors of a frontier life during a state of Indian war.

Born of Irish parents, in March, 1755, in Fauquier county, Virginia, he spent the first fifteen years of his life in the humble labors of the field and in the domestic avocations of a frontier life. His father being poor, and belonging to one of the degraded classes of the British empire, from whom the lordly aristocracy of England exclude even the first glimmerings of learning and science, Simon grew up to manhood in the aristocratic province of Virginia utterly ignorant of the English alphabet, and old age found him barely able to inscribe a scroll

---

to said remains. Thirty years since, Daniel Boone selected this spot in Missouri for the interment of his wife, with the request that his own body might be deposited by her side, which was done accordingly five years afterward. In this place they remained until July 17th, 1845, when, in the presence of the committee, and the assenting relatives of Daniel Boone, and the assembled citizens of Marthasville, the graves were opened, and the sacred relics removed. The body of Colonel Boone had been interred about twenty-five years, and that of his wife thirty years. The larger bones were entire, the smaller were moldered into dust; the coffins, except the bottom plank, were entirely decayed. The ceremonies of exhumation were honored by an eloquent and appropriate address, delivered by Mr. Crittenden, with a response and eulogy to his character, by Joseph B. Wells, Esq.—See Frankfort Commonwealth; St. Louis New Era; and Southwestern Christian Advocate.

with an autograph intended for "Simon Kenton." Yet he was not unskilled in the strategy of the hunter and the frontier soldier.

[A.D. 1771.] At the age of sixteen, an unfortunate rencounter, in which he supposed his antagonist mortally wounded, caused him to fly from the settlements, where law and order prevailed, to the remote West, where these restraints were unknown, and where obscurity might be a sure protection from the demands of law and justice. Hence, leaving his father's house and the victim of his just vengeance, he fled west of the mountains, traveling on foot all night, and lying concealed all day, living upon the most scanty forest fare, in constant fear of pursuit, until he reached the settlements upon the head waters of Cheat River. Here, almost perished with fatigue and hunger, and fearing discovery, he assumed the name of Simon Butler, and friendless, destitute, and unlettered, sought a bare subsistence by daily labor as a menial. At length, after months of arduous toil, he succeeded in supplying himself with a rifle, when he entered upon the hunter's life, and, in company with a party of hunters in a canoe, descended the Monongahela to Fort Pitt. Having secured the favor and patronage of Simon Girty, a man of talent and influence in the fort, he became special hunter for the garrison.* Here, having frequent intercourse with the friendly Indians, who then mingled freely among the whites, he learned to speak several dialects of the Indian tongue; and Yeager and Strader, two of his hunting companions, were already familiar with the Indian language. At this early date did Kenton become acquainted with the language of those who were to be his deadly foes in subsequent times.

In company with Yeager and Strader, Kenton set out down the Ohio, floating in a canoe, and visiting the Indian towns as they passed along in quest of the "cane lands" of Kentucky, of which they had heard much as a region abounding in game. At length, late in the autumn, they found themselves at the

---

* See M'Donald's Sketches, p. 201, 202. This is a small work which we have noted before. It is a duodecimo volume of two hundred and sixty-six pages, by John M'Donald, of "Poplar Ridge," near Chillicothe, Ohio, published at Cincinnati in 1838. Mr. M'Donald was a cotemporary with Simon Kenton, and has compiled his biographical sketches from oral information given by Kenton in person. We shall have occasion to refer to this little work as we progress with the history of the early settlement of the Northwestern Territory, and his authority is unquestionable. Having been cotemporary with most of those of whom he speaks, and intimately acquainted with several of them, Mr. M'Donald is to be relied on fully.

mouth of Kentucky River. Having thus far seen none of the "cane lands," they ascended the Ohio as far as the mouth of the Great Kenhawa, and ascending this stream as far as the mouth of Elk River, on the present site of Charleston, they established a "hunting-camp" for the winter's campaign.

[A.D. 1772.] After a prosperous hunt, the spring found them on the Ohio, exchanging their rich supply of hides and peltries for clothing, ammunition, and other necessaries, which they procured from a French trader.*

The ensuing summer and fall was spent by Kenton and his party in hunting excursions, roaming over the hills, plains, and mountains which lie upon the sources of the Great Kenhawa and Big Sandy Rivers. In these romantic regions of primeval forests, Kenton himself declares he spent the most happy periods of his long and eventful life. Here, in the majestic solitudes of nature, free from care, the denizen of nature in the full vigor of health, and abounding in all that a hunter's life can desire, he enjoyed that perfect independence which fears no rival in its wide domain.

[A.D. 1773.] The spring brought with it the portents of a savage war, the clouds of the American Revolution began to lower, and Indian difficulties in the West had commenced. The encroachments of the white man had become intolerable to the Indian, for cases of individual revenge were already frequent; and Kenton, in his lonely "camp," a hundred miles from the white man's settlements, was not secure from the vindictive savage. In the cold month of March, one evening just at dark, after a tedious ramble during the day, Kenton and his two friends had returned to camp, and before a cheerful camp-fire were lounging upon their bearskin pallets, thoughtless of danger, and beguiling away the dull hours of a winter evening with cheerful glee, when, like the lightning's flash, the sharp crack of the Indian's rifle laid Yeager a lifeless corpse. Surrounded by a party of lurking Indians, lest the camp-fire should direct their unerring aim, Kenton and Strader instantly fled under the shelter of night, without clothes, arms, or rifle. Thus exposed in the wilderness before the close of winter, in their shirts, without shoes, destitute of arms or ammunition, without the means of procuring food or fire, exposed to the horrors of cold and starvation, they sought their melancholy way through

* M'Donald's Sketches, p. 203.

a pathless wilderness toward the white settlements.* At length, with lacerated feet and legs, skin bruised and scratched by briers and brush, and nearly perished with hunger and cold, they fell in with a hunting party on the Ohio, by whom their wants were supplied.

[A.D. 1774.] The determined hostilities of the Indians the following spring compelled the hunting parties and traders throughout the wide frontier to retire to the settlements and posts. Kenton, with others, having disposed of his hides and peltries to a French trader on the Ohio, retired to Fort Pitt.

He is next employed as a hunter and ranger attached to Lord Dunmore's army. Selected by Major Connolly at Fort Pitt, he was employed as the bearer of dispatches from his lordship to General Lewis on the Kenhawa. Failing to meet the general's division while in his lonely search, he was attacked by Indians on the Kenhawa, and escaping, made his way through a region infested with hostile savages to Fort Pitt, in time to join the main expedition to the Scioto.

From the mouth of the Hocking River across to the Scioto, Kenton was employed as a spy, or scout, to range the forest in advance of the army, to observe the movements and "signs" of the savages, and to guard the army against surprise or ambuscade. The service of a "spy," or scout, in an Indian country, is one of great danger and great responsibility, and none but choice men are assigned to the arduous and dangerous task. None ever possessed the requisites of a spy more amply than Simon Kenton, and when he was in advance of the army it was more safe from ambuscade than if preceded by a cohort. Thoroughly acquainted with the Indian character and wiles, with deliberate courage, a steady nerve, a keen eye, ranging miles in advance of the marching column, and moving with the caution and silence of the wolf, he detected the first "signs" of a lurking enemy, himself unseen. Such was Kenton's task in the expedition to the Scioto.

[A.D. 1775.] The campaign closed, and Kenton resumed his favorite employment, and passed the winter in a hunting tour among the mountains and highland forests of that wild and romantic region on the sources of the Big Sandy. The spoils of the winter hunt having been again exchanged for a plentiful supply of ammunition, he descended the Ohio, again to explore

* M'Donald's Sketches, p. 204.

the famous "cane lands" of Kentucky. In company with Thomas Williams, early in May he encamped for the night at the mouth of Limestone Creek, but "saw no cane." Next morning, with his rifle, he commenced a hunting ramble over the highland plain, and before he had proceeded four miles from the river, to his great joy he saw "the most luxuriant cane" growing upon the richest lands he had ever seen, and which abounded in game, and was finely watered with gushing springs. Near a fine spring, bursting from the rock, he selected a tract of land, which he determined to secure under the pre-emption laws of Virginia. This was the first time Kenton had felt a desire to appropriate lands to his own use, and it became the fruitful source of perplexity and loss. His location was within one mile of the present town of Washington, in Mason county, Kentucky.*

In company with his companion, Williams, he erected his camp, cleared half an acre of ground, and planted a patch of corn, when his "right of settlement" was complete. The whole region for sixty miles south and west was the range of his hunting-grounds and his summer explorations.

In one of his solitary excursions upon the waters of Elkhorn, disguised as an Indian, he encountered Michael Stoner, a hunter from North Carolina, also in Indian guise. A silent contest of Indian strategy for mutual destruction commenced, but not a word was spoken. Each knowing himself to be a white man, and believing his antagonist an Indian, sought, by all the arts of Indian warfare, to protect himself, and draw the enemy's fire. After mutual efforts and manœuvers ineffectually to draw each other from his shelter, or to steal his fire, Stoner, suspecting that his antagonist was verily *not* an Indian, from his covert exclaimed, "For God's sake, if you are a white man, speak!" The spell was broken. They were both white men speaking the same tongue, and soon were companions in the solitary wilderness. Stoner conducted Kenton to the new settlements which had been commenced at Boonesborough and Harrodsburg. This was Kenton's first introduction to the inhabitants on the Kentucky River; and here he subsequently took up his abode as an active defender of these settlements through the Indian wars which soon commenced.†

But where was Thomas Williams? Indian hostilities had

---

* M'Donald's Sketches, p. 207. † Idem, p. 210–212.

been commenced by straggling bands of hunting warriors, and when Kenton returned to his pre-emption improvement near Limestone Creek, he found it deserted. The Indians had been there and plundered the camp, and a few rods distant he found evidences of a fire, and hard by were human bones, which told the fate of Williams, the first victim of the war in Kentucky. Returning to Harrod's Station, Kenton soon found employment congenial with his nature in guarding the inhabitants from danger and in supplying them with meat.

[A.D. 1776.] The Indians began to move against all the new settlements, most of which were soon abandoned, and their occupants retired for safety to the vicinity of Boonesborough, Harrod's Station, and Logan's Fort. These places, being securely fortified, served as places of general rendezvous. Kenton served all these stations in the capacity of a general scout, or "ranger," to detect the first approach of the enemy, during the remainder of this year. Here he commenced his pupilage in the wiles of actual Indian warfare, in which he soon became noted for his courage, skill, and stratagem against the wary Indian.

His first enterprise was one for the supply of ammunition for the general defense of the stations. A volunteer with Robert Patterson and twenty-eight other pioneers of Kentucky, he accompanied Major George Rogers Clark from Harrod's Station to the mouth of Limestone Creek, for the purpose of escorting and transporting on foot twenty-five kegs of powder to the stations on Kentucky River.

[A.D. 1777.] Kenton was now in his twenty-first year, and presented a fair specimen of a hardy, athletic young backwoods hunter. In stature he was above the middle size, standing in his moccasins six feet and one inch. His ordinary weight varied from one hundred and seventy to one hundred and eighty pounds; his muscle was full and firm, and free from redundant fat; his body was vigorous, active, and patient of toil, hunger, and exposure; his form was erect and graceful, his limbs well proportioned, and possessing uncommon strength. In personal prowess he had few equals, either among the American pioneers or among the native tribes of the forest.

His complexion was naturally fair, his hair flaxen brown, and his eye a soft grayish blue. In his eye there was a bewitching smile, which seldom failed to fascinate the beholder and bespeak his partiality. In his disposition he was frank and void of suspicion, generous, kind, and confiding to a fault. Careless of himself and his own interests, he was most happy when he could serve those around him.

Unskilled in the lore of schools or the refinements of polished society, he was one of nature's noblemen, uncontaminated by luxury and vice. Honest himself, he could scarcely conceive a motive for deception or dishonesty in others. Skilled in all the signs and maxims of Indian warfare, and expert in all the mysteries of the chase and in the exploration of unfrequented regions—true to his course as the needle to the pole, he was at home in the most retired valley or in the most intricate forest, and with his comprehensive knowledge of the relative bearings of remote points, he required no pathway to direct his feet.

Mild and benevolent in his feelings, he was slow to anger; but when his rage was once excited, it was a hurricane of action. When enraged, his fiery glance withered the object of his fury from his presence.*

His voice was soft and tremulous, but not unpleasant to the ear.

It was in the spring of 1777 that he commenced his fierce contests with the wily savage in Kentucky. While on a tour of duty as a scout, in company with five others, near "Hingston's Station," he was attacked by a superior party of Indian warriors, and after a vigorous defense he was defeated, with the loss of one man killed and all their horses captured by the victors.

Soon afterward, by the orders of Major Clark, the captain of each station was required to keep out three state-rangers, or spies, for the security of the settlements; and Captain Boone selected Simon Kenton as one of *his* state-spies on the part of Boonesborough. In company with five others, he was dispatched on a tour of duty, to guard the inhabitants from surprise. To accomplish this object, it was necessary to traverse the whole region from the principal forts and stations upon the Kentucky to the Ohio, and from the mouth of Licking on the north to the mouth of Kentucky River and to "the falls" on the south.†

* M'Donald's Sketches, p. 266.   † Idem, p. 215.

Kenton's first adventure in his new capacity was close at hand. One morning early, while with two companions he was just leaving Boonesborough on a morning hunt, and before he had left the gate, the alarm was given by two men who were suddenly driven back from the woods, with five Indians close at their heels. One of the men fell under the tomahawk within seventy yards of the fort. The pursuer, eager for his trophy, was tearing the scalp from his victim, when the unerring rifle of Kenton dropped him upon his fallen foe. Kenton, with his companions, gave pursuit to the remaining four Indians as they retreated to the woods. Re-enforced by Captain Boone and ten men from the fort, Kenton's party advanced until they were drawn into an ambuscade, and the whole of Boone's party became engaged in a destructive skirmish. During the deadly strife, while Indians and white men were sheltered each by his tree, Kenton perceived upon his right an Indian taking deadly aim upon Captain Boone, and, quick as thought, he dropped the savage before his aim was complete, and Captain Boone's life was the trophy of his skill. He had scarcely reloaded his piece, when the Indians in large numbers were perceived deploying from a covert on the left, in order to cut off their retreat to the fort. The fearless Boone resolved to force his way through their line to the fort; but in the advance the intrepid captain fell, having his leg fractured by a rifle-ball, when the pursuing savage raised the yell of triumph as he drew his tomahawk to give the fatal blow. But Kenton's unerring and quick-sighted aim dropped the warrior in his tracks before the tomahawk had done its work. Twice had Kenton saved the life of Boone that day; which drew from the intrepid captain, after being borne to the fort, and in the presence of the garrison, the well-earned and highly-prized plaudit of " Well done, Kenton! you have acted like a man this day!"*

[A.D. 1778.] During two subsequent sieges of Boonesborough, in which the garrison and inmates were reduced to great extremities, Kenton was a valuable and indefatigable defender; by whose skill as a hunter, and by whose fearless daring and perilous service the lives of the starving station were preserved.

The Indians, having dispersed in detached parties for miles around the fort, had killed all the cattle and stock of every kind; gardens and fields, with every other source of sustenance,

* M'Donald's Sketches, p. 216, 217.

were destroyed; even the wild game for miles was consumed or driven off; and none dared to roam the forest in search of meat. It fell to Kenton's lot to risk his life for the preservation of the whole station. Accompanied by a few choice companions, in the dead of night, eluding the beleaguering host in the gloom of darkness, he plunged into the remote forest lying south and west beyond the lurking savages, in search of the deer and the elk.

Penetrating the remote forest under cover of the night, they sought for game at the distance of nearly fifteen miles from the station, where they remained for several days, until they had secured an ample supply. The meat thus procured was carefully cut from the bones and *jerked*, or dried in small pieces upon spits before a slow fire until greatly reduced in bulk. Loaded with this substantial nutriment, the hunters made their cautious way back to the fort, and, eluding the watchful savages in the darkness of the night, arrived safely at the fort, and were admitted by their friends. Supplies thus obtained were the means of securing the beleaguered stations from famine and starvation. This substitute for better fare was eaten or made into broth, without bread, salt, or vegetables. Such was the service which Simon Kenton rendered to the Kentucky stations in the years 1777 and 1778.

But Kenton's restless genius sought a wider field of action. In June, 1778, he was the first man from the Kentucky stations who volunteered to join the hazardous expedition under Colonel Clark against Kaskaskia; he was also the first man to enter Fort Gage, the man who surprised Governor Rocheblave in his bed, and received from him the surrender of the fort, with its sleeping garrison.

No sooner had the Illinois posts and country been subdued and quietly occupied by the Virginians, than Kenton, seeking more active adventures in Kentucky, was made the bearer of dispatches to Colonel Bowman at Harrodsburg, and undertook, in his route thither, to reconnoiter the British post at Vincennes, on the Wabash, in order to furnish Colonel Clark with correct information of its condition, force, and the feelings of the people. At Vincennes, after lying concealed by day and reconnoitering by night for three days and nights, he transmitted to Colonel Clark the true state of the post, informing him of its weakness and the disaffection of the people. Thirteen days after his departure from Vincennes, he arrived in Harrodsburg and delivered his dispatches safe to Colonel Bowman.*

In August, Daniel Boone, having escaped from his long captivity among the Indians, proposed to lead an incursion against the Indian town of Chillicothe, upon the North Fork of Paint Creek, now occupied by the present town of Frankfort, in Ross county. The enterprise was one congenial with Kenton's taste, and his feelings were soon enlisted in the hazardous undertaking. In company with Boone and eighteen chosen companions, all armed with rifles, and supplied with knapsacks filled with parched corn for rations in their march, Kenton set out for the Indian town, distant one hundred and sixty miles. Within six miles of the town, Boone encountered a party of forty Indians, who were taken by surprise and routed, without loss to the assailants. But the fugitives, giving the alarm to the town, rendered surprise impracticable, and Boone ordered a speedy retreat. Kenton could not retire without another adventure. In company with Montgomery, a fearless Irishman, he laid in concealment near the town for two days and nights, until they succeeded in capturing two horses from the Indians, upon which they retreated to Boonesborough.†

In September following, Kenton planned an incursion to the Paint Creek towns in quest of horses. In company with Montgomery, and a companion named Clark, he succeeded in bringing off seven horses from the Indian town as far as the Ohio River. Here, having imprudently delayed two days in crossing his horses over to the Kentucky shore, he was overtaken by a party of Indians in pursuit. After a severe conflict, Kenton was overpowered and taken prisoner, Montgomery was killed, and Clark escaped.

The Indians were elated with their good fortune in capturing such a formidable antagonist and warrior, a future object for the vengeance of the Shawanese towns.

Kenton, deeming his case utterly hopeless, gave himself up to despair, in the fearful anticipation of all the horrors of Indian torture, and the protracted sufferings of the slow fire and the stake. Nor were these forebodings dispelled by the savage mirth over him, amid taunts and sallies of savage wit, while they ironically professed to admire his horse-stealing propensity, slapping him gently on the face with Montgomery's scalp.

* M'Donald's Sketches, p. 220. † Idem.

The horrors of his captivity during nine months among the Indians may be briefly enumerated, but they can not be described. The sufferings of his body may be recounted, but the anguish of his mind, the internal torments of spirit, none but himself could know.

The first regular torture was the hellish one of Mazeppa. He was securely bound, hand and foot, upon the back of an unbroken horse, which plunged furiously through the forest, through thickets, briers, and brush, vainly endeavoring to extricate himself from the back of his unwelcome rider until completely exhausted. By this time Kenton had been bruised, lacerated, scratched, and mangled, until life itself was nearly extinct, while his sufferings had afforded the most unbounded ecstasies of mirth to his savage captors. This, however, was only a prelude to subsequent sufferings.*

Upon the route to the Indian towns, for the greater security of their prisoner, the savages bound him securely, with his body extended upon the ground, and each foot and hand tied to a stake or sapling; and to preclude the possibility of escape, a young sapling was laid across his breast, having its extremities well secured to the ground, while a rope secured his neck to another sapling. In this condition, nearly naked, and exposed to swarms of gnats and musquetoes, he was compelled to spend the tedious night upon the cold ground, exposed to the chilling dews of autumn.

On the third day, at noon, he was within one mile of old Chillicothe, the present site of Frankfort, where he was detained in confinement until the next day. Toward evening, curiosity had brought hundreds, of all sexes and conditions, to view the great Kentuckian. Their satisfaction at his wretched condition was evinced by numerous grunts, kicks, blows, and stripes, inflicted amid applauding yells, dancing, and every demonstration of savage indignation.

This, however, was only a prelude to a more energetic mode of torture the next day, in which the whole village was to be partakers. The torture of a prisoner is a school for the young warrior, to stir up his hatred for their white enemies, and keep alive the fire of revenge, while it affords sport and mirth to gratify the vindictive rage of bereaved mothers and relatives, by participating in the infliction of the agonies which he is compelled to suffer.

* M'Donald, p. 223.

Running the gantlet was the torture of the next day, when nearly three hundred Indians, of both sexes and all ages, were assembled for the savage festival.

The ceremony commenced. Kenton, nearly naked, and freed from his bonds, was produced as the victim of the ceremony. The Indians were ranged in two parallel lines, about six feet apart, all armed with sticks, hickory rods, whips, and other means of inflicting pain. Between these lines, for more than half a mile, to the village, the wretched prisoner was doomed to run for his life, exposed to such injury as his tormentors could inflict as he passed. If he succeeded in reaching the council-house alive, it would prove an asylum to him for the present.

At a given signal, Kenton started in the perilous race. Exerting his utmost strength and activity, he passed swiftly along the line, receiving numerous blows, stripes, buffets, and wounds, until he approached the town, near which he saw an Indian leisurely awaiting his advance with a drawn knife in his hand, intent upon his death.

To avoid him, he instantly broke through the line, and made his rapid way toward the council-house, pursued by the promiscuous crowd, whooping and yelling like infernal furies at his heels. Entering the town in advance of his pursuers, just as he had supposed the council-house within his reach, an Indian was perceived leisurely approaching him, with his blanket wrapped around him; but suddenly he threw off his blanket, and sprung upon Kenton as he advanced. Exhausted with fatigue and wounds, he was thrown to the ground, and in a moment he was beset with crowds of savages, eager to strip him, and to inflict upon him each the kick or blow which had been avoided by breaking through the line. Here, beaten, kicked, and scourged until he was nearly lifeless, he was left to die.

A few hours afterward, having partially revived, he was supplied with food and water, and was suffered to recuperate for a few days, until he was able to attend at the council-house and receive the announcement of his final doom.

After a violent discussion, the council, by a large majority, determined that he should be made a public sacrifice to the vengeance of the nation, and the decision was announced by a burst of savage joy, with yells and shouts which made the welkin ring. The place of execution was Wappatomica, the present site of Zanesfield, in Logan county, Ohio. On his route to this place, he was taken through Pickaway and Mackacheck, on the Scioto, where he was again compelled to undergo the torture of the gantlet, and was severely scourged through the line.

At this place, smarting under his wounds and bruises, he was detained several days, in order that he might recuperate preparatory to his march to Wappatomica. At length, being carelessly guarded, he determined, if possible, to make his escape from the impending doom. In this attempt he had proceeded two miles from the place of confinement, when he was met by two Indians on horseback, who in a brutal manner drove him back to the village. The last ray of hope had now expired, and, loathing a life of continual suffering, he in despair resigned himself to his fate.

His late attempt to escape had brought upon him a repetition of savage torture, which had well-nigh closed his sufferings forever, and he verily believed himself a "God-forsaken wretch." Taken to a neighboring creek, he was thrown in and dragged through mud and water, and submerged repeatedly, until life was nearly extinct, when he was again left in a dying state; but the constitutional vigor within him revived, and a few days afterward he was taken to Wappatomica for execution.

At Wappatomica he first saw, at a British trading-post, his old friend Simon Girty, in all the glory of his Indian life, surrounded by swarms of Indians, who had come to view the doomed prisoner and to witness his torture. Yet Girty suspected not the presence of his old acquaintance at Fort Pitt. Although well acquainted with Kenton only a few years before, his present mangled condition and his blackened face left no traces of recognition in Girty's mind. Looking upon him as a doomed victim, beyond the reach of pity or hope, he could view him only as the victim of sacrifice; but so soon as Kenton succeeded in making himself known to Girty, the hard heart of the latter at once relented, and sympathizing with his miserable condition and still more horrid doom, he resolved to make an effort for his release. His whole personal influence, and his eloquence, no less than his intrigue, were put in requisition for the safety of his fallen friend. He portrayed in strong language the policy of preserving the life of the prisoner, and the advantage which might accrue to the Indians from the possession of one so intimately acquainted with all the white settlements. For a time Girty's eloquence prevailed, and a respite was granted; but suspicions arose, and he was again summoned before the council. The death of Kenton was again decreed. Again the influence of Girty prevailed, and through finesse he accomplished a further respite, together with a removal of the prisoner to Sandusky.*

Here, again, the council decreed his death, and again he was compelled to submit to the terrors of the gantlet, preliminary to his execution. Still Girty did not relax his efforts. Despairing of his own influence with the council, he secured the aid and influence of Logan, "the friend of white men." Logan interceded with Captain Druyer, a British officer, and procured, through him, the offer of a liberal ransom to the vindictive savages for the life of the prisoner. Captain Druyer met the council, and urged the great advantage such a prisoner would be to the commandant at Detroit, in procuring from him such information as would greatly facilitate his future operations against the rebel colonies. At the same time, appealing to their avarice, he suggested that the ransom would be proportionate to the value of the prisoner.

[A.D. 1779.] Captain Druyer guarantied the ransom of one hundred dollars for his delivery, and Kenton was delivered to him in charge for the commandant at Detroit. At the latter post Kenton remained a prisoner of war until June 3d, 1779, when, with the aid of Mrs. Harvey, a trader's wife, he made his escape, in company with Captain Nathan Bullitt and John Caffer, fellow-prisoners from Kentucky, and set out through the wilderness for the settlements on the Kentucky River,† having been so fortunate as to supply themselves each with a rifle.

To avoid hostile bands on the frequented route from Detroit to Kentucky, Kenton plunged into the western wilderness by way of the Wabash. Through this circuitous route, depending for sustenance upon the rifle alone, they pursued their lonely journey on foot without seeing the face of another human being until, after thirty-three days, they arrived safely at the Falls of the Ohio. Such was the termination of Simon

* M'Donald's Sketches, p. 220–225.   † Idem, p. 237, 238.

Kenton's sufferings and perils among the Indians in 1779; such, too, had been the renewed cause for eternal hostility to the Indian race.

[A.D. 1780-1792.] From this time until the close of the war Kenton was an active partisan in all the movements against the Indians in Kentucky, both offensive and defensive. First, we find him an active scout, with one companion, watching every movement of the Indian host under Colonel Bird, as they retired from the invasion of Kentucky in the summer of 1780, and faithfully reporting the same to his commander at Harrod's Station. Next, we find him commanding a choice company of riflemen in Colonel Clark's mounted regiment against the Miami towns in the autumn of the same year; and on the whole route, from the mouth of Licking, Kenton's company led the way, and conducted the invasion to the hostile towns upon the sources of the Little Miami and Scioto Rivers. Next, in 1782, we find him again a volunteer captain, commanding a choice company under Colonel Clark in his terrible incursion against the Indian towns upon the head waters of the Scioto and Miami Rivers. From 1784 to 1792 he was a frontier settler in the exposed region of Mason county, Kentucky, and took the command of all the defensive and offensive operations from his county against the savages. During these operations he was engaged in many fearful encounters with the savages, and once with the great, rising Shawanese warrior, *Tecumseh* himself.

[A.D. 1793.] Next we find him, in the autumn of 1793, acting major of a volunteer battalion of choice spirits from Kentucky, under General Scott, attached to General Wayne's army.

[A.D. 1795-1802.] After the close of the Indian war, Major Kenton retired to his farm near Washington, in Mason county, where he remained beloved by all for his generous and confiding friendship, and for his unbounded hospitality. His house was known as the stranger's home and the pioneer's welcome. He had become a wealthy frontier resident; possessed of extensive landed estates, a great number of cattle and horses, besides domestic stock of divers kinds, with abundant fields, he began to enjoy the comforts of a green old age in peace and competence. But a dark cloud was about to lower upon the evening of his life. Ignorant of the technicalities of law, and of the intricacies of land-titles, he had quietly enjoyed his possessions, unsuspicious of the requirements of law in the conveyance of lands and the formalities requisite to complete inchoate titles, until he was involved in litigation. Defending imperfect titles to lands which he believed justly his own, his whole attention was engrossed in efforts to secure himself and family from poverty and dependence in his declining age. He was now in his forty-seventh year; his ardor and physical energy abated, his spirits depressed by misfortunes which had followed in close succession, he saw himself ejected from one piece of land after another, which he had defended against the savage in his youth, and for which he had shed his blood and endured tortures indescribable. One suit after another was decided against him; one tract of land after another was lost; and one bill of costs after another stripped him of his remaining property, until he was reduced to absolute poverty.

Such was the recompense which Kentucky awarded to her pioneers and early defenders. Such was her gratitude to Boone, Clark, and Kenton.

Thus was Major Simon Kenton, in the forty-seventh year of his age, refused a resting-place in the country which he had defended against the savage, and for which he had spent the prime of his life, and had done and suffered more than any other man in Kentucky.

Hence, in 1802, he emigrated to the Northwestern Territory, and settled on the frontier, near Urbana, in Champaign county of the present state of Ohio, in a region then scarcely reclaimed from the Indian warwhoop. Here, in advance of civilization, he settled, preferring the dangers of Indian warfare to the treachery of civilized man. He became a useful member of the frontier settlements, poor and retired, but beloved by his neighbors, who subsequently elected him to the office of brigadier-general in the new militia organization of the state. In 1810 he became a worthy member of the Methodist Episcopal Church, and such he continued until his death.

[A.D. 1813.] But the patriotic fire of Kenton had not been extinguished by the ingratitude of Kentucky and the unfeeling avarice of her people. Again, in 1813, in the fifty-eighth year of his age, rejecting inglorious ease when his country required his services, his military ardor revived, and as a volunteer under Governor Shelby, he joined the Kentucky troops as they advanced through Urbana in their march to the northwestern frontier. Attached to the military family of Governor Shelby, and true to his former spirit, he adhered to the fortune of the army, and closed his military career by his intrepid aid in achieving the glorious victory of the Thames, in Upper Canada.

[A.D. 1820.] In 1820 he removed to the head of Mad River, in Logan county, near the site of the old Indian town Wappatomica, one of the places where, in 1779, he had encountered the horrors of Indian torture. Here, in a beech forest, he took up his final residence, where he lived in humble poverty through the evening of his eventful life, relieved from actual want, during the last twelve years, by a mere pension of twenty dollars per month from the Federal government. On the 24th of June, 1836, he resigned his spirit to God, in peace with all men, and in hope of a glorious immortality.*

[A.D. 1836.] Thus died General Simon Kenton, in the eighty-second year of his age, a man who, as a western pioneer, passed through more dangers, privations, perils, and hairbreadth escapes than any man living or dead; a man whose iron nerve never quailed before danger, and whose patriotism warmed up the evening of his life. After a long life devoted to his country, having passed through a thousand dangers, and having outlived the sufferings of a thousand deaths, he was permitted to die quietly in his bed at home, in peace and resignation, in the midst of a flourishing settlement, where once was the center of the Indian power. His bones repose within the bosom of the state which sheltered and protected his declining age, and well does Ohio deserve to retain them.

[A.D. 1774–1776.] 3. *Robert Patterson*, a native of Pennsylvania, was one of the most enterprising pioneers of Kentucky. At the age of twenty-one years he served as a ranger six months on the frontiers of Pennsylvania, during Lord Dunmore's Indian war.† After the treaty of Camp Charlotte he was a pioneer on the Monongahela until the autumn of 1775, when, in company with John M'Clellan and six other pioneers, he descended the Ohio from Fort Pitt to Limestone Creek, and thence traversing the country by way of the Blue Licks, proceeded to the stations then erecting on the Kentucky River. Soon afterward he joined M'Clellan in the formation of a settlement near "Royal Spring," on the present site of Georgetown, in Scott county, Kentucky. Here he contributed to the erection of the first log house built in this portion of that great

---

* M'Donald, p. 264, 265.   † American Pioneer, vol. ii., p. 343.

state, and which was subsequently fortified and known as "M'Clellan's Station." Attacked by Indians on the 29th of December following, the feeble garrison, encumbered with women and children, and unable to withstand a siege, secretly left the fort by night, and were conducted by Patterson safely to the more secure settlements near Harrodsburg. Here he became an active defender of the feeble colony first formed in Kentucky, and was called by Major George Rogers Clark, in 1776, to assist him in forwarding ammunition from Fort Pitt to be distributed among the settlements on Kentucky River.*

In the month of October, in company with Major Clark and five other companions, he engaged in the perilous enterprise of conveying powder to the Kentucky stations. Descending the Ohio River from Fort Pitt in a large canoe, with five hundred pounds of powder in twenty-five kegs, this fearless party eluded the hostile savages infesting the river until they reached the mouth of Hocking River. Here they were furiously assailed by a party of Indians on shore, when Patterson was severely wounded in the arm, and two of his companions were killed. The remainder effected their escape with the precious treasure, and succeeded in safely reaching the "Three Islands," above Limestone Creek. Here the powder was securely concealed from the lurking Indians until an ample escort from "Harrod's Station" should be able to convey it safely to the settlements.

From this time he continued an active pioneer soldier, engaged in the defense of the Kentucky settlers until June, 1778, when, with ten comrades from the stations, he volunteered to accompany Colonel Clark in his expedition against the British posts in the Illinois country. In this expedition he was an active and efficient subaltern, and took a prominent part in the capture of Kaskaskia and Fort Gage, on the 4th of July, 1778. In September following, in company with seventy others, whose term of service had expired, he returned to Kentucky and entered into the militia service at Harrod's Station.

In April, 1779, as ensign, commanding twenty-five men, he repaired to the south fork of Elk-horn, and encamped on the present site of Lexington, in Fayette county. On the 17th of April a stockade was commenced, which was the first white man's residence in the beautiful region which now surrounds the city of Lexington.

* American Pioneer, vol. ii., p. 344.

About the middle of May following, he joined the expedition under Colonel Bowman against the Shawanese towns on the sources of the Little Miami, in which he distinguished himself as a valuable and efficient officer. In August, 1780, he again served as an officer under Colonel George Rogers Clark in the expedition which spread terror and devastation throughout the Shawanese towns, from the sources of the Scioto to those of the Wabash. From this time until the close of the Indian wars, he was one of the regular defenders of the Kentucky stations in all attacks, and in every invasion of the Indian country. In the terrible and disastrous battle of the Blue Licks, on the 19th of August, 1782, he was a prominent actor,[*] and greatly distinguished himself for his generous courage. For several years subsequent to the winter of 1790, he was an active pioneer in the Northwestern Territory in establishing the first settlements made on the north side of the Ohio, between the Great and Little Miamies.

4. *George Rogers Clark*, a man whose history has not yet been written, was one of the most prominent pioneer defenders of the whole West; confined to no particular section of country, his field of operation was the whole western settlements, over which he exercised a watchful care, which secured them from utter extermination and ruin. For decision, energy, forethought, good sense, and intrepidity, he will compare favorably with any general of the Revolutionary war. In the West, he was certainly the best soldier that ever led an army against the savages, and he knew how to control those uncontrollable beings better than any other man of his day.[†]

Clark, if not the first founder of Kentucky, was certainly a principal architect in rearing the superstructure. He was the guardian angel which stood over the infant colony from 1776 until 1785 with the ægis of his protection, and his name deserves to stand enrolled high among the worthies who have been honored as the fathers of the western country comprised in the eastern half of the Valley of the Mississippi, and his bones should lie side by side with those of Daniel Boone and Simon Kenton in the capital of Kentucky, under the monument which patriotism may rear to their memories.

He has been justly esteemed as the most extraordinary mil-

---

[*] American Pioneer, vol. ii., p. 346.
[†] See North American Review, No. 105, October, 1839, p. 295.

itary genius which Virginia has ever produced, although the field of his operations was the remote wilderness of the West. Judge Hall declares him to have been " a man of extraordinary talents and energy of character, and possessed of a military genius, which enabled him to plan with consummate wisdom, and to execute his designs with decision and promptitude." His great mind* readily comprehended the situation of the country; he made himself acquainted with the topography of the whole region and the localities of the enemy's forts, as well as the strength of their forces. He possessed the rare faculty of "penetrating the designs" of his antagonist; thus becoming informed of the actual condition and movements of the enemy, he could deduce his subsequent operations and his ulterior designs, and hence was enabled to anticipate and defeat all his plans and movements before they were matured. In the execution of his plans, his movements were made with such precision and celerity, and conducted with such consummate judgment, that success was always doubly insured.

In his personal appearance Major Clark was commanding and dignified; hence, as Mr. Marshall observes, "His appearance was well calculated to attract attention; and it was rendered particularly agreeable by the manliness of his deportment, the intelligence of his conversation, and, above all, by the vivacity and boldness of his spirit for enterprise."†

Major Clark was a native of Virginia, and was engaged in the early defense of the western inhabitants of the Old Dominion; yet the most important portion of his history commences in 1776, when he was upon the Ohio frontier, engaged in the protection of the settlements against Indian hostilities consequent upon the war of the Revolution. He was upon the frontiers near the Monongahela and southward to the Kenhawa during the year 1776, and superintended the construction of Fort Fincastle for the protection of the inhabitants in the vicinity of Wheeling Creek, as well as other settlements north and south of that point, near the Ohio River. Subsequently he repaired to Kentucky, and superintended the construction and defense of the settlements in that quarter. Finding those settlements in a state of insecurity, and destitute of ammunition for defense, he procured from the executive of Virginia an appropriation of five hundred pounds of powder for the use of

* Sketches of the West, vol. ii., p. 118–121.   † History of Kentucky.

the Kentucky stations. Repairing in person to Fort Pitt, he obtained the powder, and with six men conducted it safely through the Indian territory, down the Ohio to the " Three Islands," near Limestone Creek, where it was carefully concealed from the scrutiny of the savages, who roamed the whole country. Finding it too hazardous to advance with the precious treasure without a strong guard, he returned to Harrodsburg on foot, in company with Captain Jones, and by way of " M'Clellan's Station," for a sufficient escort to conduct it safely to the forts. Having procured the aid of Simon Kenton, Robert Patterson, and twenty-seven other hunters of like mold from the stations, he set out for the place of concealment, and returned a few days afterward, each man bearing his keg of powder.

[A.D. 1777.] Shortly afterward he received his commission from the governor, authorizing him to organize the militia of the Kentucky stations. The militia of Kentucky were accordingly organized into three companies: one at Boonesborough, under Captain Daniel Boone; one at Logan's Fort, under Captain Benjamin Logan; and one at Harrod's Station, under Captain James Harrod. This was the first militia organization in Kentucky. From this time, Major Clark, as the real father of Kentucky, continued to watch over the infant settlements with paternal solicitude, which never faltered, until the close of the Revolutionary difficulties. During his service on the western frontier, he was advanced to the rank of brigadier-general, and was actual commander-in-chief of all the Virginia forces on the Ohio.

His observing eye and his military perception soon discovered that, after Detroit, the posts at Vincennes and Kaskaskia were the grand sources of Indian hostilities, the points from which emanated the plans and operations of the western savages for the destruction of the Kentucky settlements. Having been perfectly convinced of this fact, he conceived the design of putting an end to these incursions by the capture or destruction of these posts. Concealing his designs, he proceeded to Williamsburg, the capital of Virginia, to concert with the governor and Executive Council a plan for accomplishing this object. His views and plans were approved by the governor, and measures were adopted to enable him to execute his designs. It was then that Major Clark was commissioned as colonel, with authority to raise a battalion of seven companies in the western counties of Virginia for a secret expedition under his command.

Early in June his recruiting captains returned with their levies from the counties west of the Blue Ridge to Pittsburgh, and he descended the Ohio with the broken companies to "the Falls." Here, encamped on "Corn Island," he tarried some time, in hopes of recruiting his forces from the stations; but the secret expedition was unpopular in the settlements, which were entirely dependent on the protection of the militia, and it was deemed inexpedient to reduce their numbers, and thereby invite attack from the enemy.

With one hundred and fifty-three men, he descended the river below the mouth of the Tennessee; there concealing his boats, he advanced through the wilderness direct to Kaskaskia, and on the night of July 4th took possession of the British post and the town of Kaskaskia, without the loss of a man or the fire of a gun.

[A.D. 1778.] A few days sufficed to reduce the whole country to the allegiance of Virginia, and the posts to her arms. Before the lapse of many days he was master of all the British posts from the Wabash to the Upper Mississippi, had established the authority of Virginia, and had sent the governor and commandants prisoners of war to the State capital.

[A.D. 1779.] The following year, the British commandant at Detroit having advanced upon Vincennes and recovered the post, which had been without a garrison, Colonel Clark, with the same celerity as at Kaskaskia, advanced eastward to the Wabash, at the most wet and inclement season of the winter, and after an investment of thirty-six hours, captured the entire British force and recovered the place, sending Colonel Hamilton and his officers prisoners of war to Virginia.

[A.D. 1780.] Having supreme military command on the Lower Ohio and on the Mississippi, he established Fort Jefferson on the Mississippi, a few miles below the Ohio, thus extending the authority and the arms of Virginia to the remotest limit of British power in the West. For several years afterward he commanded on the Ohio above "the Falls," and became the admiration and the terror of the hostile tribes.

The history of Colonel Clark during the subsequent years, until 1786, is so intimately blended with that of Kentucky, that it is unnecessary here to trace his services further.

CHAPTER III.

EXTENSION OF VIRGINIA SETTLEMENTS AND JURISDICTION TO THE MISSISSIPPI.—INDIAN HOSTILITIES UPON THE OHIO.—A.D. 1776 TO 1780.

Argument.—Retrospect of the frontier Settlements of Western Virginia, Pennsylvania, North Carolina, and Kentucky in 1776.—Check to these Settlements by hostile Cherokees.—Cherokee War.—Three-fold Invasion of Cherokee Country.—" Treaty of Dewett's Corner."—" Treaty of Long Island," on Holston.—Cherokees retire from ceded Territory.—Hostilities of Northwestern Tribes.—Kentucky Stations supplied with Powder by Major Clark.—Posts on the Ohio.—Attack on M'Clellan's Station, December, 1776.—Hostilities in West Augusta.— County of Kentucky erected.— Militia Organization in 1777.—District of West Augusta divided into three Counties. —Ohio County organized.—Settlements in West Augusta.—The Indians attack Harrod's Station ; also, Logan's Fort and Boonesborough.—Militia organization in Ohio County.—Memorable Siege of Boonesborough from July 4th to September.— Captain Logan's Re-enforcement from North Carolina.—Colonel John Bowman's Re-enforcement.—County of Kentucky organized.—Militia Organization.—Extent of Kentucky County.—Colonel Henderson indemnified for Loss of. Transylvania.—Indian Hostilities near the Ohio.—Cornstalk, Ellinipsico, and Red Hawk killed at Point Pleasant. —Condition of Wheeling Fort.—" Fort Henry."—Situation and Importance of this Fort.—Attacked by four hundred Indians under Simon Girty.—Loss of the Garrison near the Fort.—Incidents of Indian Warfare.—Major M'Cullock.—Captain Mason.— Major Clark plans the Reduction of Kaskaskia.—The Expedition proceeds from "the Falls."—Surprise and Capture of Kaskaskia and " Fort Gage."—Suspension of Civil Government in West Augusta.—Martial Law suspended.—Courts organized.—Attorneys and Attorney-general.—Daniel Boone and twenty-seven Men captured at Blue Licks.—His Captivity among the Indians.—His Escape and Return to Boonesborough.—Makes an Incursion to Paint Creek.—Boonesborough invested by large Indian Force, August, 1778.—Defense and Incidents of the Siege.—" Fort M'Intosh" erected.—" Fort Laurens" erected.—Protracted Siege of Fort Laurens.—Court of Land Commissioners established in Kentucky, 1779.—First Settlement at Lexington, Bryant's Station, Forks of Licking, and on Sources of Salt River.—Massacre of Colonel Rodgers and ninety Men on the Ohio.—Colonel Bowman's unsuccessful Expedition to the Miami Towns.—Emigration to Kentucky.—Arrival of Immigrants in 1779. —Scarcity of Provisions.—Depreciation of Paper Currency.—Distress of Emigrants until 1780.—Defenses on the Ohio.—" Fort Nelson."—Colonel Slaughter.—Landed Interest in Kentucky.—The Indians capture Ruddle's and Martin's Stations, and retire.—Destruction of the Moravian Towns on the Coshocton.—Massacre of Captives and friendly Moravians.—Colonel Clark invades the Shawanese Country in 1780.— Militia Organization in 1780.—Colonel Clark erects " Fort Jefferson" on the Mississippi.—Southern Boundary of Virginia extended to the Mississippi.

[A.D. 1776.] DURING the period under consideration, the state of Virginia, in virtue of her royal charter, claimed all the territory which would be included by extending her northern and southern boundaries due west to the Mississippi. This would comprise all the lands east of the Mississippi between the parallels of 36° 30' and 39° 40', of course including Kentucky, the southern half of Illinois, and one third of Ohio, or all that portion south of M'Connelsville, Lancaster, and Xenia; and before the close of the year 1780, her jurisdiction had been extended over the whole of her claim, besides an extensive portion of Western Pennsylvania south of Fort Pitt, upon the Monongahela and Youghiogeny, which was supposed to be within the limits of Virginia.

At this time, as we have already shown,* the settlements had extended upon all the eastern branches of the Monongahela, the Youghiogeny, and upon all the small eastern tributaries of the Upper Ohio, for one hundred and twenty miles below Pittsburgh; also, upon the sources of the Greenbrier, the Little Kenhawa, and Elk River, west of the mountains, together comprising the northwestern counties of Virginia and the southwestern counties of Pennsylvania as now established. Pittsburgh was a frontier town of Virginia, and the settlements southward upon all the tributaries of the Monongahela were considered frontier settlements of Virginia, into which the tide of emigration from Eastern Virginia, Maryland, and Pennsylvania was bearing numerous settlers and pioneers. The extensive region, however, south of the Little Kenhawa and westward to the Mississippi, was one immense savage wilderness, occupied chiefly by the native tribes. To this there was one exception, which comprised the settlements recently commenced upon the Kentucky River and its tributaries in the vicinity of Boonesborough, Logan's Fort, and Harrodsburg. This was the "dark and bloody ground" of the Indians, which had been reserved by the Northern and Southern Indians as common hunting-grounds. They looked with suspicious jealousy upon the rapid advance of the white man, as his habitations were gradually multiplying upon both sides of the Kentucky River. These settlements, which were already attracting the hostile demonstrations of the Shawanese and other northwestern tribes, were in their infancy, and almost beyond the protection of the state.

In the extreme southeastern angle of the present State of Virginia, the population had been advancing slowly for the last ten years, upon the sources of the Holston and Clinch Rivers, within the territory claimed by the Cherokees. This war-

---

* See book iii. of this work, viz.: Advance of the Anglo-American Population, &c., chapters ii. and iii.

like nation had again commenced hostilities against these frontier settlements, and the immigrants had been compelled hastily to abandon their homes, and seek safety and protection in the older settlements. At this period the vicinity of the present old town of Abington was an exposed frontier region, where several hundred of the inhabitants had collected for mutual protection and defense against the hostile Cherokees. The stockade in which they were cooped up for nearly six months was known as "Black's Station," and occupied the present site of Abington.

The whole region north and south of Kentucky River was virtually beyond the civil jurisdiction of Virginia, although, by an act of the Legislature, it had been annexed to the jurisdiction of Fincastle county. The authority of the Transylvanian Republic had failed, and the civil organization had not been extended over the settlements.

In the mean time, the colony which had been commenced upon the Kentucky River had been harassed by straggling parties of hostile Indians, who infested all the settlements, occasionally killing those who were passing from one habitation to another, destroying the cattle, and stealing horses. So frequent had these murders and depredations become toward the close of the year, that no family was considered safe beyond the limits of the "stations," to which all retired for mutual protection and defense. Individuals passing from one station to another were armed, or an armed guard escorted them to their destination, as a protection from Indian massacre. No one was safe to walk beyond the stockades; for death, in the shape of an Indian, might lurk in every thicket, behind every tree, or under every bush. Were the fields to be tilled, was firewood or timber for building to be procured from the forest, or were the cattle to be penned outside the stockade, an armed sentinel stood by to give alarm of danger, or an armed guard was ready to resist any sudden assault. To accomplish his purpose of capturing a prisoner, of taking a scalp, or of stealing a horse, the wily Indian, in his silent approaches, would lurk near the stations and settlements, unseen for days, until an opportunity offered to retire with his trophy.

It was not until October that the inhabitants were supplied with powder for their defense, through the intrepid perseverance of Major George Rogers Clark, the protector and patron of Kentucky. Having visited the capital of Virginia, and procured the appropriation of five hundred pounds of powder, to be delivered at Pittsburgh, for the settlements of Kentucky, he proceeded in a boat with six companions, two of whom were killed by the Indians on the way, to convey it down the river, through a region infested with hostile savages. With great precaution and secrecy, he succeeded in conveying it to the vicinity of the Limestone Creek, near the present town of Maysville, where it was concealed until he could proceed on foot to M'Clellan's Station in search of a sufficient escort for its safe delivery at Harrod's Station. Having procured a guard of twenty-seven men, including Simon Kenton, Robert Patterson, and others of like character, he returned to Limestone Creek, whence the twenty-five kegs of powder were safely conveyed by the escort to the principal stations.*

The nearest military post was that at the mouth of the Great Kenhawa, where Captain Arbuckle commanded a garrison of militia, not less than two hundred miles from the isolated settlements of Kentucky.† The people, under the direction of Major Clark, were compelled to provide for their own safety, and unite for the common defense. No civil government by the state had been yet organized in this remote region.

Although the Shawanese from the Miami and Wabash had annoyed the inhabitants on the waters of the Kentucky River with their depredations and secret murders, yet it was not until the last of December that a regular war party advanced against the settlements. On the 29th of December, a party of forty-seven warriors, led on by "Black Fish," a noted Shawanese chief, made an unexpected attack upon M'Clellan's Station, on the north fork of Elk-horn, and near the site of the present village of Georgetown. On the first attack, M'Clellan and two other men were killed before the fort was placed in a state of defense. The remainder of the settlers defended themselves, being closely cooped up in the stockade until the Indians had dispersed to attack other points. The whole number subsequently abandoned the station, and escaped by night to the more secure and populous one at Harrodsburg.‡

In the mean time, the hostile Indians of the Mingo tribes, as well as the Shawanese, had not been idle in their operations

---

* Butler's Kentucky, p. 40.   † American Pioneer, vol. ii., p. 344.
‡ Butler's Kentucky, p. 42.

against the settlements on the Upper Ohio and Monongahela Rivers. Numerous hostile bands had infested this portion of Virginia with their robberies, outrages, and murders upon the unprotected families. Many exposed habitations near the Ohio River, below "Wheeling Fort," were abandoned until greater security could be enjoyed. Among those then abandoned was the one near Big Grave Creek, and another near the mouth of the Little Kenhawa.

At the next session of the Legislature, the jurisdiction of Virginia was formally extended over the settlements on the Kentucky River. At the recommendation of Major George Rogers Clark, the "county of Kentucky" had been formally organized, embracing all the country west of Big Sandy Creek, and extending to the Mississippi River. To this extension of the civil jurisdiction over the Transylvania purchase and the little republic organized therein, strong opposition was urged by Colonels Henderson and Campbell, but ineffectually.

To Major Clark was committed the military organization of the county, and the superintendence of the defensive operations for the protection of the inhabitants. Without loss of time, he repaired to his post, and entered upon the duties of his station.

[A.D. 1777.] Early in the spring, the militia were organized into three companies, one at Boonesborough, under Captain Daniel Boone; one at Logan's Fort, under Captain Benjamin Logan; and one at Harrod's Station, under Captain James Harrod. The different stockades were placed in a state of complete defense, with the resident militia and occasional re-enforcements derived by way of the "wilderness road," both from the Holston settlements, and other portions of North Carolina.

The settlements on the Kentucky River had already begun to contract their limits, and the pioneers had retired from the danger which awaited them, or had fortified themselves in the most commanding stations. "Leestown," a general rendezvous for explorers and surveyors, situated upon the Kentucky River, one mile below the present town of Frankfort, was abandoned early in the summer of 1776. Explorers, surveyors, and settlers, who had been traversing the country and opening preemption settlements on the north side of the Kentucky River, and upon the branches of Elk-horn Creek, now retired under the protection of the general " Rendezvous" of Harrod's Station. Georgetown, on the north fork of Elk-horn, has since sprung up on the site of M'Clellan's Station, which was soon afterward abandoned to the savages. The present site of Lexington was then a desolate forest, upon which the white man had not entered. A few scattered habitations had been erected east of the sources of Elk-horn, but they were broken up during the same year, when most of the surveyors and explorers retired from Kentucky to the old settlements of Virginia, or to those on the Monongahela.*

The most extensive and populous frontier settlements of Virginia, however, were those upon the waters of the Monongahela and the Upper Ohio, and sparsely distributed upon the eastern sources of the Great and Little Kenhawas. These remote settlements, until near the close of 1776, had been beyond the organized limits of Virginia, but they had been attached to the jurisdiction of Augusta county, as the "District of West Augusta."

Meantime, the Legislature of Virginia, during the autumn of 1776, had been active in providing for the protection and civil government of the remote settlements upon the Ohio frontier. The district of West Augusta was divided into three large counties, designated as the counties of " Ohio," " Youghiogeny," and " Monongahela," which were organized during the following spring, when the first civil government was extended formally over this portion of the state.

Ohio county was first organized by the appointment of John M'Cullock, sheriff, his commission bearing date November 9th, 1776. His instructions required him to hold an election on the 27th of December, to decide by the votes of the landholders the location of the county seat of justice. The choice fell upon " Black's Cabin," on Short Creek, at which place was held the first county court ever organized upon the Ohio. The court opened on the 7th of January, 1777, constituted of seven associate justices, of whom David Shepherd was " presiding justice," and John M'Cullock, sheriff.† On the first day of the court, an order was issued for the erection of a court-house

---

* Marshall's Kentucky, vol. i., p. 46.

† The " Court" was constituted as follows : David Shepherd, *presiding justice;* Silas Hodges, William Scott, James Caldwell, Zachariah Spriggs, Thomas Weller, and Daniel M'Clain, *associate justices ;* James M'Mechan, *clerk ;* John M'Cullock, *sheriff.*— See American Pioneer.

and jail. Other counties were organized in like manner soon afterward.

At this time the county of Ohio contained several large settlements, the most important of which were those on Buffalo Creek, Beech Bottom, Cross Creek, at the Forks of Wheeling Creek, on Big Grave Creek, Fish Creek, and Middle Island Creek. That on Short Creek was the largest settlement, and comprised the county seat. In nearly all of these settlements there was at least one block house, or fort, in which the families could be sheltered from Indian barbarity in case of imminent danger.* The whole number of inhabitants in this county was small compared to the older counties east of the mountains. Nearly twelve months afterward, when the population had doubtless been considerably augmented, the whole number of tithables, or males over sixteen years of age, amounted to only three hundred and fifty-two.†

Since the Declaration of Independence, the Cherokees, instigated by John Stuart, Esq., his majesty's "Superintendent of Indian Affairs" in the South, in obedience to his instructions, had been active in their hostilities against the frontier population of Virginia and North and South Carolina. The Legislature of Virginia, co-operating with the authorities of the Carolinas, had been actively engaged in providing for the protection and defense of her extreme southwestern frontier. During the autumn of 1776, active preparations were in operation throughout the southwestern counties of Virginia for a formidable invasion of the Cherokee country on the north, at the same time that it was invaded in two opposite directions by the troops of North and South Carolina from the southeast. While the preparations for this three-fold invasion were in progress for the effectual chastisement of this warlike and implacable nation, the whole of the border settlements of Virginia and the Carolinas in this quarter were broken up and deserted by the inhabitants, who had hastily fled from their homes to the older settlements, while others retired to more secure situations, where they were compelled to remain cooped up in crowded forts and stockaded stations for months together. During this time the

---

* American Pioneer, vol. ii., p. 303–306; also, 377.

† The poll-tax levied for the state at this time was twenty-four shillings for all males over sixteen years, provided they adhered to the government of the "Commonwealth;" but from those who refused to take the prescribed oath of allegiance, the sheriff was required to collect double that amount, or forty-eight shillings.—Pioneer, ibidem.

frontier settlements of Virginia, upon all the sources of the Holston and Clinch Rivers, were entirely abandoned to the savages. The same was true of the settlements of South Carolina, which had been advancing upon the sources of the Savannah, the Broad, and Saluda Rivers, and their tributaries, until they were relieved in the winter of 1776-7 by the simultaneous advance of the invading forces.

Each of the contiguous states, notwithstanding they were engaged near the seaboard in contending with the myrmidons of Great Britain for their lives and property, had organized a strong military force for the protection of their western frontier from the ravages of her savage allies. Late in the autumn of 1776, these different invading divisions were in motion for the Indian country. The division from South Carolina, commanded by Brigadier-general Andrew Williamson, invaded the country upon the Keowe and Tugalo Rivers, comprising a large portion of the southeastern frontier of the nation. The whole of the Indian towns in this quarter were totally destroyed, and their fields ravaged by fire. The division from North Carolina, commanded by General Rutherford, advanced against the country upon the southern and eastern tributaries of the Holston, comprising the eastern portion of the nation. The towns and fields in this quarter, upon the branches of the south fork of Holston and upon the French Broad, were utterly destroyed, and the savages reduced to great suffering from extreme want.

About the same time, the division from Virginia, commanded by Colonel Christian, consisting of fifteen hundred men, advanced upon the country and towns on the waters of the north fork of Holston and of Clinch Rivers, comprising the northwestern portion of the nation. This division, in like manner, had laid waste the whole of their towns and fields as it advanced. After completing the destruction of all the towns in this quarter, Colonel Christian advanced his division to the south fork of Holston, and took up his winter-quarters upon Long Island, a few miles above the junction of the north and south forks. Here he erected "Fort Henry," so called in honor of the patriotic Governor of Virginia.* This fort was situated on the main south fork of Holston, about one hundred and fifty miles by the river above the mouth of French Broad, and at that time near the heart of the Cherokee nation.

* American Pioneer, vol. i., p. 336.

The whole Cherokee nation, by this prompt and powerful invasion of their country in every direction, had been reduced to great want and suffering. At length, their national pride being humbled, and their martial spirit subdued, they made overtures for peace, which were readily met by the victorious commanders. Preliminary arrangements required both portions of the Cherokee nation to send delegates, or representatives, to treat separately with the commissioners of South Carolina and those of Virginia. Having complied with this preliminary, two separate treaties were subsequently entered into.

The *first* treaty was that of " Dewett's Corner." This treaty was conducted with the commissioners of South Carolina and Georgia, on the part of those states respectively. The Cherokees, by this treaty, signed in December, ceded and relinquished, by right of conquest, to those states large tracts of country upon the head branches of the Savannah and Saluda Rivers, free from any future claim on the part of the Indians.

The *second* treaty, held in January, 1777, on " Long Island," was conducted by commissioners on the part of Virginia and North Carolina. In this treaty, also, the Indians ceded large tracts of country to those states respectively upon the head waters of the north fork of Holston, and upon the branches of Clinch River. The ceded country embraced the frontier settlements west of Abington, and southeast of the Cumberland range of mountains, at present partly in Virginia and partly in East Tennessee.*

After these treaties, the Cherokees retired further south and west, relinquishing the country upon Powell's River, and other head branches of Clinch River and the north fork of Holston, and occupying the country on the south fork, and upon the Tennessee River as far south and west as the Muscle Shoals. In less than two years after the treaty, the inhabitants of Virginia had advanced into the conquered country.

Meantime, the Shawanese and their confederates had commenced a regular Indian war against the new settlements upon the waters of Kentucky River. By the 1st of March, a large party of Indian warriors had advanced across the Ohio River, and on the 6th of March they were before Harrod's Station, having killed several persons and dispersed divers parties of pioneers on their advance. The fortunate escape of James

---

* See American State Papers, *Indian Affairs*, vol. i., p. 431, 432, folio edition.

Ray, a mere lad, from one of these parties, and his speed in reaching the station with the alarm, saved the post from surprise and a disastrous defeat. The Indians, having perceived that one of the party which they had surprised near the station had escaped to give the alarm, immediately resolved to defer the contemplated attack, which was not made until next day, when the station was in a complete state of defense, the men having been all called in from the vicinity. On the morning of the 7th the savages appeared before the fort, and commenced the attack by secretly setting fire to an outbuilding a short distance from the stockade. Supposing the fire had been communicated accidentally, as no Indians were seen, several men sallied out to extinguish it; but they were immediately attacked by the Indians, who suddenly appeared and attempted to intercept their retreat to the fort. The men, being hard pressed by the Indians in their retreat, took shelter behind a copse of trees near at hand, when a sharp skirmish by the savages commenced. The fire of the Indians was promptly returned from the fort, and the savages soon afterward withdrew, having lost one warrior killed and several wounded. After a desultory fire with small arms for a few hours longer, they retired and abandoned the attack. The whites lost one man killed and three wounded.* For several days the Indians continued to infest the woods in the vicinity, cutting off all communication between the fort and other settlements. They intercepted the arrival of all supplies from a distance, and prevented the hunters from procuring game in the forest, although wild meat constituted an important item in their daily fare. The domestic cattle also were killed, which thus cut off this necessary source of future supply.

On the 5th of April, a party of about one hundred Indians surrounded the station at Boonesborough, and immediately commenced a brisk attack. Their fire was promptly returned from the fort, and after a few hours the Indians retired, carrying off their dead and wounded. In the fort one man was killed and four wounded.

The same party, re-enforced, invested Logan's Fort on the 20th of May. The garrison, consisting of only fifteen men, made a vigorous defense for several hours, after which the Indians retired, carrying off their dead and wounded. In the fort two men were killed and one wounded.[†]

* Butler's Kentucky, p. 42. Also, Marshall.   † Marshall, vol. i., p. 49.

For a time the inhabitants of Kentucky were exempt from hostile attacks, although the country in the vicinity of the stations continued to be infested by lurking savages, compelling the occupants to remain within their stockades.

In the mean time, the border inhabitants on the Monongahela and upper Ohio had been less exposed to the incursions of the war parties, although not wholly exempt from nocturnal depredations by marauding bands.

Civil government had been established, and the threatening attitude of the savages north and west of the Ohio made it expedient to organize the militia. Commissions had been forwarded from the governor for the organization of a regiment in the counties comprised in the former district of West Augusta. On the second day of June, the several commissioned officers appeared in open court, received their commissions, and took the required oath of allegiance and fidelity to the state, preparatory to entering upon their respective duties. David Shepherd, presiding justice, was colonel-commandant, and Samuel M'Cullock, major, with five captains.* The old provincial fort at Wheeling, formerly known as Fort Fincastle, relinquished its colonial name, and assumed that of "*Fort Henry*," in honor of Patrick Henry, the governor of Virginia. A garrison, under the command of Colonel Shepherd, was to occupy it as a regular military state post.

The militia rolls were to be immediately filled, and every able-bodied man over sixteen years was required to hold himself in readiness to take the field at a moment's warning.

On the 4th of July, a force of about two hundred savages appeared before Boonesborough, and commenced one of the most memorable sieges in the early annals of Kentucky. This was a regular Indian siege, kept up without intermission for nearly nine weeks, or from the 4th of July until the 4th of September. During this whole period the people and garrison were reduced to great extremities of both mental and physical suffering. They were harassed with continual watchings; excited by constant alarms and fearful apprehensions, cut off from all supplies of food to sustain life, destitute of ammunition to

---

* The following were some of the company officers, viz.: *Captains:* Samuel Mason, John Mitchell, Joseph Ogle, Samuel Teter, and Jacob Leffler. *Lieutenants:* Samuel Tomlinson, John Biggs, Derrick Hoagler, and Thomas Gilleland. *Ensign*, William Sparks.—See Pioneer, vol. ii., p. 303–306, and 317.

maintain a protracted siege, confined to the narrow limits of the stockade, cut off from communication with other stations, alarmed by repeated attacks and fearful yells of the savages, life itself was almost a burden to them.

While the main body of savages invested Boonesborough, detachments were constantly scouring the country near Logan's Fort and Harrod's Station, to intercept supplies, to prevent communication, and to excite fears of attack, which might deter the garrison from a division for the relief of Boonesborough.

Such were the incessant efforts of the savages, and such the variety and perseverance of their stratagems and their wiles, that the forts must certainly have fallen under their repeated attacks and the privations of the defenders, had they not received timely relief and supplies, about the 25th of July, by a party of forty riflemen, who forced their way through the wilderness from North Carolina. These brave men, fortunately, reached the fort in safety, restored confidence to the desponding, replenished their stores of ammunition, and shared with them the toils of their perilous defense. Yet the relief was temporary; the Indians continued the siege, and a few weeks found them as exhausted and destitute as before. The second relief came, most opportune, on the first of September, when Colonel John Bowman arrived, with one hundred men, from the Holston settlements. To the Indians, already impatient to return to their towns, this unexpected re-enforcement was an event of ominous import, and they soon afterward abandoned the siege and retired north of the Ohio.

During the whole of this protracted siege, the regular force at any one time was only twenty-two men at Boonesborough, fifteen at Logan's Fort, and sixty-five at Harrod's Station. At Boonesborough only one man was killed; and two wounded in the fort. A number of Indians were known to have been killed by the riflemen when they extended their approaches within rifle-shot.

Upon the body of one of the Indians, killed near the fort, was found a copy of a proclamation by Henry Hamilton, British lieutenant-governor, and commandant at Detroit, in which he offers protection to such of the inhabitants of Kentucky as would abandon the cause of the revolted provinces, but denounces vengeance against those who adhere to them.

To illustrate the hardy daring of the early pioneers of Kentucky, their own actions are the best examples. The last re-enforcement, about the first of September, as before observed, was led on by Captain Logan, who, with a select party of woodsmen, had departed from the fort by night, and set out for the Holston settlements for aid and supplies. Traveling all night on foot, concealed in deep, secluded valleys by day, to avoid the hostile savages who infested the road, often leaving the beaten trace for the unfrequented routes, supplied with only a sack of parched corn for his fare, and enduring fatigues incredible, he at length, after ten days, reached the Holston settlements, two hundred miles from Boonesborough. The enterprise, and the daring perseverance which could accomplish this hazardous journey, could not fail to rouse his countrymen to relieve the beleaguered forts, and he soon returned with supplies, and one hundred pioneer riflemen.*

Although the county of Kentucky had been laid off by law nearly twelve months, no regular organization of the civil government had taken place until after the termination of the siege of Boonesborough. Such had been the incessant alarms and dangers from the savages, that the militia organization alone had been carried into effect.

Late in the autumn, however, when Indian incursions had been in a good degree suspended, the first legal county court was regularly convened at Harrod's Station. It was constituted of John Todd, *presiding justice;* and John Floyd, Benjamin Logan, John Bowman, and Richard Calloway, *associate justices.* Levi Todd was *clerk.* The sheriff opened the court, and the justices entered upon their duties. Militia officers were commissioned for the organization of a regiment, and Lieutenant-colonel John Bowman proceeded immediately to enroll all the able-bodied men in the county.†

Thus was the jurisdiction of Virginia extended to the Mississippi on the south side of the Ohio; and the infant Republic of Transylvania, established nearly two years previously, was swallowed up in the county of Kentucky, and became an integral part of the State of Virginia. The laws of the Commonwealth and the state jurisdiction superseded all the former legislation by the proprietors.

The county of Kentucky, as first laid off, comprised all the

---

* See Marshall's Kentucky, vol. i., p. 54.   † Ibidem, p. 47.

country south of the Ohio River, and west of Big Sandy Creek and the Cumberland Mountains, with the boundary of North Carolina as its southern limit. Of course it comprised within its jurisdiction the whole country south of the Kentucky River, which had been purchased of the Cherokees by Colonel Richard Henderson and company. Colonel Henderson could be recognized only as a private individual, having no right to make treaties with the Indian tribes, or to purchase lands from them.* Virginia was now an independent state, and in virtue of her royal charter she claimed the right and sovereignty in the soil to the whole of the regions comprised in Transylvania. The Legislature of Virginia had accordingly refused to recognize Colonel Henderson's purchase further than as an extinguishment of the Indian title in favor of Virginia; in consideration of which, he was subsequently allowed a grant of two hundred thousand acres of land on Green River, near the Ohio, as a remuneration to him and his associates for their expenditures previous and subsequent to the treaty of Watauga.†

In the course of the summer, the northwestern settlement of Virginia, upon the Monongahela and Ohio Rivers, were harassed by the incursions of scalping parties, which prowled through the country, committing such depredations and outrages upon the weak and unprotected settlers as chance and accident threw in their power. But their chief object was to supply themselves with horses, great numbers of which were stolen by them during the summer.

Cornstalk, the great Shawanese warrior, who had commanded the confederate Indians in the battle of the Kenhawa in the fall of 1774, had remained an idle spectator in the present war, and was even a friend of the white men; but he fell a victim to the natural enmity between the two races.‡ Desirous to avert the effusion of blood, he visited the military post at Point Pleasant, in company with a young Delaware chief called "Red Hawk," to warn the commander of approaching danger. In an interview with Captain Arbuckle, Cornstalk "declared that, in consequence of the British influence, the current was setting so strong against the Americans, that his people would float with it in spite of his exertions." The commandant deemed it proper to retain the two chiefs as hostages until he

---

* See book iii., chap. iii., of this work.   † Marshal, vol. i., p. 14, 15.
‡ American Pioneer, vol. i., p. 95.

could receive instructions from his government. Some time afterward, the son of Cornstalk, Ellinipsico, who had fought by his side at the Point, came to the fort to inquire the cause of his father's delay. He was received into the fort, and detained also. A few days afterward, several murders were committed in the vicinity by hostile Indians; whereupon a number of militia men, with Captain Hall at their head, highly exasperated at the murders, in a fit of fury determined, in retaliation, "to kill the Indians in the fort." With their guns cocked, breathing vengeance and death to any who dared to interfere, they proceeded to execute their horrid design. Cornstalk was engaged conversing with some of the officers, and delineating the region north of the Ohio upon the ground, when he was apprised of their murderous intent. At their approach, Ellinipsico appeared agitated, but the veteran chief bade him not to fear death: "My son, the Great Spirit has seen fit that we should die together, and has sent you here to that end; it is his will, let us submit." The murderers had now arrived; the old chief turned around to meet them, when, shot through the body with seven balls, he fell and expired without a struggle. Ellinipsico met his fate with great composure, and was shot upon the seat in which he was sitting when he first received the announcement of his fate. Red Hawk endeavored to escape, but was soon slain by his pursuers.*

The murders in this case were perpetrated by individuals from a detachment of militia which had arrived a few days before, and whose martial fire exhausted itself in the cowardly act which threw disgrace upon the arms of Virginia. They returned from their tour of service without once facing an enemy in the field.

But such is the spirit of inveterate hostility which burns in the breasts of the frontier people, that the murder of their friends seems to cry continually for vengeance against every individual of the race. Thus died ingloriously, by the hand of violence, one of the most talented, and one of the bravest Indian warriors that ever lived. In cool courage and commanding talents he has never had his superior, and seldom his equal.

A few weeks more convinced the people of the newly-organized counties of Northwestern Virginia that they were not forgotten by the hostile warriors. The savages had looked

---

* Drake's Book of Indians, book v., p. 29.

with a jealous eye upon the fort at Wheeling, and its destruction had engaged the attention of the British commandant at Detroit. A strong expedition for its reduction had been committed to the command of the notorious renegade, Simon Girty. This had been one of the oldest and strongest settlement forts on the Ohio, and had been too strong for attack by any of the war parties which had scoured the frontier settlements. To reduce it, a regular Indian army must be collected, and well provided with the means of offensive warfare.

This fort, formerly known as "Fort Fincastle," and now called "Fort Henry," stood on the east bank of the Ohio River, nearly five hundred yards above the mouth of Wheeling Creek, and about three hundred yards from the base of the abrupt hill which rises east of the present city of Wheeling. The immediate site of the fort was upon an elevated plateau, rising twenty or thirty feet above the surrounding creek and river bottom, which was then cultivated as a corn-field. Between the fort and the base of the hill stood the straggling village, composed of about thirty small log dwelling houses and outbuildings. The fort was a parallelogram, with two blockhouses at corners, and surrounded by a strong palisade eight feet high. The principal gateway opened on the east side, next the village. The garrison was a small detachment of militia, kept in active service under the direction of the colonel commandant.

About the first of June, the Indian incursions and depredations had been made with such boldness and frequency, that the civil jurisdiction ceased, and martial law prevailed over all the settlements; and such was the apprehension of imminent danger from the Indians, that the common safety was a paramount object; people threw aside their private pursuits, and every man became an energetic soldier.

Early in September it was ascertained that an immense Indian army was concentrating on the Sandusky River, under the direction of Simon Girty, who exercised unbounded influence over the Wyandots and their confederates. It had been ascertained, also, that this Indian army was well supplied with arms and ammunition by Governor Hamilton at Detroit. By this enlightened functionary Girty was empowered, if he saw proper, to grant protection from the tomahawk and scalping-knife to such of the western settlers as would espouse the cause of England, and swear allegiance to the British crown.*

The force under Girty amounted to about four hundred warriors. With these duly provided, he set out, and, to conceal his real destination, he marched toward Kentucky. Although Colonel Shepherd suspected his object, and kept out a detachment of the most active and experienced scouts, Girty succeeded in eluding them, and appeared suddenly before the walls of the fort before his advance was discovered. This was on the 27th of September.† Not an Indian had been seen, nor a sign observed, until late in the evening of the previous day, when suspicions were first aroused as to Indians in the vicinity. The fort was put in a state of defense, the women and children in the vicinity were collected into it, and preparations were matured to repel an attack. The store-house was well supplied with small arms, but deficient in ammunition. The garrison numbered only forty-two effective soldiers, including old men and boys.

On the following morning, the first man who ventured out was shot down by the Indians in sight of the fort. A negro in company escaped to the fort and gave the alarm, and reported six Indians in the corn-field. Colonel Shepherd detached Captain Mason, with fourteen men, to dislodge the Indians. He proceeded through the field, and finding no Indians, was about to return, when he was furiously assailed on every side by nearly the whole of Girty's army. The captain and his men endeavored to cut their way through the savages to the fort. In accomplishing this object, he lost more than half of his command, and was severely wounded himself. Captain Ogle, at the head of twelve volunteers, in his attempt to cover the retreat of Captain Mason, was led into an ambuscade, in which two thirds of his men were killed. The Indians pressed forward to the fort in two extended lines; and as they advanced the war-whoop rang through the lines until the welkin echoed with the wild and startling chorus.

The action commenced by a brisk fire of rifles and musketry. The garrison, in the two sallies, had already lost more than half their original number, including two of the best officers. None of the parties succeeded in reaching the fort, but were lying, wounded and concealed, beyond reach of aid

* American Pioneer, vol. ii., p. 305.   † Idem, p. 314.

from the garrison. The effective force in the fort was now only twelve boys, who on that day performed prodigies of valor.

The Indians surrounded the fort in every direction, keeping up a brisk fire by parties stationed in the houses of the village, and behind fences, and in the corn-field, from which they could securely annoy the garrison.

After an active firing of an hour, Girty suspended a white flag from the window of a house, and demanded the surrender of the fort in the name of his Britannic majesty. He read the proclamation of Governor Hamilton, and promised protection to such as would swear allegiance to the British crown. He warned the garrison of the danger of resistance, and added the usual threat of his inability to restrain his savages in case the fort fell by assault. Colonel Shepherd returned for answer that he could not obtain possession of the fort while an American soldier remained to defend it. Girty renewed his proposition for surrender, which being disregarded, he retired, and a brisk fire was again opened upon the fort.*

It was now about nine o'clock in the morning, and the fire was kept up, with but little intermission, for about six hours. The Indians, elated with the early successes of the day, and furiously impatient to complete the work of butchery in the fort, fired at random against the pickets, houses, and every thing which seemed to shelter a man. The garrison, on the contrary, was cool and deliberate with their fire, and every man and boy was a marksman and a soldier. Many of the Indians, at length, in their fury, rushed up to the block houses for the purpose of firing through the logs and openings; but they were soon compelled to retire.

An intermission of an hour occurred about two o'clock, after which the Indians renewed their exertions. The fire was resumed with great activity, and about twenty Indians, with rails and blocks of wood, rushed to the gate for the purpose of forcing it open or of breaking it down. They were repulsed, with the loss of several of their warriors killed; but the attack was continued until night. Soon after dark the Indians advanced within sixty yards of the fort with a large log, which they had converted into a cannon, charged to the muzzle with chains, stones, slugs of iron, and other hard substances taken

* See American Pioneer, vol. ii., p. 307–310.

Vol. II.—G

from the blacksmith shop of the station. This was directed so as to discharge its contents full against the gate. A crowd of Indians stood near to witness the discharge. The match was applied, and the explosion burst the iron-bound cannon into a hundred fragments, killing several of the Indians, but inflicting no injury on the fort. A loud yell proclaimed their disaster, and the failure to injure the fort. The main body of the Indians soon afterward retired from the siege to take food and repose, while a few prowled about the fort all night to annoy and harass the garrison.

Next day the garrison was fortunately re-enforced by Colonel Swearengen, who succeeded in reaching the fort safely with fourteen men. The Indians still remained dispersed over the surrounding country, committing such depredations and murders as presented to their rapacity.

Next morning, about daybreak, Major Samuel M'Cullock, already a distinguished frontier soldier, arrived at the fort with a troop of forty horsemen from Short Creek. The gate was thrown open, and the troop dashed in through a shower of bullets and crowds of Indians, who attempted to intercept them. The troop succeeded in entering the fort in safety; but their brave commander, by the press of the Indians, had been separated from his men, and excluded from the gate. He was well known to many of the Indians, and was deemed well worthy the honor of being taken alive as one of the greatest trophies. Twenty Indians were eager to intercept him; and after several ineffectual attempts to pass his pursuers and dash into the fort, he wheeled his charger and dashed swiftly toward Wheeling Hill, east of the fort. He reached the top of the hill, and took down the ridge, determined to reach the Short Creek settlement, if possible; but here he was met by another party of Indians on the eastern side of the hill, who quickly joined in pursuit of the flying hero. He immediately wheeled and retraced his steps, in hope of finding some other opening for his escape; but he soon met his first pursuers in full chase, who had already gained the top of the ridge. His situation was now exceedingly critical; surrounded on two sides by his pursuers, hemmed in on the third side by impending cliffs and rocky steeps, and the fourth side presenting a precipice, nearly perpendicular, of one hundred and fifty feet to the channel of Wheeling Creek. An instant decided his course. Supporting his rifle in one hand, and carefully adjusting his reins with the other, he urged his horse to the brink of the bluff, and made the leap which decided his fate. Having, by the activity of his horse, reached the base of the hill in safety, he dashed across the creek, and was soon beyond the reach of his pursuers. This is only a specimen of the many adventures and hair-breadth escapes incident to Indian warfare.*

The escape of Major M'Cullock and the re-enforcement received by the garrison decided the siege. The Indians soon afterward assembled near the foot of the hill, set fire to all the houses and inclosures outside of the fort, killed about three hundred head of cattle, and then took up the line of march for some other theatre of action.

During this siege not a man in the fort was killed, and only one slightly wounded by the enemy. But the whole loss sustained by the whites in this incursion was severe. Of forty-two men in the fort on the morning of the 27th, twenty-three were killed in the corn-field before the siege commenced. Two men, who had been sent down the river in a canoe on the evening of the 26th, were killed by the Indians. Mr. Duke, son-in-law of Colonel Shepherd, had been killed by the Indians on the evening of the 27th, in attempting to reach the fort. Thus the whole loss of the whites was twenty-six killed and five wounded. The loss of the enemy was not correctly known, as they always remove their dead; but it was variously estimated from sixty to one hundred killed.

Those who took a conspicuous part in the defense of Wheeling Fort, and distinguished themselves for courage and intrepidity, were Colonel Shepherd, Silas and Ebenezer Zane, John Caldwell, men of the first standing and influence in the western settlements; also, Abram Rogers, John Linn, Joseph Biggs, and Robert Lemmon, expert Indian fighters, and noted on the frontiers. Nor must we omit that heroic and devoted girl, Elizabeth Zane, who offered herself a willing sacrifice to bring a keg of powder, during the siege, from a building sixty yards distant into the fort, to which she fortunately returned unhurt, amid a shower of bullets.† During the remainder of the siege she was continually engaged, with other females, in running bullets, rendering assistance in every quarter, and by words and example infusing new life and courage into the soldiers.

* American Pioneer, vol. ii., p. 312, 313.   † Idem, p. 310.

In the mean time, Major Clark had taken great interest in the defense of the whole northwestern frontier of Virginia, as well as of Kentucky. Auxiliary to his contemplated operations during the summer of 1777, he had dispatched secretly two spies by the names of Moore and Dunn, and from them had learned the state of things at the remote British posts of Detroit, Vincennes, and Kaskaskia. He was convinced that they were the true source of all the Indian hostilities against the settlements of Kentucky, and he had conceived the secret design of leading an expedition against them. Accordingly, on the 1st of October, he left Kentucky on a visit to the capital of Virginia, to consult with the Executive Council relative to the protection of the western inhabitants. He proceeded to Williamsburg, and on the 10th of December he first disclosed to Patrick Henry, the governor of Virginia, his proposed plan of a secret expedition against those British posts, and especially against Kaskaskia. After several conferences with the governor and Executive Council, and after due consideration of all his plans for the reduction of those posts, they approved the plan, and pledged themselves to sustain him in the attempt. He was commissioned as a colonel in the service of Virginia, with authority to raise troops on the credit of the Commonwealth. They also obligated themselves to use their efforts and influence with the Legislature to procure a bounty of three hundred acres of land for each man who should serve in the expedition.*

[A.D. 1778.] Having received authority for supplies and transports from General Hand at Fort Pitt, he set out for that post, preparatory to further operations toward organizing his expedition.

On the 4th of February Colonel Clark set out for Fort Pitt to make arrangements for his expedition, and to levy troops in the western settlements near Fort Redstone, which was then claimed by Virginia. Major William B. Smith had been dispatched to the Holston settlements, while Captains Leonard Helm, Joseph Bowman, William Harrod, and several others were sent to other counties west of the Blue Ridge to recruit men for the expedition. Each of these was instructed to meet him, with his respective company, on the Monongahela. At length Colonel Clark descended the river in boats from Fort

* Butler's Kentucky, p. 47.

A.D. 1778.]   VALLEY OF THE MISSISSIPPI.   101

Pitt, with his recruits, to the Falls of the Ohio, where he was detained several weeks, encamped upon "Corn Island," recruiting his forces and completing his preparations for the ultimate object of his commission. Here he received an important accession to his little army of twenty volunteers from Kentucky, under Captain Montgomery.

All things being in readiness, about the middle of June he descended the river with less than two hundred men in barges, until they arrived at a point within sixty miles of its mouth. Here Colonel Clark determined to disembark his troops, and make a rapid and secret march across the country, so as more certainly to surprise the post of Kaskaskia. After a hazardous and tedious march through the unfrequented wilderness of wet lowlands, he at length reached Kaskaskia in safety.

The further consideration of the military operations of this division of the army of Virginia, in the reduction of the British posts on the Upper Mississippi and Wabash, agreeably to the plan of this work, will be found in book iii., chap. iv. Suffice it to say here that the whole of the British posts north of the Ohio and west of Detroit were subdued by Colonel Clark and his brave associates during the following month of July. The authority of Virginia was acknowledged by the inhabitants, and the country was embraced as an integral portion of the State of Virginia, under the name of the "county of Illinois." Many of the hostile tribes of Indians between the Wabash and the Upper Mississippi entered into treaties of peace and amity with Colonel Clark, and ceased their hostilities against the frontier settlements of Virginia.* Captain John Todd was appointed first civil and military commandant and lieutenant-colonel of the county.†

The capture of Kaskaskia and other northwestern British posts served to rouse the commandant at Detroit to greater exertions in harassing the frontier population east and south of the Ohio. Although, for a time, his operations in Kentucky and Illinois were paralyzed by this unexpected disaster to his majesty's arms, he resolved to retrieve the honor of the British flag, and add new laurels to his own brow.‡

With this resolution he concentrated all his forces, and called in all his savage allies, for the contemplated recapture of the British posts on the Wabash and in the Illinois country, together with

* Butler's Kentucky, p. 66.   † Idem, p. 65.   ‡ Idem, p. 80, 81 the rebel Virginians who held possession of them. With eighty British regulars, and a large force of Indian warriors, he advanced to Vincennes, and took possession of the post without resistance ; but it was only a few weeks afterward when he was compelled to surrender his whole force to Colonel Clark, and proceed a prisoner of war to the capital of Virginia, where he and others of his subordinates were put in close confinement as a retaliation for their past cruelties.*

The Cherokees, instigated by his agents, had again resumed hostilities against the frontier settlements of North Carolina, and Colonel Shelby, at the head of a victorious army, had overrun their country with fire and sword, destroying no less than eleven towns, besides twenty thousand bushels of corn, and the capture of a large supply of stores and goods, valued at £20,000, which had been provided by his "majesty's agents" for distribution at a general council of the northern and southern Indians, which was to convene at the mouth of Tennessee in the spring of 1779.†

Thus were terminated forever the hostile operations of Great Britain in the Illinois country, from the Wabash to the Mississippi; yet many years elapsed before the strong-holds of her power were demolished northeast of the Wabash.‡

The settlements on the Monongahela and Upper Ohio, although erected into counties as early as January, 1777, had been so continually harassed by Indian hostilities, that courts and civil government had been entirely neglected until April of the following year. During this period of more than fifteen months, the militia of the three newly-organized counties had been held under marching orders, with but little intermission, until the 6th of April, 1778. Martial law superseded the civil authority; and the District of West Augusta was again, to all intents, a military colony, wholly absorbed in defensive operations for the general safety.

Yet at this early period, and in the infancy of the western settlements, the people, true to the principles of liberty, were jealous of military power, although its exercise had been necessary for the public safety and the protection of the inhabitants

---

* Jefferson's Correspondence, Randolph's edition, p. 164–169.   † Idem, p. 163.

‡ The last remnant of British power south of the western lakes was "Fort Miami," just below the Rapids of the Maumee, and about fifty miles south of Detroit. These forts were surrendered or evacuated in 1796, in conformity with the treaty of London, 1794. They had been held ten years in violation of the treaty of 1783.

from savage incursions. After the first respite from Indian alarms and danger, the Court of Quarter Sessions held its regular term early in April. On the second day of court, Colonel Shepherd was formally arraigned before the court, charged with having established martial law during the recess. The colonel pleaded the public danger and the necessity of the times as his justification, and the court, satisfied that he did not intend to encroach upon the prerogatives of the civil authorities, discharged him, and the complaint was dismissed.*

In these early times, licensed attorneys, as a necessary appendage to a court of justice, were unknown. While courts are unsophisticated by legal quibbles and technicalities, the administration of justice is simple and easy; but as civilization and legal lore pervert the ends of justice, the other adjuncts become necessary to clear away the mist thrown before the mental vision. It was not until the second day of November, 1778, that Philip Pendleton and George Brent were admitted as the first attorneys, and licensed to practice in the court of Ohio county. At the same time, the state required an attorney to enforce the penalties of the law, and Philip Pendleton was appointed first attorney-general† for the District of West Augusta.

During the spring and summer of 1778, Indian hostilities upon the Upper Ohio and upon the Monongahela were partially suspended, and civil government resumed its supremacy. Released from imminent danger and constant alarm, the people had leisure to apply themselves to domestic concerns, in the improvement of their farms and dwellings, in cultivating fields and gardens, and in rearing their stock and multiplying domestic animals.

The people of Kentucky were less fortunate. In this quarter the Indians commenced their incursions early in January; and, with occasional remissions, they were continued until the close of the year. Their principal operations, however, were directed against the Fort of Boonesborough. This was the most exposed of the three principal stations, and appeared to be an object of peculiar aversion to the savages, who directed all their efforts to its destruction.

Among their first operations was the capture of Captain Daniel Boone, with a detachment of twenty-seven men, at the

* American Pioneer, vol. ii., p. 377. † Idem.

Blue Licks, while making salt for the inhabitants. Such had been the harassing incursions of the savages during the past year, that most of the settlements near the Kentucky River had become almost destitute of the requisites for sustaining life. Among the privations most sensibly felt was the want of salt. As the Indians generally abstain from their incursions during the winter, Captain Daniel Boone proposed to take a party of thirty men and go to the Lower Blue Licks, on Licking River, and make salt to supply the stations. He set out on this expedition about the 1st of January, and continued making salt and sending it in to the settlements until the 7th of February, when he was surprised and taken prisoner by a large body of Indians on their way to Boonesborough. Alone in the woods, in quest of game for his salt-makers, he was taken prisoner, and deemed it expedient to enter into a capitulation for the surrender of his men, to the number of twenty-seven, who were at the salt-lick. The Indians promised to spare their lives and to give them good treatment while prisoners. Nor did they violate the stipulations into which they had entered.

This band of Indians, exceeding one hundred in number, elated with their success, without any loss, determined to return with their prisoners to their towns on the Little Miami River. In March following, Boone and ten of his men were marched to Detroit, the headquarters of Governor Hamilton, the British commandant.* During his captivity, Boone had succeeded in warmly ingratiating himself with the Indians, so that they refused to deliver him up to Governor Hamilton for a ransom of one hundred pounds; and soon after their return to their towns on the Miami, he was adopted as a son into the family of one of the principal chiefs. He remained among them greatly caressed, and accompanied them in many of their hunting excursions and rambles within the limits of the present State of Ohio. Yet no proper opportunity for escape occurred until the middle of June. At this time there were at their town of Chillicothe four hundred and fifty warriors, armed and painted in the most frightful manner, and ready to march against Boonesborough. He now resolved to make his escape, and to apprise his countrymen and friends of the danger which threatened them. On the 16th of June, he set out early in the morning, as usual, for a hunt. With the utmost expedition, he directed his course to-

* Marshall's Kentucky, vol. i., p. 56, 57. Also, Butler, p. 95.

ward Boonesborough, where he arrived in five days, a distance of one hundred and sixty miles, sustained by one single meal, which he had concealed under his blanket.* Every preparation was immediately made to place the fort in a proper state of defense, toward which his presence was equal to the aid of a host. Boone's escape caused the Indians to defer their intended expedition for nearly a month. This postponement being known to Captain Boone, he set out with a party of nineteen chosen men to surprise Chillicothe, an Indian town on Paint Creek, a tributary of the Scioto. Having advanced within four miles of the town, he encountered a party of twenty Indians, and after killing one and wounding two of them, he captured all their plunder and horses, without losing a man, and returned by a forced march to Boonesborough. In his return he fell upon the trail of the main Indian army, commanded by Captain Duquesne, a French officer, within one day's march of their destination.

On the 8th of August this formidable force was before the fort, with a demand for its surrender in the name of his "Britannic majesty." Two days' consideration was requested and granted. The garrison did not exceed fifty men; the subject was considered in all its bearings, and at length the answer returned was, "We are determined to defend our fort as long as a man of us lives." This answer was proclaimed aloud by Captain Boone from one of the bastions of the fort to the listening commander of the Indian host. To this Captain Boone subjoined his own personal thanks for the notice given him of the intended attack, and the time allowed to prepare his defense.† Captain Duquesne then stated that he did not wish to injure or rob them; that his orders from Governor Hamilton were to take the garrison prisoners of war; and that, if nine of the principal persons would come out and treat with him, he would do them no violence, but return home with the prisoners, or, if they would swear allegiance to his Britannic majesty, he would release them. Every artifice failing to decoy the garrison from their strong-hold, the attack, at length commenced, was kept up with but little intermission for nine days. During this time an attempt was made, under the direction of the French engineers, to lay a mine under the fort from the river bank.

* Marshall's Kentucky, vol. i., p. 58. Also, Butler, p. 96.
† Marshall, vol. i., p. 60.

This was discovered and prevented. At length, on the 20th of August, the siege was abandoned, and the Indian army returned without having accomplished the great object of their campaign.* During the investment, the defense had been vigorous and unremitting. Only two men were killed, and four wounded in the fort. The Indians had thirty-seven killed, and many more wounded. After the Indians retired the people picked up one hundred and twenty-five pounds of leaden bullets which had fallen, besides those which had buried themselves in the logs and palisades.† Such are the evidences of the untiring efforts with which the savage host urged their attacks.

This was the only important Indian incursion during this year on the extensive frontier of Western Virginia, other operations being most probably diverted by Colonel Clark.

For the protection of the settlements upon the Upper Ohio and upon the Monongahela more effectually, General M'Intosh, of the Federal army, early in the spring of 1778, had descended the river from Fort Pitt, with a detachment of regulars and militia, and erected a stockade fort on the north side of the Ohio, half a mile below the mouth of Big Beaver Creek, and about thirty miles below Fort Pitt. The fort was defended by strong bastions, and mounted with one six-pounder cannon. The post was called "Fort M'Intosh," in honor of the general. It was situated upon an elevated plain, terminating in a rocky parapet, two hundred feet above the river, and having a most commanding position. It was directly in the line of the war-path leading to the settlements on the west side of the Monongahela.‡

Late in the autumn, General M'Intosh received orders from the Federal government to march a strong force against the Wyandot towns on the head waters of the Sandusky River, situated about one hundred and seventy miles west of Fort M'Intosh. It was not until late that the troops were put in motion, when the general set out with one thousand men. Advancing by slow and regular marches, he was overtaken by winter, about sixty miles from Fort M'Intosh, and upon the head waters of the Tuscarawas. Here, on account of the lateness of the season and the inclemency of the weather, the council of war deemed it expedient to suspend the march, and defer further operations until spring.

* Marshall's Kentucky, vol. i., p. 62. † Idem. ‡ See Doddridge, p. 243, 244.

The expedition against the Sandusky towns was accordingly postponed, and a stockade post was erected upon the Tuscarawas, just below the mouth of Sandy Creek, and, in honor of the President of Congress, it was called "Fort Laurens." Colonel John Gibson, with one hundred and fifty men, detached as a garrison, took command of the fort, and General M'Intosh, with the residue of the troops, returned to Fort Pitt.*

This was the first advance of the white man's power west and north of the Ohio; and although the Indians had relaxed their operations against the frontier settlements, it was not their intention to permit the enemy thus quietly to occupy their country, and they left untried no effort to capture the post and destroy the feeble garrison.

[A.D. 1779.] It was early in January following when they made their first hostile movement against Fort Laurens, and the investment was continued without intermission until spring. Early in January the first party of Indians appeared before the fort, and before they had been seen succeeded in drawing a portion of the garrison into a disastrous ambuscade. Concealing themselves in the high grass, they sent a number of horses, with bells on their necks, to graze near the fort. The horses continued for some time in sight of the fort, and no Indians appearing, the commandant was induced to order out a fatigue party of sixteen men to secure the horses. They had advanced but a few hundred yards, when, by a sudden fire from the concealed Indians, fourteen of them were killed on the spot, and the remaining two were taken prisoners. Such was the beginning of the siege of Fort Laurens.

The same evening the savages appeared in great force, numbering, according to estimate, at least eight hundred and forty warriors. They continued to surround the fort with detached parties for nearly six weeks, entirely cutting off all communication with Fort M'Intosh or the settlements below Fort Pitt. During this time they kept the garrison in continual alarm and constant watching by their incessant attacks and threatened assaults.

In March they had disappeared for some days, and the commandant, in the vain hope that they had retired to their towns, permitted Colonel Clark, of the Pennsylvania line, with a guard, to escort twelve invalids to Fort M'Intosh. But the party had

* See Doddridge's Indian Wars, p. 246.

not advanced two miles from the fort, when they were surprised by a party of Indians, and at the first fire fourteen men were killed; four only escaped. Their bodies, horribly mangled, were left unburied on the plain, to be devoured by wolves.

So close had been the siege during the winter, that the bones of those killed in January, in sight of the fort, remained unburied, and were devoured by wolves.*

Settlements had extended rapidly in Kentucky, and the resident population in all the region south of the Ohio could not be less than five thousand souls, besides hundreds of visitors and transient persons. Organized civil government had been in operation nearly two years, hundreds of settlements had been made, and the whole country was covered with improvements barely sufficient to establish a claim, or inchoate title, to the land; the extent and bounds of each claim were undefined, and conflicting interests of individuals required adjudication to confirm and ratify the claims in the order of their precedence. For this purpose, the Legislature of Virginia, at its last session, had created a Court of Commissioners to examine and adjudicate upon all claims, or inchoate titles, having their inception anterior to the first day of January, 1778. This court held its sessions alternately in the different settlements during the summer of 1779, and at the close of the year the commissioners had adjudicated no less than three thousand claims. Such had been the progress of pioneer emigrants up to the beginning of the year 1778 in Kentucky. Other acts of the Legislature had made ample provision for pre-emption rights subsequent to that time.†

It was about the first of April, this year, that the first permanent settlement was made on the present site of Lexington, in Fayette county. It was begun by Ensign Robert Patterson and twenty-five men from Harrod's Station. The houses, or log cabins, were arranged in parallel rows, and connected by a strong picket inclosure. It was soon occupied by the families of James Masterson, Major John Morrison, the M'Connels, Lindsays, and others.‡ About the same time, Bryant's Station,

---

* Doddridge's Notes, p. 246.

† The Court of Land Commissioners in Kentucky, in 1779, was constituted of William Flemming, Edmund Lyne, James Barbour, and Stephen Trigg, *commissioners;* and John Williams, Jr., *clerk.* Their first session was held at St. Asaph's.—See Butler, p. 100, 101. Also, Marshall, vol. i., p. 101.

‡ Marshall, p. 101, 102. Also, Butler, p. 101.

five miles northeast of Lexington, was begun, and several others in the vicinity of Danville. Many other stations on the southwest side of Licking River, and thence westward to the sources of the Elk-horn, and upon the sources of Green River, and Rolling Fork of Salt River, were also commenced about this time.

The older stations became the principal resort of emigrants and new-comers, and their population was thus rapidly increased. The region near the Ohio River, except near the falls, was avoided by emigrants as an exposed frontier, where families were not safe from Indian outrage.

About midsummer the Indians resumed their incursions, distributed in small marauding parties from five to twenty in number, which penetrated every settlement, infested the roads near the stations, occasionally capturing a prisoner, taking a scalp, or firing upon such as came within their reach. By such means the Indians succeeded in keeping the inhabitants in a state of continual alarm, and compelling the families to concentrate around the stations for protection from secret attacks.

But the most disastrous event upon the frontiers of Kentucky, during this summer, was the defeat and massacre of Colonel Rodgers and a detachment of ninety men, near the mouth of the Little Miami. This defeat, in its effects upon the frontier settlements, was far more disastrous than any thing which had been experienced from the Indians since the hard-fought battle of the Kenhawa. Colonel David Rodgers and Captain Robert Benham, agents for the supply of the western posts, had returned from New Orleans in charge of two large keels freighted with an abundant supply of military stores, ammunition, and provisions for the western posts, with a complement of one hundred men. About the first of June, having recovered from the fatigue of a long and toilsome voyage up the Mississippi and Ohio Rivers, Colonel Rodgers set out from the "falls" to conduct the supplies up the Ohio to Fort Pitt. Near the mouth of the Little Miami, he beheld a number of Indians in canoes and upon rafts floating out of the Miami, which was then in flood from recent rains. As he approached, the Indians retired behind a copse of willows near the mouth, and the brave but unfortunate Colonel Rodgers resolved to attack them. The boats were landed, and his men were ordered to attack the savages on shore. In their advance they were soon led into a dangerous ambuscade just beyond the willows, where his men were instantly surrounded by more than four hundred Indians. Colonel Rodgers, at the head of his men, fought to the last; but the Indians, in a furious onset with tomahawk and scalping-knife, soon dispatched about ninety men, including their commander. Only two escaped to the boats, and six or eight subsequently made their way to the falls. The whole amount of stores and supplies fell into the hands of the savages; one boat was ultimately recovered.

To revenge this disaster, and to protect the settlements from the frequent incursions of marauding parties, known to be Shawanese from the head waters of the Miami and Scioto Rivers, the people of Kentucky planned a mounted expedition, under the command of Colonel John Bowman, against these Shawanese towns, and especially that known as Chillicothe. About the middle of July, the expedition, comprising nearly two hundred of the best men in Kentucky, set out for the devoted town. After a rapid march, they arrived near the first Indian town unobserved. The town and all its inhabitants might have been sacrificed to their vengeance; but by some extraordinary mismanagement or indecision of the commander, they utterly failed to accomplish this object. Assailed by a panic more formidable than the savage warriors, Colonel Bowman ordered a retreat, which was maintained under a galling pursuit and fire from a few savages for nearly one hundred miles, until they reached the Ohio River. Several of their number had fallen under the Indian fire during the retreat, and left their bones in the wilderness, and many others were severely wounded. The injury sustained by the enemy was inconsiderable.*

Yet one of the great sources of Indian invasion and of hostile instigation had been broken up by the capture of the British posts on the Wabash and in the Illinois country, and the captivity of Colonel Hamilton, who was now secure in the dungeons of Williamsburg.† Many of the western tribes had entered into treaties of peace and friendship with Colonel Clark, which presaged a temporary quietude to the frontier people.

The news of these successes had reached the Atlantic settlements, and the spirit of emigration, which for months had

---

* See Butler, p. 102–104. † See book iii., chap. iv., of this work.

languished, began to revive with renewed ardor. The terrors of the Indian waned in the distant horizon, and autumn found hundreds of families again on the road for the Monongahela, besides hundreds who had advanced from that region down to Kentucky, admitted to be the paradise of all the West. Already, during the last spring, while Indian hostilities for a time had been suspended, more than a thousand emigrants had reached Kentucky from the Monongahela; and before the recession of the spring floods, three hundred large family boats had arrived at the falls, all freighted with emigrants for the interior of Kentucky. For months together, trains of wagons, ten or fifteen in number, might be seen daily departing from "the falls" for different parts of the interior settlements. Before the last of October there had been established six "stations" on Bear-grass Creek, with a population of six hundred men.*

The rapid increase of population exhausted the limited supplies of food in the country, and a dearth ensued. Corn, and every article of provisions for family consumption, became remarkably scarce, with the price increased in due proportion. In December, corn was worth fifty dollars per bushel in Continental money, and before the first of March following its value had increased to one hundred and sixty-five dollars, which price was sustained until opening spring supplied other means of sustenance. This was a memorable period for emigrants to Kentucky. In the midst of an inclement winter, without meat, except that obtained from the forest, without bread, for the store of wheat was exhausted, and corn, the only substitute, one hundred and sixty-five dollars a bushel! This, indeed, was in depreciated paper money; but this was their circulating medium. The condition of all classes of people was alarming in the extreme; all were compelled to subsist upon such roots and vegetables as could be procured; upon the flesh of the deer, the bear, and the wild turkey, or such other animals as the hunter could procure. Milk, butter, and curd, to those possessed of domestic stock, afforded a grateful variety in their daily fare; but bread, however coarse, was the luxury of but few.†

The same state of scarcity prevailed throughout the whole frontier line for five hundred miles. The pressure was not

* Butler's Kentucky, p. 99.   † Marshall's Kentucky, vol. i., p. 103.

relieved until the last of May, when corn fell to thirty dollars per bushel.*

[A.D. 1780.] The winter of 1779–80 had been uncommonly severe and protracted. Emigrants had continued to arrive on the Monongahela and in Kentucky until mid-winter. Many had been overtaken by the severity of winter while in the midst of the wilderness, and there many of them were compelled to encamp, exposed to hardships and privations almost incredible. Hunger and cold, in their extremes, were the lot of all; their domestic stock of all kinds, designed for their new settlements, died from cold and starvation. The store of provisions for the journey became exhausted, and those camps which could not produce an experienced hunter, reduced to the verge of starvation, were obliged to sustain life by killing their remaining stock of cattle and hogs, already reduced to living skeletons. The ground was covered several feet deep with snow, drifted in many places to the depth of six or eight feet. The rivers and springs were congealed to solid ice, or entirely dried up. Wild beasts and game of all kinds were poor, emaciated, and sickly; many died from inanition. When winter began to break up, such were the enormous floods from rains and melting snows, that many of the beasts of the forest, such as the bear, the elk, the deer, and game of less magnitude, were drowned or killed by drifting ice. To such extremities, in many cases, were migrating families reduced before they reached Kentucky, that they were compelled to sustain life by eating the dead carcasses of such animals as were found floating on the river floods. Having arrived in Kentucky, they

---

* The prices of other articles were in proportion to corn; but as this was an article of prime demand, it is given as a criterion for estimating the value of other things. In June following, when corn had fallen to thirty dollars per bushel, the tavern rates in Ohio county, Virginia, were established by the county court, in Continental paper money, as follows:

1. Breakfast or supper $4 00
2. Half a pint of whisky 6 00
3. Dinner 6 00
4. Lodging, with clean sheets 3 00
5. Horse to hay over night 3 00
6. One gallon of corn 5 00
7. One gallon of oats 4 00
8. Half a pint of whisky, with sugar 8 00
9. One quart of strong beer 4 00

The currency, Continental money, continued to diminish in value until 1781, when the charge for dinner was fixed by court at twenty dollars; breakfast and supper at fifteen dollars.—See American Pioneer, vol. ii., p. 378.

were able to procure a scanty supply of vegetables, of milk, and animal food of divers kinds; but the corn and wheat had been exhausted, and, consequently, bread was an article rarely seen.*

Settlements were advancing over the central parts of Kentucky, and the population of each was rapidly increasing. The same was true upon the waters of the Monongahela, the Kenhawa, and the Ohio itself. But Indian hostilities had not ceased. Incursions by hostile bands continued to harass the exposed inhabitants in both regions and along the whole course of the Ohio. Covered boats, for the protection of their inmates from the fire of the Indian rifle, seldom arrived at the "falls" without having encountered an attack from the savages who infested the shores; often family boats were plundered and destroyed, and their inmates were fortunate to escape with their lives.

To protect the emigrants advancing by this great route to Kentucky, troops were stationed at suitable places on the river, but chiefly at Fort Pitt, at Fort M'Intosh, Wheeling, and Point Pleasant.

About this time, Colonel George Slaughter, from Virginia, descended the Ohio with one hundred and fifty state troops for the protection of Kentucky. He established his headquarters near the mouth of Bear-grass Creek, just above the falls. Here he erected a stockade fort, after the western manner, defended by several pieces of cannon, and known as "Fort Nelson." For several months public attention was directed to this point, which was strongly fortified, under a belief that the British commandant at Detroit designed to lead a strong expedition for its destruction. Other points, deemed more secure, were less prepared to resist a hostile attack, and public attention in the interior, notwithstanding occasional instances of Indian hostilities, seemed wholly engrossed in the acquisition of land, as if it were the only subject of interest, the only great business of life.

In the mean time, the British commandant at Detroit, to offset the former successes of Colonel Clark in the Illinois country, had prepared a strong military expedition for the reduction of Ruddle's and Martin's Stations on the forks of Licking River. The expedition was prepared with great secrecy, and about the first of June the whole allied British force, consisting

---

* See Marshall's Kentucky, vol. i., p. 91, 92; also, p. 102, 103.

of six hundred Indians and Canadian French, under the command of Captain Bird, a half-breed British officer, began to descend the Great Miami, with six pieces of artillery, and a large supply of military stores and ammunition. This British and Indian host advanced with such caution and secrecy, that they had ascended the Licking River, with their cannon, unperceived; and on the 22d of June they suddenly made their appearance before Ruddle's Station, on the south fork of Licking. This fort was a common stockade, without artillery, and the feeble garrison, encumbered with many women and children, was beyond the reach of aid from any quarter. Resistance was vain, and the garrison was compelled to surrender at discretion to the "arms of his majesty," with the guarantee of their lives only. Having demolished the fort, the victors loaded the prisoners with the spoils, and pursued their route to Martin's Station, on Stoner's Fork. The fort and garrison here shared the same fate, and were led into hopeless captivity.

Elated by their unexpected success, and without loss, the invading host quickly retired with their prisoners and booty to the north side of the Ohio. Such of the women and children as could not keep up with their rapid march were sacrificed to the tomahawk and scalping-knife.

About this time a formidable invasion of the Coshocton towns was preparing on the waters of the Monongahela, to proceed from Wheeling, the point of general rendezvous. The whole number of troops collected for this expedition amounted to eight hundred men, including regulars and militia, under the command of General Broadhead. About mid-summer they set out from Wheeling, and after a rapid march by the most direct route, they reached the vicinity of the lower Moravian town, called "Salem." Here the commander halted, and sent an express to the missionary, the Rev. John Heckewelder, requesting of him an interview at his camp, and desiring him to bring a small supply of provisions for the army. The missionary attended accordingly, when the general communicated to him the object of the expedition, and informed him that it was designed against the hostile Indians, and not against the peaceable Moravians under his charge, who had conducted themselves with propriety as neutrals during the war; that it would be a source of pain to him to learn that any of the peaceable Indians, his disciples, should suffer any injury from the troops;

to prevent which, he advised them not to be found in the route of their march.

The militia, however, had been highly incensed against Indians indiscriminately, on account of the continued and harassing incursions and murders committed upon the frontier settlements east of the Ohio. They had, moreover, secretly resolved to destroy the Moravian villages with those of the hostile bands, and with difficulty were prevented from accomplishing their object only by the influence of General Broadhead and Colonel Shepherd.*

Although they receded from their purpose, their fury was not appeased; it was only suppressed for the time. The army made a forced march to the hostile towns on the Coshocton, a few miles above, and succeeded in surprising one village on the east side of the river, and capturing every soul found in it; but, owing to a sudden flood in the river, from a recent heavy rain, the Indians of another village, on the west bank, escaped. Ten or twelve prisoners were picked up from some other towns in the vicinity. The prisoners, among whom were sixteen warriors, were placed under guard until night, when a council of war was held to determine their fate. The decision of the council doomed the whole sixteen warriors to death. By the order of the commander, they were bound, and marched a short distance below the town, where they were immediately dispatched by the bayonet, the tomahawk, and the spear;† after which they were all scalped according to the Indian custom. Such are the horrors of savage warfare, although waged by a civilized people.

On the following morning a fine-looking chief presented himself on the bank of the river as a messenger of peace, and, after having been introduced into camp, was treacherously murdered by a man named Wetzel while conversing with the commander. Wetzel approached with a tomahawk concealed under his hunting-shirt, which he suddenly drew, and cleft open the head of the chief with a single blow, so that he instantly expired.

At noon the army took up the line of its retrograde march. The Indian prisoners, about twenty in number, were committed to the custody of the militia, whose thirst for blood had not been satiated. After proceeding half a mile, the men began to

* Doddridge, p. 291, 292. † Idem, p. 292.

kill the prisoners, and in a short time they had dispatched all of them except a few women and children, who were spared to be subsequently exchanged for an equal number of white prisoners held by the Indians.*

Such is the insatiable revenge which exists between the two races of men, in whom the utter extermination of each other is the only sufficient revenge. In all the invasions made into the Indian country for the last three years, the savage chiefs omitted no opportunity of deploring the existing state of feelings between the white and the red men, and professing their earnest desire of peace; yet they could not accede to a peace which did not protect their country from the occupation of their enemies.†

The people of Kentucky, smarting under the defeat of Colonel Bowman last summer, and the more recent invasion of their country by the savages under Captain Bird, determined to invade the Shawanese towns on the Great Miami with a force adequate to the object in view. For this purpose, a regiment of mounted volunteers had assembled at the falls; and in the month of August they placed themselves under the command of Colonel George Rogers Clark, ready to take up the line of march for the Miami towns.‡

The regiment proceeded up the Ohio, on the Kentucky shore, until they reached the mouth of Licking River. Here they crossed over to the present site of Cincinnati, where they erected a block house for the protection of some military stores and a few wounded men of Captain M'Gary's company, who had been imprudently and rashly led by their commander into an Indian ambuscade on the north side of the river. This block house was the first building ever erected by white men on the site of Cincinnati. This being completed and provided with a suitable guard, the army proceeded northwardly toward the head waters of the Great Miami. With the celerity so characteristic of all Colonel Clark's military movements, they reached the object of their destination unperceived. The town was taken by surprise, and the troops rushed to the assault. After a fierce conflict, the brave warriors who defended the town were compelled to fly, leaving seventeen of their number dead on the field. The town was consumed with fire, and their fields of growing corn were utterly destroyed.

* Doddridge, p. 293. † Idem, p. 245.
‡ American Pionter, vol. ii., p. 377, 378.

In this engagement Colonel Clark's regiment lost seventeen men killed, besides several severely wounded, a certain evidence of the resolute resistance of the savages.*

Captain Hugh M'Gary, who, by his rashness, had exposed his men, foolishly crossing the river and marching upon the Indian shore, was the man who, two years afterward, brought on the disastrous defeat at the Blue Licks. He was courageous to a fault, but rash in the extreme.

After the destruction of the principal town and its fields, the expedition ravaged several other towns upon other head waters of the Miami, and spread consternation wherever they appeared. A British trading-post, on a branch of Mad River, was likewise taken and unceremoniously destroyed. The regiment returned to the falls, having fully accomplished the object of the expedition, and having, for the present, put an effectual check to the Indian incursions from this quarter.

This year the militia of Kentucky were organized into a brigade, under Brigadier-general Clark. The brigade officers were Colonels Benjamin Logan and John Todd; Lieutenant-colonels John Floyd, William Pope, Stephen Trigg, and Daniel Boone.† General Clark's command extended to the banks of the Mississippi.

At the same time, emigrants from Virginia and North Carolina, by hundreds, were advancing by way of the "wilderness road" into Kentucky, through Cumberland Gap, as well as by the northwestern routes to the Ohio River. The Commonwealth of Virginia never receded from her western limits, and the county of Illinois was still a military dependence of Virginia, under the command of a civil commandant, appointed by the executive of the state.

At the same time, Virginia was anxious to extend her authority to the Mississippi, south of the Ohio River. General Clark was accordingly instructed to take military possession of the extreme western limit of Kentucky. Obediently to this order, he descended the Ohio with a detachment of troops, and took possession of a point of high land on the east bank of the Mississippi, five miles below the mouth of the Ohio, upon which he erected "Fort Jefferson."‡ This post was strongly fortified, and well supplied with light artillery. After its completion,

---
* Marshall, vol. i., p. 110.   † Butler's Kentucky, p. 114–119.
‡ See Flint's History and Geography, vol. ii., p. 461, first edition.

Colonel Clark placed it under the command of Captain George, with a garrison of one hundred men. This occupancy on the Lower Mississippi was discontinued the following year.

This arrangement completed, General Clark, with two companions, Josiah Harland and Harmon Connolly, all dressed and painted in Indian style, traversed on foot the wilderness eastward nearly three hundred miles to Harrodsburg. Armed with rifle, tomahawk, and scalping-knife, sustained by jerked beef and parched corn, he plodded the tedious route through desolate forests, swamps, and swollen rivers, crossing the Tennessee on a frail raft, evading the hunting parties of the savages, and finally reaching his destination in safety.*

But Fort Jefferson, was within the territory claimed by the Chickasâ Indians; the fort had been erected without their consent, and their relinquishment had never been obtained to any portion of the western territory. The Chickasâs immediately remonstrated against the aggression upon their domains. But the commandant had no authority to negotiate with them on the subject, although, as it subsequently appeared, the Governor of Virginia had directed the purchase of a site for the fort from the Indians. Their remonstrances being disregarded, under the promptings of Colbert, a Scotch half-breed, they prepared to repel the invaders by force.

During the past year, difficulties had arisen between the States of Virginia and North Carolina relative to their respective limits, and the rights of the inhabitants as to property and jurisdiction in the western settlements. The settlements south of Kentucky River had been made under a doubt whether they would fall under the jurisdiction of Virginia or North Carolina. So rapidly had they advanced to the West, and so much had the state government been engrossed with the protection of the eastern frontier from British invasion, and the western from savage warfare, that the lines of her northern and southern limits had been alike neglected, and had never been properly surveyed and designated.

The line which divided Virginia and North Carolina was the parallel of 36° 30' north latitude, and this had never been ascertained. To ascertain the latitude, and to designate the proper boundary line between the two states, each state appointed one commissioner: Colonel Richard Henderson on the part of North Carolina, and Dr. Walker on that of Virginia.

* Butler, p. 115, 116.

These gentlemen disagreed in their respective lines, and the question of boundary was not conclusively settled for several years afterward. Colonel Henderson abandoned his survey before it was completed, while Dr. Walker completed his line westward to the Tennessee River, about sixty miles above its mouth. Descending the Tennessee and Ohio to the Mississippi, he there ascertained that the parallel of 36° 30' would intersect the Mississippi, and not the Ohio.* This line is the basis of the present southern limit of Kentucky.

CHAPTER IV.

INDIAN WARS ON THE OHIO. — EXTENSION OF THE AMERICAN SETTLEMENTS EAST AND SOUTH OF THE OHIO.—A.D. 1781 TO 1784.

Argument.—Severe Winter of 1780–81.—Scarcity in Kentucky.—Kentucky divided into three Counties.—Indian Hostilities on Bear-grass Creek.—Attack on Boone's and M'Afee's Stations. — Indians contemplate utter Destruction of Kentucky Settlements.—Chickasâs attack Fort Jefferson in 1780.—Counties of Kentucky organized. —General Clark's gun-boat Defense on the Ohio River.—Abundant Crops of 1781. —Indian Hostilities renewed in the Spring of 1782.—Estill's Defeat.—Last Survivor of his Party.—Indian Hostilities continued.—Laherty's Defeat.—Indian Invasion, under Simon Girty, on Bryant's Station.—Disastrous Battle of Blue Licks.—Colonel Logan buries the Dead. *Upper Ohio.*—Settlements of West Augusta harassed.— Wheeling Campaign against the Moravian Towns.—Horrible Massacre of peaceable Indians.—Former Position of the Moravian Towns.—Previous Admonitions neglected. —Disastrous Campaign against Moravians on Sandusky.—Colonel Crawford and Dr. Knight captured. — Execution and horrid Torture of Colonel Crawford. — British Agency the Source of Indian Hostilities.—Attack on Wheeling Fort, and on Rice's Fort. *Lower Ohio.*—General Clark invades the Indian Country in 1782.—Effects of this Invasion.—Domestic Prosperity of Kentucky.—Settlements extend North of Licking.—Flood of Emigration sets into Kentucky.—The "District of Kentucky" organized.—Peace with Great· Britain announced.—Extent of the Kentucky Settlements in 1783.—Population and Moral Condition of the Settlements.—Settlements extend North of Licking River in 1784–85.—Settlements in Western Virginia.

[A.D. 1781.] THE winter of 1780–81 was unusually protracted and severe; Indian depredations and murders for a time were suspended, and the people enjoyed a temporary respit from harassing alarms; the crops of the previous year had been greatly injured, and, in many cases, entirely destroyed by the Indians; the domestic stock of cattle and hogs had been killed; the supplies of salt, and other indispensable requisites

* Marshall, vol. i., p. 113.

of new settlements, had been exhausted, and the whole population of Kentucky was now on the verge of absolute want. Such was the state of things in the settlements, when opening spring enabled the savages to resume hostilities. The whole line of frontier settlements in Pennsylvania, Virginia, and Kentucky was simultaneously assailed by marauding parties of Indians distributed along this extensive frontier. Terror and consternation were only the precursors of havoc and desolation. The whole country was again thrown into a state of preparation to repel the invaders at every point.

Agreeably to the provisions of an act of the Legislature of the preceding year, the county of Kentucky was divided into three counties, designated by the act as the "counties of Jefferson, Fayette, and Lincoln." The county of Jefferson comprised all the country lying on the Ohio River, between the Kentucky and Green Rivers, presenting a frontier of more than two hundred miles along the Ohio. The county of Fayette comprised the country on the northeast side of Kentucky River, and extending to the Big Sandy, presenting a frontier coast of equal extent on the Ohio. The county of Lincoln comprised all the southeastern portion of the present State of Kentucky. These extensive counties were organized with a civil and military government, similar to other counties in Virginia, and, like many of the western counties, they comprised extensive regions of uninhabited country.*

The first Indian incursions into Kentucky took place early in March, and were directed against Jefferson county. Several persons were killed during that month. Among the most conspicuous of those who suffered in the opening campaign were Colonel Lynn, and Captains Tipton and Chapman, of the Bear-grass settlements. A party of fifteen men having set out in pursuit of one of the marauding bands of Indians, was surprised near the Ohio, on the waters of Bear-grass Creek, and were severely defeated by the Indians, with the loss of nine men killed, and one wounded.

In April, a station settled by Squire Boone, near the site of the present town of Shelbyville, was alarmed by signs of Indians, and the occupants deserting it, sought safety at the stronger settlements on Bear-grass Creek. While on this route, a party of men, encumbered with the women, children, house-

* Butler, p. 118.

hold goods, and cattle, were attacked by the Indians, who killed several persons, and dispersed the remainder in the recesses of the forest. To revenge this outrage, Colonel John Floyd, with twenty-five men collected from the vicinity of the falls, went in pursuit of the Indians, but soon fell into an ambuscade, and was defeated with the loss of half his men.*

Early in May, a party of Indians appeared before M'Afee's Station, and, after a brisk skirmish with a few men, who retreated to the fort, a fierce attack was commenced, and continued with vigor for nearly two hours, when persons from other stations in the vicinity, apprised of the attack, came to the relief of their friends, who were thus enabled to defeat the Indians within one mile of the fort. In this affair, one white man was killed and one mortally wounded; the Indians lost six or seven killed, besides their wounded.†

M'Afee's Station, although a frontier post, was not again molested by them. The hostile incursions of these marauding bands against other points of the settlements also became less frequent during the remainder of this year, and Kentucky again, for a time, enjoyed comparative tranquillity from Indian invasions; but it was only the deceptive calm before the desolating storm; the savages were only preparing for more important operations.

The Indians had perceived that their detached predatory incursions by small parties, however harassing they might be to the whites, did not check the increase of their settlements. They saw that, in spite of all their hostilities, all their marauding incursions, and all their persevering efforts in this way to check the advance of the whites from the east side of the mountains, their numbers daily increased by the arrival of additional emigrants; the number of dwellings and fortified stations likewise increased, and the surveyors were again busily employed measuring the land. This latter circumstance, from the first occupancy by the whites, had always been a hated omen and a sure precursor of the entire loss of their territories. Nor had the whites been satisfied in defending their settlements east and south of the Ohio; they had sent several expeditions into the heart of the Indian country north of the Ohio, and had burned their towns, laid waste their fields, and reduced their women and children to wretchedness and want. Their favorite hunt-

* Marshall, vol. i., p. 118. † Idem.

ing-grounds south of the Ohio were already in the occupancy of the whites, who were never known to recede from their advances; and so long as their forts remained, the people would hold the country, and the surveyors would measure off the land for fields and residences. It was in vain to invade their settlements by small bands, who could not take and destroy the forts. Hence it was evident to them that they must give up the contest in Kentucky, or they must bring their whole united force, and, by one grand effort, recover the country, with the destruction of the forts and the extermination of the whites. The latter plan was adopted by the leading chiefs of the Shawanese tribe, and during the remainder of the year they were unremitting in their efforts to bring about a general concert of action among all the northwestern tribes for a grand exterminating invasion during the next summer. In this they had the approbation and encouragement of British agents and officers at Detroit and on the Maumee, who assured them of the powerful aid of their great ally "George III., by the grace of God king of Great Britain," &c.*

While the plan of this grand invasion was in contemplation, and the preparations were secretly progressing, it was deemed expedient to keep the frontier settlements in a state of alarm and apprehension, with a renewal of desultory hostilities by detached bands.

In the mean time, Kentucky was threatened with a war from the Southern Indians. Fort Jefferson, as has been before observed, had been built the previous year upon the territory of the Chickasâ Indians, without their consent. So soon as it had been known to them, they had formally remonstrated against this invasion of their territory. This remonstrance being disregarded, they prepared to repel the invaders by force. Accordingly, early in the following autumn, when the garrison was reduced to about thirty men, most of whom were invalids, the fort was invested by a large force of Chickasâ Indians, led on by Colbert, a half-breed chief of Scotch extraction. During six days the siege was pressed with much vigor, and frequent assaults were made by the savages, who were as often driven back by the artillery loaded with grape and musket-balls. At length the garrison was relieved from its perilous condition by the arrival of General Clark, with a re-enforcement from Kas-

* Marshall's Kentucky, vol. i., p. 118.

kaskia, and a supply of ammunition and provisions. The Indians were thus compelled to abandon the siege and retire.*

Soon afterward, the Governor of Virginia issued instructions to General Clark to abandon and dismantle the fort, it being unnecessary for defense, and serving only as a source of hostility with the Indians. The order was obeyed, and the hostility of the Chickasâs ceased.†

The ultimate plans of the northwestern savages were unknown to the people of Kentucky until late in the following winter. In the mean time, emigrants continued to arrive in great numbers from the western parts of Virginia, Pennsylvania and Maryland. Population extended, under the protection of new stations, in the more exposed frontier settlements, while organization of the civil government was gradually extended over them, in the establishment of regular county courts, with a qualified jurisdiction in common-plea cases, reserving to the jurisdiction of the district courts near the capital all important civil cases, together with criminal and capital offenses.

General Clark having been appointed to superintend the general defense of Kentucky, and relieved from his command on the Mississippi, now began to put in operation his plans of frontier defense for the settlements near the Ohio River.

A portion of his plan of defense comprised a large floating battery of gun-boats, mounted with several pieces of artillery, and garrisoned by a strong detachment of light troops and riflemen, who could debark at any point to encounter the savages hovering near the Ohio. This battery was removed from point to point on the Ohio, between the mouth of Licking River and the "falls," which had now become the most exposed frontier of Kentucky. This new species of defense greatly interrupted the operations of the Indians against the Kentucky settlements, and afforded comparative security against their frequent incursions.

The year 1781 had yielded abundant crops of wheat, corn, and vegetables of all kinds, and plenty once more smiled upon the new settlements. The autumn brought with it great numbers of emigrants for permanent residence; and many of them were in good circumstances, and well qualified to be valuable members of the new and rising state, whose intellect and talents contributed greatly toward the building up of the new commonwealth a few years afterward.

* Butler, p. 119.   † Marshall's Kentucky, vol. i., p. 112.

[A.D. 1782.] Early in the following spring, the Indians resumed their hostile incursions against the settlements, and predatory bands began to infest the vicinities of the frontier stations in March and April. On the 20th of March a party of twenty-five Wyandots invested "Estill's Station," on the south side of Kentucky River. Having killed Miss Gass, and all the cattle in the vicinity, they retired with one captive negro. Captain Estill, ignorant of their numbers, proceeded to raise a party of twenty-five men, and set off in pursuit of the retiring enemy. Following their trail as far as Hingston's Fork, a few miles below Little Mountain, and in the vicinity of Mount Sterling, Montgomery county, on the 22d of March he came suddenly upon the enemy. The Indians were Wyandots, a tribe that are never known to retreat or to surrender. A desperate contest immediately commenced. Each opposing party being equal in numbers, the contest was, indeed, so many individual rencounters, "each man to his tree, and every man to his man." A more sanguinary conflict has not been seen in all the West. For two hours the deadly strife raged, and half the combatants were among the slain. Victory leaned toward the white man, when an unfortunate manœuver, if not "an inglorious flight," deprived Captain Estill of one half his surviving force. Lieutenant Miller, with six men, supposed to have been endeavoring to gain the enemy's flank, disappeared from the contest. This gave the Indians the ascendency, and the strife was soon finished. Captain Estill, in a deadly struggle with a powerful warrior, received the knife of his antagonist in his heart, just after his arm gave way at a former fracture, and that instant the Indian received his death from Joseph Proctor's unerring rifle.*

The survivors were compelled to make a precipitate retreat, leaving nine of their companions and their commander dead upon the ground.

Nearly one half of the Indians had likewise fallen, when Miller's defection turned the scale in their favor.

The usefulness and popularity of Captain Estill; the deep and universal sensibility excited by the premature death of a

---

* See biographical sketch and obituary notice, in the "Western Christian Advocate," February 7, 1845. In Flint's Life of Boone, the name of "Ashton" is erroneously used instead of Estill. The biographical sketch, in the Western Christian Advocate, from the pen of W. G. Montgomery, assumes the 22d of March, 1782, as the precise date of Estill's defeat. Marshall and Butler give it in May.

citizen so gallant and so beloved; the character of his associates in the battle; the masterly skill and chivalric daring displayed in the contest; the grief and despondence produced by the catastrophe, all contribute to give to "Estill's defeat" a most signal notoriety among the early settlers.

The memory of the brave but unfortunate Captain Estill is perpetuated by the state in the name of one of her counties.*

The last surviving hero of this memorable defeat was Joseph Proctor, who had distinguished himself by his deliberate courage in the contest. He lived, beloved by all, until the 2d of December, 1844, when he died, in the ninetieth year of his age, full of honors, in Estill county, Kentucky, where he had been a Christian minister more than fifty years. In commemoration of his youthful valor and his heroic deeds, he was buried with military honors by the volunteer companies of two counties, and attended by a concourse of one thousand of his fellow-citizens. A native of North Carolina, he had been a prominent and courageous defender of Kentucky from 1778 to 1782, and had fought side by side with Boone, Calloway, and Logan.

Among the disasters which befell the Ohio frontier this spring, we must not omit the melancholy fate of a detachment of regular troops, which was descending the river to Fort Steuben, at the Falls of Ohio, to re-enforce the garrison at that place. Captain Laherty, with one hundred and seven men, had advanced as far as the mouth of the Great Miami, when he was attacked by a large body of Indians a short distance below that stream. After a brave resistance, he was finally compelled to escape with the loss of nearly half his detachment, slain by the savages. This defeat is commemorated on the Ohio by a small creek near the scene of the disaster, which is still known as Laherty's Creek.

The Shawanese, Delawares, and Wyandots continued to make their incursions, and to spread terror among the frontier stations. A party of more than twenty Indians presented themselves before Hoy's Station, destroyed the cattle, took several prisoners, and then retired. Soon after, Captain Holder, with seventeen men, set out in pursuit of them, and after following their trail about twenty miles, he overtook the Indians on the second day, near the Upper Blue Licks. A sharp conflict ensued, when Captain Holder and his party were com-

* See Marshall, vol. i., p. 128-130. Also, Butler, p. 122-124. 5 Marshall's Reports.

pelled to retreat precipitately, with the loss of four men killed and wounded. The loss of the Indians was not ascertained.*

Indian depredations and successes against Kentucky became alarming. They were effected generally by parties of five or six penetrating into the heart of the country, prowling unseen for days until a fatal stroke could be made. Large bodies of savages, however, hovered near the Ohio River, whose spies observed all the movements on the river, and, when opportunity offered, never failed to make a bold effort before they retired.

Early in the spring, a man was shot by an Indian in a field adjoining the present site of Lexington; the Indian, however, was killed while scalping his victim.† Another white man was killed and scalped by an Indian about one mile from Lexington, on the road to M'Connel's Station. Other occurrences of a similar character were only the preludes to more important movements on the part of the hostile Indians.

In the mean time, the grand confederate army of Indians was assembling at Chillicothe, from which they were to proceed to the invasion of Kentucky. About the first of August, the savages, to the number of five hundred warriors, collected from the northwestern tribes, as well as from the Cherokees, were assembled at Old Chillicothe, all painted and equipped for war. They were led on by two degenerate white men, known as Simon Girty and Colonel M'Key, men in the British interest at Detroit, and who had been active in stirring up the northwestern Indians to commit their horrid atrocities upon the border population.

On the eve of their departure for the invasion of Kentucky, Simon Girty made a harangue in the presence of the Indian host, and encouraged them, with all his powers of eloquence, to seize upon the present occasion to exterminate the *long-knife* rebels, the enemies of their father, the British king, from their favorite hunting-grounds, which the Great Spirit had prepared for his red children. After inflaming their avarice and revenge to the highest pitch, he ceased, and the deep tones of the war-whoop were their approving response.‡

In a few days, the frontier settlements, ignorant of the extent of the hostile preparations against them, as well as of the route by which they were approaching, were alarmed

---

* Marshall, vol. i., p. 130. † Life of Boone, p. 193. ‡ Marshall, vol. i., p. 130–132.

by the advanced parties of the invading army. On the 15th of August this formidable host of savage warriors presented themselves before Bryant's Station, on the south bank of Elk-horn Creek, not far from the present road leading from Lexington to Maysville. The station comprised about forty cabins, in three parallel lines, and connected by strong palisades, in the usual form of a stockade fort. The garrison consisted of about fifty men, some of whom were absent at different points in the vicinity when the attack was first made. The fort was closely invested for two days, during which time the besiegers killed all the cattle, and kept up a continual fire of small arms upon the fort, besides numerous attempts to fire the buildings, by shooting blazing arrows upon the roofs, and throwing burning torches upon the wooden inclosures. On the fourth day, after having sustained a loss of about thirty warriors in their different assaults, and having failed to effect any serious injury to the fort and garrison, they retired toward the lower Blue Licks, passing along the Great Buffalo Trace, by the way of Martin's and Ruddle's Stations, which they had destroyed two years before. In their retreat, contrary to the customary Indian tactics, they made no effort to conceal their trace, but rather seemed to invite pursuit and encounter.

In the mean time, Colonel Todd, of Lexington, had assembled several companies, under their respective officers, amounting in all to one hundred and eighty-two mounted men, for the relief of the station. On the 18th they reached the station, and found the Indians had retired. Without waiting for further re-enforcements, which were expected, it was resolved to march in immediate pursuit of the enemy. Not an Indian was seen until the troop reached the banks of Licking River, at the Lower Blue Licks. After some delay, disregarding the prudent counsel of Colonel Daniel Boone, who believed an ambuscade near, the whole army marched forward across the river, under the fatal influence of Major M'Gary's example: he, spurring his horse forward, exclaimed, "Those who are not cowards, follow me, and I will show you where the Indians are!" The whole troop passed the ford without order or concert, and entered upon a narrow ridge almost encircled by the river, and covered with stunted forest-trees and cedar undergrowth. The Indians, who lay concealed on each side of the ridge, opened a heavy fire upon the advancing column, which was placed fairly between two fires, each of which more than equalled their own number. The men fought bravely for about ten minutes, when they were thrown into confusion, and every man used his utmost exertions to force his way back to the opposite side of the river, through the narrow descent to the ford. As they crowded promiscuously along, the fire of the pursuing Indians did prodigious execution, mowing down the men by scores. The Indians pressed forward in every direction, and, crossing the river above and below the ford, attempted to intercept their retreat. The flight necessarily became a perfect rout, and the victorious Indians continued the pursuit for twenty miles. Such was the "disastrous battle of the Blue Licks," which continued only about ten minutes. Sixty men were killed on the spot, and seven were taken captive by the savages. Among the slain were Colonel Todd, Lieutenant-colonel Trigg, and Majors M'Bride and Harlan.

On the 20th of August, Colonel Logan, who was only a few hours behind the advanced detachment, reached the battle-ground with his command of four hundred and fifty men; but the work was done; the fate of his friends and fellow-soldiers was sealed. The most he could do was to view and weep over the scene of carnage, and bury the mangled and disfigured bodies of the slain.* The loss of the Indians was said to be about equal to that of the Kentuckians, or about sixty killed and wounded. This was the severest blow that Kentucky had yet experienced from the hostile Indians. The whole country was filled with consternation, grief, and mourning, for in this bloody tragedy every family near Lexington had lost a member.

While these things were transpiring south of the Ohio, hostilities had been almost incessant upon the eastern side of the river, above and below Wheeling. The settlements along the river and upon the Monongahela had been greatly harassed by repeated incursions, which had not been intermitted, as usual, during the winter months. The weather, during the greater part of February, had been uncommonly fine, so that the war parties from the Sandusky River had visited the settlements earlier than usual. Several families had been killed in the latter part of February. From the early period at which these fatal visitations had taken place, many were led to believe that

* Butler's Kentucky, p. 128-130.

the murderers were either Moravians from the Muskingum, or that the war parties had spent the winter at the Moravian towns, to be convenient for their spring operations. If either conclusion were correct, the Moravian towns were dangerous to the safety of the settlements, and should be destroyed. Under this impression, an expedition was hastily prepared for the fatal enterprise. Each man furnished himself with his own arms, ammunition, and provisions, and some with horses. In this manner, nearly ninety volunteers assembled, under the command of Colonel David Williamson, in the Mingo Bottom, on the west side of the Ohio River. The second day's march brought them to the middle Moravian town, called Gnadenhutten, where they encamped for the night. In the morning, having ascertained that there were Indians on each side of the river, the men were divided into three parties, so as completely to surround the town from both sides of the river. When they reached the town, they found a large party of Indians in the field gathering corn. Professing peace and friendship for the Indians, they informed them that they had come to take them to Fort Pitt for their protection. The Indians immediately surrendered, delivered up their arms, and, appearing highly pleased with the prospect of their removal, began immediately to prepare breakfast for the white men and for themselves previous to their journey. A detachment was sent to Salem, another town not far off, to bring the Indians of that town also. They, like those of the first town, were found gathering their corn, and were carried to Gnadenhutten. The whole number from both towns were confined in two houses under a strong guard.

After the prisoners were thus secured, a council of war was held to decide upon their doom. The officers, unwilling to incur the whole responsibility of the terrible decision, agreed to refer the question to the whole number of men engaged in the expedition. The men were accordingly paraded in a line, and the commandant, Colonel Williamson, then put the following question to them: "Shall the Moravian Indians be taken prisoners to Pittsburgh, or shall they be put to death? All those who are in favor of saving their lives, step forward and form a front rank." Only sixteen or eighteen stepped forward. The line for vengeance greatly outnumbered that of mercy, and the fate of the innocent and defenseless Indians was sealed. They were informed that they must prepare for death. They were not surprised at the summons; for, from the moment they were placed in the guard-house, they anticipated their fate, and had commenced their devotions with hymns, prayers, and exhortations to each other to place a firm reliance upon the mercy of the Savior of men.

"When their fate was announced to them, these devoted people embraced and kissed each other, and, bedewing each other's faces and bosoms with their tears, asked pardon of the brothers and sisters for any offense they may have committed through life. Thus at peace with God and each other, they replied to those who, impatient for the slaughter, demanded 'whether they were ready to die,' that, having commended their souls to God, they were ready to die."*

"Suffice it to say, that in a few minutes these two slaughter-houses, as they were then called, exhibited in their ghastly interior the mangled and bleeding remains of these poor unfortunate people, of all ages and sexes, from the aged, gray-headed parent down to the helpless infant at its mother's breast; all dishonored by the fatal wounds of the tomahawk, war-club, mallet, spear, and scalping-knife."†

"The number of the slain, as reported by the men on their return from the campaign, was about eighty-eight; the Moravian account, which is more correct, no doubt, makes it ninety-six. Of these, sixty-two were grown persons, of whom one-third were women; the remaining thirty-four were children. Of this entire number, about five were shot on their first approach to surround the town. A few of the men, who were supposed to be warriors, were taken from the slaughter-houses to be tomahawked." These suffered without resistance, except one, who resisted and attempted to escape, after turning upon his executioner; but he was at length dispatched by several shots from the fire-arms.

After the massacre was finished, fire was set to the town, which consumed the whole village, including the two slaughter-houses and the dead bodies within them.

The Indians of the upper town, called Schoenbrunn, having received intelligence of what was transpiring at the lower towns, fortunately made their escape by deserting their town. The detachment sent to secure them, finding the town deserted, loaded themselves with plunder and returned to their companions.

* See Doddridge's Indian Wars, &c., p. 248-265.   † Doddridge's Notes.

As this is a memorable instance of the horrors of Indian warfare, and of the excesses and barbarities into which men raised in a civilized country may be carried by rage, prejudice, or fear, it may merit a further passing remark.

As Dr. Doddridge remarks, the whole campaign evinced a perfect disregard of military discipline and of military foresight. Had the Indians been disposed to make a firm resistance, in all probability the whole number in the expedition might have been cut off. Nothing would have been easier, had the Indians been so disposed; and yet they submitted to be "led like sheep to the slaughter," by men who well knew that no resistance would be made. Some of the men under the command of Colonel Williamson were probably the last who could have been induced to march against the hostile towns. They knew the pacific principles of the Moravians, and knew that blood and plunder might be their recompense, without incurring danger.

The situation of these Indians, both as respects the whites and their native countrymen, was one of peculiar danger. These villages had been commenced, under the superintendence of the Moravian missionaries, in the year 1772, and were first composed partly of emigrants from the missions of these people on the Big Beaver, at Freidenshutten, and from Wyalusing and Sheshequon, on the Susquehanna.* They soon increased in numbers and prosperity, until they comprised four hundred people. In the summer of 1774, during Lord Dunmore's war, they had been much annoyed by the parties of hostile Indians, in their passage to and from the white settlements, as well as by frequent rumors of hostile intentions against them by the whites; yet they continued their labors, their schools, and their religious exercises without intermis-

* The Moravians on the Muskingum were originally from the Susquehanna River, and were comprised in several towns, or villages, under the superintendence of the Moravian missionaries. They had occupied their villages on the Susquehanna some years, when the Indian war of Pontiac broke out, in 1763. In consequence of the extensive outrages and massacres by the hostile Indians on the frontier settlements of Pennsylvania, a portion of these peaceable Indians were massacred, as we have before observed, by the lawless Paxton Boys. The remainder of them, having been preserved with great difficulty from the infuriate vengeance of those zealots, and the same hostility, on the part of those who had composed this lawless band, continuing after the close of the war, without much prospect of change, it was at length "deemed high time they should retire to some Indian country beyond the Ohio." They accordingly left the Susquehanna for the Muskingum in the year 1773.—See Gordon's Pennsylvania, p. 473, &c.

sion. During the Revolutionary war, their situation became more critical and dangerous. In this war England had associated the tomahawk and scalping-knife of the savage with her own arms against the frontier settlements near the Ohio; and these allies had spread the most horrid barbarities along the whole extent of the western border. From this cause, the settlers of Western Pennsylvania and Virginia had endured the severest hardships and privations. They had been cooped up in small stockade forts; they had cultivated their little fields under the protection of armed guards; they had lived from day to day with sentinels on duty; they had been compelled to hear, if not to witness, the rumors of almost daily murders, or the still more horrid captivity of their friends and neighbors, the burning of their houses, and the plunder of their property. Almost unprotected by the eastern population, who were fully absorbed in resisting the civilized armies of Great Britain, they were compelled to bear the whole burden of the western war, and supply their means, choose their officers, and to conduct the war in their own manner. In this way they were often driven to acts which the government was bound to disavow. Constantly habituated to violence and insubordination, the people naturally became wanton and lawless in their contests with the Indians.

The Moravian villages were situated nearly midway between the white settlements and the hostile towns, being from sixty to eighty miles from each. Thus they were viewed by the whites as the "half-way houses of the warriors." Situated, as they were, between two contending races, it was no easy task to preserve a strict neutrality. Their pacific feelings and their aversion to the shedding of blood brought them into difficulties with both parties. When they sent their runners to Fort Pitt to inform our people of the approach of the war parties; when they received and fed, secreted and sent home such of our people as had escaped from savage captivity, they were guilty of breaches of their neutrality to the hostile Indians. If they afforded the warriors a resting-place and food, it was a breach of neutrality to the whites; yet they were so situated that the war parties could compel them to furnish all they had, and the whites required the same.

They were first suspected by the hostile Indians and the English commandant at Detroit as being confederates of the

American Congress, and to have induced the Delawares and others not to espouse the cause of Great Britain against the provinces. The frequent failure of their war parties was ascribed to the Moravians, who had sent runners to Fort Pitt to give the alarm.

A Delaware chief, during the spring of 1781, had fully informed the missionaries and their flocks of their imminent danger, both from Indians and from the whites, and had advised a removal to a place of safety. They disregarded the admonition; and in the fall of the same year a party of three hundred warriors broke up their settlements, plundered their towns, and took the missionaries prisoners. The Moravian Indians were carried to the Sandusky Plains, and there turned loose to shift for themselves, while the missionaries were carried to Detroit. In February following, about one hundred and fifty of these Moravian Indians had returned to their deserted villages on the Muskingum, to procure corn to keep their families and cattle from starving. Of these, ninety-six fell into the hands of Williamson's party, and were murdered. Under a similar jealousy on the part of the hostile Indians, they had been on the point of being murdered once or twice before. In the fall of 1781, such had become the exasperation of the whites against the position occupied by the Moravians, that the militia had determined to go and break up their settlement. For this purpose, a detachment had been sent out under Colonel David Williamson, to induce them to move further off, or to bring them to Fort Pitt. The few Indians found in their villages had been carried to Fort Pitt, and, after a short detention, had been dismissed. The people had censured Colonel Williamson for his lenity toward them. This may account for his non-interference in the next campaign.

As a palliation to the massacre of these Indians, it may be said that many of those engaged in the campaign, who were men of standing and worth, had lost one or more of their families or friends by the hands of the savages. In their towns several articles were found which had been plundered from their own houses or from those of their neighbors. One man is said to have found the bloody clothes of his wife and children, who had been murdered a few days before. Those articles, no doubt, had been purchased of the hostile Indians.

The majority of those in the expedition took no hand in the

massacre, but turned away with horror from the scene, their voice and their displeasure being silenced by the clamor and violence of a lawless minority.* Colonel Williamson himself was a brave and honorable man.

The next hostile movement on the part of the white inhabitants on the Upper Ohio and on the Monongahela took place late in May following. As we have already observed, less than half of the Moravian Indians were at their old towns on the Muskingum when Colonel Williamson and his party marched against them. The remainder, who had been carried off by the hostile Indians to Sandusky, had settled themselves upon that river, not far from the towns of the hostile Wyandots. The plan of destroying the remainder of the Moravians, together with the Wyandots, was conceived soon after the return of the expedition under Colonel Williamson. Preparations for a campaign against the Sandusky towns were immediately put in operation, with the design of making "a dash" upon them early in the summer.

The long continuance of the war and the innumerable outrages perpetrated by the Indians upon the settlements, the horrid murders which had been so often committed upon their families, neighbors, and relatives, whenever they ventured out of the forts and fortified stations, had at length produced in the minds of the frontier people a thirst for indiscriminate revenge, with a proportionate debasement of the moral feeling toward the authors of all their troubles; and having once tasted the sweets of a bloody revenge, obtained without risk or loss, they determined to wreak their vengeance indiscriminately upon every Indian, whether a professed friend or foe.

A strong force was accordingly raised to make a rapid and secret march to the Sandusky towns. For the sake of secrecy and dispatch, the whole were to be mounted upon the best horses they could procure; each man furnished himself with arms and every necessary outfit except ammunition, which was supplied by the lieutenant-colonel of Washington county. On the 25th of May, four hundred and eighty volunteers from the vicinity of the Ohio, and from Washington county, in Pennsylvania, mustered at the old Mingo towns,† on the west side

---

* See Doddridge, p. 260–264.

† This town, in 1766, was the only Indian village on the Ohio River, at which time it contained sixty Indian families.—Old Navigator, p. 25.

of the Ohio, seventy-five miles below Fort Pitt. Here they elected their commander for the expedition. The candidates were Colonel Williamson and Colonel Crawford. The latter was elected to command, although with reluctance he accepted the office.

All things being in readiness, the expedition commenced its march westward along "Williamson's Trail" to the old Moravian towns on the Muskingum. Here, finding plenty of corn in the fields for their horses, they encamped during the night. Soon after the army had halted near these towns, Colonel Crawford had a presage of evil in the utter disregard of military order by the men under his command. To illustrate this, one fact will suffice. Three men having walked beyond the encampment, discovered two Indians and fired upon them. This brought the men from the camp, regardless of military discipline and the authority of their commander, in a most irregular and tumultuous manner, to see what had happened. Next morning they continued their march without any important incident, and on the 6th of June their guides conducted them to the site of the Moravian villages; but the place was deserted, and the Indians had removed to the Scioto. A few huts among the high grass were all that remained. This was on the upper branches of the Sandusky. They were at the ultimate destination of the expedition, and neither blood nor plunder had slaked their fury. A council of officers was held, and they determined to march one day further toward Upper Sandusky, and, if no Moravians were found, they were to retreat immediately. They proceeded a little over half a day's march, when the advanced guard was driven back by a large body of Indians concealed in the high grass. A general fire from both sides immediately ensued, and continued incessantly until dark, when night separated the combatants. During the evening the Indians had been completely dislodged from a copse of woods in the prairie, which they had perseveringly attempted to hold. During these movements, the vigilance and bravery of Major Leet were conspicuous; and the detachment had lost but three men killed, and several wounded.

At night both armies retired behind a line of fires, mutually to avoid surprise and lay upon their arms. During the next day the Indians seemed busily engaged traversing the plains in every direction, but made no attack upon the whites. In the mean time, another council of war was held, and a speedy retreat was decided to be the only path of safety, as the Indians were hourly increasing in numbers. Colonel Williamson, who accompanied the expedition, had proposed to march with a strong detachment and attack the Upper Sandusky towns; but the commander prudently declined to divide his forces, saying, "We must stay together, and do the best we can." The dead were buried, and their graves concealed from the search of the Indians, and every thing was in readiness to retreat after night. The Indians perceived the object in contemplation, and about sunset attacked the army in every direction except that next the Sandusky, with great fury and in great force. Early in the night, after a circuitous march of two miles, they changed their direction, eluding their assailants in the dark, and retreated rapidly toward the trail by which they had advanced the day before. During the next day they pursued their retreat without loss of time, and were but little annoyed by pursuit. But the army became divided into small parties, in hope of eluding Indian pursuit. This was a most disastrous resolve: it was the very thing desired by their savage enemies. The Indians, during the whole retreat, paid but little attention to the main body, but dispersed over the whole country, from the Sandusky to the Muskingum, actively pursuing and cutting off the small parties, nearly all of whom were killed, and some almost in sight of the Ohio River. The number killed in this retreat was never known.*

At the commencement of the retreat, Colonel Crawford, missing his son and several of his family connections, halted to search for them as the line passed on. They were not in the line; and, having fallen behind the retreating column, he was never able to overtake it, on account of the wearied condition of his horse. He traveled all night, first toward the north and then toward the east, to avoid the Indian parties dispersed along the trail in pursuit. Having fallen in company with Dr. Knight and several others, they proceeded until the third day, when they were attacked by a party of Indians, who made Dr. Knight and Colonel Crawford prisoners; the remainder of the party, who were unable to escape, were killed. Dr. Knight and Colonel Crawford were conducted to an Indian camp not far distant, where they found nine fellow-prisoners in charge of seventeen Indians.†

* Doddridge, p. 272. † Idem, p. 275.

The next day Colonel Crawford and Dr. Knight were conducted by two Delaware chiefs, Pipe and Wingemond, to an Indian village, while four of the other prisoners were tomahawked and scalped at different places on the way. Five others were tomahawked and scalped by a party of squaws and boys near the place designed for Colonel Crawford's execution.

After the colonel was conducted to the place of execution, a post about fifteen feet high was set in the ground, and a large fire of hickory poles was made about eighteen feet from it. He was stripped and ordered to sit down; when he was severely beaten with sticks, and afterward tied to the stake by a rope just long enough to allow him to walk two or three times around the post and then back again. The torture began by shooting a great number of loads of powder upon his body from head to foot. Next they applied the burning ends of the firebrands to different portions of his body, with fiendish mirth at the agony produced; at the same time, the squaws amused themselves by pouring hot embers and coals over his naked body, until the ground within the limit of his tether became covered with live coals and embers, over which he was compelled to walk barefoot.

In the midst of his protracted sufferings, he cast an imploring look at the notorious Simon Girty, whom he had known many years before, and entreated him to take pity upon him, and in mercy shoot him. But Girty, true to his savage nature, taunted him, and with a fiendish smile bade him "entreat some one else."*

After three hours of this kind of torture, he became faint, and fell upon his face; an Indian stepped up and scalped him, after which an old squaw threw a quantity of burning coals on the raw and bloody skull from which the scalp had been torn. After this, he rose and walked once or twice around the post,

* No injustice should be done Girty, degraded as he stands before the tribunal of posterity. His conduct at the execution may have been assumed as a consideration of personal security from the suspicion which any interference or evidence of disapprobation might excite in the minds of the Indian chiefs. It is affirmed that Simon Girty, on the day previous to the burning of Crawford, proposed to purchase the prisoner from Captain Pipe, the Delaware chief, for a ransom of three hundred and fifty dollars, with a design of preserving his life; but Captain Pipe indignantly refused the offer, and severely menaced him for his interference. It has also been ascertained that Girty, on the night previous to the fatal defeat, had an interview with Colonel Crawford, and privately apprised him of the contemplated movements of the Indians, and advised him to escape that night. A suspicion of treachery or partiality for the white man might have brought destruction upon his own head.—See American Pioneer, vol. ii., 284, 285.

and soon after expired. His body was thrown into the flames and consumed to ashes. His son and his son-in-law, Major Harrison, were executed at the Shawanese towns.

Dr. Knight was more fortunate. He was doomed to be burned at a town about forty miles distant, whither he was sent in charge of a young Indian. On the way he sought the first opportunity to rebel, and escaped from his guard. In his subsequent hazardous advance, after suffering all but death and the extreme of famine, he reached the settlements on the Ohio after twenty-one days of toil and hunger.*

Most of the prisoners taken in this campaign were burned to death with cruel tortures, in retaliation, it is supposed, for the massacre of the Moravian Indians. Incidents of personal adventure and imminent peril, among some of those who finally escaped from Indian captivity to the white settlements, are full of thrilling interest, but can not be detailed within the limits of this work.

Thus ended this disastrous campaign, in which the Indians severely retaliated the cruel massacre of the Moravians on the Muskingum. It was the closing campaign on the part of the whites into the Indian country during the Revolutionary war. Undertaken for the purpose of blood and plunder, and not for necessary defense; carried on without the sanction of the government, it was conducted without judgment or strict military discipline, and could not have terminated otherwise than disastrously. If it were presumed that the hostile Indians would not protect their pacific brethren, a wrong estimate was placed on human nature. It was also ascertained that the hostile Indians had observed all their movements, from the first rendezvous on the old Mingo fields until their final disastrous defeat, and had, accordingly, made all their preparations to receive them.

All the horrors of this Indian war, without doubt, are to be ascribed to the inhuman policy of England in employing the savages to murder the defenseless frontier settlements, because they were a portion of the revolted provinces. Thus the most powerful of civilized nations, and whose subjects are most active in disseminating the Gospel, prostituted her power and her resources to encourage the most inhuman barbarities upon innocent women and children, and authorized the com-

* Doddridge, p. 276.

mandants of the western posts to pay the Indians a stipulated price for each scalp and each prisoner, for the purpose of stimulating them to greater exertion against the helpless frontier people. Thus the scalps of the white man, and of his wife and children, under this diabolical policy, were, in the hands of the savages, a current coin, which, at the British posts, served to purchase powder, arms, clothing, and the other necessaries for savage comfort.* This policy has been denounced and discarded invariably by the government of the United States, which would not permit it among those Indians who chose to range themselves under its banners.

The policy pursued by this more than savage enemy on the western frontier had the effect of debasing many of the western people to the state of savage barbarity; it produced in them that thirst for indiscriminate revenge against the Indian, which caused the commission of barbarities which the government never could approve. "It was a war of mutual but unavailing slaughter, devastation, and revenge, over whose record humanity must drop a tear of regret; but that tear can not efface its disgraceful history."†

Colonel Williamson returned safe from the disastrous Sandusky expedition. Of Colonel Crawford, we may pay him the tribute of one further notice. He was among the first emigrants to the West; he was a man of good heart and sterling worth. He had been a meritorious officer under General Forbes in his march to Fort Duquesne in 1758.‡ Colonel George Washington, at that early day, says, "I know him to be a brave and active officer." He afterward served during the war of Pontiac, in defense of the frontier settlements of Pennsylvania, in 1763–64; and he was an efficient officer in the campaign of Lord Dunmore to the Shawanese towns on the Scioto. He afterward settled on the Youghiogeny, became a colonel, and fought on the western frontiers during the Revolutionary war. He was finally selected to command the fatal expedition to the Sandusky River. The Indians, remembering his former active services against their tribes, determined to wreak the whole weight of savage vengeance upon him.

Apprehensive of a renewal of Indian incursions, after the late

* Doddridge, p. 279, 280. † Idem, p. 281.
‡ Sparks's Writings of Washington, vol. ii., p. 346.

disastrous invasion of the Sandusky country, the people near Fish Creek erected a stockade for their common protection on the east bank of the Ohio, at the head of " Cresap's Bottom." This was subsequently known as " Baker's Station."

The campaign of Colonel Crawford was the last invasion of the Indian territory from western Pennsylvania and Virginia during the war of Independence; yet it was not the conclusion of hostilities on the part of the Indians. Encouraged by their recent successes, they determined to carry the war into the white settlements, and to the very doors of those who had invaded their country. Besides the scalping parties which occasionally overrun the settlements in their secret and predatory excursions, the Indians sent a regular army of three hundred warriors to invade and lay waste the enemy's country. During the month of September, this Indian army invested the fort at Wheeling, and, after three days of ineffectual efforts to take or burn it, they retired. Having sent two hundred warriors home, a chief, with one hundred chosen men, made an attack on Rice's Fort, about twelve miles north of Wheeling, on Buffalo Creek. After four hours of fruitless attempts to capture the fort, they endeavored to burn it, setting fire to all the outhouses, barns, and stacks of grain and hay, in hopes fire might thus be communicated to the stockade. Failing in this, they collected the cattle, hogs, and sheep, and killed them near the stockade, by which means the whole air in the vicinity became tainted by the effluvia from their putrid bodies.

After having lost five of their number killed, and several wounded, they retired. This fort was defended by only six effective men, besides some boys and women. Such were the hostile operations on the upper portion of the Ohio in 1782.

Indian depredations and occasional murders were experienced in the Kentucky settlements for some weeks after the disastrous battle at Blue Licks, perpetrated, as was supposed, by a few western Indians who had joined the invading force from Detroit, and were taking the Salt River settlements in their route to the Wabash. The remainder of the Indian army had retired to their towns on the Great Miami tributaries and those of Sandusky, or had gone to Detroit to receive their supplies and presents, and to claim their premiums on their scalps taken from Kentucky.

The terrible blow struck by the savages at the Blue Licks

had roused the people to a determination to inflict signal vengeance upon the hostile towns. Hundreds were eager to engage in a formidable invasion of the Shawanese country; and the habiliments of mourning, daily presented to their view by the friends and surviving relatives of the slain, continued to impress them with the melancholy reflection concerning the late loss of many valuable citizens, who were deeply deplored by all.

To provide for the future security of the settlements against such incursions, it was the desire of the community that General Clark would take command of a mounted regiment for the destruction of the most hostile of the Shawanese towns on the upper tributaries of the Miami and Scioto Rivers. No man possessed the confidence of the people of Kentucky more than General Clark; and as an experienced and energetic commander, he certainly had no rival. He accordingly took measures for the speedy organization of a mounted brigade for the invasion of the Shawanese country.

The brigade was to consist of one thousand mounted men, to be raised partly by a draft and partly by volunteers. It was to embrace two divisions: one under Colonel Logan, from the upper settlements, to rendezvous at Bryant's Station; the other from the lower settlements, to rendezvous at "the falls," under the command of Colonel Floyd. The two divisions were to form a junction at the mouth of Licking River, preparatory to the invasion of the Indian country. The people readily contributed their aid in supplying all the requisites in the way of transportation and supplies for the contemplated expedition, and advanced the greater portion upon the faith of the Commonwealth.

All things having been arranged, the two divisions of the brigade united at the mouth of Licking on the 28th of September, when General Clark assumed the command. On the 30th the line of march was taken up, and the troops crossed the river and entered the Indian country. With the dispatch and celerity so characteristic of all General Clark's military movements, they advanced rapidly up the Miami, and arrived at the first Indian town, more than one hundred and thirty miles from the Ohio, before the enemy had intelligence of their approach. The savages fled with the utmost precipitation, leaving their deserted village to the mercy of the invaders, who were in close pursuit. The alarm spread rapidly through all the towns up Mad River and as far as the Scioto. The pursuit was continued more than one hundred miles, to the head branches of the Scioto, and in every direction the army encountered nothing but deserted fields and villages; the latter were utterly destroyed by fire, and every vestige of their growing corn was cut up and destroyed.*

The loss of the army in this expedition was only two men killed by Indians. Several Indians were killed, and seven warriors were taken prisoners. Although attended with but little loss of life on either side, this expedition resulted in great advantage to the settlements of Kentucky. It inspired confidence in the people, and struck terror into the savages, such as had not been known of any previous invasion from Kentucky. Their principal resources were cut off, and their country desolated by fire. It produced, also, a conviction in the savages that the increasing numbers and power of the whites were such that all hope of exterminating them was abandoned forever; and they never afterward attempted any formidable invasion of Kentucky. The incursions of small detachments and scalping parties also ceased to harass the country, and people began to feel security in their homes.

The attention of the inhabitants, and of the numerous emigrants who were arriving daily, was again engrossed in the selection and acquisition of lands, under every species of warrant or title which had been legalized for the last ten years. Locations of every kind were stretched over the whole country, with but little precision or accuracy of boundaries, and these as vaguely defined. Speculation in land claims became a trade, or, rather, a science, from which sprang a fruitful harvest of contention and litigation in subsequent years.†

[A.D. 1783.] Agriculture now began to flourish; commerce began to appear; the arts and manufactures connected with agriculture and domestic life became incorporated with the new state of society; labor was rewarded, and employ-

---

* Marshall's History of Kentucky, vol. i., p. 146, 147.

† During the term of service for this expedition, so much had public attention been absorbed in locating, settling, and securing lands, that, in compliance with the wishes of a large portion of the people, and in order to prevent any undue advantage over those who were engaged in the expedition, General Clark declared martial law in force, so far as to order the land-office to be closed until the return of the expedition, or until the first of November. Colonel Thomas Marshall was surveyor of Fayette county, and George May of Jefferson.—See Marshall's Kentucky, vol. i., p. 150–154.

ment given to the industrious; schools sprung up for the education of youth; ministers of the Gospel who had emigrated west consecrated the Sabbath to the service of God and teaching the truths of salvation. Farmers began to prosper; their fields were enlarged, their stock of domestic animals began to multiply, and a market was already open for their surplus produce. Money began to circulate, and property assumed a definite value.

About the first of June, immigrants began to arrive by hundreds, and spread like a flood of fertilizing water over the whole country. Merchandise from Philadelphia and Baltimore, transported in wagons across the mountains, by way of Ligonier and Cumberland, to Pittsburgh and Brownsville, and thence boated down the Ohio, in keel-boats and arks, to Limestone and the falls, began to arrive in the new settlements. The same summer Kentucky was greeted with the first dry-goods store, opened in Louisville by Daniel Broadhead, from Brownsville, on the Monongahela. The second store was not opened until the following year, when Colonel James Wilkinson, of Maryland, also from Brownsville,* opened the first dry-goods store in Lexington.

The population of all the settlements, up to the year 1783, exceeded twelve thousand souls. This number was greatly augmented by the daily arrivals during the succeeding summer; and the spring of 1784 found the entire number increased to more than twenty thousand souls.

The intercourse through the country was extended by the opening of new roads from the river to the interior settlements. Such was the prosperous condition of Kentucky when the news of peace arrived, confirming the independence of the United States, and diffusing universal joy throughout the West.

Military law ceased to be paramount to the civil authority. The garrisons in all the western posts were soon afterward reduced, and only twenty-five privates were retained at Fort Pitt, to guard the stores.†

[A.D. 1784.] Hitherto the principal settlements were north and south of Kentucky River, and upon the sources of Salt River; also upon the southwestern tributaries of Licking River, and near the Ohio, below the mouth of Kentucky, and above "the Falls." Those upon the branches of Bear-grass Creek were increasing rapidly.

* American Pioneer, vol. i., p. 101.   † Marshall's Kentucky, vol. i., p. 179.

The country on the north side of Licking had been abandoned to the Indians on account of its exposed situation. The war-path to the settlements on the Kentucky River traversed this region nearly in the route now occupied by the great road from Lexington to Maysville, and had rendered any settlements insecure in this quarter.

Early in the spring, the three counties of Kentucky, agreeably to an act of the Legislature of Virginia, had been organized into a judicial district, known as the "District of Kentucky." The district court was invested with civil and criminal jurisdiction, as other circuit courts of Virginia.* This court held its first term at Harrodsburg; the subsequent terms were to be holden at Danville, where a log court-house and a log jail were soon afterward erected, amply sufficient for the security of criminals and debtors. From this time, Danville became a noted point for public meetings, and the great political discussions which agitated this country for five years afterward.

It was early in the winter when the whole country was electrified by the news of peace with Great Britain, and the recognition of the independence of the United States.

Wearied and impoverished by a war of nearly eight years, the American people heard with rapture the news of peace, and rejoiced in the beaming prospects before them. Those upon the sterile and sandy shores of the Atlantic desired retirement and ease upon the fertile and virgin lands which lay inviting their occupancy upon the waters of the Ohio, and where they might repose in the peaceful shades of agricultural retirement. From North Carolina, by way of Cumberland Gap, the tide of emigration was rapidly pouring into Kentucky and the present State of Tennessee, while Virginia and the states north of her were sending their colonies upon the Upper Ohio, and by way of Limestone and "the Falls" into Kentucky.

As yet Kentucky was a large, isolated settlement. The region on the east, for nearly five hundred miles, through the sources of the Big Sandy and the Kenhawa, was a desolate mountain wilderness. On the west and north, the country, to a boundless extent, was in the occupancy of the native tribes. The region north of Licking, which now sustains a dense and

---

* The court consisted of John Floyd and Samuel M'Dowell, *judges*; John May, *clerk*; and Walker Daniel, *district attorney*.—See Butler's Kentucky, p. 141, 142.

wealthy population, was then an exposed, sparsely-populated frontier, liable to the continual incursions of marauding bands of savages.

A great portion of Western Virginia was then an unsettled country, having only a few habitations on the Kenhawa, Greenbrier, Elk, and Cheat Rivers, while the country near the Ohio, from Fishing Creek to Licking River, a distance of three hundred miles, was a frontier region too much exposed to Indian incursions to afford a safe residence. In Pennsylvania, north of the Kiskeminetas, and on the Alleghany River to its source, was the heart of the Six Nations, and all the extensive region south of this border was an exposed frontier. The principal settlements of Western Virginia south of Wheeling were upon the head branches of the Monongahela, upon the East and West Forks, and upon Cheat River; also, the head branches of the Great and Little Kenhawas. All that extensive region lying between the Ohio and the west branch of the Monongahela, from thirty to fifty miles in width, had been subject to the continual incursions of the hostile Indians. Clarksburg, near the west branch, was then a frontier settlement. A small military post had been maintained for several years at the mouth of the Kenhawa, known as the "Point;" yet the settlements east of it had been penetrated repeatedly by the war parties, which eluded the military posts on the Ohio, and crossed between the Muskingum and the Kenhawa.*

Before the close of the year 1784, the settlements of Kentucky had augmented their population to nearly thirty thousand souls. The people began to take a deep interest in completing the organization of civil government, and were gathering around them the elements of foreign intercourse and domestic wealth. The accumulation of personal property, as well as real estate, began to engage the energies of the recent emigrants; towns were laid off, mills and factories were erected; agriculture and trade began to develop the resources of the country; domestic stock of all kinds were introduced, and were multiplying abundantly; and all began to enjoy the comforts and luxuries of a newly-settled country.

The moral condition of the people was not neglected. Ministers of the Gospel, and religious teachers of every sect and creed, borne along on the tide of emigration, found the field

* See American Pioneer, vol. i., p. 60.

ripe for the harvest, and the laborers were not few. Societies and churches were organized by the Presbyterians, Methodists, and Baptists, and were subsequently attached to the mother-churches east of the mountains. Schools were established for the education of youth, and the rudiments of learning were freely dispensed among the rising generation.

The people east of the mountains, released from a long and unnatural war, and having only partially recovered from the consequent depression, after peace had been restored with the Indian tribes, sought ease and fortune in the West. The tide of emigration began to set with unprecedented rapidity from the Atlantic settlements across the mountains and down the Ohio River. The roads from Cumberland and Bedford to Pittsburgh and Brownsville were traversed by continued and successive groups of emigrant colonies, with their long lines of family wagons, followed by herds of cattle, hogs, and all kinds of stock, and the necessary appendages for agricultural life.

The mouth of Limestone Creek, the site of the present town of Maysville, had already become a frequented route from the Ohio to the older settlements on the waters of the Kentucky River, comprised in the counties of Nelson, Lincoln, and Fayette. Simon Kenton, the first explorer of this route, had returned from his "station" on the waters of Salt River, and resumed his tomahawk improvement made in 1774. In the autumn of 1784, he commenced a block house and other buildings for a settlement, three miles from Limestone and one mile from the present town of Washington, in Mason county. Early in the following spring, he received an accession of several families, and thus commenced the first permanent settlement in this exposed frontier. For several years subsequently it was known as "Kenton's Station." The town of Limestone soon sprung up as a noted point of debarkation for emigrants advancing to the central settlements of Kentucky.

About the same time other settlements were begun in other portions of the present county of Mason, although it was not until the year following that Simon Kenton, Arthur Fox, and William Wood laid off the town of Washington.[*]

From this time habitations began to multiply in this quarter of the country, and Indian hostilities had apparently ceased.

[*] M'Donald's Sketches, p. 250, 251.

"Lee's Station," "Warren's Station," and "Clark's Station" were formed about this time; and emigrants, as they advanced into the interior, began to settle upon all the northern branches of Licking.

CHAPTER V.

INDIAN HOSTILITIES ON THE OHIO.—PREDATORY INCURSIONS INTO KENTUCKY, AND PARTISAN WARFARE.—A.D. 1785 TO 1793.

Argument.—The Shawanese resume predatory Incursions.—Indian Horse-stealing.—Object and Extent of these Depredations.—The Continuance of them provokes Invasion of the Indian Country in 1786.—Plan of Campaign under General Clark and Colonel Logan.—Colonel Logan destroys Scioto and Mad River Towns.—General Clark advances to the Wabash.—His further Operations frustrated for Want of Supplies.—A Mutiny ensues.—He returns inglorious to Kentucky.—His Sun sets.—Virginia comes to his Relief.—The Shawanese commence active Hostilities.—Exposed Condition of Settlements in Mason County in 1787.—Colonel Todd invades the Paint Creek Towns.—Simon Kenton as a Partisan Warrior.—Emigration in 1788.—Indians harass the Ohio Frontier of Kentucky and Western Virginia.—Depredations and Murders on the Ohio from 1788 to 1790.—Population of Kentucky in 1791.—Partisan Warfare from 1790 to 1791.—General Harmar's Efforts to suppress Indian Hostilities.—The Campaigns of 1790 and 1791 divert Hostilities from the Kentucky Frontier.—Indian Hostility and partisan Warfare in Kentucky renewed in 1792-93.—Kenton makes an Incursion upon the Little Miami, and encounters Tecumseh.—Severe night Skirmish with Tecumseh in 1792.—Kenton continues his partisan Warfare in 1793.—Makes an Incursion to Paint Creek.—Intercepts and kills a marauding Party of Indians at Holt's Creek on the Ohio, and recovers a large Number of Horses.

[A.D. 1785.] NOTWITHSTANDING treaties had been formed and ratified with the principal Indian tribes on the western frontier,* and the greater portion of the hostile tribes had assumed a pacific attitude, there were parties of malcontents who rejected the treaties, and continued to harass the settlements of Kentucky contiguous to the Ohio River. The first and only murder perpetrated in Kentucky by the Indians in 1785 was in the month of March, when the settlements were thrown into a state of alarm by a murder and outrage committed by a party of Shawanese malcontents upon the person and habitation of Elliott, at the mouth of Kentucky River. Elliott was killed and scalped, his houses were burned, and his family, escaping, were dispersed into the neighboring settlements.†

Although incursions by marauding parties were made subsequently, it was not with the design of collecting scalps, but for the purpose of "stealing horses" from the settlements. This

* See chap. ix. of this book, "Indian Relations," &c.   † Butler's Kentucky, p. 140.

is one of the feats which gives distinction to the warrior, and entitles him to the character of a brave.*

The object of the savages in these incursions was not to create alarm and terror by any outrage against individuals, for this would at once have roused an armed party in pursuit; but their object was simply plunder, and to supply themselves with horses, and to deprive their late enemies of the valuable animals which had made their incursions so terrible to the Indian country. To insure success in this line of operation, it was necessary to pass unperceived through the country, leaving no certain trace of their inroad except such as might be inferred from the disappearance of the horses.

[A.D. 1786.] These depredations had annoyed the inhabitants during the autumn of 1785, and toward the close of the year they had become more frequent; and the marauders extended the field of their operations. At first a party of two or three warriors would occasionally penetrate a settlement and secretly retire with one or two horses; but at length they began to advance to the Ohio River at different points, in parties of six, ten, and twelve; and, having selected some secure and retired rendezvous near the river, they would distribute themselves in parties of one or two, penetrate far into the settlements, and supply themselves with horses, which were taken to the general rendezvous and left in charge of a keeper, while they returned to secure others. So soon as ten, fifteen, or twenty had been procured, the company secretly crossed the river with them, and made all speed for their towns.

Toward the close of the year 1786 these depredations became so frequent and annoying, that the settlements were seriously injured, being deprived of great numbers of horses, which were requisite for the agricultural necessities of the country. No man felt safe in the possession of his property; for the wily savage prowled like the wolf in the dark, alike unseen and unheard, penetrating the remotest settlements and visiting every inclosure in the dead hour of night, against which no precaution was a guarantee for the security of property.

* Mr. Wetmore says, "there is a small difference between the moral sense of the savage and the white man." "The red man is esteemed honorable in proportion to the number of grand larcenies he may have perpetrated; and this engaging quality of horse-stealing is esteemed a virtue next to that of taking scalps. An Indian, therefore, has a table on his war-club with two columns, in which he enters in hieroglyphics the number of transactions of each class, which are to render him illustrious."—See Wetmore's Gazetteer of Missouri, p. 299.

It was no uncommon occurrence for a party of five or six Indians, after an absence of a week or ten days, to return to the rendezvous with an aggregate of ten or fifteen horses; sometimes each individual would bring in one every night, until their complement was full. It was no unusual exploit for a party of five or six Indians to set out from their village, more than a hundred miles from the settlements, and, after an absence of ten or twenty days, to return with fifteen or twenty horses. Nor was it an unfrequent occurrence for a single county of Kentucky to lose one hundred horses in a single month.

To such an extent had these depredations been carried against the settlements of Kentucky and Western Virginia, during five years previous to 1791, that, from estimates based upon authentic information, it was supposed not less than twenty thousand horses had been taken by the Indians.

It was ascertained that the most active agents were the Shawanese malcontents from the towns upon the head waters of Mad River, an eastern tributary of the Great Miami, and from the towns on White River, an eastern tributary of the Wabash. Those from the former extended their incursions chiefly to the settlements near the Ohio and upon the waters of Licking River, while the latter extended their operations mostly to the settlements on Salt River and its head waters.

To prevent these depredations, and to intercept the movements or discover the trail of these marauding parties, each settlement kept out in active service one or more scouts or rangers, as had been customary during actual hostilities. These rangers used every effort to discover the trail of such parties, or to detect any "Indian sign" by which it could be ascertained that Indians were in the country. Yet so cautious was the wily savage, that their haunts were seldom discovered, unless where they had concentrated to cross the river on their departure.

The marauders at length infested the Ohio River, upon which hundreds of family boats and arks were continually descending from Fort Pitt to different points along the Kentucky shore. Occasionally family boats were attacked and plundered, and not unfrequently the occupants were killed or wounded by the fire of the Indians from the shore. At length it became hazardous for solitary boats, unarmed, to descend; and, for safety and mutual defense, emigrant families were compelled to associate in companies and descend in several boats together, with a full proportion of expert riflemen. Subsequently, it became evident that large bodies of Indians from the remote towns had assembled near the Ohio, and from the general rendezvous west of the river marauding parties were distributed at different points on the shore, while others penetrated to the remote settlements east and south of the Ohio.

Yet the Federal government discouraged every attempt to conduct partisan incursions into their country, and took active measures for an amicable settlement of all grounds for difficulty with the malcontent Shawanese. As early as the 31st of January, 1786, a council had been convened at the mouth of the Great Miami, and a treaty of peace and friendship had been concluded with the Shawanese nation by Generals Richard Butler and George R. Clark. In consideration of certain benefactions and presents from the United States, the Shawanese stipulated for the suppression of the marauding incursions.

But the malcontents, regardless of the stipulations of the treaty, continued their incursions and their depredations on the river, with increasing frequency and audacity. The settlements north of Licking River, in the line of the "old war-path," were particularly obnoxious to this species of Indian warfare. The savages continued to obstruct the river commerce and the advance of emigrants, and to plunder the settlements of the interior with unremitted perseverance.

At length it was perceived that these continual aggressions were prompted and instigated by British traders and agents at Detroit and upon the Maumee. The fur-trade in the Northwestern Territory was almost wholly controlled by these British traders, who were deeply interested in checking the advance of the American population across the Ohio, which would sound the knell of approaching dissolution to their monopoly. A state of active hostilities renewed by the savages might yet defer for many years the advance of white settlements north of the Ohio, and thus prolong the monopoly of the Indian fur-trade. Such were the views and conclusions of the British agents and traders at Detroit and at other points south of Lake Erie.

It was during the summer of 1786 that these hostilities became so frequent and daring that a recourse to arms was deemed the only mode by which the settlements and emigrants upon the river could be secured from continual danger. Murders had already been frequent, not only on the river, but in the settlements, and the people of Kentucky became clamorous for an invasion of the Indian country.

To inflict suitable chastisement upon the Shawanese nation, it was resolved to invade their country with two mounted expeditions; one against the eastern, and the other against the western portion of their towns, and completely to ravage with fire and sword the whole country from the Scioto to the Wabash. The command of the campaign was given to General Clark, whose name alone carried terror to the savages. Many of the officers who volunteered to serve under him were among the first military men of Kentucky; and among the private soldiers were some of the most fearless backwoodsmen in all the West.

The brigade was to consist of two full regiments, or nearly eighteen hundred men, which were to enter the Indian country in two divisions. The main body, under General Clark in person, was to rendezvous at "the Falls," and advance across the country by way of White River to Vincennes, at which place they were to meet their supplies forwarded by water. From this place they were to ravage the whole country upon the head waters of the Wabash, as far as Tippecanoe and Eel Rivers.

The other division, under the command of Colonel Logan, was to advance from their rendezvous at "Kenton's Station," three miles from Limestone, by way of the Little Miami, to its sources, and thence to ravage the whole country from the Scioto westward down Mad River to the Great Miami.*

Such was the general plan of the campaign for the chastisement of this warlike and restless nation. To accomplish this, all Kentucky was in commotion, and all were emulous in advancing the preparations which were to render it one of the most formidable invasions which had ever proceeded from Kentucky, and one which would strike terror into the remotest tribes. It was not expected that the expedition would encounter any formidable force of imbodied savages in arms, for the troops themselves were to bear the intelligence of their approach. The object was to inflict a severe chastisement upon the Shawanese nation for the many murders and depredations

* M'Donald's Sketches, p. 250, 251.

committed by their war-parties and marauders by destroying their towns, laying waste their fields, and destroying their resources, and breaking up their settlements within striking distance of Kentucky.

For the supply of the Wabash expedition, nine keel-boats were freighted with stores and provisions, and dispatched by way of the Ohio and Wabash for Vincennes. Such was the active state of preparation until the close of September, when the troops were ready to take up the line of march.

On the first of October Colonel Logan began to move his division, consisting of seven hundred mounted riflemen. After a rapid march of ninety miles, he surprised the Indian town of Chillicothe, upon the sources of the Little Miami. Conducted by Captain Kenton, at the head of a company of picked men from his own neighborhood, such was the celerity and precision of his movements that two Indian towns, situated one mile apart, were simultaneously surprised by two separate columns of his command. A large portion of the inhabitants of each were either captured or killed in their attempt at resistance. The towns were destroyed by fire, and the extensive fields of ripe corn were laid waste and destroyed, so as to cut off their future supplies. The few who escaped gave the alarm to other towns, from which the savages fled with great precipitation, leaving their wigwams, cabins, and fields to the mercy of the invaders. Four other towns, deserted by their inhabitants, together with their fields, were destroyed by fire. The country east and west upon the waters of the Scioto, and upon the sources of Mad River, was ravaged for nearly one hundred miles around, when Colonel Logan and his victorious companions prepared to return with their prisoners.

The whole number of Indians slain in the different skirmishes was about thirty. The troop lost ten men killed, besides several wounded, during the campaign.*

But General Clark was less fortunate. After a circuitous march of one hundred and thirty miles to Vincennes, with more than a thousand mounted riflemen, he found his supplies had not arrived, having been delayed by extreme low water in the river. His further advance was unavoidably arrested. Nine days was he compelled to remain inactive at Vincennes, awaiting the tardy arrival of supplies for his men. The troops

* M'Donald's Sketches, p. 251.

had left Kentucky full of ardor and enthusiasm, to acquit themselves by the celerity of their movements, and the sudden destruction of the Indian towns. Each day tended to damp the military spirit of the men, and impatience began to undermine military subordination, and introduce disaffection for the service. A few days elapsed, when the continued delay of the expected supplies placed them upon short allowance, and increased their impatience almost to mutiny. Still, the pervading influence of their beloved commander restrained them until the expected arrival of the supplies. But the arrival was a greater disappointment than its delay. Inspection proved too clearly that the pickled beef was highly tainted from the excessive heat; scarcely rations for three days remained in a sound condition, and the hostile towns were yet distant at least two hundred miles. General Clark would have proceeded in his march, and quartered upon the enemy; but the discontent of his men had broken out into insubordination, and many, refusing to advance, demanded to be led back to Kentucky. The fury of the savage they could encounter, but the more appalling form of famine they would not meet, and they refused to advance.*

In vain the veteran commander and the successful leader, "in the most persuasive terms of entreaty," implored the mutineers to advance to the enemy's towns. At length a body of three hundred men, encouraged by some officers of rank, regardless of the honor of the soldier, or the disgrace of an inglorious retreat, retired from the expedition.

With little more than half his original force, General Clark advanced toward the Indian towns, and after several days of fruitless search for Indians, who had received intelligence of the formidable preparations against them, he returned to the Falls, covered with shame and confusion at the unmerited disgrace which, for the first time, had rested upon his arms.†

Such had been the effect of inaction to undisciplined troops, although naturally courageous, and commanded by the most extraordinary military genius of his day. For want of timely supplies a brave army was dissolved, and the conqueror of Kaskaskia and Vincennes returned ingloriously from an enterprise which, with proper supplies, he would have surmounted without an effort.

* See Butler's Kentucky, p. 151, 152. † Idem.

But the fact of the entire failure of his division of the expedition seemed to prey upon his spirits, and he ceased to be the iron-hearted chieftain of 1778, as he began to feel the ingratitude of his fellow-citizens no less than the neglect of his native state, which had reaped all the advantages of his early toil and suffering. In his many efforts for the defense of the unprotected settlements during his most vigorous period of life, he had become involved in liabilities for money which his resources did not enable him to pay; and his creditors, regardless of the high claims which he had upon their forbearance, began to oppress him with legal coercion. At length, harassed by vexatious lawsuits and oppressive executions for the recovery of money which had been expended for the benefit of the state, he became stripped of his personal as well as his landed estate, and was left poor and destitute.

General Clark was a native of Albemarle county in Virginia. He was early engaged in defense of the frontier settlements of Virginia, and served as a captain under General Lewis in the campaign to the Scioto, and was an active participant in the sanguinary battle of "the Point." For the first eight years after the commencement of the war of Independence, he was the life of all defensive operations in Kentucky and other portions of Western Virginia. His campaign against Kaskaskia in 1778, and against Vincennes in 1779, for fortitude, daring intrepidity, and military skill, are not surpassed in the annals of war, surrounded as he was with the most limited resources. In his defense of Kentucky he shed a lustre over the chivalry of that state, and carried the arms of Virginia triumphantly to the Mississippi. To testify the exalted regard entertained for her hero, she had presented him with two swords, and at last, when old age and poverty had overtaken him, the bounty of his native state was extended to him as a support for his declining years.*

* To the honor of Virginia, although she failed suitably to reward him for his many services, or to shield him against the claims of public creditors, she did not desert him in the darkest hour, when poverty and old age had borne him down. She had repeatedly testified her exalted estimate of his services; but his necessities required something more than empty honors. In September, 1779, the Governor of Virginia, authorized by the Legislature, presented Colonel Clark an elegant sword in token of gratitude for his extraordinary services and gallantry. Several years afterward, harassed for claims created for the public service, and stripped of his property for public debts, smarting under the anguish of the injustice of his state, and the ingratitude of his country, in a fit of despair he indignantly broke this sword in pieces and threw it from him, disdaining to possess the empty mockery of his wrongs. Subsequently, in the

[A.D. 1787.] This invasion of the Shawanese country served only to exasperate that fierce and vindictive nation. They immediately commenced active hostilities against the whole line of the Kentucky frontier. During the winter and succeeding spring they infested the settlements near the Ohio, as well as those more remote, with their marauding and war parties, which did not confine their operations exclusively to the capture of horses, but exerted themselves also for the acquisition of scalps, the trophies of their efforts against the enemies of their race.

Such was the frequency of these murders and depredations during the summer of 1787, throughout the counties of Mason and Bourbon, that the inhabitants were again compelled to congregate in "stations" and forts, to avoid the danger of exposure to the vengeance of the lurking savage. The whole country was again in a state of actual Indian war; the labors of the field and the intercourse between settlements were safe only under the protection of an armed guard, while the Ohio River was under a state of savage blockade.*

Impatient of this insecure state of the settlements, Captain Kenton proposed to lead an invasion into the Indian country, and retaliate upon the hostile towns of the Scioto. Early in the autumn, Colonel Todd, of Lexington, and Major Hingston,

year 1812, the Legislature of Virginia, sympathizing with him in his misfortunes, in token of their esteem and gratitude, voted him another sword, with proper emblems and devices, to be presented by the governor.—See Butler's Kentucky, Appendix, p. 480, and 437–439. General Clark lived several years afterward, in poverty and obscurity, his only dependence being his pension from the State of Virginia as a half-pay officer, amounting to four hundred dollars per annum.

* The renewal of active hostilities by the Indians at this time was the result of instigation and intrigue on the part of the British authorities of Canada. In 1786, President Washington dispatched Baron Steuben as commissioner to Sir Frederic Haldimand, Governor of Canada at Quebec, fully authorized to receive possession of the northwestern posts, agreeably to the provisions of the treaty of 1783. But the governor informed the baron that the posts would not be surrendered; he also refused to furnish him with passports for the prosecution of his journey to Detroit. The same winter a grand council of the northwestern tribes was assembled at Detroit, which was attended by delegates from the Six Nations, the Hurons, Ottawâs, Miamis, Shawanese, Chippewas, Delawares, Potawatamies, and Cherokees. At the council convened in December were the British agents M'Key, Elliott, Simon Girty, and Sir Alexander M'Kenzie, "dressed and painted in the Indian style." At this council the Indians were urged to unite their efforts to resist the advance of the American settlements beyond the Ohio; and Sir Alexander, just from his exploring tour through remote northern tribes, assured them that their red brethren north of the Lakes were ready to join them in resisting the American claims. They also had assurance of the aid and countenance of his Britannic majesty. To give them more efficient aid, a new British fort was soon afterward erected upon the Maumee, just below "the Rapids."—See Lanman's History of Michigan.

united with Captain Kenton in organizing an expedition of three hundred mounted riflemen for the destruction of the towns on the north fork of Paint Creek. From their rendezvous, near Kenton's Station, the troop proceeded toward the Shawanese towns. Crossing the Ohio at Limestone, they arrived, after a rapid and secret march, at the town of Chillicothe, on the north fork of Paint Creek, which they surprised and destroyed, after killing several Indians and capturing some prisoners. The country for many miles round was ravaged, and the fields of ripe corn were destroyed. After an absence of ten days, the troop returned without the loss of a man.*

[A.D. 1788.] The Indian incursions continued to increase in frequency and audacity during the summer of 1788; the savages became more vindictive and blood-thirsty, making frequent attacks upon emigrants descending the river, as well as upon any parties of scouts or rangers with whom they came in collision.

Yet emigration to Kentucky did not cease. The settlements of Mason and Bourbon counties, although exposed to continual danger, continued to augment their population by the numerous arrivals of emigrant families, who erected new stations for their own security, or united with the occupants of older stations for mutual defense. To intercept the war parties in their advance or retreat, armed detachments were distributed near certain frequented routes; and in several instances parties of savages were overtaken and dispersed, while their stolen horses were recovered.†

In the partisan warfare for the defense of the settlements, no man was more active, or took a more prominent part, than Captain Simon Kenton.

At one time a marauding party of fifteen or twenty Indians had established their rendezvous within a few miles of Kenton's Station, until they had collected their complement of horses. Kenton undertook to discover their trail, and to intercept them as they retired with their booty. With a party of hunters, he set out and discovered their trail and crossing-place on the Ohio, near the mouth of Locust Creek. Crossing the Ohio, he pursued their trail for several miles with the certainty of animal instinct, and late in the evening came upon

---

* M'Donald's Sketches, p. 252. † Idem, p. 253.

the fresh trace, just as they were preparing to encamp for the night. Cautiously concealing his men until dark, he made a sudden and furious onset upon their encampment. The Indians, alarmed at the unexpected attack, and ignorant of the number of the assailants, fled precipitately at the first fire, leaving one of their number killed, all their camp equipage, some of their guns, and all their horses. The party returned home in triumph, to the great gratification of the settlement.*

As the tide of emigration continued to swell the population of Kentucky, the Shawanese malcontents became more and more exasperated; and the recent incursions by the mounted riflemen had induced many from other tribes to make common cause with the Shawanese. They were willing to assist in arresting the advance of the white settlements, and to prolong their own national existence; and the more now, since the white population was already advancing across the Ohio River in the vicinity of Fort Harmar and Fort Washington. Hence, strong hostile parties advanced to the Ohio to redouble their efforts for harassing the settlements on both sides of the river, and for arresting the descent of emigrants.

To effect these objects, atrocious murders were committed upon defenseless females and children. Emigrants for Kentucky, descending the Ohio, although protected from the rifle while floating in their family arks and covered barges, were exposed to continual danger from the bands of warriors lurking upon the shores, and ever ready to attack, decoy, or pursue any unprotected or unguarded boats. Yet the river was continually thronged with the adventurous emigrants, descending, mostly in strong parties for mutual defense, in boats, barges, and every species of river craft, freighted with families, goods, agricultural implements, horses, and domestic stock of all kinds, for their future residences. Did any one of these become separated from the rest, or did they incautiously approach the shore, or attempt to make a landing, the eye of the wily savage was upon them; and if the sharp crack of his rifle did not carry death to the pilot, or others on deck, it was because he contemplated a wholesale capture and massacre by a successful ambuscade. Was any party of emigrants too strong for open attack, the wily Indian, from his concealment on shore, with his rifle deliberately picked off, one by one,

* M'Donald's Sketches, p. 253.

those who incautiously exposed their persons above the decks. Did a party of them have occasion to go on shore for firewood, to kill the game which presented on the bank, or to give their stock temporary freedom from the narrow prison of the boat, or to enjoy an evening stroll on land, the lurking savage, from his covert, cautiously observed every movement, and so planned his ambuscade as to make a sure and easy capture, or a slaughter of the whole.

[A.D. 1789.] While parties thus waylaid the river banks, others were incessant in their roaming incursions through the settlements, waylaying every path, ambuscading every neighborhood, lurking as invisibly as the wolf near every residence, watching every family spring, ensconced in every corn-field and near every cross-road, patiently waiting whole days and nights for the approaching victim.

Although the "Northwestern Territory" had been erected into a territorial government, and the Federal authorities were nominally exercising jurisdiction over it; although several military posts had been established on the western bank, the depredations and incursions of the savages were unrestrained. Avoiding the fortified places and military stations, which could not be attacked with impunity, they passed on to feeble settlements and unprotected neighborhoods, where scalps and plunder were easily obtained, and where caution and cunning secured an easy victory.

The hostile incursions into the Kentucky settlements in 1789 commenced early in March, and were continued occasionally until May, when they became frequent and alarming. These parties consisted chiefly of warriors from the towns upon the sources of the Little Miami and of branches flowing into the Scioto and Great Miami, and the field of their operations was the whole range of settlements near the Ohio, from Fort Harmar to the mouth of Salt River.

From the first of May to the first of August there had been thirteen persons killed and ten wounded by Indians in the county of Jefferson, besides twenty horses stolen. In the county of Nelson, two persons had been killed and two wounded, besides twenty horses stolen. In Lincoln county, two persons had been killed and two wounded, and twenty-five horses stolen. In Madison county, one person had been killed and three wounded, and ten horses stolen. In Bourbon county, two persons had been wounded and fifteen horses stolen. In Mason county, two persons had been killed and forty-one horses stolen. In Woodford county, one boy had been killed and several horses stolen. Many other harassing depredations of less note had been perpetrated by lurking parties of savages, so that the whole frontier region within thirty miles of the Ohio was kept in a state of continual alarm and apprehension. Parties of Indians often penetrated unperceived into the very heart of Kentucky, at least fifty or sixty miles from the Ohio. In Woodford county, on the 10th of August, two men were fired upon by a party of Indians, but escaped with the loss of one horse, saddle, and bridle. On the night succeeding, the same party stole eleven horses in that vicinity. A party of men next day set out in pursuit of the Indians, and, having overtaken them, killed two of them, and recovered most of the horses. On the 16th of August, a party of Indians in ambuscade captured six negroes. Having retreated half a mile with the captives, and fearing pursuit, they tomahawked four of them, and the other two escaped. Two of those who were left for dead finally recovered. The same party, on the following night, stole a number of horses, with which they fled across the Ohio. Next day a party of forty men, under Lieutenant Robert Johnson, set out in pursuit, and followed them to the Ohio River, about twenty-five miles below the mouth of the Great Miami. Here part of the company returned; but twenty-six of them volunteered to cross the river and continue the pursuit. Having followed their trail about twelve miles further, they came upon the Indians, encamped at a salt lick. By a vigorous and unexpected attack in two divisions, the Indians were at length routed, and forty horses were recovered. Lieutenant Johnson lost two men killed and three wounded.* Other parties of Indians had penetrated the settlements, and served to keep up alarm and apprehension among the frontier people; and occasional murders and depredations were continued, with but little intermission, until checked by the severity of winter. In December the Indians killed three men within twelve miles of Danville, at "Carpenter's Station," and five others on Russell's Creek, besides some who were wounded and escaped.†

---

* See American State Papers, *Indian Affairs*, vol. i., p. 84, folio edition.
† Idem, p. 86.

Such was the state of Indian hostilities in the District of Kentucky. The same predatory warfare had been carried on against the western counties of Virginia, on the east side of the Ohio, over nearly three hundred miles of exposed frontier, extending as far south as the mouth of the Big Sandy.

[A.D. 1790.] The year 1790 opened with a more vigorous and extensive series of depredations and murders upon the emigrants, who were advancing in great numbers to Kentucky and to various points on the northwest side of the Ohio River.

In January, a family boat or covered barge, with ten persons on board, was captured by the Indians only about sixteen miles above Limestone. Nine of the persons were killed, and their dead bodies, scalped, were afterward found in the boat. One woman was taken captive.

About the middle of March, a party of fifty desperadoes, chiefly Shawanese, with a few Cherokees, stationed themselves near the mouth of the Scioto, on the north bank of the Ohio, for the purpose of carrying on their operations more successfully.

From this rendezvous they continued for several weeks to interrupt the navigation of the river, besides dispatching occasional scalping parties into the frontier settlements for murder and plunder. Not a boat could pass without receiving a volley from their rifles when stratagem and deception failed to bring them to shore. For the purpose of deceiving the crews and commanders of boats, they had one or more white captives, who were made to present themselves as objects of distress, to decoy boats to their relief, while the Indians laid concealed ready to kill those on board, and, when practicable, to capture the boat. By this device they succeeded in decoying several boats to shore, which fell an easy prey to the savages.

On the 20th of March they attacked and captured the boat of John May, Esq., of Virginia, with six persons on board. May and one other person were killed, and the remainder taken captive. Next day an open pirogue, with six men, was ascending the river, when the Indians fired upon it and killed every soul on board.[*]

About the last of March a party of Indians captured and carried off three persons from Brashear's Creek, near the Falls of the Ohio. A few days afterward they killed two men while working a field in the same vicinity. About the same time a

[*] American State Papers, *Indian Affairs*, vol. i., p. 86, 87.

party of Indians from the Wabash captured a boat laden with salt at the mouth of Salt River, having killed and scalped three men who had charge of the cargo.*

A short time previously two men had been killed, and one woman and five children taken captive, in Kennedy's Bottom, on the Ohio, twenty-five miles above Limestone. On the 2d of April, Colonel Ward, from Greenbrier, in company with several family boats from the Monongahela, was attacked by Indians near the same place. One man was killed; the remainder, accelerating their flight by the abandonment of one boat and its contents to the enemy, and placing the hands on the others, succeeded in effecting their escape, after a severe chase of two hours.

On the 4th of April, Colonel George Thompson, in company with three family boats, was attacked near the same place by the same Indians. After failing to decoy the boats ashore, they manned a barge, which they had captured, with thirty warriors, and set out in vigorous pursuit. To preserve the lives of the families on board, two boats were abandoned, and the hands transferred to Colonel Thompson's barge, in which, with the oars double-manned, they at length succeeded in effecting their escape, after a vigorous chase of fifteen miles. The Indians, despairing of successful pursuit, gave up the chase, and returned to take possession of the boats which had been abandoned. The boats thus lost contained twenty-eight horses, a large amount of household furniture, besides dry-goods to the value of nearly five thousand dollars.†

On the 18th of April, it being Sunday, a company of defenseless women and children returning from preaching at Hartford Town to a station on Rough Creek, were attacked by a party of Indians, who killed a boy and a girl, both of whom were tomahawked and scalped. One old woman was tomahawked and scalped alive, and her daughter was carried off captive.

On the 11th of May, nine miles above Limestone, a barge containing sixteen persons, including an officer and eight regular soldiers, in company with goods, household furniture, and horses, was captured by a party of twenty Indians from the Scioto. Five persons were murdered in the most barbarous manner, three escaped, and eight were taken captive.‡

* American State Papers, *Indian Affairs*, vol. i., p. 88.   † Idem. p. 86.
‡ Idem, p. 88.

Soon afterward the Indians captured two boys, who were hunting near "Loudon's Station," on the head waters of Drennon's Lick Creek. On the 23d of May the Indians fired upon a company of unarmed people returning from church, near Clear Creek; one man was killed on the spot; one young woman was taken prisoner, who, after having been driven ten miles on foot, and exhausted by fatigue, was tomahawked and scalped.*

Such was the state of Indian hostilities upon the Ohio River during the spring and summer of 1790. Nor were these all: many murders and outrages upon other portions of the settlements must be omitted, lest the enumeration become tedious.

To suppress these hostilities on the Ohio, General Harmar, early in April, had sent a detachment of one hundred regular troops, and two hundred Kentucky militia, under General Scott, to surprise and capture this band of desperadoes, whose camp was not far from the Scioto; but the detachment failed to accomplish that object. The Indians eluded pursuit as effectually as so many wolves, and the detachment returned to Limestone, bringing four Indian scalps as their only trophies.†

During the whole summer, volunteer companies and scouting parties had been in motion along the Kentucky shore, and detachments had been sent occasionally from Fort Harmar and Fort Washington, for the purpose of breaking up any Indian camps that might be found within striking distance of the settlements. The activity with which these defensive movements were made along the Ohio, below the Kenhawa, finally succeeded in diverting the operations of the hostile bands from Kentucky to the settlements of Western Virginia upon the waters of the Kenhawa and the Monongahela.

Western Virginia.—On the 19th of September, a party of Indians penetrated into the country within nine miles of Clarksburg, in Harrison county, where they killed and scalped four persons, and captured four others. On the 22d, they killed a woman and two children, and burned the house. The same night, in that vicinity, they burned another house, from which the family had just escaped. The same party continued in that region for several days, committing like depredations, until the 28th of September, when they departed, having stolen

---

* American State Papers, *Indian Affairs*, p. 90, 91.
† Idem, p. 91. Also, Butler's Kentucky, p. 190.

eleven horses from that county, and having killed a large number of hogs, cattle, and sheep.

Kenhawa county did not escape. Several persons were killed, and others who escaped had been fired upon by the Indians. Several negroes, and more than twenty horses, had been stolen, besides other depredations near Point Pleasant and Charleston. Such had been the hostilities of the Indians upon the northwestern frontier before the Federal government would consent to abandon fruitless negotiation for the last resort of nations.

[A.D. 1791.] The population of Kentucky, by the close of the year 1790, had increased to more than eighty thousand souls. The whole country for two years was in a state of excitement and military parade in defending her own frontier, and in giving aid to the expeditions of the Federal government under Generals Harmar and St. Clair, against the Indian tribes of the northwestern territory.* Both of these expeditions terminated disastrously to the American arms, and brought no permanent relief to Kentucky. Yet they served in some degree to divert their attention and their operations from the settlements east and south of the Ohio. Thus the people of Kentucky enjoyed a temporary respit from alarms and dangers at home, although many of her citizens were engaged in the campaigns which withdrew the seat of war from the Ohio River to the heart of the Indian country. But this respit was of short duration; for after the disastrous campaign of General St. Clair, the Indians, elated by their late successes, renewed their hostilities with increased vigor upon the exposed population of Kentucky, but especially in the counties of Mason, Bourbon, Nelson, and Jefferson.

[A.D. 1793.] These settlements were defended by volunteer detachments, which patrolled the country in every direction, to observe any Indian movements which might be attempted. Sometimes a bold spirit of partisan warfare led voluntary detachments to pursue the trail of the Indians from the vicinity of the settlements to the region north of the Ohio. Of these partisan leaders, none were more persevering and more daring than Captain Simon Kenton. One of the most important of these excursions in which he was engaged in the year 1792 was against a party of warriors commanded by the Shawanese

* See chap. xi., "Indian Wars and Military Operations of the United States," &c.

chief *Tecumseh,* who subsequently became one of the most distinguished warriors of his nation and age.

To avenge themselves upon the hostile Indians on the Little Miami, whose incursions and depredations had become exceedingly harassing to the settlements, none was so fit as Captain Kenton. With a volunteer company of thirty-seven men, all excellent hunters and woodsmen, young, bold, cautious, and trained by himself, he set out in pursuit of a band of Indian marauders, which had retired from the settlements with a large number of horses. Following their trail across the Ohio and advancing up the Little Miami, he discovered "signs" of his near approach to an Indian encampment on the East Fork, about a mile above the present town of Williamsburg, in Hamilton county, Ohio. Concealing his company from observation, he advanced to reconnoiter the camp, in company with three excellent marksmen, among whom was Cornelius Washburn, whose pulse was as regular and whose nerves were as steady while taking aim at an Indian as if he were practicing at the target, and who had never failed to distinguish himself as an intrepid soldier. An Indian on horseback, hunting for deer, with his horse-bell open,* was approaching in the distance. Kenton, concealing himself and his companions, directed Washburn to shoot the Indian so soon as fairly within reach of his rifle. The savage advanced, unconscious of danger, until he had reached an open place, when Kenton, to arrest his attention, gave a signal with his voice. The Indian instantly halted to discover whence the sound, and in a moment, at the crack of Washburn's rifle, he fell to the ground a lifeless corpse. *Such are the artifices mutually practiced by the white man and the Indian.

Kenton and his companion remained stationary, while Washburn and a comrade advanced cautiously along the trail to make further observations. A few hundred yards brought them within hearing of a large number of horse-bells, indicative of the Indian camp, near which the horses were feeding. With the utmost circumspection, Washburn quickly retired to communicate the fact to his captain. A council was immedi-

---

* The Indians have a bell attached to each horse, to facilitate their search for them when at large in the woods. If a deer hear the sound of a horse-bell in the forest, instead of flying, he will stand with wonder, and gaze steadily at the horse to which it is attached, while the hunter is enabled to take deliberate aim.—*Kenton.* See M'Donald's Sketches, &c.

ately held for the arrangements preparatory to the approaching conflict. Having determined upon the time for attack, Kenton, in company with Washburn, advanced to make a personal examination of the strength and position of the enemy. He discovered their encampment on the second bottom of the creek, comprising a large number of linen tents and markees; the number of Indians he could not discover.

Believing the savages greatly superior in numbers, he resolved to avail himself of the advantage which might result from the panic and confusion of a night attack. The evening was cloudy and drizzly, and the night would be dark and quiet. Pursuit can not be made in the night; and as he might need the protection of the night for retreat in case of defeat, he resolved to make the assault at midnight, when the enemy would be asleep and unprepared. At the appointed time, Kenton led on his little band cautiously and silently toward the sleeping host. So well had this advance been made, that they were undiscovered when within ten paces of the line of encampment and tents.* Divided into four equal parties, within striking distance, at a signal from Kenton each man at the first fire silenced a warrior, and rushed with terrific yells toward the tents. The alarm was general and the confusion instantaneous. Those who had escaped the first fire fled precipitately from the tents; but the assailants were too few to make a simultaneous attack on all the tents. The Indians rallied boldly, and returning to the unoccupied tents, seized their arms, and returned the fire with much animation. The warriors from another encampment, on a lower terraced flat, which had not been discovered in the first reconnoisance, now came to the aid of their friends, when Kenton, surprised at their numbers, and perceiving an attempt to surround him, ordered a speedy retreat, after the skirmish had continued only a few minutes. The retreat was continued without delay until they reached the south side of the river in safety.†

In this perilous enterprise only one man, John Barr, was killed, and one captured by the Indians, Alexander M'Intyre, who was executed by them next day.‡ The Indian loss in this skirmish, as was ascertained subsequently from a white

---

* M'Donald's Sketches, p. 254, 255. † Idem, p. 256.
‡ Idem, p. 257.

man living among them, was about thirty killed and several wounded. The whole number of savages was about two hundred, of whom some were women.

After the first alarm, they were rallied and brought back to the contest by a fearless chief, who inspired courage wherever he moved. This was the undaunted Tecumseh, afterward king of the Shawanese. This war party consisted of about one hundred and fifty warriors; and had it not been for the courage of their chief in checking the flight, and in rallying them by his authority and example, they would have been routed by less than one fourth of their number of "hunters from Kentucky."

The tents and markees in possession of this party were doubtless those which had been lost by Harmar and St. Clair in their disastrous defeats in 1790 and 1791.

The next important partisan enterprise within the limits of Kentucky was conducted by Captain Kenton. In June, 1793, a party of Indians had attacked and captured "Morgan's Station," from which they had retired rapidly across the Ohio to their towns upon the Yoctangee, or Paint Creek. Captain Kenton immediately raised a party of thirty men, and moved rapidly across the country to intercept them near the Scioto. Having reached Paint Creek at "Reeve's Crossings," he discovered the "fresh signs" of a large party of Indians. Pursuing the trail down the creek until close upon them, he halted his party, and, in company with Michael Cassady, proceeded to reconnoiter the enemy's camp. He found the Indians encamped upon the bank of the creek, with three fires; many were carousing and singing, with other indications of mirth and conscious security. Having viewed their position, he deferred the contemplated attack until just before daylight next morning. It was made in three opposite directions, and carried forward with a vigorous assault by three divisions of ten men each. The Indians were routed in great consternation, with the loss of four warriors, including a white man who had been captured when a child, and who to all appearance was an Indian. Kenton and his troop reached home in safety, having lost only one man, Joseph Jones, in the assault.*

Incursions by marauding parties still continued occasionally

* M'Donald's Sketches, p. 258, 259.

to annoy the settlements of Kentucky, and Kenton was ever ready to engage in any hazardous enterprise connected with the defense of the inhabitants. The regular spies had discovered the trail of twenty Indians, who were advancing through the country in quest of horses and plunder, and it fell to Kenton's lot to raise a company for the pursuit and capture of the depredators. With a party of seven men, among them Cornelius Washburn, he crossed at Limestone, and proceeded down the river to Holt's Creek. Here, on the south side of the river, he found the Indian canoes concealed in the bottom, and withdrawing his men to the opposite side, he patiently awaited the return of the Indian marauders, with their horses and plunder. On the fourth day three Indians returned with six horses, which they drove across the river. After the horses had been passed over, the Indians raised one of the canoes and followed them. As the canoe approached the shore where Kenton's party laid in ambush, perceiving that one of them was a white man, he directed his men to spare him. The first fire killed both Indians as the canoe struck the shore. To the surprise of all, the white man refused to be taken, and they were compelled to shoot him in self-defense. His ears were slit, his nose bored, and he otherwise possessed the marks of an Indian. On the same day, four hours afterward, two more Indians and one white man, with five horses, arrived, and the horses were crossed over in like manner. Another canoe was raised, and the whole party passed over in it. As they approached the shore, one simultaneous discharge killed every soul.*

During the night the main body of the party arrived, with thirty horses stolen from Bourbon county, and gave a signal by hooting like owls. The signal not being answered from the opposite side, suspicion was awakened, and, after a cautious reconnoissance, one Indian silently swam the river, and approached in the rear of the ambuscade. Suddenly he gave the signal to his party by three deep and long yells, when, in his native tongue, he warned them of the lurking danger, and bade them escape for their lives, for a party of white men were in ambuscade. The words were well understood by Kenton and several of his men, who were familiar with the Indian tongue. At the signal the Indians fled precipitately in the dark, leaving

* M'Donald's Sketches, p. 260.

all their horses in the hands of their enemies. In less than one hour a detachment of militia from Bourbon county arrived, in hot pursuit of the fugitives.

Such is the character of the daring and perilous encounters to which the frontier settlers have been exposed in innumerable instances.

CHAPTER VI.

POLITICAL CONDITION OF THE "DISTRICT OF KENTUCKY," FROM 1783 UNTIL ITS ADMISSION INTO THE FEDERAL UNION AS AN INDEPENDENT STATE.—A.D. 1783 TO 1794.

Argument.—Retrospect of the political Condition of the District.—Causes for political Discontent.—The People desire an independent State Government.—*First* Convention in 1784.—*Second* Convention in May, 1785.—*Third* Convention recommended.—Great Emigration to Kentucky in 1786.—Improved Condition of the Kentucky Settlements in 1786.—Measures adopted by the third Convention.—Action of the Virginia Legislature in favor of Separation.—Requisite Action by Kentucky unavoidably delayed.—*Fourth* Convention appointed for August, 1787.—First Newspaper in Kentucky.—Agricultural and commercial Prosperity in 1787.—Navigation of the Mississippi commenced.—*Fifth* Convention held in September, 1787.—*Sixth* Convention in July, 1788.—Diversity of political Sentiment.—Political Parties.—Action of the sixth Convention.—Prominent Men.—Corresponding Action of the Virginia Legislature.—Final Action of this Convention, and Application for Assent of Congress.—Assent of Congress granted February 4th, 1791.—Boundaries of the new State.—First State Governor and Legislature convened June 4th, 1792, for the organization of State Government.—Causes of the protracted delay of Separation.—A new Experiment in Political Philosophy.—Notice of political Parties.—Foreign Influence.—Spanish Intrigue.—Increasing Trade with New Orleans.—The fluctuating Policy of Spain with regard to the Navigation of the Mississippi.—Genet's Intrigue for the Invasion of Louisiana in 1793-94.—Measures taken by the Federal Government to suppress the contemplated Invasion.—Reluctance of Governor Shelby to interfere in the Plans of Genet.—Increasing Population of Kentucky in 1794.—New Counties organized.—Kentucky levies for the Campaign in the Northwestern Territory.—Advantages derived by Kentucky from Treaties of London and Madrid.—Last Efforts of Spain to detach Kentucky from the Union.—Progressive Wealth and Population of Kentucky.—Governors of Kentucky.

[A.D. 1783.] THE political relations of Kentucky had already become a source of great anxiety, as well as inconvenience and danger, to the people. Removed five hundred miles from the capital, their dependence upon Virginia was like that of a remote province, governed by laws enacted by strangers, too remote to appreciate their wants or their grievances. Such was the tardy intercourse between them and the state government, that months often elapsed before they could communicate with the executive authorities relative to civil or military affairs. They had a representation in the Legislature, but it was that of an isolated colony, and not of an integral portion of a great whole; they had organized county courts, with regular quarterly sessions, for the trial of misdemeanors, and persons charged with such criminal offenses as were punishable by fine and imprisonment; they might adjudicate civil cases involving an amount not exceeding twenty-five shillings; but for capital offenses there was no court of competent jurisdiction short of the state capital, and the prisoner, the prosecutor, and the witnesses must travel by land five hundred miles to Richmond, with delays and expenses which could not fail to be oppressive to all who came within the influence of the superior courts. In appeal cases the same difficulties presented, and the same delays were unavoidable.

During the existence of the Revolutionary war, it was esteemed fortunate if an order from the executive of the state reached its destination in Kentucky in less than three months; and military commanders were often unable to obey instructions, based upon certain emergencies, before it was too late to accomplish their objects. In April, 1781, Governor Jefferson issued an order to Colonel Clark, directing a military expedition into the Indian country, and the order was not received at "the Falls" until the 11th of July. But delays of this kind were viewed as trivial inconveniences compared to other embarrassments under which the people of the "District of Kentucky" labored, as to their civil and military organization, during her colonial dependence upon Virginia. They had been compelled to rely almost exclusively upon their own unaided exertions for defense against the combined savages of the northwest.

Amid the incessant incursions of the hostile savages, and the continual dangers which surrounded all the settlements, their chief defense proceeded from their own voluntary efforts for the protection of their firesides and families. A few state troops, in small detachments, were occasionally sent to re-enforce a post or station, or to aid in a hostile invasion of the Indian country; but the most efficient and the most essential service in protecting the country was rendered by individual enterprise and patriotism, without the authority of the state, and without any legal claims upon her for remuneration. The operations for the common defense fell unequally and oppressively upon the most patriotic, and the state was reluctant to assume and remunerate expenses incurred for private enterprise against the Indians.*

[A.D. 1784.] The attention of the people was first drawn forcibly to the imperfection of their military organization in the autumn of 1784. Martial law had now ceased to be paramount, and the civil authorities resumed their supremacy. Impressments for the public service could no longer be enforced with impunity. A year had now elapsed since military parade and martial law had prevailed, and citizens had mostly retired to the private walks of life, to reinstate their exhausted resources.

It was at this time that rumor represented a contemplated invasion of Kentucky by the hostile Cherokees from the South. The settlements were thrown into excitement and alarm, and Colonel Logan was urged to organize an expedition to invade the Cherokee towns. After due reflection and advice, it was discovered that the isolated community of Kentucky possessed no legal authority or military jurisdiction competent for the organization of a military expedition against the savages. Accordingly, it was deemed advisable to invite a meeting of representatives from the whole district during the succeeding month, to take into consideration the important subjects of political interest then agitating the district, in view of legislative relief to this portion of the state. This convention assembled at Danville, and after a short session adjourned, having adopted a written circular to each militia company in the district, recommending the election of one delegate from each company, to meet in convention at Danville on the 27th of December following, for the purpose of a full discussion of the subjects worthy of consideration. The delegates, twenty-five in number, convened accordingly; Samuel M‘Dowell was elected president of the convention, and Thomas Todd clerk. After a session of two days, during which business was "conducted with great decorum," the convention adjourned *sine die*.

During the session there had been a free interchange of opinion upon the important subjects connected with the prosperity of "the District." To some it was evident that many of their grievances might be removed by suitable legislation on

* Butler's Kentucky, p. 117.

the part of Virginia ; but to others it was evident that the grievances of greatest magnitude grew out of the remote distance of the state capital from the district, and that these were evils which could be removed only by a separation of the district from the parent commonwealth, and its erection into an equal and independent member of the Federal Union. The latter opinion prevailed, and, by a large majority, a resolution was adopted expressive of their sentiments " in favor of applying for an act to render Kentucky independent of Virginia." Yet, not having been delegated for a purpose so radically affecting the political condition of their constituents, the convention determined to do nothing more than offer a simple expression of their opinion for the consideration of the people at large.*

[A.D. 1785.] The convention suggested the propriety of electing other delegates to a convention to be assembled at Danville on the third Monday in May following, and that these delegates be elected with special reference to the question of " separation from the Commonwealth of Virginia."

The canvass for the April elections opened by a full and general discussion of the question of separation, and all those delegates who advocated a separation were returned to the next convention, which assembled on the 23d of May, 1785. A large majority of the former delegates having been re-elected, the organization of the deliberative body was unchanged.

The convention proceeded with great decorum to the important task assigned them. The delegates comprised a fair representation of the talent and eloquence of the district; for the people, in committing to their charge the most vital interests of the community, had selected the first men in the country, of known talent and integrity. During the session of the convention, the meetings were attended by a large concourse of people anxious to witness the proceedings and to hear their discussions.

The result of the deliberations of this convention was the adoption of the following resolution, expressive of the sense of the whole number of delegates, viz. :

"*Resolved unanimously*, as the opinion of this convention, that a petition be presented to the Assembly praying that this

* On this subject, Mr. Butler's account of the proceedings of the convention is so exceedingly confused and obscure, that it defies human acumen to unravel or to explain his narrative.—See Butler's Kentucky, p. 148–151 ; 164–167 ; and 174–181. Also, Marshall's Kentucky, vol. i., p. 194, 195.

district may be established into a state, separate from Virginia."

The convention had also recommended the election of another convention, to be assembled on the second Monday of August following at Danville, "to take under their further consideration the state of the district," and suggesting the propriety of electing the new delegates upon the "principle of population, and not of property or territory;" thus discarding a principle which had obtained in Virginia from the old colonial usages. This was the first step taken by Kentucky toward a more democratic form of government.

In the mean time, the Legislature of Virginia, at its last session, had laid out a new county, designated as the county of Nelson. This county had been duly organized early in the spring, and comprised all that portion of Jefferson county which laid south of Salt River and north of Green River. The district was now comprised in four counties, each embracing a large extent of territory, the greater portion of which was sparsely inhabited.

The people, acting upon the recommendation of the former convention, had proceeded to elect delegates from the different counties, according to the population of each, as ascertained from the muster-rolls and other records, which afforded an approximate estimate. No census had as yet been taken in Kentucky, although the number of people at this time must have amounted to thirty thousand.

According to the basis of population adopted, the following ratio of representation was selected for the new convention, viz.: to the counties of Jefferson and Nelson, each six delegates; to Lincoln, ten delegates; to Fayette, eight delegates. Thus the convention, representing the four counties of the district, was to consist of twenty-four delegates. Nearly all the former delegates were re-elected, and the deliberative body was organized as before.

The result of the August convention was the adoption of a petition to the Legislature of Virginia, praying for "a separation from the commonwealth," and the adoption of the draft of an address for circulation among the people.

The address to the people was an able statement of the views entertained by the convention as to the proper policy of the people of Kentucky in obtaining from the parent state a legalized separation, and an independent system of state government. It also recommended the election of delegates to another convention, to be assembled twelve months from that time, in order to be fully apprised of the disposition of the State Legislature at its next session. The object of this course was to give the people of the district generally an opportunity of considering the important question maturely, and enable them more fully to appreciate the advantages of separation, after the whole matter had been fully presented to the people of Virginia, as well as to their representatives in the Legislature.

The petition of the convention was laid before the executive of the state for his consideration previous to its formal introduction to the legislative bodies.

At this time, the population of Kentucky, as well as all the western portions of Virginia and Pennsylvania, was augmenting rapidly by emigration from the old settlements east of the mountains. The Ohio River was thronged with families descending in boats, barges, and Kentucky arks, freighted with their movable effects, comprising household furniture, implements of husbandry, goods and wares of all sorts, and domestic stock and supplies of every kind, all destined for Kentucky.

Among the numerous emigrants which were arriving almost daily, were many men of talent and enterprise; many had been officers and soldiers of the Revolutionary war, who sought ease and competence in the delightful regions of Kentucky, where they constituted valuable accessions to the young and flourishing colony. Some of the emigrants were from France, England, and Ireland; but by far the greatest portion were from the eastern counties of Virginia, Maryland, Pennsylvania, and New Jersey.

[A.D. 1786.] The spring of 1786 opened with an increase of emigration to the West, and to Kentucky especially. Among those who had arrived during the past year was Colonel James Wilkinson, a distinguished officer of the Revolutionary army, a man of fine address, of great talent, and of untiring industry and enterprise; qualities which never fail in the West to receive from the people the highest appointments, and the most honorable political preferment, as a mark of popular confidence. Colonel Wilkinson had been an active officer, and served under the command of Generals Washington, Gates, Wayne, and St.

Clair, and was the associate of Generals Morgan, Mercer, and Schuyler; he had fought in the battles of Trenton, Princeton, Saratoga, and Ticonderoga.* In Kentucky, he became an enterprising merchant, and traded extensively with the settlements on the Cumberland River, as well as with those on the Ohio, and from Pittsburgh to New Orleans.

Heretofore the whole western country on the Ohio south of Pittsburgh could not boast a single newspaper or periodical. The circular address to the militia companies in December, 1784, was in manuscript copies, as was also the address of the convention to the people in August, 1785. One of these was posted up in each county seat.

Previous to the year 1784, the great business of the colony, the all-absorbing interest in the settlements, was military service and military preparation for the defense of the exposed frontier, or to carry invasion into the heart of the enemy's country. Now the arts of peace had begun to appear, agriculture and commerce began to employ the industry and enterprise of many valuable citizens, and all were absorbed in the acquisition of lands either for use or speculation; and settlements were rapidly filling the country north of Licking as far as the Ohio River.

The time appointed for the assembling of the convention found the whole country involved in the excitement and parade of a military campaign for the chastisement of the Shawanese nation, whose war parties had been for several months committing a succession of murders, depredations, and outrages upon the extensive frontier. The people were determined to inflict summary punishment upon the whole nation, and the most active measures were now in progress throughout all the settlements; public attention was greatly absorbed in preparations for a formidable invasion of the Indian country from the banks of the Scioto to the head waters of the Wabash. Many of the delegates elect were deeply engaged in the arduous labors of the contemplated campaign.

Owing to this circumstance, the convention failed to secure a full attendance of the members, and after a short session it adjourned. The sense of the convention was fully expressed in a resolution reported by George Muter, chairman of a committee to whom the subject had been referred. This resolu-

* See Wilkinson's Memoirs, passim.

tion declared that "*it was the indispensable duty of the convention to make application to the General Assembly at the ensuing session for an act to separate this district from the present government forever, on terms honorable to both, and injurious to neither.*"*

This resolution was followed by an address to the Legislature of Virginia, and another to the people of the district, both written by General James Wilkinson in a style of dignity, beauty, and energy of language heretofore unknown in the public proceedings of Kentucky.

Chief-justice George Muter, and the attorney-general, Harry Innes, were instructed to present and sustain the petition before the next session of the Virginia Legislature.†

It was during the early part of this year that the counties of Bourbon, Mercer, and Madison were erected and properly organized under the authority of the Virginia Legislature, increasing the number of counties in the district to seven. The county of Bourbon, indicative of Spanish influence and partiality, was districted from Fayette; the counties of Mercer and Madison were laid off from Lincoln county.

[A.D. 1787.] The General Assembly of Virginia had received the petition and address of the convention with due consideration, indicative of that liberality and generous sentiment which has always characterized the "Old Dominion." An act of the Legislature provided that, at the next election in August, five representatives from each of the counties should be elected by the free white male inhabitants of the district; that the representatives so elected should meet and determine whether it be expedient, and the will of the people, that the district of Kentucky should be erected into an independent state.

The act provided further that these representatives, if they approved of a separation, should appoint a day, subsequent to the first of September, 1787, when the authority of Virginia should cease over the district, provided that Congress, prior to June 1st, 1787, should assent to said separation, and release Virginia from her Federal obligations arising therefrom, and also agree to admit Kentucky into the Federal Union as an independent state.‡

Meantime, political embarrassments and Indian disturbances had interfered with the action of Kentucky on the subject, until

* Butler's Kentucky, p. 148.   † Idem, p. 149.   ‡ Idem, p. 150.

it was too late to obtain the assent of the United States previous to the first of June, 1787. Thus the former act of Virginia stipulating that condition became null and void. Yet the Legislature of Virginia freely assented to the desired separation, provided the new convention, to convene in August, 1787, should consent to the separation by a majority of two thirds. Hence the period of separation was necessarily deferred for eighteen months longer, in order to obtain the assent of Congress, and the subsequent legislation by the State of Virginia.*

Such was the difficulty of disseminating political views and political communications by manuscript circulars, that public meetings and public discussions became the most obvious mode of operating upon the public mind. This difficulty, however, was removed soon after the convention of August, 1787, by John and Fielding Bradford, citizens of Lexington. These men, although not practical printers, determined to issue a weekly paper, and on the 18th of August the "Kentucky Gazette," in the shape of a small demy sheet, made its first appearance. Their stock of type being small and imperfect, several deficiencies were supplied by wooden type cut from dogwood.† Thus commenced the *second* newspaper published on the Ohio, about fifteen months after the "Pittsburgh Gazette," which was the first.

In the mean time, new objects of interest began to attract the public attention in Kentucky. As early as the year 1786, the people perceived the necessity of the free navigation of the Mississippi, as the proper outlet for the surplus products of their flourishing settlements. The agricultural produce was abundant, and New Orleans and Louisiana presented a rich market for their enterprise; but Louisiana was a foreign province, and the duty imposed upon American commerce descending the Mississippi was exorbitant, and the commercial regulations were highly oppressive. The rich market for American produce was thus withheld; or the people, in the excessive exactions levied upon their property, saw themselves robbed of one half of their profits. The subsequent difficulties and embarrassments thrown in the way of American trade by the Spanish authorities were the result of a settled policy on the part of Spain, for the purpose of effecting ultimately in the western people an alienation of feeling from the Federal Union,

* Butler, p. 150, 151. † Idem, p. 163, 164.

and a consequent alliance with Louisiana under the Spanish crown.

On the 17th of September, 1787, the fifth convention assembled at Danville. The decision was unanimous in favor of separating the "District" from the parent state, upon the terms and conditions prescribed by the Legislature of Virginia. An address was prepared for Congress, relative to the admission of the new state into the Federal Union, under the name of the "State of Kentucky." The convention provided for the election of a new convention, clothed with authority "to adopt a form of state government, and to frame and establish a state Constitution for the proposed state."

Thus the period of separation was necessarily deferred, although conceded by Virginia, until the session of Congress, which was the last under the old confederation. This Congress declined to take any decided action in the case, preferring to refer the whole subject to the new administration under the new Constitution. Thus the definite legislation of Virginia was again deferred another year.

[A.D. 1790.] The population of Kentucky in the last three years had greatly augmented by emigration from Virginia, Maryland, and Pennsylvania, and also from North Carolina by way of Cumberland Gap. According to a census taken during the year 1790 by authority of the United States, the District of Kentucky, comprising nine counties, had an aggregate population of 73,677 persons, of whom 61,103 were free whites, the remainder being chiefly slaves and free people of color.

About one half of the above number of whites, and two thirds of the slaves, were emigrants from Virginia. The remainder were chiefly from Pennsylvania, Maryland, and North Carolina.*

Various political difficulties connected with the adoption of the new Constitution of the United States, and the organization of the government under that Constitution, delayed any definite action relative to the separation of Kentucky until the year

---

* Marshall's Kentucky, vol. i., p. 441. The tide of emigration to Kentucky had been remarkably strong for two years previous to 1790. By a register kept at Fort Harmar, at the mouth of Muskingum, it appeared that in twelve months, comprising portions of the years 1788 and 1789, twenty thousand persons of all descriptions had descended the Ohio in eight hundred and fifty boats of all kinds, containing, also, six hundred wagons, seven thousand horses, three thousand cows, and nine hundred head of sheep. The greatest portion of this immense emigration was moving for Kentucky.—See Holmes's Annals, vol. ii., p. 370.

VOL. II.—M

1789, after the election of the first Congress under the new Federal Constitution. Of course no action on the part of Congress could be obtained until after the assembling of the new Congress, under the administration of General Washington.

It was on this account that the final separation of Kentucky was deferred for two years more. It was at this critical period, when disappointment, delay, and uncertainty seemed to brood over the political prospects of Kentucky, and when her numerous talented statesmen, who were ambitious of taking their rank in the new order of things, were impatient of political distinction, that the intrigue of the Spanish minister and the Governor-general of Louisiana was set on foot for encouraging disaffection in the western people, preparatory to a separation and alliance with Louisiana under the dominion of Spain.

[A.D. 1791.] At length, after an angry and spirited controversy between the district of Kentucky and the parent state, the Legislature of Virginia passed an act which, in the nature of a solemn compact between the State of Virginia and Kentucky, provided that the district of Kentucky should become "separate from, and independent of, the State of Virginia, from and after the first day of June, 1792."

The question as to the admission of Kentucky had been presented before Congress by President Washington, with a strong recommendation in favor of the independence of the new state. The president had taken a lively interest in the welfare of this rising state, and lost no time in taking measures for securing to the western people the free navigation of the Mississippi.

On the 4th of February an act of Congress was approved which provided for the admission of Kentucky into the Federal Union as an independent state. This act authorized the election, in December following, of a convention authorized to form and adopt a State Constitution, to be submitted for the approbation of Congress. The convention elected under this authority convened at Danville on the first Monday in April following. They proceeded to the task assigned them, and after a session of nearly three weeks they had completed their labors, and on the 19th day of April, 1792, the Constitution was adopted and received the signatures of the members.* It was soon promulgated, and was well received by the people.

* Marshall, vol. i., p. 395–419.

[A.D. 1792.] The boundaries of the new state, as prescribed by the Legislature of Virginia and ratified by Congress, were as follows: On the north, the Ohio River, from the mouth of Big Sandy to the Mississippi River: on the east, Big Sandy Creek, from its mouth up to the mouth of Knox Creek, on Tug Fork; thence the top of the Cumberland Mountain to the line of North Carolina, at Cumberland Gap: on the south, the line of Virginia, running due west from Cumberland Gap, as designated by Dr. Walker in 1780, to Tennessee River: on the west, the Mississippi River. The line of boundary on the east was established by commissioners, subsequently appointed by Virginia and Kentucky.

On the fourth day of June, the governor and Legislature elected under the new Constitution assembled at Lexington. Isaac Shelby was the first governor elect. The two Houses of the Legislature organized by electing Alexander S. Bullitt President of the Senate, and Robert Breckenridge Speaker of the House of Representatives. On the sixth of June, Governor Shelby, in accordance with the ancient usage of Virginia, delivered his address to the two Houses of the Legislature.* Thus commenced the state government under the first Constitution. The Legislature proceeded to complete the organization of the state government, creating the requisite offices, and making the necessary appointments. Such was the beginning of the separate political existence of the State of Kentucky, the first new state in the West.

On the part of the Eastern States, a strong opposition to the admission of Kentucky into the Union had manifested itself in Congress as early as the year 1788, when the subject was first laid before that body. This opposition, no doubt, gave encouragement to the Spanish minister, Don Guardoqui, in his plans for separating the western people from the Atlantic

* Until the administration of Thomas Jefferson, the intercourse between the President of the United States and Congress, as well as between the state governors and their respective Legislatures, was by a formal address, delivered in person, followed by a formal response and reply. This mode of intercourse, a relic of the monarchical usages of the royal governors, although calculated for the colonies of a splendid monarchy, was very inconvenient for the business intercourse of a simple form of Republican government, and not unfrequently gave rise to a premature agitation of public measures, or the committal of the legislative bodies to the approbation of measures before they had been fairly understood or properly investigated. Hence Mr. Jefferson first introduced the present mode of intercourse by written message, which has been adopted by the state governors.—See Butler's Kentucky, p. 212.

States, and the formation of independent states, in alliance with Louisiana, under the protection of the Spanish crown.*

Many in Kentucky seem to have contemplated a forcible separation from the State of Virginia, and without her consent; for the accomplishment of which they expected aid from Spain, if necessary. But as the Federal government would have resisted any illegal dismemberment of Virginia, the majority were uniformly in favor of a voluntary and legal separation from the parent state, with the sanction of the Federal government. Hence the preliminary application to Congress in 1788.

The case of Kentucky was the first instance of the formation of an independent state from territory previously embraced within the organized limits of a sovereign state; hence the experiment of separation and the mode of accomplishment did not clearly present itself to the minds of those in authority, and the road to a voluntary and legal independence from the states of the Union was an untried experiment, an unexplored route to the Federal and state politicians. But since the way has been explored by Kentucky, the mode for amicable and legal changes in the state sovereignty has become plain and easy, and the retrospect scarcely perceives a cause for former embarrassment.†

In organizing the executive and judicial departments of the government, James Brown was appointed first Secretary of State, and George Nicholas Attorney-general. John Brown and John Edwards were elected first Senators in Congress. Inferior and superior courts were organized, and commissioners for locating the state capital were appointed, who soon selected the present site of Frankfort as the permanent capital of the state.‡

At the period of the adoption of the first Constitution of Kentucky, the aggregate population of the state could not have been less than ninety thousand persons. The tide of emigration to this delightful region had not abated since 1788, and every year continued to add thousands of immigrants to the settle-

---

* Butler's Kentucky, p. 173. † Idem, p. 180.
‡ Robert Todd, John Edwards, John Allen, Henry Lee, and Thomas Kennedy were commissioners for locating the state capital. A "Court of Appeals" was organized, consisting of one chief-justice and two associate judges. The first Court of Appeals consisted of George Muter, *chief justice*, and Benjamin Sebastian and Caleb Wallace, *associate judges.*—See Butler, p. 212, 213.

ments spreading rapidly from the sources of Green River to those of the Kentucky. Notwithstanding the hostile attitude of the Indian tribes, the population had increased greatly during the next five years. Towns had grown up in various parts of the state. Lexington already had a population of about one thousand souls. Danville and Louisville were thriving towns, with more than five hundred inhabitants each.*

Here it may not be improper to take a brief retrospect of the dissensions of political parties and the foreign intrigue which had been brought to operate upon the people of Kentucky.

Isolated and unprotected as they had been under the old confederacy in all their Indian wars; cut off from trade with the East by natural obstacles; deprived, by the arbitrary will of the Spanish intendant of Louisiana, from trade on the Mississippi, their only and natural outlet for the surplus product, unless they would enter into alliance with Louisiana under the protection of Spain; harassed with the confiscation of their property by Spanish commandants, and encouraged by Spanish intrigue to separate from the United States, which had been unable to afford them redress or to obtain for them the privileges of navigation which their peculiar situation demanded, it was hardly to have been expected that the people of Kentucky should have entertained very strong predilections for the old confederation. Engaged with their own difficulties, and almost indifferent as to the new Federal Constitution, they had felt but little interest in the election which had taken place in 1788 for President of the United States under the new confederation. After the installation of the new administration, it remained to be seen whether the government was able to extend relief to them, as well as what might be the advantages of a union with the older states.

During this crisis, England and Spain were anxious spectators, awaiting the result of the political contest which agitated the people of Kentucky. Both these powers viewed Kentucky as a prize almost within their grasp. Great Britain still occupied the posts of Detroit, Maumee, and other points south of the lakes, which gave her virtual possession of the Northwestern Territory, separated from Kentucky by the Ohio River. Spain possessed and occupied the whole of Louisiana

* Imlay's America, p. 180.

and West Florida, embracing all the region west of the Mississippi, as well as its eastern bank for five hundred miles above its mouth. Besides this, she had asserted a claim to the whole eastern bank up to the mouth of the Ohio, and had taken possession of the same in virtue of her Indian treaties.

Through the governors of the respective provinces and their agents, both these courts were intriguing to produce a separation from the United States. A spirit of hostile feeling between the two governments had nearly matured into a pretext for the invasion of their respective and contiguous provinces of Canada and Upper Louisiana.*

During the summer of 1790, Doctor Connolly, who had been a British agent at Fort Pitt at the beginning of the Revolutionary war, and was now a citizen of Quebec, and an emissary of the Earl of Dorchester, honored Kentucky with a visit. He was a man of talents and fine address, and under the pretext of closing up some old unsettled business, or searching for confiscated lands, was the secret agent of the Governor-general of Canada to sound the leading men of Kentucky on the subject of an invasion of Louisiana from the Ohio River. He was authorized to give assurances of aid from Canada in case an invasion of Louisiana was attempted by the western people. Rumor had already reported "that four thousand British troops were in readiness to march from Canada at a moment's warning." The Governor of Louisiana, apprehensive of the invasion from Canada, had a pretext for new fortifications near the mouth of the Ohio, and the re-enforcement of his garrisons on the Upper Mississippi.

After a temporary sojourn in Kentucky, perceiving, from his intercourse with some of the prominent men, that a prejudice existed among the western people against British faith, and that the public feeling was not in favor of the invasion of Louisiana so much as against the occupation of the northwestern posts by British troops, and contrary to treaty stipulations, Doctor Connolly retired from Kentucky. Before his departure, he had made an imperfect disclosure of his views and propositions to some of his confidential friends; and shortly afterward suspicion was awakened, and he was suspected as a "British spy." Alarmed at his position, and aware of the danger of public vengeance, his friends conveyed him, with the

* Martin's Louisiana, vol. ii., p. 106.

A.D. 1792.] VALLEY OF THE MISSISSIPPI. 183

utmost secrecy and expedition, to Limestone, on his way to Canada.* His sudden flight, in which he had nearly been captured, alone secured him from the Tory's fate, "a coat of tar and feathers." Thus ended the first British intrigue in Kentucky, to which Colonel Marshall, Colonel J. Campbell, of Louisville, and General Wilkinson, of Lexington, were cognizant.† Governor Blount, of the Southwestern Territory, was deeply implicated in the treasonable conspiracy.

It would carry us beyond our limits to give a full account of all the plans and dissensions of the numerous political leaders and their respective adherents. It is sufficient in this place to enumerate some of the prominent views of the principal parties. It is beyond doubt that many were so swayed by interest and the future prospect of trade, that they were perfectly reconciled to a union with Louisiana under the Spanish crown. The peculiar condition of Kentucky previous to the adoption of the State Constitution, and the conflicting interests of a new and unsettled government, had reduced the people to a deplorable state of discord and anarchy. The Spanish authorities were active in their efforts to wean them from the Federal Union, by restrictions and favors alternately, as the emergency might dictate; while the court of Madrid, with an eye to the separation, delayed any decisive negotiations with the United States relative to the navigation of the Mississippi, or the surrender of the territory east of that river, agreeably to the boundary designated in the treaty of 1783. There can be no doubt that the Governor of Louisiana used all his art and finess in state intrigue through General James Wilkinson, Judge Sebastian, and others, in hope of ultimate success. Through General Wilkinson, the privilege of trade with New Orleans and Louisiana, and the right of emigration to West Florida, on the east side of the Mississippi, with liberal grants of land to each family, had been held out as means of first counteracting the prejudice of the western people against the Spanish character. General Wilkinson had descended the Mississippi to New Orleans in June, 1787, with a boat-load of tobacco and western produce, which he had disposed of to great profit. While in Louisiana, he had entered into arrangements with the governor, which secured to himself the monopoly of the tobacco trade on very lucrative

* Butler, p. 184. Marshall, vol. i., p. 346.   † Butler, p. 183, 184.

terms. He had also procured the privilege, according to his own statement, of introducing and settling several thousand families in Louisiana and West Florida.* Yet, unless the western people were prompt to avail themselves of these privileges, by complying with the terms, which were confided to certain persons, the trade and intercourse by the river with Louisiana would be prohibited.

The numerous plans and intrigues put in operation by the governors of Louisiana and Florida, and by the Spanish minister, Guardoqui, at the seat of the Federal government, are not properly within the province of the present work, but are more specially noted in another place.†

During the political excitement in Kentucky and Tennessee, from the year 1788 to 1792, the policy of Spain, and the restrictions upon western trade, together with Genet's intrigue, gave rise to the following parties, viz.:

1. In favor of forming a separate and independent Republic, under no special obligation of union, except such as might be most advantageous.

2. In favor of entering into commercial arrangements with Spain, and of annexing Kentucky to Louisiana, with all the advantages offered.

3. Opposed to any Spanish connection, and in favor of forcing the free navigation of the Mississippi by the arms of the United States, with the invasion of Louisiana and West Florida.

4. In favor of soliciting France to claim a retrocession of Louisiana, and to extend her protection to Kentucky.

5. The strongest party, however, was in favor of a separation from Virginia, and admission into the Federal Union as a free and independent state, leaving it to the general government to regulate the Mississippi question with Spain.

It may be proper here to take some notice of the state of trade and commerce of the western country about this time, and of Kentucky especially. Since the general peace of 1783, Spain had claimed the right to control the navigation of the Mississippi River, in virtue of her treaty with England, which relinquished to her the provinces of East and West Florida, as appendages to Louisiana. West Florida, under the pretensions

---

* Butler's Kentucky, p. 161; also, p. 164–190. Marshall, vol. i., p. 320–360.
† See book iv., chap. iii., "Spain in the Valley of the Mississippi."

of Spain, extended up the east bank of the Mississippi to the mouth of the Yazoo, and gave Spain virtual control of both banks of the Mississippi River, nearly five hundred miles above its mouth.

About the year 1786, the people of the western settlements of North Carolina and Virginia, upon the waters of the Holston and Clinch, and upon the Kentucky and Cumberland Rivers, began to look to the Spanish settlements on the Lower Mississippi as the natural market for the surplus products of their fine agricultural regions, and the Mississippi River as the natural high-way upon which their trade should meet the ocean through the Gulf of Mexico. The increasing population, and the prosperous condition of these settlements, rendered it expedient to seek some foreign market for their abundant products; and numerous attempts were made by enterprising men and adventurers to open a lucrative trade with New Orleans and the river settlements of West Florida. But the fluctuating policy of Spain, growing out of the peculiar situation of the western people, at length produced a high degree of prejudice and national irritation, which threatened the security of all Louisiana. The western people, again restricted in their trade, and plundered by Spanish exactions on the Mississippi, without relief from the Federal government, began to evince their impatience of the inefficient administration of the national councils, and their indignation against the Spanish restrictions by a contemplated invasion of Louisiana and Florida.

To allay this feeling of hostility among the western people, Governor Miro, of Louisiana, sought every favorable opportunity to conciliate the people of Kentucky and the Cumberland settlements, by extending to them certain commercial privileges, besides the rights of Spanish subjects to such as would emigrate to West Florida, and a general relaxation of the revenue exactions upon the river trade. By this policy he at length succeeded in effecting a partial reconciliation of the western people to the Spanish authorities. But his successor, the Baron de Carondelet, having adopted an opposite course of policy, revived the prejudices and hostility of the western people, until they again contemplated asserting their rights by the invasion and conquest of Louisiana and West Florida.

Through the judicious policy of the Federal government, this state of feeling toward the Spaniards of Louisiana had been in a great measure allayed, and the people of Kentucky had been received into the Union as an independent state, when the whole West was again thrown into a state of great excitement by a new intrigue, planned and conducted under the agency of M. Genet, the French minister in the United States.

The object of this enterprise was to invade and repossess the province of Louisiana for France, by means of an expedition raised and furnished within the United States under the authority of revolutionary France. The French minister, apprised of the political factions which had been prevailing in the West, and the renewed impatience of the western people under the rigid policy of the Baron de Carondelet, conceived the plan of uniting all parties for the expulsion of the Spanish authority from Louisiana and Florida.

It was during the excited and unsettled state of political feeling in the West that the French minister, M. Genet, arrived in Charleston. He was received with enthusiasm by the people wherever he appeared, until, elated with the marked attention of the people, who took a deep interest in the cause of France against the combined powers of Europe, he so far forgot his duty to the Federal government as to encourage the people of Charleston to fit out privateers against the commerce of England, who was at peace with the United States. From Charleston he proceeded triumphantly to the seat of the Federal government as the accredited minister of the French Republic. "Scarcely were the first ceremonies of his reception over, when M. Genet displayed a disposition to usurp and exercise within the United States the choicest and most important duties and powers of sovereignty. He claimed the privilege of arming and imbodying the citizens of America within their own territory, to carry on from thence expeditions against nations with whom they were at peace; of fitting out and equipping within their limits privateers to cruise on a commerce destined for their ports; of erecting within their jurisdiction an independent judiciary; and of arraigning their government at the bar of the people." Such was the tenor of his conduct, when President Washington, indignant at his unwarrantable interference with the prerogatives of the government, demanded his recall. "The recall of the minister was received with universal joy, as a confirmation that his whole system of conduct was attributable only to himself."[*]

---

[*] American State Papers, Boston edition, vol. iv., p. 33.

Early in October, the agents of Genet, M. Lachaise, Charles Delpeau, M. Mathurin, and Gignoux, left the city of Philadelphia in the stage for Kentucky, where they subsequently fomented great popular excitement and indignation against the Federal government.*

[A.D. 1794.] Early in January following, Mr. Jefferson, Secretary of State of the United States, in answer to inquiries directed to Governor Shelby, received from him in reply the admission that "two Frenchmen, Lachaise and Delpeau, have lately come into this state; and I am told they declare publicly that they are in daily expectation of receiving a supply of money, and that, as soon as they do receive it, they shall raise a body of men, and proceed with them down the river. Whether they have any sufficient reason to expect such a supply, or have any serious intention of applying it in that manner if they do receive it, I can form no opinion."†

Yet doubts were entertained by Governor Shelby whether there was any *legal* authority to restrain or punish them for such enterprise before it was actually accomplished, provided their operations were conducted with prudence. In his dispatch to the Federal government, he asserts, "that if it is lawful for any one citizen of a state to leave it, it is equally lawful for any number to do the same. It is also lawful for them to carry any quantity of provisions, arms, and ammunition. And if the act is lawful in itself, there is nothing but the particular intention with which it is done that can possibly make it unlawful; but I know of no law which inflicts a punishment on intention only, or any criterion by which to decide what would be sufficient evidence of that intention, even if it were a proper subject of legal censure."‡

Yet Governor Shelby, concealing his own doubts of the illegality of the enterprise, in reply to an impertinent letter from Delpeau, declaring in express terms his intention to join the expedition of the Mississippi, and inquiring his instructions from the President of the United States, condescended to reply "that *his present condition* required him to take those legal measures necessary to prevent such an enterprise."§

Early in January General Wayne had notified the Governor of Kentucky that the legionary cavalry, then stationed between

---

* American State Papers, Boston edition, vol. ii., p. 37.   † Idem, p. 39.
‡ Butler, p. 225.   § Idem, p. 224.   Also, Marshall, p. 100.

Lexington and Georgetown, and any other troops requisite, should be held ready to obey his orders in suppressing any enterprise attempted against Louisiana.*

All effectual interposition on the part of the Governor of Kentucky being precluded by his expressed opinion, the President issued his proclamation on the 24th of March, warning the people of the United States against the unlawful enterprise, and the consequences of any participation in it.

On the 31st of March an order from the War Department instructed General Wayne, commander-in-chief of the northwestern army, to send without delay to Fort Massac a respectable force, "under the command of an officer of approved integrity, firmness, and prudence," and there to " erect a strong redoubt and block-house," supplied with "some suitable cannon from Fort Washington." The object of this post was to prevent the advance of any "lawless people residing on the waters of the Ohio, who, in defiance of the national authority, had entertained the daring design of invading the territories of Spain."† Governor St. Clair had been previously authorized to call out the militia of the Northwestern Territory, to suppress any attempted expedition from Kentucky.‡

At this time, an agent of General Clark, of Georgia, was at Lexington, engaged in the purchase of five hundred pounds of powder and one ton of cannon ball, to be shipped from "the Falls" in boats, with provisions said to be ready on the Ohio, to descend by the 15th of April.§ It was represented to the Federal government that about the 8th and 9th of April preparations were active in Kentucky, and boat-builders and artificers at the Falls were busily employed on account of the expedition. Some of the United States troops deserted to join the enterprise; some persons in Kentucky sold their property, and received commissions in the French service as officers of the Legion. Among them were Charles Smith, of Kentucky, who subsequently resigned his commission. Many gave the enterprise a tacit assent, and but few opposed it boldly. Cannon were said to be ordered at the iron-works, and some of the inhabitants of Lexington had subscribed to furnish ammunition.‖

Yet such was the influence of the French party, and the hos-

---

* American State Papers, Boston edition, vol. ii., p. 49. † Idem, p. 50.
‡ Idem, p. 47.   § Idem, p. 49.   ‖ Idem, p. 54.

tility to the Spanish dominion in the West, that neither Governor Shelby nor the Legislature of Kentucky took any measures to interrupt the unlawful enterprise;* and such was the state of public feeling in Kentucky, that on the 14th of May following, a numerous and respectable public meeting was held at Lexington, at which resolutions of the most violent character were adopted, expressive of the severest censure upon the administration of President Washington, in condemnation for all the difficulties, perplexities, and disasters of the Indian war, and the British occupancy of the northwestern posts, and the procrastination of arrangements with Spain for the free navigation of the Mississippi. The virtuous and patriotic John Jay was denounced as the enemy of the West for his failure to secure greater advantages to the western people in his treaty with England and Spain.† A convention was likewise invited, "for the purpose of deliberating on the steps which will be most expedient for the attainment and security of our just rights."‡

The enterprise of Genet was wholly frustrated by the recall of the French minister, and the active efforts of the Federal authorities in suppressing any attempt to continue his schemes. Thus ended the exciting period of French intrigue in the West. The people of Kentucky, and of the West generally, were soon afterward officially informed that the Federal government had opened an active and pressing negotiation with the Spanish minister for the speedy adjustment of existing difficulties relative to the free navigation of the Mississippi. With this assurance of the energetic action of the Federal government in their behalf, the public mind became quieted, and harmony was restored to the country.§

In the mean time, the population of Kentucky had continued to increase rapidly under the new state government; the people were making rapid advances in wealth, manufactures, and commerce, no less than in arts, sciences, and intellectual refinement. The new state, which had been the theatre of strife and discord, now rose proudly in her station as the first independent state in the Valley of the Mississippi, the foster-mother of the rising empire of the West.

* Butler's Kentucky, p. 226, 227.
† Mr. Jay, in his negotiations with the Spanish minister, had entertained the proposition of surrendering the navigation of the Mississippi for twenty or thirty years, while the western settlements were comparatively small, in consideration of a free and unrestricted navigation of the river after the expiration of that period.
‡ Butler, p. 235.   § Idem, p. 228.

The first Legislature in 1793 had laid off and organized three additional counties. These were the "counties of Washington, Scott, and Shelby," the first named in honor of the President of the United States, and the father of his country; the others in honor of the two prominent defenders of Kentucky, General Charles Scott and Colonel Isaac Shelby.

In the spring of 1794 the "counties of Greene and Hardin" were laid off and organized. They were named in honor of General Nathaniel Greene, a distinguished officer of the Revolutionary war, and of Colonel Hardin, a distinguished officer of the western army, who fell a sacrifice to Indian revenge on his way to negotiate for peace with the hostile tribes in 1792.*

In the winter of 1794 the "counties of Franklin, Christian, and Campbell" were laid off, and named in honor of the patriotic philosopher Benjamin Franklin, and two prominent defenders of Kentucky, Colonel Christian, a noted and gallant defender of southwestern Virginia, and Colonel Campbell of North Carolina, who was also one of the first proprietors of Transylvania.

Colonel Christian was a veteran of the Revolution, and had distinguished himself early in the war by his noted invasion of the Cherokee country upon the sources of the Holston River in December, 1776. Having distinguished himself in defense of the western frontier of Virginia, at the close of the Revolutionary war he retired to Kentucky, and settled upon the waters of Bear-grass Creek, where he was killed by a party of Indians in April, 1785.†

The Legislature, at the next session, laid off and organized the "county of Floyd," which was named in honor of Colonel John Floyd, one of the most enterprising of the early pioneers of Kentucky.

During the Indian war which was prosecuted by the Federal government against the northwestern tribes in the years 1793 and 1794, Kentucky furnished nearly sixteen hundred volunteers and militia, chiefly under the command of her favorite general, Charles Scott. These, co-operating with the regular troops under General Wayne, carried the American arms victoriously to the confines of the British province of Upper

---

* See Flint's History and Geography of the Mississippi Valley, vol. ii., p. 289–299, first edition. Also, chapter xi., of this book.

† See Flint's History and Geography of the Mississippi Valley, vol. ii., p. 273, first edition.

Canada, and effectually humbled the power of the savages. During all the campaigns into the northwestern territory, Kentucky had been the principal store-house for the army, and the theatre of military parade and preparation, no less than for the decisive campaign conducted by General Wayne. Many of the officers of the regular army, and hundreds of recruits, besides the militia and mounted volunteers, were citizens of Kentucky.

Kentucky continued to increase in population and wealth; organized government was gradually extended to the remote limits of the state, and new counties were laid off from the larger ones as the population multiplied and the settlements reached into the unoccupied portions of the state. Each new county formed was designated by the name of some one of the early pioneers and defenders, who were occasionally leaving the stage of action; and to this day her ninety counties are so many monuments perpetuating the memory of the most prominent founders of the state.*

The population by the census of the United States in 1790 was 73,677 souls, including 12,430 slaves. The emigration of ten years augmented the number to 220,960 souls, including 40,343 slaves. This number in ten years more had increased to 406,511 souls in 1810, including 80,560 slaves. The increase of population continued rapid for thirty years more, although in a diminished ratio. The census of 1820 gave the population at 564,317 souls; that of 1830 at 688,884 souls, of whom 165,350 were slaves. The census of 1840 gave the entire pop-

---

* The governors of Kentucky are as follows:

1. Isaac Shelby, from 1792 to 1796, September.
2. James Garrard, from 1796 to 1804, September.
3. Christopher Greenup, from 1804 to 1808, September.
4. Charles Scott, from 1808 to 1812, September.
5. Isaac Shelby, from 1812 to 1816, September.
6. George Madison, from 1816.
7. Gabriel Slaughter, from 1816 to 1820, acting governor.
8. John Adair, from 1820 to 1824, September.
9. Joseph Desha, from 1824 to 1828, September.
10. Thomas Metcalfe, from 1828 to 1832, September.
11. John Breathitt, from 1832 to 1835, September.
12. James T. Morehead, from 1835 to 1836, acting governor.
13. James Clark, from 1836 to 1839: died September 27, 1839.
14. Charles A. Wickliffe, from 1839 to 1840, acting governor.
15. Robert P. Letcher, from 1840 to 1844, September.
16. William Ousley, from 1844 to 1848, September.

—*Bradford's Illustrated Atlas*, p. 124 and *American Almanac for* 1845.

ulation at 779,828 souls, including 182,258 slaves.* The state contained hundreds of large towns and villages. Louisville, the chief commercial city, contained a population of more than twenty-one thousand inhabitants, and Lexington, an inland city, contained nearly seven thousand.

CHAPTER VII.

THE EARLY SETTLEMENT AND POLITICAL CONDITION OF WESTERN PENNSYLVANIA.—A.D. 1783 TO 1796.

Argument.—Jurisdiction of Pennsylvania extended to the Ohio. — "Westmoreland County" organized.—"Washington County" organized.—Emigration to the Monongahela and Youghiogeny.—Town of Pittsburgh laid out.—Brownsville laid out; becomes an important Point.—First Newspaper in the West.—Pittsburgh becomes a Market Town in 1788.—Trade and Manufactures spring up.—It derives great Importance as a military Dépôt in 1790.—Prosperous Condition of Settlements on the Monongahela.—Pittsburgh becomes an important manufacturing and trading Town. —Agricultural Prosperity of Monongahela Settlements.—Effects of Spanish Restrictions on the Mississippi.—"Excise Law" odious.—Disaffection toward Federal Government.—French Influence in the West.—Resistance to Excise on Whisky.—Difficulties encountered by excise Officers.—General Neville appointed Superintendent of excise Customs.—His moral Worth and Popularity insufficient to sustain him.— His House burned by a Mob.—Other Outrages perpetrated by the Mob.—Character of the Insurgents.—A Meeting of the Militia.—A Convention proposed.—Measures adopted by the President of the United States.—Proposed Amnesty.—Convention at Parkinson's Ferry.—Alarm of the insurgent Leaders.—Effects of General Wayne's Victory on the Maumee.—Commissioners appointed by the President.—Troops levied to suppress the Insurrection.—Fourteen thousand Troops advance to Pittsburgh. —The Insurrection is suppressed.—Insurgents dispersed.—Inquisitorial Court established.—Three hundred Insurgents arrested.—The Troops discharged.—Pittsburgh incorporated in 1794.—Quietude of Frontiers, and Advance of Population.—Uninhabited Region west of Alleghany River.—Emigration encouraged.—"Population Company."—Their Grant. — State Grants to actual Settlers. — Conflict of State Grants with the Company's Privileges.—First Paper Mill on the Monongahela.—Manufactures increase.

[A.D. 1783.] WE have already remarked, that in the early settlement of the country west of the mountains, before the close of the Revolutionary war, the northern and southern limits of Virginia were not clearly defined and known. Virginia, however, was prompt in asserting her right to all the territory which was supposed to lie within her chartered limits on the west. It was not until the year 1780 that her southern boundary, separating her from North Carolina, had been surveyed from the mountains westward to the Mississippi.

* See Guthrie's Geography, vol. ii., p. 451. Smith's Gazetteer of the United States, p. 320.

Her northern boundary next to Pennsylvania had not been properly ascertained and designated until several years afterward.

Previous to running this line, Virginia had claimed, and had exercised, jurisdiction over Western Pennsylvania as far north as Fort Pitt, which was claimed as a post of the Old Dominion. Emigrants from Virginia and Maryland had formed settlements, and had introduced their slave property, believing themselves within the jurisdiction of Virginia. Hundreds of the best citizens, who had settled on the Youghiogeny and Monongahela Rivers, afterward finding themselves in Pennsylvania by the line of demarkation, were compelled to retire, with their slaves, to Western Virginia and to Kentucky, where they would be protected in their property by the laws of Virginia.

After the southern line of Pennsylvania had been fully designated, the Legislature proceeded to organize the country thus detached from Virginia into two counties, called Westmoreland and Washington. Westmoreland county extended from the mountains westward to the Alleghany River, including the town of Pittsburgh and all the country between the Kiskeminetas and the Youghiogeny. North of this was the Indian territory, in the possession of the native tribes. Washington county comprised all south and west of Pittsburgh, including all the country east and west of the Monongahela, now comprised in the counties of Washington, Green, Alleghany, and Fayette.

[A.D. 1784.] After the close of the Revolutionary war, the tide of immigration set with double force into the region west of the mountains. Besides hundreds of families who had suffered in their fortunes by the war, there were thousands of soldiers and officers of the Continental army, who, now disbanded, were compelled to seek homes in the West, and provide for their growing families.

As late as the year 1784, Fort Pitt was a frontier post, and the region contiguous was quite unprotected. The Indian tribes occupied the country on the north and west, and their numbers and prowess rendered them terrible to the weak settlements. The town of Pittsburgh, which had sprung up near the fort, was a frontier trading place, frequented by hundreds of friendly Indians in time of peace, eager to barter their furs, skins, and bear's grease for the rude staples of a trader's stock of goods. The Alleghany River was the Indian boundary, and in time of peace the Indian trade brought to the town hundreds of canoes and pirogues, by means of which a regular intercourse was maintained with remote towns in the country still in possession of the natives.

After the jurisdiction of Pennsylvania was formally extended over the southwestern portion of the state in the organization of counties, population began to press forward into the most exposed points contiguous to the Indian boundary, and the village of Pittsburgh now assumed the form of a regular American town. It was in the month of May, 1784, that Colonel George Woods, agent for the proprietors and heirs of William Penn, to whom the land belonged, as a portion of one of the manors of the original grantee, first surveyed and laid out the regular plan of a town, which was called Pittsburgh.*

About the same time, the settlement at "Red Stone Old Fort" had become an important point of embarkation for emigrants to Kentucky, and bid fair to be the future seat of trade for the western country. In the spring of the same year, Thomas and Basil Brown, from Maryland, having purchased the claim formerly belonging to Captain Michael Cresap, including the "Old Fort," deemed it a suitable point for a town. In May, 1785, they laid off a plot near the "Old Fort," and called it by its present name of "Brownsville."† Thus began the oldest town on the Monongahela.

[A.D. 1785.] The situation of this place, as the point to which nearly the whole western emigration concentrated previous to its descent of the Ohio, soon gave to Brownsville a trade and importance unknown then to any town in the West. Before the close of the year 1786, its population had increased to five hundred souls.‡ Many of these were engaged in the mechanic arts which contribute chiefly to boat-building, and supply the rude necessaries for barge and flat-boat navigation. Emigrants who designed taking water at Wheeling, where the voyage to Kentucky would be shortened one hundred and sixty miles, were still obliged to take Brownsville in their route, and here supply themselves for their future journey. This produced a necessity for mercantile houses, provided with the articles indispensable to the emigrants.

---

* Pittsburgh Navigator for 1814. Also, American Pioneer, vol. i., p. 302–308.
† Pioneer, vol. ii., p. 62.   ‡ Idem, vol. i., p. 305.

Heretofore the western settlers had been compelled to send their annual "caravans" across the mountains to Fort Cumberland, Hagerstown, Fredericktown, or some other point, for all their supplies, which were transported upon pack-horses several hundred miles to the West. But this usage was now about to cease, and be superseded by regular commercial houses at Brownsville, which could supply the emigrants with implements of agriculture, provisions, salt, iron, and other articles indispensable in a new country.

[A.D. 1787.] By the following year, several mercantile houses were established, and supplied with goods hauled in wagons across the mountains from Forts Cumberland and Ligonier. These tended to give additional importance to Brownsville, as a point of embarkation for the West. Emigrants could carry money with less inconvenience than the heavy articles for which they could exchange it at the end of their journey. Of course, money would seek its way to the West, instead of being carried to the East.

A good wagon road had been opened to Brownsville from the East, and a regular line of freight-wagons from Baltimore and Fredericktown had been established, each wagon making the trip to Brownsville and back, with full loads, once a month. The cost of transportation over this route was generally three dollars per hundred weight, and the great numbers of emigrants to the West soon opened a profitable commerce between these remote points. The same cause soon made Brownsville one of the most active trading and manufacturing towns in the West. The demand for mechanics and manufacturers of a certain class brought great numbers of adventurers from the East in search of profitable employment. The great demand was for carpenters and boat-builders, to supply conveyance for the hundreds of emigrants who arrived every week, seeking boats of all kinds for the voyage to Kentucky and Western Virginia, as well as to the Northwestern Territory. The boat-building and the boating business soon became an important branch of western enterprise. Hundreds of arks, keels, barges, and every variety of boats, kept up a constant intercourse between the Monongahela and the settlements on the Ohio below, and also with the city of New Orleans, and the rich settlements on the Lower Mississippi.*

* See American Pioneer, vol. ii., p. 62, 63.

In the mean time, Pittsburgh had been rapidly increasing its population and business. Already a printing-office had been established by John Scull and Joseph Hall, two industrious young men, who had embarked their whole means in the enterprise. On the 29th of July, 1786, they had issued the first number of the "Pittsburgh Gazette," and the first newspaper printed west of the mountains,* and more than a year before the first newspaper was printed in Kentucky. It was not until March, 1787, that a town meeting in Pittsburgh first resolved to establish a weekly market, and to erect a market-house.

[A.D. 1788.] As late as the year 1788, Pittsburgh was a small frontier town, thirty miles distant from the county seat of Westmoreland county, to which it pertained. Hannahstown was the county seat, to which the people of Pittsburgh had to repair on county business, twelve miles east of Chestnut Ridge. On the 24th of September of that year they were released from these journeys by the organization of "Alleghany county," taken from Westmoreland and Washington counties. From that time Pittsburgh became the county seat for Alleghany county,† and began to assume importance as a trading and manufacturing town; mercantile and trading establishments began to appear, mechanics flocked to it for employment, and manufactures and trade began to extend. The inhabitants on the Monongahela and Yough had already found agriculture a profitable employment; and the produce of their fields, in the form of flour, whisky, and other surplus products of a new country, had already passed Pittsburgh, and found its way down the Ohio and Mississippi to New Orleans. A new class of hardy pioneers, under the name of "boatmen," now sprang up, who carried the products of the Monongahela and its tributaries to the more recent settlements of Kentucky, and to the Spanish provinces of Louisiana and West Florida. Thus commenced the first regular trade between Pittsburgh and New Orleans.

Manufactures had already begun to flourish in Western Pennsylvania. Iron had been found in great abundance from its first settlement, and the great demand for it, connected with the difficulty of transporting it from the east side of the mountains, soon prompted the erection of furnaces and iron-works. The first blast-furnace west of the mountains was "Union Fur-

---

* American Pioneer, vol. i., p. 305.   † Idem, p. 306.

GROUND PLAN OF "FORT PITT" AND "FORT DUQUESNE."

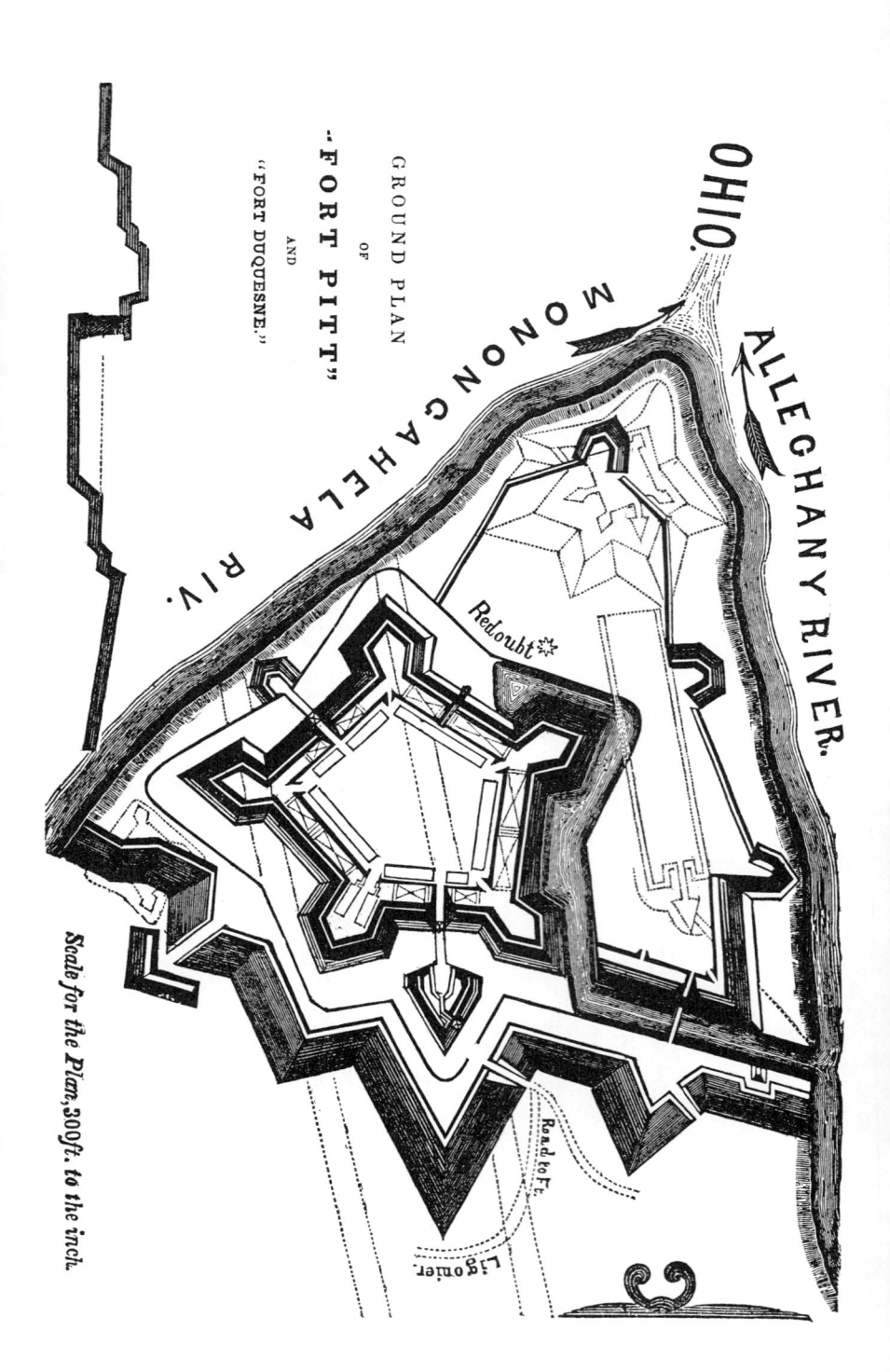

OHIO.

MONONGAHELA RIV.

ALLEGHANY RIVER.

Redoubt

Road to Ft. Ligonier

Scale for the Plan, 300 ft. to the inch.

nace," on Dunbar Creek, fifteen miles east of Brownsville. It was erected by Colonel Isaac Meason, John Gibson, and Moses Dillon. The increasing population in the West, and especially in Kentucky, created a demand which caused others to spring up in different sections of the country. Forges were erected for the manufacture of bar iron. A few years elapsed, when more than twenty forges were in operation upon the waters of the Monongahela.* As these multiplied, they gave rise to every variety of factories for the manufacture of iron into the implements of husbandry, house-building, and all the mechanic arts. Excellent mills and machinery of all kinds, propelled by water power, were early introduced upon all the branches of the Yough, from its sources near the Laurel Hill to its junction with the Monongahela. The same valuable manufactories had extended down Cheat River, from its sources near the Alleghany range in Virginia down the Monongahela to Brownsville.

[A.D. 1789.] Notwithstanding the treaties concluded by the United States with the northwestern tribes of Indians in the year 1785–86, they became impatient of the advance of the whites upon the Ohio and Alleghany Rivers. Settlements had already been made upon the west side of the Ohio, and the natives plainly foresaw their approaching destruction. For several years past lawless bands of savages had infested the Ohio River, committing frequent murders and robberies upon the emigrants, who were continually descending the river to Kentucky. The main body of the tribes had scarcely refrained from similar acts of hostility; and now these aggressions, on the part of the Indians, had become so frequent and audacious, that it was evident that a general hostile movement of the savages against the advancing settlements was contemplated. To avoid any such occurrence, negotiations had been resorted to ineffectually, and the Federal government had resolved to invade the Indian country with a strong military force.

[A.D. 1790.] At length, early in the year 1790, troops began to advance from the east by way of Bedford and Cumberland, and to concentrate at Fort Pitt, as a general rendezvous and dépôt for military stores and munitions of war, preparatory to an invasion of the Indian country west of the Ohio.† It was at this time that the town of Pittsburgh began to assume a de-

* See American Pioneer, vol. ii., p. 64. † Idem, p. 59–62.

gree of importance heretofore unknown. It became the general store-house for all the western posts, and the grand dépôt for the western army. It was also the point at which military supplies were procured, and where the principal disbursements of public moneys was made for the use of the army, as well as the distribution of annuities and supplies for the friendly Indian tribes.

[A.D. 1791.] As yet the Alleghany River was the remote frontier limit of the Pennsylvania settlements, and all its northwestern tributaries were wholly within the Indian country. A few settlements had been made near the river for forty miles above Pittsburgh by the more fearless and inconsiderate. But they paid with their lives the forfeit of their temerity. The whole of these settlements were broken up about the 9th of February, 1791, soon after the outbreak of the Indian war. On that day the settlements were simultaneously assailed and exterminated by one hundred and fifty warriors, distributed in bands assigned for the extermination of their respective neighborhoods. The settlements in this quarter were entirely broken up; some were killed, some were taken prisoners, and others escaped with their lives.*

[A.D. 1792.] Notwithstanding all the difficulties encountered in the West, the settlements on the Yough and Monongahela, comprised in the western portions of Pennsylvania and Virginia, had become prosperous and enterprising. They had extended arts and manufactures, and were rapidly increasing in numbers. The manufacture of iron had become extensive; smelting-furnaces, forges, and founderies existed in every important settlement, and the hills yielded abundance of ore. Agriculture had increased, until scarcity and want had been driven from the settlements, and the Ohio formed a magnificent outlet for their surplus products of all kinds to the new settlements, which were rapidly extending into Kentucky and the northwestern territory. Such was the abundance of the agricultural products and of manufactures, that the new settlements on the lower tributaries of the Ohio failed to afford an adequate market, and the more enterprising extended their trading voyages to the rich settlements of Spain on the Lower Mississippi. Thus a commerce, which had first sprung up in 1786, in five years had become an important item in the prosperity

* See American Pioneer, vol. i., p. 40–43.

of Western Pennsylvania. To diminish the proportionate cost of transportation for corn, rye, and other grains and products, these articles were converted into whisky, which could be sent to all parts of the world through the great avenue of the Ohio and Mississippi. Thus the value of thousands of bushels of these grains were contained in the small bulk of a few barrels of whisky, and an equal quantity was withdrawn from the grain-market. The fame of their favorite drink, "Old Monongahela," extended not only to the whole western settlements, but also to New Orleans, the Atlantic States, and to Europe. Horses, cattle, and blooded stock from the Atlantic seaboard had been introduced upon the Monongahela, and had also become an important item of western trade for the supply of the new settlements lower down the Ohio, in the Northwestern Territory, and those of Louisiana. Rude castings of all descriptions, cutlery of every variety, adapted to the use of new settlements, such as axes, hoes, drawing-knives, carpenters' tools, knives and forks, scythe-blades, reaping-hooks, and the like, were made in great abundance for the supply of the extending settlements. Navigation on the Ohio assumed an importance hitherto unknown. Besides the endless variety of small craft, and the rude arks, or "Kentucky flats," numerous well-built keel-boats, barges, and some sea vessels were conveying the produce of this region to every portion of the Ohio region; and, in return from Louisiana, supplying the commercial points with the products of the West Indies and the specie of Mexico by way of New Orleans.

It was in the year 1792 that the Spanish authorities began to embarrass this trade by the imposition of transit and port duties, which greatly reduced the profits, and sometimes resulted in the entire loss of vessel and cargo by confiscation. The western people, conscious that the free navigation of the Mississippi would greatly promote their prosperity and extend the field of their enterprise, had vainly looked to the Federal government for relief from the Spanish imposts and the arbitrary exactions of a despotic government. They expected from the Federal government, through commercial treaties with Spain, an exemption from duties upon a river, the use of which they claimed as a natural right, growing out of their relative situation and occupancy. In these respects, their condition was identical with the settlements upon the great southern tributaries of the Ohio.

[A.D. 1793.] The prevalence of eastern influence in Congress and in the cabinet of the United States was strong, and swayed the national policy as to measures affecting the western people, and these measures operated no less perniciously upon them than if they had been prompted by interested jealousy in the Atlantic States. The Spanish authorities of Louisiana had been permitted for years to obstruct and embarrass the river trade, which fell heavy upon the people of Western Pennsylvania, as well as upon those of Kentucky and Cumberland, while the commerce of the Atlantic ports was favored with a more liberal policy; and, as if to increase their burdens, Congress, in 1790, had passed a law imposing excise duties upon all spirituous liquors distilled in the United States, when it was well known that the most extensive and most important distilleries were those on the waters of the Monongahela, where the surplus grain was worthless unless it could be converted into whisky and other distilled spirits.

Besides these disadvantages, the whole burden of the Indian war, which had been improvidently planned and injudiciously conducted for more than three years, had fallen chiefly upon the western settlements. While these things were operating to weaken the ties which bound the western people to those east of the mountains, the Spanish authorities of Louisiana, sagaciously perceiving the error of the Federal government, lost no opportunity to augment the embarrassments and stimulate the discontent, while they held out in prospect ultimate relief from the Spanish crown, by a separation from the Federal Union and an alliance with Louisiana. Congress beheld the cloud in the West: the loud murmurs from the commercial classes, the open denunciations from the exposed frontiers, the spirit of insurrection in the grain districts against the iniquitous excise, convinced the Federal government that they were daily losing the confidence of the western people, and absolving them from their allegiance.

The Indian war had been waged with but little success for some time, and at great expense to the general government. The war was for the protection of the western people especially, and more particularly for those of Western Pennsylvania and Virginia. These people were the principal sufferers from Indian barbarity and revenge. They, too, were called on chiefly to fill the ranks of the armies which had been sent against the savages, until they began loudly to complain of the burdens which were thrown upon them, while the East reaped the advantages of their labors. The western people, although ardent friends of the Federal Union, could not submit to oppression by an unjust exercise of Federal power, and the attempt to enforce it roused them to resistance.

The impost upon whisky, distilled from grain in a country where grain was a surplus article, was tantamount to a tax upon grain itself, and operated oppressively upon the West. In the eastern counties and Atlantic States grain was *not a surplus* product; of course, but little of it could be distilled into spirits; consequently, the tax fell entirely upon the western people, who were otherwise embarrassed in their commerce. The enforcement of the law for collecting the revenue was considered as indicative of a disposition in the Federal government to usurp the powers of the states toward the formation of a consolidated government, whose controlling power would be east of the mountains.

The western people had become prejudiced against the Federal government, not only because the frontier settlements had been left for years exposed to Indian hostilities, almost unprotected by the national power from 1787 to 1790, but because the protection extended subsequently had been ineffectual, and had resulted in two disgraceful defeats, with the loss of many lives and great expense, without any equivalent advantage, chiefly for want of a liberal appropriation by Congress. Another cause of discontent, closely connected with Indian depredations, was the temporizing policy of the Federal government with the court of St. James, in permitting the continued occupancy of the western posts, for more than ten years after the time stipulated for their delivery, agreeably to the treaty of 1783. The whole Indian war had been the result of intrigue between agents and emissaries from the British posts along the Canada frontier, whose avowed object was to check the advance of population northwest of the Ohio.

Another prominent cause of dissatisfaction in Western Pennsylvania was the inefficient policy of the Federal government in submitting to Spanish usurpations on the Mississippi, the object of which was to embarrass the western people. Not only had Spain claimed the exclusive navigation of the river, but she held possession of the country on the east bank as far north as the Chickasâ Bluffs, nearly five hundred miles by the river above the boundary established by the treaty of 1783.

To encourage the dissatisfaction of the western people on this point, French emissaries, under the authority of the French minister, Genet, were sent to the West to foment discord and to instigate a hostile expedition against the Spanish provinces, under the patronage and authority of the French Republic, which promised to open to them the free navigation of the river, when once under the dominion of France. "Democratic clubs," or societies, under French influence, were organized in many parts of the country, with the avowed object of opposing the general measures of the Federal administration in the West. Their resolutions openly denounced the excise on distilled spirits, and the acts of the government in its attempts to enforce the law. Newspapers, filled with inflammatory speeches by members of Congress favorable to the French party, were circulated with great industry through every town and settlement, while the friends of the administration, the advocates of the Federal authorities, were few and odious.

[A.D. 1794.] Such was the state of feeling in Western Pennsylvania, which had developed itself gradually and progressively for nearly four years after the passage of the law taxing distilleries, and generally known as the "excise law."

A feeling of resistance had been manifested from the first passage of the law in 1790; and the president, aware of its pernicious tendency, had recommended a modification of its obnoxious features at the next succeeding session. Congress adopted the suggestion, and modified the law in 1791. But this concession was not sufficient; it seemed rather to strengthen opposition. The people demanded its unconditional repeal, and every expedient was resorted to for the purpose of defeating its operation. Many refused to pay the duties in any form, and resistance to the Federal government already began to assume the form of rebellion. The president proceeded to enforce the law; but, as far as practicable, he omitted no opportunity to strip the law of its obnoxious features, and sought to allay excitement and to conciliate opposition by the influence and popularity of those who were charged with its execution.

For this purpose, General John Neville was appointed collector for Western Pennsylvania, and he accepted the appointment from a sense of public duty. He accepted, however, at the hazard of his life and the loss of all his property; for he became the object of public indignation and the victim of an incensed community. All his former Revolutionary services, and his well-known benevolence and charity to the suffering frontier people for years past, were insufficient to shield him from popular indignation.

General Neville had been one of the most zealous patriots of the Revolution, a man of great wealth and unbounded benevolence. From his own resources alone, he had organized, equipped, and supplied a company of troops, including his son as an officer, which he had marched at his own expense to Boston, to re-enforce the command of General Washington in support of the Declaration of Independence. During the "starving years" of the early settlements on the Upper Ohio and Monongahela, he had contributed greatly to the relief and comfort of the destitute and suffering pioneers; and, when necessary, he had divided his last loaf with the needy. In seasons of more than ordinary scarcity, when his wheat matured, he had opened his fields to those who were destitute of bread. By blood and marriage he was related to some of the most distinguished officers of the Revolutionary armies; and such was his popularity in the West, that, had it been possible for any one to have enforced this odious law, General Neville was the man.

Having entered upon the duties of his office as collector, he appointed his deputies from among the most popular of his fellow-citizens, who proceeded to execute the law. But the first attempts were resisted. They were warned to desist, and to resign their thankless office. Some of the deputies, disregarding this admonition, were seized by the mob, and invested with "a coat of tar and feathers;" others were compelled to surrender their commissions, as the only condition of safety.

The malcontents soon proceeded to acts of open violence. Simple resistance assumed the attitude of revolt and insurrection. A mob of several hundred men proceeded to the house of General Neville and demanded the surrender of his commission; but, finding his house defended by ample force, they retired without violence. Believing that there was in the country sufficient patriotism to enable the civil authorities to sustain him and protect him in the discharge of his official duties, he continued to maintain his position. But he was mistaken:

the magistrates, who are but the emanations of popular will, as the ministers of civil liberty, were powerless in resisting the current of public displeasure. Their authority in support of the obnoxious law was set at defiance.

In the mean time, the feeling of excitement continued to increase in violence, and spread into every section of the country, and the civil authorities were utterly powerless in restraining the progress of disorder and outrage. Public meetings were held by the disaffected at Pittsburg, Brownsville, Parkinson's Ferry, "Braddock's Fields," and other places.

Many who never designed to resist the laws of the country had indirectly aided in raising a political storm which they could neither allay nor direct. The western country for many years had been receiving a large increase of population from Irish emigrants, no strangers to popular outbreaks in their native country. There was also a floating population, who had found employment heretofore in guarding the frontiers from Indian incursions, or as supernumeraries attached to the campaigns during the Indian wars, who were fond of excitement and commotion. These, as they could lose nothing by insurrection, swelled the amount of the insurgents, and their numbers gave a preponderance in favor of violent measures, against the wishes of those who were more considerate. Organized resistance to law was formed. Public meetings were held in all the malcontent districts, and officers were appointed to take the lead. Several hundred men volunteered to take General Neville into immediate custody. His friends in Pittsburgh devised plans for his protection; but it was the strength of a few men to arrest the advance of the avalanche. His house was protected by an armed guard of fifteen regular soldiers; but on the 15th of July, 1794, it was surrounded by five hundred men, organized into a lawless mob.

On the approach of the insurgents, the general, with his servant, had consented to retire from the mob. They advanced, and demanded the surrender of the general and his papers. The refusal brought on a contest, and some were killed. The outbuildings were set on fire; and the party within the splendid mansion house surrendered, to prevent its destruction. But it was in vain; the demon was unchained, and the hospitable mansion was consumed to ashes, in the view of hundreds who had shared his bounty or had enjoyed his benevolence. Insubordination walked abroad at noon-day; all law was disregarded; the peaceable and orderly members of society became obnoxious to the enraged mob and their adherents. The mail was boldly robbed, and disclosed letters which added new victims to the lawless rage. The United States marshal was compelled to escape for his life down the Ohio.

Soon afterward, a public meeting of the militia was called by the insurgents at "Braddock's Fields," and seven or eight thousand obeyed the summons. Resolutions were passed, and a committee was appointed to consult and devise measures for future action. Without a resolute and able chief, no plan of operation could be adopted; and after various efforts to act, the discordant materials of the faction began to lose its cohesive properties, and dissolution followed soon afterward. Law and order once more resumed the sway, and the guilty dreaded the recompense of their deeds. The subject was referred to a convention of delegates from the several towns for a decision as to future proceedings.*

In the mean time, the President of the United States, reluctant to use the force of arms in quelling the insurrection, had sent three commissioners to the western country, to offer pardon from the general government to all offenders who should return to their duty and peaceably submit to the law. These commissioners reached the region of disaffection about the time the convention were to meet at "Parkinson's Ferry," now Williamsport, on the Monongahela.

Among the delegates to the convention were men of distinguished ability, at the head of whom was Albert Gallatin. Although a foreigner, who could with difficulty make himself understood in the English language, yet he presented with great force the folly and danger of past resistance, and the ruinous consequences which must result from a continuance of the insurrectionary movements. He showed that the government was bound to vindicate the laws, and that an overwhelming force would be marched against them unless the offered amnesty was accepted. The insurrection by him was placed in a new light; it was shown to be a matter of much more serious import than had been apprehended. The ardor of the most reckless was abated; the commissioners of the government were admitted to a conference; in an earnest discussion

* American Pioneer, vol. ii., p. 206–210.

relative to a submission to the laws, a strong disposition was manifested to accept the proffered amnesty. Some of the leaders of the rebellion already began to tremble for the consequences. The Democratic clubs of Paris did not work so well in the western country; and, for the permanent citizens, mob-law, executed by a set of desperadoes, had proved an indifferent substitute for law regularly administered.*

Many had seen their folly, and would gladly return to their allegiance, but to retrace their steps was no easy matter. The Federal government might grant an amnesty, but they had incurred a fearful state of responsibility to their fellow-citizens and neighbors; violence against individual property and personal rights might meet a fearful retribution in the state courts. A dissolution of the Union had been agitated in the West; many were anxious to throw themselves under the protection of Spain or of France, if she resumed dominion in Louisiana. Spanish emissaries and agents of the Jacobins of France were encouraging disaffection in Kentucky and Tennessee. The British emissaries from Canada had likewise been through the western country, to ascertain the tone of public feeling.

The convention were in favor of submission; but they had not been authorized by their constituents to make any terms with the general government. They declined to act, and referred the question back to the primary town meetings.

Early in September, the country was electrified with the news of General Wayne's victory on the Maumee. The combined army of the hostile horde, and their English and Canadian allies, had been signally defeated in sight of a British fortress. The danger of Indian barbarity was over; the general government had triumphed in the arduous warfare with the indomitable savage tribes; could not this victorious army, released from foreign wars, quell the discontent of a disorganized mob at home? Be this as it may, the general government began to acquire respect and consequence among those who lately had defied its power.

The primary meetings were held near the middle of September. Resistance was no longer advocated, except by a few desperate men. The terms of submission proposed by the commissioners were printed, and distributed widely through the country. They were carried to the primary meetings, and

* See American Pioneer, vol. ii., p. 210, 211.

were signed by hundreds, who gladly accepted the proffered amnesty. The leading insurgents were deserted, discouraged, and powerless; the first of October hailed the restoration of peace and order.*

The disorganized malcontents still were sufficiently numerous to make a show of resistance, and to produce some annoyance to the tranquillity of the country. The Federal government had made active preparations to subdue the rebels by force of arms, while overtures of peace were tendered to them. Already a powerful army of fourteen thousand militia, assembled from Virginia, Maryland, New Jersey, and Pennsylvania, was on its march to the western counties of Pennsylvania. The army proceeded to Pittsburgh, and there encamped. Not a shadow of resistance was shown, and the last remains of disaffection disappeared. Bradford and a few obnoxious chiefs fled to the Spanish dominions on the Mississippi, and others to the remote settlements of the West.

An inquisitorial court was opened by General Hamilton on the part of the government, and informers flocked in by hundreds, of whom many had suffered severely from the insurgents. At length a catalogue of names was completed and handed over to a captain of dragoons, who found no lack of guides in making his arrests. A few days sufficed to place under military guard about three hundred prisoners for further examination.

The intercession of influential friends procured the discharge of many; but others, less fortunate, were detained in custody and sent to Philadelphia for trial. Some were there detained in prison for several months, and finally discharged. One individual was tried, convicted, and sentenced to death for robbing the mail, but was ultimately pardoned. Thus terminated this first resistance to the laws of the country by a regularly organized insurrection.†

The main body of the army soon afterward took up the line of march for their homes; some, at their request, were paid off and discharged at Pittsburgh. A few battalions were retained on duty through the winter. To keep down any germs of insurrectionary spirit, the government ordered the enlistment of a regiment of dragoons, to serve six months, and to be composed of such persons as were well disposed to the govern-

* See American Pioneer, vol. ii., p. 212.   † Idem, p. 212, 213

ment. Portions of this troop were kept in constant motion from point to point, or in attending the excise officers in their visits.

In the mean time, the inhabitants of the western settlements had been gradually and steadily increasing. Pittsburgh had acquired much importance by reason of the arrival and departure of the United States troops and military stores. The population was now one thousand souls, and the Legislature at its last session had incorporated it as a regular borough, by an act approved April 22d, 1794. The same year a settlement at Presque Isle had been abandoned, in order to conciliate the Indians.* It was again settled two years afterward.

[A.D. 1795.] The decisive victory of the Maumee over the combined savages and their English allies had restored the frontiers to quietude and safety. Confidence was renewed, and emigrants again began to press forward; settlements became more dense; trade and manufactures began to flourish, and prosperity smiled upon the country. About the close of this year Pittsburgh presented a population of fourteen hundred souls.†

Yet the country northwest of the Alleghany River was still an uninhabited wilderness, and its contiguity to the warlike tribes near the lakes formed but little inducement to immigrants more securely located. To procure the occupancy of this region, the state government deemed it expedient to hold out strong temptations to the poor settler as well as to the rich capitalist. Among the first measures adopted for this purpose was the grant, or the right of entering or locating a large body of lands, designated in the act of the Legislature, to a number of capitalists who had assumed the name of the "Population Company." The principal condition required of this company was, that within a certain time they should place upon every tract of four hundred acres so located at least one able-bodied settler, and cause to be made certain slight preemption improvements.

The company, to induce immigrants to settle their lands, proposed to grant in fee simple to every such settler one hundred and fifty acres of land, provided he should comply with the requisitions imposed on them. Thus the settler would secure for himself one hundred and fifty acres of land, including

* Writings of Washington, vol. xii., p. 52.   † Pioneer, vol. i., p. 306.

his improvement, while the "company," through him, would secure two hundred and fifty acres more.

Soon afterward, the Legislature passed an act giving to the individual settler, for the same improvements, four hundred acres, the same amount previously allowed to the "company." This interfered with the company's plan of aggrandizement, and was deemed by them an infringement of "vested rights." Immigrants, of course, would prefer to receive four hundred acres from the state, rather than one hundred and fifty acres from the company. The company's grants were slowly taken up; each settler made his improvement for himself, and not for the company, and some incautiously made their improvements within the district which had been appropriated exclusively to the "Population Company."

Settlements progressed in this manner for some time, when the agents of the company commenced suits of ejectment against the state settlers who had encroached upon their privilege. At length the latter harassed with suits and the expenses of litigation, and being utterly unable singly to contend with a moneyed company, voluntarily abandoned their habitations and retired westward into the "Connecticut Reserve." Here no lands were given away; but it was sold for a reasonable price, and the title was indisputable to such amounts and tracts as purchasers desired.* This is a specimen of the beauties of companies and vested rights, and their proneness to interfere with the general prosperity.

[A.D. 1796.] In the mean time, manufactures and arts had greatly multiplied since the treaty of Greenville. Trade began to stand upon a firm basis, and capital was freely invested. The first paper-mill west of the mountains was erected this year, within four miles of Brownsville. This was the "Redstone paper-mills," owned by Samuel Jackson and Jonathan Sharpless, two Quaker mechanics from "Gilpin's paper-mills," on Brandywine Creek.†

* Pioneer, vol. ii., p. 368–370.   † Ibidem.

CHAPTER VIII.

INDIAN RELATIONS AND TREATIES WITH THE UNITED STATES, FROM THE TREATY OF PARIS TO THE "TREATY OF GREENVILLE."—A.D. 1783 TO 1795.

Argument.—Retrospect relative to the Northwestern Boundary.—Reluctantly assented to in the Treaty of 1783 by Great Britain.—Disregard of Treaty Stipulations relative to the Northwestern Posts by British Cabinet.—British and Indian Alliance during the Revolutionary War.—Western Feeling toward the Indians.—Jealousy of the Indians at the rapid Advance of the White Settlements.—Measures of Congress to conciliate Indian Jealousy.—Preliminary Steps for Treaties with all the Tribes.—Treaties by individual States prior to 1784.—Treaty of Fort Stanwix, and the Treaty Line.—Treaty of Fort M'Intosh, and Boundary Line.—Treaty of the Miami with the Shawanese, and their Cession of Lands.—Treaties of Hopewell with Southern Indians.—Cherokee Treaty.—Choctâ Treaty.—Chickasâ Treaty.—Extent of Country and Number of Warriors of each Nation respectively.—Dissatisfaction of the Six Nations relative to the Treaty of Fort Stanwix.—Their Grievances.—Preparations for a new Treaty.—Treaty of Fort Harmar in 1789.—The Shawanese refuse to attend.—Shawanese encouraged to Hostilities by British Traders at Detroit.—Connivance of the British Government at these Intrigues.—Hostilities commenced upon the Ohio Frontier.—Pacific Overtures of Governor St. Clair.—Unsettled Condition of the Southern Indians.—The Cherokees.—Encroachments of the Cumberland Settlements.—Treaty of Holston, July 2d, 1791.—Creek Disturbances.—Measures to conciliate the Creeks.—The Treaty of New York with M'Gillivray and other Creek Chiefs.—Efforts of Spanish Agents to embarrass the Negotiations.—M'Gillivray's Opposition.—The Creeks instigated to War.—Cherokees commence Hostilities.—Spanish Intrigue with Creeks and Cherokees.—Creek Preparation for Hostilities against Cumberland Settlements.—Bowles, a Creek Chief.—Indian Tribes generally make Overtures for Peace and Friendship after Wayne's Victory.—Treaty with Six Nations in 1794.—Treaty of Greenville in 1795, comprising all Northwestern Tribes.—Termination of Indian Wars.

[A.D. 1783.] By the treaty of Paris, September 3d, 1783, Great Britain renounced all claim to the territory of the United States south of all the great lakes, and east of the Mississippi to its sources. That power also stipulated to withdraw her troops and military garrisons, as soon as convenient, from every part of the relinquished territory. Among the most important posts held by Great Britain within the said territory were those of Niagara, Detroit, and the Miami, on the Maumee River, below the Rapids, besides other posts of minor importance upon the head waters of the Wabash.

The stipulations for this relinquishment were made with great reluctance on the part of the British government. During the greater part of the negotiations preceding the treaty, Mr.

Oswald, the British commissioner, persisted in his demands that the Ohio River should form the northwestern boundary of the United States; and it was only after every effort had failed to move Mr. Adams and Mr. Jay that he consented to adopt the present boundary through the middle of the great lakes.

[A.D. 1784.] We have already seen that, during the war of Independence, Great Britain had armed all the northwestern tribes against her revolted colonies; that her agents and emissaries had instigated all the tribes south of the lakes, and as far west as the Mississippi, to carry the scalping-knife and the tomahawk, with all the horrors of Indian warfare, upon all the frontier settlements from the Hudson River to the western parts of North Carolina and Georgia. To carry out this plan of Indian hostilities, the agents and military officers of Great Britain at her western posts were authorized to enter into treaties of alliance with the savage tribes, with stipulations to protect and defend them, and to furnish them with arms, ammunition, and all the means necessary to their hostile operations. Still further to inflame their avarice and stimulate them to deeds of blood, the agents of Great Britain were encouraged to pay a premium upon every scalp taken from the head of the colonists, whether male or female, child or adult. Such was the spirit in which England carried on the war with her colonies.

By such means, the greater portion of the "Six Nations," inhabiting the northern and western parts of New York and Pennsylvania, had been involved in hostilities with the colonies. All the tribes south of Lake Erie, embracing the Shawanese, Wyandots, Delawares, Ottawâs, Chippewas, and many smaller tribes, had been enlisted in the British interest. The hostilities which had been incessantly waged against the frontier inhabitants during the struggle for Independence, had created and kept alive in the breasts of the western people of New York, Pennsylvania, and Virginia an undying hatred and desire of revenge against those tribes, who continued their hostility after the war with Great Britain had been terminated. Compelled to contend alone with the savages, while their eastern friends were engaged with the ruthless armies of the mother country, the western people were now anxious to conciliate the Indian power, after the support and protection of England had been withdrawn.

After a persevering negotiation in behalf of the Indians as independent allies, England, by treaty, had abandoned the savages, and left them to make such terms as they could with the United States. Yet, in order to extend partial protection to them, Great Britain, in violation of her treaty with the United States, continued to hold possession of the northwestern posts, especially those of Niagara, Detroit, and Miami,* in the heart of the Indian country. From these points British agents controlled the action of the Indians, while British traders, holding a monopoly of the fur-trade, failed not, on all occasions, to instill into the dependent savages a settled hostility to the American people on the waters of the Ohio.

To conciliate the feelings of the frontier people, as well as of the hostile tribes, Congress took the subject under the earliest consideration. The necessity for some prompt action was the more evident, as the tide of emigration had begun to set westward in every direction immediately after the cessation of hostilities with Great Britain. Thousands of emigrants were pushing westward, often regardless of any claim which the Indians asserted to the territory.

The rapid immigration alone, independent of the collisions between the border settlers and the Indians, was calculated to create and foster a spirit of hostility in the native tribes, who saw in it the certain presage of their own destruction or expulsion from the country.

The same circumstances generated a similar feeling of hostility and resistance on the part of the Southern Indians, who also saw the white settlements rapidly encroaching upon their territories. The confederated tribes, who inhabited and claimed the southwestern frontier, and who were most deeply interested in the advance of the settlements from North and South Carolina, were the Cherokees and Creeks. These were powerful and warlike tribes, and had occasionally, during the war of Independence, sent bands of warriors to join the hostile tribes on the northwest. They occupied the western parts

---

* The Miami was a British post, situated on the north side of the Maumee River, about two miles below the Rapids. This fort fell under the league of Pontiac, in 1763, and its garrison was massacred. It was reoccupied during the war of the Revolution, and was discontinued at the peace of 1783; but in November of 1793, when General Wayne was advancing into the Indian country, the British troops under Colonel Hamilton reoccupied it, under orders from the commandant at Detroit. It was strongly fortified, and maintained until 1796, as a support to the Indian tribes in alliance with Great Britain.—See Marshall's Washington, vol. v., p. 569.

of both Carolinas and of Georgia, and were each able to bring at least twenty-five hundred warriors into the field in case of a general war.

In this state of things, the Federal government adopted a humane and conciliatory course of policy toward the native tribes, while it exerted its whole power and influence to restrain the western people from aggressions upon the Indian territories. Every effort was used to prevent collisions and difficulties between the frontier people and the Indians, to cultivate harmony and friendship, by the establishment of Indian agencies, by granting annuities, and by entering into treaty stipulations for the purchase of the Indian title to such lands as they were willing to relinquish. The agents of the United States and the military commandants on the frontiers were instructed and commanded to cultivate peace and friendship with all the tribes, by a strict observance of justice and forbearance toward all the natives with whom they might have intercourse. They were required strictly to enforce all the laws of Congress prohibiting lawless white men from residing in the Indian country, and from carrying on any contraband trade with them. Agencies were to be established by the general government, well supplied with articles of Indian trade, where they could obtain, at fair and reasonable prices, such articles as they might wish to purchase, free from the impositions and extortions of private traders. Messages were sent from the war department to the different agents in the Indian nations, and to the chiefs, head men, and warriors of the frontier tribes, proposing peace and amity, by the adoption of regular and formal treaties. To conciliate, and as tokens of friendship, presents were sent to influential chiefs and warriors throughout all the tribes from the western part of New York to the southern limit of Georgia.

Great Britain had claimed the sovereignty over the region south of the Ohio, comprising the present State of Kentucky, in virtue of the cession made by the Six Nations, in the treaty of Fort Stanwix, on the Mohawk River, in the year 1768. This claim was never recognized by the Chickasâs and Cherokees, the real owners of the country, who denied the right of the Six Nations to make such cession. As the cession, if ever made, was a fraud upon the true owners of the soil, and was never intended by the Six Nations, the confederated states individually, as well as Congress, declined to set up any claim on the score of the British treaty.*

The Creeks were a powerful confederacy, inhabiting the western parts of Georgia, upon the head waters of the Savannah, Oconee, Ocmulgee, and Chattahoochy Rivers. This confederacy had maintained a hostile attitude during the whole of the war of Independence, and the states of South Carolina and Georgia had conducted the Indian wars and treaties in this region up to the termination of hostilities by Great Britain. During this time, several treaties with those Indians had been made by those states, and certain cessions of territory had been obtained from them.

Yet a large portion of the southern part of Kentucky had been disposed of by the Cherokees to Colonel Henderson and company by the treaty of Watauga in March, 1775. At the close of the Revolutionary war, the State of North Carolina obtained from the Chickasâs, in a treaty held by Colonels Donaldson and Martin, near the present site of Nashville, in the autumn of 1783, the relinquishment of a large district of country upon the Cumberland River, extending southward to the sources of Duck River. This territory was subsequently comprised in the district of Miro, and the jurisdiction of North Carolina was peaceably extended upon the Valley of the Cumberland River.†

Other portions of territory, occupied and claimed by the Chickasâs, Creeks, and Cherokees, within the present states of Tennessee, Mississippi, Alabama, and Georgia, were successively relinquished to the Federal government of the United States by the tribes respectively claiming the same, in the different treaties subsequently held and concluded with them.

The extinguishment of the Indian title to the territory in the western parts of New York and Pennsylvania, as well as in the Northwestern Territory, became an object of primary importance with the Federal government. For this purpose, preliminary measures were taken for a general treaty with the Iroquois confederacy, known as the Six Nations. The first treaty by the Federal government with the Six Nations was designated

The Treaty of Fort Stanwix.—This treaty was held at Fort Stanwix, or Fort Schuyler, on the Mohawk River, one hundred

---

* Butler's Kentucky, p. 50, 51, Introduction.
† American State Papers, *Indian Affairs*, vol. i., p. 15, folio edition.

and ten miles west of Albany. A large number of confederate tribes attended with their chiefs, head men, and warriors. On the part of the United States were Oliver Wolcott, Richard Butler, and Arthur Lee, commissioners. The treaty was concluded and signed on the 22d of October, 1784.

By this treaty, the United States grant peace to the hostile Senecas, Mohawks, Onondagas, and Cayugas, and receive them under their protection, upon condition that they deliver six hostages for the surrender of all American prisoners in their possession which had been captured by any of these tribes during the previous wars. The Oneidas and Tuscaroras nations are permitted to remain upon the lands then in their occupancy. The boundary line between the Indian territory and the white settlements was established. By this treaty, the Indian title was peaceably extinguished to a large portion of western New York.*

[A.D. 1785.] In January following, another treaty was concluded with the tribes inhabiting the northwestern territory south of Lake Erie. This was

The Treaty of Fort M'Intosh.—This treaty was conducted by George Rogers Clark, Richard Butler, and Arthur Lee, commissioners on the part of the United States, and signed on the 21st day of January, 1785, at Fort M'Intosh, in the western part of Pennsylvania. The tribes represented in this treaty were the Wyandots, Delawares, Ottawâs, and Chippewas, then inhabiting the extreme northern portions of the present State of Ohio, west of the Cuyahoga River.

In this treaty, the chiefs, sachems, and warriors of these tribes relinquish to the United States all claim to the lands lying south of Lake Erie, and east of Cuyahoga River, as well as all the southeastern portion of the present State of Ohio. The boundary line agreed upon at this treaty was as follows: " Beginning at the mouth of the Cuyahoga River, on the southern shore of Lake Erie ; thence up the east bank of the Cuyahoga River to its lake source ; thence across to the source of the Tuscarawa, and down that stream to its junction with Walhonding Creek, near the site of the old American 'Fort Laurens;'" thence in a direct line south of west, to the mouth of Mad River, a large eastern tributary of the Great Miami, or Stony River ; "it being that branch of the Stony River on

---

* American State Papers, *Indian Affairs*, vol. i., p. 10.

which the French had a fort" in the year 1752;* thence up the main branch of the Miami or Stony River, to the portage across to the St. Mary's River, or main branch of the Maumee; thence down the southwestern bank of the St. Mary's and the Maumee to Lake Erie.

East and south of this line the lands are ceded and relinquished to the United States, for the use of the people thereof. The United States grant and relinquish to the Indians all lands north and west of this line for their use and occupancy, as dwelling-places and hunting-grounds, free from encroachment by the whites, excepting certain roads therein specified, leading to the principal military posts on the northwestern frontier, and also six miles square contiguous to and including each of said posts; also, six miles square at the Rapids of the Maumee, and six miles square, also, at its mouth; also, six miles square on the Sandusky River, another at Detroit, and one on the River Raisin.*

In the fall of 1785 the United States took formal possession of the eastern portion of the country ceded by the treaty of Fort M'Intosh, by a detachment of troops under Major John Doughty, who was in the autumn ordered from Fort M'Intosh to the mouth of the Muskingum. Here he commenced a block house and other works of defense, which were finished the following summer, when he gave to the whole the name of "Fort Harmar," in honor of his commanding general at Fort M'Intosh. This was the first military post of the United States within the limits of the present State of Ohio, if we except the old Fort Laurens, built in the year 1778, on the right bank of the Tuscarawas, not far below the mouth of Sandy Creek.‡

[A.D. 1786.] The next treaty with the northwestern tribes was

The *Treaty of the Great Miami*, concluded with the chiefs, warriors, and head men of the Shawanese nation, and signed on the 31st day of January, 1786. It was conducted by General George Rogers Clark, Colonel Richard Butler, and Samuel H. Parsons, commissioners on the part of the United States, near the mouth of the Great Miami River.

---

* Mr. Gist, in his explorations in 1752, visited this French fort, a mere trading-post with a stockade. By him the stream was called "Mad Creek;" and now it is known as Mad River.—See Imlay's America, p. 120.

† American State Papers, *Indian Affairs*, vol. i., p. 7, folio edition.

‡ American Pioneer, vol. i., p. 25, 26.

In this treaty the Shawanese nation acknowledges the United States to be the sole and absolute sovereign of all the territory heretofore relinquished to them by their chiefs in the treaty of January 14th, 1784. The nation agrees to be peaceable, and to abstain from hostilities against the white settlements; to surrender three hostages for the faithful delivery of all prisoners in their possession; to punish such of their young warriors as should be guilty of murder or robbery against the whites; and to give notice to the officers of the United States of any contemplated incursion by any of the savages upon the frontier inhabitants.

The United States, upon these conditions, grant peace to the Shawanese, and receive them under their protection and friendship, and allot to them, as their hunting-grounds, the territory lying west of the Great Miami, and north of a line drawn due west from the mouth of Mad River to the River de la Panse, and down that stream to the Wabash. The United States stipulate to prevent the intrusion and settlement of white men north of this boundary, and the Shawanese relinquish all claim whatever to all lands east and south of the same.*

The next important treaty was with the great southern nations occupying the country from the settlements of Georgia westward to the Mississippi. In the preparation for this treaty, the object of the Federal government was to assemble the delegates from all the southern tribes, and thereby to establish a general peace throughout the whole southern frontier.

After due notice and preparation, the savages, in large numbers, attended at the place designated, on the Keowee River, in Georgia, known as Hopewell, for the contemplated treaty.

The *Treaty of Hopewell* commenced in October, 1785, and was continued until late in January following. The Cherokees being more convenient, were first on the ground, some weeks before the arrival of the Chickasâs and Choctâs, who came more than three hundred miles from their western towns.

At this treaty the Indian tribes were amply represented by chiefs, warriors, and sachems from each of the above-mentioned nations.

The commissioners on the part of the United States were Benjamin Hawkins, Andrew Pickens, Joseph Martin, and Laughlin M'Intosh; and also William Blount as commissioner

* American State Papers, *Indian Affairs,* vol. i., p. 11, 12.

on the part of North Carolina. Three separate treaties were negotiated, one with each of the respective nations.

The treaty with the *Cherokees* was concluded and signed on the 28th day of November, 1785, at which time the delegates from the Chickasâs and Choctâs had not arrived. By this treaty the Cherokee nation placed itself under the protection of the United States, and recognized an established boundary between the Indian territory and the lands claimed by the State of North Carolina, in the "Western District," upon the branches of Holston River, and also by the States of South Carolina and Georgia.

The Choctâ delegates having arrived, negotiations were commenced, which terminated in a treaty, which was signed on the 3d day of January, 1786. The Choctâs stipulate for peace and friendship with the United States, and the recognition of certain boundaries established between the United States and other conterminous tribes. Having no territory contiguous to the American settlements, they made no cessions of lands.*

Immediately after the conclusion of the Choctâ treaty, negotiations were opened with the *Chickasâs*, and terminated in a treaty, which was signed on the 10th of January. The Chickasâs stipulated for peace and friendship, and they agreed to ratify and confirm the treaties heretofore made in 1783 with Colonels Donaldson and Martin, commissioners of North Carolina, for the relinquishment of certain lands on Cumberland River. They also agreed to cede and relinquish, for a valuable consideration, extensive bodies of lands on the southern branches of Cumberland River, and upon the head waters of Duck River, nearly as far west as the lower portion of Tennessee River.†

At this time the Cherokee Indians were a powerful confederacy, and inhabited the region drained by all the branches of the Holston River and the whole Valley of the Tennessee above the Muscle Shoals. Their hunting-grounds formerly comprised one third of Western Virginia, all East Tennessee, one third of North Carolina and Georgia, and nearly all North Alabama. For nearly fifty years they had been the terror of the western frontier of Virginia and the two Carolinas. At the period of the treaty, their national strength was estimated at more than two thousand warriors; two years subsequently, Colonel Joseph Martin, experienced in Indian affairs, estimated their strength at twenty-six hundred and fifty warriors.

* American State Papers, *Indian Affairs*, vol. i., p. 40–44.   † Idem, p. 432.

The Chickasâs occupied and claimed the country east of the Mississippi, from the mouth of the Ohio to the mouth of the Yazoo, and westward to the Cumberland Mountains on the north, and to the Tombigby and Black Warrior on the south. The claims of this nation included all the western half of Kentucky and Tennessee, and the northern half of Mississippi. Subsequently, in the year 1787, their strength was estimated at twelve hundred warriors.*

The Choctâs, one of the most powerful nations of the South, occupied all the country south of the Chickasâs and west of the Cherokee and Creek territories. Their limits comprised all the regions drained by the Lower Tombigby and the western tributaries of the Black Warrior, and westward to the Mississippi, including the whole country drained by the Pearl and Pascagoula Rivers. Their fighting men were estimated at six thousand.

[A.D. 1787.] The treaty of Fort Stanwix, signed October 22d, 1784, had been a source of great dissatisfaction and complaint with the Six Nations. The chiefs persisted in their declarations that they had been deceived by the commissioners of the United States, both as to the amount of territory relinquished and the line fixed in the treaty, as well as in the consideration which they believed was stipulated in the same. They declared, also, that, coerced by threats of war upon their people, and the destruction of their towns, they had been induced to sign the treaty against their will; that they had been thus compelled to relinquish more territory to the United States than they were authorized to cede, and that the nations would not ratify the cession.

They declared, moreover, that they had been defrauded out of the goods stipulated in the treaty, and, consequently, the same was not binding upon them. The government endeavored, without success, to satisfy them on these points. In the mean time, notwithstanding their remonstrances and protestations, the whites continued to advance upon the lands claimed to have been ceded by the treaty. At length, finding all their efforts unavailing, they had seriously contemplated a league offensive and defensive with the western tribes, for resisting by force of arms the encroachments of the whites. To this measure they were strongly incited by the western tribes.

* See American State Papers, *Indian Affairs*, vol. i., p. 48; also, p. 432, &c.

The latter upbraided them with a want of courage in surrendering their own lands, and being compelled to fall back upon those tribes who had the courage to defend and hold their country. On this subject the British agents and traders at Niagara and Detroit neglected no opportunity to poison the minds of the savages, for the purpose of exciting animosity against the border settlements of the United States.

[A.D. 1788.] Under these circumstances, the frontiers had been almost continually harassed by depredations, murders, and thefts, constituting a series of petty hostilities, perpetrated by lawless bands of Indians, almost from the signing of the treaty of Fort M'Intosh. To allay this feeling of dissatisfaction on the part of the Six Nations, the government issued instructions to General Arthur St. Clair, governor of the Northwestern Territory, to assemble the sachems, warriors, and head men of all the northwestern tribes and nations in general convention at Fort Harmar, at the mouth of the Muskingum, for the purpose of negotiating a new treaty and satisfying any demands which they might urge for further compensation under the treaty of Fort Stanwix.

Agreeably to the invitation of Governor St. Clair, the Indians began to assemble near Fort Harmar early in the winter. Negotiations were opened and conducted by the governor as Commissioner Plenipotentiary of the United States. The sachems, chiefs, and warriors of the " Five Nations," exclusive of the Mohawks, of the Wyandots, Delawares, Ottawâs, Chippewas, Potawatamies, and Sauks, attended on the part of the hostile tribes. The negotiations resulted in the *Treaty of Fort Harmar*, signed on the 9th day of January, 1789.*

The treaty of Fort Harmar consisted of two separate parts:

---

* *Description of Fort Harmar.*—Fort Harmar was erected, under the superintendence of Major John Doughty, in the autumn of 1785. It was situated upon a second bottom, six or eight feet above the first bottom, extending across from the Ohio to the Muskingum. The outline was that of a regular pentagon, including about three fourths of an acre of ground. The curtains, or main walls, were constructed of large timbers horizontally raised to the height of twelve or fourteen feet, and were each one hundred and twenty feet long. Bastions, also pentagonal, and fourteen feet high, were made of large timbers set upright in the ground, and tied by cross timbers, tree-nailed, to each upright piece. The fifth, or inner side, was occupied by dwellings, or quarters, for the officers; and the main sides, or curtains, by the barracks, or quarters, for the soldiers. The roofs inclined inward, and each house was divided into four rooms. The quarters for the officers was a large two story house, built of hewed logs. Upon the roof of the barracks, facing the Ohio, was a cupola, or square tower, surmounted by a flag-staff and occupied by a sentinel. An arsenal of large logs, covered with earth, formed a place of security as a magazine. At a short distance were highly-cultivated gardens. *See plate*—American Pioneer, vol. i., p. 25, 26.

FORT HARMAR.

first, a treaty with the Five Nations, the Oneidas, Onondagas, Tuscaroras, Cayugas, and Senecas; *second*, a treaty with the six northwestern tribes before enumerated.

[A.D. 1789.] The treaty with the Five Nations of the Iroquois was designed to confirm and ratify the treaty of Fort Stanwix, and to establish the boundaries designated in that treaty. Therefore the United States stipulated to pay to the Indians the additional sum of three thousand dollars, to be properly distributed among them. Besides this amount, in cash or its equivalent, various presents of valuable goods and necessary articles of Indian costume were made to the chiefs and warriors. Upon these conditions, they ratified and confirmed the former treaty.

In like manner, the treaty with the six northwestern tribes stipulated for peace and friendship between their people and those of the United States, and for the recognition of the treaties of Fort Stanwix and Fort M'Intosh, and the lines established by them respectively. For and in consideration of said recognition, and relinquishment of all claim to said designated territory, the United States stipulate to pay them, for distribution, six thousand dollars, besides sundry valuable presents to the chiefs and warriors.*

The Shawanese, and some other bands upon the head waters of the Wabash and Maumee, still maintaining a hostile attitude, refused to attend the treaty or to sanction its provisions. These dissenting tribes and bands soon after resumed their hostilities against the frontier settlements of Virginia, Pennsylvania, and Kentucky, embracing the settlements east and south of the Ohio River, from the Monongahela to Green River.

From the close of the war of Independence, the Indian tribes, instigated by British agents and traders at Detroit and other western posts within the United States, had urged the Ohio River as the proper boundary between the white man and the Indian, as fixed by the English treaty of Fort Stanwix, under Sir William Johnson, in 1768. Hence it is evident that the British cabinet, in retaining the northwestern posts, had not abandoned the hope that circumstances might yet compel the United States to recognize the Ohio River as their northwestern boundary.†

* American State Papers, *Indian Affairs*, vol. i., p. 5.
† See Cincinnati in 1841, p. 167. Also, Burnett's Letters, p. 100, &c.

This policy of the British government having been defeated, the traders and agents in Canada, being fully convinced that their influence and the lucrative trade with the northwestern Indians would cease with the advance of the whites, sought every occasion to prolong their own power by instigating the Indians to arrest the advance of the settlements by a resort to open warfare.

The spirit of dissatisfaction and hostility which prevailed so extensively among the northwestern tribes soon after the treaties of Forts Stanwix and M'Intosh was clearly traced to British influence and intrigue, under the superintendence of Colonel M'Key, the British agent at Detroit, and afterward at the Rapids of the Maumee.*

Detroit had long been an important central dépôt for the British fur traders with the northwestern Indians. It was an important place of business, and many Scotch and English capitalists had large investments in the lucrative trade with the natives. To comply with the treaty stipulations would incommode these important personages, by interrupting their trade and restricting their influence over the savage tribes south and west of the lakes. A state of hostilities between the Indians and the American people of the West would be a sufficient guarantee to them that, for a time, they should be free from interruption; hence they desired to arrest the advance of immigrants across the Ohio River.

[A.D. 1790.] Although these hostile demonstrations of the Indians produced a temporary check to the advance of the whites into the territory west of the Ohio, yet large settlements had been advanced to the west and north banks of the river, under the protection of Forts Harmar and Washington. It required no great foresight in the British traders to perceive that, if the late treaties were observed, the whole country north of the Ohio would soon be filled with a white civilized population. This state of things would completely annihilate the fur trade in that region. Should the interests of a privileged monopoly be interrupted by the obligations created by treaty stipulations? Such must have been the reasoning of the British court.†

Hence Indian discontent was fanned into a flame of war.

---

* American State Papers, *Indian Affairs*, General Wayne's Dispatches.
† See Burnett's Letters, p. 49, 50.

Open hostilities were encouraged; the savages were induced to disregard the stipulations of the recent treaty of Fort Harmar; and the warrior bands, prepared for war and plunder, having obtained their outfit of arms and ammunition from British traders and agents, were sent, with the tomahawk and scalping-knife, against the defenseless border population and the tide of emigration flowing down the Ohio.

During the critical state of affairs which preceded the first military movement of the United States under General Harmar, Governor St. Clair, of the Northwestern Territory, had been unintermitting in his efforts to bring about a better state of feeling among the northwestern tribes. By negotiations and treaties, he had endeavored to convince them, not only of the justice, but of the humane policy of the Federal government. At length, finding all overtures abortive and unavailing, he had devoted his whole attention to the protection of the frontier settlements from their aggressions.

Yet the military posts, although kept in a state of complete defense, and amply garrisoned, were found wholly insufficient to protect the feeble and remote settlements from continual incursions by small detachments and straggling parties of Indians, who studiously avoided the fortified places and the military force. Hence the stationed garrisons were a protection only to those settlements within their immediate vicinity. Such was the state of Indian affairs on the northwestern frontier previous to the active military campaign of the United States in that quarter; and no settlement within fifty miles of the Ohio was safe unless within a stockade inclosure.

In the mean time, the hostile attitude of the northern tribes was fully known to the Southern Indians. Between the Shawanese on the Wabash, and the Cherokees and Creeks south and east of Tennessee River, an uninterrupted intercourse existed, and a regular interchange of feeling was sedulously cultivated by the prominent chiefs, who desired to bring about a general league against the white inhabitants both north and south of the Ohio. In effecting this object, they had so far succeeded that the government of the United States was compelled again to adopt measures for conciliating the hostile spirit among the Creeks.

The Federal government had used great exertions to settle the difficulties existing between the Creek nation and the people of Georgia; yet they had failed to conciliate the chiefs, who were believed to be under Spanish influence. No effort had been spared by the Federal government to assemble a large portion of the nation for the purpose of entering into a treaty of peace and friendship, with an adjustment of boundaries. For this purpose, the chiefs, warriors, head men, and other Indians, to the number of two thousand, were assembled during the last summer at Rock Landing, on the Oconee River. The treaty was concluded, and ready for signatures, when, under some frivolous pretext, M'Gillivray abruptly broke off all negotiation, and the treaty was not signed.*

The following spring, Colonel Marius Willet, a distinguished officer of the Revolution, and a man of great prudence and firmness, was appointed to visit the Creek nation, in order to effect an amicable arrangement. After some time spent in the nation and about the Creek agency, he succeeded in his delicate mission so far as to induce M'Gillivray and twenty-nine chiefs to accompany him to New York, for the purpose of negotiating with the heads of the Federal government. They were formally introduced to the president and the heads of departments, and entertained with marks of great distinction. On the 7th day of August a treaty was concluded, and signed by these chiefs on the part of their nation, and by General Knox, Secretary of War. This treaty, it was hoped, would produce harmony between the people of Georgia and the Creeks; but the hope was fallacious.†

The treaty stipulated for perpetual peace and friendship between the United States and the Creek nation; that the Creek nation should remain under the protection of the United States; and that their warriors should be restrained from committing outrages against the white settlements, and made to observe their obligations of friendship. The United States stipulated to restrain the encroachments of the white people upon the lands and hunting-grounds of the Creeks. A boundary line was agreed upon, and commissioners were to be appointed by both nations to run out and mark the line separating the lands of the Indians from those of the whites. M'Gillivray was honored with the title of Brigadier-general of the United States.

* See Marshall's Life of Washington, vol. v., p. 274, 275. Alexander M'Gillivray was a half-breed Creek, son of a Scotch trader, born in the Creek nation, a man of intellect and good acquirements, having received his education in Charleston, South Carolina. Being a principal chief, he exerted a strong influence over his nation.
† See Drake's Book of Indians, book iv., p. 39, 40.

As soon as it was made known to the Governor-general of Cuba that the Creek chiefs were to visit New York, he took immediate measures for observing the tendency of the negotiations, and for embarrassing the operations of the commissioners of the Federal government in conducting them. For this purpose, the Secretary of East Florida was dispatched from St. Augustine to the city of New York with a large sum of money, for the ostensible purpose of purchasing flour for the Spanish garrisons, but in fact for observing, and, as far as practicable, for the purpose of embarrassing the negotiations with the Creek chiefs. The watchful eye of the government was upon the Spanish emissary, and all interference on his part was circumvented.*

But the efforts of the Spanish authorities did not stop here. Intrigues were set on foot in the Creek nation, and with the chiefs after their return from New York, by which the objects of the treaty were for a time effectually defeated. M'Gillivray, bought over to the Spanish interest, resigned his nominal commission of brigadier-general under the United States, and accepted the same rank under the Spanish crown, with an annual salary of fifteen hundred dollars.†

The treaty was rejected by the Creek nation; the line of demarkation was never run, and a spirit of revenge against the American settlements was manifested in no ambiguous manner for several years afterward.

In the mean time the *Cherokees* had become highly exasperated at the lawless encroachment of the white population into their territory. The Chickamaugas on the Lower Tennessee had repeatedly indicated their resentment to these encroachments by depredations and acts of hostility upon the settlements, which were advancing upon the waters of Duck River and Elk River into the Indian territory. These acts of hostility by the Indians had given occasion to partisan warfare on the part of the white inhabitants south of Nashville, until a regular war had broken out between these settlements and a portion of the Creek and Cherokee Indians. Notwithstanding the efforts made by the Federal government to restrain the encroachments of the American people, and to compensate the Indians for the unlawful intrusion of

---

* See Martin's Louisiana, vol. ii., p. 106, 107.   Also, Marshall's Life of Washington, vol. v., p. 274, 275, first edition.   † Martin, vol. ii., p. 113, 114.

the whites, hostilities were not finally suspended until the spring of 1794.*

The Indians had remonstrated without effect, and the proclamations of the Federal government had been disregarded. As early as 1788, soon after the first Cherokee incursions, the old Congress issued their proclamation on the first of September, forbidding "the unwarrantable intrusions" upon the Indian territory on the waters of Duck and Elk Rivers.†

Again, in August, 1790, President Washington presented the subject to Congress in a message as one well deserving their serious attention. On this subject he says, "Notwithstanding the treaties with the Indians, and the proclamations of the Federal government against encroachments on the Indian territory, upward of five hundred families have settled on the Cherokee lands, exclusive of the settlements between the French, Broad, and the Holston Rivers."‡

Before the close of the year 1790, marauding parties of Cherokee and Creek Indians had begun to assail all the exposed settlements, from the eastern limit of Washington District, on Holston River, to the western limit of Miro District, on the Cumberland.

[A.D. 1791.] To check hostilities on the part of the Cherokees, William Blount, "Governor of the Southwestern Territory, and Superintendent of Indian Affairs," was instructed to convene the chiefs and head men of the Cherokee nation for the purpose of entering into negotiations for the amicable relinquishment of certain lands on the south side of Cumberland River. The Indians were convened accordingly, and a treaty was concluded and signed on the second day of July, 1791, near the present site of Knoxville, on the Holston River. This treaty, signed by William Blount on the part of the United States, and by forty-one chiefs and warriors of the Cherokee nation, is known as the "*Treaty of Holston.*"

By this treaty the Cherokee nation ceded to the United States extensive tracts of land situated south of the Cumberland, and upon the waters of Duck River, and as far as the sources of Elk River.

They also agreed, for a stipulated annuity, to grant to the

---

* See chap. x. of this book, "Early Settlement and Indian Hostilities in Southwestern Territory." † Sparks's Writings of Washington, vol. xii., p. 88.
‡ American State Papers, *Indian Affairs*, vol. i., p. 83.

people of the United States the right of a road through their country to the Cumberland settlements from the Southwest Point, at the junction of Holston and Clinch Rivers, and the free navigation of the Tennessee River. They also entered into obligations to observe peace and friendship with the United States.*

[A.D. 1792.] But the treaty of Holston did not restore peace to the whole Cherokee nation, and partial hostilities against the white inhabitants upon the Cumberland and the Holston Rivers continued for several years, notwithstanding all the efforts of the Federal government to establish peace.† War parties also penetrated through the country, and co-operated with the tribes north of the Ohio. The northern Indians, who had been unremitting in their efforts to engage the southern Indians in a general league, had twice encountered the Federal troops and returned triumphantly to their towns. Elated with the success of their northern friends, the Cherokees had almost consented to involve themselves in a general war with the United States. Conceiving that the only protection attainable for them, in the quiet possession of their lands, was open war, by which the invaders should be driven from their soil, they had well-nigh entered into the general league. Encouraged by two successive defeats of the Federal army, and warmly encouraged by the Spaniards of Florida and Louisiana, they were restrained only by the persevering efforts of the Federal authorities in their negotiations for peace.

The natural jealousy of the Indian character required but little prompting to induce them to resist the white man's encroachments. The American people, believing the region upon which they were advancing to be within the proper limits of the United States, and that the Indian claim was a mere nominal right of occupancy, were less scrupulous in their advances, because the encroachment was one for which the government could easily compensate them.

* American State Papers, *Indian Affairs*, vol. i., p. 124.
† A portion of the western Cherokees were more unfriendly than the eastern portion of the nation. The Chickamaugas, on the extreme west of the Cherokee country, had been peculiarly hostile, and had been instrumental in fomenting a feeling of enmity between the Indians and the whites of Tennessee. President Washington, in his message to Congress November 6th, 1792, observes: "A part of the Cherokee nation, known by the name of the Chickamaugas, inhabiting five towns on the Tennessee River, have long been in the practice of committing depredations on the neighboring settlements."—See Sparks's Writings of Washington, vol. xii.

The government of the United States invariably endeavored to maintain the utmost good faith toward the Indians, although it was not always practicable to restrain and prevent aggression by individuals. Hence, under the influence of some new alarm or popular excitement, partisan warfare has been carried on against innocent towns, and occasionally the tribe has been made to suffer for the acts of lawless individuals. But the general government, in all its intercourse with the Indian tribes, has scrupulously observed the stipulations and obligations of treaties and natural-justice.

The Spanish authorities in Louisiana and Florida had indulged a spirit of jealous hostility toward the rapid extension of the American settlements into the territory occupied by the southern tribes. As they could not occupy it themselves, they were anxious that it should remain neutral, in the exclusive possession of the savages. Foreseeing a collision between the Federal government and the native tribes, under which the latter must melt away, the Spanish authorities had taken the precaution to secure the alliance and friendship of the Indians by formal treaties, and by means of traders and agents located among them. By the same means they exerted a secret influence upon them in favor of the Spanish monarchy, while they encouraged them to resist the encroachments of the whites on the east and north.

In this manner hostilities had been instigated by the Spaniards against the settlements on Cumberland and Holston Rivers for more than two years past, until the territory was necessarily placed in a defensive attitude, and troops were advanced toward the Indian country for the protection of the inhabitants from surprise and massacre. The Indians resorted to their usual mode of operations, harassing the exposed population by sudden incursions of their scalping-parties. But it was not long before the whole nation was in arms for the entire destruction of the advanced settlers.

At length, in September, 1792, Governor Blount received certain intelligence of the intrigues of the Spanish authorities in Louisiana and Florida. This intelligence was conveyed by Richard Finnelson, a half-breed Cherokee Indian, and Joseph Deraque, a Canadian half-breed, who had been sent by the Governor of Louisiana as agents and bearers of dispatches to the Indian tribes. These men, having been well paid by the

Spanish agents for discharging their duties as emissaries, and seeing the imminent danger which might suddenly overwhelm the settlements on the Cumberland River, resolved to convey to them due notice of their danger. Therefore, while in the Indian country, and seeing the savages prepared for the sudden destruction of the white inhabitants, they desired and urged the Indians to defer their expedition for ten days, until they could return from Knoxville, alleging that the Spanish intendant had required them to convey letters to a friend of his in that town before war should be commenced. Instead of returning to the Indians, they communicated to Governor Blount the facts which had transpired in the Creek nation.

By this information, it appeared that it was the Spanish governor at New Orleans, the Baron de Carondelet, and Don O'Neil, governor of Florida at Pensacola, who had been instigating the southern Indians to hostilities against the United States. Agents had been sent to the Choctâs, Chickasâs, Creeks, and Cherokees, to distribute among them presents, and to encourage them to resist the advance of the white population into the Cumberland country, and to assure them of the aid of the King of Spain, who would see justice done to them in case of a war with the United States; that he would supply them with ammunition and arms to carry on the war; and they were instructed to urge the Indians to strike *now! that now was the time*, while the United States were engaged with the Shawanese and other northern tribes, unless the Americans would agree to give up and withdraw from the lands on the Cumberland and Oconee Rivers.

It also appeared that Alexander M'Gillivray had been on a visit to New Orleans, in consequence of a special invitation from the Spanish governor, upon matters of importance.

It also appeared that a half-breed Creek, by the name of Bowles, had returned from England or some of the British West India Islands, and that he was exerting his influence among the Creeks, encouraging them to war against the United States, and assuring them that both England and Spain were ready to aid them in the undertaking. These emissaries, moreover, declared that they had seen six hundred Indian warriors, armed and painted black, holding their war-dances preparatory to an invasion of the American settlements.

[A.D. 1793.] Thus was the Cherokee nation and the

Creeks for nearly three years wavering between war and peace, closely observing the progress of events in the Indian war north of the Ohio. Had General Wayne been as unfortunate as his predecessors, in all probability the southern Indians, from the banks of the Savannah to the Mississippi, would have been united in one general league with those of the north, under the auspices of English and Spanish diplomacy. But the successes of General Wayne during the years 1793 and 1794, and his impetuous and vigilant character, struck terror into the savage warriors, and dispelled all intentions of a general league.

[A.D. 1794.] The Cherokees at length evinced a willingness to treat with the Federal government, and sent a deputation of thirteen chiefs to Philadelphia, authorized to enter into treaty stipulations for the Cherokee nation. On the 26th of June, 1794, a treaty was concluded and signed in Philadelphia; in which, for an additional annuity, the chiefs stipulated to ratify and confirm the treaty of Holston, made in 1791, and also the treaty of Hopewell, made in 1785.*

During the latter months of this year, several treaties were concluded with the northwestern tribes by Timothy Pickering, acting as commissioner of the United States. The *first* and principal was that with the Six Nations, at Canandaigua, in New York, concluded and signed November 4th, 1794. The second was that with the Oneidas, Tuscaroras, and Stockbridges, signed at Oneida on the 2d of December following. These treaties established the boundaries between the white settlements and the Indian territory within the limits of the State of New York, and secured the frontiers of New York and Pennsylvania from the hostile incursions of these warlike bands.

[A.D. 1795.] In January following, General Wayne entered into preliminary articles of treaty with the Chippewas, Ottawàs, Potawatamies, Sauks, and Miamis, on behalf of the northwestern tribes, for a general treaty of peace and friendship, to be holden by the hostile nations of the West in the course of the following summer. Accordingly, in July, the chiefs and warriors of the northwestern tribes east of the Mississippi had convened in the vicinity of Fort Greenville. After protracted negotiations for more than six weeks, a treaty was signed on the 3d day of August, 1795, by General Wayne, commissioner plenipotentiary of the United States, and by the

* American State Papers, *Indian Affairs*, vol. i., p. 543.

chiefs of the following twelve tribes, to wit: the Wyandots, Delawares, Shawanese, Ottawâs, Chippewas, Potawatamies, Miamis, Eel Rivers, Weas, Kickapoos, Piankeshas, and Kaskaskias.* These Indians remained on the treaty-ground until the 10th of August.

The *Treaty of Greenville*, besides the usual stipulations of peace and friendship, ratifies and confirms the cessions made by the treaties of Fort M'Intosh and Fort Harmar, as also a complete relinquishment of sixteen square tracts in the vicinity of the several military posts, then held or claimed by the United States, south of the lakes, together with the right of way to and from them.

The United States delivered to the Indians at the treaty, for proper distribution, goods to the amount of twenty thousand dollars, and stipulated to pay annually forever, while the treaty was observed, an annuity of nine thousand dollars in goods.

Ever since the decisive battle of the Maumee Rapids, on the 20th of August, 1794, the Indian tribes had been reduced to great privation and suffering by the destruction of their towns and the extensive fields of corn which had lined the banks of the Au Glaize and Maumee for more than fifty miles above the Rapids. Thrown out of their villages and winter residences, destitute of every comfort which the savage is enabled to collect around him, and deprived of the sustenance which their fertile fields were so well calculated to yield, they were anxious for peace, and were obliged to receive it at the dictation of the conqueror.

The treaty of Greenville is an important epoch in the history of the Indian wars upon the Ohio region, and closes the long series of hostilities which had been kept up against the western frontier, with but few interruptions, ever since the beginning of the French war in the year 1754.

* American State Papers, *Indian Affairs*, vol. i., p. 562.

CHAPTER IX.

EXTENSION OF THE FIRST WHITE SETTLEMENTS ACROSS THE OHIO, UNTIL THE CLOSE OF THE INDIAN WARS.—A.D. 1787 TO 1794.

Argument.—Claims of Virginia and other States to "Northwestern Territory" relinquished, with certain Reservations.—" Connecticut Reserve."—Virginia military District.—" Northwestern Territory" laid off by Ordinance of 1787.—Territorial Government provided.—Partial Occupation by United States.—First Settlement on the Muskingum.—Putnam's Colony, from Connecticut, arrives at Fort Harmar April 17th, 1788.—Character of the Colonists.—Second Colony arrives July 2d.—Celebration of 4th of July in the Wilderness.—First Clergyman, Daniel Story.—Governor St. Clair and territorial Officers arrive.—Territorial Government organized.—"Washington County" laid off.—Arrival of Emigrants.—*Campus Martius.*—Settlements formed at Belpre and Newberry.—Emigration to Kentucky.—Miami Settlements.—Symmes's Purchase on the Miami.—Settlement at Columbia.—Settlement at Cincinnati.—Fort Washington commenced.—Its Form and Dimensions.—" County of Hamilton" organized.—Squire M'Millan.—Colerain Settlement.—Headquarters established at Fort Washington.—" Knox County" organized.—" St. Clair County" organized.—Population of Settlements on Muskingum and Miami in 1790.—Indian Hostilities commence. —Defensive Measures adopted.—Indians exasperated at the unsuccessful Expedition of General Harmar.—Destruction of Settlement of Big Bottom, January 2d, 1791. —Attack on Wolf Creek Settlement.—Attack on Colerain Station.—Nathaniel Massie settles Manchester, on the Ohio.—French Settlement at Gallipolis, March, 1791. —Fraud of the "Scioto Company."—General St. Clair also unsuccessful.—Indian Audacity and Hostilities increase.—President Washington adopts more energetic Measures with the Indians.—Indian Outrages multiply in 1792.—Cincinnati in 1793. —Its Importance as a military Dépôt.—First Presbyterian Pastor.—Indian Hostilities in 1793.—Martial Law paramount.—First Newspaper in Northwestern Territory.—General Wayne takes Command of the Army.—Confidence restored to the western People.—Troops concentrate in the Miami Country.—Advanced Posts established.—Indians defeated and reduced to great Distress.—Settlements again advance.

THE territory lying north and west of the Ohio was claimed partly by the States of Massachusetts, Connecticut, New York, and Virginia. The claim of the first three states was based upon their early royal charters, which left their western boundaries undefined. Virginia claimed under the same title ; and she also claimed under another title, which was indisputable, the title of conquest. For the amicable adjustment of these claims, each state consented to relinquish its individual interest to the Federal government, for the common use and benefit of the Union, excepting two principal reservations, one in favor of Connecticut, and another in favor of Virginia, for the purpose of liquidating their respective liabilities to Revolutionary soldiers. The reservation of Connecticut was laid in the northeastern section, embracing that region of the present State of Ohio lying north of latitude 41° and west of the Pennsylvania line. It was bounded on the north by Lake Erie, and was about one hundred and twenty miles in length from east to west, and its greatest breadth from north to south was about sixty-eight miles. The area comprised, by estimate, three millions of acres, and was known and designated as the "Connecticut Reserve."

Virginia, in relinquishing her claim, reserved the lands lying between the Scioto and Little Miami, to be appropriated to the liquidation of the claims of her Revolutionary soldiers. This reservation was known as the "Virginia Military District." Besides these reservations, Congress appropriated a large amount of the lands to liquidate the claims of Revolutionary soldiers upon the Federal government. This reservation was known as the "United States Military District," and laid upon the east side of the Scioto River. With these reservations, the remainder of the territory was relinquished by the states respectively to the Federal government, as the property of the whole Union, and constituting a territory of the United States, to be subsequently organized into new states when the population should be sufficient.*

[A.D. 1787.] These cessions having been completed, Congress proceeded to establish a territorial form of government for the whole territory, until the increase of population should entitle them to state governments. The jurisdiction of the United States was formally extended over this extensive region, under the provisions of an ordinance of Congress approved July 13th, 1787. This ordinance provided for the subsequent division of the territory into not less than three and not more than five states, agreeably to the stipulations of the compact with Virginia, as a condition of cession.

The following articles in the ordinance were "to remain forever unalterable, unless by common consent:"

"No person shall ever be molested on account of his mode of worship or religious sentiments.

"No law shall be passed that shall in any manner whatever interfere with or affect private interests or engagements, bona fide, and without fraud, previously formed.

---

* The relinquishment by the Legislatures of the several states was in the following order: that of New York, March 1st, 1780; that of Virginia, April 23d, 1784; that of Massachusetts, April 19th, 1785; that of Connecticut, September 13th, 1786.

"The utmost good faith shall always be observed toward the Indians. Their lands and property shall never be taken from them without their consent, unless in just and lawful wars authorized by Congress.

"No tax shall be imposed on lands the property of the United States, and in no case shall non-resident proprietors be taxed higher than resident.

"There shall be formed in the said territory not less than three nor more than five states. And the boundaries of the states, as soon as Virginia shall alter her act of cession, and consent to the same, shall become fixed and established.

"There shall be neither slavery nor involuntary servitude in the said territory, otherwise than in the punishment of crimes, whereof the party shall have been duly convicted; provided always that any person escaping into the same, from whom labor or service is lawfully claimed in any of the original states, such fugitive may be lawfully reclaimed and conveyed to the person claiming his or her labor in service, as aforesaid."

The territory was designated in the ordinance as the "Northwestern Territory," and comprised all the possessions of the United States northwest of the Ohio River. The form of government prescribed by the ordinance consisted of two grades of territorial government prior to the assumption of an independent state government.

The *first* grade of territorial dependence was to continue until the aggregate number of free white males over twenty-one years should amount to five thousand. During this period the jurisdiction was confided to a governor, appointed for three years, a secretary, appointed for four years, and three superior judges, appointed for four years.

Each judge is required to hold two terms of the Superior Court in his district every year, with the jurisdiction of a superior and appellate court. The three judges, or a majority of them, constitute the Supreme Territorial Court, which is required to meet once every year.

The governor, by the ordinance, is invested with authority as commander-in-chief of the militia, and appoints and commissions all officers in the same below the rank of general; he appoints and commissions all magistrates and civil officers for the preservation of the peace; and, with the advice and concurrence of the judges, or a majority of them, "he shall adopt and publish such laws of the original states, civil and criminal, as may be necessary and best adapted to the circumstances of the district, and report them to Congress from time to time" for their approbation. " He shall lay off counties, and organize such inferior courts" as he may deem requisite.

" The secretary of the territory shall keep and preserve the acts and laws, and the public records of the territory, and the records of the governor in the executive department, and transmit authentic copies of such acts and proceedings every six months to the secretary of Congress." In the absence of the governor, he shall exercise the authority and perform the duties of that officer.

The *second* grade provides for the election of a Legislative Assembly and a Legislative Council, which, with the concurrence of the governor, shall enact all laws and regulations necessary for the administration of justice.

The Legislative Assembly consists of representatives elected by the legal voters in the proportion of one representative to every five hundred free white males over the age of twenty-one years. The representatives, when duly elected, shall have authority to elect and nominate to Congress ten persons, from whom Congress shall select and appoint five as a Legislative Council, of whom any three shall be a quorum.

The Legislative Assembly and the Legislative Council, duly organized in co-operation with the governor, shall constitute the General Assembly, under the second grade of territorial government. The General Assembly shall be vested with all legislative powers for the good government of the territory, and enact such laws as they may deem expedient, not repugnant to the laws and Constitution of the United States. No act of the Legislature shall have the force and sanction of law until it has received the signature of the governor, who shall have power to convene, prorogue, or dissolve the General Assembly when, in his opinion, it may be expedient.

The Legislative Assembly, or House of Representatives, so soon as regularly organized, have power to elect a delegate to Congress, who shall have the right to speak, but not to vote.

The second grade of government was to continue until the whole population increased to sixty thousand souls; at which time the people, expressing their wishes through the General

Assembly, shall be entitled to the right of an independent state government, under the authority and approbation of Congress.

The Muskingum Settlement.—In the mean time, colonies were organizing on the Atlantic seaboard for the establishment of the first Anglo-American settlements within the Northwestern Territory. Congress had already entered into arrangements with Manasseh Cutler and Winthrop Sargent, agents of the "Ohio Company," for the sale of large bodies of land, to be located on the west side of the Ohio, between the Muskingum and the Hockhocking Rivers. The purchase was made at one dollar per acre, payable in land scrip and other evidences of debt for Revolutionary services.*

The company found no difficulty in procuring emigrants for their contemplated colony. Besides the proprietors, forty-seven in number, there were hundreds of Revolutionary soldiers and officers who were ready to embark for the West, to secure a permanent home and to retrieve their exhausted fortunes.

Yet the whole region west of the Ohio was in the occupancy of Indian tribes, who were jealous of the advance of the white population. Although, by treaties made after the close of the Revolutionary war, they had ceded large bodies of lands in this region, yet they still maintained a hostile attitude, and refused to permit the whites to occupy the lands ceded by former treaties. The only occupancy west of the Ohio was that of two military posts, Fort M'Intosh, at the mouth of Big Beaver, and Fort Harmar, at the mouth of the Muskingum.

Such were the inducements for the New England immigrants. Yet in the autumn of 1787, General Rufus Putnam, a son of the brave General Israel Putnam, and an enterprising pioneer, had already advanced with a colony of forty-seven persons upon the Youghiogeny, to commence the first settlement of the "Northwestern Territory." For nearly eight weeks they had toiled with their families across the mountains,

---

* The "Ohio Company" was formed by a number of officers and soldiers of the Revolutionary army, who resolved to emigrate to the West to retrieve their exhausted fortunes in a new country. Many of them had lost their property and estates during the troubles and disasters of the Revolution, and were now advanced in life and involved in debts which their means were insufficient to discharge. Their interest in the increasing value of their lands promised them the means of discharging their liabilities and securing a competence for their families. Many of them held large claims against the government, which they could obtain no other way.

and through the rugged frontier country of Pennsylvania, before they reached "Simrel's Ferry," on the Yough. The severities of a western winter, in a wilderness region, forbade them to proceed beyond that point, and the colony remained upon the Yough until returning spring.

During the winter they were diligent in preparing to reach their new homes on the Muskingum. A large covered barge, made bullet-proof against the Indian rifle, was built by Jonathan Devoll, the first ship-builder on the Monongahela and Ohio Rivers. In remembrance of their pilgrim ancestors, it was called the "May Flower;" it was well adapted to transport the families and their colonial effects to their ultimate destination, and to serve as a floating residence while more permanent ones were erecting on land.*

[A.D. 1788.] Toward the last of March the "May Flower" was freighted with the new colony at Simrel's Ferry, on the Yough. The colony, composed chiefly of officers and soldiers of the Revolutionary army, proceeded on their voyage by way of Fort Pitt and the Ohio. Early in April they arrived in the mouth of the Muskingum, and on the 7th of April the agents of the Ohio Company formally took possession of their purchase, by locating a portion of the colony, under General Putnam, upon the north bank of the Muskingum, on the point of land opposite to the military post. Some provision for their reception had been made in advance, and the "May Flower" served as a store-house until others were supplied. The colony entered at once upon the work of making a permanent settlement, and erecting the necessary houses for their families. Like the ancient Greek colonies, and unlike some of the American, the colonists of Marietta were chiefly men of science and refinement, and they carried these advantages into the western wilderness.

On the 2d day of July following, the new colony received an accession to its numbers, by the arrival of forty persons from Worcester, Massachusetts. This colony included General Edward Tupper, Major Asa Coborn, Major Nathan Goodale, Major Nathaniel Cushing, and Mr. Ichabod Nye, with their families. Nine weeks had they been toiling in the tedious journey through a rough frontier wilderness, with their wagons, cattle, and stock of every kind. Eight weeks' travel, with

* See American Pioneer, vol. i., p. 90, 91.

a regular encampment each night, brought them to Wheeling, upon the banks of the Ohio, about eighty miles above the point of their ultimate destination. After several days of preparation, they procured a large Kentucky flat-boat, into which the colonists were crowded with their personal effects, and after two days' floating upon the current, they landed at the wharf, beside the "May Flower," in the mouth of the Muskingum. Here they were welcomed by their joyful friends who had preceded them into the garden of the West. Their greetings and mutual congratulations had not ceased, when the dawn of the 4th day of July was ushered in by the roar of the artillery of Fort Harmar, reminding them of the glorious anniversary of their national independence. The whole colony, with joyful hearts, prepared to pass over to the fort, and unite with the troops in celebrating the joyful day. Thus civilization and patriotism entered the wilderness together, emblematic of the peace and harmony which have since characterized the civil and military powers of the great West.*

Nor had the proprietors and the colonists been negligent of the more benign influences of religion. Already they had engaged a pious and zealous young minister to teach, not only the principles of religion and morality to the adults and parents, but likewise the rudiments of learning and the elements of religion to their children. This was the Rev. Daniel Story, from Worcester, Massachusetts, who came out with the colonists during the following summer. He arrived, and for many years continued to labor in his vocation within the company's claim, dividing his time between the settlements at Marietta, Belpre, and Newberry, and adhering to his flock through prosperity and adversity for fifteen years.†

Early in July the officers for the new territorial government arrived at Marietta or Fort Harmar. These were General Arthur St. Clair, governor, Winthrop Sargent, secretary, and three judges for the executive council, agreeably to the *first grade* of territorial government.

A few days after their arrival, the governor published his commission, and those of his executive council, and also the ordinance of Congress under which they exercised their authority. A public meeting of the settlers and others was called, when the governor made an address to the people, in

* See American Pioneer, vol. i., p. 64. † Idem, vol. i., p. 86–88.

which he explained to them the new form of government, to which he asked their cordial support and hearty co-operation.

On the 26th of July the governor called together his council, and proceeded to organize the civil and military departments of the new government. The whole country north of the Ohio River, and between the Muskingum and the Hockhocking Rivers, was designated as the "county of Washington," in honor of the first President of the United States. Marietta was declared the seat of justice for this county.

In the mean time, it was evident, from the hostile bearing of the Indian tribes, that the colony could not expect perfect security in the midst of their savage neighbors. Prudence dictated a timely preparation for any danger which might threaten in this quarter. It was resolved to convert the block-house and other buildings into a regular stockade, or fortified station. Under the direction and superintendence of General Rufus Putnam, the work was commenced on a plan adapted to the security of the colony. The work progressed regularly until the close of the following year, when it was fully completed.

The walls of the main buildings formed a regular parallelogram of one hundred and eighty feet on each side. Each corner was protected subsequently, in 1791, by a strong projecting block-house, twenty feet square in the lower story, and twenty-four feet in the upper. Each block-house was surmounted by a tower, or sentry-box, bullet-proof; and the curtains, or sides of the parallelogram, were protected by a range of sharpened pickets, inclining outward. The whole was surrounded by a strong palisade ten feet high, and securely planted in the ground, beyond which was a range of abattis.

The buildings were constructed of whip-sawed timbers four inches thick, and neatly dove-tailed at the corners, two stories high, and covered with good shingle roofs. The rooms were large and commodious, provided with good fireplaces and brick chimneys.

A guarded gateway on the west and south front gave admission and exit to the inmates; and over the gateway, facing the Muskingum on the south, was a large room, surmounted with a belfry, in which was suspended the church-going bell. The whole range of buildings was amply supplied with portholes for defensive firing. Such is the outline of the first regular station northwest of the Ohio, known as the "*Campus Martius.*"

Its bastions and towers, all white-washed and glistening in the sun, reminded the beholder at a distance of some ancient feudal tower, with its imposing battlements, rising as if by magic in the western wilderness.*

Thus began the first settlement and the first regular town west of the Ohio River, and the first made by white men in the present State of Ohio, which now contains, after a lapse of half a century, a population of more than one million of civilized people.

The militia were organized in three companies, with three captains, three lieutenants, and three ensigns. Three justices of the peace were also appointed, and duly commissioned; also, a probate court, and clerk. A court of quarter sessions was also organized, with three associate justices, having jurisdiction over common pleas, and authority to sit as a court of quarter sessions, with a sheriff, duly commissioned for the county.†

In the mean time, the plan of a regular town was laid off on the bank of the Ohio, above the mouth of the Muskingum, to which was given the name of Marietta, in honor of the unfortunate French queen Marie Antoinette.

During the summer and autumn the settlements in Washington county increased by the arrival of numerous emigrants from east of the mountains, as well as from Western Virginia and Pennsylvania. Early in the autumn Marietta received an accession of twenty families, including those of several of the proprietors of the Muskingum purchase. In December an additional colony from Connecticut arrived by way of the Yough and Pittsburgh. Other accessions were received from the East during the following spring and summer.

* See American Pioneer, vol. i., p. 83, 84.

† It might be interesting to some readers to have the names of the individuals who constituted the first civil and military organization in the Northwestern Territory. They are as follows:

1. MILITIA. *Captains.*—Nathaniel Cushing, Nathan Goodale, Charles Knowles. *Lieutenants.*—George Ingersol, Wanton Casey, Samuel Stebbins. *Ensigns.*—James Backus, Joseph Lincoln, Arnold Colt.

2. CIVIL AUTHORITIES. *Justices of Peace.*—Rufus Putnam, Benjamin Tupper, Winthrop Sargent. *Probate Court.*—Rufus Putnam, *judge;* Return J. Meigs, *clerk.* *Quarter Sessions.*—Archibald Casey, Isaac Pierce, Thomas Lord, Esqrs., *justices;* Return J. Meigs, *clerk.* *Sheriff.*—Ebenezer Sproat. *The Supreme Court,* composed of the *Territorial Judges.*—Samuel Holden Parsons, James Mitchell Varnum, and John Cleves Symmes; and William Callis, *clerk.*—See Atwater's History of Ohio, p. 130.

CAMPUS MARTIUS

The first civil court ever held in the Northwestern Territory convened on the 2d day of September, 1788 : it was the "Court of Common Pleas," held in the hall of the Campus Martius, with Rufus Putnam and Benjamin Tupper presiding justices.

The opening of this court in the remote wilderness was attended with an imposing ceremony, for the first time seen in the West. The governor and judges of the territory having collated, examined, and adopted such of the statutes of the states as were deemed appropriate to the condition of the new colony, proceeded to assert the supremacy of the laws by the organization of a regular court.

A procession was formed on the point near the residence of the citizens ; the sheriff, with a drawn sword, in advance, followed by the citizens, officers of the garrison at Fort Harmar, the members of the bar, the judges of the Supreme Court, the governor and a clergyman, with the judges of the newly-organized Court of Common Pleas, in the order they are named.

Arriving at the hall of the Campus Martius, the whole procession was countermarched into it, and the judges Putnam and Tupper took their seats on the bench; the audience was seated, and, after the divine benediction was invoked by the Rev. Dr. Cutler, the high sheriff, Ebenezer Sproat, advanced to the door, and proclaimed aloud, "Oyes! Oyes! a court is opened for the administration of even-handed justice to the poor and the rich, to the guilty and the innocent, without respect of persons ; none to be punished without a trial by their peers, and in pursuance of the laws and evidence in the case."

Besides the crowd of emigrants and settlers, there were present to witness the ceremonies hundreds of Indians, who had their encampment in the vicinity, for the purpose of entering into a treaty with the Federal government.

The population continued to increase by the arrival of emigrants during the autumn and winter, and by other colonies which arrived subsequently.

In the spring following, it had been determined to make other settlements on the Ohio below the Muskingum, and General Putnam, with a number of families, descended the river to a beautiful level tract about twelve miles below Marietta ; and on the 11th day of April, 1789, he commenced a new settlement near a natural meadow, and called it Belpre.* The set-

---

* See American Pioneer, vol. i., p. 24. Also, Atwater's Ohio, p. 131.

tlers here were intelligent and hardy men; foremost among them was Nathan Goodale, an enterprising officer of the Revolutionary army. These colonists proceeded to erect a blockhouse and the ordinary family residences.. Subsequently, a stockade was added, to secure them from Indian outrage, and the station assumed the name of "Farmer's Castle."

Shortly afterward, a small colony was located ten miles below, upon the bank of the Ohio, and received the name of Newberry. This settlement also augmented its population during the fall and winter, and subsequently was compelled to erect a block-house for protection against the Indians.

Such were the settlements comprised in the first New England colony on the Ohio, included within the limits of the first county of Washington.

Miami Settlement.—At the same time that the settlement was made at the mouth of the Muskingum, a colony was on the route to the West for the settlement of the Miami country. Arriving at the Monongahela late in the autumn, they descended to Limestone, where most of them remained during the winter.

Soon after the purchase by the Ohio Company, Judge John Cleves Symmes, of New Jersey, had purchased of the government six hundred thousand acres of land, to be located between the Great and Little Miami Rivers. The value of the government scrip having advanced since the purchase of the former company, Judge Symmes stipulated to pay sixty cents per acre in military warrants, and in other evidences of debt against the United States.*

During the winter of 1788–89, arrangements were made at Limestone for locating the colony early in the following spring. Large portions of land were sold and distributed in smaller tracts to private companies and individuals, for the purpose of opening the settlements at different points between the Little Miami and the North Bend of the Ohio, twenty-three miles below.

The first purchase from Symmes was made by Major Benjamin Stites, from the Monongahela. This purchase comprised ten thousand acres immediately below the Little Miami River. The colony for its settlement was already on the river from Brownsville.

* See American Pioneer, vol. i., p. 98, 99. Also, Burnett's Letters, p. 135–145

The first portion of Major Stites's colony embraced some twenty families, originally from New York and New Jersey, who advanced from Limestone late in the autumn, and commenced a settlement three miles below the Little Miami about the 16th of November, 1788, upon the north bank of the Ohio. This little colony comprised some of the most intelligent of all the early emigrants to the Miami country. Among them were Colonel Spencer, Major Gano, Judge Goforth, Francis Dunlavy, Major Kibby, John Smith, and Colonel Brown, all men of enterprise and worth, who have left numerous descendants to perpetuate their names.

A few houses or log cabins were erected for dwellings, a block-house for protection against Indian hostility, and such other out-buildings as were necessary to a permanent settlement. Major Stites then proceeded to lay off a town in the woods, which he called Columbia, in honor of his country.*

Thus, about the close of the year 1788, commenced the first settlement in the Miami country, about six months after the first on the Muskingum.

The next purchase was made by Mathias Denham, of New Jersey, comprising a large body of lands immediately adjoining, and west of the former purchase. Denham lost no time in making preparations to enter upon his settlement. Forming a partnership with Robert Patterson and John Filsom, a surveyor, both of Lexington, Kentucky, he engaged the latter to survey and lay off the plan of a town immediately opposite the mouth of Licking River, and to superintend the sale of the lots, while himself and Patterson returned to Limestone to make arrangements for the new colony.

Filsom proceeded to survey the purchase of Denham, and to establish the boundaries of the same; but after a short tour he was killed by Indians, and the survey of the town for a time was delayed.

[A.D. 1789.] About the first of January, 1789, Israel Ludlow was employed to complete the survey and to lay off the plan of the contemplated town. Accordingly, about six weeks after the first location of the town of Columbia, Israel Ludlow and Robert Patterson repaired to the site selected, and, in company with twenty persons, began the first settlement in Den-

* Cincinnati in 1841, p. 15. Burnett's Letters, p. 18. Also, Atwater, p. 132.

ham's purchase, about five miles below Columbia, and opposite the mouth of Licking River.*

Three log houses were erected, and other preparations were made for the reception of families in the spring. The site was a beautiful wooded first bottom, on the immediate bank of the Ohio, about sixty feet above low-water mark, and stretched away upward of three hundred yards from the river, where a second bank, or terrace, rose gently forty feet higher. The second bottom extended back, gently declining to the base of the bluff, more than half a mile from the shore. The whole was clothed with a heavy forest; on the lower bottom was chiefly sycamore, sugar-maple, and black walnut; on the upper terrace were chiefly beech, oaks, and walnut.† The corners of streets were marked upon the trees of the lower bottom, while the corners of lots were designated by stakes driven into the ground.

Thus commenced the second settlement and the second town in the Miami country. By some freak of fancy, the village assumed the name of "Losanteville." But the point was a dangerous one. Immediately in the line of the old Indian war path, emigrants were not anxious to make it their residences; hence it received but few accessions to its population or houses until near the close of the year. In June the population was eleven families and twenty-four single men, and the whole town consisted of about twenty log cabins.

The summer witnessed a continual line of emigration from the Atlantic States to the Ohio River. Many of these, from the New England States, took up their residence in the Ohio Company's purchase, near the settlements already formed on the Muskingum and the Ohio, above the Hockhocking River. Many from New Jersey and Virginia, desirous of joining the settlers of the Miami country, were induced, by the uncertain peace of the Indian tribes, to take up a temporary residence in Kentucky. Yet the settlements of Colonel Stites and Major Denham, below the Little Miami, received several emigrant parties from New York and New Jersey.

About this time, Judge Symmes, who was indefatigable in settling his lands, laid out and commenced a town at North Bend, sixteen miles below the last settlement, to which emigrants were attracted until the following year, when the erec-

* Cincinnati in 1841, p. 15–17.   † See Burnett's Letters, p. 11.

tion of Fort Washington presented greater inducements near the mouth of Licking.*

In the mean time, these new settlements were gradually increasing, and attracting the attention of the commander of Fort Harmar, from their exposed situation and the frequent indications of approaching hostilities by the Indians. Accordingly, early in the summer, Major Doughty, a brave and efficient officer, was detached from Fort Harmar with one hundred and forty regular troops for the protection of the Miami settlements. He took up his position on the terrace, or second bottom, just above the town of Losanteville, where he encamped his troops until a selection for a post should have been made. Before the expiration of June, he decided to erect his post opposite the mouth of Licking, upon a reservation of fifteen acres belonging to the Federal government. He immediately commenced the erection of four block-houses, as the outlines of a stockade, upon the margin of the terrace above the town.†

The body of the new fort and the outline of palisades were soon in a state of perfection, indicating a formidable military post, completely impregnable to any Indian attack.

The principal building was a large two-story house, one hundred and eighty feet in length, constructed of hewed logs, the upper story projecting two feet beyond the lower, and divided off into apartments for the soldiers, and well provided with port-holes for defensive firing: the whole surrounded by an inclosure of strong palisades planted in the ground, and flanked at each corner by strong block-houses or bastions, projecting ten feet beyond the line of stockades, from which cannon could be brought to rake the walls. Through the middle of the lower story was the principal entrance, facing the river, and secured by strong wooden doors, leaving a passage twelve feet wide and ten feet high. On the north or back side it was secured by a strong picket inclosure surrounding the outbuildings, shops, and stables. The front presented a fine esplanade eighty feet wide, with a glacis of thirty feet descent. The whole exterior was thoroughly white-washed, and from a distance presented a handsome and imposing appearance. Around it were the beautiful gardens of the officers, handsomely ornamented with summer-houses, and affording a variety of vegetables in great abundance. Such was Fort Washington after

* Burnett's Letters, p. 16–18.   † Cincinnati in 1841, p. 18.

its completion in 1790, and until after the treaty of Greenville.

About the last of December, 1789, General Harmar, with three hundred regular troops, arrived, and Fort Washington shortly afterward became the headquarters of the northwestern army and the residence of the governor.*

[A.D. 1790.] In the mean time, the population in the Miami settlements had increased to such an extent that Governor St. Clair deemed it expedient to organize civil government without further delay.† In company with the territorial judges, he arrived at Fort Washington, and early in January following convened his executive council in the adjacent village, which by this time, through the influence of some of the officers in the garrison, had assumed the name of "Cincinnati." Without delay he proceeded to organize the civil and military departments of the territorial government in the same manner as Washington county had been organized at Marietta. The whole country contiguous to the Ohio, from the Hock-

* Cincinnati in 1841, p. 19.

† Previous to the arrival of Governor St. Clair at Fort Washington, no civil government existed in this portion of the country, and no judicial tribunal was open. The inhabitants were compelled to take some steps for their own protection against the vicious and unprincipled. To this effect, notice was given throughout the settlement that there would be a public meeting of the people next day to consult what was necessary for the common safety. The meeting convened, agreeably to notice, under a large spreading tree, and was organized by appointing William M'Millan chairman, and a secretary. A code of by-laws was formed, and the punishment for certain offenses was decreed. Before adjournment, every person present pledged himself to aid in carrying these provisions into execution as the laws of the settlement. William M'Millan was appointed judge, and John Ludlow sheriff. The first culprit was Patrick Grimes, for a petit larceny. A jury, summoned for his trial, the testimony and defense being heard, found him guilty, and the judge awarded to him thirty-nine lashes on his bare back, which was inflicted the same evening. Some weeks afterward another writ was issued for a culprit, but he escaped to the garrison and claimed the protection of the commandant, who next day sent to Judge M'Millan an abusive note; to which a spirited reply was returned by the judge, setting the commandant at defiance. The military pride of the subaltern was touched, and next day he dispatched a sergeant and three men to arrest the judge. The judge was a large, vigorous man, possessed of great activity. Sitting in his cabin, his first notice was the appearance of the sergeant's guard at the door. M'Millan refused to be taken alive, and forbade them entering his cabin. In the attempt to secure him, a furious contest ensued, and was continued for fifteen or twenty minutes. The sergeant and one of the guards were disabled, and the other two, more or less injured and exhausted in the struggle, withdrew, leaving the judge badly wounded, but master of his own domicil. Such was the first conflict between the civil and military authority in the Northwestern Territory, and in which the supremacy of the civil authority was fully maintained by the intrepid judge. Governor St. Clair soon afterward arrived, and, in organizing the regular government, William M'Millan was not forgotten. Although laboring under his wound, he was appointed one of the justices of the quorum.—Burnett's Letters, p. 20, 21.

hocking River to the Great Miami, was designated as the "county of Hamilton," in honor of the Secretary of the Treasury. Cincinnati was declared to be the seat of justice for this extensive county. On the 2d day of January the governor and executive committee completed the civil organization of Hamilton county, which, like that of Washington, comprised three justices of the peace, four captains of militia, four lieutenants, and four ensigns, a court of quarter sessions, constituted of three associate justices, a clerk, and a sheriff. The regular meetings of the Court of Quarter Sessions was fixed by law, ordained and enacted January 5th, to be holden on the first Tuesdays in February, May, August, and November.*

Cincinnati, being the seat of justice for Hamilton county, as well as headquarters of the army, began to assume a degree of importance unknown to similar towns which had recently sprung up in the wilderness. It became the center of fashion and refinement, and soon attracted many persons of intelligence and enterprise. Frame houses began to appear, and during the following summer nearly forty log cabins were added as the dwellings of so many new families.

A new settlement was made about this time on the Great Miami, seventeen miles north from Cincinnati. This was the settlement of Colerain, where a number of families united and erected a stockade for mutual protection and defense. Such was the exposed situation of this advanced settlement, while the incursions of the savages were becoming more frequent and daring, that a small detachment of United States troops, under the command of Lieutenant Kingsbury, with one piece of artillery, was ordered to take post in the station for its defense.†

Governor St. Clair was ever active. No sooner had he completed his public duties in organizing the civil government of Hamilton county, than he set off for the "Falls of the Ohio,"

---

* It may be satisfactory to the reader to have the names of the persons who exercised the first civil and military authority in Hamilton county, and the second in the State of Ohio. They are as follows:

1. MILITIA. *Captains.*—Israel Ludlow, James Flinn, John S. Gano, and Gresham Guard. *Lieutenants.*—Francis Kennedy, John Ferris, Luke Foster, and Brier Virgin. *Ensigns.*—Scott Traverse, Ephraim Kibby, Elijah Stites, and John Dunlap.

2. *Justices of the Peace.*—Jacob Topping, Benjamin Stites, and John S. Gano.

3. COURT OF QUARTER SESSIONS. *Associate Justices.*—William Goforth, William Wells, and William M'Millan. *Clerk.*—Israel Ludlow. *Sheriff.*—John Brown.—See Atwater's Ohio, p. 130. † Burnett's Letters, p. 31.

where he spent a few days in Clarksville, engaged in similar duties. Thence he proceeded by land across the wilderness, one hundred and thirty miles by an Indian trace, to Vincennes, on the Wabash. Here, with his council, he proceeded to organize the county of Knox, named in honor of the Secretary of War. The limits of Knox county extended from the Great Miami to the Wabash, with the Ohio on the south. Vincennes was the seat of justice.*

The governor proceeded westward; and at Cahokia, on the Upper Mississippi, he organized the county of St. Clair. This county comprised all the territory from the Wabash to the Mississippi, and southward to the Ohio, and was subdivided into three judicial districts, known as those of Cahokia, Prairie du Rocher, and Kaskaskia.†

Since the first arrival on the Muskingum, more than two years had now elapsed, and the settlements on the Ohio Company's purchase had multiplied, and the number of immigrants upon each had gradually increased. The militia rolls in the county of Washington comprised four hundred and forty-seven men fit for militia duty. Of these, one hundred and three were heads of families. A few persons had been cut off by the lurking Indians. The total population of Washington county was about twenty-five hundred souls.

Since the first arrival upon the Miami purchase, eighteen months had elapsed; and between the Little Miami and the Great Miami numerous settlements had already been commenced, and there had been a rapid increase of settlers in those first planted. The entire population of Hamilton county was about two thousand souls; and the whole number of men upon the muster rolls fit for militia duty was but little less than those of Washington county, besides the regular troops in Fort Washington.‡ But the annoyance and danger from Indian hostilities had been also gradually increasing, and the settlers were now compelled to protect themselves with more care, and confine themselves within their fortified stations and block-houses. The advance of the emigrants was, in fact, checked by the determined opposition of the Indians and the increasing danger of the settlers. Several of those within six

---
* Burnett's Letters, p. 48.
† Idem, p. 48. Also, Winterbotham's America, vol. ii, p. 486.
‡ See Atwater's Ohio, p. 157. Also, Winterbotham's America, vol. ii., p. 487.

or eight miles of Fort Washington had been so exposed to the lurking savages that General Harmar had furnished them with a few soldiers for their protection.

The Indians had from the first indicated signs of a hostile movement. They had loitered about the settlements, and appeared to observe the nature and extent of the defenses. They had committed sundry depredations on the property of the settlers. They had waylaid the paths and traces which led from one settlement to another, and several persons had been murdered by them near the larger stations. At length the murders became more frequent and daring. The settlers dared not venture out from their inclosures only at the peril of their lives. No precaution or vigilance was sufficient security from the vengeance of the insidious foe, who lurked unseen under every bush and covert. Some would insinuate themselves under the guise of friendship, to enable them the more securely to destroy. Fugitive negro slaves had taken asylum among the savages, and were sometimes emissaries of death.

Such became the dread and apprehension in the settlements on account of Indian and negro treachery, that the executive council ordained it to be a penal offense for any one to entertain any Indian or negro without first reporting him to the commandant. All male settlers and immigrants were likewise required by law to carry their arms with them on all occasions, even to public worship. When at their daily work in the fields and about the stations, one or more sentinels were posted near, upon some stump or other eminence, to give timely warning of any approach of danger.

For nearly twelve months the Federal government had resolved to invade the Indian country with a strong military force, and to destroy their fields and burn their towns, in retaliation for the murders and depredations which had been committed upon the whites on the Ohio for three years past. During the year 1790, active preparations had been in operation for concentrating at Fort Washington a sufficient force of regular troops and militia for the accomplishment of this purpose, provided negotiation and overtures of peace, in the mean time, should fail to induce a suspension of their outrages upon the settlers. The chief towns of the hostile Indians at that time were upon the great branches of the Maumee River, and especially upon the waters of the Au Glaize.

Near the close of summer, a large body of troops had been assembled at the mouth of Licking, and in the vicinity of the Miami River, north of Cincinnati, for the contemplated invasion. Many of the settlers and recent immigrants connected themselves with the army, which early in October was in motion, under General Harmar, for the Maumee towns. Hope gleamed on the new settlements, and foretold better days, with exemption from Indian dangers. But, before one month had elapsed, the remnant of the army returned to Fort Washington, if not defeated, certainly with the loss of many brave men, and with little or no injury to the savages,* who, highly exasperated, pursued and harassed the retreating army almost to Fort Washington.

The tide of immigration to the Ohio had been already checked, and the new settlements in the Northwestern Territory were greatly depressed by the unsuccessful campaign under the commander-in-chief. The settlers became more fearful, and the Indians became more audacious. They prowled secretly about the stations, and even through the streets of Cincinnati at night.

[A.D. 1791.] The first massacre upon the Muskingum was on the second day of the year 1791, and gave a fearful import of future vengeance.

This was the destruction of the settlement at Big Bottom, on the Muskingum. This situation had been imprudently occupied a few months before, and against the advice of the more experienced, by a party of young men, who had been delighted with the beauty of the lands. The whole colony consisted of about twenty-five persons, including several female heads of families. They had erected a block-house and several log cabins, and seemed to enjoy perfect impunity from Indian molestation.

On the 2d day of January a party of twenty-five Indians advanced to the brow of the eminence which overlooks the Muskingum Valley.† Here they concealed themselves, patiently observing the movements of the little colony during the day, until after the evening twilight, when, descending, they advanced to the assault. The assailants divided off in parties to attack each house simultaneously, directed by the fires within.

* For the account of General Harmar's campaign, see chap. xi., Indian Hostilities and Military Operations of the United States.—Burnett's Letters, p. 30.
† Pioneer, vol. ii., p. 109.

The tenants of the block-house were sitting around the supper-table by the cheerful fire-light, and their guns were standing in the corner of the room. The house being surrounded by the Indians, one large Mohawk gently pushed open the door, while his comrades fired upon the men at the table, who dropped one after the other. A woman seized an ax, and made a desperate blow at the Mohawk who held the door, and inflicted upon him a terrible wound. She was immediately dispatched by the tomahawk, with the remaining inmates.

Another cabin was entered at the same time by another party of Indians, who bound the inmates and took them prisoners. The occupants of a third cabin had not been secured, when, alarmed by the report of the guns at the block-house, they escaped into the woods and concealed themselves from the enemy. The Indians failing to find them, proceeded to plunder the houses of every thing valuable, and then set fire to them. They secured the prisoners and regaled themselves by the light of the burning houses. The whole number killed at this settlement was fourteen persons, of whom eleven were young men, besides one woman and two children. Five persons, including four men and one boy, were taken captive to Detroit.*

Within a few days, all the settlements on the Muskingum beyond the guns of Fort Harmar were broken up, and those who had not made a timely escape were killed or taken prisoners.

Hostile movements were made simultaneously against other neighborhoods, and those around Fort Washington were special objects of savage indignation. A large Indian force had marched for this quarter of the American settlements. Colerain was already a large station, advanced seventeen miles north of Fort Hamilton. On the 8th day of January four men from this station were exploring the lands on the west bank of the Miami, when they suddenly perceived the advance of a large Indian army. They fled with all haste; but two of them, Cunningham and Abner Hunt, were killed; the other two escaped to the station and gave the alarm. The body of Hunt was afterward found most barbarously mutilated, and with a firebrand thrust into the bowels.†

The Indians did not appear before the station until next

* Atwater's Ohio, p. 153.   † Cincinnati in 1841, p. 21.

morning, when three hundred warriors demanded its surrender. The demand was promptly refused, and the attack immediately began. The defense was made with equal spirit and perseverance for twenty-four hours. The Indians, apprehending a re-enforcement from the garrison at Fort Washington, suddenly retired, to the great relief of the station. One hour afterward, Captain Truman, with thirty regular troops and thirty-three volunteers from Cincinnati, came to the assistance of the besieged.

During the attack the defense was conducted with the usual frontier courage. Captain Kingsbury, with eighteen regular troops and fourteen other inmates of the station, conducted the defense. The women supplied the riflemen with bullets, and when the lead was expended, they melted their pewter plates and spoons into balls.

But no danger seemed sufficient to deter the emigrants from attempts to obtain a foot-hold in the delightful country which had been partly explored. New locations were still made near the banks of the Ohio, where a partial security was felt from the vicinity of the Virginia and Kentucky shores.

It was early in January, 1791, that Nathaniel Massie, one of the most enterprising pioneers of Ohio, first made a location on the north bank of the Ohio River, within the "Virginia Military District," twelve miles below the town of Limestone.

In the location at Manchester, he had obligated himself, by a written compact with his colonists, to grant in fee simple to every person who should settle and remain with his family two years, one town-lot and one out-lot, besides one hundred acres in the vicinity, until the number amounted to twenty-five families. About thirty families soon joined him under these stipulations. The settlement was immediately begun, and by the middle of March cabins were erected for their residence, and the whole inclosed with a strong stockade, with a block-house at each angle, for defense.*

The next colony located within the present State of Ohio was that of Gallipolis, direct from France. This colony, of about four hundred persons, had been made up in Paris, where the principal persons had purchased a large extent of lands from Joel Barlow, "agent of the Scioto Company." They had paid for their lands at the rate of a French crown per acre

* American Pioneer, vol. i., p. 71. Also, M'Donald's Sketches, p. 12–40.

while in France, to enable the company to consummate their contract with the government. The agent of the company had accompanied them to the Ohio River, and had selected for them a beautiful site on the west bank, two miles below the Great Kenhawa River, and within the limits, as was subsequently ascertained, of the Ohio Company's purchase. The location having been selected, the immigrants remained upon the Ohio River, whither they had arrived from Philadelphia, during the winter, ready to commence their new settlement. Early in March the colony was all action and enterprise, clearing land, erecting houses and inclosures for their future security from Indian hostility. Peace and joy seemed to smile upon them; and the arduous toils of the day were beguiled by mirth and festivity at night, cheered by the melody of the violin and the gay dance. But soon they found themselves deceived in a strange land, beset by savage foes, and, in fact, without a home and without money.* The Scioto Company could not give titles to the land, and were dissolved, and irresponsible for the one hundred thousand francs which they had received from the credulous Frenchmen.†

During the summer of 1791 the settlements on the Muskingum, and on the Ohio below Marietta, as well as the French colony of Gallipolis, were greatly harassed by Indian depredations and incursions; yet each settlement was re-enforced by a few troops, detailed for their protection by Captain Haskell, who commanded at Fort Harmar during the Indian war.‡

The summer had been spent by the officers of the United States army in preparations for another campaign against the Miami towns southwest of Lake Erie. Troops had been drawn

---

* American Pioneer, vol. i., p. 94, 95.

† The "Scioto Company" was an association of several New England men, for the purchase of a large body of lands adjacent to the Ohio Company's purchase, which had not yet been defined on the west. They had been negotiating with the government to effect their purchase; but after their sale to the French emigrants, the company failed to comply with its obligations, and never became entitled to the lands in question. The easy Frenchmen were left without remedy. Many of them left the country, after suffering much from sickness, privation, and Indian troubles. Others subsequently petitioned Congress for relief; and that body generously made them a grant of a large body of lands near the Scioto, known as the "French Grant." Many, however, had migrated to the Wabash, to join their countrymen at Vincennes; some had returned to Philadelphia, and some to France. The "French Grant" by Congress for the remainder comprised twenty-four thousand acres; besides which, Congress gave them permission to purchase any other lands at a reduced price.—See Pioneer, vol. ii., p. 182, 183. Also, Atwater's Ohio, p. 159.

‡ See American Pioneer, vol. ii., p. 25-27.

from the different states contiguous; and volunteers from Kentucky and the western parts of Virginia, as well as from the new settlements north of the Ohio River, cheerfully joined the standard of General St. Clair, who was to command the expedition in person. At length, on the 17th day of September, the army set out from Fort Washington, and, by slow and regular marches, advanced on the west side of the Great Miami northwardly as far as the extreme sources of the Wabash River, and by estimate about fifty miles from the principal Miami towns near the mouth of the Au Glaize. Here, on the 4th of November, the army was surprised by the Indians and completely routed, with the loss of nearly half of the troops left on the field of battle.* The remnant of the army reached Fort Washington on the 8th of November, spreading consternation and mourning in every family. Nearly one half of the settlers had entered the ranks of the army, and many of them had fallen in the fatal engagement, and others lost friends and relatives among the slain.

The whole settlements in the Miami country were broken up or forsaken, except those in the immediate vicinity of the forts. Many determined to retire, for greater safety, across the Ohio, to the more settled parts of Kentucky, until the imminent danger should cease.

The Indians, encouraged by their late successes, ventured into the streets of Cincinnati by night, and spied out all the movements in the town and about Fort Washington. Others lurked and prowled through the settlements, and destroyed all who were unprotected.†

[A.D. 1792.] General Washington, President of the United States, had been anxious to see the war prosecuted with that energy and force which the honor and peace of the government required; but he had met with every kind of opposition in his plans from the opponents of his administration in Congress. Now, after two disastrous campaigns, and the destruction of two armies, they had assumed more assurance, and urged the policy of withdrawing the Federal jurisdiction and forces from the Northwestern Territory, conceding the Ohio River as the boundary, and a speedy peace upon this basis with the Indians.‡

---

* See chap. xi., "Military Operations of the U. States." † Pioneer, vol. ii., p. 149.
‡ Atwater's Ohio, p. 143.

The tardy manner in which Congress met the wishes of the president in providing the means of prosecuting the war was ample evidence of its unpopularity east of the mountains.

The whole of the year 1792 had nearly elapsed without any active measures by the general government for the protection of the frontier settlements, or the chastisement of the Indians. At length, in the spring of 1793, Congress authorized and provided for the organization of a strong expedition with regular troops into the heart of the Indian country, to chastise the hostile savages and retrieve the national honor. Recruiting officers were distributed through the western counties, and also east of the mountains, preparatory to the ulterior operations on the frontier.

[A.D. 1793.] Indian hostilities, since St. Clair's defeat, became more regular and systematic; war parties penetrated into every settlement, and killed, with the most cruel barbarities, all who fell into their hands. Having acquired confidence in themselves, and contempt for their enemies on the Ohio, they became more daring in their incursions upon the settlements, as well as upon the immigrants descending the Ohio River to Kentucky.

During the year 1793, about fifty immigrants were added to the population of Cincinnati. Several cabins, three or four frames, and one Presbyterian house of worship were erected, and it began to assume the appearance of a regular place of trade and business.* As usual in all such cases, the headquarters of the army and the seat of the territorial government gave an importance and air of business to the place which many years could not have imparted without these influences. The town was now built along the lower terrace, near the river, in a straggling street of log cabins, intersected by short cross-streets extending to the second terrace, which was crowned by the imposing walls and bastions of Fort Washington. The site of the town was still a forest, partly leveled, with its logs and stumps visible in every direction, and bounded in the rear by a heavy forest in its natural state, with a few partial openings.

Religion and morals were not neglected. The rude Presbyterian church recently erected was occupied on Sabbaths by its first pastor, James Kemper, an eloquent divine. A

* Cincinnati in 1841, p. 25.

school had been opened during the summer, and was attended by thirty boys and girls, who were taught the elements of reading, writing, and arithmetic.*

The greater portion of this year had been spent in raising the new levies for the regular army, and late in the autumn detachments began to arrive on the upper portions of the Ohio, preparatory to opening an early campaign next spring. Advanced detachments of the regular army at Fort Washington and bodies of militia had been posted at Fort Jefferson, seventy miles north of Cincinnati, which served to protect that frontier.

The continual hostile movements of the war parties who scoured the country north and west of the Ohio, during the preparations for another invasion under General Wayne, were such that but few of the settlements increased their population, unless it were those in the immediate vicinity of Forts Harmar and Washington. During this time the Ohio Company's colony kept in continual service about six " spies," who ranged the woods for miles in the vicinity of the settlements, for the purpose of discovering and destroying any small parties of Indians who might be lying about for scalps or plunder. If larger bodies were discovered, they immediately gave notice, and the forts and stations were prepared to receive them. The alarm-gun fired at the fort admonished all within hearing of the danger, and all hastened to the stockade for protection. The same precautions were taken on the Miamis. Yet this year witnessed several murders near the settlements, notwithstanding these precautions. At Belpre several persons had been killed, having ventured too far into the woods when no Indian sign had been seen. Major Nathaniel Goodale, an officer of the old Continental army, having gone into the forest to haul timber, was taken prisoner by two lurking Indians, and carried captive to Sandusky, where he died six weeks afterward. Captain King, from Rhode Island, was shot while cutting wood in sight of the stockade, besides others at other points of the settlement. Newberry settlement lost one woman and two children, killed by Indians near the adjoining field.†

Notwithstanding all these dangers, civilization was taking deep root upon the north bank of the Ohio. Before the close

---

* See Flint's History and Geography, vol. ii., p. 379, first edition.
† Atwater's Ohio, p. 151, 152.

of this year, the first newspaper ever published north of the Ohio was issued in Cincinnati. This was the "Sentinel of the Northwestern Territory," the first number of which was issued on the 9th day of November, 1793, by William Maxwell. This paper, like those which had been issued in Pittsburgh in July, 1786, and in Lexington in August, 1787, was a small weekly sheet, badly printed, and of inferior materials. Like all the newspapers in the West for many years afterward, it was printed on an old cast-off press, with worn-out types, having only a few sets of new type for job-work. All the first western papers were published by young printers, who were unable to purchase new presses and type, and were compelled to use those that had been worn out, because they could be obtained cheap.*

During nearly three years past, while the settlements were driven into forts and block-houses, and harassed with continual alarms and menaced with constant attack, the civil administration of the territorial government had almost ceased, or had been only partially enforced. The military authority, as is common in all countries in time of general danger, had superseded the civil administration, and swallowed up the legislative and judicial functions in the person of the commander-in-chief.

In the mean time, General Anthony Wayne, a distinguished officer of the Revolutionary army, had been appointed commander-in-chief of the northwestern army, and to him were confided the arduous duties of organizing a powerful military force for the effectual invasion of the Indian country. The well-known character of this accomplished and energetic soldier for prudence, system, courage, and command, gave general satisfaction to the western people, and restored the confidence and drooping courage of the frontier settlers.

During the close of the year 1793, military preparations had been active throughout all the western country, and troops were rapidly concentrating upon the Ohio River from Pittsburgh to the "Falls." The ranks were filled not only with regulars enlisted during the war, but with militia and cheerful volunteers. The settlements northwest of the Ohio began to experience some relief from Indian incursions, and a gleam of hope shone again upon their future prospects.

* Atwater's Ohio, p. 320, 321.

Although the Indians had remitted their depredations partially upon the Ohio River, they were actively engaged in forming alliances with western and southern tribes, and concentrating upon the waters of the Maumee their utmost strength, to meet the hostile invasion with which they were threatened.

[A.D. 1794.] Want, privation, and distress had been experienced by the new settlements, until they had almost despaired of a change. But the movements of General Wayne, upon the opening of the campaign, early in the summer of 1794, withdrew the Indian warriors to the immediate defense of their own towns. A succession of bold advances from Fort Jefferson drove the Indian forces before him, with the loss of all their towns, fields, and possessions, until they made a stand upon the north bank of the Maumee, within two miles of the British "Fort of the Miamis." In a pitched battle, on the 20th day of August, the American army completely routed and defeated the combined army of Indians and Canadians, driving them under the protection of the guns of the British fort.*

On the other hand, the whites took fresh courage; the settlements near the Ohio began to increase their numbers by the arrival of new immigrants, and those who two years before had retired in despair to the secure settlements of Kentucky, began to return to the occupation of their former improvements.

[A.D. 1795.] Although few or no hostilities were perpetrated upon the inhabitants after the battle of the Miamis, yet suspicion of danger, and the uncertain security from Indian incursions, deterred immigrants from attempts to form new settlements.

The treaty of Greenville,† in the following summer, put an end to doubts and fears as to danger from the Indians; and hundreds were ready, waiting the result of the negotiations known to have been undertaken by General Wayne. The whole white population within the limits of the present State of Ohio at that time, exclusive of the army, did not exceed five thousand souls, distributed in the sparse settlements.

* See chap. x., "Military Operations of the United States."
† See chap. ix., "Indian Relations and Treaties."

CHAPTER X.

EARLY SETTLEMENT AND INDIAN HOSTILITIES IN THE "SOUTH-WESTERN TERRITORY," UNTIL ITS ADMISSION INTO THE FEDERAL UNION AS THE STATE OF TENNESSEE.—A.D. 1776 TO 1796.

Argument.—Retrospect of the First Settlements of East Tennessee.—First Settlements on Cumberland River.—Cherokee Hostilities in 1780.—North Carolina encourages Emigration to the Cumberland in 1783.—Military Land District erected.—Chickasá Cession in 1784.—Increased Emigration to Holston and Cumberland in 1785.—Political Difficulties in Washington District.—Attempted Organization of the "Republic of Frankland."—Colonel John Sevier attainted for Treason, and restored to his Rights.—Authority of North Carolina sustained.—Spanish Influence in the Cumberland Settlements.—Population of Washington and Miro Districts in 1789.—North Carolina cedes her Western Territory to the Federal Government.—" Southwestern Territory" organized in 1790.—Indian Hostilities commence.—Efforts of the Federal Government to maintain Peace.—Rapid Increase of Emigration Westward in 1791.—Indian Hostilities in 1791 to 1793.—Spanish Intrigue with the Indians.—Colonel Sevier and General Robertson conduct Defenses.—Population of Southwestern Territory in 1794.—Population of the Territory in 1795.—Second Grade of Territorial Government assumed.—State Constitution adopted in 1796.—" State of Tennessee" admitted into the Union.—Features of Constitution.—Progressive Increase of Population and Extension of Settlements to the Mississippi until 1840.—Displacement of the Indian Tribes.—West Tennessee and Memphis.—Population and Enterprise.—Colonies sent out from Tennessee.

[A.D. 1776.] IN another portion of this work,* we have shown that the country now comprised in the extreme eastern and southeastern counties of Tennessee, and especially the counties of Washington, Carter, Sullivan, Greene, and Hawkins, was sparsely settled by Virginians and North Carolinians as early as the beginning of the Revolutionary war. These settlements, early in the latter period, gradually extended upon the tributaries of the north and south branches of the Holston, and upon the Watauga and French Broad, for more than one hundred miles toward the southwest, along the western base of the great Alleghany range of mountains, and within the former limits of North Carolina. Soon after the Declaration of Independence, the people of these remote settlements were invited by the British authorities to espouse the royal cause against the revolted provinces; but, with noble firmness, they indignantly rejected the proffered protection of the crown, and adhered to the cause of independence.†

---

* See book iii., chap. iii., "Advance of Anglo-American Population," &c.
† Winterbotham's America, vol. ii., p. 26.

In the autumn of 1776, these settlements, as the "Western District," were entitled to a delegate in the convention for the adoption of a state constitution. Among the prominent men of this region at that early period was Captain John Sevier, who had been an active defender of the frontiers in the preceding Indian wars. The confidence reposed in him by the western people was such that they elected him to represent the Western District in the convention for adopting a state constitution for North Carolina. During the continuance of the struggle for independence, he was a prominent soldier in resisting the incursions of the British cavalry in the western settlements.

[A.D. 1777.] During the year 1777, the jurisdiction of North Carolina was formally extended over the Western District, which was organized into the "county of Washington," having a nominal jurisdiction westward to the Mississippi.*

The militia of Washington county was organized under Colonel Carter and Lieutenant-colonel John Sevier.† Before the close of the year, large bodies of land were relinquished by the Cherokees, in conformity with the stipulations in the treaty of the preceding year. The settlements began immediately to extend upon the ceded territory down the north fork of Holston, and upon the branches of the south fork, and emigration continued gradually to swell the population.

[A.D. 1778.] Only a few months elapsed from the organization of Washington county, when the adventurous pioneers began to plunge into the remote western forest, more than three hundred miles by the only route from the older settlements of the new county. A settlement was commenced on the lower valley of the Cumberland River, nearly one hundred miles west of the chain of the Cumberland Mountains. To reach this remote region, the pioneers advanced through Cumberland Gap, and, diverging from the wilderness route to Kentucky, they proceeded nearly one hundred miles through the southern part of the present State of Kentucky, and thence down the Cumberland Valley to the vicinity of the present site of Nashville. This route traversed the country which had been partly relinquished by the Cherokees to Richard Henderson and Company. South of it was the undisputed territory of the Cherokees and Creeks, who permitted no encroachment with im-

---

* Martin's Louisiana, vol. ii., p. 41.
‡ Flint's History and Geography, vol. ii., p. 21, edition of 1828.

punity. The first settlement in this remote region was that near Bledsoe's Station, in the vicinity of Bledsoe's Lick; it was occupied the first year by less than a dozen families, isolated in the heart of the Chickasâ nation, with no other protection than their own courage and a small stockade inclosure.*

About the same time, a number of French traders advanced up the Cumberland River as far as "the Bluff," near the present city of Nashville, where they erected a trading-post and a few log cabins,† with the approbation of the Chickasâs.

[A.D. 1780.] Bledsoe's Station, in the year 1779, received an accession of several additional families, who advanced by the same route from the Holston settlements. With this accession to their numbers, the little colony continued to hold undisputed possession of the country now comprised in Middle Tennessee, until the autumn of 1780, when Colonel James Robertson led out a colony of forty families, who were anxious to retire beyond the reach of the marauding incursions of the British cavalry, which had repeatedly ravaged the remote western settlements of North Carolina. So long as they remained within striking distance of Tarlton's troop, they were allowed the only alternative of submitting to the insolent ravages of the British soldiery, or of espousing the royal cause against their friends and fellow-citizens.‡

Colonel Robertson and his colony, preferring to encounter the dangers of savage warfare to the ruthless incursions of the English, set out for the remote wilderness upon the lower Cumberland Valley. His location was made not far from the present site of Nashville, where he proceeded to erect a stockade inclosure for the protection of the colony from Indian hostility. This was the beginning of "Robertson's Station," which became the nucleus of the Cumberland settlements, around which were gathered the numerous emigrants who soon afterward advanced to this region.

This remote point continued to be the object of adventurers for three years, when the flood-gates of emigration were opened by North Carolina, in establishment of a military land district in this vicinity.

In the mean time, the Cherokees had become impatient of

---

* Flint's History and Geography, vol. ii., p. 21.
† Martin's Louisiana, vol. ii., p. 41.
‡ Imlay's America, p. 14, 15. Also, Guthrie's Geography, vol. ii., p. 472.

the advance of the white population upon the Holston, and before the close of the year 1780 they commenced active hostilities upon the frontier inhabitants of Washington District. To protect the exposed colonies, and to chastise the warlike savages, Colonel Campbell, of North Carolina, invaded the Cherokee country with a force of seven hundred mounted riflemen, and spread consternation and desolation in his march. This was the first time that cavalry in the character of mounted riflemen had been employed successfully against the hostile Indians, and it was the beginning of a new era in savage warfare in the West.*

It was in the summer of 1782 that the government of North Carolina determined to establish a military land district in her western territory for the liquidation of military land-scrip and Revolutionary claims in favor of officers and soldiers of the old Continental line. The same year commissioners were appointed to explore the country upon Cumberland River, and select a suitable region for the military district. After due exploration, they reported in favor of the country south and west of the new settlements upon that river, which was still in the occupancy of the Chickasâ Indians.

[A.D. 1783.] At the next session of the Legislature, provision was made for the formal extension of the state jurisdiction over this country in the organization of a land district, with a land-office, together with a pre-emption law in favor of actual settlers. The latter opened the way of emigration to the Cumberland River, and was a virtual invitation to the people to advance to the occupancy of this valuable region of country.

To prevent collision with the Chickasâ nation, commissioners were appointed to hold a council with the chiefs, head men, and warriors of that tribe for the amicable relinquishment of the country designated. The Indians were assembled early in the year 1783, in the vicinity of Robertson's Station, where a treaty was concluded. In this treaty, the Chickasâs, for and in consideration of certain amounts to them paid, agreed to cede and relinquish to the State of North Carolina an extensive region of country extending nearly forty miles south of the Cumberland River, to the dividing ridge between the tributaries of that river and those of Duck and Elk Rivers. This cession, subsequently confirmed by the treaty of Hopewell, in the year

* See Winterbotham's America, vol. ii., p. 27.

1785, was formed into a land district for the entry and location of lands. Emigrants immediately commenced their journeys to these western regions, which offered many advantages unknown to the country east of the mountains. Among them were hundreds of officers and soldiers of the Revolutionary armies, and with them came men of talent and enterprise.

[A.D. 1784.] The tide of emigration during the year 1784 began to set strong upon the Cumberland, as well as into Washington District. In the latter, the population had greatly increased, and settlements had extended until the district contained no less than four counties.

The peace of 1783 had quieted all apprehension on the score of English depredations and partisan warfare. The restless population of the Atlantic States were left free to pursue their own inclinations for western adventure and exploration. No state in the confederacy possessed more of this roving and adventurous spirit than North Carolina. Her western regions had been explored, and the fame of their beauty and fertility were the subject of every fireside conversation, and the object of every family's ambition. The privations, the hardships, and the dangers of a frontier life to them had all the charms of romance without its novelty. There is a charm in the virgin earth and primeval forests of the West which perfectly bewilders the mind of the emigrant from old and dense settlements.

The whole Atlantic population, from Maine to Georgia, was convulsed with the tide of emigration setting toward the great Valley of the Mississippi. While Pennsylvania, Virginia, Maryland, and New Jersey were sending their colonies upon the tributaries of the Monongahela, the states of North and South Carolina, as well as Southern Virginia, were sending numerous colonies upon the waters of the Holston and Clinch, and even to the remote regions of Cumberland River and to Kentucky.

Although settlements were extending west of the Cumberland Mountains and upon the lower portion of the Cumberland River, yet such had been the inveterate hostility of the Cherokees and Creeks, that the southern tributaries of the Holston were still chiefly in their possession.

But the following year brought large accessions of emigrants from North Carolina and Georgia to the head waters of the south fork of the Holston, and upon the Watauga. The white population was rapidly extending upon the waters of the Nolichucky and French Broad, where five years before the Indian was sole lord of the soil.*

The settlements which had been made on the Cumberland River, and which had been slowly increasing for the last two years, now began to augment rapidly. Nashville, the present emporium of the state, was first laid out during this summer, and received its name in honor of the gallant General Francis Nash, who fell in the battle of Brandywine.† Many soldiers and officers of the Revolutionary army were among the emigrants for the Cumberland settlements; and these had now increased their population to more than three thousand souls. Still they were citizens of North Carolina, subject to her laws and amenable to her authority; although, like their neighbors, the pioneers of Kentucky, they were removed nearly five hundred miles from the state capital. Unprotected by the troops of the state, or of the United States, they were compelled to protect and defend themselves against the united attacks of the Cherokees and Creeks.

[A.D. 1785.] The same inconveniences which induced the separation of Kentucky operated with equal force in the western settlements of North Carolina. These inconveniences multiplied in the ratio of the increase of population, and all looked forward to a time when they would be obviated. There were many of the first men in North Carolina who had removed to the western country, and who were ambitious of political distinction in becoming the founders of a new state. The question of separation began to be examined in all its bearings, not only in the western settlements, but in the capital of North Carolina. The Legislature, willing to extend relief to the western people, proposed to cede, at the expiration of two years, all the western territory to the Federal government, for the purpose of forming an independent state. Until such time, it was to remain under the jurisdiction of North Carolina. But the people, dissatisfied with the remote period designated for their separation, and the difficulties in calling out and controlling their militia in sudden emergencies, to which their situation in an Indian country exposed them, proposed to dispense with the jurisdiction of North Carolina without further delay. A convention was called, consisting of dele-

---

* Imlay's America, p. 46–48.
† Flint's History and Geog., vol. ii., p. 36, edition of 1828.

gates from each of the western counties. The convention met, and enacted sundry regulations for the good government of the western settlements. Among these were the following: that all laws of North Carolina, compatible with the condition of the new settlements, should remain in force; that a memorial should be sent to Congress praying the speedy acceptance of the act of cession by 'North Carolina, with authority to organize an independent state government; that the political affairs of the new settlements shall in the mean time be conducted through a convention elected by the people; that the convention shall elect a delegate to Congress.

[A.D. 1786.] A second convention met in Jonesborough, composed of five members from each county. Commencing their deliberations as delegates of the sovereign people, they formally declared the Washington District independent of North Carolina, and constituting the new State of "Frankland." The new state government was put into operation by the appointment of judges and executive officers. A memorial was sent to Congress by the delegate, who carried with him a copy of the new Constitution. But Congress refused to encourage any rebellion against the mother-state, and declined to recognize the new government in any manner whatever. The delegate was obliged to return to his constituents, and report his fruitless mission.

The State of North Carolina asserted her jurisdiction, and manifested a determination to maintain it over any irregular assumption of power. Two parties, of course, soon sprung up: one for the new government, and one for the state jurisdiction. Each authority persisted in maintaining its supremacy, and collisions were unavoidable. The "State of Frankland" contained within its limits two distinct and opposing courts, each exercising jurisdiction, and each claiming for its decisions paramount authority. In some instances the sheriff of Frankland, with his "*posse comitatus*," entered the court established by North Carolina, and, having seized the papers, turned the court and its officers out of doors. The power of the mother state in due time retaliated the same courtesy upon the courts of Frankland.

Colonel John Sevier had been elected the first governor of Frankland. Soon after his inauguration he came in collision with Colonel Tipton, a stanch adherent of the old state. From words they came to blows, and a personal combat ensued. The adherents of each principal followed the example of their leaders, and a general mêlée followed. But this did not settle principles or establish the supremacy of law.

The regular state elections were held. The counties of Washington District elected their representatives to the Legislature of North Carolina. Colonel Tipton was one of these, and carried with him the names of those who were willing to accept the terms of cession by North Carolina, and to secede from the new state authority. The former law proposing a cession to the United States was repealed, and the state persisted in enforcing her authority.

In the mean time, the third convention of Frankland met, enacted laws, and levied taxes. They also selected the eloquent William Cocke, Esq., as a delegate to Congress. He was permitted to address that body on behalf of the helpless and distracted condition of Frankland. Engaged in a civil war with North Carolina on the one hand, and assailed again by the warlike Cherokees, their only protection, their only hope, was in the wisdom of Congress. That body readily interposed its influence to restore harmony in this portion of North Carolina. The authority of the state was maintained, and the new government of Frankland declared illegal. An amnesty was recommended for all past differences, and the regular state authorities were soon after re-established.

The new government very reluctantly yielded. The legislative convention of Frankland met in 1787 for the last time. Their power was at an end, and but little was attempted. The adherents of the new state gradually abandoned their leaders, and the organization of their new government wasted by degrees, until it finally became extinct.

[A.D. 1788.] Thus terminated the first attempt in the West to throw off the allegiance to a parent state in violation of law. The authority of North Carolina having been established over the western counties, her jurisdiction was also extended over the whole settlements, then spreading rapidly upon all the Holston tributaries, as well as those on the Cumberland River.

During the year 1788, the population of the Cumberland settlements had increased to more than six thousand souls, sparsely located within twenty miles of the river, for a distance of more than fifty miles along the same.

Governor Sevier, however, had been highly obnoxious to the authorities of North Carolina. His property had been declared confiscated, and himself outlawed. Colonel Tipton had been active in prosecuting the state authority against his late antagonist, until the Legislature of North Carolina, swayed by public opinion, which duly appreciated his character and services in the war of the Revolution, as well as in the Indian wars, in which he had lately distinguished himself, resolved, in 1789, to repeal the obnoxious law,* and to relieve him from all attainder. Soon after which, Colonel Sevier was elected as senator from Greene county to the Legislature of North Carolina, and was appointed brigadier-general for the western counties.

[A.D. 1789.] Since the year 1787, the people of all the Holston settlements, in common with those on the Cumberland River, had become deeply interested in the navigation of the Mississippi, which was the natural outlet for all their surplus products. On this subject they were influenced by all the motives, interests, and prejudices which operated so powerfully upon the people of Kentucky about the same time. During this period, Spain had viewed the rising Republic with jealous concern. Kentucky was presumed by Spain to be disaffected, and the Cumberland and Holston settlements were by no means contented.

It was under these circumstances that the benevolent Governor Miro, of Louisiana, through Colonel Wilkinson, tendered to the people of the Holston and Cumberland settlements, in common with those of Kentucky, the free navigation of the Mississippi, and the rights and privileges of Spanish subjects, upon conditions deemed advantageous to them. Many, lured by the tempting offers of the governor, emigrated to the district of West Florida, and became Spanish subjects.†

About the same time, the cultivation of cotton was partially introduced upon the Cumberland River; and for several years it constituted an article of trade and barter between the Cumberland settlements and those of Kentucky, under the control of Colonel Wilkinson's agents.‡

Meantime, the population on all the head branches of the Holston and Clinch Rivers, as well as on Cumberland, contin-

---

* Flint's History of Georgia, vol. ii., p. 30–36, edition of 1828. Also, Martin's Louisiana, vol. ii., p. 89. † Martin's Louisiana, vol. ii., p. 102, 103.
‡ See M'Donald's Sketches, Life of Massie.

Vol. II.—S

ued to extend and to increase in number under the jurisdiction of North Carolina. The Cumberland settlements, before the close of the year 1789, had increased their population to more than eight thousand souls, and had been erected into a judicial district designated "Miro District." Washington District comprised the counties of Washington, Carter, Sullivan, and Greene; and new settlements were extending upon the French Broad and Nolichucky, within the Indian territory. The aggregate population in this district was but little short of thirty thousand persons.

During the advance of the settlements in 1789, the Indians on the whole southern frontier began to manifest extreme impatience of the rapid encroachments upon their territory, and depredations and murders upon the inhabitants became frequent, perpetrated chiefly by Cherokees and Creeks.

[A.D. 1790.] North Carolina had not been averse to an amicable and legal separation of her western territory for the purpose of forming an independent state. Early in the year 1790 the Legislature took measures for accomplishing this desirable object. Following the example of Virginia in her relinquishment of the Northwestern Territory, the Legislature proposed to cede to the Federal government all the western territory, for the purpose of organizing in the same a territorial form of government, preparatory to an independent state government, agreeably to the provisions of the ordinance of July, 1787. In April, Congress acceded to the proposed cession, and the relinquishment on the part of North Carolina was completed.

The ceded country, by act of Congress approved May 20th, was erected into a territory of the United States, under the name of the "Southwestern Territory," agreeably to the provisions of the ordinance of 1787, excepting the clause which prohibits slavery.*

The territorial government was organized agreeably to the first grade provided by the ordinance of 1787, with a legislative assembly elected by the people, and a legislative council nominated by the Assembly, and appointed by the president. The two houses, thus constituted, elected the delegate to Congress, with the right of speaking, but not of voting, in the House of Representatives. The first territorial governor was Will-

* See chap. ix. of this book, "Extension of the First White Settlements," &c.

iam Blount, who was also superintendent of Indian affairs, which station he continued to fill until the territory passed through its dependent grades to the rank of an independent state.

The census of 1790 gave to Washington District a population of thirty-six thousand souls, including three thousand five hundred slaves; at the same time, the settlements on Cumberland River contained an aggregate of nearly ten thousand souls.

To protect the frontier people from Indian attacks, a military post of the United States was established at the "Southwest Point," the present site of Kingston, near the confluence of the Clinch and Holston Rivers, then within the Indian country.

During the same year, the territorial government went fully into operation, and the present site of Knoxville was selected as the future seat of government, within a few miles of the Indian boundary. The same year witnessed the publication of the first newspaper in the Southwestern Territory, and the first number of the "Knoxville Gazette" was issued on the 5th of November, 1790.

To secure the people of the territory from Indian hostility, the Federal government took immediate measures for conciliating the rising spirit of resistance which had been manifested by portions of the Cherokee and Creek nations. Governor Blount, as superintendent of Indian affairs, commenced a series of treaties and negotiations with different portions of the Cherokee and Creek nations for the peaceable sale and relinquishment of lands occupied by the settlements, and for the amicable adjustment of all cause of complaint on the part of the Indians. These negotiations continued at different points along the exposed border until the close of the following year.

[A.D. 1791.] By this means the Federal government succeeded in restraining the great body of warriors in these two powerful and warlike nations from open war and invasion of the settlements; but it was unable to prevent the encroachments of lawless emigrants upon the Indian lands, or to restrain the depredations and murders which were frequently committed by small parties of hostile Indians upon the exposed colonies.* Hence, notwithstanding the Federal govern-

* The following is a catalogue of the hostilities of the war parties during the year 1791, viz.:
Early in January the Cherokees commenced their incursions against the Cumberland settlements. The first man killed was Richard Withs, shot on the 16th of Jan-

ment had entered into treaties of peace and friendship with the chiefs of the Cherokee and Creek nations, a partisan warfare sprung up along the whole frontier between disorderly individuals and detached parties from both Indian nations; and although the Federal authorities forbore to plunge the country into a general Indian war, it was unable entirely to restrain the voluntary expeditions of the people.

[A.D. 1792.] The following year opened with a continuation of hostile incursions and murders by small parties of Creeks and Cherokees along the whole line of border settlements in both Washington and Miro Districts.*

Yet Governor Blount had not remitted his efforts to conciliate the savages and to restrain the unlawful aggression of the whites upon the Indian territory. The warriors of both nations were gradually preparing for a regular invasion and destruction of the white settlements, especially those on the

uary, near Papon's Creek. In February, one man was killed and another, wounded near Bledsoe's Lick. In March, several murders were committed by Indians. On the first of April, Charles Hickman was killed by them on Duck River. On the 25th of May, George Wilson was killed on the great road near Station Creek. Two days afterward, John Nicherson was killed near Smith's Fork. During the month of June, four men were killed by Creeks not far from Nashville. In July, three men were killed by Cherokees; one of these was killed within eight miles of Sumner Court-house, and one on the "new trace" across Cumberland Mountain. One man was killed in August, one in November, and one in December.

* The following catalogue comprises the principal murders and depredations committed in Miro District during the year 1792, viz.:

On the 7th of January, a Cherokee chief and party advanced into the settlements and captured two boats descending the Cumberland River, killing John Curtis, and three young men named Seviers. On the 14th, they killed a man near Clarksville. On the 17th of February, four persons were killed on the Chickasá trace. On the 25th, a party of Creeks penetrated within seven miles of Nashville, killed Mr. Thompson and two of his sons, and carried his wife and two other sons away captive. On the 5th of March, a party of twenty-five Indians attacked "Brown's Station," and killed four boys, only six miles from Nashville. The next day they burned all the out-buildings at "Denham's Station." During the next eighteen days, five persons were killed and three taken prisoners by the Cherokees not far from Nashville. On the 24th of March, General James Robertson and two other men were wounded by Indians. On the 8th of April, the family of Benjamin Williams, consisting of eight persons, were killed by them. One man was killed on the 8th, and another on the 23d of June. On the 26th, a party of Creeks, Shawanese, and Cherokees, attacked and captured "Zeigler's Station," where five persons were killed, four wounded, and twelve taken prisoners. From this time until the last of July, six men were killed and several more wounded in different portions of the Cumberland settlements. During this time, about two hundred horses had been stolen from both districts by Indians. During the same period, from January to December, sixteen persons, including men, women, and children, had been killed in the District of Washington, about Clinch Mountain and in the vicinity of the present town of Rogersville. The whole number of persons killed, wounded, and missing in both districts of East and West Tennessee, was about one hundred and twenty, nearly all of whom were scalped and otherwise mangled.

Cumberland, prompted and supplied, as was subsequently ascertained, by Spanish emissaries from Florida and Louisiana.

On the 23d of June, Governor Blount had concluded a treaty of peace and friendship with the Cherokees at Coyatee, where he distributed a large amount of goods and blankets. On the 26th, a council was held with the Cherokees at Estanaula, where the chiefs and warriors entered into an agreement to use their utmost efforts to restrain their young men from acts of hostility. On the 10th of August, a treaty of peace and friendship was concluded with the Chickasâs and Choctâs, near Nashville, accompanied with a distribution of a large amount of goods, and presents to the chiefs. On the 31st of October, a similar treaty was concluded with a portion of the Creek nation, near the site of Knoxville, on the Holston.*

Notwithstanding these negotiations, and the earnest efforts to allay all hostile feeling in the Creek and Cherokee nations, they produced no other effect than to prevent an open and general war against all the settlements in the Southwestern Territory.

On the 3d of September, a large Indian trail was discovered within four miles of Buchanan's Station. The same day a party of twenty-four Indians advanced to Fletcher's Lick, eight miles southeast of Nashville, and near the new wilderness road from Knoxville. On the 11th of September, Governor Blount greatly apprehended a descent upon the Cumberland settlements by a large body of Indians which had been discovered upon their march in that direction. On the 30th of September, Buchanan's Station, within four miles of Nashville, was attacked by four hundred Indians, who were repulsed with loss by the garrison. On the 2d of October, Governor Blount wrote to the Secretary of War that "about five hundred Creeks, within a few days, had passed the Tennessee River on their way to the Cumberland settlements, and that they were re-enforced by two hundred Cherokees near the crossing-place, thirty miles below Nicojack."

All these parties of Indians had been well supplied with arms and ammunition by the Spanish agents from Florida, by whom the savages had been urged to exterminate the Cumberland settlements while the American army was advancing north.

[A.D. 1793.] The year 1793 opened with increased activity on the part of the hostile Indians against the whole frontier, from

* See American State Papers, *Indian Affairs*, vol. i., p. 230–276, folio edition.

Holston to Cumberland.* The scalping parties advanced into the heart of the settlements, and no place beyond the stockade inclosures was deemed secure from the nocturnal inroads of the savage foe.

Those on Cumberland River had gradually extended during the year 1792, until they were distributed along the Cumberland River on both sides for a distance of eighty-five miles from east to west, with a general width of about twenty-five miles from north to south. Such was their extent, according to Governor Blount's report to the Secretary of War in 1792.† The country occupied by them was a fertile and beau-

* The following catalogue will indicate the extent of the hostile operations of the savages in the Southwestern Territory during the year 1793, viz.:
In Miro District, Colonel Hugh Tinnan was badly wounded by Indians on the 16th of January, near Clarksburg, on the north side of Cumberland River. On the 18th, Major Shelby, James Harris, and a negro were killed near the mouth of Red River, not far from Clarksville. Several horses were stolen in the same vicinity. On the 19th, two boys in a canoe, near Clarksville, were fired upon by Indians. On the 22d, two men were killed on the trace leading from Cumberland River to Kentucky, and several horses were stolen. On the 24th, a party of Indians attacked a salt-boat in Cumberland River, killing four men and wounding two. About the same time, they attacked a pirogue manned by Frenchmen, and killed three of them. On the 26th, two men were shot by Indians on the north side of Cumberland River, near Nashville.
In the month of February these hostile operations continued. On the 17th, two negroes and a son of Colonel Bledsoe were killed, and one negro taken prisoner by the Indians. On the 22d, two boys, sons of Colonel Sanders, were killed and scalped. On the 24th, Captain Samuel Hays was killed near a neighbor's house. Several horses were stolen in the vicinity of Nashville.
In March murders were less frequent in this district. On the 9th, two brothers, named Nelson, were killed by the Cherokees. On the 18th, two young men, named Clements, were killed and scalped in the settlements east of the Cumberland Mountains.
In April, Miro District suffered severely. On the 9th day, Colonel Bledsoe was killed in his own field by a party of twenty Indians, and his premises plundered. On the 11th, two men were killed near Simcoe Creek. On the 14th, two others were killed near General Rutherford's. On the 18th, Captain Benton and two other men were killed on Cumberland, near Clarksville; and soon after, two others were killed and one wounded by Indians. On the 27th, a large party of Indians attacked Greenfield Station, but were repulsed.
The next Indian murder was that of John Hacker, on the 30th of May, near Drake's Creek.
On the 2d of June, James Steele and his daughter were killed. On the 4th, three men were killed and two wounded on the Kentucky road to Big Bone. On the 29th, Joseph Heaton was killed near Heaton's Lick.
On the first of July, three men, named Castleman, were killed, and one was wounded, at "Haye's Station." On the 15th, a man was killed near Nashville, and another on the 19th, at Johnston's Lick.
Murders were frequent in August. On the first, Samuel Miller was killed at "Joslin's Station," near Cumberland River. On the 21st, the Widow Baker and a large family of children were killed, only two escaping. On the 22d, Mrs. Wells and a family of children were killed.—See American State Papers, *Indian Affairs*, vol. i., p. 450–465.   † Idem, p. 433.

tiful region, diversified with deep valleys and towering cliffs, intersected and watered by numerous deep, transparent streams flowing through lofty forests and verdant plains. Many had advanced beyond the limits of the ceded territory, and were encroaching upon the Indian lands upon the northern tributaries of Duck River, when the hostile movements of the Creeks and Cherokees in 1793 compelled them to retire and abandon their unlawful habitations.

Before the close of summer the savages had begun to make formidable demonstrations against the whole extent of the white settlements, and the militia were necessarily called into service for the general defense. In the eastern district the military operations were confided to Brigadier-general Sevier, one of the most efficient officers in the West. Bold, active, and persevering, he possessed the entire confidence of his fellow-citizens, who cheerfully rallied under his command at the first summons. In East Tennessee he was the bulwark of defense against savage invasion. Such was his energy and skill in conducting the Indian wars, that Governor Blount declared in one of his dispatches that "his name carries more terror to the Cherokees than an additional regiment would have done."*

The principal commander in the District of Miro was General William Robertson. Although he conducted the defenses with great skill and prudence, yet such was the cautious and secret movements of the savages that they never could be encountered in force upon the field of battle. They studiously avoided a general engagement, and restricted their operations to harassing the settlements by frequent incursions of small war parties, which could evade any large force sent against them.

The most formidable demonstration by the savages during this year was made by the Cherokees on the 25th of September, when a large body of warriors, estimated at one thousand, advanced toward Knoxville by night, passing within seven miles of General Sevier's camp of four hundred men; but, after committing several murders and other outrages upon defenseless families, they retired without any attempted collision with his troops.†

The successful operations of General Wayne upon the northwestern frontier evidently exerted a restraining influence upon the Cherokees and Creeks in the South. From this time their

* Flint's Hist. and Geog., vol. ii., p. 40.   † Amer. State Papers, vol. i., p. 466.

hostilities began to cease, and during the next year they made overtures for the establishment of peace and amity by formal treaties.

[A.D. 1794.] Notwithstanding the hostile attitude of the Creeks and Cherokees, the settlements continued to extend, and the population had steadily increased in numbers, from the continual arrivals of immigrants, not only from North Carolina, but also from Virginia, South Carolina, and Georgia. During the past year, the people became impatient of their dependent form of government, and the grand jury at Knoxville, in the month of November, adopted an address to the governor, claiming a more independent form of government, as provided by the ordinance of 1787, since the territory contained more than the requisite number of "five thousand free white males." In December following, the governor issued his proclamation for the election of a General Assembly, as provided by law. The Legislature, duly constituted, convened at Knoxville in February, 1794. Much of the session was occupied in providing for the opening of roads and for the protection of the inhabitants from Indian hostilities.

[A.D. 1795.] According to a census ordered by the territorial Legislature, the aggregate population of the territory in 1795 was 77,262 persons; of whom 66,490 were whites, the remainder slaves and colored persons. This amount of population, under the provisions of the ordinance of 1787, entitled the people to an independent state government, and application was made to Congress for authority to frame and adopt a state constitution.

[A.D. 1796.] The convention authorized assembled at Knoxville on the 11th of January, 1796, and after a session of four weeks a state constitution was adopted, which having been approved by Congress, the new state was on the first of June admitted into the Federal Union as the "State of Tennessee."*

The new Constitution, in its general features, was more Democratic than that of the parent state, and imposed fewer restraints not absolutely necessary for good government. In its provisions it illustrates the principle established by all subsequent constitutions, that the new states, as well as the older which have remodelled their constitutions, exhibit a uni-

* See Laws of the United States, vol. ii., p. 567.

form tendency in the public mind to render government more and more the instrument of the popular will.

From the adoption of the state government until the year 1840, the advance of population, agriculture, arts, and manufactures was unprecedented in the West. Tennessee, abounding in fertile lands and rich mineral resources, and possessing a genial climate and an enterprising population, has been surpassed by no state in the rapid development of her natural resources, and in the patriotic chivalry of her citizens.

The increase of her population continued to extend her settlements westward into the Valley of the Cumberland and upon the tributaries of the Tennessee River. Four years after the establishment of state government, the population had increased to 105,602 souls, including 13,584 slaves and colored persons. Ten years afterward the census of 1810 gave the whole population at 261,727 souls, including 44,535 slaves and colored persons.

[A.D. 1820.] In ten years more this number had almost doubled, and the census of 1820 gave an entire population of 420,813 souls, including 80,107 slaves and colored persons. The ratio of increase for the next ten years was almost as great. The census of 1830 gave the inhabitants at 681,903 souls, including 141,603 slaves and 4555 colored persons.*

Yet the whole of the present western district of Tennessee, as late as 1816, was an Indian wilderness, in the undisputed occupancy of the native savages. Until that year, the Chickasâ nation occupied the whole western portion of Tennessee, as far eastward as the Tennessee River, and northward to the southern boundary of Kentucky. The rapid advance of the civilized population made it requisite that the Indian tribes should occupy more circumscribed limits; and they retired within the present State of Mississippi, and subsequently to the Indian territory provided for them west of the present State of Arkansas.

It was on the 20th of September, 1816, that General Andrew Jackson, with David Meriwether and Jesse Franklin, concluded a treaty with the Chickasâs, after a protracted negotiation in a general council of the nation. By this treaty, the Chickasâ nation, for a valuable consideration, ceded to the United States large bodies of land lying on both sides of the

* Mitchell's World, p. 216.

Tennessee River, west of the Muscle Shoals, partly in Alabama, and partly within the present State of Mississippi.

This treaty extinguished the Indian title to a large portion of country, and opened the way for the egress of the redundant population. The treaty was ratified by the Senate on the 30th day of December following, and soon after, the lands were surveyed for market. This was the first advance of the whites into the Chickasâ country after the Creek war.

The second relinquishment of lands by the Chickasâs in Tennessee was two years afterward. In this case, negotiations were conducted by General Andrew Jackson and Colonel Isaac Shelby, of Kentucky; and the treaty was finally concluded and signed on the 19th day of October, 1818, and ratified by the Senate on the 7th of January following.

By this treaty the Chickasâ nation cede and relinquish to the United States *all their lands in the western part of Tennessee* north of latitude 35° and east of the Mississippi. The Chickasâs soon afterward commenced their gradual removal from the ceded territory. Some retired across the Mississippi to the Indian territory west of the present State of Arkansas; others retired into the heart of the nation in North Mississippi, where they remained until the treaty of Pontatoc, sixteen years afterward.

The first white immigrants advanced into the country early in the year 1820, and extended down the tributaries of the Obian, Forked Deer, Hatchy, and Wolf River, to the Mississippi. Among the first settlements upon the Chickasâ Bluffs was one by John Overton, for himself and company, near the old Fort Pickering, below the mouth of Wolf River. The site of a town was laid off in the month of May, and called Memphis,* which received its first inhabitants the following year.

[A.D. 1822.] Emigration from East and Middle Tennessee began to advance into all the late Chickasâ cession, and the jurisdiction of the state was annually extended over new counties successively erected and organized by the Legislature. Settlements continued to multiply in all the fine cotton lands upon the tributaries of the Hatchy and Wolf Rivers, until the year 1830, when the entire population of the Western District, according to the census of that year, was 94,792 souls, including 26,224 slaves, distributed over fourteen counties. Such had

---

* See Mississippi State Gazette, June 20th, 1820.

been the tide of emigration in ten years into the western district of Tennessee.

[A.D. 1840.] The population, wealth, and resources of Tennessee continued to increase almost in an equal ratio for the next ten years. The Indian claim having been extinguished to the entire territory within the state, and the whole Indian population removed from its eastern as well as its western frontier, the energies of the people of Tennessee were untrammeled, and their wealth, resources, and agricultural enterprise even outstripped their prolific population.

The census of 1840 gave the aggregate inhabitants at 829,210 souls, including 183,059 slaves and colored people The Western District alone contained a population of 193,241 persons, comprised in eighteen organized counties. The admirable agricultural resources of this portion of the state had been greatly developed, and it had become an important portion of the great cotton region of the Mississippi Valley. Memphis, the emporium of Western Tennessee, had received the impress of Tennessee enterprise, and was already the third commercial city on the Mississippi River, and the great cotton mart for West Tennessee and North Mississippi. Its population in 1840 was nearly four thousand inhabitants; but such was the enterprise awakened in 1842, that the commerce and population of the city had more than doubled before the year 1846, when it had also been selected as the location of a naval dépôt for the United States.

[A.D. 1846.] Tennessee, not inaptly, has been called the mother of states. From the bosom of this state have issued more colonies for the peopling of the great Valley of the Mississippi than from any one state in the American Union.* Her emigrant citizens have formed a very important portion of the population of Alabama, of the northern half of Mississippi, and of Florida. They have also formed the principal portion of the early population of the states of Missouri, Arkansas, and Texas.

* The following have been the governors of Tennessee, with their terms of service annexed, viz.:

I. *Southwestern Territory.*
1. William Blount, from 1790 to 1796.
II. *State of Tennessee.*
1. John Sevier, from 1796 to 1801.
2. Archibald Roane, from 1801 to 1803.
3. John Sevier, from 1803 to 1809.
4. Willie Blount, from 1809 to 1815.
5. Joseph M'Minn, from 1815 to 1821.
6. William Carroll, from 1821 to 1827.
7. Samuel Houston, from 1827 to 1830.
8. William Carroll, from 1830 to 1835.
9. Newton Cannon, from 1835 to 1838.
10. James K. Polk, from 1838 to 1841.
11. James C. Jones, from 1841 to 1844.

CHAPTER XI.

INDIAN WARS AND MILITARY OPERATIONS BY THE UNITED STATES NORTH OF THE OHIO RIVER.—A.D. 1787 TO 1795.

Argument.—Unsettled State of the Indian Tribes from 1784 to 1790.—Extent of Indian Depredation and Murders up to 1790.—General Harmar prepares to invade the Indian Country.—Advances to the Maumee.—Is defeated in two Engagements.—Retreats to Fort Washington.—Indian Hostilities renewed.—General Scott marches an Expedition against the Wabash Towns.—Colonel Wilkinson leads another against the Towns on Eel River and Tippecanoe.—General St. Clair prepares to invade the Maumee Country.—Marches toward the St. Mary's.—Meets with a disastrous Defeat. —Terrible Onset of the Savages.—Their Number and Allies.—The Remnant of the Army arrives at Fort Washington.—Colonel Wilkinson commands at Fort Washington.—He proceeds from Fort Jefferson to the Scene of the Defeat.—Overtures of Peace tendered to the Indians in 1792.—The Federal Government authorize a strong Force for the Humiliation of the Savages.—General Wayne Commander-in-chief.— Indians continue their hostile Demonstrations.—Excited by British Emissaries.— General Wayne concentrates his Forces at Fort Greenville.—The advanced Posts harassed by Indians.—Plan of Encampment at Greenville.—Lord Dorchester.—President Washington's Views of Indian Tactics.—Fort Recovery built.—Is attacked by Indians in 1793.—General Scott arrives with the mounted Riflemen.—General Wayne takes up the Line of March for the Maumee.—"Fort Defiance" commenced.—" Fort Deposit" at the Head of the Rapids.—Force concentrated at this Point.—Battle of the Miami, August 20th, 1794.—Utter Defeat of the Savages.—The Army returns to Fort Defiance, which is strongly fortified.—Army advances to Miami Villages.—Fort Wayne erected.—Army retires to Winter-quarters at Greenville.—Indians sue for Peace.

[A.D. 1787.] ALTHOUGH the northwestern Indians had resumed hostilities against the frontier settlements of Kentucky, and those in the western part of Virginia and Pennsylvania, as early as 1789, the Federal government had taken no active measures to enforce peace and the observance of their recent treaties entered into at the Great Miami and at Fort Harmar. The Federal executive studiously abstained from any military operations against the hostile savages, vainly relying upon the success of negotiation and treaty, from which they disdainfully retired. Partisan expeditions from Kentucky and other portions of the exposed settlements, for the defense of the Ohio frontier, were the only defensive measures adopted, and they were undertaken at individual expense, and sustained by individual enterprise, and without the sanction of the Federal government.

The extent and nature of the hostile operations of the savages against the frontier people, and the emigrants upon the

Ohio River, have been enumerated in another place, to which the reader is referred.*

[A.D. 1790.] To such an extent had these hostilities and depredations been carried in the spring of 1790, that in a communication from Judge Harry Innis to the Secretary of War, dated July 7th, he states that, to his knowledge, about fifteen hundred persons had been killed or captured by the Indians on and near the Ohio since the peace of 1783. The number of horses seized or stolen from the new settlements and from emigrants during that time was estimated at not less than twenty thousand, besides household furniture and other property taken or destroyed to the value of fifteen thousand pounds, or about fifty thousand dollars.

At length, all overtures and efforts at negotiation on the part of the Federal government having been rejected by the savages, the president determined to organize a strong military force for the invasion of the Indian country, and the destruction of the towns upon the head waters of the Miami and Maumee Rivers. Orders were accordingly issued by the Secretary of War to General Harmar on the 7th of June, 1790, to plan, in conjunction with Governor St. Clair, a vigorous expedition against the Indians of the Maumee. The governor was authorized to call out the militia and volunteers of Western Pennsylvania and Kentucky to co-operate with the Federal troops. Agreeably to this authority, a requisition was made by Governor St. Clair upon the western counties of these states, as follows: From the counties of Washington, Fayette, Westmoreland, and Alleghany, in Pennsylvania, five hundred men, to rendezvous at M'Mahon's Creek, four miles below Wheeling, on the 3d of September; from the District of Kentucky, embracing the counties of Nelson, Lincoln, and Jefferson, three hundred men, to rendezvous at Fort Steuben, near "the Falls," on the 12th of September; and from the counties of Madison, Mercer, Fayette, Bourbon, Woodford, and Mason, seven hundred men, to rendezvous at Fort Washington on the 15th of September.†

On the 27th of September the advanced detachments were in motion, and on the 30th the line of march was taken up for the towns on the St. Mary's River. The route pursued was the "Old War-path" of the Indians across the head waters of the

---
* See chapters v. and x. of this book.
† See American State Papers, *Indian Affairs*, vol. i., p. 105, 106, General Order.

Little Miami and Mad Rivers, where the villages had been deserted by the enemy. Thence the march was directed westward, crossing the Great Miami at Piqua, a few miles below the mouth of Loramie's Creek. Here the first three Indians were seen, and they appeared to be spies reconnoitering the force and movements of the army. A small detachment of mounted men were sent in pursuit, who succeeded in capturing one; the others escaped.* This was evidence that the enemy were observing their advance.

From Loramie's Creek the march was continued west of north, and on the west side of that stream about thirty miles, crossing the head stream of the St. Mary's River. The army was now about one hundred and thirty miles from Fort Washington, and about fifty miles from the principal town at the confluence of the St. Mary's. The whole force consisted of three hundred and twenty regular troops, and eleven hundred and thirty-five volunteers and militia.

Colonel Hardin and Major Paul of the Pennsylvania line were detached in advance with six hundred men, to surprise and capture the town at the confluence. On the second day, October 16th, Colonel Hardin approached the Indian stronghold, and found it deserted and burned by the savages. The only resistance made was from some straggling Indians, who exchanged a few shots with the advanced guard of the troops. This detachment remained four days encamped at the village, awaiting the arrival of General Harmar with the main body of the army, during which time no important movement was made against the enemy. The Indians, in the mean time, were making vigorous efforts to repel the invaders. They began to assemble in great numbers in the vicinity of the camp, and every foraging detachment was either cut off or driven back.

On the 20th, Colonel Hardin, with one hundred and fifty Kentucky militia and thirty regulars, was detached to surprise and destroy an Indian town on the St. Mary's, six miles above the confluence. This detachment marched without interruption until within half a mile of the town, when suddenly they found themselves in the midst of several hundred Indians in ambuscade, concealed by the high grass and brushwood on each side of the path in the margin of the prairie. The marching column was suddenly assailed by a destructive fire from

* American State Papers, *Indian Affairs*, vol. i., p. 105, 106.

the concealed enemy, and, being thrown into confusion, the militia fled precipitately. The regulars maintained their position with the utmost courage, defending themselves with the bayonet as the Indians rushed upon them with the tomahawk, until nearly the whole number were killed. Two privates and two officers escaped the massacre by concealing themselves behind logs in an adjacent swamp. Twenty-three regulars were killed upon the ground, and several others in their retreat. Ten of the militia were killed, and others wounded.

General Harmar, alarmed at this foreboding of disaster, resolved to take up the line of march for Fort Washington. On the following morning he broke up his encampment, and marched eight miles on the retrograde route, when he encamped for the night. While at this place, intelligence was received that the Indians had taken possession of the town immediately after it had been evacuated by the army. Colonel Hardin, mortified with his recent disaster, and in hopes of retrieving his military character, solicited permission once more to give the Indians battle, and to drive them from the town. Permission was granted, and he was dispatched with six hundred militia, and sixty regulars under Major Fontaine, to attack the town. The attack was made with skill and great courage; but the Indians had arranged matters to complete his discomfiture. At first they made a strong show of resistance, and then fell back across the Maumee, and retreated up the St. Joseph's, drawing the militia after them, and leaving the regulars to be overpowered by superior numbers in the rear. The militia continued the pursuit for nearly two miles, when, unable to bring them to an engagement, they retired. In the mean time, two ambuscades had been laid; one to fall upon the regulars after they had been abandoned by the militia, and another to intercept the militia on their return. The plan succeeded to their most sanguine expectations. The militia had pressed on after the retiring Indians, heedless of danger, while the regulars on the opposite side of the river were attacked by an overwhelming number of savages, who rushed furiously upon them with the tomahawk and war-club. They fought with desperate courage, defending themselves with the bayonet until nearly every man was killed. Lieutenant-colonel Wyllis and Major Fontaine fell valiantly fighting, the latter pierced by eighteen balls; and around them laid the bodies of fifty of their brave men. The militia on both sides of the St. Joseph's were severely harassed in their return by the Indians in ambuscade upon elevated ground near their path. The whole loss of the militia under Colonel Hardin was one hundred privates and ten officers killed, besides the wounded.* Only eight of the regulars survived.

Thus terminated the whole of General Harmar's operations against the northwestern savages upon the waters of the Maumee. In two disastrous enterprises, conducted by Colonel Hardin, he had lost in one week no less than one hundred and eighty-three men killed, besides about forty wounded, leaving no evidence of more than about fifty Indians destroyed. The town at the confluence of the St. Joseph's and St. Mary's, known as "Girty's Town," and which was consumed by the savages, contained about two hundred and fifty cabins. The entire injury sustained by the Indians was trivial compared to the number of troops in the field and the loss of life sustained by the Americans.

A portion of the orders to General Harmar, which were utterly neglected after his disasters on the St. Mary's, required him to advance westward from the Maumee for the destruction of the Wea towns upon the Upper Wabash, as well as others upon Eel River, noted as the residence of several hostile bands which had been active in their incursions against the frontier population upon the Ohio; yet, gratified in his reverses by the slightest success, and fearful of other disasters, he ordered an immediate retreat, consoling himself with the reflection "that we are able to lose ten men to their one;" also, that one great object of the expedition had been accomplished in " the destruction of the Miami towns." The retrograde march was immediately commenced for Fort Washington, leaving the slain upon the field of battle, unburied, and having the savages in his rear almost to the Ohio.

The campaign of 1790, instead of producing a salutary restraint upon the savages, served only to provoke them, and render them more confident and daring. During the winter and spring, war parties continued their incursions against the unprotected settlements near the Ohio River, from Fort Pitt down to the "Falls," while marauding parties infested the

---

* Butler's Kentucky, p. 194.   Marshall's Kentucky, vol. i., p. 364, 365.   Atwater's Ohio, p. 135.

banks of the river, greatly interrupting the intercourse between the upper and lower settlements.

[A.D. 1791.] For the restraint of the savages and the protection of the exposed frontiers, until the Federal government could concentrate a strong force for the effectual chastisement of the hostile tribes, General Charles Scott, of Kentucky, was authorized to organize and equip a volunteer brigade of mounted riflemen, not exceeding seven hundred and fifty in number, to be sent against the tribes located on the head waters of the Wabash.

The volunteers began to rendezvous at the mouth of Kentucky River about the middle of May. On the 23d, having crossed the Ohio with his whole command, General Scott took up the line of march upon the route leading to the Miami towns, until he crossed the St. Mary's, when, suddenly changing his course toward the west, after a rapid march he succeeded in surprising several towns upon the Wabash and Eel Rivers. On the 2d of June the expedition had destroyed several large towns, and laid waste extensive fields of growing corn, and otherwise ravaged the country.

On the 14th of June the expedition returned to Kentucky, without the loss of a single man killed, and having only five wounded. In the campaign, the troops had encountered the savages in numerous skirmishes, killing no less than thirty-two warriors, and taking fifty-eight prisoners, including women and children.*

Meantime, the Federal government had made provision for a second invasion of the Miami country with a strong force, under the immediate command of General St. Clair, who was actively engaged in Kentucky, making preparations for the contemplated campaign, preparatory to the arrival of new levies of regular troops from Pennsylvania, Virginia, Maryland, and New Jersey. While these preparations were in progress, General St. Clair organized a volunteer mounted expedition, consisting of five hundred and thirty men, under the command of Colonel Wilkinson, for the destruction of several large towns upon Eel River.

On the first of August, Colonel Wilkinson left Fort Washington with his command, and marched with a bold feint toward the Miami towns, until he reached St. Mary's River,

* See American State Papers, *Indian Affairs*, vol. i., p. 121.

when he marched rapidly to the northwest and west, crossing the head streams of the Wabash, and coming suddenly upon the towns on Eel River and other northern tributaries of the Wabash. Having destroyed several towns, together with their fine fields of corn, on the Eel River and Tippecanoe, the expedition set out on their return to Fort Washington with thirty-four prisoners, having lost two men killed and one wounded. Eight Indians had been killed. In this campaign, much of the Wabash and Weatanon country had been overrun and ravaged, the troops having traveled four hundred and fifty miles when they reached Fort Washington, on the 23d of August.

Early in September the new levies from the East arrived at Fort Washington, and soon afterward the arrival of the volunteers and militia from the western country increased the entire force under General St. Clair to two thousand men, including cavalry and artillery.*

At the head of this force, the general commenced his march from Fort Washington on the 3d of October, and proceeded to Fort Hamilton, an advanced post on the Miami, twenty miles from Fort Washington. Having received a small addition of three hundred militia from Kentucky, he proceeded northward twenty miles further, and erected another stockade, called Fort St. Clair. Twenty miles further he erected Fort Jefferson; each of which was furnished with a suitable garrison. About this time a company of sixty Kentucky militia deserted and returned home. After these reductions, the whole force of General St. Clair was less than eighteen hundred men, with which he continued his march for the Miami towns. He had now reached a champaign country, which was frequently wet, and heavily timbered. The roads were poor, and with great labor the baggage-wagons and artillery were slowly advanced on the route, while the infantry proceeded with scarcely less difficulty.

On the 24th of October the army was about ninety miles from Fort Washington. The advance was slow and tedious; desertions were frequent; and at last, on the 31st, sixty men deserted in a body, and set out on their return march. All efforts to restore them to their duties having failed, Lieutenant-colonel Hamtramck was dispatched with a strong detach-

* American State Papers, *Indian Affairs*, vol. i., p. 136, 137.

ment in pursuit of the deserters, reducing the main army to little more than fourteen hundred men. After the arrival of a company of about sixty men from Kentucky, under Captain Ellis, the general pursued his march. Provisions and forage became scarce, and many of the horses began to fail, which still further retarded the progress of the army, while the Indians began to make their appearance in small detachments, hovering upon the flanks of the advancing column.

On the 3d of November the army encamped in a wooded plain among the sources of a Wabash tributary, upon the banks of several small creeks, about fifty miles south of the Miami towns.* The winter had already commenced, and the ground was covered with snow three inches deep.

Next morning, November 4th, just before sunrise, and immediately after the troops had been dismissed from parade, the Indians made a furious attack upon the militia, whose camp was about a quarter of a mile in advance of the main camp of the regular troops. The militia immediately gave way, and fled with great precipitation and disorder, with the Indians in close pursuit; and, rushing through the camp, they threw the battalions of Majors Butler and Clark into confusion. The utmost exertion of those officers failed to restore complete order. The Indians, pressing close upon the militia, immediately engaged Butler's command with great intrepidity and fury. The attack soon became general both in the front and second lines, but the weight of the enemy's fire was directed against the center of each line, where the artillery was stationed. Such was the intensity of the enemy's fire, that the men were repeatedly driven from their guns with great loss. Confusion was spreading among the troops, from the great numbers who were constantly falling, while no impression was made by their fire upon the enemy. "At length resort was had to the bayonet. Colonel Darke was ordered to charge with part of the second line, and endeavor to turn the left flank of the enemy. This order was executed with great spirit. The Indians instantly gave way, and were driven back three or four hundred yards; but, for want of a sufficient number of riflemen to pursue this advantage, they soon rallied, and the troops were obliged in turn to fall back. At this moment the Indians had entered our camp by the left flank, having driven back the troops that were

* American State Papers, *Indian Affairs*, vol. i., p. 136, 137.

posted there. Another charge was made here by the second regiment, Butler's and Clark's battalions, with equal effect, and it was repeated several times, and always with success; but in each charge several men were lost, and particularly the officers; which, with raw troops, was a loss altogether irremediable."* In the last charge Major Butler was dangerously wounded, and every officer of the second regiment fell except three. The artillery being now silenced, and all the officers killed except Captain Ford, who was severely wounded, and more than half the army having fallen, it became necessary to make a retreat, if possible. This was immediately done, while Major Clark protected the rear with his battalion. The retreat was precipitous: it was a perfect flight. The camp and artillery were abandoned; not a horse was alive to draw the cannon. The men, in their flight and consternation, threw away their arms and accoutrements after pursuit had ceased, and the road was strewed with them for more than four miles. The rout continued to Fort Jefferson, twenty-nine miles. The action began half an hour before sunrise, the retreat commenced at half past nine o'clock, and the remnant of the army reached Fort Jefferson just after sunset. The savages continued the pursuit for four miles, when, fortunately, they returned to the scene of action for scalps and plunder.

The slain were left with the wounded upon the field of battle, both alike subject to the mercy of the infuriate savages, who tomahawked and scalped them indiscriminately. Some who were taken prisoners in the fight were afterward burned at the stake.

The detachment at Fort Jefferson was insufficient to restore the former numerical strength of the army, as it was previous to the attack on the 4th, and a large number of those who had escaped were without arms, and were useless as soldiers.

In this most disastrous battle, thirty-eight commissioned officers were killed on the field. Six hundred non-commissioned officers and privates were either killed or missing. Among the wounded were twenty-one commissioned officers, and two hundred and forty-two non-commissioned officers and privates. Many of the wounded died subsequently of their wounds. The Indian loss did not exceed sixty warriors killed.†

* American State Papers, *Indian Affairs*, vol. i., p. 137.
† See Butler's Kentucky, p. 205. Thatcher's Indian Biography, vol. ii., p. 249.

The grand error in this campaign was the impolicy of urging forward on a dangerous service, far into the Indian country, an army of raw troops, who were unwilling to enter upon the campaign, as was fully evinced by frequent desertions as they approached the hostile towns. The army was fatally reduced by the detachment sent to overtake the deserters from the Kentucky militia; and General St. Clair himself was quite infirm, and often unable to attend to his duties as commander-in-chief. On the fatal day of the defeat, he was scarcely able to be mounted upon his horse, either from physical infirmity or culpable intemperance.

The Indians engaged in this terrible battle comprised about nine hundred warriors. Among them were about four hundred Shawanese, commanded by Blue Jacket, and chiefly from the waters of the Wabash. The remainder were commanded by Little Turtle and Buckongahelas, consisting of Delawares, Wyandots, Potawatamies, and Mingoes. The Delawares alone numbered nearly four hundred warriors, who fought with great fury. On the ground, during the battle, were seen several British officers in full uniform from Detroit, who had come to witness the strife which they had instigated.* Simon Girty commanded a party of Wyandots.

Among the camp-followers in this campaign were nearly two hundred and fifty women, of whom fifty-six were killed during the carnage; the remainder were chiefly captured by the Indians.†

The army made but little delay at Fort Jefferson; but, leaving the wounded in charge of a suitable garrison, the main body advanced eagerly toward Fort Washington, where it arrived with its broken detachment on the evening of the 8th of November. Such was the terror and the consternation with which the troops had been impressed, that the sentinels at Fort Jefferson repeatedly deserted their posts and escaped.

Thus terminated the disastrous campaign of General St. Clair, who returned ingloriously to the civil administration of his government, surrounded with a cloud of public indignation, which was not wholly dispelled during his subsequent life.

[A.D. 1792.] Early in January he set out for the city of Philadelphia, in order to vindicate himself before the Federal

---

* See American State Papers, *Indian Affairs*, vol. i., p. 243–489.
† Atwater's Ohio, p. 142.

government, leaving Colonel James Wilkinson in command at Fort Washington. A committee of Congress, appointed to investigate his conduct during the campaign, after a full investigation acquitted him of all censure on the part of the government.

During the absence of General St. Clair, Colonel Wilkinson, who had been commissioned colonel of the second regiment of United States infantry, assumed the command of the northwestern army.

Soon after the departure of General St. Clair, Colonel Wilkinson, with a detachment of regulars, and one hundred and seventy militia commanded by Major Gano, proceeded to relieve Fort Jefferson. From that post he advanced to the scene of the late disastrous defeat, where he collected more than two hundred muskets and one piece of artillery, which had been left on the field by the savages.

The Indian war had now become a matter of serious consideration to the whole United States, and the inefficient measures adopted by the Federal authorities heretofore for its successful termination had met with but one indignant response from the whole West. The war having assumed a national character, the people of the West as well as those of the nation at large, no less than the country's honor, required some adequate provision for the defense of the frontier people, and such movements on the part of the nation as should signally retrieve the disgrace of these repeated disasters.

At the urgent recommendation of President Washington, Congress at length authorized the enlistment of three additional regiments of infantry, and one complete squadron, two thousand of cavalry, for a term of three years' service, or until peace should finally be extorted from the Indians.

While these levies were organizing and concentrating upon the Ohio River for the humiliation of the hostile savages, General Anthony Wayne, a distinguished officer of the Revolutionary war, was appointed commander-in-chief of the northwestern army. The new levies were to rendezvous at Fort Pitt and other posts on the Ohio, preparatory to an early campaign during the following year.

Meantime, Colonel Wilkinson, commanding at Fort Washington under the instructions of the president, had made frequent overtures of peace to the hostile tribes. But the savages treated with disdain every attempt at negotiation, and repeatedly put to death such as ventured to bear his dispatches.

After the failure of several messages from Colonel Wilkinson to the inimical bands during the spring of 1792, in June he determined, at the desire of the president, to send a formal embassy by an officer of rank, authorized to make preliminary arrangements for a general treaty of pacification with all the confederate tribes of the Northwestern Territory. For this hazardous mission, he selected Major Truman as the bearer of dispatches from the commander of the army, and a peace-talk from the president, under the protection of a flag of truce. Willing to advance the interests of his country even at the risk of his life, Major Truman set out upon his dangerous mission, accompanied by a French interpreter, and one other attendant in the capacity of a servant boy. On his route to the Indian towns, he fell in with two Indian warriors, who, affecting to apprehend danger by the inequality of numbers, proposed to leave the camp during the night. To quiet their apprehension on that point, and to inspire confidence in his professed object, Major Truman permitted himself to be tied, so as to leave the two parties equal without him. But no sooner was he confined by his bonds, than the treacherous savages took occasion to shoot his two companions, after which he was dispatched with the tomahawk.

At a subsequent period, Colonel Hardin and Captain Hendricks, having been sent for the same object, were in like manner killed by the Indians.*

The medals, speeches, and papers in their possession were delivered by the Indians to the officers of the British garrison at the "Rapids" of the Maumee, and by them transmitted to the commandant at Detroit. Other papers, taken from some of the flag parties who had been killed by the Indians, were carried to the Wabash. M. Vigo, from Vincennes, on the 3d of July, reported at Fort Washington that a flag party of four had been killed by the Indians on the 28th of June, and that from them the Indians had obtained a great many papers, among which was "a great and good talk from a great chief."†

During the year 1792, the advanced posts of Fort St. Clair and Fort Jefferson were occupied by the regular troops and

* American State Papers, *Indian Affairs*, vol. i., p. 243.   † Ibidem, p. 238.

detachments of militia, as a restraint upon the advance of hostile Indians against the settlements of Kentucky and the "Miami Purchase." These advanced garrisons were frequently assailed by the savages, who lurked in the vicinity to observe and cut off communication with Fort Washington, or to capture the supplies forwarded for their use. Skirmishes with detachments of regular troops or militia passing to the relief of these posts were common during the summer and autumn.

Among the skirmishes of this kind we may enumerate one on the 6th of November, in which Major John Adair, with one hundred Kentucky militia, was attacked near Fort St. Clair by a large body of Indians under Little Turtle, and after a severe skirmish was compelled to retreat, with the loss of six men killed, besides the loss of one hundred and forty pack-horses and all their camp equipage. The Indian loss was six warriors killed.

Several of the Indian parties which harassed the advanced posts and infested the frontier settlements during the summer and fall of 1792 were led or planned by Simon Girty, a renegade Pennsylvanian in the British service. During this year he had been exceedingly active in his operations among all the northwestern as well as the southern tribes, to rouse them against the American people. Under the direction of Alexander M'Key, Indian agent of his Britannic majesty, he had visited numerous tribes, and had sent emissaries and presents to the Creeks of Western Georgia, and to other portions of the southern nations, urging them to the conflict. It was during this year that Girty, exulting in his success, declared that when the next campaign opened the United States would find seventeen nations arrayed in arms against them, and that, in his rude phraseology, "he would raise all hell to prevent a peace."*

During the months of November and December, the new levies from the East were arriving at Pittsburgh, on their way to the seat of war. Such as arrived were placed in winter quarters on the Ohio, about twenty miles below Pittsburgh, where they remained until spring, when they were quartered in the vicinity of Fort Washington and at the advanced posts toward the Miami towns.

[A.D. 1793.] Early in April General Wayne began to concentrate his troops and military supplies in the vicinity of Fort

* American State Papers, *Indian Affairs*, vol. i., p. 238–243.

Washington, and was actively engaged in his preparations for the invasion of the Indian country. But it was not long before he perceived that the period for active operations would be passed ere the arrival of the whole complement of the new levies. The recruiting officers in many places had encountered much difficulty in filling their rolls, on account of the prejudice which existed against the dangerous character of the service, which had already proved so disastrous to two armies.

During this unavoidable delay, he lost no opportunity of renewing overtures of peace with the Indian foe; but the savages disdainfully rejected not only all his proposals, but those made by commissioners from the president.

At length, finding all his efforts to reconcile the savages ineffectual, he began, in September, to advance his forces toward the seat of the Indian power upon the branches of the Maumee. Having proceeded about eighty miles northward from Fort Washington, he took up his position for the winter, and erected a strongly-fortified camp, which he called "Fort Greenville." This position was about six miles in advance of Fort Jefferson, near the bank of Greenville Creek, a western tributary of the Great Miami, and near the site of the present town of Greenville, in Darke county, Ohio.

During the winter the Indians were active in their demonstrations against the troops, as well as against the frontier settlements in the rear of the army, even to Fort Washington.

On the 17th of October, a detachment of ninety men, commanded by Lieutenant Lowry and Ensign Boyd, conducting a quantity of provisions and military stores from Fort Washington, was attacked early in the morning by a superior force of savages, seven miles in advance of Fort St. Clair. After a severe skirmish, both officers were killed, and the detachment retreated to Fort St. Clair, leaving thirteen of their number on the field, together with seventy horses and the stores in twenty-one wagons, to the mercy of the enemy. The whole number killed was fifteen. The wagons and a large portion of their contents were subsequently recovered.*

On the 24th of October, General Charles Scott, with one thousand mounted riflemen from Kentucky, arrived at Greenville; but as all active operations were deferred until the close

---

* American State Papers, *Indian Affairs*, vol. i., p. 361, General Wayne's Dispatches, Official Report.

of winter, he returned with his command to Kentucky until the following spring.*

During the winter the scouting parties of General Wayne, at the head of whom was Major Simon Kenton, ascertained that the Indians were concentrating in great force on the Maumee, below the mouth of the Au Glaize, and were active in their preparations to meet their invaders.† The general became fully convinced that he should encounter the most obstinate resistance from the combined savages, and he made his movements accordingly.

Nor had the British authorities in Canada failed to take a deep interest in the success of the savages, while they encouraged them in a vigorous resistance, under the assurances of a probable co-operation of the British arms before the close of the contest.

In the autumn of 1793, Lord Dorchester had issued a proclamation to the western savages, in which he declared that, "from the manner in which the people of the United States push forward, act, and talk, I should not be surprised if we are at war with them in the course of the present year: if so, a *line* will have to be drawn by the warriors." The same fall Governor Simcoe advanced from Detroit to the foot of the "Maumee Rapids," with three companies of British troops, to occupy and erect a military post at that place, ostensibly to protect Detroit from the advance of the American army, which was about to invade the Indian country.‡ This was the first occupation of Fort Miami since its capture by the Indians at the beginning of Pontiac's war, in 1763.

[A.D. 1794.] The summer of 1794, until near the last of July, was spent in active preparations by the commander-in-chief for his advance against the combined savages. During this time, the general was indefatigable in completing the organization and discipline of his troops, and in providing ample supplies and military stores.

The president, in a military conference and personal interview with General Wayne and the Secretary of War, had urged the necessity of strictly observing certain principles of tactics in the campaigns to be undertaken against the Indian tribes.

---

* Butler's Kentucky, p. 222.   † M'Donald's Sketches, p. 262.
‡ Butler's Kentucky, p. 236. Also, American State Papers, vol. ii., p. 58–61, and 72, 73, Boston edition of 1817.

The most important of these were "a facility of forming an order of battle from an order of march," so as to be able to resist a sudden attack from any quarter; also, "a capacity of forming a line in thick woods," and "an easy mode of securing and prolonging the flanks, with a line of extreme open order," having each file more than arm's length asunder. These were considered by President Washington essential points in a war with our northwestern Indians; for no vigilance could guard against an unexpected attack in their native forests and defiles. Their object in all their tactics is to turn the enemy's flank. The president further observes: "The plan suggested above presents to the Indians, in all their attempts to turn either flank, a succession of fresh troops coming from the rear to extend the line." The plan of fighting regular troops requires the files so close that the shoulders of the men touch each other. "In fighting Indians, as no shock was to be given or received, a very open order was, therefore, attended with two very great advantages: it more than doubled the length of the lines, and in charging, which was an essential part of the system, it gave more facility to get through the obstacles which an action in the woods always presents. The camp was to be always in a hollow square, within which were to be placed all the baggage and cavalry, and sometimes the light infantry and riflemen, for the purpose of making sallies in a night attack. Ramparts of logs or fallen timber are requisite for the purpose of arresting a *night attack* until the troops can be gotten under arms. Patrols and picket guards are useless, as they are sure to be cut off by the savages. A chain of camp sentinels are placed within supporting distance of each other around the camp. The army is to be kept together as an entire whole, for detachments are generally intercepted, or surrounded and cut off by the savages."*

Such was the general outline of the plan suggested by Washington for conducting a campaign against the savages; and upon these principles General Wayne formed his fortified camp at Greenville, as well as his daily encampment, on the line of march into the Indian country.† The annexed diagram gives

---

* Butler's Kentucky, p. 217, 218.

† In the daily march, suitable ground could not always be found for this plan in full, and the plan was adhered to as far as the ground would permit. In regular marches the army generally halted about the middle of the afternoon. The quartermasters of the several sub-legions, with the quartermaster-general, surveyor, and engineer, went

a tolerably correct representation of the encampment at Greenville.

In June, a strong detachment of the army was advanced to the scene of " St. Clair's defeat." The ground was still strewed with the bleached bones of the brave men who had been slaughtered nearly three years before. After the melancholy duty of collecting and interring nearly six hundred skulls, besides other bones, in one common grave, the ground was occupied by the detachment, and a stockade was immediately commenced.* A few weeks sufficed to complete the work, when it received from the commander the significant name of " Fort Recovery."

The Indians, by their scouting parties, had observed this movement of the troops, and impatiently witnessed the erection of this post upon the field of their triumph. Encouraged by British agents and officers, they were making great preparations to encounter the invading foe. The whole of the northwestern tribes from New York to the Upper Mississippi, and many Creek and Cherokee auxiliaries, had contributed their quota of warriors to augment the allied army upon the waters of the Maumee, where the final contest was to decide the fate of the Indian tribes.

Undaunted by the formidable array preparing against them, the savages seemed to bid defiance to the power of their enemies, and invited the contest. On the last day of June, a large body of Indian warriors appeared before Fort Recovery early in the morning, and made a furious attack upon a detachment of ninety riflemen and fifty dragoons, under Major M'Mahan, encamped near the fort. The attack soon became general, extending from the detachment of Major M'Mahan to the whole garrison in every direction. The action was continued with great spirit, and the Indians were repulsed with the loss of many of their warriors; but, rallying their forces, they renewed the assault, and continued their efforts without intermission until night. Although the severe fire from the fort compelled

---

in advance with a front guard and selected the ground, laid off the encampment, and marked the bounds of each sub-legion, so that when the army arrived the troops proceeded to pitch their tents. This done, each company proceeded to fortify twenty feet in front of its position. This was effected by cutting down trees, trimming off the limbs, and putting them up from two to four logs high, according to the timber. Generally after the commencement of a breast-work, the whole was completed around the encampment before dark.—See American Pioneer, vol. ii., p. 392.

* American Pioneer, vol. ii., p. 294.

GENERAL WAYNE'S DAILY ENCAMPMENT.

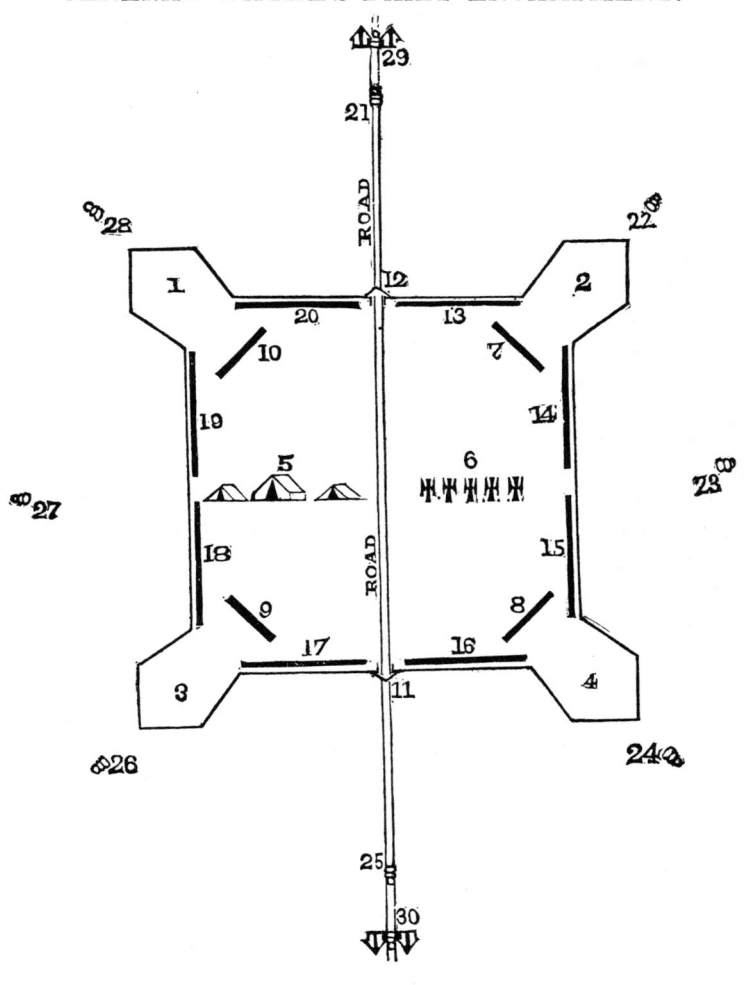

REFERENCE.

1. Lieutenant Massie's bastion.
2. Lieutenant Pope's bastion.
3. Captain Porter's bastion.
4. Captain Ford's bastion.
5. Headquarters.
6. Park of artillery.
7. Second troop of dragoons.
8. First troop of dragoons.
9. Fourth troop of dragoons.
10. Third troop of dragoons.
11. Rear gateway.
12. Front gateway.
13 and 14. Third sub-legion.
15 and 16. First sub-legion.
17 and 18. Second sub-legion.
19 and 20. Fourth sub-legion.
21, 22, 23, 24, 25, 26, 27, and 28. Picquet guards.
29. Advance guard.
30. Rear guard.

them subsequently to maintain a respectful distance, they did not abandon their design of capturing the post. They were re-enforced on the following morning, July 1st, and resumed the attack with increased fury; but having been soon repulsed, with great loss, by the small arms and artillery of the fort, they retired from the contest. Thus the savages experienced a signal reverse upon the same field where once they had been so triumphantly victorious.

The American loss in this attack was twenty-five men killed and missing, and thirty wounded. Two hundred and twenty-two horses fell into the hands of the Indians, and twenty-two were wounded.

The Indian loss in this attack was severe; but, as they labored almost incessantly during two nights in removing their dead and wounded, only ten bodies were found when they retired. The entire number engaged in the attack, as was subsequently ascertained, was nearly fifteen hundred, including many Canadian French, who, with blackened faces, took an active part in the attack. Several British officers in full uniform were also seen on the field.

Among the slain on the part of the Americans were the gallant officers Major M'Mahan, Captain Hartshorne, and Lieutenant Craig. The intrepid M'Mahan was the pride of the northwestern army, and the idol of his soldiers. In honor of his heroic defense of the post, General Wayne, in his official report, proudly refers to him as the "defender of Fort Recovery."

On the 20th of July, General Scott, from Kentucky, arrived at Fort Recovery with sixteen hundred mounted men, to re-enforce the regular army. This brigade augmented the whole effective force to nearly four thousand men; and on the 29th, General Wayne took up the line of march for the hostile towns upon the Au Glaize River. The fourth day brought them to the St. Mary's River, forty-seven miles from Greenville, and twenty-four miles in advance of Fort Recovery. Here, on the margin of a beautiful prairie, the legion remained three days, erecting a stockade fort, which was completed on the 4th of August, and called "Fort Adams." It consisted mainly of two salient block-houses, connected by a salient stockade, inclosing the quarters of the troops and the military stores. This post was left in command of Lieutenant Underhill, with a garrison of one hundred men, when the army resumed its march for the Au Glaize.*

The advance was by regular marches across the Au Glaize, and thence down that stream through extensive towns and fields which lined its banks for many miles. On the 8th of August the army encamped at the mouth of the Grand Glaize, fifty-three miles in advance of Fort Adams, and one hundred and three miles from Greenville. Next day the general ordered the erection of a strong stockade, immediately at the junction of the Au Glaize and Maumee Rivers, which he called "Fort Defiance." During the construction of this fort, the troops remained encamped in the principal Miami village, surrounded by extensive fields of corn, until the 14th, during which time the cavalry scoured the whole country for many miles round, laying waste the fields and burning the deserted towns

On the 15th, such was the progress made toward the completion of Fort Defiance, that General Wayne, leaving a detachment of troops for its defense, proceeded with the main body of the army down the Maumee by regular marches until the 18th, when he encamped near the head of the Rapids, forty-five miles in advance of Fort Defiance, and within seven miles of the British Fort Miami.

Here he erected a stockade for the security of the baggage and military stores, and called it "Fort Deposit." The army under his command assembled at this point amounted to two thousand regulars, besides eleven hundred mounted riflemen, commanded by General Scott. The troops were in fine spirits, and in a high state of discipline, all eager to be led against the allied savages, who were encamped in the rear of the British fort, and within five miles of the American army.

On the 20th, at eight o'clock in the morning, the troops in battle array advanced toward the enemy. The line of battle consisted of three columns: the "legion" on the right, next the river; General Todd's brigade of mounted riflemen on the left; and General Barbee's brigade of mounted men in the rear. Major Price, with his select corps, marched in front as an advanced detachment, to give timely notice of the approach of the enemy.

The Indians were formed in three lines, within supporting distance of each other, in the midst of a forest which was in-

* American Pioneer, vol. ii., p. 203.

terrupted with prostrate trees, and having their left resting upon the river, and their right extending nearly two miles into a dense thicket of brushwood.*

In this order the army advanced slowly five miles down the left bank of the Maumee, when Major Price sent an express to the commander-in-chief, with intelligence that he had discovered the enemy. It was only a few minutes afterward when the major was compelled to fall back from the heavy fire of a large body of Indians, concealed in the high grass and behind fallen timber. The action soon became general, and the troops advanced to their respective stations in front.

The Indians immediately began to extend their front, advancing their right into the brushwood thicket, with the design of outflanking the left of the American line, when General Scott was ordered to that quarter with General Todd's brigade, to turn the enemy's right flank. Captain Campbell, with the legion on the right, was ordered to charge the enemy's left. The order was promptly obeyed, but in the advance Captain Campbell was killed, and his command was driven back upon the infantry. The infantry were ordered to advance with trailed arms, and rouse the Indians from their covert with the bayonet, and, when roused, to deliver a well-directed fire upon their backs, and follow it up immediately with a brisk charge, so as to give no time to reload, or to form their line again.

Such was the impetuosity of this charge by the first line of infantry, that the Indians and Canadians were driven from all their coverts so rapidly, that only a part of the second line of General Scott's mounted battalion could gain their position in time to take an active part in the battle. The Indians were driven through the thick woods and fallen timber more than two miles in the course of one hour by less than half their number.†

The force of the Indians and their British allies was estimated at about two thousand combatants; the troops under General Wayne who were actually engaged did not exceed nine hundred.

The woods for a considerable distance were strewed with the dead bodies of the Indians and their white allies, the latter

---

* Butler's Kentucky, p. 237.
† American State Papers, *Indian Affairs*, vol. i., p. 491. Also, Butler's Kentucky, p. 237, 238.

having been armed with British muskets and bayonets. The loss of the American army on this occasion was comparatively small. Of the legion of cavalry, Captain Robert Mis Campbell, Lieutenant Henry B. Towles, and twenty-four non-commissioned officers and privates were killed, and eighty-seven officers and privates wounded. Of the dragoons and artillery, three were killed and eight wounded. Of the Kentucky volunteers, seven were killed and thirteen wounded. The total loss of killed and missing, including eleven who died of their wounds, was forty-four; the whole number wounded was one hundred.

In this campaign, and in the battle of August 20th, every officer and soldier behaved with that courage and promptness which drew from their commander the most unbounded approbation. Among the officers who distinguished themselves for courage and intrepidity were Brigadier-general Wilkinson, Colonel Hamtramck, Lieutenant Covington, who cut down two savages with his own hand; Captains De Butts and Lewis; Lieutenant Harrison, Major Mills, and Lieutenant Webb, who also cut down a savage with his own hand.*

This battle was fought in view of the British post, and many of the fugitive Indians and Canadians took refuge from the vengeance of the American troops under the guns of the fort. The American army encamped on the banks of the Maumee, in sight of the British post, for three days. During this time, General Wayne reconnoitered the fort and its defenses by advancing with his staff within range of the guns. The troops destroyed and burned all houses and property of every kind belonging to the Indians and Canadians, as well as the house and store of the British agent, Alexander M'Key.

After the battle, a spirited correspondence was opened between the British commandant, Major Campbell, and the American commander-in-chief. The former desired to know of the latter in what light he should view " such near approaches of an American army, almost within reach of the guns of a post belonging to his majesty, the King of Great Britain ?" General Wayne, in a tone of proud defiance, replied, "Were you entitled to an answer, the most full and satisfactory was announced to you from the muzzles of my small arms yesterday morning, in the action against hordes of savages in the vicinity of your fort, and which terminated gloriously for the American

* See General Wayne's Official Report, *Indian Affairs*, p. 491.

arms; but had it continued until the Indians were driven under the influence of the post and guns you mention, they would not much have impeded the progress of the victorious army under my command, as no such post was established at the commencement of the present war between the Indians and the United States." The correspondence was continued by several letters from each commander, in one of which General Wayne demanded, in the name of the President of the United States, that the British post should be abandoned, and the troops and military stores removed to the nearest post occupied by the British troops at the treaty of 1783. The commandant, in his reply, observed, " that the post would not be abandoned at the summons of any power whatever until orders were received from his superiors, or the fortunes of war should oblige him."

Here the correspondence terminated, and every thing in view of the fort which could be of any service to the Indians or British having been destroyed, the American army returned to Fort Deposit.

This was one of the most decisive battles ever fought with the western Indians, and tended more than any other to humble the power and spirit of the hostile tribes. The name of General Wayne alone was more terror to them than an army, for they looked upon him as a chief that never slept, and whom no art could surprise.

The army, by easy marches, returned to Fort Defiance, where it arrived on the 27th of August, having laid waste the whole adjacent country. The sick and wounded received due attention, and the regular troops were employed in completing the defenses of the post. On the 12th of September, an additional glacis and fascines, with a ditch twelve feet wide and eight feet deep, besides four bomb-proof block-houses, having been completed, the main army took up the line of march for the "Miami villages," at the confluence of the St. Mary's and St. Joseph's Rivers. A suitable garrison was detailed for the defense of the post against any Indian force which could be arrayed against it.

This fort, being in the most exposed portion of the Indian country, was completed with great labor, and was one of the strongest ever built for the defense of the frontier. The annexed diagram represents the general plan of the works.*

* Diagram and sketch furnished by John W. Vancleve, of Dayton, June 1st, 1843.—See Pioneer, vol. ii., p. 387.

On the 17th the army encamped at the Miami villages, forty-seven miles above Fort Defiance. The camp was fortified as usual, and the following day General Wayne selected the site for another stockade fort, the construction of which was begun on the 24th of September. On the 23d of October it was completed, and by Colonel Hamtramck called "Fort Wayne," in honor of the commander-in chief.

On the 18th of October the cavalry and the greater portion of the infantry set out from Fort Wayne on their march for Greenville. On the way, a detachment was left at Loramie's Creek, seventy miles from Fort Wayne, where Fort Loramie was erected. On the 20th of November the regular troops went into winter-quarters at Greenville.

The campaign of 1794 put a close to the Indian hostilities in the northwest. The spirit and power of the savages had been subdued; their country had been ravaged with fire and sword; their houses and their fields were destroyed; their supplies consumed; their hopes of checking the advance of the white population had been blasted; and now, fearing the power of the United States, they soon began to evince a disposition to enter into amicable negotiations for a permanent treaty of peace and friendship, notwithstanding the opposition urged by the British agents.

At each angle of the fort was a block-house. The one next the Maumee is marked A, having port-holes, B B B, on three exterior sides, and a door, D, and a chimney, C, on the interior side. A line of pickets on each side of the fort connected the block-houses by their nearest angles. Outside the pickets and around the block-houses was a glacis, or wall of earth, eight feet thick, sloping upward and outward from the foot of the pickets, supported by a log wall on the sides of the ditch, and by fascines, or a wall of fagots, next the Au Glaize. The ditch, twelve feet wide and eight feet deep, surrounded the whole work, except on the side next the Au Glaize. Diagonal pickets, eleven feet long and one foot apart, were secured to the log wall, and projected over the ditch. Gate-ways, E E. A bank of earth left, four feet wide, for a passage across the ditch, F. A falling gate, or draw-bridge, across the ditch, G. Officers' quarters, H. Store-houses, I. Two lines of pickets converged toward L, a ditch eight feet deep leading to the river, as a covert way for water. Small sand-bar at the point M.

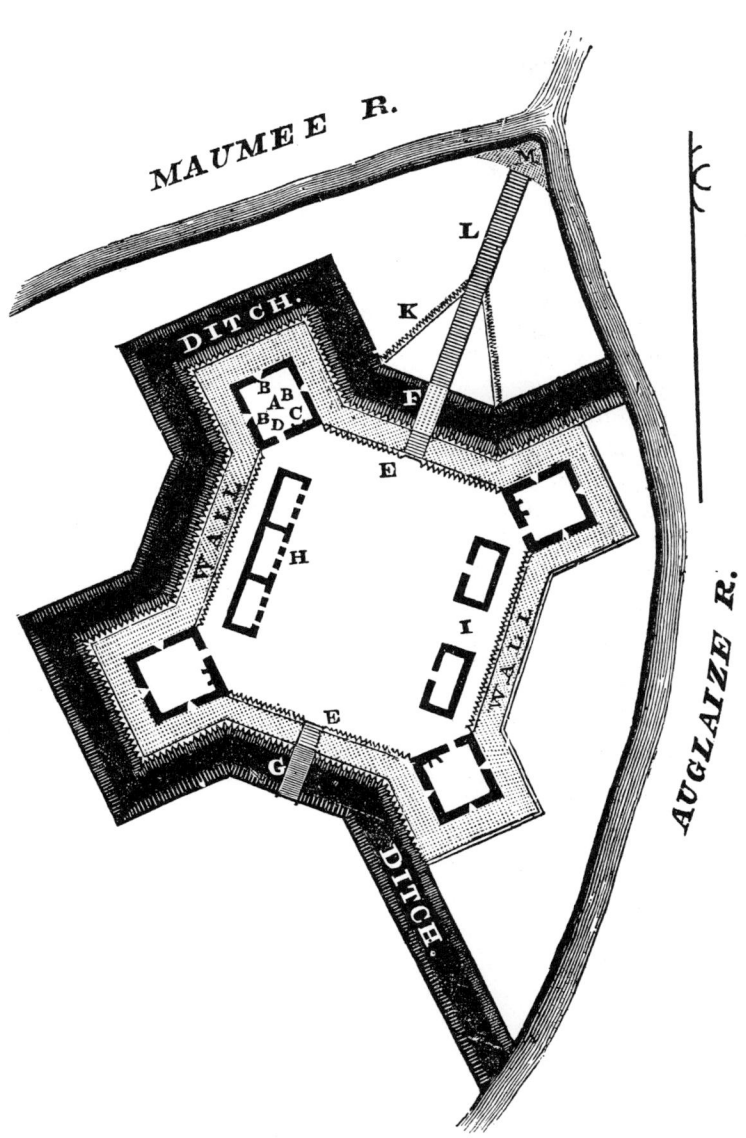

GROUND-PLAN OF FORT DEFIANCE.

CHAPTER XII.

ADVANCE OF THE WHITE POPULATION INTO THE NORTHWESTERN TERRITORY.—ADMISSION OF THE "STATE OF OHIO" INTO THE FEDERAL UNION.—A.D. 1795 TO 1804.

Argument.—Security of the frontier Population after the Treaty of Greenville.—Amicable Intercourse with the Indians.—Emigrants advance upon the Muskingum, Scioto, and Miami Rivers.—Population of Northwestern Territory in 1796.—Of Cincinnati in 1797.—Population advances into the Virginia Military District.—Nathaniel Massie, Pioneer of Scioto Valley.—Chillicothe first Settled.—Tribute to Memory of Massie.—First Mail-route opened from Wheeling to Limestone.—Population advances to the "Western Reserve:"—"County of Wayne" organized.—Old French Settlements near Detroit.—Traits of Character in French Population.—Retrospect of Northwestern Territory in 1796.—Extension of Settlements up the Scioto and Muskingum Valleys.—"Adams County" organized.—"Ross County" organized.—Condition of Chillicothe in 1798.—Extreme Settlements north of Chillicothe.—Herman Blannerhasset emigra'es to Ohio in 1798.—His Traits of Character.—Blannerhasset's Island.—Steubenville laid off and settled.—Territorial Population in 1798.—*Second Grade* of Government assumed.—First Territorial Legislature.—Public Surveys.—Counties of Trumbull and Fairfield organized.—Belmont County organized.—Indiana Territory organized into a separate Government.—Congress authorizes a Convention to form a State Constitution.—Convention assembles and adopts a Constitution.—"State of Ohio" admitted into the Union.—State Government organized March 1st, 1803.—Character and Merits of Governor St. Clair.—New Counties organized.—Governors of Ohio.—Subsequent Increase of Population and Extension of Civil Government.—Population in 1840.—Character of Emigration to Ohio.

[A.D. 1795.] THE treaty of Greenville was hailed with joy throughout the West; in Kentucky, Western Virginia, and Pennsylvania, no less than in the Northwestern Territory. The whole western population of these states was deeply interested in the peace and security of the frontier, for all had participated in the dangers and privations incident to the state of hostilities which had called forth the previous unfortunate campaigns into the Indian country.

Several months before the treaty, the greater portion of the Indian tribes had been anxious for peace, and had discontinued their incursions against the Ohio border; yet the exposed settlements in the Northwestern Territory were not altogether secure from outrages committed by a few desperate malcontents, belonging chiefly to the Shawanese nation. The apprehension of danger from such was sufficient to prevent the extension of population beyond the immediate vicinity of forts, stations, and stockades. But no sooner had the treaty of

Greenville been concluded, than the frontier inhabitants, in conscious security, began to advance; while the Indians, relieved from the toils and privations of war, confidently approached the settlements, anxious to open a friendly intercourse and trade in the sale of their furs, peltries, and game for cash, or to exchange them for powder and lead, and for such necessaries and comforts as were adapted to their mode of life. On the part of the whites, all apprehension of danger ceased, and friendly intercourse succeeded to outrage and war. The disaffected Indians who persisted in their hostility had retired either into the Far West or to their allies in Canada. Repose and security lighted up the path of the pioneers with new hopes, and renewed energy and enterprise for peopling the fertile and boundless regions before them; and again they prepared to explore the lands which lay inviting their advance in the valleys of the Muskingum, the Hockhocking, the Scioto, and the two Miamis. Forts, stations, and stockades, having lost their importance, began to crumble and decay; while the restless pioneer confidently advanced, pitched his tent, and erected his cabin in the dense forest, or the remote plains which expand near the sources of these beautiful streams. Men of capital and enterprise in the older settlements soon became interested in securing claims and titles to extensive bodies of land, and in leading forth colonies for their occupation. Emigrant families from Kentucky, from Western Virginia, and from Pennsylvania were also advancing across the Ohio, by way of Cincinnati, Marietta, and Wheeling, into the valleys of the Little Miami, Scioto, and Muskingum.

Among the most active of the early landed proprietors in the Miami country were Winthrop Sargent, Secretary of the Northwestern Territory, and General James Wilkinson, of Kentucky. These two officers, anxious to speculate in lands, associated themselves with Jonathan Dayton and Israel Ludlow, a surveyor, and made a joint purchase of a large body of lands from J. C. Symmes, lying high up the Little Miami, and extending westward to the Great Miami as high as Mad River. This purchase was made on the 20th day of August, and only seventeen days after the treaty of Greenville had been signed. Preparations were made for the early distribution of this purchase into suitable family tracts, and on the 4th day of November Israel Ludlow commenced surveying the plot of a town, which was named "Dayton," in honor of one of the proprietors.* This town was laid out at the mouth of Mad River, and about one mile below the mouth of Stillwater Creek. The following spring witnessed the erection of the first houses and the arrival of the first families in Dayton. But it was doomed to insignificance as a town for thirteen years, until it became the seat of justice for Montgomery county in the year 1809, although some settlements sprang up in the vicinity before the close of the second year.

[A.D. 1796.] *Extension of Settlements into the Miami, Scioto, and Muskingum Valleys.*—A large portion of the emigrants from the New England States, and from Pennsylvania, Maryland, New Jersey, and Virginia, advanced by the way of Brownsville and Wheeling. Here a portion descended the Ohio to Limestone, and other points in Kentucky, to make preparations for their final residence. Others proceeded across the Ohio River at Wheeling and other convenient points, and thence by land to the section of country which they had selected for their homes. The colonies for the Muskingum and Scioto valleys passed chiefly by this route into the interior of the territory.

Before the close of the year 1796, the white population of the Northwestern Territory increased to about five thousand souls of all ages, who were distributed chiefly in the lower valleys of the Muskingum, Scioto, and Miami Rivers, and upon their small tributaries within fifty miles of the Ohio River. Such were the extent and condition of the white settlements previous to the year 1797.

The Ohio Company's purchase continued to receive emigrants, and numerous settlements had been made on the banks of the Ohio and upon its small tributaries south of the Muskingum. The purchase of Symmes on the Miami presented numerous small villages, besides those near Fort Washington and Columbia, both of which had greatly increased their population since the treaty of Greenville.

Cincinnati had increased its population and improved the style of its buildings. In the year 1792 the town contained about thirty log cabins, besides the buildings and appurtenances of Fort Washington, and not above two hundred and fifty inhabitants. In the beginning of the year 1796 it contained

* Ohio Gazetteer of 1841, p. 157.

more than one hundred cabins, besides about one dozen frame houses, with a population of nearly six hundred persons.* As yet, brick houses had not been used at Cincinnati; those chimneys not built of wood and clay were made of stone. Stone abounded in the hills in the rear of the town, and supplied abundant material for all the purposes to which brick is usually applied;† and, as stone was much more easily obtained than lumber or mechanics in a new country, it soon became a substitute for wood in the construction of houses.

Within the Virginia Military District, between the Little Miami and the Scioto Rivers, were several new settlements in the vicinity of Manchester, and less than thirty miles from the Ohio. Within three years a few settlements had been extended ten miles up the Little Miami and twenty-five miles up the Scioto Rivers, or as far as the present town of Piketon. Surveys had been executed by Nathaniel Massie, the enterprising pioneer of the Scioto Valley, over most of the fertile lands westward to the Little Miami, as far north as Todd's Fork, and upon all the branches of Paint Creek, and eastward to the Scioto, near Westfall. He had done much to extend the settlements upon the Scioto, and his name deserves to be enrolled among the hardy pioneers who led the van of civilization into the western wilderness. Nathaniel Massie was an early emigrant to Kentucky; born in Goochland county, Virginia, near the close of the year 1763, he was a soldier in the Revolutionary war at the age of seventeen. A surveyor in 1783, he set out for the West in quest of employment, where, for more than two years, he was engaged in exploring, locating, and surveying the fine lands upon the north side of the Kentucky River. In the autumn of 1787 he engaged with zeal as a surveyor under Colonel Richard C. Anderson, surveyor-general for the Virginia Military Land Districts, and surveyed north of the Ohio in the Virginia Military District, between the Little Miami and Scioto Rivers. Near the close of the year 1790, he commenced the first settlement in the Virginia Military District by laying out the town of Manchester, twelve miles above Limestone. In March following his stockade was completed as a defense against Indian hostility, and contained a population of thirty families.‡

* Cincinnati in 1841, p. 28.   † Burnett's Letters, p. 11, 12.
‡ M'Donald's Sketches, p. 30, 31.

During the year 1795, Massie, having secured large bodies of excellent lands west of the Scioto, upon the branches of Paint Creek, led out an exploring party for the purpose of laying off a town at some advantageous point on the Scioto; but encountering hostile Indians near Reeve's Crossings, on Paint Creek, he returned to Manchester.* But the design of laying off a town was not abandoned. Early in March, 1796, he assembled another party, and again advanced up the Scioto to the mouth of Paint Creek, where he erected a "station," and, early in April, planted a crop of corn. The colony was well supplied with horses, stock, farming utensils, and all the requisites of a new settlement. Cabins were erected, and in May three hundred acres of fertile prairie had been turned up by thirty plows, ready for pitching a crop of corn.†

Thus commenced the first settlement on the waters of Paint Creek, at "Station Prairie," three miles below the present city of Chillicothe. While the settlers were employed in the duties of a pioneer colony, Massie, assisted by Duncan M'Arthur, was engaged in the selection of a site for the contemplated town upon the banks of the Scioto River. The elevated alluvial plain three miles above was selected for the town, and was soon laid off into two hundred and eighty-seven town lots, and one hundred and sixty-nine out-lots, regularly intersected at right angles by wide streets and lanes alternately. According to the original plan of settlement, one hundred town lots and one hundred out-lots were selected by lot as a donation to the first hundred settlers. To others, the price of a choice town lot was ten dollars, and each owner proceeded to erect upon his lot the stipulated house or tenement for future residence. The town sprang up almost, as it were, by magic. Before the close of the year, it contained, besides private residences, several stores, taverns, and mechanical shops. The arts of pioneer life began to multiply, and to give competence in the midst of the wilderness. Emigrants constantly arrived; the population, trade, and enterprise of the place continued to increase under the liberal policy of its enterprising founder.‡

The town was called "Chillicothe," a term which in the Indian dialect signifies *town*. It was the first town west of the mountains which was built in peace and quietude, and not requiring the protection of stockades and forts against Indian hostility.

---

* M'Donald's Sketches, p. 56–58.　　† Idem, p. 60, 61.　　‡ Idem, p. 62, 63.

Nathaniel Massie continued to retain the confidence and respect of the new settlements until the day of his death, November 3d, 1813. Under the territorial government, enjoying the entire confidence of Governor St. Clair, he was commissioned colonel for the proper organization of the territorial militia. He was subsequently a prominent member of the convention which formed the state constitution; he was a senator from Ross county in the first General Assembly under the constitution, and speaker of the Senate; and he was subsequently elected major-general of the second division of Ohio militia.* Although a large landholder, his liberality and kindness to the western emigrants were proverbial.

Emigrants from Virginia advanced in great numbers into the Scioto Valley, and settlements were extended rapidly upon all the fine lands in the vicinity of Chillicothe, upon the branches of Paint Creek and Deer Creek, as well as upon the smaller tributaries of the Scioto, within twenty miles of Chillicothe.

Such was the advance of population into the wide and fertile Valley of the Scioto in less than three years after the restoration of peace with the Indians.

At the same time, settlements were advancing upon all the beautiful tributaries on the eastern side of the Great Miami. Sparse settlements were formed as high as Dayton; but the principal population in this quarter was near Cincinnati, and in the Valley of the Little Miami. Settlements, likewise, were gradually extended up the Muskingum as far as the mouth of Licking. It was in this year that Ebenezer Zane obtained a grant for one section of land, in compensation for opening a bridle-trace from the Ohio River at Wheeling across the country to Limestone, in Kentucky.† The first United States mail traversed this route in the following year; but it was not until two years afterward that the town was laid off, when the first cabins were erected, and the village assumed the name of "Zanesville."‡

Extension of Settlements into the Connecticut Reserve.—About the same time, emigrants from the New England States began to arrive in the northeastern part of the territory, and to form settlements in "New Connecticut," or the "Western Re-

---

* M'Donald's Sketches, p. 64, 65.
† Atwater's Ohio, p. 160. Also, American Pioneer, vol. i., p. 204.
‡ Ohio Gazetteer, 1841, p. 489.

serve." During the same year the first settlement was made at the mouth of Conneaut Creek, near the western line of Pennsylvania, upon the shore of Lake Erie; a few months after, the town of Cleveland had been laid out, near the mouth of the Cuyahoga.*

The claim of the State of Connecticut to the lands comprised in the "Connecticut Reserve" had been formally transferred and confirmed to the Connecticut Land Company, by deed bearing date September 5th, 1795, two months after the Indian title to the same had been extinguished by the Federal government. This land company was constituted of fifty-six individuals, acting through a board of directors. During the next summer, the company sent out forty-three surveyors, to lay off and subdivide that portion lying east of the Cuyahoga into townships five miles square.†

It was on the 16th of September, 1795, that the agents of the company advanced to the lake shore, selected and laid off the plot of a town, upon a beautiful, dry, alluvial, wooded plain, comprising a peninsula between the Cuyahoga River and the lake, and elevated about eighty feet above the water. The site was one well adapted for a commercial town. The original plot represented two hundred and twenty lots, seven streets, and four lanes. In honor of General Moses Cleveland, the enterprising agent of the Connecticut Company, the town was called "Cleveland."

Although emigrants continued to arrive in the Western Reserve, yet Cleveland attained no importance as a town until May, 1806, when it became the county seat of Geauga county, organized in March preceding. Such it continued until May, 1810, when it became the seat of justice for Cuyahoga county, which had been erected two years before. In this county the first presiding justice of the Court of Common Pleas was Benjamin Ruggles.

Settlements near Detroit.—In the mean time, the northwestern posts, including the country west and south of Lake Erie, had been evacuated by the British troops, and were now in the occupancy of the United States. The settlements near the Detroit River and upon the Maumee were annexed to the jurisdiction of the Northwestern Territory, and were comprised in the "county of Wayne," which included all the southeastern

* Atwater's Ohio, p. 160. † American Pioneer, vol. ii., p. 24.

portion of Michigan and the northwestern portion of the present State of Ohio, eastward to the Cuyahoga, and the "portage path" to the Tuscarawas. The town and post of Detroit was the county seat of justice.* Detroit having become the headquarters of the northwestern army, the troops were removed from Fort Washington to the more remote stations of Fort Wayne, Miamis, and Detroit.

Two full regiments of troops were retained upon this frontier until the spring of 1798, when they were chiefly removed to the posts near the Upper and Lower Mississippi. A road, or trace, had been opened from Cincinnati, through the wilderness, by way of Forts Wayne and Miami, to Detroit, and to other remote posts in the territory.

Detroit, and other western posts occupied by the British troops within the boundaries of the United States, agreeably to the stipulations in the treaty of 1783, were to have been surrendered, "as soon as convenient," to the authorities of the United States; yet they had been retained for more than ten years after the treaty, notwithstanding the earnest remonstrances of the American government. This infraction of the treaty, and other difficulties of a kindred nature, was deemed a matter of such vital importance to the peace and welfare of the country, that a special minister had been sent to England to urge the amicable evacuation of them. The minister, John Jay, after a difficult and tedious negotiation, succeeded in obtaining the treaty of November 19th, 1794, containing a stipulation for the surrender of all the military posts within the United States, and the withdrawal of all British troops and munitions of war prior to the first day of June, 1796. †

In conformity with this stipulation, the military posts at Detroit and upon the Maumee were formally surrendered to General Wayne early in that year.

Detroit was one of the oldest French settlements in the western country, having been occupied by the French as early as the year 1700. Since the fall of Canada, it had been a regular British military post, and the great western dépôt of the American Fur Company, until its delivery to General Wayne.‡ The inhabitants who remained were mostly Creole French, speaking

---

* Burnett's Letters, p. 48, 49.
† American State Papers, *Foreign Relations*, vol. i., p. 520, edition of 1832.
‡ Burnett's Letters, p. 49, 50.

a corrupt dialect, and ignorant of the English tongue, which was a foreign language to them.

Their ignorance of the language of their new rulers for a time was a source of much inconvenience to both parties. This made public business, and especially the administration of justice in the Federal courts, slow and tedious. Every word must necessarily pass from mouth to ear through an interpreter for the benefit of the French citizens. The progress in business was not only slow and tedious, but novel, and often amusing; but it was seldom satisfactory to the French. Another cause of dissatisfaction to them was the mode of administering justice through the mummery and tedious process of court forms, and, as they conceived, that useless appendage to a court, *a jury.** It created delay; nor could they comprehend its advantages. Formerly, both under the French and English dominion, they had been accustomed to more prompt and speedy action, when the will of the commandant was law, and his decision final, to which all bowed with due submission. This mode possessed the advantage of being prompt without expense or delay, and the decisions were often more correct than the verdicts of juries, and free of the embarrassing quibbles of law.

Another source of dissatisfaction prevailed, which also sprang from the American mode of conducting litigated questions. Attorneys were of course interested in encouraging litigation, especially where doubts arose concerning points of law relative to real estates. The attorneys were anxious to test the correctness and validity of the late commandant's decisions, and hence they stirred up questions of law at the expense and cost of the litigants. The attorneys were a new appendage to the forms of judicial proceedings with the French, and, what was more annoying, they encouraged litigation whether the cause was good or bad, provided the parties were good for their fees. Cases of this kind, relative to real estate or landed property, in the course of a few years became numerous, prominent upon the records of the courts, and highly profitable to the attorneys.† The expenses of courts, the costs of counsel, and the national or provincial abhorrence of the Americans, or "*Bostonais*," had but little effect in creating a predilection for American justice or for the Federal government.

* Burnett's Letters, p. 63–66, note.   † Ibidem.

The settlements on the Raisin, Detroit, and Maumee Rivers. as well as those on the Wabash and in the "Illinois country," were composed almost exclusively of Creole French, or French Canadians, remains of the old French colonies. They lived in the old Creole style, each settlement or homestead having a narrow front on the river bank, near which ran the public road, passing each man's door successively. They were generally poor, indolent, illiterate, and credulous, if not superstitious. They were Catholics, as their fathers had been before them, in whose footsteps they had trodden for three generations without change or desire of change.* Ignorant, poor, and contented, it is not surprising that they should deprecate the authority of the Federal government, and what they considered the delays and useless forms of their judicial proceedings.

The Counties of the Northwestern Territory in 1796.—The whole of the Northwestern Territory not in the actual possession of the Indian tribes was now organized into five extensive counties, as has been before observed. Washington county comprised all that portion of the present State of Ohio within forty miles of the Ohio River, and between the Muskingum and the Little Miami; Marietta was the seat of justice. Hamilton county comprised all that portion of the state between the Little and the Great Miami, within the same distance of the Ohio River; and Cincinnati was the county seat. Knox county embraced the region near the Ohio River, between the Great Miami and the Wabash Rivers; and Vincennes was the county seat. St. Clair county embraced the settlements upon the Illinois and upon the Kaskaskia Rivers, as well as those upon the Upper Mississippi; and Kaskaskia was the seat of justice. Wayne county, recently organized, embraced all the settlements upon the Maumee, Raisin, and Detroit Rivers; and Detroit was the seat of justice.

The jurisdiction of each of these counties extended over a territory but little less in extent than some of the New England States. The settlements were few, comparatively small, and widely separated by an uninhabited wilderness of not less than one hundred miles in extent, except where the solitary hut of the frontier hunter broke the uniformity of the scene. The only routes of intercourse between these remote settlements were either the liquid high-ways of nature, or bridle-paths and

* Burnett's Letters, p. 63, 64, note.

"blazed-traces," through the deep forests which covered the southern portion of this extensive territory. A cabin, a hunter's hut, or a solitary family residence might be seen on these routes at the distance of ten or fifteen miles from each other, where man and horse might obtain imperfect shelter and scanty fare. In other directions, the traveler might traverse the wilderness for thirty or forty miles without house or shelter, or food for man or beast, except the prolific herbage which covered his route on every side.

[A.D. 1797.] *Extension of Population in* 1797 *and* 1798.— The settlements had extended sparsely up the Scioto Valley and River; a village of more than fifty cabins, log houses, and frames, had sprung into existence upon the site where Chillicothe had been laid out twelve months before ; a few scattering settlements were found along the river for twenty miles below, and also upon some of the tributaries within fifty miles of the mouth. Forty-five miles by land above Chillicothe, on the Scioto, were three or four cabins, recently erected near the site of the present town of Franklinton, opposite the present location of Columbus, and not far from the Indian boundary. But this remote portion was a perfect wilderness of woods and wet prairies, and the few settlers were such hunters as live only on the extreme verge of civilization, or who, like John Brickell, had lived with the Indians until they had been "weaned" from civilized life.* Two years afterward, a cabin might be seen in this region every ten or twelve miles upon the principal routes and traces.

Upon the Muskingum but few settlements had extended above the present site of Zanesville, which was near the limits of the Indian country, and was occupied by a few squatters with their half-formed cabins, barely giving them a shelter from the inclemency of the seasons.

In the mean time, since the treaty of Greenville, a large number of emigrants from Kentucky and Virginia had advanced into the extreme eastern portion of Hamilton county, on the west side of the Scioto River, within the limits of the "Virginia Military District." Hundreds of settlements had been already made, and the population had augmented until it became expedient to divide the county of Hamilton. The governor and council, accordingly, on the 10th day of July laid

* American Pioneer, vol. i, p. 55.

off and organized Adams county, which comprised the eastern half of what had been Hamilton county. Manchester was made the seat of justice, and the first court was held in September following. The same year the seat of justice was fixed at "Adamsville," four miles above the mouth of Brush Creek, by Secretary Sargent.* Nathaniel Massie was colonel of militia, and Thomas Worthington, Hugh Cochran, and Samuel Smith were the first magistrates for these settlements.

Emigrants from New England and from Pennsylvania continued to arrive in the eastern portion of the territory, and had already formed numerous settlements west of the Ohio for more than fifty miles north of the Muskingum, and beyond the Ohio Company's purchase. This region was organized into the county of Jefferson, and embraced the country upon the Ohio for more than thirty miles above Wheeling, and as far below.

For nearly eight years past, Cincinnati had presented an animated scene of military parade, with the pomp and circumstance of war, and the thrilling music of the drum and fife, diversified by the roar of the morning gun as its echo reverberated along the hills which form the shores of the Ohio; but Fort Washington having ceased to be the headquarters of the army, and the general rendezvous of all the troops destined for the northwestern campaigns and frontier posts, Cincinnati lost much of its former consequence, which had been imparted by the arrival of droves of pack-horses, with all the attendant business of the commissary department. Stripped of all these incitements to life and enterprise, Cincinnati began to assume the appearance of a quiet commercial town,† and Fort Washington, with its imposing outworks and block-houses, lay useless and neglected.‡

[A.D. 1798.] The year 1798 found the population of Hamilton county greatly augmented by recent emigration. The same increase by emigration existed at different points on the Ohio, from Hamilton eastward to Jefferson county. But the strongest tide of population was beginning to flow into the Scioto Valley, not only from the East, but also from Kentucky and Tennessee. The Scioto country had become noted

---

* Ohio Gazetteer, p. 51, 52.   † American Pioneer, vol. ii., p. 98, &c.
‡ American Pioneer, vol. i., p. 158.

for its fine wooded bottoms, no less than for its level plains, which spread out almost boundless in extent a few miles north of Chillicothe. Hence it became a center of attraction to the advancing emigrants. Before the midsummer of 1798, the governor deemed it expedient to organize the country north of Adams, to comprise the upper settlements on the Scioto; and, on the 20th of August, in council, he laid off and organized the county of "Ross," named in honor of James Ross, an enterprising agent of the Ohio Company. Chillicothe, having about two hundred inhabitants, was the county seat. The first Court of Common Pleas was held in Chillicothe during the same autumn, and the first case on the docket was conducted by William Creighton, Jr., a lawyer of great worth and talents.

As yet Chillicothe was in the midst of an isolated settlement of not more than ten miles in extent, and Ross county contained large regions of country unexplored. The "Piqua Plains," intersected by "Zane's Trace," twenty miles from Chillicothe, presented only one cabin near the eastern margin, and three miles south of it was another; thence to the present site of Lancaster one more cabin was seen near the trace; from thence to the mouth of Licking Creek several improvements were commenced; but from that point eastward to Indian Creek, near the Ohio, the route was through an unsettled region. A "blazed trace" of sixty miles opened a communication between the frontier settlements of Western Virginia, near Clarksburg and Marietta. About the first of October, 1798, Felix Renick and Joseph Harness, surveyors from the south branch of the Potomac, and Leonard Stump, set out on a tour of exploration in the Scioto Valley in search of the fine lands seen by their friends more than twenty years previous in Lord Dunmore's campaign. Provided each with a good rifle, a pack-horse laden with supplies, and ammunition, they passed by way of Clarksburg, on the west branch of the Monongahela, to the Muskingum Valley, and thence westward to the Scioto Plains. Advancing upon Zane's Trace, they found upon the present site of Zanesville only a wilderness house of entertainment, near which were encamped a few white hunters, surrounded by Indian wigwams, occupied by the native savages employed in hunting, fishing, trading, and drinking. The region near Columbus, the present state capital, was a dense forest; one mile distant, near the present town of Franklinton, were a number of newly-erected log cabins without chinking or daubing, and having only a blanket in the doorway instead of a wooden door. In the same vicinity was the cabin of John Brickell, a white captive, adopted into the Indian tribes from childhood, but surrendered at the treaty of Greenville, and still more wedded to savage life than to the comforts of civilization. From the mouth of Whetstone Creek to Chillicothe the trace passes a new cabin or improvement "about every eight or ten miles."*

Among the emigrants to the Northwestern Territory during this year was Herman Blannerhasset, an accomplished gentleman and a man of fortune, from Ireland. Driven from his native country by political difficulties, he sought an asylum on the bosom of the beautiful Ohio. He purchased from Colonel Devoll, of Virginia, the island in that river, one mile below the mouth of the Little Kenhawa, and soon afterward commenced his improvements.† As this has become classic ground in Ohio, it is worthy of a more detailed notice. Before the year 1801 had closed, Mr. Blannerhasset had erected a splendid mansion on the upper end of the island, and had surrounded it with fine pleasure-grounds, gardens, and orchards of choice fruit. His study was furnished with a large and well-selected library, an extensive philosophical apparatus, and every thing which taste and learning could desire. A fine scholar, and well versed in languages, he spent much of his time in study, when not engaged in social intercourse with his intelligent neighbors from Belpre and Marietta. So tenacious was his memory, that he is said to have been able to repeat some of the books of Homer by rote in the original Greek. His wife was accomplished in all the acquirements of female elegance and learning: music, painting, drawing, and dancing were her amusements, and the social converse of cultivated minds and festive amusements of the young beguiled the happy hours. Surrounded with every thing that could make existence desirable and happy, and cheered by a rising and brilliant family, his seat was almost a terrestrial paradise, as described by Wirt, until the acquaintance of Aaron Burr blasted every hope and ruined every source of enjoyment. This former paradise is now faintly commemorated in the solitary and desolate spot remaining of "Blannerhasset's Island." The mansion was consumed by

---

* See American Pioneer, vol. i., p. 174, 175; also, p. 55, 56.   † Idem, p. 92, &c.

fire in 1810, and since then every vestige of improvement has disappeared.

Settlements continued to extend upon all the lower tributaries of the Miami, Scioto, and Muskingum Rivers, while their head branches were still inhabited by the Indian tribes. Numerous towns sprung up, but their population did not augment rapidly. Cincinnati, with all its advantages of location, scarcely numbered eight hundred souls. Chillicothe, after two years, now numbered two hundred and fifty souls. These were the largest towns in the territory.

About the close of the year 1798, James Ross and Basil Wells, Esquires, having purchased a large tract of land in the northern portion of Jefferson county, laid out a town on the west bank of the Ohio, which was named "Steubenville," in honor of the Baron Steuben,* who had nobly volunteered his services in the cause of American independence.

Second Grade of Territorial Government. — In the mean time, the population of the territory had gradually increased, and a census, taken during the summer of 1798, proved that the whole number of free white males amounted to full *five thousand*.† This condition, agreeably to the ordinance of July, 1787, entitled the people to the *second grade* of territorial government. Accordingly, on the 29th day of October, Governor St. Clair issued his proclamation, ordering an election to be held in the several counties on the third Monday in December following, for the selection of twenty representatives to serve as a Lower House, or popular branch of the territorial Legislature.

Those elected to compose this Legislature were such as are not excelled in point of talent by the members of any legislative body in the United States, even at this late day. Among the pioneers of Ohio were men of the first order of talent and of finished education, improved and polished by much intercourse with the most refined population of the Atlantic States. Hamilton county sent a strong representation. Of these, William M'Millan was a native of Virginia, a man of strong and commanding talent, and a finished scholar. John Smith was a man of strong mind, native talent, and great energy of character. His laudable ambition and rectitude of pur-

---

* Pittsburgh Navigator of 1814, p. 81. Also, American Pioneer, vol. i., p. 157.
† Burnett's Letters, p. 99.

pose placed him above many of the talented leaders of his day. Jacob Burnett, another representative from Hamilton, was a prominent member of the territorial government, and continued to fill responsible offices under the state government for many years.

Solomon Sibley, of Detroit, and representative from Wayne county, possessed a sound mind, improved by a liberal education, and a stability of character which commanded general respect, and made him rank as one of the most talented men in the House. Return J. Meigs and Paul Fearing, both lawyers of Marietta, and representatives of Washington county, were men of talent and great worth. The former subsequently filled more important offices than commonly falls to the lot of one man, both in the State and Federal governments. Nathaniel Massie and Joseph Darlington, representatives of Adams county, were among the earliest and most enterprising citizens of Ohio. Ross county sent a representation not excelled by any county in the territory for intelligence and talent. Worthington, Tiffin, Finley, and Langham were qualified to exert an influence in any deliberative body. They, too, were natives of Virginia, excepting Tiffin, and all were conspicuous in the subsequent state government. Edward Tiffin was an Englishman by birth, having arrived in the United States as surgeon in Burgoyne's army.*

[A.D. 1799.] The representatives elected convened at Cincinnati on the first Monday of February, 1799, and nominated ten persons to the President of the United States, from whom he appointed five to serve as a "legislative council." The first legislative council, appointed by the president on the 22d of January, 1799, consisted of the following persons, viz.: Henry Vanderburg, of Vincennes; Robert Oliver, of Marietta; James Finley and Jacob Burnett, of Cincinnati, and David Vance, of Vanceville.†

The new territorial Legislature met, agreeably to the governor's proclamation, at Cincinnati, on the 16th day of September.‡ In a very elegant address the governor laid before that

---

* Burnett's Letters, 101–103. † Idem, p. 70, 71.

‡ The first territorial Legislature of the Northwestern Territory was constituted as follows:

1. *Legislative Council.*—Jacob Burnett, of Cincinnati; Henry Vanderburg, of Vincennes; David Vance, of Vanceville, in Jefferson county; and Robert Oliver, of Marietta. Henry Vanderburg, *president;* William C. Schenck, *secretary;* George Howard, *door-keeper;* and Abram Carey, *sergeant-at-arms.*

body his views of such measures as were worthy its consideration. Among these, the most important duty was the revision of the former laws, and the formation of a regular territorial code, adapted to the condition of the territory, under its new form of government. The former laws required to be altered, amended, repealed, or otherwise modified, so as to adapt them to the present state of the territory. After a laborious session of nearly three months, the Legislature was prorogued by the governor, to meet again on the first Monday in November following. Captain William H. Harrison had been elected first delegate to Congress.

At this first session of the territorial Legislature, Governor St. Clair began to manifest his high-toned aristocratic feelings and his imperious disposition. The misfortunes which attended the campaign against the Maumee towns, while under his immediate command seven years before, had any other effect than to create respect and submission to his arbitrary demands. Conscious of his power and the moral rectitude of his intentions, he in turn disregarded the opposition of his adversaries.

Inconvenience had been experienced already by emigrants, on account of the large continuous bodies of fine lands held by private companies and individual proprietors, which tended to exclude the former class of people.

To prevent such unfavorable influences in future, and to place the emigrant beyond the power of the capricious monopolist, Congress devised a new mode of survey and sale, by which the public lands should be laid off in small tracts, and be held open for sale to any individual. The investigations on this subject resulted in the present enlightened and eligible plan of survey, which has been in general use for more than forty years.

[A.D. 1800.] The "Connecticut Reserve" continued to receive numerous emigrants from the New England States, who

---

2. *House of Representatives.* From *Hamilton county.*—William Goforth, William M'Millan, John Smith, John Ludlow, Robert Benham, Aaron Cadwell, and Isaac Martin. From *Ross county.*—Thomas Worthington, Samuel Finley, Elias Langham, and Edward Tiffin. From *Wayne county.*—Solomon Sibley, Charles F. Chobert de Joncaire, and Jacob Visger. From *Adams county.*—Joseph Darlington and Nathaniel Massie. From *Knox county.*—Shadrach Bond. From *Jefferson county.*—James Pritchard. From *Washington county.*—Return J. Meigs and Paul Fearing. *Speaker.*—Edward Tiffin. *Clerk.*—John Reily. *Door-keeper.*—Joshua Rowland. *Sergeant-at-arms.* —Abram Carey. Joseph Carpenter was appointed public printer on the 30th day of September.

formed settlements chiefly near the shore of Lake Erie. The population in this region having greatly increased, the governor laid off and organized the county of Trumbull on the 6th of December, 1800. It was about this time that a large number of settlers upon the Pennsylvania state grants, northwest of the Alleghany River, abandoned their improvements, to avoid litigation, and retired to the "Connecticut Reserve."*

The high, rolling, and broken country upon the upper branches of the Hockhocking River, between the Scioto and Muskingum, had also received a numerous population of German emigrants from Europe and from Pennsylvania, forming an interesting colony. Industry and frugality were their characteristic traits, and their settlements soon evinced the great accession to the moral worth of the territory. The county of Fairfield was accordingly organized on the 9th day of December, and the town of Lancaster was made the seat of justice, around which sprang up, soon afterward, one of the most wealthy settlements in Ohio.

During the same summer the country directly north of Fairfield was settled by enterprising immigrants from Western Pennsylvania and Virginia, and subsequently by others from New England. Hence this region had already received the elements of an industrious and frugal population. These settlements were soon afterward comprised in the newly-organized "county of Licking."†

The population was rapidly increasing in all the settlements within sixty miles of the Ohio, from the county of Jefferson on the east to the Great Miami on the west, and the people were becoming impatient for the adoption of a state government under the ordinance of 1787, when Congress proceeded to set apart a portion of the territory preparatory to the formation of such a government. The eastern part was separated by act of Congress from the western, by a line to be run due north from the mouth of the Great Miami, until it should intersect the parallel of latitude which passes through the southern extremity of Lake Michigan.‡ The District of Detroit was to continue under the jurisdiction of the eastern portion of the territory, which was still designated as the Northwestern Territory. The northern boundary of the proposed state remained undefined by actual survey for several years.§ Thus the

---

* American Pioneer, vol. ii., p. 368–371.   † Atwater's Ohio.
‡ See Atwater's Ohio, p. 158.   § See Burnett's Letters, p. 77.

Northwestern Territory was restricted on the west to the limits of the present State of Ohio.

The rapid extension of settlements on the Ohio near the Pennsylvania line made it expedient to lay off another county in that part of the territory. The county of Jefferson was therefore divided, and the northern portion was organized as the county of "Belmont," and St. Clairsville was made the seat of justice.*

[A.D. 1801.] *Indiana Territory organized.* — Meantime, Congress had provided for the organization of a new territorial government for the western division, designated as the "Indiana Territory," by the appointment of Captain William H. Harrison, the former delegate to Congress, as governor and "Superintendent of Indian Affairs." From this time Captain Harrison became identified with the early history of the Indiana Territory.

The Indiana Territory comprised all the country from the Great Miami westward to the Mississippi River, and from the Ohio on the south, to the sources of the Mississippi and Lake Superior on the north. The name by which it was designated was indicative of the principal inhabitants, consisting of the native Indian tribes, who still occupied the greater portion of the country.

[A.D. 1802.] *Congress authorizes a Convention.*—The leading politicians of that day, warmly opposed to the governor, resolved to abolish the territorial form of government; and, believing that their wishes on this subject were not sufficiently advocated by the territorial Legislature, they pressed forward by direct means to the accomplishment of their purpose.† Determined to displace Governor St. Clair by abolishing the territorial form of government, they were unwilling to subject their favorite object to the danger of legislative finesse, where the governor had influential friends, and where his absolute veto could paralyze every successful effort. Hence, during the winter of 1801–2, the advocates of a state government, to prevent the delays of indirect application to Congress, prepared a petition and secured hundreds of signers, praying Congress to authorize the people of the territory to elect delegates to a convention empowered to frame and adopt a state constitution. The prayer of the petitioners was warmly advocated

* Atwater's Ohio, p. 160, 161. † Burnett's Letters, p. 108.

in Congress, and on the 30th of April, 1802, the president approved the act entitled " an act to enable the people of the eastern division of the territory northwest of the River Ohio to form a constitution and state government, and for the admission of such state into the Union on an equal footing with the original states, and for other purposes."*

This act defined the limits of the territory, agreeably to the present boundaries of Ohio, designated the number of delegates from each county, prescribed the qualification of the electors and the day of holding the election, as well as the time and place of holding the convention. The act also empowered the members of the convention, when properly assembled and organized, "first to determine, by a majority of the whole number elected, whether it be or be not expedient at that time to form a constitution and state government for the people within said territory." The act also provided "that, if it were determined to be expedient, the convention shall be, and hereby are, authorized to form a constitution and state government; or, if it be deemed more expedient, the same convention shall provide by ordinance for electing representatives to form a constitution or frame of government, which said representatives shall be chosen in such manner and in such proportion, and shall meet at such time and place as shall be prescribed by said ordinance, and shall form for the people of said state a constitution and state government; provided the same shall be Republican, and not repugnant to the ordinance of July 13th, 1787, between the original states and the people and states of the territory northwest of the Ohio River."

In assenting to the admission of Ohio into the Union as an independent state, Congress required the exemption of all the public lands from taxation by the state for five years from the date of sale, including such as had been sold since the 30th day of June, 1802. In consideration of this privilege, Congress appropriated permanently, for the use of schools in the state, the *sixteenth section* in every township of the public lands, subsequently to be sold within the state, or one thirty-sixth part of the whole. The same conditions have been extended to all other new states upon their admission into the Union; and

---

* Laws of Ohio, vol. i., p. 37–39. Also, Land Laws of the United States, vol. iii., p. 497.

hence originated the appropriation of one section of *school lands* in every township.

Although, by many, this act in its provisions was deemed an unwarrantable assumption of power on the part of Congress, and an infringement of the Constitutional rights and prerogatives of the territorial Legislature, yet the members of that body deemed it expedient to submit quietly to the operation of the law. The election of delegates to the Convention was accordingly held on the second Tuesday of October, and the Convention assembled at Chillicothe on the first Monday in November following. Having organized, the Convention determined that it *was expedient* to proceed forthwith to form a constitution and state government. The territorial Legislature having been prorogued until the third Monday in November, the President of the Convention was authorized to desire the governor to prorogue the General Assembly indefinitely.* But this was unnecessary; for the members, as if by common consent, agreed to absent themselves, in accordance with the will of the Convention. Although Governor St. Clair had been reappointed by President Adams, the Legislature evinced no disposition to interfere in any manner with the movements of the newly-organized body.

Yet Governor St. Clair desired to participate in the deliberations of that body. As the chief executive of the territory, he wished to address the Convention in his official capacity; but the proposition was resisted; and after a warm discussion as to the impropriety of permitting any official influence to interfere with their deliberations, the Convention decided, by a majority of five votes, to receive a communication from him in his private capacity; and a resolution was adopted declaring "that *Arthur St. Clair*, Senior, Esquire, be permitted to address the Convention on those subjects which he deems of importance."†

Constitution adopted.—The Convention consisted of thirty-five members, elected in the ratio of one to every twelve hundred white inhabitants, agreeably to the returns of the territorial census taken during the summer of 1802. By this census it had been ascertained that the aggregate white inhabitants in all parts of the eastern division of the territory amounted to forty-five thousand persons.

* Burnett's Letters, p. 111. † Idem, p. 110

The Convention proceeded to the important duty of forming a constitution for the state government, which was finally completed, adopted, and signed by all the members on the 29th day of November, 1802, after an arduous session of three weeks.* The Constitution, as adopted, was declared obligatory without the assent of the people; and a resolution to submit it to the people for adoption or rejection was lost by a vote of twenty-seven to seven.†

· The Convention of Ohio, like the first territorial Legislature, was composed of men of superior talent. As a whole, they were not surpassed, probably, by any body which has since convened for a similar purpose in the West. Many of them had been distinguished for talent and enterprise in the Atlantic States, and had proved themselves men of intelligence and worth in their new station. Some of them became distinguished in the subsequent history of the state.†

Although the framers of this Constitution, in the language of Caleb Atwater, " were generally young men who had been little engaged in legislation, and could not take a very wide survey of human societies," " they were, perhaps, better qualified for the task than any other men then in the territory."

But the Constitution was peculiarly Democratic: it gave the Legislature all the power, and to the governor none. " Owing to their ill-will toward Governor St. Clair, the members of the Convention made the governor a mere cipher : he can pardon criminals, appoint the adjutant-general, sign commissions, and fill temporary vacancies ; but he has no voice in making laws,

---

* Burnett's Letters, p. 108. Also, Laws of Ohio, vol. i., p. 42–67, edition of 1805.
† Idem, p. 110.
‡ The Convention organized by electing Edward Tiffin *president*, and Thomas Scott *secretary*. The delegates from the several counties represented in the Convention were,
1. *Hamilton county*.—Francis Dunlavy, John Paul, Jeremiah Morrow, John Wilson, Charles Willing Bird, William Goforth, John Smith, John Reily, John W. Brown, and John Kitchell.
2. *Adams county*.—Joseph Darlington, Thomas Kircher, and Israel Donaldson.
3. *Ross county*.—Edward Tiffin, Nathaniel Massie, Thomas Worthington, Michael Baldwin, and James Grubb.
4. *Jefferson county*.—Randolph Blair, John Milligan, George Humphrey, Bazaleel Wells, and Nathan Updegraff.
5. *Trumbull county*.—Samuel Huntington and David Abbott.
6. *Belmont county*.—James Caldwell and Elijah Woods.
7. *Fairfield county*.—Emanuel Carpenter and Henry Abrahams.
8. *Washington county*.—Ephraim Cutler, Rufus Putnam, John M'Intire, and Benjamin Ives Gilman.
9. *Clermont county*.—Philip Gatch and James Sargent.

no *veto power*, nor has he any power to interfere in the appointment of officers."*

Wayne County excluded.—The people of Wayne county, who had been included in the previous territorial government, were sorely disappointed when they learned that the new boundary prescribed for the state excluded them from the anticipated advantages of a state government, and left them to serve out a tedious territorial probation for many years, while their fellow-citizens further south were in the enjoyment of independent state privileges. They remonstrated with much warmth, and claimed the right to become a part of the new state until their numbers should entitle them to a separate state government of their own: they complained of the separation as unconstitutional and oppressive, to which they could not submit. It was not long, however, before their views underwent a change, and they became convinced that their interests required a separate territorial government, the offices of which would be filled with their own citizens. Jacob Burnett, of Cincinnati, by advocating the cause of the discontented in Wayne county, drew upon himself the displeasure of the Federal executive.†

[A.D. 1803.] *Ohio admitted into the Union.*—The Constitution at length was duly approved by Congress. Although the ordinance of July, 1787, required a population of sixty thousand inhabitants, yet Congress waived that requirement, and on the 19th of February, 1803, an act was approved by the president fully recognizing the admission of the "State of Ohio" into the Federal Union as a free and independent state.

Party politics ran high; many were still opposed to the adoption of state government, as premature and impolitic for the true interests of the territory; they objected to the restriction of the boundary on the north, which excluded the settlements in the vicinity of Detroit. The majority were in favor of the new government; but the feelings and passions on both sides were highly excited, and much personal rancor was indulged. The arguments of the minority were rejected; they were denounced as aristocrats and enemies of the people; their motives were questioned; their patriotism and fidelity to the interests of the territory were impeached. On the other hand, the minority alleged that their opponents were influenced by

* Atwater's Ohio, p. 171–173.   † Burnett's Letters, p. 129.

personal considerations of interest, by a love of popularity, and a desire of office, for which they would sacrifice the ulterior interests of the territory. These criminations and recriminations, in some instances of the most bitter character, produced between many of the leading men a personal enmity which ceased only with their lives.

State Government organized.—On the first of March, 1803, the first "General Assembly of the State of Ohio" under the Constitution convened in Chillicothe, for the purpose of organizing the state government. The Legislature, having organized, proceeded to the appointment of the principal executive and judicial officers for carrying into operation the provisions of the Constitution.*

Judges of the new courts were appointed, and all the courts under the territorial form of government were abolished, or so changed as to conform to the new order of things. Most of the powers formerly exercised by the Court of Quarter Sessions regulating the internal police of the counties were transferred to the Court of Common Pleas. Provision was made for the election of justices, and for transferring to them the unfinished business under the territorial magistrates. The tax laws under the territorial Legislature were continued in force with slight modifications. A secretary of state, an auditor of public accounts, and a state treasurer were appointed, with their appropriate duties assigned to each. Senators to Congress were elected, and provision was made for the election of a representative. Other minor provisions for state and county police and good government were enacted.

* Michael Baldwin was elected *Speaker* of the House of Representatives, and Nathaniel Massie *President* of the Senate.

The appointments by the Legislature for conducting the state government were as follows:

Secretary of State.—William Creighton, Jr., of Chillicothe, who continued to serve until 1808.

Auditor of State.—Colonel Thomas Gibson.

Treasurer of State.—William M'Farland.

Judges of the Supreme Court.—Return J. Meigs, Jr., Samuel Huntington, and William Sprigg.

Presiding Judges of Districts.—First District, Francis Dunlavy; Second District, Wyllys Silliman; Third District, Calvin Pease.

United States Senators.—Thomas Worthington, John Smith.

The elections subsequently held by the people resulted in the election of Edward Tiffin as *first Governor* of the State; also, first *Representative to Congress*, Jeremiah Morrow.

First Adjutant-general.—Samuel Finley.—See Atwater's Ohio, p. 176; also, p. 357, &c.

In due time the new order of things under the Constitution superseded the old. The state government, as organized by the first General Assembly, was accordingly put into operation.

Character of Governor St. Clair.—It may be well to review the causes which produced the strong opposition to Governor St. Clair during the last two years of his administration as governor of the Northwestern Territory. The feelings of the West were still revolutionary, and highly averse to arbitrary authority. Previous to the year 1798, the governor was invested with extensive powers, and until after the adoption of the *second* grade of territorial government. After this change, scrupulous of his prerogatives in his intercourse with the territorial Legislature, he created enemies and excited prejudices by his firmness and his close adherence to the privileges of his office, and the authority which he claimed as the chief executive of the territory. On these points he, not very erroneously, supposed the co-ordinate branches of the Legislature were strongly inclined to encroach. The Legislative Assembly had claimed for itself all the powers and prerogatives which were not expressly withheld by law. On the other hand, the governor, having possessed almost absolute power from his first appointment until the election of the Legislative Assembly, laid claim to all those powers which were not expressly taken away by law. Among these was that of laying off and organizing new counties. On the other hand, the Legislative Assembly claimed the same power independent of the governor's control.

Governor St. Clair was a stanch Federalist of the John Adams and Hamilton school; but, before the adoption of the state Constitution, the majority of prominent men in the territory had warmly espoused the Republican principles of Jefferson, and, under these circumstances, it was impossible that harmony could prevail in the legislative departments.

It is but a tribute of merited respect to Governor St. Clair to sum up his general character in a few words. During his long term of service, from the year 1788 to 1802, from the first organization of the Northwestern Territory until it was ready to become an independent state, he enjoyed the confidence and esteem of the people generally. He was plain and unassuming in his manners; but, placing a high estimate upon his own judgment and intellect, he rarely yielded his opinions to those of other men. In his dress he was plain and simple, without ostentation or gaudy equipage; in his deportment, easy, frank, and accessible to persons of every rank, he presented a strong contrast with the austere, haughty, and repulsive bearing of his secretary, Colonel Winthrop Sargent. As Judge Burnett justly observes, he was a man of superior native talent, " of extensive information, and great uprightness of purpose."* Accustomed from early life to mingle in circles of taste and refinement, and among the first orders of society, he was well acquainted with the proper courtesy to which his station entitled him. He had acquired a polish of manners and a habitual respect for the feelings of those around him, which were referred to as a standard of genuine urbanity, known to but few of his political adversaries.†

Among the legislative acts of the first General Assembly was the laying off and organizing of seven new counties, which had been attempted before the adoption of the Constitution, but had been vetoed by Governor St. Clair. These new counties were designated Gallia, Scioto, Geauga, Warren, Green, Montgomery, and Butler.‡ They were, as yet, sparsely settled, but were gradually increasing their population.

The number of counties in the state was now about fifteen, many of them large and thinly settled, with extensive districts of uninhabited country in different parts of the state south and east of the Indian line, while all north and west of that line, comprising about one third of the state, was uninhabited by whites, and chiefly occupied by the Indians. The last remnant of these, the Wyandots, were not removed from their "Reserve" on Sandusky River until the summer of 1843. With this exception, the Indian title to the whole area of the state had been extinguished by successive treaties previous to the year 1820.§

Since the adoption of the state Constitution, the State of Ohio

* Burnett's Letters, p. 79.
† GOVERNORS OF THE STATE OF OHIO.

Territorial:
1. Arthur St. Clair, *governor of Northwestern Territory.*

State:
1. Edward Tiffin, from 1803 to 1808.
2. Samuel Huntington, from 1808 to 1810.
3. Return J. Meigs, from 1810 to 1814.
4. Thomas Worthington, from 1814 to 1818.

5. Ethan A. Brown, from 1818 to 1822.
6. Jeremiah Morrow, from 1822 to 1826.
7. Allen Trimble, from 1826 to 1830.
8. Duncan M'Arthur, from 1830 to 1832.
9. Robert Lucas, from 1832 to 1836.
10. Joseph Vance, from 1836 to 1840.
11. Wilson Shannon, from 1840 to 1844.
12. Thomas W. Bartley, from 1844 to 1846.

‡ Ohio Gazetteer, p. 95, edition of 1841.
§ See chapter xvi. of this book, *note*, Indian Treaties in "Northwestern Territory."

has increased in population, wealth, arts, manufactures, and internal improvements beyond all parallel in the history of nations. From the close of the war in 1815, when the northern half of the state was an uninhabited wilderness, the settlements have advanced to its extreme limits; a dense population has extended to the shores of Lake Erie, as well as over all the former unoccupied portions of the older counties. Towns have sprung up, as if by magic, in every part of the state; agriculture and trade have penetrated to the most secluded recesses; and arts and manufactures have multiplied in the same ratio.

[A.D. 1810.] The census of 1810 gave a population of more than 230,000 souls, showing an increase of about 185,000 persons in the previous seven years, or an annual increase of over 26,000 persons. Cincinnati, in the same time, had increased from about 1000 to more than 2300 inhabitants. Five years afterward, this number was more than doubled. Chillicothe in 1815 had augmented its population from about 500 souls in 1803, to more than 1500; and in 1830 its population was 2800 inhabitants.*

[A.D. 1840.] In 1840 the aggregate population of the state had increased to one million five hundred and fifteen thousand souls:† the number of counties had been augmented to seventy-nine. The principal towns and cities had increased their population in an equal ratio. By the census of 1840, the city of Cincinnati presented an aggregate of 46,300 inhabitants, and was one of the most extensive manufacturing and commercial cities in all the West. Chillicothe contained 4000 inhabitants, Zanesville 4000, and Steubenville 4000.‡ Hundreds of smaller towns had increased in the same proportion. Nor had the growth of Cincinnati ceased in 1840: each year witnessed a progressive increase of population, manufactures, and commerce. During the year 1845 nearly two thousand buildings were erected in the city and suburbs.

The war with Great Britain, which closed in 1815, had been waged with great energy by that power against the northern frontier of Ohio, which was then occupied by a few sparse white settlements; but the advance of troops, and munitions of war for defense against hostile invasion, opened to the gov-

---

* Ohio Gazetteer for 1841, p. 109.   † Census of 1840.
‡ Ohio Gazetteer for 1841, p. 561–567; also, 577.

ernment and the people the unbounded advantages of this beautiful region, for the extension of agriculture, manufactures, and commerce. The efforts of Great Britain from Canada to check the advance of the American settlements northwest of the Ohio River, resulted in ultimate advantage to the country; for this, more than all other causes, subsequently drew population upon the lake frontier.

The great Ohio Canal, which intersects the state from north to south, was commenced in 1825, and completed a few years afterward. It has given an impulse to manufactures and commerce unparalleled in the history of civilization, and has raised the state in wealth and population to a rank second only to the Empire State of New York.

The population of Ohio, besides the natural increase, has been derived from emigration. The first settlements previous to the adoption of the state Constitution were formed chiefly by emigrants from the older states near the Atlantic. The northeastern portion, south of Lake Erie and northeast of the Muskingum River, was settled chiefly by emigrants from Connecticut and other New England States, besides numerous accessions from New York, Pennsylvania, New Jersey, and Delaware. The southern portion, between the Hockhocking and Great Miami Rivers, was settled chiefly by emigrants from Virginia, Maryland, and Kentucky, as well as by numerous colonies from New Jersey, Pennsylvania, and Delaware.

In the eastern portion of the state, including Columbiana county, adjoining Pennsylvania, a large population was derived from colonies of Germans, Scotch, English, and Irish, from Pennsylvania and from Europe.

Emigration from the Atlantic seaboard has continued to send annual colonies to different portions of Ohio; and since the year 1830, not less than two hundred thousand frugal, industrious emigrants from Germany have been distributed over every part of the state. The influx of foreign immigrants, especially those from Germany, after the year 1840, continued to increase the population of Ohio and the whole West. Not a town or village, not a city or capital, not an agricultural district in the great State of Ohio in 1844, which did not present a copious admixture of Germans who had not yet acquired a fluency in the English language.

CHAPTER XIII.

"THE MISSISSIPPI TERRITORY" FROM ITS FIRST ORGANIZATION TO THE COMMENCEMENT OF THE CREEK WAR. — A.D. 1798 TO 1813.

Argument.—Original Extent of the Mississippi Territory.—First Governor and Territorial Judges.—Authority and Jurisdiction of the same.—Arrival of the United States Troops under General Wilkinson.—*First* Grade of Territorial Government organized in 1799.—Extent of the White Settlements and Indian Territory.—Adams and Pickering Counties organized. — Population in 1799. — Washington County organized on the Mobile River.—*Second* Grade of Territorial Government in 1800.—The Federal Army in the Mississippi Territory.—Indian Treaties in 1801.—Treaty of Fort Adams.—Treaty of Chickasâ Bluffs.—Governor Claiborne enters upon his Duties.—The Counties of Claiborne, Jefferson, and Wilkinson organized in 1802.—First System of Jurisprudence.—First Newspapers in Mississippi.—"Articles of Agreement and Cession" by Georgia.—Extent of Georgia Claim.—Adjudication of Private Claims by Commissioners.—Land Offices.—Surveyor-general's Office organized.—Enlargement of Territorial Limits.—Indian Nations included.—Legislative Care for the Encouragement of Education.—First College and first Academy chartered.—The Robber Mason killed.—Emigration in 1803, in anticipation of the Occupation of Louisiana.—Governor Claiborne Commissioner.—Commissioners and Troops advance toward New Orleans.—Protestant Religion introduced in Mississippi Territory.—Washington County erected into a Judicial District.—Harry Toulmin, Judge.—First Delegate to Congress.—Robert Williams, Governor.—First City Charter of Natchez.—Spanish Exactions on the Mobile.—First Natchez Hospital.—Border Collisions.—Abduction of the Kempers.—Indian Treaties in 1805 : with the Chickasâs ; with the Cherokees ; Creeks ; Choctâs. — First "Choctâ Purchase."— Extent of White Settlements in 1806.—Spanish Encroachments on the Sabine.—Militia Movements in Mississippi.—Burr's Conspiracy in the West.—Burr prepares to descend the Mississippi.—President's Proclamation.—General Wilkinson protects New Orleans.—Defensive Measures of Governor Mead in the Mississippi Territory.—Burr appears before the Superior Court.—Patriotic Citizens of Wilkinson County.—Abortive Attempt to arraign Burr.—He escapes from Custody.—Is arrested near Fort Stoddart.—Sent to Richmond, Virginia.—Emigration to Mississippi induced by Burr's Plans.—Agriculture in the Territory in 1807.—Cotton the Staple Product.—Cotton Receipts negotiable by Law.—First Digest of Territorial Laws.—First Road across to Tombigby.—Lands on the Upper Tombigby.—Condition of the Tombigby Settlements.—Patriotism of the Inhabitants.—Governor Williams.—First White Settlements in "Madison County."—First Bank in the Territory in 1809.—Population in 1810.—Revolution in District of Baton Rouge.—First Brigade of Militia in 1812.—Tennessee Volunteers under General Jackson.—General Wilkinson occupies Fort Charlotte.—Mobile District annexed to the Mississippi Territory.

[A.D. 1798.] *Original Limits.*—The territory heretofore surrendered by the Spanish authorities, and lying north of the thirty-first degree of latitude, with the consent and approbation of the State of Georgia, was erected into a territory of the United States by act of Congress, approved April 7th, 1798, entitled "an act for the amicable settlement of limits with the State of Georgia, and authorizing the establishment of a government in the Mississippi Territory."*

The territory comprised in the new organization, or the *original* Mississippi Territory, embraced that portion of country between the Spanish line of demarkation and a line drawn due east from the mouth of the Yazoo to the Chattahoochy River. The Mississippi River was its western limit, and the Chattahoochy its eastern. The organization of a territorial government by the United States was in no wise to impair the rights of Georgia to the soil, which was left open for future negotiation between the State of Georgia and the United States.

The sixth section of the act of April 7th provided "that from and after the establishment of said government, the aforesaid territory shall be entitled to and enjoy all and singular the rights, privileges, and advantages granted to the people of the United States northwest of the Ohio River, in and by the aforesaid ordinance of July 13th, 1787, in as full and complete a manner as the same are possessed and enjoyed by the said last-mentioned territory."†

Organization of Territorial Government.—Agreeably to the provisions of this act, President Adams appointed Winthrop Sargent, former secretary of the Northwestern Territory, as governor, and John Steele, secretary of the new government; Thomas Rodney, of Delaware, and Daniel Tilton, of New Hampshire, were appointed territorial judges of the Superior Court. Other subordinate officers under the *first grade* of territorial government were subject to the governor's appointment.

The governor and judges, with their friends, arrived at Natchez in August following, in company with a number of emigrant families from the Northwestern Territory. The governor shortly afterward, with the advice of the judges, proceeded to make provision for the regular administration of justice, and the preservation of order in the territory; magistrates and inferior civil and militia officers were appointed for the respective settlements within the Natchez District.

---

* See Toulmin's Digest of the Statutes, &c., of the Mississippi Territory, p. 467–477, edition of 1807, where the ordinance may be seen at length. This was the first regular digest of the laws of the Mississippi Territory, compiled by Judge Harry Toulmin, of Washington county, and published in 1807. Timothy Terrell, territorial printer.

† See Poindexter's Code. Also, Toulmin's Code, p. 456–459. Also, Walker's Reports of the Supreme Court of Mississippi, p. 56, 57.

The powers of the governor, with his legal advisers, were extensive and multifarious. He was empowered to exercise supreme executive jurisdiction within the prescribed limits of his government; he appointed and commissioned all magistrates, inferior judges, and all other civil officers, and all militia officers below the rank of general; he could lay off counties, subdivide or create new ones, adopt and ordain laws for the territory with the consent of the judges, who, in their judicial capacity, were empowered to execute and enforce the same in their respective districts.

On the 26th of August, General Wilkinson, commander-in-chief of the army, arrived at Natchez with the United States troops. They were quartered in cantonments in the vicinity of Washington, and near the Half-way Hill, on the road leading to Second Creek, until the following year, when a military post was erected at the first highland point on the Mississippi, a few miles above the Spanish line of demarkation. This post, which was occupied by the United States troops until the close of the year 1807, was situated upon an elevated plateau near the river, and was called "Fort Adams," in honor of John Adams, the second president of the United States.*

[A.D. 1799.] In April following, Governor Sargent proceeded to complete the organization of the territorial government by laying off counties, and organizing county courts having subordinate jurisdiction.† By his proclamation, dated April 2d, the Natchez District was divided into the counties of Adams and Pickering, named in honor of the President of the United States and the Secretary of State. The dividing line was nearly the same as the present boundary between Adams and Jefferson; Adams being on the south, and Pickering on the north of the line.‡

The principal white population within the limits of the ter-

* Martin's Louisiana, vol. ii., p. 256.
† The County Court was a Court of Common Pleas holding quarterly sessions. The first Court of Common Pleas in Adams county consisted of three associate justices, of whom Daniel Clark, Sen., was presiding justice until 1800, when he was succeeded by Bernard Lintot. In 1801, John Ellis succeeded as presiding justice; after him William Kenner. In 1810, the County Court consisted of five associate justices, and the presiding justice of the quorum was, *ex officio*, judge of probate. The County Court had jurisdiction in all civil cases where the amount in litigation did not exceed one thousand dollars; also, in all criminal cases wherein slaves were the offenders; also, in all matters of county police. Alexander Covington succeeded as presiding justice of the quorum in 1810.—See Circuit Court Records of Adams county.
‡ Toulmin's Digest, p. 3, 4.

ritory at this early period was that of the "Natchez District," comprising about six thousand inhabitants, including slaves. These were distributed in several large settlements upon the waters of the Bayou Pierre, Cole's Creek, St. Catharine, Second Creek, Homochitto and Buffalo Creeks, and chiefly within ten or fifteen miles of the Mississippi River. Besides these, a few inhabitants were distributed near the Walnut Hills, and near the Big Black. Another isolated settlement of about eight hundred inhabitants existed on the Tombigby and Mobile Rivers. The aggregate white population in all these settlements, after the evacuation by the Spaniards, scarcely exceeded five thousand persons, exclusive of slaves and Indians.

Many of these were Anglo-Americans, remnants of the former British colonies of West Florida, and a few were individuals of Spanish and French descent. Some had emigrated from the United States after the termination of the Revolutionary war, under the inducements held out by the Spanish governor previous to 1792. Others from the Western States, and from North Carolina and Georgia, had arrived subsequently to the treaty of Madrid, which recognized the country as a portion of the United States.

The whole region extending north and east of the Natchez District for nearly five hundred miles, to the settlements on Cumberland River of Tennessee, and to those on the Oconee, in Georgia, was Indian territory, in the sole occupancy of the native tribes, except the small district on the Tombigby and Mobile Rivers, to which the Indian title had been extinguished by the former governments of France and England. The Natchez District extended upon the east side of the Mississippi River for about one hundred miles, and was bounded on the east by a line extending direct from the sources of the Tickfaw, in a direction west of north to the Yazoo River, ten miles above its mouth. No portion of this district extended more than twenty-five miles direct from the river.

Such was the country which was then placed under the first grade of territorial government. The only route of intercourse with the United States was that of the Mississippi and the Ohio Rivers to the settlements of Kentucky and Tennessee; or by the lonely route of a solitary Indian trace, leading for five hundred miles, either to the Cumberland settlements or those of the Oconee, in Georgia.

[A.D. 1800.] The counties of Adams and Pickering comprised the whole Natchez District until the 4th of June, 1800, when the governor again issued his proclamation, countersigned by John Steele, secretary, laying off the "County of Washington" on the Tombigby River. The limits of this county were the territorial boundaries on the north and south, the Pearl River on the west, and the Chattahoochy on the east ;* and the Mississippi Territory comprised only three large counties until the following year.

Meantime, in consequence of an increase of population, and also on account of dissatisfaction among the people, and remonstrances against the arbitrary measures of Governor Sargent and his council, Congress, by special favor, passed an act authorizing the establishment of the *second grade* of territorial government at an earlier period than the population of the territory would authorize under the provisions of the ordinance of July 13th, 1787. Thus, the second grade of representative government commenced in the Mississippi Territory before the free white males had increased to five thousand in number.

A House of Representatives, or Legislative Assembly, was duly elected, and members of the "Council" having been appointed, the General Assembly was organized for business in December following. The Legislative Assembly consisted of four representatives from Adams, four from Pickering, and one from the Tombigby settlements, elected in the ratio of one representative to every five hundred free white males; and the Legislative Council consisted of five members. The first General Assembly thus organized convened at Natchez on the first Monday in December, which was fixed as the time for each annual meeting thereafter. All bills enacted by the two houses received the force of law only after the approbation and signature of the governor, who held an unqualified *veto* upon

* The style of this proclamation was in this form, viz.: "Know all men," &c. " In virtue of the authority vested in me by the sovereign authority of the United States, and for the purpose of extending the administration of equal justice to the inhabitants upon the Tombigby and other eastern settlements, I have thought proper, therefore, to erect a new county; and by these letters made patent, do ordain and order that all and singular the lands lying and being within the following limits, to wit," &c., "shall constitute the same; to be named, and to be hereafter called, the ' *County of Washington ;*' and unto the said county of Washington is hereby granted all and singular the jurisdictions, rights, liberties, privileges, and immunities to a county belonging and appertaining, and which any other county that is or may hereafter be erected or laid off shall or ought to enjoy, conformably to the laws and ordinances of the United States and of this territory."—See Toulmin's Digest, p. iv.

all their acts, when, in his opinion, they were impolitic or unconstitutional.

The Superior Court was required by law to hold two terms annually.*

[A.D. 1801.] *Indian Treaties.*—While the headquarters of General Wilkinson were at Natchez and Fort Adams, he was engaged in conducting negotiations with the Indian tribes south of Tennessee. Previously to his departure on this service, detachments of troops were stationed at different points on the line of demarkation from Fort Adams eastward to Pearl River, for the preservation of order and neutrality along the border settlements. A detachment was also stationed at Fort Stoddart, near the line, on Mobile River, and another at Fort Florida, a few miles above.†

The object of negotiations with the Indian tribes was the establishment of amicable relations, confirmed by treaty stipulations, and to procure their consent to the opening of roads and mail-routes from the frontier settlements of Tennessee and Georgia, to those on the Mobile and in the Natchez District, in order to facilitate intercourse with those remote places, and to encourage emigration to the Mississippi Territory.

The first treaty was held with the Chickasâ nation at the Chickasâ Bluff, on the Mississippi. By this treaty, the Chickasâs conceded to the United States the right of opening a wagon-road from Miro District, in Tennessee, to the American settlements in the Natchez District, and that this road should be at all times free to the people of the United States passing and repassing from the settlements on Cumberland River to those near Natchez; also, for the transportation of the United States mail between the same points, free from molestation.

This road crossed the Tennessee River a few miles below the Muscle Shoals, at "Colbert's Ferry," and thence led through the Chickasâ nation to the "Grindstone Ford," on the Bayou Pierre. The Indians reserved to themselves the privileges and emoluments pertaining to all ferries on the route, and the establishing of public houses for the entertainment of travelers.

The next treaty was with the Choctâ nation, concluded on the 17th of December, at Fort Adams. In this treaty, besides

---

* The Superior Court in 1802 consisted of three judges, viz.: Daniel Tilton, Peter B. Bruin, and Seth Lewis. In 1803 David Kerr succeeded Seth Lewis. In 1804 Thomas Rodney was reappointed; the judges in 1810 were Thomas Rodney, Walter Leake, and O. Fitz. † Martin's Louisiana, vol. ii., p. 179, 180.

other stipulations, the Choctâs consent to the exploration and opening of a convenient wagon-road through their country, from the vicinity of "Fort Adams" to the Chickasâ boundary near the Yazoo River. The old British boundary, extending from the Tickfaw northwest to the Yazoo, was confirmed and marked anew as the proper boundary between the white settlements and the Indian territory.* This road, communicating with the Chickasâ trace, opened the first direct communication between the settlements on the Lower Mississippi and those of Cumberland, near Nashville.

In the mean time, Thomas Jefferson, having succeeded as President of the United States, early in his administration appointed William C. C. Claiborne,† of East Tennessee, governor of the Mississippi Territory, and Cato West secretary. Governor Sargent retired from office, and was not again called into public service during his subsequent life.

A corresponding change was made in the territorial authorities, when those who adhered to the late administration were superseded by those attached to the Republican party, which had become predominant.

Since the first organization of the American government in the territory, the population had been greatly increased by emigration. The census of 1800 gave the aggregate of the white inhabitants at eight thousand eight hundred and fifty persons, exclusive of about two thousand slaves. In January, 1802, the entire population was probably not less than twelve thousand souls.

Governor Claiborne entered upon the duties of his office with zeal and patriotic devotion. Although a man of strict integrity, and an undoubted patriot, yet, possessing all the graces of a polished courtier, he delighted more in the pomp and display of military parade than was congenial with the plain, unaffected simplicity of many of his associates.

* Martin's Louisiana, vol. ii., p. 179–180.

† William Charles Cole Claiborne was a native of Virginia, from an ancient family. In 1793, when quite a youth, he removed to Sullivan county, East Tennessee, where he was subsequently elected a delegate to form the state Constitution, where he began his public career. After the adoption of the state Constitution he was appointed Judge of the Supreme Court of Law and Equity by Governor Sevier. About two years afterward he was elected a member of Congress from Tennessee, in the 25th year of his age. To this post of honor and trust he was re-elected for a second term. From this station he was selected by Mr. Jefferson to serve as governor of the Mississippi Territory in 1801.—See "Notes on the War in the South," &c., by Nathaniel H. Claiborne, p. 91–102.

[A.D. 1802.] Early in the year 1802 the territory was erected into five counties by the division of both Adams and Pickering. On the 11th of January an act of the General Assembly changed the name of Pickering county to that of "Jefferson," in honor of the newly-elected president. On the 27th of January, another act divided the county of Jefferson, by a line varying but little from the present one between Jefferson and Claiborne counties, and which extended eastward to the western bank of Pearl River. That portion of the territory on the north of this line was called "Claiborne county," in honor of the new governor.* The seat of justice was located permanently, on the 5th of March, at "Gibson's Landing," on the south fork of Bayou Pierre.

On the 30th of January another act of the General Assembly divided the county of Adams by the Homochitto River, from its mouth up to "Richard's Ferry," and thence eastward by an imaginary line to Pearl River. That portion of the territory south of this line was called "Wilkinson county," in honor of General James Wilkinson, commander-in-chief of the Federal army.†

The first regular code of jurisprudence and judicial proceedings for the use of the territory were adopted during the session of 1801 and 1802. An act of the same session, passed February 1st, removed the seat of the territorial government to the town of Washington. This session had organized with Joshua Baker speaker of the Legislative Assembly, and John Ellis president of the Council. Each of these received as salary five dollars *per diem* during the session, and the members of both houses four dollars *per diem*.

The first weekly newspaper in the Mississippi Territory was published in the spring of 1802, by Colonel Andrew Marschalk, formerly a lieutenant in General Wayne's army. Having descended the river with General Wilkinson, he continued in the service until 1802, when he commenced the publication of the "Natchez Gazette." This paper, under different forms and names, such as the "Mississippi Herald and Natchez Gazette," the "Washington Republican," and "Mississippi State Gazette," was published by this father of the press in Mississippi for nearly forty years afterward.

The second weekly paper in the territory was the "Mis-

---

* See Toulmin's Digest, p. 5. † Idem.

sissippi Messenger," published by Samuel and Timothy Terrell, and which was continued under Dr. John Shaw and others until the year 1810.

Compromise with Georgia.—Agreeably to the provisions of the Compromise Act, the commissioners of Georgia and those of the United States had entered into "Articles of Agreement and Cession," which were signed on the part of their governments respectively on the 24th day of April, 1802.* The stipulations in these articles provided that for and in consideration of the cession by Georgia of all her claim to lands south of the State of Tennessee, the United States should pay to Georgia one million two hundred and fifty thousand dollars out of the first nett proceeds of lands lying in said ceded territory; and also to recognize in favor of the inhabitants all grants of land regularly made and authenticated by the authorities of England, Spain, or Georgia previous to the 27th day of October, 1795.

The sovereignty over all the territory south of Tennessee, and north of the Spanish line of demarkation, and eastward to the Chattahoochy River, was now vested in the Federal government, excepting only the right of occupancy reserved to the native tribes then in possession.

[A.D. 1803.] Emigration from Georgia, Tennessee, and Kentucky, as well as from Western Pennsylvania, had begun to augment the population in all the old settlements of the five organized counties, and men of capital and enterprise were ready to invest their capital in valuable land. A large portion of the lands within the limits of the white settlements was claimed and occupied by virtue of grants or titles derived through the authorities of England, Spain, and Georgia, and required adjudication before confirmation by the United States; and Congress proceeded to make the necessary provisions through a board of commissioners, appointed to examine and adjudicate the respective claims. The first and most important act for the accomplishment of this object was approved March 3d, 1803, and was entitled "An act regulating grants of land, and providing for the disposal of the lands of the United States south of the State of Tennessee."

---

* A copy of the "Articles of Agreément and Cession" may be seen in Toulmin's Digest, p. 462–467; also, in Poindexter's Code, p. 502–505. This compact was signed on the part of the United States by James Madison, Albert Gallatin, and Levi Lincoln; and on the part of Georgia by James Jackson, Abraham Baldwin, and John Milledge, commissioners.

This act provided for a surveyor-general's department, connected with two district land-offices, for the record and sale of all lands duly surveyed. One of these was established at Fort Stoddart, for the "district east of Pearl River," and the other at Washington, Adams county, for the "district west of Pearl River." To each of these offices was attached a "board of commissioners," to receive and adjudicate private claims.*

The land-office west of Pearl River was organized on the 9th day of July, with Edward Turner as register, and Thomas Rodney and Robert Williams as commissioners of claims. This board convened at the town of Washington on the 1st of December, 1803, and continued open for the reception of claims until the 3d of July, 1807, when it was adjourned *sine die*, after having received for record two thousand and ninety claims. Some of these claims were subsequently contested in the high courts of the United States.†

* The *first* section of the act of March 3d, 1803, provides that all persons, heads of families, actually residing in the territory, and having claims, by grants or orders of survey, from the English, Spanish, or Georgia government, for lands, to which the Indian title had been extinguished prior to October 27th, 1795, shall be confirmed in their titles. The *second* section provides that every person, twenty-one years of age, who actually inhabited and cultivated any land on the 30th day of March, 1797, the day on which the Spanish troops finally evacuated the territory, and not claimed under the first section, or by any British or Georgia grant, shall have said land granted to him or her, to any amount not exceeding six hundred and forty acres. The *third* section provides that every such person, over twenty-one years, who at the passage of the act inhabited and cultivated any land, not secured as above, shall be entitled to a pre-emption right to their said lands. The time allowed for the presentation of claims was limited to the 31st of March, 1804, but was subsequently extended by Congress.

† The claim of Georgia to the Western Territory, as far as the Mississippi and north of latitude 31°, has been deemed by the Supreme Court of the United States to have been valid; and that Spain exercised an unlawful jurisdiction over the same, while Georgia was the rightful proprietor of the domain.—See 12 *Wheaton*, 523–530.

It was further decreed, that the grants of Spain to portions of the soil "have, in themselves, no intrinsic validity, because at the very time Georgia possessed the right of soil and sovereignty." Spain had the actual occupancy; but "that occupancy was wrongful," and was never acquiesced in by Georgia or by the United States. From the treaty of 1783 until October 27th, 1795, Georgia passed many laws claiming the right of soil and jurisdiction over the country; and the United States, during the same time, by many official acts, sustained the claim of Georgia both here and at the court of Spain, until finally, on the 27th of October, 1795, Spain, by treaty with the United States, *acknowledged* their right "to said territory," *not as a cession by Spain*, but as a *pre-existing right*. On this point the Supreme Court of the Union thus concludes the reasoning, viz.: "It follows that Spanish grants made after the treaty of 1783 can have no intrinsic validity, and the holders must depend for their titles upon the laws of the United States."—12 *Wheaton*, 535. * * * * * "Georgia, by the cession of 1802 to the United States, stipulated for the confirmation of certain Spanish, British, and Georgia titles, but never sanctioned the introduction of the Spanish laws." * * * * "Now, during the Spanish occupancy, Georgia had extended her laws over this country; not over detached portions of it, but over the whole territory; and her legislation was general and

The office for the district east of Pearl River was established at Fort Stoddart, with Joseph Chambers as register, and Ephraim Kirby and Robert Carter Nicholas as commissioners. This board convened for business first on the 2d of February, 1804, and continued open for the presentation of claims until September 21st, 1805, when it adjourned *sine die*, after receiving for record two hundred and seventy-six claims.

The surveyor-general's office was established at Washington, and Isaac Briggs was first surveyor-general. He soon afterward commenced the public surveys in the territory.

The whole of the extensive territory ceded by Georgia, lying north of the Mississippi Territory, and south of Tennessee, was, by the seventh section of the *act supplementary* to the "act regulating the grants of land south of Tennessee," approved March 27th, 1804, annexed to the Mississippi Territory, and was subsequently included within its limits and jurisdiction. The

exclusive. The power to regulate the transfer of all the lands within the territory was vested in Georgia; and, in the language of the Supreme Court of the Union, 'The existence of this power must negative the existence of any right which may conflict or control it.'"

"The commencement of the occupation of this country by the Spanish forces was as our ally during the war of the Revolution. Surely this could give to Spain no right of sovereignty over the territory of her ally; nor could the subsequent occupancy by the Spanish troops, under the pretense that it was a part of Florida, introduce here the laws of Spain." "When there is a wrongful and a rightful sovereign, both legislating at the same time over the same territory, the laws of the latter must prevail." "Neither Georgia nor the United States ever acquiesced in this wrongful Spanish occupancy." The legislation asserting the title of Georgia to this territory is chiefly comprised in the following acts:

1. Statute of Georgia, February 17, 1783, extending her laws and jurisdiction over it.
2. Statute of Georgia, February 7, 1785, creating a county of "Bourbon," and the land laws of the state.
3. Statute of South Carolina, 1787, relinquishing to Georgia all her claim.
4. Act of Georgia Legislature, selling a portion of the lands; sustained by the Supreme Court of the United States.—6 *Cranch*, 87.
5. Act of Georgia Legislature, February 13, 1796, relative to this territory.
6. Resolutions of Congress, October 20, 1787, consenting to South Carolina's relinquishment.
7. Report of Mr. Jefferson, Secretary of State, recognizing Georgia claim.
8. Report of commissioners to Spain in 1793, asserting same.
9. Mr. Pinckney's report to Spanish court, August, 1795, asserting same.
10. Spanish treaty, 1795, October 27, recognizing boundary of 1783.
11. Spanish evacuation of the Natchez District, March 30th, 1798.
12. Recognition of the claim by United States in act of April 7th, 1798, organizing government for the Mississippi Territory, saving "the right of the State of Georgia."— N.B. The Spanish posts on the Mobile were evacuated finally on the 5th of February, 1799.
13. Recognition by Congress, May 10, 1801.
14. Cession to United States, by compact, April 24, 1802.—See *Walker's Reports of Supreme Court of Mississippi*, p. 52, 53, &c.

boundaries of the Mississippi Territory, consequently, were the thirty-first degree on the south, and the thirty-fifth degree on the north, extending from the Mississippi River to the western limits of Georgia, and comprised the whole territory now embraced in the States of Alabama and Mississippi, excepting the small Florida District between the Pearl and Perdido Rivers. Four fifths of this extensive territory were in the possession of the four great southern Indian confederacies, the Choctâs, the Chickasâs, the Creeks, and the Cherokees, comprising an aggregate of about seventy-five thousand souls, and at least ten thousand warriors. The only portions of this territory to which the Indian title had been extinguished was a narrow strip from fifteen to fifty miles in width, on the east side of the Mississippi, and about seventy miles in length, and a small district on the Tombigby.

Education.—The subject of education was one which had engaged the early attention of the Territorial Legislature. A large portion of the recent emigrants to the territory, and especially those connected with the government, were men of education, enterprise, and talent, who were duly impressed with the importance of providing for the " encouragement of learning," and " the dissemination of useful knowledge." To aid in the accomplishment of this desirable object, a literary society was organized, which received its incorporation on the 8th of November, 1803, under the name of " the Mississippi Society for the Acquirement and Dissemination of Useful Knowledge." The society originally comprised eighteen members, including the governor, secretary, judges, and several members of the Legislature.

About the same time, the first college in the territory was chartered, under the control of twenty-five trustees, including several members of the Mississippi Society. The new college, in honor of the President of the United States, was called " Jefferson College." The trustees were authorized to receive for its support the proceeds of a " lottery," and " to collect donations from citizens of the territory and elsewhere." The charter required a book to be kept, in which should be inscribed the " names of the donors, with their donations annexed," which book " should be preserved in the archives of the college, in order that posterity might know who were the benefactors of the institution." The first of these were John and James Foster, and Randall Gibson, who made the "donation of a parcel of land, including a spring, commonly called 'Ellicott's Spring,' and 'situated in the vicinage of the town of Washington.'" On the 11th of November following, this tract of land by law was declared to be "the permanent site of Jefferson College."

Such was the origin of the oldest and best endowed college in the State of Mississippi. But its subsequent history has been disastrous and mortifying. Although liberally endowed by Congress, soon after its first charter, with the use of the territorial escheats for ten years, with liberal and gratuitous loans by the state in 1817 and 1820, and with a most bountiful relief or second endowment by Congress in 1832, it has failed to accomplish the object of its creation. After having realized ample funds in 1836, and having attracted the notice of the whole Union for its wealth in 1838, yet, without concert of action in its numerous trustees, for the wise appropriation of its ample resources, at the end of forty years from its first endowment, after many abortive attempts to build up an institution of learning, after a few partial successes and repeated failures, it presented to the eye of history only the emaciated skeleton of a college, bereft of its power to benefit posterity, or to advance the cause of science and literature.

Other institutions, chartered by the early territorial government for the advancement of learning, unlike Jefferson College, being destitute of any liberal endowment, either by public or private munificence, struggled through a short period of unsuccessful efforts to promote the cause of education, when they sunk into oblivion. Such was the "Franklin Society," instituted "for the purpose of establishing an academy in the town of Greenville or its vicinity, in the county of Jefferson."

Among the incidents in the early history of the Mississippi Territory was the violent death of the notorious robber Mason. This fearless bandit had become the terror of the routes from New Orleans and Natchez through the Indian nations. After the organization of the territorial government, and the opening of roads through the wilderness to Tennessee, the return of traders, supercargoes, and boatmen to the northern settlements with the proceeds of their voyage was on foot and on horseback, in parties for mutual protection, through the Indian nations; and often rich treasures of specie were packed on mules and horses over these long and toilsome journeys. Nor was it a matter of surprise, in a dreary wilderness, that bandits should infest such a route. It was in the year 1802, when all travel and intercourse from New Orleans and the Mississippi Territory was necessarily by way of this solitary trace, or by the slow-ascending barge and keel, that Mason made his appearance in the Mississippi Territory.

"Long accustomed to robbery and murder upon the Lower Ohio, during the Spanish dominion on the Mississippi, and pressed by the rapid approach of the American population, he deserted the 'Cave in the Rock,' on the Ohio, and began to infest the great Natchez Trace, where the rich proceeds of the river trade were the tempting prize, and where he soon became the terror of every peaceful traveler through the wilderness. Associated with him were his two sons and a few other desperate miscreants; and the name of Mason and his band was known and dreaded from the morasses of the southern frontier to the silent shades of the Tennessee River. The outrages of Mason became more frequent and sanguinary. One day found him marauding on the banks of the Pearl, against the life and fortune of the trader; and before pursuit was organized, the hunter, attracted by the descending sweep of the solitary vulture, learned the story of another robbery and murder on the remote shores of the Mississippi. Their depredations became at last so frequent and daring, that the people of the territory were driven to adopt measures for their apprehension. But such was the knowledge of the wilderness possessed by the wily bandit, and such his untiring vigilance and activity, that for a time he baffled every effort for his capture.

"Treachery at last, however, effected what stratagem, enterprise, and courage had in vain attempted. A citizen of great respectability, passing with his sons through the wilderness, was plundered by the bandits. Their lives were, however, spared, and they returned to the settlement. Public feeling was now excited, and the governor of the territory found it necessary to act. Governor Claiborne accordingly offered a liberal reward for the robber Mason, dead or alive! The proclamation was widely distributed, and a copy of it reached Mason himself, who indulged in much merriment on the occasion. Two of his band, however, tempted by the large reward, concerted a plan by which they might obtain it. An opportunity soon occurred; and while Mason, in company with the two conspirators, was counting out some ill-gotten plunder, a tomahawk was buried in his brain. His head was severed from his body and borne in triumph to Washington, then the seat of the territorial government.

"The head of Mason was recognized by many, and identified by all who read the proclamation, as the head entirely corresponded with the description given of certain scars and peculiar marks. Some delay, however, occurred in paying over the reward, owing to the slender state of the treasury. Meantime, a great assemblage from all the adjacent country had taken place, to view the grim and ghastly head of the robber chief. They were not less inspired with curiosity to see and converse with the individual whose prowess had delivered the country from so great a scourge. Among those spectators were the two young men, who, unfortunately for these traitors, recognized them as companions of Mason in the robbery of their father.

"It is unnecessary to say that treachery met its just reward, and that justice was also satisfied. The reward was not only withheld, but the robbers were imprisoned, and, on the full evidence of their guilt, condemned and executed at Greenville, Jefferson county.

"The band of Mason, being thus deprived of their leader and two of his most efficient men, dispersed and fled the country. Thus terminated the terrors which had infested the route through the Indian nations, known to travelers as the 'Natchez and Nashville Trace.'"

Emigration from the Western States, by way of the Mississippi River, for two years past had gradually augmented the population of the four counties organized near this river. The sparse pastoral population on the Mobile and Tombigby Rivers had likewise been increased to nearly fifteen hundred souls, by emigrants from West Florida and from Georgia.

During the autumn of 1803, numerous emigrants and men of enterprise pressed forward to the Mississippi Territory, in anticipation of the expected occupancy of the province of Louisiana by the Federal government. Among the arrivals at Natchez were several volunteer companies of patriotic Tennesseans, impatient of the dominion of Spain. The contemplated occupancy of the province by the United States had diffused hope throughout the whole West, and its final delivery

Vol. II.—Z

was expected to take place in December. Fired with zeal and ardor for the aggrandizement of their country in the extension of the Federal dominion over the whole Valley of the Mississippi, hundreds and thousands of enterprising men—merchants, traders, laborers, mechanics, men of the three learned professions, and those who had been bred to arms—flocked to the Mississippi Territory, ready to seize the first advantages' of citizenship in the rich province. Volunteer companies, fully equipped, coveted the honor of accompanying the Federal troops and witnessing the ceremony of the national transfer.

Hence the close of the year 1803 was a memorable epoch in the early history of Mississippi. . Within its limits were assembled the army of the United States, as well as the patriotic volunteers, at the head of which the commander-in-chief and Governor Claiborne, commissioners of the United States, were to advance to the consummation of the purchase, by extending over it the authority and jurisdiction of the Federal government. All were eager to witness this glorious termination to the dominion, extortion, and perfidy of the Spanish authority on the Mississippi.

About the 2d of December, Governor Claiborne took his departure from Natchez, in company with his friends and the volunteer troops, to join the Federal army under General Wilkinson at Fort Adams.* Leaving the secretary, Cato West, in charge of the territorial government, he proceeded on his way to New Orleans. His military escort consisted of a company of volunteer cavalry, under the command of Captain Benjamin Farrar, the first troop ever formed in the territory, and one which, for many years afterward, maintained an elevated character for patriotism and chivalrous bearing.

The province of Louisiana was formally surrendered to Governor Claiborne on the 20th day of December, 1803, as we have more fully detailed in another place.†

Although the official duties of Governor Claiborne had ceased, he was nevertheless the actual governor of the Mississippi Territory until his successor, Robert Williams, entered upon the duties, near the close of the following year. During the same time, he exercised the prerogatives and powers of governor-general of the province of Louisiana, until Congress provided for it a regular form of territorial government.

---
* See Mississippi Herald, December 5, 1803.
† See book iv., chap. v. Also, Martin's Louisiana, vol. ii., p. 183.

During his administration in the Mississippi Territory, he ceased not to enjoy the confidence and esteem of the patriotic, the intelligent, and the virtuous. Yet, during his whole administration, he encountered active opposition to many of his official acts and executive measures; but it was chiefly that opposition which springs from a party spirit and political difference of opinion.

It has been said that he was unpopular, but it was only with a certain class of men. With the majority of the people no one was more esteemed for his intelligence, virtue, and patriotism as a man; and as the chief executive, his course was patriotic, dignified, and urbane, securing him the confidence of the intelligent and good. By the interested and designing, attempts had been made to embarrass his measures and destroy his usefulness soon after his departure for New Orleans. But the people of Mississippi spoke for themselves. While discharging the responsible duties of Governor-general of Louisiana, he received, in March, 1804, from the citizens of Washington and its vicinity, a flattering address, with the signatures of nearly three hundred respectable persons of the county of Adams, who testified to his " talents, benevolence, universal philanthropy, and sense of justice," and who tendered " their undivided approbation of the firm and dignified measures of his late administration in this territory." They also expressed " an earnest desire for the return of his excellency." About the same time, a correspondent from New Orleans, who had made special observation on this point, declares that the attempts to render Governor Claiborne unpopular in that place " have originated with certain *disaffected* and *unprincipled* characters, whose views are insidious, and whose conduct can not stand the test of investigation."*

On the 18th of March, an address from a number of citizens of Wilkinson county was forwarded to him in New Orleans, expressing " their fullest approbation of the wise and virtuous measures of his late administration in the Mississippi Territory, with assurances of the firm support which is due from a patriotic community to a public functionary whose only object is the happiness of the people." They also declare that " the simplicity of manners and the dignified conduct observed by his excellency in discharging the important trust of Commis-

* Mississippi Herald, March 25. 1804.

sioner of the United States for receiving possession of the province of Louisiana will remain a lasting monument of honest fame, not to be corroded by the breath of faction." They declare, moreover, that "they earnestly regret the loss sustained by this section of the Union, should the President of the United States require a continuance of his services in the high station which he now fills."

The friends and admirers of the governor did not hesitate to declare that the opposition proceeded from a "faction, formed by the union of opposite principles and characters, fomented and encouraged by the party *out of power* and patriots out of place;" among whom were classed "ex-attorney-generals, ex-sheriffs, ex-clerks, and ex-officers" of divers grades, and their dependents.*

Introduction of the Protestant Religion.—Previous to the extension of the American jurisdiction over the Natchez District, the Catholic religion alone was tolerated, and all Protestant denominations whatever were strictly prohibited from inculcating their tenets or in any manner exercising parochial duties. Hence, when the American authority was introduced, there existed nothing like a Protestant church or meeting-house. No religious association or society had been organized; public preaching had been unknown; and the only mode of observing the Sabbath had been the morning solemnization of mass in the chapel before a few devout Catholics, from which they could retire to spend the residue of the day with the giddy throng in the recreations of balls, theatres, military parades, or festive exhibitions.

The first public preaching by Protestant ministers was from those among the promiscuous emigrants who might possess the gift of speaking. The only regular Sabbath exercises were by those who early came as missionaries from the Protestant churches of Kentucky and Tennessee.

The first Methodist missionary was Tobias Gibson, from the South Carolina Conference, who advanced by way of East Tennessee and the Cumberland River, and arrived at Natchez in the summer of 1799. He at once entered upon the work of organizing societies in Washington and its vicinity, where he continued until his departure next spring. Late in the autumn of 1800, he again descended the river from Tennessee

* Mississippi Herald, May 2, 1804

as a missionary of the Tennessee Conference. He entered upon his work, and continued diligently employed in forming and building up societies throughout the settlements from the Bayou Pierre to the line of demarkation. During three years prior to his death, in 1804, he had formed societies at Washington, Kingston, on Cole's Creek, near Greenville, and on the Bayou Pierre, together comprising two hundred church members. These, after his death, were left without a shepherd until the arrival of Learned Blackburn in 1806, who undertook to gather up the lost sheep. Thus was Methodism first introduced into the Mississippi Territory.

One of the most useful missionaries at Natchez was the Rev. Mr. Bowman, of the Methodist Episcopal Church, who came from Tennessee in the year 1803, and confined his labors chiefly to the city and vicinage of Natchez. Zealous as a missionary, and devoted to the intellectual culture, as well as the religious instruction of the people, he was still preaching and lecturing on scientific subjects and ethics in the city of Natchez as late as the year 1807.

It was about the year 1802 that the first Presbyterian missionaries, the Rev. Messrs. Hall and Montgomery, arrived in the territory. Hall labored several years in his ministerial duties in Natchez. Montgomery became a permanent resident, and more than forty years afterward he was exercising his pastoral calling as the patriarch of the Scotch settlement in Jefferson county.

The first Baptist missionary was David Cooper, a most excellent and pious man, who arrived in the year 1802, and continued to build up his churches for more than thirty years, when he was gathered home to his fathers in great peace triumphantly. The Rev. Dr. Cloud, of the Episcopal Church, entered upon his missionary duties about the same time, and, after nearly thirty-five years, he was still officiating within the limits of Jefferson county.

[A.D. 1804.] The Spaniards still held a footing on the eastern side of the Mississippi.

Louisiana, as surrendered to the United States, embraced only the Island of New Orleans on the east side of the Mississippi, and the Spaniards continued to occupy and exercise dominion over all the remaining country east of the river, and south of the line of demarkation. The port of Mobile, as well as the town and district of Baton Rouge, including one hundred miles of the eastern bank of the river, was still occupied as a portion of West Florida. Along the line of demarkation from the Mississippi eastward to the Chattahoochy, a distance of more than three hundred miles, the only barrier between the jurisdiction and settlements of the Mississippi Territory and the province of West Florida was an open avenue through the forest, or a surveyor's line and mile-posts through the prairies and open woods. The manners and customs, the races and their characteristic traits, their feelings, prejudices, and national antipathies, as well as their government, laws, and civil jurisprudence, were opposite and altogether antagonistical. In such a state of things, could border difficulties between the scattered dwellers of the forest be avoided? Each, placed beyond the reach of the strong arm of the civil authorities, revenged his own wrongs, and vindicated his own rights.

Hence border difficulties, broils, and private animosities had occasionally presented from the first establishment of the line of demarkation; but a few detachments of troops, stationed at intervals along the border, served to suppress any important outbreak.

Washington District.—In the mean time, the population on the Tombigby and Mobile Rivers had increased, and it was deemed expedient to erect the county of Washington into a judicial district, with an "additional judge." Agreeably to an act of Congress, approved March 27th, 1804, an additional judge was appointed, and required to reside in or near the principal settlements of Washington county, where he should hold two regular terms of the Superior Court annually on the first Mondays in May and September.* The court was soon afterward organized, with the Honorable Harry Toulmin as judge. Judge Toulmin entered upon his duties with zeal and energy, and contributed greatly to the complete organization of the new territorial government, and the establishment of a regular system of judicial proceedings throughout the territory. Such was the confidence reposed in his talents and integrity as a legislator, that he was employed by the General Assembly, within two years after his appointment, "to compile a digest of the statutes now in force," and also to prepare a "set of forms and brief general principles for the information of justices of

* See Toulmin's Digest, p. 480–482.

the peace and inferior courts." The task committed to his charge was completed during the year 1806, and formally approved by an act of the Legislature in February following.*

[A.D. 1805.] By the beginning of the year 1805, the population of the territory had so far been augmented that Congress assented to the election of a delegate from the territory under the provisions of the ordinance of 1787.†

In the mean time, Robert Williams, of North Carolina, having been appointed governor of the territory, arrived at the seat of the territorial government on the 26th of January, 1805. His appointment was greeted with a cordial reception and a public dinner.‡

Having made his appointments,§ he issued his proclamation for the assembling of the Legislature on the first of July for the dispatch of important business. He continued to discharge the duties of his office for more than twelve months, when, leaving the secretary, Cowles Mead, "executing the powers and performing the duties of governor," he was absent some months on a visit to North Carolina.

First City Charter of Natchez.—Natchez had already become an important commercial point for the western people. It was a large village, consisting chiefly of small wooden buildings of one story, distributed over an irregular, undulating surface, with but little regard to system or cleanliness. Impressed with its growing importance as a great commercial point, the Legislature, as early as the 10th of March, 1803, had incorporated it with ample municipal power, under the style of "The Mayor, Aldermen, and Assistants of the City of Natchez." The city authorities consisted chiefly of a mayor, a recorder, three aldermen, six assistants, a clerk, and a marshal; all except the marshal and six assistants exercising the authority of justices

---

* See Toulmin's Digest, p. 19–27.

† The *first* delegate, elected in May, 1805, was Dr. William Lattimore, of Wilkinson county; he was succeeded by George Poindexter, of Jefferson, elected in February, 1807.—See Mississippi Messenger, February 4th, 1807.

The third delegate was Thomas M. Green, of Greenville, who served until 1811, when he was succeeded by Dr. William Lattimore.

‡ At this public dinner by the citizens of Washington, the Hon. Thomas Rodney acted as president, and Thomas H. Williams as vice-president.—See Mississippi Herald and Natchez Gazette, June 7th, 1805.

§ The following persons constituted the governor's military staff, viz.:
William Scott, aid-de-camp, with the rank of *colonel*.
William B. Shields, William Wooldridge, and John F. Carmichael, aids-de-camp, with the rank of *major*. Thomas H. Williams served as secretary until the arrival of Cowles Mead, May 31st, 1806.

of the peace. In the selection of the city authorities popular suffrage was not entirely excluded by the charter. "Citizens and freeholders" might elect the six assistants, the city treasurer, and the assessor and collector; but the Federal government reserved to itself the appointment of the remainder. The governor appointed the mayor, the recorder, the three aldermen, and the marshal, all of whom were subject to his removal. The powers of the "Mayor's Court" were extensive and summary. The mayor might hold his court for the hearing of civil cases three days in every month, with a jury empanneled, if desired by either party. Cases were to be adjudicated and judgment enforced in a summary manner. The jurisdiction extended to all civil cases in the city wherein the subject of controversy did not exceed one hundred dollars in value, and to all criminal cases in which the penalty did not exceed one month of imprisonment, fifty dollars' fine, or thirty-nine lashes on the bare back.

Such were some of the powers and provisions of this charter, which went into operation early in the summer of 1803. If it leaned to the despotism of monarchy, it resulted from the nature of the circumstances under which it was enacted. Such was the number of lawless adventurers and boatmen from the Ohio region which annually infested the city and habitually defied the municipal authorities, that no man was safe from their depredations and assaults until the city authorities were clothed with ample powers for their punishment.

Yet each session of the Legislature conferred additional powers upon the municipal authorities, until the year 1805, when the mayor and aldermen, with the common council, were authorized to appoint the times for holding the Mayor's Court, the jurisdiction of which was also enlarged to the adjudication of all civil cases within the city, where the amount in controversy did "not exceed five hundred dollars." The arbitrary proceedings of this court at length became so oppressive that public opinion was roused against it, until it was denounced in a public meeting, and finally made the object of a presentment by the grand jury, "as a public grievance."

Spanish Difficulties.—In the mean time, Congress had erected the District of Washington into a revenue precinct, known as the "District of Mobile;" and Fort Stoddart was declared a port of entry, for the commerce of the Mobile and Tombigby settlements. Hence began a series of vexatious exactions, searches, and delays to all American trade or produce passing up or down the river. The Spaniards at Mobile, twenty miles below the line, claimed the right to control the entire navigation of the bay and river within their limits. They therefore imposed a heavy duty upon all American produce exported, as well as upon all other commodities of trade passing to and from the settlements, as well as the military posts on the river, above the line. Even the military supplies and the Indian annuities from the Federal government were not exempt. Hence the national government, no less than the citizens individually, was compelled to pay tribute to a foreign power for the privilege of entering its own ports, and navigating its own waters.

This transit duty was levied and collected in the port of Mobile, at the rate of *twelve and a half per cent. ad valorem,* by Spanish estimate, upon all articles without exception. Thus the crops seeking the market of New Orleans, and the proceeds invested in the necessary articles of domestic use, paid an aggregate duty of *twenty-five per cent.* for the privilege of passing through the Spanish waters.* Nor was this duty an idle ceremony. Every boat and vessel was compelled to pass under the guns of Fort Charlotte, and was required, on penalty of instant destruction, to make land and submit to a vexatious search, often by overhauling the whole cargo, in order that an estimate, arbitrary in the extreme, might be affixed to each article, for the collection of the imposed revenue. Vessels were often required to unload, for the purpose of taking a full inventory of the cargo, in order to ascertain the requisite duties. Such had been the arbitrary course of the Spanish officers, under this oppressive system, that Governor Claiborne, of New Orleans, in his dispatches of August, 1805, declared " that the settlements will be abandoned unless this exaction terminates."

The same year gave rise to the first public charitable institution in the city of Natchez. The increasing numbers of indigent boatmen who were annually thrown helpless upon the city prompted the humane members of the medical profession to set on foot the plan of erecting a charity hospital for their relief, by means of private donations and contributions throughout all the organized counties near the Mississippi. The plan

---

* American State Papers, vol. v., p. 94–96. Also, vol. iii., p. 344, 345, Boston edition.

was so far matured in 1804, that a bill of incorporation was obtained in January following for the "Natchez Hospital."

The preamble to the bill proceeds: "Whereas great numbers of sick and distressed boatmen, employed in the navigation of the Mississippi River, and other indigent persons destitute of the means of procuring medical assistance, are found in the city of Natchez and other parts of the territory, for the relief of whose wants private charity and the present legal regulations are inadequate, and subscriptions to a considerable amount having been raised, and the sum of *one thousand dollars* bequeathed by the late George Cochrane, Esq., for the purpose of establishing a hospital in said city; and whereas David Lattimore, Garrett E. Pendergrast, William Lyon, Joseph Macreary, James Speed, Andrew Macreary, and Frederic Seip, physicians of that place, have humanely proffered their professional services *gratis* for the benefit of such institution," &c. Such is the origin of the present "Natchez Hospital," which yet stands an honorable memorial of the early benevolence of Adams county.*

Before the close of the summer, the border animosities between the American and Spanish population had broken out into acts of open violence and mutual aggression.

The first violation of American soil by these lawless persons was on the 12th of August, when Lieutenant John Glasscock, with twelve Spanish light-horse, crossed the line two miles into the territory, where he captured William Flannagan and wife, who were forcibly abducted, together with his horse, saddle, and bridle, fifteen miles into the Spanish dominion; but subsequently finding he had seized the wrong man, he permitted them to return; the horse, however, was retained.†

On the 3d of September one of these border feuds terminated in an open violation of the American territory by an armed detachment from the Spanish border. Samuel, Reuben, and Nathan Kemper, brothers, residing within the limits of the Mississippi Territory, near Pinckneyville, having become highly

---

* See Toulmin's Digest, p. 422–426.

† Lieutenant Glasscock and his party were Anglo-Americans, and subjects of the Spanish crown, who had been English subjects of West Florida, and still retained all their hostility to the authority of the United States, and some of them had retired with the Spanish authorities from the Mississippi Territory. Among them were Benjamin Lanear, Abram Jones, —— Kennedy, Jun., Obiel Brewer, —— Connor, and others.—See American State Papers, vol. v., p. 111, 112, Boston edition.

obnoxious to the Spanish authorities, were unlawfully seized at night in their own houses by a party of twelve white men in disguise and seven negroes. After great personal violence and abusive language, they were forcibly abducted beyond the line, and placed in the custody of a party of twelve Spanish light-horse, under the command of Captain Alston, who had been waiting to receive them. They were hurried off to the river, near Tunica Bayou, and, in charge of Captain William Barker and five men, were embarked on board a boat as prisoners, to be delivered into the custody of Governor Grandpre at Baton Rouge.

But their captivity was of short duration. In the morning, soon after daylight, as the boat passed the American post at Point Coupée, the prisoners gave the alarm to a person on shore, and before the boat had traversed the bend, Lieutenant Wilson, with a file of soldiers, having crossed the isthmus and taken his station below, succeeded in capturing the boat, with the prisoners and their abductors.* The whole party was sent under guard to the civil authorities at Washington. After a hearing before Judge Rodney, they were finally sent to the Spanish line, and their offense was formally represented to the Spanish governor.†

To secure quiet on the border, and to prevent future violations of the American territory, Governor Williams, soon after this outrage, directed two full companies of militia to be stationed near the line, with orders to patrol the country and arrest all trespassers from the Spanish settlements, preserve the peace, and prevent any violation of territory.‡

---

* This circumstance by Martin is erroneously given as transpiring on the 23d of September. The whole circumstances are fully detailed in the several affidavits taken on the trial at Washington.—See American State Papers, vol. v., p. 104–123, Boston edition.

The disguised white men, who, in company with the negroes, abducted the Kempers for the Spanish officer, were subsequently ascertained to have been Lewis Ritchie, Minor Butler, Abraham Horton, James Horton, Doctor Bomar, Henry Flowers, Jun., and ——— M'Dermot, citizens of the Mississippi Territory, but accessaries and accomplices in the outrage. The guard under Captain Barker, in charge of the prisoners, was composed of Charles Stuart, John Morris, Adam Bingaman, John Ratcliff, and George Rowe, a portion of them being citizens of the Mississippi Territory.—See American State Papers, vol. v., p. 123.

† American State Papers, vol. v., p. 98–104. Also, Martin's Louisiana, vol. ii., p. 245. For a full and detailed account of these transactions, and the entire correspondence between Governor Williams and Governor Grandpre, see Mississippi Messenger, February 4th, 1806.

‡ The governor's order was directed to Colonel John Ellis, of Wilkinson county, commanding him to detail two companies of eighty men each, with officers and musicians

Indian Treaties in 1805.—The eastern half of the territory was still an unbroken savage wilderness in the possession of the Creek nation, except the district on Tombigby and Mobile Rivers. The routes from this district to Georgia and East Tennessee were only Indian trails, traversed and occupied by the Creeks and Cherokees. The principal intercourse between these settlements and those on the Mississippi was by way of the road leading from New Orleans to Fort Stoddart. To open a direct communication between these settlements and the populous portions of Tennessee and Georgia, and to afford mail facilities to the remote portions of the Union, the Federal government entered into treaties with the Indian nations.

The first treaty of this year was with the Chickasâs, wherein they ceded the extreme eastern portion of their country lying north of the "Great Bend" of Tennessee River, and comprising about three hundred and forty-five thousand acres in the vicinity of Huntsville, and which was subsequently organized into the "county of Madison."

The next was with the Cherokees at Tellico, on the 7th of October, 1805. By this treaty the Cherokees ceded to the United States a mail-route through their country, from Knoxville, in East Tennessee, to New Orleans, by way of the Tellico and the Tombigby Rivers. They also conceded to the people of the United States the free and unmolested use of this road in traveling from one extreme to the other. This was the first public road from East Tennessee to the Tombigby, and it opened the way for emigration to the settlements on the banks of that river below the Indian boundary.*

By a convention concluded at Washington city on the 14th of November, 1805, certain Creek chiefs, about thirty in number, in behalf of the Creek nation, guarantied to the United States forever the right of a horse-path through the Creek country, from the Ocmulgee to the Mobile River, upon which the people of the United States shall have a right at all times peaceably to travel. They stipulated, also, that the Indians would keep up suitable ferries and ferry-boats upon the different rivers, for the convenience of travelers, and maintain houses of public entertainment at suitable distances on the road.†

complete, with twelve rounds of cartridge, and instructions that, "if any hostile intention were evinced by any party, to repel force by force."—See Mississippi Messenger, September 13th, 1805.   * Martin's Louisiana, vol. ii., p. 258.

† Martin's Louisiana, vol. ii., p. 258. Also, Land Laws of the United States, Indian Treaties.

About the same time, a treaty was concluded by General James Robertson and Silas Dinsmoor with the Choctâ nation, at " Mount Dexter," for the sale of a large extent of country, comprising about five millions of acres, contiguous to the line of demarkation. This cession was bounded on the north by a line running nearly east by north from the intersection of the old Choctâ boundary near the sources of the Homochitto River, along " M'Leary's Path" to the Pearl River, and thence east by north to the Chickasâhay River, near the Hiyoowanee towns, and thence northeast by east across the Tombigby River to the eastern limit of the Choctâ nation.

By this treaty, in consideration of the sum of fifty thousand five hundred dollars in hand paid, besides a perpetual annuity of three thousand dollars, and other sums formerly paid, the Indians conveyed their title to the whole territory lying west of Washington county, on the Tombigby, and east of the old Choctâ boundary. Thus the whole southern portion of the present State of Mississippi, near the line of demarkation, was thrown open to the white population, and the Choctâ nation was virtually removed from the Spanish border by an intervening strip of more than fifty miles in width.* This purchase was soon afterward erected into three large counties, named Marion, Wayne, and Greene, when the territorial jurisdiction was formally extended over all that portion of country now comprised in the counties of Lawrence, Covington, Jones, Wayne, Pike, Marion, Perry, and Greene, at a period when the entire white population of the whole territory scarcely exceeded twenty thousand souls.

[A.D. 1806.] The Mississippi Territory, for several years afterward, with its wide extent of Indian country, was traversed by only three principal roads, or horse-paths. These were, first, the road from the Cumberland settlements through the Chickasâ and Choctâ nations to the Natchez District; second, from Knoxville through the Cherokee and Creek nations, by way of the Tombigby, to Natchez; third, that from the Oconee settlements of Georgia, by way of Fort Stoddart, to Natchez and New Orleans. The Chickasâ, or Nashville Trace, was frequented more than any other, it being the traveled route for the return journeys of all the Ohio boatmen and traders from New Orleans and Natchez.†

---

* See Mississippi Messenger, December 24th, 1805.

† The old Nashville Trace extended from the settlements on D--ck River, in West

The country recently purchased from the Choctâs comprised a large extent of sterile pine lands, of which the uplands were unprofitable for agricultural purposes, and the greater portion of the low grounds were subject to frequent inundations from heavy rains and spring floods. Such was the condition of the Mobile, Tombigby, and Pascagoula bottoms; and many years did not elapse before the pioneers began to covet the fine lands beyond the Indian boundary, and upon the Upper Tombigby.

This subject was brought before the Superior Court by the grand jury as early as May, 1806. The grand jury represents " that nearly four fifths of the lands in Washington county are unfit for cultivation; that the Tombigby is navigable within sixty miles of the Tennessee River; that the Choctâs are willing to sell lands high up the Tombigby," and they desire to have permission to settle them.*

Spaniards on the Sabine.—Meantime, the Spanish commander, General Herrera, having advanced from Texas with a force of twelve hundred men, had taken his position on the Bayou Pierre, in the vicinity of Natchitoches, claiming the Arroyo Hondo as the eastern boundary of Texas. Having occupied this position during the summer, notwithstanding the remonstrances of Governor Claiborne against the intrusion, General Wilkinson had been ordered to take his position at Natchitoches with the troops of the United States.†

Preparatory to the advance of the regular army, the general had made a requisition upon the governors of the territories of Orleans and Mississippi for detachments of militia, to be held in readiness to co-operate with the regular army on the Spanish frontier.

On the 6th of September, while General Wilkinson was in the county of Adams conferring with the governor relative to the requisition, he issued orders to the commandant at Fort Stoddart, requiring him to hold himself in readiness to invest Mobile with his command, supported by two hundred militia

---

Tennessee, to the Grindstone Ford of Bayou Pierre. The distance, as then traveled, was as follows: From Duck River to Tennessee River, at Colbert's Ferry, one hundred miles; thence to the Chickasâ towns, ninety miles; thence to Grindstone Ford, one hundred and eighty miles. George Colbert was a half-breed Chickasâ, and resided nearly thirty miles below the Muscle Shoals; he had four or five brothers. The principal Chickasâ town contained two hundred cabins, or houses.—See Bowman's Description of Country south of Tennessee.   * Messenger, June 17th, 1806.

† See book v., chap. xv., of this work, "Territory of Orleans," &c.

from Washington county, under Colonel James Caller, who was then actively engaged in preparations for the capture of Mobile.

About the last of September, the militia and volunteers from Mississippi advanced toward Natchitoches. Two fine cavalry troops, under Captains Farrar and Hinds, proceeded from Natchez to Natchitoches. Soon afterward, Major F. L. Claiborne, at the head of a battalion of militia from Adams county, consisting of two hundred and fifty men,* besides the "Mississippi Blues," an independent company, commanded by Captain Poindexter,† advanced to Alexandria. Here they were met, late in October, by an order from the commander-in-chief, directing them to return to Natchez, the Spaniards on the Sabine having agreed peaceably to retire to Nacogdoches. The volunteer cavalry, commanded by Captains Farrar and Hinds, were ordered to join the troops on the Sabine, where they remained until the American army retired in November.

Aaron Burr's Movements.—It was in November, 1806, that Kentucky was thrown into great excitement and apprehension relative to the designs of Aaron Burr.‡ Joseph H. Daviess,

---

* Major Claiborne was a brother of Governor Claiborne, formerly of the Mississippi Territory. He had been an officer in the regular army under General Wayne in 1794, and descended the river with General Wilkinson in 1798: having retired from the army in 1803, he entered the militia service.

† The "Mississippi Blues" were organized into a company in the town of Washington early in March, 1806, in anticipation of hostilities with the Spaniards.

‡ See Mississippi Messenger, December 9th, 1816.

"*Motion in the Federal Court of the Kentucky District against Aaron Burr, Esquire, late Vice-president of the United States, for Crimes of high Misdemeanors.*

"On Wednesday, about noon, on the fifth instant, J. H. Daviess, Esquire, attorney of the United States for the above district, rose, and addressing the court, said that he had a motion to make of the utmost magnitude and extraordinary nature, and which regarded the welfare of the Union at large. That the unhappy state of his health alone had prevented him from making it on the first day of the term. That he should ground his motion on an affidavit which he would present to the court. He then made oath to the following affidavit:

"UNITED STATES OF AMERICA, KENTUCKY DISTRICT, *sct.*—J. H. Daviess, attorney for the United States in and for said district, upon his corporeal oath, doth depose and say, that the deponent is informed, and doth verily believe, that a certain Aaron Burr, Esquire, late Vice-president of the United States, for several months past hath been, and is now, engaged in preparing and setting on foot, and in providing and preparing the means, for a military expedition and enterprise within this district, for the purpose of descending the Ohio and Mississippi therewith, and making war upon the subjects of the King of Spain, who are in a state of peace with the people of these United States—to wit, on the provinces of Mexico, on the westwardly side of Louisiana, which appertain and belong to the King of Spain, a European prince with whom these United States are at peace.

"And said deponent further saith, that he is informed, and fully believes, that the above charge can be, and will be, fully substantiated by evidence, provided this honorable court will grant compulsory process to bring in witness to testify thereto.

District Attorney of the United States, having failed in his laudable attempts to bring Burr to trial upon a treasonable indictment, against the tact of his counsels, Henry Clay and John Allen, Esquires, abandoned the prosecution, and Burr was discharged.

This premature attempt to bring Burr to justice, without sufficient evidence for his conviction, had produced a popular

"And the deponent further saith, that he is informed, and verily believes, that the agents and emissaries of the said Burr have purchased up, and are continuing to purchase, large stores of provisions, as if for an army; which the said Burr seems to conceal in great mystery from the people at large, his purposes and projects; while the minds of the good people of this district seem agitated with the current rumor that a military expedition against some neighboring power is preparing by said Burr.

"Wherefore said attorney, on behalf of said United States, prays, that due process issue to compel the personal appearance of the said Aaron Burr in this court, and also of such witnesses as may be necessary on behalf of the said United States, and that this honorable court will duly recognize the said Aaron Burr, to answer such charges as may be preferred against him in the premises; and, in the mean time, that he desist and refrain from all further preparation and proceeding in the said armament within the said United States, or the territories or dependences thereof.

"J. H. DAVIESS, A. U. S.

"Having read this affidavit, the attorney proceeded in the following words:

"The present subject has much engaged my mind. The case made out is only as to the expedition against Mexico; but I have information on which I can rely, that all the western territories are the next object of the scheme; and, finally, all the region of the Ohio is calculated as falling into the vortex of the new proposed revolution. What the practicability of this scheme is I will not say; but, certainly, any progress in it might cost our country much blood and treasure to undo; and, at the least, great public agitation must be expected.

"I am determined to use every effort in my power, as an officer and as a man, to prevent and defeat it.

"Having made the affidavit myself, I shall make no comments on its sufficiency.

"In cases of felony, the affidavit must be positive as to a felony actually committed, but in a misdemeanor of this nature, where the sole object of the law is prevention, such an oath can not be required; the thing must rest on belief as to the main point of guilt.

"I could easily prove positively the purchase of supplies of various kinds, but this is no offense. Mr. Burr may purchase supplies; he may import arms; he may engage men, which I am told is actually begun; yet all these things being proved make no offense; neither can proof of the declarations of his known confidants, of which abundance might be had, attach guilt to him: it is the *design*, the *intent* with which he makes these preparations that constitute his misdemeanor.

"There must be a great exertion of supposition to imagine a case in which positive proof of the illegal *design* can be had; it must rest in information and belief.

"The court ought, therefore, to issue a warrant or capias for the accused, and examine witnesses, when the court will be able to decide whether Mr. Burr should be bound to good behavior on the premises, or recognized to appear here and answer an indictment."—Western World, Nov. 8th, 1806.

On the second day of court, Colonel Daviess, well aware of the popular feeling and the strong efforts contemplated, and already in operation, to defeat his attempt to procure a *true bill* from the grand jury, made a formal motion for the discharge of the grand jury, stating that the absence of a material witness would prevent him from proceeding to establish the facts intended by him. Upon this motion, the gratification of the crowd was evinced in sneers and laughter at the abortive attempt to arraign Colonel Burr.—See Mississippi Messenger, Dec. 6th, 1806.

impression in his favor, and a general disbelief of his guilt. This gave him an opportunity of hastening his equipments for descending the Mississippi River.

After his discharge at Lexington, Burr proceeded to Nashville, in Tennessee, where his late honorable acquittal secured him a hearty welcome and numerous friends. Encouraged by his good fortune, he lost no time in expediting the preparations for his contemplated enterprise. Friends and money were at command, and active preparations were prosecuted with vigor. Boats adapted to the low stage of the river were erecting at various points on the Cumberland;* provisions, arms, and ammunition were provided for descending the Mississippi to Natchez before the 20th of December. General John Adair, from Kentucky, was a warm and active adherent in the enterprise.†

He, with other agents and emissaries, advanced, by different routes, to Natchez and New Orleans, to prepare matters for the arrival of their leader and his van-guard of three hundred men. In arranging their plans, and in gaining the influence of prominent men, they did not fail to court the favor and adherence of the commander-in-chief of the army, then on the Sabine. At the same time, it was rumored mysteriously that Burr, with three hundred men, would arrive at Natchez about the 20th of December, in the prosecution of his enterprise, which was represented as laudable and advantageous to the American people, and pre-eminently so to those engaged in the enterprise.‡

* "At Marietta, Ohio, also, Colonel Burr had in a forward state no less than forty-feet batteaux, which were to be finished in a few weeks, besides stores, provisions," &c. These were all captured and confiscated by order of the Governor of Ohio. —See *letter* from Marietta, Oct. 20th, 1806, in Mississippi Messenger, Dec. 2d, 1806.

† See chap. xv., "Territory of Orleans," &c., Dr. Carmichael's affidavit.

‡ *The Deposition of William Eaton, Esquire, January 26th,* 1807. — "Early last winter, Colonel Aaron Burr, late Vice-president of the United States, signified to me, at this place, that, under the authority of the general government, he was organizing a secret expedition against the Spanish provinces on our southwestern borders, which expediton he was to lead, and in which he was authorized to invite me to take the command of a division. I had never before been made personally acquainted with Colonel Burr, and having for many years been employed in foreign service, I knew but little about the estimation this gentleman now held in the opinion of his countrymen and his government; the rank and confidence by which he had so lately been distinguished left me no right to suspect his patriotism. I knew him a soldier. In case of a war with the Spanish nation, which, from the tenor of the president's message to both Houses of Congress, seemed probable, I should have thought it my duty to obey so honorable a call of my country, and under that impression I did engage to embark in the expedition. I had frequent interviews with Colonel Burr in this city, and, for a

Vol. II.—A a

Among the confidents it was asserted that four thousand men were in readiness to follow as soon as their leader should considerable time, his object seemed to be to instruct me, by maps and other information, in the feasibility of penetrating to Mexico, always carrying forward the idea that the measure was authorized by government. At length, some time in February, he began by degrees to unveil himself. He reproached the government with want of character, want of gratitude, and want of justice. He seemed desirous of irritating resentment in my breast by dilating on certain injuries he felt I had suffered from reflections made on the floor of the House of Representatives concerning my operations in Barbary, and from the delays of government in adjusting my claims for disbursements on that coast during my consular agency at Tunis; and he said he would point me to an honorable mode of indemnity. I now began to entertain a suspicion that Mr. Burr was preparing an unauthorized military expedition, which to me was enveloped in mystery; and, desirous to draw an explanation from him, I suffered him to suppose me resigned to his counsel. He now laid open his project of revolutionizing the western country, separating it from the Union, establishing a monarchy there, of which he was to be the sovereign, New Orleans to be his capital; organizing a force on the waters of the Mississippi, and extending conquest to Mexico. I suggested a number of impediments to his scheme, such as the Republican habits of the citizens of that country, and their affection toward our present administration of government; the want of funds; the resistance he would meet from the regular army of the United States on those frontiers; and the opposition of Miranda in case he should succeed to Republicanize the Mexicans.

"Mr. Burr found no difficulty in removing these obstacles. He said he had, the preceding season, made a tour through that country, and had secured the attachment of the principal citizens of Kentucky, Tennessee, and Louisiana to his person and his measures; declared he had inexhaustible resources as to funds; assured me the regular army would act with him, and would be re-enforced by ten or twelve thousand men from the above-mentioned states and territory, and from other parts of the Union; said he had powerful agents in the Spanish territory.

"Mr. Burr talked of the establishment of an independent government west of the Alleghany as a matter of inherent constitutional right of the people; a change which would eventually take place, and for the operation of which the present crisis was peculiarly favorable. There was, said he, no energy in the government to be dreaded, and the divisions of political opinions throughout the Union was a circumstance of which we should profit. There were very many enterprising men among us who aspired to something beyond the dull pursuits of civil life, and who would volunteer in this enterprise; and the vast territory belonging to the United States which offered to adventurers, and the mines of Mexico, would bring strength to his standard from all quarters. I listened to the exposition of Colonel Burr's views with seeming acquiescence. Every interview convinced me more and more that he had organized a deep-laid plot of treason in the West, in the accomplishment of which he felt fully confident; till at length I discovered that his ambition was not bounded by the waters of the Mississippi and Mexico, but that he meditated overthrowing the present government of our country. He said if he could gain over the marine corps, and secure the naval commanders, Truxton, Preble, Decatur, and others, *he would turn Congress neck and heels out of doors; assassinate the president; seize on the treasury and the navy, and declare himself the protector of an energetic government.* The honorable trust of corrupting the marine corps, and of sounding Commodore Preble and Captain Decatur, Colonel Burr proposed confiding to me. Shocked at this proposition, I dropped the mask, and exclaimed against his views. He talked of the degraded situation of our country, and the necessity of a *blow* by which its energy and its dignity should be restored; said if that blow could be struck here at this time, he was confident of the support of the best blood of America. I told Colonel Burr he deceived himself in presuming that he, or any other man, could excite a party in this country who would countenance him in such a plot of desperation, murder, and treason. He replied that he, perhaps, knew

give the order, and that Burr was compelled to reject the services of more than half the applicants, and that twelve thousand, were it desirable, could be obtained as easily as four thousand; those who were accepted would appear suddenly in arms, at a moment's notice. Such was the tenor of the rumors which reached the executive of the Mississippi Territory about the last of November. Nor were these idle rumors, for there were portents and visible indications of some unusual movement from the regions upon the Ohio. About this time, it appeared that the thousands of adherents of which Burr boasted, instead of imbodying on the Ohio, in readiness to follow their chief at the word of command, had been sent before him singly, as emigrants, traders, and private adventurers, and they were dispersed into every town and settlement, unobserved and unsuspected, patiently awaiting the arrival of their leader and his chosen band of three hundred men.

Yet, from some cause, Burr did not leave the Cumberland River until the 22d of December, at which time the president's proclamation, bearing date of November 27th, had preceded him to the Lower Mississippi. In this proclamation the president warned all good citizens against the unlawful enterprise which was contemplated by certain citizens of the United States against the dominions of the King of Spain, and " com-

better the dispositions of the influential citizens of this country than I did. I told him one solitary word would destroy him. He asked, what word? I answered, *Usurper!* He smiled at my hesitation, and quoted some great examples in his favor.

"Satisfied that Mr. Burr was resolute in pushing his project of rebellion in the west of the Alleghany, and apprehensive that it was too well and too extensively organized to be easily suppressed, though I dreaded the weight of his character when laid in the balance against my solitary assertion, I brought myself to the resolution to endeavor to defeat it by getting him removed from among us, or to expose myself to all consequences by a disclosure of his intentions. Accordingly, I waited on the President of the United States; and after some desultory conversation, in which I aimed to draw his view to the westward, I used the freedom to say to the president I thought Mr. Burr should be sent out of this country, and gave for reason that I believed him dangerous in it. The president asked where he should be sent. I mentioned London and Cadiz. The president thought the trust too important, and seemed to entertain a doubt of Mr. Burr's integrity. I intimated that no one, perhaps, had stronger grounds to mistrust Mr. Burr's moral integrity than myself, yet I believed ambition so much predominated over him, that, when placed on an eminence and put on his honor, respect to himself would insure his fidelity. His talents were unquestionable. I perceived the subject was disagreeable to the president, and, to give it the shortest course to the point, declared my concern that if *Mr. Burr were not in some way disposed of, we should, within eight months, have an insurrection, if not a revolution, on the waters of the Mississippi.* The president answered, *that he had too much confidence in the information, the integrity, and the attachment to the Union* of the citizens of that country to admit an *apprehension* of that kind."

manded all civil and military officers of every grade and department to be active and vigilant in searching out and bringing to condign punishment all persons engaged or concerned in such enterprise, by all the lawful means within their power."*

The whole military force of the United States on the Lower Mississippi had already been distributed for the protection of New Orleans. General Wilkinson, having received early intimations, while at Natchitoches, of the designs and plans of Burr, through the confidential emissaries sent to solicit his co-operation, at once determined to take measures to defeat the whole enterprise. ·Hence, intimating to the Spanish general the contemplated enterprise against Mexico, he was readily induced to enter into an armistice and agreement to withdraw his troops to Nacogdoches, upon condition that General Wilkinson should exert his whole official influence and authority, as com-

---

* The following is a copy of the president's proclamation, viz.:

Whereas information has been received that sundry persons, citizens of the United States, or residents within the same, are conspiring and confederating together to begin and set on foot, provide and prepare the means for a military expedition or enterprise against the dominions of Spain; that for this purpose they are fitting out and arming vessels in the western waters of the United States, collecting provisions, arms, military stores, and other means; are deceiving and seducing honest and well-meaning citizens, under various pretenses, to engage in their criminal enterprises; are organizing, officering, and arming themselves, contrary to the laws in such case made and provided: I have therefore thought fit to issue this my *proclamation*, warning and enjoining all faithful citizens who have been led, without knowledge or consideration, to participate in the said unlawful enterprises, to withdraw from the same without delay; and commanding all persons whatsoever, engaged or concerned in the same, to cease all further proceedings therein, as they will answer the contrary at their peril, and incur prosecution with all the rigors of the law. And I hereby enjoin and require all officers, civil and military, of the United States, or of any of the states or territories, and especially all governors and other executive authorities, all judges, justices, and other officers of the peace, all military officers of the army or navy of the United States, and officers of the militia, to be vigilant, each within his respective department, and according to his functions, in searching out and bringing to condign punishment all persons engaged or concerned in such enterprise, in seizing and detaining, subject to the dispositions of the law, all vessels, arms, military stores or other means provided or providing for the same, and in general in preventing the carrying on such expedition or enterprise by all lawful means within their power; and I require all good and faithful citizens, and others within the United States, to be aiding and assisting herein, and especially in the discovery, apprehension, and bringing to justice of all such offenders, in preventing the execution of their unlawful designs, and in giving information against them to the proper authorities.

In testimony whereof, I have caused the seal of the United States to be affixed to these presents, and have signed the same with my hand. Given at the city
[L. S.] of Washington, on the 27th day of November, 1806, and in the year of the sovereignty and independence of the United States the thirty-first.
    (Signed)   THOMAS JEFFERSON.
        By the president,
    (Signed)   JAMES MADISON, Secretary of State.

mander-in-chief, to suppress and defeat the operations of Burr and his adherents.

On the 23d of December, Cowles Mead, acting governor of the Mississippi Territory, issued his proclamation against the contemplated unlawful enterprise, and requiring all officers, civil and military, in the territory to be vigilant and active in their efforts to suppress the treasonable movements, and to bring all offenders to justice. The Governor of Louisiana had issued his proclamation to the same effect on the 16th of December.

On the 25th Governor Mead issued his orders as commander-in-chief of the militia, ordering the four regiments of the western counties to assemble for parade and organization in their respective counties between the 10th and 20th of January.

[A.D. 1807.] In the mean time, the whole country was in a state of great excitement and apprehension on account of the danger which seemed to threaten the settlements with the horrors of anarchy and civil war. This apprehension was further increased by the continual arrival of strangers and emigrants at this unusual period, and who, apparently, were unconcerned at the dangers which threatened.

At the same time, there were some who affected to deride and pity the timidity of those who magnified trivial incidents into portents of treason and civil war. Such persons seemed anxious to quiet public apprehension by denouncing the unnecessary steps of precaution taken by the commander-in-chief, and by the executive departments of the two territories. Bollman and Swartwout had already been arrested in New Orleans by General Wilkinson, and were in the custody of the law, the general having sent them under a military guard to the proper authorities of the United States near the Federal government.

On the 10th of January an express from Washington city arrived at Natchez with dispatches for the executive of the territory; after a short delay, he proceeded by way of Fort Adams to New Orleans, with dispatches for Governor Claiborne.

These dispatches contained important information relative to the designs of Colonel Burr and his contemplated movements on the Mississippi River. Accordingly, on the 12th, the governor ordered a guard of sixty men to be stationed on the bank of the river, with instructions to board and examine every boat descending. The same day, Governor Mead, in view of the impending danger, prorogued the General Assembly until the 19th, for the purpose of taking active measures for averting the approaching storm, " which presaged an explosion dangerous to domestic safety, and insulting to national dignity."

On the 14th of January, intelligence was received at Natchez that Colonel Burr, with about sixty men, had arrived at the mouth of the Bayou Pierre, when the acting governor immediately issued his orders for imbodying the militia. In twenty-four hours, two hundred and seventy-five men, under Colonel Ferdinand L. Claiborne, were ready for marching orders. The same evening, under a most inclement sky, they embarked in boats, and commenced their voyage to the mouth of Cole's Creek, twenty-five miles above Natchez. At this point they were joined by a troop of cavalry from Jefferson county; and the acting governor dispatched his two aids, Majors Shields and Poindexter, immediately to Burr's encampment, near the Bayou Pierre, with a message, notifying him of the formidable military movements against him, and inviting him to surrender himself and his adherents into the hands of the civil authorities. An armistice was arranged at Burr's camp, by which Colonel Burr agreed to meet Governor Mead next day at the house of Thomas Calvit, near Colonel Claiborne's encampment, attended by his friend Colonel Fitzpatrick, of Jefferson county. Next day, Colonel Burr, accordingly, descended the river to the mouth of Cole's Creek, and having spent an hour in the camp at that place, proceeded, escorted by several officers of the Jefferson troop, to the appointed interview with the acting governor. Having entered into a capitulation for the surrender of himself, thirteen boats, and sixty men, at discretion, he proceeded, a prisoner, in company with the governor, to Washington.

A detachment of cavalry from the Jefferson troop the same day proceeded to the mouth of the Bayou Pierre, to receive the prisoners, and to take charge of the boats containing his stores and military supplies, which were conducted to Natchez.[*]

It was affirmed by some, that, previous to the departure of Burr from the Bayou Pierre, he had given orders for the concealment of a large portion of military stores, and some cannon which were contained in boats near the mouth of Bruin's Bayou, on the west side of the river.

[*] Mississippi Messenger, January 14th, 1807.

Colonel Burr appeared before Judge Rodney, of the Superior Court, and, having entered into recognizance with his sureties, Lyman Harding, Esq., and Colonel Benajah Osmun, in the sum of ten thousand dollars for his appearance at the called session of that court, to be holden on the 3d of February, was discharged from custody.* His men, to the number of sixty, were liberated upon parole in Natchez.

About this time, Herman Blannerhasset and Comfort Tyler, two prominent adherents of Burr, arrived at Natchez, and commenced their residence in the Mississippi Territory, some weeks after the arrival of Mrs. Blannerhasset.

In the mean time, many persons evinced a strong disapprobation to the course pursued by the executive authorities in their efforts to frustrate the plans which Burr and his adherents may have contemplated. This feeling of disapprobation, which discovered itself in various ways, sought to shield itself under the pretext of patriotic devotion to the untrammeled liberties guarantied by the Constitution and laws of the United States. In New Orleans, it had manifested itself through the grand jury on the 24th of January, in a presentment of General Wilkinson for the arrest of certain emissaries of Burr. The same disapprobation had displayed itself early in January, through James Workman, judge of the court of the county of Orleans, in a writ of *habeas corpus* for the release of Peter V. Ogden from the custody of the commander-in-chief; and subsequently, by his resolution to issue a writ of attachment from the same court against the person of the general for an alleged contempt of court.†

About this time, the patriotic citizens of Wilkinson county, in an address, signed by ninety-six of the principal inhabitants, to the acting governor, assured him of their devotion to the cause of their country, and their readiness to sustain him in his efforts for the prompt suppression of any treasonable conspiracy against the government of the United States. They declared themselves firmly resolved; "and, being zealously attached to the government of the United States of America, they deemed it their indispensable duty to support, protect, and defend the Constitution thereof, at the risk of their lives and prop-

---

* Mississippi Messenger, January 27th, 1807.
† See chapter xv., "Territory of Orleans," &c. Also, the Mississippi Messenger, January 14th, 1807. Also, Idem, January 21st, 1807.

erty." They declared that "this government is now our own; we may exchange it for a worse, but a better, as relates to the people in general, we can not expect; the designing only wish for a change." They expressed their warmest gratitude to Governor Mead and Colonel Claiborne for the zeal and energy with which they had suppressed the insidious designs of ambitious men.*

In the mean time, Burr remained in the settlements, and received every attention and respect which is usually shown to men of talent and distinction; nor did he fail to exert his influence, by impressing his acquaintances with his patriotic devotion, and the futility of the charges which had been made against his fidelity to the Union.†

On Monday, the 3d of February, the extra session of the Superior Court was held in the town of Washington; and Colonel Burr, attended by his counsel, William B. Shields and Lyman Harding, Esquires, appeared upon his recognizance. "The grand jury having been duly impanneled, Judge Rodney delivered an impressive and comprehensive charge, and the court adjourned until next day, when the case was taken up. The attorney-general, George Poindexter, moved the court to discharge the grand jury.‡ He stated that, after examining the depositions submitted to him by the court, he did not discover any testimony which brought the offenses charged against Colonel Burr within the jurisdiction of the courts of the Mississippi Territory; that the Supreme Court of the Mississippi Territory was not a court of original jurisdiction, either criminal or civil, and could take cognizance only of points reserved at the trial in the respective Circuit Courts, where all criminal prosecutions must originate, according to the statutes of the territory. He further observed, that, in order to secure

* Mississippi Messenger, January 27th, 1807.

† The "Natchez Herald" May 6th, 1807, in commenting upon Burr's trial at the town of Washington, asserts that "Burr and his men were *caressed* by a number of the wealthy merchants and planters of Adams county; several balls were given to them as marks of respect and confidence; none of his men were confined until after his trial before the Superior Court;" that "the proceedings against the accused were more like a 'mock trial' than a criminal prosecution; that, during the trial, Judge Bruin appeared more like his advocate than his impartial judge. as he ought to have been;" and that "both before and on the day of trial he advocated his cause as a laudable and just one."

‡ The grand jury consisted of Philander Smith, *foreman*, Lewis Evans, Ebenezer Rees, James Spain, James Andrews, John Brooks, Looe Baker, George Overaker, H. Turner, John Rabb, Nathaniel Hoggatt, E. Newman, James Dunbar, and John Wood.
—*Mississippi Messenger*, February 10th, 1807.

the public safety, the territorial judges ought immediately to convey the accused to a tribunal competent to try and punish him, if guilty of the charges alleged against him; which they might legally do, and thereby effectually prevent the contemplated military expedition against Mexico, and maintain inviolate the laws and Constitution of the United States. He therefore hoped that, inasmuch as the attorney prosecuting for the United States had no bills for the consideration of the grand jury, it would be discharged."

Colonel Burr made several observations against the motion, and remarked that if the *attorney-general* had no business for the grand jury, *he had*, and that, therefore, it ought not to be dismissed. On this motion the court was divided. Judge Bruin declared himself opposed to discharging the grand jury, unless Colonel Burr was also instantly discharged from his recognizance.

"The attorney-general then withdrew, and the grand jury were directed to retire to their room." The next day the grand jury appeared in court, with several presentments of a negative character, which were not founded on any bill exhibited to them. After an appropriate reproof from the court for the "particularly improper interference" of the grand jury at that time, it was discharged the same evening, and no other notice was taken of their presentments.*

Colonel Burr demanded a release from his recognizance, which the court promptly refused. On the opening of court next morning, Thursday the 6th, Colonel Burr did not make his appearance, and it was soon ascertained that he had made his escape.

The same evening, Governor Williams, who had returned from North Carolina, issued his proclamation, offering a reward of two thousand dollars for the apprehension and delivery of Aaron Burr, either to him in Washington, or to the Federal authorities of the United States. A troop of cavalry was dispatched to Claiborne county in search of the fugitive; yet no intelligence from Burr was received in Washington until near the last of February, when the governor was informed by Cap-

---

* See Mississippi Messenger, February 10th, 1807. The substance of these presentments were equivalent to a censure upon the action of the governor and militia in arresting Burr; asserting that it was "their opinion that Aaron Burr *has not been guilty* of any crime or misdemeanor against the laws of the United States or of this territory."

tain E. P. Gaines, commanding at Fort Stoddart, that Colonel Burr had been arrested near that post, and was then a prisoner in his custody.* He had been making his way down the Tombigby, traveling by night, in order to reach Pensacola and obtain the protection of a British vessel in the harbor. Governor Williams was strongly suspected of conniving at Burr's escape; and he was not the only one who entertained for the prisoner a sympathy which facilitated his escape.

Colonel Burr was sent under a military guard by sea to Charleston, and from thence to Richmond by land, in charge of Major Perkins, by whom he had been arrested. He arrived at Richmond on the 30th of March, 1807, and was delivered over to the civil authorities to await his trial.

General Wilkinson, having succeeded in arresting the whole plan of the conspiracy, was assailed by Burr and his satellites as implicated in the conspiracy itself. Although Wilkinson was actively instrumental in frustrating the whole conspiracy, it is evident that for years before he did entertain the idea of invading the Mexican provinces with the army of the United States; but there is no evidence of any design on his part to turn his arms against his country, or to invade Mexico without authority.

Meantime, the excitement in the West, connected with Burr's movements on the Mississippi, brought hundreds, if not thousands, of enterprising emigrants to the Mississippi Territory, greatly increasing its population, and augmenting the talent and moral worth in the country.

Cotton Staple.—Agriculture within the territory had just emerged from that state of depression which existed at the time when the American jurisdiction was established over the country. Indigo had been a principal staple of export up to the year 1807, when the invention of the saw cotton-gin, by Whitney, was introduced, and imparted an impulse to the cultivation of cotton which produced a corresponding decline in the indigo crop. Cotton now became the engrossing staple of the

* Colonel Burr was arrested under the following circumstances, viz.: In company with Major Ashley, a man of bad character, he designed to reach the residence of Colonel Caller, who was known to be inimical to the Spaniards of Florida, and who had been anxious for their expulsion from Mobile. Not being able to reach Colonel Caller's, on account of high waters, he took the road down the Tombigby, toward Fort Stoddart. It was on his way that he was met by Major Perkins, with a file of men from Fort Stoddart, who had been apprised of his approach.

fine agricultural settlements; and the comparatively easy and speedy mode of divesting the lint from the seed gave a presage of future wealth and prosperity to the country.

Yet cotton-gins were few; and, like mills in a new country, one public cotton-gin performed the work of ginning the crops for a whole neighborhood. The large estates, which produced from one to two hundred bales of cotton, could afford to keep a gin for their own use; but the cotton crop of the territory was produced chiefly by small planters, whose entire crops seldom exceeded twenty-five or thirty bales. Such were compelled to carry their crops to the public gins and wait their turn, in the order of their application, for their ginned crops. The toll paid for ginning and pressing was one tenth of the nett cotton, besides an extra charge for bagging and rope.

To regulate this new species of trade, it became necessary to enact laws applicable to the changes thus introduced. Planters might be seriously injured in the price and sale of their crops by delays and disappointments at the gin, and by postponing their crops out of their order. Hence the time for delivering a crop ready baled to the owner was limited by law to four months from the date of the "cotton receipt" for its delivery at the gin. A longer delay rendered the gin-holder liable for any damage which might accrue to the owner from such cause; and the owner might claim *twenty per cent.* damage for *any delay* after legal notice and demand of his cotton. The "cotton receipt," as early as March, 1806, was "made negotiable" by law, and vested in the holder all the rights and privileges pertaining to the original owner. Thus, "cotton receipts" became domestic bills of exchange; and the staple of the country, stored in the public gins, supplied a circulating medium to the people. This was the first attempt, and a laudable one it was, to convert the staple of the country into exchange and domestic currency, untainted by the lust of speculation under chartered privileges.*

As has been before observed, the statutes of the territory, revised and condensed by Judge Toulmin, were adopted by the Legislature on the 10th of February, 1807, when two hundred copies were ordered to be published. The edition was completed during the summer by Timothy Terrell, "territorial printer," and was known as "Toulmin's Digest." This code

* See Toulmin's Digest, p. 232–235.

comprised not only a digest of the laws then in force, but it presented them arranged and digested into a regular system of "judicial proceedings," in the *first* part of which were comprised the "laws establishing courts of justice, defining the duties of their officers, and regulating judicial proceedings, chiefly in civil cases;" in the *second* part were comprised "laws relating to crimes, misdemeanors, and the public police;" besides a general "militia law." This is the oldest digest of Mississippi laws, and formed the basis of the present system of jurisprudence in the State of Mississippi.*

Tombigby Settlements.—About the close of the year 1806, a settlement had been commenced on the north side of the Tennessee River, in the vicinity of the present town of Huntsville. About the same time, another was commenced on the Lower Tombigby, near the present site of St. Stephen's, on the route leading from Georgia, through the Creek country, to New Orleans.

In the summer following, agreeably to an act of the Legislature, approved February 4th, 1807, Harry Toulmin, James Caller, and Leonard Henry had completed the duty assigned them as "commissioners to view, mark, and open a good road on the nearest route from the city of Natchez to Fort Stoddart, so as to intersect the new Creek road on the line of demarkation east of Pearl River."† This was the first road from Natchez to St. Stephen's.

At the same session of the Legislature, by an act approved January 8th, John Baker, James Morgan, and John F. M'Grew, as commissioners, were authorized to lay off a town on the lands of Edwin Lewis, near Fort St. Stephen, reserving for the public use the lands near the fort, where a land-office was subsequently established. On the 7th of December following, public notice was given that "the ferry is now complete over the Alabama River, above Little River, and on the Tombigby, just above Fort St. Stephen. The way is now completely opened and marked with causeways across all boggy guts and branches, so that strangers can travel the road with safety, by observing the three notches, or three-chopped way, which cuts off a great distance in traveling from Natchez to Georgia."‡ This was the first road opened from the western to the eastern part of the territory.

---

* See Toulmin's Digest, edition of 1807, printed by Samuel Terrell, territorial printer.
† Toulmin's Digest, p. 397, 398.   ‡ Mississippi Messenger, Jan. and Feb., 1808.

The settlements on the Tombigby and Mobile Rivers labored under many privations and disadvantages. They were an advanced guard into the Indian Territory, remote and isolated, cut off from every other American community, surrounded on all sides by the most powerful tribes of Indians then existing within the original limits of the United States, and occupying but a limited district, which had been relinquished by the native tribes. They were not only cut off from intercourse with their fellow-citizens in other parts of the territory by an Indian wilderness, but were subjected to heavy exactions in the shape of transit duties to a foreign government on their commercial intercourse with the nearest ports of the United States. Yet their patriotism was unshaken, and, although chiefly composed of the remaining colonists of English Florida, who had been successively the subjects of the English and Spanish monarchies, they were true Americans in principle and feeling. And when the outrage perpetrated by the British frigate "Leopard" upon the American ship Chesapeake had produced a general burst of popular indignation from Maine to Louisiana, in no portion of the Union was the patriotic response more hearty and indignant than from the people of Washington county. At a public meeting held at Wakefield, the county seat, on the 8th day of September, 1807, resolutions were unanimously adopted expressive of their indignation at the "outrage which has been committed on our national rights by the arrogant representatives of British despotism."

The preamble declares, "That if England counts upon our divisions, she is mistaken: her violence has united America. Our settlements originally consisted, and still, in a great measure, consist of those who adhered to England in the Revolutionary war. They were led by principle: the elders taught them that resistance was sinful; and they imbibed from their infancy a deep veneration for their king; but the delusion lasts no longer. We have since seen that king engaged in almost incessant wars against the liberty and happiness of man; while the government which has succeeded his in America has preserved us in peace with all the world, and has been pre-eminently occupied in promoting our national prosperity. Old factions are forgotten; old Whigs and old Tories will cordially unite in devoting their lives and fortunes to avenge the wounded dignity of America against the insults and oppression of any government on earth." Such was the tenor of the sentiments of Washington county, expressed at Wakefield, and certified by James Caller, chairman, and T. Malone, secretary.*

At the same meeting they declared, " We have suffered multiplied injuries, inflicted upon us in a regular system, by the agents of the Spanish government. We have been the objects of oppression from the officers of his Catholic majesty for a series of years. The produce of our lands, before it could reach a market even in our own territories, has been subjected to a duty of *twelve and a half per cent. ad valorem* to a foreign monarch; we have been constantly the sport of vexatious searches and arbitrary seizures; we have been compelled to pay twelve and a half per cent. to the King of Spain on every thing which we have imported even from the next town within the American limits. Through the joint operation of the revenue systems of Spain and the United States, we have frequently been obliged to pay from forty-two to forty-seven per cent. ad valorem, on the price when first imported into the United States, of such articles as are most essential to family comfort."

" But we will discard all personal jealousies; we shall cease to regard our local grievances, until those of the nation are redressed; we will give the Spaniard his twelve and a half per cent.; we will continue to pay double price for the commodities of Europe; we will continue to pay, if need be, sixteen dollars a barrel for Kentucky flour, while our neighbors at Natchez, unencumbered by Spanish obstacles, are paying four dollars for the same article."†

The multiplied difficulties operating against the settlements of Washington were duly represented to the American Congress in a memorial from the General Assembly in December following, in which the interference of the Federal government was invoked in their behalf.

[A.D. 1808.] *Williams's Administration.*—In the mean time, the executive department of the territorial government continued under the administration of Governor Williams, who had, in a great measure, within the last two years, lost the confidence, if not the respect, of a large and influential party in the old and populous settlements of the territory. In all the counties from the Yazoo, west of the "old Choctâ boundary,"

* Mississippi Messenger, November 5th, 1807. † Idem.

he was decidedly unpopular, and a majority of the people impatiently awaited the close of his official career.*

The 4th of March was expected to close the administration as well as the political career of Robert Williams. Although received with due respect and cordiality upon entering upon the duties of his office in 1805, he had soon rendered himself odious to his political opponents, and scarcely respected by his friends. Destitute of refined sensibility and generous feeling, and governed in his official intercourse by a narrow and selfish policy, he knew not how to conciliate his enemies, or to secure the attachment and esteem of his friends. With strong prejudices and an uncultivated mind, his disregard of the courtesy due from a statesman, and his arbitrary disposition, created difficulties innumerable to his administration, while his inconsistency raised up enemies among his friends.

[A.D. 1809.] Meantime, settlements had advanced from Tennessee into the country north of the "Great Bend" of Tennessee River, in the vicinity of the present town of Huntsville, upon lands in the Chickasâ cession by treaty of July 23d, 1805. These settlements, during the past year, had been organized into the "County of Madison" by the territorial Legislature. This county received its population almost entirely from Tennessee, and was separated from others of the territory by a wilderness of three hundred miles in extent, in the entire occupation of the savages.

The first joint-stock bank in the territory was chartered on the 23d of December, 1809. The capital stock was five thousand shares of one hundred dollars each, making an aggregate of five hundred thousand dollars, when speculation was in its infancy in Mississippi. The books were opened subsequently in Natchez, under the superintendence of thirteen commissioners, among whom were the prominent men in the territory. They were Francis X. Martin, Ferdinand L. Claiborne, John Steele, Abner Green, Abijah Hunt, Samuel Postlethwaite, Ebenezer Reese, Cowles Mead, Joseph Sessions, William B. Shields, Winthrop Sargent, Alexander Montgomery, and Lyman Harding. The style of the company was, "The President, Directors, and Company of the Bank of Mississippi;" and its privileges were to remain inviolate twenty-five years, or until the year 1834. But this bank was established upon cor-

* Mississippi Messenger, November 27th, 1807.

rect principles, making the *directors* liable in their individual capacity for *any emission of notes or bills* over three times the amount of their capital stock during their administration ; those who might be absent during such emission, and were free from any connection in the transaction, were entitled to exemption by a timely disclosure of the facts. No bill or note was negotiable at said bank unless expressly so written on its face.*

But chartered associations are insatiable. No sooner had the state Constitution been adopted, and the new state government formally organized, than the company, desirous of monopolizing the whole banking privileges of the state, procured from the Legislature an act, approved February 4th, 1818, increasing the capital stock, making the state a stockholder, and extending the monopoly until the year 1840, with authority to establish branches in other parts of the state.† The bank was expressly prohibited from trading or dealing, either directly or indirectly, in any thing except bills of exchange, discounted notes, or "current money," and was subject to a strict supervision by the Legislature. Such was the first bank in the State of Mississippi. The principles embraced in this charter were those to which the state was compelled to recur twenty-five years afterward, when all confidence had been destroyed, and the prosperity of the state had been prostrated by a temporary departure from them in the years 1836 and 1837.

[A.D. 1810.] For the last three years the population of the territory had been gradually increasing in all the older settlements, and new counties had been organized in the district purchased of the Choctâs, north of the line of demarkation, with sparse settlements extending from the eastern limits of Franklin and Amité counties eastward to the Tombigby. The entire population in the white settlements, by the census of 1810, was 40,352 souls.‡ Of these, Washington county contained about six thousand, of whom a large portion were recent emigrants from Tennessee and Georgia. The Tombigby settle-

---

* See Poindexter's Code, p. 467, section 7.

† See Poindexter's Code, p. 468, 469. The branches were soon afterward established: one at *Port Gibson,* where books were opened by Israel Loring, Daniel Vertner, and Benjamin Smith; another at *Woodville,* where books were opened by Richard Butler, Edward Randolph, Charles Stewart, and Moses Liddell. A branch was also established at *Pearlington,* on Pearl River.

‡ Darby's Louisiana, p. 289, and United States Census.

ments had extended on both sides of the river as far up as Mount Sterling, more than sixty miles above Fort St. Stephen. Instead of the few pastoral French and Spaniards of former years, an active agricultural population was springing up, impressed with the enterprise and indomitable perseverance of the Anglo-Saxon race.

Near the close of the year 1810, the territory was thrown into some excitement by the revolution in the western parishes of West Florida, near the Mississippi, and within the government of Baton Rouge. The dissatisfaction of the people under the Spanish authority had been gradually ripening into revolt, which, on the 7th of December, terminated in a formal renouncement of the Spanish authority. Under instructions from the Federal government, Governor Holmes ordered out a detachment of militia from Adams and Wilkinson counties, together with some volunteer companies, which were marched under Colonel Claiborne, to take possession of the country in the name of the United States. The American flag was hoisted at St. Francisville; the Spanish authorities retired, and the district was subsequently annexed to the Territory of Orleans.*

[A.D. 1812.] Thus the Spanish influence and intrigue, aided by British agents and emissaries from Mobile and Pensacola, was restricted from active operation upon the banks of the Mississippi; but the Spaniards, restrained in this quarter, began to operate more actively in the eastern portion of the territory, by instigating the savages to commence hostilities against the American settlements. Thus, in the war which had commenced between Great Britain and the United States, the Spaniards of Florida became the secret allies of the former, and promoted the views of the English cabinet in arraying the powerful tribes of Florida against the unprotected inhabitants of the United States.

The president, apprehensive of a descent by the British fleet on some portion of the coast of Louisiana or of the Mississippi Territory, caused troops to be concentrated at suitable points to repel such invasion. Besides the regular army under his immediate command, General Wilkinson was authorized to call upon the governors of Louisiana and the Mississippi Territory

---

* Martin's Louisiana, vol. ii., p. 299. Also, chapter xv. of this book, viz., "Territory of Orleans," &c.

for quotas of militia and volunteers in any case of emergency, to re-enforce his command.

On the 16th of July, Governor Holmes, in consequence of a requisition from General Wilkinson, issued his general orders for a draft of the militia, requiring the quotas from each regiment to hold themselves in readiness to rendezvous under their respective officers at Baton Rouge on or before the 1st of October, to be organized into a brigade under the command of Brigadier-general Claiborne, heretofore colonel of the first regiment.

The patriotism of the Mississippi Territory has always been exalted and pure; they have ever been ready and willing to face danger and encounter privations in defense of their common country, whether against British aggression or the murderous warfare of the savages. The call of the governor was cheerfully obeyed; the complement required was supplied chiefly by voluntary enrolment, without recourse to a draft. On the 18th of August, 1812, General Claiborne reports to the governor the alacrity with which the citizens enrolled themselves for service. "With infinite satisfaction," he writes, "I have the honor to report to you that the lieutenant-colonels commandant of the first, second, third, fourth, fifth, tenth, eleventh, and thirteenth regiments have in readiness, to march at the shortest notice, the number required from their respective regiments, under your order of the 16th ultimo; and I am persuaded it will be particularly gratifying to your excellency to be informed that the requisition has been filled principally by voluntary enrolment. The counties of Wilkinson, Jefferson, Claiborne, Warren, and Marion had no occasion to resort to a draft. Amité and Franklin drafted but a few privates. Adams was completed by a draft principally. All await your orders with solicitude; and from the thorough knowledge of the patriotism of the brigade, I am confident that they will march, when ordered, with great promptitude, and in all situations will discharge their duty with fidelity and zeal."*

Such was the spirit and patriotism which animated the first brigade of Mississippi militia called into the service of the United States during the last war with Great Britain.

[A.D. 1813.] *Tennessee Volunteers.*—To aid in the defense of the southern frontier against apprehended invasion, Major-gen-

* Claiborne MS. Papers.

eral Jackson, of Tennessee, had imbodied a force of two thousand and seventy volunteers at Nashville, consisting of fourteen hundred infantry and riflemen, and six hundred and seventy mounted riflemen.* On the 7th of January, 1813, he broke up his camp at Nashville; the mounted infantry took up the line of march through the Indian country to Natchez, during inclement weather, and over roads almost impassable. The infantry embarked in thirteen boats, and set off in the midst of a severe winter on their perilous voyage down the Cumberland, Ohio, and Mississippi Rivers, more than fifteen hundred miles. After a tedious and hazardous voyage of five weeks, they arrived at Natchez on the 15th of February, and encamped on the west side of Washington.† Here they were joined by the mounted troops, which had arrived a few days before.

But, instead of encountering the enemies of their country, they were destined to great disappointment and embarrassment, through the imbecility of the Secretary of War, and the indecision of President Madison. Shortly after the arrival of this patriotic army under their chivalrous commander, an order was received from John Armstrong, Secretary of War, requiring General Jackson to discharge his men from service, under the alleged pretext that the imminent danger of invasion had vanished from Louisiana. This order of the imbecile, if not traitorous, secretary, issued before General Jackson's departure from Nashville, required him "to deliver all the public stores and property in his possession into the hands of General Wilkinson, commander of the seventh district."‡

To obey the order under present circumstances would inflict great injustice upon the brave men who had placed themselves under his command, and were now more than five hundred miles from their abodes, wholly dependent upon the government for sustenance and means of returning through a savage wilderness. Many of them were sick, and about two hundred were upon the invalid roll. Few or none of them were able, from their own resources, to reach their homes; and to have discharged them here, remote from their friends, and destitute,

---

* The general staff was composed of Andrew Jackson, *major-general;* William B. Lewis, *assistant deputy quartermaster;* William Carroll, *brigade inspector;* James Henderson, *brigade quartermaster;* Colonel Thomas H. Benton, *first aid;* John Reid, *second aid.* A regiment of cavalry was commanded by Colonel John Coffee. See Kendall's Life of Jackson, p. 134–138. † Kendall's Life of Jackson, p. 138, 139.

‡ Waldo's Life of Jackson, p. 55. Eaton, p. 19, 20.

would have been to reward their patriotic devotion with the grossest injustice.

Under these circumstances, General Jackson assumed the responsibility of disobeying the unreasonable order; he determined to retain his men in the service until they reached their homes in Tennessee.*

General Wilkinson, of the regular army, conceiving it a fine opportunity of recruiting his command by the enlistment of the discharged volunteers, endeavored to dissuade General Jackson from his purpose, and reminded him of the great responsibility which would rest upon him in carrying out his determination; but the "commander of the Tennessee volunteers," nothing daunted, persisted in his determination to do justice to his troops, relying upon the purity of his motives as his justification with the Federal government.

At length, having been greatly harassed by the interference and machinations of General Wilkinson and his recruiting officers, General Jackson issued his orders to the quartermaster and commissary, requiring them to continue in the performance of their duties, under the penalty of military coercion.† The interference on the part of General Wilkinson's officers was discontinued only after General Jackson had threatened to disgrace them by drumming them out of his camp.

The line of march was at length taken up for Tennessee through the Choctâ and Chickasâ nations, the commander "refusing to leave behind a single man who had life in him." After a fatiguing march of nearly five hundred miles through the Indian country, they were discharged near their homes, in Tennessee, on the 19th and 22d of May. The government, approving the course of the general, allowed his accounts, and the whole expense was paid out of the public treasury.‡ Such is the brief history of the first expedition of the "Tennessee volunteers" to the Mississippi Territory.

Occupation of Mobile District.—In the mean time, the attention of the Federal government was seriously directed to that portion of the original province of Louisiana which was still in possession of the Spaniards between the Pascagoula and the Perdido Rivers, including the bay and port of Mobile. Although the western extremity of West Florida, from the Mis-

---

* Kendall, p. 144–146. † Eaton's Life, p. 23.
‡ Waldo's Life of Jackson, p. 58. See, also, Kendall's Life of Jackson, p. 150–152.

sissippi eastward to Pascagoula, had been occupied in 1810, and was subsequently annexed to the State of Louisiana, no attempt had been made forcibly to occupy the country included in the district and government of Mobile. This region was still in the occupancy of the Spanish commandant of Fort Charlotte.

Since the beginning of the war with Great Britain, there had been repeated evidence of the danger of permitting a part of the United States to be occupied by a power which was unable to maintain its neutrality against an enemy which was then waging a war of extermination against the American people. In view of this danger, Congress, by an act approved February 12th, had authorized its occupancy by the troops of the United States, and General Wilkinson was instructed by the president to take forcible possession of Fort Charlotte, and the district eastward to the Perdido. Accordingly, having completed his preparations, the general, at the head of a strong land and naval force, took possession of the fort and district on the 13th of April, 1813.*

The fort was left in command of Colonel Constant, with a suitable garrison, when the general proceeded to erect a strong fortification at Mobile Point, to prevent the entrance of vessels of war into the bay. This fortification was left in command of Lieutenant John Bowyer, and, in honor of him, it was subsequently called "Fort Bowyer." The works had not been completed in September following.

By an act of Congress, approved May 12th, the Mobile District, dependent upon Fort Charlotte, was annexed to the Mississippi Territory.†

For months afterward, the Spaniards, in their interviews with the hostile Creeks, asserted that Mobile had been basely surrendered by a cowardly commandant, and that his Catholic majesty's troops expected orders for its recapture, when they should expect the aid of the Creek warriors.

The occupation of all Florida had been an event ardently desired by the great mass of the southwestern people, and by the officers of the United States army. As early as January, 1813, General Jackson, in a communication to the Secretary of War, observes, "If the government orders, I will rejoice at

---

* See book i., chap. v., of this work.
† Land Laws of the United States, p. 612, edition of 1827.

the opportunity of placing the American eagle on the ramparts of Mobile, Pensacola, and St. Augustine, effectually banishing from the southern coast all British influence." In June, General Wilkinson's instructions from the war department directed him that, "if the Spaniards should attempt to dislodge him from Mobile or the Perdido, it will be an act of hostility, and, as such, will warrant you, not only in repelling it on the spot, but *in pursuing and punishing the perpetrators* of it wherever they may be found. The same law will govern in case of Indian invasion." This was, in substance, the course pursued by General Jackson eighteen months afterward.

Although the British fleet had been hovering near the Florida coast occasionally for several months, they made no decided effort to invade the territory of the United States. They were not yet ready for this measure, but rather desired to await the result of their intrigues with the powerful tribes of Indians in the interior of Florida and the Mississippi Territory, and to furnish them, through their agents and emissaries from Pensacola and St. Mark's, with supplies of arms and ammunition.

CHAPTER XIV.

THE "MISSISSIPPI TERRITORY," FROM THE BEGINNING OF THE CREEK WAR UNTIL THE ADMISSION OF THE STATES OF "MISSISSIPPI" AND "ALABAMA" INTO THE FEDERAL UNION.—A.D. 1813 TO 1819.

Argument.—British Policy of instigating savage Warfare.—Population and Settlements in 1813.—Origin of Creek Hostilities.—Prosperous Condition of the Creeks in 1812.—British Instigation from Canada.—Tecumseh stirs up a war Party in the Creek Nation. —Tombigby Settlements menaced by hostile Creeks.—Deluded Security of Colonel Hawkins and General Flournoy.—General Claiborne advances to the Tombigby.—Judge Toulmin's Opinion of the true State of the Indian Affairs.—Disposition of Troops under General Claiborne.—Condition of Affairs on the Alabama in August.—General Claiborne's Letter.—Major Beasly admonished of Danger.—Attack and Massacre of Mims's Fort.—Number of Whites slain.—Loss of Indians.—Consternation produced by the Disaster.—Wretched Condition of the Inhabitants.—Marauding Bands of Indians ravage the Country.—Employment of the Choctâs urged as indispensably necessary.—General Claiborne secures the Co-operation of the Choctâs under Mushulatubbe and Pushmataha.—Spanish Treachery detected.—British Supplies for Indians sent to Pensacola.—The Army advances to Fort Claiborne.—Advances to the Holy Ground, and defeats Creeks under Weatherford.—The Georgia Troops under General Floyd invade eastern Part of the Creek Nation.—Tennessee Troops invade the northern Part.—General Jackson advances to Fort Strother, on the Coosa.—Battle of Tallushatches.—Battle of Talladega.—Creeks supplied for the War by British Agents.—Battle of Emuckfaw.—Battle of Enotochopco.—Battle of the Horse-shoe, or Tohopeka.—The Power of the Creeks humbled.—Invasion of the Hickory Grounds.—"Fort Jackson" built.—Submission of the hostile Chiefs.—Surrender of Weatherford.—Treaty of Fort Jackson.—Its Conditions and Requirements.—Colonel Nichols in Florida.—General Jackson Commander-in-chief in 7th military District.—British Emissaries among the Florida Indians.—Jackson advances to Mobile.—Defense of Fort Bowyer against British Fleet.—Expels the British Forces from Pensacola.—Tribute of Esteem to General Jackson.—Advance of white Population into the Indian Country.—Settlements north and south of Tennessee River; upon Sources of Tombigby.—Monroe County organized.—Population of Madison County in 1815.—The Creeks instigated by British Emissaries to reject the Treaty of Fort Jackson.—Population of the Territory in 1816.—Application for Authority to form a state Government.—Indian Treaties in 1816.—Territory divided.—"State of Mississippi" admitted into the Union.—Choctâ Cession by Treaty of Doak's Stand.—Ceded Territory organized into Counties.—Permanent state Capital selected.—"City of Jackson."—County of Monroe annexed.—Final Extension of the state Jurisdiction within the entire Limits.—Summary of Indian Treaties within the Mississippi Territory.—Governors of Mississippi.—*Alabama Territory* organized.—State of Alabama admitted into the Union.—Subsequent increase of Population.

[A.D. 1813.] In the war of 1812–1815, Great Britain, not content to lay waste the seaboard of the United States, by burning the cities, towns, and private property of individuals within reach of her fleets and armies, together with the monuments of art and genius, again adopted the disgraceful and inhuman policy of instigating the savages, and supplying them with the means of carrying on a murderous warfare of indiscriminate destruction against the feeble frontier settlements which were remote from the seat of war, and were not, properly, parties in the contest. The Indian barbarities of the Revolutionary war were to be revived against the northern and southern frontiers.

As late as the close of the year 1813, the American settlements within the Mississippi Territory were comprised in three distinct portions of the country, each remote from the other, with extensive Indian territory intervening. The principal population was to be found in the Natchez District, which included the counties of Warren, Claiborne, Jefferson, Adams, Wilkinson, Amité, and Franklin, containing in the aggregate about twenty-two thousand persons. In the eastern portion were the Tombigby settlements, including the annexed portion of Florida near the Mobile Bay. These settlements composed four counties, Washington, Clark, Mobile, and Baldwin, with an aggregate population of about seven thousand persons. West of these were the large counties of Hancock, Marion, Greene, and Wayne, extending to the eastern portion of Amité, and containing a sparse population, in the aggregate not exceeding five thousand persons. The third important settlement was north of the "Great Bend" of Tennessee River, and was comprised in the county of Madison, with a population of about eight thousand persons.

The aggregate white population did not exceed forty thousand, and scarcely forty-two thousand, including slaves. The remainder was occupied wholly by powerful tribes of Indians, known as the Chickasâs, Choctâs, Cherokees, and Creeks. The two latter nations, and especially the last, were numerous and warlike.

Origin of Creek Hostilities.—Although the Creeks, as a nation, for many years after the close of the Revolutionary war, under Spanish influence, had been occasionally hostile to the American people, yet, after the occupancy of Louisiana by the United States, their enmity had been subdued by the conciliatory policy of the Federal government, confirmed by formal treaties of peace and friendship. Missions had also been established in the nation for the purpose of improving their moral condition, opening schools for the education of their children, and teaching the useful arts and employments of civilized life. To encourage these aids to domestic comfort, and to introduce among them useful employments, and gradually wean them from the uncertain support and destitution of savage life, Congress made liberal appropriations toward the introduction of agriculture and manufactures; agencies were established for supplying them by government with all the articles of Indian trade at fair prices, excluding the introduction of whisky, and protecting them from the extortion of designing individuals.

One of the principal agents of the government, Colonel Benjamin Hawkins, on the frontiers of Georgia, who had been zealously engaged for years in the laudable enterprise of introducing the arts and usages of civilized life among them, had succeeded in greatly meliorating their condition. Many towns were large, with buildings and improvements, which indicated a degree of comfort and domestic independence previously unknown among the Indians. Some of the industrious Creeks were wealthy, possessing large plantations, a great variety of domestic stock, and numerous slaves. The leading chiefs were pleased with the improved condition of their people, and gave their full influence to measures which were gradually to place them above the precarious dependence of savage life.

Such was the condition of the Creek nation after the commencement of the war with Great Britain, until the summer of 1813; and such, in all probability, it would have continued, with a progressive improvement, had it not been for the inhuman course of Great Britain, which seeks to accomplish her purposes regardless of the means employed.

Pursuing the barbarous policy which has characterized that government for the last three centuries, agents and emissaries were dispatched to instigate the northern and southern Indians to resume hostilities against the whole southern and western frontier of the United States.

Under the direction of Elliott, a British trader of Canada, and relative of the notorious Elliott, formerly British agent on the Maumee, the revengeful Tecumseh was employed as an emissary to rouse up the southern as well as the northern savages for the destruction of the border settlements.

This warlike Indian, in the winter of 1812–13, empowered by the British authorities of Canada, commenced his enterprise of uniting all the powerful nations south of the Ohio into a league with those of the north for a general war with the United States.

Accompanied by his brother, the "Prophet," and about thirty warriors from the northern tribes, Tecumseh set out from the Wabash on his mission to the great tribes of the South. With his fiery eloquence, and his vindictive hatred of the American people, he soon created a party in the Creek nation which began to defy all restraint and all subordination to their constituted authorities, and soon spread conflagration and havoc from the frontiers of Georgia to the banks of the Mississippi.*

* Among the evidences of Tecumseh's visit and agency in exciting the Creek war, and inducing the Creeks to take up the hatchet as allies of Great Britain, the following affidavit of Samuel Manac, a respectable and wealthy half-breed Creek, may be taken as one which is corroborated by undoubted testimony, viz.:

The Deposition of Samuel Manac, of lawful age, a Warrior of the Creek Nation.
MISSISSIPPI TERRITORY, WASHINGTON DISTRICT:
About the last of October, 1812, thirty northern Indians came down with Tecumseh, who said he had been sent by his brother, the Prophet. They attended our council at the Tuccabache, and had a talk for us. I was there for the space of three days; but every day, while I was there, Tecumseh refused to deliver his talk; and, on being requested to give it, said that the sun had gone too far that day. The next day I came away, and he delivered his talk. It was not until about Christmas that any of our people began to dance the war-dance. The Muskhogees have not been used to dance before war, but afterward. At that time about forty of our people began this "northern custom;" and my brother-in-law, Francis, who also pretends to be a "prophet," was at the head of them.

Their number has very much increased since, and there are probably now more than one half of the Creek nation who have joined them. Being afraid of the consequences of a murder having been committed on the mail-route, I left my house on the road, and had gone down to my plantation on the river, where I remained some time. I went to Pensacola with some steers; during which time my sister and brother, who have joined the war party, came and took off a number of my horses, and other stock, and thirty-six of my negroes. About twenty-two days ago I went up to my house on the road, and found some Indians encamped near it, and I tried to avoid them, but could not. An Indian came to me, who goes by the name of High-headed Jim, and who, I found, had been appointed to head a party sent from the Autossee town, on the Tallapoosa, on a trip to Pensacola. He shook hands with me, and immediately began to tremble and jerk in every part of his frame, and the very calves of his legs were convulsed, and he would get entirely out of breath with the agitation. This practice was introduced in May or June last by "the Prophet Francis," who says that he was so instructed by the Spirit. High-headed Jim asked me what I meant to do. I said that I would sell my property, and buy ammunition, and join them. He then told me that they were going down *to Pensacola to get ammunition,* and they had got a *letter from a British general,* which would enable them to receive ammunition from the governor; that it had been given to the Little Warrior, and was saved by his nephew when he was killed, and by him sent to Francis. High Head told me that, when they went back with their supply, another body of men would go down for another supply of ammunition; and that ten men were to go out of each town, and they calculated on *five horse-loads for every town.* He said they were to make a general attack on the American settlements; that the Indians on the waters of the Coosa, Tallapoosa, and Black Warrior were to attack the settlements on the Tombigby and Alabama, particularly the Tensas and Fork settlements; that the Creek Indians bordering on the Cherokees were to attack the people of Tennessee, and that the Seminoles and Lower Creeks were to attack the Georgians; that the Choctâs also had joined them, and were to attack the

This party soon began to increase both in numbers and violence. Imbued with all the insatiable malice, and the well-known contempt for civilized life, which was entertained by that ferocious savage, his adherents became violent in their opposition to every attempt to introduce any change in the national habits and customs of the Creek nation. They denounced any attempted innovation upon their long-established customs and usages as only an artifice of the whites for the ultimate acquisition of their country, after having deprived them of their ability to subsist on the resources so bountifully provided by Nature. Still, the party in favor of civilization, sustained by the principal chiefs, the United States agents, and by the missionary influence, resisted the efforts of the hostiles until they were finally overwhelmed by increasing numbers.

The war spirit spread rapidly from town to town, until the whole nation was thrown into the greatest state of excitement and phrensy. Elated with the assurances given by Tecumseh of efficient aid from the British king, they commenced their war-dances, their incantations, and national preparations for making common cause with England in the extermination of the frontier settlements of Georgia and Tennessee, with those of the Mississippi Territory.

At length the hostile Creeks conceived a bitter enmity to the ruling chiefs of the party in favor of peace and civilization. A rebellion was fomented against their authority, because the friends of civilization were the friends of peace; they were denounced as the enemies of their country, and confederates of the white man for the extinction of their nation. If so, they

Mississippi settlements; that the attack was to be made at the same time in all places, when they had become furnished with ammunition.

I found from my sister that they were treated very rigorously by the chiefs; and that many, especially the women, among them two daughters of the late General M'Gillivray, who had been induced to join them in order to save their property, were very desirous of leaving them, but could not.

I found from the talk of High Head that the war was to be *against the whites*, and not between the Indians themselves; that all they wanted was to kill those who had taken the talk of the whites, viz.: the Big Warrior, Alexander Curnels, Captain Isaac, William M'Intosh, the Mad Dragon's son, the Little Prince, Spoke Kange, and Tallassee Thicksico. They have destroyed a large quantity of my cattle, have burned my houses and my plantation, as well as those of James Curnels and Leonard M'Gee.

                                                                                      his
(Signed)   SAMUEL (S. M.) MANAC.
                                                                                           mark.

Sworn to and subscribed before me, one of the United States judges for the Mississippi Territory, this 2d day of August, 1813.   HARRY TOULMIN.
    (A true copy.)   GEORGE T. ROSS, Lieutenant-colonel of Volunteers

deserved to die, and each hostile warrior conceived himself the chosen instrument to execute the sentence.

The opposing parties at length became organized under their respective leaders, and a civil war commenced. At the head of the peace party was the "Big Warrior," one of the legitimate chiefs; at the head of the hostile party was the "Little Warrior," a violent and sanguinary man. Acts of violence ensued, and several of the friendly chiefs were murdered in cold blood. As the hostiles gained strength, they proceeded to new acts of violence; regardless of the legitimate authorities, they deposed and put to death the friends of peace, until the nation was involved in general bloodshed. The war party at length prevailed, and all opposition was suppressed by arbitrary force.

The war-dances introduced by Tecumseh and the Prophet were celebrated generally, and served to rouse the enthusiasm of the savages into a perfect phrensy.*

Parties of hostile warriors began to assemble in various parts of the Creek nation, with the avowed purpose of commencing hostilities against the white settlements of the Mississippi Territory, and of Georgia and Tennessee. Emissaries were employed in efforts to induce the Choctâs to unite with them in the general league, Tecumseh having been unsuccessful in his efforts among the chiefs of that nation.

Meantime, the settlements on the Alabama and Tombigby Rivers were harassed by continual alarms of divers incursions, which threatened to involve them in one promiscuous massacre. Tormented with the most exaggerated reports of approaching danger, and believing themselves menaced with speedy destruction, the people of Washington District made their urgent appeals to Governor Holmes for protection against the hostile savages. To quiet these apprehensions, the governor lost no time in organizing a brigade of nine hundred volunteers and militia, which he placed under the command of Brigadier-general F. L. Claiborne.

Although many of the Choctâ warriors were inclined to join the Creeks in their contemplated hostilities, the prudent counsel of Mushulatubbe, Pushmataha, and Pitchlynn, three influen-

---

* Before the mission of Tecumseh, it had been the custom of the Creeks and Choctâs to celebrate the war-dances *after* the war was finished, or after any signal victory, *not before* hostilities commenced.

tial war chiefs, prevailed, and the Choctâ nation remained friendly to the Americans. Yet the influence of these chiefs would have been of little avail, had it not been for the influence, address, and prudence of General Claiborne, who finally secured not only their neutrality, but their co-operation.

Although the people on the Tombigby and Alabama frontier had been kept in a state of continual alarm and apprehension by the commotion and civil discord in the Creek nation, and the continual rumors of hostile designs against the American settlements, no actual warlike demonstration had been made against them until July. Early in this month the hostiles proceeded to acts of violence against the ruling chiefs who advocated peace and friendship with the whites. About the same time they began to burn the houses and destroy the property of the half-breeds living near the white settlements who were suspected of being friendly to the United States.

On the 20th of July information was received by Captain Gaines, Choctâ agent at St. Stephen's, from Mushulatubbe, a friendly Choctâ chief, apprising him of the disposition and movements of the Creek nation.* It thus became evident that

---

* The following is a copy of Mushulatubbe's letter to Captain Gaines:

"*Choctâ Nation, July* 15*th*, 1813.

"FRIEND AND BROTHER,—

"On the 15th of June I thought proper to call my friends and warriors together, to judge of the improper proceedings of the Muskhogees, and on that day wrote my sentiments, and sent four of my captains to their nation; but, I am sorry to inform you, my warriors, who returned four days since, could not deliver my letter, owing to the disturbance among the villanous Muskhogees. My captains, whom I can depend upon, inform me that part of sixteen towns have rebelled, and killed eight of the chiefs who were friendly to the United States. They also inform me that the Big Warrior and Captain Isaacs are secreted together, and protected by a few friends.

"Colonel Hawkins and Alexander Curnels have left the nation at the request of the Big Warrior, to solicit the assistance of the white people to quell those who have rebelled.

"They are making every arrangement to attack the frontier of Tombigby. They have also received *letters from Canada*, demanding of the *English store in Pensacola arms and ammunition*, to obtain which, my captains inform me, the party, with their pack-horses, must be in Pensacola about this time.

"I am sorry, also, that thirty of the Yannubbe town warriors have joined Tala-bola, whom the Muskhogees have made a chief, and are certainly on the Black Warrior at present, holding their dances, and making preparations to attack the frontiers.

"In two days I shall call the warriors belonging to my district, and make them acquainted, and obtain their opinions respecting the business.

"I assure you and the rest of my white brethren that you have my friendship; and should there be any depredations committed against the white people within my district, I certainly shall seek satisfaction.   Yours, &c.,

"(Signed)   MUSHULATUBBE, + his mark.

all the disturbance and violence in the Creek nation was only the harbinger of a contemplated attack upon the frontier settlements, for which they were receiving supplies of ammunition from the Spaniards of Florida.

At this time no efficient measures had been taken by the commander-in-chief of the Seventh Military District to protect the border inhabitants of Washington District from Indian revenge. General Flournoy, who had succeeded General Wilkinson, having his headquarters occasionally at New Orleans, or the Bay of St. Louis, rarely visited the exposed frontier, and was deaf to all the representations and entreaties, not only of the people, but also of the militia officers on duty in that quarter. With two or three full regiments of United States regular troops under his command, he permitted these settlements to be harassed by constant alarms, while the third and seventh regiments were in cantonments at Washington, Baton Rouge, and New Orleans.

Trusting in the perverted judgment, and guided by the mistaken declarations of the Creek agent, Colonel Hawkins, he remained at New Orleans and other points remote from the Indian region, ignorant of the true state of Indian feeling and hostile preparations, neglectful of the appeals for aid and protection from the exposed people, and apparently regardless of the storm which was about to burst over them. Notwithstanding the daily evidences of hostility in the Creek nation, and the repeated acts of violence by those in favor of war; and notwithstanding the same spirit was now extending to the Choctâs, and threatened to involve them with the Creek nation, he refused to give his sanction to any efficient measures for arresting the designs of the inimical Creeks, or securing the friendship of the Choctâ nation. Thus, by his incompetence for the station he occupied, and by his misdirection of the military resources under his control, he contributed in no small degree to all the horrors of the Indian war which soon afterward broke forth.

Meantime, Colonel Hawkins, at a period when the Creeks were ripe for the execution of their plans and the destruction of the exposed population infatuated by his misguided judg-

---

"I do certify the within and above statement to be agreeably to the report made by the Indians now from the Creek nation.

"P.S.—The statement of the Indians is, that two thousand of them are in arms in the United States.
JOHN PITCHLYNN."

ment, denied there was any hostile party in the Creek nation, Under this false impression, he omitted no effort to inculcate his belief among the white inhabitants, as well as upon the credulous commander-in-chief. He asserted that all the disturbance, commotion, and violence in the Creek nation was without any hostile design against the United States, but solely the result of a domestic faction opposed to civilization; that the alarm and distrust on the Alabama and Tombigby Rivers were without any real foundation, and that all precautions and means of defense were uncalled for and superfluous; that no hostile movement against the whites could be made until the civil war in the nation was finally settled.

Such were the views entertained by Colonel Hawkins, and which were imbibed by General Flournoy, controlling the defenses of the southern frontier; views which were not changed until the agent was compelled, early in July, to fly for his life from the Creek nation; and the commander-in-chief was astounded by the massacre of Fort Mims.*

In the mean time, the British fleet had been cruising in the Gulf of Mexico for months, and had made its appearance several times off the coast of Florida, whence vessels had been dispatched to Pensacola and to other neutral ports in East Florida, to discharge supplies for their savage allies, together with munitions of war, and emissaries to superintend their distribution, and to expedite the hostile organization of the Creek nation.

It was not until the first week in July that General Claiborne received orders from General Flournoy, in New Orleans, requiring him to advance with his brigade from Baton Rouge and take post at Mount Vernon, three miles east of Fort Stoddart. Colonel Carson, with the advanced guard, set out immediately for the designated point, where he arrived and established a cantonment for the troops. On the 30th of July, General Claiborne, with the rear guard, arrived and took charge of the army for the protection of the exposed settlements. The greatest energy was then required to enable him to distribute his forces in such a manner as to give a tolerable security to the defenseless inhabitants and the recent stockades which they had hastily constructed for their preservation.

* The MS. papers of General Claiborne furnish incontestable evidence of these facts in great abundance.

Upon his arrival at Fort Stoddart, General Claiborne took every measure to ascertain the true condition of the Creek nation, and their designs toward the United States. The following day he received from Judge Toulmin a written opinion, assuring him that hostilities were already commenced against the frontier people.*

* The following is a copy of the opinion of Judge Toulmin, which fully illustrates the condition of affairs on the Mobile and Tombigby frontier at this time, viz.:

"*Fort Stoddart*, 31*st July*, 1813.

"Dear Sir,—

"You have done me the honor to request my opinion relative to the hostile dispositions of the Creek Indians. My own apprehensions on this subject have grown out of transient circumstances as they have occurred, but are not founded on what would be deemed legal evidence.

"I may safely say that I am sufficiently satisfied; but as I would not express opinions which may influence, on so important an occasion, the conduct of others, without bringing into view the grounds and reasons of those opinions, I will endeavor to trace back the impressions which have been made upon my own mind, and will lay before you the result.

"1. I think it is about two months since Colonel Hawkins informed me that he anticipated a civil war among the Creeks, which was notoriously originating, in a great degree, in the vigorous measures taken by the heads of the nation to punish those of their tribe who had made war on the people of the United States.

"Where the cause of the white people was the primary source of domestic disturbances in the nation, it was reasonable to suppose that the interests and safety of white people would be materially involved in the progress and issue of those disturbances. Colonel Hawkins, accordingly, soon after sent his family from the nation, and has since removed himself.

"2. A few weeks after this, General Wilkinson was about to pass through the nation, but found the prospect of disturbances so alarming that he halted for a guard.

"As soon as he had an opportunity, he made himself acquainted with the spirit prevailing in the Indian nation, and, satisfied that hostilities were intended, he sent an express back to me, with a letter on the subject, a copy, or the substance of which, I immediately did myself the honor to transmit to you, to General Flournoy, to Governor Holmes, and to Colonel Bowyer. This letter evinced his conviction that we were on the eve of an Indian war, and that immediate measures of defense ought to be adopted.

"3. Mr. Samuel Manac, a half-breed, well known to all persons conversant with the Creek nation, whose veracity I never heard impeached, and who has certainly as much at stake as any man in the country, assured me that he had had a conversation with High Head, one of the chiefs, who has lately been at Pensacola (and who was then on his way), in which High Head acknowledged to him that their object was to make war on the American people; that they had no animosity against the half-breeds, but wished to have them as partners in the general scheme; and that as to going to war with their own people, they had no idea of the kind, but merely wished to put about eight chiefs out of the way, who had signalized themselves by their anxiety to preserve peace with the whites.

"4. The letter from the Choctâ chief Mushulatubbe to Mr. George Gaines fully corresponds with the account given by Mr. Manac. He had sent messengers into the Creek nation, who had clearly ascertained their hostile dispositions toward the people of the United States, and had seen them dancing the war-dance—a national ceremony preparatory to warlike operations. No suggestion existed that their hostilities were intended against any other Indians. They avowed that they were to be against us; and some few restless, misguided Choctâs had unhappily imbibed the spirit of the Muskhogees.

"5. It is a fact, concerning which, I believe, there is no doubt, that some of the

The general proceeded to distribute his troops in such a manner as would best promote the security of the exposed population, who were now in the greatest alarm and apprehension of a speedy attack from the hostile warriors, who were reported upon the march for the Tensas settlements. Two hundred men, under Colonel Carson, were allotted for the defense of the large settlement in the "Forks" of the Alabama and Tombigby, where the people had erected a stockade for protection, which was known as "Easley's Station." Major Beasly, with one hundred and eighty men, was dispatched to the Tensas settlement, where the inhabitants were also collected into a stockade, known as "Mims's Fort." Captain Scott, with one company, was dispatched to Fort St. Stephen, to reenforce the garrison for the protection of that settlement, and for the security of the United States agency at that place. The mounted dragoons of Major Hinds were employed to scour the country in every direction, to discover the first approach

Creeks have participated in the northern warfare from the time of its commencement. They have committed murders on our peaceable citizens in their passage to and from the north. Some of them, and particularly the Little Warrior, have been put to death since their return. Their friends, their confederates, and their relatives survive. These are the men who have organized the present confederacy, and overthrown the legitimate government of the Creek nation.

"They are well known to the British, and have been patronized by them. The Little Warrior was furnished with a letter from a British general to the Governor of Pensacola, containing, as *they* say, a requisition for arms and ammunition, and, as *he* says, merely an introduction and recommendation of them to his notice. On the strength of this, however, they applied for ammunition, and have obtained it. While in Pensacola, they avowed their intention of making war on the American people. They danced the war-dance: they told the governor that nineteen towns had joined them, and that in those towns there were 4800 men.

"6. A party of the Indians going to Pensacola attacked the post-rider and robbed him of his mail; they shot at him and killed his horse; they carried the mail to Pensacola, and said that they had killed the post-rider; they refused to give it up when the governor informed them that he would send it to Mobile.

"7. There is a general impression that hostilities are meditated against the United States.

"No one travels through the Creek nation. All intercourse between this country and Georgia has ceased. The carrying of the mail is completely suspended.

"8. The general commotion through the Creek nation is a matter of notoriety. Their plantations are in a great degree neglected and uncultivated, and the houses of all who resided near the road are abandoned. This state of things seems a prelude to war.

"I believe that all the circumstances which I have stated can be established on oath; and, under this belief, I submit it to you, sir, whether I am not warranted in the opinion that war exists between a part of the Creek nation and the people of the United States.

"I have the honor to be, dear sir, very respectfully, your most obedient and most humble servant,
(Copy.) "HARRY TOULMIN."

of the Indians. The militia of Washington county were distributed to re-enforce the exposed stockades.

Such was the precautionary measures taken to guard against any sudden attack which might be contemplated by the savages during the month of August. The settlements which were deemed greatly exposed were entirely abandoned by their inhabitants, many of whom fled westward as far as the Chickasâhay River, and some as far as the vicinity of Natchez.

We can not give a better idea of the condition of things on the Tombigby at this period than is contained in a letter of General Claiborne to the Governor of Georgia, dated "Cantonment, near Fort Stoddart, August 14th, 1813." The general says, "On my arrival here on the 30th ult., I found the inhabitants on Tombigby and Alabama in a state of the utmost confusion and alarm. They were flying from all quarters to the west side of the Tombigby, leaving behind them rich and highly cultivated farms, with immense crops and stocks of cattle, an easy prey to the hostile Indians. I took every possible pains to ascertain the disposition of the Creeks toward the American government; and, from the unquestionable testimony of many respectable planters and half-breed Indians who reside on the east side of the Alabama, and who are perfectly acquainted with the disposition and intentions of the unfriendly Creeks, I deemed it advisable to make such a disposition of the disposable force under my command as would best secure protection to the most exposed part of the eastern frontier of this territory.

"Some time previous to my arrival, information which could be relied on was received that M'Queen, who appears to be a leading man among the unfriendly Creeks, was on his way to Pensacola with a party of about three hundred Indians, who were going to procure powder and other warlike stores from the governor of that place.

"Immediately on the receipt of this intelligence, two gentlemen of respectability were dispatched to Pensacola, to ascertain whether the governor of that place would furnish munitions of war to the Indians, and also to discover their intentions toward us. Their report was, that the governor had supplied them with a considerable quantity of powder, lead, flints, and the like, and that the Indians did not hesitate to declare openly and at all times that their objects were hostile to the whites, and that they were determined to attack and destroy the settlements on Tombigby and Alabama. Information was also brought that this party of M'Queen's would proceed from Pensacola north to the Whetstone Hill, about eighty miles east of Tombigby, where they were to be met by a party from the nation, when they would distribute their stores, and immediately attack our defenseless frontier.

"When these things were known, Colonel Caller, of the militia, hastily collected about one hundred and seventy-five mounted men, and proceeded to the trace leading from Pensacola into the nation, with a view to prevent the junction of these two parties, and also to destroy the stores which they were conveying into the nation.

"On the 27th of July, Colonel Caller, with his militia, met the Indians on the edge of the Escambia low grounds, where he gave them battle. The savages were soon driven, and when every thing declared for the colonel's party, contrary to his express orders and expectations, a retreat was ordered by a junior officer; and, notwithstanding every exertion of Colonel Caller, and some of his officers and men, the militia could not be rallied, but retreated in confusion, with the loss of two killed, and seven or eight wounded. The loss of the enemy was much greater.

"From the information which I have collected, there can be no doubt but that the civil war between the Creeks has originated with the British in Canada. It is stated to me by some of the most intelligent half-breeds, that the Little Warrior, who had been with the British army in Canada, had written orders from the commanders in that quarter to the governor at Pensacola to furnish the Indians with whatever arms and ammunition they might require. These orders, when the Little Warrior was killed, fell into the hands of M'Queen, and on them there is no doubt he was supplied. From a letter of John Innerarity, of the house of John Forbes and Co., of Pensacola, it appears that the Indians have obtained, by threats and otherwise, considerable warlike supplies. It shows, too, that the Spanish government at that place is too weak to support their authority.

"When we are at war with a savage nation, who are thus able to procure warlike supplies from the Spanish government immediately on our borders, and which enables them to commit depredations on our frontier, and to support a contest with our troops at great expense to our government, sound policy would dictate that such dispositions should be made as would effectually destroy these resources. This can only be done by taking possession of Pensacola and such other places in East Florida as border on our lines. This measure, I hope, will be adopted.

"I have now at the different frontier stations about seven hundred men, and expect in a few days to be re-enforced by the seventh regiment. I sincerely hope that I may then be ordered by General Flournoy, under whose orders I act, to penetrate the Creek nation. More could be effected now by one thousand men than could be accomplished three months hence by double that number."*

In order to prevent the apprehended incursion of the savages, General Claiborne solicited re-enforcements of regular troops from General Flournoy, with authority to invade the Creek country. But the latter withheld re-enforcements, and declared the Creek difficulties would soon be terminated. Conscious of the impending danger, General Claiborne having re-enforced the different garrisons with his feeble force, enjoined the most ceaseless vigilance and untiring industry in completing the stockades and block-houses.

In the mean time, the storm of Indian warfare was about to burst with savage fury upon the defenseless inhabitants east of the Tombigby. Rumor asserted that more than fifteen hundred Creek warriors were imbodied, and were already on their march in two divisions against the frontier settlements; one party, of nearly eight hundred warriors, was destined to lay waste those of Tennessee, from Georgia on the east to the Muscle Shoals on the west; another body, of more than seven hundred warriors, designed the destruction of the settlements on the southwest, from the Alabama and Mobile to the Pascagoula on the west. This party was led by the ferocious Weatherford, who delayed his advance for a few days in the vicinity of Pensacola, procuring supplies of ammunition from the Spaniards.†

Yet General Flournoy, as if fearful to approach the scene of danger without express orders, and fearful of "transcending his authority," even to the discomfiture of the enemy, still enjoined upon General Claiborne to act strictly on the defensive.

Apprehensive of an attack on the lower settlements, General Claiborne dispatched orders to Major Beasly at Fort Mims,

* MS. Claiborne Papers. † Eaton's Life of Jackson, p. 30.

urging him to the utmost vigilance and caution; requiring him to complete the block-houses, to strengthen the stockades, to respect the prowess of the enemy, and prepare for a vigorous resistance, and to guard against a sudden attack by employing scouts throughout the settlements.

These apprehensions on the part of General Claiborne and the citizens generally were not without good cause. On the 30th of August, near eleven o'clock A.M., the savages first made their appearance before Mims's Fort, when about sixty warriors, suddenly deploying from a thicket, rushed furiously to the gate, which was open. Before they were perceived they were within thirty yards of the gate, which they endeavored to possess before they could be assailed by the garrison within. Although the attack was unexpected, the whole garrison was immediately in arms, and each man bravely defending the fort. The slaughter at the gate was terrible; nearly every Indian who first approached was killed in the onset; but increasing numbers crowded on, and a furious mêlée was maintained for half an hour by the commingled combatants, with the bayonet, sword, and the clubbed rifle on one side, and the tomahawk, scalping-knife, and the war-club on the other, amid the deafening yells of the infuriated savages, until the garrison, reduced in numbers and borne down by superior force, retreated within the gate, and sought safety in the buildings and blockhouses. A scene of indescribable confusion and carnage ensued within and around the fort while the contest continued, and subsequently in the wholesale massacre of the helpless families who had taken shelter within it. The following extract is from the official report of the massacre:

"In the contest for the gate many fell on both sides. Soon, however, the action became general, the enemy fighting on all sides in the open field, and as near the stockade as they could get. The port-holes were taken and retaken several times. A block-house was contended for by Captain Jack, at the head of his brave riflemen, for the space of an hour after the enemy were in possession of a part of it, when, finally, they succeeded in driving this company into a house in the fort, and, having stopped many of the port-holes with the ends of rails, possessed themselves of the walls. From the houses our troops made a most gallant defense; but the enemy set fire to the roofs, and an attempt to extinguish the flames proved unsuccessful. The few who remained now attempted a retreat under the direction of Captain Bayley of the militia, and Ensign Chambliss of the rifle company, both of whom had been badly wounded. Previously to their retreat, they threw into the flames many of the guns of the dead men. Few of them succeeded in escaping. A few citizens who fought in the stockade, but were not enrolled in any company, also escaped; one of them leaving a wife and six children, who were probably burned to death.

"Major Beasly fell, gallantly fighting at the head of his command near the gate, at the commencement of the action. Captain Jack was killed about the close of the scene, having previously received two wounds. Captain Middleton also distinguished himself, having received four or five wounds before he fell. He was active, and fought bravely from the commencement of the action until he died. Lieutenant Spruce M. Osborn, of Wilkinson county, after receiving two wounds, was taken into a house, but requested to die on the ground, that he might, as long as possible, see the men fight. The other officers fell nobly doing their duty, and the non-commissioned officers and privates deserve equally well. The action continued until five o'clock in the evening.

"Our loss is great; sixty-five, including officers and men, were killed, belonging to the first regiment of Mississippi Territory Volunteers, and twenty-seven volunteer militia, officers included. Many respectable citizens with numerous families, who had abandoned their farms for security, were also killed or burned in the houses into which they had fled."*

The whole number of persons slain in the fort, including about twenty respectable families, which were massacred or burned in the houses, was over two hundred and fifty. Only seventeen escaped, most of them severely wounded.†

---

* See Martin's Louisiana, vol. ii., p. 316. Compare, also, Breckenridge's History of the Late War, p. 181, 182.

† Manuscript papers of General Claiborne.

The official list of killed in the tragedy of Fort Mims was, of volunteers, as follows:

1. Of *Captain Middleton's company*.—Captain H. Middleton; Ensign Swan; Sergeant Edward Steers; Corporal Levi Holliday; musician, Zechariah Shaw; privates, H. Wade, Peter Tierney, William Hamilton.

2. *Captain Painbœuf's company*.—Ensign Y. R. M'Donald; sergeants, John Lowe and Charles Lee; and six privates.

3. *Captain Engil's company*.—Five men.

4. *Captain Jack's company*.—Captain William Jack; Sergeant James H. Gowan; and twelve privates.

Besides militia and citizens who had taken refuge in the stockade.

The loss of the Indians was but little less. Their whole number was subsequently ascertained to have been seven hundred and twenty-five warriors, chiefly Alabamons, commanded by the ferocious Weatherford. The detachment sent to bury the bones of the white victims, subsequently, on their return, reported that the woods adjacent presented nearly two hundred Indian graves. The loss of the enemy had previously been estimated over one hundred and fifty.

Such was the melancholy catastrophe of Fort Mims. In the massacre the fury of the savages was unbounded. Perfectly intoxicated with rage and vengeance, after they had gained the fort they murdered in cold blood, amid the heart-rending screams and entreaties of their victims, the crowd of women and children.

The stockade of Mims's Fort was amply sufficient to have been defended by the garrison, had a proper degree of vigilance been enforced by the commandant; but he seemed to have been incredulous of the imminent danger to which he was exposed. On the morning of the 30th, a few hours before the attack, he had written to General Claiborne, declaring his ability to maintain the post against any number of Indians.*

Such was the penalty for despising an enemy. That Major Beasly was brave, can not be doubted; but his courage was devoid of that ceaseless vigilance which alone gives victory to the brave, by detecting the movements and secret operations of an enemy. When cautioned from several sources of the impending danger, he treated the information as an idle tale, unworthy of his attention; and, instead of preparing to meet the storm, his gates were carelessly thrown open to admit the savage foe.

This melancholy catastrophe spread gloom and consternation throughout the whole territory. The country north and south of the post at Mount Vernon was abandoned by the inhabitants, except the few posts occupied by troops. A spectator at Mount Vernon writes, on the sixth of September, "Never in my life did I see a country given up before without a struggle. Here are the finest crops my eyes ever beheld, made and almost fit to be housed, with immense herds of cattle, negroes, and property, abandoned by their owners almost

---

* This letter, dated August 30th, in the hand-writing of Major Beasly, is among the papers of General Claiborne.

on the first alarm. Many have run from this neighborhood particularly, and have literally abandoned their property. The country is in a deplorable state. It is full of Indians, and the force on the frontier admits only of defensive operations. The Indians which took Mims's station are on the Alabama, only ten miles from that place."*

Nor did the Indians cease from their hostilities after the destruction of Fort Mims. Every station, every block-house, and every fort was assailed by the open foe or by lurking bands of concealed savages. During the month of September, the distress of the people in the midst of the sickly season was extreme; hundreds of families were lying around the stockades, unable to get within the walls. At Mount Vernon, both forts were so crowded that no more could be admitted.

On the seventh of September, Rankin's Fort, a stockade for the protection of the fugitive people, contained five hundred

---

* MS. Claiborne papers.

The following account of the principal hostilities in Washington District, after the massacre at Fort Mims, will give the reader some general idea of the state of the settlements:

On the 1st of September, two families, consisting of twelve persons, women and children, were killed near Sinkfields, in the Fork. On the next day, Sinkfields Fort was furiously assailed by a party of sixty or seventy Indians, by whom the attack was continued two hours, until they had lost ten or eleven of their number, killed by the fire from the fort, when they retired, carrying with them seven dragoon horses, which were tied outside. In the fort one man and one woman were killed, and one boy was wounded.

September 3d. After the Indians disappeared, the inmates of the fort abandoned it, and fled to Fort Madison, a place of greater safety. Other temporary stockades in the Forks were likewise abandoned by their occupants, who fled to Fort Madison. This fort, on the 6th of September, contained more than one thousand souls crowded together, including Colonel Carson's command of two hundred and twenty men.

September 6th. Two men were wounded by lurking Indians near Fort Madison; and on the 7th, Colonel Carson writes that sixty or seventy Indians were lurking in that neighborhood, doing considerable mischief, and probably waiting for re-enforcements preparatory to an attack.

At the same time, the town and Fort of St. Stephen was in continual apprehension of an attack. Lieutenant-colonel Joseph Skinner was endeavoring to organize a volunteer company to accompany General Claiborne into the Creek nation.

On the 9th of September, Colonel James Powell, of the eighth regiment of Mississippi militia, writes that he is "forted at a place commonly known as Gullet's Bluffs, on the east side of Tombigby. This stockade, called Fort Hawn, contains three hundred and ninety-one souls, including sixty men capable of bearing arms, all of whom will be sacrificed to Indian vengeance unless timely aid is afforded."

On the 11th, the people in their crowded forts were very sickly, but were fearful to leave their coverts and go down to Dauphin Island for health and safety.

Colonel Bowyer, from Mobile Point, "regrets the state into which our stars have thrown us, preventing offensive movements, because "our force is insufficient," and "our powers do not permit us to take offensive measures." He "fears Governor Holmes will not be here in time to enable us to save any posts in this territory."

and thirty white persons, of whom only eighty-seven were capable of military duty. Others were arriving every hour, and it was feared the number would be doubled in a few days.

Consternation pervaded the whole country, from the town of Mobile to the extreme northern settlements near the Choctâ boundary, and westward to the Tombigby. Parties of Indians spread themselves in every direction over the whole country, burning and destroying every thing in their reach. After burning the houses, they herded the stock together, and drove them off or destroyed them on the spot. The hogs were driven into the corn-fields to fatten for their use; the horses were taken for their marauding detachments, to enable them the better to spread their ravages; while their camp was furnished with all the luxuries requisite for the continuance of their bacchanalian orgies and nocturnal revelries.

People, prizing their lives above all worldly possessions, fled from their homes utterly destitute, leaving every thing, even their wardrobe and household furniture, to the mercy of the Indians, and with their families sought the nearest stockade.

Employment of the Choctâs.—In these perilous times, in the infancy of the State of Mississippi, Judge Toulmin was always active in his patriotic efforts to defend the settlements from acts of aggression, whether by a savage or a civilized foe. To conciliate the wavering Choctâs, he had been first to urge the employment of them against the unfriendly Creeks; he declared that they would take part on one side or the other; and that, if the American commander lost the opportunity then offered, the Choctâs, in self-defense, would be compelled to join the Creeks, who already looked upon their neutrality as cause of war, and for which they designed to treat them as enemies.

On the 23d of September, a "committee of safety" had prepared an address for the consideration of General Flournoy, setting forth the imminent danger of the inhabitants, and the necessity of conciliating the Choctâs by employing them in the service of the United States against the hostile Creeks. It urges, in view of the impending danger, that the public stores of the Choctâ agency at that place shall be opened for the supply of the Choctâ warriors who are ready to take up arms in defense of the American settlements, and it presents the names of many citizens who voluntarily obligated themselves to indemnify the agent for any loss which he might sustain by so doing. It represented that such is the condition of that nation, urged and menaced by the Creeks, and lured by the liberal supplies of arms and military stores promised by British emissaries to those who espouse the British interests and unite with the Creeks, that they are compelled to take sides in the war either with their old enemies, the Muskhogees, or with the American people.

The committee further represented that "the Choctâs, through a principal chief of one of the three districts of the Choctâ nation, and a captain from another, have manifested a disposition to engage in the war, upon condition of being supplied by the United States with the means of carrying it on; that, upon these conditions, they will co-operate with our troops against the hostile Creeks, who, unless promptly checked, will ruin the settlements in this part of the territory." It represents further, that a number of the Choctâs have been already seduced to join the Muskhogees; and that, as the nation will embark in the war on one side or the other, the success which has heretofore attended the Creeks, in the only two battles yet fought, will exert a strong influence in making their final decision lean to the Creeks; and so strong was the conviction of many in the settlements that *this would be their decision*, that they are already deserting the country for more secure places.

It represents further, that it is now well known that a British vessel has arrived on the coast of West Florida laden with stores and presents to be distributed among the Indians, in order to attach them to the British interests;* that the hostile

---

* About this time the following letter from Lieutenant-colonel Bowyer, commanding at Mobile Point, was received by General Claiborne, viz.:

"*Mobile Point, September* 14*th*, 1813.

"SIR,—I have information from a source in which I place every confidence, that a British armed schooner from the Bahamas arrived at Pensacola on the 10th instant with a large supply of arms, ammunition, clothing, and blankets for the Creek Indians; also, that the old Seminole chief Perriman, and his son William, the latter lately appointed a brigadier-general in the British service, are at Pensacola. They drove into that place two hundred head of fine cattle, and sacrificed them at the heretofore unknown price of from one to eight dollars per head; fifty cows and calves sold for fifty dollars, so anxious were they to get supplies to join the hostile Indians. I am well acquainted with those chiefs, and know they have great influence with their people. It appears the arms, &c., were forwarded in consequence of an address sent to the Governor of Jamaica some time since by the Creek Indians. The schooner is the property of a well-known freebooter (a Captain Johnston, of the Bahamas), who has made his fortune by preying on the commerce of France, Spain, and the United States; I recollect his breaking out of the prison in New Orleans in the year 1809.

"I hope the arrival of these supplies will give you a short respite, and enable you to

portion of the Creeks amounts to four fifths of the nation, all burning with mad enthusiasm for the destruction of the American settlements in this quarter, which they will abandon only with their lives.

It recounts the inadequate protection now furnished to that portion of the territory, the troops from the Mississippi not yet arrived, no intelligence of assistance from Tennessee, and only a rumor that the Georgia militia had taken the field. Under these circumstances, the committee believe a *crisis* has arrived when it is absolutely necessary, for the future safety and peace of the country, to close with the propositions of the Choctâs, to invade the Creek country, and completely subdue or exterminate the Creek nation. Those best acquainted with Choctâ affairs deem it indispensable to make no delay in securing the co-operation of these Indians, lest they cease their friendly overtures, and yield to the seductions of the enemy. Such are the reasons urged for the employment of the Choctâs in the war against the hostile Creeks.* In the emphatic language of

prepare for any force the whole confederation can possibly bring against your posts. I am, sir, respectfully, your obedient servant, JOHN BOWYER,
" Lieutenant-colonel commanding."
"Brigadier-general Claiborne."

* The Spaniards continued their seductive efforts with the Indians up to this time, as may be seen by the following copy of a letter from the Governor of Pensacola to the hostile Creeks, with whom he was in regular correspondence, viz.:

"*Pensacola, September* 29*th*, 1813.

"GENTLEMEN,—I received the letter which you wrote me in the month of August; by which, and with great satisfaction, I was informed of the advantage which your brave warriors obtained over your enemies. I represented, as I promised you, to the Captain-general of Havana, the request which, the last time I took you by the hand, you made of me for arms and munitions; but until now I can not yet have an answer; but I am in hopes that he will send me the effects which I requested, and, as soon as I receive them, I shall inform you.

"I am very thankful for your generous offers to procure me the provisions and warriors necessary, in order to retake the post of Mobile; and you ask me, at the same time, if we have given up the post of Mobile to the Americans? To which I answer, that, for the present, I can not profit by your generous offer, not being at war with the Americans, who did not take Mobile by force, since they purchased it from the miserable officer, destitute of honor, who commanded there, and delivered it without authority, by which means the sale and delivery of the place is totally null and void.* I hope that the Americans will return it again to us, because no one can dispose of a thing that is not his own property; in consequence of which, the Spaniards have not lost their right to it. I hope you will not put in execution the project of which you spoke to me, that of burning the town, since those houses and properties do not belong to Americans, but to true Spaniards.

"To the bearers of your letters I have ordered some small presents to be given, and I remain forever your good father and friend,
(Signed) "MAXEO GONZALEZ MANXIQUE."

* See book i., chap. v., year 1813.

Major Gibson, the point was narrowed down to this, "We must engage the Choctâs, or fight them!"

Pushmataha, a medal Choctâ chief, had been active in his efforts to restrain the inimical feelings of his people toward the whites, and to induce them to abandon the contemplated alliance with the Creeks in the approaching war. He had succeeded in causing several Choctâ warriors to burn the war-club and abandon the Creeks.

To carry out his friendly designs in favor of the United States, this chief, with a few attendants, had visited Fort St. Stephen, to lay his views before the American commanders. A formal interview with General Claiborne was held on the 23d of September, when the first step was taken to enlist the Choctâ warriors in defense of the American settlements. The measures adopted were subsequently approved by General Flournoy.

Up to the 1st of October, nothing had been done by General Flournoy to secure the peace and friendship of the Choctâs. The whole country was deeply concerned at the position occupied by this nation in the contest which had commenced. Strongly urged by the Creeks to make common cause with them, and exposed to their resentment for refusal, and yet without any assurance of protection from the American commander, it was evident to all that, without some decided measures on the part of the American commanders, they must shortly ally themselves to the Creek nation. Many of the best men in the country, among whom was Judge Toulmin, believed the Choctâs would soon embark in the war on the side of the hostile Creeks, and thus place the settlements of Washington county between two opposing tribes.

General Claiborne had been impatient to invade the Creek country from the first outbreak of hostilities, and, at the same time, he had been anxious to secure the friendship and co-operation of the Choctâs; but General Flournoy, "fearful of trans-

---

"We certify that the foregoing is a true copy from the original, transmitted to the war office by Brigadier-general Claiborne."   "BENJAMIN S. SMOOT,
"JOHN T. WIRT, Captain,
"Assistant Deputy Quartermaster-generals.
"St. Stephen's, 9th January, 1814."

This letter was found in the house of Weatherford, after the capture of Eccanachaca, December 23d, 1813.

cending his authority," declined any decisive action in the case until the month of October.

In the mean time, a confidential agent had been sent into the Choctâ nation with instructions to conciliate their feelings, and to induce them, if possible, to accept the tomahawk, and unite with us in chastising their old enemies the Muskhogees. The hostiles were conciliated by friendly talk, and several principal chiefs consented to visit St. Stephen's, and hold a conference with General Claiborne. From this place, they were induced to visit General Flournoy at Mobile, to impress him with the importance of some speedy and decisive action. But it was at Fort St. Stephen that the first efficient measures were taken to imbody the Choctâs in arms against the unfriendly Creeks; there, also, the first arrangements were made, and the first definite action taken, which resulted in the complete pacification of the Choctâs, and secured the settlements upon the Mississippi, as well as those upon the eastern frontier, from the revenge of the Choctâ nation.

Arrangements having been made for the co-operation of the Choctâs with the troops under General Claiborne, Pushmataha arrived at Mount Vernon on the 4th of November with a detachment of fifty-one warriors. Here they remained, waiting for arms and ammunition, until the 10th; Mushulatubbe, with another portion of the Choctâ warriors, was advancing toward the Black Warrior. By the first of December, Mushulatubbe's captains, the "Talking Warrior" and the "Old Leader," had commenced operations against the Creek towns on the Black Warrior, and their first trophies were the scalps of four Creek warriors.

On the first of November, General Claiborne was still at "Pine Levels," near St. Stephen's, awaiting the arrival of supplies and equipments for his Indian auxiliaries, his troops being impatient to advance into the strongholds of the Creeks, beyond the Cahaba.

At length, after great indecision and delay on the part of General Flournoy, he issued orders on the 10th of November for General Claiborne to advance with his command* to Weath-

* The immediate command of General Claiborne consisted, besides the third regiment of regular troops under Colonel Russell, who was to follow, of Colonel Carson's regiment of three hundred and seventy-five volunteers, eighty militiamen, the Mississippi dragoons under Major Hinds, and a large body of Choctâ warriors under Pushmataha and Mushulatubbe.

erford's Bluff, on the east side of the Alabama River, eighty-five miles by land above Fort Stoddart, and one hundred and fifty miles below the junction of the Coosa and Tallapoosa, and there erect a stockade cantonment as a dépôt for supplies and military stores for the relief of the Tennessee troops under General Jackson, who was advancing down the Coosa.

Accordingly, on the 13th of November, General Claiborne took up the line of march from "Pine Levels," and traversed the region between the Tombigby and the Alabama until the 16th, when he encamped upon the west bank of the Alabama, opposite Weatherford's Bluff. Next day, having crossed the river, he took his position and commenced the stockade on the bluff, which was completed before the close of the month, and called "Fort Claiborne." It consisted of a strong stockade two hundred feet square, defended by three block-houses and a half-moon battery, which completely commanded the river. It was near the middle of December before General Flournoy permitted the army to advance against the Creeks.

The Creek war was now fully opened in every quarter of their wide, extended country, and the hostile Creeks were inflamed with the most vindictive rage against such of their own people as were neutral or favorable to peace. Hence the latter were compelled to seek safety against their enraged countrymen either by flying to the white settlements and joining the American troops, or by fortifying themselves in their towns as against an opposing foe.

The Georgia troops, advancing from the east, were accompanied by large numbers of the friendly warriors, who were compelled to seek the protection of the whites. On the north, each division of the Tennessee troops was also accompanied by large numbers of friendly Creeks, who were likewise compelled to take up arms against their own countrymen, who had become their most inveterate enemies. In like manner, the contiguous Choctâs, Chickasâs, and Cherokees, in self-defense, were compelled to take sides with the whites. The revengeful Creeks tolerated no suspicious neutrals; and, at a subsequent date, General Jackson adopted the same policy with rigor. Thus the war, in fact, shortly became to the Creeks a war of self-extermination.

On the 13th of December, General Claiborne, at the head of nearly one thousand men, including a portion of the third regiment under Lieutenant-colonel Russell, and the Choctâs under Pushmataha, took up the line of march for the Creek country on the Alabama, above the mouth of the Cahaba River. Advancing eastward, on the south side of the Alabama, after a march of more than one hundred miles from Fort Claiborne, he approached the strong-hold of Weatherford, a town of about two hundred houses, situated in a swamp near the south bank of the Alabama River, and known as *Eccanachaca,* or " Holy Ground."

This town was attacked on the 23d of December by the army in three divisions, with great spirit and impetuosity. The Indians, encouraged by their chiefs and prophets, Weatherford, Josiah, Francis, and Sinquister, as firmly defended their town against the assault. But they were soon compelled to submit to a total defeat, with the loss of thirty of their warriors. Weatherford, in the midst of the battle, fought like a demon until overpowered, when he fled.

Meantime, the Georgia troops had advanced into the Creek nation. About the middle of October, General Floyd, at different points on the western frontier of Georgia, had under his command about twenty-five hundred troops; and early in November, at the head of nearly one thousand troops and about four hundred friendly Indians, he advanced from the Chattahoochy against the Creeks living upon the Tallapoosa and its tributaries. On the south side of the Tallapoosa, thirty miles above its mouth, and near Autossee Creek, he came upon a fortified town, defended by nearly four hundred Creek warriors. On the 29th of November, after a severe conflict of several hours, the town was carried by storm, and the hostile Indians were defeated and completely routed, with the loss of two hundred warriors killed on the field. Among the slain were two of their kings. Two towns, comprising four hundred houses were destroyed and burned, including many of a superior order not common among the Indians.*

The Autossee towns were situated upon the " beloved ground" of the Creeks, where they had supposed no white man in hostile array could come without certain death; but the whole eastern portion of their country was subsequently overrun and terribly ravaged by the Georgia troops in other

---

* See Waldo's Life of Jackson, p. 88–90. Drake's Book of the Indians, b. iv., p. 45. Also, Martin's Louisiana, vol. ii., p. 319–322.

campaigns. Yet this was only the beginning of the retribution which awaited them during the following year from another quarter.

Operations of the Tennessee Troops.—The people of Tennessee had been no idle spectators of the infuriate vengeance which impelled the savages to the destruction of the American settlements in the beginning of the war. The success at Fort Mims and other points on the Mobile waters had imboldened the savages, and accelerated their destiny by prompting their advance against the confines of Tennessee, and against that portion of Tennessee where the energy and skill of the commander and the courage of the troops were equal to the emergency of the conflict.*

The exposed condition of the inhabitants in the Tennessee Valley, west of Huntsville, had presented a favorable opportunity for another savage triumph, and in the month of September the Indian warriors began to concentrate near the advanced settlements north of the Tennessee River. The rumor of their approach spread alarm throughout the exposed population, and hundreds of families on the advanced frontiers fled from their homes, and sought safety more remote from the Indian border.

Meantime, active preparations had been in progress for imbodying a strong military force in Tennessee for the invasion of the Creek country. Major-general Jackson, in West Tennessee, and General John Cocke, in East Tennessee, were each advancing with twenty-five hundred men toward the Indian Territory, for its simultaneous invasion from two opposite directions.

On the 10th of October, General Jackson commenced his march from Huntsville, with two thousand choice volunteers, for the Indian country. Marching the infantry toward the Coosa, he detached Brigadier-general Coffee, with nearly one thousand mounted volunteers, to make a circuit and scour the country upon the head waters of the Black Warrior, for the dispersion of the hostile Creeks who were supposed to be in that quarter.

In his advance into the Indian country, General Jackson encountered great difficulties in procuring supplies for his troops; yet, overcoming all obstacles by his indomitable energy and

* Kendall's Life of Jackson, p. 185-188.

perseverance, he continued to advance toward the Indian towns, near the "Ten Islands" of Coosa.

Learning that a large body of Indians had posted themselves on Tallushatches Creek, southeast of the Coosa, and about thirteen miles from his encampment, General Jackson dispatched General Coffee with his mounted brigade to attack and disperse them. Conducted by the Indian pilot, General Coffee crossed the Coosa four miles above Ten Islands, and encamped a few miles distant from Tallushatches. Early next morning he advanced to the attack. Within one mile and a half he divided his troops into two divisions, each marching so as to unite their fronts beyond the town. An hour after sunrise the battle was commenced by two companies of spies, thrown within the circle of alignment for the purpose of drawing the Indians from their houses.

In a few minutes the action became general, and the Indians were immediately driven into the town, where they fought with the most obstinate fury as long as they could stand or sit, disdaining to ask quarter. The principal missiles used by the Indians after their first fire were bows and arrows, each warrior being furnished with a bow and quiver, which was used when no opportunity occurred for reloading. The savages were utterly defeated with great slaughter, and their town, with all its effects, was consumed with fire.

Upon the ground were found one hundred and eighty-six Indians killed, besides eighty-four taken prisoners. The Tennesseans lost five men killed, and had forty-one wounded.* Such was the first regular engagement of the Tennessee volunteers with the Creek Indians, and such the issue of the battle of *Tallushatches*, on the 2d of November.

General Jackson concentrated his force near Ten Islands, on the Coosa, where he established a strong post, which he called "Fort Strother," and made it his headquarters. On the 8th of November he took up his line of march for Talladega, with his whole disposable force, consisting of twelve hundred infantry and eight hundred mounted riflemen. At this point the hostile Creeks were in great strength.

After a rapid march, the army arrived within six miles of the enemy late in the evening, and there encamped with the

---

* Eaton, p. 50. See, also, Martin's Louisiana, vol. ii., p. 317; and Kendall's Life of Jackson, p. 198, 199.

utmost circumspection. Soon afterward, the scouts reported the Indians posted in great force within a quarter of a mile, but their numbers could not be ascertained. Orders were given about midnight to prepare the troops for marching. By four o'clock in the morning the whole line was in motion. The infantry proceeded, as usual, in three columns; the cavalry in the same order in the rear, with flankers on each wing. At seven o'clock, having arrived within a mile of the enemy's position, the columns were displayed in order of battle. At eight o'clock the battle was commenced by a heavy fire from the savages, throwing the advance into some confusion. Order was soon restored in every part except in the regiment of Colonel Bradley, who failed to advance.* The action soon became general along the whole line, and in fifteen minutes afterward the Indians were seen flying in all directions. They were pursued, with great slaughter, to the mountains, a distance of three miles. In this engagement, Colonel Carroll, Lieutenant-colonel Dyer, and many other brave officers distinguished themselves, and were highly applauded by their commander for their gallantry and deliberate courage during the action.

The force of the Indians in this engagement was one thousand and eighty warriors. The battle continued, with occasional remissions, for nearly two hours. The Indian loss was three hundred warriors left dead upon the field. The Tennessee troops lost fifteen men killed and eighty-five wounded.†

Such was the result of the battle of *Talladega;* and had it not been for the defection of Colonel Bradley with his regiment, and the retreat of three companies of militia, which opened a space for the flight of the enemy, it is more than probable that scarcely a warrior would have escaped.

No other operations of importance were undertaken by General Jackson for want of supplies and re-enforcements, the term of service having expired with many, until January following.

Thus terminated the first campaign of the Tennessee troops in the Creek war. The only severe contests and honorable victories were achieved by the western division, which, under their active and skillful commander, had they not been paralyzed in their efforts by the want of provisions and supplies, would well-nigh have terminated the war in a single campaign.

* Eaton, p. 56. Also, Kendall's Life of Jackson, p. 203-205.
† Waldo's Life of Jackson, p. 82, 83. Eaton, p. 57, 58. Kendall, p. 205.

[A.D. 1814.] In the mean time, the British fleet had been off the coast of Florida, and through the Spanish ports had abundantly supplied the Seminoles and Creeks with arms and ammunition, and all the requisites for maintaining an Indian war. Thus sustained and assisted, the Creeks imbibed new life and new energy in their preparations to renew the conflict, and to compel the co-operation of their own nation.

Second Campaign of the Tennessee Troops.—At the distance of fifty miles from Fort Strother, in a southeast direction, the hostile Indians had concentrated in great force at the Horseshoe Bend of the Tallapoosa River. The isthmus and peninsula formed by this bend had been fortified in such manner as to bid defiance to the militia without the aid of artillery. This fortified peninsula was near the mouth of a creek which the Indians called Emuckfaw, and included an island in the river, the whole situated just below the Indian village of New Youka. Toward this place General Jackson began his march on the 18th of January, and on the evening of the 21st he encamped on the Emuckfaw Creek, about twelve miles from the Indian citadel.* Here, perceiving that the Indians in great force were within a few miles of his position, and scouts had been discovered reconnoitering his movements, he adopted an expedient which prevented the horrors of a night attack from the wily savages, who were anticipating an easy victory. Encircling his camp with a cordon of camp-fires beyond the line of sentinels, he effectually protected the army, as well as the sentinels, from surprise by the lurking enemy. The sentinels, being double-manned, and securely posted within the circle of reflected light, were enabled plainly to discern every Indian enemy who might approach the camp, and, from their position in the dark, could deliberately shoot down the lurking foe, while vainly searching for the encampment. Thus protected, the troops were held in readiness for battle until the morning light.

The Indians, apprised of his design against Tohopeka, had resolved to intercept his march, and, if possible, cut off the advancing enemy. But the wary commander had defeated the prompt execution of the chief design of the warriors from the Tallapoosa. The savage host resolved not to abandon the ultimate object of their advance, but prepared to attack the camp at the first dawn of day.

* Waldo's Life of Jackson, p. 105, 106. Also, Kendall's Life. Eaton, p. 125.

About six o'clock on the morning of the twenty-second, a while before daylight, the Indians made a vigorous assault upon the left flank of the army. The attack was resisted with great firmness for half an hour, when a furious charge of the cavalry, under General Coffee, completely routed the Indians, and drove them nearly two miles from the field, with great slaughter.

During the first half hour, General Coffee, Colonel Carroll, Lieutenant-colonel Sitler, the adjutant-general, and Colonel Higgins, distinguished themselves for their cool and deliberate courage in sustaining the assault and in pursuing the flying enemy.*

Not long afterward the camp was attacked with great vigor on the right, where the principal attack was intended from the first. Against this General Jackson had duly provided, he having from the first believed the attack on the left only a feint to confuse and weaken the right. This second attack was accordingly sustained with firmness and courage until the mounted volunteers were prepared to charge. The first charge, under Colonel Carroll and Colonel Higgins, put one division of the Indians to flight, and a second charge, under General Coffee, completely routed the remainder of their forces, with the loss of forty-five of their warriors left upon the ground.

General Jackson next encountered the savages on his return to Fort Strother, on the 24th of January. The retrograde march was taken up at ten o'clock on the forenoon of the 23d. Late in the evening the army reached their encampment on *Enotochopco* Creek. Here they spent the night in constant apprehension of an attack from the Indians, who had followed in their trail. The march was resumed on the morning of the 24th, with increasing evidence of a contemplated attack by the Indians at the defile in crossing the creek. Just as the first columns had crossed the creek, and the artillery was entering the ford, the rear columns were furiously attacked by the savages, and thrown into temporary disorder and flight. A short time, however, served to restore order, when the troops fought with great courage. The artillery was soon brought to bear upon the enemy by Lieutenant Armstrong and his brave company, who advanced in the face of a most galling fire from ten times their number of Indians. They were soon supported by the

---

* Eaton's Life of Jackson, p. 126–129. Also, Kendall's Life of Jackson, p. 253, 254

columns of infantry, which were brought up to take the place of the right and left columns, which had given way. In a short time the Indians were routed in every direction, and were pursued by the cavalry more than two miles, under the greatest consternation. Twenty-six warriors were left dead on the field.

The loss of the Tennessee troops in these several engagements, on the 22d and on the 24th of January, was twenty-four men killed and seventy-five wounded.* The whole number of Indians found dead on the several battle-grounds was one hundred and eighty-nine warriors, and there is no doubt but that many had been removed.†

Early in March, General Jackson having been appointed major-general in the United States service, was re-enforced by the thirty-ninth regiment of United States Infantry, under the skillful and intrepid Colonel John Williams. This regiment numbered about six hundred effective men, and possessed ample supplies. Several detachments of militia and volunteers had also joined his standard before the middle of March, when his entire force amounted to nearly four thousand men, besides Indian auxiliaries to the number of nearly one thousand.‡

At this time, the Choctâs from the Tombigby and Black Warrior, the Chickasâs, and the Cherokees, as well as the friendly Creeks, had rallied to his standard.

The enemy was encountered again, and for the last time in a general engagement, at the strong-hold of Tohopeka, upon the Tallapoosa River. It was on the 27th of March, about ten o'clock in the forenoon, when the army reached the vicinity of the Indian fortress.

The savages, aware of the approach of General Jackson's

---

* After the army retired, as was subsequently ascertained, the savages, in their fury, dug up the slain who had been buried on the fields of Emuckfaw and Enotochopco, for the purpose of obtaining their scalps, and exhibiting their ferocity in mutilating the lifeless bodies of their enemies. Hence General Jackson, after the battle of Tohopeka, took the precaution of having his dead sunk in the river, to secure their remains from the indignity of savage ferocity.—See Kendall's Life of Jackson, p. 282.

† See Waldo's Life of Jackson, p. 110–115. Eaton, p. 137.

‡ See Waldo's Life of Jackson, p. 124. Eaton, p. 147. Kendall, p. 267.

The first re-enforcement consisted of two thousand men from East Tennessee, commanded by General George Doherty, who arrived about the 3d of February. Soon afterward, Brigadier-general Thomas Johnston, with seventeen hundred men, arrived from West Tennessee. A part of General Coffee's volunteer cavalry again entered the field, organized into a regiment under Colonel Henry Dyer. Another mounted regiment from East Tennessee, under Colonel John Brown, also arrived.

forces, had made every preparation for defense, and had assembled their warriors, to the number of about one thousand, from their different towns. The peninsula enclosed by the bend was a place of great natural strength, being surrounded on all sides but one by a deep river, with high and steep banks. The isthmus, or neck which separated the extremes of the bend, was defended by a strong wall or breast-work, from five to eight feet high, and pierced with numerous port-holes.

Preparations for an attack were made without delay. General Coffee, with his brigade of mounted volunteers, and with the friendly Indians, had been detached to cross the river, two miles below the bend, and to encompass the bend on the opposite side, so as to cut off from the enemy all opportunity of retreat. Soon afterward the infantry were put in motion, and advanced slowly along the isthmus toward the breast-work; one six-pounder cannon and one three-pounder were planted in an advantageous position, within two hundred yards of the enemy's line. The cavalry under General Coffee and the Indian allies had attained their position, and had commenced an attack on the rear from the opposite side of the river, when the cannon opened a very brisk fire upon the breast-work. The infantry slowly advanced, and poured in volleys of musketry and rifle-balls whenever the Indians presented themselves above the breast-work. In this manner the attack was kept up with but little intermission for two hours, when a part of the mounted volunteers and some of the friendly Indians crossed the river in canoes, and set fire to some buildings in the rear of the hostile Indians, and opened a brisk fire upon the enemy's rear. At this time General Jackson resolved to carry the place by storm. The infantry in front of the breast-work had been in readiness for some time, and were impatient for the order to storm the works. The order was given, and received by the troops with acclamation, and " the history of warfare furnishes few instances of a more brilliant attack. The regulars, led on by their intrepid and skillful commander, Colonel Williams, and by the gallant Major Montgomery, soon gained possession of the works, in the midst of a most tremendous fire from behind them; and the militia of the brave and venerable Doherty's brigade accompanied them in the charge, with a vivacity and firmness which would have done honor to regulars. The enemy were completely routed. Five hundred and fifty-seven were left dead upon the peninsula, and a great number were killed by the horsemen in their attempt to cross the river. It is believed that not more than twenty have escaped."*

"The fighting continued with some severity for five hours; but we continued to destroy many of them, who had concealed themselves under the banks of the river, until we were prevented by night. The morning following, sixteen men were killed who had been concealed. We took two hundred and fifty prisoners, all women and children. The power of the Creeks is forever broken."† Such is the general's brief account of the terrible *battle of Tohopeka*.

The loss of the Americans was twenty-five killed and one hundred and five wounded. Among the slain were the brave, accomplished, and lamented Major D. P. Montgomery, and Lieutenants Moulton and Somerville. The friendly Indians under Major M'Intosh, the Cowetan, lost twenty-nine killed and fifty-four wounded.‡

The memories of Lieutenants Moulton and Somerville are perpetuated in the flourishing towns of Moulton and Somerville, in the counties of Lawrence and Morgan, in North Alabama. That of the lamented Montgomery is perpetuated in the county and town of Montgomery, southeast of the Alabama River. Major Montgomery, a native of Virginia, had been an eminent lawyer and an accomplished gentleman in Tennessee at the commencement of the war with Great Britain, when he assumed the profession of arms, and entered the regular service of the United States. In this capacity he was the idol, and the model for imitation to his junior officers and men. Attentive to the wants of his men, to their health and comfort he was looked upon as a father and friend. Strictly obedient to the orders of his superiors, and punctilious in the performance of his promises, he secured the most implicit obedience from those under his command. In his person tall and graceful; in his manners, polite, reserved, and modest, he was the favorite of all who knew him. Ardent, brave, and patriotic, he hastened to the field of danger in defense of his country; and, scarcely expecting to return alive, he faltered not, observing, "If I fall in battle, I hope I shall die gloriously."§

* General Jackson's official Report, Waldo's Life of Jackson, p. 125. Eaton, p. 150, 151, and 154. † General Jackson's official Report, p. 126, 127.
‡ General Jackson's official Report, p. 127. Also, Martin's Louisiana, p. 318, 319
§ Claiborne's Notes on the War in the South, p. 41.

In the mean time, Colonel Pearson, with two hundred and fifty militia from North Carolina, scoured the banks of the Alabama, and captured six hundred and twenty-two Indians, including men, women, and children. Several other skirmishes with parties of Indians had resulted in the death of some, and the capture of many others.

These victories completely prostrated the Creek power. They had heretofore been a powerful confederacy, and for more than thirty years had been inveterate in their hatred of the white settlers. In this they had been instigated by Spanish emissaries ever since the close of the war of Independence. During this time, no permanent peace, no complete security, no sincere friendship could be obtained for the white population of Georgia and Tennessee, or for those of the Mississippi Territory.

On the 1st of April General Jackson marched to Fort Williams, where he remained a few days to refresh his troops and to recruit their horses.* Convinced, however, of the necessity of reducing the remainder of the Creeks to peace, or of exterminating them, he again prepared to take up the line of march for the "Hickory Grounds," comprising the region lying between the Coosa and Tallapoosa Rivers, commonly known as the Forks. This region was the favorite resort of the Creeks, and their prophets had assured them it was sacred against the footsteps of the white man. In this region, extending more than thirty miles up the Tallapoosa, there were a number of hostile towns, whose inhabitants were said to be furious with desperation. To animate his soldiers to further toils and new achievements, the general issued the following address: "You have entitled yourselves to the gratitude of your country and your general. The expedition from which you have just returned has, by your good conduct, been rendered prosperous beyond any example in the history of our warfare; it has redeemed the character of your state, and of that description of troops to which most of you belong.

"The fiends of the Tallapoosa will no longer murder our women and children, or disturb the quiet of our borders. Their midnight flambeaux will no more illuminate their council-house, or shine upon the victims of their infernal orgies. In their places a new generation will arise, who will know their duty

* Waldo's Life of Jackson, p. 130–134. Eaton, p. 150–152.

better. The weapons of warfare will be exchanged for the utensils of husbandry, and the wilderness, which now withers in sterility, and mourns the desolation which overspreads it, will blossom as the rose, and become the nursery of the arts. But, before this happy day can arrive, other chastisements remain to be inflicted. It is indeed lamentable that the path to peace should lead through blood, and over the bodies of the slain; but it is a dispensation of Providence, and perhaps a wise one, to inflict partial evils, that ultimate good may be produced."

With rations for eight days packed upon the backs of the soldiers, the army set out for the hostile towns over the rugged country which forms the dividing ridges between the Coosa and Tallapoosa. In less than ten days, the whole country on both sides of the Tallapoosa, for fifty miles above its mouth, was severely scoured and ravaged by fire and sword. But the Indians fled in every direction on the approach of the victorious army; the towns were all deserted, with their fields, to the mercy of the invader. On the 17th of April the army arrived at old Fort Talassee, on the Coosa, six miles above its mouth. This is the site of the old French Fort Toulouse, upon an isthmus between the Coosa and Tallapoosa, which approach within one hundred rods of each other. Here the last chain of military posts was erected, and, in honor of the victorious commander, it was called "Fort Jackson."

In the mean time, the Georgia troops, under Colonel Milton, had advanced to the east side of the Tallapoosa with provisions and supplies; and having formed a junction with General Jackson's army, advanced to the general rendezvous at Fort Jackson. Many of the Indian auxiliaries had been discharged at Fort Williams on account of the scarcity of provisions, and others were also discharged at Fort Jackson, as the war was now terminated.

The savages were humbled, and they had sued for peace and mercy from their conquerors. From the day that the general arrived at Fort Jackson, the Creek warriors and chiefs had been daily arriving from every quarter, imploring peace for their nation and for their families. Among the distinguished chiefs was the notorious *Weatherford*, chief of the Alabamons, a principal instigator of the outbreak, the leader in the capture and massacre of Fort Mims, and an active commander during the war. Vanquished, but not subdued, the proud warrior and fearless chief, disdaining to be led a captive, boldly advanced through the American camp into the presence of his victorious enemy, surrounded by his staff officers, and, bearing in his hands the emblem of peace, thus addressed General Jackson:

"I am in your power; do with me as you please. I am a soldier. I have done the white people all the harm I could; I have fought them, and fought them bravely. If I had an army, I would yet fight, and contend to the last; but I have none; my people are all gone. I can do no more than weep over the misfortunes of my nation. Once I could animate my warriors to battle; but I can not animate the dead. My warriors can no longer hear my voice: their bones are at *Talladega*, *Tallushatches*, *Emuckfaw*, and *Tohopeka*. I have not surrendered myself thoughtlessly. While there were chances of success, I never left my post nor supplicated peace; but my people are gone, and I now ask it for my nation and for myself. On the miseries and misfortunes brought on my country, I look back with deepest sorrow, and wish to avert still greater calamities. If I had been left to contend with the Georgia army, I would have raised my corn on one bank of the river and fought them on the other; but your people have destroyed my nation. You are a brave man: I rely on your generosity. You will exact no terms of a conquered people but such as they should accede to: whatever they may be, it would be madness and folly to oppose. If they are opposed, you shall find me among the sternest enforcers of obedience. Those who would still hold out can be influenced only by a mean spirit of revenge; and to this they must not, and shall not, sacrifice the last remnant of their country. You have told us where we might go and be safe. This is a good talk, and my nation ought to listen to it: they *shall* listen to it."

In the mean time, arrangements were in progress by the Federal government for holding a regular treaty with the Creeks at Fort Jackson, on the Tallapoosa River. For the accomplishment of this desirable object, no one was so well calculated to impress the savages with the power and justice of the United States as the "commander of the Tennessee volunteers." Hence General Jackson, in conjunction with Colonel Benjamin Hawkins, the Creek agent, was appointed commissioner to negotiate and conclude a permanent treaty of peace and amity with the Creek nation. The whole country of the Creeks having been overrun, and the nation entirely subdued by the American troops, they were completely at the mercy of the conquerors, both as to territory and their own personal safety.

On the 9th day of August the treaty was regularly concluded and signed by the American commissioners and the chiefs representing the Creek nation, which thereby ceded to the United States all the Creek territory lying east of the Tombigby and west of the Coosa Rivers.

The "treaty of Fort Jackson" bears upon it the impress of the great soldier, and the forbearance of a nation outraged by savage cruelty, yet kind and indulgent to the conquered.

The preamble of the treaty sets forth that the Creeks had commenced an unprovoked, inhuman, and sanguinary war against the people of the United States, which had been repelled, prosecuted, and determined by the United States successfully, and agreeably to the principles of national justice and honorable warfare; that prior to the outbreak of the war, and the subsequent conquest of the whole Creek country, numberless aggressions had been committed by hostile Creeks against the property, safety, and lives of American citizens, and against such Creeks as were friendly to the United States, at the mouth of Duck River, Fort Mims, and elsewhere, contrary to national faith and express treaty stipulations. That the United States, previous to the perpetration of these outrages, had endeavored to secure the peace and future harmony of their people respectively, by a strict conformity to former articles of treaty, while the Creeks, their chiefs, and warriors, had been induced, by foreign emissaries, impostors, and agents, to commence hostilities against the American people.

Wherefore, the United States claim, as an indemnity for the expenses of the war, a cession of the Creek territory within certain limits, while they guarantee to the Indians the integrity and occupancy of the residue, provided the Creek nation abstains from all intercourse with English or Spanish agents not authorized by the United States to trade with them.

The United States also claim and require the right to establish trading-houses and military posts, and to navigate all the waters of the Creek territory, and to open and use such roads as may be deemed expedient. The United States demand the immediate surrender of all prisoners and property in their possession, and also the capture and delivery of all prophets and instigators of the war, whether natives or foreigners.

And whereas the Creek nation is reduced to extreme want, without the means of subsistence, the United States, out of pure benevolence and humanity, agree to furnish gratuitously to the Creek nation the necessaries of life until their crops shall be matured.

Under the foregoing provisions and considerations, the United States ratify and confirm the peace with the Creek nation, and between them and the Cherokees, Chickasâs, and Choctâs. Such are the leading provisions and stipulations of the "treaty of Fort Jackson."*

Such was the close of the Creek war; a war of extermination commenced by them against the American settlements, instigated and sustained by British revenge, but which resulted in the loss of nearly four thousand of their people, slain in battle, and the complete devastation of their country.

British Emissaries in Florida.—In the mean time, British officers and emissaries had been actively engaged in rousing the Indians of Florida to renewed hostilities. This province was inhabited by portions of the Creek nation, and by a numerous tribe known as the Seminoles, within the limits of the Spanish dominions. These were to be armed against the frontier population of the United States, to renew the scenes at Fort Mims. For this purpose, the British brig Orpheus, early in August, landed several British officers, with a few men, and several pieces of artillery, at Appalachy Bay, near St. Mark's, in East Florida. These officers in advance were to stir up the Creeks and Seminoles; to imbody, train, and drill a large force of them, to assist in the reduction of Mobile Point, and other posts and settlements in the vicinity of Mobile Bay.† The avowed object was to restore to Spain that portion of country which had been seized and occupied by the United States west of the Perdido River.

These agents and officers at St. Mark's at length succeeded in imbodying a large number of Indians, who were drilled in the field exercise, and supplied with arms and ammunition. Soon

---

* Martin's Louisiana, vol. ii., p. 320–322. Drake, book iv., p. 44.
† Martin's Louisiana, vol. ii., p. 322, 323.

afterward, Colonel Nichols arrived with a British squadron at Pensacola, where he established his headquarters, and from which he soon issued his famous proclamation to the people of Louisiana.* Copies of this fulsome and presumptuous document, dated "Headquarters, Pensacola," were distributed in various border portions of Louisiana and the Mississippi Territory. An address, drawn up in a similar strain, was to the troops and "allies" of Great Britain; and to the savages he promised a bounty of *ten dollars for every scalp*, as a stimulus to active operations.†

It was not long before his emissaries returned to him at Pensacola, accompanied by several hundred Indian allies recruited from Florida, who were subsequently engaged with the British troops in their abortive attack upon "Fort Bowyer," on Mobile Point.

Early in the autumn, General Jackson was appointed commander-in-chief of the Seventh Military District in place of General Flournoy. Proceeding without delay to the seat of

---

* In this bombastic document, which was filled with ridiculous promises, he announced, in the name of the King of Great Britain, to the native Louisianians, that on them was made the first call to aid in liberating their native soil from a weak and faithless government. The same call was made equally to Spaniards, Frenchmen, Italians, and Englishmen in Louisiana, whether sojourners or residents. He announced that he had brought a fine train of artillery, and every thing requisite for heading a large organized body of Indians commanded by British officers, and that he was supported by a numerous British and Spanish fleet. His object, he asserted, was to put an end to the usurpations of the United States, and restore the country to its lawful owners.

He reminded the people of the good faith and disinterestedness of Britains in Europe, which was an ample warrant for confidence in America. He would guarantee to them the free enjoyment of their property, their laws, their religion, the peace and tranquillity of the country, free from taxes imposed to support an unnatural war. The Indians, he said, had pledged themselves in the most solemn manner to injure none but the enemies of their Spanish and British fathers. The flag of Spain, France, or England upon any house would be a sure protection to the inmates.

Above all, he had the assurance to address himself to the Kentuckians. He said they had too long borne with grievous impositions from the general government, and the whole brunt of the war had been thrown upon them. He informed them they might observe the strictest neutrality, or they might now revenge their wrongs under the standard of their forefathers; the free navigation of the Mississippi would be granted to them, and they might open a lucrative trade with his majesty's forces in the supply of provisions.

He reminded them of the atrocious conduct of the United States in declaring war against Great Britain at the time when she was spending all her energies, her blood, and her treasure in defense of liberty in Europe, which, by her arms, had at length been disinthralled in the restoration of the Bourbons, and the banishment of Napoleon to Elba.

All his promises were guarantied upon the "*sound honor of a British officer!*"
† Williams's Florida, p. 200.

war, near the Gulf of Mexico, he immediately took active measures to protect the coast of Louisiana and the Mississippi Territory from British invasion. At his summons the Tennessee volunteers again rallied under his standard for the defense of the country from foreign invasion, as they had already done for the humiliation of savage power.

The fort which had been commenced by General Wilkinson at Mobile Point was the only defense against the entrance of the enemy's vessels into the Bay of Mobile, and General Flournoy had considered the post too much exposed to admit of successful defense in case of a vigorous attack. As such, it had been partially abandoned to its fate; but General Jackson immediately ordered its reoccupation by a suitable garrison, and proceeded to augment and strengthen the defenses, so as to close the pass against the entrance of the enemy's vessels. This post, known as Fort Bowyer, was placed under the command of Major Lawrence, with a garrison of one hundred and thirty men and twenty pieces of cannon; and with such success was the defense conducted, that on the 15th of September it successfully repulsed a combined attack by Colonel Nichols and Captain Woodbine with six hundred Indians on land, and the fleet of Sir W. H. Percy, consisting of four vessels and ninety-two pieces of cannon.* In the assault the enemy lost one hundred and sixty men killed, about seventy wounded, with the destruction of one vessel of war.†

The British troops and vessels engaged in the attack on Fort Bowyer having retired to the port of Pensacola, General Jackson resolved to drive the enemy from the neutral port, and to enforce an observance of neutrality on the part of the Spanish authorities, and, if necessary, to take military possession of the port and fortresses.

Having concentrated a strong force in the vicinity of the line of demarkation, he advanced toward Pensacola, and on the 6th of November encamped before the place with nearly four thousand men, including Indian auxiliaries. The same evening he dispatched a flag by his aid, Major Piere, with a communication to the Spanish governor; but as he advanced, the fort opened her fire, and compelled him to return. The tenor of the communication was to inform the Spanish gov-

---

* See Eaton's Life of Jackson, p. 214, 215.
† Martin's Louisiana, vol. ii., p. 330. Also, Eaton's Life of Jackson, p. 214–217.

ernor that the army of the United States did not approach with any hostile designs against Spain, but for the purpose of dislodging the British army from a position from which they were carrying on war against the territories and people of the United States, and requiring the Spanish governor to admit, from the army of the United States, a sufficient number of troops to garrison the Forts St. Michael, Barancas, and St. Rose, until the Spanish authorities could supply a force sufficient to enable the government of Pensacola to support the neutrality of his Catholic majesty's territory. Having reconnoitered the forts at Pensacola, he ascertained distinctly that they were occupied by British troops. The Spanish flag at that time was displayed, but on the day previous both the Spanish and British flags had been hoisted.*

No satisfactory assurances having been given by the Spanish governor, the army was put in motion to take the town and forts by storm on the seventh. Three thousand men, in three different columns, with artillery, were marched along the beach, in order to avoid the fire of Fort St. Michael. When approaching the town, the advance of the artillery being retarded by the deep sand, the middle column was ordered to charge with the bayonet. This column advanced briskly; and as it entered the principal street, a Spanish battery of two guns opened its fire upon them; but it was immediately carried by the Americans at the point of the bayonet, when the town was surrendered, and the British troops, with their Indian allies, retired from Fort Barancas to their shipping, having first laid a train by which the fort was blown up soon after it was evacuated.

The American army retired to Mobile, from which General Jackson proceeded westward to superintend the defenses of the Louisiana coast, and especially the passes to the city of New Orleans, which was the ultimate object of the enemy. A few weeks afterward the troops were concentrated near Baton Rouge, preparatory to their advance to New Orleans, which was then threatened by a formidable British fleet and army.†

[A.D. 1815.] Meantime, the war with Great Britain, as well as with the savages, having been conducted to a successful termination, the people of Mississippi, secure alike from savage

* Martin's Louisiana, vol. ii., p. 331.   † See chap. xv. of this book.

and British barbarity, through the extraordinary courage and energy of General Jackson, made no delay in publicly bearing testimony to his merits as a military commander. The people of the territory, through the General Assembly, in March, with great unanimity, awarded to him a splendid sword, embellished with suitable devices, as a token of their gratitude and affectionate regard for his extraordinary services during the war. This testimonial of an admiring people, accompanied with the cordial congratulations of Governor Holmes, was dispatched to Governor Blount, of Tennessee, by whom, on the 25th of May, it was formally presented to the general at a public meeting in Nashville, amid the felicitations of his friends and companions in arms.

Extension of the white Population into the Indian Country.—Meanwhile, the people of Tennessee, and other states contiguous to the Indian nations, relieved from apprehension of savage hostility, began to advance into the Indian country. The treaty of Fort Jackson had extinguished the claim of the Creek nation to all the country south of Tennessee River, from the Black Warrior eastward to the Coosa, and beyond Fort Jackson on the Tallapoosa; and the tribes of that nation had begun to retire within their new boundary; but the country south and west of the county of Madison was in the possession of the Chickasâ nation, as far south and west as the Choctâ boundary; yet, before the close of the year 1815, the white population was gradually advancing and forming settlements west of Madison county and south of the Tennessee River, within the Chickasâ territory.

At the same time, population was crowding into the country north of the Tennessee River, eastward and westward from Madison county, into that portion of the Chickasâ and Cherokee country which has since been organized into the counties of Jackson, Limestone, and Lauderdale, in North Alabama. While these regions were receiving a rapid increase of immigrant population, the country within twenty miles of the southern limit of Madison county was likewise receiving its advanced pioneer settlements in all that portion of the Tennessee Valley now comprised in the counties of Franklin, Lawrence, and Morgan, of North Alabama. Before the close of the year 1816, all this portion of country north and south of the Tennessee River was fairly in the exclusive occupation of the white population. Nor was this the limit of emigration; hundreds were advancing down the Tombigby to the settlements on the lower portion of the river, near Washington county; others advanced westward upon the head waters of the Tombigby, coveting the fertile and virgin lands still in the occupancy of the Chickasâs. The advanced pioneers from Tennessee, who had explored the country upon the sources of the Tombigby and Black Warrior, "considered it the 'land of promise,' and they impatiently awaited the completion of the surveys by the United States, when they were ready to cover it with their tens of thousands."*

It was early in the summer of 1815 that the first white emigrants advanced upon the tributaries of the Buttahatchy and the eastern sources of the Tombigby. The same summer a settlement was made on the main stream of Tombigby, near the site of Cotton-gin Port. By the first of June, such was the number who had arrived in this quarter and lower down the Tombigby, and in the vicinity of Columbus, that it was deemed expedient, "for the preservation of good order, and to prevent the laws of the territory from being infracted with impunity," to extend the jurisdiction of the government over them, when Governor Holmes, by his proclamation, dated June 9th, 1815, "in virtue of the powers vested in him as Governor of the Mississippi Territory, erected all the country to which the Indian title had been extinguished upon the Tombigby and Black Warrior Rivers into the 'county of Monroe.'" The laws of Congress and those of the Mississippi Territory were declared in full force over the same.†

The same year, Madison county, north of the Tennessee River, was the most populous county in the territory, it having given at the June election, for delegate to Congress, fifteen hundred and seventy votes. At the same election, the whole number of votes polled in the three counties of Adams, Jefferson, and Claiborne yielded an aggregate of only fourteen hundred and twenty.‡

Near the close of this year, a writer in the Washington Republican observes, that "Madison county, which is less than thirteen miles square, has within six years obtained a population of more than ten thousand inhabitants, many of

---

* Washington (Miss.) Republican, Dec. 13, 1815.
† Idem, July 5. ‡ Idem, June 14.

whom are wealthy planters from Georgia and South Carolina." The same year, this county sent three representatives to the General Assembly. These were Gabriel Moore, William Winston, and Hugh M'Vey. Washington District, on the Mobile and Lower Tombigby, sent only two representatives. Such was the relative population of these remote points in the territory at the close of the year 1815.*

Origin of the Seminole War.—But the advance of the whites was premature. The Indian tribes had not yet abandoned the country. The boundary line stipulated in the " Treaty of Fort Jackson" had not been established ; and the Indians, reluctant to yield up so large a portion of their territory, under the promptings of British emissaries from Florida, refused to abandon the country, or to permit the line to be established. Influenced by these emissaries and agents, they denied the obligation of the treaty, because its terms were dictated by the victorious general, and was disapproved by a fraction of the Creek nation. They asserted their unimpaired title to the country, and forbade the advance of the white population. " The Big Warrior declared he was deceived in the extent of country to be ceded by the treaty ; and that the restriction of the Creek nation to the limits of the treaty line would lead to the inevitable destruction of his nation, as it would leave their country too limited for a subsistence by hunting, and that they might as well die by the sword as by famine."

Before the 16th of October, the Creek Indians had commenced hostilities upon the frontiers of Georgia, and had broken up all the military cantonments on the line from Fort Jackson eastward to Fort Mitchell, on the Chattahoochy.† The pioneer settlers were compelled to retire from the exposed situations, and seek safety in the older settlements.

On the 12th of December, the president issued his proclamation forewarning all persons against entering upon the lands of the United States and making settlements thereon, when such lands had not been surveyed and thrown open to them ; he also commanded the marshal in any state or territory where such trespass shall have taken place, to remove, if necessary, by military force, all persons unlawfully remaining upon any such lands after the 10th of March, 1816.‡ Meantime, the Federal

---

* Washington Republican, November 6th, 1815. † Idem, November 11th.
‡ Idem, January 17th, 1816, and sequent.

government omitted no effort for the amicable adjustment of the contested boundary; but the intrigues of British and Spanish emissaries defeated the humane policy of the government, and ultimately involved the hostile portion of the Creek nation and the Seminoles in another war of extermination.

[A.D. 1816.] Until the beginning of the year 1816, the Mississippi Territory continued to include the immense regions extending from the Mississippi to the Chattahoochy River. The greater portion of this extensive country was as yet in the virtual occupancy of the Indian tribes, the white population being still contained in three separate and remote districts. The first of these was that on the Mississippi, lying south of latitude 33°, and extending eastward to Pearl River. The *second* was comprised in the counties on the Tombigby and Mobile Rivers; the *third* was the isolated county of Madison, distant nearly four hundred miles from Natchez, and separated by two tribes of Indians. Between the settlements on the Mississippi and those on the Tombigby, an unsubdued wilderness of nearly three hundred miles intervened, with a few scattering settlements on the route of communication. Between these districts there was no natural or commercial connection; no community of interests or pursuits; and between the first and the second, the sterile character of the lands interposed an insuperable barrier to a continuous population; the Indian nations intervening between the first and the third precluded an intimate and safe intercourse. Hence the inhabitants of each of these sections were strangers to those of the others; but, being all within the limits prescribed for the Mississippi Territory, they were included in one territorial government for temporary convenience.

The great distance of Madison county and the Tombigby settlements from the seat of the territorial government gave rise to much dissatisfaction, and the plan of dividing the territory into two portions, with two separate governments, was warmly discussed during the year 1815. One of the first and most plausible plans devised by politicians was the annexation of the counties west of Pearl River, and south of latitude 33°, to the State of Louisiana, giving that state a uniform shape, and embracing both banks of the Mississippi River. Another government, extending from the mouth of the Tombigby northward to the southern boundary of Tennessee, was desired, having its seat on the Tennessee River.*

Meantime, before the close of the year 1815, a memorial from the General Assembly, as well as one from the people upon the Tombigby and Alabama, had been laid before Congress, representing the inconveniences of the existing government, and praying the division of the territory and the establishment of two separate governments. The county of Monroe, east of the Tombigby, had been organized, and formed a connecting link between the eastern settlements on the Upper and Lower Tombigby, and those further north, contiguous to Madison county.

Indian Treaties in 1816.—The advanced population in all the new settlements, and especially those upon the head waters of the Tombigby and Black Warrior, was encroaching upon the contiguous territories of Choctâs, Chickasâs, and Cherokee nations, which were in friendly alliance with the United States. To facilitate the advance of these settlements chiefly north and east of the Creek nation, the Federal government took immediate measures to obtain a formal relinquishment of the claims of the three coterminous nations. For this purpose, commissioners were appointed on the part of the United States, who, during the autumn of the year, concluded three several treaties for the cession of all the territory from the head waters of the Coosa, westward to the Tombigby at Cotton-gin Port, and to a line running thence direct to the mouth of Caney Creek, on the Tennessee River. These were the last treaties for the relinquishment of Indian lands within the Mississippi Territory previous to its division into two separate territorial governments.

Immediately after these treaties, the white population pressed forward with great rapidity from the Tennessee Valley into the fertile and beautiful plains comprised within the limits defined by the late treaties. Before the close of the year 1816, the civilized inhabitants of the Mississippi Territory had increased to more than seventy-five thousand persons, including slaves. Of these, about forty-six thousand were distributed in the counties situated west of Pearl River; the remainder were in the Tennessee Valley, and upon the Tombigby and Mobile Rivers.

* Washington Republican, December 6th, 1815.

[A.D. 1817.] *The Territory divided.*—On the 21st of January Congress adopted the views contained in the memorial from the General Assembly, and assented to the formation of a state Constitution. The subject having been duly considered, on the first of March following a bill was passed authorizing the people of the *western portion* of the Mississippi Territory to form a state government, preparatory to its admission into the Union as an independent state.* The eastern limit of this portion was " a line to be drawn direct from the mouth of Bear Creek, on the Tennessee River, to the northwestern corner of Washington county, on the Tombigby, thence due south with the western limit of said county to the sea."

State of Mississippi admitted into the Union.—Agreeably to the provisions of the act of Congress, the General Assembly proceeded to provide for the election of delegates to a convention which was to assemble on the first Monday in July. The convention was to consist of forty-four members, representing fourteen counties, and to be convened and held in the town of Washington. After a session of more than five weeks, the Constitution was finally adopted on the 15th of August, 1817, and on the 10th of December following it was approved by Congress, when the " State of Mississippi" was admitted into the Federal Union.†

At this time the whole white population of the new state was restricted to fourteen large counties, sparsely inhabited, and situated chiefly in its southern extremity, immediately north of the old Spanish line of demarkation, and south of the old Choctâ line, established by the treaty of Mount Dexter in 1805.

---

* See Land Laws of United States, compilation of 1827, p. 705. Also, Land Laws, vol. vi., p. 176.

† The members of the convention which formed the first Constitution of the State of Mississippi were as follows:

David Holmes, president, and delegate from Adams county.

Adams county: Josiah Simpson, James C. Wilkins, John Taylor, Christopher Rankin, Edward Turner, Joseph Sessions, John Steele.—*Jefferson county:* Cowles Mead, Hezekiah J. Balch, Joseph E. Davis, George W. King.—*Marion county:* John Ford, Dougal M'Laughlin.—*Hancock county:* Noel Jourdan, Amos Burnett.—*Wayne county:* James Patton, Clinch Gray.—*Green county:* Laughlin M'Kay, John M'Rea.—*Jackson county:* John M'Leod, Thomas Bilbo.—*Lawrence county:* Harmon Runnels.—*Claiborne county:* Walter Leake, Thomas Barnes, Daniel Burnett, Joshua G. Clark.—*Warren county:* Henry D. Downs, Andrew Glass.—*Franklin county:* James Knox.—*Wilkinson county:* George Poindexter, Daniel Williams, Abram M. Scott, John Joor, Gerard C. Brandon, Joseph Johnson.—*Amité county:* Henry Hanna, Thomas Batchelor, John Burton, Thomas Torrence, Angus Wilkinson, William Lattimore.—*Pike county:* David Dickson, William J. Minton, James Y. M'Nabb. Louis Winston, secretary.

The county of Monroe, then lying chiefly on the east side of the Tombigby River, was not represented in the convention of Mississippi, but remained attached to the State of Alabama until the winter of 1820, when the boundary line, established by actual survey, assigned it to Mississippi.

The first session of the " First General Assembly of the State of Mississippi" convened in the town of Washington on the first Monday in October, 1817.* The session continued, for the organization of the state government, until February following. During this time many of the territorial laws were remodeled; inferior and superior courts were established and organized; a general militia law, and a law establishing a regular system of state revenue, were enacted.† The first senators to Congress were David Holmes and Thomas H. Williams; and the first representative elected by the people was George Poindexter, of Wilkinson county, who succeeded William Lattimore, the last territorial delegate. Such was the first organization of state government in Mississippi.

[A.D. 1820.] The new state continued to receive annual accessions to its population by emigrants from North Carolina, Tennessee, and the western states upon the Ohio; and in 1820, the number of inhabitants, exclusive of Indians, was seventy-five thousand four hundred, of whom thirty-three thousand were slaves. The inhabited portion had been subdivided into seventeen counties,‡ lying south of the Choctâ boundary, established at Mount Dexter.

Yet more than two thirds of the country comprised within the limits of the state were in the possession of the native tribes. The Choctâs claimed the largest portion, extending northward from the limit of the white settlements, while the Chickasâs occupied all the territory on the north beyond them. The claims of both nations extended from the Tombigby to the Mississippi.

To facilitate the extension of the white settlements into valuable and fertile lands lying north of the Choctâ boundary, the Federal government entered into negotiations with the Choctâ nation for the purchase of another large district of country.

---

* The first session of the General Assembly organized with Thomas Barnes *speaker* of the House of Representatives; D. Stewart, *lieutenant-governor*, and president of the Senate; David Holmes, *governor*.

† See Acts of " First Session of First General Assembly," 1817, 1818.

‡ Darby's Gazetteer, article " Mississippi."

Major-general Jackson, of Tennessee, and Major-general Thomas Hinds, of Mississippi, were appointed commissioners on the part of the United States to treat upon the subject. The chiefs, head men, and warriors of the Choctâ nation were assembled at Doak's Stand, near the eastern limit of the present county of Madison, and on the 20th of October a treaty was signed for the relinquishment of nearly five and a half millions of acres. This cession comprised all the lands, except a few reservations which lie west of a line drawn northwardly from a point on the former Choctâ boundary, near the southeast corner of the present county of Simpson, "to the source of Black Creek, a tributary of the Yazoo ; thence along said creek westward to its mouth; thence by a direct line to the Mississippi, one mile below the mouth of the Arkansas River."

The Legislature at the next session erected the ceded territory, for temporary government, into the "county of Hinds," in honor of the commissioner from Mississippi. During the same session a joint resolution was adopted, tendering "the thanks of the General Assembly and of the state to Major-general Andrew Jackson, and our distinguished fellow-citizen, Major-general Thomas Hinds, 'commissioners plenipotentiary on the part of the United States to treat with the Choctâ tribe of Indians,' for their patriotic and indefatigable exertions in effecting a treaty with said Indians, whereby their claim has been extinguished to a large portion of land within this state, and whereby a fund has been provided for public exigencies, our settlements on the Mississippi rendered more contiguous, and the state we represent more powerful in its resources and more respectable as a member of the confederacy."*

The territory acquired by this treaty for many years subsequently was known and designated as the "New Purchase;" and hundreds from the old counties, lured by the prospect of securing large bodies of fine lands at cheap rates, began to prepare for settling the country. Subsequently this purchase was erected into the counties of Hinds, Simpson, Copiah, Rankin, Madison, Bolivar, Yazoo, Washington, and Holmes.

Heretofore the General Assembly had convened at Natchez or Washington, near the extreme southwestern part of the state, and at least two hundred and fifty miles from the newly-erected county of Monroe, east of the Tombigby. It had been deter-

* Acts of 1821, p. 113, 114.

mined to establish the future seat of the state government at some point nearly central to the geographical limits of the state. Hence, at the autumnal session of the General Assembly, on the 28th of November, a bill was passed, authorizing "Thomas Hinds and William Lattimore, the commissioners heretofore appointed, and Peter A. Vandorn, to locate the future capital of the state" upon certain lands near the Pearl River, within the "New Purchase," and to prepare suitable buildings for the next session of the General Assembly. The same act declares that the future capital "shall be called and known by the name of "Jackson," in honor of Major-general Andrew Jackson."* Thus was the name of the early patron and defender of Mississippi perpetuated to posterity as identified with her future progress as an independent state.†

* "Acts of the General Assembly" of winter session, 1820, p. 137.

† General Jackson died at the Hermitage, on the Cumberland River, in Tennessee, on the 8th of June, 1845, mourned by the whole nation, and honored by the civilized world. The following general order contains the national notice of his death:

"GENERAL ORDER.

"*Washington, June* 16, 1845.

"The President of the United States, with heartfelt sorrow, announces to the army, the navy, and the marine corps, the death of ANDREW JACKSON. On the evening of Sunday, the eighth day of June, about six o'clock, he resigned his spirit to his heavenly Father. The nation, while it learns with grief the death of its most illustrious citizen, finds solace in contemplating his venerable character and services. The Valley of the Mississippi beheld in him the bravest, and wisest, and most fortunate of its defenders. The country raised him to the highest trusts in military and in civil life, with a confidence that never abated, and an affection that followed him in undiminished vigor to retirement, watched over his latest hours, and pays its tribute at his grave. Wherever his lot was cast, he appeared among those around him, first in natural endowments and resources, not less than first in authority and station. The power of his mind impressed itself on the policy of his country, and still lives, and will live forever, in the memory of its people. Child of a forest region, and a settler of the wilderness, his was a genius which, as it came to the guidance of affairs, instinctively attached itself to general principles, and, inspired by the truth which his own heart revealed to him in singleness and simplicity, he found always a response in the breasts of his countrymen. Crowned with glory in war, in his whole career as a statesman he showed himself the friend and lover of peace. With an American heart, whose throbs were all for Republican freedom and his native land, he yet longed to promote the widest intercourse and the most intimate commerce between the many nations of mankind. He was the servant of humanity. Of a vehement will, he was patient in council, deliberating long, hearing all things, yet, in the moment of action, deciding with rapidity. Of a noble nature, and incapable of disguise, his thoughts lay open to all around him, and won their confidence by his ingenuous frankness. His judgment was of that solidity that he ever tempered vigor with prudence. The flushings of anger could never cloud his faculties, but rather kindled and lighted them up, quickening their energy without disturbing their balance. In war, his eye at a glance discerned his plans with unerring sagacity; in peace, he proposed measures with instinctive wisdom, of which the inspirations were prophecy. In discipline stern, in a just resolution inflexible, he was full of the gentlest affections, ever ready to solace the distressed and to relieve the needy; faithful to his friends, fervid for his country. Indifferent to other rewards, he aspired

Meantime, by an act of the Legislature, approved February 9th, 1821, the county of Monroe had been recognized as within the limits of the state; and the state authority was extended over it by an act entitled " An act to form a county east of the Tombigby River, and for other purposes."* Since that time, Monroe county has formed an integral part of the State of Mississippi.

Yet the county of Monroe was separated from the counties near the Mississippi by the territory of the Choctâ nation, which had been reduced in width at this point, by the "new purchase," to about one hundred and twenty miles from Jackson. To connect these remote settlements, a public road was opened from the old "Nashville Trace," in a northeast direction, through the Choctâ nation, until it intersected the military road leading from Florence, on the Tennessee River, to the city of Orleans. This road passed through the new purchase, by way of the old Choctâ agency and Raymond, to the town of Columbus, thus connecting the settlements on the Tombigby with those near the Mississippi. For several years this road was known as the "Robinson Road," after its projector, Raymond Robinson, who erected the first house, and gave name to the present town of Raymond.

Population began to crowd rapidly into the "New Purchase,"

throughout life to an honorable fame, and so loved his fellow-men, that he longed to dwell in their affectionate remembrance. Heaven gave him length of days, and he filled them with deeds of greatness. He was always happy: happy in his youth, which shared the achievement of our national independence; happy in his after years, which beheld the Valley of the West cover itself with the glory of free and ever-increasing states; happy in his age, which saw the people multiplied from two to twenty millions, and freedom and union make their pathway from the Atlantic to the Pacific; thrice happy in death, for, while he believed the liberties of his country imperishable, and was cheered by visions of its constant advancement, he departed from this life in full hope of a blessed immortality, through the merits and atonement of his Redeemer.

" Officers of the army, the navy, and marine corps will wear crape on the left arm and on their swords, and the colors of the several regiments will be put in mourning for the period of six months. At the naval stations, and on public vessels in commission, the flags will be worn at half-mast for one week; and on the day after this order is received, twenty-one minute guns will be fired, beginning at 12 o'clock. At each military station, the day after the reception of this order, the national flag will be displayed at half-staff from sunrise to sunset; thirteen guns will be fired at daybreak; half-hour guns during the day, and at the close of the day a general salute. The troops will be paraded at 10 o'clock and this order read to them, on which the labors of the day will cease.

" Let the virtues of the illustrious dead retain their influence, and when energy and courage are called to trial, emulate his example.
" GEORGE BANCROFT,
"Acting Secretary of War and Secretary of the Navy."

* Acts of Mississippi in 1821, p. 35, 36.

from which the Indians gradually retired, some into the nation northward, and many westward, across the Mississippi River, thus leaving forever the homes of their ancestors.

[A.D. 1830.] *Extension of the State Jurisdiction over the Indian Country.*—After the organization of the state government, the population gradually increased, and extended into all the counties south of the former Indian boundary, until the close of the year 1820, when the aggregate number, exclusive of Monroe county, amounted to more than seventy-five thousand souls. From this time emigration was more active, and contributed to augment the population rapidly until the year 1830, when the " New Purchase," with its seven new counties, had received a large agricultural population, increasing the inhabitants of the state to one hundred and thirty-six thousand souls, exclusive of Indians. About this time the rage for the fine cotton lands of Mississippi, both in the upland regions of the Yazoo and Pearl Rivers, no less than the lowlands of the Mississippi, began to rouse the spirit of exploration in search of other lands beyond the limits of the white settlements. The white people had again begun to press upon the Indian territory, and the Indians themselves began to find their country too circumscribed to admit of further restrictions. The Chickasàs had already been compelled to retire from the limits of the State of Tennessee to the occupancy of a district in North Mississippi, less than one tenth of their limits in the year 1800.

The Choctâs, occupying the middle portion of the state, were restricted to less than one tenth of the territory occupied by them thirty years before. The impatient white population, which was crowding into the state from Tennessee, Alabama, and Georgia, demanded the final withdrawal of the Indian tribes to the west side of the Mississippi, and the subsequent survey and sale of the lands occupied by them. In order to constrain them to emigrate west of the Mississippi, the jurisdiction of the state was extended over their country, and themselves made amenable to its laws. The savage can not be forced into civilization; and abhorring the restraints of civil government and the steady advance of the white man, they agreed to enter into negotiations with the Federal authorities for the final cession and relinquishment of their country east of the Mississippi, and to accept in lieu of it the lands provided for them west of the Arkansas Territory. The " Treaty of Dancing Rabbit," concluded on the 27th day of September, 1830, completed the stipulations for the sale and relinquishment of all the remaining lands of the Choctâ nation on the east side of the Mississippi.* Two years were allowed for their final removal from the country, and every assistance by

* It may be well here to enumerate the principal treaties of the Federal government with the native tribes of the original Mississippi Territory for the relinquishment and sale of lands previous to the "Treaty of Dancing Rabbit" and that of Pontotoc, which finally extinguished the last remains of Indian title within the State of Mississippi:

1. The *Treaty of Fort Adams*, concluded December 17th, 1801.—By this treaty the Choctâs relinquished the southern portion of the present State of Mississippi, near the West Florida line, between the Pearl and Chickasâhay Rivers, comprising 2,245,720 acres.

2. The *Treaty of Chickasâ Bluffs*, concluded October 24th, 1801.—By this treaty the Chickasâs ceded to the United States the right of way for a public road through their country, formerly known as the "Nashville Trace," leading from Nashville to the Natchez settlements.

3. *Treaty of Fort Confederation*, concluded October 17th, 1802.—By this treaty the Choctâs ceded to the United States the lands east of the Chickasâhay River, extending to the Tombigby, near the Florida line.

4. *Treaty of Chickasâ Country*, concluded July 23d, 1805.—By this treaty the Chickasâs ceded to the United States 345,600 acres in the eastern portion of their country, north of the Tennessee River, and comprising the original "county of Madison," in the great bend of the Tennessee River.

5. *Treaty of Mount Dexter*, concluded November 16th, 1805.—By this treaty the Choctâs ceded to the United States large bodies of land in the southern portion of the territory between the Amité and Tombigby Rivers, comprising 5,987,000 acres. This treaty ratifies and confirms preceding treaties.

6. *Treaty of City of Washington*, concluded January 7th, 1806.—By this treaty the Cherokees ceded to the United States 1,209,000 acres, chiefly in Tennessee and upon the Holston River, and partly in the Mississippi Territory, comprising a portion of Madison county.

7. *Treaty of Fort Jackson*, concluded August 9th, 1814.—By this treaty the Creek nation, humbled and subdued, are compelled to cede to the United States 14,692,000 acres in the eastern half of the Mississippi Territory, west of the Tallapoosa River, and 7,500,000 acres in Georgia.

8. *Treaty of Chickasâ Council-house*, concluded September 20th, 1816.—By this treaty the Chickasâ nation ceded to the United States 408,000 acres on their eastern, or Creek frontier, lying upon the eastern tributaries of the Upper Tombigby, embracing the country originally comprised in the large "county of Monroe." The Creek claim to the same lands had been relinquished by the treaty of Fort Jackson.

9. *Treaty of Turkey Town*, concluded October 4th, 1816.—By this treaty the Cherokees ceded to the United States 1,395,200 acres of land in the eastern half of Tennessee, including the head waters of Elk River, and as far south as the Great Bend of Tennessee River, above the Muscle Shoals, east of Madison county.

10. *Treaty of Choctâ Trading-house*, concluded October 24th, 1816.—By this treaty the Choctâs ratify and confirm the treaties previously entered into before the Creek war.

11. *Treaty of Doak's Stand*, concluded October 20th, 1820.—By this treaty the Choctâs ceded to the United States an extensive scope of country lying north of the Mount Dexter treaty line, and bounded on the north by a line drawn northwestwardly from the Ocktibbeha Creek to the Mississippi River, one mile below the mouth of the Arkansas River. This cession, for many years, was called the "New Purchase," and comprised 5,447,267 acres.—See Land Laws of the United States, compilation of 1827.

the government, with bountiful supplies, was tendered to facilitate emigration to their new homes; yet it was with reluctance they consented to take their leave.

[A.D. 1832.] Two years after the treaty of Dancing Rabbit, the Chickasâs, to avoid the jurisdiction of the state authority, agreed to enter into negotiations for the cession of all their remaining lands east of the Mississippi, preparatory to their departure for the country set apart for them in the West. The "Treaty of Pontotoc," concluded on the 20th of October, 1832, completed the stipulations for the cession and final relinquishment of all the Chickasâ territory within the limits of the State of Mississippi, and their subsequent removal west of the present State of Arkansas. Bountiful advantages were extended to them in the shape of large appropriations of land, and ample time was allowed for their change of abode.

To the Choctâs, also, liberal reservations of lands were allowed, provided they preferred to remain under the jurisdiction of the state. But these privileges have resulted more to the advantage of the land speculator than to the Indians themselves. Several hundred of the Choctâs remained in the sparsely-settled counties south of the Chickasâ line, for the purpose of claiming the reservation rights until the year 1845, when they were conducted by the United States agent to their destination west of the Mississippi River.

[A.D. 1834.] After the ratification of the treaty of Pontotoc, the tide of emigration from Tennessee began to set toward the Indian country; but the Chickasâs were reluctant to abandon their ancient homes and the graves of their ancestors. Many resolved to remain, and, by submitting to the state authority, secure the reservations of land allowed to those who were so inclined; yet, before the close of the year 1839, the Chickasâs had taken up their residence west of the Mississippi.

[A.D. 1845.] Finally, it was about the year 1836, when the tide of emigration not only from the older counties of the state, but from Tennessee, North Alabama, and even from Georgia, began to crowd into this region with all the ardor of enthusiasm. All hearts appeared set upon the fine lands of the Chickasâ country, which had been erected into twelve large counties. Before the close of the year 1845, these counties had become the most populous in the state. The population of the state in 1840 had increased to more than three hundred and seventy-five thousand souls, exclusive of Indians still remaining. Of these, one hundred and ninety-five thousand were slaves, engaged chiefly in agriculture, and rendering Mississippi one of the largest cotton-producing states in the Union. The treaty of Pontotoc comprised a stipulation, that certain of the Chickasâ lands should be sold at a reduced price, even below the minimum of the government; the consequence was, that hundreds of landholders in Tennessee and North Alabama, anxious to profit by the enhanced value of their lands in the older settlements, began to convert their estates into cash, for investment in the fertile regions of the Chickasâ cession. The advance of emigration continued to swell the number of whites in these regions until the close of the year 1845, when not only all the Chickasâs, but the last lingering remains of the Choctâs, were finally removed to the Indian territory upon the Arkansas River. The last removal of the Choctâs was completed under the superintendence of Colonels Anderson and Forester, Cobb and Pickens. Such has been the increase of population in the State of Mississippi.*

The same year, the last remnant of the Creeks in Alabama, reduced to one hundred and sixty in number, were also removed to their new homes in the reserved Indian territory west of the Mississippi.†

[A.D. 1817.] *Alabama Territory.*—A brief retrospect of the advance of emigration into the eastern portion of the Mississippi Territory, and the admission of the State of Alabama into the Union, will close this chapter.

* *Governors of the Mississippi Territory.*
1. Winthrop Sargent, from 1798 to 1802.
2. William C. C. Claiborne, " 1802 to 1804.
3. Robert Williams, " 1805 to 1809.
4. David Holmes, " 1809 to 1817.

Governors of the State of Mississippi.
1. David Holmes, from 1817 to 1820, one term.
2. George Poindexter, " 1820 to 1822, "
3. Walter Leake, " 1822 to 1826, "
4. David Holmes, " 1826 to 1828. "
5. Girard C. Brandon, " 1828 to 1832, two terms.
6. Abram M. Scott, " 1832 to 1834, one term.
7. Hiram G. Runnels, " 1834 to 1836, "
8. Charles Lynch, " 1836 to 1838, "
9. A. G. M'Nutt, " 1838 to 1842, two terms.
10. Tiglman M. Tucker, " 1842 to 1844, one term.
11. Albert G. Brown, " 1844 to 1846, "

† See Report of Commissioners of Indian Affairs, Globe appendix. Documents accompanying President's Message, November, 1845, No. 3, p. 40, 41.

After the Mississippi Territory, under the provisions of the act of March 1st, 1817, the remaining or eastern portion was erected into a separate territorial government by an act approved March 3d, 1817, and was to be known and designated as the "Alabama Territory," after the principal river within its limits. The seat of the new territorial government was established temporarily at St. Stephen's, on the Lower Tombigby River, and the first governor was William W. Bibb.

The Alabama Territory, thus districted, contained a population of more than thirty-three thousand souls, exclusive of the native tribes. There were also seven organized counties, including Monroe, on the Upper Tombigby River. The principal old settlements were those in the Tennessee Valley, on the north, comprised in the original county of Madison, besides others extending for fifty miles east and west, south of the Muscle Shoals. The remaining population was upon the Lower Tombigby and upon the Mobile Rivers.

The former organized counties remaining in the Alabama Territory after the division were those of Mobile, Baldwin, Washington, and Clark, in the southern portion, comprising, in the summer of 1817, about twenty thousand inhabitants. In the northern portion were the counties of Madison, Limestone, and Lauderdale. In these counties, seven in number, all the authorities, legislative, executive, and judicial, remained as they were previous to the division, clothed, with all their powers unimpaired, in the full exercise of their respective duties. The act of Congress of March 3d, 1817, provided "that all offices which may exist, and all laws which may be in force within said boundaries, shall continue to exist and be in force until otherwise provided by law." The members of the former General Assembly, who represented these counties, when convened by the governor immediately after entering upon the duties of his office, were authorized to elect six persons, from whom the president should appoint three to complete the Legislative Council. Thus was the new territorial government fully organized, agreeably to the provisions of the ordinance of July, 1787.

A new land-office was organized in the northern part of the territory, for the survey and sale of lands in the "Northern Land District," and located at Huntsville, in Madison county.*

[A.D. 1819.] The population of the Alabama Territory in-

* Land Laws of the United States, edition of 1827, p. 74, 712.

creased rapidly; in 1816 the aggregate was short of thirty thousand souls, exclusive of Indians; but before the close of the year 1818 it had increased to more than seventy thousand persons, and the people desired an independent state government. In compliance with an application from the General Assembly, Congress, on the 2d of March, 1819, passed an act " to enable the people of the Alabama Territory to form a state Constitution, and for the admission of such state into the Union on an equal footing with the original states."*

Agreeably to the provisions of this act, a convention of forty-four delegates from twenty-two counties convened at Huntsville, Madison county, on the first Monday in July following. Of these delegates the county of Madison sent eight; the county of Monroe, on Tombigby, four; Tuscaloosa, two; Washington, two; Montgomery, two; and others one, in proportion to their population respectively. The Constitution was adopted on the 2d day of August, and on the 14th of December following the " State of Alabama" was formally admitted into the Union by a joint resolution of Congress.

Meantime, the northern land-office at Huntsville had been in operation, and extensive surveys in the " Northern District" had been completed; the land-sales were proclaimed, and thousands of eager purchasers flocked into the country from every portion of the Southern and Western States in search of lands, not only for settlement, but as a profitable investment for future speculation.

[A.D. 1820.] Before the close of the year 1820, the population of the State of Alabama had increased to 127,900 persons; and in less than seven years afterward, immigration had augmented it to 244,000 souls. This number in 1830, twelve years after its admission into the Federal Union, had increased to 309,756 souls.† In 1844 it amounted to 625,000 persons.

* Laws of the United States, edition of 1827, p. 744–746.
† The Governor of the Alabama Territory was William W. Bibb, from 1817 to 1819.

Governors of the State of Alabama.

1. William W. Bibb, from 1819 to December, 1821.
2. Israel Pickens, " 1821 " 1825.
3. John Murphy, " 1825 " 1829.
4. Gabriel Moore, " 1829 " 1831.
5. John Gayle, " 1831 " 1835.
6. Clement C. Clay, " 1835 " 1839.
7. Arthur P. Bagby, " 1839 " 1841.
8. Benj. Fitzpatrick, " 1841 " 1845.
9. Joshua L. Martin, " 1845 " 1847.

CHAPTER XV.

THE "TERRITORY OF ORLEANS" FROM ITS FIRST ORGANIZATION UNTIL AFTER ITS ADMISSION INTO THE UNION AS THE "STATE OF LOUISIANA."—A.D. 1804 TO 1815.

Argument.—William C. C. Claiborne Governor-general of the Province of Louisiana.—General James Wilkinson Commander-in-chief of the Army.—Emigrants from the United States.—Governor Claiborne's judicious Administration.—Territorial Government provided for the "Territory of Orleans."—Plan of Government obnoxious to the People.—Volunteer Companies patronized by the Governor.—Expressions of popular Discontent by the French Population.—Territorial Government instituted.—First Territorial Legislature.—First Bank created.—Territorial Legislature modified.—Discontent in Baton Rouge District.—Abduction of the Kempers.—Their Release.—Spanish Exactions on the Mobile River, and Aggressions West of the Mississippi in 1805.—Spanish Officers in New Orleans.—They contemplate the Mississippi south of Red River as their eastern Boundary.—Re-enforcements in Texas and Florida.—Policy of the Federal Government.—Advance of the Spanish Troops to Red River.—Movements of United States Troops.—Spanish Troops on the Bayou Pierre and Arroyo Hondo.—Remonstrances of Governor Claiborne.—General Wilkinson advances the Army to Natchitoches.—His Negotiation with General Herrera.—Spaniards retire West of the Sabine.—Wilkinson proceeds to New Orleans to intercept Burr's Operations.—His energetic Measures against the Conspirators.—Zealous co-operation of Governor Claiborne.—His Proclamation.—Arrest of Dr. Bollman and others.—Great popular Excitement.—Conflict of the civil and military Authorities.—Affected Zeal of Judges Workman and Hall for the Supremacy of the civil Power.—Efforts made by Persons clothed with civil Authority to embarrass General Wilkinson, and to protect the Conspirators.—Burr utterly circumvented in the Mississippi Territory.—Lieutenant Pike's exploring Party returns from Santa Fé.—Object of his Exploration.—Wilkinson's Position relative to Burr's Enterprise *not criminal.*—The Organization of the Territorial Government completed.—Great Mortality of the Troops under General Wilkinson.—Revolt in District of Baton Rouge in 1810.—Spanish Authority expelled.—A Provisional Government established by the People.—The Baton Rouge District annexed to the Territory of Orleans.—Revolt among Slaves above New Orleans in 1811.—State Government authorized.—Constitution adopted.—Some of its Features.—"State of Louisiana" admitted into the Union.—Baton Rouge District annexed.—State Government organized.—General Wilkinson acquitted by a Court of Inquiry.—Advance of American Population into Louisiana.—General Wilkinson's Activity in providing for maritime Defense of Louisiana against British Invasion.—Louisiana threatened by a powerful Armament.—General Jackson Commander-in-chief.—He arrives at New Orleans.—His extraordinary Efforts for the effectual Defense of the City.—Suppresses a Spirit of Despondency by efficient Measures.—The Enemy advances by Way of the Lakes.—Encounters American Gun-boats.—Martial Law proclaimed.—The Enemy advances through Bayou Bienvenu.—American Army concentrated at New Orleans.—Active Hostilities commence.—Efforts of the Enemy previous to January 8th.—Patriotic Devotion of American Citizens in New Orleans.—Grand Attack upon the American Lines on the 8th.—Repulse of the Enemy's bombarding Squadron at Fort St. Philip.—The British Army retires from the Scene of its Disasters.—The Watchword "Booty and Beauty."—Arbitrary Exercise of civil Authority by Judge Hall.—The unjust Fine disclaimed by the American People after thirty Years.—Population of Louisiana in 1815.—Extent of Settlements.—Agricultural Resources.—Governors until 1846.

[A.D. 1804.] AFTER the transfer of Louisiana, Governor Claiborne entered upon the duties of his office as governor-general of the province, invested with nearly the same powers and prerogatives which pertained to the former Spanish governor-general, until Congress should have provided a regular form of territorial government. Meantime, the former authorities in the several departments of the civil government continued to retain their situations, and to perform the duties of their offices, until their places were otherwise supplied by Governor Claiborne. The different military posts were taken possession of by the troops of the United States, under the immediate command of Brigadier-general James Wilkinson, commander-in-chief of the army.*

From the first extension of the Federal authority over the province, emigrants by hundreds, from the Atlantic and Western States, advanced into the settlements of both Upper and Lower Louisiana. Many had arrived in New Orleans with the American commissioners, and large numbers had preceded them in anticipation of the transfer.

Trade and speculation had brought many to New Orleans, during the period which had elapsed since the treaty of Madrid, in order to avail themselves of the privileges secured by its articles. These were ready to accept office and employment under the authority of the United States, and hence but little delay was encountered by the governor in substituting American citizens for the former Spanish authorities where prudence dictated a change. A wide field for enterprise and speculation was thrown open to the people of the United States, and not a few were eager to share the advantages which so abundantly presented.

Governor Claiborne, from his first entrance upon the duties of his office, had devoted himself with assiduity to the arduous labors of his station, in which he was cordially supported by the patriotic Americans who had taken up their residence in the province. On the 10th of April a temporary government had been organized by the governor, and the approbation of the people was manifested in a public dinner given in honor of himself and General Wilkinson as American commissioners. The sentiments of the people were elegantly expressed by Dr. Watkins,† presiding on the occasion, when, with patriotic fervor, he remarked, that " the eagle of Liberty has extended its

---

* See vol. i., book iv., chap. v., of this work.
† Natchez Herald and Mississippi Gazette, May 10, 1804.

flight to Louisiana, and will cover its virtuous inhabitants with its protecting wings. We hail a new and enterprising people as friends, brothers, and fellow-citizens. The seeds of agriculture, commerce, and the arts are already sown among them, and will grow, unrestrained by the hands of Wisdom, into wealth, power, and national greatness." Relative to the acquisition of Louisiana, he continued : " The prudence which has governed the latter part of this great transaction has been equal to the wisdom which originally planned it. To execute with ability and address important trusts is the particular privilege of exalted minds ; and you, gentlemen, are entitled to all the praise and all the recompense due to distinguished and arduous services. Your manly, dignified conduct ; your firmness and perseverance in a difficult, troublesome transaction ; your affable, conciliating manners ; and, above all, your constant scrupulous attention to the interests of your country, entitle you to the love of all honest men, and the approbation and confidence of the United States. The 20th of December last will ever be remembered as the birth-day of the liberties of Louisiana, and will be celebrated by the lovers of freedom and equal rights as long as time shall last. The names of Claiborne and Wilkinson will be consecrated in the annals of Louisiana, and command the respect of posterity."

As one of the duties imposed upon the governor-general by the Federal government, it was expected that he " should obtain all the information in his power relative to the customs, habits, and dispositions of the inhabitants of the said territory, and communicate the same from time to time to the President of the United States." This duty he performed with such fidelity and discretion as gained for him the most unbounded confidence of the Federal executive, and exalted him in the estimation of his friends and all admirers of American liberty.

Meanwhile, the Federal authorities had been anxiously preparing a form of territorial government adapted to the peculiar condition of the people of Louisiana. An act of Congress, approved March 26th, provided for erecting the whole province into two territorial governments. The first section of the act declared, that " all that portion of country ceded by France to the United States under the name of Louisiana, which lies south of the Mississippi Territory, and of an east and west line to commence on the Mississippi River at the thirty-third degree of north latitude, and extending westward to the western boundary of said cession, shall constitute a territory of the United States, under the name of the 'Territory of Orleans.'" The formation of the same was similar to that of the Northwestern Territory under the provisions of the ordinance of July, 1787, with such modifications as the peculiar condition of the people of Louisiana seemed to require, they being altogether of foreign origin and language, while those of the Northwestern Territory were principally native Americans.

The plan of government provided for the Territory of Orleans, and promulgated for the information of the people, was, accordingly, less democratic than that of the Northwestern Territory. Instead of conferring upon the people the privilege of electing the Legislative Assembly, the act provided that the legislative power should be confided to the governor and a legislative council; the latter to consist of " thirteen of the most fit and discreet persons in the territory, nominated by the governor annually to the president for his appointment, from among the resident inhabitants holding real estate therein, and holding no office of profit under the territory or the United States."

This feature was objectionable, especially to the native American citizens, because it deprived them of one of the rights guarantied by the Constitution of the United States, in excluding them from the advantages of popular suffrage in the election of their Legislature. Hence the act created active opponents, who exerted every effort to prevent the provisions from being enforced. On this account, Governor Claiborne subsequently met with much difficulty in procuring persons willing to serve as members of the Legislative Council.

The French population were dissatisfied with the act for a different reason. They had expected to be admitted speedily into all the rights and privileges of citizens of an independent state, and deprecated the division of the province, because, by dividing the people between two territorial governments, the period of their admission into the Union would necessarily be delayed, which would be contrary to the stipulation in the treaty of cession. They also objected to extending over them those laws of the United States which prohibited the introduction of African slaves into the territory. This they deemed a blow at the agricultural prosperity of the province. At length public meetings were held and remonstrances were adopted against the provisions of the act, and demanding immediate admission into the Federal Union as an independent state. A deputation of three Frenchmen, MM. Derbigny, Detrehen, and Sauve, was dispatched to Washington to protest against these grievances, and to urge their favorite measure.

No militia system existing in the province, Governor Claiborne was active in his efforts to encourage the formation of numerous volunteer military companies composed of American citizens, and chiefly of such as had recently arrived from the Western States. By means of these companies he had been able to give character and efficiency to his government; but the measure was unpopular with the Creole French, who viewed it as an invidious distinction drawn between the American and French citizens; and hence a portion of the prejudice which many of the Creoles of Louisiana entertained against the patriotic governor.

Meantime, the 1st of October arrived, and the territorial government was organized, agreeably to the stipulations of the act of March 26th. William C. C. Claiborne was reappointed governor; Dr. Samuel Brown was secretary of the territory; Duponceau, Kirby, Prevost, and Dominic A. Hall were territorial judges; Mahlon Dickinson was district attorney; and Le Breton d'Orgeney marshal.

Members of the Legislative Council were nominated and appointed by the president, but, from some latent dissatisfaction, a majority of them declined serving. After various delays and embarrassments, Governor Claiborne succeeded in completing the organization of the Legislative Council by means of blank commissions forwarded by the president. It was on the 4th of December that the legislative body, duly formed, convened in the city of New Orleans. The members entered upon the arduous duties before them with zeal and energy, until the civil authority was fully established according to the act of Congress.

[A.D. 1805.] During this first session the Territory of Orleans was divided into twelve counties, with a county court organized in each. A code of judicial proceeding, for the regulation of the inferior and superior courts, was enacted, similar to that of the Mississippi Territory, besides many wholesome laws and provisions for the good government of the people.*

* Martin's Louisiana, vol. ii., p. 252-260.

Among other creations of this Legislature was that of the first bank in Louisiana, with a capital of six hundred thousand dollars, with the privilege of increasing it to two millions, with a legal existence of sixteen years, and known as the "Bank of Louisiana." The successful operation of this bank greatly relieved the embarrassments caused by a depreciated paper currency in the shape of *liberanzas*, or government scrip, left in circulation by the Spaniards; yet the French inhabitants, having suffered severely by paper circulation, were distrustful of the new expedient for relief.*

Meantime, Congress having duly considered the grounds of dissatisfaction with the former act for organizing the territory, repealed the obnoxious law and substituted another, agreeably to the provisions of the ordinance of 1787, and which gave to the people the right of electing their representatives in the General Assembly. This act was approved March 2d, 1805, and placed the people of the Orleans Territory upon the same footing with others.

The first Legislature under the new act convened for business on the 20th of June, 1805, in the city of New Orleans. During this session the territorial laws and judicial proceedings were greatly modified, and received the impress of the leading features of the Louisiana code, which were retained for forty years afterward, until superseded by the new Constitution in 1845.

In the mean time, the Anglo-Americans residing in the Baton Rouge District, and government of West Florida, had become greatly dissatisfied with their condition, being subjects of Spain, although inhabitants of a portion of Louisiana as claimed by the United States, under the cession from France. Although claiming the rights of American citizens, they were compelled to submit to the colonial authority of a despotic and foreign power. Thus, disappointed in their expectation that the District of Baton Rouge would have been included in the surrender of Louisiana, and impatient of the Spanish authority, many became discontented and vindictive. Believing the Spanish government at Baton Rouge weak and isolated, and confidently expecting the sympathy, if not the co-operation, of the Americans in the adjoining territories of Orleans and Mississippi, they determined to resist by force of arms. The entire population of the Baton Rouge District, at this time known

* Martin's Louisiana, vol. ii., p. 247.

as "New Feliciana," was about twelve hundred persons. They were chiefly the descendants of the former British colonists, consisting of English, Irish, and Scotch emigrants, together with many who had emigrated recently from the United States.* A design was formed to expel the Spanish garrison from Baton Rouge, and with them to drive the civil authorities from the district.

A few resolute men, who were resolved to throw off the Spanish yoke, endeavored to stir up a spirit of rebellion among the people, and several prominent leaders, having armed themselves, traversed the country in order to engage volunteers in the enterprise. About two hundred men were at length collected ; but a difference between the principal leaders caused the failure of the entire scheme, and brought upon them the vengeance of the Spanish governor.

Those who had taken an active part in the abortive attempt to subvert the Spanish power, having become obnoxious to the constituted government, were compelled to seek safety beyond the Spanish jurisdiction. Among the most prominent of these offenders were three brothers by the name of Kemper, who were citizens of the Mississippi Territory, residing near Pinckneyville, in Wilkinson county. To seize and punish these men, the Spanish authorities neglected no opportunity and spared no effort.

At length, on the 3d of September, in order to secure their victims, they did not hesitate to violate the American territory in a forcible and unlawful manner. The Kempers, in their own houses, and at the hour of midnight, were seized by a party of armed men in disguise, and after severe personal violence and abuse, were forcibly carried off, in close confinement, across the line of demarkation, and delivered to a troop of Spanish light-horse, acting under orders from Governor Grandpre, of Baton Rouge. Having been placed on board a boat at Tunica Bayou, they were conveyed down the river as far as Point Coupée, when the party was discovered and arrested by Lieutenant Wilson, of the United States army, stationed at that point. Having captured the whole party, he sent them under guard to answer before the proper tribunals at Washington, in the Mississippi Territory.†

* Stoddart's Louisiana, p. 115.
† See this subject more fully noted in chapter xiii. of this book, viz.: "Mississippi Territory," year 1805.

On the west side of the Mississippi, similar violations of territory and outrages upon the rights of American citizens had been perpetrated by armed patrols under the Spanish authorities. Claiming all the region west of Natchitoches, the Spanish armed patrols prohibited all travel and intercourse of American citizens beyond that point. Early in the year, an exploring expedition of the United States, under the command of Major Thomas Freeman, had been intercepted on Red River, above Natchitoches, by a detachment of Spanish troops, and compelled to return, leaving the object of the expedition unaccomplished.

Spain had been compelled reluctantly to surrender Louisiana into the hands of the French prefect, for the use of the United States. She still held the Floridas, and thus controlled the ports, harbors, and rivers east of the Mississippi, and still looked forward to some change of fortune which might yet restore Louisiana, and thus preserve the integrity of her North American possessions. Hence the Spanish officials of Louisiana continued to delay their departure from New Orleans for more than eighteen months after its formal transfer to the American commissioners; and finally retired reluctantly only when compelled, in obedience to instructions from the Federal government. As late as the 7th of August, 1805, Governor Claiborne says, "The Spaniards are so wedded to Louisiana, that necessity alone will induce them to depart." The Marquis de Casa Calvo, after he had been informed by Governor Claiborne that "so many Spanish officers continuing in Louisiana so long beyond the right occasion for it was viewed by the general government with disapprobation," still claimed further indulgence, and desired his property and his attendants to be exempted from municipal taxation.* On the 26th of August, Governor Claiborne wrote to the president "that he had been informed by the Marquis de Casa Calvo that the court of Spain desired to make the Mississippi River the boundary line, and that in time this object would be obtained."

It was in the same communication that Governor Claiborne desired authority to compel the Spanish officers and troops to leave the country immediately, as they were insidiously exerting themselves to raise up a Spanish party. He proceeds, "The *prospect of a retrocession* of the west bank of the Mississippi is

* American State Papers, vol. v., p. 97, Boston edition.

now, and has always been, the theme of the Spanish officers who remain in this territory; and many citizens seem to view it as an event likely to happen: an impression which I greatly regret, since it tends to lessen their confidence in the American government, and to cherish a Spanish party among us. Next, therefore, to a final adjustment of limits with the Spanish government, I most desire to see every Spanish officer removed from the ceded territory. There certainly must be a power somewhere vested, to cause to be executed the clause in the treaty which directs '*the Spanish forces to be withdrawn in three months from the ceded territory.*' I should, indeed, be pleased to have it hinted to me that, in my character as 'commissioner' or governor, I could on this occasion (if necessary) use compulsory measures."*

At length the Marquis de Casa Calvo, in September, 1805, having embarked the Spanish troops under his control for Pensacola, took his departure by land westward, through the Mexican provinces, to Chihuahua. Yet many of the remaining Spaniards, as well as some others, could not believe that the country was lost to Spain, but had only been conveyed to the United States in trust until the close of the European wars, when they hoped for its restoration.

Meantime, every effort had been made by the Spanish authorities of Mexico to extend their settlements east of the Sabine. The village and settlement of Adaës, fourteen miles west of Natchitoches, was one of the oldest in this part of Louisiana, and was coeval with Natchitoches itself; and as late as the summer of 1805 it was the most important one west of Alexandria. To maintain the influence of the Spanish viceroy, and to confirm the people in the Catholic faith, the Bishop of New Leon, Don Feliciano Mariro, made his annual visit, and having performed high mass, and consecrated a graveyard, administered the ordinance of baptism to two hundred neophytes.

Subsequently, during the summer and autumn, several additional colonies of Spanish settlers were located in the eastern portion of Texas, and new military posts were established west of the Sabine. The first of these colonies had arrived at San Antonio on the 5th of July, and consisted of five hundred

---

* American State Papers, vol. v., p. 102, Boston edition. Also, Mississippi Herald and Natchez Gazette, November, 1806.

Spanish emigrants and one hundred and fifty troops. Soon afterward, a similar colony arrived at Nacogdoches, for the extension and security of the settlements in that quarter.

Again, during the autumn strong military re-enforcements from Mexico and Havana were sent to West Florida and Texas. The first arrival at Pensacola, on the 24th of October, consisted of four hundred troops; and on the 30th an additional force of three hundred arrived at the same port, and were ordered to the District of Baton Rouge, to strengthen the garrisons in that quarter. About the same time, Spanish agents from Mobile had contracted for four thousand barrels of flour, besides other supplies for the army in Florida and Texas. The number of regular troops at the different points in Texas, west of the Sabine, at this time amounted to eight hundred.*

Such was the state of affairs on the frontiers of the Territory of Orleans until the beginning of the year 1806. Every indication presaged a speedy rupture between the United States and Spain, and the whole West was impatient for the collision.

But it was not the policy of the Federal government to engage in open war with the waning power of Spain. Although Mr. Jefferson, as early as 1786, had expressed a belief that the United States were ultimately to occupy all North America, yet he deemed it the best policy to permit the Spaniards peaceably to occupy the immense territories until the American population, by its constant increase, should advance and occupy the country gradually as it might be required for new states. In one of his letters at that early period he says, "Our confederacy must be received as the hive from which all America, north and south, is to be peopled. We should take care, too, not to think it for the interest of that great continent *to press too soon upon the Spaniards.* Those countries can not be in better hands. My fear is that they are too feeble to hold them until our population can be sufficiently advanced *to gain it from them piece by piece.* The navigation of the Mississippi we *must have soon.* This is all we are as yet ready to receive." Such was the policy of this great American statesman in 1786; and the same policy has been regularly pursued by the Federal authorities ever since. Such were the views of Mr. Jefferson in 1805, when directing the affairs of the national government. At that time the population was rapidly advancing over

* American State Papers, vol. v., p. 94, 95, Boston edition.

the great Valley of the Mississippi. The Federal government had, by a cautious perseverance in amicable negotiations, acquired all the territory claimed by Spain east of the Mississippi, from the mouth of the Ohio to the thirty-first degree of north latitude; it had also secured the free navigation of the Mississippi for American commerce as early as 1798. Again, in 1803, it had obtained the actual occupancy of both banks of the Mississippi, including the port of New Orleans, together with an indefinite claim to all the country west of the Mississippi and east of the Rio Bravo del Norte. Why press the final adjustment of the western boundary so long before the American population were ready to take actual possession? It was evidently for the interest of the United States to hold possession of what they already occupied east of Natchitoches, leaving the remainder, with its unsettled limits on the west, for the time, wholly with the Spaniards.

Hence it was the policy of the Federal government to avoid, by all means, a war with Spain, by running a conventional line west of the American settlements, leaving the whole subject of the actual and rightful boundary on the west open to future discussion. Such was the policy which prompted its course in restraining the western people, as well as the troops of the United States, from actual hostilities against the Spaniards during the events which subsequently transpired.

The Spaniards had become exasperated at the rapid advance of the Anglo-Americans, and the destiny which seemed to threaten them unless the tide were arrested. Instead of provoking further irritation, the government of the United States had omitted no effort in its attempts to insure an amicable adjustment of all old difficulties with Spain, as well as the establishment of a temporary boundary west of the Mississippi. In order to settle the controversy relative to the Feliciana parishes of Florida, the United States proposed a friendly negotiation for the purchase of both the Floridas entire, connected with a permanent arrangement for the western confines of Louisiana; yet all efforts at agreement on this point were unsuccessful, and the president, in his annual message, announced to Congress that "with Spain our negotiations for a settlement of differences have not had a satisfactory issue. On the Mobile, our commerce passing through that river continues to be obstructed by arbitrary duties and vexatious searches. Propositions for adjusting amicably the boundaries of Louisiana have not been acceded to. While, however, the right is unsettled, we have avoided any change in the state of things by taking new posts, or strengthening ourselves on the disputed territories, in the hope that the other power would not, by a contrary course of conduct, oblige us to meet the example, and endanger conflicts of authority, the issue of which may not be easily controlled. But in this hope we have now reason to lose our confidence."

Meantime, the president had caused a military post to be erected at Natchitoches, with a garrison of two hundred men, to restrain any advances of the Spaniards east of that place. Major Porter, commanding at Natchitoches, was instructed to observe closely the movements of the Spanish troops on the western frontier.

[A.D. 1806.] On the first of January following, after an absence of less than three months, the Marquis de Casa Calvo returned to Louisiana on his route to Pensacola. As he advanced, he tarried several days in the vicinity of Natchitoches, in social intercourse with the Spaniards of that settlement, and friendly communication with the officers of the American garrison. But, his object being suspected, the commandant, Major Porter, extending to him the courtesy due his rank, refused to admit him into the fort. His object was, doubtless, to assure the Spanish inhabitants of the efforts in contemplation for the restoration of the Spanish authority to the west bank of the Mississippi, and to ascertain the condition of the American defenses.

Soon after his departure for Pensacola, a small garrison of Spanish troops proceeded from the Sabine to the town of Adaës, fourteen miles from Natchitoches, for the purpose of establishing a post at that place. Rumor likewise gave notice of the advance of six hundred men under Don Antonio Codero, governor of Texas, as far as the Trinity River. This force, accompanied by a detachment of militia and a few Indian auxiliaries, well supplied with stores and munitions of war, remained several weeks upon the Trinity, awaiting the arrival of reenforcements, under Don Simon Herrera, from New Leon, when they continued to the town of Nacogdoches, on the head waters of the Neches. The march of such a force toward the frontier of the Territory of Orleans in time of peace was ample ground for apprehension on the part of the American government of a design in the Spanish officer to interrupt the amicable relations between the two powers.

Accordingly, on the 24th of January, Major Porter, in obedience to instructions, dispatched a messenger to the Spanish commander at Nacogdoches, requiring from him assurances that all inroads of Spanish troops, and all violence and restraint toward American citizens east of the Sabine, should cease forthwith; and informing him that, in case such assurances were withheld, he should proceed to protect the citizens of the United States in the lawful pursuit of business within the Territory of Orleans westward to the Sabine; that, agreeably to his instructions, he should distribute patrols through the country east of the Sabine, and prevent armed men, not under the authority of the United States, from advancing east of that stream; repel invasion by pursuing and arresting the invaders, always avoiding the effusion of blood, unless absolutely necessary; that in case those assurances were given in good faith, he should not interrupt the peaceable intercourse between the settlements of the Bayou Pierre and those of Nacogdoches; but otherwise he should cut off all communication.*

To this message Don Rodriguez promptly made answer, that no encroachment had been intended, nor had any violence been offered by his troops, except so far as was requisite for the suppression of contraband trade and the exportation of horses. He added, that duty forbade him to give the assurances required, and that he had ordered his parties to patrol as far as the Arroyo Hondo; and that, in obedience to instructions from the Spanish commander, he had established a frontier post, garrisoned by fifteen men, with directions to observe the Arroyo Hondo as the provisional boundary between Louisiana and the Spanish possessions.† At the same time, he sent

* Martin's Louisiana, vol. ii., p. 263.

† The Arroyo Hondo was a deep ravine seven miles west of Natchitoches, and about an equal distance from the town of Adaës. The town of Natchitoches had been first occupied as a trading-post by St. Denys in 1712, and in 1717 it was made a military post. To occupy the country also, the Spaniards, in May following, established the settlement and "Mission of San Miguel de los Adaës," under the protection of a military force. During the contentions of the French and Spanish commandants in this quarter, a mutual agreement established the Arroyo Hondo as a conventional boundary, which was observed until 1762, when the whole of Louisiana west of the Mississippi was ceded to Spain. From that time until the transfer of Louisiana to the United States in 1803, no adverse claim was agitated relative to the western boundary of Louisiana. This transfer revived the controversy as to the real boundaries of Louisiana on the west.

an order to the people on the Bayou Pierre, reminding them of their allegiance to his Catholic majesty, who required them to join his standard whenever commanded by his officers. He also gave them assurances of the protection of his Catholic majesty, and that Red River would soon be made the boundary between Louisiana and the Spanish provinces.*

Upon the reception of this intelligence, Major Porter detached sixty men under Captain Turner, with orders forthwith to remove the Spanish garrison from Adaës to the west side of the Sabine. This object having been effected, Captain Turner established his patrol on the east side of the Sabine.

Meantime, General Wilkinson was instructed to take the necessary measures to prevent the invasion of the Territory of Orleans by the troops of Spain. Lieutenant Kingsbury, from Fort Adams, was accordingly ordered to advance with a detachment of three companies and four field-pieces to Natchitoches, to re-enforce the garrison at that post.

The Spanish minister at Washington city had been formally notified that, while negotiations were pending relative to the boundaries of Louisiana, the military posts of each power should remain as they were; that neither power should make any military operation, or advance any posts beyond their former positions; that the United States designed no movement which would change the existing state of things, and that any attempt on the part of Spain to occupy new posts east of the Sabine would be viewed as an invasion, and as such resisted.

Early in June, the Spanish army, to the number of twelve hundred men, under the command of General Herrera, took position near the Bayou Pierre settlement, about twenty miles from Natchitoches. General Herrera continued to occupy this station without any hostile movement until the 20th of September, when he retired with his command to the east bank of the Sabine, upon the approach of the Federal troops under General Wilkinson.†

Upon the first advance of the Spanish troops to the vicinity of Nacogdoches, Governor Claiborne had opened a spirited correspondence with the Spanish authorities, and remonstrated against the unwarrantable intrusion upon the limits of the territory under his jurisdiction. Receiving no satisfactory

* Martin's Louisiana, vol. ii., p. 262, 263.
† See Mississippi Messenger at Natchez, September 6th, 1806.

assurance of a disposition to retire, the governor called out a portion of the militia to strengthen the garrison at Natchitoches.

Meantime, Colonel Cushing, with the first regiment of United States infantry, had proceeded to Natchitoches, and taken charge of that post, under instructions to act strictly on the defensive until offensive measures were unavoidable. Hence the two armies remained several months within a few miles of each other without collision.

During this time General Wilkinson prosecuted his military preparations actively in the city of New Orleans. The forts were put in a complete state of defense, and several stockades near the city were nearly completed; nine gun-boats had arrived from the Ohio; and additional troops having been ordered from the northwestern posts, were concentrating in the vicinity of Fort Adams and New Orleans,* and detachments of militia advanced from the Mississippi Territory, and also from the Territory of Orleans, to re-enforce the army at Natchitoches.

It was on the 24th of September that General Wilkinson arrived at this place, and assumed the chief command of the army. Without delay he dispatched Colonel Cushing with a communication to Governor Codero, at Nacogdoches, demanding the immediate withdrawal of all Spanish troops to the west side of the Sabine. Codero, in reply, informed him that he would transmit his communication to the captain-general, without whose orders he could not act in the matter. General Wilkinson rejoined, and informed him that the troops of the United States would march to the Sabine, but without any hostile intention against the troops or territory of his Catholic majesty; that his sole object was to settle the western boundary of the United States, and to observe the movements of the Spanish forces near that river.

It was after the middle of October when the secret emissaries of Burr made a visit to the headquarters of General Wilkinson, at Natchitoches, to sound his views and feelings upon the subject of the contemplated enterprise. The general with great circumspection, elicited from them much information relative to the proposed movements of Burr, and then dismissed them with promises and evasive answers. Scarcely half satisfied with the result of their mission, they retired to the settlements in the Mississippi Territory, near Fort Adams, to await further developments.

* Martin's Louisiana, vol. ii., p. 266.

On the 22d of October General Wilkinson took up the line of march from Natchitoches to the Sabine, where he designed to establish his headquarters. As he advanced, he received notice from the Spanish commander that he should endeavor to prevent the occupation of the east bank of the Sabine River by the American army; yet General Wilkinson, regardless of this threat, continued his march, and reached the Sabine on the 24th, when he found the Spaniards encamped on the west side of the river.

The American army took position upon the left bank of the Sabine, while the Spanish occupied the right. These positions were held by the respective armies until about the 6th of November, when both commanders agreed to withdraw their forces and submit the settlement of the boundary question to the friendly action of their respective governments. This is the first time that the Sabine was ever considered as a limit of the Mexican provinces on the east.

General Wilkinson made no delay in opening a negotiation with Governor Codero relative to the establishment of a provisional boundary between the province of Texas and the Territory of Orleans. For this purpose, Major Walter Burling was dispatched as a special agent to treat with the governor for the peaceable settlement of the existing difficulties. The specific object of this mission has remained a mystery; but its general tenor and object was the amicable arrangement for a provisional boundary, and the voluntary withdrawal of the Spanish forces from the territory east of the Sabine.* From subsequent events, it was strongly believed that the mission had been instituted by General Wilkinson as much for his own pecuniary emolument as for the peaceable adjustment of a boundary. It was impossible for him to divest himself of the suspicion which settled over him, that he had extorted money from the Spanish governor by exciting his fears as to the powerful invasion contemplated by Burr, and which could be arrested only by the most energetic movements of the American commander-in-chief, with the whole of the army and means at his disposal.†

---

* See Martin's Louisiana, vol. ii., 272.

† The substance of this suspicion, which is certainly not without some foundation, is contained in the following "extract of a letter from New Orleans, dated April 23d, 1807," first published in the New York Spectator of June 10th, and copied in the Mississippi Messenger of August 11th, 1807. The author of this work has conversed with

Having completed his arrangements with the Spanish governor and General Herrera for the mutual withdrawal of the troops from the Sabine, General Wilkinson prepared to concentrate his forces upon the Mississippi, and the following order was issued to the American troops:

"MORNING ORDER.

"Camp, east bank of the Sabine, November 5th, 1806.

"His Excellency General Herrera, the military chief immediately opposed to this corps, having agreed to withdraw his troops to Nacogdoches, and to prohibit their re-crossing the Sabine River pending the negotiations between the United States and Spain, the objects of this expedition are accom-

some of the survivors of Captain Farrar's troop on the Sabine, and they corroborate the statement contained in the extract, viz.:

"The intendant said that General Wilkinson first communicated intelligence of the general nature of this plot to Governor Cordero upon the Sabine, and proposed to him, that if he would withdraw his forces from that river, and prevail upon the vice-king to furnish him (General Wilkinson) with $300,000, he would undertake to frustrate the designs of the conspirators, and save the provinces of his Catholic majesty from invasion, employing for that purpose the forces and other resources, naval and military, of the United States. Governor Cordero, knowing Wilkinson to have been for a long time in the interests of his king, lent a favorable ear to his propositions. He immediately consented that both armies should retire from the banks of the Sabine; the Spanish force for the purpose of re-enforcing their posts on the frontiers of New Mexico, and the American troops to defend the passes of the Mississippi. He also dispatched couriers to the vice-king in Mexico, and furnished Wilkinson forthwith with $120,000, *which were sent from St. Antoine upon mules.* The intendant further informed this gentleman that, before the arrival of Cordero's dispatches, the vice-king was by no means inclined to place full confidence in Wilkinson, and refused to transmit $180,000, the balance of the sum which Cordero had undertaken to promise him. Soon after this refusal, the intendant said that Wilkinson had dispatched a confidential aid-de-camp, Major Burling, to Mexico with further proofs of the conspiracy, and with further disclosures relating to the part taken in it by the inhabitants of the Spanish provinces, and with a request for the immediate payment of the $180,000 to General Wilkinson. The vice-king refused to receive the information from Burling, and referred him for the payment of the money to the intendant at La Vera Cruz, for which place he immediately ordered him to depart. Upon his arrival here, the intendant refused to furnish him with any thing but a guard, and ordered him to take his passage immediately to New Orleans.

"When the gentleman to whom this was spoken returned to this place, about a fortnight or three weeks ago, he mentioned the circumstances and the substance of this conversation to some of his friends, who immediately gave it circulation. It at last reached the ears of Wilkinson, and, after some hesitation, he was compelled to take notice of it. He sent an officer to the gentleman, with three written interrogatories, to which he requested an answer in writing. 1st. He demanded whether he had authorized the report of such conversation with the intendant at La Vera Cruz. 2d. Whether such conversation actually took place of the nature and name reported; and, 3d. Whether he believed the relation of the intendant to be true. To each of which this gentleman answered by a laconic *Yes!* and he has since heard nothing further from the general. From the weight of this gentleman's name and character, as well as from a thousand other corroborating circumstances, his report is almost universally accredited."

plished, and the camp will be, of course, evacuated to-morrow or next day, and Colonel Cushing will lead the troops to Natchitoches.

(Signed) "WALTER BURLING, *Aid-de-camp*."

Thus terminated the Sabine expedition. The object in view by the Federal government was the withdrawal of the Spanish army from within the present limits of the State of Louisiana. This object was certainly effected by General Wilkinson; and his friends congratulated the country "that all the noise and trouble on the western frontier had been settled quietly, by the intelligence, temper, and firmness of the general, without bloodshed."* Yet his troops retired indignantly from the Sabine, many of them fully convinced that they had been robbed of their anticipated laurels by the cupidity of their commander, who had entered into dishonorable negotiations, and that money, and not the sword, had terminated the campaign.

Ten days afterward, General Wilkinson dispatched Colonel Burling to Mexico upon a secret mission, avowedly to apprise the viceroy of the danger which menaced the dominions of his Catholic majesty west of the Mississippi, but, as he subsequently alleged, for a different purpose.†

Leaving the troops to be advanced to Fort Adams under their respective commanders, General Wilkinson, with his staff, proceeded to New Orleans, to make such arrangements as prudence and circumtsances might dictate for the defense of the city against the revolutionary designs of Aaron Burr and his confederates.

On the 24th of November he arrived in the city of New Orleans, and immediately commenced the most active measures for employing the resources of the country and the government in the defense of the nation against the contemplated movements for the invasion of Florida and Mexico. Of these, General Wilkinson had been apprised by the special agents sent from Burr himself, urging his active co-operation with the troops under his command. These confidential agents were Samuel Swartwout and Dr. Erick Bollman, who had obtained an interview at Natchitoches, and who renewed their

---
* See Mississippi Messenger, November 11th, 1806.
† Martin's Louisiana, vol. ii., p. 272–275.

efforts with the general again in more than one interview in New Orleans.

During the early part of December, the commander-in-chief was actively employed in the arduous duties devolving upon him for the defense of Louisiana and the city of New Orleans. As a part of the measures for this purpose, he assumed the responsibility of dispatching Lieutenant Swan to Jamaica, ostensibly to apprise the several British commanders at that station of the designs of Burr, in which he professed to expect aid from the British naval forces, and against which the commander-in-chief entered his formal protest.

On the 9th of December, Governor Claiborne, in view of the alarming danger which appeared to threaten the country from an unlawful combination on the Ohio, called a meeting of the principal citizens of New Orleans, which was assembled at the government house. At this meeting, Governor Claiborne and General Wilkinson personally attended, and announced to the people the imminent peril which required the active military preparations in progress for the defense of the city, in order to protect it against a powerful conspiracy of seven thousand men, who designed the subversion of the government, the dissolution of the Union, and the plunder of the city, preparatory to the establishment of a new government under the direction of one of the most influential and designing men in the Union.*

General Wilkinson spoke of the intended co-operation of the British navy in accomplishing the ultimate designs of Aaron Burr against the Spanish provinces of Mexico. The contemplated invasion, he asserted, had been communicated to him, by a special messenger from the conspirators, on the 18th day of October, at the moment when he was preparing to proceed to the Sabine. The object in making him acquainted with the plot, he said, was the hope of his co-operating with them; and that, without disclosing his determination, he set out for the Sabine, settled the Spanish affairs, and, with all expedition, repaired to New Orleans, where he intended to concentrate his forces for its defense or perish in its ruins: that, while at Natchitoches, he received a message on the same subject from New Orleans, and added, that there were several persons in the city who were concerned in the plot, and who were known to him, and whom he should have arrested long

* Martin's Louisiana, vol. ii., p. 277.

since had he been duly authorized. He informed them that his object in entering the city was to prepare for its security; but subsequent advices had determined him to change his plans, and attack the conspirators before they arrived, as their numbers were much greater than he had expected. To this end, he was preparing the flotilla to meet the foe above Natchez, compel them to land, and thus cut them off; to effect which, it was requisite that immediate measures should be taken, as the enemy, by all advices, was to arrive at Natchez on the 20th of December, with two thousand men. He also informed them that the leaders of the plot were supported by some of the first characters in the Union, that it was extensive in its object, and that, more effectually to accomplish its execution, armed vessels in disguise would enter the river to serve as convoys to the expedition to the port of Vera Cruz. To protect the mouth of the river, vessels were procured to occupy the passes, and he concluded by pledging his life in defense of the city and country.*

On the 10th of December the troops from Natchitoches arrived in the city; martial law was declared and rigorously enforced throughout the military district. Guards and patrols were distributed through the city, and upon the principal roads leading to the Mississippi Territory; and men who were *known* to belong to Burr's party, as well as those who were suspected, were unceremoniously arrested, and held in the custody of the commander-in-chief. Fort Adams, on the Mississippi, was placed in a state of complete military defense, and commanded the descent of the river. The officers of detachments and patrols were required to arrest, examine, and deliver to the civil authorities for further trial all strangers and suspicious persons not having passports from the commander-in-chief or some commissioned officer.

Rumors of the most alarming description were daily received from the Ohio River, magnifying the force and the resources of the conspirators in proportion to the fears and apprehensions of the informant. Nor were these rumors idle fabrications. The whole West was in a feverish excitement, and thousands were ready to embark in any enterprise against the Spanish power in the southwest, and not a few were willing to enlist in any undertaking which their leaders might require. New Or-

* Louisiana Gazette, December 12th, 1806.

leans was certainly in imminent danger, and was infested with hundreds of Burr's emissaries and adherents, who were distributed through the city and the country adjacent to the Mississippi, from the Walnut Hills to New Orleans. Suspicion fastened upon every emigrant from the Ohio or Western States, and every man who could not satisfactorily explain his arrival in the South. Hence arrests, discharges, and vexatious delays were frequent, even to the great annoyance of peaceable citizens. Those who at heart were favorably inclined to Burr's undertaking, as well as those who were secret emissaries and agents, complained bitterly of the intolerable annoyance, and dealt out wholesale denunciations against the useless precautions and the arbitrary conduct of General Wilkinson (although he was known to be acting under the orders of the President of the United States) as violations of individual rights secured by the Federal Constitution. Nor was it strange that they should charge him with a desire to promote his own aggrandizement in the substitution of martial law and arbitrary rule for the civil jurisdiction guarantied by the Constitution, seeing they alone were obnoxious to its operation.

About the same time, the patriotic citizens of New Orleans, as an evidence of their attachment to the Federal government and approval of the measures of General Wilkinson, and the zeal and energy evinced by him in defeating the designs of the conspirators, made a tender of their services for any duty to which he might assign them. To aid the government in suppressing the unlawful enterprise, " the inhabitants, merchants, captains, and supercargoes of vessels in the port evinced great zeal in favor of the efforts of the commander-in-chief, readily agreeing to the most laudable exertions and sacrifices for manning the vessels with seamen, while the citizens generally manifested unequivocal fidelity to the Union, and a spirit of determined resistance to the expected assailants."*

The patriotic governor of the Orleans Territory was also indefatigable in his efforts to sustain the views and measures of the commander-in-chief; and, to give efficient support, he called into service the militia and volunteers of the city, who were speedily organized into the " Battalion of New Orleans," and continued on duty until March following, when tranquillity was restored to the city.

* Jefferson's Message, December 16th, 1806.

On the 14th of December General Wilkinson arrested the fearless deliverer of La Fayette, Dr. Erick Bollman, a conspicuous emissary of Burr, and sent him to a place of security below the city. Soon afterward he caused the arrest of Samuel Swartwout, of New York, and Peter V. Ogden, of New Jersey, known adherents of Aaron Burr. These men were retained in the custody of the commander-in-chief until an opportunity presented of sending them to Richmond, Virginia, to stand their trial before the supreme tribunal of the country.

On the 16th of December Governor Claiborne issued his proclamation as "Governor of the Territory of Orleans, and Commander-in-chief of the Militia thereof," in which he denounced the "*traitorous project* to subvert the authority of the government of the United States over a portion of the territories thereof, and to invade the dominions of the King of Spain, a prince in amity with the United States," and made known the law and the penalty against such an offense.*

* The following is the proclamation of Governor Claiborne:

A PROCLAMATION,

By *William C. C. Claiborne, Governor of the Territory of Orleans, and Commander-in-chief of the Militia thereof.*

Whereas I have received information that certain persons are combining and confederating in a *traitorous project* to subvert the authority of the government of the United States over a portion of the territories thereof, and to invade the dominions of the King of Spain, a prince in amity with the United States, I have thought proper to issue this my proclamation, hereby solemnly cautioning the citizens of this territory against entering into, or in any manner countenancing, the conspiracy aforesaid; and that no one may remain ignorant of the fatal consequences which may await the parties concerned, I do now make it known that the law of the United States declares, "that if any person, or persons, owing allegiance to the United States of America, shall *levy war against them, or shall adhere to their enemies,* giving them aid and comfort within the United States, or elsewhere, and shall be thereof convicted, on confession in open court, or on the testimony of two witnesses, to the same overt act of the treason whereof he or they shall stand indicted, such person, or persons, shall be adjudged guilty of treason against the United States, and *shall suffer death;*" and that "if any person, or persons, having knowledge of the commission of any of the treasons aforesaid, shall conceal, and not as soon as may be disclose and make known the same to the President of the United States, or some one of the judges thereof, or to the president or governor of a particular state, or some one of the judges or justices thereof, such person, or persons, on conviction, shall be adjudged guilty of misprision of treason, and shall be imprisoned not exceeding seven years, and fined not exceeding one thousand dollars."

And I do further make it known, that the law of the United States has also declared, "that if any person shall, within the territory or jurisdiction of the United States, begin or set on foot, or provide or prepare the means of any military expedition or enterprise to be carried on from thence against the territory or dominions of any foreign prince or state with whom the United States are at peace, every such person so offending shall, upon conviction, be adjudged guilty of high misdemeanor, and shall suffer fine and imprisonment at the discretion of the court in which the conviction shall be had, so as that such fine shall not exceed three thousand dollars, nor the term of imprisonment be more than three years."

Meantime, great efforts were made by the friends of Dr. Bollman for his release from the military custody of General Wilkinson. In his efforts to effect this object, none was more zealous and indefatigable than James Alexander, Esq., acting as attorney in his behalf. On Tuesday, the 16th of December, having applied to Judge Dominic A. Hall, of the Superior Court of the Territory, upon the affidavits of himself, Leonora d'Avergne, and Edmund Forrestal, relative to the arrest of Dr Bollman at the command of General Wilkinson, an order was granted " that a writ of *habeas corpus, ad subjiciendum,* on behalf of Dr. Bollman, do issue, directed to General Wilkinson, returnable to-morrow at eleven o'clock in the morning; it was *further ordered,* that the general be served with copies of the affidavits filed in this behalf."

Next day the return made thereto was in the following words, viz.:

"*The undersigned, commanding the army of the United States, takes to himself all responsibility for the arrest of Errick Bollman, on a charge of misprision of treason against the government and laws of the United States, and has adopted measures for his safe delivery to the executive of the United States. It was after several consultations with the governor and two of the judges of this territory, that the undersigned has hazarded this step for the national safety, menaced to its base by a lawless band of traitors, associated under Aaron Burr, whose accomplices are extended from New York to this city. No man can hold in higher reverence the civil institutions of his country than the undersigned, and it is to maintain and perpetuate the holy attributes of the Constitution against the uplifted hand of violence that he has interposed the force of arms, in a moment of extreme peril, to seize upon Bollman, as he will upon all others, without regard to standing or station, against whom satisfactory proof may arise, of a participation in the lawless combination.*

"JAMES WILKINSON.

"*Headquarters, Army of the United States, New Orleans, December* 17, 1806."*

About the same time, General Wilkinson was served with an-

Given at New Orleans, the 16th December, 1806, and of the sovereignty and independence of the United States the thirty-first.

[L. S.] In testimony whereof, I have undersigned my name, and caused the public seal to be hereunto affixed.   WILLIAM C. C. CLAIBORNE.

By the Governor,   R. CLAIBORNE, Secretary *pro tem.*

* New Orleans Gazette, December 18th, 1806.

other writ of *habeas corpus* from Judge James Workman, of the court of the county of Orleans, for the release of Peter V. Ogden, in the custody of the general. The prisoner was produced, and the judge, deeming his imprisonment illegal and unconstitutional, ordered his release.

But General Wilkinson persisted in making other arrests of persons suspected to be in the confidence of Burr, and active in their efforts to insure the successful issue of the undertaking. It was not long afterward when he again caused the arrest of Peter V. Ogden, who was immediately sent down the river, beyond the reach of judicial interference. With him was arrested his late attorney and advocate, James Alexander, who was also secured under the custody of a military guard near Fort St. Philip, until an opportunity offered of transmitting them by sea to the port of Baltimore, where they were placed in the custody of the commandant of Fort M'Henry.

While these things were transpiring in the Territory of Orleans as well as in the Mississippi Territory, Governor Grandpre, at Baton Rouge, alarmed at the threatening aspect of affairs, and well apprised that West Florida was one of the Spanish provinces against which the conspirators designed to march, conferred with the officers of his government and the principal inhabitants, to whom he recommended the prompt organization of the militia for active service, ready to march at the first notice.*

[A.D. 1807.] Such was the state of public anxiety and suspicion until the middle of January following. During this time General Wilkinson had been actively and zealously engaged in giving additional strength to the defenses of the city, and in defeating the plans of the conspirators, by arresting and securing the prominent leaders for a legal investigation before the Supreme Court of the United States. Among those placed under military arrest during this time were James M. Bradford, editor of the New Orleans Gazette, Lewis Kerr, an Irish barrister, a man of enterprise and restless activity, and an ardent advocate for the invasion of Mexico. Many others, who had taken an active part in opposing the prosecution of Burr's adherents, were also arrested by General Wilkinson, and sent to the Federal authorities near the city of Washington.†

* Mississippi Messenger, January 13th, 1807.
† See Mississippi Herald and Natchez Gazette of January 27th, of April 15th, 22d, and 29th, and of May 6th, 1807.

It was on the 14th day of January that General John Adair, of Kentucky, one of the most fearless of men, was arrested at the dinner-table of his hotel by Colonel Kingsbury, at the head of one hundred men, by whom he was taken to the headquarters of General Wilkinson, whence he was removed to Fort St. Philip for security, where he remained until an opportunity offered, when, in company with Peter V. Ogden, he was shipped to Baltimore on board the schooner Thatcher, Ezra Hows master, in charge of Lieutenant Luck and a corporal's guard. General Adair had been an active participant in the enterprise of Burr for the invasion of the Spanish provinces; yet, like all the others who were indicted for the high misdemeanor, he was finally discharged for want of sufficient proof.*

* The following affidavit of Dr. John F. Carmichael, formerly surgeon in General Wilkinson's army, and the statement of Dr. Claiborne, comprise the principal testimony obtained against General Adair, viz.:

"*County of Orleans, ss.*

"Personally appeared before me, the subscriber, one of the justices of the peace in and for the said county, Doctor John F. Carmichael, who on his solemn oath declares that, on the evening of the 11th of January instant, Mr. Ralston and Mr. Floyd, the son of Captain Floyd, of Louisville, Kentucky, called at the house of this deponent, spent the evening and breakfasted with him the next day; that the conversation during the evening and morning generally related to the various opinions in circulation respecting Colonel Burr, and the situation of this country; that after breakfast Mr. Ralston opened his business with this deponent, stating that he had descended the Mississippi as far as New Madrid in company with Colonel Burr, where he left him; that General Adair had gone to New Orleans by a circuitous route, and that his intention was to communicate with General Wilkinson, and to return so as to meet them at my house about that time, if possible; that it was an object with them to obtain the exact situation of the fort at Baton Rouge, the state of the works, the number of men, its weak situation; and that Fort Adams was of some consequence; what United States troops were there, and who commanded them; where the gun-boats were, and who individually commanded them; who was the commanding officer of marines, &c. All these questions were answered by this deponent as far as he had been acquainted with them. The said Ralston and Floyd proposed to this deponent to visit Baton Rouge to ascertain the exact situation of that fort, but declined when the orders of Colonel Grandpre were stated, and the difficulty attending such an enterprise. Mr. Ralston informed me that Colonel Burr was to be, on the 12th day of January instant, at Bayou Pierre, where he was to wait for his re-enforcement and to receive his information from his agents, who were circulated through the country in that time; that the first object of Colonel Burr was *to take Baton Rouge*, where he was to *raise his standard*, and to make his communication to the government of the United States, and where he was to be joined by a number of men already engaged, to the number of ten thousand men, if necessary; that the number at present with Colonel Burr did not exceed one hundred and fifty, but Colonel Burr's arrangements were so made that the men already engaged in Kentucky and Tennessee should join without show, so that no possible alarm or suspicion on the part of the general government might take place *before he had left* the government and *taken possession of Baton Rouge*. Mr. Ralston further stated to this deponent that it was not the intention of Colonel Burr to promote and make a separation of the Union, but to act against the Spanish government; and stated the intended expedition against Mexico. When this deponent mentioned the name of Captain Shaw

General Adair had long been known as one of the most active and fearless men in the United States; his courage was proverbial, even in Kentucky; and no man entertained a stronger aversion to the power of Spain in the South and West. Hence the expulsion of the Spaniards from Florida, and the invasion of Mexico, were not repugnant to his feelings.

In his route through the Indian nations to New Orleans in the autumn of 1806, he traversed the country from Nashville southward to the new settlements, on the Lower Tombigby; thence, by way of Pascagoula and Pearl River, to New Orleans.

During the month of January great excitement prevailed in New Orleans; the troops were kept continually marching through the streets of the city, the volunteer " Battalion of New Orleans" was upon constant duty, and the city and its envi-

Mr. Ralston observed that, if he was one of the Mediterranean officers, he was friendly to their measures; and it was well understood that a large proportion of the officers of the army and Mediterranean officers were already engaged in their interests. Mr. Ralston expressed great surprise at the conduct of General Wilkinson in arresting certain characters, Swartwout, Ogden, Bollman, and Alexander, and repeatedly asked this deponent what he thought of the conduct of General Wilkinson, and whether he believed he had deserted the interests of the party, or was it only to cover his greater objects. This deponent further declares that Mr. Ralston and Mr. Floyd visited the fortifications of Fort Adams on the evening of the 12th of January instant, between sunset and dark, and walked round the said fort.

(Signed)   " JOHN F. CARMICHAEL.
"Sworn and subscribed before me on this 18th day of January, 1807.
(Signed)   " B. CENAS, *Justice of Peace.*"

The statement of Dr. Claiborne is as follows:
" *General James Wilkinson,*

" SIR,—In compliance to your request of yesterday, relative to the period of General John Adair's arrival and departure from the city of Nashville, Tennessee, and the conversation that passed between us while there, I hasten to make the following statement, which I believe to be a correct one: General John Adair and Colonel Burr arrived at Nashville about the middle of December last from Kentucky; I know not whether they came together. They lodged at the same house, and occupied, I understood, one room. They left Nashville within a few days of each other, General Adair by land and Colonel Burr by water. From a previous conversation with Adair, an impression was made on my mind that he had either returned to Kentucky, or had gone to visit the tract of country lately ceded to the United States by the Chickasâ Indians, on the waters of Duck River, having expressed a determination of making a purchase in that quarter, if the land answered the description.

" He mentioned his intention of visiting New Orleans in the course of three weeks from the time of his arrival at Nashville, and that he would be happy if I could be ready to accompany him. I heard no more of the general for a week, when I was informed by a gentleman from Natchez that he met him and his servant in the Chickasâ nation, traveling with great rapidity in a direction to the Mississippi Territory. His business in this quarter I know not. I believe the above to be all that passed between us.

"I have the honor to be, respectfully, your obedient servant,
"THOMAS A. CLAIBORNE."

rons presented the appearance of a besieged town, with numerous gun-boats and armed vessels in port, and stationed at different points upon the river and adjacent lakes. In all the active measures of defense, Governor Claiborne sustained the commander-in-chief by the whole weight of his influence and authority. The proceedings of both officers were approved by a large majority of the resident inhabitants of the city and the adjacent territories.

Yet there were hundreds of transient persons and a few resident citizens, some holding high offices of trust and honor, who joined in the clamor against the usurpations of the governor and the commanding general.

Such denounced in no measured terms the military arrests as unwarrantable assumptions of power and gross violations of the Federal Constitution, meriting the severest vengeance of the law; they declared that military despotism had superseded the civil authority, and had trampled the Constitution under foot upon the idle pretext of a plot to overthrow the government. Hundreds of emigrants and strangers, comparatively, were suddenly inspired with a deep concern for the inviolability of the Constitution, and a sacred regard for the personal liberty and the right of trial by jury guarantied by that instrument. Even men clothed with the superior judicial authority of the United States were found ready and willing to protect the conspirators with their individual influence in the community, and also with their official power, by means of the writ of "habeas corpus."

Among the violent and vindictive opposers of the measures adopted by Governor Claiborne and General Wilkinson for the suppression of Burr's enterprise, James Workman, judge of the county of Orleans, stands pre-eminent; and second to him may be named Dominic A. Hall, judge of the Superior Territorial Court. Judge Workman was a naturalized Englishman, who had been concerned in the stormy politics of Europe, and had witnessed the scenes which had disgraced Paris during the Reign of Terror, and still retained a bias in favor of revolutionary principles in America. After his collision with General Wilkinson, he omitted no opportunity, and spared no effort, officially as well as in his private capacity, to embarrass his operations for the apprehension of the conspirators and the suppression of the conspiracy, which was then agitating the whole western country.

Such had been the obnoxious character of his opposition early in January, that on the 14th he was himself arrested by a military order, and carried to the headquarters of General Wilkinson, from whose custody he was released next day by a writ of " habeas corpus," issued by Judge Hall of the Superior Territorial Court. From that time he redoubled his efforts, by the exercise of the power of his office, under the guise of imperative duty, and his personal influence, to bring General Wilkinson to condign punishment; but, after weeks of unavailing effort to induce Governor Claiborne to sustain his course, finding that the governor remained firm against his remonstrances, entreaties, and reproaches, in disgust, after a public and undignified appeal to the governor, he adjourned his court *sine die*, and on the 23d of February, 1807, sent in his resignation; and thus terminated his official authority and his influence in the territory. A few days afterward he was indicted by the grand jury for a high misdemeanor, and charged with being an adherent of Aaron Burr, "in setting on foot a military expedition against the Spanish provinces of Florida and Mexico," for which he was tried on the 4th of March; but the evidence being insufficient for conviction, like his associates, he was discharged.*

Judge Hall, also an Englishman by birth and predilection, omitted no opportunity to interpose the weight of his official station, as well as his personal influence, to protect the conspirators from the power of the commander-in-chief. The same judge, eight years afterward, as if unconquerably averse to the interests and prosperity of his adopted country, interposed his official authority to arrest the vigorous efforts of Major-general Andrew Jackson in his masterly defense of New Orleans against a powerful British army, thereby contributing to the probable success of the enemy, and facilitating, so far as he was able, their advance against the city.

The result of the conflicting interests, opinions, and feelings of the people, during the excitement of Burr's enterprise, proves the possibility that the judiciary, the great bulwark of freedom, in improper hands, may be converted into a shield for the protection of the most dangerous enemies of the country; far more to be feared than military power itself in virtuous hands. Such had been the use made by unworthy men of the cautious

* See Mississippi Herald and Natchez Gazette, April 1st and 15th, 1807.

delay in the administration of justice, as originally provided by American legislators, when brought to bear upon a powerful conspiracy and a popular enterprise. The authority of the highest courts, the forms of making the grand inquest, and the officers of justice for the execution of the laws, may become only so many means of evading the very laws themselves. Courts, judges, attorney-generals, and grand juries may become only so many avenues or instruments for the escape of great offenders. Such might have been observed in the various arrests and discharges, commitments and acquittals, indictments and trials which grew out of the government prosecutions connected with Burr's noted scheme in Kentucky, Mississippi, Louisiana, and Virginia. Such was the case especially in the city of New Orleans.

Even the grand jury, forgetting that the general safety of the country was a paramount consideration, and that the commander-in-chief was acting under the superior authority and instructions of the President of the United States, attempted to embarrass the operations of General Wilkinson, and to throw censure upon his official conduct, as subversive of the civil authority. Thus, at the January term of the Supreme Court of the territory, holden in the City Hall of New Orleans, the grand jury,* among other presentments within the limits of their duties, made one against General Wilkinson for his measures of public safety, which were termed "illegal military despotism," the "forcible suspension of the writ of *habeas corpus*," contrary to the Constitution of the United States. The fact upon which this presentment was based was the arrest of Samuel Swartwout, Dr. Erick Bollman, Peter V. Ogden, and James Alexander, known agents and emissaries of Aaron Burr.†

---

* The grand jury was constituted of Evan Jones, *foreman*, George Pollock, William Davis, William Nott, John Poultney, William Kenner, J. M'Neal, S. B. Davis, Waters Clark, F. Armaud, Edmond Foriestall, William Munford, D. Urquhart, P. F. Dubourg, N. Girod, J. Touro, and F. Duplessis.—See *Mississippi Herald, Natchez, February* 4th, 1807.

† The following is an extract from the opinion delivered by Judge Fitzhugh, on the commitment of Messrs. *Bollman* and *Swartwout*, on a charge of treason, copied in the Mississippi Messenger, March 21st, 1807, and in the papers generally, viz. :

"These inquiries obviously occur: 1st. Is there probable cause to believe that any treason has been committed against the United States, and this supported by oath, &c.? 2d. Are the prisoners implicated in the treason? and, 3d. How, whether as principals, or only guilty of misprision of treason?

"That there is probable cause to believe that treason has been committed by Colonel

The precaution of the commander-in-chief, in establishing military patrols for the apprehension of suspicious persons Burr, the public rumor and universal alarm which seem to have convulsed our country from the extremity to the center; the president's communication to Congress and to the court, afford at least grounds of suspicion, and this is supported by the positive oaths of General Eaton, General Wilkinson, Mr. Donaldson, Mr. Mead, and Mr. Wilson, all going to show the origin, existence, and progress of Burr's treasonable projects and acts. But here the counsel for the prisoners have insisted that none of this mass of evidence criminates Burr, and have contended that the president's communications are inadmissible. It is not generally by detached parts of evidence, but by a well-connected chain of circumstances that we arrive at proof; nor can a crime be made out by the proof of any solitary fact. In a charge of murder it would not be sufficient to show that a blow was given from which death ensued; but it is necessary to prove and disclose a particular state of mind. There must be deliberate resentment, or ill will; there must be malice prepense. So in treason (the case now under consideration), no degree of violence, however atrocious, no enlisting or marching men; no injury, if limited in its object to personal rivalship, or even extensive enough in point of locality to contemplate and threaten the opposition and destruction of the laws, or government of any one of the United States, will amount to treason against the United States. It is the intention alone which fixes the grade of the offense. This intention is only to be collected from circumstances; and though the communications of the president do not of themselves furnish full evidence of Burr's treason against the United States, yet they must be considered entitled to some weight in leading to the conclusion that there is probable cause; but when, in addition to this, it is considered that the most solemn obligation is imposed by the Constitution on the president to make communications of this nature to Congress, and that he has also, in further discharge of his constitutional duties, ordered out the militia, which on ordinary and trivial occasions he is not justifiable in doing, a person must be *strangely incredulous* who will not admit that there is probable cause of suspicion that a dangerous insurrection or treason exists in our country. A report thus sanctioned by duty and oath, if made to this court by one of its officers, would be respected, and why shall not a communication from the first executive officer of the Union be credited, when he announces to the nation information in the line of his duties ? But this general ground of alarm is rendered more specific by the affidavits which have been exhibited to us. If the persons who have been sworn on this occasion are to be believed (and no one has yet questioned their credibility), they prove a scheme laid by Burr to usurp the government of the United States, to sever the Western States from the Union, *to establish an empire west of the Alleghany Mountains*, of which he, Burr, was to be the sovereign, and New Orleans the emporium, and *to invade and revolutionize Mexico*. That in prosecution of those projects he wrote a letter to General Wilkinson, the commander-in-chief of the American army, with the avowed object and design of alienating him from his duty, and inviting him to embark in the undertaking, and holding out to him the most flattering and sanguine assurances and prospects of success. Horrid as this attempt was, yet if the information had reached no further, I should have no hesitation in saying that it would have been nothing more than a conspiracy to commit treason, or some other offense. But when Burr assures Wilkinson that he had obtained funds, and *actually commenced* the enterprise; that detachments from various points and under different pretenses would rendezvous on the Ohio the 1st of November; that his plan was to move down rapidly from the Falls the 15th of November, with first 500 or 1000 men in light boats *now constructing for that purpose:* when, in addition to this, Wilson and Mead swear that when they left New Orleans, the one the 15th, the other the 19th of December, the strongest apprehension and belief universally prevailed among the inhabitants that Burr and his confederates had prepared an armed force, and were marching to attack and plunder the city; and that they knew that Wilkinson was decidedly of opinion, from the most satisfactory information, that Burr was advancing, and under that belief he was putting the place in a posture of defense: when this coinci-

and others who at this time infested the country, and had suddenly appeared from unknown parts, was also presented as a nuisance.

Nor did the malcontents confine themselves to mere verbal remonstrances and denunciations: many, through the press, continued to assail the conduct of the general as arbitrary and despotic, "not required by the exigency of the times," and proceeding from improper motives. To give themselves the semblance of respectability in point of numbers, they were active, indefatigable, and persevering in the clamor raised against the patriotic and faithful execution of the laws.

The *mass of the people* sustained the governor, as well as the commander-in-chief, although they entered not into the noise and strife of political contention and angry denunciation.

Yet there were many who openly approved his course, and justified him in the exercise of military power for accomplishing his object. By those who were zealous for the suppression of any treasonable enterprise, and were solicitous for the protection of the city and country from anarchy and bloodshed, by the enforcement of the president's commands, such sensibility to military rule, and such affected zeal for the supremacy of the civil authority, were viewed only as an evidence

dence of circumstances and this strength of testimony appear, there can be little doubt of the existence and the extent of Burr's views, and of his having imbodied and enlisted men with views hostile to the government of his country, and that he has done acts which amount to levying war on the United States.

"Burr's treason, then, being established, we are to inquire whether the prisoners were his confederates. They are represented, under oath, to have been the bearers of the duplicates of Burr's letters in cipher to Wilkinson, and to possess Burr's confidence; they use arguments, in addition to those in the letter, to invite Wilkinson to accede to their views; admit that they have corresponded with Burr on the subject since the delivery of the letter; that Swartwout informed Wilkinson that Burr, with a powerful association, extending from New York to New Orleans, was levying an armed body of 7000 men from New York and the Western States and Territories, with a view to carry an expedition against the Mexican provinces, and that 500 men under Colonel Swartwout and Major Tyler were to defend the Alleghany, for whose accommodation *light boats had been built and were ready*; said that New Orleans would be revolutionized when the people were ready to join them, and that there would be some *seizing*.

"Here, then, is evidence of a connection with Colonel Burr of a treasonable nature. What is it? The act of Congress defines misprision of treason to be a neglect to disclose the knowledge of a treason. But the prisoners have not only known of the treason, but carried a treasonable letter, knowing its contents; endeavored to further Burr's views and wishes, and to seduce Wilkinson from his duty. The offense exceeds misprision of treason, and as there is no intermediate class of offenses of a treasonable nature between misprision and treason, it must be treason.

"I am, therefore, of opinion, that the prisoners should be committed for treason against the United States, in levying war against them."

of their concurrence or participation in the designs of the conspirators, disguised under the cloak of avowed patriotism. It was with the view to sustain the execution of the president's orders that Governor Claiborne, about this time, in his address to the Legislative Council, urged the necessity and the expediency of *suspending* the constitutional right of the "writ of *habeas corpus*," until affairs should assume a more tranquil condition. But the council refused to comply.

The governor's zeal and patriotism were approved by the majority of the good citizens, as was likewise the active measures of General Wilkinson for the suppression of any contemplated conspiracy. Among the many evidences of this approbation was an address in behalf of the commercial interests, signed by thirty-one captains of vessels in the port.*

Meanwhile, Aaron Burr, with a number of boats, a small supply of arms and ammunition, and less than one hundred men, had arrived at the mouth of the Bayou Pierre, in the Mississippi Territory, and had surrendered himself and his immediate attendants into the hands of the civil authorities; had entered into recognizance, had forfeited his bonds, had been proclaimed a fugitive from justice, had been captured upon the Tombigby, delivered into the hands of the commander-in-chief, and was then on his way to stand his trial at Richmond, Virginia, under a charge for "a high misdemeanor."†

---

* The following is a copy of this address:

"*His Excellency Brigadier-general* JAMES WILKINSON,

"SIR,—The subscribers, masters of vessels in the port of New Orleans, beg leave to express to you, through this channel of communication, the high sense they entertain of your services in the present alarming crisis.

"Surrounded as we are by suspicious or deluded persons, more than ordinary means are requisite to frustrate their nefarious designs; and although we deprecate military ascendency in a free government, yet at *this juncture we consider it the only alternative* to preserve the peace of the country, and *maintain inviolable the interests of the United States*.

"In all your measures, sir, we have perceived the arm of power guided by the dictates of *patriotism;* and we are well convinced that the civil authority is set aside *only because it is incompetent*, from the nature of its process, to avert the storm which was ready to burst over us.

"That your exertion may be crowned with success, and your services meet the reward which they so justly merit, is the sincere wish of, sir, your admirers and friends."

(Here follows the signatures of thirty-one captains.)

"RICHARD STITES,
"LLOYD JONES,   } *Committee to wait on the general.*"
"W. J. PIGOT,

† Martin's Louisiana, vol. ii., p. 290–295.

Thus terminated the excitement and alarm which had pervaded the whole West relative to the contemplated separation of the Union, and the invasion of the Spanish provinces.

While these events were transpiring in the vicinity of the Lower Mississippi, the agents and officers of Spain and the United States were active in their explorations upon the upper tributaries of the Arkansas and Red Rivers. During the years 1805 and 1806 the Spanish cavalry had penetrated into the country north of the Upper Arkansas, for the purpose of establishing missions, and forming friendly alliances with the native tribes in that quarter, claiming the regions drained by those rivers. Nor had the agents and officers of the Federal government been idle. After the jealousy of the Spaniards had precluded an examination of Red River by way of Natchitoches, an exploring party was fitted out to advance across the country from the Missouri River to the head waters of the Arkansas and Red Rivers, and thence to examine them to their junctions with the Mississippi. By order of the president, Lieutenant Z. M. Pike, of the first regiment of United States Infantry, on the 24th of June, 1806, received from General James Wilkinson, at St. Louis, his instructions for conducting these explorations. The principal object was to establish a good understanding with the *Tetaus*, or Camanche Indians, and to examine the country.

The instructions proceed as follows: "As your interview with the Camanches will probably lead you to the head branches of the Arkansas and Red Rivers, you may find yourself approximated to the settlements of New Mexico; and there it will be necessary you should move with great circumspection, to keep clear of any hunting or reconnoitering parties from that province, and to prevent alarm or offense, because the affairs of Spain and the United States appear to be on the point of amicable adjustment; and, moreover, it is the desire of the president to cultivate the friendship and harmonious intercourse of all the nations of the earth, and particularly of our neighbors, the Spaniards."*

It is evident that a military invasion of Mexico had been deemed a possible event; for Lieutenant Pike, in his communications to General Wilkinson from the "Pawnee Republic," upon the Arkansas, observes, "Any number of men (who may

* Pike's Expedition, p. 108.

reasonably be calculated on) would find no difficulty in marching the route we came, with baggage wagons, field artillery, and all the usual appendages of a small army; and I would pledge my life (and, what is infinitely dearer, *my honor*) for the successful march of a reasonable body of troops into the province of New Mexico."*

Meantime, while General Wilkinson was operating upon the Lower Mississippi, for the suppression of Burr's plan for the invasion of the Spanish provinces, Lieutenant Pike, with his exploring detachment, had penetrated across the sources of the Arkansas and Red Rivers, when he ascertained that himself, with a portion of his party, were upon the sources of the Rio del Norte, within the Spanish dominions. Having been conducted, unwillingly, by a Spanish troop, to the interior provinces, he was detained by the governor for several months, in company with his attendants; in the following summer he was escorted to the province of Texas, and from thence he proceeded toward the American settlements, and arrived at Natchitoches in July, 1807. Another portion of his party having descended Red River, had reached Fort Adams, on the Mississippi, in the month of February preceding.

The position held by General Wilkinson, in regard to Burr's contemplated invasion of Mexico, has been a subject of doubt and mystery with many, who were but partially acquainted with the history of his political and military life in the West. His intimate connection with the Spanish authorities of Louisiana during his commercial career in Kentucky, from 1787 to 1792; his subsequent epistolary correspondence with the Spanish governor and his agents, while holding a command in the western army of the United States, until the year 1796; and the reception of large sums of money, even at that late period, from the Spanish agents, as also at previous dates, which fact is fully established, all concurred to fix a suspicion upon his conduct, and upon the motives by which he was influenced, and to raise up numerous active enemies to his peace and reputation as an officer in the service of the United States.

During the political troubles and excitement which prevailed in Kentucky previous to the adoption of the state Constitution, there is ample evidence that he belonged to that portion of Kentucky politicians which was known as the Spanish party.

* Pike's Expedition, Appendix to Part II., p. 47-49.

This party, like several others, contemplated a separation of the western country from the Atlantic States on the east and north, and a distinct and independent government, which would secure them the uninterrupted navigation and trade of the Mississippi River.

After the acquisition of Louisiana, he conceived the plan of revolutionizing the Spanish provinces of Mexico and Florida, and took every opportunity of promoting its accomplishment. It was a matter in which he felt a deep interest, and of which he often spoke to his confidential friends as an object worthy of their ambition, and one which, as commander-in-chief of the American army, he expected ultimately to achieve. The plan of this undertaking had been communicated to Colonel Burr and to General Adair, two men of undoubted courage and ambition, as an enterprise in which military distinction and great riches would be the reward of success. At this time difficulties between the Spanish court and the Federal government had increased to such an extent, and border difficulties, east and west of the Mississippi, were so frequent, and so irritating to the impatient people of the West, that the most discerning politicians were in daily apprehension of an open rupture with Spain; and the Spanish authorities, in view of such an event, had re-enforced all the garrisons in Florida and Texas, which latter was claimed as extending to the Arroyo Hondo, in the vicinity of Natchitoches. The western people had imbibed these views, and were impatient to engage in the war, and to embark in an expedition against the Mexican provinces. This expedition, it was hoped, would be organized and conducted under the authority and auspices of the Federal government. The high position occupied by General Wilkinson led him to believe that he should be appointed its leader, in which case he hoped to immortalize himself as the liberator of Mexico. In anticipation of such an event, he had planned the exploring party of Lieutenant Pike, to obtain a more perfect knowledge of the country.*

* The following is the substance of the deposition of Judge Timothy Kibby, of the "Louisiana Territory," an acting chief-justice of the Court of Common Pleas for the District of St. Charles, also colonel of militia, taken before Judge Otho Shrader, territorial judge of the United States, on the 6th of July, 1807, published in the Mississippi Herald, September 15th, 1807.

This deponent declares, "That in July, 1805, he was introduced to General Wilkinson at St. Charles, and after a private and confidential interview, the general inquired into the views, feelings, and prejudices of the people of St. Charles as regarded the

This accounts for a paragraph contained in one of his letters to General Adair, in the spring of 1806, and which was subsequently produced as evidence of his connection with Burr's contemplated invasion. In this he remarks, respecting Mexico and Santa Fé, " Do you not know that I have reserved these places for my own triumphal entry? that I have been reconnoitering and exploring the route for sixteen years? that I not only know the way, but all the difficulties, and how to surmount them? *I wish I could get leave, and Mexico would soon be ours,*" &c.*

Thus it is that General Wilkinson, ignorant of events which were subsequently to transpire, may have used expressions which, with some of his acts at a later period, after Burr's disgrace, might be construed into a participation in his guilt.

On this important and trying occasion, relative to his operations for the defeat of Burr's enterprise, General Wilkinson merits, at the hands of posterity, such judgment as must be sustained by his uniform patriotism, and the tenor of his service in defense of his country both before and after this transaction.

American government; whether they were pleased with the change. He inquired, whether the greater portion *would not prefer a government separate from the government of the United States.* The general said that, as the greater portion of the people in Upper Louisiana had left the United States, and removed to this country while it was under the Spanish dominion, he was convinced that they could not be pleased with their own government, &c.

"The general desired him to make the acquaintance of Mr. Burr, who was then at St. Louis, and who was one of the most *enterprising men* in the United States.

"In a subsequent interview, in October following (1806), the general avoided the name of Burr; said we should before long have enough to do; for in eighteen months there would be an attack upon the Spanish provinces of Mexico; that he should lead the expedition, and personally make the attack. He tendered to Colonel Kibby a handsome command in the campaign; inquired how many men could be obtained in the St. Charles District, intimating that Spain was about to declare war against the United States, and that the latter would attack Mexico and Peru.

"Similar conversations were subsequently held at divers times. The general speaking of Lieutenant Pike's expedition, upon inquiry, replied, smiling, that it was of a *secret nature,* and that Lieutenant Pike himself was not apprised of the ultimate object of his expedition; but that his destination was Santa Fé, treating with the Indians as he advanced. He intimated that Lieutenant Pike had been dispatched by *his orders;* that the plan was *his own;* not emanating from the government, but assented to; and stated, 'That, if he should succeed, he *should be in a situation to call his d—d enemies to account for their deeds.*'

"Upon learning that Colonel Kibby was attached to the government of the United States, and would march wherever ordered for the interests of the country, the general seemed surprised, and subsequently was more reserved."

The whole tenor of this statement is altogether compatible with General Wilkinson's fidelity to the government in 1806, he believing that it secretly contemplated an invasion of the Spanish provinces. The last paragraph of this affivadit will be duly appreciated by the reader when he is informed that Judge or Colonel Kibby was a zealous adherent of Aaron Burr as late as November, 1806.

* See Mississippi Messenger, June 30th, 1837.

When his military services are reviewed, whether in the revolutionary struggle for independence, or during the subsequent campaigns in the Northwestern Territory against the savages and their Canadian allies, or during his command in the West after the cession of the province of Louisiana, until the occupancy of Fort Charlotte on the Mobile, and his activity and zeal at a later period in preparing for the defense of the southern borders against British invasion, or his conduct while on the Niagara frontier, no one transaction can be adduced which savors of treachery to his government. Whatever may have been his indiscretions, his pecuniary exactions, and his commercial intrigues with the credulous Spaniards, he never was a traitor to his country, or deserted her in the hour of danger.

In resisting the enterprise of Burr and his adherents, Wilkinson necessarily encountered the hostility and the strong opposition of those whom he had formerly esteemed as friends; and so far as his duty to the Federal government was concerned, it is only necessary to witness the fidelity and firmness with which he encountered danger and opposition in suppressing the conspiracy, in obedience to the proclamation of the president and the orders of the executive departments. The finesse of diplomacy which could extort from the Spaniards a ransom for the safety of their provinces does not change this feature of the question.

Meantime, while these events were engrossing the public attention, the territorial Legislature had been engaged in a long and arduous session of more than three months. The important duties of framing and organizing a system of state polity adapted to the Constitution and laws of the United States, and yet so modified as to be acceptable to the Creole population, who had their predilections for the prompt and efficient government of Spain, were completed late in April. County courts were abolished, and in their stead a species of court was organized partaking of the nature of a Spanish commandant's court, and known as parish courts. From these originated the more perfect system of the parish judge's court, which continued in use for nearly forty years afterward. The judge was, *ex officio*, judge of probate, and performed the duties of sheriff, clerk, and notary public. In the parishes of Lafourche, Point Coupée, at Alexandria, Opelousas, and Attakapas, semi-annual courts were established, and regular provision made for the due administration of justice. The House of Representatives consisted of twenty-five members, of whom six were elected from the county of Orleans. The territory was divided into nineteen parishes, some of them of great extent; and a committee was appointed to prepare and report to the next Legislature a digest of laws and practice adapted to the new order of things. At the next session, which convened on the 8th of January, 1808, a code of laws was adopted, and the English language was by law introduced into the courts, with the aid of such interpreters as were necessary. This code was based on the "Code Napoleon" of France.*

[A.D. 1808.] During the summer of 1808, difficulties with Great Britain began to presage an actual outbreak between the two powers. Strong apprehensions of a speedy rupture with that power caused the executive of the United States to provide for the protection of Louisiana against hostile invasion. For this purpose, a large body of regular troops were ordered to the vicinity of New Orleans under the immediate command of General Wilkinson. The exposure of unacclimated troops to the malarious atmosphere of the Terre aux Bœufs at length spread disease among them, and they were removed to the highlands near Fort Adams and Natchez. Embarking in boats on the Mississippi in the middle of September, the most pestilential month in the year, death made sad ravages in their ranks before they reached their destination. During a tedious voyage in boats and barges, propelled up the stream by human strength, after a lapse of forty-seven days, two hundred and forty men had died, and six hundred and thirty-eight were upon the sick-list. Scarcely one hundred men remained fit for duty upon their arrival at Fort Adams and Natchez.† The disease which had so terribly thinned their ranks was a malignant scurvy, a most loathsome and fatal disease, which rendered the victims before death a mass of living putrefaction. Doctor Samuel Brown, surgeon to the division, has often declared that he has seen the men, in despair, pluck their putrid tongues from their mouths, and exult in the temporary relief from the corrupt mass. The survivors were cantoned at Fort Adams and at Fort Dearborn, near Washington. Such is the picture of disease and death, induced by a total disregard of the danger

* Martin's Louisiana, vol. ii., p. 292.   † Idem, p. 295.

of exposing unacclimated men in the marshes of Louisiana during the autumnal months.

The troops under the command of General Wilkinson during the spring of 1808 had amounted to nearly two thousand of all ranks and grades. Of these, seven hundred and sixty-four had died, and one hundred and sixty-six had deserted, giving a total loss of nine hundred and thirty men sacrificed to a reckless want of prudence in the commander. In the month of August, five hundred and sixty-three had been on the sick-list at one time.

[A.D. 1809.] Soon after the accession of Mr. Madison to the presidential chair commenced that fatal interference with the military organization of the war department which was so disastrous to the American arms until the second year of the war with Great Britain. Such had been the mortality among the troops under General Wilkinson, that he was suspended from his command by the appointment of General Wade Hampton on the 19th of December, when he was summoned to appear in Washington city, and submit his official conduct for the last five years to the scrutiny of a court of inquiry. After the necessary delay, he resumed his command on the Lower Mississippi.

[A.D. 1810.] The Spaniards still held possession of the district and government of Baton Rouge, embracing the east bank of the Mississippi, from the line of demarkation to the Bayou Iberville, and extending eastward to the Pearl River. As has been before observed, this district comprised many Anglo-Americans and emigrants from the United States, who, as early as 1805, had made efforts to throw off the Spanish authority and to place themselves under the protection of the United States. Although they had failed in a former attempt, they had not abandoned the object of their desire. Meantime, many emigrants from the Ohio region, and from the adjacent territories of Mississippi and Orleans, had taken up their residence within the Spanish limits, carrying with them no small degree of repugnance to the Spanish authority, of which they gradually became more and more impatient.

The summer of 1810 presented a favorable opportunity to renew their attempt to throw off their allegiance. The garrison at Baton Rouge was at this time reduced to a mere detachment of troops, too feeble to offer any serious resistance to a vigorous revolt. Under these circumstances, the people of the settlements near the Bayou Sara took up arms, and, having formed themselves into a company, were soon re-enforced by volunteers from the Mississippi Territory. This force, under the direction of daring leaders, took up the line of march for Baton Rouge. The garrison at that place, unable to offer any effectual resistance, surrendered at discretion.* The troops and the civil authorities were permitted to retire peaceably to Pensacola.

A provisional government was established and a convention ordered, which was to consist of delegates from the different settlements, for the formation of a constitution preparatory to the adoption of a state government. This Convention constituted the supreme legislative authority of the " Florida Territory " until superseded by the authority of the United States.

The Convention assembled at Baton Rouge late in September, and after a full discussion of the political condition of the country, a Declaration of Independence was adopted upon the 26th of September. In this declaration the Convention recited their former fidelity to their legitimate sovereign, the King of Spain, which had been manifested by repeated instances of devotion to the royal government while any hope remained of receiving protection to their property and lives; that they had voluntarily, adopted certain regulations, in concert with their chief magistrate, for the express purpose of preserving that territory and showing their attachment to the government which had heretofore protected them; but measures intended

---

* The Patriot forces of the Baton Rouge District were commanded by two intrepid men, both inveterate in their hatred of the Spanish authorities. The expedition against the Spanish post of Baton Rouge was organized near St. Francisville. Captain Thomas led about eighty riflemen from the pine woods, and rendezvoused in the plains south of Baton Rouge; and Captain George Depassau headed about forty of the St. Francisville dragoons, and advanced to the attack. The Spanish garrison, about one hundred and fifty in number, was drawn up within the gates to receive the cavalry as they advanced. Dashing in among them, Captain Depassau demanded of them the surrender of the fort: alarmed at his reckless daring, the garrison retired to the guard-house, where they were rallied by the commandant, Colonel de Grandpre. Captain Depassau demanded of him the surrender of the fort, when he ordered his men to fire. At the same instant, Grandpre was shot down and Depassau charged the Spaniards, who, at the same time, hearing the war-whoop from Captain Thomas and his riflemen, who were rushing in at the southern gate, called out for quarters and surrendered. The town soon followed the example of the garrison, and the Patriots took possession of the whole country south of the line. Captain Depassau died in the spring of 1846. Captain Thomas, a veteran of 80 years, was then living.—*New Orleans Commercial Times*, March, 1846.

for their preservation were, by the governor, perverted into an engine of destruction, by a most perfidious violation of ordinances sanctioned and established by himself as the law of the land. They therefore declared themselves absolved from all allegiance to a government which no longer protected them, and declared "the territory of West Florida a free and independent state."*

A Constitution was adopted, and a form of state government organized under the name of the "State of Florida," and Fulwar Skipworth was appointed governor.

On the 11th of October the Convention ordered a formal application, through its president, John Rhea, to the Federal authorities of the United States for admission into the Union. This application was transmitted through Governor Holmes of the Mississippi Territory, to the acting Secretary of State for the United States. It "expresses the hope and desire that this commonwealth may be immediately acknowledged and protected as an integral part of the American Union," and requests "the most direct and unequivocal assurances of the views and wishes of the American government without delay, since our weak and unprotected situation will oblige us to look to some foreign government for support, should it be refused by the country which we have considered as our parent state."†

In case "the United States recognize their claim to protection," the Convention, in behalf of their constituents, claims

---

* Extract from the "DECLARATION of the people of West Florida, in Convention assembled."—See American State Papers, vol. vii., p. 486, 487, Boston edition.

"We, therefore, the representatives aforesaid, appealing to the Supreme Ruler of the world for the rectitude of our intentions, do solemnly publish and declare the several districts composing this territory of West Florida to be *a free and independent state*, and that they have a right to institute for themselves such form of government as they may think conducive to their safety and happiness; to form treaties; to establish commerce; to provide for their common defense; and to do all acts which may of right be done by a sovereign and independent nation: at the same time declaring all acts within the said territory of West Florida, after this date, by any tribunal or authorities not deriving their powers from the people, agreeably to the provisions of this Convention, to be null and void; and calling upon all foreign nations to respect this our declaration, acknowledging our independence, and giving us such aid as may be consistent with the laws and usages of nations.

"This declaration, made in Convention at the town of Baton Rouge, on the 26th day of September, in the year of our Lord 1810, we, the representatives, in the name and on behalf of our constituents, do hereby solemnly pledge ourselves to support with our lives and fortunes.

"By order of the Convention.

"JOHN RHEA, *President.*
"ANDREW STEELE, *Secretary.*"

† American State Papers, vol. vii., p. 482 and 484.

immediate admission into the Union as an independent state, or as a territory of the United States, with permission to adopt their own form of government, or to be annexed to one of the adjacent territories, more especially to that of Orleans. They solicit, also, a loan of one hundred thousand dollars, upon the guarantee of the public lands, and permission to be governed by their own laws, enacted by the Convention, until annexation is consummated.

The Federal government had never ceased to regard this part of West Florida as properly a portion of Louisiana, ceded by the treaty of Paris. The continued occupancy by the Spanish authorities had been permitted only from a conciliatory policy toward Spain, in hopes that his Catholic majesty would ultimately yield possession by amicable negotiation; but now the dominion of Spain had been renounced by the people themselves; and Congress, deeming it expedient for the good government and tranquillity of the country, directed the president to take immediate possession, and extend over it the authority and jurisdiction of the United States. Accordingly, on the 27th of October, 1810, he issued his proclamation, announcing that William C. C. Claiborne, governor of the Territory of Orleans, was empowered to take possession of the same in the name of the United States, as a portion of the territory under his jurisdiction; to organize the militia, prescribe the bounds of parishes, establish parish courts, and otherwise fully to incorporate the people of this territory with those already under his rule, and to place them, as far as practicable, on the same footing with the inhabitants of the other districts.*

The same day, instructions were issued to Governor Claiborne to carry out the requisitions of the proclamation.

The authority of the United States was peaceably extended over the country about the 7th of December following. Gov-

* American State Papers, vol. vii., p. 479.

The work of Judge Martin is very erroneous in regard to this territory and the general proceedings relative to the same. He places the meeting of the Convention at St. Francisville, and makes the date of the president's proclamation to be October 16th instead of 27th. Other similar errors abound.

The territory comprised in the proclamation extended from the Mississippi eastward to the Perdido, bounded on the north by the parallel of latitude 31°, or Ellicott's line, and by the Iberville, Lake Pontchartrain, the Rigolets, and the sea-shore eastward to the Perdido. But the Spaniards continued to hold possession of Mobile and its district until April 13th, 1813, when it was invested by the troops of the United States, under General Wilkinson.—See book i., chap. v.; also, book v., chap. xiii., of this work.

ernor Claiborne, returning from a visit to the Middle States, called on Governor Holmes, of the Mississippi Territory, who promptly furnished him with a detachment of militia and a volunteer troop of cavalry. At the head of these he advanced to St. Francisville, where he raised the flag of the United States in token of possession.

The people submitted cheerfully to his authority, and his proclamation issued soon afterward made the event generally known. By a subsequent proclamation, the "Florida District" was annexed to the jurisdiction of the Territory of Orleans, subdivided into the parishes of Feliciana, East Baton Rouge, St. Helena, St. Tammany, Biloxi, and Pascagoula.* The district and town of Mobile, with Fort Charlotte, were not included or disturbed, Governor Claiborne having been specially instructed to make no forcible occupancy of any post or district occupied by any Spanish garrison, or wherein the Spanish authority was respected.

Thus was the limit of the present State of Louisiana first extended northward, on the east side of the Mississippi, to the old Spanish line of demarkation.

The population of the Territory of Orleans had been augmented annually by emigration from the United States. According to the census of 1810, the whole territory, exclusive of the Florida parishes, contained an aggregate of 76,550 souls. Of this number, the city of New Orleans and its precincts contained 24,552 persons, leaving 52,000 souls for the remainder of the territory.† Besides these, the inhabitants of the Florida parishes amounted, probably, to not less than twenty-five hundred, including slaves.

[A.D. 1811.] Early in January following, the territory was

---

* Martin, vol. ii., p. 298, 299.
† The population of the different parishes was as follows:

1. Parish of Plaquemines	1,549 souls.		Brought forward	23,633 souls.
2. " St. Bernard	1,020 "	11. Parish of Point Coupée	4,539 "
3. " St. Charles	3,291 "	12. " Concordia	2,895 "
4. " St. John Baptist	2,990 "	13. " Ouachita	1,077 "
5. " St. James	3,955 "	14. " Rapides	2,200 "
6. " Ascension	2,219 "	15. " Catahoola	1,164 "
7. " Assumption	2,472 "	16. " Avoyelles	1,209 "
8. " Lafourche	1,995 "	17. " Natchitoches	2,870 "
9. " Iberville	2,679 "	18. " Opelousas	5,040 "
10. " Baton Rouge	1,463 "	19. " Attakapas	7,369 "
Carried forward	23,633 "		Total,	51,996 "

—See Martin, vol. ii., p. 297, &c.

thrown into a state of alarm and agitation by a rising among the slaves in the parish of St. John Baptist, about thirty-six miles above New Orleans. Soon after the first outbreak, they formed into companies on the east bank of the Mississippi, and marched toward the city, with flags displayed, to the sound of martial music. The slaves of such plantations as they passed were compelled to join their ranks. The whole number engaged in this outbreak was estimated at nearly five hundred, before they were arrested by the militia of the adjoining parishes. General Hampton immediately ordered the regular troops from Baton Rouge and Fort St. Charles to advance toward the seat of revolt. The insurgents succeeded in destroying only a few plantations before they were subdued. They encountered the militia, but were soon surrounded and routed, with the loss of sixty-six killed, or hung immediately afterward. Many fled to the swamps to avoid pursuit, and a number of the wounded subsequently died. Sixteen others, who had taken a prominent part in the insurrection, were carried to New Orleans, where they were tried, convicted, and executed in an exemplary manner, after which their heads were exposed on poles at different points along the river. A detachment of the regular troops was stationed in the vicinity until tranquillity was fully restored.*

The next session of the General Assembly, on account of the late insurrection, was deferred until the fourth Monday in January, when the first attention was directed to the newly-annexed Florida parishes. An act provided for a representation from each of these parishes in the General Assembly. Two new judicial districts were organized, one for the Florida parishes, designated Feliciana District, and one on Black River, known as Catahoola District. The same session Vidalia was made the seat of justice for Concordia Parish, then extending from the mouth of Red River to the northern limit of the present state, and comprising the west bank of the Mississippi for two hundred and fifty miles. Two banks were also chartered the same session, the "Planters' Bank" and the "Bank of Orleans;" the first with a capital of six hundred thousand dollars, for a period of fifteen years; the second, with a capital of five hundred thousand dollars, for fifteen years also.†

Meantime, Congress, by an act approved February 11th,

* Martin, vol. ii., p. 301. † Idem.

1811, had authorized the election of a convention to adopt a Constitution, preparatory to the admission of the territory into the Union as an independent state.

The Convention, consisting of sixty delegates from the original parishes, met according to law, on the first Monday in November, and concluded its labors on the 22d day of January following, having adopted a Constitution for the proposed new "State of Louisiana."*

This Constitution contained the general features of other state constitutions which had preceded it, except those peculiarities resulting from the institution of slavery, which was strongly protected and sustained. Clergymen or priests were made ineligible to seats in the Legislature and to the office of governor. The boundaries of Louisiana were restricted to the Sabine on the west. On the east side of the Mississippi the territory represented in the Convention included only the Island of New Orleans, exclusive of the annexed Florida parishes.

By this Constitution, the legislative powers were vested in a General Assembly, composed of a Senate and House of Representatives. The number of representatives was to be regulated by the number of qualified voters, or electors, to ascertain which, a census was directed every four years. The state was divided into fourteen senatorial districts, which were to remain forever indivisible, and each district was entitled to one senator. Senators were to be elected for six years, and one third of the number go out every two years. In each house a majority of the members constituted a quorum; but a less number could adjourn and compel the attendance of members.†

The governor is elected every four years by the Legislature, on the second day of the session, from the two highest candidates returned by the popular vote: he must be at least thirty-five years old, holding in his own right a landed estate worth five thousand dollars, and have resided in the state six years next preceding his election.

The subordinate officers, executive and judicial, are mostly appointed by the governor, with the approbation of the Senate. In many respects the Constitution of Louisiana was much less

---

* Martin's Louisiana, vol. ii., p. 302. Also, Land Laws of United States, compilation of 1827, p. 581. † Martin's Louisiana, vol. ii., p. 306, 307.

Democratic than that of Kentucky, after which it was modeled.* This Constitution continued in force until January, 1846, when it was superseded by a new one thoroughly Democratic in its general features, restricting the patronage of the governor by placing the election of judicial and executive officers chiefly in the hands of the people.

[A.D. 1812.] The Constitution was accepted by Congress, and the State of Louisiana was formally admitted into the Union on the 8th day of April, 1812, upon an equal footing with the original states, from and after the 30th day of April, it being the ninth anniversary of the treaty of Paris.†

A few days subsequently, a "supplemental act" of Congress extended the limits of the new state by the addition of the Florida parishes. This gave it the boundaries it has at present; the Pearl River on the east, and Ellicott's line on the north. This act was entitled "An act to enlarge the limits of the State of Louisiana," and was approved April 14th, 1812. The supplemental act required the Legislature of Louisiana, provided it assented to the proposed union, to make provision at its next session for giving the people of the above parishes a fair and equal representation in their body, and place them in all respects upon the same footing with other portions of the state.‡

The proposed annexation was readily assented to by the Legislature, and the act thereby completed. Thus it happened that the inhabitants of the Florida parishes had no voice in framing the first Constitution of the state, which had been formed and approved by Congress previous to the consummation of the above measure.

In June following, the first election was held under the Constitution for a governor and the two Houses of the Legislature. The Legislature convened on the first Monday of July, and the next day the two Houses proceeded to elect the governor from the two highest candidates returned by the people. These were William C. C. Claiborne and M. Villère; from whom the Legislature chose the former as the first governor of the State of Louisiana.

The Legislature proceeded to the important duties of organ-

---
* Martin, vol. ii., p. 310.
† Land Laws of the United States, vol. iv., p. 403. Also, Martin.
‡ Martin, vol. ii., p. 304.

izing the state government, by the appointment of executive and judicial officers, and the passage of such acts as were requisite.

Meantime, General Wilkinson had been restored to his command of the seventh military district. The charges which had been preferred against him had been formally investigated by a court of inquiry, at Fredericktown, in Maryland, and after a protracted trial he was honorably acquitted, none of them having been sustained.

The charges, of which a copy had been furnished to him on the 11th of July, embraced the following leading points, viz. :

1. Collusion with the Spanish authorities for the separation of the western people from the Atlantic States, and receiving large sums of money from Spain.

2. Collusion with Aaron Burr in his design of invading Mexico while at peace with the United States, and being accessary to the conspiracy.

3. A prodigal waste of public money, as commander-in-chief; and, finally,

4. Disobedience of orders.

[A.D. 1813.] At this time there had been quite a large emigration from Kentucky and other states of the Union to Louisiana, yet the greater portion of the permanent residents were Creole French and foreigners. The people of France, under the treaty of cession, were entitled to certain commercial privileges for twelve years, without becoming citizens of the United States. This term had not yet expired.

The principal American population, speaking the English language, were to be found in New Orleans, and at some towns on the coast; a few Americans had settled upon the bayous of Red River, near Alexandria, and in the parish of Opelousas. The inhabitants distributed on the Washita were chiefly French; those east of the Washita, and north of the mouth of Red River, were mostly American emigrants. The largest Anglo-American settlements in the state speaking the English language were those on the east side of the Mississippi River, in the uplands, between Baton Rouge and Ellicott's line.

The French were concentrated principally in New Orleans, on the river-coast below Baton Rouge, on the Bayous

Lafourche, Plaquemines, Atchafalaya, Teche, and other connecting bayous, and in the prairies south and west of the Mississippi, below the mouth of Red River. The whole population of the state, exclusive of Indians, in all probability exceeded eighty-five thousand persons at the beginning of the year 1813. The number of people increased but little until after the close of the contest with Great Britain.

During the war, which raged with great violence on the northwestern borders, as well as upon the Atlantic coast, Louisiana, although in constant apprehension of danger, was not molested by the enemy until the close of the year 1814.

From the first indication of a hostile disposition on the part of Great Britain, and several months previous to the declaration of war, General Wilkinson had urged upon the Federal executive the vast importance of adequate fortifications on the whole coast of Louisiana, and especially on the east side of the Mississippi River as far as Mobile. As early as the 28th of March, 1812, the general had fully apprised Mr. Madison of the assailable nature of the coast, and had designated the defenses requisite for the protection of New Orleans, which would require a complement of ten thousand men with ample munitions of war, in case of a formidable invasion.* But Mr. Madison, strangely infatuated relative to the security of the country, disregarded the admonition. After the declaration of war, General Wilkinson continued to urge upon the president and the war department the danger to be apprehended from British troops occupying the Spanish ports of Mobile and Pensacola, upon the southern frontier. He also urged the importance of providing a principal dépôt of military stores and arsenals at Cantonment Dearborn, in the Mississippi Territory, or at some other secure place at a convenient distance from the assailable points ;† also strong fortifications on the passes of the Mississippi River, especially at the Balize, Fort St. Philip, and the English Turn, for preventing the advance of a hostile squadron against the city of New Orleans. He pointed out, too, the necessity of defending the passes of Chef Menteur, Terre aux Bœufs, Bayou Bienvenu, Petite Coquilles, Rivière au Chene, and Mobile Point, to prevent the entrance of small vessels into the lakes and bays along the coast.‡ He likewise pressed the establishment of a flotilla of gun-boats, to guard the

* Wilkinson's Memoirs, vol. i., p. 472-488.   † Idem, p. 489-493.   ‡ Idem, p. 503-505.

passes in the shoal water of the lakes and bayous; and the use of steam-boats on the Mississippi, and in high tides, for the transport of troops, munitions, artillery, and provisions. " Without these boats," said he, " the obstructions from the currents, calms, and adverse winds must forbid all calculations of punctuality on the Mississippi and the lakes."

In August, 1812, after war had been declared, and an invasion of the southern coast threatened, such was the danger and the exposed position of his command, as regards every thing like permanent protection, that General Wilkinson called a "council of war" to devise the future course of defensive operations. The decision of the council was unanimous in favor of the plan above indicated.* Yet such was the unaccountable neglect, or the want of capacity in Mr. Madison's cabinet, that little or nothing was accomplished for the security of this portion of the country, while their whole attention was devoted to futile efforts at points not endangered.

The same incapacity, willful blindness, or incorrigible "obstinacy," as General Wilkinson termed it, in the conduct of Mr. Madison's counselors, continued to embarrass every subsequent effort for the safety of New Orleans. Under the pretext of "economy," the Secretary of War, John Armstrong, was permitted to withhold the means of defense, to disconcert every measure, and mar every proposition for the protection of New Orleans.† At length, in June, 1813, at the most critical period of affairs on the southern borders, as if to remove all obstacles to the successful advance of the British forces and their savage allies, and to expose the whole southern frontier to an easy conquest, the treacherous Secretary of War was allowed to remove General Wilkinson from his command, and substitute General Flournoy, a man without military talent, or the slightest pretensions to the qualifications of commander-in-chief.

[A.D. 1814.] During the next twelve months General Flournoy signalized himself in the seventh military district by holding the troops under his command in inglorious inactivity, and throwing obstacles in the way of the territorial authorities for the speedy termination of the Creek war, while General

---

* Wilkinson's Memoirs, vol. i., p. 501–505. The "council of war" consisted of Brigadier-general Wilkinson, Commodore Shaw, Lieutenant-colonel Purdy, Major Cammack, Captain Patterson, of U. S. N., Captain Blakely, U. S. N., Colonel Shaumburg, and Benjamin Morgan, Dep. Comm. General.

† Wilkinson's Memoirs, vol. i., p. 545.

Wilkinson, with military talents and undoubted courage, was detained an idle spectator at the seat of government, to witness its destruction by a British army, and the ignominious flight of the president and his cabinet from the capital of the Union, and this, too, all under the pretext that "the South and New Orleans were not safe in his keeping," when the courage and talents of Wilkinson, even at the head of the militia assembled for its security, would have driven the foe ingloriously from the soil, and have preserved the Capitol from desecration.

Hence it was that toward the close of the year 1814, when the British fleet, with a powerful army, finally approached the coast, prepared for the contemplated attack, the South was unprotected; the defenses were weak; the magazines were empty; there was a deficiency of munitions and stores, of clothing and ammunition, and all the requisites of defensive warfare.*

Such was the condition of Louisiana in the autumn of 1814, when General Andrew Jackson took command of the seventh military district. It was only after almost incredible efforts to surmount the obstacles to success, and, as it were, in spite of the indecision of the president, and the criminal neglect in the war department, that he, with a mere handful of men, succeeded in defending the country, and driving back the invader with unparalleled slaughter and defeat.†

Having terminated the Creek war with brilliant success, and completely humbled the hostile Creeks, and forced the remnant of the nation east of the Coosa and Tallapoosa, General Jackson had retired to his residence in Tennessee; but the clouds of war were gathering in the South, and Louisiana was menaced with foreign invasion, when he was again called to the field. Hastening to the seat of war, he issued his call to the Tennessee volunteers again to follow him to the camp, while he advanced to direct the movements of the troops on the southern frontier.

Before the last of November he had given a signal repulse to a division of the British fleet and army before Fort Bowyer, on Mobile Point, and had effectually enforced neutrality upon the perfidious Spaniards of Pensacola, when he turned his face toward New Orleans, the ultimate object of a powerful British armament in the Gulf of Mexico.

* Wilkinson's Memoirs, vol. i., p. 500–502.   † Idem, p. 484.

To arrest the progress, and to defeat the ultimate designs of the enemy, General Jackson lost no time in repairing to the city to superintend the requisite preparations for defense. While his cavalry, under General Coffee and Major Hinds, advanced from the Pine Barrens, near Mobile, to recruit their horses in the vicinity of Baton Rouge, and Woodville, he ordered the artillery to proceed by slow and easy marches to New Orleans.

On the 2d of December he established his headquarters in the city, from which he conducted his operations with incredible energy and skill for the security and safety of the commercial emporium of the Southwest.

At this time Louisiana contained a large mixed population, besides the Americans and patriotic French. The citizens were ill supplied with arms, with little or no organization of the militia, and without any effectual means to repel invasion. No troops, arms, or ammunition had yet arrived from the Ohio. The only means of resistance on which General Jackson could rely were the few regular troops at that place, and the patriotic volunteers of the city, until the arrival of the cavalry and infantry from Mobile, and other new levies expected from Kentucky and Tennessee. At such a time as this, it required all the cool decision, the energy, and fearless tranquillity of General Jackson to inspire confidence and courage in the people of Louisiana.

In all his plans for the protection of the city, the general found Governor Claiborne ready to co-operate, and to lend, not only his official influence and authority, but also his individual services in frustrating the designs of the foe.

On the 9th of December intelligence was received in New Orleans that a British fleet of sixty sail of war vessels, with numerous transports, was lying off the mouth of the Mississippi. A public meeting was held in the city, with Edward Livingston presiding, for the purpose of devising means to aid the civil and military authorities in the defense of the country. A resolution was unanimously adopted, declaring, in emphatic language, the firm attachment of the people to the American government, and their determination to oppose the enemy by every means in their power.*

Yet there were many foreigners, Spaniards, and other disaffected persons, insidiously moving about the city in the mixed

---

* Breckenridge's History of the War, p. 278.

population, who evinced no desire to offer any opposition to the approach of the enemy. Notwithstanding the citizens of New Orleans, even the free persons of color, manifested the greatest alacrity in organizing volunteer companies, and in preparing to take the field, yet it was far otherwise in many of the agricultural districts among the Creole French. They took scarce any interest in the war, and evinced but little disposition to resist the invader. Notwithstanding a general order of the governor, issued several weeks previously, upon a requisition of General Jackson while at Mobile, requiring the two divisions of the Louisiana militia, under Major-generals Villère and Thomas, to hold themselves in continued readiness to march at the first call, they had disregarded the order so far that scarcely any militia organization existed, and discipline was unknown.

To remedy this defect, General Jackson was unremitting in his exertions to rouse the people to a sense of their danger, and to complete the formation of the different volunteer companies for active service. A patriotic appeal was made to the people in an animated address from the governor, calling upon them to rise *en masse* for the defense of their homes and families. Orders were issued for the immediate advance of the cavalry from their rendezvous at Baton Rouge and Woodville; a demand was made for troops and arms from the Governor of the Mississippi Territory, and measures were taken to expedite the new levies from Kentucky and Tennessee.

The chief security of New Orleans from immediate danger was found in the nature of the surrounding country. The shoal coast, with its shallow lakes and bays, and the narrow inlets on every side, was of itself a barrier to the near approach of large vessels of war. Many of the inlets and passes were susceptible of such obstruction as would preclude the entrance of large boats and barges; or they might be effectually guarded by a proper force. The river itself afforded the only channel by which heavy vessels of war could approach the city; this channel, by means of the tortuous course of the river, and the impetuosity of the current, was susceptible of being strongly defended against ascending vessels. Yet the means and resources at the command of the general were inadequate to the accomplishment of all these objects, and for guarding every avenue through which the enemy might enter.*

* Breckenridge's History of the War, p. 279.

The Legislature having been convened, was already in session, but their counsels were no support to the commanding general. Instead of providing actively for the defense of the city, they wasted time in idle discussions, which tended to embarrass judicious measures. But for the perseverance and firmness of General Jackson, and the zealous co-operation of the patriotic governor, New Orleans would have fallen an easy prey to the enemy. But General Jackson, by his presence and energy, inspired confidence in the people to sustain him in the plans he had adopted.

Personally inspecting all the places to be fortified, as well as all the bayous and inlets, he caused all the latter situated near the river, from the Atchafalaya to Chef Menteur Pass, to be obstructed, so as to prevent the passage of boats and military stores. The points below the city on the river were strongly fortified, so as to prevent vessels from ascending. A battery with a sufficient guard was erected on Chef Menteur Pass. On the arrival of the troops from Mobile, one thousand regulars were stationed in the city, which, with the co-operation of the volunteers and militia of Louisiana, were distributed for the security of the most assailable points.

Meantime, the enemy had been unremitting in his preparations for the capture and destruction of New Orleans. His vessels, boats, and spies were engaged in exploring the country south and east of the city, and searching for the most practicable avenues to the banks of the river, and acquainting themselves with the general topography of the country, being aided by the Spanish fishermen and others frequenting the place.

On the 12th of December the enemy's fleet was discovered in great force off Cat Island, near the entrance of Lake Borgne. The commander of the naval station, Commodore Patterson, dispatched a flotilla of five gun-boats, under Lieutenant Jones, to observe the enemy, and to impede his advance by way of the lakes. Lieutenant Jones sailed for the Bay of St. Louis, where, having observed the enemy's position, he determined to occupy the pass which communicates with Lake Pontchartrain, for the purpose of opposing the entrance of the British barges and light craft. Before this resolution could be effected, the enemy attacked the flotilla in the Bay of St. Louis, and one of the gun-boats, the Sea-horse, after a gallant resistance, was captured. On the 14th, the gun-boats, while becalmed, were again attacked by an overwhelming force of forty-three barges, carrying twelve hundred men. After a severe contest of one hour with this superior force, they were compelled to surrender at discretion. In this engagement the loss of the Americans was six men killed and thirty-five wounded. Among the latter were Lieutenants Spidden, Jones, and M'Keever. The loss of the English is believed to have been not less than three hundred killed and wounded.*

The capture of the gun-boats placed the enemy in a condition to choose the point of attack, and at the same time deprived the Americans of the principal means of observing his movements upon the lakes lying east and north of New Orleans. Thus circumstanced, the commander-in-chief ordered the battalion of colored men under Major Lacoste, together with the Feliciana dragoons, to take post on the Gentilly Road conducting to the city, and to defend the pass Chef Menteur, leading from Lake Borgne into Lake Pontchartrain. Captain Newman, of the artillery, commanding the fort on the Rigolets, was ordered to maintain that post to the last extremity.

Meantime, General Jackson, convinced that the enemy would soon make a demonstration against the city, became extremely solicitous for its safety, on account of the inadequate means of defense placed within his control. General Coffee having been delayed in his progress from Baton Rouge by high waters and inclement weather, an express was dispatched to meet him, with orders to hasten to the seat of danger with the utmost celerity, and "*not to sleep until he arrived.*" Every effort was used to expedite the advancing troops from Louisiana, the Mississippi Territory, and those expected from Kentucky and Tennessee. The few steamers which then plied between New Orleans and Natchez were employed in meeting the advancing flat-boats and barges, and transporting their troops, arms, and munitions to the points of attack. General Coffee, who received the express from the commander-in-chief on the 17th of December, at Baton Rouge, took up the line of march without delay, and on the 19th he encamped within fifteen miles of New Orleans, having marched one hundred and fifty miles, with twelve hundred mounted volunteers, in two days. Major Hinds, with the Mississippi dragoons, hastened from Woodville with equal celerity.‡

---

* See Breckenridge's History of the War, p. 280. Also, Eaton's Life of Jackson, p. 261.   † Breckenridge, p. 281.   ‡ Eaton's Life of Jackson, p. 268–270.

The enemy was already in possession of the lakes, and was indefatigable in his efforts to approach the banks of the Mississippi through some of the numerous bayous which intersected the country. To his great mortification and disappointment, all those above the city had been completely obstructed by General Jackson, or so securely defended that no advance could be made in that quarter.

Other measures were adopted with great expedition. Colonel Fortier, one of the principal merchants of the city, who had the superintendence of the colored volunteer companies, formed a second battalion, which was placed under the command of Major Daquin. By means of bounties, a number of persons were induced to serve on board the schooner Caroline and the brig Louisiana, thus in part supplying the places of the sailors who had been lost in the gun-boats.

On the 18th, the commander-in-chief reviewed the city regiments, and was particularly gratified with the uniform companies under Major Plauche. The battalion of the latter, with a company of light artillery under Lieutenant Wagner, was ordered to Fort St. John, for the protection of the Bayou St. John, which presented an accessible route from Lake Pontchartrain to the upper part of the banks of the Mississippi, above the city. An embargo for three days was decreed by the Legislature; a number of persons confined in the prisons were liberated upon condition of their serving in the ranks; and at length, the commander-in-chief conceived it indispensable for the safety of the country to proclaim *martial law*, a measure which greatly contributed to the salvation of the city, and has since been sanctioned by the verdict of one generation.*

About the same time, Lafitte and his band of Baratarian smugglers and pirates, who had carried on their illicit operations from an almost inaccessible island in Lake Barataria, availed themselves of the amnesty and pardon offered them by Governor Claiborne, on condition that they would come forward and aid in the defense of the country. They also joined the American forces, and took position under General Jackson. These men, under their daring leader, rendered important services during the subsequent attack on the city, and well merited the pardon of the civil government. The whole number of troops of every description in New Orleans and its vicin-

* Breckenridge, p. 281.

ity on the 20th of December was upward of four thousand men.*

All the principal bayous which communicated between Lake Pontchartrain and the river had been closed or obstructed by order of General Jackson. There was a bayou, known as Bayou Bienvenu, which opened a communication from Lake Borgne nearly to the Mississippi, at the plantation of General Villère, seven miles below the city. Although this was known to only a few fishermen, and was supposed to afford but few facilities for the approach of an invading army, General Jackson ordered it to be blocked up by fallen timber and securely guarded. A small force, for observation, was accordingly placed near its mouth, on the lake, at the cabins of some Spanish fishermen, who, as afterward appeared, were in the interest of the British; but the obstruction of the bayou was neglected or forgotten by General Villère, to whom it was referred. This proved to be the route selected by the foe for his passage to the Mississippi below the city.

On the 22d, guided by those fishermen, a division of the enemy under General Keane, amounting to three thousand men, advancing in boats, came suddenly upon the American guard about dark, and took them all prisoners. By four o'clock on the morning of the 23d, they had reached the end of Villère's Canal, near the head of the bayou, with five barges full of troops, and some artillery. Here they disembarked and rested some hours, after which they proceeded to the left bank of the Mississippi, where they arrived at two o'clock P.M. General Villère's house was immediately surrounded, as was also that of his neighbor, Colonel La Rondé. But Colonel La Rondé, as well as a son of General Villère, were so fortunate as to escape; and, hastening to headquarters, they communicated the first intelligence of the approach of the English.†

The commander-in-chief resolved instantly upon the only proper course to be pursued. This was, to attack the enemy in their new position without the loss of a moment. In one hour's time, Coffee's riflemen, stationed above the city, were at the place of rendezvous; the battalion of Major Plauche had arrived from the bayou; and the regulars and city volunteers were ready to march. At six o'clock in the evening the different corps were united at Rodrigue's Canal, six miles below

---

* Martin, vol. ii., p. 351. † Idem, vol. ii., p. 352.

the city. The schooner Caroline, Captain Henley, bearing the broad pendant of Commodore Patterson, at the same time dropped down the river, and the Louisiana was ordered to follow. General Coffee's division, together with Captain Beale's riflemen, was placed on the extreme left, toward the woods; the city volunteers and the men of color, under Plauche and Daquin, both commanded by Colonel Ross, were stationed in the center; and on the right were the seventh and forty-fourth regiments of United States troops, while the artillery and marines, under Colonel M'Rae, occupied the road. This whole force scarcely exceeded two thousand in numbers.

The British troops, amounting to three thousand men, upon their arrival on the bank of the Mississippi, instead of pushing directly toward the city, had bivouacked, with their right resting upon a wood and their left on the river, in the full conviction that the most difficult part of the enterprise had already been achieved.

General Coffee was ordered to turn their right and attack them in the rear; General Jackson in person, with the main body of the army, assailed them in front and on their left. A fire from the Caroline was to be the signal for the attack. The river was nearly on a level with the banks; and at half past seven o clock, it being already dark, the action commenced by a raking broad-side of grape and canister from the schooner, directed by the light in the enemy's camp; and this gave him the first intimation of the approach of the Americans. Coffee's men, having dismounted, with their usual impetuosity rushed to the attack and entered the British lines; those in the front and on the right, under the immediate command of General Jackson, advanced with equal ardor.

The enemy, engaged in camp duties, was taken by surprise at the terrible discharge from the schooner, which actually drove the troops from the exposed part of the camp, after nearly one hundred of them had been killed. All the lights were immediately extinguished, to conceal the troops from the fire of the vessel. The confusion which at first spread through the camp at length ceased, and order was restored; not, however, until nearly four hundred men had been killed, wounded, and taken prisoners. The battle continued with great vivacity for about one hour, at which time the enemy had fallen back nearly a mile. During the action, he had been re-enforced by a detachment of one thousand men, who were advancing from the lake.

At length the darkness of the night, and the uncertainty of any effective movement, induced General Jackson to call off the troops from prosecuting the attack.

At the commencement of this engagement, General Morgan, with a detachment of three hundred and fifty Louisiana militia, was stationed at the English Turn, upon the left bank of the river. When the guns of the Caroline announced the contest with the enemy, finding it impossible to restrain the ardor of his men, he led them toward the scene of action. About eleven o'clock at night he reached the plantation of M. Jumonville, adjoining that of General Villère, where his advanced guard came in collision with a picket of the enemy, which, after a few fires, retreated to the main line. Before daylight, General Morgan retired from this critical position.*

Next morning, at four o'clock, General Jackson fell back nearly two miles nearer the city, and took up a position on the left bank of the river, where the swamp approaches within some half a mile of its shore. Here he determined to make a stand, and erect his line of defense on the upper side of a millrace canal leading from the river to the lake.

In the action of the night of the 23d of December, the Americans lost twenty-four men killed and one hundred and fifteen wounded. Seventy-four men were taken prisoners, including many of the principal citizens of New Orleans. Among the slain was Colonel Lauderdale, of Tennessee, a brave soldier, greatly regretted. The loss of the British was estimated at four hundred, killed, wounded, and missing.†

This prompt and energetic attack taught the British commanders a lesson of caution, and was virtually the salvation of the city. Believing the American force much more numerous than it was, they suspended any further advance until their main force was received from the lake.

General Jackson, without delay, commenced his defenses on the upper side of the ditch, which was enlarged. An embankment of earth, and such materials as were accessible, was commenced, and urged forward with great vigor, extending from the river to the low swamp, a distance of nearly one

* Martin's Louisiana, vol. ii., p. 354–356.   † Breckenridge, p. 283.

mile. The ground was flat and wet; the ditches were filled with water within a few feet of the surface; the river was on a level with its banks, and in many places the levee alone protected the adjacent marshes from inundation. Under these circumstances, it was difficult to procure dry earth for a heavy embankment; but the commander, ever fruitful in resources, was not without an expedient. In the city of New Orleans were several thousand cotton-bales in store, which, in case of defeat, would fall into the hands of the British. To secure his own troops from the enemy's fire, and to deprive him of a portion of his anticipated "booty," the American general resolved to appropriate it to his own use. The cotton was pressed into the service, and, with the aid of hundreds of drays from the city, an impenetrable wall of earth and cotton-bales began to extend from the river to the swamp. Built up in regular order, and cemented with earth, like bricks in a wall, the cotton-bales soon formed an impregnable barrier, not only to small arms and light artillery, but against the most impetuous charge of infantry, while on its inner side it afforded a firm and useful banquette. The front was protected by a deep and wide ditch, filled nearly to the top with water. Such was the line of defense on the fields of Chalmette.*

The enemy was indefatigable in fortifying his position and in expediting the advance of his remaining troops from the lakes, while he kept up an incessant cannonade against every part of the American works.

In the mean time, General Jackson caused the levee to be cut about four hundred yards below his line, so as to discharge a broad stream of water, which, by flooding the whole plain in front of the enemy, embarrassed his advance. The following day orders were sent to General Morgan, at the English Turn, to send a detachment of men up the river, as near the enemy's encampment as prudent, and there cut the levee, so as to inundate the lands below his camp, and thus to insulate him, and prevent him from marching either up or down. After executing this order, General Morgan was instructed to destroy the fort at the English Turn, retire across the river, and take a stand nearly opposite the American army.†

---

* Breckenridge's History of the War, p. 283. Eaton's Life of Jackson, p. 299, 300.
† Eaton's Life of Jackson, p. 309.

The Louisiana had joined the Caroline, and both continuing to annoy the British from the opposite shore, the latter began to construct hot-shot batteries for their destruction. On the 27th these were completed, and commenced throwing their fiery missiles. A strong north wind prevented the vessels from escaping up the river, and the Caroline was soon set on fire, and blew up about an hour after she had been abandoned by her crew. The Louisiana next sustained the fire of their batteries, and was in imminent danger of sharing the same fate as the Caroline; but her commander, Lieutenant Thompson, after encountering many difficulties, finally succeeded in extricating her from her perilous situation, soon after which she was anchored on the right flank of General Jackson's position.*

After the burning of the Caroline, Sir Edward Pakenham, commander-in-chief of the British army, having landed the main body of his forces, with a heavy train of artillery, proceeded in person to superintend the arrangements for attacking the American lines. On the 28th he advanced up the bank of the river along the levee, with the intention of driving Jackson into the city. At the distance of half a mile, he commenced the attack with a furious display of rockets, bombs, and artillery. When he came within reach, the Louisiana and the batteries along the American works opened upon him a most destructive fire. For seven hours the cannonade and bombardment was continued, when the British general, having his columns broken and driven back, relinquished the attack, and retired to his intrenchments. The loss of the Americans in this attack was seven men killed and ten wounded. Among the former was Colonel Henderson, of Tennessee, a highly meritorious officer. The loss of the British forces during the operations of this day was not less than two hundred and fifty men killed and wounded.†

During the next three days the British commanders were actively engaged in bringing up their re-enforcements and in making preparations to storm the American lines. The American commander daily became more confident of his strength, and infused new confidence into his companions in arms.

[A.D. 1815.] On the morning of the first day of January,

---
* Breckenridge's History of the War, p. 284.
† Idem. Also, Martin's Louisiana, vol. ii., p. 361.

Sir Edward Pakenham had succeeded in erecting, during the night, and within six hundred yards of the American works, three heavy batteries, from which, about nine o'clock in the forenoon, so soon as the dense fog disappeared, he opened a heavy cannonade against the American lines, with a terrible display of congreve rockets. The fire from the batteries on the American center and left was returned with great spirit and effect.

About the same time a bold attempt was made to turn the American left; but in this the enemy was signally repulsed by the Tennessee volunteers. About three o'clock in the afternoon the fire of the British batteries was completely silenced, having been entirely dismounted by the American artillery. Soon afterward the British abandoned them, and retreated to their camp, having suffered a severe loss near both extremities of the American line. That of the Americans was eleven men killed and twenty-three wounded.

On the 4th General Jackson was joined by twenty-two hundred and fifty Kentuckians, under General Adair.* On the 6th the British were re-enforced by a reserve of four thousand men, under General Lambert. The British force now amounted to nearly fifteen thousand men, the flower of their European army. The Americans numbered about six thousand, most of them untried militia, many of whom were unarmed, badly clothed, and unprovided. Many of those who were armed were supplied with private arms, collected from the citizens. On this occasion, the patriotism of the citizens, and the ladies especially, of New Orleans, was displayed most conspicuously. The latter, with devoted zeal, were employed in making apparel to supply the destitute militia and volunteers, who had been hurried from home at this inclement season, without time for proper equipment or clothing suited to the severity of the weather. The patriotic ladies volunteered for their relief; and in a few days, with their own hands, made twelve hundred blanket-coats, two hundred and twenty-five waistcoats, eleven hundred and twenty-seven pairs of pantaloons, and eight hundred shirts.† The whole of the resident population were fired with enthusiasm, all emulous to excel in their efforts to sustain the heroic commander in the defense of the city, which was already doomed by the British commanders to rapine and

---

* Eaton's Life of Jackson, p. 332.   † Martin's Louisiana, vol. ii., p. 372.

blood, in order to stimulate the courage of their soldiers. The noble-hearted mayor of the city devoted his whole energies, in his private and public capacity, in promoting the patriotic efforts of his fellow-citizens.

The British general was now ready for a serious attempt on the American works. Great preparations had been made, and the trench from the Mississippi to the head of Bayou Bienvenu had been deepened and enlarged, so as to enable the troops to transport the boats and barges from the first point of disembarkation. By this route the British general provided transports to cross a portion of his forces to the west side of the river.

The works of the American general, by this time, were completed on the left bank of the river. The front consisted of a breast-work, about one mile in length, reaching from the shore, at right angles, to the swamp, and extending into the latter several hundred yards beyond where it was passable, and inclining to the left for the last two hundred yards. The whole was defended by upward of three thousand infantry and artillerists. The ditch in front was flooded with five feet of water from the river, which was even with its banks; and beyond the ditch the ground was wet and slippery from the river and rains. Along the breast-work eight distinct batteries were judiciously distributed, mounting in all twelve guns of different calibers. On the opposite side of the river was stationed another of fifteen guns, with intrenchments occupied by some Louisiana militia and a strong detachment of Kentuckians under General Morgan.

The memorable 8th of January dawned upon the vigilant troops of the opposing armies. A rocket ascended on the left, near the swamp; soon after another on the right, near the river. About daylight, General Pakenham, after having detached Colonel Thornton with eight hundred men to the west side of the river, to attack the works on the right hand, moved with his whole force in two columns, commanded by Generals Gibbs and Keane, and with a front of sixty or seventy deep. The right and principal division, under General Gibbs, was to attack the center of the works. The British advanced deliberately to the assault in solid columns, over the even plain in front of the American intrenchments, the men carrying, besides

* Breckenridge, p. 285.

their muskets, fascines made of sugar-cane, and some of them ladders. A dead silence prevailed as they advanced, until they approached within reach of the batteries, when an incessant and destructive cannonade opened upon them. Yet they continued to move on in tolerable order, closing up their ranks as fast as they were opened by the American artillery, until they came within reach of the musketry and rifles. At this time such dreadful havoc was produced that they were instantly thrown into the utmost confusion. Never was there so tremendous a fire as that kept up from the American lines. It was a continual stream, or blaze, along their whole extent, those behind loading for those in front, and thus enabling them to fire almost without intermission. The British columns were literally swept away; hundreds fell at each discharge, until, broken, dispersed, and disheartened, they fled from the field.[*]

The most active efforts were made to rally them. General Pakenham was killed in front of his troops, endeavoring to animate and encourage them by his presence and example. Around him lay nearly a thousand men, dead, dying, and wounded. Generals Gibbs and Keane succeeded in bringing the troops to a second charge; but the second advance was more fatal than the first. The continued roll of the American fire resembled peals of thunder; it was such as no troops could stand. The approaching columns again broke, a few platoons only reaching the ditch, there to meet certain destruction.[†]

An attempt was made, unavailingly, to lead them to the attack a third time by the officers, whose gallantry on this occasion deserved a better fate in a better cause. Generals Gibbs and Keane were carried from the field, the latter severely, the former mortally, wounded. The narrow field of strife between the American and British armies was strewed with dead and dying. A carnage so dreadful, considering the length of time and the numbers engaged, has seldom been recorded in history. Two thousand, at the lowest estimate, pressed the earth, besides such of the wounded as were able to escape The whole number of killed and wounded from the British forces in front of Jackson's lines, on the 8th of January, was fully three thousand men. The loss of the Americans was seven killed and six wounded.[‡]

---

[*] Breckenridge, p. 286. Martin, ii., p. 375.   [†] Breckenridge, p. 286.
[‡] Idem. Also, Martin, ii., p. 377.

General Lambert, who succeeded to the command, met the retreating columns with the reserve, but, being unable to restore the fortune of the day, he withdrew them from the reach of the American artillery, and, finally, from the scene of their discomfiture. The whole field, for half a mile in front of the American lines, was literally strewn with the dead and dying, where thousands were weltering in their blood.

On the right bank of the river the success of the Americans was less flattering. Colonel Thornton had succeeded in making a landing there, and marched immediately against the works of General Morgan. The advanced guard of the Americans was taken by surprise, and retreated to the main body. The enemy, without loss of time, proceeded to attack the principal position of General Morgan. As he approached, a well-directed discharge from the batteries caused a momentary check to his progress; he returned to the charge, and received a severe fire for a few minutes, when he began to outflank the American right; confusion having spread among the militia and raw troops, they gave way, and fled two miles up the river, leaving the works in the hands of the enemy. The Kentucky militia, on the extreme right, having given way, soon drew the Louisiana militia after them; the left, finding themselves deserted by the right wing, and pressed by superior numbers, spiked their guns and retired also.*

In the attack, Colonel Thornton was severely wounded, and Colonel Gubbins succeeded to the command. The occupancy of the works by the enemy was of short duration; for, while General Jackson was preparing re-enforcements to dislodge them, an order from General Lambert required them to retreat across the river to the main army. The American troops immediately re-occupied the works.

Soon afterward General Lambert dispatched a flag to General Jackson, proposing a cessation of hostilities for twenty-four hours, requesting permission to bury the dead, and bring off the wounded lying near the American works. These terms were readily granted.

In the mean time, it had been intended by the British commander-in-chief that the fleet should have co-operated in the grand attack. For this purpose, a squadron of bombarding vessels had been sent around to the Balize to ascend the

* Martin, vol. ii., p. 376, 377. Breckenridge, 287.

Mississippi, after reducing the Forts St. Philip and Jackson at Plaquemines, seventy miles below the city. These points had been securely fortified and re-enforced by General Jackson early in December, and proved impregnable. From delays and difficulty in ascending the river, the bombarding squadron did not reach Fort St. Philip until the 9th of January, at ten o'clock in the forenoon. This squadron consisted of two bomb-vessels, a brig, a schooner, and a sloop, well manned and supplied with heavy artillery. Soon after they came in sight of the fort, they took position, and commenced a tremendous cannonade and bombardment against it; but a severe and well-directed fire from the water-battery very soon compelled the ships to retreat to the distance of two miles, and beyond the reach of its guns; and from this position, with their long guns and largest mortars, the enemy continued to bombard the fort until the 17th, when a heavy mortar having been mounted and turned upon them, they hastily retreated, and abandoned the enterprise on the 18th of January.* Fort St. Philip was garrisoned and defended by three hundred and sixty-six men, under the command of Major Overton, of the United States army.†

On the night of the 18th of January the whole British force precipitately abandoned the encampment on Villère's plantation, and returned to their ships through Lake Borgne. In their retreat they left fourteen pieces of artillery and a large quantity of shot, besides sixteen wounded men and two officers, commended to the mercy of the victors.

Thus terminated the attempted invasion of Louisiana, and the destruction of New Orleans, as contemplated by the British cabinet. It was one of the most powerful and expensive ex peditions ever sent out by that plunderer of the world, Great Britain, and it resulted in the entire failure of its object, with a most disastrous loss of life and military supplies.

The whole loss of the British fleet and army in this unfortunate expedition, from its first arrival upon the coast of Louisiana until its final departure on the 19th of January, was at least four thousand men, besides munitions of war and naval and military stores to an almost unlimited amount.‡

In the mean time, peace had been concluded on the 24th of

---

* Martin, vol. ii., p. 378. Breckenridge, p. 287. † Idem.
‡ Martin's Louisiana, vol. ii., p. 379.

December by the plenipotentiaries of Great Britain and the United States at Ghent. The official intelligence of the treaty of peace did not reach New Orleans until about the middle of February; yet, on the 12th, when the British fleet must have been in full possession of the intelligence, the ferocious and unscrupulous Cockburn, in violation of the treaty stipulations, which required an immediate cessation of hostilities, insatiate of plunder and slaughter, concerted an overwhelming attack upon Fort Bowyer, on Mobile Point, when the feeble garrison of three hundred men, and the well-served batteries, which had spread death and disaster in the British fleet in September, after a brave resistance of four days, were compelled to surrender to the superior force of the enemy, comprising twenty-five sail of vessels, and five thousand land troops.*

Meantime, the principal portion of the fleet had been employed in plundering and ravaging the coast of South Carolina, where the crews were permitted to enrich themselves with the booty stripped from the plantations within their reach.†

The British navy, or many of its recognized commanders, from the days of Sir Francis Drake and Captain Davis, the most noted English buccaneers of former times, down to the infamous Cockburn, has been disgraced by the plunder of feeble colonies and unprotected rich settlements. The latter had rendered his name a curse and a by-word in America by his atrocities upon the Chesapeake in 1813; and in consummating the invasion of Louisiana, the pillage and ravishment of New Orleans and the river coast were to have been the reward of his piratical crews and the British soldiery for their perseverance and privations in the siege. To stimulate them to the terrible contest of the 8th of January, they had been promised the rapine and lust of the city, which, upon the successful issue of the battle, was to have been delivered up to the infuriate troops. To keep this prize continually in their view, the watchword on the day of battle was "*Booty and Beauty!*" Several years afterward, some of the surviving officers of the defeated army, smarting under the exposure of their inhuman depravity, caused a statement to be published in some of our own papers, in which the charge was denied; but the American commander was in possession of undoubted evidence, which can not be success-

* Martin's Louisiana, vol. ii., p. 383.
† Notes on the War in the South, by Nathaniel Herbert Claiborne, p. 78.

fully controverted; and it is useless for the ferocious Britons to deny a specific charge here which, in principle, is proved by the united testimony of mankind in other parts of the world.*

Such was the issue of the boasted armament which, with twelve thousand veteran troops from the command of Wellington, victorious from the defeat of Napoleon, was to spread desolation and slaughter throughout the whole southwestern frontier. The indignant West had been aroused, and its patriotic yeomanry, united to the chivalry of Tennessee and Kentucky, suddenly called from their homes, met the invaders at Chalmette, and with the energy of freemen hurled defiance against them.

The people of New Orleans, relieved from all apprehension of foreign invasion, and the ruthless sacking of the city, returned offerings of devout gratitude to Almighty God for his protecting providence in rescuing them out of the hands of a brutal enemy, while all eyes were turned to General Jackson as the efficient instrument of their deliverance.

But would it be believed that, in the midst of this general rejoicing, there could be found an individual in the city, and one clothed with the highest judicial authority of the Federal government, who could descend to mar the general happiness by a malignant exercise of arbitrary power against the deliverer of the city under the *guise of official duty?* Yes! Dominic A. Hall, judge of the United States District Court, an Englishman by birth and feelings, having failed in his efforts to paralyze the energetic actions of Jackson, persisted in arraigning the victorious general before *himself* upon a charge of *his own* for a *contempt of court,* in disregarding the frequent writs of " habeas corpus" issued by the judge during the investment of the city, with the intent to embarrass the general's plans of defense in the establishment of *martial law.* The judge, persisting in his vindictive course, and disregarding all answers, and overruling all pleas, proceeded to pronounce sentence by a fine of one thousand dollars, which was rigidly enforced, and was paid from the private funds of the general. The judge retired from the court amid the contempt of the assembled multitude, protected from their vengeance only by the efforts and entreaties of the magnanimous hero, who inter-

* See Claiborne's Notes on the War in the South, p. 73.

posed his authority and his commanding influence with the people for the preservation of the unworthy judge, assuring them that, having set them an example of patriotism by repelling foreign invasion, he now desired to evince his respect to the civil power by a voluntary submission to the constituted authorities. The people bore him off in joyful triumph, while the judge was permitted to pass unmolested, and all were emulous of the honor of contributing toward the liquidation of the unjust fine; but the general, refusing thus to be released from the penalty of the law by the kindness of his friends, hastened to liquidate the demand from his own resources. Thirty years afterward, in the year 1845, upon the recommendation of John Tyler, President of the United States, the whole subject was taken up by Congress, and, after a full examination by an impartial committee, that body, refusing longer to sanction the arbitrary and unjust exaction of the malicious judge, by law required the original amount of the fine, with interest for thirty years, to be paid to the aged soldier, as an atonement for the wrong imposed on him by Judge Hall; the national Legislature thus concurring in the argument eloquently advanced by Mr. Douglass, of Indiana, and maintained by the general himself, that the " law of self-preservation, the first law of Nature," above all law and all constitution, *required* the declaration of *martial law* with authority paramount even to the Constitution itself. The Legislature of Louisiana, upon the theatre of Judge Hall's former power, at the same time instituted a thorough inquiry by committee, upon whose report resolutions were passed by an overwhelming majority approving the conduct of General Jackson, and generously proposing to refund the unjust exaction from the state treasury.

This closes our sketch of the early history of Louisiana under the jurisdiction of the United States, and the first years after her admission into the Federal Union as an independent and sovereign state. We shall conclude with a rapid survey of the subsequent increase of inhabitants, the extension of settlements, and the growth of her agricultural and commercial importance.

Near the close of the year 1815, the entire population of Louisiana did not exceed ninety thousand souls, of whom one half were blacks. The greater portion of this number were concentrated in the city of New Orleans, and upon the river coast, for thirty miles below, and seventy miles above the city. The inhabitants of these river settlements were chiefly Creole French, with a small intermixture of Anglo-Americans. On the Lafourche, for fifty miles below its efflux, and upon the Teche, for fifty miles below Opelousas, was also a dense French population. Several bayous west of the Atchafalaya were likewise occupied by the same people, and others in the delta of Red River, and extending as high as Natchitoches, but chiefly below Alexandria. A few scattering French habitations had been formed on Red River, many miles above Natchitoches, and also upon the Washita, as high as the post of Washita, and above the present town of Monroe. In all these settlements west of the Mississippi but few Anglo-Americans had arrived before the purchase of Louisiana. As late as the admission of that state into the Federal Union, the French were the most predominant class in the vicinity of Alexandria, as well as on the river coast below Baton Rouge.

It was only after the year 1815, when Louisiana was relieved from the dangers of foreign invasion, and began to reap the advantages of steam navigation on the river, that the state and New Orleans began to take the proud rank they now enjoy in population, commerce, agriculture, and arts. Enterprising emigrants and capitalists began to develop the unbounded resources of this great agricultural state. Since that time the Anglo-Americans have advanced into every portion of the state, and intermixed, by settlement and marriage, with the French, until, at last, the English language has nearly superseded the French, even in the concentrated settlements near New Orleans, as well as in one half of the old French part of the city.

In the Florida parishes the number of French was comparatively small at the cession of the province of Louisiana, and the proportion had greatly diminished in 1810, when the Spanish authority was rejected by the inhabitants, previous to their annexation to the State of Louisiana. Since that period the increase of population has been effected chiefly by emigrants from the State of Mississippi, and from the Western States generally; and the French language is almost unknown as a colloquial dialect.

[A.D. 1840.] That portion of the state on the west side of the Mississippi, north of latitude 31°, and westward to the Sabine, has been settled by emigrants from the States of Mississippi, Alabama, Tennessee, and Kentucky, besides a portion from Carolina and Georgia. These, of course, are the native Anglo-Americans, and are mostly strangers to the French tongue. The American population in 1840 had spread, also, upon all the arable lands in the bayou regions and prairies southwest of the Teche.

The whole portion of the state west of the Washita and north of Red River in 1830 contained scarcely two thousand inhabitants. The same region in 1845 had been subdivided into several large parishes, with an aggregate population of not less than fourteen thousand souls. In the mean time, the state had increased in numbers in 1830 to 215,740 persons, including 126,300 blacks. The census of 1840 gave an aggregate of 352,400 souls, including 168,452 slaves, which in 1845 had increased to more than 400,000. In point of agricultural and commercial importance, Louisiana had advanced to an elevated rank as early as 1830. In mercantile transactions, New Orleans, in 1840, had attained a standing which placed her second only to the city of New York, and the staple productions of the state were probably inferior in value to none in the United States.

Louisiana is the only state in the Union which has made sugar one of its principal staples of export, and in the production of this article it greatly exceeds all the other states in the Union. The sugar crop of Louisiana in 1836 had increased to 55,000 hogsheads, each weighing not less than one thousand pounds, besides 1547 barrels of molasses. The crop of 1838 yielded 75,000 hogsheads of sugar, and molasses in proportion. The next largest crop of sugar in Louisiana was that of 1842, when the favorable season and the activity of the planters, with the wonderful facilities afforded by the introduction of steam power in all the operations of the manufacturing process, yielded a crop of about 140,000 hogsheads. The agricultural enterprise and resources of the country, stimulated by the success of former efforts, and favored by the fine season of 1844, was rewarded by the largest crop ever made in the state, amounting to 200,000 hogsheads.*

Louisiana, at the same time, had become an important cot-

---

* See "New Orleans Annual Statement" of the prices current, and Merchant's Transcript, for 1844, 1845.

ton-producing state. For several years subsequent to 1836, the American population from Mississippi, Alabama, Tennessee, Carolina, and Georgia had been advancing into the fine cotton regions on the Red River and Washita, and upon the Black River and Tensas north of Red River, as far as the northern limit of the state; and the original parish of Concordia had become densely inhabited, and subdivided into four new ones. In 1845 it constituted one of the most important cotton regions in the state.

As early as the year 1840 the subject of a revisal of the state Constitution had been agitated among the people, and, in obedience to the popular will expressed at the ballot-box, the Legislature had made provision for a convention to assemble at Baton Rouge in 1844, for the purpose of forming a new Constitution upon a more liberal basis, and more Democratic in its general features and provisions. The Constitution subsequently submitted to the people was approved by them in the usual way, and the new government went formally into operation in January, 1846, with Isaac Johnston as governor.* The Legislature was engaged until near the 1st of June following in reorganizing the administration of public affairs.

[A.D. 1846.] Such is the harmony and ease with which forms of government in the United States may be altered and established upon a new basis, without violence or bloodshed. The first Constitution of Louisiana, formed in 1812, under a strong national prejudice of the French inhabitants in favor of monarchical forms and powers, and partaking, in many of its features, of the aristocratic character of the old Spanish dominion, had fallen far behind the liberal and Democratic spirit which had

---

* *Governor of the Territory of Orleans.*
1. William C. C. Claiborne, from 1804 to 1812.

Governors of the State of Louisiana.
1. William C. C. Claiborne, from 1812 to 1816.
2. James Villère, " 1816 to 1820.
3. Thomas B. Robinson, " 1820 to 1824.
4. Henry Johnson, " 1824 to 1828.
5. Peter Derbigny, " 1828 to 1829.
6. A. Beauvais, " 1829 to 1830, acting governor.
7. Jacques Dupré " 1830 to 1831, " "
8. A. B. Roman, " 1831 to 1835.
9. Edward D. White, " 1835 to 1839.
10. A. B. Roman, " 1839 to 1843.
11. Alexander Mouton, " 1843 to 1846.
12. Isaac Johnson, " 1846 to 1849.

overspread the Valley of the Mississippi, and of course became obnoxious to the majority of the people, who in 1842 were mostly emigrants from adjoining states, where liberal and Democratic constitutions existed in successful and salutary operation. The year 1846 found Louisiana protected by and enjoying the advantages of a liberal Constitution, upon the same basis as other Western States, where all offices have a definite term of tenure, and where all are, directly or indirectly, at stated periods, responsible to the people for the faithful discharge of the duties of their offices respectively.

CHAPTER XVI.

PROGRESSIVE EXTENSION OF THE FEDERAL JURISDICTION OVER THE "NORTHWESTERN TERRITORY" TO THE MISSISSIPPI.—A.D. 1800 TO 1845.

Argument.—The Origins of three States in Northwestern Territory.—Indiana.—Illinois.—Michigan.—" Indiana Territory" organized.—Indian Treaties.—" Illinois Territory" organized.—Michigan Territory organized.—Condition of these Territories in 1811.—Shawanese threaten Hostilities.—United States Troops advance with Governor Harrison toward the Prophet's Town.—Harrison contemplates a Treaty.—Unfortunate Battle of Tippecanoe.—Beginning of the Indian War in the West.—Emigration to Indiana and Illinois in 1816.—" State of Indiana" admitted into the Union.—" State of Illinois" admitted into the Union.—Progressive Increase of Population in these States.—Treaties for Extinguishment of Indian Title.—Michigan Territory until 1832.—Emigration to Michigan and Wisconsin.—Commercial and Agricultural Advantages of Michigan discovered.—Increase of Population.—Extension of Settlements.—" State of Michigan" admitted.—" Wisconsin Territory" organized.—Population and Resources of Wisconsin.—" Territory of Iowa" organized in 1838.—Rapid Extension of Population into Wisconsin and Iowa.—Aggregate Population of the States and Territories comprised in original Limits of Northwestern Territory.—Commerce on the Lakes.—Advance of Population and Education in the State of Michigan.—Emigration to Wisconsin and Iowa Territories in 1840-43.—Wisconsin applies for Admission into the Union.

[A.D. 1800.] WE have shown that previous to the admission of the State of Ohio into the Union, the Northwestern Territory, in its greatest extent, contained the germs of three other independent states, in which the *first* grade of territorial government had been instituted, and which were comprised in the Indiana Territory as originally organized. This territory included the county of Knox, upon the Wabash, from which has sprung the State of Indiana; the county of St. Clair, on the Upper Mississippi, or Illinois River, from which has sprung the

State of Illinois; and the county of Wayne, upon the Detroit River, from which has sprung the State of Michigan.

In each of these large counties, surrounded by immense regions of uninhabited country or Indian territory, the nucleus of the white population was the remains of old French colonies, which had been settled at these points early in the eighteenth century, about twenty years after the first settlement at Detroit.

From the first organization of state government in Ohio, when the Indian title to the southern half of the state had been extinguished by the treaty of Greenville, the Federal government omitted no opportunity, by treaty and purchase, to prepare the way for the progressive march of the whites, by extinguishing the Indian claim to other portions of territory. For this purpose, numerous and successive treaties were concluded with the resident tribes for the sale and relinquishment of lands, still in advance of the civil jurisdiction. In this manner the advanced settlements on the Wabash, the Illinois, the Upper Mississippi, and the Detroit River were protected from Indian resentment, and were restrained from encroachment upon lands still in the possession of the Indian tribes. After the close of the war with Great Britain, in the years 1812–15, the Federal executives redoubled their efforts for the peaceful purchase of the Indian right to lands which would soon be required by the rapid spread of immigration.

Indiana Territory.—When the eastern portion of the Northwestern Territory was organized into a separate territorial government, by act of Congress, approved May 7th, 1800, the remaining part of it, extending westward to the Mississippi and northward to the lakes, was denominated the "Indiana Territory," and was subsequently formed into the *first* grade of territorial government, as prescribed in the ordinance of July, 1787. Captain William H. Harrison received the appointment of governor and "Superintendent of Indian Affairs;" and the town of Vincennes was selected as the capital and seat of government.

The Indiana Territory, under this organization, embraced all the white settlements upon the Illinois and Upper Mississippi, as well as those in the vicinity of Detroit. At this time, the inhabitants contained in all of them did not amount to more than 5640 souls, while the aggregate number of the Indian tribes within the extreme limits of the territory was more than one hundred thousand.

[A.D. 1802.] *Extinction of Indian Title.*—After the treaty of Greenville, the northwestern tribes had continued peaceable, and the white inhabitants in the isolated settlements began to increase by emigration from the western country, and by those who were connected with the army, or were concerned in the administration of the territorial government and the Indian department. Roads, or traces, through the Indian country were opened, to facilitate intercourse between the remote counties, in the execution of the laws, and the discharge of the executive duties of the governor and the agents of the Indian department. The rambling disposition of the western people, the propensity for Indian trade and traffic, and the innate curiosity to see and explore new and beautiful regions, by plunging still further into the boundless wilderness, stimulated them to seek out these remote and lonely abodes. Hence the number of whites gradually augmented around the French nucleus on the Wabash, Illinois, and Detroit Rivers.

As the population increased and the settlements extended, it became necessary to obtain the peaceable consent of the Indian tribes for the occupancy of additional territory, and to compensate them for the relinquishment of their title to the soil. Hence, arrangements were entered into for extending by negotiation the boundary of the land already ceded by the treaty of Greenville.*

* The following is an authentic abstract from the principal *Indian treaties for the sale and relinquishment of lands in the territory northwest of the Ohio, from the treaty of Greenville inclusive.*

1. *Treaty of Greenville*, concluded on the 3d of August, 1795, with the Wyandots, Delawares, Shawanese, Ottawâs, Chippewas, Potawatamies, Miamies, Eel Rivers, Miamies, Kickapoos, Piankeshas, and Kaskaskias.—By this treaty the tribes concerned cede and relinquish to the United States, within the limits of the present States of Ohio and Indiana, 17,724,489 acres of land; of this quantity, 1,726,000 acres were within the limits of the Connecticut Reserve, and 794,072 acres were within the present State of Indiana.

2. *Treaty of Fort Wayne*, concluded June 7th, 1803, with the Delawares, Shawanese, Potawatamies, Eel Rivers, Weas, Kickapoos, Piankeshas, and Kaskaskias.—This treaty was ratified at the council held in Vincennes, August 7th, 1803, by the Eel Rivers, Wyandots, Kaskaskias, and Kickapoos. By it the tribes concerned cede to the United States, within the limits of the present States of Indiana and Illinois, 1,634,000 acres, of which 1,297,920 acres were in Indiana, and 336,128 acres were in Illinois.

3. *Treaty of Vincennes*, concluded August 13th, 1803.—By this treaty the Kaskaskias cede to the United States, within the present State of Illinois, 8,608,167 acres.

4. *Treaty of Vincennes*, concluded August 18th, 1804, at Vincennes.—This treaty

[A.D. 1804.] By successive treaties, the Indian title was extinguished gradually to all the country lying upon the waters of the White River, and upon all the lower tributaries of the Wabash, upon the Little Wabash, the Kaskaskia, and east of the Mississippi, below the mouth of the Illinois. Thus, before the close of the year 1805, nearly all the southern half of the present State of Indiana, and one third of the State of Illinois, was open to the advance of the enterprising pioneer; the great obstacle having been removed by the peaceable extinction of the Indian claim to the same.

[A.D. 1805.] By the same means, the Indian right was extinguished to the greater portion of the Western Reserve in the northeastern part of Ohio. In 1807, the Federal government, in like manner, purchased from the Indians extensive regions west of Detroit River, and within the present State of Michigan, far beyond the limits of the white settlements in that quarter.

was made with the Delawares, who thereby ceded, within the limits of the present State of Indiana, 1,910,717 acres of land. This cession was ratified by the Piankeshas, at Vincennes, on the 27th of August, 1804.

5. *Treaty of St. Louis*, concluded November 3d, 1804.—By this treaty the Sauks and Foxes ceded to the United States 14,000,000 acres of land, situated principally within the limits of the present State of Illinois, but partly in Missouri, west of the Mississippi.

6. *Treaty of Fort Industry*, concluded July 4th, 1805.—This treaty was made with the Wyandots, Ottawâs, Chippewas, Munsees, Delawares, Shawanese, and Potawatamies, by which they ceded to the United States 2,726,812 acres of land, all within the northern limits of the present State of Ohio, east of the Sandusky River, and chiefly within the Connecticut Reserve.

7. *Treaty of Grouse-land*, near Vincennes, concluded August 21st, 1805.—This treaty was made with the Delawares, Potawatamies, Miamies, Eel Rivers, and Weas. They ceded to the United States 1,244,211 acres of land, within the limits of the present State of Indiana.

8. *Treaty of Vincennes*, concluded December 30th, 1805.—This treaty was made with the Piankeshas, who ceded their claim to 2,616,921 acres of land, within the limits of the present State of Illinois.

9. *Treaty of Detroit*, concluded November 17th, 1807.—By this treaty the Ottawâs, Chippewas, Wyandots, and Potawatamies ceded to the United States 5,937,760 acres of land, chiefly within the present limits of Michigan, and partly within the northwestern limits of Ohio.

10. *Treaty of Brownstown*, concluded November 25th, 1808, at Brownstown, Michigan.—By this treaty the Chippewas, Ottawâs, Wyandots, Potawatamies, Miamies, and Eel Rivers ceded to the United States certain lands in the State of Ohio for the use of a road, &c.

11. *Treaty of Fort Wayne*, concluded September 30th, 1809.—This treaty was made with the Delawares, Potawatamies, Miamies, and Eel Rivers. They ceded thereby to the United States 2,136,266 acres of land, within the northern portion of the present State of Indiana.

This cession was subsequently confirmed in convention, at Vincennes, by the Weas, on the 26th day of October, 1809. Also, by the Kickapoos, in a treaty at Vincennes, concluded December 9th, 1809.— *See Land Laws of United States, compilation of* 1827, *by M. St. Clair Clarke, passim.*

Michigan Territory.—Meantime, the settlements formerly comprised in Wayne county, having increased in inhabitants and importance, had been erected into a separate territorial government, known and designated as the "Territory of Michigan." On the first of July, 1805, the territory entered upon the first grade of territorial government, under the provisions of the ordinance of 1787; and William Hull, formerly a lieutenant in the Revolutionary army, was made the first governor. The judges and other officers appointed soon afterward entered upon the discharge of their respective duties at Detroit, which was made the seat of the territorial government. The southern limit of "Michigan Territory," according to the act of Congress, was to be a line running due east from the most southern part of Lake Michigan to the Maumee Bay.

Meantime, Louisiana, purchased from France, had been occupied by the American troops, and Upper Louisiana, comprising the settlements on the west side of the Mississippi, from the Arkansas to the Missouri River, had been annexed to the jurisdiction of the Indiana Territory as the "District of Missouri." A treaty had been held at St. Louis on the 3d of November, for the extinction of the Indian title to extensive tracts in this district also. Thus, as early as 1805, the whole region north of the Ohio, and south of a line drawn southwest from Greenville to St. Louis, on the Upper Mississippi, was released from the claim, if not from the occupancy, of the native tribes, and thrown open to the explorations of the western pioneers.

[A.D. 1807.] But these countries were too remote, and too much exposed to the precarious friendship of the savages, and too destitute of the comforts of civilized life, to attract many emigrants, while lands equally good, and much more secure from danger, were more convenient. Hence the settlements on the Wabash, on the Illinois, on the Upper Mississippi, and near the Detroit River, increased in numbers slowly. The Indians still lingered around their homes and familiar hunting-grounds, as if reluctant to abandon the scenes of their youth and the graves of their ancestors, although they had received the stipulated payment, and had consented to retire from them.

[A.D. 1809.] *Illinois Territory.*—Yet the tide of emigration set strongly to the West, and the redundant population began to reach the Wabash and the Illinois. By the close of the year

1808, the Indiana Territory east of the Wabash had received such an increase in numbers that it was desirable to assume the second grade of territorial government. Having a population of five thousand free white males, Congress, with a view to a future state government, by an act approved February 3d, 1809, restricted its limits, and authorized a territorial Legislature, agreeably to the provisions of the ordinance of 1787. The Indiana Territory, from this time, was bounded on the west by a line extending up the middle of the Wabash, from its mouth to Vincennes, and thence by a meridian due north to the southern extremity of Lake Michigan. On the north, it was bounded by the southern line of the Michigan Territory. That portion west of the Wabash was erected into a separate territorial government of the *first* grade, known and designated as the "Illinois Territory."*

[A.D. 1810.] The inhabitants of the Indiana Territory soon began to augment more rapidly, and emigration to seek the fine lands on White River, and upon the Wabash, as well as the regions near the banks of the Ohio, between Cincinnati and New Albany. In 1810 the people had increased in numbers to twenty-four thousand five hundred, and in the newly-erected Territory of Illinois there was an aggregate of twelve thousand three hundred persons.†

The population of Michigan Territory, upon its first organization in 1805, exclusive of the troops of the western army, did not exceed three thousand souls. As late as the year 1810, the increase by emigration from the western settlements had been comparatively small, and the census of 1810 gave an aggregate of only eight thousand four hundred souls.‡ At the opening of the war in 1812, the whole number of people could not have exceeded six thousand souls.

[A.D. 1811.] Thus, at the beginning of hostilities near the close of the year 1811, these three territories together scarcely contained forty thousand inhabitants, including the Creole French on the Detroit, Wabash, and Illinois Rivers. The whole northern half of Michigan still belonged to the Indians, and was in their sole occupancy. Of Indiana, two thirds of its entire area, on the north, were likewise territory to which

---

* Land Laws of United States, compilation of 1827, p. 563.
† Mitchell's World, p. 221. Census of United States.
‡ Idem, p. 224. United States Census for 1810.

the Indian title had not been extinguished. A still greater portion of the whole area of Illinois was in the possession of the natives.

Yet, notwithstanding the right of soil had been purchased of the Indians, the further progress of the whites was checked by the very first act of open warfare. Many who had already advanced too far for safety, retired from their new homes; hence, during the war with Great Britain and her savage "allies," the advanced settlements were abandoned. It was not until the summer of 1815 that population began to extend into the wilderness of these three territories, and into the northern half of the State of Ohio.

The first indication of aggression shown by the Indians northwest of the Ohio was from the Shawanese, controlled by their great war-chief, Tecumseh, aided by his brother, the "Prophet." The former was an extraordinary man, possessed of great talent, energy, and perseverance; endowed with eloquence and a commanding influence, which enabled him to control not only his own, but many other tribes. He had been a noted warrior from the close of the revolutionary struggle, and, like his prototype Pontiac, seemed to devote the whole of his great energies to arresting the advance of civilization into the Indian country. In this object he derived aid and counsel from British agents and officers in Canada, who, believing a rupture between the United States and England inevitable, had used every effort to induce him to stir up the tribes of the northwest, as well as of the south, to engage in the approaching contest. During the year 1812 he was zealously engaged in exciting a general Indian war, having visited the Chickasâs, the Cherokees, and the Creeks, in order to rouse them in the common cause against the American people. His brother, by operating upon the credulity and superstition of the Indians, greatly promoted his plans, and gave him additional influence over the savages.

Tecumseh had opposed the sale and cession of lands to the United States, and now contended that the treaties and sales were null and void; as such, he refused to permit their occupancy by the whites. Toward the autumn of the year 1811 he had stirred up the northwestern Indians to such a degree, that an outbreak of hostilities was constantly apprehended in the settlements of the Indiana Territory. To avert the danger, and to appease the anger of the savages, Governor Harrison, of the Indiana Territory, and agent for Indian affairs, had convened a council of chiefs and warriors at Vincennes, for the purpose of friendly negotiations.

This council was attended by Tecumseh and twenty or thirty chiefs and warriors, but no arrangement was accomplished, on account of the violence of Tecumseh, who broke up the assembly by his impetuous insolence.

Campaign of Tippecanoe.—In the mean time, the Federal government, preparing for the worst, had concentrated a military force in the vicinity of Vincennes, for the protection of the inhabitants, and to chastise any outbreak that might occur. The fourth regiment of United States troops, under Colonel Boyd, was stationed at that place, and was re-enforced by detachments of volunteers and militia from Kentucky and Indiana.

As the year drew toward a close, the frontier settlers became seriously alarmed at the threatening aspect of Indian affairs, which clearly indicated approaching hostilities. Under these circumstances, Governor Harrison advanced with the troops toward the principal towns of the Shawanese, on the Wabash, near the outlet of the Tippecanoe Creek.

On the 5th of November he was in the vicinity of the Prophet's Town, with about twelve hundred men, including regulars, militia, and mounted volunteers. His object was to demand satisfactory explanations for the hostile appearances, or to enforce the observance of existing treaties by force of arms.*

On the 6th the troops were within a few miles of the Prophet's Town, on the northwest side of the Wabash River, near the mouth of the Tippecanoe Creek. During this day, as well as upon the whole march, the Indians continued to manifest every indication of aggression except an actual attack, which they seldom make without great advantages in their favor. They continued to hover upon the flanks and front of the army, in warlike array, and to elude every attempt to approach them, and to reject all overtures to meet in council. Several peace-flags had been sent to them for an amicable conference, which they declined by sullenly retiring toward their towns. The army continued to advance until within one mile of the Prophet's Town, when, becoming alarmed for their safety,

* Breckenridge's Late War, p. 24.

they sent a delegation of warriors to Governor Harrison, proposing to meet in council next morning. Colonel Boyd urged the expediency of advancing immediately upon the town, to take possession of it, and to chastise them severely, when they would be able to dictate the terms of peace on their own ground. He knew the perfidious character of the savages, and was unwilling to afford them time to concert means of defense, or to mature any treacherous designs.

But Governor Harrison had been instructed to avoid actual hostilities as long as possible, and he resolved to accede to the proposition for holding a council with them on the next day. The army was accordingly directed to halt, and take up its position for the night in a piece of woods on the margin of a prairie. Aware of the Indian character for studied duplicity, the troops were ordered to repose upon their arms, with a numerous guard on duty within the line of sentinels. The order of encampment was designed to resist any sudden attack at night, so far as their unprotected situation permitted.*

In this condition they remained undisturbed until about four o'clock next morning, when, the night being cloudy and drizzly, the Indians made their attack with great impetuosity, in that part of the camp near the regular troops. They had crept upon their hands and knees, unobserved, nearly to the sentinels, whom they designed to kill before any alarm could be given; but they were discovered, and the alarm was immediately sounded. The Indians sprang to their feet, gave the terrible war-whoop, and rushed to the assault with the tomahawk against the advanced guard of militia on the left flank. The guard, panic-stricken, fled in confusion upon the regulars under Colonel Boyd. The assault was first received by Captain Barton's company of infantry, and Captain Guiger's company of mounted riflemen, who maintained their position with great firmness. While the commander-in-chief was endeavoring to re-enforce this point, and to dislodge the Indians from their covert by means of the cavalry, a furious attack was made on the right wing, which was received by two companies of United States infantry under Captains Spencer and Warwick. Captain Spencer and all his lieutenants were killed, and Captain Warwick was mortally wounded. This line was strengthened by Captain Robb's company, which maintained its position with

* Breckenridge, p. 25.

great courage. While Governor Harrison was bringing up this company, his aid, Colonel Owen, was killed by his side. Colonel Daviess, of Kentucky, and Colonel White, of Indiana, were killed in leading a charge against the Indians on the left flank.

The camp fires had been extinguished, and the whole army was closely engaged in the action. The Indians, concealed behind logs and trees, and in the grass, kept up an incessant and galling fire upon the compact bodies of troops, who suffered severely, until the savages were routed by a charge of cavalry, led on by Captain Snelling.

The contest was now maintained with great valor on both sides, and on every part of the field. The Indians advanced and retreated alternately, fighting desperately, and with a fury seldom seen or equalled. Their yells, and the terrific rattling of deer-hoofs and Indian drums, served to render the scene one of the most fearful import. Such it continued until about daybreak, when several companies were ordered to charge simultaneously from the right and left wings upon the enemy, aided by such of the dragoons as could be mounted. The savages fled in every direction, and were pursued by the horsemen into the swamps as far as they could proceed. Thus terminated this sanguinary and unfortunate battle.*

The loss of the Americans in this engagement was but little short of two hundred men killed and wounded. Among them were Colonels Daviess and Owen, highly distinguished and greatly lamented. The whole of the troops, both of the regular army and the volunteers and militia, behaved with great courage and prudence, and merited the thanks of their countrymen. The loss of the Indians was unknown; but, from their advantages and concealment, it is probable their loss did not exceed fifty or sixty warriors.

This battle was, in fact, the beginning of the war which was declared against Great Britain in June following. The whole of the western frontier was thrown into a state of alarm, and many retired to the older settlements for safety. The Indian tribes inhabiting the country on the waters of the Wabash, and the regions south and west of all the great lakes, immediately flew to arms, and sought the aid of their allies, the English in Canada. They had previously received assurance of

* Breckenridge, p. 26. Official returns give 62 killed, 126 wounded.—Drake's Book of Indians, book v., p. 103.

aid from Great Britain in case of hostilities, and they now began to threaten all the American border population and posts in the Michigan, Indiana, and Illinois Territories, as well as the northwestern confines of New York, Pennsylvania, and Ohio.*

It would carry us entirely beyond the limits prescribed for this work to attempt to give an account of the military operations and the horrors of savage warfare conducted by the British commanders upon the northwestern frontier during three years, from 1812 to 1815; we shall, therefore, pass them by, and pursue the subject of the gradual extension of the white inhabitants after the war.

[A.D. 1815.] The year 1815 was ushered in with the news of peace between the United States and Great Britain. The Indian tribes in the northwest, deprived of their great civilized ally, were comparatively powerless, and readily suspended operations. A short time served to banish fear from the western emigrants and to restore confidence to the frontier settlements. With the death of Tecumseh all hope of resisting the onward march of the whites had vanished from the Indian tribes. They contented themselves with the privilege of making peace with them, and living upon their own soil, until the settlements should encroach upon them. The gradual relinquishment of their lands, as they retired westward, created for them a fund, in the shape of annuities from the American government, which supplied them with many of the comforts of life, which they could not procure otherwise.

State of Indiana.—The various campaigns and mounted expeditions which had traversed the regions of the Illinois, Indiana, and Michigan Territories for the last three years, were virtual explorations of the fertile and beautiful country by thousands of

* While the government of the United States had adopted every prudential measure which humanity and natural justice might dictate for the preservation of neutrality and peace with the northwestern Indians, as Mr. Madison declared in his message of November 4th, 1812, "The enemy has not scrupled to call to his aid the ruthless ferocity of the savages, armed with instruments of carnage and torture, which are known to spare neither age nor sex. In this outrage against the laws of honorable war, and against the feelings sacred to humanity, the British commanders can not resort to the plea of retaliation, for it is committed in the face of our example. They can not mitigate it by calling it 'self-defense' against men in arms, for it embraces the most shocking butcheries of defenseless families. Nor can it be pretended that they are not answerable for the atrocities perpetrated; for the savages are employed with a knowledge, and even with menaces that their fury can not be controlled. Such is the spectacle which the deputed authorities of a nation boasting its religion and morality have not restrained from presenting to an enlightened age."—See American State Papers, Boston ed., vol. ix., p. 51.

young, hardy, and enterprising pioneers. The enchanting prospects, and the fertile valleys upon all the branches of the Wabash and of the Illinois and Kaskaskia, had filled many with enthusiasm for adventure into those desirable regions. Those who had traversed this country in hostile array now advanced with their families in the peaceful garb of husbandmen, and habitations began to multiply and extend upon all the water-courses. The older settlements of Kentucky and Ohio began to send forth young colonies to these beautiful localities, where the land was both productive and cheap.

[A.D. 1816.] Early in the following year it was ascertained that the Indiana Territory possessed a population which entitled it to an independent state government. Congress authorized the election of a convention to form a state Constitution, agreeably to the provisions of the ordinance of 1787. The Convention formed a Constitution similar to that which had been adopted by the State of Ohio nearly fifteen years before. This Constitution having been approved by Congress, the new "State of Indiana" was formally admitted into the Union on the 19th of April, 1816.*

The new state government went into operation by the election of Jonathan Jennings first governor,† and a General Assembly, which proceeded to the formation of the various departments, agreeably to the provisions of the Constitution.

In the mean time, the same tide of immigration had set equally strong into the Illinois Territory. The inhabitants began to increase in all the old settlements, and gradually to extend into the country west of the Wabash and upon the lower tributaries of the Illinois, as well as upon the region between the mouth of the Illinois and Ohio Rivers, and east of the Mississippi.

State of Illinois.—Before the close of the year 1817, it was ascertained that the population of the Illinois Territory was equal to that of Ohio previous to its admission into the Union.

---

* See Land Laws of United States, vol. vi., p. 68. Also, Senate compilation of 1827, p. 682. Also, Darby's Gazetteer, p. 336.

† GOVERNORS OF INDIANA.
Territorial.
1. Wm. H. Harrison, from 1800 to 1813. | 2. Thomas Posey, from 1813 to 1816.

State.
1. Jonathan Jennings, from 1816 to 1822. | 4. Noah Noble, from 1831 to 1837.
2. Wm. B. Hendricks, " 1822 " 1825. | 5. David Wallace, " 1837 " 1843.
3. James B. Ray, " 1825 " 1831. | 6. James Whitcomb, " 1843 " 1846.

The territorial Legislature at its next session, representing the will of the people, made application to Congress for authority to establish a state government. Congress, granting a ready assent, on the 18th of April, 1818, passed "An act to enable the people of the Illinois Territory to form a state Constitution, and for the admission of such state into the Union upon an equal footing with the original states." The act provided for the election of delegates to a convention, which was held in July following. The Constitution adopted early in August was approved by Congress on the 3d day of December following, when, by a joint resolution, the "State of Illinois" was admitted into the Union in less than two years after the admission of Indiana.

[A.D. 1820.] The inhabitants increased slowly during the next two years, and the census of 1820 gave the entire number at 55,210 souls. The state census, five years afterward, indicated the population at 72,817, being an annual increase of nearly ten thousand persons.*

Indiana had increased in an equal or greater ratio, having received a large number of immigrants from the adjoining State of Ohio. Such had been the unprecedented emigration to Indiana, that the census of 1820, four years after the adoption of the state government, presented a population of 147,178 souls, including 1420 blacks. The state census, five years afterward, gave an aggregate of 250,000 souls.† The people continued to increase in numbers in a similar ratio during the next five years, and in 1830 the census presented an aggregate of 341,582 souls, of whom 3562 were blacks. But, what is most surprising, the same ratio of increase was maintained for five years longer, and in 1835 the whole number of inhabitants was estimated at six hundred thousand persons.‡

* See Laws of United States, vol. vi., p. 294. Bradford's Illustrated Atlas, p. 97. Also, Emigrant's Guide, p. 334.

GOVERNORS OF ILLINOIS.
Territorial.
1. Wm. H. Harrison, as Governor of Indiana until 1809.
2. Ninian Edwards, from 1809 to 1818, three terms.
State.

1. Shadrach Bond, from 1818 to 1822.
2. Edward Coles,   " 1822 " 1826.
3. Ninian Edwards, " 1826 " 1830.
4. John Reynolds, " 1830 " 1834.

5. Joseph Duncan, from 1834 to 1838.
6. Thomas Carlin, " 1838 " 1842.
7. Thomas Ford,   " 1842 " 1846.

† Darby's Gazetteer, p. 336.

‡ Mitchell's World, p. 219

Meantime, since the close of the war in 1815, the Federal government had perseveringly pursued the policy of gradually removing the Indian tribes from all the habitable portions of the northwestern states and territories. By successive treaties, the different tribes and nations had relinquished their claim to and occupancy of the lands within the jurisdiction of the respective states, and had entered into agreements to remove ultimately to the west side of the Mississippi, there to occupy lands provided for them by the United States.*

Michigan Territory.—The remainder of the Northwestern Territory, as formerly organized, was the Territory of Michigan. This territory at the beginning of the war was comparatively unknown to the western people, and had but little attractions for emigrants. A much larger portion of its surface was also in the actual possession of the native tribes. But few settlements had been made beyond the region of the Detroit and Raisin Rivers; and these, in a great measure, had been broken up by the savages and their English allies during the war.

Huron District.—Lying in a more rigorous climate, remote from the dense settlements of the Western States, and exposed to the dangers of an Indian frontier, years elapsed after the war before the tide of immigration had set strong into the Michigan Territory. At the close of the war the whole white

---

* The principal Indian treaties with the northwestern tribes, after the peace of 1815, for the cession of lands, are as follows:

1. *Treaty of the Maumee Rapids*, concluded September 29th, 1817.—By this treaty the Wyandots, Senecas, Shawanese, Ottawâs, Delawares, Potawatamies, and Chippewas ceded to the United States 4,776,971 acres of land near the Lakes Erie and Michigan, but chiefly in Ohio; some in Indiana and Michigan Territory.

2. *Treaty of Edwardsville*, concluded September 26th, 1818.—By this treaty the Peorias, Kaskaskias, Michigamies, Cahokias, and Temarois ceded to the United States, within the Territory of Illinois, 7,138,398 acres of land.

3. *Treaty of St. Mary's*, concluded October 3d, 1818.—By this treaty the Delawares ceded all their lands in Indiana, in exchange for others west of the Mississippi.

4. *Treaty of Edwardsville*, concluded July 30th, 1819. 5. *Treaty of Fort Harrison*, concluded August 30th, 1819.—By these treaties the Kickapoos ceded to the United States 3,312,450 acres of land, chiefly in Illinois, but partly in Indiana.

6. *Treaty of Saginaw*, concluded September 29th, 1819.—By this treaty the Chippewas ceded to the United States 7,451,520 acres of land in the Territory of Michigan. Other treaties, by the same tribes, concluded at Sault St. Marie, June 16th, 1820; and at L'Arbre Croché, July 6th, 1820, ceded other smaller portions of territory near the St. Mary's River.

7. *Treaty of Chicago*, concluded August 29th, 1821.—By this treaty the Chippewas, Ottawâs, and Potawatamies ceded to the United States, chiefly in Michigan and partly in Indiana, 4,933,550 acres.—*See Land Laws of United States, compilation of* 1827, *by M. St. Clair Clarke.*

population in this territory was but little, if any, over six thousand souls. Five years afterward, the census of 1820 gave to the territory an aggregate of only 8900 souls, distributed over seven counties, which embraced the entire organized portion of the territory, including the "Huron District," on the west side of Lake Michigan. The inhabitants increased slowly and gradually for ten years more ; and the census of 1830 presented the number of people at only 28,000 souls, distributed over twelve counties, exclusive of the "Huron District." This district, comprising four counties west of the southern portion of Lake Michigan, contained about 3640 souls.* At this time, that part of Michigan Territory over which the civil jurisdiction had been extended included only about one third of the peninsula, or that portion lying south of the forty-third parallel of north latitude. The remainder, as far north as the Straits of Michillimackinac, was Indian territory, in the undisturbed occupancy of more than eight thousand savages.

[A.D. 1832.] About the year 1832 the tide of emigration began to set toward Michigan Territory. Steam-boat navigation had opened a new commerce upon the lakes, and had connected the eastern lakes and their population with the Illinois and Upper Mississippi. This immense lake navigation encircled the peninsula of Michigan. It became an object of exploration. Its unrivalled advantages for navigation, its immense tracts of the most fertile arable lands, adapted to the cultivation of all the northern grains and grasses, attracted the attention of western immigrants. The tide soon began to set strong into Michigan. Its fine level and rolling plains, its deep and enduring soil, and its immense advantages for trade and commerce had become known and duly appreciated. The hundreds of canoes, pirogues, and barges, with their half-civilized *couriers du bois*, which had annually visited Detroit for more than a century, had given way to large and splendid steam-boats, which daily traversed the lakes from Buffalo to Chicago, from the east end of Lake Erie to the southwestern extremity of Lake Michigan. Nearly a hundred sail of sloops and schooners were now traversing every part of these inland seas. Under these circumstances, how should Michigan remain a savage wilderness?† The New England States began to send forth their numerous colonies, and the wilderness to smile.

* Emigrant's Guide, p. '78, 179. † Mitchell's World, p. 224.

[A.D. 1834.] At the end of two years more, or in 1834, the population of Michigan had increased to 87,273 souls, exclusive of Indians. The following year the number amounted to more than ninety thousand persons, distributed over thirty-eight counties, comprised in the southern half of the peninsula, and the "attached Huron, or Wisconsin District," lying west of Lake Michigan. The town of Detroit, which in 1812 was a stockade village, had now become "a city," with nearly twenty-five hundred inhabitants.

[A.D. 1835.] *State of Michigan.*—The humble villages and wigwams of the Indians, sparsely distributed over a wide extent of wilderness, had now given way to thousands of farms and civilized habitations. Towns and smiling villages usurped the encampment and the battle-field. The fertile banks of the "River Raisin" were crowned with hamlets and towns instead of the melancholy stockade. A Constitution had been adopted on the 15th of June, 1836, and the "State of Michigan" was admitted into the Union* on the 26th day of January, 1837.†

[A.D. 1836.] The area of the peninsula of Michigan is but little short of twenty-two millions of acres. One third of this yet remained in the occupancy of the native tribes, embracing all that part of it extending west and north of Saginaw Bay. This portion was still occupied by no less than eight thousand roving savages; but, under the eager advance and enterprise of the New England emigrants, it could not long remain so.

Wisconsin Territory.—In the mean time, the "Huron District," west of Lake Michigan, after the organization of the state government, had been erected into a separate territorial government, under the name of the "Wisconsin Territory." This territory comprised within its limits and jurisdiction the whole

---

* See Laws of the United States, vol. ix., p. 377. Emigrant's Guide, p. 185. Also, American Almanac for 1838, p. 256.

† *Governors of the Territory of Michigan.*
1. William Hull, from 1805 to 1812.
2. Lewis Cass, " 1814 to 1832.
3. George B. Porter, " 1832 to 1834.
4. Stephens T. Mason, " 1834, acting governor.
5. John S. Horner, " 1835 to 1836.

Governors of the State of Michigan.
1. Stephens T. Mason, from 1836 to 1840, two terms.
2. " 1840 to 1842.
3. John S. Barry, " 1842 to 1846, two terms.
4. Alpheus Felch, " 1846 to 1848.

region from Lake Michigan to Lake Superior, extending westward to the Missouri River, including all the sources of the Upper Mississippi. Its southern limits were the northern boundaries of the States of Illinois and Missouri, and its extent from north to south was five hundred and eighty miles, and from east to west six hundred and fifty miles.*

The territorial government was organized in 1836. The first "Governor and Superintendent of Indian Affairs" was Henry Dodge; and John S. Horner was territorial secretary.† The first General Assembly consisted of a Legislative Council of thirteen members, appointed for two years, and a Legislative Assembly of twenty-six members, elected for one year, in the ratio of one member to every five hundred free white males.

The settled portions of the territory were chiefly near the western shore of Lake Michigan, and the organized counties extended westward and southwestwardly to the banks of the Fox River of Green Bay, as far as Fort Winnebago, and thence down the Wisconsin River, on the southeastern side, for thirty miles below the "portage." At the same time, immigrants, by way of Milwaukie and Racine, were advancing upon the upper tributaries of Rock River, as far west as the "Four Lakes" and Fort Madison. A few settlements had extended, likewise, westward to the banks of the Mississippi, north of Galena and the Illinois state line. Others had been slowly, for more than three years, extending west of the Mississippi, upon the waters of the Des Moines, Skunk River, Lower Iowa, and Waubesapinacon, as well as upon the immediate banks of the Mississippi itself. These settlements, for temporary government, were annexed to the jurisdiction of the Wisconsin Territory as the "District of Iowa."

The remainder of the Territory of Wisconsin, north and west of the Wisconsin River and of Fox River, as well as the northern and western portions of the present State of Iowa, was a savage waste, still in the partial occupancy of the remaining tribes of Indians, and in a great degree unknown to civilization. Such were the extent and population of the Wis-

* Mitchell's World, p. 228.
† The governors of Wisconsin Territory are as follows:
1. Henry Dodge, Governor and Superintendent of Indian Affairs, from 1836 to 1841.
2. James M. Doty,   "   "   "   "   " 1841 to 1844.
3. Nathaniel P. Tallmage, "   "   "   "   " 1844 to 1845.
4. Henry Dodge,   "   "   "   "   " 1845 to 1848.

consin Territory upon its first independent organization. The District of Iowa, in August, 1836, contained two large counties, those of Dubuque and Des Moines, with an aggregate population of 10,531 persons. These two counties, in less than two years afterward, were divided into sixteen others,* containing about 22,860 souls.

[A.D. 1838.] But after the organization of a separate territorial government, and especially after the final extinction of the Indian title in 1837, the new settlements began to extend in a remarkable manner, not only upon the western shores of Lake Michigan, but in an equal degree westward to the Mississippi River, and on its western side, into the District of Iowa. The tide of emigration continued to flow into these regions during the years of 1837 and 1838 ; population increased, new counties were laid off and organized, in the gradual extension of the territorial jurisdiction over the newly-occupied country, both east and west of the Mississippi. Such was the increase of inhabitants, and the extension of civil government on the west side of the Mississippi, that Congress, for the convenience of the people, and the equal administration of justice, proceeded to divide the territory, by erecting the " District of Iowa" into a separate territorial government, to be known and designated as the " Territory of Iowa."

The act authorizing this division was approved June 12th, 1838, and was to take effect from and after the 4th day of July following.

The " Territory of Iowa" at this time comprised thirteen counties, with a General Assembly elected by the people, a governor, secretary, superior judges, and other Federal officers appointed by the president, similar in all respects to the original Territory of Wisconsin.†

About this time immense numbers of foreign immigrants from Europe, but chiefly from Germany, began to arrive at the ports of New York and New Orleans. Those from New York proceeded by way of the lakes, and settled in the northwestern parts of New York and Pennsylvania, in the northern parts of Ohio, in Michigan, and the Wisconsin Territory. Those by way of New Orleans ascended the Mississippi by

---

* See Newhall's Sketches of Iowa, p. 247, &c.

† Territory of Iowa is continued under the head of chap. xvii., *i. e.,* " Extension of Federal Jurisdiction west of the Mississippi," &c.

thousands, on crowded steam-boats, and settled themselves in the southern and middle portions of Ohio, Indiana, and Illinois. Many of them advanced into the fine country of the Wisconsin Territory, upon the tributaries of the Wisconsin River, and the small branches of the Mississippi.

Nor did those who went to the Wisconsin Territory consist of foreigners only. Thousands of the early settlers of Ohio and Indiana, as well as of Kentucky and Tennessee, or their offspring, were seeking homes in the regions of the Upper Mississippi, both on the east and west sides of that noble river.

[A.D. 1840.] During the year 1839 the emigration to Iowa began to rival that to Wisconsin itself; and before the census of 1840 was completed, the Iowa Territory contained a larger number of inhabitants than that of Wisconsin. This census gave to Iowa a population of 43,112 persons, distributed over eighteen counties;* while to Wisconsin it gave only 30,845 persons, distributed over twenty-two counties.

Illinois had increased in numbers in the same manner, and almost as rapidly. This large state had also been relieved of its Indian population, whose claim to the right of soil had been entirely extinguished by the Federal government by purchase and treaty. The jurisdiction of the state had been extended over its whole territory, which had been organized into eighty-five counties, with an aggregate of 476,183 souls.

The town of Chicago, on the shore of Lake Michigan, had become an important mercantile city, the great lake port of Illinois. Situated on both sides of Chicago Creek, where it opens like a canal basin, with a fine harbor, to the lake, and spreading over a beautiful level plain, sufficiently elevated above tides and floods, it had become the commercial emporium of Illinois, and one of the most important ports on Lake Michigan. Of Chicago, Judge Peck, in 1841, observes :†

"Its growth, even for western cities, has been of unparalleled rapidity. In 1832 it contained five small stores and 250 inhabitants. In 1831 there were four arrivals from the lower lakes, two brigs and two schooners, which were sufficient for all the trade of the northeastern part of Illinois and the northwestern part of Indiana. In 1835 there were about 267 arrivals of ships, brigs, and schooners, and 9 of steam-boats, which

---

* See chap. xvii., "Extension of Federal Jurisdiction west of the Mississippi," &c.
† See Gazetteer of Illinois, art. Chicago.

brought 5015 tons of merchandise and 9400 barrels of salt. The value of merchandise imported was equal to two and a half millions of dollars ; there was also a vast number of emigrant families, with their furniture, provisions, &c. Owing to the vast influx of emigration, the exports have been but small."

During the next three years the commercial importance of this city continued to augment in a still greater ratio, as will appear from the following table :*

Commerce of Chicago.

Exports.		Imports.	
1836	$1,000 64	1836	$325,203 90
1837	11,065 00	1837	373,667 12
1838	16,044 75	1838	579,174 61
1839	33,843 00	1839	630,980 26
1840	228,635 74	1840	562,106 20
1841	348,362 24	1841	564,347 88
1842	659,305 20	1842	664,347 88
1843	1,008,207 00	1843	1,433,886 00

The amount of tonnage employed in the trade the past season was 1,826,950.

The exports in this short period show an increase of more than one thousand per cent., and the imports nearly four hundred per cent. No other port in the western country can produce an official statement so favorable as the above. This great increase comprised chiefly the productions of the soil, and is an addition of so much wealth.

[A.D. 1842.] During the years 1841, 1842, and 1843, emigration from the Northeastern States began to send its floods into the Wisconsin Territory, both by way of the akes and by way of the Ohio and Mississippi Rivers, to the b ks of the Wisconsin River. Thousands, especially in the la ter years, crowded into the beautifully undulating lands along the western shore of Lake Michigan, south of Green Bay, to the Illinois line ; and population extended rapidly from the lake shore westward to the banks of Fox River, and along the region south of the Wisconsin River as far as the banks of the Mississippi. Settlements soon spread over this delightful country, diversified by lakes and prairies, in which all the crystal tributaries of Rock River take their rise.

A few years before, this had been called the " Far West," beyond the advance of white settlements and civilized life, in the sole occupancy of the most degraded and improvident of the savages, the Winnebagoes, Sauks, and Foxes. Now

* See New York Weekly Herald, Feb. 17th, 1844.

towns and commerce occupy the seats and haunts of the degraded Indian, upon which the rays of civilization had never beamed. A large mercantile town, with an active and enterprising community, had sprung up at Milwaukie Bay; a town which, three years afterward, in 1845, became an incorporated city, with extensive powers and privileges, designed to render it the commercial emporium of the future State of Wisconsin. Other trading towns lined the beautiful shore of the lake for many miles north and south of this central dépôt.

[A.D. 1843.] During the year 1843, the aggregate number of persons who arrived in the Wisconsin Territory has been estimated at more than sixty thousand, embracing all ages and sexes. Of these, about fifty thousand arrived by way of the lake route.* The remainder advanced by way of the Mississippi and Wisconsin Rivers, and comprised a great proportion of foreign emigrants from the German States. These emigrants spread over the country south and east of the Wisconsin River, and opened new settlements upon its northern and western tributaries. In 1845 Wisconsin Territory contained more inhabitants than any other new state possessed upon her admission into the Union; yet the people, satisfied with the territorial form of government, desired not, in the recent state of the principal settlements, to incur the additional expenses of an independent state government. Hence, with a population of more than one hundred and forty thousand souls, the Wisconsin Territory had not, in 1845, made application to Congress for authority to establish a state government.

The commercial, agricultural, and manufacturing resources of the Wisconsin Territory are unrivaled in that latitude, either in Europe or America. But it is in her mineral resources that Wisconsin excels any other portion of the West. Besides other mineral productions of value, the lead mines of Wisconsin are inexhaustible, and embrace nearly half of the great lead region east of the Mississippi. According to the census of 1840, the whole amount of lead produced in the United States and territories was 31,239,453 pounds. Of this the Territory of Wisconsin, with a capital of $664,600, produced one half, or 15,000,000 pounds.

Michigan had already become a great agricultural state, supplying the city of New York with immense quantities of wheat,

* National Intelligencer, 7th December, 1843.

flour, and various grains, not only for domestic consumption, but for export to foreign countries. The Indian claim to the whole peninsula had been completely extinguished, and the white inhabitants had spread over the entire region to the extreme north, distributed in sixty-two organized counties. The population, according to the census of 1840, was 212,251 souls. In five years more it had augmented to upward of 300,000 white citizens.

The city of Detroit had increased in numbers and commerce in an equal ratio. In 1840 it had become an important manufacturing place, as well as the commercial emporium of the state, and contained nearly ten thousand inhabitants. Three years afterward this amount had swelled to fifteen thousand.

Internal improvements had advanced rapidly, and the state was intersected by a "central rail-road," extending from the city of Detroit to St. Joseph's, on Lake Michigan. A state university had been established at Ann Arbor, with a valuable cabinet of natural history, and a well-selected library of four thousand volumes; as well as a system of common schools, and five preparatory schools or academies. The common schools of the state in full operation comprised, in 1844, no less than 66,818 scholars.* Such is the provision made by the State of Michigan for education; a fair indication of the intelligence and enterprise introduced by the early emigrants from the New England States, and their wise provision for the rising generation.

Commerce and navigation are active in these regions about eight months in the year, during which time Detroit is an important commercial point. As early as 1840, the tonnage of that port was 11,432 tons. The arrivals and clearances of vessels and steam-boats were then about 300 annually.†

Meantime, the continued emigration from the Western States of Ohio, Kentucky, and Tennessee, as well as from the Atlantic and New England States, by the lake route, had swelled the number of people in "Indiana," the oldest subdivision of the former Northwestern Territory, after the State of Ohio, to 685,886 persons in 1840, distributed over eighty-six organized counties. The Indian population had been removed from

* See American Almanac for 1845, p. 281, 282; also for 1844, p. 282, 283.
† See Smith and Haskell's Gazetteer of the United States, p. 176.

the whole region embraced within its original limits; instead of which, in 1845, the whites amounted to but little short of 700,000 souls.

[A.D. 1844.] During the years 1843 and 1844 an immense number of foreigners arrived at the port of New York, principally from the German States and from Ireland, of whom the greater portion advanced by way of the lake route to the regions west of Lake Michigan, and chiefly to the territories of Wisconsin and Iowa. Scarcely a day elapsed during the months of June and July in which crowds of immigrants were not making their advance from New York on rail-roads, canals, and steam-boats, for their destination in the West. In the interval from the first till about the middle of the month of June, 1844, no less than eight thousand two hundred and fifty foreign immigrants, chiefly Germans, arrived in the city of New York.*

[A.D. 1845.] At the close of the year 1845, such had been the general increase of inhabitants in the states and territories comprised within the limits of the original "Northwestern Territory," as organized in 1787, that the regions which, fifty years before, had been occupied as the abodes and hunting-grounds of a few naked, roving bands of savages, were now inhabited by three millions and a half of the most active, enterprising, and commercial people in the world, producing and enjoying all the luxuries and comforts of civilized life, with the improvements, refinements, and intelligence of the oldest nations in the world.†

Such is the change which American colonization and American freedom have wrought upon this portion of the Valley of the Mississippi within the last half century; and the march is onward. Already their pioneers are on the Rio del Norte, and their videttes are on the shores of the Pacific Ocean.

It was not until the year 1846 that the people of Wisconsin, with an aggregate population of more than one hundred and fifty-five thousand persons, desired to assume an independent state government. Agreeably to the application of the terri-

* See New York Weekly Herald, June 15th, 1844.

† By the state census for the year 1845, the entire population of the states and territories is as follows:

1. State of Ohio, 1,732,832 souls.	4. State of Michigan,	304,285 souls.
2. " Indiana, 854,321 "	5. Territory of Wisconsin,	150,000 "
3. " Illinois, 705,011 "		

The above states, in 1845, had forty members of Congress, and Wisconsin one delegate.—See New Orleans Jeffersonian of February 14th, 1846.

torial Legislature, Congress authorized a convention to form and adopt a state Constitution preparatory to the admission of the State of Wisconsin into the Union. On the 7th of September, 1846, the election was held for delegates to said convention.

CHAPTER XVII.

EXTENSION OF THE FEDERAL UNION WEST OF THE MISSISSIPPI, AND THE RE-ANNEXATION OF TEXAS.—A.D. 1803 TO 1846.

Argument.—Retrospect of the Province of Louisiana.—" Territory of Orleans" and District of Louisiana.—Increase of Population in the Territory of Orleans and District of Louisiana.—Remote Missouri Regions explored by Lewis and Clark.—Lieutenant Pike explores the Upper Mississippi and the Arkansas Rivers.—Population advances into the District.—Settlements extend upon the Arkansas and Missouri.—Missouri Territory organized in 1812.—New Impulse to Emigration in 1815.—Indian Treaties.—Population of Missouri Territory in 1817.—" Territory of Arkansas" organized in 1819.—French Settlement incorporated with the American Population.—St. Louis as a commercial Point.—The People of Missouri Territory apply for a State Government in 1819.—Strong Opposition in Congress.—Stormy Debates on the "Missouri Question" in 1819-1829.—Convention and State Government authorized in 1820.—Constitution adopted, and State Government organized.—"State of Missouri" admitted into the Union under Restriction in 1821.—Population, Agriculture, and Commerce of Missouri until 1836.—Emigration to Arkansas Territory in 1835-36.—"State of Arkansas" admitted into the Union.—Features of the Constitution.—Governors of Arkansas.—State of Missouri, and City of St. Louis from 1838 to 1845.—Emigration west of the Mississippi; to Louisiana; to "Iowa District."—"Territory of Iowa" organized.—"Iowa City."—Increased Emigration to Territory of Iowa, from 1839 to 1844.—State Constitution authorized.—Features of Constitution.—Iowa rejects Terms of Admission.—Florida and Texas admitted.—Iowa forms another Constitution in 1846.—Emigration through Nebraska Territory to Oregon, from 1842 to 1845.

Re-annexation of Texas.—Former Condition of Texas as a Spanish Province.—Adheres to the Mexican Confederation of 1824.—Departments and Settlements in 1832.—Mexican Grants for European and American Colonies.—Population in 1834.—Texas and Coahuila form one Mexican State.—Texas secedes from the dictatorial Authority of Santa Anna, and is invaded by General Cos.—Texas declares herself Independent in 1836.—Is invaded by Santa Anna.—Santa Anna recognizes her Independence.—It is recognized by United States and the European Powers.—Emigration to Texas greatly increases.—The People of Texas desire Annexation to the United States.—Second Application in 1837.—Mexico, prompted by Santa Anna, repudiates his Acts in Texas.—Third Application of Texas met by an Overture from the United States in 1844.—President Tyler's Treaty of Annexation.—Mr. Shannon, Minister to Mexico.—His fruitless Mission.—Mr. Thompson sent as Envoy.—Returns unsuccessful.—Captain Elliott becomes an active Diplomatist against Annexation.—Hostile Attitude of Mexico.—Captain Elliott's Zeal in Diplomacy.—Intrigue of the British and French Ministers.—Annexation consummated.—The Protection of United States invoked against Mexican Invasion.—Army of Occupation at Corpus Christi.—Advances to the Rio del Norte.

[A.D. 1803.] THE purchase of the province of Louisiana from the French Republic in 1803 gave to the United States a claim to the jurisdiction over this vast region, which comprised the coast from the Perdido to the Rio del Norte, and from the sources of that river to the Pacific Ocean on the west, and from the Gulf of Mexico on the south, to the British possessions on the north.

As has been elsewhere observed,* the most considerable settlements of European descent in this extensive territory were located principally in what are now the States of Louisiana and Missouri, and contained an aggregate population of but little over forty-five thousand.

District of Louisiana.—After the "Territory of Orleans" was laid off, the remainder of the province was known and designated as the "District of Louisiana," until a separate government could be established by Congress. During this period the country near the Mississippi River was occupied by the troops of the United States, under military and civil commandants, stationed in the vicinity of the largest settlements. The jurisdiction of the Federal courts of the Indiana Territory was temporarily extended over it.

[A.D. 1804.] The first military commandant and civil governor of the "District of Louisiana" was Major Amos Stoddart, an intelligent and highly meritorious officer of the United States army, and author of a valuable work on the early history and resources of Louisiana. His headquarters were at St. Louis, the capital of Upper Louisiana.†

At this time the District of Louisiana contained the germs of two independent states on the west side of the Mississippi, comprised in the few detached settlements upon the Arkansas River and upon the west side of the Upper Mississippi, south of the Missouri River. These settlements were composed mostly of French Creoles and traders, with a few emigrant Anglo-Americans from the United States. Those on the Arkansas River were distributed chiefly within fifty miles of the Mississippi, at a point where a military post was subsequently established and known as the "Post of Arkansas." The pop-

---

* See book iv., chapter v., "Close of Spanish dominion in Louisiana."

† Major Stoddart was an accomplished scholar, and was attached to the first regiment of artillery, and distinguished himself on the Northwestern frontier during the campaign of 1812 and 1813. He died at Fort Meigs in the spring of 1813, of *tetanus*, produced by a wound received during the siege from a fragment of a shell. His work, published in 1810, is a valuable compilation of the early history, settlements, resources, and population of Louisiana and Florida, commonly known as "Stoddart's Sketches of Louisiana."

ulation of this settlement in 1804, exclusive of the garrison in the post, was three hundred and sixty-eight persons; that of Upper Louisiana was much greater, and was situated chiefly between the settlement of Cape Girardeau and those near St. Louis, comprising more than six thousand persons, not including the garrison in the post of St. Louis.*

Exploring Expeditions.—The remainder of this immense district was an unknown savage wilderness of forests and prairies, traversed by a few roving bands of savages, and explored only by a few French traders, with their attendant *couriers du bois* and *voyageurs*, engaged in the fur-trade with the remote Indian tribes. The first authentic American explorations were those conducted by Lewis and Clark, in the years 1804 and 1805, to the sources of the Missouri, and thence to the Pacific Ocean through the Columbia River. Next were those conducted by Lieutenant Pike in the years 1805 and 1806, for the exploration of the sources of the Mississippi, and subsequently, in 1806 and 1807, for the exploration of the regions near the sources of the Arkansas and Red Rivers.†

One important object of all these explorations was to conciliate the numerous tribes of Indians then inhabiting the country watered by all the western tributaries of the Mississippi, and to establish amicable relations with those in the immediate vicinity of the frontier settlements. In his explorations upon the Upper Mississippi, upon the lower tributaries of the Missouri and Arkansas, no less than upon the sources of the Arkansas and Red River, Lieutenant Pike had omitted no opportunity for entering into treaties of friendship and peace with the native tribes through which he passed; thus preparing the way for the subsequent sale and relinquishment of lands in advance of the adventurous pioneer.

[A.D. 1805.] *Territory of Louisiana.*—Meantime, the District of Louisiana had been erected into the "Territory of Louisiana," with the first grade of territorial government administered by a governor and territorial judges. The first governor was General James Wilkinson, who held the office until the close of the year 1806, when he was succeeded by Colonel Meriwether Lewis. Under his administration, assisted by the territorial judges, the Territory of Louisiana remained a

---
* See Martin's Louisiana, vol. ii., p. 205. Also, Drake's Life of Harrison, p. 74.
† See Pike's Expedition, passim.

dependence of the United States until the year 1812, when the "State of Louisiana" was admitted into the Union. During this period the town and post of St. Louis continued to be the seat of the territorial government. The territory was divided into six judicial districts, or large counties, viz.: those of St. Charles, St. Louis, St. Geneviève, Cape Girardeau, New Madrid, and Arkansas.

[A.D. 1808.] The limits of the white settlements, as late as the beginning of the year 1808, had been extended but little beyond the boundaries claimed by the Spanish authorities in virtue of former treaties with the native tribes; but the Federal government had made ample provision for the extension of settlements by future emigration.

On the 10th of November, 1808, at a grand council of the western Indians, convened at "Fort Clark," a treaty was concluded, by which the Osage tribes ceded to the United States an extensive portion of territory between the Missouri and the Arkansas Rivers. These lands were to be gradually relinquished by the tribes in advance of the white settlements. Hence the way was first opened for the extension of the white population into the eastern portions of the present States of Missouri and Arkansas.

[A.D. 1809.] Soon after the occupation of Louisiana by the United States, people from the Western States began to move slowly into this remote region, gradually augmenting the number in all the old French settlements, and in the vicinity of the American posts.

The greatest emigration was to the settlements in the vicinity of Cape Girardeau, St. Geneviève, St. Louis, and St. Charles; those of New Madrid and the post of Arkansas were also augmented, but in a less degree, by frontier settlers.

[A.D. 1810.] In the year 1810, the number of people in the Territory of Louisiana had, in six years, increased to nearly twenty-one thousand souls, including about three thousand slaves.* Of this aggregate population about fifteen hundred were within the limits of the present State of Arkansas; the remainder were comprised chiefly within the confines of the present State of Missouri.

[A.D. 1811.] At this time the frontier population had ex-

* See Darby's Universal Gazetteer, p. 495, edition of 1827. Also, Bradford's Illustrated Atlas of United States, p. 154.

tended sparsely, and at remote intervals, to the distance of nearly sixty miles west of the Mississippi River, but chiefly near the military posts on the frontiers and around the old French villages. Many new settlements had been opened since the relinquishment of frontier lands by the Indians, agreeably to the treaty of Fort Clark; and the territory during the year 1811 had increased its population, until the number justified the organization of a representative territorial government.*

[A.D. 1812.] The Territory of Orleans, in assuming the rank of an independent state, had adopted the name of the "State of Louisiana," and it was deemed expedient to change the name of the Territory of Louisiana. An act of Congress, passed June 4th, 1812, provided for the organization of a representative grade of territorial government upon the west side of the Mississippi, including all the settlements north of the western portion of the present State of Louisiana.† This territory extended from latitude 33° to 41° north, and was known and designated as the "Missouri Territory." Its western limit was the Indian and Mexican Territories in the remote West, five hundred miles beyond the Mississippi. St. Louis was made the seat of the territorial government, and headquarters of the "Governor and Superintendent of Indian Affairs."

[A.D. 1813.] The first governor was General William Clarke; the first territorial assembly consisted of a "Legislative Council," composed of nine members, appointed by the president, and a House of Representatives, elected by the people in the ratio of one to every five hundred free white males. The first delegate to Congress was Edward Hempstead. Such was the first step in the establishing of a representative government within the present State of Missouri.

Under the new state of things, the number of people on the Upper Mississippi began to augment rapidly, by the advance of the Anglo-American emigrants from the Western States and territories. The language, manners, customs, laws, and usages of the American people began to extend over the French settlements, and to change the aspect of the country. Yet, as late as the year 1814, St. Louis had not lost either its French population, aspect, or usages. Up to the year 1815,

---

* Mitchell's World, p. 227. Also, Guthrie's Geography, vol. ii., p. 503, edition of 1815. † See Land Laws of United States, compilation of 1827, p. 614-15.

St. Louis was a French town, extending along the river in long, narrow, and sometimes filthy streets, lined with frail wooden tenements, contrasting strongly with the few large stone houses, plastered and white-washed, near the river, and the romantic circular stone forts in the rear, also white-washed with lime.

[A.D. 1815.] *Emigration to Louisiana Territory.*—The whole northwestern frontier was involved in open war with Great Britain and her Indian allies, and the French population, still wedded to their ancient laws, manners, and customs, seemed to consider themselves as a neutral party, equally exposed to two enemies, and scarcely able to choose between them a protector.* But success finally crowned the arms of the United States with victory, and the Indians of the Northwestern Territory, deprived of their civilized allies, suspended hostilities along the frontier.

About the close of the year 1815 a new impulse was given to emigration west of the Mississippi. The war had terminated; the northwestern tribes of Indians had been humbled and pacified, and were now on terms of friendly intercourse with the American people. The American settlements began to extend rapidly, and literally to overrun those of the French in their course. The French, becoming gradually weaned from their partiality for a wilderness life, for Indian associates, and Indian trade, began to entertain a common feeling, as American citizens, with their new neighbors who had settled among them.

[A.D. 1816.] A valuable class of emigrants from Kentucky and Tennessee began to arrive in great numbers, who, with others from the north side of the Ohio River, greatly increased the population in all the organized portion of the territory as far as the Indian title had been extinguished by the Osage purchase in 1808.†

---

* See Flint's Mississippi Valley, edition of 1828, vol. ii., p. 109.

† The following are some of the principal Indian treaties in the Territory of Louisiana, and the Missouri Territory, viz.:

Indian Treaties for the Cession of Lands West of the Mississippi.

1. *Treaty of Fort Clark*, concluded November 10th, 1808.—This treaty was with the Great and Little Osage tribes, which ceded to the United States 33,173,383 acres within the present State of Missouri, and 14,830,432 acres within the present State of Arkansas. This cession comprised all the lands lying between the Missouri and Arkansas Rivers, as far west as the limits of the States of Missouri and Arkansas.

2. *Treaty of St. Louis*, concluded September 25th, 1818.—This treaty was also with

Adventurous pioneers, before the close of 1816, had advanced into many portions of the present State of Missouri, between eighty and ninety miles west of the Mississippi River, and at many points on the Missouri, two hundred miles above its mouth. Settlements and organized counties had also spread over a considerable portion of the northern half of the present State of Arkansas, west of the St. Francis, and upon the waters of White River. Emigration continued to augment the population in all the new settlements, and to send new colonies toward the frontiers, until the close of the year 1817, when the territorial jurisdiction had been extended over twenty large counties, comprising an aggregate population of sixty thousand souls, including a large number of slaves.

This number of inhabitants being sufficient to entitle the territory to an independent state government, the General Assembly made application to Congress for authority to form a state Constitution, preparatory to admission into the Federal Union.* During the next two years, the number of people gradually increased by the arrival of settlers, who extended themselves into all the new counties as far as the Indian boundary.

French Population in Missouri.—The American people, with American enterprise, laws, and institutions, were now prevalent; the old French inhabitants yielded their influence, and became Americanized. Abandoning their former habits of an indolent village life, devoted to ease and amusement, they dispersed upon the fine alluvial lands, entered upon the active labors of agriculture and trade, and zealously engaged in the Anglo-American passion for the accumulation of wealth by an energetic and persevering course of industry. Thus the Creole French assumed new life and enterprise, and, gradually co-

---

the Great and Little Osages, and ceded 7,392,000 acres within the limits of the present State of Arkansas and west of it, for the use of emigrating tribes.

3. *Treaty of St. Louis*, concluded August 24th, 1818.—This treaty was with the Quapaws of the West, and ceded 26,698,560 acres west of Arkansas, and 2,492,000 acres within Louisiana, south of Arkansas, upon Verdigris River, for the use of the emigrant Indians.

4. *Treaty at Harrington's*, concluded November 15th, 1824.—The Quapaws by this treaty ceded to the United States 1,500,000 acres, within the State of Arkansas, which had been reserved at the treaty of St. Louis, August 24th, 1818.

5. *Treaty of Washington City*, concluded January 20th, 1825.—By this treaty the Choctâs ceded to the United States 5,031,000 acres of land within the present State of Arkansas.—*See Land Laws of the United States, compilation of* 1827, *by M. St. Clair Clarke.*

* See Darby's Gazetteer, p. 496, and seq.

alescing with the Anglo-Americans, became incorporated into one homogeneous people, reciprocally modified in character and feeling.

The Catholic religion, the exclusive creed of French Louisiana, made its impress upon a large portion of the early emigrants from the Western States, and is partly transmitted to their common offspring. Hence the prevalence of Catholic influence, Catholic piety, and Catholic institutions in the vicinity of St. Louis, and other districts first occupied by the French colonists. In those settlements which are purely American, the Protestant forms, tenets, and usages are maintained.

The town of St. Louis, from its admirable situation, and its great commercial advantages for domestic and foreign trade by the Mississippi, as well as for the Santa Fé trade, and the fur trade with the western tribes, had already increased its inhabitants to nearly five thousand souls. The quick perception of western enterprise had selected it as the future emporium of the Upper Mississippi, and one hundred buildings were erected during the year 1818.*

In 1804, upon its first occupancy by the United States, St. Louis did not contain more than one thousand inhabitants. This number had increased gradually to two thousand in 1816; in the next four years the increase was unusually rapid, and the census of 1820 gave the entire population at four thousand six hundred inhabitants.

The "Missouri Question."—The application of the Missouri Territory for authority to assume a regular state government raised one of the most alarming political storms ever witnessed in the United States. The "Missouri Question," as it was called, continued to agitate the Union from one extreme to the other, until many experienced statesmen were apprehensive that even a dissolution of the Union might result from the untempered zeal of the enemies of slavery.

Louisiana, from its earliest colonization, had not only tolerated and sustained the institution of negro slavery, but its very existence as a province, as well as its agricultural prosperity and commercial importance for nearly a century, had been inseparably connected with the institution. By the laws and usages of Louisiana, under the dominion both of France and Spain,

---

* See Darby's Gazetteer, article "St. Louis."

African negroes had been *recognized as property* no less than real estate. The treaty of cession secured for the inhabitants of Louisiana protection from the United States, in the full enjoyment of their liberty, property, and religion, as inalienable rights. Hence Congress possessed no just right to disturb the relation existing between master and slave.

Yet, regardless of the sacred obligation contained in a solemn treaty stipulation, the enemies of slavery, chiefly in the non-slaveholding states, opposed the legal extension of servitude beyond the limits of the original slaveholding states of the Union, and required the Federal government to restrict its extension west of the Mississippi, as had been done north of the Ohio. They zealously and perseveringly urged that the new states, by their constitutions, should exclude slavery. Hence they required the people of Missouri to renounce it, or forfeit their right to admission into the Federal Union as an independent state.

The friends of the South resisted the usurpation as a gross violation of vested rights guaranteed to the people of Louisiana by the treaty of cession, and over which Congress had no rightful jurisdiction. The capital of the United States was the arena where the contending parties met in fierce debate. The halls of Congress continued to be agitated for two years, while the angry conflict of opposing feelings and interests held the fate of Missouri in suspense, and for a time withheld from her the right of state government.

At length law and justice prevailed over prejudice and error, and the rights of Missouri were recognized, and the Missouri Question was put to rest. It was mutually agreed that the institution of slavery on the west side of the Mississippi should be recognized in the present State of Missouri, and no further north or west, but only south of latitude 36° 30′.

[A.D. 1819.] *Arkansas Territory laid off.*—Preparatory to the assumption of state government, the limits of the Missouri Territory were restricted on the south by the parallel of 36° 30′ north. The restriction was made by an act of Congress, approved March 3d, 1819, entitled "An act establishing a separate territorial government in the southern portion of the Missouri Territory." The portion thus separated was subsequently organized into the second grade of territorial government, and Colonel James Miller, a meritorious and distinguished officer of the Northwestern army, was appointed first governor. This territory was known and designated as the "Arkansas Territory," and, at the period of its first organization, contained an aggregate of nearly fourteen thousand inhabitants.* Its limits comprised all the territory on the west side of the Mississippi between the parallels 33° and 36° 30', or between the northern limit of Louisiana and the southern boundary of the State of Missouri. On the west it extended indefinitely to the Mexican territories at least five hundred and fifty miles. The Post of Arkansas was made the seat of the new government.

[A.D. 1820.] The population of this extensive territory for several years was comprised chiefly in the settlements upon the tributaries of White River and the St. Francis; upon the Mississippi, between New Madrid and Point Chicot; and upon both sides of the Arkansas River, within one hundred miles of its mouth, but especially in the vicinity of the " Post of Arkansas."

Missouri Constitution authorized.—It was not until the 6th of March, 1820, that the act of Congress was passed which authorized the people of the Missouri Territory to form a state Constitution, preparatory to their admission into the Union as an independent state, with the boundaries as they exist at this time. The convention was to consist of forty delegates, duly elected from fifteen counties.†

The convention authorized by this act met at St. Louis on the 12th day of June, 1820, and organized by the election of David Barton as president, and William G. Pettus as secretary.‡

* The first territorial Legislature districted the settlements into seven large counties, and the census of 1820 gave the population of each as follows:

    1. Lawrence, with a population of 5,602 souls.
    2. Phillips, " " " 1,201 "
    3. Arkansas, " " " 1,260 "
    4. Pulaski, " " " 1,923 "
    5. Clark, " " " 1,040 "
    6. Hempstead, " " " 2,248 "
    7. Miller, " " " 999 "
                                      13,671 "

Of these, seventeen hundred were slaves and people of color.—See Darby's Universal Gazetteer, p. 44.

† See Land Laws of United States, edition of 1827, p. 764.

‡ The members of the convention which framed the Constitution of Missouri were as follows:

Cape Girardeau county: Stephen Byrd, James Evans, Richard S. Thomas, Alex-

After a session of five weeks, the Constitution of the "State of Missouri" was finally adopted, and signed on the 19th day of July. Under its provisions an election was held, which resulted in the selection of Alexander M'Nair as the first governor; a "General Assembly" was chosen at the same time, which soon afterward convened for the organization of the new state government.

The population of the new state, by the census of 1820, was found to comprise 66,586 souls, including 10,222 slaves.

Proviso in Admission of Missouri.—The Constitution of Missouri had been duly submitted to Congress for its approbation, and for admission into the Federal Union as an independent state. After some opposition and delay, an act of Congress finally passed on the 2d of March, 1821, providing for the admission of the "State of Missouri" into the Union upon an equal footing with the original states. Yet the undying hostility of the anti-slavery spirit in the non-slaveholding states demanded a burnt-offering to the idol of their adoration, and an offensive condition was made the proviso for admission. This proviso required the Legislature of the new state to declare by a solemn act of legislation, " That the Constitution should never be construed to authorize the passage of any law (and that no law shall be passed in conformity thereto) by which any citizen of either of the states in this Union shall be excluded from the enjoyment of any of the privileges and immunities to which such citizen is entitled under the Constitution of the United States."[*]

The Legislature of Missouri, indignant at the implied imputation, which had been permitted as an offering to appease sectional feeling, assented to the condition,[†] but asserted with bold-

ander Buckner, and Joseph M'Ferron.—*Cooper county:* Robert P. Clarke, Robert Wallace, and William Lillard.—*Franklin county:* John G. Heath.—*Howard county:* Nicholas S. Burkhart, Duff Green, John Ray, Jonathan S. Finlay, Benjamin H. Reeves.—*Jefferson county:* S. Hammond.—*Lincoln county:* Malcolm Henry.—*Montgomery county:* Jonathan Ramsay and James Talbot.—*Madison county:* Nathaniel Cook.—*New Madrid county:* Robert D. Dawson, Christopher G. Houts.—*Pike county:* Stephen Cleaver.—*St. Charles county:* Hiram H. Baber, Benjamin Emmons, Nathan Boone.—*St. Geneviève county:* R. T. Brown, H. Dodge, John D. Cook, John Scott.—*St. Louis county:* Edward Bates, Alexander M'Nair, William Rector, John C. Sullivan, Pierre Chouteau, Junior, Bernard Pratte, Thomas F. Riddick.—*Washington county:* John Rice Jones, Samuel Perry, John Hutchings.—*Wayne county:* Elijah Bettis.—See Wetmore's Gazetteer of Missouri, p. 376–378. Also, Darby's Universal Gazetteer, p. 495.

[*] See Land Laws of United States, edition of 1827, p. 793.

[†] See Act of General Assembly of Missouri, passed June 26th, 1821. This act is certified by H. S. Geyer, Speaker of the House of Representatives, and William H.

ness the true construction of the Federal Constitution, which was repugnant to the enfranchisement of negro slaves or their remote descendants.

The president's proclamation of August 10th, 1821, announced the compliance of Missouri, and the full consummation of her admission into the Union as an equal and independent state.

Such was the fiery ordeal through which the State of Missouri passed in her advance to the rank of an independent state in the American Union, and the second within the original limits of the ceded province of Louisiana.

[A.D. 1830.] *Missouri after her Admission.*—From this time the population of Missouri continued to increase by the constant tide of emigration from Kentucky, Tennessee, Virginia, and North Carolina, as well as from other Western States north of the Ohio. The interior of the state became occupied by an active and industrious population; new counties were organized, and the jurisdiction of the state was extended to her western limit. In the lapse of ten years from the adoption of the state government, the number of people had increased to **140,455** souls, distributed over thirty-two large counties, including nearly 26,000 slaves and persons of color, as indicated by the census of 1830.*

[A.D. 1833.] Trade and commerce had sprung up in all the river towns; numerous flourishing villages had grown up throughout the interior; agriculture, manufactures, and arts had extended to the extreme frontier settlements; the rich staple of hemp, manufactured into bagging and rope, but chiefly the raw material for export to Kentucky, began to attract the attention of the farmers, as a product admirably adapted to the virgin lands of Missouri, especially on the north side of the

Ashley, President of the Senate, approved by Alexander M'Nair, the first state governor.—See *Land Laws* of 1827, p. 228–30. Also, *Land Laws*, vol. vi., p. 599.

The following is a summary of the several governors of Missouri, and the terms of their service respectively.

GOVERNORS OF MISSOURI.
Territorial.

1. Amos Stoddart,   from 1804 to 1805. | 3. Meriwether Lewis, from 1807 to 1813.
2. James Wilkinson,   "   1805 to 1807. | 4. William Clarke,   "   1813 to 1820.

State.

1. Alexander M'Nair, from 1820 to 1824. | 5. Lilburn Boggs,   from 1836 to 1840.
2. Frederic Bates,   "   1824 to 1828. | 6. Thomas Reynolds,   "   1840 to 1844.
3. John Miller,   "   1828 to 1832. | 7. John C. Edwards,   "   1844 to 1848.
4. Daniel Dunklin,   "   1832 to 1836. |

* See Wetmore's Gazetteer of Missouri, p. 267. Also, Flint's Geography, p. 284.

Missouri River. Wheat became another valuable staple, and large quantities, manufactured into flour, began to crowd the market of New Orleans.

The production of these agricultural staples had not ceased to extend ten years afterward, when they were deemed superior to the same articles from Kentucky and the Ohio region.

Emigration from New England supplied Missouri with hundreds of enterprising men by way of the lakes and the Illinois River, anxious to embark in trade and manufactures in the West. Emigrants from Kentucky were also continually advancing to Missouri in search of cheap lands, and a profitable employment of their slaves. Before the close of the year 1833 the state had also received the accession of nearly thirty thousand frugal and industrious Germans, distributed in the towns and upon productive farms.

Such were the sources of increased population, when the census of 1833 indicated the aggregate number at 176,286 persons, including over 32,000 slaves.

The enterprise of the state was only beginning to develop the inexhaustible wealth of the country in the mineral regions upon the tributaries of the Maramec and Gasconade, as well as upon the sources of White River. The never failing supplies of lead, zinc, copper, iron, manganese, antimony, and other useful minerals, gave ample presage of the extension of arts and manufactures far beyond what had yet been seen in Missouri. It was also ascertained that coal abounded in the hills near the Missouri River, especially on the north side.

Such was the condition of Missouri until the year 1836, when the inhabitants had increased to 244,208 persons, distributed over fifty-eight organized counties.*

Emigration to Arkansas Territory.—Meantime, population advanced slowly into the Territory of Arkansas. For a number of years subsequently to the organization of the second grade of territorial government, Arkansas was considered to be on the extreme confines of civilization in the southwest; and its inhabitants were supposed to consist chiefly of the hardy, fearless, and restless spirits of Kentucky and Tennessee, who had retired from the wholesome restraints of law and good morals. So feeble was the attraction, in this remote region, for the active, industrious, and well-disposed portion of the western pi-

---

* Bradford's Comprehensive Atlas, p. 50. Mitchell's World, p. 225. Wetmore, p. 267.

oneers, that the Arkansas Territory, in 1830, ten years after its organization, had acquired an aggregate of only 30,388 souls, including 4576 slaves. The jurisdiction of the territorial government had been extended over twenty-three large counties, of which sixteen had been laid off and organized since 1820, in that portion of the country to which the Indian title had been extinguished. The western half of the territory had been erected, in 1824, into a separate district, to be reserved for the future residence of the Indian tribes, and to be known as the Indian territory.*

From this time the tide of emigration began to set more actively into Arkansas, as well as into other portions of the southwest. Population began to advance up the Arkansas River in the vicinity of Little Rock, and as far as the western boundary of the present State of Arkansas; also upon the numerous tributaries of White River, south of the State of Missouri; upon the Little Red River, the Big Black, the St. Francis and its upland tributaries. Settlements began to extend, also, south of the Arkansas River, upon the Bayou Barthelemy, the Saline of the Washita, the deep mountain defiles of the main Washita and its tributary, the Little Missouri. In the year 1835, they had extended into the southwestern portion of the territory, upon the fertile lands north and south of Red River, upon its small tributaries, where the genial climate invited the farmer to the cultivation of grain and the more valuable staple of cotton.

[A.D. 1835.] *Emigration West of the Mississippi.*—It was in the year 1834 that the American people became enthusiastic in their search for western lands; and the advance of their explorations was not checked by the Mississippi River, for hundreds extended their researches beyond the Rocky Mountains. While the State of Tennessee was pouring her redundant population into the northern half of Mississippi, she did not withhold her numerous emigrants from the Arkansas Territory. Wealthy planters and capitalists from Mississippi, Louisiana, Tennessee, and even from Georgia, had their faces turned to the fertile and salubrious regions upon Red River, in the southwest corner of the Arkansas Territory. Surveys and explorations were progressing rapidly in this region, and numbers were advancing to the occupancy of choice locations for their future homes. Nor was it long before the Federal

* Darby's Universal Gazetteer.

government caused the surveyed lands free from Indian claim to be exposed to public sale, when not reserved to the actual occupants.

Nor was the western portion of the Arkansas Territory the limit of American progress in that quarter. Hundreds of adventurous families from the Western and Southern States, attracted by the liberal offer of lands in Texas, advanced to swell the colonies established by American proprietors within grants profusely made by the Republic of Mexico. Settlers for these remote colonies advanced from the western frontier of the United States, descended the Mississippi to the mouth of Red River, and thence, ascending that stream to Shreevesport, proceeded by a direct route into the eastern portion of Texas, and sought their favorite colony.

Emigrants from Kentucky and Tennessee, and from North Alabama, crowded into the alluvions of the Mississippi, on the eastern margin of the Arkansas Territory, as well as into the fine rolling uplands and alluvions of Red River, where they found the same climate and a productive soil, adapted to the agriculture common in Tennessee and Kentucky, and situated upon the navigable waters of one of the noblest rivers in the West. Such was the tide of emigration on the lower portions of the Arkansas and Red Rivers during the year 1836 and subsequently.

State of Arkansas.—Under these favorable circumstances, the territory increased rapidly for several years, and the census of 1835 gave the whole number of inhabitants at 58,134 souls, including 9630 slaves. Thus the Arkansas Territory in the last five years had doubled its population. The increase in the number of slaves was in the same proportion with the increase of the whites, and afforded a good index to the advance of agricultural prosperity.

[A.D. 1836.] The population, as indicated by the census of 1835, entitled the people to all the rights and privileges of an independent state government, agreeably to the principles established by the ordinance of 1787. Since the year 1830, seven large counties had been added to the jurisdiction of the territory, and the people, through the General Assembly, made application to Congress for authority to establish a regular form of state government. The assent of Congress was not withheld, and a Convention was authorized to meet at Little

Rock on the first day of January, 1836, for the purpose of forming and adopting a state Constitution. The same was approved by Congress, and on the 13th of June following the "State of Arkansas" was admitted into the Federal Union as an independent state, and was, in point of time and order, the twenty-fifth in the confederacy.*

The elections for governor and the state Legislature took place early in August following, and the state government was organized the same year. The first governor of the state was James S. Conway, with Robert A. Watkins secretary of state.

Like the Missouri Territory, Arkansas had been a slave-holding country from the earliest French colonies. Of course, the institution of negro slavery, with proper checks and limits, was sustained by the new Constitution.

The progress of Democratic principles in the West was evinced in the bold and liberal features of the new Constitution. By its provisions every white male citizen of the United States who has been six months resident in the state is a qualified elector, and all votes are given *viva voce*. The number of senators, which can not be less than seventeen, is limited to thirty-three; and the number of representatives, which shall not be less than fifty-four, is restricted to one hundred. The judges of the Circuit Courts hold their term of office for four years, and those of the Superior Court for a term of eight years. Neither lotteries nor the sale of lottery tickets are allowed. Only one state bank, with branches, and one banking institution for the promotion of agriculture in the state, are ever to be established by the Legislature; and the Legislature have no power to emancipate slaves without the consent of the owners. Slaves are entitled to an impartial trial by jury for capital offenses, with counsel for their defense, and, upon conviction, shall suffer the same punishment prescribed for white persons. Citizens shall not be imprisoned for debt without strong presumption of fraud.†

After the admission of the State of Arkansas into the Federal Union, her population and wealth continued to increase; settlements gradually extended over the unoccupied districts, and rapidly occupied the fertile regions upon all the tributaries

---

* See Land Laws of the United States, vol. ix., p. 378.

† See American Almanac for 1837, p. 272, 273. Also, Smith and Haskel's Gazetteer, article "Arkansas."

of the White River and the St. Francis, north of the Arkansas River, as well as those upon the tributaries of the Washita and Red River, south of that river. New counties had been laid off annually to embrace the advancing settlements; and the census of 1840 gave the state an entire population of 97,574 persons, including 19,935 slaves, comprised within the limits of forty organized counties.*

[A.D. 1838.] Meantime, the State of Missouri was increasing in numbers and wealth; settlements had been extended over her waste territory; and civil government was organized in sixty-two counties, comprising in 1840 an aggregate population of 383,702 persons, including 58,240 slaves. The state was already an important agricultural and commercial community, abounding with infant manufactures in all the older settlements, and rural villages of independent and happy people, extending up the Missouri for nearly three hundred miles to her western limit, as well as upon the sources of the St. Francis, and the great branches of White River, the Maramec, Gasconade, and Osage Rivers, and also upon the waters of Salt River, Chariton, and Grand River.

St. Louis had become the great emporium of the Upper Mississippi in trade, arts, and manufactures; second only to New Orleans in point of mercantile importance as well as population, it controlled the commerce of the Upper Mississippi, as New Orleans did that of the Lower. Besides its advantages as a commercial port, and the dépôt of the American Fur Company, it carried on a valuable trade with Santa Fé and the Mexican States, by means of caravans across the great American Desert by way of Independence, on the Missouri River.

The introduction of steam-power in the navigation of the Mississippi and its tributaries at an early period had greatly increased the importance of St. Louis, which, in a commercial point of view, had advanced in a direct ratio to the successful extension of steam-navigation upon the western waters. About the year 1840, the manufactories for the supply of materials used in the construction of steam-boats and steam machinery

---

* The governors of Arkansas, from its earliest territorial organization, are as follows:

Under the Territorial Government.	Under the State Government.
1. James Miller, from 1819 to 1825.	1. James S. Conway, from 1836 to 1840.
2. George Izard, " 1825 to 1829.	2. Archibald Yell, " 1840 to 1844.
3. John Pope, " 1829 to 1835.	3. Samuel Adams, acting until Nov., 1844.
4. William S. Fulton, " 1835 to 1836.	4. Thomas J. Drew, 1844.

began to rival those of Pittsburgh, Cincinnati, and Louisville; and before the year 1844 the most splendid specimens of western steam-engines and western boat-building issued from the port of St. Louis.

In the year 1831, sixty different steam-boats, with an aggregate tonnage of 7769 tons, were engaged in the commerce of St. Louis; and the whole number of steam-boat arrivals for the same year was five hundred and thirty-two. In 1835 the number of steam-boats engaged in this trade was one hundred and twenty-one, with an aggregate tonnage of 15,470 tons; and the whole number of arrivals was eight hundred and three.* The commercial importance of the city continued to advance steadily as late as 1846, having become the great entrepôt for all the new settlements which were extending over the whole region of the Upper Mississippi.

The population augmented in proportion to its importance as a commercial dépôt and entrepôt for the new states of the West. In the year 1830, the aggregate number in the city was 6252 persons of all kinds; in 1831 it began to increase in a remarkable manner, with the new impulse given to western emigration and steam-boat navigation; and from this time the growth of the city was regularly progressive. In the year 1843, the number of inhabitants had increased to more than twenty-eight thousand; and three years afterward, in 1846, the entire population was forty thousand.† During the year 1845, nearly one thousand buildings of all kinds had been erected within the limits of the city.

Subsequent to the year 1840, the tide of emigration began to set again into Missouri, not only from the Eastern and Western States, but from Europe. Thousands of German immigrants, seeking homes in the region of the Upper Mississippi, selected Missouri as the place of their residence, and crowded into the fertile and healthy regions near its northern and western limits.

Emigration to Louisiana and Iowa Territory.—The tide of western emigration was not restricted by the limits of Missouri and Arkansas. After the year 1836, the advance of population began to reach both extremes of the former province of Louisiana, heretofore occupied by a few sparse and remote settlements. All that portion of the State of Louisiana lying

---

* American Almanac for 1837, p. 270.   † St. Louis Reporter, April, 1845.

southwest of the Teche, and north of Red River, had been thinly settled and imperfectly explored as late as the year 1834, when the spirit of enterprise and land speculation first began to develop the extent of her agricultural resources. The alluvial regions southwest of the Lafourche and the Teche, and east and west of the Atchafalaya, and in the deltas of Red River and the Washita, became the theatre of explorations and new habitations. The lapse of five years found these regions occupied by a succession of dense settlements, which now constitute the most valuable cotton plantations in Northern Louisiana, opened chiefly by enterprising planters from Mississippi and Alabama, as well as by many from Georgia and South Carolina.

The beautiful and fertile upland prairies and unrivalled plains west of the Upper Mississippi, and north of the Des Moines River, had remained in the occupancy of the native tribes, which had gradually retired west of the great lakes, until they commenced their aggressions against the people of Illinois, under the fierce and vindictive Black Hawk, in 1829. After a disastrous war of nearly three years on the northern frontier of the State of Illinois, Black Hawk, with his confederates, utterly routed, and driven from the Wisconsin Territory, retired, with their destitute and crest-fallen followers, across the Mississippi River, and sought safety and peace in the remote west, beyond the northern boundary of Missouri.

Here, upon the waters of the Iowa River, the vanquished warriors and their indomitable chief made overtures for a cessation of hostilities and negotiations for peace. Before the close of September, 1832, a treaty of peace and amity was concluded between the discomfited savages and the Federal government, providing for the sale and relinquishment, on the part of the Indians, of nearly all the lands owned or claimed by them within fifty miles from the west bank of the Mississippi, and extending from the Des Moines River on the south to the Yellow River on the north, and designated by a certain specified boundary on the west. This cession contained not less than one third of the present State of Iowa, and was subsequently known as the "Black Hawk Purchase." The Indians, by this treaty, stipulated to retire from the country thus relinquished on or before the first day of June, 1833.

No sooner had the stipulated period expired, than the white

population began to advance into the ceded territory, which was speedily overrun by pioneers and exploring parties, in search of choice lands, desirable sites for towns, and water-power, for future locations.

District of Iowa.—The first white settlement in the Black Hawk Purchase was made near the close of the year 1832, at Fort Madison, by a colony introduced by Zachariah Hawkins, Benjamin Jennings, and others.

In the summer of 1835 the town-plat of "Fort Madison" was laid off by General John H. Knapp and Colonel Nathaniel Knapp, the first lots in which were exposed to sale early in the year 1836.* From that time the place continued to augment its population, and in less than two years the beautiful location was covered by a flourishing town, containing nearly six hundred inhabitants, with a large proportion of enterprising merchants, mechanics, and manufacturers.

The second settlement was made in 1833, at Burlington, seventy-nine miles below Rock Island. This settlement was conducted by Morton M. M‘Carver and Simpson S. White, who located their families at this point when it was still in the occupancy of the Indians. Here they erected their cabins in the midst of the wilderness, braving all the dangers, privations, and sufferings incident to every new settlement remote from the older states. The same autumn the plat of a town was laid off by A. Doolittle and Simpson S. White, upon the beautiful area of some sloping eminences and gentle declivities, comprised within a natural amphitheatre formed by the surrounding hills, which were crowned with luxuriant forests, and presented the most picturesque scenery. The same autumn witnessed the opening of the first dry-goods stores, by Dr. W. R. Ross and Major Jeremiah Smith, each

* This name was selected to commemorate the first American post established upon the same ground as early as the year 1808, soon after the first Indian treaty in this quarter. This post was "Fort Madison," erected as a frontier post and Indian agency upon a site selected by Lieutenant Pike in 1805, during his expedition to the sources of the Mississippi. This post was occupied in the heart of the Indian country until the year 1813, when it was abandoned, after having been reduced to the last extremity of suffering and famine by the combined savages of the Northwestern Territory, in alliance with the British forces of Canada. The beleaguered garrison, reduced by privation and famine, and beyond the reach of succor from the American settlements, was compelled to abandon the fort, and make good their retreat by night down the river. Having opened a covert way from the southeast block-house to the river, they succeeded in effecting their escape, leaving the fort in flames.—See Newhall's Sketches of Iowa, p. 122–124.

well supplied with western merchandise. Such was the origin of the town of "Burlington," which in less than four years became the seat of government for the Territory of Wisconsin, and in three years more contained a population of fourteen hundred persons.*

About the same time the city of Dubuque, four hundred and twenty-five miles above St. Louis, received its first Anglo-American population; and before seven years had elapsed it had become a rich commercial town, with an enterprising population of fourteen hundred persons. The new emigrants designated this frontier town by the name of "Dubuque," in honor of Julien Dubuque, the early proprietor of the "mines of Spain" upon the Upper Mississippi. An enterprising Canadian, he had visited this region as early as 1786; and, having fully explored its mineral wealth, he returned two years afterward, and at a formal council of the Indians in 1788, obtained from them a grant comprising no less than one hundred and forty thousand acres of land on the west bank of the Mississippi River. This grant was subsequently, in 1796, confirmed by the Baron Carondelet, and the king's title was issued for eighteen square leagues of land, having three leagues front on the Mississippi, by six leagues in length.†

Before the close of the year 1833, settlements of less note were commenced at many other points near the western shore of the Mississippi,‡ within two hundred miles of the northern limit of the State of Missouri.

It was in the autumn of 1834 that Aaron Street, a member of the "Society of Friends," and son of the Aaron Street who emigrated from Salem, in New Jersey, founded the first Salem in Ohio, and subsequently the first Salem in Indiana, on a tour of exploration to the Iowa country, in search of "a new home," selected the "beautiful prairie eminence" south of Skunk River as the site of another Salem in the "Far West." In his rambles thirty miles west of Burlington, over the uninhabited regions, in all their native loveliness, he was impressed with the

---

* Newhall's Sketches of Iowa, p. 112–116.

† Julien Dubuque acquired great wealth by his mining operations, and lived until March 24th, 1810. His grave is indicated by a stone monument, situated on a high bluff near the bank of the Mississippi, one mile below the city of Dubuque, and upon which is the following inscription, viz.: "*Julien Dubuque, mineur des les mines, d'Epagne, mort mars* 1810, *agée de* 45 *ans.*"—See Newhall's Sketches of Iowa, p. 121 Also, p. 78–122. ‡ Idem, p. 115.

great advantages presented by the " beautiful and fertile prairie country, which abounded in groves of tall forest trees, and was watered by crystal streams flowing among the variegated drapery of the blooming prairies." Transported with the prospect, the venerable patriarch exclaimed, " Now have mine eyes beheld a country teeming with every good thing, and hither will I come, with my children and my children's children, and my flocks and herds; and our dwelling-place shall be called 'Salem,' after the peaceful city of our fathers."*

Next year witnessed the commencement of the town of Salem, on the frontier region of the Black Hawk Purchase, the first Quaker settlement in Iowa. Five years afterward this colony in the vicinity of Salem numbered nearly one thousand souls, comprising many patriarchs bleached by the snows of seventy winters, with their descendants to the third and fourth generations.

Such was the first advance of the Anglo-American population west of the Upper Mississippi, within the " District of Iowa," which, before the close of the year 1834, contained nearly five thousand white inhabitants.

Meantime, for the convenience of temporary government, the settlements west of the Mississippi, extending more than one hundred miles north of the Des Moines River, had been by Congress erected into the " District of Iowa," and attached to the District of Wisconsin, subject to the jurisdiction of the Michigan Territory.

The District of Iowa remained, with the District of Wisconsin, attached to the jurisdiction of Michigan Territory until the latter had assumed an independent state government in 1836, when the District of Wisconsin was erected into a separate government, known as the Wisconsin Territory, exercising jurisdiction over the District of Iowa, then comprised in two large counties, designated as the counties of Des Moines and Dubuque.† The aggregate population of these counties in 1836 was 10,531 persons. It was not long before the District of Iowa became noted throughout the West for its extraordinary beauty and fertility, and the great advantages which it afforded to agricultural enterprise.

---

* Newhall's Sketches of Iowa, p. 141–143.
† Newhall's Sketches, p. 247. See, also, chap. xvi. of this volume; *i. e.*, " Progressive Extension of the Federal Jurisdiction over the Northwestern Territory."

Already the pioneer emigrants had overrun the first Black Hawk Purchase, and were advancing upon the Indian country west of the boundary line. Such was their restless impatience to enter upon the territory still in possession of the savages, that the Federal government was constrained to take measures for extending the limits established by the treaty of 1833. For this object, a new treaty was concluded with the Sauks and Foxes on the 21st of October, 1837, in which they consented to the extension of the western boundary, in latitude 45° 40', so as to include the principal sources of the Iowa River, not less than twenty miles west of the present "city of Iowa." The Indians began to retire still further west, and the country upon the principal sources of the Iowa was thrown open to the enterprise of the whites.

Thus the warlike Sauks and Foxes, from the Wisconsin and Rock River regions, east of the Upper Mississippi, who had been the most formidable enemies to the early French colonies of Canada, and to the American settlements of Ohio, Michigan, Indiana, and Illinois, for more than a century past, were at last compelled to retire still further before the steady advance of the American pioneer, and to seek a last asylum among the Dahcotas west of the Mississippi.

Settlements continued to extend, emigration augmented the population, and land-offices were established at Dubuque and Burlington for the sale of such lands as were surveyed. These, by the surveyors as well as the explorers, were reported as "a beautiful, fertile, healthy, undulating region, interspersed with groves and prairies, abounding in springs of pure water, with numerous streams flowing through a soil abounding with limestone of divers varieties, and other kind of rock, and some coal."

Iowa Territory.—Meantime, the District of Iowa, before the close of the year 1838, had been subdivided into sixteen counties, with an aggregate population of 22,860 souls, distributed sparsely over the whole territory to which the Indian title had been extinguished. The same year, on the 4th of July, agreeably to the provisions of an act of Congress, approved June 12th, 1838, the District of Iowa was erected into an independent territorial government, known as the "Territory of Iowa." The first "Territorial Governor and Superintendent of Indian Affairs" was Robert Lucas, former Governor of Ohio, with

James Clark secretary of the territory. Charles Mason was chief justice of the Superior Court, and judge of the first judicial district; Joseph Williams was judge in the second district, and Thomas S. Wilson in the third. The first delegate elected by the people to represent them in Congress was Augustus C. Dodge.*

The Iowa Territory, as first organized, comprised "all that region of country north of Missouri which lies west of the Mississippi River, and of a line drawn due north from the source of the Mississippi to the northern limit of the United States."

[A.D. 1839.] The first General Assembly of the Iowa Territory made provision for the permanent seat of government. On the first of May, 1839, the beautiful spot which is now occupied by the "city of Iowa" was within the Indian hunting-grounds, from which the tribes had not then retired, and within twenty miles of the new Indian boundary, and seventy-five miles west of the Mississippi River. On the fourth it was selected by the commissioners as the site of the future state capital. On the first of July the survey of the "city" was commenced upon a scale of magnificence rarely equalled. The streets and avenues were wide, and spacious lots and squares were designated for the public use, and the "city of Iowa" commenced. Twelve months afterward it contained a population of seven hundred persons.†

During the year 1839, emigration from New England, and from New York by way of the lake route from Buffalo to the ports on the western shore of Lake Michigan, and from Ohio, Indiana, and Illinois, began to set strongly into the Iowa Territory, and numerous colonies advanced to settle the beautiful and fertile lands on both sides of the Des Moines River and its numerous tributaries, as well as those upon the small tributaries of the Mississippi for two hundred miles above.

Population increased in a remarkable manner; aided by the unbounded facilities of steam navigation, both on the great lakes and upon the large tributaries of the Mississippi, the emigration to the Iowa and Wisconsin Territories was unprecedented in the history of western colonization. The census of 1840 exhibited the entire population of Iowa Territory at 43,017 persons, and that of the Wisconsin Territory at 30,945 persons.‡

---

* See Newhall's Sketches of Iowa, p. 60–62. † Idem, p. 125–128.
‡ Idem, passim.

[A.D. 1840.] Among the emigrants were thousands from foreign countries, but chiefly from the states of Germany. The frugal and industrious people from these states arrived in great numbers at the ports of New York and New Orleans, whence they secured a speedy conveyance to the West; from the former port by way of the Hudson River, and by railroads and canals to Buffalo, and thence in steam-boats by way of the lakes to the ports of Chicago, Racine, and Milwaukie for Wisconsin; and from New Orleans by the Mississippi in steam-boats the conveyance was speedy and direct to any point of Iowa or Wisconsin.

[A.D. 1843.] Such were the routes by which population swarmed to these remote territories; and such had been the increase of emigration previous to 1843, that the Legislature of Iowa made formal application for authority to adopt a state Constitution. At the following session of Congress, an act was passed to "enable the people of the Iowa Territory to form a state government." A convention assembled in September, and on the 7th of October, 1844, adopted a Constitution for the proposed "State of Iowa;" it being the fourth state organized within the limits of the province of Louisiana.

[A.D. 1844.] The population of Iowa, in the mean time, had increased to 81,921 persons; yet the people were subjected to disappointment in the contemplated change of government. The Constitution adopted by the convention evinced the progress of Republican feeling, and the strong Democratic tendency so prominent in all the new states. The Constitution for Iowa extended the right of suffrage to every free white male citizen of the United States who had resided six months in the state, and one month in the county, previous to his application for the right of voting. The judiciary were all to be elected by the people for a term of four years, and all other officers, both civil and military, were to be elected by the people at stated periods. Chartered monopolies were not tolerated, and no act of incorporation was permitted to remain in force more than twenty years, unless it were designed for public improvements or literary purposes; and the personal as well as the real estate of the members of all corporations was liable for the debts of the same. The Legislature was prohibited from creating any debt in the name of the state exceeding one hundred thousand dollars, unless it were for defense in case of war, invasion, or insurrection; and in such case, the bill creating the debt should, at the same time, provide the ways and means for its redemption. Such were some of the prominent features of the first Constitution adopted for the State of Iowa. Yet the state was not to be finally organized under this Constitution, and the people of Iowa remained under the territorial form of government until the close of the year 1846.*

[A.D. 1845.] The Constitution of Iowa having been approved by Congress, an act was passed, March 3d, 1845, for the admission of the "State of Iowa" into the Federal Union simultaneously with the "State of Florida," upon the condition that the people of Iowa, at a subsequent general election, assent to the restricted limits imposed by Congress, in order to conform with the general area of other Western States; but the people of Iowa refused to ratify the restricted limits prescribed for the new state, a majority of nearly two thousand in the popular vote having rejected the terms of admission. Hence Iowa remained under the territorial government until the beginning of 1846, when the people, through their Legislature, acquiesced in the prescribed limits, and Congress authorized the formation of another Constitution preparatory to the admission of Iowa into the Union.†

It had been the desire of the Northern States to restrain the extension of the slave states without a corresponding extension of the free states. Hence, the Territory of Florida had been excluded from admission into the Union for several years, to restrict the southern representation in Congress, until the balance of power could be preserved by the simultaneous admission of a free state. Yet destiny decided for the South. Florida assented to the terms of admission, and took her sta-

* The people of Iowa, in 1846, assented to the restriction of limits, and the formation of a territorial government over the remaining waste territory lying north and west of the limits prescribed by Congress. Petitions, with numerous signatures, demanded the proposed restriction by the organization of a separate territory, to be designated and known as the "Dahcota Territory," comprising the Indian territory beyond the organized settlements of Iowa. Congress accordingly authorized a second convention for the adoption of another state Constitution, and this convention assembled in May, 1846, and adopted another Constitution, which was submitted to Congress in June following. In August the State of Iowa was formally admitted into the Union, and the first state election was, by the proclamation of Governor Clarke, to be held on the 26th day of October following.

† The *territorial governors* of Iowa were as follows:
      1. Robert Lucas, term of service from 1838 to 1841.
      2. John Chambers,   "   "   1841 to 1844.
      3. John Chambers, reappointed   1844.

tion as an independent state, while Iowa, rejecting the terms, remained a territorial dependence.

Nor was this the only accession to the weight of southern influence. The same year witnessed the admission of the great "State of Texas" into the Union as an independent and equal member.

Florida and Texas were slaveholding states in virtue of their original rights as French and Spanish provinces, which were secured to their inhabitants by subsequent treaties made by the United States with those powers in the purchase of Louisiana and the Floridas. But in Iowa the extension of slavery was prohibited in virtue of the Missouri compromise in 1820, which restricted slavery to that portion of the province of Louisiana lying and situated south of the parallel of 36° 30', excepting from these limits only the State of Missouri. Moreover, the State of Iowa was in a latitude where slave labor was unprofitable, and but few inducements presented for its introduction. Hence Iowa, in her Constitution, was bound to exclude negro slavery from the limits of her jurisdiction; and thus it was that the greater portion of emigrants to Iowa and Wisconsin* came from the free states of New England, New York, and those north of the Ohio River, as well as a large proportion of foreign immigrants from Germany, France, and Great Britain. These together form one of the most economical, frugal, and industrious communities in the West.

After the organization of Iowa Territory, and especially after the year 1840, the tide of emigration began to set strongly into the Valley of the Columbia River, on the extreme western confines of the former province of Louisiana. The indefatigable explorations of Lieutenant J. C. Fremont, in the Nebrasca Territory, upon the sources of the Platte and those of the south fork of the Columbia or Lewis River, opened the way for emigrants through the "South Pass" to the Pacific Ocean. As early as the year 1840, several colonies, lured by the glowing descriptions given by the missionaries upon the Wallamette, had taken up the line of march, or pilgrimage, to the remote regions of Oregon and California. Two years afterward, a good wagon-road had been marked out to the South Pass, by which emigrants imperceptibly passed beyond the great ranges

---

* For "Wisconsin Territory," see chapter xvi., "Progressive Extension of the Federal Jurisdiction over the Northwestern Territory to the Mississippi," &c.

of the Rocky or Oregon Mountains. During the year 1844, emigration had so far augmented the settlements upon the south fork of the Columbia, that the people proceeded in the spring of 1845 to organize for themselves a provisional government, and claimed the protection of the United States as a portion of their territorial jurisdiction.* The summer of 1846 witnessed the final settlement of the long-contested Oregon question, by a formal treaty between Great Britain and the United States, whereby the United States acquired the undisputed sovereignty to the Oregon Territory as far north as the 49th degree of latitude. This removed all fears of foreign jurisdiction from the settlers, and opened the way for the United States to extend an unequivocal authority over the country, and to encourage its growth by the liberal grant of lands to the families of occupants.

RE-ANNEXATION OF TEXAS.

[A.D. 1821.] It has been shown in another place, that by the treaty of 1819 with Spain for the cession of the Floridas, the United States relinquished all claim to the western portion of Louisiana lying south of Red River and west of the Sabine.* After the final ratification of that treaty by both governments, and the cession and delivery of the Floridas to the United States, the Spaniards took formal possession of the country west of the Sabine, and erected it into the "Province of Texas," under the authority and jurisdiction of the Viceroy of Mexico. From that time the Sabine River was the western boundary of the United States, near the Gulf of Mexico.

The province of Texas at this time was occupied by the native tribes of savages, interrupted only by a few Spanish settlements, located chiefly at the remote points of San Augustine, thirty-five miles west of the Sabine; at Nacogdoches, forty miles west of San Augustine; besides other settlements upon the Trinity, Brazos, Colorado, Guadaloupe, and as far westward

---

* The emigration to Oregon by the Great Platte and South Pass is stated at one hundred and thirty-seven, men, women, and children, in 1842. In 1843 the number of emigrants, men, women, and children, was eight hundred and seventy-five, besides one thousand three hundred head of cattle. In 1844 the emigrants were one thousand four hundred and seventy-five, including men, women, and children, besides three thousand head of cattle and sheep. In 1845 the number was three thousand, men, women, and chilren, and seven thousand five hundred head of cattle and sheep. Total of American emigrants in 1845, eight thousand; British emigrants, one thousand two hundred and fifty. Such was the increase of American population in Oregon.—See Weekly Union, vol. i., No. 45, p. 708, 709.   * See vol. i., book i., chap. v., p. 99, 100.

as San Antonio de Bexar. The country between these remote settlements was almost uninhabited, being occupied solely by a few roving savages, and some French and Spanish Creoles, or Anglo-Americans, who had taken up their solitary residence among the Indians. The whole population, including some settlements in the vicinity of the sea-coast, scarcely exceeded five thousand souls, of whom the greater portion were the remains of old colonies formed during the Spanish dominion over the province of Louisiana.

Each principal settlement, from San Antonio de Bexar to Nacogdoches, was placed under the government of a military commandant, who exercised civil and military authority within the limits of his *presidio*. At each presidio was established a "mission," which generally preceded the formation of settlements, and was, in fact, the nucleus around which population concentrated in the wilderness.

The old "missions," or ancient edifices, whose remains are yet seen in Western Texas, were of massive stone, and resembled the feudal castles of Europe. Several of them were erected by the Spaniards from Mexico early in the eighteenth century; some of them are coeval with the oldest cities in the United States. They were nearly all built upon the same general plan, consisting of a church in a fort. Of these, the most ancient are those of San Antonio de Bexar and Goliad. The former has become memorable in the recent history of Texas, on account of the bloody tragedy of the Alamo, and the fall of Travis and his heroic band.

Such was the province of Texas under the Spanish monarchy until the year 1821, when Mexico became an independent nation. Up to this period Texas was almost an unknown wilderness, and foreigners of all nations were prohibited, under the penalty of indefinite imprisonment at the caprice of the military commandant, from emigrating to the province. The few Spanish subjects who had sufficient enterprise to encounter the toils and privations incident to a new country, were constrained, by their habitual indolence and timidity, to congregate in small, compact settlements around the garrisoned posts or fortified missions. Under such circumstances commenced the city of San Antonio de Bexar; also the town of Goliad, or La Bahia, Refugio, Espiritu Santo, and Nacogdoches. Around each of these *presidios* small portions of land were brought into cultivation for the support of the little colony,* while all beyond was but one remove from savage life. The principal articles cultivated by these colonies were corn, sugar-cane, beans, and other culinary vegetables, barely sufficient for home consumption.

The remainder of the country was left in its primitive condition, and such it remained, without any effort on the part of the government to reclaim it by emigration and settlement, until the final subversion of the regal power, and the emancipation of Mexico from the imbecile and improvident dominion of Spain.

[A.D. 1824.] On the 24th of October, 1824, the Mexican States adopted a Republican form of government, embracing "a confederation of independent states," known and designated as the "United States of Mexico." In this confederation the departments of Texas and Coahuila were admitted as one state, and were jointly represented in the Congress of Mexico.

Soon after the establishment of independence in the United States of Mexico, the colonization and settlement of Texas became a favorite subject of national policy with the new government. To attract population for the settlement of the country, colonization laws were enacted, to encourage enterprising individuals from foreign countries to establish large colonies of emigrants within the limits of Texas. Under the provisions of these laws enterprise was awakened in the United States and in some portions of Europe. Founders of colonies, or *Empresarios*, were induced to enter into engagements for the occupancy and settlement of large tracts of country, designated in their respective "grants;" the extent of the grant being proportionate to the number of colonists to be introduced. The first grant was made to Moses Austin, a native of Durham, Connecticut, in 1821, and under its provisions he was required by the Mexican authorities to introduce three hundred families from the United States. This enterprising man, having departed from Bexar for the introduction of his colony, died on his journey through the wilderness, leaving his plans of colonization to be prosecuted by his son, Colonel Stephen F. Austin, who possessed the talents, energy, and judgment requisite for the arduous undertaking. Having succeeded to his father's enterprise, he subsequently acquired more influence

* Bradford's Comprehensive Atlas, art. "Texas," p. 64.

with the Mexican government than any other *empresario* in the province.

The difficulties, privations, and dangers of a new colony in the wilderness of Texas were such as had been experienced by the pioneer settlements upon the waters of the Ohio in the first occupancy of Kentucky and Tennessee, alike remote from the aid and resources of a civilized country. Yet the native tribes of savages in Texas were less numerous and warlike than those which were encountered in the settlement of Tennessee and Kentucky.

[A.D. 1832.] But a few years had elapsed when nearly the whole area of the department of Texas had been parceled out into extensive grants for settlement by the different *empresarios*, with their colonies. The country was also organized into four separate jurisdictions, or subordinate departments, each comprising a number of "grants." These were,

I. DEPARTMENT OF NACOGDOCHES: Comprising five grants, viz.: those of *Zavalla, Whelin, Burnett, Filisola,* and *Milam*.

II. DEPARTMENT OF BRAZOS: Comprising the first and second grants of *Austin*, and that of *Austin* and *Williams*.

III. DEPARTMENT OF BEXAR: Comprising the grants of *De Witt, De Leon, Power, M'Mullen,* and *M'Elone*.

IV. NORTHWESTERN DEPARTMENT: Comprising the first and second grants of *Cameron*, and that of *Woodbury*, &c.

Under this policy, emigration from the United States, as well as from Great Britain and Ireland, continued to augment the population in all the departments until the year 1834, when political troubles began to convulse the Mexican Republic.

[A.D. 1835.] At this time the whole Anglo-American population of Texas was about twenty thousand; of this number General Austin's colony comprised no less than thirteen thousand, or more than half the entire population. These were chiefly emigrants from the United States; almost every city, village, and hamlet from Maine to Florida, and from the Alleghanies to the base of the Rocky Mountains, having furnished its proportional quota.

The Mexicans within the limits of Texas at this period scarcely exceeded three thousand, most of whom resided in the vicinity of Bexar.*

Meantime, Texas and Coahuila, comprising the territory from

---

* See Moore's *Texas*, edition of 1840, p. 26.

the Sabine westward to the Rio del Norte, and including the "Presidio de Rio Grande," on the west side of that river, had been constituted one independent state, duly represented in the Mexican Congress. But they were not formed, it seems, to exist in harmony together. The active enterprise and innate energy of the Anglo-American people, who constituted a large proportion of the inhabitants of Texas proper, required the introduction of the arts and manufactures, together with implements of husbandry, machinery, and colonial supplies, which were indispensable to agricultural prosperity and domestic comfort. In the infancy of their settlements, these indispensable supplies could be procured in the greatest abundance from the United States and other countries, by importation, and of better quality and at far less cost than they could be produced in a new settlement. The colonists who had emigrated from the United States had been familiar with the use and advantages of such supplies, and without which prosperity was hopeless. Yet by the Mexican tariff the articles which were most indispensable to them as successful agriculturists and intelligent farmers were excluded, or were so augmented in their cost by prohibitory duties as to be virtually banished from popular use. Among the articles thus excluded from the new settlements were to be found many which could not be produced in a new country still in its infancy as to arts and manufactures. Thus the honest and industrious emigrant was exposed to the avarice of the monopolist and speculator, who could extort from him his whole available resources in exchange for a few necessaries of domestic use.

As a relief from these embarrassments, the people of Texas, in numerous petitions to the Mexican Congress, represented their condition, and respectfully prayed "that certain articles indispensable to the prosperity of Texas" might be "admitted *free of duty* for three years," until manufacturing establishments could be erected within the limits of Texas.* The Mexican government turned a deaf ear to their entreaties, and also to a petition "that Texas, as a state, should be separated

---

* The articles enumerated in the Texan petition as indispensable to the prosperity of Texas were provisions, iron and steel, machinery, farming utensils, tools of the various mechanic arts, hard-ware and hollow-ware, nails, wagons and carts, cotton bagging and bale rope, coarse cotton goods and clothing, shoes, hats, and household furniture, powder and lead, shot, books and stationery, medicines, and tobacco in small quantities.—See Bradford's Comprehensive Atlas, p. 64.

from Coahuila," and be represented separately in the Mexican Congress.

Before the close of the year 1835 the different grants in Texas had received important accessions to their population, comprising many active and enterprising Irish, English, and German emigrants, who were distributed over the country in separate colonies, or were incorporated with the Americans from the United States.

The liberties of Mexico had begun to totter under the dictatorial sway of General Santa Anna, and several of the states openly renounced his authority. Texas was among the first to protest against the arbitrary measures of the existing government, the arms of which were turned against those provinces that dared to assert their rights.

The Mexican Congress at length were driven from their halls by the armed soldiery of Santa Anna, and soon afterward his servile troops entered the capital of Texas, captured and dispersed the Legislature of Texas and Coahuila, and drove forth the judges and courts at the point of the bayonet. Several states resisting his usurpations, were in turn subdued by his arms; and a general order was issued, and the lawless decree of a military despot was enforced, for disarming the free citizens of Texas. But the people of Texas, having the Anglo-Saxon blood in their veins, and the germs of American freedom in their hearts, defied the commands of the treacherous tyrant. Having remonstrated against the violation of the Federal Constitution of 1824, they threw off the yoke of the dictator, and established a provisional government, which, on the 7th of November, 1835, issued a manifesto, of which the following is an extract:

"Whereas, General Antonio Lopez de Santa Anna, and other military chieftains, have, by force of arms, overthrown the Federal Constitution of Mexico, and dissolved the social compact which existed between Texas and the other members of the confederacy, Now the good people of Texas, availing themselves of their natural right, do solemnly declare:

"That they have taken up arms in defense of their rights and liberties, which were threatened by the encroachments of military despots, and in defense of the Republican principles of the Federal Constitution of Mexico of 1824."*

* Senator Walker's Speech, delivered in Senate of United States, May 20th, 1844

The war was immediately prosecuted against Texas. Martin Perfecto de Cos, lieutenant commandant under Santa Anna, invaded the State of Texas at the head of a mercenary army, for the subjugation of the people, who were arrayed in defense of the Constitution which they had sworn to support. Heaven frowned upon the ruthless invaders, and General Cos and his whole force were made prisoners of war. Granting him the privileges of civilized warfare, on the 11th of December, 1835, the Texan commander, presuming upon the honor of a soldier, stipulated for the release of his barbarian captives upon the condition "that General Cos and his officers retire with their arms and private property into the interior of the Republic, under parole of honor, and that they will not in any way oppose the re-establishment of the Federal Constitution of 1824."

[A.D. 1836.] But the faithless Spaniard, regardless of his plighted honor, returned a few months afterward, accompanied by the dictator, Santa Anna himself, at the head of a formidable army of hireling soldiers, with the avowed purpose of indiscriminate slaughter to all those who resisted the reign of the usurper.

Then it was that the people of Texas, on the 2d of March, 1836, by their delegates in General Convention, assembled at Washington, issued their "Declaration of Independence," which, after reciting a long train of grievances and usurpations unparalleled in the history of civilized nations, and terminating with the usurpation of Santa Anna and invasion by his mercenaries in 1835, concluded as follows:

"We then took up arms in defense of our national Constitution. We appealed to our Mexican brethren for assistance; our appeal has been made in vain; though months have elapsed, no sympathetic response has yet been heard from the interior. We are, therefore, forced to the melancholy conclusion that the Mexican people have acquiesced in the destruction of their liberty and the substitution of a military government; that *they are unfit to be free,* and incapable of self-government.

"The necessity of self-preservation, therefore, now decrees our eternal political separation.

"W E, *therefore, the delegates, with plenary powers of the people of Texas, in solemn convention assembled, appealing to a candid world for the necessities of our condition, do hereby resolve and declare that our political connection with the Mexican* nation has forever ended, and that the people of Texas do now constitute a FREE, SOVEREIGN, AND INDEPENDENT REPUBLIC, and are fully invested with all the rights and attributes which properly belong to independent nations; and, conscious of the rectitude of our intentions, we fearlessly and confidently submit the issue to the Supreme Arbiter of the destinies of nations."

The appeal was sustained by an overruling Providence, and the sanguinary tyrant, with his mercenary host, advanced to his inevitable doom. On the plains of San Jacinto, north of Galveston Bay, the dictator and his army were overthrown in a most disastrous battle, and himself, a suppliant captive, was compelled to receive his life at the hands of his conquerors.*

* Santa Anna, who was acting president of Mexico, as well as military dictator and commander-in-chief of the armies, then a captive in the Republic of Texas, procured his release from captivity, and his safe conveyance from the United States in a national vessel, and also the lives and liberty of his captive army, by a voluntary agreement on his part, confirmed by two formal treaties, stipulating for the recognition of the independence of Texas, with the Rio del Norte as its western boundary. The two treaties are as follows, viz.:

1. *Secret Treaty.*

Antonio Lopez de Santa Anna, general-in-chief of the army of operations, and President of the Republic of Mexico, before the government established in Texas, solemnly pledges himself to fulfill the stipulations contained in the following articles, as far as concerns himself:

Article 1. He will not take up arms, nor cause them to be taken up, against the people of Texas during the present war of independence.

Art. 2. He will give his orders that, in the shortest time, the Mexican troops may leave the territory of Texas.

Art. 3. He will so prepare matters in the cabinet of Mexico, that the mission that may be sent thither by the government of Texas may be well received; and that, by means of negotiations, all differences may be settled, and the independence that has been declared by the Convention may be acknowledged.

Art. 4. A treaty of commerce, amity, and limits will be established between Mexico and Texas. *The territory of the latter not to extend beyond the Rio Bravo del Norte.*

Art. 5. The prompt return of General Santa Anna to Vera Cruz being indispensable, for the purpose of effecting his solemn engagements, the government of Texas will provide for his immediate embarkation for said port.

Art. 6. This instrument being obligatory on one part as well as on the other, will be signed by duplicate, remaining folded and sealed until the negotiation shall have been concluded, when it will be restored to his Excellency General Santa Anna; no use of it to be made before that time, unless there should be an infraction by either of the contracting parties.

Port of Velasco, May 14th, 1836.
(Signed) DAVID G. BURNET.
ANTONIO LOPEZ DE SANTA ANNA.
JAMES COLLINSWORTH, Secretary of State.
BAILY HARDIMAN, Secretary of the Treasury.
P. H. GRAYSON, Attorney-general.

2. *Open Treaty.*

Articles of agreement entered into between his Excellency David G. Burnet, presi-

It was on the 21st of April that Santa Anna encountered the Texan forces, under General Samuel Houston, in the battle which annihilated his army, gave freedom to the Republic of Texas, and established the Rio del Norte as her western boundary.

On the 17th of March the Convention unanimously adopted a Constitution for a Republican government, similar in its fea-

dent of the Republic of Texas, of the one part, and his Excellency General Antonio Lopez de Santa Anna, president and general-in-chief of the Mexican army, of the other part:

Article 1. General Antonio Lopez de Santa Anna agrees that he will not take up arms, nor will exercise his influence to cause them to be taken up, against the people of Texas during the present war of independence.

Art. 2. All hostilities between the Mexican and Texan troops will cease immediately, both on land and water.

Art. 3. The Mexican troops will vacate the territory of Texas, passing to the other side of the Rio Grande del Norte.

Art. 4. The Mexican army, in its retreat, shall not take the property of any person without his consent and just indemnification, using only such articles as may be necessary for its subsistence, in cases when the owner may not be present, and remitting to the commander of the army of Texas, or to the commissioners to be appointed for the adjustment of such matters, an account of the value of the property consumed, the place where taken, and the name of the owner, if it can be ascertained.

Art. 5. That all private property, including cattle, horses, negro slaves, or indentured persons of whatever denomination, that may have been captured by any portion of the Mexican army, or may have taken refuge in the said army since the commencement of the last invasion, shall be restored to the commander of the Texan army, or to such other persons as may be appointed by the government of Texas to receive them.

Art. 6. The troops of both armies will refrain from coming into contact with each other; and, to this end, the commander of the army of Texas will be careful not to approach within a less distance of the Mexican army than five leagues.

Art. 7. The Mexican army shall not make any other delay on its march than that which is necessary to take up their hospitals, baggage, &c., and to cross the rivers. Any delay not necessary to these purposes to be considered an infraction of this agreement.

Art. 8. By express, to be immediately dispatched, this agreement shall be sent to General Vicente Filisola, and to General T. J. Rush, commander of the Texan army, in order that they may be apprised of its stipulations; and, to this end, they will exchange engagements to comply with the same.

Art. 9. That all Texan prisoners now in possession of the Mexican army or its authorities be forthwith released, with free passports to return to their homes; in consideration of which, a corresponding number of Mexican prisoners, rank and file, now in possession of the government of Texas, shall be immediately released. The remainder of the Mexican prisoners that continue in the possession of the government of Texas to be treated with due humanity; any extraordinary comforts that may be furnished them to be at the charge of the government of Mexico.

Art. 10. General Antonio Lopez de Santa Anna will be sent to Vera Cruz as soon as it shall be deemed proper. The contracting parties sign the instrument for the above-mentioned purpose, by duplicate, at the port of Velasco, this fourteenth day of May, 1836.

(Signed) DAVID G. BURNET.
JAMES COLLINSWORTH, Secretary of State.
ANTONIO LOPEZ DE SANTA ANNA.
BAILY HARDIMAN, Secretary of the Treasury.
P. H. GRAYSON, Attorney-general.

tures to that of the United States, in which the people assume the name and title of the "Republic of Texas."

[A.D. 1842.] From this time until the year 1842, for more than six years, the Republic of Texas continued to maintain the rank and station of an independent nation, and had been formally recognized as such, not only by the government of the United States, but also by those of Great Britain, France, and Holland. As Mr. Webster, Secretary of State of the United States, declared in an official dispatch of July 8th, 1842, " From the time of the battle of San Jacinto, in April, 1836, to the present moment, Texas has exhibited the same external signs of national independence as Mexico herself, and with quite as much stability of government. Practically free and independent, acknowledged as a political sovereignty by the principal powers of the world, *no hostile foot* finding rest within her territory *for six or seven years*, and Mexico herself refraining, *for all that period*, from any further attempt to reestablish her own authority over that territory."

In confirmation of this declaration, Mr. Vanzandt, the Texan chargé, two years afterward, in May, 1844, declared that " There has been no war waged by Mexico against Texas, and there is now no war, and for a long time past there has been uninterrupted peace, with the exception of three marauding expeditions, for the purpose of harassing and pillaging the weak and isolated settlements, neither of which was able to maintain its position within the settlements longer than eight days, all of which occurred in 1842."*

Meantime, the United States, as well as several European powers, had entered into treaties of friendship and commerce, thus ratifying fully their formal recognition of independence.

But the feeble and distracted government of Mexico, although unable to wage a war of subjugation against the Republic of Texas, had still persevered in the absurd declaration that it was yet an integral portion of the Mexican Republic.

Soon after the victory of San Jacinto, emigration from the United States, as well as from other countries, had begun to produce a rapid augmentation of inhabitants in Texas. Organized counties were annually multiplied; new settlements were opened, and population extended over a large portion of the country upon the waters of the Trinity, Brazos, and Colorado.

* Speech of Senator Walker, May 20th, 1844.

In the year 1840 emigration began to increase rapidly, not only from the United States, but from the western states of Europe; and before the close of the year 1843, the population, exclusive of Indians, had increased to more than two hundred and fifty thousand souls, distributed over more than forty large counties,* chiefly east of San Antonio de Bexar.

Meanwhile, the people of Texas, at the declaration of independence, having been principally emigrants from the United States, and the subsequent increase of population having been derived chiefly from the same source, had never ceased to solicit admission into the American Union as an equal and independent member of that confederacy. A union, or, rather, a re-union with that great Republic, was the object of their constant desire, the consummation of their security and happiness as a member of the great family of nations. As early as the year 1836, and within seven months after they had achieved their independence by the battle of San Jacinto, the supreme government of Texas sought admission into the Union of the United States, as set forth in the following resolution, adopted almost unanimously on the 16th of November, 1836, viz.:

" Whereas, the good people of Texas, in accordance with a proclamation of his Excellency Daniel G. Burnet, president, *ad interim*, of the Republic, did, on the first Monday of September last past, at an election held for president, vice-president, senators, and representatives of Congress, vote to be annexed to the United States of America, with a unanimity unparalleled in the annals of the elective franchise, only ninety-three of the whole population voting against it:

" *Be it therefore resolved, by the Senate and House of Representatives of the Republic of Texas, in Congress assembled,* That the president be, and he is, authorized and requested to dispatch forthwith to the government of the United States of America a minister vested with ample and plenary power to enter into negotiations and treaties with the United States government for the *recognition of the independence of Texas, and for an immediate annexation to the United States,* a measure required by the almost unanimous voice of the people of Texas, and fully concurred in by the present Congress."

But General Jackson, then President of the United States, refused to give occasion of complaint to Mexico. " Too early

---

* See Moore's Texas, passim.

a movement," said he, "might subject us, however unjustly, to the charge of seeking to establish the claims of our neighbors to territory, with a view to its subsequent acquisition by ourselves."

Again, in August, 1837, Texas, through her minister, General Memucan Hunt, a second time desired to be annexed to the United States. Yet the president, Mr. Van Buren, for similar reasons, declined to encourage the proposition. It was the policy of the American government to acknowledge her independence as existing in fact, and to wait the progress of events to seal the permanence of the change. Hence Texas was excluded from the proffered union for nearly six years longer, that her independence should be fully established and recognized by the nations of Europe, independently of any agency from the government of the United States; for, said General Jackson, although "the title of Texas to the territory she claims is identified with her independence, yet she asks us to acknowledge that title to the territory with the avowed design of its transfer to the United States."

Yet the government of the United States did not hesitate to protest against the barbarous species of warfare which had been waged against the people of Texas, and which was still threatened. But the intercession of the United States was rejected by the government of Mexico, and the American minister was treated with unmerited neglect and indignity.

Meantime, notwithstanding the stipulations entered into by General Santa Anna in Texas, his government in Mexico, with his approbation, renounced the acts of the captive dictator, and, repudiating the obligation therein contained, still continued to proclaim Texas as a revolted province, for the ultimate subjugation of which the whole power and resources of the Mexican government were to be arrayed in a barbarous war of extermination. Meanwhile, the border population was to be harassed, and the country desolated by predatory incursions, until preparations were effected for its final invasion.

[A.D. 1844.] Meantime, the people of Texas, through their government, still sought annexation to the United States, and, early in the year 1844, the president, considering the independence of Texas fully established, and her sovereignty having been sustained among the nations of the earth for eight years, notwithstanding the hostile menaces of Mexico, entered into negotiations, and concluded a treaty with Texas, preparatory to the ultimate annexation of its territory to the United States.

At the opening of the Congress of the United States in December following, President Tyler communicated the result of his negotiations with Texas, and presented, for the ratification of the Senate, a formal treaty for the annexation of Texas.* In order to render this step less obnoxious to Mexico, the government of the United States, as a preliminary measure, had dispatched the Hon. Wilson Shannon as minister plenipoten-

* That portion of Mr. Tyler's message which refers more especially to this subject was in the following words :
"Since your last session Mexico has threatened to renew the war, and has either made, or proposes to make, formidable preparations for invading Texas. She has issued decrees and proclamations preparatory to the commencement of hostilities, full of threats, revolting to humanity, and which, if carried into effect, would arouse the attention of all Christendom. This new demonstration of feeling, there is too much reason to believe, has been produced in consequence of the negotiation of the late treaty of annexation with Texas. The executive, therefore, could not be indifferent to such proceedings; and it felt it to be due, as well to itself as to the honor of the country, that a strong representation should be made to the Mexican government upon the subject. This was accordingly done, as will be seen by the copy of the accompanying dispatch from the Secretary of State to the United States envoy at Mexico. Mexico has no right to jeopard the peace of the world, by urging any longer a useless and fruitless contest. Such a condition of things would not be tolerated on the European continent. Why should it be on this? A war of desolation, such as is now threatened by Mexico, can not be waged without involving our peace and tranquillity. It is idle to believe that such a war could be looked upon with indifference by our own citizens, inhabiting adjoining states; and our neutrality would be violated, in despite of all efforts on the part of the government to prevent it. The country is settled by emigrants from the United States, under invitations held out to them by Spain and Mexico. Those emigrants have left behind them friends and relatives, who would not fail to sympathize with them in their difficulties, and who would be led by those sympathies to participate in their struggles, however energetic the action of government to prevent it. Nor would the numerous and formidable bands of Indians, the most warlike to be found in any land, which occupy the extensive regions contiguous to the States of Arkansas and Missouri, and who are in possession of large tracts of country within the limits of Texas, be likely to remain passive. The inclination of those numerous tribes lead them invariably to war whenever pretexts exist.

"Mexico had no just grounds of displeasure against this government or people for negotiating the treaty. What interest of hers was affected by the treaty? She was despoiled of nothing, since Texas was forever lost to her. The independence of Texas was recognized by several of the leading powers of the earth. She was free to treat; free to adopt her own line of policy; free to take the course which she believed was best calculated to secure her happiness. Her government and people decided on annexation to the United States; and the executive saw, in the acquisition of such a territory, the means of advancing their permanent happiness and glory. What principle of good faith, then, was violated? What rule of political morals trampled under foot? So far as Mexico herself was concerned, the measure should have been regarded by her as highly beneficial. Her inability to reconquer Texas had been exhibited, I repeat, by eight—now nine—years of fruitless and ruinous contests. In the mean time, Texas has been growing in population and resources. Emigration has flowed into her territory from all parts of the world in a current which continues to increase in strength."

tiary to the Mexican government, in order to enter into negotiations for a settlement of all former difficulties, and to provide for an amicable adjustment of the western boundary of Texas. The minister was instructed to protest against a further prosecution of war against the people of Texas, and to use every effort to reconcile the government of Mexico to a recognition of the independence of Texas, with a view to its annexation to the United States.

The Mexican minister of foreign affairs, M. Rejon, in the most offensive terms, charged the government of the United States with instigating the revolt in Texas, with a view to its ultimate annexation to the American Union; he also charged the people of the United States with the design of emigrating to Texas as early as 1830, for the purpose of detaching it ultimately from the Mexican confederation. He declared that the American government had been guilty of gross duplicity toward Mexico, with a fixed purpose of dismembering her empire; that the President of the United States had sent General Houston to Texas for the express purpose of revolutionizing the country.

After ineffectual efforts to bring the Mexican government to a dignified negotiation, by conciliating the bitter hostility evinced toward the United States, and to placate the unconquerable resolution of the Mexican government to provoke the United States to actual hostilities by menace and insult, accompanied by an utter refusal to arrange former difficulties, and the arrearages for indemnities withheld in violation of former treaty stipulations, the American minister demanded his passports, and returned to the United States.*

* To the general tenor of M. Rejon's offensive charges, Mr. Shannon replied partly as follows:

* * * * * * * *

"The undersigned repeats, that to make such a charge argues an utter ignorance of the history of Mexico, or a deliberate purpose of making a false charge against the government of the United States.

* * * * * * * *

"That there may not be further cavil on this point, and to prove that the government of Mexico, and not the government of the United States, is responsible for the proceedings in Texas, which resulted in the declaration of independence, and the subsequent application to be annexed to the United States, the undersigned refers to the well-known facts of Mexican history; and to show the state of things on which the government of the United States recognized the independence of Texas, the undersigned refers his Excellency M. Rejon to the report made by a special agent sent by President Jackson to ascertain and report upon the condition and facts in relation to the independence of Texas. The following are extracts from that report:

"'The present political condition of Texas has been produced by a series of alleged aggressions upon the laws of colonization; a refusal on the part of Mexico to protect

[A.D. 1845.] Although the elections in the United States had been decisive in favor of the annexation of Texas to the the colonial settlements from the depredations of the Indian tribes; by laws excluding citizens of the United States of the North from admission into the country; by a refusal to incorporate this province into the Federal system, as provided by the Constitution; and, finally, by the establishment of a central or consolidated government, and the destruction of the Constitution itself. Such are the reasons assigned by the old inhabitants, with whom I have conversed, for the separation of this State from Mexico.

* * * * * * * *

"'The history of the events leading to the Revolution, as I find it in the public documents, is this: In 1824 a convention was held by representatives from all the provinces, and a Federal system and Constitution adopted, by which all Mexico became a Republic. Texas at that time did not contain the required population to become a state, but was provisionally united with the neighboring province of Coahuila to form the State of Coahuila and Texas, until the latter should possess the necessary elements to form a separate state for herself. This law was understood and intended to guaranty to the latter a specific political existence as soon as she should be in a condition to exercise it.

"'In 1833, the inhabitants having ascertained that their numbers were equal to most, and exceeded several of the old states, and that the resources of the country were such as to constitute the required elements for a state, they held a convention and formed a constitution upon the principles of that of the Mexican Republic. This was presented to the general Congress, with a petition to be admitted into the Union. The application was rejected and the delegate imprisoned.

"'In 1834 the Constitutional Congress was dissolved by a military order of the president, Santa Anna, before the expiration of its appointed term, and in the following year a new Congress was assembled, by virtue of another military order, which is said to have been "aristocratical, ecclesiastical, and central in its politics." Numerous applications were made by meetings of the citizens and by some of the State Legislatures, to restore the Constitution and Federal government, and protests were presented against the subversion of the laws; but they were disregarded, and in many instances the authors were prosecuted and imprisoned.

"'The central government deposed the constitutional vice-president without trial, elected another in his place, united the Senate and House of Representatives in one chamber, and, thus constituted, declared itself invested with all the powers of a legitimate constitution. Under this assumption, it abolished the Federal Constitution and established a consolidated government.

"'In September, 1835, General Cos invaded the province of Texas by land, with orders to disarm the citizens, and to require an unconditional submission to the central government, under penalty of expulsion from the country. At the same time, all the ports were declared to be in a state of blockade, and a military force having been sent to Gonzales, to require from the citizens a surrender of their arms, a battle ensued, which terminated in the retreat of the Mexicans.

"'The Texans assert that this resistance was not because they even *then* wished to separate from the confederacy, but, on the contrary, because they were desirous to bring back the government to the terms of the Constitution of 1824.

"'They, therefore, held a convention at San Philippi, in November, 1835, composed of fifty-six representatives from all the municipalities, in which they declared that, as Santa Anna and other military chieftains had, by force of arms, overthrown the Federal institutions of Mexico, and dissolved the social compact which existed between Texas and the other members of the confederacy, they had taken up arms against the encroachments of military despots, and in defense of the Constitution.

"'This was considered as an absolute separation from Mexico; and on the 3d of March, 1836, delegates of the people, from all the districts, declared Texas "a free, sovereign, and independent state."'

"In communicating this report to Congress, President Jackson, referring to the recognition of the independence, and the application of Texas to be annexed to the United

Union, and although a large majority of the members in both Houses of Congress were favorable to annexation, a strong opposition was made to the ratification of President Tyler's treaty. The opposition was made, not to the act of annexation, but to the manner in which it had been accomplished, and to the terms comprised in the treaty. The strongest opposition was made specially to that stipulation which required the United States to assume the public debt of Texas, in consideration of the public lands belonging to the Republic.

After a protracted discussion in both branches, Congress determined to consummate the annexation by means of "joint resolutions," containing the conditions upon which Texas should be received into the Union.

It was not until the first of March, 1845, that the joint resolutions finally passed both Houses, and received the signature of the president.

The conditions contained in these resolutions provided for the annexation of Texas without any *definite boundary* on the west, and without any liability on the part of the United States for her debt, which was left to be liquidated subsequently by the proceeds of the public lands.

The full and complete assent and ratification of these reso-

States, advised that the government of the United States should maintain its 'present attitude until the lapse of time, or the course of events, should have proved, beyond cavil or dispute, the ability of the people of that country to maintain their separate sovereignty, or to uphold the government constituted by them.'

* * * * * * * *

"Spain first invited citizens of the United States to Texas, and the government of Mexico renewed that invitation, by tendering large grants of land. These invitations were accompanied by pledges of protection of person and property; and the Mexican government should have foreseen that natives of the United States, well informed as to what their rights were, and accustomed to a government in which just laws and good faith prevail, would resist the attempt of the Mexican government to subvert the constitutional government and laws; and it is, therefore, manifest, from this statement of the case, that their removal to Texas and their declaration of independence were the work of the government of Mexico, and not of the government of the United States, as is unjustly charged by his excellency.

* * * * * * * *

"She was entitled to, and enjoyed, her own local Legislature, and was only bound to the general government according to the express terms of the Constitution of 1824. When the army, therefore, destroyed that Constitution, the State of Coahuila and Texas was remitted to its original sovereignty; and the Constitution of 1824, which bound the states together, being destroyed, and, consequently, Texas, owing no allegiance to that which had no existence, was left free to choose and adopt her own form of government, as best suited to her interests. The other states had no right to force upon her a form of government of which she did not approve, and much less had the army, without consulting the will of the people, the right to do so."—See *Official Documents accompanying President's Message of November*, 1844.

lutions by the existing government of Texas, and by the people thereof, prior to the first of January, 1846, entitled the Republic to admission into the Federal Union as an independent state, provided her state Constitution, modified and adapted to her new station as an American state, should not be repugnant to the Constitution of the United States.

No sooner had the joint resolutions for the annexation of Texas become a law of the country, than the Mexican minister at Washington city entered a formal protest against it, and demanded his passports. Soon afterward he took his departure, and, on the part of the Mexican government, threatened war against the United States.

In May following, the government of the United States, anxious to conciliate the Mexican authorities, and with a view to the amicable adjustment of pre-existing difficulties, no less than the establishment of a permanent boundary between Texas and Mexico, dispatched Gilbert L. Thompson as minister plenipotentiary to the government of Mexico, fully empowered to treat on all points in controversy. After an ineffectual effort at negotiation with the President of Mexico, General Santa Anna, the American minister was compelled to return, unsuccessful, to the United States.

Meantime, Captain Elliott, British chargé in Texas, had conceived a lively interest for the future independence and welfare of the Republic of Texas, and, with an ardent solicitude to regain the confidence of the British cabinet, which had been withdrawn on account of his humanity in China, he immediately put in requisition the whole weight of his diplomatic influence and skill, in the confident expectation of defeating the contemplated annexation to the United States. Every argument was employed, and every effort was made, to induce the government and the people of Texas to renounce the proposed annexation, and to maintain their separate national independence, under the protection and friendly alliance of Great Britain, secured by advantageous commercial treaties with England and France, both of whom had taken a deep interest in the separate existence of Texas as an independent nation.

While these negotiations were urged in Texas, the government of Mexico denounced war against the United States and the invasion of Texas as the penalty for any attempt to consummate the plan of annexation. To give effect to the idle boast, troops were levied throughout the Republic of Mexico, and every hostile preparation was made, with the avowed object of commencing the war so soon as any consummation of the measure should be attempted. At the same time, the rulers of Mexico employed every effort and sought every occasion to inflame the prejudices and to rouse the national hatred of their people against the people and government of the United States, who were designated, opprobriously, as the " Northern Invaders," ready at all times to invade and dismember the Mexican Republic.

This circumstance was eagerly seized by Captain Elliott as a fortunate coincidence for his diplomatic enterprise. In order to remove all apprehension on the part of Texas as to any ulterior designs of Mexico, upon condition that she would give her decision to remain a separate and independent government, the indefatigable British chargé engaged to visit the government of Mexico in his official capacity, and, through the influence of the British and French ministers, procure from Mexico a formal recognition of independence, and a relinquishment of all intention of reducing the Republic again to the condition of a Mexican province. The authorities of Texas, seeing no good reason why this concession might not be desirable, even should annexation to the United States be the choice of the people, determined to indulge him in his benevolent designs for the reconciliation of Mexico.

Aware of the inveterate prejudice of the Mexican government toward the people of the United States, Captain Elliott set out on his voluntary mission to the city of Mexico. Convinced that the hostility of the Mexican authorities toward the United States was even more inveterate than against Texas itself, and believing that, for the sake of defeating what they deemed a favorite scheme of national aggrandizement, they would not hesitate to concede the claims of Texas, and recognize her as an independent nation, provided she would stipulate to abandon all idea of annexation to the United States, he entered upon the Utopian enterprise. Nor was he wrong in this conclusion. Mexico, seizing every occasion to embarrass the pending negotiations with the United States, was willing to give assurances to Texas that, in rejecting the overture from the United States, she would secure the recognition of her independence by Mexico, to be ratified subsequently by a formal treaty of peace, for the amicable adjustment of boundaries.

Such was the extreme solicitude of the indefatigable chargé for the accomplishment of his favorite measure, that the Mexican government was assailed by the united importunities of the whole British and French legations, composed of the Texan envoy, and the more dignified ministers plenipotentiary.

At the urgent solicitation of the British minister, Mr. Charles Bankhead, and of the French minister, the Baron Alleye de Cyprey, the Mexican government consented to recognize the independence of Texas, and thereupon enter into a formal treaty of peace and adjustment of boundaries, upon the condition that she should agree and stipulate to remain independent of all other powers, and abandon the proposition of annexation to the United States.

The "articles preliminary" to a treaty of peace between Mexico and Texas, transmitted by the Texan Secretary of State through Captain Elliott, were formally submitted by the English and French ministers to the Mexican Minister of Foreign Affairs, by whom they were laid before the Congress of Mexico.* That body, on the 19th of May, adopted a resolution "authorizing the government to hear the propositions which Texas had made, and to proceed to the arrangement or celebration of the treaty that may be fit and honorable to the Republic, giving an account to Congress for its examination and approval."

Fortune seemed to smile upon the officious envoy, and he believed his mission crowned with success. Elated with the bright prospect of consummating a diplomatic measure which he fain believed was forever to decide the fate of annexation, and identify him with the destiny of the "lone star" of Texas,

---

* The following is a copy of the articles preliminary to a treaty of peace between Mexico and Texas:
 1. Mexico consents to acknowledge the independence of Texas.
 2. Texas engages that she will stipulate in the treaty not to annex herself, or become subject to any country whatever.
 3. Limits and other conditions to be matter of arrangement in the final treaty.
 4. Texas will be willing to remit disputed points respecting territory and other matters to the arbitration of umpires.
 Done at Washington (on the Brazos) the 29th March, 1845.
   [L. S.]   ASHBEL SMITH, *Secretary of State.*

he hastened to lay his dispatches before the government and people of Texas.* Fortified with an official copy of the act

* The following are copies of some of the important dispatches borne by Captain Elliott to the President of Texas:

[TRANSLATION.]

The Minister of Foreign Affairs and government of the Mexican Republic has received the preliminary propositions of Texas for an arrangement or definitive treaty between Mexico and Texas, which are of the following tenor:

" *Conditions preliminary to a Treaty of Peace between Mexico and Texas.*

" 1st. Mexico consents to acknowledge the independence of Texas.

" 2d. Texas engages that she will stipulate in the treaty not to annex herself, or become subject to any country whatever.

" 3d. Limits and other conditions to be matter of arrangement in the final treaty.

" 4th. Texas will be willing to remit disputed points respecting territory and other matters to the arbitration of umpires.

" Done at Washington (on the Brazos) the 29th March, 1845.

[L. S.] "ASHBEL SMITH, *Secretary of State.*"

The government of the Republic has asked, in consequence, of the national Congress the authority which it has granted, and which is of the following tenor:

"The government is authorized to hear the propositions which Texas has made, and to proceed to the arrangement or celebration of the treaty that may be fit and honorable to the Republic, giving an account to Congress for its examination and approval."

In consequence of the preceding authority of the Congress of the Mexican Republic, the undersigned, Minister of Foreign Affairs and government, declares, that the supreme government receives the four articles above-mentioned as the preliminaries of a formal and definitive treaty; and further, that it is disposed to commence the negotiation as [soon as] Texas may desire, and to receive the commissioners which she may name for this purpose.

[L. S.] LUIS G. CUEVAS.
Mexico, May 19, 1845.

The above is a correct translation of the original.

STEPHEN Z. HOYLE, *Translator.*

[TRANSLATION.]

ADDITIONAL DECLARATION.

It is understood that, besides the four preliminary articles proposed by Texas, there are other essential and important points which ought, also, to be included in the negotiation; and that if this negotiation is not realized on account of circumstances, or because Texas, influenced by the law passed in the United States on annexation, should consent thereto, either directly or indirectly, then the answer which under this date is given to Texas by the undersigned, Minister for Foreign Affairs, shall be considered as null and void.

[L. S.] LUIS G. CUEVAS.
Mexico, May 19, 1845.

The above is a correct translation of the original.

STEPHEN Z. HOYLE, *Translator.*

[TRANSLATION.]

Legation of France in Mexico.

MR. PRESIDENT: I am happy to be able to announce to your excellency that the Mexican government, after having obtained the authorization of the two Chambers of Congress, has acceded to the four preliminary articles which the Secretary of State of Texas had remitted to the chargés des affaires of France and England, near your government, and which these last had transmitted to me and to the minister of H. B. M., to be presented to the executive power of Mexico.

The act of acceptation, clothed with the necessary forms, will be handed by Mr. Elliott to the Secretary of State of the Texan government; and your excellency will

of the Mexican Congress, and the self-applauding congratulations of the French minister, who coveted the honor of its accomplishment as one of the triumphs of "his diplomatic career," he hastened to electrify all Texas with its announcement to the government and people.

But after all his zeal, and all his efforts at diplomacy, he was doomed to the mortifying disappointment of witnessing the cold indifference with which all his labors were received by the government of Texas, under the veil of official courtesy.

Meantime, President Jones could do no less than to reciprocate the courteous congratulations of the Baron de Cyprey, returning thanks "for his kindness and courtesy," no less than for "his valuable services, in producing a result" so fraught with advantage to Texas. "Should the result," said President Jones, "be the establishment of a good understanding and a lasting peace between the governments of Texas and Mexico, with the concurrence of their people, the cause of humanity will assuredly be greatly indebted to his efforts in its behalf."

Still further to humor the vanity of the French minister, to thence find yourself in a situation to name commissioners to negotiate with Mexico the definitive treaty between Mexico and Texas.

The success which has crowned our efforts has only been obtained by much management of susceptibilities. But I should say that the dispositions of the executive power have never appeared doubtful to me, and that they give me the hope of a solution proper to satisfy the two parties and to assure their reciprocal well-being.

If, in the course which must be given to this affair, I can contribute to the wise views and sound policy which animate your excellency, I shall lend myself to it with so much the more zeal that it relates to the accomplishment of a work useful to humanity; and if the result answers to our hopes, I shall consider the part which I have taken in it as one of the deeds for which I may most applaud myself in my diplomatic career.

Receive, Mr. President, the assurances of the high consideration with which I am your excellency's
Very humble and most obedient servant,
Baron Alleye de Cyprey.

Mexico, 20th May, 1845.
His excellency Mr. Anson Jones, President of the Republic of Texas, &c., &c.
The foregoing is a correct translation of the original.
Stephen Z. Hoyle, Translator.

[TRANSLATION.]

The undersigned, envoy extraordinary and minister plenipotentiary of his Majesty the King of the French, and minister plenipotentiary of her Britannic majesty, certify that the above copy conforms with the original, which has been presented to them by Mr. Elliott, H. B. M. chargé d'affaires to Texas.
[L. S.]   Baron Alleye de Cyprey,
[L. S.]   Charles Bankhead.
Mexico, 20th May, 1845.

These documents are among the official papers accompanying the ratification of the final act of annexation, published in the Weekly Union at Washington city.

flatter the officiousness of the intermeddling British chargé, and to lull apprehension with the treacherous Mexicans, the President of Texas, in a proclamation to the people of Texas, announced the cessation of hostilities between the two governments, consequent upon the agreement of the Mexican government to the "articles preliminary to a definitive treaty of peace." The Mexican government accordingly suspended its hostile demonstrations against Texas.

Meantime, the President of Texas, well convinced of the unconquerable aversion of the Congress and people of Texas to any political connection with Mexico, and of their unchangeable attachment to the government and people of the United States, and conscious, also, of "the very ridiculous position in which Elliott had placed his government by his *ex parte* negotiation of this treaty," determined to submit the whole negotiation, together with the joint resolutions from the United States, to the Congress of Texas, as well as to the people in general convention subsequently, for their final action and decision upon the same.

On the 21st of June, the government of Texas, by a joint resolution of both Houses, unanimously adopted, ratified, and confirmed the assent of Texas to the propositions for annexation contained in the joint resolutions of the United States, which had been transmitted by the hands of Andrew J. Donelson, American chargé des affaires to Texas.

The Texan Congress proceeded to make provision, by law, for the consummation of the annexation so far as Texas was concerned. The British chargé, perceiving the futility of all his schemes of diplomacy, retired into his proper sphere, stripped of the imaginary honors which he, with Sir Charles Bankhead and the Baron Alleye de Cyprey, had gained by their diplomatic proficiency.

Among the provisions enacted by the Texan Congress for the final ratification of the annexation, was that of a general convention of delegates, representing the whole Republic, for the purpose of adopting a state Constitution for the contemplated "State of Texas," preparatory to its formal admission into the American Union "upon an equal footing with the original states."

The Convention assembled at the town of Austin on the 4th day of July, and at one o'clock P.M. of that day the unanimous vote of that body declared the assent of the sovereign people of Texas to the terms and conditions contained in the joint resolutions of the United States. This assent, in fact, consummated the annexation on the part of Texas, and made that country an integral portion of the United States.*

* The following copy of the "Ordinance" of the Convention of Texas comprises also the joint resolutions of the United States:

AN ORDINANCE.

Whereas, the Congress of the United States of America has passed resolutions providing for the annexation of Texas to that Union, which resolutions were approved by the President of the United States on the first day of March, one thousand eight hundred and forty-five; and whereas the President of the United States has submitted to Texas the first and second sections of the said resolutions as the basis upon which Texas may be admitted as one of the states of the said Union; and whereas the existing government of the Republic of Texas has assented to the proposals thus made, the terms and conditions of which are as follows:

Joint Resolution for Annexing Texas to the United States.

"Resolved, *by the Senate and House of Representatives of the United States of America in Congress assembled,* That Congress doth consent that the territory properly included within, and rightly belonging to, the Republic of Texas, may be erected into a new state, to be called the State of Texas, with a Republican form of government, to be adopted by the people of said Republic, by deputies in convention assembled, with the consent of the existing government, in order that the same may be admitted as one of the states of this Union.

" 2. *And be it further resolved,* That the foregoing consent of Congress is given upon the following conditions, and with the following guarantees, to wit:

"*First.* Said state to be formed subject to the adjustment by this government of all questions of boundary that may arise with other governments; and the Constitution thereof, with the proper evidence of its adoption by the people of said Republic of Texas, shall be transmitted to the President of the United States, to be laid before Congress for its final action, on or before the first day of January, one thousand eight hundred and forty-six.

" *Second.* Said state, when admitted into the Union, after ceding to the United States all public edifices, fortifications, barracks, ports, and harbors, navy, and navy-yards, docks, magazines, arms, and armaments, and all other property and means pertaining to the public defense belonging to the said Republic of Texas, shall retain all the public funds, debts, taxes, and dues of every kind which may belong to, or be due and owing to the said Republic; and shall also retain all the vacant and unappropriated lands lying within its limits, to be applied to the payment of the debts and liabilities of said Republic of Texas; and the residue of said lands, after discharging said debts and liabilities, to be disposed of as said state may direct, but in no event are said debts and liabilities to become a charge upon the government of the United States.

" *Third.* New states of convenient size, not exceeding four in number, in addition to said State of Texas, and having sufficient population, may hereafter, by the consent of said state, be formed out of the territory thereof, which shall be entitled to admission under the provisions of the Federal Constitution. And such states as may be formed out of that portion of said territory lying south of thirty-six degrees thirty minutes north latitude, commonly known as the Missouri compromise line, shall be admitted into the Union, with or without slavery, as the people of each state asking admission may desire. And in such state, or states, as shall be formed out of said territory, north of said Missouri compromise line, slavery or involuntary servitude (except for crime) shall be prohibited."

Now, in order to manifest the assent of the people of this Republic, as required in the above recited portions of the said resolutions,

The Convention proceeded to the labors of framing a state Constitution, which was finally adopted, and submitted to the consideration of the American Congress for their approval and ratification at the session of 1845 and 1846.

Meantime, the government of Mexico, apprised of the determination of the Texan Congress on the subject of annexation, and which was a just criterion for the decision of the Convention, had resolved to take active measures for the invasion of the country east of the Rio del Norte. Chagrined that all the means put into operation had been unsuccessful in defeating the annexation to the United States, the government of Mexico began to make every demonstration of active hostilities against the United States for the recovery and subjugation of Texas eastward to the Sabine. Great military preparations were made in all the departments subject to the central government, while large bodies of troops were gradually advanced toward Matamoros on the Rio del Norte. Before the middle of August, the advanced detachments of the Mexican army had arrived at Monterey, within two hundred and twenty miles of Matamoros, while the declarations of the Mexican government, published at and near the city of Mexico, asserted that war would be prosecuted vigorously for the recovery of Texas.*

We, the deputies of the people of Texas, in convention assembled, in their name and by their authority, do ordain and declare, that we assent to and accept the proposals, conditions, and guarantees contained in the first and second sections of the resolutions of the Congress of the United States aforesaid.

THOS. J. RUSK, *President.*

Phil. M. Cuny, H. G. Runnels, Robert M. Forbes, Sam. Lusk, Jno. Caldwell, Jose Antonio Navarro, Geo. M. Brown, George T. Wood, G. W. Wright, H. R. Latimer, John M. Lewis, James Scott, Archibald M'Neill, A. C. Horton, Gustavus A. Everts, Lemuel Dale Evans, J. B. Miller, R. E. B. Baylor, J. S. Mayfield, R. Bache, James Love, William L. Hunter, John D. Anderson, Isaac Parker, P. O. Lumpkin, Francis Moore, Sr., Isaac W. Brashear, Alexander M'Gowan, Isaac Van Zant, S. Holland, Edward Clark, Geo. W. Smyth, James Armstrong, Francis W. White, James Davis, Israel Standefer, Jos. L. Hogg, Chas. S. Taylor, David Gage, Henry S. Jewett, Cavitt Armstrong, James Bower, Albert H. Latimer, Wm. C. Young, J. Pinckney Henderson, Nicholas H. Darnell, Emery Rains, A. W. O. Hicks, James M. Burroughs, H. L. Kinney, William L. Cazneau, A. S. Cunningham, Abner S. Lipscomb, John Hemphill, Van R. Irion.

(Attest) JAS. H. RAYMOND, *Secretary of the Convention.*
Adopted July 4th, 1845.

The first state Legislature of Texas assembled at Austin on Friday, Feb. 20th, 1846. General Burleson was elected President of the Senate, and Mr. Crump, of Austin county, Speaker of the House of Representatives.

* On the 21st of July the Mexican minister of foreign affairs addressed a report to the Congress in behalf of the government, strongly recommending war for the recovery of Texas in case the plan of annexation to the United States is consummated. This report closes with submitting the following proposition by the minister:

To secure the border inhabitants from the horrors of war, and the country from hostile invasion, the Convention, on the 7th of August, by a resolution of their body, in the name of the people of Texas, had requested the President of the United States to send troops without delay to the western frontier.

Under these circumstances, the president, viewing Texas as an integral part of the Union, threatened with foreign invasion, caused a portion of the Federal troops to concentrate near the western frontier of Texas, as an army of observation and occupancy. Before the middle of August, detachments of mounted dragoons, infantry, and field artillery were advancing into Texas in every direction from the Valley of the Mississippi. On the 27th of August, General Taylor, from Fort Jessup, at the head of about two thousand men, including Colonel Twigg's regiment of dragoons, and Major Ringgold's flying artillery, arrived at Corpus Christi, on the west side of the Nueces, where his headquarters were established until the middle of March following, when, in obedience to orders from the government, he advanced toward the Rio del Norte.

Meantime, the assent of Texas, as expressed through the existing government and the sovereign people in convention assembled, having been given to the terms proposed by the United States, the president proceeded to take the necessary steps and measures for consummating the annexation for the final ratification of Congress, and the formal admission of Texas into the Union on an equal footing with the original states. In his annual message of December, 1845, President Polk submitted the whole subject to Congress for their consideration. The following is a brief extract from the message:

" The terms of annexation which were offered by the United States having been accepted by Texas, the public faith of both parties is solemnly pledged to the compact of their union.

"His excellency, the president, at a council of the ministers, and with their full assent, has been pleased to order me to address the chamber in the following terms, as approved by the council:

"Article 1. From the moment when the supreme government shall know that the department of Texas has annexed itself to the American Union, or that troops from the Union have invaded it, it shall declare the nation at war with the United States of North America.

"Article 2. The object of this war shall be to secure the integrity of the Mexican Territory, according to its ancient limits, acknowledged by the United States in treaties from the year 1828 to 1836, and to insure the independence of the nation.

"God and Liberty!   Luis G. Cuevas.

"*Mexico, July* 21, 1845."

Nothing remains to consummate the event but the passage of an act by Congress to admit the State of Texas into the Union upon an equal footing with the original states.   *   *   *
As soon as the act to admit Texas as a state shall be passed, the union of the two Republics will be consummated by their own voluntary consent.

" This accession to our territory has been a bloodless achievement. No arm of force has been raised to produce the result. The sword has had no part in the victory. We have not sought to extend our territorial possessions by conquest, or our Republican institutions over a reluctant people. It was the deliberate homage of each people to the great principle of our federative Union.

*   *   *   *   *   *   *   *   *   *

" Since that time Mexico has, until recently, occupied an attitude of hostility toward the United States; has been marshalling and organizing armies, issuing proclamations, and avowing the intention to make war on the United States, either by an open declaration, or by invading Texas. Both the Congress and Convention of the people of Texas invited this government to send an army into that territory, to protect and defend them against the menaced attack.   *   *   *   Our army was ordered to take position in the country between the Nueces and the Del Norte, and to repel any invasion of the Texan territory which might be attempted by the Mexican forces. Our squadron in the Gulf was ordered to co-operate with the army. But though our army and navy were placed in a position to defend our own and the rights of Texas, they were ordered to commit no act of hostility against Mexico unless she declared war, or was herself the aggressor by striking the first blow. The result has been, that Mexico has made no aggressive movement, and our military and naval commanders have executed their orders with such discretion that the peace of the two Republics has not been disturbed.

"Texas had declared her independence, and maintained it by her arms for more than nine years. She has had an organized government in successful operation during that period. Her separate existence as an independent state had been recognized by the United States and the principal powers of Europe. Treaties of commerce and navigation had been concluded with her by different nations, and it had become manifest to the whole world that any further attempt on the part of Mexico to conquer her, or overthrow her government, would be vain. Even Mexico herself had become satisfied of this fact, and while the question of annexation was pending before the people of Texas during the past summer, the government of Mexico, by a formal act, agreed to recognize the independence of Texas, on condition that she would not annex herself to any other power." Such was the state of affairs in December, 1845.

Early in the session of Congress, the Constitution of the "State of Texas". was approved, and the annexation was finally consummated in the formal admission of the new state as an equal and independent member of the Federal Union.

[A.D. 1846.] The new state government was organized by the election of a governor and General Assembly, which convened on the 20th of February following. General Henderson, who was elected first governor by an overwhelming vote, in his inaugural address congratulated the people of Texas upon the reunion of their country to the sovereignty of the United States, as the result of the extending influence of Republican freedom in America. "We again," he observes, "hail the incorporation of Texas into our Union as one of the most remarkable events of the age. It was accomplished by no violence of the sword, no effusion of blood, no corruption of the people, no constraint upon their inclinations, but in the best spirit of the age, according to the purest principles of free government, by the free consent of the people of the two Republics. It was left for the Anglo-American inhabitants of the Western Continent to furnish a new mode of enlarging the bounds of empire by the more natural tendency of free principles."

It was about the middle of March when the American troops, under General Taylor, took up the line of march for the east bank of the Rio del Norte, and on the 28th they pitched their camp opposite the city of Matamoros, where they erected strong field-works, comprising a fortified camp extending nearly three miles along the river.

THE END.

The First American Frontier
AN ARNO PRESS/NEW YORK TIMES COLLECTION

Agnew, Daniel.
A History of the Region of Pennsylvania North of the Allegheny River. 1887.

Alden, George H.
New Government West of the Alleghenies Before 1780. 1897.

Barrett, Jay Amos.
Evolution of the Ordinance of 1787. 1891.

Billon, Frederick.
Annals of St. Louis in its Early Days Under the French and Spanish Dominations. 1886.

Billon, Frederick.
Annals of St. Louis in its Territorial Days, 1804-1821. 1888.

Littel, William.
Political Transactions in and Concerning Kentucky. 1926.

Bowles, William Augustus.
Authentic Memoirs of William Augustus Bowles. 1916.

Bradley, A. G.
The Fight with France for North America. 1900.

Brannan, John, ed.
Official Letters of the Military and Naval Officers of the War, 1812-1815. 1823.

Brown, John P.
Old Frontiers. 1938.

Brown, Samuel R.
The Western Gazetteer. 1817.

Cist, Charles.
Cincinnati Miscellany of Antiquities of the West and Pioneer History. (2 volumes in one). 1845-6.

Claiborne, Nathaniel Herbert.
Notes on the War in the South with Biographical Sketches of the Lives of Montgomery, Jackson, Sevier, and Others. 1819.

Clark, Daniel.
Proofs of the Corruption of Gen. James Wilkinson. 1809.

Clark, George Rogers.
Colonel George Rogers Clark's Sketch of His Campaign in the Illinois in 1778-9. 1869.

Collins, Lewis.
Historical Sketches of Kentucky. 1847.

Cruikshank, Ernest, ed,
Documents Relating to Invasion of Canada and the Surrender of Detroit. 1912.

Cruikshank, Ernest, ed,
The Documentary History of the Campaign on the Niagara Frontier, 1812-1814. (4 volumes). 1896-1909.

Cutler, Jervis.
A Topographical Description of the State of Ohio, Indian Territory, and Louisiana. 1812.

Cutler, Julia P.
The Life and Times of Ephraim Cutler. 1890.

Darlington, Mary C.
History of Col. Henry Bouquet and the Western Frontiers of Pennsylvania. 1920.

Darlington, Mary C.
Fort Pitt and Letters From the Frontier. 1892.

De Schweinitz, Edmund.
The Life and Times of David Zeisberger. 1870.

Dillon, John B.
History of Indiana. 1859.

Eaton, John Henry.
Life of Andrew Jackson. 1824.

English, William Hayden.
Conquest of the Country Northwest of the Ohio. (2 volumes in one). 1896.

Flint, Timothy.
Indian Wars of the West. 1833.

Forbes, John.
Writings of General John Forbes Relating to His Service in North America. 1938.

Forman, Samuel S.
Narrative of a Journey Down the Ohio and Mississippi in 1789-90. 1888.

Haywood, John.
Civil and Political History of the State of Tennessee to 1796. 1823.

Heckewelder, John.
History, Manners and Customs of the Indian Nations. 1876.

Heckewelder, John.
Narrative of the Mission of the United Brethren. 1820.

Hildreth, Samuel P.
Pioneer History. 1848.

Houck, Louis.
The Boundaries of the Louisiana Purchase: A Historical Study. 1901.

Houck, Louis.
History of Missouri. (3 volumes in one). 1908.

Houck, Louis.
The Spanish Regime in Missouri. (2 volumes in one). 1909.

Jacob, John J.
A Biographical Sketch of the Life of the Late Capt. Michael Cresap. 1826.

Jones, David.
A Journal of Two Visits Made to Some Nations of Indians on the West Side of the River Ohio, in the Years 1772 and 1773. 1774.

Kenton, Edna.
Simon Kenton. 1930.

Loudon, Archibald.
Selection of Some of the Most Interesting Narratives of Outrages. (2 volumes in one). 1808-1811.

Monette, J. W.
History, Discovery and Settlement of the Mississippi Valley. (2 volumes in one). 1846.

Morse, Jedediah.
American Gazetteer. 1797.

Pickett, Albert James.
History of Alabama. (2 volumes in one). 1851.

Pope, John.
A Tour Through the Southern and Western Territories. 1792.

Putnam, Albigence Waldo.
History of Middle Tennessee. 1859.

Ramsey, James G. M.
Annals of Tennessee. 1853.

Ranck, George W.
Boonesborough. 1901.

Robertson, James Rood, ed.
Petitions of the Early Inhabitants of Kentucky to the Gen. Assembly of Virginia. 1914.

Royce, Charles.
Indian Land Cessions. 1899.

Rupp, I. Daniel.
History of Northampton, Lehigh, Monroe, Carbon and Schuykill Counties. 1845.

Safford, William H.
The Blennerhasset Papers. 1864.

St. Clair, Arthur.
A Narrative of the Manner in which the Campaign Against the Indians, in the Year 1791 was Conducted. 1812.

Sargent, Winthrop, ed.
A History of an Expedition Against Fort DuQuesne in 1755. 1855.

Severance, Frank H.
An Old Frontier of France. (2 volumes in one). 1917.

Sipe, C. Hale.
Fort Ligonier and Its Times. 1932.

Stevens, Henry N.
Lewis Evans: His Map of the Middle British Colonies in America. 1920.

Timberlake, Henry.
The Memoirs of Lieut. Henry Timberlake. 1927.

Tome, Philip.
Pioneer Life: Or Thirty Years a Hunter. 1854.

Trent, William.
Journal of Captain William Trent From Logstown to Pickawillany. 1871.

Walton, Joseph S.
Conrad Weiser and the Indian Policy of Colonial Pennsylvania. 1900.

Withers, Alexander Scott.
Chronicles of Border Warfare. 1895.